Lecture Notes in Computer Science 10923

Commenced Publication in 1973
Founding and Former Series Editors:
Gerhard Goos, Juris Hartmanis, and Jan van Leeuwen

More information about this series at http://www.springer.com/series/7409

Fiona Fui-Hoon Nah · Bo Sophia Xiao (Eds.)

HCI in Business, Government, and Organizations

5th International Conference, HCIBGO 2018
Held as Part of HCI International 2018
Las Vegas, NV, USA, July 15–20, 2018
Proceedings

Springer

Editors
Fiona Fui-Hoon Nah
Missouri University of Science
   and Technology
Rolla, MO
USA

Bo Sophia Xiao
University of Hawaii at Manoa
Honolulu, HI
USA

ISSN 0302-9743   ISSN 1611-3349   (electronic)
Lecture Notes in Computer Science
ISBN 978-3-319-91715-3   ISBN 978-3-319-91716-0   (eBook)
https://doi.org/10.1007/978-3-319-91716-0

Library of Congress Control Number: 2018944302

LNCS Sublibrary: SL3 – Information Systems and Applications, incl. Internet/Web, and HCI

This Springer imprint is published by the registered company Springer Nature Switzerland AG
The registered company address is: Gewerbestrasse 11, 6330 Cham, Switzerland

Foreword

The 20th International Conference on Human-Computer Interaction, HCI International 2018, was held in Las Vegas, NV, USA, during July 15–20, 2018. The event incorporated the 14 conferences/thematic areas listed on the following page.

A total of 4,373 individuals from academia, research institutes, industry, and governmental agencies from 76 countries submitted contributions, and 1,170 papers and 195 posters have been included in the proceedings. These contributions address the latest research and development efforts and highlight the human aspects of design and use of computing systems. The contributions thoroughly cover the entire field of human-computer interaction, addressing major advances in knowledge and effective use of computers in a variety of application areas. The volumes constituting the full set of the conference proceedings are listed in the following pages.

I would like to thank the program board chairs and the members of the program boards of all thematic areas and affiliated conferences for their contribution to the highest scientific quality and the overall success of the HCI International 2018 conference.

This conference would not have been possible without the continuous and unwavering support and advice of the founder, Conference General Chair Emeritus and Conference Scientific Advisor Prof. Gavriel Salvendy. For his outstanding efforts, I would like to express my appreciation to the communications chair and editor of *HCI International News*, Dr. Abbas Moallem.

July 2018   Constantine Stephanidis

Foreword

HCI International 2018 Thematic Areas and Affiliated Conferences

Thematic areas:

- Human-Computer Interaction (HCI 2018)
- Human Interface and the Management of Information (HIMI 2018)

Affiliated conferences:

- 15th International Conference on Engineering Psychology and Cognitive Ergonomics (EPCE 2018)
- 12th International Conference on Universal Access in Human-Computer Interaction (UAHCI 2018)
- 10th International Conference on Virtual, Augmented, and Mixed Reality (VAMR 2018)
- 10th International Conference on Cross-Cultural Design (CCD 2018)
- 10th International Conference on Social Computing and Social Media (SCSM 2018)
- 12th International Conference on Augmented Cognition (AC 2018)
- 9th International Conference on Digital Human Modeling and Applications in Health, Safety, Ergonomics, and Risk Management (DHM 2018)
- 7th International Conference on Design, User Experience, and Usability (DUXU 2018)
- 6th International Conference on Distributed, Ambient, and Pervasive Interactions (DAPI 2018)
- 5th International Conference on HCI in Business, Government, and Organizations (HCIBGO)
- 5th International Conference on Learning and Collaboration Technologies (LCT 2018)
- 4th International Conference on Human Aspects of IT for the Aged Population (ITAP 2018)

19. LNCS 10919, Design, User Experience, and Usability: Designing Interactions (Part II), edited by Aaron Marcus and Wentao Wang
20. LNCS 10920, Design, User Experience, and Usability: Users, Contexts, and Case Studies (Part III), edited by Aaron Marcus and Wentao Wang
21. LNCS 10921, Distributed, Ambient, and Pervasive Interactions: Understanding Humans (Part I), edited by Norbert Streitz and Shin'ichi Konomi
22. LNCS 10922, Distributed, Ambient, and Pervasive Interactions: Technologies and Contexts (Part II), edited by Norbert Streitz and Shin'ichi Konomi
23. LNCS 10923, HCI in Business, Government, and Organizations, edited by Fiona Fui-Hoon Nah and Bo Sophia Xiao
24. LNCS 10924, Learning and Collaboration Technologies: Design, Development and Technological Innovation (Part I), edited by Panayiotis Zaphiris and Andri Ioannou
25. LNCS 10925, Learning and Collaboration Technologies: Learning and Teaching (Part II), edited by Panayiotis Zaphiris and Andri Ioannou
26. LNCS 10926, Human Aspects of IT for the Aged Population: Acceptance, Communication, and Participation (Part I), edited by Jia Zhou and Gavriel Salvendy
27. LNCS 10927, Human Aspects of IT for the Aged Population: Applications in Health, Assistance, and Entertainment (Part II), edited by Jia Zhou and Gavriel Salvendy
28. CCIS 850, HCI International 2018 Posters Extended Abstracts (Part I), edited by Constantine Stephanidis
29. CCIS 851, HCI International 2018 Posters Extended Abstracts (Part II), edited by Constantine Stephanidis
30. CCIS 852, HCI International 2018 Posters Extended Abstracts (Part III), edited by Constantine Stephanidis

http://2018.hci.international/proceedings

Conference Proceedings Volumes Full List

1. LNCS 10901, Human-Computer Interaction: Theories, Methods, and Human Issues (Part I), edited by Masaaki Kurosu
2. LNCS 10902, Human-Computer Interaction: Interaction in Context (Part II), edited by Masaaki Kurosu
3. LNCS 10903, Human-Computer Interaction: Interaction Technologies (Part III), edited by Masaaki Kurosu
4. LNCS 10904, Human Interface and the Management of Information: Interaction, Visualization, and Analytics (Part I), edited by Sakae Yamamoto and Hirohiko Mori
5. LNCS 10905, Human Interface and the Management of Information: Information in Applications and Services (Part II), edited by Sakae Yamamoto and Hirohiko Mori
6. LNAI 10906, Engineering Psychology and Cognitive Ergonomics, edited by Don Harris
7. LNCS 10907, Universal Access in Human-Computer Interaction: Methods, Technologies, and Users (Part I), edited by Margherita Antona and Constantine Stephanidis
8. LNCS 10908, Universal Access in Human-Computer Interaction: Virtual, Augmented, and Intelligent Environments (Part II), edited by Margherita Antona and Constantine Stephanidis
9. LNCS 10909, Virtual, Augmented and Mixed Reality: Interaction, Navigation, Visualization, Embodiment, and Simulation (Part I), edited by Jessie Y. C. Chen and Gino Fragomeni
10. LNCS 10910, Virtual, Augmented and Mixed Reality: Applications in Health, Cultural Heritage, and Industry (Part II), edited by Jessie Y. C. Chen and Gino Fragomeni
11. LNCS 10911, Cross-Cultural Design: Methods, Tools, and Users (Part I), edited by Pei-Luen Patrick Rau
12. LNCS 10912, Cross-Cultural Design: Applications in Cultural Heritage, Creativity, and Social Development (Part II), edited by Pei-Luen Patrick Rau
13. LNCS 10913, Social Computing and Social Media: User Experience and Behavior (Part I), edited by Gabriele Meiselwitz
14. LNCS 10914, Social Computing and Social Media: Technologies and Analytics (Part II), edited by Gabriele Meiselwitz
15. LNAI 10915, Augmented Cognition: Intelligent Technologies (Part I), edited by Dylan D. Schmorrow and Cali M. Fidopiastis
16. LNAI 10916, Augmented Cognition: Users and Contexts (Part II), edited by Dylan D. Schmorrow and Cali M. Fidopiastis
17. LNCS 10917, Digital Human Modeling and Applications in Health, Safety, Ergonomics, and Risk Management, edited by Vincent G. Duffy
18. LNCS 10918, Design, User Experience, and Usability: Theory and Practice (Part I), edited by Aaron Marcus and Wentao Wang

5th International Conference on HCI in Business, Government, and Organizations

Program Board Chair(s): **Fiona Fui-Hoon Nah and Bo Sophia Xiao, USA**

The full list with the Program Board Chairs and the members of the Program Boards of all thematic areas and affiliated conferences is available online at:

http://www.hci.international/board-members-2018.php

HCI International 2019

The 21st International Conference on Human-Computer Interaction, HCI International 2019, will be held jointly with the affiliated conferences in Orlando, FL, USA, at Walt Disney World Swan and Dolphin Resort, July 26–31, 2019. It will cover a broad spectrum of themes related to Human-Computer Interaction, including theoretical issues, methods, tools, processes, and case studies in HCI design, as well as novel interaction techniques, interfaces, and applications. The proceedings will be published by Springer. More information will be available on the conference website: http://2019.hci.international/.

General Chair
Prof. Constantine Stephanidis
University of Crete and ICS-FORTH
Heraklion, Crete, Greece
E-mail: general_chair@hcii2019.org

http://2019.hci.international/

Contents

Electronic Commerce and Consumer Behavior

Social Media and Social Communities in Business

Social Innovation

Business Analytics and Visualization

Information Systems in Business

In AI We Trust: Characteristics Influencing Assortment Planners' Perceptions of AI Based Recommendation Agents

Emilie Bigras[1]([✉]), Marc-Antoine Jutras[1], Sylvain Sénécal[1],
Pierre-Majorique Léger[1], Chrystel Black[2], Nicolas Robitaille[2],
Karine Grande[2], and Christian Hudon[2]

[1] HEC Montréal, Montréal, Canada
emilie.bigras@hec.ca
[2] JDA Labs, Montréal, Canada

Abstract. While creating an optimal assortment of products, assortment planners need to take into account an important amount of information, which leads to a certain level of uncertainty. These trade-offs can diminish the quality of the assortment decisions made by the planners. To reduce their impact, assortment planners can now use artificial intelligence (AI) based recommendation agents (RAs) throughout their decision-making process, thus benefiting from their ability to process a large quantity of information to improve their decisions. However, research on user-RA shows that there are some challenges to their adoption. For instance, RA adoption depends on the users perceived credibility of its recommendations. Hence, this study investigates how the richness of the information provided by the RA and the necessary effort to access this information influences the assortment planners' usage behavior (visual attention) and perceptions (credibility, satisfaction, performance, intention to adopt the RA). A within-subject lab experiment was conducted with twenty participants. The results show the importance of the RA's recommendations that include easily accessible explanations of the variables included in their calculations on the usage behavior, perceptions, and decision quality of the assortment planners. These findings contribute to the HCI literature and the theory of RA adoption in B2B contexts by providing insights on features enhancing employee adoption.

Keywords: Recommendation agent · Artificial intelligence · Credibility
Perception · Behavior · Eye tracking

1 Introduction

Creating an optimal assortment of products is one of the most basic yet critical decision assortment planners must make for retailers [1]. In order to create an optimal assortment of products, assortment planners need to take into consideration qualitative and quantitative criteria [2]. These criteria include a great number of variables (e.g., past sales, retail trends, inventory, customers' needs, sales forecast) that must be taken into account by the assortment planners, which creates a certain level of uncertainty. This level of uncertainty results from the important amount of information that needs to be

© Springer International Publishing AG, part of Springer Nature 2018
F. F.-H. Nah and B. S. Xiao (Eds.): HCIBGO 2018, LNCS 10923, pp. 3–16, 2018.
https://doi.org/10.1007/978-3-319-91716-0_1

considered by the assortment planners throughout their decision-making process. Hence, the information load could negatively impact the assortment decision quality [3] which could lead to losses in both current and future sales due to customers exits [1].

To reduce the impact of these trade-offs, artificial intelligence (AI) based recommender systems can be used as an aid by assortment planners throughout their decision-making process [4]. By processing a large quantity of decision relevant information, AI based recommendation agents (RAs) can help assortment planners define an optimal assortment more easily [5]. Though AI based RAs are becoming more present in the workplace, most research on RA adoption has focused on consumer adoption, not employee adoption [6, 7]. Understanding the way professionals use and perceive RAs, and more importantly, what RA characteristics encourage their adoption and continuous usage will contribute to advancing knowledge in the human-computer interaction (HCI) literature. In addition, it will inform the human interaction community on how to best present decision recommendations in order to create better RA interactions.

Therefore, the main objective of this study is to investigate how assortment planners' usage behavior and perceptions of RAs are influenced by the way recommendations are presented. This study contributes to theory on RA adoption in B2B contexts and has implications for RA developers by providing insights on features that would enhance RA adoption by employees.

2 Development of Hypotheses

In the RA literature, two main factors have been investigated [8, 9]. The first factor, information richness, is associated with the amount of information provided by the RA to assist assortment planners throughout their decision-making process. The scientific literature shows that user acceptance towards RAs increases with perceived transparency [10]. The perception of transparency is recognized when the logical reasoning behind an RA is explained [11, 12]. The need for explanations and justifications are specifically triggered when users are supporting their decisions through knowledge-based systems [13]. The second factor, effort, is related to the number of steps required to get to the information (e.g., number of screens). Thus, in a high effort condition, the number of steps required to get to the information is greater than in a low effort condition. In addition to processing information, assortment planners need, in order to make an assortment decision, to gather the decision-relevant information which can lead to information load [10]. Due to the limited capacity of individuals to process information, information overload can result in cognitive fatigue and confusion [14]. Hence, processing and obtaining a large quantity of information can negatively affect the assortment planners' decision-making process by reducing the quality of their decisions [3].

According to the literature, explanations about the recommendations presented have been demonstrated to positively influence the RA's perceived credibility [15], satisfaction [16], and performance (i.e., decision quality) [8]. In this study, the source credibility dimensions of trustworthiness (i.e., the recommendations of the RA are identified by the users as reliable) and expertise (i.e., the RA is recognized by the users as knowing the right answer) have been observed [17]. In order to establish trust and show the expertise behind the recommendations of the RA, transparency of the recommendation process is crucial [18]. Explaining this process increases users trust in the RA's recommendations [10]. Furthermore, the perceived ease of use of the RA is also related to RA trust [19]. According to Pereira [20], the cognitive load of gathering and processing information can negatively impact the perceived satisfaction and performance of the decision-making process. Therefore, finding a balance between information richness and effort seems to be crucial.

H1: Assortment planners' perceptions toward the RA regarding credibility (H1a), satisfaction (H1b), and performance (H1c) will be more positive when the RA's recommendations include easily accessible explanations.

Moreover, trust towards RAs is needed to foster their adoption, but trust in RAs is difficult to build [21]. Initial trust is thus essential in influencing users' continuous usage [22, 23]. However, users experiencing information overload, even in the absence of trust, are likely to consult the RA's recommendations more frequently [9]. Thus, accepting the recommendations of the RA due to cognitive fatigue of confusion [14].

H2: Assortment planners will consult each recommendation of the RA more frequently when the RA's recommendations are enhanced with explanations that are difficult to access.

Research also shows that when trust is built, the risk perceived in adopting the RA's recommendations is then diminished [23]. Hence, when RA trust increases, the usage of the RA follows [24]. Without knowledgeable explanations that are perceived as credible by the users, the recommendations of the RA are expected to be ignored [19, 25]. Therefore, understanding the logical reasoning behind the recommendations of the RA seems to be important for users.

H3: When the RA's recommendations are explained, assortment planners will allocate their visual attention more towards the information explaining these recommendations at the beginning of the decision-making process, rather than at the end.

According to the literature, the presence of information load diminishes users' reluctance towards using RA recommendations [9]. By perceiving the usefulness of the RA's recommendations through explanations, users are more inclined in adopting these recommendations during their decision-making process [19, 26]. The users' intention in adopting the RA also increases when RA credibility is perceived [21, 23, 27]. Hence, users are known to prefer transparent recommendations to non-transparent recommendations [18].

H4: Assortment planners will have a higher intention of adopting the RA throughout their decision-making process (i.e., RA used as a delegated agent or as a decision aid) when the RA's recommendations include explanations.

Furthermore, the important number of trade-offs made by the assortment planners during their decision-making process, trying to balance a great number of variables (e.g., past sales, retail trends, inventory, customers' needs, sales forecast), indicates that the product assortment created by an assortment planner will always vary from one assortment planner to another [1]. Consequently, an optimal product assortment might not be fully optimal, which in turn diminishes the performance of the assortment planners. The cognitive load of gathering and processing information can negatively impact the quality of the decisions taken by users [20]. With the help of RAs, this cognitive load can be reduced through recommendations [28]. However, in order to increase the quality of the decisions taken by the users, the RA's recommendations need to be considered [20, 29].

> H5: When the RA's recommendations are complemented with easily accessible explanations, assortment planners will have a higher performance (i.e., decision quality).

3   Method

To test our hypotheses, a within-subject laboratory experiment was conducted. A total of twenty logistics and marketing professionals ($M_{age} = 26$, SD = 3.92; 9 women) participated in the study. During the experiment, participants used the experimental RA prototype for assortment planning developed by JDA Labs (Montreal, Canada). Overall, the experiment lasted two hours and each participant received a $30 gift card as a compensation. This project was approved by the Institutional Review Board (IRB) of our institution and each participant completed a consent form.

3.1   Experimental Design and Protocol

Participants had to make assortment decisions in six tasks and were allowed to take as much time as they needed for each task (about 5 min per task). These tasks were divided into two similar fictitious scenarios that were counterbalanced, three tasks per scenario. The three tasks of each scenario were counterbalanced and each task was exposing participants to a particular recommendation representation condition based on the two experimental factors (i.e., effort required to access information and information richness). Task 1 represented a low richness & low effort condition (T1), Task 2 reflected a high richness & low effort condition (T2), and Task 3 was a high richness & high effort condition (T3). Due to time constraints in the experiment and to avoid participant fatigue, the low richness & high effort condition was not included in the experiment. In order to familiarize participants with the assortment planning software, each scenario began with a practice task with no RA.

A total of 24 distinctive products per task were presented to participants for each scenario (24 products × 6 tasks). Participants were required to make an assortment decision by selecting the optimal assortment of products from the 24 displayed products (see Fig. 1). Each scenario specified the total number of products (ranging from 6 to 7) that needed to be selected for each task. Figure 1 represents the elements that were displayed for each product and in each condition to the participants. The product score, RA's recommendation, was generated using AI. This product score varied between 0 to 100 and was surrounded by a circle that changed colour depending on the score number (i.e., green > 66, 66 $\geq$ orange > 33, and red $\leq$ 33).

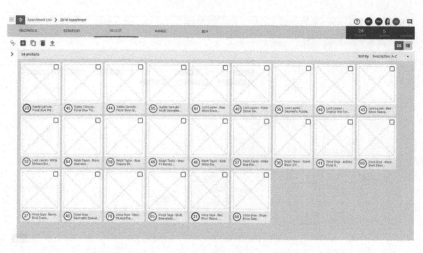

Fig. 1. For each task, 24 products were presented to the participants. Each product was presented with an image, its name including its brand, and its product score (i.e., RA's recommendation). (Color figure online)

For T1 (low richness & low effort), the product score represented in Fig. 1 was the only source of information made available to the participants. For T2 (high richness condition & low effort) and T3 (high richness & high effort), the product score was also made available to participants, however, participants could also acquire further product information by clicking on each product. Additional information included various product characteristics, e.g., attributes, past sales, margin and comparative products. The effort required to access additional information varied between T2 and T3. For T2,

Fig. 2. For T2, each product had a modal window that was used to access the explanations of its product score (i.e., RA's recommendation).

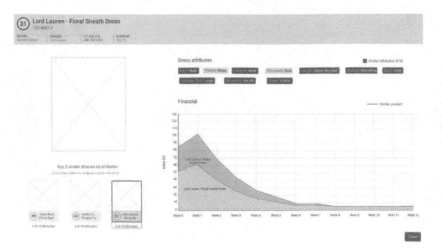

Fig. 3. For T3, each product had a new page presenting an additional layer of difficulty to access explanations of the RA's recommendation.

the information was made available through a modal window (see Fig. 2). As for T3, accessing the information necessitated additional navigation through a different page, thus requiring more effort from participants (see Fig. 3).

3.2 Apparatus and Measures

The experimental prototype for assortment planning by JDA Labs (Montreal, Canada) was made available to the participants through a 1680×1050 resolution monitor. This prototype was developed with Axure RP 8. All statistical analyses were performed with SAS 9.4.

Psychometric Measures. After each task, participants completed a questionnaire. This questionnaire used validated measurement scales to assess the participants' perceptions towards the RA regarding credibility [17], satisfaction [30], and type of future usage (i.e., RA used as a decision aid or as a delegated agent [24]). Participants were also asked to rate their perceived task performance (from 1 to 10).

Performance Measures. The performance of the participants was measured exclusively for the first scenario, because JDA Labs was only able to provide predetermined optimal assortments for this scenario. The guidelines of the first scenario, combined with all the additional information made available to the participants, led to a predetermined optimal assortment for each task. Each final assortment, for each task and each participant, was compared to the predetermined optimal assortment. When a product in the final assortment of the participant was also in the predetermined optimal assortment, one point was given. For each participant and each task, results were calculated as percentages. Thus, a performance score was created.

Behavioral Measures. During each task, the visual attention of the participants was captured at a 60 Hz sampling rate with a Smart Eye Pro system (Gothenburg, Sweden). A 9-point calibration grid was used. For each participant, calibration was repeated until sufficient accuracy was obtained ($\pm$ 2 degrees of accuracy). The MAPPS 2016.1 software was used to analyse the eye tracking data. For each RA product score (see Fig. 1) and for each modal window or new page with additional information that was consulted by the participants, areas of interest (AOIs) were generated. The number and duration of ocular fixations, for each AOI, were collected. An ocular fixation was accepted at 200 ms [31] (Fig. 4).

Fig. 4. Experimental set-up.

4 Results and Analysis

H1 stipulates that the assortment planners' perceptions toward the RA regarding credibility (H1a), satisfaction (H1b), and performance (H1c) will be higher in the high richness & low effort condition. A linear regression with random intercept and a two-tailed level of significance adjusted for multiple comparisons was used to test the difference between the means of assortment planners' perceptions for each combination of conditions (see Table 1). First, results suggest that the perceptions of the participants toward the RA regarding credibility and satisfaction are positively affected when information on the different variables included in the calculations of the RA's recommendations is present (T2 and T3 greater than T1 with one-tailed level of significance, respectively 0.7055, p $\leq$ .0001 and 0.6139, p $\leq$ .0001; 0.6068, p = .0027 and 0.5103, p = .0077). However, no difference was found between the high richness conditions (T2 and T3) and the low richness condition (T1) for the participants' perceived performance toward the RA. Second, although results show that the assortment planners' perceptions toward the RA in terms of performance is impacted negatively by the effort required to access information (T2 greater than T3 with one-tailed level of significance, 0.4706, p = .0474), no difference between high richness & low effort (T2) and high richness & high effort (T3) was found on the perceptions of the participants toward the RA regarding credibility and satisfaction. Hence, H1a, H1b, and H1c are partially supported.

Table 1. Participants' perceptions results

	Hypothesis	Result	Estimate	p-value[a]
Credibility	H1a	T2 > T1	0.7055	< .0001
		T3 > T1	0.6139	< .0001
Satisfaction	H1b	T2 > T1	0.6068	0.0054
		T3 > T1	0.5103	0.0154
Performance	H1c	T2 > T3	0.4706	0.0948

[a] Two-tailed level of significance

In order to test H2, a Poisson regression with a mixed model adjusted for multiple comparisons with a two-tailed level of significance was performed. Thus, the difference between the least square means of the number of fixations for the AOIs of the different conditions was tested (i.e., the number of fixations on all the product scores of one condition versus another). Results revealed that participants, when in the high richness & high effort condition (T3), are consulting the product scores more frequently than when in the low richness & low effort and high richness & low effort conditions (T1 and T2), which provides strong support for H2 (T3 is greater than T1 and T2 with one-tailed level of significance, respectively 1.1617, p = .0054; 0.7471, p = .0225).

We also hypothesized that assortment planners, when in a high richness condition (i.e., high richness & low effort and high richness & high effort), will allocate their visual attention more towards the information explaining the different variables included in the product score (i.e., RA's recommendation) at the beginning of the decision-making process, rather than at the end (H3). To test H3, the difference between the first 25% and the last 25% of the number of fixations and the task duration for each AOI of each condition was compared by using a Wilcoxon signed rank test with a two-tailed level of significance. Results revealed no difference through time concerning frequency and the time spent by the participants on the RA's recommendations. In addition, results showed that participants, when in the high richness & low effort condition (T2), consulted more frequently and for a longer period of time the information on the different variables included in the calculations of the RA's recommendations at the beginning of the task (p = .0137 and p = .0171, respectively with a one-tailed level of significance). Furthermore, results also revealed that when in the high richness & high effort condition (T3), participants consulted this additional information for a longer period of time, but not more frequently, at the beginning of the task (p = .0279 with a one-tailed level of significance and p = .1104, respectively). These results were also in line with a similar test that was conducted to compare the difference between the first 40% and the last 40% of the number of fixations and the task duration for each AOI of each condition. Hence, these results partially confirm H3.

Moreover, the difference between the means of assortment planners perceived intention to adopt the RA throughout their decision-making process (i.e., RA used as a delegated agent or as a decision aid) for each combination of conditions was analyzed with a linear regression with random intercept and a two-tailed level of significance adjusted for multiple comparisons (see Table 2). Results show that, when in a high richness condition (i.e., high richness & low effort and high richness & high effort), participants had a higher intention of adopting the RA as a delegated agent and as a decision aid than when in the low richness & low effort condition (T2 and T3 are greater than T1 with one-tailed level of significance, respectively 0.8503, p = .0001; 0.5647, p = .008 and 1.0705, p = .0001; 0.9681, p = .0002). These results confirm H4.

Table 2. Participants' intention to adopt the RA for future usage results

	Hypothesis	Result	Estimate	p-value[a]
The intention to adopt the RA as a delegated agent	H4	T2 > T1	0.8503	0.0003
		T3 > T1	0.5647	0.016
The intention to adopt the RA as a decision aid		T2 > T1	1.0705	0.0002
		T3 > T1	0.9681	0.0005

[a] Two-tailed level of significance

To compare the difference between the intention to adopt the RA as a delegated agent and the intention to adopt the RA as a decision aid for each condition, a Wilcoxon signed rank test with a two-tailed level of significance was conducted. For all three conditions, results propose that participants are more inclined to adopt the RA as a decision aid than as a delegated agent (T1: p ≤ .0001; T2: p ≤ .0001; T3: p ≤ .0001).

H5 specifies that the assortment planners' performance will be higher in the high richness & low effort condition compared to the other two conditions (i.e., low richness & low effort and high richness & high effort conditions). In order to test this hypothesis, a linear regression with a mixed model adjusted for multiple comparisons with a two-tailed level of significance was used. Results show that participants had a higher performance in the high richness & low effort condition, which confirms H5 (T2 is greater than T1 and T3 with one-tailed level of significance, respectively 1.0500, p = .0001 and 0.2330, p = .0001). Furthermore, no difference between low richness & low effort (T1) and high richness & high effort was found (T3) (Table 3).

Table 3. Participants' performance results

	Hypothesis	Result	Estimate	p-value[a]
Performance	H5	T2 > T1	1.0500	0.0002
		T2 > T3	0.2330	0.0002

[a] Two-tailed level of significance

To explore different AOIs which most attracted the visual attention of the high-performance and the low-performance participants, a Poisson regression with a mixed model, and a linear regression with a mixed model, both with a two-tailed level of significance adjusted for multiple comparisons, were performed. Thus, testing the difference between the least square means of the number of fixations and the duration of the AOIs for the different conditions for each level of performance. Results revealed that when in a high richness condition (T2 and T3), high-performance participants consulted the product scores more frequently but not for a longer period of time (T2 and T3 greater than T1, respectively 1.6405, p $\leq$ .0001 and -0.5500, p = 0.2052; 1.6323, p $\leq$ .0001 and -0.8942, p = 0.1145). In addition, no difference between high richness & low effort (T2) and high richness & high effort (T3) was found concerning the frequency, or the period of time in which the information explaining the different variables included in the product score was consulted. Compared to the high-performance participants, the low-performance participants spend the same amount of time and consulted the product scores as frequently throughout the different conditions. Moreover, a significant difference between high richness & low effort (T2) and high richness & high effort (T3) was found concerning the frequency but not the period of time in which the information explaining the different variables included in the product score was consulted (0.7539, p = 0.005 and 0.1535, p = .7379), thus indicating the effort required to access information impacted the low-performance participants.

5   Discussion and Concluding Comments

Results revealed that: (1) an RA providing rich information is perceived as more credible (H1a) and satisfactory (H1b); (2) users' perceived performance is negatively influenced by the effort required to access information (H1c); (3) the RA's recommendations are consulted more frequently by the assortment planners when the product scores are enhanced with difficult to access explanations (H2); (4) users are consulting consistently the product scores throughout their decision-making process; (5) when the RA provides additional information, planners are consulting this information more often at the beginning of their decision-making process (H3); (6) the intention to adopt the RA significantly increases with the richness of information, thus indicating that assortment planners seem to favor the recommendations of an RA when they are enhanced with additional information about the variables included in their calculations (H4); (7) users are more willing to adopt the RA as a decision aid than as a delegated agent; (8) the performance of the users is significantly higher when the RA provided rich information that was easily accessible (H5).

This paper's main theoretical implication is related to the advancement of RA adoption in B2B contexts. As AI is becoming more common in the workplace [32], it is essential to understand how to best present AI based recommendations in order to positively influence professionals' usage behavior and perceptions toward a RA. The findings in this study show the importance of RA's recommendations that are enhanced with easily accessible information. A RA providing rich information on the variables included in the calculations of its recommendations (i.e., product scores) increases assortment planners' perceptions toward the RA regarding credibility and satisfaction. These findings are in line with the literature focusing on the RA adoption of consumers [15, 16]. Furthermore, the intention of the professionals to adopt this RA also increases with information richness. However, planners seem more willing to adopt the RA as a decision aid than as a delegated agent. Though in a consumer RA adoption context, this could be explained by the importance of a product purchase [24]. In a professional context, assortment planners could feel that following only the RA's recommendations in their decision-making process would diminish their performance, thus negatively affecting the quality of their assortment decisions [33]. Moreover, the RA's recommendations, when enhanced with additional information that is accessible through an increased effort, are consulted more frequently by the users. This indicates the degree of importance that is given by the assortment planners to the product scores [34] when experiencing information overload [9]. This could also explain why the planners perceived a higher performance when the additional information was easily accessible. In addition, the performance (i.e., decision quality) of the assortment planners increases with information richness and decreases with the effort to access this information.

This study also has implications for RA developers and UX designers. First, results show that professional users need to have access to information about the variables included in the calculations of the RA's recommendations in order to increase perceived credibility and satisfaction. That being said, the tremendous amount of data behind the AI based recommendations needs to be brought forward to the users in a condensed intuitive form [35]. Hence, a visual representation of this condensed form must be created by designers. Second, this additional information seems to be a key element in the adoption of a RA. Results revealed that assortment planners consulted the additional information that was easily accessible to them more frequently and for a longer period of time at the beginning of their decision-making process. This usage behavior indicates that the degree of importance [34] and cognitive engagement [36] toward this information decreases over time, emphasizing the importance of initial trust. Explaining the recommendation process increases professionals' initial trust towards the RA's recommendations, which then influences positively their continued usage of this RA [10, 22]. These insights can contribute to building best practices in UX design for AI.

Before applying these results, two limitations of this study need to be acknowledged. First, the low richness & high effort condition has not been tested in this experiment, due to time constraints and to avoid participant fatigue. Thus, future research should include this condition in order to extend the results of this study. Second, the two fictitious scenarios, in this experiment, informed participants that they were working for a fashion company which entailed that clothes were used as products (i.e., dresses and male upper body clothing). Hence, additional studies using a more complex category of products could help generalize the results of this study.

In conclusion, more research is needed to better understand the way RAs are used by professional users. For example, emotional and cognitive state at fixation on RA could be assessed using techniques proposed by Léger et al. [37] and Courtemanche et al. [38]. These additional studies could provide further guidelines to RA developers and UX designers. Results of this study revealed that the usage of the assortment planners changed throughout their decision-making process, which confirms that user behavior changes over time [39, 40] However, understanding how the user-RA relationship changes in terms of behaviors and perceptions over time could show that the explanations of the RA's recommendations become decreasingly significant and indeed unnecessary after a while, with the users then relying predominantly on the RA's recommendations to make decisions.

Acknowledgments. We are thankful for the financial support of the Natural Sciences and Engineering Research Council of Canada (NSERC).

References

1. Mantrala, M.K., Levy, M., Kahn, B.E., Fox, E.J., Gaidarev, P., Dankworth, B., Shah, D.: Why is assortment planning so difficult for retailers? A framework and research agenda. J. Retail. **85**(1), 71–83 (2009)
2. Brijs, T., Swinnen, G., Vanhoof, K., Wets, G.: Using association rules for product assortment decisions: a case study. In: Proceedings of the Fifth ACM SIGKDD International Conference on Knowledge Discovery and Data Mining (KDD 1999), pp. 254–260. ACM, New York (1999)
3. Lurie, N.H.: Decision making in information-rich environments: the role of information structure. J. Consum. Res. **30**(4), 473–486 (2004)
4. Wang, L., Zeng, X., Koehl, L., Chen, Y.: Intelligent fashion recommender system: fuzzy logic in personalized garment design. IEEE Trans. Hum. Mach. Syst. **45**(1), 95–109 (2015)
5. Dellaert, B.C., Häubl, G.: Searching in choice mode: consumer decision processes in product search with recommendations. J. Mark. Res. **49**(2), 277–288 (2012)
6. Senecal, S., Nantel, J.: The influence of online product recommendations on consumers' online choices. J. Retail. **80**(2), 159–169 (2004)
7. Wang, W., Benbasat, I.: Interactive decision aids for consumer decision making in e-commerce: the influence of perceived strategy restrictiveness. MIS Q. **33**(2), 293–320 (2009)
8. Wang, W.: Design of trustworthy online recommendation agents: explanation facilities and decision strategy support. Doctoral dissertation. University of British Columbia (2005)
9. Aljukhadar, M., Senecal, S., Daoust, C.-E.: Using recommendation agents to cope with information overload. Int. J. Electron. Commer. **17**(2), 41–70 (2012)
10. Pu, P., Chen, L.: Trust building with explanation interfaces. In: Proceedings of the 11th International Conference on Intelligent User Interfaces (IUI 2006), pp. 93–100. ACM, New York (2006)
11. Nilashi, M., Jannach, D., Ibrahim, O.B., Esfahani, M.D., Ahmadi, H.: Recommendation quality, transparency, and website quality for trust-building in recommendation agents. Electron. Commer. Res. Appl. **19**, 70–84 (2016)
12. Swearingen, K., Sinha, R.: Beyond algorithms: an HCI perspective on recommender systems. In: ACM SIGIR 2001 Workshop on Recommender Systems, pp. 1–11. ACM, New York (2001)
13. Gregor, S.: Explanations from knowledge-based systems and cooperative problem solving: an empirical study. Int. J. Hum. Comput. Stud. **54**(1), 81–105 (2001)
14. Eppler, M., Mengis, J.: The concept of information overload: a review of literature from organization science, accounting, marketing, MIS, and related disciplines. Inf. Soc. **20**(5), 325–344 (2004)

15. Heesacker, M., Petty, R.E., Cacioppo, J.T.: Field dependence and attitude change: source credibility can alter persuasion by affecting message-relevant thinking. J. Pers. **51**(4), 653–666 (1983)
16. Xiao, B., Benbasat, I.: E-commerce product recommendation agents: use, characteristics, and impact. MIS Q. **31**(1), 137–209 (2007)
17. Ohanian, R.: Construction and validation of a scale to measure celebrity endorsers' perceived expertise, trustworthiness, and attractiveness. J. Advert. **19**(3), 39–52 (1990)
18. Sinha, R., Swearingen, K.: The role of transparency in recommender systems. In: Extended Abstracts on Human Factors in Computing Systems (CHI 2002), pp. 830–831. ACM, New York (2002)
19. Wang, W., Benbasat, I.: Trust in and adoption of online recommendation agents. J. Assoc. Inf. Syst. **6**(3), 72–101 (2005)
20. Pereira, R.E.: Influence of query-based decision aids on consumer decision making in electronic commerce. Inf. Resour. Manag. J. **14**(1), 31–48 (2001)
21. Lemoine, J.-F., Cherif, E.: Comment générer de la confiance envers un agent virtuel à l'aide de ses caractéristiques? Une étude exploratoire. Manag. Avenir **58**(8), 169–188 (2012)
22. Wang, W., Benbasat, I.: Recommendation agents for electronic commerce: effects of explanation facilities on trusting beliefs. J. Manag. Inf. Syst. **23**(4), 217–246 (2007)
23. Hengstler, M., Enkel, E., Duelli, S.: Applied artificial intelligence and trust - the case of autonomous vehicles and medical assistance devices. Technol. Forecast. Soc. Change **105**, 105–120 (2016)
24. Komiak, S.Y., Benbasat, I.: The effects of personalization and familiarity on trust and adoption of recommendation agents. MIS Q. **30**(4), 941–960 (2006)
25. Zanker, M.: The influence of knowledgeable explanations on users' perception of a recommender system. In: Proceedings of the Sixth ACM Conference on Recommender Systems (RecSys 2012), pp. 269–272. ACM, New York (2012)
26. Qiu, L., Benbasat, I.: Evaluating anthropomorphic product recommendation agents: a social relationship perspective to designing information systems. J. Manag. Inf. Syst. **25**(4), 145–181 (2009)
27. Xiao, S., Benbasat, I.: The formation of trust and distrust in recommendation agents in repeated interactions: a process-tracing analysis. In: Proceedings of the 5th International Conference on Electronic Commerce (ICEC 2003), pp. 287–293. ACM, New York (2003)
28. Häubl, G., Trifts, V.: Consumer decision making in online shopping environments: the effects of interactive decision aids. Mark. Sci. **19**(1), 4–21 (2000)
29. Huseynov, F., Huseynov, S.Y., Özkan, S.: The influence of knowledge-based e-commerce product recommender agents on online consumer decision-making. Inf. Dev. **32**(1), 81–90 (2016)
30. Sirdeshmukh, D., Singh, J., Sabol, B.: Consumer trust, value, and loyalty in relational exchanges. J. Mark. **66**(1), 15–37 (2002)
31. Rayner, K.: Eye movements in reading and information processing: 20 years of research. Psychol. Bull. **124**(3), 372–422 (1998)
32. Andrews, W., Sau, M., Dekate, C., Mullen, A., Brant, K.F., Revang, M., Plummer, D.C.: Predicts 2018: Artificial Intelligence. Gartner (2017)
33. Spreitzer, G.M., Mishra, A.K.: Giving up control without losing control: trust and its substitutes' effects on managers' involving employees in decision making. Group Organ. Manag. **24**(2), 155–187 (1999)
34. Chen, S., Epps, J.: Automatic classification of eye activity for cognitive load measurement with emotion interference. Comput. Methods Program. Biomed. **110**(2), 111–124 (2013)
35. Nilsson, N.J.: Principles of Artificial Intelligence. Morgan Kaufmann, Burlington (2014)

36. Just, M.A., Carpenter, P.A.: Eye fixations and cognitive processes. Cogn. Psychol. **8**(4), 441–480 (1976)
37. Léger, P.M., Sénécal, S., Courtemanche, F., de Guinea, A.O., Titah, R., Fredette, M., Labonté-LeMoyne, É.: Precision is in the eye of the beholder: application of eye fixation-related potentials to information systems research. J. Assoc. Inf. Syst. **15**(10), 651–678 (2014)
38. Courtemanche, F., Léger, P.M., Dufresne, A., Fredette, M., Labonté-LeMoyne, É., Sénécal, S.: Physiological heatmaps: a tool for visualizing users' emotional reactions. Multimed. Tools Appl., 1–28 (2017)
39. Knijnenburg, B.P., Willemsen, M.C., Gantner, Z., Soncu, H., Newell, C.: Explaining the user experience of recommender systems. User Model. User Adapt. Interact. **22**(4–5), 441–504 (2012)
40. Sénécal, S., Fredette, M., Léger, P.-M., Courtemanche, F., Riedl, R.: Consumers' cognitive lock-in on websites: evidence from a neurophysiological study. J. Internet Commer. **14**(3), 277–293 (2015)

Activity Simulation for Experiential Learning in Cybersecurity Workforce Development

John Burris[1(✉)], Wesley Deneke[2(✉)], and Brandon Maulding[1]

[1] Southeastern Louisiana University, Hammond, LA 70402, USA
jburris@southeastern.edu
[2] Western Washington University, Bellingham, WA 98225, USA
Wesley.Deneke@wwu.edu

Abstract. A significant challenge to maintaining security within an organization is the training of a non-technical workforce to respond appropriately to cybersecurity threats. This work describes an online environment that utilizes experiential learning to give non-technical workers an increased exposure to issues in cybersecurity. We present a simulation-based approach that provides a better understanding of specific cybersecurity threats through experiential learning. The presented interface uses simulations of cybersecurity threats to provide concrete experiences rather than descriptions. While moving through the simulation, the user can attempt multiple actions and is provided with an "awareness" measure. For each, the system provides continuous feedback to allow active experimentation. After each threat has been exposed, the environment provides a narrative of the user's actions with suggested improvements to allow for reflective observation. This work includes a user study of the interface, shows the results of usability testing, and evaluates the effectiveness of the training through simulation.

Keywords: Cybersecurity · Experiential learning · Workforce development
Simulation

1 Introduction

Cybersecurity has been described by the National Science Foundation as a defining issue of our time [1]. Entities such as the "Shadow Brokers" have highlighted cybersecurity as a significant weakness in the United States' national security by obtaining classified documents through cyberattack [2]. Global businesses face an estimated cost of $400 billion (US) each year due to cyberattacks [3]. Cybersecurity awareness has become a critical concern not only to organizations, but among individuals as well. Over eight million adults in the United States were victims of identity theft in 2005, with 56% of the victims not even knowing how their personal information was taken from them [4].

A popular response has been the introduction of frameworks that provide standards, guidelines, and best practices to help organizations understand and manage cybersecurity risks. These frameworks have led to national certifications such as CompTIA Security+, Certified Ethical Hacker (CEH), and Certified Information Systems Security

© Springer International Publishing AG, part of Springer Nature 2018
F. F.-H. Nah and B. S. Xiao (Eds.): HCIBGO 2018, LNCS 10923, pp. 17–25, 2018.
https://doi.org/10.1007/978-3-319-91716-0_2

Professional (CISSP) that train and certify security professionals on the policies and responses. This has provided organizations with a means to bolster the cybersecurity awareness of their technical workforce. According to the National Institute of Standards and Technology (NIST), however, these efforts to improve cybersecurity are undermined by a lack of comparable training for the non-technical workforce [5]. Non-technical workers often lack knowledge of how to recognize and respond to cybersecurity threats. Consequently, they become the 'weakest link' in the security circle. Techniques such as shoulder surfing, phishing, dumpster diving, and impersonation are all established techniques that could be addressed with additional awareness and training, but national certifications for the non-technical workforce do not exist today [5].

The problem this work explores is how to expose the non-technical workforce to key cybersecurity threats so that they will have an increased awareness of these threats. Training content must be presented in a way that is natural to the intended trainee. Due to their lack of technical expertise, a trainee may be familiar with checking their email, but may not understand statements used to describe recognizing a potential threat, like "check the sender's domain". Similarly, a trainee may recognize a potential threat, but not be aware of the severity of the threat or how to respond appropriately. Existing solutions for workforce cybersecurity education largely target technical workers, such as security professionals, or lack hands-on training [6–9]. Hands-on training like [10–15] provide effective training through experiential learning, but as before target technical workers.

The focus of this work is the presentation of the training content. This paper introduces a simulation-based approach that emphasizes experiential learning to provide non-technical workers a better understanding of how to recognize and respond to cybersecurity threats. Learning has been the focus of significant research and debate. The theory of Experiential Learning was introduced as early as 1938, but has been increasing in popularity as it has been shown to increase retention and enrich the learning experience. Kolb give four "modes" of learning: (1) concrete experiences, (2) reflective observation, (3) abstract conceptualization, (4) active experimentation. The proposed certification process uses these modes to provide a better understanding of specific cybersecurity threats [16]. Users are presented with simulations of cybersecurity threats to provide concrete experiences. While moving through the simulation, the user can attempt multiple actions and is provided with an "awareness" measure. For each, the system provides continuous feedback to allow active experimentation. After each threat has been exposed, the environment provides a narrative of the user's actions with suggested improvements to allow for reflective observation.

The rest of this paper is organized as follows: the approach for simulating cybersecurity threats is described in Sect. 2. Section 3 evaluates the results gathered from a system prototype. Finally, conclusions and next steps are summarized in Sect. 4.

2 Using Experiential Learning for Cybersecurity Workforce Development

2.1 Approach for Simulating Cybersecurity Threats

This work describes a prototype of a system that uses simulations of cybersecurity threats to provide concrete experiences rather than traditional descriptions such as videos or textual narratives. While moving through the simulation, the user is able to attempt multiple actions and provide an "awareness" measure. For each, the system provides continuous feedback to allow active experimentation. After each threat is exposed, the environment provides a narrative of the user's actions with suggested improvements to allow for reflective observation.

As an example, the user could select "Phishing" as a cybersecurity threat. Phishing is the process of sending emails to manipulate recipients into providing personal information. To simulate such a scenario, the user would progress to a simulated email client. The user's email address is shown as user@example.com. They receive an email from boss@example.com with an "important" attachment. Note the domain of the "boss" account is misspelled. This provides a concrete experience of a real-world phishing attempt. This simulation is conceptualized in Fig. 1. The simulation shown in Fig. 1 will progress the user through emails that are not at risk of being phishing attempts to judge the competency of the user both when a threat is present and when there are no threats. In addition, the simulation will repeat scenarios until the responses demonstrate a determined level of competency.

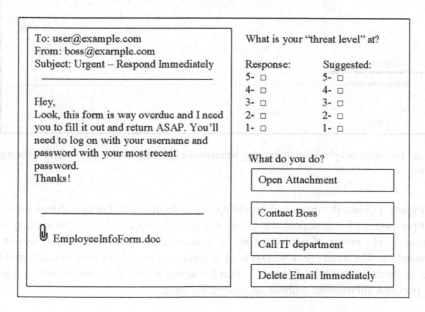

Fig. 1. A mockup of a simulated cybersecurity threat - phishing

The implementation of the prototype focused on increasing the amount of feedback during experimentation to maximize retention. Using previous guidelines for color selection and components, a traditional green/red color scheme was used for positive and negative feedback respectively [17]. The prototype design also considered the possible reasons for non-use [18]. The text of emails were chosen so that it would seem relevant to any industry or position to avoid issues such as disenfranchisement or disenchantment. The vocabulary and traditional design were chosen to prevent active resistance to the training. These issues were addressed to increase usage and engagement for the purpose of increased learning and retention. The initial prototype can be seen in Fig. 2. Figure 2 displays the beginning of a threat simulation. The colors are homogenous to draw attention first to the content being displayed to the user for evaluation and response. At this point, the instructional text has been minimized. Audio instructions provide additional details to the user.

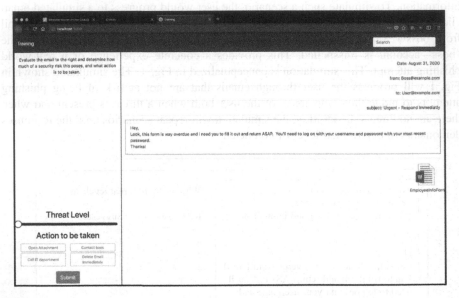

Fig. 2. Prototype of cybersecurity training simulation as initially displayed to user. (Color figure online)

Figure 3 shows the prototype providing active feedback to the user. Since there are multiple points of interaction, the consistent use of colors is key to preventing user confusion. The points of interaction are all concentrated on the bottom left section of the interface. The three provided points of interaction are: a slider used to determine the level of threat, a multiple choice selection for action to be taken, and a submit button that prevents submission without an acceptable input.

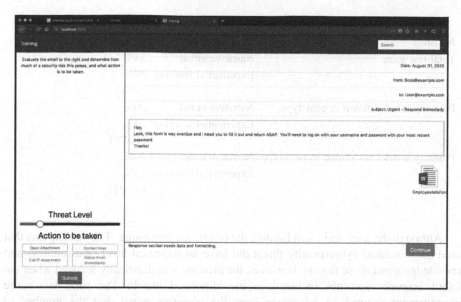

Fig. 3. Prototype of cybersecurity training simulation with active feedback displayed. (Color figure online)

3   Evaluation

A small-scale user study with twenty-nine participants was performed to determine the performance of this approach when compared to a traditional approach for introducing non-technical workers to cybersecurity threats. All twenty-nine participants were given a pretest to determine their awareness of the threat and knowledge of appropriate actions. As a control, fourteen participants were given an email about phishing as sent from a company IT department. Fifteen participants used the prototype for experiential learning as an introduction to phishing. All participants were then given the same questions from the pretest as a posttest.

The test included multiple choice and true/false questions about phishing scams. Six questions were on the types of phishing attacks that were included in the simulation. Four questions were on phishing techniques that were not included in the simulation. The study was designed this way so that the control would maintain the benefit of having the capacity for more information and not having to have the detail required for simulation.

The user study does not include a second posttest to measure the retention for users after an extended period of time. The pretest, training, and posttest were all done in a lab at a single sitting. The process lasted no more than 20 min to complete.

Highlighted increases in scores for each method are shown in Table 1. The results are shown as the total increase in scoring for the key points of interest in the study: the overall increase in performance, the increase in performance for attacks included in the simulation and the increase in performance for attacks not included in the simulation.

Table 1. Results of user study.

Measure	Training type	Change in score (rounded)
Total test score	Narrative email	34%
	Experiential learning	39%
		(+5%)
Phishing attacks shown in prototype	Narrative email	30%
	Experiential learning	54%
		(+24%)
Phishing attacks not shown in prototype	Narrative email	39%
	Experiential learning	15%
		(−24%)

Although the user study was limited, the results are promising. The participants that used the simulated cybersecurity threat did have an increased level of awareness and knowledge about those threats. However, the increase was drastically reduced when the tested scenario was not included in the simulated attack. The total test score improvement showed an advantage over the narrative email, but the number of questions were weighted to phishing attacks that were included in the simulation.

The narrative email resulted in an increased the level of awareness and knowledge on all variations of phishing. The improvements were consistent for both question types and the total test score.

The most significant result is the improvement shown by the questions on phishing attacks that were included in the prototype. A 54% improvement compared to the 30% improvement shown by the control shows that the approach does improve learning. The inverse improvements shown by the approach for questions on phishing attacks not included in the simulation are not as significant since it is more important to show that the improvements are a result of the simulation.

4 Conclusion

4.1 Summary of Results

This work presents an approach for non-technical, cybersecurity workforce development that uses experiential learning to increase the effectiveness of training. A prototype as developed that focused on a single cyber attack. The goal of prototype was to be an interface for education that provided the user with an approachable lesson with potential for experimentation and personal reflection. A user study was conducted to determine the increased awareness and knowledge resulting from the presented approach when compared to a traditional method for preventing cybersecurity attacks.

While significant challenges remain in the development of a comprehensive cybersecurity workforce development system, the initial results show that for non-technical workers, the increase in awareness can be substantial. Possible reasons for these results are the increased level of engagement and decreased disenfranchisement.

4.2 Future Work

Cybersecurity threats continue to evolve and diversify, which makes providing a wide variety of simulation-based training scenarios more desirable. However, training content is currently created manually, which is a time-consuming process that limits the diversity of the content. Future work should explore providing tools that support the rapid development of diverse simulation-based training content for experiential learning. An authoring tool like [19–22] can present authors with an intuitive, visual-based domain-specific language to specify desired simulation content in a declarative manner. The technical specifications of simulation design can be abstracted behind buttons, checkboxes, sliders, and other user interactions of a visual dashboard, such as depicted in Fig. 4. The benefit is that it removes the need to have a human user design content.

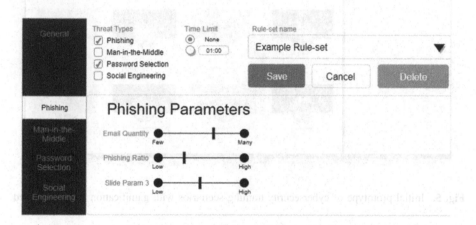

Fig. 4. A mockup of a visual authoring tool

While authoring tools can provide a high-level approach to create and modify training content, a human user must still design and validate the content produced. Another area of future work then is a simulation generator that can dynamically create diverse simulations. Specifications from the authoring tool can feed into an engine that employs procedural generation and AI planning to dynamically produce diverse simulations. Such a solution could provide variation in training content, without the need for manual, human design.

In addition to the authoring and generation tools, future work will include an element of gamification to encourage the completion of the workforce development process. This encouragement to gain exposure to multiple threats and improved response will lead to a more comprehensive understanding of cybersecurity in the non-technical workforce. Gamification is the addition of elements of traditional gameplay to areas outside of gaming. These elements can include scoring, awards, and competition. It is primarily used to increase user engagement in a process [23]. The proposed process for workforce development will use an award system similar to the system used in the internationally recognized award system for the Olympic Games. While not indicative of performance in relation to any other user, it is indicative of the demonstrated level of competency for a particular cybersecurity scenario. An initial component for gamification is shown in Fig. 5.

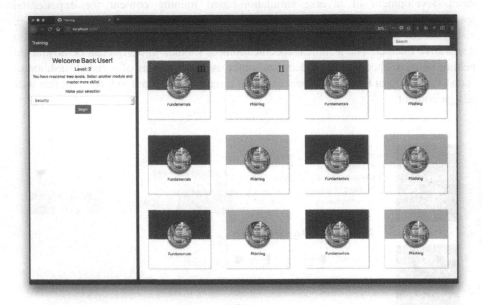

Fig. 5. Initial prototype of cybersecurity training scenarios with gamification aspect included.

References

1. National Science Foundation: Cybersecurity: tech, tools, and training to safeguard the future (2017). https://www.nsf.gov/news/special_reports/cybersecurity/index.jsp. Accessed Nov 2017
2. Aftergood, S.: Cybersecurity: the cold war online. Nature **547**, 30 (2017)
3. Okenyi, P.O., Owens, T.J.: On the anatomy of human hacking. Inf. Syst. Secur. **16**(6), 302–314 (2007)
4. Federal Trade Commission: About Identity Theft (2006). http://www.ftc.gov/bcp/edu/microsites/idtheft/consumers/about-identity-theft.html. Accessed Nov 2017
5. NIST: NIST Impacts: Cybersecurity (2017). https://www.nist.gov/industry-impacts/cybersecurity. Accessed Nov 2017
6. Newhouse, W.: NICE cybersecurity workforce framework: national initiative for cybersecurity education. Special Publication (NIST SP)-800-181 (2017)
7. Paulsen, C., McDuffie, E., Newhouse, W., Toth, P.: NICE: creating a cybersecurity workforce and aware public. IEEE Secur. Priv. **10**(3), 76–79 (2012)
8. Conklin, W., Cline, R., Roosa, T.: Re-engineering cybersecurity education in the US: an analysis of the critical factors. In: IEEE 47th Hawaii International Conference on System Sciences (HICSS) (2014)

 9. Sensato Education & Simulation: Sensato Cybersecurity Solutions. http://www.sensato.co/sensato-education-simulation. Accessed Dec 2017
10. Cheung, R., Cohen, J., Lo, H., Elia, F.: Challenge based learning in cybersecurity education. In: Proceedings of the 2011 International Conference on Security and Management (2011)
11. Assante, M., Tobey, D.: Enhancing the cybersecurity workforce. IT Prof. **13**(1), 12–15 (2011)
12. Abraham, S., Shih, L.: Instructional perspective: towards an integrative learning approach in cybersecurity education. Inf. Secur. Educ. J. **2**(2), 84–90 (2015)
13. Irvine, C., Thompson, M., Allen, K.: Active learning with the CyberCIEGE video game. In: Federal Information Systems Security Educators' Association Conference (2005)
14. Benjamin, C., Irvine, C., Thompson, M.: A video game for cyber security training and awareness. Comput. Secur. **26**(1), 63–72 (2007)
15. Fite, B.: Simulating cyber operations: a cyber security training framework (2014). https://www.sans.org/reading-room/whitepapers/bestprac/simulating-cyber-operations-cyber-security-training-framework-34510. Accessed Dec 2017
16. Kolb, D.A.: Experiential learning: experience as the source of learning and development. Prentice-Hall, Englewood Cliffs (1984)
17. Wright, P., Mosser-Wooley, D., Wooley, B.: Techniques & tools for using color in computer interface design. Crossroads **3**(3), 3–6 (1997)
18. Satchell, C., Dourish, P.: Beyond the user: use and non-use in HCI. In: Proceedings of the 21st Annual Conference of the Australian Computer-Human Interaction Special Interest Group: Design: Open 24/7 (OZCHI 2009), pp. 9–16. ACM, New York (2009)
19. Learning Management System. https://www.agylia.com. Accessed Dec 2017
20. Cyber Security eLearning. https://www.delta-net.com/compliance/cyber-security. Accessed Dec 2017
21. Benjamin, P., Patki, M., Mayer, R.: Using ontologies for simulation modeling. In: IEEE Winter Simulation Conference (WSC 2006) (2006)
22. Miller, J.A., Baramidze, G., Sheth, A., Silver, G., Fishwick, P.: Ontologies for modeling and simulation: an initial framework. In: Computer Science Department, University of Georgia, Athens, GA (2004)
23. Deterding, S., Sicart, M., Nacke, L., O'Hara, K., Dixon, D.: Gamification: using game-design elements in non-gaming contexts. In: CHI 2011 Extended Abstracts on Human Factors in Computing Systems (CHI EA 2011), pp. 2425–2428. ACM, New York (2011)

Relation Extraction in Knowledge Base Question Answering: From General-Domain to the Catering Industry

Hung-Chen Chen[1], Zi-Yuan Chen[1(✉)], Sin-Yi Huang[1], Lun-Wei Ku[1], Yu-Shian Chiu[2], and Wei-Jen Yang[2]

[1] Institute of Information Science, Academia Sinica, Taipei, Taiwan
{hankchen,hsy1106,lwku}@iis.sinica.edu.tw, b02902017@ntu.edu.tw
[2] Institute of Digital Transformation Institute, Institute for Information Industry, Taipei, Taiwan
{samuelchiu,wjyang}@iii.org.tw

Abstract. Knowledge base question answering (KBQA) can be decomposed into entity linking and relation extraction. In KBQA relation extraction, the goal is to find the appropriate relation given the question and its linked entity. Previous work used neural network models to process entities in a pairwise manner, which is well-suited to large relation sets in KBQA. However, such models must execute the same relation detection procedure multiple times for each question to complete an exhaustive search of the relation combinations. In this paper, we propose treating relation extraction in KBQA as a classification problem. Moreover, we introduce a masking layer which filters out less probable relations in advance. Experiments show that the masking mechanism benefits the proposed model by improving the accuracy from 72% to 77%. In addition, a catering knowledge base is constructed automatically in this paper, on which the proposed model yields an accuracy of 89%, demonstrating its effectiveness.

Keywords: Question-answering · Relation detection
Deep learning application · Knowledge-base question answering
Knowledge-base relation extraction

1 Introduction

It has been shown that knowledge bases (KBs) such as DBpedia [1], Freebase [2], and WordNet [3] are effective sources of knowledge for applications such as hypernym detection [4], machine translation [5], and question answering [6–8]. Among these applications, knowledge-based question answering (KBQA), the process of requesting knowledge over a KB using natural language questions, is the most direct approach to access KB knowledge. As the common representation of knowledge graph beliefs is a discrete relational triple showing one relation between two entities, such as LocatedIn (NewOrleans, Louisiana), where the

© Springer International Publishing AG, part of Springer Nature 2018
F. F.-H. Nah and B. S. Xiao (Eds.): HCIBGO 2018, LNCS 10923, pp. 26–41, 2018.
https://doi.org/10.1007/978-3-319-91716-0_3

two entities are two nodes and their relation is the edge between them in the knowledge graph, the procedure of answering a question can be transformed into a traversal that starts from the question entity and searches for the appropriate path to reach the answer entity. Therefore, KBQA can be divided into two major tasks: entity linking and relation extraction. The former discovers the topic entity in the question and then locates this entity in the KB; the latter attempts to discover all the relations in the path which connects the question topic entity and the answer entity. These two tasks are illustrated in Fig. 1. Given the question "What is the name of Justin Bieber brother?", the entity linking process identifies "Justin Bieber" as the topic entity and begins to search for candidate relations from it; the relation extraction process identifies "sibling_s" and "sibling" as the relations in the form of a relation path between the topic entity and the answer entity. In this paper, we focus on relation extraction.

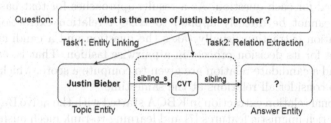

Fig. 1. Two KBQA tasks

Most previous work [6,9] treats the relation extraction task of KBQA as a ranking problem. In contrast, we attempt to solve this task in a more straightforward fashion by regarding it as a multi-class classification task. The challenge then comes from the model optimization with a relatively large search space. Fortunately, some candidate relations can be filtered out in advance by traversing the whole KB to remove unlikely relations and reduce the search space. In this paper, we propose a masking mechanism to prevent our model from selecting these impossible relations. In this paper, we develop and discuss three models: (1) a convolutional neural network-based model (CNN), (2) a convolutional neural network-based model with a masking layer (CNN + masking) and (3) a hybrid convolutional neural network/recurrent neural network model (CNN + RNN). We evaluate the performance of these models on the WebQuestions Semantic Parses Dataset (WebQSP) [10].

In addition to providing effective models, we hope to offer a strong baseline for companies and government agencies who seek to build their own knowledge-based question-answering systems efficiently. Therefore, we describe the construction of the KB for the catering industry for which we apply the proposed models to demonstrate adaptation from the general domain to a specific domain.

The major contributions of this paper are: (1) We propose an effective relation extraction model to extract relations in both general KBs and domain-specific KBs. (2) We demonstrate strong performance on the catering KB and describe details when adapting this general model to a specific domain.

2　Related Work

Determining the relation between two entities is critical for natural language understanding. With the text evidence and the given two mentioned entities, the aim of text-based relation extraction is to predict the relation indicated by the text evidence. Previous methods include labor-intensive feature engineering with SVM [11] and clustering words before relation classification [12] for more sophisticated management of semantics. With the advance of deep learning techniques, relation extraction models have evolved from machine learning models based on word embeddings [13,14] to deep neural networks such as CNNs or LSTMs [15–17] and even more complicated models [18,19]. One of the assumptions in the text-based relation extraction task is that a fixed set of candidate relations is given, with a relatively small size. However, in the KBQA relation extraction task, thousands of relations are included in the KB and all are to be considered for each question. As a result, approaches for text-based relation extraction cannot be directly applied to KBQA relation extraction. Instead, KBQA relation extraction usually takes the question and a candidate relation as the input for its decision process in a pairwise fashion. That is, each time, a question and a candidate relation are given to compute a score, which eliminates the need to consider all relations at the same time.

Traditional relation extraction in KBQA started with the naive Bayes method considering rich linguistic features [7] and learning-to-rank mechanism with hierarchical relations [20]. These were followed by neural network models [6,21,22] with the attention mechanism [18,23] and the residual network [9] in recent years. Though these models are able to handle all relations in a KB sequentially, they must repeat the same process for each candidate relation many times for the final decision. Moreover, when processing one relation, other relations are neglected. This is clearly a drawback for a selection process. To address this problem, we propose a model that combines the advantages of both text-based and KBQA relation extraction, and that considers the large KB relation set using only one forward pass for each question.

3　Method

We first implemented a CNN-based multi-class classifier, the output layer of which is the probability of all the relations in the training data. After we analyzing the errors in this first model, we observed that the major errors were domain errors and semantic meaning errors.

Each relation in Freebase is composed of the following three fragments (tokens): Domain.Type.Property. A domain error indicates the wrong domain field in the predicted relation. For example, the predicted relation is "film.performance.actor" for the question "Who plays ken barlow in coronation street?" when the correct relation is "tv.regular_tv_appearance.actor", where the domain field "tv" is mis-identified as "film".

From our observations, domain errors arise from considering all of the relations in KB, a relative large relation set, regardless of the topic entity. In the above example, "coronation street" is obviously a TV show and will not connect to a relation whose domain is "film". Therefore, we attempt to reduce domain errors by ignoring those highly unlikely relations in advance: we propose a masking mechanism to filter out relations which are not connected to the topic entity within two hops, i.e., relations in the relation path whose length is not greater than two.

Semantic errors, in turn, indicate semantic mismatches between the question and the relation. For example, for the question "Where did they find Jenni Rivera's body?" our model predicts "people.place_lived.location" while the correct answer is "people.deceased_person.place_of_death". In this example, the model did not learn that "find the body" is related more to "death" than to "live". This may due to the design in which the proposed model considers each relation independently as one class but ignores the semantic meaning of its name. In order to solve this problem, we propose the third model, the hybrid CNN/RNN model (CNN + RNN).

For this hybrid model, we collect the relation paths connected to the topic entity whose lengths are equal or less than two (within two hops) and view these relation paths as the candidate answers. Then we perform a binary classification on all the candidate paths.

3.1 CNN

The first proposed model is a CNN-based multi-class classifier. To fully utilize the deep neural network and to achieve better language understanding, we use several different features as the input of this model. In addition, we use two channels to offer features from the raw question and its dependency-parsed question. The architecture of the proposed CNN model is illustrated in Fig. 2.

With the first channel we consider the following types of features:

– **Lexical:**
  We use public pretrained GloVe word embeddings to turn words into fixed-length vectors. Given the $D \times d$ word embedding matrix W, the i-th row indicates the embedding of the i-th word, yielding a d-dimensional vector x_{glove}.
– **WordNet:**
  To gain more information on the semantic type, we use WordNet to generate another set of word embeddings as features. Each word, together with its hypernyms, forms a sequence in their hierarchical order: this is termed the hypernym path. Ten hypernym paths are generated by a random walk for each word in WordNet. All the generated paths are then treated as sentences for GloVe to train the embedding for each word in WordNet, yielding a d-dimensional vector $x_{wordnet}$.
– **POS:**
  We randomly initialize an embedding matrix for the POS tag vocabulary. The weights in the matrix are updated during the training process. For each POS the embedding matrix yields a d-dimensional vector x_{pos}.

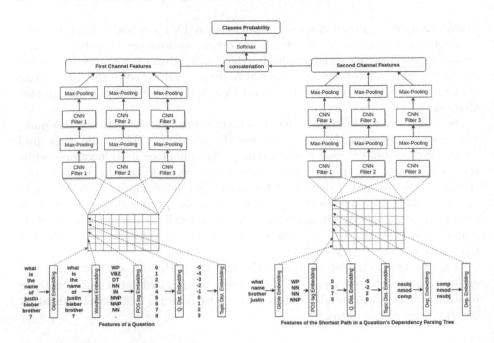

Fig. 2. Architecture of proposed CNN model

- **Distance:**
  For each word, we compute two distances to the current question: its distance to the question word (e.g., Who, What, How) and its distance to the topic entity. For example, in the question "What is the name of Justin Bieber's brother?", the question entity distance, i.e., the distance from the word "name" to "What", is 3 and the topic entity distance, i.e., that from "name" to "Justin Bieber", is 2. After the two distances are computed, the randomly initialized embedding matrix turns them into the d-dimensional vectors x_{ques} and x_{topic}, respectively. The weights of the embedding matrix are also updated in the training process.

Once these features are extracted, we concatenate and feed them into the first channel of the proposed CNN model. These concatenations are shown as follows:

$$X = X_{glove} \oplus X_{wordnet} \oplus X_{pos} \oplus X_{ques} \oplus X_{topic}$$
$$X_{glove} = x_{glove}^0 \oplus x_{glove}^1 \oplus x_{glove}^2 \oplus \cdots \oplus x_{glove}^{n-1} \oplus x_{glove}^n$$
$$X_{wordnet} = x_{wordnet}^0 \oplus x_{wordnet}^1 \oplus \cdots \oplus x_{wordnet}^{n-1} \oplus x_{wordnet}^n$$
$$X_{pos} = x_{pos}^0 \oplus x_{pos}^1 \oplus x_{pos}^2 \oplus \cdots \oplus x_{pos}^{n-1} \oplus x_{pos}^n$$
$$X_{ques} = x_{ques}^0 \oplus x_{ques}^1 \oplus x_{ques}^2 \oplus \cdots \oplus x_{ques}^{n-1} \oplus x_{ques}^n$$
$$X_{topic} = x_{topic}^0 \oplus x_{topic}^1 \oplus x_{topic}^2 \oplus \cdots \oplus x_{topic}^{n-1} \oplus x_{topic}^n$$

where $\oplus$ is the concatenation operator, X is the input of channel one, x_k^i denotes the i-th vector of feature k, and n is the number of words in the question.

For the second channel, we use the Stanford CoreNLP [24] dependency parser to generate the question's dependency parse tree. From the parse tree, we extract the shortest path from the topic entity to the question word, and then use words on the shortest path to generate the following types of features:

- **Lexical:**
  The pretrained word embedding matrix for channel one is used here as well. For each word in the shortest path, from the matrix we extract a d-dimensional vector s_{glove}.
- **POS:**
  For POS tags, we use the embedding matrix from channel one to transform the POS vocabulary. Each POS tag in the shortest path yields a d-dimensional vector s_{pos}.
- **Distance:**
  As in channel one, we extract the question entity distance and the topic entity distance. The distance between the question entity and the topic entity in the original question is computed for each separate word in the shortest path. Again, the distance embedding matrix from channel one is used to turn the distance into d-dimensional vectors s_{ques} and s_{topic}.
- **Dependency tag:**
  Words in the dependency parsed tree are connected by dependency tags, which indicate their mutual relationship. We randomly initialize a dependency tag embedding matrix for later training, and turn each dependency tag appearing in the shortest path into a d-dimensional vector s_{dep}.
- **Reversed dependency tag:**
  In the end, we reverse the dependency tag feature above, indicating a traversal of the dependency parse tree from the topic entity to the question entity. The same dependency embedding matrix is used to generate d-dimensional vectors s_{rdep}.

Given these features, we concatenate them and feed them into channel two of our models.

$$S = S_{glove} \oplus S_{pos} \oplus S_{ques} \oplus S_{topic} \oplus S_{dep} \oplus S_{rdep}$$

$$S_{glove} = s_{glove}^0 \oplus s_{glove}^1 \oplus s_{glove}^2 \oplus \cdots \oplus s_{glove}^{m-1} \oplus s_{glove}^m$$

$$S_{pos} = s_{pos}^0 \oplus s_{pos}^1 \oplus s_{pos}^2 \oplus \cdots \oplus s_{pos}^{m-1} \oplus s_{pos}^m$$

$$S_{ques} = s_{ques}^0 \oplus s_{ques}^1 \oplus s_{ques}^2 \oplus \cdots \oplus s_{ques}^{m-1} \oplus s_{ques}^m$$

$$S_{topic} = s_{topic}^0 \oplus s_{topic}^1 \oplus s_{topic}^2 \oplus \cdots \oplus s_{topic}^{m-1} \oplus s_{topic}^m$$

$$S_{dep} = s_{dep}^0 \oplus s_{dep}^1 \oplus s_{dep}^2 \oplus \cdots \oplus s_{dep}^{m-1}$$

$$S_{rdep} = s_{rdep}^0 \oplus s_{rdep}^1 \oplus s_{rdep}^2 \oplus \cdots \oplus s_{rdep}^{m-1}$$

where S is the input of channel two of our model, s_k^i denotes the i-th vector of feature k, and m is the number of words in the dependency shortest path.

After providing our model with the feature vectors, for each channel, we use three filters of size 1, 2, and 3 to capture features using different window sizes. Assume a sequence of feature vectors fed into channel k is represented as

$$V^k = v_1^k \oplus v_2^k \oplus \cdots \oplus v_{n-1}^k \oplus v_n^k,$$

and $v_{i:i+j}^k$ refers to the concatenation of $v_i^k, v_{i+1}^k, \ldots, v_{i+j}^k$. The filter $w \in R^{hd}$ in our model generates new d-dimensional features from each window of size h, where h is either 1, 2, or 3. For instance, feature c_i is generated from a window of words $v_{i:i+h-1}$:

$$c_i = f(\mathbf{w} \cdot v_{i:i+h-1}), \tag{1}$$

where f is a linear activation function. This filter is applied to each possible window in the sentence $\{v_{1:h}, v_{2:h+1}, \ldots, v_{n-h+1:n}\}$ to produce a feature map $\mathbf{c}$:

$$\mathbf{c} = [c_1, c_2, \ldots, c_{n-h+1}]. \tag{2}$$

Then two max pooling layers are applied on these feature maps to obtain the max value of each feature map. The first max pooling layer is of length 3, and the second is designed to produce the single-length feature map. After this convolution process, 6 feature maps are generated from 2 channels and 3 filters. We then concatenate these feature maps and pass them through a dense layer and then a softmax layer to calculate the class probabilities. The model is optimized by minimizing the categorical cross-entropy loss.

3.2   CNN + Masking

Further observations indicate that some candidate relations can be filtered out in advance: in the WebQSP dataset, there are 5,210 different relations in the training data, while on average there are only 141.6 relations connected to a topic entity. This substantial difference indicates that searches performed on unconnected relations of the topic entity by the proposed CNN model are inefficient.

To take into account only connected relations, we propose a masking mechanism. The masking layer is added before the output layer in the proposed CNN model to drop disconnected relations from the final prediction. Given a question and its topic entity, we retrieve these possible relations from the KB. In this work, we enumerate the possible relations R' by traversing the KB from the topic entity and recording relations within two hops. With the total relation set R, we define the masking layer M as

$$M = \{1 \text{ if } r \in R' \text{ else } 0, \forall r \in R\}. \tag{3}$$

As illustrated in Fig. 3, the output vector of the probabilities of relation classes is then multiplied element-wise with the masking layer to yield only the probabilities of the connected relations.

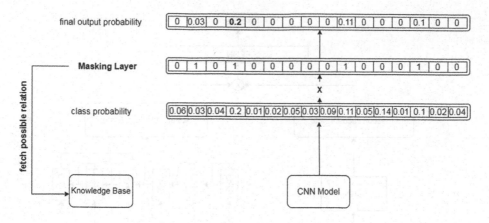

Fig. 3. Proposed CNN + masking model

3.3 CNN + RNN

Since the relations are organized hierarchically from domain, type, to property, we propose a third model, which not only encodes information from a question, but also considers information from candidate relations using a recurrent neural network (RNN). In this model, we treat the relation extraction task as a ranking problem. As illustrated in Fig. 4, we use the model to encode the question. For candidate relations, we first segment them into tokens according to their hierarchy, and then apply a gate recurrent unit (GRU) [25] to encode these tokens sequentially.

Consider t_i as the i-th relation token: we start by passing it through a randomly initialized embedding matrix to generate its embedding representation y_i. Then the whole y sequence is processed using the GRU layer, which is formulated as

$$h_t = (1 - z_t)h_{t-1} + z_t\tilde{h}_t \qquad (4)$$

$$z_t = \sigma(W_z x_t + U_z h_{t-1}) \qquad (5)$$

$$\tilde{h}_t = tanh(W x_t + U(r_t \odot h_{t-1})) \qquad (6)$$

$$r_t = \sigma(W_r y_t + U_r h_{t-1}), \qquad (7)$$

where W and U are trainable parameters, σ is an arbitrary non-linear activation function, and x_t denotes the t-th relation token.

The hidden vector of the question and the candidate relation are then concatenated and passed onto a *relu* [26] activated feed-forward neural network (FFNN), which outputs a single-digit score indicating the fitness of the question and candidate relation. As with previous work that treats relation extraction

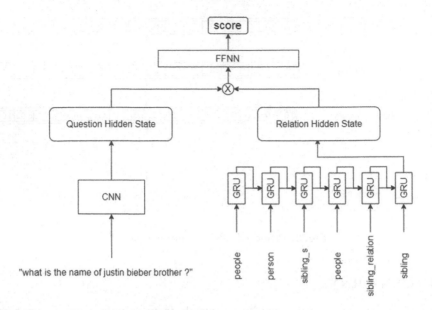

Fig. 4. Proposed CNN + RNN model

as a ranking test, hinge loss is applied to optimize the model, which can be formulated as

$$loss = max(0, -(score^+ - score^-) + margin),$$

where $margin$ is an arbitrary value and $score^+$ and $score^-$ stand for the output scores of the correct and incorrect relations, respectively.

As this model considers relations semantically, it has the potential to relate the relation to the question more correctly. Moreover, with hinge loss, we can train the model not only with positive samples but also with negative ones.

4   Experiment

4.1   The WebQSP Dataset

For experiments, we use WebQSP [10], a public QA dataset which is an annotated version of WebQuestion [27], another public QA dataset which contains question entity and answer entity pairs from the Freebase KB. Questions in WebQuestion were generated based on suggestions from the Google Search Suggestions API and were labeled with semantic parses by experts who are familiar with Freebase. In the WebQSP dataset, in addition to the question and its linked entity with the corresponding MID in Freebase, there is the annotated inferential chain which we refer as the relations (relation path) in this paper. WebQSP specifies 3,098 questions for training and 1,639 questions for testing. From these 3,098 training questions we further set aside 305 for validation.

4.2 Results and Discussion

We evaluated the three proposed models in terms of accuracy. As shown in Table 1, compared to previous works, the proposed models show comparable performance with a smaller search space. The state-of-the-art HR-BiLSTM [9] achieves 83% accuracy by incorporating both relation tokens and relation words.

Table 1. Accuracy of proposed models

Method	Accuracy
BiCNN [6]	78%
BiLSTM + words [9]	80%
BiLSTM + relation_names [9]	79%
HR-BiLSTM [9]	**83%**
CNN	72%
CNN + masking	77%
CNN + RNN	71%

Comparing the three proposed models, it is surprising that the CNN + masking model outperforms the others. The architecture of the CNN + RNN model is similar to the other related work. Moreover, the CNN + RNN model, the BiCNN model, and the BiLSTM + relation_names model all use the same features. Therefore, we expected it to yield comparable performance. Instead, this model yielded the worst performance in our experiment; the BiCNN model and the BiLSTM + relation_names model both far outperformed this model. This suggests that the recurrent model cannot extract information on relations effectively in the CNN + RNN model.

However, we found that masking benefits the proposed model. To the best of our knowledge, this is the first attempt to treat the relation extraction task as a classification problem. The main challenge in making it a classification problem is the large search space for selecting possible relations. Results show that simply adding a masking layer can solve this problem efficiently.

4.3 Error Analysis

We further analyzed the errors found in the results from the CNN + masking model. The first major type of error observed was ambiguous relations. For example, consider the question "What are the major languages spoken in Greece?": whereas the correct relation for this question is "location. country.official_language", our model predicts the "location.country.languages_ spoken" relation. About 16% of the errors are of this type.

The second major error type is due to the model's understanding the question not as a whole but in pieces. For example, the question "What state is Mount St. Helens in?" is classified as "geography.mountain.mountain_type" relation, instead of the gold relation "location.location.contained_by". The model understands the concept "mount", but wrongly recognizes that the question is asking the type of mountain instead of its location. Another example is the question "What town did Justin Bieber grow up in?" being classified to the relation "people.person.place_of_birth", while the correct relation should be "people.person.places_lived people.place_lived.location". To avoid this kind of error, a more sophisticated language encoding model may help such as the deeper CNN model [28,29], the attention mechanism [30,31], or the residual network [32].

5 KBQA on a Catering Knowledge Base

5.1 Constructing CaterKB from iPeen

CaterKB is a Freebase-style knowledge base generated from iPeen[1], the biggest Taiwanese restaurant ranking website. Each restaurant has its own webpage

Table 2. Relations of CaterKB

Chinese	English	Chinese	English
餐廳類型	Restaurant Type	消費方式	Payment
推薦菜色	Recommended Dish	聯絡方式	Contact
客人短評	Customer Comment	類似餐廳	Similar Restaurant
營業時間	Opening Time	媒體推薦	Media Recommendation
地理位置	Location	席位	Seat
消費價位	Price		

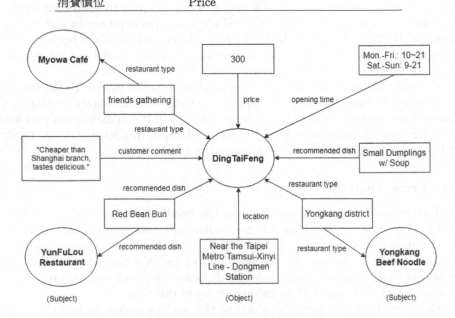

Fig. 5. CaterKB sample

---

[1] www.ipeen.com.tw.

in iPeen from which most of the information can be collected. Each relation representation is a RDF triple in the form of <Subject> <Relation> <Object>. A total of 11 relations are defined in CaterKB, as shown in Table 2. We collected a total of 2,371,397 triples from 147,868 restaurants. Figure 5 shows a sample partial CaterKB knowledge graph.

5.2 Generating Questions for Catering

As people usually search for information they need on the Internet using keywords rather than complete questions, especially with catering information, we failed to collect enough questions with the Google Search Suggestion API. Therefore, we recruited 15 native Chinese speakers to generate 200 questions about restaurants and foods. As it is challenging to generate high-quality questions for all types of relations, six types of restaurant relations were selected for experiments: restaurant type, recommended dish, customer comment, opening time, price, and location.

5.3 Experimental Settings

We applied the CNN + masking layer model to the generated 200 questions. As for data preparing, we performed ten-fold cross validation to make sure low variance between each setting. The result reported is the average of the testing accuracy of the ten folds. The learning rate was set to 0.00005, the batch size 4, and the hidden layer size 128. We adopted the Stanford CoreNLP parser [24] for word segmentation, POS tagging and dependency parsing. To utilize the parser, we use OpenCC toolkit[2] to translate sentences from traditional Chinese to simplified Chinese. After parsing, we translate the parsed result from simplified Chinese to traditional Chinese, and we use Skip-Gram [33] to train on the Chinese Gigaword Second Edition (CG2) [34] as the pre-trained word embedding.

5.4 Results and Discussion

Results are shown in Table 3. The accuracy is unchanged in three different dropout rates and only achieves 75%. As we investigate the results and errors, we find that the relation "餐廳類型 (restaurant type)" is not easily identified by the model; questions of this type bring in much noise. These questions include various terms such as "brunch", "Japanese", "secret place", "historic", and "Taipei", which are too diverse to learn. Hence in terms of KB construction principles, "restaurant type" may not be a good relation.

To evaluate the impact of the error-prone "restaurant type" relation, we excluded questions of this type, keeping 167 questions with other five types of relation, and conducted the experiment again with 147 questions for training, 10 for validation, and 10 for testing. The performance improved considerably: the best performance was now 89%, from which we conclude that (1)

---

[2] https://github.com/BYVoid/OpenCC.

Table 3. CNN + masking accuracy on CaterKB questions

200 questions		167 questions	
Dropout	Accuracy	Dropout	Accuracy
0.0	75%	0.0	88%
0.2	75%	0.2	88%
0.4	75%	0.4	**89%**

carefully designing the relation types in a domain-specific knowledge base may considerably improve performance (2) the 89% accuracy indicates that the proposed CNN + masking model can be used in real-world domain-specific KBQA applications.

Overall, the best performance – an accuracy of 89% – is observed when the dropout rate is set to a relatively high value of 0.4.

5.5   Error Analysis

From the error results of the CNN + masking model with a 0.4 dropout rate, we noticed that the questions for the "location" relation which contain the Chinese word "開 (open/locate/drive)" tended to be classified as questions for the "opening time" relation, such as "鼎泰豐開在哪？(Where is DingTaiFeng located?)". This error is due to polysemy in the questions, in this case, 開 (open/locate/drive). As we did not perform word sense disambiguation before relation extraction, the most commonly used sense "開 (open)" is always adopted by the model. Other questions using this word include "鼎泰豐每天都有開嗎？ (Is DingTaiFeng open everyday?)" and "鼎泰豐早上9點開了嗎？(Is DingTaiFeng open at nine o'clock?)", where 18 of 19 appearances of the word are of the sense "open". This shows that word sense disambiguation is relatively important for domain-specific KBQA.

Questions for "recommended dish" relation such as "鼎泰豐要怎麼點菜最好？ (How to make the best order in DingTaiFeng?)" are also challenging for the proposed model. These questions involve the question word "怎麼 (how)", which is also a challenging question type in the conventional question answering task. The results showed that the model confused these questions with those for the "customer comment" relation, as the latter are common connected with the question word "怎麼 (how)". Usually when one word is found in questions for different relations, its context can aid disambiguation. However, as how-type questions are expressed using a wide variety of words, the context of the question word "how" may not help in relation extraction.

Finally, we note that the vocabulary of the specific domain is small; hence some words are common in questions. For example, in catering questions words such as "菜 (dish)", "價錢 (price)", "營業 (open)", "評價 (comment)", and "哪裡 (where)" are often seen, and are strong features for relations "recommended dish", "price", "opening time", "customer comment", and "location" respectively. We believe this is a worthy direction for improving domain-specific relation extraction.

6   Conclusion and Future Work

Relation extraction plays an important role in KBQA. However, the greatest challenge comes from the large search space of relations. In this paper, we propose three models to extract relations for KBQA, as well as a masking mechanism to reduce the search space. Results show that it is comparable to the state of the art in the general domain and yields superior performance for domain-specific KBs.

In the future, we will investigate automatic question collection for relations in domain-specific KB and useful features for domain adaptation. We believe the proposed model can serve as a simple but strong tool for real-world applications.

Acknowledgements. This study was conducted under the "Big Data Technologies and Applications Project (3/4)" of the Institute for Information Industry which is subsidized by the Ministry of Economic Affairs of the Republic of China.

References

1. Auer, S., Bizer, C., Kobilarov, G., Lehmann, J., Cyganiak, R., Ives, Z.: DBpedia: a nucleus for a web of open data. In: Aberer, K., et al. (eds.) ASWC/ISWC - 2007. LNCS, vol. 4825, pp. 722–735. Springer, Heidelberg (2007). https://doi.org/10.1007/978-3-540-76298-0_52
2. Bollacker, K., Evans, C., Paritosh, P., Sturge, T., Taylor, J.: Freebase: a collaboratively created graph database for structuring human knowledge. In: Proceedings of the 2008 ACM SIGMOD International Conference on Management of Data, pp. 1247–1250. ACM (2008)
3. Miller, G.A.: WordNet: a lexical database for English. Commun. ACM **38**(11), 39–41 (1995)
4. Liang, J., Zhang, Y., Xiao, Y., Wang, H., Wang, W., Zhu, P.: On the transitivity of hypernym-hyponym relations in data-driven lexical taxonomies. In: AAAI, pp. 1185–1191 (2017)
5. Agrawal, R., Shekhar, M., Misra, D.: Integrating knowledge encoded by linguistic phenomena of indian languages with neural machine translation. In: Ghosh, A., Pal, R., Prasath, R. (eds.) MIKE 2017. LNCS (LNAI), vol. 10682, pp. 287–296. Springer, Cham (2017). https://doi.org/10.1007/978-3-319-71928-3_28
6. Yih, S.W., Chang, M.W., He, X., Gao, J.: Semantic parsing via staged query graph generation: question answering with knowledge base (2015)
7. Yao, X., Van Durme, B.: Information extraction over structured data: question answering with freebase. In: Proceedings of the 52nd Annual Meeting of the Association for Computational Linguistics (Volume 1: Long Papers), vol. 1, pp. 956–966 (2014)

8. Dong, L., Wei, F., Zhou, M., Xu, K.: Question answering over freebase with multi-column convolutional neural networks. In: Proceedings of the 53rd Annual Meeting of the Association for Computational Linguistics and the 7th International Joint Conference on Natural Language Processing (Volume 1: Long Papers), vol. 1, pp. 260–269 (2015)
9. Yu, M., Yin, W., Hasan, K.S., dos Santos, C., Xiang, B., Zhou, B.: Improved neural relation detection for knowledge base question answering. In: Proceedings of the 55th Annual Meeting of the Association for Computational Linguistics (Volume 1: Long Papers), vol. 1, pp. 571–581 (2017)
10. Yih, W., Richardson, M., Meek, C., Chang, M.W., Suh, J.: The value of semantic parse labeling for knowledge base question answering. In: Proceedings of the 54th Annual Meeting of the Association for Computational Linguistics (Volume 2: Short Papers), vol. 2, pp. 201–206 (2016)
11. GuoDong, Z., Jian, S., Jie, Z., Min, Z.: Exploring various knowledge in relation extraction. In: Proceedings of the 43rd Annual Meeting on Association for Computational Linguistics, Stroudsburg, PA, USA, ACL 2005, pp. 427–434. Association for Computational Linguistics (2005)
12. Sun, A., Grishman, R., Sekine, S.: Semi-supervised relation extraction with large-scale word clustering. In: Proceedings of the 49th Annual Meeting of the Association for Computational Linguistics: Human Language Technologies, vol. 1, pp. 521–529. Association for Computational Linguistics (2011)
13. Nguyen, T.H., Grishman, R.: Employing word representations and regularization for domain adaptation of relation extraction. In: Proceedings of the 52nd Annual Meeting of the Association for Computational Linguistics (Volume 2: Short Papers), vol. 2, pp. 68–74 (2014)
14. Gormley, M.R., Yu, M., Dredze, M.: Improved relation extraction with feature-rich compositional embedding models. arXiv preprint arXiv:1505.02419 (2015)
15. Zeng, D., Liu, K., Lai, S., Zhou, G., Zhao, J.: Relation classification via convolutional deep neural network. In: Proceedings of COLING 2014, the 25th International Conference on Computational Linguistics: Technical Papers, pp. 2335–2344 (2014)
16. dos Santos, C.N., Xiang, B., Zhou, B.: Classifying relations by ranking with convolutional neural networks. arXiv preprint arXiv:1504.06580 (2015)
17. Vu, N.T., Adel, H., Gupta, P., Schütze, H.: Combining recurrent and convolutional neural networks for relation classification. arXiv preprint arXiv:1605.07333 (2016)
18. Wang, L., Cao, Z., de Melo, G., Liu, Z.: Relation classification via multi-level attention CNNs. In: Proceedings of the 54th Annual Meeting of the Association for Computational Linguistics (Volume 1: Long Papers), vol. 1, pp. 1298–1307 (2016)
19. Zhou, P., Shi, W., Tian, J., Qi, Z., Li, B., Hao, H., Xu, B.: Attention-based bidirectional long short-term memory networks for relation classification. In: Proceedings of the 54th Annual Meeting of the Association for Computational Linguistics (Volume 2: Short Papers), vol. 2, pp. 207–212 (2016)
20. Bast, H., Haussmann, E.: More accurate question answering on freebase. In: Proceedings of the 24th ACM International on Conference on Information and Knowledge Management, pp. 1431–1440. ACM (2015)
21. Xu, K., Reddy, S., Feng, Y., Huang, S., Zhao, D.: Question answering on freebase via relation extraction and textual evidence. arXiv preprint arXiv:1603.00957 (2016)
22. Dai, Z., Li, L., Xu, W.: CFO: conditional focused neural question answering with large-scale knowledge bases. arXiv preprint arXiv:1606.01994 (2016)

23. Golub, D., He, X.: Character-level question answering with attention. arXiv preprint arXiv:1604.00727 (2016)
24. Manning, C.D., Surdeanu, M., Bauer, J., Finkel, J., Bethard, S.J., McClosky, D.: The Stanford CoreNLP natural language processing toolkit. In: Association for Computational Linguistics (ACL) System Demonstrations, pp. 55–60 (2014)
25. Cho, K., Van Merriënboer, B., Bahdanau, D., Bengio, Y.: On the properties of neural machine translation: encoder-decoder approaches. arXiv preprint arXiv:1409.1259 (2014)
26. Nair, V., Hinton, G.E.: Rectified linear units improve restricted Boltzmann machines. In: Proceedings of the 27th International Conference on Machine Learning (ICML-2010), pp. 807–814 (2010)
27. Berant, J., Chou, A., Frostig, R., Liang, P.: Semantic parsing on freebase from question-answer pairs. In: Proceedings of the 2013 Conference on Empirical Methods in Natural Language Processing, pp. 1533–1544 (2013)
28. He, K., Zhang, X., Ren, S., Sun, J.: Deep residual learning for image recognition. In: Proceedings of the IEEE Conference on Computer Vision and Pattern Recognition, pp. 770–778 (2016)
29. Conneau, A., Schwenk, H., Barrault, L., Lecun, Y.: Very deep convolutional networks for text classification. In: Proceedings of the 15th Conference of the European Chapter of the Association for Computational Linguistics: Volume 1, Long Papers, vol. 1, pp. 1107–1116 (2017)
30. Bahdanau, D., Cho, K., Bengio, Y.: Neural machine translation by jointly learning to align and translate. arXiv preprint arXiv:1409.0473 (2014)
31. Vaswani, A., Shazeer, N., Parmar, N., Uszkoreit, J., Jones, L., Gomez, A.N., Kaiser, Ł., Polosukhin, I.: Attention is all you need. In: Advances in Neural Information Processing Systems, pp. 6000–6010 (2017)
32. Liao, Q., Poggio, T.: Bridging the gaps between residual learning, recurrent neural networks and visual cortex. arXiv preprint arXiv:1604.03640 (2016)
33. Mikolov, T., Sutskever, I., Chen, K., Corrado, G.S., Dean, J.: Distributed representations of words and phrases and their compositionality. In: Advances in Neural Information Processing Systems, pp. 3111–3119 (2013)
34. Graff, D., Chen, K., Kong, J., Maeda, K.: Chinese Gigaword Second Edition (LDC2005t14). Linguistic Data Consortium, Philadelphia (2005)

Risk and Information Disclosure in Google Drive Sharing of Tax Data

Craig C. Claybaugh[1(✉)], Langtao Chen[1], Peter Haried[2],
and Dale Zhou[3]

[1] Missouri University of Science and Technology, Rolla, USA
{claybaughc, chenla}@mst.edu
[2] University of Wisconsin - La Crosse, La Crosse, USA
pharied@uwlax.edu
[3] Washington University in St. Louis, St. Louis, USA
dale.zhao@wustl.edu

Abstract. Risk abounds as individuals engage in activities involving the sharing of sensitive information through a third-party cloud storage tool. In this research, we investigate the storage and sharing of very sensitive information (an individual's tax filing information) through a specific third-party technology provider, Google Drive. Within the specifics of such a potentially risky act we argue that information assurance mechanisms implemented by the cloud storage service provider reduce risk perceptions of individuals even when very sensitive information is being shared. Previous positive experience with a cloud service is likely to mitigate concerns on information sharing on the cloud. To elaborate this proposed relationship a research model of information assurance is proposed and tested in the context of tax filing sharing intention.

Keywords: Information assurance · Risk · Tax filing data · Cloud storage

1 Introduction

More and more organizations and people today are using cloud storage services for the centralized storage of their financial information. While participants enjoy the service's convenience and ease of use, the sharing of sensitive financial information on the cloud has raised many concerns regarding the safety of the information shared. Such concerns might be even more serious when these services are a mandatory part of how modern financial services conduct business [1]. To take an example, the Equifax security breach of summer 2017 has shown that there are considerable risks with utilizing the cloud from both a consumer and business model perspective [2].

One financial action requiring an individual to share sensitive information is their annual tax filing [3]. This action is required by law and a majority of individuals have to share their information with a third party as part of this process [4]. Given the prevalence of data breaches and their severe consequence, do individuals feel that this traditional act is risky? Do assurance mechanisms of a trusted third party (e.g., Google Drive) reduce these risk perceptions and influence the intention to share? Drawing on past literature on information assurance and risk the authors propose a research model

© Springer International Publishing AG, part of Springer Nature 2018
F. F.-H. Nah and B. S. Xiao (Eds.): HCIBGO 2018, LNCS 10923, pp. 42–50, 2018.
https://doi.org/10.1007/978-3-319-91716-0_4

of continuance intention in this setting. To empirically validate this proposed model of risky behavior a survey instrument will be developed and tested.

2 Financial Services and Tax Filing

The financial systems of a nation play a pivotal role in the proper functioning of modern economies [1]. While running smoothly they can contribute to the nurturing of economic growth [5]. In contrast, failures within the financial system, as have been crystallized by the recent financial crisis, can be devastating for the economy. Proper execution requires an orchestration framework of highly interconnected economic agents and services connected through government regulation [6]. One of these required integrations is for tax filings between governments and individuals in the United States of America. This annual filing requirement is often processed through a key financial service: tax preparation companies.

The tax filing process has come a long way from the paper-based system used for decades. In the past, tax preparation companies collected clients' information in paper form and mailed the tax forms to Internal Revenue Service Department. Now tax preparation companies provide the service for individuals to submit their forms and be paid in short order through the use of the Internet and cloud services [7]. With the advancement of the Internet, the cloud storage services enable individuals to store their information in the cloud and instantaneously on-demand share information with tax preparation companies. By using the cloud storage services, tax preparation companies do not need to store their client's information in their computer system. As a result, the security and privacy issues regarding using cloud services become the major concerns for the users [8].

Given the mandatory nature of tax filing and the encouraged use of these third-party tax filing service, the access provided to sensitive information should not be over-looked. By requiring this annual activity, the government is in effect encouraging a significant risk-taking behavior [9]. The storage of this information and its transmission cannot be guaranteed to be risk-free similar to other kinds of trusting behaviors [10, 11]. The nature of the internet leaves it vulnerable to a number of privacy and security attacks [12]. It is the nature of these limitations which inhibit the adoption of this process for tax filing.

This proposed study seeks to look at how participants perceive this risk-taking behavior through a well-known third-party cloud provider, Google Drive. The study seeks to understand how tax filers in a country perceive this risk and their likelihood to engage in the behavior.

3 Proposed Model of Sharing Intention

The proposed model of risk in cloud storage sharing shown in Fig. 1 below. Prior studies on online sharing suggest that the intention to share is influenced by the information assurance mechanisms of the third party, the individual's perception of risk in the behavior, and the benefit of using the service [13–15]. The factors driving the intention of these participants to perform this act with a specific service will change based on the users' perceptions of the provider's authenticity and ability to protect their data. The proposed study will look at Google Drive storage and how Google Drive builds technological and institutional assurance of competence in the ability to be used for this service.

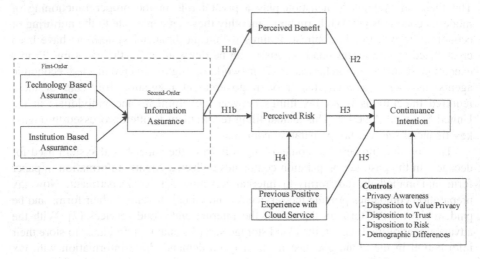

Fig. 1. Proposed model of risk in cloud storage sharing of tax documents.

3.1 Continuance Intention

The continued use of a cloud service provider will be based on the perception of benefits to the use of the service relative to the risk of undertaking the action. When a user feels the benefits outweigh the risks then the actions are continued [16]. This might be influenced by the history of the individual having any issues with sharing sensitive information in the past. It is also possible the fact that the sharing behavior is mandatory and regulated might mean the participants feel the use of sharing is not that large of a risk. At the same time, some individuals might have become immune to the threat of data breaches due to their prevalence over the last few years. The third-party provider of the sharing service can also influence the risk perception through many trust-building mechanisms [17]. Google Drive has a strong incentive to be assured users come back and use the service repeatedly like other technology providers [18].

3.2 Information Assurance

Prior studies suggest that information assurance mechanisms, such as privacy-preserving technologies [19] and institutional policies [20] may enhance user perceptions of control and decrease the perception of risk. Following previous literature [21, 22] this study looks at two broad categories of information assurance: technology-based assurance and institution-based assurance. The use of certain technologies such as encryption and using current versions of software are some of the ways a cloud service provider can show it is providing technology-based assurance [23]. At the institutional level, we see actions done by a firm to assure users their data is being protected and continued use of a company's service is warranted [24].

A number of technology-based assurance mechanisms can enhance a person's willingness to use a particular technology service [25]. Data storage and transmission safeguards and the ability to manage data being collected and shared enhance the ability of the user to share information [26]. This might include third-party certifications and a prominent security policy displayed for the user [27]. The technologies provide safeguards to my personal information which is being shared in this context (i.e. tax filing). In general, these privacy enhancing technologies (PET) add to a sense of empowerment to the user of these services [28]. The ability of Google Drive to set up a robust technological environment will enhance the ability of a participant to share personal information.

The organizations providing the cloud storage services can also provide a number of assurance mechanisms such as privacy policies and joining in industry self-regulation associations to reduce risk concerns [29]. By engaging in these actions, the cloud storage provider demonstrates their commitment to privacy and the protection of data stored on their service. The reputation of the cloud storage provider can also enhance trust [30]. Those providers with a better reputation would not want to lose this status and as such would actively protect data it stores [31]. In this sense, there is a business need for Google Drive to protect personal information from getting into the wrong hands. A failure to do will result in lost business and revenue.

In the proposed model, we formulate that information assurance is a second-order factor derived from technology- and institution-based factors. The combination of these two factors together is seen as a more comprehensive framework of information assurance from the perspective of the service user. In the context of this study, this includes a participant's perspective of Google's technology and of Google as a company. Both of these perspectives are expected to create a sense of a person's information assurance related to using Google Drive.

> *Hypothesis 1a*: Information assurance is positively associated with perceived benefits of cloud sharing of tax documents.
> *Hypothesis 1b*: Information assurance is negatively associated with perceived risk perception in cloud sharing of tax documents.

3.3 Perceived Risk and Benefits

Due to the considerable economic and usage-based benefits cloud-based file sharing technologies provide; more and more users are considering the use of these services. The associated economies of scale, on-demand continuous availability, flexibility and agility benefits has made cloud services an indispensable tool for users across many aspects of their computing activities [32]. For many cloud service clients, the perceived economic benefits are based on the fact that economies of scale of delivering computing from a centralized, shared infrastructure are often significantly lower than those incurred when compared to providing and supporting one's own computing infrastructure. With the growing dependence on mobility and need for on-demand access, utilization of cloud-based services is the access method needed for flexible on-demand file access. However, cloud service clients cannot only consider the benefits without evaluating the risks involved. In order to ensure the adoption of cloud services, several perceived risks centered around security, privacy, trust, performance and other quality attributes need to be considered [32]. The inherent flexibility involved with cloud services has left these services vulnerable to potential malicious intrusion and security risks. Cloud services are subject to continuous attacks by adversaries and malicious intruders' intent on exploiting critical databases and the theft of intellectual property (IP) and other resources [33]. Thus, consideration of both the benefits and risks involved in the adoption decision are needed.

The evaluation and management of perceived risks and benefits between clients and vendors are often noted to be significant in the use and ultimate success of sourcing relationships [34]. In this research, we consider the utilization of a cloud-based file service as an example of a client/vendor relationship. The client must make an evaluation of the perceived risks involved in the utilization of the cloud-based service. Clients must determine if the perceived benefits outweigh the perceived risks. Perceived risk is the product of the probability of an undesirable outcome and the loss due to the undesirable outcome [35]. The perceived risks of using a cloud service vendor revolve around security and privacy as noted above. In many cases, it may be difficult for the cloud services client to effectively check the data handling practices of the cloud vendor and thus to be sure that the data is handled in a secure and lawful way [36]. Consequently, the client must make a determination if the use of a cloud-based service to share tax information is more or less risky than other non-cloud based sharing options. As a result, we hypothesize the following:

Hypothesis 2: Perceived benefit is positively associated with intention to use cloud sharing of tax documents.
Hypothesis 3: Perceived risk perception is negatively associated with intention to use cloud sharing of tax documents.

3.4   Previous Positive Experience with Cloud Service

Previous positive experience refers to the overall satisfaction and quality of previous experience with the service. Prior experience is an important cognitive factor that affects users' perceptions of the cloud service as well as the intention to use it. Studies have shown that previous positive experience helps to build the trust of users with an online service provider and increases the use of the service [e.g., 27, 37]. Pires et al. [38] found that prior positive experience is negatively associated with the perceived risk of online purchase. In the setting of a cloud service, a user who has a prior positive experience is more likely to have favorable trusting beliefs on the cloud service, thus alleviating the concern on the potential risks associated with confidential information disclosure. Overall satisfaction with prior cloud service experience strengthens users' intention to use the service. Therefore, the following hypotheses are proposed:

Hypothesis 4: Previous positive experience with cloud service is negatively associated with perceived risk.

Hypothesis 5: Previous positive experience with cloud service is positively associated with the intention to use cloud sharing of tax documents.

3.5 Controls

A number of individual differences are expected to influence the intention to engage in this potentially risky behavior. These include privacy awareness, disposition to value privacy [29], disposition to trust [39], and disposition to engage in risk behaviors [40], and demographic differences [24]. Including these measures will provide a clear sense of who would be more likely to engage in this behavior of confidential information disclosure. In the suggested research model, we control for these factors in order to rule out alternative explanations of the proposed theoretical relationships.

4   Method (Proposed)

A survey will be conducted to evaluate the perception of Google Drive as an appropriate way to share tax information with a third-party tax preparation company. Since every citizen is required to file taxes and most users are familiar with Google Drive we should have a large pool of respondents to sample. The specific focus will be on sharing a specific item (latest tax filings) into a cloud storage location to facilitate a service exchange with a tax preparing agency.

The subjects are expected to be US residents who are filing personal income tax. MBA and undergraduate students will be used for the data sample collection process as they meet the criteria for a valid user of Google Drive and an obligation to file taxes each year. The respondents will be asked to respond relating to the current filing year for their income earned in the last calendar year.

Data will be analyzed by using partial least squares structural equation modeling (PLS-SEM) as the PLS-SEM can easily analyze a research model containing formative items [e.g., 41] and non-normal variables [42, 43]. Information assurance will be modeled as a formative second-order construct.

5   Expected Contribution and Discussion

This study has the potential to validate how tax filers in the US view potential data security concerns when using a cloud based service. Of course, not all tax filers will see issues with the sharing of sensitive data via the cloud. Some might not see any risk due to a lack of assets (students for example) while others may have already been a victim of data theft and thus are more vigilant. Understanding how customers approach the problem and antecedents of their intention to adopt the cloud storage service will provide guidance for Google Drive to find innovative ways to mitigate the potential information sharing risk.

The provider of a data share between the two parties, such as Google Drive, has a number of approaches to safeguard data as they are stored and shared. There is a strong incentive on the part of cloud service provider to minimize data breaches in order to maintain a market share among competitors. This proposed study will look at how a set of users perceive this set of safeguards (both technological and institutional) in this setting.

A future study might also expand on these proposed contributions and look at other types of mandatory data sharing activities through a cloud provider. One potential study might look at the sharing of education data. Education data provides an example of a common but not as critical scenario of personal information share. Another direction is to look at sharing health data through a cloud provider or online health communities [44]. Future studies are encouraged to investigate the challenges involved with sharing health data through the cloud. The popular press has a number of stories related to unauthorized disclosure or accessing of health information. Another study might look at comparing different cloud providers such as Google Drive, Amazon cloud, and Microsoft cloud to see how users evaluate the information assurance, benefits and risks involved with these popular cloud service providers.

References

1. Bernal, O., Gnabo, J.Y., Guilmin, G.: Assessing the contribution of banks, insurance and other financial services to systemic risk. J. Bank. Financ. **47**, 270–287 (2014)
2. CNN 2017: Giant Equifax data breach: 143 million people could be affected. http://money. cnn.com/2017/09/07/technology/business/equifax-data-breach/index.html. Accessed 7 Feb 2018
3. Chen, J.V., Jubilado, R.J.M., Capistrano, E.P.S., Yen, D.C.: Factors affecting online tax filing–an application of the IS success model and trust theory. Comput. Hum. Behav. **43**, 251–262 (2015)
4. Venkatesh, V., Thong, J.Y., Chan, F.K., Hu, P.J.: Managing citizens' uncertainty in E-government services: the mediating and moderating roles of transparency and trust. Inf. Syst. Res. **27**(1), 87–111 (2016)
5. Levine, R.: Financial development and economic growth: views and agenda. J. Econ. Lit. **32**(2), 668–726 (1997)
6. Salampasis, D., Mention, A.L., Torkkeli, M.: Open innovation and collaboration in the financial services sector: exploring the role of trust. Int. J. Bus. Innov. Res. **8**(5), 466–484 (2014)
7. Albring, S., Robinson, D., Robinson, M.: Audit committee financial expertise, corporate governance, and the voluntary switch from auditor-provided to non-auditor-provided tax services. Adv. Account. **30**(1), 81–94 (2014)
8. Thilakanathan, D., Chen, S., Nepal, S., Calvo, R.A.: Secure data sharing in the cloud. In: Nepal, S., Pathan, M. (eds.) Security, Privacy and Trust in Cloud Systems, pp. 45–72. Springer, Heidelberg (2014). https://doi.org/10.1007/978-3-642-38586-5_2
9. Guo, J.T., Harrison, S.G.: Tax policy and stability in a model with sector-specific externalities. Rev. Econ. Dyn. **4**(1), 75–89 (2001)
10. Claybaugh, C.C., Haseman, W.D.: Understanding professional connections in LINKEDIN— A question of trust. J. Comput. Inf. Syst. **54**(1), 94–105 (2013)

11. Claybaugh, C.C., Haried, P., Chen, L., Twyman, N.: Dueling for trust in the online fantasy sports industry: fame, fortune, and pride for the winners. In: Nah, F.F.-H., Tan, C.-H. (eds.) HCIBGO 2017. LNCS, vol. 10294, pp. 203–212. Springer, Cham (2017). https://doi.org/10. 1007/978-3-319-58484-3_16
12. Kshetri, N.: Big data's impact on privacy, security and consumer welfare. Telecommun. Policy **38**(11), 1134–1145 (2014)
13. Hajli, N., Lin, X.: Exploring the security of information sharing on social networking sites: the role of perceived control of information. J. Bus. Eth. **133**, 111–123 (2016)
14. Hu, W., Yang, T., Matthews, J.N.: The good, the bad and the ugly of consumer cloud storage. ACM SIGOPS Oper. Syst. Rev. **44**(3), 110–115 (2010)
15. Li, H., Sarathy, R., Xu, H.: Understanding situational online information disclosure as a privacy calculus. J. Comput. Inf. Syst. **51**(1), 62–71 (2010)
16. Yang, H.L., Lin, S.L.: User continuance intention to use cloud storage service. Comput. Hum. Behav. **52**, 219–232 (2015)
17. Haried, P.J., Claybaugh, C.C.: Evaluating information systems offshore project success: can success and failure coexist? J. Glob. Inf. Technol. Manag. **20**(1), 8–27 (2017)
18. Claybaugh, C.C., Srite, M.: Factors contributing to the information technology vendor-client relationship. JITTA: J. Inf. Technol. Theory Appl. **10**(2), 19 (2009)
19. Chakraborty, R., Ramireddy, S., Raghu, T.S., Rao, H.R.: The information assurance practices of cloud computing vendors. IT Prof. **12**(4), 29–37 (2010)
20. Sunyaev, A., Schneider, S.: Cloud services certification. Commun. ACM **56**(2), 33–36 (2013)
21. Li, X., Hess, T.J., Valacich, J.S.: Why do we trust new technology? A study of initial trust formation with organizational information systems. J. Strateg. Inf. Syst. **17**(1), 39–71 (2008)
22. Hsu, M.H., Chang, C.M., Chu, K.K., Lee, Y.J.: Determinants of repurchase intention in online group-buying: the perspectives of DeLone & McLean IS success model and trust. Comput. Hum. Behav. **36**, 234–245 (2014)
23. Wang, G., Liu, Q., Wu, J.: Hierarchical attribute-based encryption for fine-grained access control in cloud storage services. In: Proceedings of the 17th ACM Conference on Computer and Communications Security, pp. 735–737. ACM (2010)
24. Smith, H.J., Dinev, T., Xu, H.: Information privacy research: an interdisciplinary review. MIS Q. **35**(4), 989–1016 (2011)
25. Boritz, J.E., No, W.G.: E-commerce and privacy: exploring what we know and opportunities for future discovery. J. Inf. Syst. **25**(2), 11–45 (2011)
26. Chandra, S., Srivastava, S.C., Theng, Y.L.: Evaluating the role of trust in consumer adoption of mobile payment systems: an empirical analysis. Commun. Assoc. Inf. Syst. **27**(1), 561–588 (2010)
27. Bansal, G., Zahedi, F.M., Gefen, D.: The impact of personal dispositions on information sensitivity, privacy concern and trust in disclosing health information online. Decis. Support Syst. **49**(2), 138–150 (2010)
28. Kokolakis, S.: Privacy attitudes and privacy behaviour: a review of current research on the privacy paradox phenomenon. Comput. Secur. **64**, 122–134 (2017)
29. Xu, H., Dinev, T., Smith, J., Hart, P.: Information privacy concerns: linking individual perceptions with institutional privacy assurances. J. Assoc. Inf. Syst. **12**(12), 798 (2011)
30. Dillon, T., Wu, C., Chang, E.: Cloud computing: issues and challenges. In: 2010 24th IEEE International Conference on Advanced Information Networking and Applications, AINA, pp. 27–33 (2010)
31. Claybaugh, C.C., Ramamurthy, K., Haseman, W.D.: Assimilation of enterprise technology upgrades: a factor-based study. Enterp. Inf. Syst. **11**(2), 250–283 (2017)

32. Chun, S., Choi, B.: Service modes and pricing schemes for cloud computing. Clust. Comput. **17**, 529–535 (2014)
33. Haimes, Y., Horowitz, B.M., Guo, Z., Andrijicic, E., Bogdanor, J.: Assessing systemic risk to cloud-computing technology as complex interconnected systems of systems. Syst. Eng. **18** (3), 284–299 (2015)
34. Kern, T., Willcocks, L.: Exploring information technology outsourcing relationship: theory and practice. J. Strateg. Inf. Syst. **9**, 321–350 (2000)
35. Aubert, B.A., Patry, M., Rivard, S.: A framework for information technology outsourcing risk management. Database Adv. Inf. Syst. **36**(4), 9–28 (2005)
36. ENISA (European Network and Information Security Agency) Cloud Computing: Benefits, risks and recommendations for information security. http://www.enisa.europa.eu/. Accessed 7 Feb 2018
37. Gefen, D., Karahanna, E., Straub, D.: Trust and TAM in online shopping: an integrated model. MIS Q. **27**(1), 51–90 (2003)
38. Pires, G., Stanton, J., Eckford, A.: Influences on the perceived risk of purchasing online. J. Consum. Behav. **4**(2), 118–131 (2004)
39. Bélanger, F., Carter, L.: Trust and risk in e-government adoption. J. Strateg. Inf. Syst. **17**(2), 165–176 (2008)
40. Kull, T.J., Oke, A., Dooley, K.J.: Supplier selection behavior under uncertainty: contextual and cognitive effects on risk perception and choice. Decis. Sci. **45**(3), 467–505 (2014)
41. Chen, L.: Essays on health information technology: insights from analyses of big datasets. Dissertation, Georgia State University (2016)
42. Gefen, D., Rigdon, E.E., Straub, D.: An update and extension to SEM guidelines for administrative and social science research. MIS Q. **35**(2), iii–xiv (2011)
43. Hair, J.F., Hult, G.T.M., Ringle, C., Sarstedt, M.: A Primer on Partial Least Squares Structural Equation Modeling (PLS-SEM). SAGE Publications, Incorporated, Thousand Oaks (2013)
44. Chen, L., Straub, D.: The impact of virtually crowdsourced social support on individual health: analyzing big datasets for underlying causalities. In: Proceedings of the 21st Americas Conference on Information Systems, Puerto Rico (2015)

Automated Leadership: Influence from Embodied Agents

Douglas C. Derrick$^{(\boxtimes)}$ and Joel S. Elson$^{(\boxtimes)}$

University of Nebraska at Omaha, 6001 Dodge Street, PKI, Omaha,
NE 68182, USA
{dcderrick, jselson}@unomaha.edu

Abstract. It is widely held that leadership consists of behaviors that should be applied strategically and systematically to motivate individuals and teams to perform. It is also self-evident that we live in a world of automation, artificial intelligence, and expert systems. Given these two assertions, we propose that some aspects of leadership are candidates for automation. This paper briefly reviews relevant leadership literature and describes three leadership behaviors that may be possibly automated: goal setting, performance monitoring, and performance consequences. The paper also explores the relationship of different embodiments of the artificial leaders and the impact of these embodiments as varying degrees of social presence and the effect of this presence on performance and satisfaction outcomes.

Keywords: Transactional leadership · Intelligent agents · Social presence
Hologram · Embodied agents

1 Introduction

In the movie "The Terminator", a computer system in the future has become self-aware and is leading an onslaught against the human race. This theme of intelligent robots has been consistently played out in various books, movies, etc. Similarly, leadership has been a topic of study and reflection for thousands of years, but it is almost always thought of in a human context – humans leading other humans. Recently, some studies have examined the relationship between, and performance of human-agent teams and others examined the role of humans leading these artificial agent teams [1, 2]. This current examination is unique in that explores if an artificially intelligent machine is capable of providing limited leadership to a person for a specific task.

There are many different definitions of leadership. As Stogdill [3] points out in a review of leadership research, there are almost as many definitions of leadership as there are people who have tried to define it. Peter Northouse offers the following observations and definition that will serve as the working definition of leadership in this paper: "leadership is a process whereby an individual influences a group of individuals to achieve a common goal" [4]. The main difference in this study is that an artificially intelligent agent will influence a group of individuals to achieve the goal. Recent leadership research has concentrated on transformational leadership [5, 6] and a charismatic human leader creating a vision that people will want to follow. However, as

© Springer International Publishing AG, part of Springer Nature 2018
F. F.-H. Nah and B. S. Xiao (Eds.): HCIBGO 2018, LNCS 10923, pp. 51–66, 2018.
https://doi.org/10.1007/978-3-319-91716-0_5

important as transformational leadership is, it has some weaknesses [4, 7]. Transactional leadership is still required in a vast set of circumstances and is closely aligned with effective management [8, 9]. A transformational leader needs to create the vision and a transactional leader will ensure that the vision is implemented and both are necessary and complementary [10]. A transactional leader does not individualize the needs of subordinates or focus on their personal development. Transactional leaders exchange things of value with subordinates to advance their own and their subordinates' agendas [11–13].

As intelligent systems advance and become more ubiquitous, we need to explore new dimensions of human-computer interactions based on natural communication patterns and consideration of human individual differences. Next generation information systems will involve both the automated delivery of human-like communication and the interpretation human verbal and non-verbal messages [14–17]. Given these assertions, the ability for a computer system to have a knowledge base on which to draw in order to deliver appropriate messages to a human user is an ambitious undertaking and is a novel conceptualization for information systems [18].

In this paper, we focus on transactional leadership and propose that this form of leadership need not be confined to human-to-human interactions. We take the position that transactional leadership can be automated. In other words, a system can be developed and/or trained to provide leadership to human counterparts in a computer-to-human interaction for a limited project. We propose to automate three leadership behaviors and explore the social presence of the automated leader as a moderating variable.

2   Research Background

At the macro-level, this research paper proposes to examine the relationship between automated leadership, social presence and task performance, and follower satisfaction. Figure 1 shows the proposed relationships between each of these constructs. The very essence of leadership is to improve performance and develop followers. Leadership theories posit that leadership consists of behaviors that should be applied strategically and systematically to motivate individuals and teams to perform [19–25].

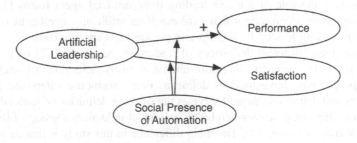

Fig. 1. Basic research model

2.1   Automated Leadership

There are multiple supervisory behaviors that have shown a positive impact on performance [22, 26–28]. We propose to apply an automated leadership style, which highlights the importance of certain behaviors, such as providing information and developing goals [29]. Research in virtual teams has shown that effective leaders in distributed teams are extremely efficient at providing regular, detailed, and prompt communication with their peers and in articulating role relationships (responsibilities) among the virtual team members [30]. Three leadership behaviors have been selected for automation: goal setting, performance monitoring, and performance consequences.

Goal Setting. A goal is a desired state or outcome [31]. According to Locke and Latham, goals affect performance through four mechanisms. First, they serve a directive function. Second, goals have an energizing function. Third, goals affect persistence. Fourth, goals affect action indirectly by leading to the arousal, discovery, and/or use of task-relevant knowledge and strategies. Locke and Latham showed that the highest and most difficult goals produced the highest levels of effort and performance [31]. They also found that specific, difficult goals led to consistently higher performance than urging people to do their best. Atkinson [32] showed that there was an inverse, curvilinear relationship between task difficulty (measured as probability of success) and performance. The highest level of effort occurred when the task was moderately difficult. Therefore, effective leaders will set goals of appropriate difficulty to stimulate the optimal performance according to a given team's capability. For the ad hoc nature of this leader and follower experiment, effective goal setting involves formulating specific, challenging and time-constrained objectives [33].

Performance Monitoring. Antonakis et al. [19] noted that transactional leadership is the ability to control and monitor outcomes. Research by Larson and Callahan [34] looked at the role of monitoring on performance. They hypothesized that performance monitoring would have an independent effect upon work behavior and found that monitoring improved subjects work output independent of other factors. Similarly, Brewer [35] found that the quantity of work improved when monitored. Aiello and Kolb [36] examined the role of electronic performance monitoring and social context on productivity and stress. They found that individually monitored participants were vastly more productive than those monitored at the group level for a simple task. More recent research has evaluated how electronic performance monitoring systems impact emotion, performance, and satisfaction [37, 38]. Therefore, effective leaders will actively monitor the performance of individual team members and the team as a whole.

Performance Consequences. Bass [39, 40] argued that theories of leadership primarily focused on follower goal and role clarification and the ways leaders rewarded or sanctioned follower behavior. Similarly, Larson and Callahan [34] found that monitoring along with consequences (feedback to the subjects about their performance during the task) significantly increased subjects' work output and that this provided the largest increase in productivity. Thus, how well a leader is able to monitor performance and influence the team's behavior is a measure of transactional leadership ability. Follower behavior can be shaped by effectively providing feedback and appropriate consequences. Consequences can be defined as either motivating/reinforcing events or as disciplining/punishing ones [41, 42]. Komaki et al. [27, 28] expanded this definition to include consequences that are neutral and informational in character. For this study, we use their definition of performance consequences, which is defined as communicating an evaluation of or indicating knowledge of another's performance, where the indication can range from highly evaluative to neutral. This type of communication is vital for performance and compliance [27, 43]. An artificial system can operate by creating clear structures that make it certain what is required of the subordinate team members, and the rewards that they will receive for following instructions. Punishments can also be clearly stated and then a computer system can be coded to use operant conditioning on followers. Komaki provides several examples of positive, negative, and neutral consequences. Several examples are listed below:

Positive

- "You have done good work; no signs of errors!"
- "Great, you have done it so quickly."

Negative

- "You have made a great deal of errors."
- "Oh no. You have done this all wrong."

Neutral

- "You have over 300 open cases."
- "He made a call yesterday for those materials."

2.2 Social Presence

Social presence is the sense that one is together with another. It encompasses the idea that embodied agents have a persona that causes natural reactions from human beings. Heeter [44] said that this phenomenon relates to the apparent existence of and feedback from the other entity in the communication and that social presence is the extent to which other beings in the world appear to exist and react to the user. Biocca et al. [45] posit that social presence may be the byproduct of reading or simulating the mental states of virtual others and that social presence is related to the theory of the mind. They state that when users interact with agents or robots, they "read minds" and respond socially, even when they know that no mind or social other really exists. They continue that although humans know that the "other" is just ink on paper or patterns of light on a screen, the social responses are automatic [45]. Similarly, Computers as Social Actors (CASA) theory proposes that human beings interact with computers as though computers were people [46]. In multiple studies, researchers have found that participants react to interactive computer systems no differently than participants react to other people [47]. It is suggested that people fail to critically assess the computer and its limitations as an interaction partner [48] and as a result, the norms of interaction observed between people occur no differently between a person and a computer [49]. CASA has been used in multiple studies to provide structure for experimentation. Some similar studies include instances were computers have been specifically designed to praise or criticize performance [50], to display dominant or submissive cues [51, 52], to flatter participants [53], explored the role of gender and flattery [54] or to display similar or dissimilar interaction cues with participants [51]. More recent studies have shown how individuals may form group relations with computer agents [55], how social presence affects interaction in a virtual environment [56], and that social presence factors contribute significantly to the building of the trustworthy online exchanging relationships [57].

2.3 Text-Based Automated Agents

One level of interaction for the automated leaders is simply to send a text-based message. Each of the leadership behaviors described above can be put into an agent that is "unembodied" and communicates with the follower through text messages that appear on the screen. We propose to use several levels of social presence/embodiment with text-based being the least "present". There are several reasons to use an embodied face over only sound and text when communicating and interacting with individuals. People interacting with embodied agents tend to interpret both nonverbal cues and the absence of nonverbal cues. Embodied agents can effectively communicate an intended emotion through animated facial expressions [58]. The nonverbal interactions between individuals include significant conversational cues and facilitate communication. Incorporating nonverbal conversational elements into an automated leader may increase the engagement and satisfaction of individuals interacting with the agent [59–63]. We anticipate that this lowest level of presence will moderate both performance and satisfaction and should provide greater performance than no leadership at all.

2.4 Embodied Automated Agents

The next level of presence for the adaptive intelligent agent in our experiment will be a "flat", embodied agent. The primary means the automated leader has for affecting its follower are the signals and messages it sends to the human via its rendered, embodied interface. For this paper, embodied agents refer to virtual, three-dimensional human likenesses that are displayed on computer screens. While they are often used interchangeably, it is important to note that the terms avatar and embodied agent are not synonymous. If an embodied agent is intended to interact with people through natural speech, it is often referred to as an Embodied Conversational Agent, or ECA [17]. The signals available to the agent take on three primary dimensions, which are appearance, voice, and size. The appearance can be manipulated to show different demeanors, genders, ethnicities, hair colors, clothing, hairstyles, and face structures. One study of embodied agents in a retail setting found a difference in gender preferences. Participants preferred the male embodied agent and responded negatively to the accented voice of the female agent. However, when cartoonlike agents were used, the effect was reversed and participants liked the female cartoon agent significantly more than the male cartoon [64].

Embodied Conversational Agents are becoming more effective at engaging human subjects as though they were intelligent individuals. Humans engage with virtual agents and respond to their gestures and statements. When the embodied agents react to human subjects appropriately and make appropriate responses, participants report finding the interaction satisfying. On the other hand, when the agents fail to recognize what humans are saying, and respond with requests for clarification or inappropriate responses, humans can find the interaction very frustrating [65]. It has been proposed that Embodied Conversational Agents could be used as an interface between users and computers [66]. While humans are relatively good at identifying expressed emotions from other humans whether static or dynamic, identifying emotions from synthetic faces is more problematic. Identifying static expressions was particularly difficult, with expressions such as fear being confused with surprise, and disgust and anger being confused with each other. When synthetic expressions are expressed dynamically, emotion identification improves significantly [58].

In one study on conversational engagement, conversational agents were either responsive to conversational pauses by giving head nods and shakes or not. Thirty percent of human storytellers in the responsive condition indicated they felt a connection with the conversational agent, while none of the storytellers to the non-responsive agents reported a connection. In this study, embodied conversational agent responsiveness was limited to head movement, and facial reactions were fixed. Subjects generally regarded responsive avatars as helpful or disruptive, while 75% of the subjects were indifferent towards the non-responsive avatars. Users talking to responsive agents spoke longer and said more, while individuals talking to unresponsive agents talked less and had proportionally greater disfluency rates and frequencies [67] (Fig. 2).

Fig. 2. Sample flat automated agent

Agents that are photorealistic need to be completely lifelike, with natural expressions, or else individuals perceive them negatively, and a disembodied voice is actually preferred and found to be clearer. When cartoon figures are utilized, three-dimensional characters are preferred over two-dimensional characters and whole body animations are preferred over talking heads [61]. Emotional demeanor is an additional signal that can be manipulated as an effector by the automated leader based on its desired goals, probable outcomes, and current states. The emotional state display may be determined from the probability that desired goals will be achieved. Emotions can be expressed through the animation movements and facial expressions, which may be probabilistically determined, based on the agent's expert system [61]. There are limitless possible renderings that may influence human perception and affect the agents operating environment. Derrick and Ligon [68] showed that these types of agents could use influence tactics such as impression management techniques to change user perceptions of the automation. Moreover, it has been shown that these perceptions change user/follower behavior include how people speak and interact with the agent [69]. Finally, Nunamaker and colleagues review how these types of agents have been tested and deployed in various contexts [16].

2.5 Hologram-Based Automated Agents

An alternate technology that is widely deployed in interactive entertainment environments is a projection display known as Pepper's Ghost. While often referred to in the mainstream media as a hologram, this is a form of 2D display technology that creates an illusion of depth under limited viewing conditions and angles. Technological advancements have produced impressive visualizations and immersive experiences, as evidenced by recent highly publicized "live" stage performances by celebrities who are not present (e.g. Narendra Modi), animated characters (e.g., Hatsune Miku, Madonna with the Gorillaz), and digital recreations of deceased celebrities (e.g., Tupac, Michael Jackson). These visualizations are also used at high-end amusement parks where the immersive experience is critical to the visitor's experience, such as Disney World's "Haunted Mansion" and "Phantom Manor" and Universal Studios' Harry Potter "Hogwarts Express" ride. We have developed a prototype limited viewing angle pseudo-hologram (LVAH) based system from readily available 2D COTS systems to use as the automated leader with the most social presence.

Technological trusting beliefs result from social presence, or the warmth, sociability, and feeling of human contact, and can be achieved through simulating interaction with another real person [70]. Trust in technology also depends upon machine accuracy, responsivity, predictability, and dependability [71]. We propose that the more socially present leader that is created using a LVAH will moderate performance and satisfaction of the followers. We will measure the followers' perceptions of social presence in each of the types of leadership agents and test how this moderates the outcome variables. Figure 3 shows the apparatus to create the hologram agent and Fig. 4 shows the embodied hologram agent that will be used in the study.

3   Method

We have created a task where students have to input fake alumni information into an online system. We generated 500 fake names, addresses and phone numbers, and printed them out on sheets of paper. We ran a control study with no leadership where students were told, "We are capturing addresses and contact information for recent UNO Alumni that will be used to send information, fundraise, and help build the UNO community. In front of you, there is a sheet of alumni's information that must be input into the system. Please use the data entry screen on the computer to input this data.

Fig. 3. Hologram apparatus

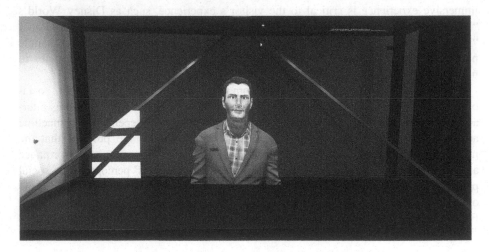

Fig. 4. Embodied hologram leader agent

Work as quickly and as accurately as possible, as your performance is based on both the number and quality of the data that you have captured. After you have input each person's contact information, please press the submit button to store it to the database. You will input data for thirty minutes and then we will ask you about your experience". The students then input the data for thirty minutes and were thanked for their participation. Based on this control group, the average user could input approximately 26 names in 30 min (25.7) with a standard deviation of 4.9. We measured the accuracy of the data input against the gold standard of the generated names stored in the database by comparing each field entered to the actual data. Figure 5 shows the user input screen.

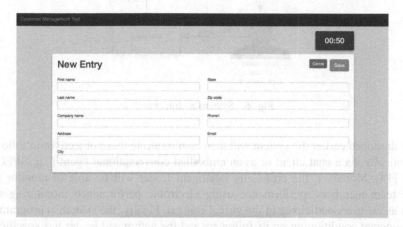

Fig. 5. User input screen

For the control group, the average accuracy was 86.4% with a standard deviation of 6.3%. Using this baseline data, we programmed the automated leaders to set an objective for the new followers that was two standard deviations higher than the average (i.e., 35 names input in 30 min) and one standard deviation higher for quality (i.e., 93%). For any of the leadership conditions regardless of embodiment, the follow script was used and was delivered either in text (for the text-based leader) or by voice in case of the embodied leaders:

> "Hello. I am a new automated manager and will be your leader for this task. We are capturing addresses and contact information for recent UNO Alumni that will be used to send information, fundraise, and help build the UNO community. In front of you, there is a sheet of alumni's information that must be input into the system. Please use the data entry screen on the computer to input this data. Work as quickly and as accurately as possible, as your performance is based on both the number and quality of the data that you have captured. After you have input each person's contact information, please press the submit button to store it to the database. You will input data for thirty minutes and then we will ask you about your experience. **I will monitor your performance. The average person can input about 30 people's contact information in 30 min. Based on your education and personality profile, I think that 35 is a reasonable goal for you. Please don't let me down.** When you press the OK button on the screen, I will start the timer. Please ask my human assistant if you have any questions".

The bolded sections in the text highlight where the agent is establishing itself as the leader and is setting a performance objective for the follower. The non-bolded text is the same as the control group instructions. Once the user starts the experiment, the systems monitors performance and provides appropriate feedback at defined intervals. The system architecture is shown in Fig. 6 below.

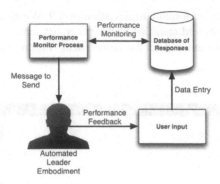

Fig. 6. System architecture

As described earlier the system will then communicate these objectives to followers electronically via a chat client or as an embodied conversational agent (e.g. SPECIES agent) [14]. Moreover, the artificially intelligent leader will be able to monitor individual team members' performance using electronic performance monitoring techniques as the users participate in the virtual context. Finally, the system is programmed to use operant conditioning on its followers and the automated leader has specific and proper pre-programmed statements that it will send to followers at appropriate intervals depending on their performance. There are multiple studies that evaluate leadership from an operant perspective [26–29, 41]. Transactional leadership from an operant perspective was chosen for automation because it can be limited to inducing only basic exchanges with followers. In essence, the programmed psychology of the artificial leader will be operant conditioning [72]. Figure 7 shows the experiment flow. The initial and second feedback are measured against progress towards the stated goal. All subsequent feedback is based on the performance of the prior five minutes. This allows the user to get more positive feedback if his or her performance improves over their initial baselines but are still short toward the goal.

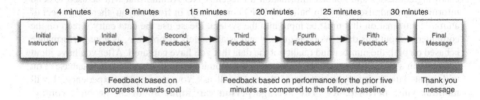

Fig. 7. Experiment flow

The leader has a battery of possible feedback based on performance. Below are two samples of the feedback. The first is an example of feedback at 9 min where the participant has good speed, but poor accuracy and the second is an example of positive feedback for both speed and accuracy at 15 min.

Example 1. Your speed is excellent, and you are on track to make our goal! However, I have also checked the quality of your data entries and they are not acceptable. You need to be more precise. Being fast is not good, if your data quality is so poor. Thank you for your effort, but you need to improve. Your quality is worse than most of the people that have worked on this task. Please be more accurate.

Example 2. Thank you so much for your effort! You are really doing a fantastic job. Your speed and accuracy are in the top tier of all of the people that have worked on this task. You are doing a remarkable job and are on pace to be one of the best participants.

The experiment concludes with the leader delivering a thank you message and telling them that they have done an excellent job. After the completion of the task, the participants are given a post-survey that measures outcome and process satisfaction [73], Leader-Member Exchange (LMX) [74], Leader Behavior Description Questionnaire [4], and degree of social presence [45, 75] of the artificial leader.

Transactional leadership theory indicates that leadership is an exchange process based on the fulfillment of contractual obligations and is typically represented as setting objectives and monitoring and controlling outcomes [19]. The object of our study is to measure the effectiveness of an information system in providing this type of leadership. We control for natural team capability by random assignment to the various embodied artificial leaders. We will perform comparisons between the control group (no leader) and the presence of leadership with the manipulations being the embodiment. Transactional leadership has been operationalized as setting goals, performance monitoring and performance consequences. These behaviors should directly affect the team performance. Figure 8 shows the final operationalized model.

Summary of hypotheses:

Automated Leadership Will Improve Follower Performance

1. Automated Leadership will increase the number of data entries
2. Automated Leadership will increase the accuracy of data entries
3. Social presence will have a positive moderating effect on performance outcomes.

Follower Satisfaction

4. Automated Leadership will decrease process satisfaction
5. Automated Leadership will increase outcome satisfaction.

Perceptions of the Leader

6. The greater the social presence of the artificial leader the better the follower perception of the leader.

The automated leader obviously has several limitations many of which are grounded in its assumptions. First, it assumes a rational follower, who is largely motivated by simple reward, and who exhibits predictable behavior. Its programmed psychology is Behaviorism, including classical conditioning [76] and operant conditioning [72]. Similarly, it is a very narrow task with limited interaction and consequences.

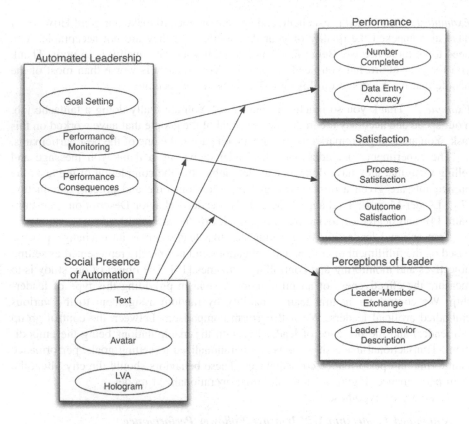

Fig. 8. Final operationalized research model

4 Conclusion

As technology advances, and virtual leadership becomes the norm, our view of leadership must evolve. Similarly, the ability of machines to exhibit leadership traits needs to be evaluated. Our overarching proposition is that an information system can perform equal to or better than a human at providing transactional leadership to a human follower. We propose to explore these propositions and questions by conducting experiments where leadership is clearly defined and consistently measured [77]. Charles Darwin said, "In the long history of humankind (and animal kind, too) those who learned to collaborate and improvise most effectively have prevailed". This new phenomenon of machine leadership is part of this next evolution we must understand how it impacts individual and team dynamics. Humans and machines are collaborating in new ways and organizations are increasingly leveraging human-automation teams. Siri (the Apple iPhone conversational assistant), Alexa (Amazon's conversational agent), physical robots, virtual customer-service agents, and many other pseudo-intelligent agents, use text clues, vocal cues, or other environmental sensors to retrieve information from the user, process it, and respond appropriately. These agents help individuals complete everyday tasks such as find directions, ask for help when ordering goods or services on a website, or understand additional information about a topic or idea. Humans still use automated agents for simple, utilitarian tasks, but these types of assistants are able to undertake larger and more important tasks. While intelligent agents present a potential solution, it is not fully understood about how humans will actually interact with digitized experts or if humans utilize intelligent agents in ways different from traditional human-to-human collaboration.

References

1. Few, D.A., Bruemmer, D.J., Walton, M.C.: Dynamic leadership for human-robot teams. In: Proceedings of the 1st ACM SIGCHI/SIGART Conference on Human-Robot Interaction, pp. 333–334. ACM, New York (2006)
2. Jones, H., Hinds, P.: Extreme work teams: using SWAT teams as a model for coordinating distributed robots. In: Proceedings of the 2002 ACM Conference on Computer Supported Cooperative Work, pp. 372–381. ACM, New York (2002)
3. Stogdill, R.M.: Handbook of Leadership: A Survey of Theory and Research. Free Press, New York (1974)
4. Northouse, P.G.: Leadership: Theory and Practice. Sage Publications, Thousand Oaks (2018)
5. Avolio, B.J.: Promoting more integrative strategies for leadership theory-building. Am. Psychol. 62, 25–33 (2007)
6. Ng, T.W.H.: Transformational leadership and performance outcomes: analyses of multiple mediation pathways. Leadersh. Q. 28, 385–417 (2017)
7. Yukl, G.: An evaluation of conceptual weaknesses in transformational and charismatic leadership theories. Leadersh. Q. 10, 285–305 (1999)
8. Deichmann, D., Stam, D.: Leveraging transformational and transactional leadership to cultivate the generation of organization-focused ideas. Leadersh. Q. 26, 204–219 (2015)
9. McCleskey, J.A.: Situational, transformational, and transactional leadership and leadership development. J. Bus. Stud. Q. 5, 117–130 (2017)
10. Kanji, G.K., Sã, P.M.E.: Measuring leadership excellence. Total Qual. Manag. 12, 701–718 (2001)
11. Kuhnert, K.W., Lewis, P.: Transactional and transformational leadership: a constructive/developmental analysis. Acad. Manag. Rev. 12, 648–657 (1987)
12. Kunhert, K.W.: Transforming leadership: developing people through delegation. In: Bass, B., Avolio, B. (eds.) Improving Organizational Effectiveness Through Transformational Leadership, pp. 10–25. Sage, Thousand Oaks (1994)
13. Tyssen, A.K., Wald, A., Spieth, P.: The challenge of transactional and transformational leadership in projects. Int. J. Proj. Manag. 32, 365–375 (2014)
14. Derrick, D.C., Jenkins, J., Nunamaker Jr., J.F.: Design principles for special purpose, embodied, conversational intelligence with environmental sensors (SPECIES) agents. AIS Trans. Hum.-Comput. Interact. 3, 62–81 (2011)
15. Elkins, A., Derrick, D.: The sound of trust: voice as a measurement of trust during interactions with embodied conversational agents. Group Decis. Negot. 22, 897–913 (2013)
16. Nunamaker, J.F., Briggs, R.O., Derrick, D.C., Schwabe, G.: The last research mile: achieving both rigor and relevance in information systems research. J. Manag. Inf. Syst. 32, 10–47 (2015)

17. Nunamaker Jr., J.F., Derrick, D.C., Elkins, A.C., Burgoon, J.K., Patton, M.W.: Embodied conversational agent (ECA) based kiosk for automated interviewing. J. Manag. Inf. Syst. **28**, 17–49 (2011)
18. Burgoon, J.K., Derrick, D.C., Elkins, A.C.: Sociocultural intelligence and intelligent agents. IEEE Intell. Syst. **26**, 84–87 (2011)
19. Antonakis, J., Avolio, B.J., Sivasubramaniam, N.: Context and leadership: an examination of the nine-factor full-range leadership theory using the Multifactor Leadership Questionnaire. Leadersh. Q. **14**, 261–295 (2003)
20. Falbe, C.M., Yukl, G.: Consequences for managers of using single influence tactics and combinations of tactics. Acad. Manag. J. **35**, 638–652 (1992)
21. Hiller, N.J., Day, D.V., Vance, R.J.: Collective enactment of leadership roles and team effectiveness: a field study. Leadersh. Q. **17**, 387–397 (2006)
22. Komaki, J.L., Citera, M.: Beyond effective supervision: identifying key interactions between superior and subordinate. Leadersh. Q. **1**, 91–105 (1990)
23. Mawhinney, T.C.: Effective leadership in superior-subordinate dyads: theory and data. J. Organ. Behav. Manag. **25**, 37–78 (2005)
24. Waldman, D.A., Javidan, M., Varella, P.: Charismatic leadership at the strategic level: a new application of upper echelons theory. Leadersh. Q. **15**, 355–380 (2004)
25. Yukl, G., Tracey, J.B.: Consequences of influence tactics used with subordinates, peers, and the boss. J. Appl. Psychol. **77**, 525–535 (1992)
26. Goltz, S.: A review of J. L. Komaki's leadership from an operant perspective. J. Organ. Behav. Manag. **25**, 73–81 (2005)
27. Komaki, J.L., Minnich, M.L.R., Grotto, A.R., Weinshank, B., Kern, M.J.: Promoting critical operant-based leadership while decreasing ubiquitous directives and exhortations. J. Organ. Behav. Manag. **31**, 236–261 (2011)
28. Komaki, J.L., Desselles, M.L., Bowman, E.D.: Definitely not a breeze: extending an operant model of effective supervision to teams. J. Appl. Psychol. **74**, 522–529 (1989)
29. Horner, M.: Leadership theory: past, present and future. Team Perform. Manag. **3**, 270–287 (1997)
30. Kayworth, T.R., Leidner, D.E.: Leadership effectiveness in global virtual teams. J. Manag. Inf. Syst. **18**, 7–40 (2002)
31. Locke, E.A., Latham, G.P.: Building a practically useful theory of goal setting and task motivation: a 35-year odyssey. Am. Psychol. **57**, 705–717 (2002)
32. Atkinson, J.: Towards experimental analysis of human motivation in terms of motives, expectancies, and incentives. In: Atkinson, J. (ed.) Motives in Fantasy, Action, and Society, pp. 288–305. Van Nostrand, Princeton (1958)
33. Berson, Y., Halevy, N., Shamir, B., Erez, M.: Leading from different psychological distances: a construal-level perspective on vision communication, goal setting, and follower motivation. Leadersh. Q. **26**, 143–155 (2015)
34. Larson, J.R., Callahan, C.: Performance monitoring: how it affects work productivity. J. Appl. Psychol. **75**, 530–538 (1990)
35. Brewer, N.: The effects of monitoring individual and group performance on the distribution of effort across tasks. J. Appl. Soc. Psychol. **25**, 760–777 (1995)
36. Aiello, J.R., Kolb, K.J.: Electronic performance monitoring and social context: impact on productivity and stress. J. Appl. Psychol. **80**, 339–353 (1995)
37. Kahn, D.: Impact of electronic performance monitoring on call centre employees performance (2016)
38. Nicolaou, N.: Electronic performance monitoring: the crossover between self-discipline and emotion management (2015)
39. Bass, B.M.: Leadership and Performance Beyond Expectations. Free Press, New York (1985)

40. Bass, B.M.: The Bass Handbook of Leadership – Theory, Research & Managerial Applications. Free Press, New York (2008)
41. Ashour, A.S., Johns, G.: Leader influence through operant principles: a theoretical and methodological framework. Hum. Relat. **36**, 603–626 (1983)
42. Luthans, F., Rosenkrantz, S.A., Hennessey, H.W.: What do successful managers really do? An observation study of managerial activities. J. Appl. Behav. Sci. **21**, 255–270 (1985)
43. Rost, K.A., Wilmer, D.R., Haas, E.J.: An operant analysis of leadership practices in mining. J. Saf. Health Environ. Res. **11**, 234–241 (2015)
44. Heeter, C.: Being there: the subjective experience of presence. Presence: Teleoper. Virtual Environ. **1**, 262–271 (1992)
45. Biocca, F., Harms, C., Burgoon, J.K.: Toward a more robust theory and measure of social presence: review and suggested criteria. Presence: Teleoper. Virtual Environ. **12**, 456–480 (2003)
46. Nass, C., Steuer, J., Tauber, E.R.: Computers are social actors. In: Proceedings of the SIGCHI Conference on Human Factors in Computing Systems: Celebrating Interdependence, pp. 72–78. ACM, Boston (1994)
47. Nass, C., Moon, Y., Morkes, J., Kim, E.-Y., Fogg, B.J.: Computers are social actors: a review of current research. In: Human Values and the Design of Computer Technology, pp. 137–161. Cambridge University Press, Stanford (1997)
48. Nass, C., Moon, Y.: Machines and mindlessness: social responses to computers. J. Soc. Issues **56**, 81–103 (2000)
49. Hall, B., Henningsen, D.D.: Social facilitation and human-computer interaction. Comput. Hum. Behav. **24**, 2965–2971 (2008)
50. Nass, C., Steuer, J.: Voices, boxes, and sources of messages. Hum. Commun. Res. **19**, 504–527 (1993)
51. Moon, Y., Nass, C.: Are computers scapegoats? Attributions of responsibility in human-computer interaction. Int. J. Hum.-Comput. Stud. **49**, 79–94 (1998)
52. Nass, C., Moon, Y., Fogg, B.J., Reeves, B., Dryer, C.: Can computer personalities be human personalities? In: Conference Companion on Human Factors in Computing Systems, pp. 228–229. ACM, Denver (1995)
53. Fogg, B.J., Nass, C.: Silicon sycophants: the effects of computers that flatter. Int. J. Hum.-Comput. Stud. **46**, 551–561 (1997)
54. Lee, E.-J.: Flattery may get computers somewhere, sometimes: the moderating role of output modality, computer gender, and user gender. Int. J. Hum.-Comput. Stud. **66**, 789–800 (2008)
55. Xu, K., Lombard, M.: Persuasive computing: feeling peer pressure from multiple computer agents. Comput. Hum. Behav. **74**, 152–162 (2017)
56. Greenwald, S.W., Wang, Z., Funk, M., Maes, P.: Investigating social presence and communication with embodied avatars in room-scale virtual reality. In: Beck, D., Allison, C., Morgado, L., Pirker, J., Khosmood, F., Richter, J., Gütl, C. (eds.) Immersive Learning Research Network. CCIS, pp. 75–90. Springer, Cham (2017). https://doi.org/10.1007/978-3-319-60633-0_7
57. Lu, B., Fan, W., Zhou, M.: Social presence, trust, and social commerce purchase intention: an empirical research. Comput. Hum. Behav. **56**, 225–237 (2016)
58. Katsyri, J., Sams, M.: The effect of dynamics on identifying basic emotions from synthetic and natural faces. Int. J. Hum.-Comput. Stud. **66**, 233–242 (2008)
59. Bailenson, J.N., Swinth, K., Hoyt, C., Persky, S., Dimov, A., Blascovich, J.: The independent and interactive effects of embodied-agent appearance and behavior on self-report, cognitive, and behavioral markers of copresence in immersive virtual environments. Presence: Teleoper. Virtual Environ. **14**, 379–393 (2005)

60. Fox, J., Ahn, S.J., Janssen, J.H., Yeykelis, L., Segovia, K.Y., Bailenson, J.N.: Avatars versus agents: a meta-analysis quantifying the effect of agency on social influence. Hum.-Comput. Interact. **30**, 401–432 (2015)
61. Gratch, J., Rickel, J., Andre, E., Cassell, J., Petajan, E., Badler, N.: Creating interactive virtual humans: some assembly required. IEEE Intell. Syst. **17**, 54–63 (2002). https://doi.org/10.1109/mis.2002.1024753
62. Gratch, J., Okhmatovskaia, A., Lamothe, F., Marsella, S., Morales, M., van der Werf, R.J., Morency, L.-P.: Virtual rapport. In: Gratch, J., Young, M., Aylett, R., Ballin, D., Olivier, P. (eds.) IVA 2006. LNCS, vol. 4133, pp. 14–27. Springer, Heidelberg (2006). https://doi.org/10.1007/11821830_2
63. Bailenson, J.N., Yee, N.: Digital chameleons: automatic assimilation of nonverbal gestures in immersive virtual environments. Psychol. Sci. **16**, 814–819 (2005)
64. McBreen, H.M., Jack, M.A.: Evaluating humanoid synthetic agents in e-retail applications. IEEE Trans. Syst. Man Cybern. Part A Syst. Hum. **31**, 394–405 (2001)
65. Kenny, P., Parsons, T.D., Gratch, J., Rizzo, A.A.: Evaluation of Justina: a virtual patient with PTSD. In: Prendinger, H., Lester, J., Ishizuka, M. (eds.) IVA 2008. LNCS, vol. 5208, pp. 394–408. Springer, Heidelberg (2008). https://doi.org/10.1007/978-3-540-85483-8_40
66. Deng, Z., Bailenson, J., Lewis, J.P., Neumann, U.: Perceiving visual emotions with speech. In: Gratch, J., Young, M., Aylett, R., Ballin, D., Olivier, P. (eds.) IVA 2006. LNCS, vol. 4133, pp. 107–120. Springer, Heidelberg (2006). https://doi.org/10.1007/11821830_9
67. Gratch, J., Okhmatovskaia, A., Lamothe, F., Marsella, S., Morales, M., van der Werf, R.J., Morency, L.-P.: Virtual rapport. In: Gratch, J., Young, M., Aylett, R., Ballin, D., Olivier, P. (eds.) IVA 2006. LNCS, vol. 4133, pp. 14–27. Springer, Heidelberg (2006). https://doi.org/10.1007/11821830_2
68. Derrick, D.C., Ligon, G.S.: The affective outcomes of using influence tactics in embodied conversational agents. Comput. Hum. Behav. **33**, 39–48 (2014)
69. Pickard, M.D., Burgoon, J.K., Derrick, D.C.: Toward an objective linguistic-based measure of perceived embodied conversational agent power and likeability. Int. J. Hum.-Comput. Interact. **30**, 495–516 (2014)
70. Hess, T., Fuller, M., Cambell, D.: Designing interfaces with social presence: using vividness and extraversion to create social recommendation agents. J. Assoc. Inf. Syst. **10**, 889–919 (2009)
71. Merritt, S.M., Ilgen, D.R.: Not all trust is created equal: dispositional and history-based trust in human-automation interactions. Hum. Factors **50**, 194–210 (2008)
72. Skinner, B.F.: The phylogeny and ontogeny of behavior. Science **153**, 1205–1213 (1966)
73. Briggs, R.O., Reinig, B.A., de Vreede, G.-J.: Meeting satisfaction for technology-supported groups: an empirical validation of a goal attainment model. Small Group Res. **37**, 585–611 (2006)
74. Graen, G.B., Uhl-Bien, M.: Relationship-based approach to leadership: development of leader-member exchange (LMX) theory of leadership over 25 years: applying a multi-level, multi-domain perspective. Leadersh. Q. **6**, 219–247 (1995)
75. Bente, G., Rüggenberg, S., Krämer, N.C., Eschenburg, F.: Avatar-mediated networking: increasing social presence and interpersonal trust in net-based collaborations. Hum. Commun. Res. **34**, 287–318 (2008)
76. Pavlov, P.I.: Conditioned reflexes: an investigation of the physiological activity of the cerebral cortex. Ann. Neurosci. **17**, 136–141 (2010)
77. Pfeffer, J.: The ambiguity of leadership. Acad. Manag. Rev. **2**, 104–112 (1977)

Head-Mounted Displays in Industrial AR-Applications: Ready for Prime Time?

Hitesh Dhiman[1], Sascha Martinez[1], Volker Paelke[3],
and Carsten Röcker[1,2(✉)]

[1] Fraunhofer IOSB-INA, Lemgo, Germany
{hitesh.dhiman, sascha.martinez,
carsten.roecker}@iosb-ina.fraunhofer.de
[2] Ostwestfalen-Lippe University of Applied Sciences, Lemgo, Germany
carsten.roecker@hs-owl.de
[3] Bremen University of Applied Sciences, Bremen, Germany
volker.paelke@hs-bremen.de

Abstract. The latest generation of head-mounted displays such as HoloLens provide mixed reality capabilities that claim to better integrate the real and virtual worlds. In this paper, we would like the share our experiences in implementing a user interface for an assembly assistance system using the HoloLens. We carried out a preliminary evaluation of the applicability of mixed reality using the perspective of developers and expert users in an assembly scenario that allows us to operate and compare two interfaces - a state-of-the-art projector display system and the HoloLens. We believe our findings may contribute towards a better understanding of the effects of new display technologies such as the HoloLens in developing and using assistance systems in other fields as well. Areas that may be of future research are also highlighted.

Keywords: Human machine interaction · Assembly assistance system
Qualitative study · HoloLens

1 Introduction

It is anticipated that trends like shorter innovation and product life cycles as well as an increase in mass customization will result in highly complex products that have to be produced in relatively small batches [3, 4]. The complexity of assembly typically leads to a complexity in automation, which might be too expensive to implement given the short life cycle [5]. Consequently, manual assembly is another viable option for many companies.

The assembly operation is designed to be a part of a larger product manufacturing environment (Fig. 1). Custom parts are loaded onto a moving conveyor prior to the assembly station, while regular parts are available in the bins directly in front of the user. Once the assembly station receives an order, the user is guided through the assembly process. Each assembly tutorial consists of various steps which are divided into two categories, pick and assemble. In the pick step the user is shown the right component to pick, and in the assembly step the components are assembled followed

© Springer International Publishing AG, part of Springer Nature 2018
F. F.-H. Nah and B. S. Xiao (Eds.): HCIBGO 2018, LNCS 10923, pp. 67–78, 2018.
https://doi.org/10.1007/978-3-319-91716-0_6

by a confirmation. Some parts of the assembly station are designed to be user configurable, for example the height of the workplace can be adjusted at any time. Several such systems are available commercially (see, e.g., [6] or [7] for an overview).

Fig. 1. Use case of an assembly assistance system, image taken from [10].

The proliferation of Augmented Reality (AR) in industrial applications [15] has enlarged the choice of display and interaction technologies that can be used on these systems. Early approaches in this field made use of head-mounted displays (HMDs) in the form of data glasses. Although the use of HMDs showed improvement in speed for picking tasks in comparison with paper instructions [3], they were shown to have various usability issues, such as the inaccuracy of stereoscopic projection, limited field of view, focusing issues and physical discomfort [1]. As a result, most state-of-the-art assembly assistance systems in the last years have utilized projection-based displays [9, 10, 16]. For instance, the Ulixes 'Der Assistent' system uses a projector in conjunction with a touch screen display.

Projection-based systems, however, also come with a few disadvantages. Firstly, the area of the workplace in such a system is limited to the area of projection. Any objects, parts and boxes that lie outside this zone cannot be augmented. Secondly, the placement of the assembly bins needs to be designed such that the projection is not blocked. Although the height of the worktable is adjustable, the placement and configuration of the boxes is fixed. In short, projection-based systems suffer from a lack of flexibility that may limit their use scenarios other than assembly assistance.

In the context of Industry 4.0, when looked at from the employees' point of view, a flexible workplace is considered as one which is networked, personalized, and mobile [2], as it may be necessary to retool and reconfigure both the entire production line as well as the assembly stations in order to respond to variations in customer orders. In addition, every employee may prefer a particular placement and arrangement of tools and parts. In this case it would be desirable if the display technology is aware of the user's environment, such that it is able to respond to the changes in configuration. Not many AR devices were able to achieve this ability until recently, when Microsoft released the HoloLens display which uses depth sensors to map the user's surroundings and make them a part of the digital augmentation. Our focus in this paper is to find out if the HoloLens offers a more flexible display technology than projection, and if it reduces the usability issues of HMDs as reported above.

2   State of the Art

Most of the work in the field of assembly assistance has applied various display technologies, which we broadly categorize into two groups: dynamic systems and static systems.

Static systems use some form of AR technology that is installed onto the system itself. For instance, some systems make use of a light that is affixed in front of, or above, every bin on the rack; this light indicates the part to be picked and feedback to the system is provided via integrated touch or proximity sensors [20]. A second class of systems [16] uses a projector located above the assembly station that projects images onto the workplace and bins. In this case, hand gestures are detected via an additional 3D sensor placed close to the projector. The projector-based system was demonstrated to be faster and more accurate in comparison to a smart glass-based system [1].

Nonetheless, an obvious limitation of these systems is that physical installation limits their flexibility and scalability, both of which cannot be achieved without considerable economic and manual effort. Further, the placement of bins has to take into account the nature of projection – bins can only be placed within the area of projection, which itself is limited per workstation. For instance, an area of 100 cm × 60 cm while sufficient for a single major assembly may not be suitable for multiple minor assembly stations spanning across a few meters. Using multiple projectors and 3D sensors to achieve the desired result becomes considerably expensive.

Dynamic systems make use of a head mounted device [10–13]. Ideally, this type of a system allows itself to be adjusted and scaled since the display and the workplace are decoupled. Most of the research work in this area has been conducted using smart glasses which overlay 2D or 3D images onto a display. Although smart glasses have been shown to improve productivity as compared to paper-based instructions [21], in comparison to projection-based systems, they have considerable drawbacks, namely, reduction of wearing comfort due to high weight, need for optical adaptability, and a narrow field of view [1, 14].

The studies mentioned previously have compared in-situ projection with HMDs that vary in their technical capabilities. For instance, Zheng et al. [11] used a Google Glass device which is a form of peripheral display, while Khuong et al. [12] used a Vuzix Wrap 920AR which is capable of displaying "stereoscopic 3D video content" but lacks the capability to render content on its own [8]. Although commercial projection technology has been available for a couple of decades now, the market for commercial HMDs is still evolving. The latest generation of HMDs such as HoloLens classify themselves as 'Mixed Reality' glasses, where Mixed Reality is defined as a combination of Augmented Reality (AR) and Augmented Virtuality (VR) [22]. In our literature review, no study has thus far compared a MR HMD to a projection-based display.

3 Overall Research Goal and Procedure

The aim of this paper is to explore the advantages and disadvantages of using an MR capable HMD as compared to a projection-based display on an assembly assistance system. We would like to firstly understand the effect of MR on information representation, and secondly, if MR brings an obvious improvement or feature add to the existing state of the art assembly assistance system such that it can possibly replace a projector as the primary display. Further, we also wish to define research questions that were until now not possible to be studied in our application scenario due to the technical limitations in HMD display technology.

For the purpose of this study we developed two instances of one and the same assembly assistance system, the only difference being the way in which information is presented. One system consists of a projection-based display, the other system uses a HoloLens (Fig. 3). A preliminary evaluation is carried out by expert users who have developed and used these assembly assistance systems.

4 Design and Implementation of Evaluation Prototype

4.1 General Setup of Evaluation Prototype

The prototype systems consist of two height adjustable workbenches, each with two rows of workbins whose height, tilt and depth can be adjusted (Fig. 2).

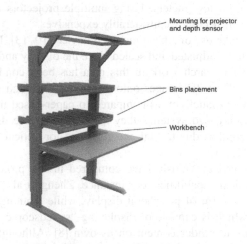

Mounting for projector
and depth sensor

Bins placement

Workbench

Fig. 2. Assistance system setup.

Fig. 3. System setup with projection-based display (left) and HoloLens (right).

The first system contains a projector and a depth sensor attached vertically above the workbench, whereas on the second system only the depth sensor is used (Fig. 3). Data from the depth sensor is processed via a hand recognition algorithm as developed by Büttner et al. [16]. The algorithm can detect if the correct part has been picked, or it can be used to make specific areas on the table touch sensitive. On both the systems, an LCD touchscreen is mounted above the bins in order to choose specific assembly instruction tutorials. The assembly system software runs on a PC that also acts as a server and is able to connect to multiple clients.

4.2 Prototype Using the Projection-Based Display

The projector displays content directly onto the workbench (Fig. 3, left). Along with the depth enabled gesture recognition, this transforms the entire workbench into a touchscreen display, where specific, predefined areas are configured as touch inputs. In the pick step the correct bin is highlighted, and in the assembly step the assembly instruction and a confirmation icon are projected. Once the physical setup is configured, the projection is stable in repeated usage with change in table height or lighting conditions.

4.3 Prototype Using the HoloLens

The hardware of the HoloLens consists of an inertial measurement unit (IMU), 4 environment understanding cameras, 1 depth camera, 1 ambient light sensor, a 12 MP photo/video camera and 4 microphones. The display contains two see through holographic lenses utilizing waveguide technology. The entire unit weighs 579 g. On the software side, libraries that provide gaze tracking, gesture recognition, speech recognition and spatial understanding are available for developer use. Applications are programmed via the Unity game engine which provides ray casting, graphics, physics and interaction support.

The main feature that sets the HoloLens apart from other VR and Immersive headsets is "Spatial Mapping". According to Microsoft, "Spatial mapping provides a detailed representation of real-world surfaces in the environment around the HoloLens,

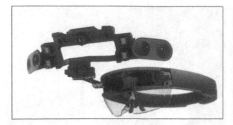

Fig. 4. HoloLens: sensor assembly (left) and display assembly (right), images taken from [17].

allowing developers to create a convincing mixed reality experience. By merging the real world with the virtual world, an application can make holograms seem real. Applications can also more naturally align with user expectations by providing familiar real-world behaviors and interactions" [18]. Spatial mapping allows holograms to exhibit physical behavior, for example occlusion and physics.

A second related, but important feature is that of a "Spatial Anchor". As stated on the Microsoft website, "A spatial anchor represents an important point in the world that the system should keep track of over time. Each anchor has a coordinate system that adjusts as needed, relative to other anchors or frames of reference, in order to ensure that anchored holograms stay precisely in place" [19]. One anchor point can serve as a frame of reference for more than one hologram in a local proximity. A typical use case is that of a board game, in which holographic objects need to be placed on a flat surface. In our use we observed that anchor placement is primarily vision based, achieved through the environment understanding cameras.

4.4   System Operation with HoloLens

Two 'virtual screens' placed in front of the user display a picture or video of the assembled part, and an additional, larger screen in the middle shows text instructions (Fig. 5, left). A green holographic arrow indicates where the correct component is located (Fig. 5, right), which the user picks to advance to the next step. The assembly step displays the intended assembly, which the user needs to confirm by tapping on a holographic buzzer button placed on the table (Fig. 6, left).

Fig. 5. Instruction screens (left) and picking instruction (right). (Color figure online)

The user can navigate through the tutorial steps, or cancel a tutorial by tapping on the touchscreen placed in front left (Fig. 4). The position of the arrow and the virtual button is user configurable prior to starting the assembly tutorial.

Fig. 6. Confirmation button (left) and calibration setup (right). (Color figure online)

One of the primary requirements of the assembly application is that the visual instructions need to be stable in all conditions of use. This implies that the placement of the visual objects should not be affected by factory conditions or physical adjustments by the user. With a top mounted projector this requirement is easily met; with the HoloLens this is achieved by making use of a QR code which serves as a physical marker. Prior to using the assembly station, the user needs to perform a 'calibration' where a digital image of the QR code is superimposed onto the physical code (Fig. 6). The calibration makes use of feature points and OpenCV to perform the alignment, after which the position of the QR code is saved as a spatial anchor. All the holograms displayed in the workplace use this anchor as a reference point.

5   Preliminary System Investigation

To evaluate this setup, we constructed a scenario in which the HoloLens replaces the projector in everyday use for our application. In order to achieve that, the HoloLens would have to surpass both the technical and functional capabilities of the projection-based display. From a technical perspective, we compared the stability of the MR display of the HoloLens with the existing 2D projection implementation under different everyday scenarios. For a functional evaluation, expert users were asked to use the system, complete an assembly task, and their responses were recorded.

Display Stability. By stability is meant the ability of the system to maintain a stable projection. A test was conducted by simulating typical workplace use cases. Each situation was repeated 10 times and the results recorded.

(a) *Start/stop Scenarios and Pauses*

This test simulates beginning a shift, taking a break and resuming work. The HoloLens is taken off and placed on the desk without quitting the assistance application. Work is resumed after 5 min of inactivity. In 8 out of 10 cases, the projections were stable. In the remaining 2 cases a drift was observed and a recalibration was needed to correct this behavior.

(b) *Table Height Adjustment*

The table's height can be changed anytime during the assembly. This is where we found the HoloLens had most trouble. The holograms would stick to the workplace in only 5 out of 10 cases, that is, only 50% of the time, in the remaining 5 cases they did not follow the desk, i.e. they were left either floating in air or intersecting with the physical workplace. In order to bring the holograms back into place a re-calibration had to be performed.

Subjective Evaluation. In order to compare the HoloLens with previous smart glass implementations, we use the same metrics as in the prior study conducted by Büttner et al. [1]. The results here were obtained via observation and discussion with expert users following the completion of the assembly task. The following points were considered:

(a) *Robustness under Bright Lighting Conditions*

The evaluation was conducted in a factory like environment with a mix of both natural and artificial light. In the previous study it was reported that users had difficulty when the background lighting was set to above 500 lux, with the HoloLens, users did not report any issues due to ambient lighting.

(b) *Restrictions of Field of View*

The Vuzix Star 1200 glasses used in the previous study had a field of view of 35°, while the HoloLens offers a field of view of 70°. Compared to the projection display this amounts to about 70% coverage of the workstation at a distance of 0.5 m from the assembly bins. Still, most users noticed the restriction in the field of view immediately.

(c) *Fixation of the Overlay*

In the previous study the users reported discomfort due to a misalignment of the interpupillary distance, and also because the position of the glasses on the nose bridge affected the digital overlays. In the case of the HoloLens no such issue was observed.

(d) *(Un-)Natural Overlays*

It was noted in the previous study that "HMD are beneficial for showing virtual objects in a free space, but when augmenting existing physical objects, the overlay may still be perceived as a separate entity and therefore be perceived as unnatural" [1]. When using the HoloLens, however, the integration between the real and the virtual world was unnoticed. In fact, the level of realism created other UI quirks - users expected the virtual objects to behave as real-world objects, for instance most users expected that the buzzer button (Fig. 6) needs only be tapped and not pressed or clicked, which led us to re-adjust the 3D camera's sensitivity to detect a tap at a certain height above the desk.

(e) *Stereoscopic View and Focusing Issues*

No problems due to focal distance were reported. The holograms appeared to be in focus at all virtual distances.

(f) *Smart Glasses and Optical Aids*

The HoloLens' placement on the head can be adjusted such that the display sits in front of optical glasses, all users in our evaluation were able to use the HoloLens without any discomfort.

(g) *Drawbacks of Wearable Devices in Industrial Settings*

In the prior study the HMD was wired, which was noted to restrict mobility. Since the HoloLens has an on-board battery, it can be used wirelessly. Users could perform tasks such as picking up a custom piece from the assembly line situated a few meters away, however, at 579 g the weight of the HoloLens is high compared to other smart glasses. The on-board battery life is 2–3 h of active use which makes it infeasible for use in an 8-h shift. Although it is possible to use the HoloLens while charging, it comes at the cost of reduced mobility.

6 Discussion

In our view, the HoloLens is a significant step up from existing smart glasses. It is still too heavy and has a battery life unsuitable for regular shift use in manufacturing environments, and the limited field of view can hinder the workflow in cases when UI elements go out of view. In our case, when the green holographic arrow pointing to the correct bin was outside the field of view, some users thought that the UI was inactive.

A related issue was regarding the distance of hologram placement. Microsoft recommends that the holograms be placed "in the optimal zone – between 1.25 m and 5 m" from the user [18], but this may not be possible if the bins are to be kept within arm's reach.

We also realized that the design of the workplace itself was also proving to be a hindrance in using the HoloLens effectively. For instance, the coexistence of 2D and 3D objects in the same space puzzled users as to which objects were interactable. In addition, users expected holograms to follow the rules of object placement in the real world, and drifts in hologram positions were particularly confusing.

Another problem was noticed when users wanted to discuss or ask questions about the UI. With the projection-based display it is possible to have more than one user interact with the UI. On the HoloLens this ability needs to be programmed into the application, and more than one HoloLens is required, which means more development effort and costs.

On the positive side, in the course of development and use, we found several features of the HoloLens had an obvious advatage, predefined areas are configured as touch inputs. over a projection display. While a projector is mounted on the work-station, the HoloLens has no such limitation as long as an anchor can be located in the visible environment. A projector needs a 2D plane to display information, therefore a

3D space needs to be constructed as a staggered collection of non-overlapping 2D planes. For instance, each new row of bins needs to be placed a few cm behind the row below, which restricts the number of rows of bins that can be used before the 2D area available extends beyond the projector's reach. In case of the HoloLens, the 3D space around a physical object is available for augmentation, therefore any kind of bin arrangements can be used as long as there is enough space for virtual objects to exist along with real objects. With a HMD such as the HoloLens the workplace can be reconfigured in real time.

A benefit of dissociating the display from the physical space is the possibility to allow more than one device to exist in the same space. In the course of our development we were able to use 2 HoloLens devices in the same workspace. This opens up the opportunity to segment the UI to cater to specific roles. For instance, the assembly supervisor may wish to see a different view of the assembly process than the assembly operator.

Lastly, the HoloLens extends the interaction modalities of the workstation as it supports speech, gaze and gesture-based interaction on its own. Along with the 3D sensor and the touch screen display, this amounts to more options from a usability perspective.

7   Topics for Future Work

This preliminary study was carried out by expert users to compare two display technologies, however, it remains to be seen if the use of MR displays such as HoloLens actually results in usability and productivity improvements in assembly tasks of various levels of difficulty. In future we would like to conduct a more detailed study with larger user groups.

The technological advancements which the HoloLens offers also brought to light the lack of usability research in using MR HMDs. Design guidelines in this regard are few and far between, the only resource available so far is Microsoft's own set of guidelines which are based on the experience of HoloLens' development.

The effect of MR technology on industrial workplace design may also be an area of future research. As this technology matures, it may be worthwhile to investigate how the workplaces of the future may be designed to accommodate both real and MR environments.

Studies on using HMDs such as the HoloLens in 8-h shifts in industrial settings have not been carried out, therefore the occupational health effects of these displays are also unknown.

8   Conclusion

In this paper, we presented an early expert evaluation of two different display types for an assembly assistance system – a HoloLens mixed reality head mounted display and an existing state of the art projection-based display. Preliminary feedback indicates that the HoloLens has greatly improved on the limitations of HMD displays, but due to its weight and low battery life, it cannot replacement projection-based displays in assembly assistance at present. However, assistance systems are also used in other areas of factories, for instance training systems, where the HoloLens may fulfill the technical and functional requirements. Nonetheless, a deeper investigation is needed to understand the effects of mixed reality-based displays in industrial settings.

References

1. Büttner, S., Röcker, C., Sand, O.: Using head-mounted displays and in-situ projection for assistive systems – a comparison. In: Proceedings of the 9th ACM International Conference on Pervasive Technologies Related to Assistive Environments (PETRA 2016), Article No. 44. ACM New York, USA (2016)
2. Gold, S.: Tomorrow's Factory Jobs (2017). https://www.siemens.com/innovation/es/home/pictures-of-the-future/industry-and-automation/digital-factories-personalized-workstations.html
3. Guo, A., Raghu, S., Xie, X., Ismail, S., Luo, X., Simoneau, J., Gilliland, S., Baumann, H., Southern, C., Starner, T.: A comparison of order picking assisted by head-up display (HUD), cart-mounted display (CMD), light, and paper pick list. In: Proceedings of the 2014 ACM International Symposium on Wearable Computers, pp. 71–78 (2014)
4. Lasi, H., Fettke, P., Feld, T., Hoffmann, M.: Industry 4.0. Bus. Inf. Syst. Eng. 6(4), 239–242 (2014)
5. Orfi, N., Terpenny, J., Sahin-Sariisik, A.: Harnessing product complexity: step 1— establishing product complexity dimensions and indicators. Eng. Econ. 56(1), 59–79 (2011)
6. https://www.assemblysolutions.de/index_en.html
7. https://www.boschrexroth.com/de/de/produkte/produktneuheiten/montagetechnik/activeassist
8. https://www.vuzix.com/Products/LegacyProduct/6
9. Paelke, V., Büttner, B., Mucha, H., Röcker, C.: A checklist-based approach for evaluating augmented reality displays in industrial applications. In: Trzcielinski, S. (ed.) Advances in Ergonomics of Manufacturing: Managing the Enterprise of the Future, pp. 225–234. Springer, Heidelberg (2017). https://doi.org/10.1007/978-3-319-60474-9_21
10. Sand, O., Büttner, S., Paelke, V., Röcker, C.: smARt.Assembly – projection-based augmented reality for supporting assembly workers. In: Lackey, S., Shumaker, R. (eds.) VAMR 2016. LNCS, vol. 9740, pp. 643–652. Springer, Cham (2016). https://doi.org/10.1007/978-3-319-39907-2_61
11. Zheng, X.S., Foucault, C., Silva, P.M., Dasari, S., Yang, T., Goose, S.: Eye-wearable technology for machine maintenance. In: Proceedings of the 33rd Annual ACM Conference on Human Factors in Computing Systems (CHI 2015), pp. 2125–2134. ACM Press, New York (2015)
12. Khuong, B.M., Kiyokawa, K., Miller, A., Viola, J.J., Mashita, T., Takemura, H.: The effectiveness of an AR-based context-aware assembly support system in object assembly. In: Proceedings of the IEEE Conference on Virtual Reality (VR 2014) (2014)
13. Biocca, F., Tang, A., Owen, C., Xiao, F.: Attention funnel: omnidirectional 3D cursor for mobile augmented reality platforms. In: Proceedings of the Conference on Human Factors in Computing Systems (CHI 2006), pp. 1115–1122. ACM Press, New York (2006)
14. Grubert, J., Hamacher, D., Mecke, R., Bockelmann, I., Schega, L., Huckauf, A., Tumler, J.: Extended investigations of user-related issues in mobile industrial AR. In: Proceedings of the IEEE International Symposium on Mixed and Augmented Reality (ISMAR 2010), pp. 229–230. IEEE Computer Society Press (2010)

15. Fellmann, M., Robert, S., Büttner, S., Mucha, H., Röcker, C.: Towards a framework for assistance systems to support work processes in smart factories. In: Holzinger, A., Kieseberg, P., Tjoa, A.M., Weippl, E. (eds.) CD-MAKE 2017. LNCS, vol. 10410, pp. 59–68. Springer, Cham (2017). https://doi.org/10.1007/978-3-319-66808-6_5

16. Büttner, S., Sand, O., Röcker, C.: Exploring design opportunities for intelligent worker assistance: a new approach using projetion-based AR and a novel hand-tracking algorithm. In: Braun, A., Wichert, R., Maña, A. (eds.) AmI 2017. LNCS, vol. 10217, pp. 33–45. Springer, Cham (2017). https://doi.org/10.1007/978-3-319-56997-0_3

17. https://developer.microsoft.com/en-us/windows/mixed-reality/HoloLens_hardware_details

18. https://developer.microsoft.com/en-us/windows/mixed-reality/hologram

19. https://developer.microsoft.com/en-us/windows/mixed-reality/spatial_anchors

20. http://flexmation.com/components/pick-to-light-systems/

21. Tang, A., Owen, C., Biocca, F., Mou, W.: Comparative effectiveness of augmented reality in object assembly. In: Proceedings of the Conference on Human Factors in Computing Systems (CHI 2003), pp. 73–80. ACM Press, New York (2003)

22. Milgram, P., Kishino, F.: A taxonomy of mixed reality visual displays. IEICE Trans. Inf. Syst. **77**(12), 1321–1329 (1994). Special Issue on Networked Reality

The Service Design of Material Traceability System in the Smart Manufacturing Theme

Rich C. Lee[(⊠)]

Institute of Applied Economics,
National Taiwan Ocean University, Keelung, Taiwan
richchihlee@gmail.com

Abstract. In the emerging era of Industry 4.0, many factories have launched a series of initiatives to enhance their lean production by adopting the information technology and the business analytics as the tool of business transformation [1]. Among these initiatives, continuously improving the quality assurance is the compelling driver and the cornerstone of rival differentiation [2]. But the satisfaction of a product significantly depends on its components' quality which were procured from the different suppliers at different times; thus, to increase the customer's confidence in using the product, the more effective collaboration in the supply chain plays the key role to success. The material traceability system is a part of the supply chain information visibility [3]; not only putting the accountability in place, but also disclosing the whole journey of each lot of production. This paper revisited the current collaboration model and to explore where went wrong in the past, proposes the feasible traceability requirement taking framework, and presents the appropriate data model for such a system.

Keywords: Material traceability · Supply chain management
Business experiments · Firm choices · Enterprise Architecture

1 Introduction

Nowadays the emerging smart business emphasizes deliver the overall service quality considering the aspects from better security, outcome consistency, professional attitude, task completeness, specific conditions, available as needed, and comprehensive training [4]. These services, apply and integrate a number of components, play as the conveyer to deliver the continuous values to the recipients. The unique features of these components are the cornerstone to differentiate with the rivals. The common core of these smart businesses, illustrated in Fig. 1, who provides a number of customer-centric touch-points to the customers; each touch-point incorporates service components collaborated by machines and people. The backend support is a composite functional unit, covering the **social**—understanding the needs, **technological**—facilitating the business processes, **economic**—scheming the revenue and profit models, and **strategic**—positioning the competitive service in the marketplace—perspectives [5] to identify and create value to the customers. The customer service maintains the intimacy and collects the complaints and the potential needs of the customers. Lastly, the quality measurements are applied throughout the processes to evaluate the performance and the effectiveness of the initiatives and recommends the proactive improvement amendments.

© Springer International Publishing AG, part of Springer Nature 2018
F. F.-H. Nah and B. S. Xiao (Eds.): HCIBGO 2018, LNCS 10923, pp. 79–90, 2018.
https://doi.org/10.1007/978-3-319-91716-0_7

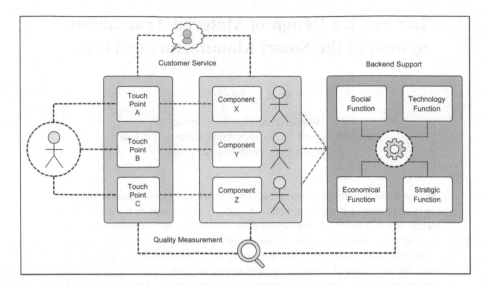

Fig. 1. Smart business operation

These smart business innovative services adopt the technology to strengthen the interoperability among their value chain though: (1) more complex, bundled, and fast delivered products and services; (2) adopting boundary spanned value co-creation model; (3) systematically orchestrating the coordination and control; (4) endeavoring the information and knowledge sharing; (5) building a business operation supportive infrastructure; and (6) always incorporate the customer experiences into the heart of the service design and delivery [6]. Obviously, the successfulness of collaboration determines the quality of the service owing to the effectiveness of establishing the shared vision about the market positioning and the efficiency of group problem-solving proactive actions taken. In order to pertain the customers, not just delivering the products and the services, but also giving the confidence of using them by providing the material traceability as a significant mean of improving the branding.

It is an agreeable strategy for smart business that the technology-enabled interoperability-strengthen initiatives are a part of smart business experiments in which it is an exploratory journey in creating the rare, imperfectly imitable, and non-substitutable competence as resources, from the resource-based view perspective [7], against the rivals. Many innovative concepts—applying the out-of-box thinking and measuring everything that matters—have injected into the new business model, such as using the analytics to find the tacit knowledge of business activities or employing the smart sensors to give a new customer experience [8]. But how to effectively build a value chain, cultivating the non-imitable resources, to maintain the products and services are at consistent quality level through the material traceability system as a business experiment to improve branding?

This paper, aiming to the perfection of supply chain management, presents the feasible approach of conducting the material traceability project through a rigorous requirement soliciting process, it introduces a novel perspective of supply chain competition dynamic model in which it disclosed why such a value chain is not easy to build because of there is potential business completion within the chain; and from those conflict factors, it proposes a better value co-creating model for the supply chain. Most importantly, this paper arguably suggests a more efficient data model of the material traceability system to simplify the design in contrast with the current commonly used schema-oriented approach.

2 Supplier Competition

There are two simple business logics of firms, shooting for either the profit maximization or/and cost minimization [9]. It seems to be a duality problem—same purpose but different angles to cut in, but their essences are different. In fact, the profit maximization goal is more related on the sales end, for example, the firm places a higher pricing strategy by delivering a product with unique features, better design and quality to the customers is a common approach; on the contrast, the cost minimization goal is more on the supply end, under the current production configuration—the execution efficiency and the product structure, the firm acquires the material from the qualified vendor list and asking for lower price. Under the cost minimization model, when the material is not from a single source and it can be provided by multiple suppliers, it will cause supply chain competition.

If cost is the major concern, the suppliers have no better way to win the competition but keep pushing downward the material price. No supplier has the definite confidence to will the order. During the multiple order biddings of various buyers, the total quality of these material requisitions might exceed the supplier's production capability. That is one of the reasons why, from time to time, the production is suspended awaiting the arrival of the required material. When the material is emergently short during the production cycle, the firm has to solicit the material from the market in time, the price and the quality might not be expected as it should.

The supply chain partners will be motivated by the firm's business logics, seeking for customer perceived value—profit maximization or the higher quality/cost benefit—cost minimization. As mentioned before, the supplier competition is inevitable under the cost minimization scenario. Supposedly, illustrated in Fig. 2, a factory is going to produce the product X, it procures the materials in order to build it. The factory invites a couple of qualified suppliers from the approval vendor list, say they are three suppliers, S, A, and D in this game; then the factory releases the material specifications and requesting the invited suppliers for bidding. These three suppliers are seeking the opportunity to maximizing their profits, also bidding for the product Y which competes against X with some product differentiated features of another factory at the same time. Because the three suppliers are on the same approval vendor list, it implies that their quality levels are also above the specifications; therefore, the price dominates the factory's choice. Luckily for the supplier D who wins both bids for better quality/cost; however, these material needs will impose the material delivery pressure—might be less expected by its planner—to its production.

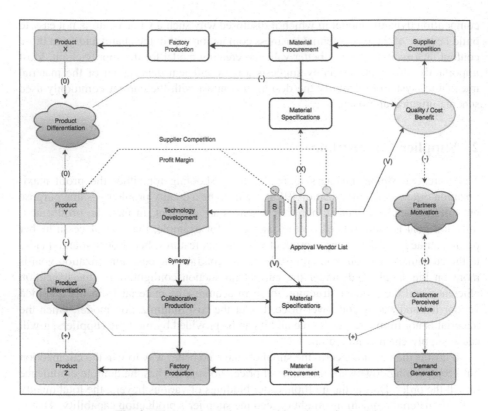

Fig. 2. The supply chain competition dynamic model

Since the model is valued for lower cost, the winning supplier is also looking for its cost minimization; the potential risk for the procurer is either the delivery is delayed, or/and the quality is compromised. When business is booming during the hot season, the suppliers have less motivation of joining this less confident bidding opportunities; this will cause the procurer to provision the material with higher buying prices and the incurred extra inventory staging costs.

To avoid the potential side-effect of the supplier competition, many firms are seeking for increasing the customer perceived value through innovation as the mean of profit maximization [10]. A product Z applying the cost minimization contrast model, instead of releasing the material specifications to a couple of suppliers after the product design, the firm encourages the selected suppliers to participate the design in the early phase and closely collaborating in production. The innovation comes from the synergy of all participants; since this model putting the product differentiation in the first place, the supplier's competition game rule has been changed from the lowest price to who can offer better value to the product. The innovation always prevails, thus the true profit winner in the market will go to the product Z; and it expels the other products X and Y out of the high profit market segment. The relentless cutting the cost scenario causes low profit margin; this is the nightmare that no firm would want to have.

3 Material Traceability

The material traceability is a process about recording the source of where the material came from and how the component was built appropriately. The information system makes the objective of material traceability achievable. Under the current business model, the product and the service delivery are synergies efforts of the integrator and the component suppliers making. There are non-technical critical challenges must be resolved before such a system can be in place: (1) asymmetric bargain power—not all integrators have the dominating power to ask their suppliers to comply with the instructions for improvements; from time to time, the key component suppliers hold the calling cards at hand that makes them superior during the negotiation; (2) credible proof—the integrity is above all; the whole system depends on the correct and non-manipulative data reported; (3) shareable data repository—many firms are still using less efficient ways of exchanging the data, such as sending the spreadsheet files over the emails; it is very hard to track and maintain the versions of data especially when multiple parties involved in the communication loop; (4) collaboration—the value of traceability depends on the degree of information visibility and the disclosure in depth; the traceability involves all parties to participate the improving process; the participants have different business priority when a jointly-communication is needed, this will make the collaboration more difficultly and less effectively; and (5) obligation to comply—in many occasions, the integrator procures the components majorly according to their lower prices; the suppliers will hesitate to comply the costly quality improvement instructions under such a short-term and no-commitment business relationship.

Effectively tracking the material sources is not as simple as it appears to be but more complicated rather. A product is made through a series of steps; each step requires the associated components to complete the process. These components were procured by purchase orders from various suppliers. From the components supplier's view, the components were also made through a series of steps; each step adopted a number of materials to build. It is worth noted that these components and materials may come from different suppliers at different times. The goal of traceability is not just giving the information about the material sources; it is very important that in case of the defect occurred, the system will reveal the responsible components and the associated materials information sufficient enough to support the following amendment process can be undertaken.

The finish good is built based on the production steps; each step may employ a number of materials to produce the final or the semi-product. The Fig. 3 illustrates a general case about the material traceability. A finished good is made of a series steps from P1 to Pn. The step P1 requires the material M11 and M12 in order to build the intermediate product Pb1 which will be used in the following step P2 as the input. The step P2 requires M21 and M22 in order to build the intermediate product Pb2 which will be used in the following step P3 as the input; and so on to the step Pn. The material suppliers are also taking the similar processes to fulfil the production. Obviously, the traceability data schema is not easy and efficient to be described as common two-dimensional—simple spreadsheet-like table—approach, it has to use several master-and-detail tables to serve the purpose. This will make data traversing recursively in order to track a suspicious material usage.

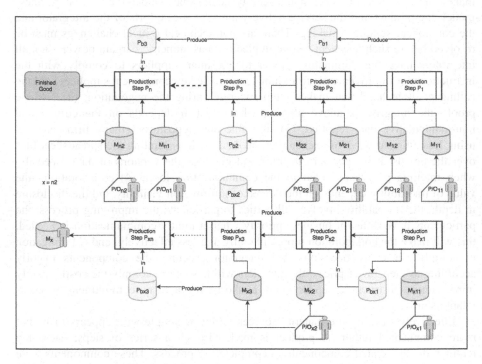

Fig. 3. The complexity of material traceability

4 Data Model

The production is lot-driven; in the just-in-time model, when a sales order is received, the planner assigns a/several lot number(s) to fulfil the order. Each lot number represents a production order and triggers material procurement if the stock quantity is shy. The supply chain department proceeds the procurement process; some certain criteria are in place to qualify the suppliers, such as price, quality, and delivery time, etc. There is no guarantee that the material is procured from the same supplier as before. In fact, it is a common practice that the material came from various suppliers at different times within the single production lot. Therefore, the data model for the traceability is not a row-based record—each row at least contains the following fields: (1) material identifier; (2) quantity needed; (3) lot identifier; and (4) supplier identifier—this model fails to keep tracks on the suppliers, but a graph/tree one in rather [11].

While in the graph/tree data model, a sample material requisition graph illustrated in Fig. 4, each lot is a node containing: (1) lot identifier; (2) production date time; (3) product quantity required; and (4) a sub-tree of material sources. Each material source has its children nodes, each child node contains: (1) lot identifier; (2) production date time; (3) supplier identifier; (4) quantity needed; and (5) material procurement order identifier. And these material source nodes link to their associated procurement order details in another table.

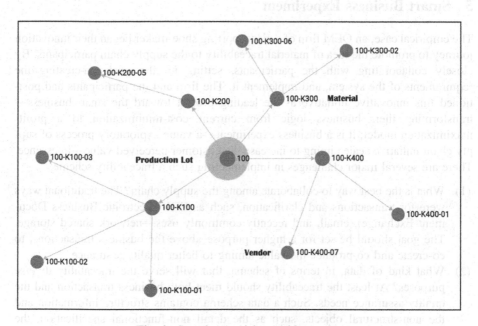

Fig. 4. Sample material requisition graph

By observing the above sample graph, the start node, marked as 100, contains production lot information. The start node links to four material nodes, marked from 100-K100 to 100-K400, contain the material information required in this lot. Each material node, marked with their associated supplier identifier with the suffix from -01 to -07, contains the requisition information. Another worth-noted point is that in this sample model, the lot 100, material K200 only has one supplier -05 and the supplier -02 provides the material of K100 and K300 in this lot.

The benefits of using the graph model are: (1) readability—the planner can easily visually understand how the material requisition is in the lot; (2) preference—a derived supplier perspective view, also a graph, can reveal who the critical suppliers are; (3) tracking—since each material node links to the associated procurement orders, in case of quality issue occurs, the material requisition graphs can be extracted to show the production lots were using this material and to calculate the potential impact imposed from this supplier; (4) alternative—when product changes its configuration due to cost/quality preference or design simplification reason, the planner can calculate the cost saving and the stock provision level for the coming sales orders; and (5) management—once the material supply routes are clear, many operations can also be optimized, for example, the warehouse can re-arrange the material bins to fulfil the production smoothly; the logistic staffs can make a better shipping schedule in terms of delivery time and saving the transportation costs.

5 Smart Business Experiment

The empirical case, an OEM firm of a giant sporting shoe-maker began their innovation journey to promote the idea of material traceability to the supply chain participants. By closely collaborating with the participants, setting up the goal, co-creating the requirements of the system, and implement it. The firm and the participants had positioned this innovative initiative as the leading project toward the smart business—transforming their business logic from current cost-minimization to a profit-maximization model; it is a business experiment—a value exploratory process of supply chain initiative scale aiming to increase the customer perceived value—in essence. There are several major challenges in implementing such a traceability scheme:

(1) What is the best way to collaborate among the supply chain? The traditional ways were for transactions and clarification, such as EDI (Electronic Business Document Exchange), email, and recently commonly uses—network shared storage. The goal should be set for a higher purpose above the business transactions, to co-create and co-produce the value aiming to better quality assurance.

(2) What kind of data, in terms of schema, that will serve the traceability diverse purposes? At least the traceability should meet both business transaction and the quality assurance needs. Such a data schema contains structure information and the non-structural objects, such as the detail non-functional specification, the images of the items, or the audio effect during the reliability tests.

(3) Recording the production history—from the customer order taking, via procurement, to the distribution—is a complicated process. The product inventory serves the customer orders first; if it is insufficient, then places further production schedule to build in a cost-effective way. This implies that a customer order may contain the information from several production lots, and each lot may also contain the material from various procurement orders and even from different suppliers.

(4) How to extend this traceability value to benefit the customers—turning the investment into potential revenue? What kind of the traceability information that the customers matter the most? What will the service model be to increase the brand equity through disclosing the material traceability?

To reach the consensus about the aforementioned challenges among the supply chain members is not an easy task; this paper presents a requirement solicitation framework, an external expert team shall facilitate the whole process.

6 Implementation

The project implementation framework adopted the methodology of the Enterprise Architecture iterative approach [12], illustrated in Fig. 5. This framework consists of three parts, the first part (the left-top portion) is to identify the problem frame—the boundary of the mission to accomplish; the second part (the right-top portion) is to outline the top-down layers, from business, operation, to the system, described in a consistent modeling semantics (the architecture description language, ADL) so that them can be used throughout the journey; the third part is the execution planning (the bottom portion), in which it embeds with an outcome measurement scheme to see if the initiative is heading the expected direction and to acquire the findings as the baseline to the next phase improvement.

First, the project manager invited several participants playing the key roles in the product production cycle, from the bottom of raw material supply to the top of whole-shoe assembly. A project executive board was formed with the help of the selected consulting firm as the steering committee regularly shared the thoughts, discussed the managerial tasks, resolved the issues, and monitored the project progress. The executives defined the service scope as: (1) positioned this was a pilot project; (2) picked the product models with minimal suppliers involved; (3) limited the material tracking level to three—product, components, and row material; and (4) focused on the material that the customers would concern the more. The initiative goal had three folds: (1) to design a material traceability system; (2) to set up the standard operation procedures for the system; and (3) to train the staffs the best practice.

Deriving the tasks from the service scope and the initiative goal, the executive board defined the problem frame—a requirement soliciting terminology, setting up the role and the responsibility facing toward the potential problems as follows: (1) service—elaborating the value, supply chain awareness, promoting the system, and conducting the training; (2) science—designing the system architecture, data schema, efficient ways of adding and querying the traceability data; (3) management—managing the project schedule, resources allocation, making reports; and (4) engineering—based on the design blueprint writing the programs, interfacing with the sensing devices to facilitate the inputs of tracking data, sustaining the system, and deploying the system.

The project team, grouped into the aforementioned four subject matters, cooperatively presented the whole picture of the material traceability in three hierarchical layers: (1) business architecture—describing the context of the system, the perceived value to the customers and the supply chain, the return of investment; (2) operation architecture—setting the corresponding procedures from the sales order taking, procurement process, component/material delivery, to the fingerprints and certificates of the source; and (3) system architecture—designing the information system architecture, including the servers, data storage, networking, and the budget/time estimation. Based on these blueprints, the team made recommendations to the executive board so that they could discuss with, reach the consensus, adjust the content of these architectures, and come out with tangible decisions. The executives brought these architectures back to their firms to conduct further evaluation and came out the gap analysis respectively.

The consulting team consolidated these gap analysis reports and design a series of sequencing plans to mitigate these gaps and deliver to the project team to execute. An outcome measurement scheme was in place to ensure the plans had been well conducted by the principles and meeting the set expectations. Finally, by examining the open issues of the problem frame, a strategy alignment analysis was brought out to the executive board to see if those missions were met in what degree after the project completion. The board set separate initiatives for individual participants to keep up with the goal and continuously to improve the precision of the material traceability.

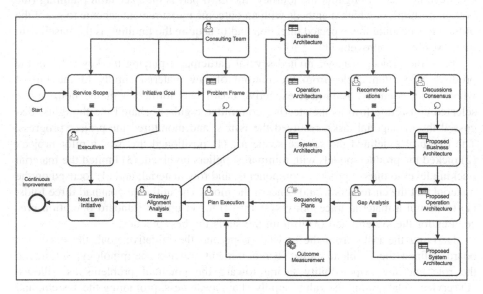

Fig. 5. The requirement solicitation framework

7   Conclusion

Although the material traceability is not a new story; from the simplest form of the material traceability just stating the origin of the material to few products being willing to disclose their components' manufactured dates; most material traceability systems are for in-house tracking purpose not in supply chain scale as the empirical case was. Establishing a shared vision and optimizing the collaboration, setting up the material traceability, across loose-coupled firms is a challenging task.

There are much to learn from the case: (1) leadership—it is common that the material suppliers lack of motivation to initiate the optimization, awaiting the brander to call on the coalition; but the enthusiasm came from the key component suppliers to take the lead is rare; (2) priority—each supplier has its own hidden agenda and business priority especially when its model falls into the cost-minimization scenario is reluctant to participate this business experiment unless the benefit is obvious; has multiple; (3) method—the participants were from various disciplines and the knowledge backgrounds; it was very difficult in consolidating their described facts and elaborated ideas into a systematic form until the Enterprise Architecture methodology was introduced in; (4) knowledge—the participating suppliers did not have all the experiences and knowledge that the traceability initiative required; it was necessary to expand their boundary by recruiting the consulting team to guide the initiative; to assemble a cross-firms virtual teams—the knowledge circle—to deal with the problem frame needed strong commitment from their executives; (5) training—it was the most critical core of the business experiment, not just disseminating the knowledge and the value of the traceability, but also realigning the different perspectives into a clear and executable initiative; and (6) awareness—the optimal goal of the traceability is to increase the customer perceived value of the product; it is evenly important than the system itself to let the customers aware the profound meaning—safe to use, green to Earth, commitment in quality perfection—of this investment.

The supply chain was meant to optimize the overall processes and to reduce the inefficiency waste in the 20th century. Unfortunately, the harsh business environment forced some manufacturers to play the cost minimization game, especially, the relentlessly seeking for the lowest labor cost region caused the bad name of exploitation. In the recent years, many firms began the business transformation journey pursuing another angle of doing the business—profit maximization. The continuous innovation and persistent in quality to make the product better than ever creating the customer perceived value becomes the proven solution of business survival competition. The material traceability is one of these value generators.

References

1. Lee, J., Bagheri, B., Kao, H.-A.: A cyber-physical systems architecture for industry 4.0-based manufacturing systems. Manuf. Lett. **3**, 18–23 (2015)
2. Schlechtendahl, J., Keinert, M., Kretschmer, F., Lechler, A., Verl, A.: Making existing production systems industry 4.0-ready. Prod. Eng. **9**(1), 143–148 (2015)
3. Tse, Y.K., Tan, K.H.: Managing product quality risk and visibility in multi-layer supply chain. Int. J. Prod. Econ. **139**(1), 49–57 (2012)
4. Yarimoglu, E.K.: A review on dimensions of service quality models. J. Mark. Manag. **2**(2), 79–93 (2014)
5. Haaker, T., Bouwman, H., Janssen, W., Reuver, M.: Business model stress testing: a practical approach to test the robustness of a business model. Futures **89**, 14–25 (2017)
6. Vervest, P., van Heck, E., Preiss, K. (eds.): Smart Business Networks. Springer, Heidelberg (2005). https://doi.org/10.1007/b137960
7. Chen, C.-D., Zhao, Q., Wang, J.-L., Huang, C.-K., Lee, N.C.A.: Exploring sharing economy success: resource based view and the role of resource complementarity in business value co-creation. In: Pacific Asia Conference on Information Systems, Langkawi Island, Malaysia (2017)
8. Anderson, E.T., Simester, D.: A step-by-step guide to smart business experiments. Harv. Bus. Rev. (2011)
9. Chan, F.T., Qi, H., Chan, H., Lau, H.C., Ip, R.W.: A conceptual model of performance measurement for supply chains. Manag. Decis. **41**(7), 635–642 (2003)

10. Gautam, N., Singh, N.: Lean product development: maximizing the customer perceived value through design change (redesign). Int. J. Prod. Econ. **114**(1), 313–332 (2008)
11. Jansen-Vullers, M.H., Dorp, C., Beulens, A.J.M.: Managing traceability information in manufacture. Int. J. Inf. Manag. **23**(5), 395–413 (2003)
12. Choi, Y., Kang, D., Chae, H., Kim, K.: An enterprise architecture framework for collaboration of virtual enterprise chains. Int. J. Adv. Manuf. Technol. **35**(11–12), 1065–1107 (2008)

The Application of IS Success Model on Continuous Intention and Information Sharing for Caller ID Apps Usage

Cho-Fan Lin(✉) and Yen-Jung Chang

Department of Graphic Arts Communication,
National Taiwan Normal University, Taipei 08544, Taiwan
60472021h@ntnu.edu.com

Abstract. The development of mobile application software has grown explosively in conjunction with the worldwide use of smartphones in recent years. Since new forms of cyber crime and fraud are also emerging, Caller ID apps are also becoming more popular in recent years. Despite abundant research on users' behavior intention for mobile app usage, the influential factors in the information sharing intention of apps have never been significantly explored to date. In this study, theoretical foundation is built based upon the IS success model, and empirical data obtained from 230 users who had experience with Caller ID app were discussed by using PLS-SEM as an analytical tool. The results indicated that information quality, technical quality and service quality are the main factors that affect users' trust and satisfaction. The findings of this study provide several vital implications for researchers to further examine phone-call-related applications, especially Caller ID apps.

Keywords: Caller ID app · Continuance intention · Information sharing

1 Introduction

Smartphones have become a vital element for modern society, and have been changing how we communicate and maintain relationships with others. Despite the fact that smartphones have advanced tremendously, the principles of interpersonal communication are still unchangeable. People may encounter strong ties, weak ties, and mostly temporary ties [1, 2]. Communication with those ties is important because it can act as conduits for diverse information and new ideas that come from different social groups. However, communicating with unfamiliar people might come with some risk.

In Taiwan, telecommunication fraud crimes have been a developing crime in recent years. Taiwan has high telecoms technology, as well as high unemployment rate, leads to lots of young people join fraud syndicates, and the rate of fraud is still exacerbating. Criminals often impersonate officials of police bureaus or authority figures (such as Internal revenue service) to prey on elderlies, students, farmers, manual labourers or the unemployed. According to Taiwan crime statistics, it was estimated that more than ten billion TWD has lost since 2004 [3]. To avoid being caught from Taiwan police force, criminals began to disperse into the neighboring countries – first to China and then to

© Springer International Publishing AG, part of Springer Nature 2018
F. F.-H. Nah and B. S. Xiao (Eds.): HCIBGO 2018, LNCS 10923, pp. 91–105, 2018.
https://doi.org/10.1007/978-3-319-91716-0_8

ASEAN, the South Pacific, Korea, Japan, Spain and even as far as to East Africa [4, 5]. As swindlers are still at large, many people are highly suspicion about the information provided by strangers or even afraid to answer phone calls from unknowns.

Using Caller ID apps is a great solution to solve this problem. The word "Caller ID" was abbreviated from "caller identification". There are different types of Caller ID apps incorporating various models, methods, detection mechanisms, and protecting against spam over telephony, such as Whoscall, Truecaller, Hiya, Mr. Number [6, 7]. When the call comes, the apps can identify important incoming call and automatically filter out unwanted annoying fraudsters, robocallers or telemarketers. Those apps help user to safely contact the network of weak (e.g., colleagues, classmates) and temporary ties (e.g., strangers), works as a complement for the network of strong ties (e.g., close friendships, family) such as Facebook Messenger, WhatsApp, WeChat, Line.

These apps allow users to search for owner information of income phone number by using their smartphone with internet or offline database, and build a blacklist by themselves. The database relies on crowd annotations, web crawlers (internet search results), and yellow/white pages to achieve call-blocking functionality. Since more companies and developers had launched similar Caller ID apps, with the condition of market competition, how to retain existing users has become an important issue. This also raises some issues for this study: What are the major factors that influence users' continuance intention of Caller ID apps? How satisfied are users with their currently used apps? Are the apps qualities can influence users' share intention? Will users continue using the Caller ID apps they are currently using?

However, to the best of authors' knowledge, very few publications can be found in the literature that discusses the issue of Caller ID apps. To date, existing research has focused on the benefit of Caller ID apps adoption, such as used it to evade harassment [8]. Other researches has focused on what approach can efficient fraudulent phone call detection [9]. In short, there is no academic research that have discussed the Caller ID apps user adoption specifically. According to previous research on mobile applications, mobile applications can be divided into two categories, one is utilitarian (e.g., stock trading, online banking, online payment, etc.), the others are hedonic services (e.g., social networking, messaging, streaming music/TV, gaming, etc.) [10]. Caller ID apps can be considered a utilitarian app which it provides user to identification number information.

Researches on utilitarian apps have used TAM, UTAUT, IS success model to examine factors that influence users' acceptance and continuance usage. Recently, those model has been widely used to discuss mobile banking [11], mobile instant messaging [12], and mobile payment services [13]. Most of them have used these factors: perceived usefulness, value, and efficiency to discuss the user adoption motivations. But these factors are primarily instrumental beliefs, which represent extrinsic motivations. The effect of intrinsic motivations on Caller ID apps user behavior has seldom been considered. Extrinsic motivation emphasizes behavioral outcomes, whereas intrinsic motivation emphasizes the process itself [14]. To fill the research gap, this research will focus on intrinsic motivation and identified what are effective factors.

The paper is organized as follows: In Sect. 2, a reviews of the related literature and develop hypotheses for Caller ID apps. In Sect. 3, we propose a research Model. Methodologies employed for the implementation of the study are outlined in Sect. 4.

Section 5 reports the results, discuss in Sect. 6. The limitations and suggestions for future studies in Sect. 7, and the conclusion is presented in Sect. 8.

2 Theoretical Background and Hypotheses Development

2.1 IS Success Model

The IS success model is seeking to describe the information system success measure [15]. It dictates that system quality and information quality affect use and adoption, which further leads to individual impact and organizational impact. In order to explain the information system success more comprehensive, Delone and Mclean developed a revised model, which included service quality in 2004 [16]. In a nutshell, the IS success model has been widely used to examine user adoption of various information systems, especially in mobile user adoption [17]. For example, IS success model has been applied for discuss the impact of trust and satisfaction in mobile banking [18] and understanding user satisfaction, trust, flow and continued use intention with mobile payment systems [19], mobile purchase [17]. Elliot et al. use the IS success model to examine site stickiness and intention to transact in virtual travel communities [20]. Since IS success model has been well supported, we chose IS success model as our theoretical foundation.

2.2 Trust

Trust is a critical factor which plays an important role in the adoption of most information systems [21]. Trust is usually defined as an individual's willingness to depend on another party because of the characteristics of the other party [22]. According to the prior studies, trust often includes three sub-dimensions: ability, benevolence and integrity. Ability means that apps developers have necessary knowledge and skills to fulfil their tasks. Benevolence means that apps developers keep users' interests in mind, not just their own benefits. Integrity means that apps developers keep their promises and do not deceive users [23]. Previous research has noted the effect of trust on user continued intention on mobile shopping continuance [24] and mobile payment [25].

More over, previous studies indicate that trust extremely affected information sharing. Higher trust could encourage sharing and enhance the quality of information sharing [26, 27]. Caller ID apps rely on numerous user phone share information in which to build a virtual community-based spam list. If caller ID apps have sufficient security mechanism to let users feel safe, they will have a positive intention to share the data to the developers and other users, also develops the sense of duty to engage in sharing behavior and help the community achieve its visions [28]. Hence, we believe that higher level of trust will influence Caller ID apps continued intention and sharing intention. The above argument leads to the following hypotheses:

H1a: Trust positively affects continued intention.
H1b: Trust positively affects sharing intention.

2.3   Satisfaction

If users are not satisfied with the mobile developer and mobile apps quality, they may cease their usage [19]. Recent studies suggested that satisfaction is a strong factor of mobile technologies and applications continuance behavior. Mobile social media [29], mobile banking [30] and mobile instant messaging are among the addressed technologies [31]. Base on the previous studies, we expected a positive effect of satisfaction on user's continued intention in Caller ID apps. Within information sharing context, previous researches have shown that satisfaction influences members decision to constantly share their information [32]. If users have high level of satisfaction with platforms, they will involve in activities within the community by unceasingly facilitate and participate in information-sharing activities [33]. Hence, this study forecasts that users' information sharing intention is influenced by their level of satisfaction towards the Caller ID apps. The above argument leads to the following hypotheses:

H2a: Satisfaction positively affects continued intention.
H2b: Satisfaction positively affects sharing intention.

2.4   Information Quality

Information quality reflects information accuracy, completeness, adequacy, relevance and timeliness [23]. Users expect to use Caller ID apps can identify and search for unknown number information when the phone ring. If this information is inaccurate, incompleteness, insufficient, irrelevant, or even antiquated, users may not be building trust with the apps. They may also assume that operation will swindle them and disregard their needs. This may affect their trust in developer. Researches indicate that information quality has a positive effect on user trust in a mobile bank [18], also has been in a mobile payment [19]. Furthermore, poor information quality cannot lead to user's satisfaction as they expect to having timely and accurate information from Caller ID apps. Previous literature suggests that the effect of information quality on user satisfaction with mobile banking [34]. The above argument leads to the following hypotheses:

H3a: Information quality positively affects trust.
H3b: Information quality positively affects satisfaction.

2.5   Technical Quality

Technical quality is an area of research that manifested how the system performance and measured by individuals' perceptions. It often reflects system's loading speed, ease of use, usefulness, navigation [35]. Just as with interpersonal relationships, first impressions of a system performance can be exceedingly important. It stands to reason that system performance with high quality, user will be having great extent of trust in the developer's competence, benevolence and integrity. Furthermore, users will be willing to spend money to support app [36]. The effect of technical quality has been supported in previous research. [18] revealed that affects user trust in mobile banking. Thus, this study attempts to test the following hypotheses:

H4a: Technical quality positively affects trust.
H4b: Technical quality positively affects satisfaction.

2.6   Aesthetic Quality

Aesthetic quality is an area of research that examines how information is displayed [37]. As the developer of Caller ID apps, it is necessary to elevate the aesthetic standards. Because user need to easily recognize and search the number information in the apps which have intuitive symbol and icon. Besides, numerous studies have assessed such factors as display formats, colors, graphics and how these factors affect user satisfaction. [38, 39] said that aesthetic quality such as presentation, layout enhance the formation of trust. Especially in the case of Caller ID apps, inappropriately designed style and interfaces can make a poor impression on users. In short, appealing interface brings about a wonderful user experience [40]. The above argument leads to the following hypotheses:

H5a: Aesthetic quality positively affects trust.
H5b: Aesthetic quality positively affects satisfaction.

2.7   Service Quality

Service quality reflects reliability, responsiveness, assurance and personalization. Providing quality services will signal service provider's ability and benevolence. In contrast, if developer present unreliable services and leisurely responses to users, users cannot build trust in them [17]. Furthermore, poor responsiveness could irritate users, and impel them to use another similar apps. Users expect the operation respond to their inquiries, requests and feedback on time [41]. Caller ID app's database does not only rely on its community sharing phone number information (crowd annotations), but also two more ways: web crawler and yellow/white page. As time goes by, information accuracy would become a huge problem. For example: a phone number was transfer to another person, but the annotations on database are still out-of-date. When the user requests customer service to update the data information, it may affect user trust if the customer service provides real-time and quality services. Previous literature suggests that effect of service quality on user trust in mobile purchase [17], and would lead the app more appealing and gain higher level of user satisfaction [42]. The above argument leads to the following hypotheses:

H6a: Service quality positively affects trust.
H6b: Service quality positively affects satisfaction.

3   Theoretical Background and Hypotheses Development

The conceptual model is shown in Fig. 1.

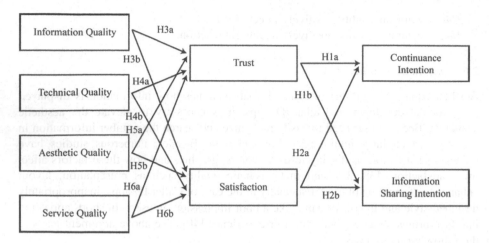

Fig. 1. Research framework

4 Methodology

In this research, the items used in the survey were adapted from existing studies to suit the context of Caller ID apps, in order to make sure of its logical consistency, contextual relevance and question clarity of all measurements. We followed the generally accepted suggestion on wording questions, Appendix A lists the measure items and their related sources. Items were measured on five-point Likert scales with 1 being "strongly disagree" and 5 being "strongly agree". At first, all construct items were developed in English. Due to the fact that our research was conducted in Taiwan, all instrument items were translated into Traditional Chinese. One pilot study with initial questionnaire was carried out on 20 participants which included our graduate students and friends for the refinement of the test. To collect data, an online survey created on Google Forms was applied for the present study. As the experiment involved mobile application, recruited participants were mainly mobile phone users who had experience on using Caller ID apps. We put the survey link in PTT's boards "MobileComm" and "iOS". PTT is the largest terminal-based bulletin board system (BBS) in Taiwan. It is similar to reddit, which includes a diverse variety of discussion groups.

In this research, to test our measurement and structural model, we choose the structural equation modeling by using Partial Least Squares (PLS) estimation. Smart-PLS 3.0 were used as a software tool to analyze the data and to yield reports. PLS algorithm calculated the path coefficients and R^2 for the endogenous variables in our study. The bootstrapping was used to calculate the t-values for this study by setting as sample 5000.

5 Results

5.1 Descriptive Statistics

After we had eliminated 8 data that showed unusual patterns in the replies (such as repeating answer questionnaire, reverse questions), 230 valid questionnaires remained.

Analysis was conducted on 230 responses. Most of the respondents were males (66.52%), between 20 and 39 in age, and nearly 80% educated at least college level. Table 1 represents the distribution in terms of age, gender, education.

Table 1. Demographics of respondents

Demographics	Male (n = 153, 66.52%)		Female (n = 77, 33.48%)	
	Frequency	Percentage	Frequency	Percentage
Age				
19 or below	10	6.54%	9	12%
20–29 years	101	66.01%	45	58%
30–39 years	36	23.53%	16	21%
40–49 years	6	3.92%	7	9%
Education				
High school or below	18	11.77%	16	21%
College	101	66.01%	48	62%
Postgraduate	34	22.22%	13	17%

5.2 The Measurement Model

The outer loading for each construct was calculated through the SmartPLS algorithm (see Appendix A). All indicators were convergent, as their correlation coefficients were great [43]. The calculation in regard to reliability including Cronbach's alpha, CR and AVE values is presented in Table 2. The internal consistency of the model was confirmed by SmartPLS for the values of Cronbach's alpha are greater than 0.711, which suggests a good reliability [44]. The Average Variance Extracted (AVE) exceeds the cut-off threshold level of 0.5 for constructs. Hair et al. indicates sufficient convergent validity, and the composite reliability (CR) above the threshold of 0.7 indicates sufficient internal consistency and reliability of constructs [45, 46]. In this research, the AVE of each construct was larger than 0.5, and the CR value was greater than 0.8.

Table 2. Cronbach's alpha, component reliability and AVE values

Construct	Cronbach's alpha	Component reliability	AVE
Trust (TRU)	0.891	0.932	0.82
Satisfaction (SAT)	0.867	0.918	0.788
Information quality (IQ)	0.851	0.9	0.693
Technical quality (TQ)	0.859	0.914	0.781
Aesthetic quality (AQ)	0.924	0.946	0.815
Service quality (SQ)	0.959	0.973	0.924
Continuance intention (CI)	0.92	0.95	0.863
Information sharing intention (ISI)	0.711	0.806	0.509

Accordingly, AVE is the common test of discriminant validity. To examine discriminant validity, we followed the method suggested by Fornell and Larcker [47]. They have validated that the square root of AVE was greater than the correlation coefficient. Hence, we compared the square root of the AVE of each construct and its correlation coefficients with other constructs. The results in Table 3 presents that the square roots of the AVEs were higher than the corresponding correlation coefficients. In brief, the measurement model demonstrated adequate reliability, convergent validity, and discriminant validity.

Table 3. Discriminant validity of measurement model

	TRU	ISI	TQ	SQ	SAT	CI	AQ	IQ
TRU	0.906							
ISI	0.635	0.713						
TQ	0.698	0.568	0.884					
SQ	0.569	0.514	0.572	0.961				
SAT	0.678	0.649	0.731	0.581	0.888			
CI	0.747	0.702	0.64	0.429	0.705	0.929		
AQ	0.605	0.511	0.638	0.607	0.552	0.506	0.903	
IQ	0.697	0.498	0.693	0.502	0.691	0.594	0.479	0.832

5.3   The Structural Model

The coefficient of determination, R^2 is a part of the variance of the dependent variable that is explained by the independent variables. Continuance intention's R^2 is 0.631, which is considered adequate [48]. Information sharing intention is 0.491, which is close the 0.5 [49], which is discussed further in next section. For each path in the model, the t-values were calculated by bootstrapping with 5000 samples. In summary, eight out of twelve hypotheses were supported with $p < 0.05$, and $p < 0.01$ as shown in Table 4.

Table 4. Summary of measurement model

No	Construct	Path coeff.	t-statistic	P-value	Supported
H1a	TRU→CI	0.545	5.764	0	$p < 0.01$**
H1b	TRU→ISI	0.37	3.077	0.002	$p < 0.01$**
H2a	SAT→CI	0.366	3.64	0	$p < 0.01$**
H2b	SAT→ISI	0.45	3.689	0	$p < 0.01$**
H3a	IQ→TRU	0.456	3.566	0	$p < 0.01$**
H3b	IQ→SAT	0.321	2.389	0.017	$p < 0.05$*
H4a	TQ→TRU	0.231	1.271	0.204	
H4b	TQ→SAT	0.49	2.812	0.005	$p < 0.01$**
H5a	AQ→TRU	0.196	1.906	0.057	
H5b	AQ→SAT	−0.009	0.107	0.915	
H6a	SQ→TRU	0.091	1.41	0.159	
H6b	SQ→SAT	0.151	2.667	0.008	$p < 0.01$**

6 Discussion

The scope of this research is to increase the understanding of internal quality of trust and satisfaction on continuance intention, as well as information sharing intention on caller ID app. To do so, we conducted an empirical investigation that focuses on internal variables and those intentions.

Trust and satisfaction are significant factors $p < 0.01$, which is found to positively affect user continuance intention and information sharing intention, supported by H1a, H1b, H2a, and H2b. The two important factors imply that multinational application developer should be aware user's cultural custom and negative reviews, regardless of nationally, age or class and concerns to improve user experience, further promoting their trustworthy and satisfaction. Furthermore, information sharing intention items 1to 4 (ISI 1-4) has showed that social awareness and privacy concern affect users' satisfaction and trust of the app. As for the item 4 (ISI 4), most participants do not share their family and friends phone information to contribute virtual community. But for items 1-3 (ISI 1-3), result indicates that most participants are willing to share phone information other than family and friends to help the community.

Information quality is a significant factor to trust (H3a, $p < 0.01$) and satisfaction (H3b, $p < 0.05$). Almost certainly, for the majority of people who adopt Caller ID app look for its accurate, complete, sufficient, relevant and fresh information. The positive relationship between information quality, trust, satisfaction is consistent with previous research [18]. Based on ourfindings, providing reliable and appropriate information are effective ways to keep users. We suggest developers of Caller ID app should emphasize on updated and comprehensive database to filter out unwanted calls. Even if people turn to social media and messenger apps to communicate, they still need to use traditional phone call. Caller ID app can immediately identify those phishing and criminality to avoid fraudulent activity and spam. That is, information quality is more important than all the other aspects of Caller ID app.

In our study, technical quality is how the app can be easily navigated, as well as the app works stably. Previous research has documented that technical quality had a positive effect on trust and satisfaction [18]. Stability of the program is vital because users will answer the phone anytime. If the app has bugs and even freezes when they receive phone call, or are unable to use functions intuitively, they will cause disappointment and distrust. However, our results show that technical quality was not significant in trust (H4a), but user satisfaction was (H4b, $p < 0.01$). The different result is possibly because the language or comprehension between different society. However, stability and an easy-to-use system are significant in user satisfaction.

Previous research has documented that aesthetic quality had a positive effect on trust, but did not effect satisfaction [18]. Surprisingly, our results show that aesthetic quality was not effect in trust (H5a) and satisfaction (H5b). We assumed that caller ID app is a very utilitarian oriented application, aesthetic quality has a relatively minor impact compared to other quality. However, most of mobile apps are different from websites, for they are accessed on small screens that relatively difficult for users to search for information. Therefore, the developers should still think holistically to contribute to high-level layout design. The design for elements of homescreen such as color, font, icon and composition have to be user friendly.

Finally, service quality reflects reliability, responsiveness, assurance and personal instruction. Caller ID apps rely on users of virtual-community that provides annotations phone number data. Accordingly, customer service have to solve issue when some people slander specific phone number, or fix phone number that is transferred to another person. We assume great service quality can effect trust and satisfaction. Research by Gao et al. [17] showed that service quality effect trust, but not satisfaction. Nevertheless, our research shows that service quality dose not effect trust (H6a), but is significant to satisfaction (H6b, $p < 0.01$). The disagreement needs to be further investigated.

7 Limitations and Future Research

There are four issues in regard to the limitations in this research. Firstly, we used the BBS platforms (PTT) to conduct the questionnaire survey, and the participants would receive PTT virtual currency as gift. Therefore, the recruited participants would be those who like to respond to survey questionnaires in return for a monetary reward.

Secondly, PTT is based on a national academic internet channels. That is, many users created their own account because they are or have been students, so they are likely highly educated. In addition, Caller ID apps are still developing. Even though some early adopters have used with self-motivation, many people such as elderly and rural residents may not have much experience with them. This research is not able to present the situation for the general population. Furthermore, the survey was conducted in Taiwan where Caller ID apps are developing rapidly. A broader area including neighboring countries such as China, India, South Korea and Japan need to be further investigated.

Thirdly, the research did not comprehensively reflect the potential influence of cultural idiosyncrasy and social factors. Future researchers may employ objective measurements to analysis user behavior and explore in different cultural dimensions, regions and countries.

Finally, this study adopted cross-sectional design, which does not allow for a longitudinal analysis of the observed effects. Thus, the results should be that taken seriously, that cross-sectional result could not show the causality clearer; future research can observe the adoption of user's attitudes and behaviors with a longer period of time.

8 Conclusion

Retaining users and attracting potential adopters of Caller ID app is becoming important for the developers. Previous researches have seldom examined the quality on continued intention and information sharing intention for apps. Combining DeLone and McLean information systems success model [15, 16] and Knowledge sharing concept from Hansen [50]. This research identified the elements of app that affect user trust and satisfaction on continuance intention and information sharing intention.

Our results show that information quality is the main factor of trust. The results also point that information quality, technical quality and service quality affect satisfaction. Aesthetic quality has no significant influence in trust and satisfaction. In addition, even moderate effect on trust and satisfaction has significant effect on continuance intention and information sharing intention.

In summary, our study provides evidence that IS success as a foundation theory is possibly suitable for understanding mobile applications. Even though this study disregards external factor such as social fact and culture dimensions, we propose that most users strongly consider to continue using and sharing information data to help community and enhance the internal quality of the app. It would help service providers to realize user's usage and develop appropriate strategies to form a virtuous cycle.

Appendix A – Questionnaire Items

Construct	Item	Survey questions[a]	Outer loading	Source
Information quality	IQ1	Caller ID apps provides the precise information you need	0.8631	[51, 52]
	IQ2[b]	The information content is not meets your needs	0.7602	
	IQ3	Caller ID app provides up-to-date information	0.8462	
	IQ4	Caller ID app has sufficient information	0.8552	
Technical quality	TQ1	Caller ID app is easy to use	0.9024	[17, 52]
	TQ2	Caller ID app is easy to navigate	0.8808	
	TQ3	Caller ID app is always up and running	0.8670	
Aesthetic quality	AQ1	Caller ID app is visually appealing	0.9147	[40, 53]
	AQ2	The visual design of Caller ID app is attractive	0.9002	
	AQ3	The layout of Caller ID app is intuitive	0.8884	
	AQ4	The design of Caller ID app is harmonious	0.9068	
Service quality	SQ1	When you have a problem, Caller ID app shows a sincere interest in solving it	0.9609	[51]
	SQ2	The Caller ID app gives you individual attention	0.9587	
	SQ3	The Caller ID app understands your specific needs	0.9645	
Satisfaction	SAT1	I am satisfied with the performance of Caller ID app	0.8947	[54]
	SAT2	I am pleased with the experience of using Caller ID app	0.8871	

(continued)

(continued)

		My decision to use Caller ID app was not a wise one	0.8814	
Trust	TRU1	Caller ID app is trustworthy	0.9027	[55]
	TRU2	Caller ID app keeps its promise	0.9182	
	TRU3	Caller ID app keeps customers' interests in mind	0.8963	
Information sharing intention	ISI1	I expect to share fraud phone information contributed by other users	0.8999	[56]
	ISI2	I expect to share telemarketing phone information by other users	0.9232	
	ISI3	I expect to share merchant phone information by other users	0.8467	
	ISI4	I expect to share family and friends phone information contributed by other users	−0.2668	
	ISI5	I intend to share phone information in the future	0.5859	
	ISI6	I plan to share phone information in regularly	0.5091	
Continuance intention	CI1	I will use Caller ID app on a regular basis in the future	0.9232	[54]
	CI2	I will frequently use Caller ID app in the future	0.9535	
	CI3	I will strongly recommend others to use it	0.9007	

[a]All measures employ a five-point Likert scale from "strongly disagree" to "strongly agree."
[b]Reverse question.

References

1. Granovetter, M.S.: The strength of weak ties. Am. J. Sociol. **78**(6), 1360–1380 (1973)
2. Li, E.Y. (ed.): Organizations and Social Networking: Utilizing Social Media to Engage Consumers. IGI Global, Hershey (2013)
3. Apple Daily: Taiwan fraudsters have rampaged around the world. Nearly 70 percent Taiwanese agree the decision to deport fraudsters to China for judgment. (in Traditional Chinese). https://tw.appledaily.com/new/realtime/20171230/1266647. Accessed 31 Dec 2017
4. Ge, Y.: International police cooperation in fighting telecommunication fraud crimes between China and ASEAN countries. In: Proceedings of International Symposium on Policing Diplomacy and the Belt and Road Initiative, pp. 178–184. American Scholars Press, Inc., Hangzhou (2016)
5. Blanchard, B., Yu, J.M.: China jails 44 Taiwanese for fraud in case denounced by Taipei. https://www.reuters.com/article/us-china-taiwan-crime/china-jails-44-taiwanese-for-fraud-in-case-denounced-by-taipei-idUSKBN1EF078. Accessed 31 Dec 2017

6. Sung, C.S., Kim, C.H., Park, J.Y.: Development of humming call system for blocking spam on a smartphone. Multimed. Tools Appl. **76**(16), 17371–17383 (2017)

7. Mele, C.: Robocalls Flooding Your Cellphone? Here's How to Stop Them. https://www.nytimes.com/2017/05/11/smarter-living/stop-robocalls.html. Accessed 31 Dec 2017

8. Schiemer, L.J.E.E.: Mobile Technology and Women's Empowerment in Post-Revolution Egypt. Royal Roads University, Canada (2017)

9. Ying, J.J.C., Zhang, J., Huang, C.W., Chen, K.T., Tseng, V.S.: PFrauDetector: a parallelized graph mining approach for efficient fraudulent phone call detection. In: International Conference on Parallel and Distributed Systems (ICPADS). IEEE 22nd International Conference 2016, Wuhan, China, pp. 1059–1066. IEEE (2016)

10. Kim, D.J., Hwang, Y.: A study of mobile internet user's service quality perceptions from a user's utilitarian and hedonic value tendency perspectives. Inf. Syst. Front. **14**(2), 409–421 (2012)

11. Al-Ghazali, B.M., Rasli, A.M., Yusoff, R.M., Mutahar, A.Y.: Antecedents of continuous usage intention of mobile banking services from the perspective of DeLone and McLean model of IS success. Int. J. Econ. Financ. Issues **5**(1S), 13–21 (2015)

12. Gan, C., Li, H.: Understanding continuance intention of mobile instant messaging: motivators and inhibitors. Ind. Manag. Data Syst. **115**(4), 646–660 (2015)

13. Chen, X., Li, S.: Understanding continuance intention of mobile payment services: an empirical study. J. Comput. Inf. Syst. **57**(4), 287–298 (2017)

14. Zhou, T.: An empirical examination of the determinants of mobile purchase. Pers. Ubiquitous Comput. **17**(1), 187–195 (2013)

15. DeLone, W.H., McLean, E.R.: Information systems success: the quest for the dependent variable. Inf. Syst. Res. **3**(1), 60–95 (1992)

16. DeLone, W.H., McLean, E.R.: Measuring the business value of information technology in e-business environments. Int. J. Electron. Commer. **9**(1), 31–47 (2004)

17. Gao, L., Waechter, K.A., Bai, X.: Understanding consumers' continuance intention towards mobile purchase: a theoretical framework and empirical study–a case of China. Comput. Hum. Behav. **53**, 249–262 (2015)

18. Lee, K.C., Chung, N.: Understanding factors affecting trust in and satisfaction with mobile banking in Korea: a modified DeLone and McLean's model perspective. Interact. Comput. **21**(5–6), 385–392 (2009)

19. Zhou, T.: Understanding the determinants of mobile payment continuance usage. Ind. Manag. Data Syst. **114**(6), 936–948 (2014)

20. Elliot, S., Li, G., Choi, C.: Understanding service quality in a virtual travel community environment. J. Bus. Res. **66**(8), 1153–1160 (2013)

21. Mcknight, D.H., Carter, M., Thatcher, J.B., Clay, P.F.: Trust in a specific technology: an investigation of its components and measures. ACM Trans. Manag. Inf. Syst. (TMIS) **2**(2), 12 (2011)

22. Rousseau, D.M., Sitkin, S.B., Burt, R.S., Camerer, C.: Not so different after all: a cross-discipline view of trust. Acad. Manag. Rev. **23**(3), 393–404 (1998)

23. Zhou, T.: An empirical examination of continuance intention of mobile payment services. Decis. Support Syst. **54**(2), 1085–1091 (2013)

24. Hung, M.C., Yang, S.T., Hsieh, T.C.: An examination of the determinants of mobile shopping continuance. Int. J. Electron. Bus. Manag. **10**(1), 29 (2012)

25. Xin, H., Techatassanasoontorn, A.A., Tan, F.B.: Antecedents of consumer trust in mobile payment adoption. J. Comput. Inf. Syst. **55**(4), 1–10 (2015)

26. Pinjani, P., Palvia, P.: Trust and knowledge sharing in diverse global virtual teams. Inf. Manag. **50**(4), 144–153 (2013)

27. Chang, H.H., Chuang, S.S.: Social capital and individual motivations on knowledge sharing: participant involvement as a moderator. Inf. Manag. **48**(1), 9–18 (2011)
28. Liou, D.K., Chih, W.H., Hsu, L.C., Huang, C.Y.: Investigating information sharing behavior: the mediating roles of the desire to share information in virtual communities. Inf. Syst. e-Bus. Manag. **14**(2), 187–216 (2016)
29. Ofori, K.S., Larbi-Siaw, O., Fianu, E., Gladjah, R.E., Boateng, E.O.Y.: Factors influencing the continuance use of mobile social media: the effect of privacy concerns. J. Cyber Secur. Mobil. **4**(3), 105–124 (2016)
30. Yuan, S., Liu, Y., Yao, R., Liu, J.: An investigation of users' continuance intention towards mobile banking in China. Inf. Dev. **32**(1), 20–34 (2016)
31. Oghuma, A.P., Libaque-Saenz, C.F., Wong, S.F., Chang, Y.: An expectation-confirmation model of continuance intention to use mobile instant messaging. Telemat. Inform. **33**(1), 34–47 (2016)
32. Jin, X.L., Lee, M.K., Cheung, C.M.: Predicting continuance in online communities: model development and empirical test. Behav. Inf. Technol. **29**(4), 383–394 (2010)
33. Hashim, K.F., Tan, F.B.: The mediating role of trust and commitment on members' continuous knowledge sharing intention: a commitment-trust theory perspective. Int. J. Inf. Manag. **35**(2), 145–151 (2015)
34. Kim, G., Shin, B., Lee, H.G.: Understanding dynamics between initial trust and usage intentions of mobile banking. Inf. Syst. J. **19**(3), 283–311 (2009)
35. Gao, L., Waechter, K.A.: Examining the role of initial trust in user adoption of mobile payment services: an empirical investigation. Inf. Syst. Front. **19**(3), 525–548 (2017)
36. Delone, W.H., McLean, E.R.: The DeLone and McLean model of information systems success: a ten-year update. J. Manag. Inf. Syst. **19**(4), 9–30 (2003)
37. Bharati, P., Chaudhury, A.: An empirical investigation of decision-making satisfaction in web-based decision support systems. Decis. Support Syst. **37**(2), 187–197 (2004)
38. Everard, A., Galletta, D.F.: How presentation flaws affect perceived site quality, trust, and intention to purchase from an online store. J. Manag. Inf. Syst. **22**(3), 56–95 (2005)
39. Wang, Y.J., Hernandez, M.D., Minor, M.S.: Web aesthetics effects on perceived online service quality and satisfaction in an e-tail environment: the moderating role of purchase task. J. Bus. Res. **63**(9), 935–942 (2010)
40. Xu, C., Peak, D., Prybutok, V.: A customer value, satisfaction, and loyalty perspective of mobile application recommendations. Decis. Support Syst. **79**, 171–183 (2015)
41. Song, L., Lai, H.: Identifying factors affecting customer satisfaction in online shopping. In: 4th Multidisciplinary International Social Networks Conference on Proceedings, Bangkok, Thailand, p. 17. ACM (2017)
42. Ayo, C.K., Oni, A.A., Adewoye, O.J., Eweoya, I.O.: E-banking users' behaviour: e-service quality, attitude, and customer satisfaction. Int. J. Bank Mark. **34**(3), 347–367 (2016)
43. Henseler, J., Ringle, C.M., Sinkovics, R.R.: The use of partial least squares path modeling in international marketing. In: New Challenges to International Marketing, pp. 277–319 (2009)
44. Cronbach, L.J., Meehl, P.E.: Construct validity in psychological tests. Psychol. Bull. **52**(4), 281 (1955)
45. Lee, E.Y., Lee, S.B., Jeon, Y.J.J.: Factors influencing the behavioral intention to use food delivery apps. Soc. Behav. Pers. Int. J. **45**(9), 1461–1473 (2017)
46. Hair Jr., J.F., Black, W.C., Babin, B.J., Anderson, R.E., Tatham, R.L.: Multivariate Data Analysis, 7th edn. Prentice-Hall, Upper Saddle River (2009)
47. Fornell, C., Larcker, D.F.: Evaluating structural equation models with unobservable variables and measurement error. J. Mark. Res. **18**(1), 39–50 (1981)
48. Hair, J.F., Ringle, C.M., Sarstedt, M.: PLS-SEM: indeed a silver bullet. J. Mark. Theory Pract. **19**(2), 139–152 (2011)

49. Hair, J.F., Hult, G.T., Ringle, C.M., Sarstedt, M.: A Primer on Partial Least Squares Structural Equations Modeling (PLS-SEM). SAGE Publications, Thousand Oaks (2014)
50. Hansen, M.T.: The search-transfer problem: the role of weak ties in sharing knowledge across organization subunits. Adm. Sci. Q. 44(1), 82–111 (1999)
51. Wang, Y.S., Liao, Y.W.: Assessing eGovernment systems success: a validation of the DeLone and McLean model of information systems success. Gov. Inf. Q. 25(4), 717–733 (2008)
52. Kim, H.W., Xu, Y., Koh, J.: A comparison of online trust building factors between potential customers and repeat customers. J. Assoc. Inf. Syst. 5(10), 13 (2004)
53. Cai, S., Xu, Y.: Designing not just for pleasure: effects of web site aesthetics on consumer shopping value. Int. J. Electron. Commer. 15(4), 159–188 (2011)
54. Roca, J.C., Chiu, C.M., Martínez, F.J.: Understanding e-learning continuance intention: an extension of the technology acceptance model. Int. J. Hum.-Comput. Stud. 64(8), 683–696 (2006)
55. Lee, T.: The impact of perceptions of interactivity on customer trust and transaction intentions in mobile commerce. J. Electron. Commer. Res. 6(3), 165 (2005)
56. Hur, K., Kim, T.T., Karatepe, O.M., Lee, G.: An exploration of the factors influencing social media continuance usage and information sharing intentions among Korean travellers. Tour. Manag. 63, 170–178 (2017)

Conducting Cost-Effective User Research in China Remotely

Shuang Liu$^{(\boxtimes)}$ and Shuang Xu

Lexmark International, Lexington, KY, USA
shuangliu12@gmail.com, shuang.xu@lexmark.com

Abstract. For companies that want to be successful in China, it is necessary to understand the needs and behaviors of Chinese consumers. However, the UX community in the US has yet to develop the best practices for conducting remote user research in China. Existing guidance seldom discuss the feasibility of the research plans, such as cost or time constraint. As a small User Experience design team with limited resources, we strived for conducting user research on Chinese users in a cost-effective way. This paper summarized our experience of exploring research methods and tools for studying printer users in China from the US, and provided advice to the UX community that faces similar challenges.

Keywords: User experience research · Chinese users · Cross-cultural study

1 Introduction

The rapid economic growth and significant market potential of China attract a growing number of global companies. Brejcha's studies on cross-cultural User Experience (UX) design pointed out that Chinese users have different preferences for user interface from European users [1]. Companies aspiring to enter the Chinese market should understand the needs and behaviors of Chinese consumers. Even though many of these companies have mature UX teams, they have minimal data or experience conducting UX research in China. The UX community in the US still lacks industry best practices for international user research [2]. Ethnography studies are usually recommended as the first step for studying users in another country, however, many companies do not have the time or budget to carry out long-term qualitative studies.

Following the acquisition by a Chinese Consortium in 2016, Lexmark shifted its focus to the Chinese market. However, lacking previous research efforts, teams at Lexmark had little data about printer users in China. The marketing team, information development team and the design teams have all been asking questions about the preferences and behaviors of our Chinese consumers but answers were not available. The User Experience Design (UX) team at Lexmark decided to take on the lead to conduct user research. As a small team with limited resources, the UX team had to explore practical ways to initiate UX research on users in China.

In the effort to develop an overall understanding of printer user needs in China, our team planned two survey studies and a diary study. The survey studies were used to define target users and understand their printing needs. The diary study was designed to

F. F.-H. Nah and B. S. Xiao (Eds.): HCIBGO 2018, LNCS 10923, pp. 106–114, 2018.
https://doi.org/10.1007/978-3-319-91716-0_9

examine how Chinese users use printers in real life settings. The first round of survey focused on collecting data on printer usage, printing needs and preferences. The second survey aimed to follow up on observations and questions generated from the first survey that require further clarification. Diary study is an economical alternative to field studies [3], where researchers can study user behaviors in context without travelling to observe users. The diary study would help us complete our data collection by probing into users' reasons and attitudes. We planned to carry out the two survey studies first, followed by the diary study. We would recruit participants for the diary study based on the user data drawn from the survey studies.

We completed the first survey study in December 2017, where we encountered and resolved many challenges. These challenges included finding the right services to reach out to the target population, developing a localized research toolkit, and overcoming logistics issues. In this paper, we shared our experiences in how to identify research tools suitable for UX research in China, and how to examine the feasibility of potential research tools. At the end of this paper, we proposed guidelines for conducting remote user research in China. We hope the learning from our research journey could provide help to UX teams in the US at the early stage of planning user studies on Chinese users.

2   Related Work

A few research papers discussed how to conduct international user research. The International Research Toolkit [4] from Facebook Research centered around field studies without discussing budget or time constraints that most UX teams in the industry must face. Biesterfeldt and Capra [5] offered a step-to-step guide for conducting international UX research. The authors proposed high-level approaches from each stage of the research projects, from planning the research, designing the research, conducting fieldwork, to data analysis and reporting. Recommendations from these studies were useful, but they gave little guidance on the feasibility of each step. When it comes to research planning, we have to stay pragmatic. Some ideas might sound great, such as Biesterfeldt and Capra's suggestions on establishing a long-term relationship with local vendors, but would not work well as we were tasked to gather reliable user data within a limited time frame. We were at the early stage of our research journey with a small budget. In addition, our team did not have established methods to handle international payments or vendor relationship with research firms in China. These logistics details might not seem to be a part of UX research, but we had to resolve these issues before we could execute our research plans.

Existing studies on international UX research usually compared user groups from different countries. Walsh et al. [6] found online storyboards to be an effective way to help participants from different cultures understand the targeted use cases. But we wanted to focus on Chinese users only, without comparing user behaviors from different countries. To fill in the gap of practical guidance on remote user studies in China, this study solely focused on conducting early user research in China. Some of the challenges and roadblocks discussed in this paper were very China-specific. Our goal was to provide detailed recommendations and practical suggestions to help other research teams find resources and avoid pitfalls.

3 Methods

3.1 Our Team

Lexmark has a small in-house User Experience Design team led by veteran UX researchers. Our team has done user interviews and usability testing for the past 20 years. We have profound knowledge in UX design and research for the printer-related market. However, our team has minimal knowledge about the Chinese market that Lexmark is entering. Our bilingual team members who are fluent in both Chinese and English led the efforts in researching and comparing the available local research platforms, communicating with local agent for logistics, and handling the definition and translation of the research materials.

3.2 Research Goals and Plans

Lexmark sells printers to enterprise customers and individual consumers. It is imperative for Lexmark to know the specific needs for both kinds of users. Surveys are a cost-effective tool for collecting data from a large sample in a short amount of time [7]. Our first survey study is designed to help us understand user segments and their printing behaviors. We defined three types of printer users: (1) people who primarily use printers at home, (2) people who primarily use printers at work, and (3) people who primarily use printing services, like printing shops. We didn't limit the type or brand of printers, because our interest was in the existing printing behaviors.

The first survey started with questions about participants' printing needs: "How often do you use printers?" and "Where do you use printers?" Based on each user's responses, we classified the user into one of the four categories (home users with one printer, home users with multiple printers, work users, and printing service users) and asked questions specific to the user category:

- For home users, we asked about their printer (brand, type, display type), what they use the printer for, how they use the printer ("How do you send documents to your printer?") and printer ownership related questions ("How much did your printer cost?").
- For work users, we asked about their usage of features related to enterprise printers, how much they print and what they use printers for.
- For printing service users, we asked them about where they satisfy their printing needs ("Where do you usually go to perform printing jobs?") and printer ownership ("Why don't you have your own printer?").

We asked demographic questions, such as age, location and smartphone brands to all of our participants.

For this survey, we planned to recruit 800 printer users in China with at least 100 respondents in each of the defined categories. We needed to find a survey platform with a large user base in China. Also, the survey platform should provide sampling services that allow us to limit participants to printer users.

The second survey and the diary study were defined but not carried out yet. The second survey was designed to follow up on observations from the first survey. We planned to collect at least 800 responses from the second survey. We used the diary study as a complementary tool to the survey studies. Diary studies are useful for collecting in-context data on users' behaviors and thoughts over a period of time [9]. We were interested in conducting a one week-long diary study to study how users interact with printers and how they deal with troubleshooting if applicable. We planned to recruit 10 to 20 printer users in China and collect data through a cloud-based collaboration tool.

3.3 Research Preparation

In order to properly develop the survey questions, we examined qualitative data from Chinese forums, Q&A sites and news articles. We read printer-related threads on Chinese forums, such as ZOL.com, online customer reviews on Lexmark printers, and printer purchase and printer repairment related discussions on Q&A sites such as Zhihu.com. We also read news articles relevant to the printer and printing business. From forums and Q&A sites, we learned customers' preference and pain points about printers, which provided important guidance for our survey study.

Translation is another key component for overseas research. Our bilingual team members decided to translate all research materials and data instead of hiring external translators. The benefit of having the same researcher as the translator is that the researcher knows the content and thus is less likely to have critical information lost in translation. We drafted our survey questions in English, so that all team members could review the questions and provide feedback. After finalizing the questions, our bilingual team member translated the survey into Chinese. Different from English, Chinese language has honorifics. We carefully selected the proper tone when phrasing the questions. We also chose terminologies with extra caution. For example, we were not sure how Chinese consumer would interpret the meaning of "打印机 (printer in Chinese)". Would they think a 打印机 (printer) is a machine that only does printing or makes copies as well? We did guerilla interviews with seven Chinese users and asked them about how they would define printers, copiers and scanners. We received seven different answers from these users. Therefore, we added definitions of terminologies in the survey to avoid potential misinterpretation of the questions.

3.4 Localization of Research Toolkit

Our UX research team has a defined research toolkit for the US market, with a partner vendor for participants screening and recruiting. We typically use survey distribution platforms such as Survey Monkey to collect nation-wide user data. Communicating with vendors and participants is usually done through emails and phone calls. We also use Google Drive for document-sharing and collaboration.

Unfortunately, these commonly used tools and methods are not available for research in China. Our vendor does not have any international connections. In addition, Google Drive and Survey Monkey are not available in China. We considered three factors when developing our research toolkit: (1) How laws and regulations in China affect the availability of tools, (2) Habits and behaviors of Chinese users, as it is unlikely for them to adopt new tools just for this study, and (3) Cost effectiveness: the qualified tools should be free for the participants to use, and can also generate reliable output at a reasonable cost for us.

The Great Firewall and Real-Name Registration Law

We are aware that the "Great Firewall" in China has blocked a list of websites including some of the most popular products in the world such as Google, Facebook, WhatsApp and YouTube. We had to find the Chinese substitutes for the handy research toolkit we were used to.

During the exploration of different products in China, the first roadblock we encountered was the real-name registration law enforced in 2017 [8]. This law requires internet services providers and companies to verify users' identities. Since 2010, China adopted the real-name registration law for phone numbers. All phone numbers have to be linked to users' true identity. To comply with the real-name registration law, the general practice of internet services in China is to ask users to use a phone number during registration, with confirmation code sent back via text message to that number. International phone numbers are not always accepted. Our team did not have a mobile number to receive the confirmation code. We initially tried to set up a Google Voice virtual number and soon found out that Google Voice also requested a real mobile number for sign-up as well. We eventually discovered TracFone, which provided a low-cost SIM card with a flexible short-term (as short as one-month) mobile plan.

User Preferences

Although sometimes a tool or product is not blocked by the "Great Firewall", the tool might not be a proper choice for the Chinese study. For example, Chinese have access to Skype, but Skype is not a popular communication tool in China. To best reach out to the Chinese users, we explored tools prevalent in China. Our criteria for research tool selection are: (1) make use of products that Chinese users are already using and familiar with. (2) If we need to ask users to adopt a new tool, the tool should be easy to set up and easy to learn.

WeChat as the Communication Tool

We selected WeChat as our primary communication tool. WeChat, the mega mobile app developed by the Chinese company Tencent, has 980 million active users [8]. WeChat is not only a social media app, but also the primarily mobile payment method in China. During our research, we also found that even businesses use WeChat for business inquiries and customer service.

Survey Platforms

To reach out to a large and diversified population, we decided to use a local survey platform in China. We looked into three popular survey platforms in China: Wen Juan Xing (which means "survey star" in Chinese), Wen Juan Wang (which means "survey website" in Chinese) and Tencent Wen Juan (which means "Tencent survey" in Chinese). We compared the three services based on user base, sampling service and, payment methods (as shown in Table 1). Since Wen Juan Xing was the only platform that allowed researchers to define screening criteria, which in our case are printer users, we selected Wen Juan Xing. Also, Wen Juan Xing was the only service that accepted international bank transactions.

Table 1. Comparison of survey platforms

Survey platform	Number of users	Screening	Payment methods
Wen Juan Xing (Survey star)	2.6 million	Demographic data, self-defined screening criteria	Alipay, WeChat Pay, Bank transaction, International bank transaction
Wen Juan Wang (Survey website)	N/A	Demographic data	Alipay, WeChat Pay
Tencent Wen Juan (Tencent survey)	2 million	N/A	Free

4 International Payment

Payment was the biggest roadblock in our research journey. Like many companies in the US, our team only has a corporate credit card for business purchases. Despite of the ubiquity of credit card usage in the US, credit cards are not a popular payment method in China. With the rapid growth of the smartphone market, mobile payments have started to dominate the payment market in China. Alipay and WeChat Pay, the two most prevalent mobile pay methods, allow Chinese users to transfer money to one another, buy groceries, pay bills, and purchase internet services. During our investigation, we found that all three of the survey platforms we investigated only accepted Alipay and WeChat Pay. Wen Juan Xing was the only service that also accepts international bank transactions.

The finance department at Lexmark did not have any knowledge regarding mobile payments, because it is not a business-to-business payment method commonly used in the US. Our team explained the cultural difference to the accounting department and received approval on using mobile pay. However, setting up and using WeChat Pay from US was unexpectedly difficult.

To enable WeChat Pay, users need to link their WeChat Wallet to a credit card, a debit card, or a Chinese bank account. For non-Chinese credit cards or debit cards, users have to make sure that the card supports international payment. A linked credit card account would allow the user to transfer money via "Red Packet", but the user cannot withdraw from or deposit to the linked credit card. Therefore, although our corporate credit card was linked, we were still not able to pay China survey service via WeChat Pay.

We tried an alternative solution to refill our WeChat Wallet. There are online services that accept credit card payments from the US and transfer money to WeChat wallets with a service fee. For example, Kavip.com provides such service at a service charge of 7% of the transaction amount. However, Kavip required the user to upload a photo of the cardholder holding the card for identity verification. This unusual request prevented us from loading WeChat Wallet via Kavip's service. The only methods remaining for the Wen Juan Xing payment were (1) international bank transaction, or (2) adding Wen Juan Xing as a vendor. Since we planned to use Wen Juan Xing for future surveys, we decided to add Wen Juan Xing as a vendor.

Successful Data Collection

We have collected 855 responses for our first survey through Wen Juan Xing. The data collection process took about two weeks. The cost of the sampling service was calculated based on sampling criteria and the number of questions. Researchers needed to have the survey questions ready and send the survey to Wen Juan Xing to get a quote. If the cost is deemed too high, the researchers can adjust the screening criteria to lower the quote. Wen Juan Xing also tells researchers the estimated time needed to collect data.

As part of the sampling service, Wen Juan Xing automatically filtered out invalid responses, such as repetitive responses from the same IP or responses that took an unusually short amount of time. Wen Juan Xing automatically collected data on users' location (city and province), how the user found out about the survey, when the user filled out the survey, overall time each user spent on the survey, and their IP addresses. We were able to see the data collection progress in real time in the user portal.

We have also used Wen Juan Xing's built-in analytics tool for data analysis. Wen Juan Xing's analytics tool allowed us to create contingency tables, compare subsets of our data and generate charts in the user portal. The data analytics tool is great for dataset exploration. It is easy to learn and simple to use. However, this tool does not allow users to aggregate data from more than one questions. To gain further insights, researchers will need to download the dataset and use other statistics analysis tools, such as: Excel, Tableau or Python. Our team used Python Pandas to aggregate data and plot out charts.

5 Recommendations

We have identified the challenges we experienced during our research planning and execution, and developed workarounds to address these challenges. Although logistics are not typically part of research planning, small UX teams sometimes have to take care of logistics to pave the road for study implementation. Logistics problems, including getting approvals from different departments within the company, processing time for transactions, shipping time for purchases, can take time and delay research progress. We advise researchers to plan the study in advance, detail the potential roadblocks and solutions, and work on logistics and study planning at the same time. We summarized the following recommendations for researchers who are new to conducting user research in China.

- Get a team mobile number. Having a mobile number is the essential first-step to have access to almost all Chinese internet products. We recommend researchers to get a burner phone and a short-term mobile plan in advance. If the research team decides to order anything online, the team should take shipping time into consideration.
- Build long-term relationship with reliable local vendors. Local vendors can help researchers take care of recruitments and international payments. As we mentioned earlier, international payment was our biggest roadblock. Research teams should consider what kinds of help they need from the vendors and define clear criteria to review, compare and select vendors in China.

- Research payment methods. Payment methods should be part of the selection criteria when choosing services. If the service provider limits payment methods to certain options, such as Alipay or WeChat Pay, the research team might have to consider other options. Meanwhile, understanding the company's policies on available payment options is also important. The research team will have to educate other departments of the company on the importance of adapting to the payment customs of the target market. Planning for unusual resources needed to conduct user research in China can be helpful. For example, a Chinese debit card that allows researchers to use WeChat Pay. If necessary, the research team should spend time in advance to help stakeholders understand why certain resources are essential for conducting UX research in China.
- Research the target population. We recommend that the US-based UX team conduct literature review on technology usage in China to ensure proper language and questions are used in the survey. It is also important to understand the popular services and products used in China, as well as the demographics of the target participants. The research team should also factor into time differences and holiday schedules in China during timeline planning.

6 Limitation and Future Studies

For our survey study, the Chinese survey platform Wen Juan Xing was our only channel for participants recruitment and data collection. We had little control over the screening process of participants or quality of survey responses we collected. We fully relied on Wen Juan Xing to filter out participants who failed to meet our criteria and eliminate invalid responses. In the end, we still saw a few responses with random strings filled in our open-ended questions. Since we outsourced the participants recruiting process to Wen Juan Xing, we would not be able to run follow-up studies with the same group of users.

Ideally, we would like to conduct additional studies to cross-check the results from this survey, as it was the first time we tried this approach. We could conduct user interviews and contextual inquiries to validate the current findings. We could also try to outsource the research work to a reputable vendor in China. However, as mentioned earlier, we had very limited time and budget to complete this research project. Running comparison studies would defeat the purpose of taking this journey in the first place. This paper aims to share the learning from our exploration of potential solutions of conducting cost-effective remote research in China. We hope to encourage more UX teams in the US to join this exploration without being intimidated by the time and cost international UX research typically requires.

As part of our research plan, we have scheduled to carry out our second survey and the diary study. The second survey would allow us to dive deeper into user preferences and behavior patterns. The results from diary study would help us understand the reported user preferences and pain points in contexts. These three studies are just a start. Our efforts on learning about Chinese printer users still have a long way to go. We hope that the learning from planning and executing these studies would streamline our remote research projects in China moving forward.

References

1. Brejcha, J.: Cross-Cultural Human-Computer and User Experience Design: A Semiotic Perspective. Taylor & Francis, London (2015)
2. Quesenbery, W., Szuc, D.: Global UX Design and Research in a Connected World. Morgan Kaufmann, Los Altos (2012)
3. Diary Studies: Understanding Long-Term User Behavior and Experiences. https://www. nngroup.com/articles/diary-studies/. Accessed 01 Feb 2018
4. Embarking on International Research. https://medium.com/facebook-research/embarking-on-international-research-a485cc160f22. Accessed 01 Feb 2018
5. Biesterfeldt, J., Capra, M.: Leading international UX research projects. In: Marcus, A. (ed.) DUXU 2011. LNCS, vol. 6769, pp. 368–377. Springer, Heidelberg (2011). https://doi.org/10. 1007/978-3-642-21675-6_43
6. Walsh, T., Nurkka, P., Koponen, T., Varsaluoma, J., Kujala, S., Belt, S.: Collecting cross-cultural user data with internationalized storyboard survey. In: Proceedings of the 23rd Australian Computer-Human Interaction Conference, pp. 301–310, Canberra, Australia (2011)
7. Martin, B., Hanington, B.: Universal Methods of Design. Rockport Publishers, Beverly (2012)
8. China doubles down on real-name registration laws, forbidding anonymous online posts. https://techcrunch.com/2017/08/27/china-doubles-down-on-real-name-registration-laws-forbi dding-anonymous-online-posts/. Accessed 01 Feb 2018
9. Statista.   https://www.statista.com/statistics/255778/number-of-active-wechat-messenger-accounts/. Accessed 01 Feb 2018

Kansei Operation: The Application of Kansei Engineering Technology to the Operating Activities of Financial Products in the Big Data Era

Miao Liu[1](✉) and Yili Wang[2]

[1] East China University of Science and Technology, Shanghai 200237, China
183787975@qq.com
[2] Shanghai Pudong Development Bank, Shanghai 200001, China
wangyll0@spdb.com.cn

Abstract. The challenge of big data era to the operation and management of financial products boil down to how to turn data operation capacity into the core competitiveness. Under the existing operation and management model of financial products, the unity between the efficiency and benefits of operating activities can be hardly achieved in big data era. Kansei engineering technology is targeted at better coordinating the relationship between consumers and products and providing a solution to the contradiction between the width and precision of big data information while conveying the usage requirements of products. This paper takes the lead in applying the Kansei engineering thoughts in non-industrial fields to the optimization of financial products operation. It proposes the concept of Kansei operation by analyzing the product lifecycle management of financial products, which is of prime importance to correctly process the structured and semi-structured Kansei information, reduce data mixture and achieve operational excellence. With the differential customer perceptual analysis as the research basis, this concept applies the conversion of sentimental demand quantification into real values to the optimization of financial products operation, thus putting into use the operational excellence in the big data era.

Keywords: Kansei engineering · Financial products · Kansei operation
Product lifecycle management · Big data

1 Introduction

Mckinsey Global Institute pointed out that big data would have much to offer in the future six years ago when data finance was gaining momentum in China and the notion of "financial management" became a household name. Over the years, data information and internet channel have been regarded as an important production factor and distribution channel, extending its influence to each product and work flow, including financial products. With Asia becoming the global center for wealth management, the investable assets of mainland Chinese had already reached 213 trillion yuan (RMB, same below)

© Springer International Publishing AG, part of Springer Nature 2018
F. F.-H. Nah and B. S. Xiao (Eds.): HCIBGO 2018, LNCS 10923, pp. 115–131, 2018.
https://doi.org/10.1007/978-3-319-91716-0_10

by the end of 2016 and are expected to amount to 415 trillion yuan in 2020, in which, financial products still take up a small proportion. The total scale of assets management in China grew at the rate of 30.07% at the end of 2016, a sharp drop compared with the growth rate of 50% over the past four years, reflecting the poor market adsorption of financial products.

With broader access to information and transmission channel, the directional transmission of product information favored by the previous industrial age has evolved into bidirectional or even multidirectional transmission of information flow. Consumers living in the big data era also begin to take the initiative both in purchasing products and designing products. The manufacturers can carry out their further research and development according to the feedback from the information channel. For the wealth management market in China, the big data ushers in the times of financial management, in which, financial products and industrial products are undergoing tremendous commercial and management revolution brought about by big data.

As one of the information-intensive industries, the financial industry makes profits through the production and sales of financial products. In addition to not having a physical form, financial products are no essentially different from the production model of industrial products in terms of design, production and sales. As known to all, financial products have higher requirements for data value. Despite the high total value of big data, the unit value is relatively low. Its real utilization value is dependent on the reliability degree of metadata. For this reason, the financial product manufacturers who are able to explore, reorganize and expand the potential values of data on the basis of the basic value of metadata will stand out in the big data era.

2   Financial Products and Industrial Products

In a broad sense, financial products refer to the publicly-traded or liquidated assets that carry economic values, such as currency, gold, foreign exchange and negotiable securities. These financial products are the buying and selling objects in the financial market, whose prices are manifested by the interest rate or rate of return. The buying and selling of financial products can promote the accommodation of funds. In spite of the fact that different financial products have different specific stipulations, they have the same product elements, such as issuer, subscriber, deadline, price, earnings, risks, negotiability and rights and interests. According to different forms, financial produces fall into currency, tangible products and intangible products; in which, the intangible product, as a financial service, means that entrusted by the investors, financial institutions provide them with financial services that manage their assets. Financial institutions shall perform their duties diligently and responsibly and charge the relevant management fees while consignors are at their own risks and get returns. Such financial products can also be called asset management products, or the narrow-sense financial product discussed in this paper.

If industrial products were said to be the outcomes of the production and operation of the secondary industry, financial products can be likened to the outcome of the tertiary industry. The development of human society goes through three stages, namely, agricultural society, industrialization stage and postindustrial stage. The major characteristic of postindustrial stage is that the tertiary industry features prominently in this stage. At present, the output value of the tertiary industry in western developed countries account for 60% to 70% of GDP, and the proportion of output value of the tertiary industry exceeded 51% from the third quarter of 2015, facts eloquently demonstrating that the products of tertiary industry, particularly the financial products, have ushered in a flourishing innovation-driven era.

Table 1 offers a comparison of the properties of the financial products listed on the basis of the basic elements of the industrial products. Financial products are intangible with simple utilization value (for appreciation in asset value). It is essentially homogeneous with industrial products in terms of the most important functional characteristics, which makes it possible to apply the industrial production technology to the field of financial products.

- Both of them must possess the basic core functions so as to provide consumers with the basic utility or interests.
- Both of them must possess the intermediary functions. The product features, determined by the perceptual requirements of consumers, must also meet their needs for expansion.
- Both of them must possess certain additional functions, which are also the associated use functions required by modern society, such as the demonstration, guidance, pre-sale and after-sale services of products.

On the basis of the above-mentioned comparison, the concept of product life cycle (PLC) is introduced to directly reveal the homogeneity of financial products and industrial products in the process of production. The management of PLC, as an integrated information channel, is used to manage the life cycle of products and all the people, technological process/activity and technology related to its peripheral design, ranging from product design and manufacturing, deployment and maintenance, service, waste disposal to the end of the product life cycle. Based on the comparison between the properties of financial products and industrial products, it is of importance to appropriately adjust the PLM model of industrial products (the left in Fig. 1) to establish the Product Life-Cycle Management (PLM) model applicable to financial products (the right in Fig. 1).

In spite of the fact that the subdivision process of the four stages of financial product life cycle is different from that of industrial products, their stage characteristics are similar. At the stage of creation, financial products should be turned from an idea or a consumer demand into an exploitable state with the Kansei value improved to a product concept. At the stage of construction, the product manufacturing method and resource consumption are determined according to the planning and output of the last stage. System development and test experience can generate specific products that can meet the requirements for specifications and functional design. The stage of service support, or the stage of marketing or maintenance is targeted at providing consumers with sufficient information to inform them of the perceived values of their products and to guarantee the continuity of this Kansei value. The last stage means scrapping for industrial products but disposal for financial products due to their non-physical property. Specifically, this stage is characterized by the termination of sales of old products and the replacement with new products, or the upgrading of old products through

Table 1. Basic elements of industrial products and financial product.

	Industrial products	Financial products
Appearance characteristics	Different physical forms and colors	No physical form
Characteristics of consumer demand	Emphasize materialistic consuming demand	Emphasize spiritual consuming demand
Functional characteristics	Basic function, mental function and additional function	
Characteristics of sales channel	Physical store and network	Counter of financial institutions and network

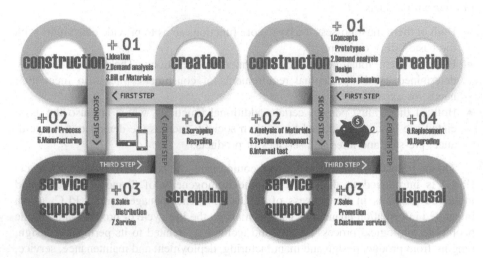

Fig. 1. PLM model of industrial products and financial products

optimization approaches. Each stage of the life cycle of financial products and different stages are connected by a series of operation activities. These activities are carried out, just like the industrial products, to find out the mode of production that can optimize the customer satisfaction, time, cost and quality to the largest extent.

3   Kansei Engineering and Operation of Products

3.1   Kansei Engineering Technology in the Operation of Industrial Products

Kansei is a Japanese word, stressing the relationship between product modality and Kansei. It is both a static concept and a dynamic process. The static Kansei refers to the feelings of people and the impression obtained while the dynamic Kansei means people's cognitive psychological activities, their perception of things and their judgment of unknown, polysemantic and ambiguous information. The Kansei technology in the engineering field is manifested as a human engineering and a technology of studying the customer demands. The emergence of Kansei engineering has ushered the engineering field into a stage of redevelopment. This engineering technology has yielded enormous economic returns in the sector of home appliance, clothing, automobile and decoration. It is the core value of Kansei engineering to analyze the Kansei characteristics between people and products, set up standard database system for the following product design, combine the user senses, emotions, the essence of products and design characteristics and center around the Kansei demands of users. Such characteristics will be made the development trend of future design.

At present, Kansei engineering has been applied not only to the stage of product design, or the stage if creation and construction mentioned above, but also to the quality evaluation of product design so as to provide reference for the design and production of enterprises and make products more adaptive to the modern flexible production and requirements of network age. In accordance with the SIPOC organizational system model proposed by Dr. W. Edwards Deming[1], operating activities can be defined as a process of "input-conversion-output". The application of different methods, be it quantitative analysis method, qualitative analysis method and product evaluation method, to product operating activities can be regarded as the "conversion" stage in this process (Fig. 2), which complies to the concept of man-machine interaction. For example, when designing a dining table, one can understand the superiority of different schemes (output) and choose the final production scheme through the input of user data, analysis and conversion with Kansei words, output of design consideration and material selection schemes and finally the input of comprehensive index for evaluation analysis (conversion) (Fig. 3). In the life cycle of PLM of industrial products, Kansei technology places more stress on the application of "Kansei design". However, whether it is applicable in other stages and how to apply have not aroused extensive discussion.

3.2 Analysis of the Operating Activities of Financial Products

In the big data era, "Kansei" has become the symbolic capacity of era development, including the capacity to perceive and exchange data information, or the capacity to extract the information needed and to transmit these data information to others in an appropriate way, which are urgently needed by the operation of financial products. Before the introduction of Kansei engineering technology to the field of financial product demands, it is necessary to analyze the characteristics of operating activities of financial products in the big data era.

Financial institution is the designer, manufacturer and retailer of financial products. The production activities of financial products are the combination of a series of intangible innovative services. Financial institutions perform their basic functions of capital settlement, account information management and asset trusteeship. In the big data era, the input content of the operating activities of financial products displays

---

[1] Dr. W. Edwards Deming proposed that any organization is a system consisting of 5 interrelated and interactive parts: supplier, input, process, output, and customer.

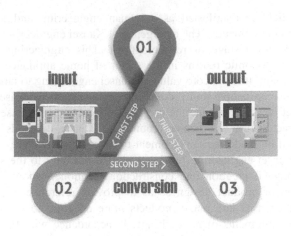

Fig. 2. The concept of SIPOC model

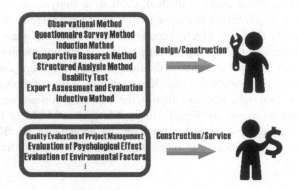

Fig. 3. The SIPOC model of a dining table's design and sale

statistical characteristics. It means that both the external and internal structural and non-structural information from the financial institutions, including the trade information, customer behavior information, demand information and industrial information, are packaged into pools. After being "converted" through data mining, creation and reorganization, these information are transmitted to other functional departments inside the financial institution and the social departments and individuals inside the financial institutions, thus achieving the data value and acting on each stage of the life cycle of financial products. Only through rapid transmission, analysis and processing will mass data be able to timely respond to user behavior. Due to the high total value but low unit value of these data, the operating activities of financial products are manifested as environmental complexity and non-linearity of data transmission.

Environmental Complexity. In the operating activities of financial products, different departments of the financial institutions should perform their own functions of handling internal customers (from other departments) and external customers (consumers) at the same time. To this end, it is of prime importance to reconcile and perfectly convert the demands of these two kinds of customers, or it will be very difficult to follow the characteristics of big data era of "accepting the mixture of data". The production and operation system of financial products, which is very complicated, stretches across different departments of financial institutions and different branches of financial groups, horizontally involving departments of the same level but different types (such as Headquarter A, Headquarter B and Headquarter C) and vertically involving departments of the same type but different levels (such as a1, a2 and a3, the branches in other places under Headquarter A). Requiring different "input" information and "conversion" method in the operation system of financial products, these departments also generate different "output" outcomes. To achieve the effective conversion of final results and give full play to the overall functions, all the roles and their SIPOC sub-models must be placed in a SIPOC master pattern. It is seen from Fig. 4 that these departments, which may appear in the operation of different stages, differ from each other in their operating activity contents. An optimal "translation" method must be found out for their correlation and exchange to guarantee the best conversion effect in case of hybridity in the information flow received.

Non-linearity of Data Transmission. Just like the industrial product PLM model, the cohesive relationship of PLM stages of financial products is manifested by the information sharing mechanism between roles of the same level and different types and information feedback mechanism between roles of different levels and same types (Fig. 5). From the perspective of the headquarter of financial institutions, it is necessary to receive (input) the information about the financial product demand and the corresponding operation support from the information sharing mechanism and the customer or market demand data from information feedback mechanism. After integrating, minting and analyzing (conversion) these data, financial institutions assign (output) new business solutions or optimization schemes of the original businesses. This scheme information, as the output content for the next stage, will be subject to a new round of process of "input-conversion-output". In the big data era, the first key point in the process of data information transmission is the accuracy of information input, such as the consistency of data mining aperture and the reliability of data itself; the second key point is the data conversion mode, or how to avoid the loss of more data value in the second data information conversion, which is a problem that must be properly handled in the operating activities of financial products.

With the rapid social development, financial products can not only bring out the new functions of products, but also integrate the demands of internal management, market and consumers. Products based on Kansei engineering and "user-centered" concept, be it industrial products or financial products, are needed by our times. Therefore, the homogenization of financial products and increase of customer experience have made the financial product producers or service providers take full note of the Kansei values that go beyond the demands of market function values in the big data era. If all the information were converted and quantified into data usage and analysis, Kansei value becomes the potential value that transcends the basic uses of data, which is data's real value and the ideal output outcomes of SIPOC model of financial products.

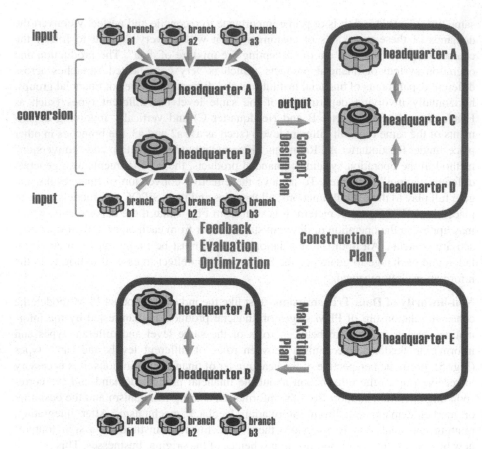

Fig. 4. The SIPOC and PLM concept in financial products' operation activity

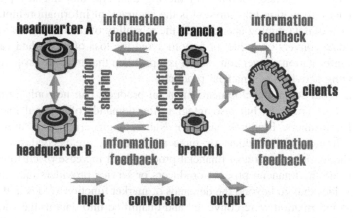

Fig. 5. The information sharing & feedback mechanism during financial products' operation

4 The Kansei Operation of Financial Products

Based on the preceding analysis, Kansei operation aims at probing into the relationship between the Kansei demands of the external and internal customers of financial institutions and operating activities through industrial production research methods. With the differentiated Kansei analysis results as the research basis, the Kansei demands are quantified into real values in order to apply them to the creation, construction, service and optimization of financial product operation, achieve the sustainability of life cycle chain of financial products and bring out the flexible production and optimization of financial products. To investigate the application of Kansei engineering technology to the operating activities of financial products, it is demanding to make certain the differentiated operation focuses of financial institutions on financial products of different types. As analyzed above, financial products have simple use value of, to be specific, increasing the assets of consumers. On this basis, the original use value is provided not by consumers, but by product designer who create and construct the product service life, rate of return, means of purchase, dividend distribution and mode of payment. Product designers have different positioning for different consumer groups. As the use values of financial products are circulatory, or characterized by rolling release or no fixed expiry date (open products), the financial products from the same financial institution can fall into the following three categories according to their operation focus (as showed in Table 2):

It is important to increase the number of consumers on the basis of maintaining the classical brand name products; to accurately transmit the product information to customers, particularly the new products generated as a result of the change in external factors, such as regulatory policies and scientific and technological innovation; to bring the product optimization and upgrading based on historical evaluation data in line with the real demands of consumers.

Classical Products. This kind of products, usually known as the well-developed brand name products or reputed products of the financial institutions, have entered into the service stage via the creation stage and construction stage. Under such circumstances, these products are targeted at further expanding customers, drawing their attention through marketing means and attracting them to make purchasing decisions, thus increasing the sales volume of products. At the same time, financial institutions should also keep an eye on the market feedback so as to make prompt handling decisions (termination or improvement).

Innovative Products. This kind of products are brand-new for the market and consumers, most of which originate from the products uniquely created as a response to the change in the environmental factors, such as regulatory policies and scientific and technological innovation. Having crossed the creation stage and most of the construction stage, these products are in the second half of the construction stage and about to enter into the service stage. For this reason, these products should guarantee the accurate transmission of all the design concepts and functions of products to consumers through effective process design and service design. Product designers can also timely adjust their operation according to the early market feedback for the smooth follow-up promotion.

Table 2. Categories of financial products according to the operation focus

	Operation focus	Periodical focus	Explanation
Classical products	Maintenance	Service	Will it be accessible to more consumers?
Creative products	Promotion	Creation	Can consumers understand the production information?
Burgeoning products	Design	Construction	Are the products needed by the consumers?

Burgeoning Products. This kind of products are not completely unfamiliar for consumers. They may grow out of a financial product which were terminated because of poor sales volume and then be improved according to the market feedback data collected. As they have just left the disposal stage and entered into the creation stage, they should make the final production decision according to the accurate analysis results. These products should place their operation focus on how to obtain accurate demand analysis results in order to guarantee the effective and feasible decision-making and schemes for the construction and service stages.

The aforesaid analyses come to the conclusion that as a result of the differences in the operational priorities, different financial products have different "output" demands even in the same product life stage. However, one financial institution cannot customize an exclusive life cycle system for each product. The application of Kansei engineering technology to the operating activities of financial products aims at effectively utilizing the "transmission" methods, such as the configuration of methods with different weights and flexible method combination.

4.1 The Creation Stage

This stage focuses on demand interpretation and analysis and promotes product design through demands. The demands of financial products are jointly advanced by the product demand side and producers. However, these demands usually contradict each other. For example, consumers may prefer the financial products that can be purchased all week long; in contrast, restricted by fund operation arrangement, system structure and flow design, product providers are unable to provide non-stop services. The market trend suggests that for one thing, as people are getting increasingly familiar with financial products, there is also an increasingly complicated and sophisticated demands from consumers; for another, the regulatory policies have raised increasingly stringent requirements for product providers, thus narrowing down the scope of the subjective initiative of the designers. Therefore, demands must be subject to verification, such as test, analysis, simulation or qualitative evaluation, so as to guarantee the evaluability of the results. The information obtained can be expanded to the follow-up PLM stage and fed back to the design stage, thus improving the future design. This verification process is just like the "conversion" link in the "input-conversion-output" model. This stage is aimed at finding out the "transmission" method appropriate for product demand analysis.

The combination of qualitative inference and quantitative analysis method is conducive to resolving the major problems of this stage. This combination method is adopted to obtain the first-hand Kansei intention data of consumers in the stage of market investigation and consumer Kansei analysis. Other quantitative means are also employed to quantify the Kansei intentions of consumers and to build up the correspondence between the Kansei intention of consumers and the product design elements. Different from the industrial products, the consumers of financial products are more delicately classified, thus obtaining more Kansei information about the product. As designers cannot design products according to each Kansei information, a few sets of products that could represent the general Kansei appeals of consumers should be provided to help consumers find their favorite Kansei characteristics. In this way, the design elements that can most represent Kansei information is generated, thus charting the course for the future development of product design.

4.2 The Construction Stage

The main task of this stage is to complete the manufacturing and production of products. As financial product is not a physical product, this stage mainly determines which system, operation and order will be applied to accomplish periodical development goals instead of considering the selection of manufacturing raw materials and consumable items in this stage. In this process, much attention should be paid to the Kansei demand information of system users and flow participants. If such information were called the internal Kansei information of the financial institution, the Kansei information obtained from the creation stage is more likely to be an external Kansei information of the financial institution. Therefore, it is essential to acquire the internal Kansei information through appropriate "input" method and effectively combine the external Kansei information through suitable "conversion" method with a view to achieving the operation target of the stage.

First, the Kansei design elements of products obtained from the last stage should be integrated into Kansei words according to the degree of importance and the field involved, which will be provided for the participants of the construction stage of financial products (hereinafter referred to as participant of the second stage) for evaluation. It is worth-noticing that the number of Kansei words and the evaluation method of participants can directly influence the quality of research data. A missing of an important word will impact the effectiveness of the research results. The semantic differential analysis method can help each design element choose the most representative Kansei word. The participants of the second stage, as members of the panel, can cut and sort the Kansei words, thus acquiring the Kansei words that can facilitate the effective development of products. What's more, participants of the second stage carry out system design and process design on the basis of these effective Kansei words. Coming from different departments of the financial institutions, the participants of the second stage are mainly categorized into the developers and operators of the operating system. It is the operators who determine the demand plans and completion flow in accordance with the early research results; on the basis of which, designers can complete the system development. The systematic development of the effective Kansei words can, to a large extent, fulfill the product demand target and operational target. In addition, after development, all the participants take part in the simulation test for further optimization of the process and the relevant system. The works of this link will be incorporated into work instruction to provide guidance for future actual production inspection.

4.3 The Service Stage

The physical time of financial products in this stage ranges from one month to several years, the longest period in product life cycle. The operational task of financial institutions in this stage is to guarantee that products can constantly provide consumers with perceived values. For one thing, consumers will be able to make purchasing decisions on this basis. At the same time, financial institutions will continue to supply information to potential consumers, such as product propaganda, marketing and consulting, to expand sales volume; for another, financial institutions offer product operation information to consumers to put into practice the Kansei services agreed in the selling period, such as the product dividend and the increase or decrease of purchasing capitals. Considering the fact that the financial products are mostly distributed through the propaganda album and posters of the sales networks of financial institutions or online advertising, online presentation or SMS reminder serves as the major operation and maintenance channel of product information. Under such conditions, the Kansei operation scheme of this stage boils down to the completion of the tasks of this stage, accurate transmission of product Kansei values to the consumers and optimization of Kansei service strategies according to market response.

In light of the speciality of financial products, it is difficult to obtain effective suggestions from consumers in advance. The marketing programs of new products are mainly formulated and introduced by the financial institutions and then flexibly adjusted according to the market response. The financial product service schemes mainly focus on whether the consumers can be immediately attracted by the information through the obviously presented or marked product characteristics. For this reason, visual factors and psychological factors are two Kansei factors that must be taken into consideration when formulating service schemes, in which, man-machine interaction is the most frequently-seen scene of this stage. In order to judge whether the product information can be accurately transmitted to the consumers, the most appropriate Kansei evaluation method is the two-phase analytic evaluation method. At the first phase, the analysis is carried out before products are formally introduced with the staff of financial institutions (apart from the product designers) as the subjects of the draft of service program. Considering the limited number of subjects and their higher professionalism, the eye tracking technology and expert evaluation method are employed to complete the scheme optimization work of this phase. The analysis of the second phase for ordinary consumers does not begin until the products are introduced to the market. In light of the large number of subjects and different types, direct evaluation methods, such as questionnaire method, interview method and observational method can be adopted to obtain the Kansei evaluation words from consumers as the basis for the program optimization of the second phase.

4.4 The Disposal Stage

The last stage of PLC is disposal. According to the analysis in the preceding part, the disposal of financial products is characterized by the feedback, evaluation and summary of the existing products. The final target of this stage is that financial institutions determine the termination of sales of these products (the first generation products) and replace with the new products or optimized products (the second generation products). Different from industrial products, financial products can never introduce the second generation products when consumers are still using the first generation products. It is worth-noticing that only after the termination of the first generation products will be the second generation products be launched. As known to all, the withdrawal of the first generation products is an unstoppable trend. Therefore, the operating activities of this stage mainly focuses on the "filing" of the knowledge assets generated in the PLC of the first generation. The negligence of this work means that the same mistakes will be repeatedly made in the research and development of new products. As a result, many resources will be wasted on the product elements that consumers do not care about at all. The high degree similarity between new products and old products, however, will not bring too much actual value to financial institutions or consumers. This stage mainly focuses on how to establish an information base through filing and extract the information related to the research and development, test and usage of previous products so as to tell financial institutions the dos and don'ts in their future works.

This information base is just like the Kansei operation system, whose structure must facilitate the input of information of the products to be disposed. There must be an appropriate conversion method that can output the reference information valuable to the design of new products before the start of the life cycle of second generation products. Kensei operation system should be composed of several sub-information bases, which are established based on the analysis of the basic characteristics of financial products, Kansei evaluation of consumers and Kansei evaluation of designers and their correlation characteristics, such as Kansei word information, image information base, consumer kanser demand information base and product design element information base. This system mainly applies computer technology, artificial intelligence and fuzzy logic to provide Kansei reference for the creation stage of PLC and bring second generation products closer to the tendency of consumers through its periodic renewal according to the technological and economic development and changes in social demand.

5   Case Study

As introduced in the last part, the financial products under the same financial institution are classified into classical products, innovative products and burgeoning products according to the focuses of operating activities. Taking innovative products for example, this part offers a brief introduction to and analysis of the Kansei operation method used by financial products in the creation stage and construction stage. In this case, the financial institution is X, a national bank. Apart from the headquarter, it also sets up branches in all provinces and cities, including X1, X2 and X3. In the operation of financial products (the bank financial products in this case), it is the headquarter that takes charge of the product research and development, system construction and formulation of sales scheme and the branches that executes marketing promotion and after-sales service according to the scheme provided by the headquarter. In accordance with function division, the financial institution encompasses Department of Product Research and Development A, Technological Development Department B, Sales Department C and Back-office Operation Department D. These departments also have their corresponding institutions at the branches in each province and city. This organizational relationship is reflected as a dendritical structure (Fig. 6). As mentioned above, innovative products refer in particular to the unprecedented financial products that consumers never heard of before and whose concepts do not stem from the optimization and upgrading of other products. The initial period of PLM cycle of such products is also known as creation stage with no link of extracting effective Kansei information from the disposal stage of other products, which makes it easier to gain a preliminary knowledge of the application of Kansei engineering technology.

The determination of the concept of product is the basis for research and development. The product innovation of X institution is aimed at resolving consumers' needs for unplanned fund. The market investigation conducted by X institution shows that after purchasing the financial products, consumers could only take back their principals and get returns on the date specified by the sales contract. It is impossible for consumers to terminate the contract before the date of expiration to meet their demands for unplanned funds even in case of emergency. It is not sufficient to simply take into consideration innovation to establish a financial product with complete elements. Therefore, the research personnel from a department of X institution first carry out product design and background analysis in the creation stage in order to obtain a complete innovative product model. After conducting the background analysis of product design from the perspectives of market status, industrial characteristics of product, the influence of Kansei engineering on product design and the special design of this product, research personnel obtain the design considerations of this product and sort them according to the research and development focus (Fig. 7). In light of the different Kansei value degree of different design considerations to the internal operational staff of X institution, system and external consumers, one to four alternative proposals are chosen for some of the design considerations (time limit, yield characteristics, operation mode and brand) as the options for the Kansei evaluation in the construction stage participated by other departments.

In the construction stage, Technological Development Department B, Sales Department C and Back-office Operation Department D join the evaluation team to settle the major two problems facing this stage together, namely, product design considerations and product manufacturing. Each department has its own Kansei vocabulary library. For example (the lower part in Fig. 8), Back-office Operation Department D is responsible for the operation management after consumers have purchased the financial products, including registration of consumers' purchase share, returns calculation, accounting treatment of product investment end and release of data

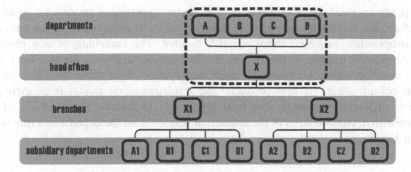

Fig. 6. The dendritical structure of financial institution X

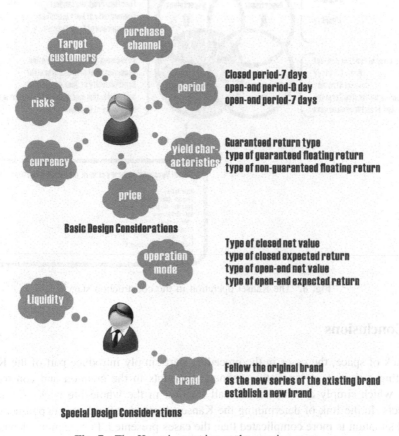

Fig. 7. The Kansei operation at the creation stage

information. All these works have to be achieved on the professional computer system. The multiple professional systems form an operation treatment platform through the business process and the corresponding data interface. The back-office operation of new products must be conducted on the same operational processing platform. Therefore, the Kansei requirements of department D, to a large extent, are based on system operation, process control and risk control. The launching of new products should not cause troubles to the existing product operation, or lack the necessary links for its own operation. Likewise, all these departments have made decisions on the design considerations of new products and implementation model from their perspective of Kansei demands. The final scheme is formulated on the basis of the comprehensive consideration of the evaluation results of all the departments (the upper part in Fig. 8).

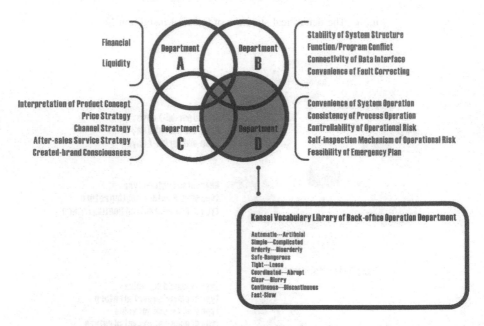

Fig. 8. The Kansei operation in the construction stage

6 Conclusions

For lack of space, the cases in the preceding part simply introduce part of the Kansei operating activities of innovative financial products in the creation and construction stage, which simply account for a small fraction in the whole life cycle of financial products. In the link of determining the Kansei demands of different departments, the actual situation is more complicated than the cases presented. For example, department C serves as both the "evaluation expert" in the construction stage and the "executor" in the service stage. It is worth-noticing that these two roles are sustained in the constant information input and output with its branches C1, C2 and C3. In each department's verification and feedback of the final scheme and manufacturing outcomes, more Kansei engineering methods will be employed. In department D's Kansei evaluation of the new system functions, the application of eye movement technique can help the developers of department B gain an understanding of whether the new product functions can facilitate back-office operators' identification of key information and know more about the essential elements of information concerned by the back-office operators, thus reaching the goal of bringing the system development achievements in line with the actual operational effect through constant iteration tests. At the service and disposal stage of financial products, more Kansei operational model and Kansei engineering technology are worth further discussions. For example, after the classification of product concept and required elements, it is necessary to conduct in-depth and detailed investigation of the different parts of products. In order to improve the feasibility and integrity of the Kansei operation model theory of financial products in the big data era, it is of prime importance to collect more cases to analyze how to help financial institutions pay more attention to the Kansei demands of the insiders of the institutions and the external consumers in their product operation with systematic Kansei engineering data and how to satisfy the emotional demands of consumers by detecting the new products with Kansei engineering technology in the final test phase.

In this information age, compared with industrial products, the operation of financial products depend more on the production factor of "information", which will turn Kansei engineering into the operation media and approach for financial products. If Kansei design could create a lifestyle that meets the needs of consumers and help consumers have dialogues with producers, the Kansei operation of financial products can promote the standardization of design information and product information and create a brand-new lifestyle. If cooperative relationship were established between the operation of financial products and usage of industrial products, consumers are able to enjoy a more colorful digital modern life. For all of these reasons, financial institutions should hold internal and external dialogues and establish a dialogue-based Kansei operation model in the process of product operation.

References

1. Ba, S.S., Yang, L.: Annual Report on the Development of China's Assets Management Industry. Zhejiang People's Publish House, Hangzhou (2017)
2. Wang, G.G.: Annual Report on China's Financial Development. Social Science Academic Press, Beijing (2017)
3. Huang, M.X.: Research on Mechanism of Virtual Products' Socialized Diffusion. Peking University Press, Beijing (2017). (in Chinese, Semantic Translation)
4. Grieves, M.: VIRTUALLY PERFECT-Driving Innovative and Lean Product Lifecycle Management. China Machine Press, Beijing (2017)
5. Luo, L.X., Hong, L.: Kansei Engineering Design. Tinghua University Press, Beijing (2015)
6. Li, L.X.: Explore the Truth of Art Design. China Electric Power Press, Beijing (2008). (in Chinese, Semantic Translation)
7. Li, Y.Z.: Selected Readings of Classic Works about Art Design. Tinghua University Press, Beijing (2006). (in Chinese, Semantic Translation)

Testing the Convergent Validity of Continuous Self-Perceived Measurement Systems: An Exploratory Study

Sébastien Lourties[✉], Pierre-Majorique Léger, Sylvain Sénécal,
Marc Fredette, and Shang Lin Chen

HEC Montreal, Tech3Lab, 3000 Chemin de la Côte-Sainte-Catherine, Montreal,
QC H3T 2A7, Canada
sebastien.lourties@hec.ca

Abstract. This paper explores the convergent validity of instruments that can provide higher temporal resolution when measuring user experience: the continuous self-perceived measurement system and psychophysiological measures. Specifically, we explore the extent to which primacy and recency effects may have an impact on the convergent validity of two constructs: valence and arousal. Using a Wilcoxon signed rank test, results suggest that users self-evaluate their valence more accurately at the end of each of the sequences than at the beginning while they evaluate their arousal more accurately at the beginning of each of the sequences. This suggests that the recency effect has more impact on valence and the primacy effect has more impact on arousal. These findings contribute to human-computer interaction research by providing more information about the psychophysiological measures that cause recency and primacy.

Keywords: Continuous self-perceived measurement system
Physiological measurement · Primacy effect · Recency effect

1 Introduction

Research is calling for a multimethod approach in human computer interactions [26, 48, 53]. Multiple measurement approaches offer a richer perspective on user experience context and can enable UX researchers to gain better insight on what the user really experiences in a given task [11, 21].

Amongst the new methods proposed in the literature, new instruments offer better temporal resolution on user experience, i.e. measures that can provide a continuous measure of the experience over time. In contrast, non-continuous measure such as psychometric scales only provide a measure at a precise moment in time. Continuous measures can be very useful to designers as they can help to identify the timing of non-optimal experiences (in other words, pain points in an interactive experience). This article focuses on two of those measures: continuous self-perceived measurement systems (CSP) [12, 22, 23, 33, 41] and continuous psychophysiological measures [2, 18, 25, 32]. CSP are retrospective measurements that "let the observer track the

© Springer International Publishing AG, part of Springer Nature 2018
F. F.-H. Nah and B. S. Xiao (Eds.): HCIBGO 2018, LNCS 10923, pp. 132–144, 2018.
https://doi.org/10.1007/978-3-319-91716-0_11

emotional content of a stimulus as they perceive it over time, allowing the emotional dynamics of speech episodes to be examined" [12] (p. 1). Psychophysiological measures are "an unobtrusive and implicit way to determine the user's affective or cognitive state on the basis of mind-body relations" [14] (p. 1362).

It is of high importance to UX researchers to understand the extent to which these new instruments converge in measuring the same constructs. As those signals can evolve over time, they may not to coevolve in the same manner over time. Thus, the objective of this paper is to explore the convergent validity of two important constructs in UX research: valence and arousal. Specifically, we explore the extent to which primacy and recency effect may have an effect on the convergent validity of these constructs.

To answer this research question, we have conducted laboratory experiment with 13 participants performing a series of utilitarian tasks on an insurance company website for 15 min. Our results suggest that users self-evaluate their valence more accurately at the end of each of the sequences than at the beginning and evaluate their arousal more accurately at the beginning of each of the sequence. This could suggest that valence has more impact on recency effect and arousal has more impact on primacy effect.

This paper is organized as follows. First of all, in the literature review, we will introduce emotion in user experience, then we will talk about psychophysiological measures of emotion, then its self-perceived evaluation. After that, we will develop our hypothesis and we will explain our research methodology. Finally, we will present the results and discuss the implications.

2   Literature Review: Measuring UX with High Temporal Resolution Instruments

This article focuses on two types of UX measurements that provide high temporal resolution: Neurophysiological measure and CSP measure. High temporal measures offer precision with respect to time during an experience. High temporal resolution measures are characterized by a sampling rate that defines the number of measures per minutes.

2.1   Continuous Self-Perceived Measures of User Experience

Continuous self-perceived measurement systems have been proposed as a novel way to enable a user to dynamically report on its experience. The simplest tools to use are composed of only one dimension of the emotion (e.g. emotional valence). The CARMA software and the Emotion Slider [22, 33] were developed with one dimension in order to facilitate the report of basic emotion (negative vs positive), so participants just have to push up or down to report their affective state. For instance, Girard and Wright [23] propose a measurement system in which users operate a joystick to indicate their reactions to a stimulus on two dimensions (e.g., emotional arousal and valence). Before that, other systems have been proposed to measure in a such way emotion. Feel-Trace [12] and EmuJoy [41] were the first software packages to propose a CSP on two dimensions. Software with two dimensions were only tested in a hedonic context: FeelTrace, Emu-joy and DARMA were tested in the music or commercial ad context that had extreme (negative or positive) arousal and valence. Furthermore, even if the authors suggest the use of the tools for retrospection in a utilitarian context, they were mainly tested directly to evaluate music or commercials.

Although these systems provide richer information than self-reported scales due to their continuous nature, to our knowledge, no research has investigated their validity. Since research suggests that any self-reported measure is subject to biases, e.g., retrospective bias, efforts to validate these continuous measurement systems will inform researchers and practitioners using such systems to evaluate user experience.

Then, we could wonder why some researchers have focus their activity on CSP. It comes from the limitations of the traditional self-reported measurement system [3]. However, as Lallemand and Grenier [31] report, the limited number of emotions reported in some tools could make it difficult for the participant to clearly express what they feel. Finally, many tools provide a scale and a score that doesn't explain what really happened during the interaction with the product/interface even if much progress has been made by researchers with the succession of tools put at our disposal. All of the self-reported tools provide the overall grade that the participant experience without explaining positive and negative emotions selected during their interaction [7, 8]. Moreover, this last limitation motivated researchers to explore CSP measurement systems. Also, it should be noted that, depending on the tool we use, important biases such as primacy and recency effects, could occur during the retrospection of the participant.

2.2 Continuous Neurophysiological Measures of User Experience

In the last decade, there has been a wide range of studies that employed tools and theories from neurosciences to inform the design of information systems in a user-computer interaction context [42, 48]. More specifically, measures of valence and arousal have been very informative [34]. Valence and arousal measurements are part of psychophysiological measures that are already defined above as "an unobtrusive and implicit way to determine the user's affective or cognitive state on the basis of mind-body relations" [14] (p. 1362). Over the years, psychophysiological measures have received a lot of attention as they provide a large quantity of information to pose an accurate diagnostic on an emotional reaction caused by a stimuli [19]. Researcher such as Plutchik, [44] proposed that there are from two to twenty different emotions. In this article, we will focus our intention on the circumplex model that was created to represent emotions with arousal and valence in two dimensions [45, 49], because it has been reused for the construction of the continuous self-perceived system DARMA [23].

Arousal is the reaction to an emotional stimuli characterized by neurophysiological level of vigilance or a state of attention [29]. The arousal construct is used to contrast states of low arousal (e.g., calm) and high arousal (e.g., surprise) [2] and is a useful construct in the human computer literature. For example, Ravaja et al. [46], in a video game context, find that the nature of the opponent (computer, friend, stranger) varied the impact on the arousal of the participant. To measure arousal, electrodermal activity (EDA) has been proposed as an accurate way to collect data using the variation of the electrical properties of the skin in response to the secretion of sweat from the palm of the hands in our case [2, 25].

Valence usually refers to "the 'positive' and 'negative' character of an emotion and/or of its aspects such as behavior, affect, evaluation, faces, adaptive value, etc." [9]. The valence construct is used to contrast states of pleasure (e.g., happy) and displeasure (e.g., angry) [2]. For example, in the IT field, this construct was used as a determinant factor to create an intelligent tutoring system (AutoTutor) that measures the frustration of the student learning the content and interacting with it [39]. Detecting this negative valence makes it possible to improve the learning curve of the student. Sas et al. [50], conducted an experiment to test most memorable moments and the attachment to the Facebook website and positive valence common denominators for all the participants. One way to measure this valence, is to use facial expression [15] because most individuals express their emotion with micro-movements of the facial muscles. Automatic facial analysis tools such as Facereader (Noldus, Wageningen, Netherlands) permit to determine with relative precision, valence change in an experience and this, in real time with a high temporal precision (6 times per second) [52].

There are several advantages to taking psychophysiological measures into consideration when studying emotion. First, you can capture the unconscious or automatic reactions of a participant without interrupting the experiment to get the most natural reaction because it is non-intrusive [42]. Then, you can have data on the user reaction in real time which is a real advantage to avoid the common bias of memory [26]. Finally, you can combine different measures with neurophysiological tools to limits the common method bias [34].

In this article, we are measuring the neurophysiological states of the user using valence and arousal dimensions of emotion because we are then able to use these two dimensions that are well accepted by research [3], characterized by a two-dimensional cartesian plane. The arousal dimension goes from calm to excited whereas valence ranges from negative to positive.

3 Hypothesis Development

While remembering an experience could be hard for someone, there exist some biases that consciously or unconsciously make this step harder.

This article aims at exploring the convergent validity of neurophysiological measures and CSP measures. Specifically, we explore to what extent the convergent validity is affected by primacy and recency bias. Primacy effect refers to the increased memory and over-weighted influence of the first moment of an experience [40, 51, 54] and recency effect correspond to the important influence of the last moment of an experience [28]. These two biases have the same root and are part of the larger topic of memory bias. To be concerned by the primacy and the recency effect you have to exercise a retrospection which is the capacity to remember the context of an experience and to explain the intention [10]. Several factors can influence the ability to remember an experience; valence and arousal are important ones.

Fredrickson and Kahneman [20] have suggested that the duration of an experience has little effect on the retrospective evaluation. They call it the "duration neglect". They conducted an experiment with video clips, but also with physical experiences [28] suggesting the same results. Overall, in a free recall context, primacy and recency effect play a U-shape curve described in the serial position curve of Craik and Lockhart [13]. After the experience, items at the beginning and at the end of a series are better reported than those in the middle.

We Posit H1: Primacy and Recency Effect Have the Same Influence on the Accuracy of Self-reported Evaluation

Fredrickson and Kahneman's results [28] suggested that adding a positive experience at the end of the task improve the retrospective evaluation. Furthermore, researchers have found that an experience with a strong emotional relevance is more likely to be remembered than a more neutral experience [4, 24]. Valence and arousal contribute in different ways to the formation of memory, but studies have shown that arousal is a much more important factor when it is time to re-member an experience [6]. First, the neural processes of memory are different for valence and arousal [30]. When remembering an experience with high arousal, different sub-stances such as glucose are released into the bloodstream [38] and the memory using emotional arousal leads to peripheral and central nervous systems activation and intensively involves the amygdala [37] whereas the prefrontal cortex hippocampal network is used for valence [30].

Moreover, recency and primacy effects are part of the selectivity bias. As Mather and Sutherland [36] explained, we are surrounded by information every day and there's a "battle for a share of our limited attention and memory, with the brain selecting the winners and discarding the losers" (p. 114). Indeed, arousal is enhancing the memory for specific details but is removing other collateral details [5]. Selectivity bias is common, our brain cannot recall each information that we have absorbed during the day, this is why recency and primacy effect have been found as one of the answer of this selection. Recency effect has been studied much more than the primacy effect due to the peak-end rule, characterized by the most intense moment at the end of an experience [28]. Different stimuli were used to test the recency effect such as medical pain [47] they found a strong relation between the intensity of pain recorded during the last 3 min of the treatment and the self-perceived evaluation.

We Posit H2: Arousal Has More Influence than Valence on the Recency Effect

4 Research Method

To test our hypothesis, we conducted a laboratory experiment with 13 subjects (7 males and 6 females), between the age of 21 and 48 (mean of 32). We provide a 100$ compensation to each participant upon completion of the experiment. Participants had normal or corrected-to-normal vision and were pre-screened for glasses, laser eye surgery, astigmatism, epilepsy, neurological and psychiatric diagnoses. This project was approved by the Ethics Committee of our institution.

4.1   Stimuli and Procedure

First, a scenario about an incident or a situation was presented to participants. Then, they had to perform a series of utilitarian tasks on website for 15 min in order to prepare a claim about an incident (e.g., provide details of the incident, make an appointment). Finally, they had to view their recorded interaction with the website and use a joystick to indicate their level of self-reported emotional arousal and valence continuously during the recording (Fig. 1). Every participant had the same task to perform and the same instruction to use the joystick. Moreover, we trained the participants to be sure that they understood the use of the joystick and the use of the dial. To make sure that the experiment was going well, we conducted two pre-tests to make sure the tools were working and recording the right data. Also, we wanted to be sure that the tasks performed as well as the instructions were understood by the participants. Minor changes were then made to finalize the protocol.

Fig. 1. The set up during the self-perceived measure using DARMA software [23]

4.2   Instruments and Measures

According to Ortiz de Guinea et al. [43] physiological measures and self-perceived evaluations interact together. Thus, to test the validity of CSP measurement systems, we assess them with neurophysiological inferences of the same constructs (emotional valence and activation) using physiological activation and automatic facial analysis [42].

We first of all measure emotion with physiological tools. Users' emotional and cognitive states can be measured with physiological signals such as electrodermal activity, heart rate, eye-tracking and facial expressions [42]. It allows researchers and practitioners the possibility of collecting real time information on what the user is experiencing through the interaction. Regarding electrodermal activity (EDA), it has been used to measure physiological arousal [2, 25]. Emotional valence represents the direction of an emotional response negative vs. positive [32]. In our case, facial expression and automatic facial analysis provide interesting insights for measuring human emotion [1, 16].

Participants physiological activation (i.e., electrodermal activity) during their interaction with the website was measured with the Acknowledge software mp150 sampled at 500 Hz (BIOPAC, Goleta, USA). The FaceReader software (Noldus, Wageningen, Netherlands) was used to measure emotional valence, calculated using the value of the positive emotion minus the strongest of the negative emotions which results in a valence score from −1 to +1 [17]. Media Recorder (Noldus, Wageningen, Netherlands) was used to record participants' interaction with the website. Observer XT (Noldus, Wageningen, Pays-Bas) was used to synchronize the signals of these three recording devices as per guidelines provided by Léger et al. [35]. Finally, participants self-reported continuous emotional reactions (arousal and valence) were measured using the DARMA software [23] (p. 1), which "synchronizes media play-back and the continuous recording of two-dimensional measurements through the manipulation of a computer joystick to indicate changes in their emotional state" (see Fig. 2). The output of DARMA is an Excel file in which each line begins with a time code, then gives the valence and activation evaluation coordinates of the joystick at that time. All of the measures and instruments are summarized in Table 1.

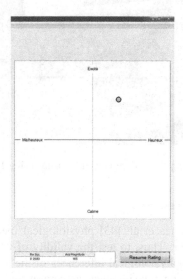

Fig. 2. The two-dimension self-report window during media playback [23].

Table 1. Measures used for the experiment

	Self-reported (retrospective)	Physiological (during interaction)
Valence	Participant's joystick position on the valence axis at time t (Darma)	Facial emotional valence at time t (Facereader)
Arousal	Participant's joystick position on the arousal axis at time t (Darma)	Electrodermal activity for time t (Acqknowledge)

As you can notice, the software was set at 30 Hz, a bin size of 0.25 s and an axis magnitude of 100. These measures are summarized in the Table 1.

5 Results

To test the convergent validity of CSP measurement, we compared the retrospection performance of the first and last time interval between self-reported and physiological measures.

The validity of CSP emotion, i.e. the degree to which it accurately measures the emotions it was designed to measure, was assessed by recording sessions, broken down into short sequences. Each participant had to report their emotional valence and arousal for 14 short sequences for a total of 182 sequences for the overall sample. Sixty percent of tasks lasted less than 30 s. To test the convergent validity of CSP measurement, we compared the retrospection performance of the first and last time interval of each one of the 14 sequences between self-reported and physiological measures. Thus, we calculate the distance between physiological valence and CSP valence in the first and last time interval and the same calculation was done with the distance between physiological arousal and CSP arousal (respectively dis_valence_first vs dis_valence_last and dis_arousal_first vs dis_arousal_last in Table 2). When the movement of the joystick was less than .001, we considered it as static and these data were excluded from the analysis. The 2-tailed p-value from the Wilcoxon signed rank test indicates whether the difference is significant or not.

Table 2. Results for 1 s interval between the beginning and the end of each one of the sequences

Pair of variables (first and last 1 s)		Mean at beginning	Mean at end	P-value
distance_valence_first	distance_valence_last	.155	.1215	.0173
distance_arousal_first	distance_arousal_last	.0191	.0377	.0635

With an interval of 1 s, we find that participants report more accurately their valence at the end of the task compared to the beginning with a mean difference of .0335 (.155–.1215) and p-value = .0173. Also, participants report with more precision their arousal at the beginning of the task compared to the end with a mean difference of

.0186 (.0377–.0191) and p-value = .0635. Because sequences were short, the data analysis was performed using one-second time periods (e.g., comparing the first second of self-reported valence vs. physiological valence), but also with two-second periods.

Significant results were found for both time periods, the results for the one and two seconds time periods are reported in Tables 2 and 3.

Table 3. Result for 2 s interval between the beginning and the end of each one of the sequences

Pair of variables (first and last 2 s)		Mean at beginning	Mean at end	P-value
distance_valence_first	distance_valence_last	.153	.1235	.0143
distance_arousal_first	distance_arousal_last	.0133	.0216	.0436

Below you can find the name of the variables and their meaning:

- distance _valence_first: the reported valence minus the experienced valence at the first moment of each sequence
- distance _valence_last: the reported valence minus the experienced valence at the last moment of each sequence
- distance _arousal_first: the reported arousal minus the experienced arousal at the first moment of each sequence
- distance _arousal_last: the reported arousal minus the experienced arousal at the last moment of each sequence

6 Discussion

The objective of this first exploratory study was to test the convergent validity of CSP measurement systems with physiological emotional measures. First of all, results suggest that users self-evaluate their valence more accurately at the end of each of the sequences than at the beginning and more accurately their arousal at the beginning of each sequences. A second study will be conducted in the spring to further validate the results.

This paper confirms that continuous measurement allows for a richer self-perceived evaluation of emotion than traditional methods. Also, we show that there is a link between psychophysiological measurements such as facial expression analysis or electrodermal activity with the self-perceived evaluation of the participant. Regarding the primacy and recency effects our results confirm that they have the same influence, biasing the retrospection of participants [10, 13]. However, participants were more accurate at the beginning and at the end of their interaction, when reporting their emotion. Moreover, arousal has been proposed as the most influential factor regarding the self-evaluation of recency effect [28, 47]. With our experimental design, using continuous self-perceived measurement, we found that that users self-evaluate their valence more accurately at the end of each of the sequences than at the beginning, so our results do not converge with Cahill and McGaugh [6], proposing arousal as more important factor than valence for retrospection in this specific context. This implies that primacy and recency effect have an influence in the way participants reported their emotion. It is important for researchers to have this result in mind when using tools such as DARMA software to explore the self-perceived evaluation because it could lead to the overestimation or underestimation of the results of an experiment.

Our findings can also be useful for the marketing or entertainment industry. With many tools to evaluate subjective emotion, our paper allows a better understanding of all the instruments that could be available for practitioners to conduct (continuous) self-reported measurement. Our results could also be interesting to have in mind when practitioners design their product/service. Indeed, if the valence is best reported at the end of the interaction with the website, you should probably focus on minimizing negative emotion and maximizing positive emotion during this sequence of time, and all the more so knowing that negative information have stronger influence on memory [27]. Regarding the arousal result that is more accurate at the beginning of the session, it depends on your goal, maximizing or minimizing arousal in accordance with the area of activity. Overall, designers could influence the user's memory of an experience when focusing on the beginning and the end of the task. Finally, during user experience testing, designers should first of all pay attention to these two periods of time.

Our experiment faced different limitations. Starting with technical limitations, when participants did not touch the joystick, it would automatically go back by default to the center which represents neutrality in terms of emotions. It is possible that some participants were influenced by this default position.

Regarding the experimental design, this initial study was performed in a specific utilitarian context, future research could use a different context in order to validate the results in a broader range of contexts.

For the results, with our data and tools that we used, we cannot know if participant under or overestimated their emotion when reporting. During our second data collection for this research project, we used IAPS pictures in order to calibrate emotional reaction with extreme stimuli in order to gain knowledge on the under/overestimated part. At this moment, we are still analyzing the results from this second phase.

7 Conclusion

Emotions and the way we measure them are destined to endless debate [9]. As Cockburn et al. [8] explained, an experience is internally composed of several sequences and is influenced by the most intense moment. Such an understanding accords more importance to psychophysiological measures and continuous self-perceived measures, as traditional post-task self-perceived measurements are more subject to bias [31]. In this paper, results suggest that an experience lived by a participant is not exactly the same as it is reported. Different biases may influence this misalignment of the "story". Primacy and recency through the influence of valence and arousal play an important role is the experience that is reported. Researchers in user experience have much to gain through a deeper understanding this topic.

Acknowledgments. We are thankful for the financial support of the Natural Sciences and Engineering Research Council of Canada.

References

1. Bartlett, M.S., Littlewort, G., Lainscsek, C., Fasel, I., Movellan, J.: Machine learning methods for fully automatic recognition of facial expressions and facial actions. In: IEEE International Conference Systems, Man Cybernetics, pp. 592–597 (2004)
2. Boucsein, W.: Electrodermal Activity. Springer, Heidelberg (2012). https://doi.org/10.1007/978-1-4614-1126-0
3. Bradley, M., Lang, P.J.: Measuring emotion: the self-assessment semantic differential manikin and the semantic differential. J. Behav. Ther. Exp. Psychiatry 25(1), 49–59 (1994)
4. Bradley, M.M., Greenwald, M.K., Petry, M.C., Lang, P.J.: Remembering pictures: pleasure and arousal in memory. J. Exp. Psychol. Learn. Mem. Cogn. 18(2), 379–390 (1992)
5. Burke, A., Heuer, F., Reisberg, D.: Remembering emotional events. Memory Cogn. 20(3), 277–290 (1992)
6. Cahill, L., McGaugh, J.L.: A novel demonstration of enhance memory associated with emotional arousal. Conscious. Cogn. 4, 410–421 (1995)
7. Cockburn, A., Quinn, P., Gutwin, C.: Examining the peak-end effects of subjective experience. In: CHI 2015, pp. 357–366 (2015)
8. Cockburn, A., Quinn, P., Gutwin, C.: The effects of interaction sequencing on user experience and preference. Int. J. Hum.-Comput. Stud. 108, 89–104 (2017)
9. Colombetti, G.: Appraising valence. J. Conscious. Stud. 12(24), 103–126 (2005)
10. Conway, M.A.: Cognitive Models of Memory. MIT Press, Cambridge (1997)
11. Courtemanche, F., Léger, P.-M., Dufresne, A., Fredette, M., Labonté-LeMoyne, É., Sénécal, S: Physiological heatmaps: a tool for visualizing users' emotional reactions. Multimed Tools Appl. 77, 1–28 (2017)
12. Cowie, R., Douglas-Cowie, E., Savvidou, S., Mcmahon, E., Sawey, M., Schröder, M.: "Feeltrace": an instrument for recording perceived emotion in real time. In: ISCA ITRW on Speech and Emotion, pp. 19–24 (2000)
13. Craik, F.I.M., Lockhart, R.S.: Levels of processing: a framework for memory research. J. Verbal Learn. Verbal Behav. 11(6), 671–684 (1972)
14. Dirican, A.C., Göktürk, M.: Psychophysiological measures of human cognitive states applied in Human Computer Interaction. Procedia Comput. Sci. 3, 1361–1367 (2011)
15. Ekman, P.: Facial expression and emotion. Am. Psychol. 48(4), 384–392 (1993)
16. Ekman, P., Friesen, W.: Constants across cultures in the face and emotion. J. Pers. Soc. Psychol. 17(2), 124–129 (1972)
17. Ekman, P., Friesen, W.V.: Unmasking the Face. Prentice Hall, Cambridge (2003)
18. Foster, I., Kesselman, C.: The Grid: Blueprint for a New Computing Infrastructure, 2nd edn. Morgan Kaufmann, Amsterdam (2004)
19. Fredette, M., Labonté-LeMoyne, É., Léger, P.-M., Courtemanche, F., Sénécal, S.: Research directions for methodological improvement of the statistical analysis of electroencephalography data collected in NeuroIS. In: Davis, F.D., Riedl, R., vom Brocke, J., Léger, P.-M. (eds.) Information Systems and Neuroscience. LNISO, vol. 10, pp. 201–206. Springer, Cham (2015). https://doi.org/10.1007/978-3-319-18702-0_27
20. Fredrickson, B.L., Kahneman, D.: Duration neglect in retrospective evaluations of affective episodes. J. Pers. Soc. Psychol. 65(1), 45–55 (1993)

21. Georges, V., Courtemanche, F., Sénécal, S., Léger, P.-M., Nacke, L., Pourchon, R.: The adoption of physiological measures as an evaluation tool in UX. In: Nah, F.F.-H. (eds.) HCIBGO 2017. LNCS, vol. 10293, pp. 90–98. Springer, Cham (2017). https://doi.org/10.1007/978-3-319-58481-2_8

22. Girard, J.M.: CARMA: software for continuous affect rating and media annotation. J. Open Res. Softw. **2**, 1–11 (2017)

23. Girard, J.M., Aidan, A.G.: DARMA: software for dual axis rating and media annotation. Behav. Res. Methods 1–8 (2017)

24. Hamann, S.: Cognitive and neural mechanisms of emotional memory. Trends Cogn. Sci. **5** (9), 394–400 (2001)

25. Hassenzahl, M., Tractinsky, N.: User experience - a research agenda. Behav. Inf. Technol. **25**(2), 91–97 (2006)

26. Ortiz de Guinea, A., Webster, J.: An investigation of information systems use patterns: technological events as triggers, the effect of time, and consequences for performance. MIS Q. **37**(4), 1165–1188 (2013)

27. Ito, T.A., Larsen, J.T., Smith, N.K., Cacioppo, J.T.: Negative information weighs more heavily on the brain: the negativity bias in evaluative categorizations. J. Pers. Soc. Psychol. **75**(4), 887–900 (1998)

28. Kahneman, D., Fredrickson, B.L., Schreiber, C.A., Redelmeier, D.: When more pain is preferred to less: adding a better end. Psychol. Sci. **4**(6), 401–405 (1993)

29. Kandel, E.R., Schwartz, J.H., Jessell, T.M.: Principles of Neural Science, 4th edn. McGraw-Hill, Health Professions Division, New York (2000)

30. Kensinger, E.A., Corkin, S.: Two routes to emotional memory: distinct neural processes for valence and arousal. Proc. Natl. Acad. Sci. U.S.A. **101**(9), 3310–3315 (2004)

31. Lallemand, C., Gronier, G.: Méthodes de design UX: 30 méthodes fondamentales pour concevoir et évaluer les systèmes interactifs. Eyrolles (2015)

32. Lane, R.D., Chua, P.M.-L., Dolan, R.D.: Common effects of emotional valence, arousal and attention on neural activation during visual processing of pictures. Neuropsychologia **37**(9), 989–997 (1999)

33. Laurans, G., Desmet, P.M.A., Hekkert, P.: The emotion slider: a self-report device for the continuous measurement of emotion. In: Affective Computing and Intelligent Interaction and Workshops, ACII 2009, 3rd International Conference on Affective Computing and Intelligent Interaction and Workshops, pp. 1–6 (2009)

34. Léger, P.-M., Davis, F.D., Cronan, T.P., Perret, J.: Neurophysiological correlates of cognitive absorption in an enactive training context. Comput. Hum. Behav. **34**, 273–283 (2012)

35. Léger, P.-M., Titah, R., Sénecal, S., Fredette, M., Courtemanche, F., Labonté-LeMoyne, É., De Guinea, A.O.: Precision is in the eye of the beholder: application of eye fixation-related potentials to information systems research. J. Assoc. Inf. Syst. **15**(1), 651–678 (2014). Suppl. Special Issue on Methods, Tools, and Measurement

36. Mather, M., Sutherland, M.R.: Arousal-biased competition in perception and memory. Perspect. Psychol. Sci. **6**(2), 114–133 (2011)

37. McGaugh, J.L.: The amygdala modulates the consolidation of memories of emotionally arousing experiences. Annu. Rev. Neurosci. **27**, 1–28 (2004)

38. McGaugh, J.L., Cahill, L., Roozendaal, B.: Involvement of the amygdala in memory storage: interaction with other brain systems. Proc. Natl. Acad. Sci. U.S.A. **93**(24), 13508–13514 (1996)

39. Mello, S.K.D., Craig, S.D., Gholson, B., Franklin, S., Picard, R., Graesser, A.C.: Integrating affect sensors in an intelligent tutoring system. In: Affective Interactions: The Computer in the Affective Loop Workshop at 2005 International conference on Intelligent User Interfaces, pp. 7–13. ACM Press, New York (2005)

40. Murdoch, B.B., Lissner, E., Marvin, C.: The serial position effect of free recall. J. Exp. Psychol. **64**(5), 482–488 (1962)

41. Nagel, F., Kopiez, R., Grewe, O., Altenmuller, E.: EMuJoy: software for continuous measurement. Behav. Res. Methods **39**(2), 283–290 (2007)

42. Ortiz de Guinea, A., Titah, R., Leger, P.-M.: Explicit and implicit antecedents of users' information systems behavioral beliefs: a neuropsychological investigation. J. Manag. Inf. Syst. **30**(4), 179–210 (2014)

43. Ortiz de Guinea, A., Titah, R., Léger, P.-M.: Measure for measure: a two study multi-trait multi-method investigation of construct validity in IS research. Comput. Hum. Behav. **29**(3), 833–844 (2013)

44. Plutchik, R.: A general psychoevolutionary theory of emotion. In: Emotion: Theory, Research, and Experience, pp. 189–217. Academic Press, New York (1980)

45. Posner, J., Russell, J.A., Peterson, B.S.: The circumplex model of affect: an integrative approach to affective neuroscience, cognitive development, and psychopathology. Dev. Psychopathol. **17**(3), 715–734 (2008)

46. Ravaja, N., Saari, T., Turpeinen, M., Laarni, J., Salminen, M., Kivikangas, M.: Spatial presence and emotions during video game playing: does it matter with whom you play? Presence Teleoper. Virtual Environ. **15**(4), 381–392 (2006)

47. Redelmeier, D.A., Kahneman, D.: Patients' memories of painful medical treatments: real-time and retrospective evaluations of two minimally invasive procedures. Pain **66**(1), 3–8 (1996)

48. Riedl, R., Léger, P.-M.: Fundamentals of NeuroIS. Studies in Neuroscience, Psychology and Behavioral Economics, pp. 1–115. Springer, Heidelberg (2016). https://doi.org/10.1007/978-3-662-45091-8

49. Russel, J.A.: A circumplex model of affect. J. Pers. Soc. Psychol. **39**(6), 1161–1178 (1980)

50. Sas, C., Dix, A., Hart, J., Ronghui, S.: Emotional experience on Facebook site. In: CHI 2009 Extended Abstracts on Human Factors in Computing Systems, pp. 4345–4350 (2009)

51. Shteingart, H., Neiman, T., Loewenstein, Y.: The role of first impression in operant learning. J. Exp. Psychol. Gen. **142**(2), 476–488 (2013)

52. Den Uyl, M.J., Van Kuilenburg, H.: The FaceReader: online facial expression recognition. In: Proceedings of Measuring Behavior, pp. 589–590 (2005)

53. Vermeeren, A.P.O.S., Law, E.L., Roto, V.: User experience evaluation methods: current state and development needs. In: Proceedings of the 6th Nordic Conference on Human-Computer Interaction: Extending Boundaries, pp. 521–530 (2010)

54. Zauberman, G., Diehl, K., Ariely, D.: Hedonic versus informational evaluations: Task dependent preferences for sequences of outcomes. J. Behav. Decis. Mak. **19**(3), 191–211 (2006)

Towards Measuring the Potential for Semantically Enriched Texts in Knowledge Working Environments

Gerald Petz(✉), Dietmar Nedbal, and Werner Wetzlinger

University of Applied Sciences Upper Austria, Steyr, Austria
{gerald.petz,dietmar.nedbal,
werner.wetzlinger}@fh-steyr.at

Abstract. Knowledge work often requires people to read and comprehend documents in order to fulfill their tasks. To support knowledge workers in their real working environment semantically enriched texts can be leveraged. One technical basis is Named Entity Linking (NEL), which provides the capabilities to identify entities in a text and link them to a knowledge base that provides further information about them. This provides several opportunities to improve the outcome (e.g. text comprehension). In this paper, we lay the foundations for evaluating such semantic text enrichment environments that can be used in different business cases. The main result is an approach for measuring the effects of semantically enriched texts in the working environment comprising the five dimensions text, enrichment, reader, activity, and output.

Keywords: Named Entity Linking · Semantic enrichment · NEL
Reading comprehension · Multimedia comprehension · Use case

1 Introduction

Knowledge work is often to a large extent document-centered work. People receive documents and have to process these documents by reading, extracting information, assessing the relevance of the document and inferring conclusions about the next steps in the context of their work. The documents are often in electronic form (e.g. emails) and may be related to persons, things or other topics. Therefore, the comprehension of the documents is an important factor in order to be able to fulfill the work task [1]. In order to support knowledge workers in their real working environment, current technical possibilities that arise from the research area of Named Entity Linking (NEL) offer interesting possibilities for semantically enriching texts for knowledge workers. Furthermore, many factors that influence reading comprehension and multimedia learning have been identified in education, cognitive psychology, or sociolinguistics literature. However, less literature can be found on applying semantically enriching text in the business context.

The objective of this paper therefore is to (i) identify dimensions for the comprehension of semantically enriched hypertexts, (ii) identify potential business cases for

© Springer International Publishing AG, part of Springer Nature 2018
F. F.-H. Nah and B. S. Xiao (Eds.): HCIBGO 2018, LNCS 10923, pp. 145–161, 2018.
https://doi.org/10.1007/978-3-319-91716-0_12

this purpose, and (iii) to develop an approach for measuring the effects of semantically enriched texts in working environments.

After an analysis of the state of the art of reading and hypertext comprehension and text enrichment based on Named Entity Linking (Sect. 2), the paper identifies business cases that could utilize text enrichment technologies (Sect. 3). Section 4 lays out the approach for measuring the effects of text enrichment in working environments using semantically enriched texts. Finally, Sect. 5 concludes with a brief discussion about the outcome of the paper and future work.

2   Reading and Comprehension in Semantically Enriched Hypertexts

Several scientific fields deal with reading comprehension and comprehension assessment, of these the following are particularly important: education/learning, cognitive psychology, sociolinguistics (and more general sociocultural perspectives) and literary theory (in the form of reader response theory) [1].

2.1   Foundations of Reading Comprehension

Reading comprehension is the ability to read text, process it and simultaneously extract and construct meaning through interaction and involvement with written language [2]. Successful understanding of text requires bottom-up identification of the words and top-down analysis of the semantic and syntactic relationships among the words. Lack of bottom-up skills will cause lower comprehension because words are misidentified and fewer cognitive resources are used for processing the semantic meaning. Lack of top-down skills results in the fact that the text will not be understood, because the meaning of the words are unknown or the logical and structural relationships between the words cannot be processed. Even if the text was read out loud the lack of understanding will remain [3].

Reading comprehension comprises three dimensions that occur within a larger sociocultural context [2]:

- The *reader* who is doing the comprehension. Each reader has their individual characteristics and preferences. The reader needs a wide range of competences (e.g. reading speed [4], symbol naming speed [5], verbal memory [6], inferential and reasoning skills [7, 8], attention [9, 10]) and abilities (e.g. vocabulary, prior domain and topic knowledge, linguistic and discourse knowledge, knowledge of specific comprehension strategies, motivation, reading skills [11, 12]).
- The *text* that should be comprehended. A couple of authors state that the material the reader is required to read is a major determinant of comprehension. Texts differ in terms of several characteristics: e.g. narrative vs. expository texts, sophisticated vocabulary, complex syntactic patterns, variety of included subject area topics [13–17].
- The *activity* in which the comprehension is required. Activities may be e.g. learning or knowledge work [18].

2.2   Reading Comprehension in Hypertext Based Multimedia Learning

Hypertext is a text that contains references to other texts and is usually displayed on an electronic screen. The reader can follow the hyperlinks and explore additional information. Most of the research papers in this area are based on the C-I-model (construction-integration model [19]) of text comprehension. The C-I-model proposes (i) a construction phase in which a text base is constructed from the text and the reader's knowledge base and (ii) an integration phase, in which the text phrase is integrated into a coherent whole. Hypertext documents usually include multimedia content such as graphics or video that needs to be processed by the reader. Research work on multimedia learning therefore proposes the following three phases: (i) learners have to select relevant visual and verbal information, (ii) the learners must organize this information in visual and verbal mental representations, and finally (iii) the learners must integrate the visual and verbal mental representations [20].

Many factors influence text/hypertext comprehension, but prior knowledge and coherence are the most important ones. Coherence describes to what extent a reader is able to understand relationships between ideas in the text. However, empirical work on comprehension does not yield a clear conclusion about processing and comprehension of hypertexts [21]: Some authors found that the availability of annotations leads to improved learning (e.g. [22]), other authors found that added material and hyperlinks increased the learners' cognitive load and decreased learning outcomes (e.g. [23]). Unfortunately, the results of the papers can only be compared with each other to a limited extent due to different settings and measurements. Moreover, similar to the reading comprehension, the hypertext comprehension is also influenced by several factors, e.g. reading strategies (whether a reader follows the hyperlink), prior knowledge, and navigational path [21].

Some research work focuses on the comparison of comprehension between reading texts on paper and reading texts on computer screens. E.g. [24] point out, that people who read texts in print scored significantly better on a reading comprehension test than those who read the texts digitally.

Regarding the comprehension of hypertexts, many authors discuss the effects considering the cognitive load theory. The theory assumes a limited capacity working memory that is used for processing a provided material and an unlimited long-term memory. The cognitive load theory differentiates between intrinsic cognitive load, extraneous cognitive load and germane cognitive load [25, 26]. Research work is also carried out on the split-attention effect. Split attention occurs when learners have to split their attention between several sources of information. This leads to increased cognitive load, because learners have to mentally integrate these sources and it is likely to have a negative impact on learning [27]. Zumbach and Mohraz [28] investigated learning with text and hypertext and compared the differences in knowledge acquisition: non-linear presentation of narrative texts leads to increased cognitive load and decreased knowledge acquisition compared to linear representation of the same text. Therefore, learning from a text with a non-linear navigation is not beneficial. Interestingly, the effect of increased cognitive load and decreased knowledge acquisition was only observed with narrative texts. This effect did not occur with less-structured encyclopedia texts. The authors used a system that presented the linear presentation on the left side of the application window, the hypertext presentation on the right side. The links in the hypertext setting obviously lead to a new page and the user had to actively navigate back to the previous page.

Wallen et al. [20] experimented with hypertext comprehension and different types of annotations. Based on the learning phases in multimedia learning the authors propose three types of annotations that should support the respective phase, namely the support of (i) selecting, (ii) organizing, or (iii) integrating the information. Selection-level annotation is a base for the higher-level processes and supports the encoding of factual knowledge. Organization-level annotation supports the connection of words into ideas, and integration-level annotations focus on relationships between visual and verbal information and prior knowledge. In order to evaluate the effects of the different types of annotations, the authors compared the results of the recognition tests, comprehension tests and transfer tests. Recognition tests showed that participants recognized significantly more words (with any of the three annotation types) from the text than those without annotation. The test results show that selection-level annotations are the most effective ones to support the processes of selecting information, organizing and integrating information. It turned out, that support in the earlier stages of processing improves higher-level learning [20].

2.3 Text Enrichment Using Named Entity Linking

As described above, the difficulty of understanding texts depends also on factors inherent in the text, on the relationship between the text and the knowledge and abilities of the reader and on the activities in which the reader is engaged [2]. We focus on improving the text to be comprehended for the following reasons [29]:

- text modifications are easy to do and therefore relatively inexpensive;
- understanding effects of this modification might allow better design of texts independently of the reader;
- there has been almost no research examining the impact of text modifications on improving text comprehension in working environments;

There are different ways to improve the text to be comprehended: *simplification, elaboration* [29] and *enrichment* [30, 31]. The purpose of simplification is to reduce the challenge concerning vocabulary and complexity in the sentence structure. Simplification can be achieved by limiting the vocabulary, by shortening sentences, and by avoiding complex sentence construction like nominalizations or embedded relative clauses. With elaboration, the text is modified to improve the coherence by clarifying relationships and explaining concepts. Both ways involve a modification of the text in order to improve comprehension. In contrast, enrichment of text involves enhancing explicitness by describing terms and underlying thematic relationships in more detail without changing the original text. In other words, we see text enrichment as a form of elaboration through clarification, repetition, and explicit definition of important text passages. In a classic non-linear hypertext, this is achieved by linking certain passages by changing the context (i.e. it is linked to a new page). It has been shown that this can be counterproductive for text comprehension as it increases cognitive load and decreases knowledge acquisition, especially in narrative text structures [28].

We therefore use a text enrichment approach where the reader is not forced to break out of the context of reading (e.g. navigate to different site) while additional information on certain text passages is shown. This preview information is displayed optionally as "tooltips"/mouse over balloons that pop up next to the relevant text passage only if the reader requests more information [30, 31]. The effects of this method are to be explored and measured.

For text enrichment, we use techniques known from the research field Named Entity Linking (NEL). The main goal of NEL is to spot text fragments and link them correctly to entities of a target knowledge base [32]. This process usually starts with a recognition of the text fragments, also called mentions or named entity candidates. This first step is also referred to as Named Entity Recognition (NER) which can be further broken down into the two subtasks entity detection (or "spotting") and entity classification. This step identifies names of entities such as people, locations, organizations and products [33, 34]. In many application scenarios, however, it is not only of interest which types of entities are contained in a text, but also how the entities can be semantically linked to a knowledge base. In this step, the recognized named entities are correctly disambiguated and linked into a knowledge base with an external definition and description [35]. The aim is to provide further information on the entities as well as semantic browsing or recommendation [32] in the context of an application domain [36]. As NER precedes entity linking and entity linking requires previously detected entities, we subsequently use the term Named Entity Linking as synonym for the whole process. The following figure shows an excerpt from a CV and possible linked entities to the term "WPF" (Fig 1).

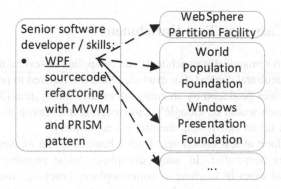

Fig. 1. Illustration of the named entity linking task

The overall process is strongly dependent on the knowledge base used to train the named entity extraction algorithm [37]. In the last decade, most approaches for linking entities leverage on the use of Wikipedia (wikipedia.org), Dbpedia (dbpedia.org), Freebase (freebase.com), BabelNet (babelnet.org) or YAGO (yago-knowledge.org) as the knowledge base [38]. Applications in the field identify and disambiguate entities of texts at high levels of accuracy. The output can be used in many different ways, which we detail in the following section.

The authors of this paper developed a NEL system called "TOMO Entity Linker" that can automatically detect entities in a text and link the entities to a corresponding knowledgebase [39]. Figure 2 shows the approach of enriching text: the mouse over balloons are only displayed when the user actively requires more information on a word or word phrase.

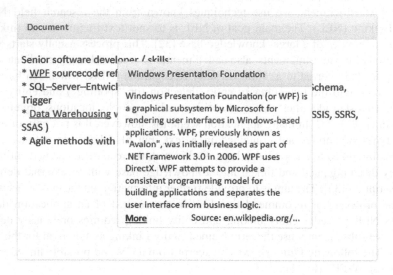

Fig. 2. Screen of TOMO Entity Linker

3   Business Cases for Text Enrichment

The use of NEL to semantically enrich texts can be applied to several different business scenarios as sociocultural context. For example, NEL can be used to provide fact-based summaries of entities produced by an entity summarization system [32]. A prominent example on the web would be Google's knowledge graph feature displaying summarized information on an entity from the user's search query.

By having a look at text enrichment from a business point of view, we exemplify several use cases hereinafter. In many disciplines, most prominently in business studies, the use of cases in teaching is commonplace. Teaching cases allow abstract theory of formal course content to be translated into a more vivid account of what actually happens in real life scenarios [40]. Use cases are also often used in software development as common means to capture early system requirements by driving a user-centric view of a system [41]. The use cases are examples the authors experienced during their academic work and in workshops with industry partners in the context of knowledge workers. Although they are incomplete, personally biased and academic centric, the applicability of the examples was also discussed with partners of three different sectors (production industry, energy sector, and software development).

In software engineering, use cases are understood as a description of an action or a sequence of actions constituting a complete task. Use case diagrams have explicitly been introduced as one of the key modeling constructs in Unified Modeling Language (UML) [42]. Owing to space constraints, we use a text-based description of the use cases in the following with a focus on the dimensions *reader, text, activity, enrichment* and *output*. The dimensions *reader, text* and *activity* are derived from the heuristic for reading comprehension (cf. Sect. 2.1) and the dimensions *enrichment* and *output* refer to the technique we use to improve the overall outcome (cf. Sect. 2.3). Table 1 provides an overview of the use cases.

The table shows twelve different cases within the business context aiming to illustrate the different characteristics of the dimensions. Each case may have multiple sources as they were discussed with different industry partners. As stated earlier, the examples are covered by the production industry (case #2, #3, #6, #7, #10, #11, #12), academia (case #4, #5, #7, #10, #12), the software development branch (case #1, #4, #7, #8, #10), and the energy sector (case #9). Due to space limitations, we explain only the first three cases in more detail.

Case #1 is centered in the *human resources* (HR) department of an organization. An employee usually needs to spend a lot of time in the evaluation of curriculum vitae (CV) because CVs often contain many domain specific details on skills, knowledge, certificates, etc. With the help of annotations in the CV, the process of pre-selecting, i.e. matching potential candidates with demands from the organization within the recruiting process could be improved in terms of speed and quality of the outcome. As a special knowledgebase, the HR department could make use of e.g. Microsoft or Oracle certificates and their abbreviations.

In case #2 we see potential for text enrichment in the *technical documentation*. As an example, available software licenses (vendor, purchase dates, license codes, license restrictions and abbreviations such as "GPL") are part of the IT infrastructure documentation. Even small businesses typically have a surprisingly long list of software licenses from different software vendors that they frequently use. An IT administrator in the need to match an available software license with one which is needed could make use of additional previews on software vendor and their available license models. This would support the decision as to whether any more licenses are needed for the purpose.

The use of text enhancement in *project documentation* is explained in case #3. The project charter is usually he initiation document for any project. The information in the charter should clearly communicate the scope of the project, as well as any associated information needed to be considered when defining additional requirements (like timeline, human and financial resources) for the project. Project charters are submitted to the appropriate project manager/director once prioritized by the user's department/division. Enrichment of certain terms would help understanding of the scope of the project when a manager in charge needs to make the go or no-go decision for the project.

Table 1. Example business cases

Case	Reader	Text (input)	Activity (goal)	Enrichment (example)	Output
#1	Employee in human resources department	Curriculum vitae	Find suitable applicants for a job	Certificates from Microsoft or Oracle	Decision about considering job applicant
#2	IT administrator	Technical IT infrastructure documentation	Match available with needed software license	Software vendor and their available license models	Decision if any more licenses are needed
#3	Project manager	Project documentation: project charter	Understand the scope of the project	Important specialized terms	Go/no-go decision
#4	Track chair	Paper (esp. title, abstract, keywords)	Assignment of reviewers for the reviewing process of a conference	Explanation of terms used (match reviewer skills)	Assignment of reviewers
#5	Student	Learning material of a course	Text comprehension of the available material in teaching	Explanation of terms in learning material	Knowledge acquisition for a formal test
#6	Quality manager	Quality guidelines and quality standards of organization	Text comprehension of the quality management guidelines	Explanation of terms in guidelines	Knowledge acquisition for assuring good quality of process/product
#7	New employee	Knowledge transfer (e.g. documentation of a process)	Text comprehension of the document	Explanation of terms (esp. use within organization)	Familiarization for daily work
#8	Software developer	Cross-department knowledge sharing	Cross-department knowledge sharing (e.g. marketing/product management and software development)	Marketing terms	Knowledge acquisition for changes in software
#9	SAP user	Working instructions	Fulfill a working task	SAP abbreviations and terminology	Familiarization for current task
#10	Office user	Security information about ransomware	Read and follow instructions per email	Explanation of ICT Terms (esp. ransomware)	Awareness of security threat
#11	Employee	Idea generation board	Understand the innovativeness of the idea	Explanation of terms (esp. current terms)	Post a reply, vote up/down idea
#12	Middle Management	Monthly sales report	Understand facts and figures of the report	Show details on abbreviations (esp. financial measures)	Interpret the report

4 An Approach for Measuring the Effects of Semantically Enriched Texts

Based on the dimensions derived from Sect. 2 and the business cases from Sect. 3, in this section we develop an approach for measuring effects of semantically enriched texts in working environments. The following figure shows the approach and the connection of the derived dimensions (Fig. 3).

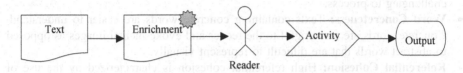

Fig. 3. Approach for measuring the effects of semantically enriched texts

4.1 Text

This dimension describes the material the reader is required to read. In the identified business cases, texts can vary based on multiple aspects like length, structure or readability. These aspects may be a major determinant of outcomes (e.g. comprehension).

Descriptive Measures. Texts can be characterized by descriptive measures that are based on the number of occurrences of elements like letters, syllables, words etc. These basic measures provide a rough overview of the structure of a text. Descriptive measures like word frequency or density scores are important to measure when looking at comprehension [43]. However, studies show a mixed picture. Some find an effect, [44] others do not [45]. Measures to analyze a text may include [46]:

- Number of words, sentences, paragraphs
- (Standard deviation of the) mean length of paragraphs
- (Standard deviation of the) mean length of sentences
- (Standard deviation of the) mean number of syllables in words
- (Standard deviation of the) mean number of letter in words

Cohesion and Coherence can have an impact on comprehension of texts. Cohesion refers to the presence or absence of links between ideas in a text on a grammatical level. These links (e.g. words like *because*, *therefore*, and *consequently*) provide cues to the reader to make connections between parts of a text like sentences or paragraphs [47]. Studies show that a higher cohesion of a text facilitates and improves text comprehension for many readers [48], particularly for low knowledge readers [49].

Coherence refers to the understanding that the reader derives from the text. This may depend on factors which are not linked to the text but to the reader, such as prior knowledge and reading skills [49, 50].

Text Difficulty. Based on the concept of cohesion McNamara et al. [46] have identified components of "text easability" that are based on linguistic characteristics of texts.

- **Narrativity:** Narrative texts use familiar vocabulary and tell stories about characters, events, places, and things that are familiar to the reader. They are similar to everyday, oral conversations.
- **Syntactic Simplicity:** Syntactic simplicity is characterized by using fewer words and simpler, familiar syntactic structures. Syntactically simpler texts are less challenging to process.
- **Word Concreteness:** Texts containing concrete words are easier to understand. Concrete words are meaningful to the reader and evoke mental images as opposed to abstract words that are difficult to represent visually.
- **Referential Cohesion:** High referential cohesion is characterized by the use of overlapping words across sentences, paragraphs and the entire text. These words provide paths for the reader that connect the text. High cohesion texts are easier to process because there are more connections that tie the ideas together for the reader.
- **Deep Cohesion:** Deep cohesion is characterized by causal and intentional connections due to causal and logical relationships within the text. These connections help the reader to form a more coherent and deeper understanding of the causal events, processes, and actions in the text. If there are many relationships but few explicit connections, the reader has to infer the relationships between the ideas in the text. Consequently, in a text with deep cohesion these relationships are more explicit and overall cohesion is high.

4.2 Enrichment

The *enrichment* of texts involves enhancing explicitness by describing terms and underlying thematic relationships in more detail without changing the original text. The result is a semantically enriched text that allows the reader to preview additional information optionally as "tooltips"/mouse over balloons that pop up next to the relevant text passage (see Sect. 2.3). This enrichment implies several challenges of NEL applications in the aforementioned business cases. To maximize the business value, these challenges need to be addressed by a state-of-the-art NEL system. The system therefore would need: (i) a configuration to optimize against precision and/or recall, (ii) to be able to use custom knowledge bases, (iii) to support multiple languages, and (iv) to cope with timely changes in knowledge bases in near real-time.

Irrelevant or Wrong Information. NEL systems are never 100% accurate. In order to deal with irrelevant or wrong entities (e.g. due to ambiguity), NEL systems often aim at a low-recall, high-precision strategy or the opposite [51]. A low recall means that in the entity detection ("spotting") step fewer entities are spotted, in order to avoid errors. As a consequence, the precision increases as the system identifies substantially more relevant entities than irrelevant ones. Precision is therefore seen as a measure of quality, whereas recall is a measure of quantity. Other approaches involve a two-step method. The first step is recall-oriented where the aim is to obtain a ranked list of candidate entities and the second step enhances precision by determining which of the candidate entities should be kept [52]. Thus, entity detection is an important task in the area of NEL and authors emphasize the importance of correct entity spotting in order to avoid errors in later stages of NEL [53, 54]. A system that shows wrong entities would decrease information quality and might lead to an increased seductive detail effect. Moreover, the amount of text enrichments could also have effects on the reader's motivation, although Madrid et al. [55] report no effects.

Domain Specific, Custom Datasets. Text enrichment relies on the dictionary being used. While large datasets contain millions of entities, the coverage of particular domains is often low and not all relevant entities can be found [38]. For enriching organization-specific texts, individual knowledge base (e.g. SAP terminology as in case #9) may be necessary and therefore a NEL system needs to be able to use domain specific datasets as well. A single knowledge base may be too specific or too generic for a certain text. Thus, a system needs to cope with several datasets, including custom-built ones, which is often not supported.

Multilinguality. The majority of research is based on the English language. It was shown that a NEL system implementing language-dependent features improves the overall quality of the spotter [39]. In real life business settings, a system needs to be able to cope with multilingualism.

Timely Changes. A knowledge base is usually updated quite often. For example, the English Wikipedia has a rate of over 10 edits per second with an average of 600 new articles per day (https://en.wikipedia.org/wiki/Wikipedia:Statistics). NEL systems do not usually consider such changes in real-time or even anywhere near real-time, as they work with graphs based on dumps of the knowledge base (e.g. DBPedia dumps are usually created once a month). This leads to inconsistent information as time goes by. A real-time synchronization would be preferable in a business setting (e.g. innovative ideas often use current terms as seen in case #11), but this is currently not usually supported by NEL systems.

4.3 Reader

The dimension *reader* refers to the person who is undertaking an activity. The reader needs to understand and comprehend the text in order to achieve a target output. Each reader needs a wide range of individual competences capacities and specialized abilities for the specific business context. Within the business case, the reader can have the role of the employee, IT administrator, project manager, chair of a conference, student, etc.

Individual differences can have an impact on comprehension of texts: age of the reader, gender, attention, reading skills, etc. As mentioned above, the reader needs a wide range of competences capacities (e.g. attention, memory, critical analytic, ability, inferencing, visualization ability) and abilities (e.g. vocabulary, linguistic and discourse knowledge, etc.) [28].

Prior Knowledge. The business context is always focused on a specific domain for which the reader has some individual prior knowledge, which needs to be taken into account. Several authors report prior knowledge as one of the most important factors that influence comprehension. In general, there is a positive correlation between comprehension and prior knowledge [21, 56, 57].

Reading Strategies. In the context of hypertext reading, reading strategies can be considered as a decision rule whether the reader follows a link. A lot of research work has investigated the relationship between strategy and reading comprehension in linear texts as well as reading strategy in hypertexts. Mainly based on the analysis of navigational paths readers can be assigned to different navigational groups [21].

4.4 Activity

In a business scenario the *activity* in which the reader is engaged is usually described as a step within a business process. Regardless of the type of activity, e.g. learning or knowledge work, a process (or an activity within a process) can be measured by its efficiency, effectiveness and quality.

Efficiency of the Activity. Maes et al. report a decisive overall advantage for preview enabled websites in terms of efficiency [31]. It assists readers in their selection process or in a business task at each subsequent step in their activity. Therefore, we see considerable improvements in task efficiency through text enrichment.

Efficiency of an activity in our case can be measured by the mean time needed for the activity, mean reading time, mean number of annotations viewed, mean number of unique annotations viewed, and mean number of navigation steps.

Effectiveness of the Activity. Although it was reported that there are no effects on the effectiveness of preview enabled websites [31], in the context of task fulfillment, the business cases suppose potential in other activities like knowledge sharing as well. We propose that semantically enriched text annotations positively influence the efficiency of the activity. Effectiveness can, for example, be measured here by the mean number of successfully finished tasks and the mean number of correctly recognized terms.

Quality of the Activity. One of the main factors for a successful activity is its quality. In the fulfillment of a task, it is possible to conceive the quality of the *process* that has led to the fulfillment as well as the quality of the task *result* [58]. We see the quality of the result within the dimension output (cf. next section).

4.5 Output

In order to understand the outcome the text needs to be understood as is seen in several business cases. We therefore see measures for reading comprehension as a way to measure the output dimension.

Text Comprehension. In the literature, a large number of test methods for measuring reading comprehension can be identified. There is a variety of widely used tests, e.g. Gates-MacGinitie Reading Test, Gray Oral Reading Test, Wechsler Individual Achievement Test, Woodcock-Johnson Language Proficiency Battery-Revised (WLPB-R) Passage Comprehension subtest, Woodcock Reading Mastery Test (Revised), Nelson-Denny advanced reading comprehension test, Form E. [3, 16, 59, 60].

There are also a number of less known test methods, e.g. the Diagnostic Assessment of Reading Comprehension (DARC). The comprehension tests vary in the demands required by the task and conceptual substantiation. Furthermore, differences arise due to different contributions to bottom-up and top-down factors across the tests, as well as different response formats [3, 15].

5 Conclusions and Future Work

The paper discusses the potential for semantically enriched texts in the business context. We deduce the five dimensions *text, enrichment, reader, activity*, and *output*, and discuss an approach to measure these dimensions in the working environment. The dimensions used in our text enrichment approach have only rarely been discussed in literature in such a holistic way. NEL literature has a clear system focus, trying to optimize the accuracy of the software. HCI and usability literature focuses on the interaction of the reader and the system in fulfilling an activity. Furthermore, reading comprehension literature does not emphasis the system's view and another research area focuses on the text itself by identifying ascendants of the ease with which a text can be read etc. Each of the individual research areas has developed a different set of measures according to the dimension(s). By analyzing and discussing these dimensions, the paper contributes to a more complete view of the overall approach needed in the business context.

As this paper is a primarily conceptual paper, a limitation lies in the fact that there is no actual proof of the appropriateness of this approach. Nevertheless, the approach is grounded on several established research areas and although the use cases are incomplete and personally biased, they show its applicability in the business context as an additional contribution. In the next step, we have planned to perform different experiments. A first experiment is planned with our partner from the software development industry focusing on improvements in the decision about considering job applicants (case #1). The experiment will be set up as follows: we want to investigate the influence of the independent variable (text with/without enrichment) on dependent variables as defined in the dimensions of the paper (e.g. text comprehension, efficiency, effectiveness and quality of activity). In order to keep complexity low we plan to use a two-group design. Results of this future research are used to provide evidence for applicability of this approach in these different business areas.

Acknowledgements. This research was supported by HC Solutions GesmbH, Linz, Austria. We have to express our appreciation to Florian Wurzer, Reinhard Schwab and Manfred Kain for discussing these topics with us.

The TOMO Entity Linker is part of TOMO ® (http://www.tomo-base.at), a big data platform for aggregating content, analyzing and visualizing content.

References

1. Duke, N.K., Pearson, P.D.: Effective practices for developing reading comprehension. J. Educ. **189**, 107–122 (2008)
2. Snow, C.: Reading for Understanding: Toward an R&D Program in Reading Comprehension. Rand Corporation (2002)
3. Cutting, L.E., Scarborough, H.S.: Prediction of reading comprehension: relative contributions of word recognition, language proficiency, and other cognitive skills can depend on how comprehension is measured. Sci. Stud. Read. **10**, 277–299 (2006)
4. Jenkins, J.R., Fuchs, L.S., van den Broek, P., Espin, C., Deno, S.L.: Sources of individual differences in reading comprehension and reading fluency. J. Educ. Psychol. **95**, 719–729 (2003)
5. Joshi, R.M., Aaron, P.G.: The component model of reading. simple view of reading made a little more complex. Read. Psychol. **21**, 85–97 (2010)
6. Perfetti, C.A., Marron, M.A., Foltz, P.W.: Sources of comprehension failure: theoretical perspectives and case studies. In: Cornoldi, C., Oakhill, J.V. (eds.) Reading Comprehension Difficulties, pp. 137–166 (1996)
7. Cain, K., Oakhill, J.V., Barnes, M.A., Bryant, P.E.: Comprehension skill, inference-making ability, and their relation to knowledge. Mem. Cogn. **29**, 850–859 (2001)
8. Catts, H.W., Adlof, S.M., Weismer, S.E.: Language deficits in poor comprehenders. a case for the simple view of reading. J. Speech Lang. Hear. Res. **49**, 278 (2006)
9. Ghelani, K., Sidhu, R., Jain, U., Tannock, R.: Reading comprehension and reading related abilities in adolescents with reading disabilities and attention-deficit/hyperactivity disorder. Dyslexia **10**, 364–384 (2004)
10. McInnes, A., Humphries, T., Hogg-Johnson, S., Tannock, R.: Listening comprehension and working memory are impaired in attention-deficit hyperactivity disorder irrespective of language impairment. J. Abnorm. Child Psychol. **31**, 427–443 (2003)
11. Laufer, B.: What percentage of text-lexis is essential for comprehension. In: Special Language: From Humans Thinking to Thinking Machines (1989)
12. Hsueh-Chao, M.H., Nation, P.: Unknown vocabulary density and reading comprehension. Read. Foreign Lang. **13**, 403–430 (2000)
13. Deane, P., Sheehan, K.M., Sabatini, J., Futagi, Y., Kostin, I.: Differences in text structure and its implications for assessment of struggling readers. Sci. Stud. Read. **10**, 257–275 (2006)
14. Francis, D.J., Snow, C.E., August, D., Carlson, C.D., Miller, J., Iglesias, A.: Measures of reading comprehension. a latent variable analysis of the diagnostic assessment of reading comprehension. Sci. Stud. Read. **10**, 301–322 (2006)
15. Fletcher, J.M.: Measuring reading comprehension. Sci. Stud. Read. **10**, 323–330 (2006)
16. Rayner, K., Chace, K.H., Slattery, T.J., Ashby, J.: Eye movements as reflections of comprehension processes in reading. Sci. Stud. Read. **10**, 241–255 (2006)
17. Hiebert, E.E.: Standards, assessments, and text difficulty. In: Farstrup, A.E., Samuels, S. J. (eds.) What Research Has to Say About Reading Instruction, pp. 337–369 (2002)
18. van Elst, L., Kiesel, M., Schwarz, S., Buscher, G., Lauer, A., Dengel, A.: Contextualized knowledge acquisition in a personal semantic Wiki. In: Gangemi, A. (eds.) EKAW 2008. LNCS (LNAI), vol. 5268, pp. 172–187. Springer, Heidelberg (2008). https://doi.org/10.1007/978-3-540-87696-0_17
19. Kintsch, W.: The role of knowledge in discourse comprehension: a construction-integration model. Psychol. Rev. **95**, 163–182 (1988)

20. Wallen, E., Plass, J.L., Brünken, R.: The function of annotations in the comprehension of scientific texts. Cognitive load effects and the impact of verbal ability. Educ. Tech. Res. Dev. **53**, 59–71 (2005)
21. Salmeron, L., Canas, J.J., Kintsch, W., Fajardo, I.: Reading strategies and hypertext comprehension. Discourse Process. **40**, 171–191 (2005)
22. Jones, L.C., Plass, J.L.: Supporting listening comprehension and vocabulary acquisition in french with multimedia annotations. Mod. Lang. J. **86**, 546–561 (2002)
23. Brünken, R., Plass, J.L., Leutner, D.: Assessment of cognitive load in multimedia learning with dual-task methodology. auditory load and modality effects. Instr. Sci. **32**, 115–132 (2004)
24. Mangen, A., Walgermo, B.R., Brønnick, K.: Reading linear texts on paper versus computer screen. Effects on reading comprehension. Int. J. Educ. Res. **58**, 61–68 (2013)
25. Sweller, J.: Cognitive load theory, learning difficulty, and instructional design. Learn. Instr. **4**, 295–312 (1994)
26. Sweller, J., van Merrienboer, J.J.G., Paas, F.G.W.C.: Cognitive architecture and instructional design. Educ. Psychol. Rev. **10**, 251–296 (1998)
27. Ayres, P., Sweller, J.: The split-attention principle in multimedia learning. In: Mayer, R.E. (ed.) The Cambridge Handbook of Multimedia Learning, vol. 2, pp. 206–226. Cambridge University Press, Cambridge (2014)
28. Zumbach, J., Mohraz, M.: Cognitive load in hypermedia reading comprehension. Influence of text type and linearity. Comput. Hum. Behav. **24**, 875–887 (2008)
29. Kim, Y.-S., Snow, C.E.: Text modification. Enhancing English language learners' reading comprehension. In: Hiebert, E.H., Sailors, M. (eds.) Finding the Right Texts. What Works for Beginning and Struggling Readers, pp. 129–148. Guilford, New York (2009)
30. Antonenko, P.D., Niederhauser, D.S.: The influence of leads on cognitive load and learning in a hypertext environment. Comput. Hum. Behav. **26**, 140–150 (2010)
31. Maes, A., van Geel, A., Cozijn, R.: Signposts on the digital highway. The effect of semantic and pragmatic hyperlink previews. Interact. Comput. **18**, 265–282 (2006)
32. Thalhammer, A., Rettinger, A.: ELES: combining entity linking and entity summarization. In: Bozzon, A., Cudre-Maroux, P. (eds.) ICWE 2016. LNCS, vol. 9671, pp. 547–550. Springer, Cham (2016). https://doi.org/10.1007/978-3-319-38791-8_45
33. Petasis, G., Spiliotopoulos, D., Tsirakis, N., Tsantilas, P.: Large-scale sentiment analysis for reputation management. In: Gindl, S., Remus, R., Wiegand, M. (eds.) 2nd Workshop on Practice and Theory of Opinion Mining and Sentiment Analysis (2013)
34. Derczynski, L., Maynard, D., Rizzo, G., van Erp, M., Gorrell, G., Troncy, R., Petrak, J., Bontcheva, K.: Analysis of Named Entity Recognition and Linking for Tweets. Preprint Submitted to Elsevier (2014)
35. Rizzo, G., van Erp, M., Troncy, R.: Benchmarking the extraction and disambiguation of named entities on the semantic web. In: 9th International Conference on Language Resources and Evaluation (LREC 2014), pp. 4593–4600 (2014)
36. Holzinger, A.: Introduction to machine learning and knowledge extraction (MAKE). Mach. Learn. Knowl. Extr. **1**, 1–20 (2017)
37. Rizzo, G., Troncy, R., Hellmann, S., Brümmer, M.: NERD meets NIF: lifting NLP extraction results to the linked data cloud. In: LDOW, 5th Workshop on Linked Data on the Web, Lyon, France, 16 April 2012
38. Sasaki, F., Dojchinovski, M., Nehring, J.: Chainable and extendable knowledge integration web services. In: van Erp, M., et al. (eds.) ISWC 2016. LNCS, vol. 10579, pp. 89–101. Springer, Cham (2017). https://doi.org/10.1007/978-3-319-68723-0_8

39. Petz, G., Wetzlinger, W., Nedbal, D.: Improving language-dependent named entity detection. In: Holzinger, A., Kieseberg, P., Tjoa, A.M. (eds.) CD-MAKE 2017. LNCS, vol. 10410, pp. 330–345. Springer, Cham (2017). https://doi.org/10.1007/978-3-319-66808-6_22

40. Salmons, J.: How to Use Cases in Research Methods Teaching. An Author and Editor's View. SAGE Publications, London (2014)

41. Jacobson, I., Ng, P.-W.: Aspect-Oriented Software Development with Use Cases. Addison-Wesley, Boston (2005)

42. Dobing, B., Parsons, J.: The role of use cases in the UML: a review and research agenda. In: Siau, K. (ed.) Advanced Topics in Database Research, vol. 1, pp. 367–382. IGI Global, Hershey (2002)

43. Graesser, A.C., McNamara, D.S., Louwerse, M.M., Cai, Z.: Coh-Metrix: analysis of text on cohesion and language. Behav. Res. Methods Instrum. Comput. 36, 193–202 (2004)

44. Leow, R.P.: The effects of input enhancement and text length on adult L2 readers' comprehension and intake in second language acquisition. Appl. Lang. Learn. 8, 151–182 (1997)

45. Mehrpour, S., Riazi, A.: The impact of text length on EFL students' reading comprehension. Asian EFL J. 6, 1–13 (2004)

46. McNamara, D.S., Graesser, A.C., McCarthy, P.M., Cai, Z.: Automated Evaluation of Text and Discourse with Coh-Metrix. Cambridge University Press, New York (2014)

47. Crossley, S., McNamara, D.: Cohesion, coherence, and expert evaluations of writing proficiency. In: Proceedings of the 32nd Annual Conference of the Cognitive Science Society, Austrin, Texas, pp. 984–989 (2010)

48. Gernsbacher, M.A.: Language Comprehension as Structure Building. L. Erlbaum, Hillsdale (1990)

49. McNamara, D., Kintsch, E., Songer, N.B., Kintsch, W.: Are good texts always better? Interactions of text coherence, background knowledge, and levels of understanding in learning from text. Cogn. Instr. 14, 1–43 (1996)

50. O'Reilly, T., McNamara, D.S.: The impact of science knowledge, reading skill, and reading strategy knowledge on more traditional "high-stakes" measures of high school students' science achievement. Am. Educ. Res. J. 44, 161–196 (2007)

51. Kulkarni, S., Singh, A., Ramakrishnan, G., Chakrabarti, S.: Collective annotation of Wikipedia entities in web text. In: Proceedings of the 15th ACM SIGKDD International Conference on Knowledge Discovery and Data Mining, pp. 457–466. ACM, New York (2009)

52. Meij, E., Weerkamp, W., de Rijke, M.: Adding semantics to microblog posts. In: Proceedings of the Fifth ACM International Conference on Web Search and Data Mining, pp. 563–572. ACM, New York (2012)

53. Piccinno, F., Ferragina, P.: From TagME to WAT: a new entity annotator. In: Proceedings of the First International Workshop on Entity Recognition & Disambiguation, pp. 55–62. ACM, New York (2014)

54. Hachey, B., Radford, W., Nothman, J., Honnibal, M., Curran, J.R.: Evaluating entity linking with Wikipedia. Artif. Intell. 194, 130–150 (2013)

55. Madrid, I.R., van Oostendorp, H., Puerta Melguizo, M.C.: The effects of the number of links and navigation support on cognitive load and learning with hypertext. The mediating role of reading order. Comput. Hum. Behav. 25, 66–75 (2009)

56. Kendeou, P., van den Broek, P.: The effects of prior knowledge and text structure on comprehension processes during reading of scientific texts. Mem. Cogn. 35, 1567–1577 (2007)

57. Amadieu, F., Tricot, A., Mariné, C.: Prior knowledge in learning from a non-linear electronic document. Disorientation and coherence of the reading sequences. Comput. Hum. Behav. **25**, 381–388 (2009)
58. Overbeek, S.J., van Bommel, P., Proper, H.A.: Statics and dynamics of cognitive and qualitative matchmaking in task fulfillment. Inf. Sci. **181**, 129–149 (2011)
59. Ouellette, G.P.: What's meaning got to do with it. The role of vocabulary in word reading and reading comprehension. J. Educ. Psychol. **98**, 554–566 (2006)
60. Pearson, P.D., Hamm, D.N.: The assessment of reading comprehension: a review of practices - past, present, and future. In: Paris, S.G., Stahl, S.A. (eds.) Children's Reading Comprehension and Assessment, pp. 13–69 (2005)

Evaluating the Two-Speed IT Concept for Digitalization

Christian Remfert[(✉)] and Jan Stockhinger

University of Muenster, Muenster, Germany
{christian.remfert, jan.stockhinger}@wi.uni-muenster.de

Abstract. Digitalization fundamentally changes the way business is conducted, since economies of scale and scope are delivered at an unbridled speed in the digital age. These circumstances induce a quest for ambidexterity among the IT department: the contemporary IT function is expected to deliver reliable and stable services as well as rapid innovation - at the same time. The two-speed IT concept aims at harmonizing these vastly different requirements by decomposing the IT function into a traditional and an agile mode. While benefits of the concept are widely acknowledged in theory, little is known about its real-world application. Our study captures notions from a practitioners. Specifically, we want to elaborate how practitioners evaluate the concept against the backdrop of the challenges induced by digitalization. By conducting semi-structured interviews with people responsible for IT, we were able to gather rich insights on the perceived benefits and perils of bimodal IT setups and highlight important topics for future academic research.

Keywords: Bimodal IT · Two-speed IT · Digitalization
Strategic IT management

1 Digitalization and Its Challenges for Business

The digital revolution is in its full swing. The fast pace of technological development, the expansion and digitalization of public IT-based infrastructures such as the Internet, as well as changes in the IT market and the overall business environment have transformed the situation for most businesses dramatically. These changes culminate in a new business situation that is often referred to as "digital business" in both, practice and academia. On the one hand, characteristic features of businesses in the digital age are the utilization of so-called "SMACIT-Technologies" (social, mobile, analytics, cloud and Internet-of-Things) [1]. On the other hand, looking beyond the mere technologies reveals that successful digital companies leverage economies of scale and scope in a speed that is in stark contrast to traditional businesses: "Instead of linear rates of change, digital companies are showing mastery over non-linear, exponential expansion in scale and scope" [2]. It is thus not surprising that pundits already declared an era of "digital Darwinism", in which only those companies are said to survive that adapt best to the circumstances as outlined above [3]. These circumstances entail the necessity of a "digital transformation" for many traditional organizations. Embarking on such a transformation is a particularly difficult endeavour for incumbent companies

© Springer International Publishing AG, part of Springer Nature 2018
F. F.-H. Nah and B. S. Xiao (Eds.): HCIBGO 2018, LNCS 10923, pp. 162–174, 2018.
https://doi.org/10.1007/978-3-319-91716-0_13

that prospered during the industrial age, as those are to scrutinize their business and operating model, while it is still running well. Otherwise, they run into danger to fall into a competency trap, like Nokia did in 2012 [4].

It becomes clear that IT becomes a key resource to manage this kind of transformation. As organizations recognize the imperative for IT agility and innovation to thrive in the digital age, corporate IT functions receive considerable attention. In fact, their self-conception becomes subject to a paradigm shift. Whereas IT units formerly have been treated as cost centers based on the provision of efficient and reliable services, they are nowadays charged with exploring, advancing and implementing digital innovations as well [5]. For IT executives, this results in a quest for ambidexterity. On the one hand, backend systems and the information contained are the firm's backbone and thus are required to be stable, secure and reliable. On the other hand, flexible frontend systems are of utter importance for companies to respond quickly to market changes and to realize competitive advantages through emerging technologies. Apparently, most contemporary IT functions are not suitably organized to handle these highly distinct tasks at the same time [6].

The so called "two-speed IT" design (sometimes also "bimodal IT") is a fashionable approach to address the conflicting challenge of harmonizing reliable and stable IT services with digital innovation tasks. The underlying idea is to divide the IT function into separate operational modes for the purpose of implementing and governing each of those modes according to their own requirements and needs. While the concept of a two-speed IT design might be a viable approach to cope with the challenges of digitalization in theory, little is known about its real-world application. The aim of our research is to explore how IT managers across different industries and company sizes understand and evaluate the two-speed IT concept. Prior to describing methodological details, the following chapter sets out relevant literature and basic premises of the concept.

2 Two-Speed IT: History and State of the Art

While first mentions of organizational ambidexterity for innovation date back to the 1970's [7], the two-speed IT concept gained vital momentum in 2014 due to the publication of Gartner's "CIO Agenda 2014" [8]. To address the challenges of digitalization, the advisory firm recommends reorganizing the corporate IT function by dividing it into two separate modes of IT delivery. Following their logic, contemporary organizations still need to be able to exploit predictable and well-understood areas to improve efficiency. This is what Gartner refers to as "mode 1", or "traditional IT". However, as digitalization changes economies of scale, scope and especially speed, organizations are also required to build an exploratory capability. In this second mode, emphasis is not on cost savings and efficiency but rather on experimenting and venturing on a high pace and thus requires a radical different skillset. Still, according to Gartner, "both modes are essential to create substantial value and drive significant organizational change, and neither is static" [9].

Derived from their different purposes, the two modes can also be distinguished with regard to management methodologies, foci and cultural differences [10]. As the overarching objective in the traditional mode is to deliver reliable and efficient IT services, the established "plan, build, run" paradigm is adequately suited for this mode [11]. Typically, requirements for application systems are known in advance in this context and may be elicited by analysis processes. Tasks could for example embrace security enhancements or improvements of business processes performances. For those tasks, a waterfall-driven IT project management approach and a risk-averse culture dovetails nicely [12]. Hence, mode 1 of the two-speed IT concept is primarily associated with process standardizations and the operations and maintenance of backend systems. Those "systems of records" are planned and updated in long cycles and prioritize reliance, compliance and governance principles over speed and flexibility. Nevertheless, to meet the requirements of the digital age, even traditional IT landscapes need to comply with the principle of periodical renewal, such as i.e. the creation of micro-services and standard-APIs, which help to ensure a flawless integration with the second mode [13]. Mode 2 – the "agile IT" – in contrast, addresses unknown areas, where application system requirements are not known in advance. It is designed to solve novel problems and to explore new business frontiers by means of digital innovation. A typical instrument representing the stance of the agile IT mode is the "minimum viable product (mvp)", which describes the first minimal working iteration of a continuously evolving product [14]. As this mode focuses on customer-oriented IT solutions and business outcomes, it requires a different project management methodology. Due to ever-changing customer demands and vastly emerging market trends, agile software development methods like SCRUM or Kanban are critical success factors in this realm. Thus – in contrast to the traditional mode – the agile mode aims at building flexible frontend systems with short release cycles ("systems of engagement") that can adapt to altered environmental circumstances at a fast pace.

With due regard to the academic literature, research as of now is in a nascent stage. The humble academic discourse available may be subdivided into two kinds of research streams: On the one hand, there are publications that promote reasons for and benefits of the bimodal IT concept. To sum up, central arguments disseminated in the literature are improved business-IT alignment, enhanced digital innovation capabilities and a stronger customer orientation [5, 11]. Limitations and shortcomings, such as inefficiencies or bloated overhead costs on the contrary are largely dismissed in the academic debate and can only be found in practitioners' literature [15]. The second research stream centers around design options for the organizational implementation of the two-speed IT concept [12, 16, 17]. The underlying premise in these publications is that companies already advocate the idea of a two-speed IT, but struggle with the implementation as specific design options are missing. HAFFKE ET AL. [12] addressed this perspective through providing a comprehensive recommendation. Based on empirical insights from 19 firms, the researchers were able to identify four distinct archetypes of bimodal IT (see Fig. 1). They found that the majority of the organizations employed either a "project-by-project (type A)" or a "subdivisional (type B)" design. While both archetypes have a single IT function in common, the subdivisional design introduces an organizational split between the agile and traditional mode, whereas the adequate mode in type A is selected on a project-by-project basis. Archetype C, in contrast, implements the agile mode via a "digital division", that is self-contained and independent from the IT function. The most extreme level of bimodality is embedded in archetype D, as the IT function is run in an agile fashion, whereas the traditional mode is outsourced or at least remains fully in the background.

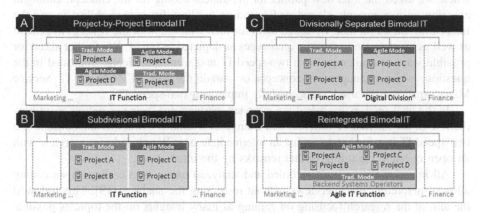

Fig. 1. Four archetypes of two-speed IT [12].

Since current research is either about benefits or design options of two-speed IT, we think there is a research gap in between. As long as practitioners do not agree with the benefits as proposed in the academic literature, discussions about design options become redundant. An often-quoted study addressing the practical relevance of the topic indicates that 45% of the responding CIOs already embarked on the topic [16, 18]. The share implies that the majority of CIOs are still unfamiliar or not engaged with the concept. Therefore, it seems to be helpful to take a step backward and let practitioners evaluate the idea of a bimodal IT in the light of digitalization.

3 Research Method

To answer our research question, we opted for a qualitative approach, using semi-structured interviews. The aim of the study is to get first insights how digitalization is understood by experts that are responsible for digital transformation within their company instead of providing a representative, quantitative study. We decided to include IT representatives of companies across different industries, as they are supposed to have profound knowledge in their companies' IT structure and are familiar with new trends in the field, such as the concept of two-speed-IT. The semi-structured interview guideline included four main sections: an introductory section, a section on digitalization, a section on the concept of two-speed-IT as well as a final summarizing section. The introductory section covers all statistical questions regarding the company itself, like branch and size of the company in terms of revenue and employees.

The second section is focusing on digitalization itself. Here, the first intention was to learn about how the interview partners understand digitalization in general and in the light of their companies. Based on this, we were interested in whether digitalization initiatives have already been started and which challenges and opportunities arose in the interviewee's company. We further questioned for counter activities addressing the challenges and how successful new opportunities are implemented. After discussing those general digitalization aspects, we moved over to the concept of two-speed-IT where we asked the interview partner for his understanding for the concept, aiming at agreeing on a commonly shared understanding to allow for comparability among the interviews. Based on that, we asked them for their evaluation of the concept in general as well as in reference to the four archetypes as depicted in Fig. 1. We further asked for possible ways of implementing a two-speed-IT and were specifically interested in the question, which management concepts or paradigms like SCRUM or IT Service Management can be used to successfully implement two-speed-IT.

In the final section, we asked the interview partners for their perception about how the role of the internal IT function will change over time and whether the concept of a two-speed-IT is a final state or just an intermediate one. We closed our interview with an open question regarding further remarks by the interviewee.

All interviews have been recorded and analyzed using open coding. Open coding allows interpreting the interviews without restricting the analysis [19]. This followed the aim of the research focusing on gaining as many insights on the topic as possible without setting limitations through predefined structures.

4   Cases

As mentioned above, we are interested in a diverse representation of companies that are currently working on digital transformation. This is mainly given in mid-sized and large companies that have enough resources to set up own digitalization programs and initiatives. Hence, we concentrated on those. In terms of the branches, we aimed at finding a diverse sample in order to examine possible differences across industries. Within these companies, we first identified those people who are responsible for digitalization. In all cases, these were either the CIO, the CDO or the CEO. In seven of the eight companies included in the research, the interview partner was a CIO or CDO and hence was assumed to have a very high technical knowledge. Luckily, the only CEO was responsible for the e-commerce sub-division and hence was also very technical-affine. Accordingly, all interview partners were able to answer questions regarding digitalization and the concept of two-speed-IT. In the following, we will give more details on each case. The names of the companies have been anonymized.

Case 1: PubliCo
PubliCo is a publishing company that produces special interest magazines. They started with magazines for the agricultural sector. Although the company has a long tradition in this field (with more than 100 years), new mass-market magazines about lifestyle, gardening and traveling were added to the company's portfolio around 2008. Those magazines made up a complete market for PubliCo and raised the company's yearly revenue above the 100 million euro level. In addition, new digital products like online trading platforms or special interest community platforms allowed to increase the revenue even further and makes PubliCo one of the most successful publishing companies in Europe. To create this success, PubliCo employs around 500 people, the majority in Germany and only a few in neighboring companies like Austria or Poland.

Case 2: MediaCo
MediaCo is a media publishing and content creation company. Founded as a print-publications only company at the middle of the last century, it enhanced its portfolio by online platforms, which nowadays make up around 70% of the whole revenue (around 3 billion Euro in 2016). MediaCo mainly concentrates on mass-market publications and platforms. Their overall strategy is to further grow the "digital" revenue share by developing and acquiring further digital platforms. For this, different activities have been started, e.g. the set-up of a company internal incubator. Hence, MediaCo has started its digitalization efforts as one of the first in its sector.

Case 3: FashionIT
FashionIT is one of the largest textile discounters in Europe with an annual revenue of around 2 billion Euro in 2016. FashionIT has grown traditionally with local stores. These stores sell nearly all types of clothing, but also other textiles like beddings. Furthermore, also food articles like sweets are in their product portfolio. The stores are mostly located out of the city center, which is a new challenge in modern days as fewer people are coming to the stores, as they either shop in the city center or online. To counter this, FashionIT has set up an online store as a complement to the local stores. FashionIT has set up a new strategic initiative in 2018, to bring both channels, local and online stores, together and establish digitalization within the company.

Case 4: LandMachine
LandMachine is an internationally leading manufacturer of land machines, with an annual revenue of around 4 billion Euro in 2015. LandMachine employs around 11,000 people and its products stand for high-quality in the agricultural sector. Traditionally, this agricultural sector is less digitalized, but LandMachine started a range of digitalization efforts a few years ago and tries to adapt the company culture to the "modern digital times". For example, LandMachine opened its own co-working space, allowing employees to try out new ways of working. Furthermore, first steps to "digitalize" their products have been made, for example, through equipping land machines with diagnostic sensors and connect them to a data center of LandMachine so that support employees can help customers even better by having real-time health data of their machines.

Case 5: PolyCo
PolyCo is an internationally acting company that is specialized in polymer processing. The company has an annual revenue of around 3 billion Euro in 2016 and employs around 20,000 employees around the world. PolyCo processes polymer for different sectors, mainly automotive, industry, construction, and medicine. Since PolyCo's products are getting more and more a commodity on the international market, new products and business models, especially digital ones, are examined. Hence, PolyCo has found its own Accelerator to develop new digital business models and strategies.

Case 6: AutoSup
AutoSup is an internationally acting manufacturer of electronic components for the automotive industry. The company has been founded in the middle of the last century and employs around 60,000 employees internationally. With an annual revenue of

around 3.5 billion Euro, AutoSup is one of the most successful automotive suppliers worldwide. AutoSup has a two-folded understanding of digitalization: on the one hand, digitalization is the gain of efficiency in internal processes by the use of information technology. On the other hand, it allows creating new business models and opportunities that the company can benefit from.

Case 7: Plastico
Plastico is an international company that processes plastics to create intermediate and end products that are used in mechanical engineering as well as in the automotive, aviation and medical industry. With an annual revenue of around 400 million Euros in 2016, approx. 2,500 employees and more than 25 fabrics around the world, Plastico is one of the leading players in their industry globally. As one of the most successful mid-sized companies within Europe, the company understands itself as a "hidden champion".

Case 8: MediTech
MediTech is a globally acting producer of medical equipment with an annual revenue of around 3 billion Euro in 2015. Their main company focus lies on care and surgery. The company employs around 15,000 employees worldwide and. In terms of digitalization, the company is currently exploring new opportunities, how digitalization efforts can help to develop the business further and how to react on new threats that arise due to digitalization, for example, new disruptive products. There are no current digitalization programs or concrete initiatives set up but awareness is given that digitalization will change the business as it is.

Table 1 summarizes the core characteristics of all cases.

Table 1. Case overview

Case	Company industry	Revenue in Euros (approx)	Employees (approx.)	Role of interviewee	Two-speed-IT used? (Archetype)
PubliCo	Print publications	80 million	500	CIO	Yes (C)
MediaCo	Print publications and media creation	3 billion	15.000	CIO	Yes (D)
FashionIT	Textile and fashion	2 billion	25.000	CEO of IT subsidiary	Yes (C)
LandMachine	Land machines/mechanical engineering	3.5 billion	11.000	CDO	Yes (A)
PolyCo	Polymer processing	3 billion	20.000	CIO	Yes (A)
AutoSup	Automotive supply	3.5 billion	60.000	CDO	Yes (A)
Plastico	Plastics processing	400 million	2.500	CIO	Yes (A)
MediTech	Medical equipment	3 billion	15.000	CIO	Yes (A)

5   Findings

As set out in chapter 3, we divided our interviews into four sections. The presentation of the findings is sequenced accordingly, whereas the results of the first section is already depicted in Table 1.

5.1   Section "Digitalization"

Not surprisingly, the interviews did not reveal a unison comprehension of digitalization and its challenges, as concrete concerns depend heavily on the respective industry and its stage of digitalization. However, six out of eight experts declared scrutinizing the recent business model and enhancing it with digital technologies as one of the main challenges in the digital age. Digging deeper for the reasons, our interviewees mostly mentioned the fear of facing severe competition from new entrants like innovative start-ups or "digital giants" like Amazon, Google and co. For three companies, this threat has already come into force. The representative of FashionIT, for example, referred to an application called "Wish", a digital platform that directly connects low-budget textile manufacturers from Asia to end customers all around the world, which leads to a disintermediation of the classic fashion discount retailer. Land-Machine, by the same token, has already initiated counter-measures by establishing a software solution/platform that allows managing nearly every aspect of the agricultural enterprise, including the integration of partners and suppliers along the supply chain, online. In addition, all CIOs perceived the constitution of new capabilities in respect of digital technologies a major challenge. In this context, PolyCo mentioned: *"a challenge is that the IT function needs to engage with new technologies. Keywords are IoT platforms, big data technologies, new databases, edge computing and machine learning. Nowadays, these competencies are not available in the IT [function]"*. Interestingly enough, neither the CDOs nor the CEO in our sample mentioned these technological competencies as a severe challenge. Instead, they emphasized the requisite of a "digital culture", i.e. an experimental, cross-functional and customer-oriented mindset that requires an ample change management program. Lastly, we were astonished that half of our interviewees mentioned process optimization/process digitalization as one of their top priorities. The CIO of PubliCo said: *"for me, the focus is on processes and the question how business processes can be adjusted to be really digital, meaning without media or system disruptions"*. This was surprising for us since academic literature with respect to digitalization usually deals with strategic topics like digital business strategies or digital business models, whereas operational tasks are mostly left out.

5.2   Section "Two-Speed IT"

The concept of a two-speed IT was known to all of the experts. All interviewees shared a common understanding of two-speed-IT as an organizational structure that has a "fast", agile mode and a slow, traditional one. Interestingly, the agile mode was associated with software development in nearly all cases, while the traditional mode has been associated with IT operations, such as server or network operations. Only the

CIO of MediaCo mentioned that he could also imagine an agile approach for the IT operations. Taking this perspective as having the agile mode for software development and the traditional mode for IT operations, some of the experts, like the CIO of PubliCo, mentioned the concept of DevOps as related to two-speed IT. This is backed by the fact that the concept of DevOps aligns development activities with operations to ensure that developed software is operable in production after completion.

Viability of the Concept Against the Background of Digitalization
With regard to the question if a two-speed IT helps to counteract the challenges of digitalization as mentioned before, we got different answers. Some of the experts – like AutoSup, MediTech and Plastico – judge a two-speed IT as a valid approach to react to the challenges of digitalization. They believe that the implementation of a two-speed IT organization allows establishing mindsets that are necessary to be successful in the digitalization. The CIO of Plastico further mentioned that the concept of a two-speed IT allows to *"analyze the status-quo of the IT function and derive how to react to the challenges of digitalization"*.
However, the implementation of a two-speed IT might also have downsides. Seven out of the eight interviewees agreed that the implementation of a two-speed IT approach bears the risk that a "two-class-society" within the IT function arises. This means that the people of the fast mode can be seen as *"winners while employees in the traditional mode might feel like losers"*, as stated the CIO of Plastico, a fact that from his perspective needs to be avoided by all means. Although he agrees with this, the CEO of FashionIT mentioned that this is a question of leadership: the head of the IT function has to ensure that such a perspective of "winners" and "losers" does not come up. This might be done by appreciating the work of employees in the fast and the traditional mode equally. This view is also supported by the CIO of MediaCo, who furthermore added that this is not only a question of leadership but also of the workforce itself. He mentioned the example of a database administrator that is short before retirement. Such an employee does not want to be part of the "winners", he just wants to do his job as usual.

Evaluation of Two-Speed IT Archetypes
When it comes to the organizational implementation of two-speed IT, four different archetypes are named by HAFFKE ET AL. (see Fig. 1). We asked all experts for their opinion, whether these archetypes are implementable or not. Interestingly, we got very different answers. Regarding the archetype A, the CDO of LandMachine said that this is the way how his company is working currently. His employees are switching modes from project to project, which enables a high flexibility due to the chance to re-assess the "best mode" for each project. In contrast, the CIO of MediaCo mentioned that archetype is not feasible as employees are not able to change from one mode to another. This goes in line with the statement of PubliCo's CIO. His main point of critique is that employees are not able to master both modes completely, which then leads to inefficiency. The other pundits were more critically in this point, as they did not judge this archetype as very reasonable. The archetypes B and C have been discussed by most of our pundits. This is based on the fact that both types are distinguishing strictly into the agile and the traditional modes, but differ in terms of the organizational implementation. Where B is a separation within the IT function, C is characterized by the set-up of an own division.

The pundits of AutoSup, Plastico, and MediTech mentioned that these archetypes allow them to establish new mindsets (especially for the management and implementation of projects), specifically in the agile mode. Furthermore, the CIO of MediTech mentioned that this also gives him the chance to hire new employees with specialist knowledge. Especially for archetype C, the CDO of AutoSup sees a chance to break free from established structures, as he believes that this type gives him more freedom in terms of budgeting and governance mechanisms. This goes in line with the opinion of Plastico's pundit, who even goes one step ahead: he said that archetype C even allows forming new guidelines for the whole company, as the new division could be seen as a prototype to test new ways of working. However, all experts also see disadvantages for the archetype B and C. The pundit of PolyCo criticized that his employees are working on different projects that cannot be distinguished strictly into agile and traditional mode. Hence, an implementation of archetype B or C is not realizable from his point of view. While this critique stems from a project perspective, the CDO of AutoSup elaborates from an employee perspective: his employees should have the chance to engage themselves in both mode to avoid a "two-tier society". The emergence of such a good-bad-culture is also what hinders the CIO of PubliCo to implement such archetypes. He wants to avoid establishing a "winner" and a "loser" class. This is highlighted also by LandMachine's CDO who stated that a division or group, *"where I put in the ten greatest talents and set-up a great, wild agile IT team"* leads to *"political difficulties"*. MediaCo's CIO is not that critical but considers archetypes B and C as an intermediate mode on the way to a final implementation of archetype D that MediaCo achieved when we conducted the interview. The CIO ironically told us that his company is back to a *"one-speed IT"* that has implemented the agile mode for all areas of the IT function. That this is the future is also believed by PubliCo's CIO. However, for the time being, he does not have a "secret recipe", how to implement agile ways of working with critical backend systems. This crucial point is also highlighted by LandMachine's CDO. He does not believe that an agile mode can be used for core systems of the company, like the central ERP system. He believes that in this point, traditional modes will survive, at least for the next years.

Methodological Implementation
With regard to the methodological implementation of the two-speed IT concept, we asked the pundits for the approaches that might be valid for the fast as well as the traditional mode. The pundit of FashionIT as well as the MediaCo CIO mentioned that Kanban is their method of choice for the fast mode. Having the view that the fast mode is for software development, Kanban allows to prioritize tasks and have an overview of the status quo at each time. Beside Kanban, the CIO of PubliCo mentioned the use of SCRUM within his organization. For the traditional mode, he named the IT Infrastructure Library (ITIL) or IT Service Management (ITSM) in general to be a suitable approach for the organization. This was also supported by the CIO of MediaCo, but with the limitation that not the full set of ITIL processes is applicable for the traditional mode and that an appropriate set of those needs to be selected. However, he understands non-agile methods like ITIL or ITSM only as an intermediate solution. In his vision for the future of IT functions, the traditional mode can be operated by agile methods like Kanban or SCRUM as well, albeit this needs to be adapted slightly then to suit the specific characteristics of IT operations.

5.3   Section "Outlook"

75% of the pundits considered a distinct split of the IT function to be an intermediate state. The CEO of FashionIT further distinguished between traditional organizations from the industrial age and what he called "modern companies", born in the digital age. Due to historical grown structures and path dependencies, former companies might consider a two-speed architecture as a final stage. However, modern companies with sufficient resources and with the possibility to choose employees accordingly will even go beyond the two-speed scale and act on a more fine-grained multi-speed scale. PolyCo's CIO confirms this point of view: *"in my opinion there is no bimodal IT, but instead there is a multimodal business pace that has to be addressed by the IT in the future"*. Since MediaCo's IT function is already run in an agile fashion predominantly, the expert expects future IT departments to operate on an 80% agile/20% traditional ratio, at least in the media publishing industry. The most radical view stems from the representative of LandMachine. According to the CDO, the IT function will only be responsible for governance structures and backend systems in near future. He arguments that operating departments increasingly consider IT capabilities as one of their core competencies, which requires a conflation between the IT and remaining departments. In his remarks, he refers to an exemplary project of a famous German automotive manufacturer that recently set up an innovation lab to approach digital transformation, which is led by an interdisciplinary team from IT, finance and sales. Instead of reporting to the CIO, this team directly reports to the head of sales. Consequently, the current IT department is disintermediated and needs to reinvent itself, according to our interviewee.

Regarding further expected IT changes induced by digitalization, FashionIT expects data and process quality to gain in importance fundamentally as well as sensor technology and thus automated processes. Concomitant with this, a concrete IT architecture strategy is a prerequisite to thrive in the digital age. In this context, he argues: *"For example, does SAP have to be traditional or can we make it agile? If it is not possible to do it all agile, can we build single modules in an agile mode? This is what the IT department has to ask for every aspect of the infrastructure in the future"*.

6   Summary and Conclusion

To avoid competitive disadvantages, IT departments in the digital age are confronted with the tough endeavor to deliver reliable services and rapid innovations at the same time. The two-speed IT concept is said to be a suitable solution to cope with this challenge since it decomposes the IT department into an agile and a traditional operating mode. However, academic research on this topic is scarce, especially with respect to empirical investigations. Hence, we contribute to this research domain by conducting an interview-based qualitative study with experts (CIOs, CDOs and one CEO) across various industries and company sizes. Our aim was to capture the diversity of practitioners' perspectives on the evaluation of the concept. Specifically, we aimed at exploring the company-specific challenges that digitalization brings as well as sentiments on the two-speed IT concept's viability of coping with these challenges.

Summing up, one of the main challenges for the companies in the sample is to rethink their business model by augmenting it with digital technologies. Furthermore, the executives perceive an increased pressure due to shorter release cycle requirements and more frequent business demands that often encompass the necessity to build new competencies with respect to digital technologies. While all CIOs mentioned process digitalization as one of the core topics, the remaining interviewees remained silent in this regard. We consider this as a finding deserving further academic attention, because the academic literature on CIO tasks is mainly engaged with strategic topics like creating competitive advantage through IT or information as a strategic resource [20]. However, taking into account that the CIOs polled have a rather technical background and are responsible for operational tasks mostly, this result might also stem from our specific sample. Relating to the two-speed IT concept, there seems to be a difference in comprehension between practitioners and academics. While most of the interviewees claimed that they do not draw on a bimodal IT, the interviews provided evidence that all companies followed one of the archetypes as presented in Fig. 1. Obviously, practitioners do not consider archetype A as an embodiment of two-speed IT. Besides that, we faced a rather sanguine mindset, at least in theory. Practically, the concern highlighted by the practitioners lies in the danger of creating a "two-class IT". Even though this is comprehensible, we think it is not a shortcoming of the concept itself. As stated by one of our interviewees, we agree that it is, in fact, a management task to establish the conditions for an appropriate culture. In that sense, future research should put emphasis on concrete change management programmes and actions that help overcome this concern. Employees need to understand that there is no "good or bad IT" but instead realize the complementary nature of both modes, making them equally important.

References

1. Sebastian, I.M., Ross, J.W., Beath, C., Mocker, M., Moloney, K.G., Fonstad, N.O.: How big old companies navigate digital transformation. MIS Q. Executive **16**, 197–213 (2017)
2. Venkatraman, V.: Digital Matrix. Greystone Books, Vancouver (2017)
3. Kreutzer, R., Land, K.-H.: Digital Darwinism. Branding and Business Models in Jeopardy. Springer, Heidelberg (2015)
4. Heracleous, L., Papachroni, A., Andriopoulos, C., Gotsi, M.: Structural ambidexterity and competency traps. Insights from Xerox PARC. Technol. Forecast. Soc. Change **117**, 327–338 (2017)
5. Horlach, B., Drews, P., Schirmer, I.: Bimodal IT: business-IT alignment in the age of digital transformation. In: Multikonferenz Wirtschaftsinformatik (MKWI) 2016, pp. 1417–1428 (2016)
6. Urbach, N., Drews, P., Ross, J.: Digital business transformation and the changing role of the IT function. MIS Q. Executive **16**, i–iv (2017)
7. Duncan, R.B.: The ambidextrous organization, designing dual structures for innovation. The Manag. Organ. Des. **1**, 167–188 (1976)
8. Gartner: Taming the Digital Dragon: The 2014 CIO Agenda. https://www.gartner.com/imagesrv/cio/pdf/cio_agenda_insights2014.pdf. Accessed 20 Feb 2018

9. Gartner: Gartner IT Glossary: Bimodal. https://www.gartner.com/it-glossary/bimodal. Accessed 20 Feb 2018
10. Haffke, I., Kalgovas, B., Benlian, A.: The transformative role of bimodal IT in an era of digital business. In: Proceedings of the 50th Hawaii International Conference on System Sciences (HICSS), Hawaii (2017)
11. Urbach, N., Ahlemann, F.: Die IT-Organisation im Wandel. Implikationen der Digitalisierung für das IT-Management. HMD **54**, 300–312 (2017)
12. Haffke, I., Kalgovas, B., Benlian, A.: Options for transforming the IT function using bimodal IT. MIS Q. Executive **16**, 101–120 (2017)
13. Pettey, C.: Smarter With Gartner. Busting Bimodal Myths. https://www.gartner.com/smarterwithgartner/busting-bimodal-myths/. Accessed 20 Feb 2018
14. Ross, J., Sebastian I., Beath, C., Mocker, M., Moloney, K., Fonstad, N.: Designing and executing digital strategies. In: 37th International Conference on Information Systems (ICIS), Dublin (2016)
15. Forrester: The False Promise Of Bimodal IT. BT Provides A Customer-Led, Insights-Driven, Fast, And Connected Alternative. https://go.forrester.com/wp-content/uploads/Forrester-False-Promise-of-Bimodal-IT.pdf. Accessed 2018/02/20
16. Jöhnk, J., Röglinger, M., Thimmel, M., Urbach, N.: How to implement agile IT setups: a taxonomy of design options. In: Proceedings of the 25th European Conference on Information Systems (ECIS), pp. 1521–1535 (2017)
17. Horlach, B., Drews, P., Schirmer, I., Böhmann, T.: Increasing the agility of IT delivery: five types of bimodal IT organization. In: Proceedings of the 50th Hawaii International Conference on System Sciences (HICSS), Hawaii (2017)
18. Sondergaard, P.: Bimodal Business leads to Bimodal IT. https://blogs.gartner.com/peter-sondergaard/bimodal-business-leads-to-bimodal-it/. Accessed 20 Feb 2018
19. Saldaña, J.: The Coding Manual for Qualitative Researchers. Sage, Los Angeles (2009)
20. Teubner, R.A., Pellengahr, A.R., Mocker, M.: The IT Strategy Divide: Professional Practice and Academic Debate. ERCIS Working Papers (2012)

System Response Time as a Stressor in a Digital World: Literature Review and Theoretical Model

René Riedl[1,2(✉)] and Thomas Fischer[1]

[1] University of Applied Sciences Upper Austria, Steyr, Austria
rene.riedl@fh-steyr.at
[2] Johannes Kepler University, Linz, Austria

Abstract. The time delay between a user's initiation of a command on a digital device (e.g., desktop computer, tablet, smartphone) and the system's task completion, including the display of the result on the screen, is referred to as system response time (SRT). This specific system property has been the object of study since the 1960s, predominantly in the field of human-computer interaction. In most usage scenarios, SRT ranges from milliseconds to several minutes, and SRT is a function of various factors, including technical system capabilities such as processing power. One would assume that technological progress has reduced the relevance of investigations into the physiological and stress-inducing effects of long and/or variable SRT. However, as a result of the ever increasing complexity of information systems and digital devices, SRT is still a significant stressor in today's society. One could even argue that, due to the ubiquity of digital devices in almost every corner of life and the resulting frequent human-computer interactions, the relevance of SRT as a topic in scientific research and practice has even increased in the last years. Against this background, the present article conceptualizes SRT as a stressor in a digital world, reviews major research results, and, based on that review, develops a theoretical model. This model is intended to guide future research on SRT.

Keywords: Digital stress · NeuroIS · Response time · Stress · Technostress

1 Introduction

The time delay between a user's initiation of a command on a digital device and the system's task completion, including the display of the result on the screen, is referred to as system response time, hereafter SRT. This specific system property has been the object of study since the 1960s (e.g., [1, 2]), predominantly in the field of human-computer interaction (HCI). SRT typically ranges from milliseconds to several minutes. Moreover, SRT depends on numerous factors, such as the complexity of the task or processing power of the system [3]. Importantly, evidence indicates that long and/or variable SRT may increase stress in users of digital devices [4].

One would assume that technological progress has diminished the relevance of investigations into the physiological and stress-inducing effects of long and/or variable

© Springer International Publishing AG, part of Springer Nature 2018
F. F.-H. Nah and B. S. Xiao (Eds.): HCIBGO 2018, LNCS 10923, pp. 175–186, 2018.
https://doi.org/10.1007/978-3-319-91716-0_14

SRT. However, due to the ever increasing complexity of information and communication technology, SRT is still a significant stressor in today's society (e.g., [5]). One could even argue that in a highly digitalized world, the relevance of SRT as a topic in scientific research and practice has even increased in comparison with previous epochs. Considering the relevance of SRT for users' stress and well-being, along with the impact of SRT on other important outcome variables in HCI (e.g., user satisfaction, technology acceptance, performance, or productivity), the present article conceptualizes SRT as a stressor in a digital world and reviews major research results which have shown that long and/or variable SRT may lead to notable physiological stress reactions. Based on that review, we develop a theoretical model which is intended to guide future research on SRT. Ultimately, it is hoped that the insight which can be developed based on this model and corresponding empirical investigations help to mitigate, or even eliminate, the negative physiological consequences of long and/or variable SRT. In other words, it is hoped that the theoretical foundation developed in this paper helps to develop effective interventions in practice.

2   Method

Riedl [6] indicates that "[d]irect human interaction with ICT, as well as perceptions, emotions, and thoughts regarding the implementation of ICT in organizations and its pervasiveness in society in general, may lead to notable stress perceptions—a type of stress referred to as technostress" (p. 18). Based on a comprehensive review of academic literature which has been published since the 1970s, Riedl [6] identified a number of negative biological effects that may emerge from human interaction with information and communication technology (ICT). Importantly, this review also identified long and/or variable SRT as major stressor. In a more recent paper on the potential of blood pressure measurement for technostress research, Fischer et al. [7] also identified research on SRT as one of the most important fields where neurophysiological devices are used in the context of technostress. Based on these findings, in the current paper we a look into selected technostress studies which report on the physiological and stress-inducing effects of SRT.

Drawing upon 12 papers on SRT that were included in these reviews (i.e., 10 empirical papers [8–17] and 2 review papers [3, 4]), we conducted a forward search in Google Scholar on 12/22/2017 and 12/23/2017 in order to identify more recent empirical research (the most recent empirical paper included in these reviews was by Trimmel et al. [16] from 2003). This procedure led to a total of 678 hits, of which 7 were empirical papers that dealt with SRT using neurophysiological measures. Hence, we ended up with a sample of 19 papers, which we analyzed in detail. The results of this analysis are presented below.

3   Results of Reviewed Studies

In Table 1, we offer an overview of the empirical studies that are part of our review, including the main characteristics of the sample, the SRT conditions, and the effects on individual physiology.

In a two-stage case study, Johansson and Aronsson [11] measured by means of multi-item survey instruments, in the first stage, stressors (e.g., rush) and symptoms (e.g., irritation) related to computer work. In the second stage of the study, users with extensive computer work and users with a low degree of computer work were investigated in detail. In essence, this study found notable degrees of technostress (based on self-report instruments and biological measures). Importantly, the authors concluded that "stress and strain in computerized work may be counteracted ... by reducing the duration and frequency of breakdowns [and] by reducing response times in the system" (p. 159). Thus, research already indicated more than three decades ago that stress resulting from long SRT constitutes a significant issue.

Trimmel et al. [16] experimentally investigated SRT, and the authors argued that long SRT causes uncertainty, which, in turn leads to arousal and stress. Twenty-five students participated in the study, 14 skilled and 11 unskilled Internet users (age range: 20–30 years). The task was to answer questions, based on an online information search (e.g., booking a hotel). SRT was manipulated as independent variable: short (2 s), medium (10 s), and long (22 s). Heart rate and skin conductance were used as dependent variables and investigated at three periods: the 10th to 5th second before the waiting time (baseline), during waiting (2, 10, or 22 s), and the 5th to 10th second after waiting (post-baseline). Also, mental load was measured based on a 163-mm analog scale.

The study revealed significant physiological stress responses. Longer SRT led to increased heart rates and enhanced electrodermal activity (note that no significant differences were found between the baseline and post-baseline conditions). Moreover, results indicate that increased activity of the physiological signals were independent of expertise, suggesting that no long-term habituation to long SRT takes place. Furthermore, in post-hoc analyses, the sample was split into two groups: low and high mental load. It was found that individuals experiencing high mental load do have a higher overall heart rate. Specifically, a heart rate of 114 beats per minute was observed for the 22-s condition. Considering that the heart rate of healthy humans is between 60–100 beats per minute at rest [25–27], such an increase is significant.

Interpreting their findings, Trimmel et al. surmise that the elevation of heartbeat and skin conductance may reflect increased attention, as well as active mental performance, because the participants might have given thought to potential reasons for delayed response times. In their recommendation for practice, the authors write that "short SRTs should be provided for the Internet user. For cases in which a long SRT cannot be avoided, a coping mechanism, such as changing the focus of attention, could be suggested" (p. 620).

In a seminal research program, Boucsein and colleagues studied the effects of the length and variability of SRT on physiological signals. In essence, long SRT (though what is considered long is task-dependent) and/or a high degree of variability in SRT

Table 1. Overview of empirical SRT studies using neurophysiological measures

Study	SRT conditions	Effects
Johansson and Aronsson [11] Sweden, 21f	–	Mainly anecdotal
Kuhmann et al. [17] Germany, students, 22f/46 m	Short: 2 s Long: 8 s 7 steps of variability	Longer SRT: higher systolic BP, more spontaneous SCR, higher SCL No effect of SRT variability
Kuhmann [13] Germany, students, 10f/38 m	SRT: 2 s; 4 s; 6 s; 8 s	No effect of SRT
Schleifer and Okogbaa [14] USA, typists, 45f	Short: .35 s Long: 3-10 s	No effect of SRT
Schaefer [18] Germany, students, 10f/38 m	SRT: 2 s; 4 s; 6 s; 8 s	No effect of SRT
Emurian [8] USA, students, 11 m	Constant: 8 s Variable: 1–30 s	No effect of SRT variability
Emurian [9] USA, students, 16f/16 m	Short: 1 s Long: 10 s	Shorter SRT: higher systolic BP
Harada et al. [10] Japan, students, 6f/6 m	Short: < .1 s Long: .3-7 s	Shorter SRT: higher diastolic BP, lower HR
Thum et al. [15] Germany, students, 20f/20 m	Short: .5 s Medium: 1.5 s Long: 4.5 s	Longer SRT: higher HRV (mean square of successive differences), higher SCR (nonspecific electrodermal responses), lower systolic BP, lower diastolic BP, lower respiration rate, lower facial EMG activity
Kohlisch and Kuhmann [12] Germany, students, 15f/27 m	Short: 1 s Medium: 5 s Long: 9 s	Shorter SRT: higher mean BP, more frequent non-specific SCR
Trimmel et al. [16] Austria, students, 14f/12 m	Short: 2 s Medium: 10 s Long: 22 s	Longer SRT: higher HR Shorter SRT: more non-specific SCR SRT (general): higher SCL

(continued)

Table 1. (*continued*)

Study	SRT conditions	Effects
Kohrs et al. [21] Germany, 9f/8 m	Short: 0 s Long: .5 s Omitted feedback	more pronouned activation in putamen in response to delayed feedback (vs ommitted feedback)
Kohrs et al. [19] Germany, 16f	Short: .5 s Medium: 1 s Long: 2 s	Longer SRT: more non-specific SCR, lower HR
Taylor et al. [20] USA, 13f/11 m	SRT: 0; .025 s; .050 s; .1 s; .2 s; .4 s	No individual effects reported, only performance of prediction model for individual frustration levels
Yang and Dorneich [22] USA, students, 7f/14 m	Short: 0 s Long: 2 s or 3 s	Longer SRT: anger (Facereader), increased electro-dermal activity
Kohrs et al. [23] Germany, 10f/11 m	Unexpected, infrequent delays: Short: 2 s Medium: 4 s Long: 6 s	Longer SRT: left and right anterior insular cortex, posterior medial frontal cortex, left inferior parietal lobule, right inferior frontal junction and default network, medial prefrontal and posterior cingulate cortex
Kohrs et al. [23] Germany, 7f/12 m	Frequent delays: Short: 0 s Long: .5 s (.3-7 s)	No differences in brain activations
Kohrs et al. [23] Germany, 9f/8 m	Frequent delays: Short: 0 s Long: .5 s (.3-7 s) & Omissions of Feeback	Longer SRT: bilateral anterior insula, posterior medial frontal cortex, and left inferior parietal lobule
Yang and Dorneich [24] USA, students, 7f/14 m	Short: 0 s Long: 2 s or 3 s	Longer SRT: anger (Facereader)

BP = blood pressure; EMG = electromyography; HR = heart rate; HRV = heart rate variability; SCL = skin conductance level; SCR = skin conductance response; s = seconds

may result in considerable physiological stress reactions, such as skin conductance elevation (e.g., [17]). Boucsein and colleagues conducted several laboratory experiments on the physiological effects of SRT length. Table 2 summarizes the findings of this research group with respect to SRT length [4].

Table 2. Summary of research findings on SRT and time pressure (source: Boucsein [4])

Short SRT (0.5–2 s) with time pressure
Systolic and diastolic blood pressure increases
Heart rate variability decreases
Respiration rate increases
Muscle tension on the forehead increases
Frequency of nonspecific electrodermal responses increases
Short SRT (0.5–2 s) without time pressure
Systolic and diastolic blood pressure increases
Heart rate increases
Long SRT (8 s or longer) with time pressure
Skin conductance level increases
Frequency of nonspecific electrodermal responses increases
Amplitude of nonspecific electrodermal responses increases
Systolic and diastolic blood pressure decreases
Respiration rate decreases
Long SRT (8 s or longer) without time pressure
Amount of electrodermal activity increases
Frequency of nonspecific electrodermal responses initially increases and later decreases

In two studies, Yang and Dorneich [22, 24] investigated the effects of varying system delays on the interaction of individuals with robots. Twenty-one students were instructed to operate a robot through a simple or more difficult maze while their inputs were implemented with or without a time delay. In the trials reported in the earlier study, they found significant differences in arousal based on task difficulty (higher task difficulty led to more arousal reflected in electro-dermal activity) and SRT (longer SRT led to more arousal reflected in electro-dermal activity), as well as a significant interaction of both (i.e., high task difficulty and long SRT together led to the highest physiological arousal). However, Yang and Dorneich were not able to replicate these findings in the more recent study.

Against the background of these findings, it can be concluded that long SRT may significantly activate the sympathetic part of the autonomic nervous system (ANS). The ANS consists of two parts: sympathetic and parasympathetic. While the former is responsible for implementation of a "fight-or-flight" (stress) response, the latter is the underlying structure of a "rest-and-digest" (relax) response. It follows that the sympathetic division is stimulatory, while the parasympathetic division is inhibitory. In stressful situations, the sympathetic part of the ANS becomes active and stimulates a number of responses, such as (Riedl and Léger [28], p. 41): pupil dilation (i.e., elevated attention), skin conductance increase (i.e., higher arousal), airway relaxation, heartbeat acceleration, intense glucose release, and muscle tension.

Moreover, recent research also shows that certain parts of the central nervous system (CNS), specifically parts of the brain, may become activated by varying SRT. Kohrs et al. [21, 23] report on laboratory experiments which utilized fMRI (functional magnetic resonance imaging) to investigate the brain regions that are activated during different SRT conditions. The task of their participants was to categorize tones, depending on their modulation (upward or downward). Response times were varied for the feedback participants received when entering their answer. In their first experiment, the delays were infrequent and therefore unexpected. In the case of delayed feedback, a number of brain areas were more profoundly activated (e.g., the left and right anterior insular cortex (aI), the posterior medial frontal cortex (pMFC), the left inferior parietal lobule (LPI), and the right inferior frontal junction (IFJ)), including the medial pre-frontal and posterior cingulate cortex, which are involved in the attentional control of individuals, indicating that individuals did not focus on the task any longer, when delays lasted too long. This effect disappeared in their second experiment though, when delays occurred frequently and individuals therefore managed to adapt to them. In their third and last variation, they kept the delays frequent, but also included omissions of feedback, which basically mimicked a short breakdown of the system. In this case, the initial activations of the first experiment were prevalent again, particularly when delays occurred after an omission event, this is likely to be because participants expected further "breakdowns" and thus are not able to trust the system any longer. Conse-quently, the authors recommend that breakdowns should be avoided at any cost and that delays, if still present and above a noticeable threshold (.2 s), should at least be kept consistent so that users can adapt to them. This recommendation can also be supported by evidence involving the autonomic nervous system, which clearly indi-cates profound stress reactions in response to perceived system breakdowns (e.g., [29, 30].

4 Theoretical Model

Previous research has revealed interesting findings on the impact of length and vari-ability of SRT on individual physiology. Yet, as can be seen in Table 1, there are still some inconclusive results that warrant further investigation. For example, while Kuhmann et al. [17] report lower levels of systolic blood pressure during conditions with short SRT, Emurian [9] reports the exact opposite finding. In addition, in some studies that utilized blood pressure measurements, diastolic blood pressure changed during different SRT conditions [10, 12, 15], but not always in conjunction with systolic blood pressure [9, 10, 17]. The same holds true for heart rate measurements (Trimmel et al. [16] report higher heart rates during conditions of long SRT, while Kohrs et al. [19] report the exact opposite) and electro-dermal activity, where some studies report more electro-dermal activity due to long SRT [15, 22], while others report more electro-dermal activity due to short SRT [12, 19].

An early indication for the potential reasons behind such different findings was given by Kuhmann [13] who had also investigated the effect of SRT length (2 s, 4 s, 6 s, 8 s). In conclusion, having not found any significant effects, he hypothesized that this might be due to a lack of time pressure that study participants felt during the laboratory experiment. This finding draws attention to the importance of moderators in the context of SRT.

In his review of previous work on SRT, Boucsein [4] also reports on important moderators of the relationship between length and/or variability of SRT and ANS activity. Specifically, he outlines the following major moderators: user experience, SRT expectations of a user, task (e.g., data entry versus complex decision making with a computer), and context factors (e.g., time pressure).

Variables that are part of one of these three categories (user, task, or context) have also been investigated in our reviewed studies. Regarding *user characteristics*, Emurian [9] found that gender had an important impact on physiological measures, with men having an overall higher blood pressure, while women had a higher heart rate, independent of the SRT condition. Regarding SRT, women showed particular masseter activity (indicative of annoyance) during short SRT conditions. Based on structured interviews, it was also investigated whether personality characteristics (Type A/B) could have an impact on physiological changes in response to different SRT conditions. Yet, this categorization was done post-hoc and only used to hypothesize that personality characteristics might also have an impact on the perception of SRT. Also, expectations of SRT can be of importance, with Johansson and Aronsson [11] reporting that study participants would accept a delay of up to 5 s, but only a small fraction would be willing to accept a delay of more than 10 s, independent of the task or system.

Regarding *task characteristics*, Johansson and Aronsson [11] reported that they were surprised that it was not the group of customer service employees who reported most problems due to computer misbehavior, but the group of individuals who spent their day feeding in data. This could, presumably, point to the dependence on technology used or monotony of computer-related tasks as potential moderators. Such an assumption regarding task monotony was also made in other studies [12, 14, 15] and was confirmed in a study by Schleifer and Okogbaa [14] who found that more monotonous tasks led to lower heart rates and higher heart rate variability, this is likely to be because study participants did not put as much effort into the completion of a task as in the beginning of the study (i.e., mental fatigue). In addition, Yang and Dorneich [22] also showed an interaction effect for task difficulty and SRT, with physiological arousal being highest when tasks are difficult and SRT is long.

Finally, we also need to pay attention to *characteristics of the context* of a study when investigating the effects of SRT. A number of studies included incentives that were connected to the performance of an individual (e.g., monetary), which put additional pressure on them to complete a task in time [8, 9, 12, 14, 15]. In the case of Schleifer and Okogbaa [14], incentivized pay (i.e., better pay for better task performance), led to reduced heart rate variability and increased overall blood pressure, which are indicators of stress. A factor that is often included in studies on SRT as well, but has, for example, been lacking in the study by Kuhmann [13], is the time pressure that is prevalent in almost every work context today [10, 17]. The effect that the presence or absence of such a moderator can have in the study of SRT is illustrated in the review by Boucsein [4]. He summarized the effects that short and long SRT had in the presence or absence of time pressure in previous studies that his research group had conducted (see Table 2).

Based on the evidence discussed in this paper, we developed a theoretical model, which is shown in Fig. 1. In essence, the model conceptualizes SRT as independent variable, with the properties length and variability. The dependent variable in the model is autonomic nervous system (ANS) activity, with five important ANS parameters (blood pressure, heart rate, respiration, skin conductance, muscle tension). Moreover, the model conceptualizes three categories of moderators: user characteristics (e.g., SRT expectation), task characteristics (monotony of the HCI task), and context factors (e.g., time pressure to complete a HCI task).

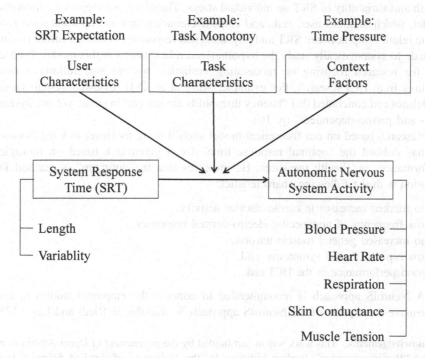

Fig. 1. Theoretical model on the stress-inducing effect of system response time (SRT)

We focus particularly on ANS activity, because related tools have also become accessible to researchers outside of neuroscience and psychology, particularly in Information Systems (IS) research, HCI, and software engineering [31, 32]. Tools such as chest belts to measure heart rate or self-measurement devices to collect blood pressure values could be used by software developers to improve SRT with regard to individual stress levels, thereby improving individual well-being, performance, and productivity. In contrast, brain measurement tools are more difficult to apply in natural settings and their application could be perceived as too resource-intensive in development projects [33]. However, it will be rewarding to see what insight future research and development projects will reveal with regard to the application potential of both self-measurement devices and brain measurement tools in software engineering.

5 Conclusion

In this paper, we have outlined the link between SRT conditions and physiological responses, mainly related to the autonomic nervous system. Based on a review of the literature, we found that there are inconclusive findings regarding the impact of the length and variability of SRT on individual stress. Therefore, we proposed a theoretical model, which includes user, task, and context characteristics as important moderators of the relationship between SRT and physiological responses. A call for future research is made to systematically study the hypothesized relationships in this model. With this call for research focusing on moderating variables, we are also following recent findings from HCI research. For example, Attig et al. [34] reviewed system latency guidelines and concluded that "latency thresholds are not cast in stone, yet, are system-, task- and person-dependent" (p. 10).

Research based on our theoretical model should bring us closer to what Boucsein [4] has dubbed the "optimal response time" for a given task based on biological, performance, and health measures. He indicates that the "optimum" is reached in a situation with the following characteristics:

- no marked increases in cardiovascular activity,
- low frequency of nonspecific electro-dermal responses,
- no increased general muscle tension,
- low reports of pain symptoms, and
- good performance in the HCI task.

A NeuroIS approach is recommended to conduct the empirical studies (a comprehensive description of the NeuroIS approach is available in Riedl and Léger [28]).

Acknowledgements. This work was in part funded by the government of Upper Austria as part of the "Basisfinanzierung" funding initiative by the University of Applied Sciences Upper Austria, project title: "Digitaler Stress in Unternehmen". This research was also funded by the Upper Austrian government as part of the PhD program "Digital Business International", a joint initiative between the University of Applied Sciences Upper Austria and the University of Linz.

References

1. Miller, R.B.: Response time in man-computer conversational transactions. In: Proceedings of the Fall Joint Computer Conference, pp. 267–277. ACM Press, New York (1968)
2. Ferrell, W.R.: Remote manipulation with transmission delay. IEEE Trans. Human Factors Electron. **6**, 24–32 (1965)
3. Dabrowski, J., Munson, E.V.: 40years of searching for the best computer system response time. Interact. Comput. **23**, 555–564 (2011)
4. Boucsein, W.: Forty years of research on system response times – what did we learn from it? In: Schlick, C.M. (ed.) Industrial Engineering and Ergonomics, pp. 575–593. Springer, Berlin Heidelberg, Berlin, Heidelberg (2009). https://doi.org/10.1007/978-3-642-01293-8_42
5. Stokel-Walker, C.: The biggest time suck at the office might be your computer. Sometimes it seems like we're still living in a dial-up world. https://www.bloomberg.com/news/articles/2017-04-20/the-worst-thing-about-work-is-slow-office-computer-equipment

6. Riedl, R.: On the biology of technostress: literature review and research agenda. DATA BASE for Adv. Inf. Syst. **44**, 18–55 (2013)
7. Fischer, T., Halmerbauer, G., Meyr, E., Riedl, R.: Blood pressure measurement: a classic of stress measurement and its role in technostress research. In: Davis, F.D., Riedl, R., vom Brocke, J., Léger, P.-M., Randolph, A.B. (eds.) Information Systems and Neuroscience. LNISO, vol. 25, pp. 25–35. Springer, Cham (2018). https://doi.org/10.1007/978-3-319-67431-5_4
8. Emurian, H.H.: Physiological responses during data retrieval: comparison of constant and variable system response times. Comput. Hum. Behav. **7**, 291–310 (1991)
9. Emurian, H.H.: Cardiovascular and electromyograph effects of low and high density work on an interactive information system. Comput. Hum. Behav. **9**, 353–370 (1993)
10. Harada, H., Okabe, K., Katsuura, T., Kikuchi, Y.: Effects of time stress on psychophysiological responses during data entry tasks. Appl. Hum. Sci.: J. Physiol. Anthropol. **14**, 279–285 (1995)
11. Johansson, G., Aronsson, G.: Stress reactions in computerized administrative work. J. Organ. Behav. **5**, 159–181 (1984)
12. Kohlisch, O., Kuhmann, W.: System response time and readiness for task execution the optimum duration of inter-task delays. Ergonomics **40**, 265–280 (1997)
13. Kuhmann, W.: Experimental investigation of stress-inducing properties of system response times. Ergonomics **32**, 271–280 (1989)
14. Schleifer, L.M., Okogbaa, G.O.: System response time and method of pay: cardiovascular stress effects in computer-based tasks*. Ergonomics **33**, 1495–1509 (1990)
15. Thum, M., Boucsein, W., Kuhmann, W., Ray, W.J.: Standardized task strain and system response times in human-computer interaction. Ergonomics **38**, 1342–1351 (1995)
16. Trimmel, M., Meixner-Pendleton, M., Haring, S.: Stress response caused by system response time when searching for information on the internet. Hum. Factors **45**, 615–621 (2003)
17. Kuhmann, W., Boucsein, W., Schaefer, F., Alexander, J.: Experimental investigation of psychophysiological stress-reactions induced by different system response times in human-computer interaction*. Ergonomics **30**, 933–943 (1987)
18. Schaefer, F.: The effect of system response times on temporal predictability of work flow in human-computer interaction. Hum. Perform. **3**, 173–186 (1990)
19. Kohrs, C., Hrabal, D., Angenstein, N., Brechmann, A.: Delayed system response times affect immediate physiology and the dynamics of subsequent button press behavior. Psychophysiology **51**, 1178–1184 (2014)
20. Taylor, B., Dey, A., Siewiorek, D., Smailagic, A.: Using physiological sensors to detect levels of user frustration induced by system delays. In: ACM (eds.) Proceedings of the 2015 ACM International Joint Conference on Pervasive and Ubiquitous Computing, pp. 517–528. ACM Press (2015)
21. Kohrs, C., Angenstein, N., Scheich, H., Brechmann, A.: Human striatum is differentially activated by delayed, omitted, and immediate registering feedback. Front. Hum. Neurosci. **6**, 243 (2012)
22. Yang, E., Dorneich, M.C.: The effect of time delay on emotion, arousal, and satisfaction in human-robot interaction. Proc. Hum. Factors Ergon. Soc. Ann. Meet. **59**, 443–447 (2015)
23. Kohrs, C., Angenstein, N., Brechmann, A.: Delays in human-computer interaction and their effects on brain activity. PLoS One **11**, e0146250 (2016)
24. Yang, E., Dorneich, M.C.: The emotional, cognitive, physiological, and performance effects of variable time delay in robotic teleoperation. Int. J. Soc. Robot. **9**, 491–508 (2017)
25. Kannel, W.B., Kannel, C., Paffenbarger, R.S., Cupples, L.: Heart rate and cardiovascular mortality. Framingham study. Ame. Heart J. **113**, 1489–1494 (1987)

26. Benetos, A., Rudnichi, A., Thomas, F., Safar, M., Guize, L.: Influence of heart rate on mortality in a french population. role of age, gender, and blood pressure. Hypertension **33**, 44–52 (1999)
27. Okamura, T., Hayakawa, T., Kadowaki, T., Kita, Y., Okayama, A., Elliott, P., Ueshima, H.: Resting heart rate and cause-specific death in a 16.5-year cohort study of the Japanese general population. Am. Heart J. **147**, 1024–1032 (2004)
28. Riedl, R., Léger, P.-M.: Fundamentals of NeuroIS: Information Systems and the Brain. Springer, Berlin, Heidelberg (2016). https://doi.org/10.1007/978-3-662-45091-8
29. Riedl, R., Kindermann, H., Auinger, A., Javor, A.: Technostress from a neurobiological perspective - system breakdown increases the stress hormone cortisol in computer users. Bus. Inf. Syst. Eng. **4**, 61–69 (2012)
30. Riedl, R., Kindermann, H., Auinger, A., Javor, A.: Computer breakdown as a stress factor during task completion under time pressure: identifying gender differences based on skin conductance. Adv. Hum. Comput. Interact. **2013**, 1–8 (2013). Article ID 420169
31. Fischer, T., Riedl, R.: Lifelogging as a viable data source for NeuroIS researchers: a review of neurophysiological data types collected in the lifelogging literature. In: Davis, F.D., Riedl, R., vom Brocke, J., Léger, P.-M., Randolph, A.B. (eds.) Information Systems and Neuroscience. LNISO, vol. 16, pp. 165–174. Springer, Cham (2017). https://doi.org/10. 1007/978-3-319-41402-7_21
32. Riedl, R., Randolph, A., Vom Brocke, J., Léger, P.-M., Dimoka, A.: The Potential of Neuroscience for Human-Computer Interaction Research. In: AIS (eds.) Proceedings of SIGHCI 2010, p. 16 (2010)
33. Dimoka, A., Banker, R.D., Benbasat, I., Davis, F.D., Dennis, A.R., Gefen, D., Gupta, A., Ischebeck, A., Kenning, P.H., Pavlou, P.A., et al.: On the use of neurophysiological tools in is research: developing a research agenda for NeuroIS. MIS Q. **36**, 679–702 (2012)
34. Attig, C., Rauh, N., Franke, T., Krems, J.F.: System latency guidelines then and now – is zero latency really considered necessary? In: Harris, D. (ed.) EPCE 2017. LNCS (LNAI), vol. 10276, pp. 3–14. Springer, Cham (2017). https://doi.org/10.1007/978-3-319-58475-1_1

Health Belief Model and Organizational Employee Computer Abuse

Mario Silic[1(✉)], Mato Njavro[1], Dario Silic[2], and Goran Oblakovic[2]

[1] University of St. Gallen, St. Gallen, Switzerland
{mario.silic,mato.njavro}@unisg.ch
[2] Zagreb School of Economics and Management, Zagreb, Croatia

Abstract. This study is set out to examine the determinants that drive preventive/protective as well as abusive behaviors among employees in the context of information security by extending the health belief model - a model set out to explain and predict healthy behaviors in human beings. A field experiment, accompanied by online surveys in two financial organizations in the US and India is conducted, measuring employees' actual security behaviors. We identified factors (perceived susceptibility, perceived barriers, and self-efficacy) that have the largest effect on employee's security behaviors. We offer several theoretical contributions and implications for practice.

Keywords: Health belief mode · Employee compliance · Computer abuse
Security compliance · Employee security

1 Introduction

1.1 A Subsection Sample

Computer abuse stemming from the inside of the organization has been identified as one of the major—if not the biggest—concern for Information Systems (IS) security managers [1]. Studies have found that more than half of all security breaches are caused by low-level of employees' IS security compliance [2, 3] and offenders include current as well as former employees, costing the organization more in damages than those attributed to external hackers [4].

Irrespective of the intentions, insider abuse necessitates two premises: Employees have to have *"access privileges and ... [an] intimate knowledge of internal organizational processes that may allow them to exploit weaknesses"* [1], and can take form of non-volitional (e.g. accidental entry of data) or volitional actions (employee is deliberately doing an action but without any malicious intentions). The threats arising from organizational insiders are identified as one of the greatest concerns for Information Systems (IS) security managers [1]. Various studies confirmed that the individual user with an organization is the least secured link in the entire organizational IT security ecosystem [5–9]. The Global State of Information Security survey of 9,700 CxOs [4] found that top offenders of insider crimes are current and former employees where insider crimes seem to be more costly or damaging than incidents perpetrated by external attackers.

© Springer International Publishing AG, part of Springer Nature 2018
F. F.-H. Nah and B. S. Xiao (Eds.): HCIBGO 2018, LNCS 10923, pp. 187–205, 2018.
https://doi.org/10.1007/978-3-319-91716-0_15

Information security research has examined several different theories, methods and techniques (e.g., deterrence techniques, anti-neutralization techniques, SETA training programs, etc.) for persuading employees to behave securely in organizations. Despite the fact that many of these techniques are rather efficient in mitigating the security risk, in reality, employees still continue to violate IT security policies [10–22]. For instance, organizations developed security education, training, and awareness (SETA) programs so that users can make a conscious decision to comply with organizational security policies in order to adopt compliant computer security behavior. While the importance of SETA programs is widely acknowledged and accepted both by scholars and practitioners [9, 23–25], little empirical research was conducted to understand the effectiveness of SETA initiatives [24–26].

Thus, a valid question we could ask is: *"Can we influence and shape employee's security behavior before it becomes non-compliant?"*. By better understanding the employee security behavior, defined as *"the behavior of employees in using organizational information systems (including hardware, software, and network systems, etc.), and such behavior may have security implications"* [27], organizations could increase their organizational security and leave less opportunities for IT security policy violations. One way to achieve this would be to influence employee's actions by stressing the protective (e.g. using a strong password) and preventive behaviors (e.g. locking the PC screen when not working). One model that is particularly interesting when it comes to the individual's protective and preventive behaviors comes from the medical area – health beliefs model (HBM) [28]. HBM is mainly used to explain and predict preventive health care behavior by focusing on the attitudes and beliefs of individuals. In the IT security context, the employee security behavior can be seen as a security practice, which, if not managed well, can lead to a security incident. Similarly, in the medical context the preventive health care behavior (e.g. wearing sunscreen to avoid skin cancer) will help to avoid the event from occurring.

We argue that health beliefs model can explain preventive and protective employee's behaviors and as such can be useful to better understand which factors influence and shape employee's behaviors. This study, therefore, provides three unique contributions to the information security literature by (1) extending health belief model; (2) studying the effects of health belief core constructs on behavioral intentions and actual behavior; and (3) examining US and India cultural dimension impact on preventive and protective employee's security behaviors.

In the following, we will present the theoretical background and develop our research model. Then, we will describe the approach and context chosen to empirically test our model, and report our findings. The paper concludes with a discussion on the results, implications and limitations of our study.

2 Theoretical Background

Important number of studies has dealt with the employee security-behavior phenomenon. Various behavior models have been suggested, such as rational choice and beliefs [29], fear [30], accountability [31], self-control and moral beliefs [32], disgruntlement [1], and leadership and organizational culture [33]. This research draws on the health belief model to understand employee security behavior.

2.1   Employee Security Behavior

Organizations are trying to tackle employee security behavior by implementing numerous security measures that include software or hardware protections (e.g. anti-virus software or firewalls), data and information encryption safeguards, monitoring systems or network detection systems. Despite all different measures in place, security attacks are significantly increasing [34]. The report from Checkpoint [34] that surveyed more than 1,300 companies and organizations worldwide found that on average 106 malicious software (malware) attacks are affecting companies where users downloaded infected files from almost 63% of companies and in 52% of cases this was caused by PDFs, and 3% for Office documents. This high number of non-compliant employee's security behaviors can be explained by the fact that employees in their quest of being more productive and efficient look to use tools, software and hardware that were not previously approved by the organizational IT department. This practice is called Shadow IT and represents all hardware, software, or any other solutions used by employees inside of the organizational ecosystem that did not receive any formal IT department approval [35]. In this context there has to be a right balance between what an employee needs in terms of systems (e.g. tools, software, hardware) and what organization can provide. This balance between needs and possibilities needs to be carefully studied in order not to jeopardize the organizational IT system.

IS research has extensively researched the security behavior that an individual will have during the technology adoption process through various theoretical lenses such as Technology Acceptance Model [36] or Theory of Planned Behavior [37], which, were focusing on the individual's intention to use security technology [38]. However, security behavior is not guided only by protective technologies (e.g. firewall that prevents unauthorized access) but also by positive technologies (e.g. technology that that is used to increase job productivity, efficiency, competitiveness, or entertainment) [39]. In this context, security behavior is not just about the technology adoption but encompasses a much wider range of conscious decisions such as choosing the right level of password security or regularly backing up important data. All these actions are not about the technology adoption or use, but are more about how to take the right decision where an employee in the organization has to reflect and take an action, for which he or she is accountable. Clearly, adoption theories such as Technology Adoption Model are not appropriate in this context where individual's conscious decision-making process is of central interest. Hence, theories from other fields such as criminology or psychology can provide a solid foundation to better understand the cognitive individual's behavioral process. A particularly interesting model, coming from the health care, is health beliefs model that we use as theoretical basis for this study.

2.2   Health Belief Model

Health belief model is a psychological model that attempts to explain and predict health behaviors [28] and as such is of one the best known and most widely used theories in health behavior research [40]. Its core assumption is that an individual will take a health-related action if the person believes that a negative health condition can be avoided, has a positive expectation that the undertaken action will lead to negative health condition avoidance and believes that his or her action will result in a successful health action. According to the health beliefs model, to change users' behavior, three conditions have to be met: (1) the individual must be personally susceptible to the health problem; (2) the individual should understand that risk can lead to serious harm; and (3) the individual must understand what actions can be taken to avoid harm and the costs or benefits of those actions [41–44].

In the IS context, to the best of our knowledge, only three studies used HBM. Ng et al. [26] studied workplace user secure behavior and found that perceived suscepti-bility, perceived benefits, and self-efficacy are significant predictors and determinants of use behavior when it comes to email attachments. Study also hypothesized perceived severity to have moderating relationship with other constructs (e.g. susceptibility, benefits) which is not supported by past HBM studies from the health field. Williams et al. [46] used HBM to study Indian working professionals and found that HMB constructs are mainly validated except barriers and self-efficacy. Study also introduced two levels of severity: organization and individual. Davinson and Sillence [45] study used HBM to explore user's perceptions of 'being safe and secure' when conducting financial transactions. Study used interviews recruited from the university and several organizations and found the level of the users' perceived threat to be low which was explained by the fact that users' generally do not believe they would be victim of fraud whilst conducting transactions online or at the ATM.

All three studies offered some first evidence when it comes to applicability and efficacy of using HBM to further understand employee security behavior antecedents. However, there are a couple of challenges with past studies which could potentially limit their findings. First, the past studies measured intentions rather than actual behavior which could be a limiting factor especially taking into account that HBM comes from the health area where intentions and actual behaviors can have important consequences on individual's health condition (e.g. it is much more realistic that a patient will really take the medicament in order to avoid illness rather than the fact that patient will have or not the intention to do it). Hence, we believe that including actual behavior in the model could bring important insights about the employee security behavior. Also, by focusing only on intentions rather than on actual behavior can lead to social desirability bias, as it does not assess real-world behavior. Indeed, several studies suggest that in an information security context, it is better and more realistic to measure actual behaviors rather than intentions [10, 47, 48] because intentions do not always lead to behavior [10]. Second, past studies focused on a single culture (one country) and it would be interesting to understand how HBM would apply and behave between different countries and cultures. We argue that since health views may be very different from country to country, HBM would also provide different results. For instance, in USA individuals are probably much more careful about their health con-dition and would react differently to various risks related to health challenges when compared to a different culture where these values could be quite different – example in India individuals could be less susceptible to fear of getting sick and consequently, may be less eager to reject or accept the action to be treated. In a study on beliefs about medicines among students that identified themselves as having Asian or European cultural background a significant association between cultural background and beliefs about the benefits and dangers of medicines was found [49]. Third, past studies did not focus on one single organization (or more) but used participants from variety of organizations (for instance Williams et al. [46]'s 237 study participants are potentially working in 237 different organizations) which could be a limiting factor as the overall security management can be very different from organization to organization. This can lead to different individual's interpretation of different constructs such as perceived severity or perceived susceptibility. Finally, past studies modified the original HBM as they did not include the modifying socio-demographic variables of, for instance, gender, age, and ethnicity.

3 Hypothesis Development

We are using the original health belief model, including the socio-demographic factors (gender, age and ethnicity). We added the actual behavior construct which, especially in the health context, should bring more precision and realism to the results. While the study done by Ng et al. [26] did use the actual behavior construct, the construct itself was based on the self-reported user's evaluation which is subject to self-report bias. Our study, uniquely, introduces the actual behavior construct, which reports the user actual security behavior. Our research model is depicted below in Fig. 1. In our research we omit the cues to action concept as empirical findings, related to cue to action construct, have been quite inconsistent which was attributed to poor operationalization and a lack of psychometric rigor [46].

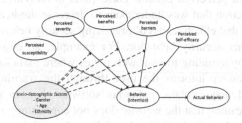

Fig. 1. Research model

3.1 Hypotheses

Perceived susceptibility refers to "subjective risks of contracting a condition" [28]. In the IS context, susceptibility is expressed as the likelihood of a security event to take place. The More an employee feels possibility of experiencing the consequences of the negative outcome, the more likely he or she will look to avoid and prevent his or her behavior from occurring. The same applies in the opposite direction where he or she will less likely be engaged in the preventive behavior if the possibility of the negative outcome is low. For instance, Windows users are advised to install and actively use anti-malware software to safeguard them against malware dangers. On the other side, Linux users are less likely to install any anti-malware software as Linux is known of being the malware free operating system. Similarly, when an employee is accessing internet web sites from organizational PC, often, he or she is informed, through web browser warning message, about the dangers of getting malware as website's security is compromised. In this content, employee will most likely stop his or her surfing activity as the risk of the negative outcome is high. Hence, we hypothesize that:

H1. Perceived susceptibility to security incidents is positively related to intentions to carry out computer security behavior.

In the health context, this construct refers to an individual's conviction regarding the serious ness of a given health problem. Similarly in the IS context, perceived severity represents individual's belief about the seriousness of being affected with a particular security event. For instance, if employee's action leads to security event where organizational data and systems are damaged, the consequences may not be limited only to these security issues but they could be extended to implications related to employee's job (e.g. employee would be fired as consequence to his or her actions). More importantly, another consequence could impact larger organizational assets where loss of confidentiality, integrity, or availability could have much more serious consequences for the entire organization. For example, all employees could be prevented from working. However, employees may have different perceptions of the level of severity as they could have different interpretations of the negative outcomes their actions may produce. Consistent with HBM, we hypothesize that:

H2. Perceived severity to security incidents is positively related to intentions to carry out computer security behavior.

HBM suggests that perceived benefits correspond to individual's beliefs about the effectiveness of the action that was undertaken to decrease the health threat. Hence, if an employee believes that effectiveness of practicing security behavior is high, then this will lead to the higher security behavior. For example, an employee may practice preventive behavior by avoiding to visit web pages where malicious software resides. However, if web browser informs the user through the warning message that the website to be visited may contain malicious software, but, in reality, it is a false positive warning – meaning that the website does not contain any malicious software – then employee may be less likely inclined to follow the web browser warning advice. Conversely, if the effectiveness of the application (e.g. anti-virus) is high, then employee will more likely use it to prevent the threat from occurring. Hence, we hypothesize:

H3. Perceived benefits to security incidents are positively related to intentions to carry out computer security behavior.

Perceived barriers to action represent an obstacle in performing a specific action that is related to the fact that the action can be inconvenient or unpleasant for the individual. This negative aspect occurs as consequence of an action that can lead to the threat reduction, and as such is seen as efficient, but creates also the situation which is uncomfortable for the individual. In the IS context, this can be translated as practicing safe behavior that will create situation where employee's task will be not convenient, harder to execute, time consuming, etc. despite the effectiveness such situation leads to.

Example is when employee needs to use two-factor authentication (get access to organizational system with the combination of password and physical token) instead of the previous simple task that corresponded to username/password combination. Clearly, two-factor authentication will lead to higher security decreasing possible risks, but will require from an employee an additional step which he or she can find inconvenient as token is something that employee has to use each time a new log in occurs. Consequently, perceived barriers will increase an individual's level of inconvenient and associated perceived cost (effort to perform the action) which will lead to a reduced security behavior level. Hence, we hypothesize:

H4. Perceived barriers to security incidents are negatively related to intentions to carry out computer security behavior.

Perceived self-efficacy was added to the original HBM and was found to be an important and useful antecedent of the healthcare behavior [50]. It comes from the social cognitive theory and corresponds to individual's self-confidence in his ability to perform a behavior [51]. It is about the confidence that the individual has in implementing the safeguard. In the security context, an individual's ability to take recommended security precautions will play an important role in preventing the risk from occurring. Clearly, individuals that show high self-efficacy will be more likely to start the desired behavior by spending more time on resolving and understanding the threat [51]. Past studies found that self-efficacy had a positive relationship with intentions to perform the behavior [29]. We also expect that, following the HBM, higher level of the perceived self-efficacy will lead to higher intentions to perform the security behavior. Hence, we hypothesize:

H5. Higher perceived self-efficacy is positively associated to intentions to carry out computer security behavior.

The HBM theorizes that socio-demographic factors will influence and moderate their relationship with the core HBM constructs (perceived susceptibility, perceived barriers, perceived self-efficacy, perceived benefits and perceived severity). For Liang and Xue [87] avoiding IT threats provides "ample evidence demonstrates that risk tolerance is a personal trait related to demographics variables including age, gender… race". In this research, we focus on age, gender and culture (or ethnicity) as demographic moderators. Reason is that the corresponding moderating relationships were successfully tested and modeled in IS research by Venkatesh, Morris, Davis and Davis [52] when creating UTAUT model. Hence, we hypothesize:

H6abcde. Age significantly moderates the relationship between perceived susceptibility, perceived barriers, perceived self-efficacy, perceived benefits, perceived severity and computer security behavior.
H7abcde. Gender significantly moderates the relationship between perceived susceptibility, perceived barriers, perceived self-efficacy, perceived benefits, perceived severity and computer security behavior.
H8abcde. Culture significantly moderates the relationship between perceived susceptibility, perceived barriers, perceived self-efficacy, perceived benefits, perceived severity and computer security behavior.

A strong relationship between intentions and actual behavior is theorized in the Theory of Reasoned Action [53], the Theory of Planned Behavior [37] and several other studies which empirically tested these studies. According to these theories, behavior corresponds to individual's deliberate intentions to act in a certain way. Consequently, behavioral intention affects an individual's actual behavior to perform the action. In the IS context, scholars such as Limayem et al. [54] suggest that actual behavior should be used in order to avoid wrong conclusions about the results where intentions may not always lead to actual behaviors. Moreover, in the IS security context to get a higher degree of realism it is far better to measure actual behaviors rather than intentions [10, 47, 48] as behavioral intentions may not always be the same as the actual behavior [10]. Hence, we hypothesize:

H9. Intentions to carry out computer security behavior are positively associated with actual security behavior.

4 Research Design

4.1 Participants

To test our research hypotheses, we conducted a field experiment and survey with two organizations: a financial company located in USA and a financial company located in India. We did not restrict our sample to any category (e.g. only managers) but preferred to include various employee levels.

Our sample size, following the "rule of ten" [55], which suggests that the sample size for nine constructs should be at least 90, largely exceeded the recommended number, ensuring good power and reliability of the results.

4.2 Measures

We measured all items (except actual security behavior) on an 11-point Likert scale from 0 to 10 that we adapted from previously validated instruments. Behavior was adapted from [26], perceived severity from [57], perceived susceptibility from [56], perceived benefits [26, 58], perceived barriers [56, 57] and perceived self-efficacy from [59]. All items were reviewed by 4 information security professionals. After a consensus was reached (three rounds), the survey was pretested with pre-selected employees from the US organization. We received 35 responses. The pre-test enabled us to conclude that our model yielded acceptable results (we tested reliability of measurement items for each construct using Cronbach's α; convergent and discriminant validity using principal components analysis).

4.3 Procedures

As we did not want to rely on vignette-based scenarios, we aimed to minimize bias by assessing real-life situations. Similar to past studies [e.g. 60] we used deception to increase the realism of the results. This was achieved by using the following procedure:

- In the two participating organizations, employees were invited to evaluate a new financial product image where they would need to choose which product image they like the most.
- In the second step, the employee would click on the Start button after what a warning message would appear informing the employee about the potential risk if he or she continues to visit the website.
- Employees could choose either to 'Exit' or 'Continue' which allowed us to measure their actual behavior whether they chosen to stop their activity (actual behavior value is 0) or continue (value is 1). In both cases, participants were taken to the online survey.

In the first initial phase (product photo evaluation) we collected participant's IP and MAC addresses that enabled us match them against the unique IP/MAC addresses we received through the online survey (the survey was anonymous for all participants; however, each survey participant was tracked by their IP/MAC address). Prior to starting the online survey we explained to participants that we collected some information in the initial phase (IP/MAC addresses) and asked for their consent to use this information. Also, we explained the purpose and objective of the study. All employees provided their consent.

Finally, with this approach we were able to get a very reliable list of participants, who completed the initial phase of photoproduct evaluation, followed by the online survey, which we identified through the unique combination of IP/MAC addresses.

4.4 PLS Analysis

Our research was built on the survey data (phase 2), and employs variance-based structural equation modeling (SEM) techniques [61, 62]. SEM is particularly useful in the IS research where often the key concepts are not directly observable [63]. Also, it is considered be a "silver bullet" for estimating causal models in many model and data situations [64]. The research model was tested using the partial least squares (PLS) approach. Our initial assumption was that all hypothesized relations are linear. Hence, due to the possible non-linear relationships that may be present in our model, standard PLS software packages based on a linear assumption may not be suitable for testing and analyzing our model. We opted for WarpPLS 3.0 [65], a powerful PLS-based structural equation modeling software that has the capability to test both linear and non-linear relationships (e.g. U shaped and S shaped functions). Also, it can perform Logistic regression that we used in this study. Furthermore, covariance-based SEM requires a larger sample size, whereas PLS can produce stable path coefficients and significant p-values with lower sample sizes (usually less than 100) [65].

5 Analysis and Results

5.1 Descriptive Statistics and Measurement Model Results

In total, we received 260 responses from the sample frame of 950. Seven responses were removed for implausible response times (less than 2 min) needed to complete the survey (average 8 min). Hence, our final sample size was 253 with 169 responses for US sample and 84 for Indian sample.

In order to assure that our model has acceptable convergent and discriminant validity and reliability we performed tests detailed in the following paragraph.

First, we assessed the research model fit checking the recommended p-values for the average path coefficient (APC) and the average r-squared (ARS) which should be lower than 0.05. Also, the average variance inflation factor (AVIF) should be lower than 5 [65]. All values for both models (US and India) indicated that all three criteria are met. Thus, our model has good explanatory quality.

Next, we reviewed the reliability results. We found that the composite reliabilities (CR) range from 0.825 to 0.953 for US sample, and from 0.889 to 0.918 for India sample, which is above the recommended threshold value of 0.70. Finally, we examined the average variance extracted (AVE) for each variable construct and found that it exceeded the 0.5 value as per Fornell and Larcker [66] recommendation.

Further, we wanted to establish discriminant validity. We checked the results from the test where we entered the square root of the reflective construct's AVE on the diagonal. Corresponding correlations between the constructs are placed in the lower left triangle. As it can be observed from the results the AVE of each latent construct is higher than the construct's highest squared correlation. We can conclude that the discriminant validity test has been established.

Next, we calculated Stone-Geisser Q-squared coefficients [67, 68] and performed a full collinearity check. Results showed following Q-squared coefficients: BEH 0.608, ACT 0.041 for US sample and BEH 0.365, ACT 0.025 for India sample. As all coefficients were greater than zero we can conclude that they present acceptable predictive validity [65]. For the full collinearity check we used variance inflation factors (VIFs) for each of the latent variables. As per recommendation of [69, 70] the recommended VIFs value should be lower than 5. As we did not observe any value higher than 5 we concluded that full collinearity check provided enough evidence to reject the existence of multicollinearity. In addition we checked for Simpson's paradox as wanted to be sure that path coefficient of a predictor latent variable with respect to a criterion latent variable have opposite signs [71]. We proceeded by examining all links between the predictor and criterion variables. Our examination did not reveal any instances of Simpson's paradox. Finally, we checked the cross loadings to establish the discriminant validity. This is done when loading of an indicator on a construct is higher than any other cross-loading of the indicator with other constructs. All constructs, except CS3 in India model (we decided to delete it), were higher than 0.7. Hence, we can conclude that the model findings are meaningful.

Finally, we have checked for common method bias and found that the common method bias is not a concern for this research.

5.2   Analysis of Full Model

Figure 2 shows the result of the full model.

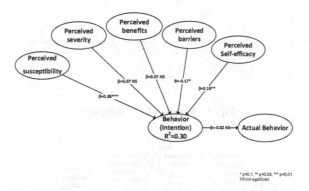

Fig. 2. Results of full model analysis

The results indicate an R^2 value of 0.30, which means that the theoretical model explained a substantial amount of variance in the adoption intention. Taking into account the 10% criterion, which suggests that the R^2 value of a dependent variable should be at least 10% in order to make a meaningful interpretation, our theoretical model shows good explanatory power.

Our structural model results indicate that perceived susceptibility to security incidents is positively related to intentions to carry out computer security behavior ($\beta = 0.38$, $p < 0.001$). Perceived self-efficacy (H5) is also positively associated to intentions to perform security behavior ($\beta = 0.18$, $p < 0.05$). The model results show that perceived barriers have negative relationship with intentions ($\beta = -0.17$, $p < 0.1$). However, H2 and H2, where we hypothesized that perceived severity ($\beta = 0.07$, $p = 0.12$) and perceived benefits ($\beta = 0.07$, $p = 0.13$) would be positively linked to intentions to carry out computer security behavior are not supported. In addition, H9 where we argued that intentions to carry out computer security behavior will be positively associated with actual security behavior is also not supported ($\beta = -0.02$, $p = 0.35$). Finally, we did not find that age or gender significantly moderates the relationship between perceived susceptibility, perceived barriers, perceived self-efficacy, perceived benefits, perceived severity and computer security behavior. Hence, hypotheses H7abcde and H8abcde are not supported.

Further, to compare moderating effects of culture we conducted multi-group comparison.

5.3   Analysis of US vs India Sample

Figures 3 and 4 shows the results for US and India sample respectively.

To conduct multi-group analysis we followed method as suggested by Kock [72]. We found that there are significant differences in relationships between perceived

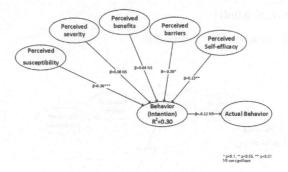

Fig. 3. Results of US subgroup

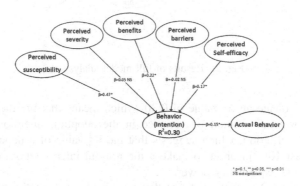

Fig. 4. Results of India subgroup

barriers → behavior (intention) and behavior (intention) → actual behavior. Interestingly, we can see that in India sample, behavior intention is positively associated with the actual behavior (β = 0.15, p < 0.1), while in US sample the relationship is negative and not significant.

6   Discussion

6.1   Interpretation of Findings

Our research has several interesting findings. First, we did not find any positive relationship between behavior intention and actual behavior. This is a quite unexpected result and in contrast with many past studies [e.g. 73, 74] which found intention to be linked to the actual behavior. However, when analyzing US and India samples, we found that this relationship is positive and significant in India case, but non-significant in US subgroup. This could be explained by the fact that culture was found to affect how an individual responds to a potential risk of being exploited by others [22, 75–78]. According to Tse et al. [79] the cognitive propensity to risk is likely to affect the perceptions of the presence of risks as well as the evaluation of the risks. Consequently, in US and India sample, which, according to Hofstede [80] are two representatives of individualism and collectivism dimensions of culture, behavior intention could lead to a different actual behavior. This confirms that behavioral intentions may not always be the same as the actual behavior [10]. Second, contrary to the findings of Williams et al. [46]'s study, where their subjects were relatively computer savvy which could explain their different finding, we found a significant relationship between perceived barriers and intentions. This is in line with the HBM literature [41]. In our context, participants are coming the financial industry, which should bring more precision and generalizability to this finding. Further, we found self-efficacy to have a positive relationship with behavior intention. This is in line with past studies on the preventive security behavior where this relationship was also significant and positive [26, 81]. While we found perceived susceptibility to be positively linked to behavior intention, we did not find any significant relationship between perceived severity, perceived benefits and behavior intention. It is quite surprising, and contrary to past results [26, 46], that perceived benefits do not affect employee's security behavior. This could be explained by the fact that employees may not have an easy and effective way to check if, for instance, the web site they are visiting is authentic or that it makes sense. It could be also that organizational (especially in the financial industry) systems are well protected through, for instance, firewall protection, which limits employee's exposure to insecure websites. Another explanation could be that users often tend to put their security concerns aside if the benefits of using internet are made pertinent [82]. When it comes to the perceived severity our finding confirms previous studies which found severity to be a weak predictor of health behavior [83]. It is interestingly to notice that the risks related to the severity do not seem to be an issue for employees. This can be explained by the fact that employees are well trained and cautioned against risks that they may encounter while conducting online surfing activities. In terms of the perceived susceptibility users tend often to show certain form of unrealistic optimism [84], where they believe that nothing bad would happen to them. In our case, susceptibility positively affects behavior intention which is conform to past health belief literature.

Overall, we can see that perceived susceptibility, perceived barriers, and self-efficacy are important determinants of the user's security behavior.

6.2 Implications for Practice

Our study offers several implications for practitioners. First, in order to design an efficient intervention program that aims at implementing preventive information security behaviors, organizations should seek to look at perceived susceptibility, perceived barriers, and self-efficacy, which have the largest effect on user's security behavior. Clearly, information security awareness programs should look at these factors in order to design a more appropriate, efficient and persuading message, which could warn and inform employees about the risks of not being compliant with organizational security policies. These risks could be expressed as the susceptibility to become victim where user should be clearly given instructions how to behave in uncertain situations where outcomes may bring negative consequences. The same applies to the perceived barriers where user needs to understand that despite the fact that preventive actions may be time-consuming or require an effort from the user's side, it is necessary to be more vigilant in order to take conscious decision to perform the appropriate preventive behavior. Second, educating users by taking an approach where security communication would be designed in such a way that it incorporates susceptibility, benefits and self-efficacy content could further increase protective security behavior. Many users that have high self-efficacy, often, may not be motivated to behave in a compliant way as they could argue that the security is not their concern but the concern of the organization [85]. Clearly, users often delegate security to their organization which are expected to take appropriate security measures [45]. However, one challenge in highlighting the risks through the protective security communication approach, could be that too much of the negative communication may lead to higher fear among users to take any action (good or bad). Consequently, users' decision-making process could be impacted where conscious decision to perform the appropriate preventive behavior would be negatively affected. From the theoretical standpoint, this calls for further research to understand the motives and reasons behind these opposite results.

6.3   Theoretical Contributions

Our research offers several new contributions to the information systems security literature. First, we reduced the gap in our understanding of the user computer security behavior. By applying health belief model, we found that some of the core model's concepts exercise significant influence on user's conscious decision to behave securely in order to perform the appropriate preventive behavior. Hence, we established an analogy between health core constructs and information security behaviors. This not only contributes to the existing body of knowledge by providing new insights into the employee compliance problem, but also opens new directions to further understand how findings from the health sector can be used to better scope and understand employee's compliance challenges. Second, our study extends on the few initial studies that used health belief model [e.g. 46], by introducing the cultural aspect where two different culture (US and India) provided new insights that help to better generalize the results. To the best of our knowledge, this is the first study that introduces cultural dimension that offers a different view on employees' protective security behaviors in different countries. Indeed, by comparing strongly individualism (US) to collectivism (India) cultures we could observe significant differences between the findings from past studies and ours. Moreover, we found that perceived barriers in a different cultural context, behaves differently. For instance, we identified barriers to be negatively associated with behavior intention in US, but to be not significant in India. Third, our research measured user's actual behavior, which strengthens our findings. However, surprisingly, we did not find any strong relationship between behavioral intention and actual behavior. This mismatch between behavioral intention and actual intention was highlighted by Crossler et al. [10]. Our research confirms that behavioral intention when it comes to preventive security behavior may not be the most realistic measure. In other words, behaviors may not lead to actual compliant actions. This is even more pronounced when cultural dimension is introduced where in US sample behavioral intention relationship with actual behavior is not established, while in India sample the link is positive and significant. The cultural aspect seems to influence the behavioral decision making process. This represents an important finding that should be taken into a basis for further theorizing regarding the security preventive behavior. Finally, our research has applied the original health belief model adding the socio-demographic factors (age, gender and culture) and as such, provides new insights into employee's compliance issues. By doing so, we added new theoretical understandings of preventive and protective employee's behaviors and how they can be applied and extended to existing information security countermeasures with the objective to influence, shape and improve employee's security behaviors.

6.4   Future Research and Limitations

One of the limitations of this study is that we focused on a single type of the policy violation that refers to the malicious software. This may lead to incorrect interpretations and we suggest that future research further examines this by introducing other types of violations that can be, for instance, related to the Shadow IT usage, which is particularly widespread in the organizational context [35, 86].

Another limitation of this study is that our sample was based on two cultures only, which are quite different in terms of different cultural dimensions. In order to have higher generalizability future studies could compare other cultures (e.g. introducing a culture from Africa) to further understand how culture influences preventive security behaviors.

References

1. Willison, R., Warkentin, M.: Beyond deterrence: an expanded view of employee computer abuse. MIS Q. **37**, 1–20 (2013)
2. Dhillon, G., Moores, S.: Computer crimes: theorizing about the enemy within. Comput. Secur. **20**, 715–723 (2001)
3. Stanton, J.M., Stam, K.R., Mastrangelo, P., Jolton, J.: Analysis of end user security behaviors. Comput. Secur. **24**, 124–133 (2005)
4. http://www.pwc.com/gx/en/consulting-services/information-security-survey/key-findings.jhtml
5. Leach, J.: Improving user security behaviour. Comput. Secur. **22**, 685–692 (2003)
6. Warkentin, M., Willison, R.: Behavioral and policy issues in information systems security: the insider threat. Eur. J. Inf. Syst. **18**, 101–105 (2009)
7. Posey, C., Bennett, R.J., Roberts, T.L.: Understanding the mindset of the abusive insider: an examination of insiders' causal reasoning following internal security changes. Comput. Secur. **30**, 486–497 (2011)
8. Greitzer, F.L., Moore, A.P., Cappelli, D.M., Andrews, D.H., Carroll, L.A., Hull, T.D.: Combating the insider cyber threat. IEEE Secur. Priv. **6**, 61–64 (2008)
9. D'Arcy, J., Hovav, A., Galletta, D.: User awareness of security countermeasures and its impact on information systems misuse: a deterrence approach. Inf. Syst. Res. **20**, 79–98 (2009)
10. Crossler, R.E., Johnston, A.C., Lowry, P.B., Hu, Q., Warkentin, M., Baskerville, R.: Future directions for behavioral information security research. Comput. Secur. **32**, 90–101 (2013)
11. Maimon, D., Alper, M., Sobesto, B., Cukier, M.: Restrictive deterrent effects of a warning banner in an attacked computer system. Criminology **52**, 33–59 (2014)

12. Anderson, B.B., Vance, A., Kirwan, B., Eargle, D., Howard, S.: Why users habituate to security warnings: insights from fMRI. In: 2014 IFIP 8.11 Dewald Roode Security Workshop (2014)
13. Vance, A., Siponen, M.T.: IS security policy violations: a rational choice perspective. J. Organ. End User Comput. (JOEUC) **24**, 21–41 (2012)
14. Vance, A., Lowry, P.B., Egget, D.: Increasing accountability through user-interface design artifacts: a new approach to addressing the problem of access-policy violations. MIS Q. **39** (2), 345–366 (2015)
15. Silic, M., Njavro, M., Oblakovic, G.: Understanding color risk appropriateness: influence of color on a user's decision to comply with the IT security policy—evidence from the U.S. and India. In: Nah, F.F.-H., Tan, C.-H. (eds.) HCIBGO 2017. LNCS, vol. 10294, pp. 412–423. Springer, Cham (2017). https://doi.org/10.1007/978-3-319-58484-3_32
16. Silic, M., Cyr, D., Back, A., Holzer, A.: Effects of color appeal, perceived risk and culture on user's decision in presence of warning banner message. In: Proceedings of the 50th Hawaii International Conference on System Sciences, January 2017
17. Silic, M.: Understanding colour impact on warning messages: evidence from us and India. In: Proceedings of the 2016 CHI Conference Extended Abstracts on Human Factors in Computing Systems, pp. 2954–2960. ACM (2016)
18. Silic, M., Silic, D., Oblakovic, G.: Restrictive deterrence: impact of warning banner messages on repeated low-trust software use. In: 18th International Conference on Enterprise Information Systems (ICEIS 2016), vol. 2, pp. 435–442. SCITEPRESS (2016)
19. Silic, M., Silic, D., Oblakovic, G.: The effects of colour on users' compliance with warning banner messages across cultures. In: ECIS 2016, Istanbul (2016)
20. Silic, M., Cyr, D.: Colour arousal effect on users' decision-making processes in the warning message context. In: Nah, F.F.-H., Tan, C.-H. (eds.) HCIBGO 2016. LNCS, vol. 9752, pp. 99–109. Springer, Cham (2016). https://doi.org/10.1007/978-3-319-39399-5_10
21. Silic, M., Barlow, J., Ormond, D.: Warning! A comprehensive model of the effects of digital information security warning messages. In: The 2015 Dewald Roode Workshop on Information Systems Security Research, IFIP, pp. 1–32. IFIP, Dewald (2015)
22. Silic, M., Back, A.: Information security: critical review and future directions for research. Inf. Manag. Comput. Secur. **22**, 279–308 (2014)
23. Albrechtsen, E., Hovden, J.: Improving information security awareness and behaviour through dialogue, participation and collective reflection. An intervention study. Comput. Secur. **29**, 432–445 (2010)
24. Puhakainen, P., Siponen, M.: Improving employees' compliance through information systems security training: an action research study. MIS Q. **34**, 757–778 (2010)
25. Karjalainen, M., Siponen, M.: Toward a new meta-theory for designing information systems (IS) security training approaches. J. Assoc. Inf. Syst. **12**, 518–555 (2011)
26. Ng, B.-Y., Kankanhalli, A., Xu, Y.C.: Studying users' computer security behavior: a health belief perspective. Decis. Support Syst. **46**, 815–825 (2009)
27. Guo, K.H.: Security-related behavior in using information systems in the workplace: a review and synthesis. Comput. Secur. **32**, 242–251 (2013)
28. Rosenstock, I.M.: The health belief model and preventive health behavior. Health Educ. Monogr. **2**, 354–386 (1974)
29. Bulgurcu, B., Cavusoglu, H., Benbasat, I.: Information security policy compliance: an empirical study of rationality-based beliefs and information security awareness. MIS Q. **34**, 523–548 (2010)
30. Johnston, A.C., Warkentin, M.: Fear appeals and information security behaviors: an empirical study. MIS Q. **34**, 549–566 (2010)

31. Vance, A., Eargle, D., Ouimet, K., Straub, D.: Enhancing password security through interactive fear appeals: a web-based field experiment. In: 46th Hawaii International Conference on System Sciences (HICSS), pp. 2988–2997. IEEE (2013)
32. Myyry, L., Siponen, M., Pahnila, S., Vartiainen, T., Vance, A.: What levels of moral reasoning and values explain adherence to information security rules? An empirical study. Eur. J. Inf. Syst. **18**, 126–139 (2009)
33. Hu, Q., Dinev, T., Hart, P., Cooke, D.: Managing employee compliance with information security policies: the critical role of top management and organizational culture. Decis. Sci. **43**, 615–660 (2012)
34. Checkpoint: Threats are on the rise. Know your landscape (2015)
35. Silic, M., Back, A.: Shadow IT–a view from behind the curtain. Comput. Secur. **45**, 274–283 (2014)
36. Davis, F.D., Bagozzi, R.P., Warshaw, P.R.: User acceptance of computer technology: a comparison of two theoretical models. Manag. Sci. **35**, 982–1003 (1989)
37. Ajzen, I.: The theory of planned behavior. Organ. Behav. Hum. Decis. Process. **50**, 179–211 (1991)
38. Dang-Pham, D., Pittayachawan, S.: Comparing intention to avoid malware across contexts in a BYOD-enabled Australian university: a protection motivation theory approach. Comput. Secur. **48**, 281–297 (2015)
39. Dinev, T., Hu, Q.: The centrality of awareness in the formation of user behavioral intention toward protective information technologies. J. Assoc. Inf. Syst. **8**, 386–408 (2007)
40. Carpenter, C.J.: A meta-analysis of the effectiveness of health belief model variables in predicting behavior. Health Commun. **25**, 661–669 (2010)
41. Janz, N.K., Becker, M.H.: The health belief model: a decade later. Health Educ. Behav. **11**, 1–47 (1984)
42. Rogers, R.W.: A protection motivation theory of fear appeals and attitude change. J. Psychol. **91**, 93–114 (1975)
43. Witte, K.: Putting fear back into fear appeals: the extended parallel process model. Commun. Monogr. **59**, 329–349 (1992)
44. Witte, K.: Fear control and danger control: a test of the extended parallel process model (EPPM). Commun. Monogr. **61**, 113–134 (1994)
45. Davinson, N., Sillence, E.: Using the health belief model to explore users' perceptions of 'being safe and secure' in the world of technology mediated financial transactions. Int. J. Hum.-Comput. Stud. **72**, 154–168 (2014)
46. Williams, C.K., Wynn, D., Madupalli, R., Karahanna, E., Duncan, B.K.: Explaining users' security behaviors with the security belief model. J. Organ. End User Comput. (JOEUC) **26**, 23–46 (2014)
47. Anderson, C.L., Agarwal, R.: Practicing safe computing: a multimedia empirical examination of home computer user security behavioral intentions. MIS Q. **34**, 613–643 (2010)
48. Mahmood, M.A., Siponen, M., Straub, D., Rao, H.R., Raghu, T.: Moving toward black hat research in information systems security: an editorial introduction to the special issue. MIS Q. **34**, 431–433 (2010)
49. Horne, R., Graupner, L., Frost, S., Weinman, J., Wright, S.M., Hankins, M.: Medicine in a multi-cultural society: the effect of cultural background on beliefs about medications. Soc. Sci. Med. **59**, 1307–1313 (2004)
50. Sheeran, P., Abraham, C.: The health belief model. Predict. Health Behav. **2**, 29–80 (1996)
51. Bandura, A.: Self-efficacy: toward a unifying theory of behavioral change. Psychol. Rev. **84**, 191 (1977)
52. Venkatesh, V., Morris, M.G., Davis, G.B., Davis, F.D.: User acceptance of information technology: toward a unified view. MIS Q. **27**, 425–478 (2003)

53. Ajzen, I., Fishbein, M.: Understanding Attitudes and Predicting Social Behavior. Prentice-Hall, Englewood Cliffs (1980)
54. Limayem, M., Hirt, S.G., Cheung, C.M.: How habit limits the predictive power of intention: the case of information systems continuance. MIS Q. **31**, 705–737 (2007)
55. Barclay, D., Higgins, C., Thompson, R.: The partial least squares (PLS) approach to causal modeling: Personal computer adoption and use as an illustration. Technol. Stud. **2**, 285–309 (1995)
56. Champion, V.L.: Instrument development for health belief model constructs. Adv. Nurs. Sci. **6**, 73–85 (1984)
57. Woon, I., Tan, G.-W., Low, R.: A protection motivation theory approach to home wireless security. In: ICIS 2005 Proceedings, p. 31 (2005)
58. Paternoster, R., Simpson, S.: Sanction threats and appeals to morality: testing a rational choice model of corporate crime. Law Soc. Rev. **30**, 549–583 (1996)
59. Compeau, D.R., Higgins, C.A.: Computer self-efficacy: development of a measure and initial test. MIS Q. **19**, 189–211 (1995)
60. Boss, S.R., Galletta, D.F., Lowry, P.B., Moody, G.D., Polak, P.: What do systems users have to fear? Using fear appeals to engender threats and fear that motivate protective security behaviors. MIS Q. **39**(4), 837–864 (2015)
61. Chin, W.W.: The partial least squares approach to structural equation modeling. Mod. Methods Bus. Res. **295**, 295–336 (1998)
62. Chin, W.W., Marcolin, B.L., Newsted, P.R.: A partial least squares latent variable modeling approach for measuring interaction effects: results from a Monte Carlo simulation study and an electronic-mail emotion/adoption study. Inf. Syst. Res. **14**, 189–217 (2003)
63. Roldán, J.L., Sánchez-Franco, M.J.: Variance-based structural equation modeling: guidelines for using partial least squares. In: Research Methodologies, Innovations and Philosophies in Software Systems Engineering and Information Systems, p. 193 (2012)
64. Hair, J., Ringle, C., Sarstedt, M.: PLS-SEM: indeed a silver bullet. J. Mark. Theory Pract. **19**, 139–152 (2011)
65. Kock, N.: WarpPLS 4.0 User Manual. ScriptWarp Systems, Laredo, Texas, USA (2010)
66. Fornell, C., Larcker, D.F.: Evaluating structural equation models with unobservable variables and measurement error. J. Mark. Res. (JMR) **18**, 39–50 (1981)
67. Geisser, S.: A predictive approach to the random effect model. Biometrika **61**, 101–107 (1974)
68. Stone, M.: Cross-validatory choice and assessment of statistical predictions. J. R. Stat. Soc. Ser. B (Methodol.) **36**, 111–147 (1974)
69. Hair, J.F.: Multivariate Data Analysis. Prentice Hall, Upper Saddle River (2009)
70. Kline, R.B.: Principles and Practice of Structural Equation Modeling. Guilford Press, New York (2011)
71. Wagner, R.K., Torgesen, J.K., Rashotte, C.A.: Development of reading-related phonological processing abilities: new evidence of bidirectional causality from a latent variable longitudinal study. Dev. Psychol. **30**, 73 (1994)
72. Kock, N.: Advanced mediating effects tests, multi-group analyses, and measurement model assessments in PLS-based SEM. Int. J. e-Collab. (IJeC) **10**, 1–13 (2014)
73. Siponen, M., Mahmood, M.A., Pahnila, S.: Employees' adherence to information security policies: an exploratory field study. Inf. Manag. **51**, 217–224 (2014)
74. Siponen, M., Pahnila, S., Mahmood, M.A.: Compliance with information security policies: an empirical investigation. Computer **43**, 64–71 (2010)
75. Weber, E.U., Hsee, C.: Cross-cultural differences in risk perception, but cross-cultural similarities in attitudes towards perceived risk. Manag. Sci. **44**, 1205–1217 (1998)

76. Yamagishi, T., Yamagishi, M.: Trust and commitment in the United States and Japan. Motiv. Emot. **18**, 129–166 (1994)
77. Silic, M., Back, A.: The influence of risk factors in decision-making process for open source software adoption. Int. J. Inf. Technol. Decis. Mak. **15**, 1–35 (2015)
78. Silic, M., Back, A.: Information security and open source dual use security software: trust paradox. In: Petrinja, E., Succi, G., El Ioini, N., Sillitti, A. (eds.) OSS 2013. IAICT, vol. 404, pp. 194–206. Springer, Heidelberg (2013). https://doi.org/10.1007/978-3-642-38928-3_14
79. Tse, D.K., Lee, K.-H., Vertinsky, I., Wehrung, D.A.: Does culture matter? A cross-cultural study of executives' choice, decisiveness, and risk adjustment in international marketing. J. Mark. **52**, 81–95 (1988)
80. Hofstede, G.: Culture's Consequences. Sage, Beverly Hills (1980)
81. Herath, T., Rao, H.R.: Protection motivation and deterrence: a framework for security policy compliance in organisations. Eur. J. Inf. Syst. **18**, 106–125 (2009)
82. Spiekermann, S., Grossklags, J., Berendt, B.: E-privacy in 2nd generation E-commerce: privacy preferences versus actual behavior. In: Proceedings of the 3rd ACM Conference on Electronic Commerce, pp. 38–47. ACM (2001)
83. Milne, S., Sheeran, P., Orbell, S.: Prediction and intervention in health-related behavior: a meta-analytic review of protection motivation theory. J. Appl. Soc. Psychol. **30**, 106–143 (2000)
84. Weinstein, N.D.: Reducing unrealistic optimism about illness susceptibility. Health Psychol. **2**, 11 (1983)
85. Weir, C.S., Douglas, G., Carruthers, M., Jack, M.: User perceptions of security, convenience and usability for ebanking authentication tokens. Comput Secur. **28**, 47–62 (2009)
86. Silic, M.: Dual-use open source security software in organizations – Dilemma: help or hinder? Comput. Secur. **39**(Part B), 386–395 (2013)
87. Liang, H., Xue, Y.: Avoidance of information technology threats: a theoretical perspective. MIS Q. 71–90 (2009)

Deception Detection in Online Automated Job Interviews

Nathan W. Twyman[1(✉)], Steven J. Pentland[2], and Lee Spitzley[3]

[1] Missouri University of Science and Technology, Rolla, MO, USA
nathantwyman@mst.edu
[2] Boise State University, Boise, ID, USA
spentland@cmi.arizona.edu
[3] University at Albany, SUNY, Albany, NY, USA
lspitzley@cmi.arizona.edu

Abstract. This research-in-progress paper presents a conceptual system for automated deception detection in online interviewing. The design proposes video recordings of responses to predefined, structured interview question sets variously selected based on the desired behavioral metric of interest, such as competence, social skills, or in this case, veracity. Raw behavioral data extracted from video responses is refined to produce indicators of behavioral metrics. A prototype implementation of the design was built and tested experimentally using a job interview scenario. Results of the experimental analysis provide evidence of the potential of the concept.

Keywords: Behavioral assessment · Automated interviewing
Deception detection · Human risk assessment · Virtual agent-based interviewing

1 Introduction

Automated interviewing research is trying to bring information about potential human deception to more people in more places. Reliability has been a key hurdle to collecting and making use of deception assessments in job interviews, audit reviews, and other relevant applications. Identification of reliable human indicators of deception has been a major theme of this area of research. Linguistic, vocalic, oculometric, kinesic, and facial movement variations are among the sources of indicators that have been explored. Such human signal variations are referred to as *deception indicators* to the extent they are shown to be reliably correlated with deceptive but not truthful communication [1, 2].

Deception detection research has traditionally focused on identifying and exploring the robustness of specific indicators of deception, such as skin conductance or respiration rate. Automated human risk assessment research has followed a similar pattern, finding evidence for the potential of indicators such as movement freeze [3], pupil dilation [4], and vocal pitch [5].

Relatively little research has examined automated analysis of exploratory interviewing such as job interviews. The exploratory nature of these interviews precludes

F. F.-H. Nah and B. S. Xiao (Eds.): HCIBGO 2018, LNCS 10923, pp. 206–216, 2018.
https://doi.org/10.1007/978-3-319-91716-0_16

exclusive use of short answer or binary yes-or-no questions, thereby falling outside the scope of some published design concepts [e.g. 6].

The knowledge proposition for this study is to outline concepts and constraints for a theoretical class of interview system that could derive behavioral metrics from open-ended interviewing scenarios, using an automated approach under the general framework of virtual agent-based interviewing [7, 8].

From the employer standpoint, the objective of the job interview is to determine if an interviewee is the most suited for a specific position. The interviewee in-turn seeks to present themselves in a way that makes the employer believe they are the best fit for the position. There is an expectation by the employer that only the most sought-after characteristics are being presented by the interviewee. And to some degree, there is an expectation that qualification enhancement or puffery is occurring. Levashina and Campion [9] found that 95% of undergraduate job seekers engage in some form of image creation or ingratiation when interviewing.

When an interviewee presents themselves to be more qualified than they are, they significantly increase the probability of making it to the next round of interviews [9]. Skillful self-presentation tactics may even be a quality that is necessary for specific types of work such as sales or customer service. However, interview performance does not necessary correlate with actual job performance [10] – meaning that employers aren't getting the quality of worker that they expected based on the interview process. This can be especially problematic when companies seek specific technical skills and expect new-hires to possess a certain level of competency. When skill enhancement becomes exaggeration or fabrication, the long-term performance of a company can suffer when unqualified employees are hired.

2 Conceptual Development

The first property we propose for the concept is a structured questioning technique. Structured approaches to interviewing have been shown to curb the effects of self-presentation tactics [10], as interviewees simply have fewer opportunities to self-present in a manner that will sway the interviewer. Some IS research has used similar structured interviewing techniques to uncover concealed knowledge during screening interviews: Twyman et al.'s [6] *autonomous scientifically controlled screening systems* (ASCSS) class of systems use binary yes-or-no questions to remove variation due to question or response type from the interview process.

However, the interviewing scenarios that are the interest of this study require the use of open-ended questions. We propose that for these contexts, open-ended questions be generated in groups of three or more, with each group of questions possessing attributes similar in type, level, personalness, and importance. Each question set should contain questions of interest, but also at least two baseline questions, or in other words, questions for which responses are reasonably verifiable. Because they only request information that is already available or easily inferred, baseline questions are often excluded from these types of interviews. However, we propose they be purposely included for the current design.

For instance, in job interviews, a set of expected skills can be used as the basis for generating a set of interview questions about the interviewee's skills in that area. Some skills such as the use of basic office software might be so prevalent among applicants that they are virtually guaranteed. Yet questions about such skills could serve as the baseline questions in this design. If desired, greater certainty of the presence of these baseline skills could be obtained by pairing objective performance assessments with the automated interview.

Ultimately, open-ended responses to baseline questions should be compared to the questions of interest. For this stage, we propose taking an approach similar to prior IS research that has used non-invasive sensors to collect useful behavioral and psychophysiological data. Sensors used in this area of research include cameras (normal or specialized), microphones, platforms, and human-friendly lasers. In interview settings, these sensors have been used to generate raw oculometric, vocalic, linguistic, kinesic, proxemic, and even cardiorespiratory data, with varying degrees of fidelity [3, 4, 11–14].

This kind of data is subject to influence from many mechanisms besides deception, which is a key reason for using baseline questions. Large variations in behavioral responses to target questions as compared to baseline questions serve as flags or indicators of deception. Some related research has taken a data-driven approach when identifying indicators that are most diagnostic for the context of interest, while others have chosen a top-down theoretical approach. The former is excellent for discovery and exploration, while the latter provides greater confidence in reproducibility and generalizability.

In most cases, the theoretical explanation for automated veracity assessment has relied on the concept of leakage or strategic behaviors. *Leakage* theory asserts that lying produces natural human responses that the deceiver typically tries to mask or otherwise control. The theory suggests that such behavioral or psychophysiological responses "leak" out because of an inherent inability to control or mask them all [15]. Some later theories additionally proposed strategic behaviors as an explanation for some indicators. *Strategic* indicators are abnormal behaviors purposely exhibited by deceivers in an attempt to appear truthful [16]. Whether leaked or strategic, observed behavior when deceiving is compared to normal (i.e., truthful) behavior to gauge potential as a deception indicator [17].

The magnitude of these indicators varies from person to person. For instance, where one individual is naturally stoic in their speech or body movement, another may be naturally dynamic. A small drop in movement may be a major variation for one but minor for the other. Prior research has addressed this issue by requiring within-interviewee standardization prior to classification [6].

Neither leakage theory nor strategic explanations necessarily guarantee particular behaviors that will be displayed. Presumably, different deception indicators may be displayed depending on interpersonal, group, or cultural nuances. For instance, a person who is less worried about self-image may focus more on portraying believable linguistic content in their deception, while an image-conscious deceiver may put more effort into appropriate body language. With theories that provide no specific indicator guarantees, it is little wonder that no "Pinocchio's nose" or highly reliable indicator of deception has been found or is expected to be found. We therefore propose that an effective design will necessarily measure and incorporate a breadth of potential deception indicators. A classification that fuses many indicators should more reliably catch deception when predicting which of many indicators will be present is not possible. Table 1 summarizes each property of the proposed class of systems.

Table 1. Summary of concepts for online interviewing system for deception detection

	Proposed system properties
1	Structured questioning technique, using homogenous question sets, each containing baseline questions and target questions of interest
2	Questions delivered by a virtual agent
3	During responses, collect raw psychophysiological and/or behavioral data using non-invasive sensor(s)
4	Scale data by interviewee prior to analysis
5	Fuse multiple disparate signals to generate a risk score reflecting deception likelihood

3 Method

To examine the potential of the proposed class of systems, we first instantiated the concepts in a prototypical system design. An experiment was conducted to evaluate the concept. Explanatory analyses were conducted to evaluate the potential of various behavioral indicators of deception. Performance analyses are currently in progress.

3.1 Prototype Implementation

To provide evidence toward proof-of-concept, we instantiated the design guidelines in an example prototypical system dubbed the Asynchronous Video-based Interviewing System, or AVIS.

AVIS displays interview questions sequentially in a text-based form, allowing respondents a limited amount of time to consider the question and a limited amount of time for a response. The amount of time for each is displayed to the interviewee between each question (see Fig. 1). Upon advancing, the interviewee considers the question for 60 s (see Fig. 2), then begins responding. Video recording does not occur except during response time (see Fig. 3), and this fact is made clear to the interviewee by showing a black screen where they would normally see themselves via a webcam.

Interviewee response recordings are tagged by question set, and stored for post-processing. AVIS extracts audio from each response, and extracts vocalic features from vocalic signal. Text is generated by applying IBM's Watson speech-to-text function to the audio signal, and linguistic features are generated by applying the text to SPLICE, a program that processes text and returns quantitative summaries of language and measurements of linguistic cues [18].

The video is currently processed using Intraface [19], a facial point mapping program, and Affectiva, a facial emotion classification system. These generate raw facial emotion measures and Cartesian coordinates of various points on the face for each frame of video.

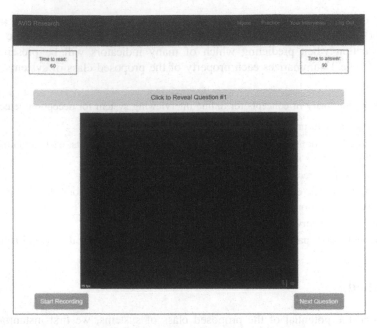

Fig. 1. Information screen displayed between questions

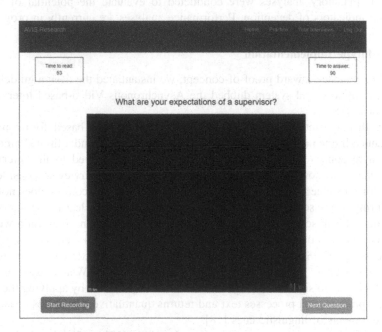

Fig. 2. Example question "pondering" stage, prior to response time. Interviewees have the option of starting the response whenever they are ready (via the green button)

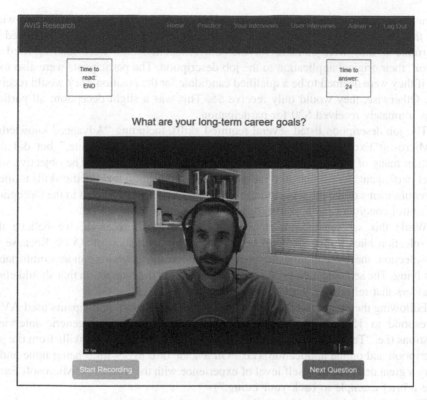

Fig. 3. Example interview question response

Whereas some prior research has used specialized hardware such as eye tracking systems and 3D cameras, such equipment is commonly not available in many potential application scenarios, and were not incorporated in this version of AVIS.

3.2   Experimental Evaluation

A mock job interview experiment was conducted with undergraduate students at a large university in the United States. The experiment employed AVIS as the interviewing mechanism for screening job applicants.

Experimental Procedure. Prior to arriving for the study, participants were asked to complete an online questionnaire. The questionnaire was designed to mirror a basic employment application and contained questions about education, work experience, and skills. The skill-related questions asked participants to rate their level of experience with common software packages, including Microsoft Excel, Microsoft Word, Adobe Photoshop, R Studio, and Oracle SQL. Additionally, participants were asked to rate their level of experience with StatView, a statistical package that does not exist.

When participants arrived for the study, they were told that they would be participating in a mock job interview using a one-way interview system. They were then given a description of the job for which they would be interviewing. Participants were told that both their online application and interview responses would be evaluated to determine if they were suitable for the job. All participants were then allowed to "tailor" their original application to the job description. The participants were also told that if they were deemed to be a qualified candidate for the position, they would receive $20. Otherwise, they would only receive $5. This was a slight deception: all participants ultimately received $20 for participation.

The job description listed several required skills, including "Advanced knowledge of Microsoft Excel" and "Proficiency with StatView Software Suite," but did not mention many of the other skills outlined on the online application. The objective was to get participants to self-select to fabricate their qualification for specific skills to meet the requirements of the job description. Thus, there was no assignment to the Deception or Control condition; participants chose their condition.

While this self-selection is unusual for this type of research, we believe the self-selection bias in this case will be beneficial for evaluation of AVIS. Because of self-selection, the Deception group probably reflects those who are more comfortable with lying. The self-selection preserves a naturalness to the interaction that should elicit behaviors that reflect real-world lies.

Following the opportunity to tailor their online application, participants used AVIS to respond to 15 interview questions. The interview contained generic interview questions (i.e. "Tell me about yourself") and a question set mirroring skills from the job description and online application. (i.e. "On a scale of 0 to 5 with 0 being none and 5 being a great deal, rate yourself level of experience with the following: Microsoft Excel Give a brief example to back your rating.")

The design of the experiment allowed researchers to track exaggerations and fabrications made to an application to appear qualified for a job. The online application completed prior to viewing the job description was treated as ground truth. After the interview, participants took a post-task survey.

Participants. A total of 89 undergraduate students participated in the experiment (Male = 35; Female = 54). Of the total number of participants, 26% reported having previously used a similar one-way interviewing system during employment activities. When given the opportunity to tailor their online application, 43.8% of participants increased their self-rating for Microsoft Excel; 21.3% of participants increased their self-rating for Microsoft Word; and 31.4% reported having at least some level of experience with StatView, when previously reporting that they had never used the software.

3.3   Analysis and Results

Raw signals were averaged for each response. The averages for the responses to the skills questions were standardized within subjects to control for interpersonal differences. Video, audio, and linguistic data were separately submitted to principal components analysis for both key component identification and dimension reduction. A promax rotation was used because of the expected correlation between components. The final rotated components were labeled according to the behavioral trait they seemed to be reflecting, based on the items that loaded heavily. The labeled components and example items are shown in Table 2.

Table 2. Labeled behavioral components

Vocal and linguistic components	Facial components
Vocal power trend	Mouth position
Vocal excitement	Facial affect
	Facial anger and contempt
Word complexity	Facial fear
Descriptive language use	Mouth openness
Language complexity	Main mouth movement
Present tense use	Upper eyelid movement
Word count	Bottom of nose movement
Negative word use	Nose bridge movement
Past tense use	Outer brow movement
	Inner brow movement
	Lower eyelid movement
	Mouth corners movement
	Main mouth acceleration
	Upper eyelids acceleration
	Bottom of nose acceleration
	Inner brow acceleration
	Outer brow acceleration
	Lower eyelid acceleration
	Mouth corners acceleration
	Nose to mouth corners vertical distance
	Inner brows to lower lids vertical distance
	Upper lips to lower lips vertical distance
	Upper lids to outer brows vertical distance
	Right outer brow vertical position
	Left outer brow vertical position
	Nostrils vertical position

A multivariate regression model was specified with Deception as the independent variable and the components in Table 2 as dependent variables. The linguistic variables were still undergoing data preparation and were not included. Deception had a significant impact on the twelve components displayed in Fig. 4. The units of measurement in Fig. 4 are standard deviations, so an interpretation for fear would be that on average, interviewees showed about half of a standard deviation more fear than normal when fabricating a response, as compared to their own baseline responses.

The results indicate that compared to the baseline questions, deceptive responses were associated with the total amount of movement dropping in locations across the face, and the acceleration of the facial movement that did occur was also slower. At the

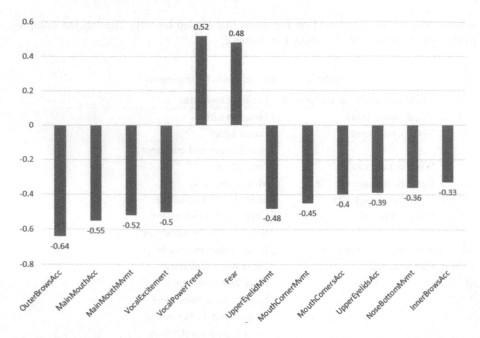

Fig. 4. Graphical representation of the coefficient estimates of significant (p < .05) behaviors during deceptive responses

same time, the amount of fear expressed on the face rose significantly. From a vocalic perspective, there was a significant drop in what we termed "Vocal Excitement," which means the pitch, intensity and jitter of the voice decreased. Probably relatedly, the response marked a low point in a trend toward increased vocalic power in later responses.

4   Discussion

The goal of this study was to investigate the potential of a new class of system that could identify deception during interviews that required open-ended questions. Results of the experimental evaluation of the AVIS provide evidence that in this type of scenario, at least some behavioral variations do manifest that are diagnostic of deception. Specifically, facial animation decreases, both in terms of overall movement and the speed of change of that movement. Decreased facial movement has been identified as a potential deception indicator in a prior research study in a related context [20], and this study provides further evidence of this indicator, and indicates some level of robustness to a context with less control in terms of the allowance of open-ended questions. This is the first study identifying decreased facial acceleration as a potential deception indicator and its cause is unclear, but may be related to the facial freeze associated with both psychophysiological and behavioral mechanisms theorized to accompany deception. Additional research is needed to determine whether this is so.

Exaggeration. A follow-up investigation identified instances of exaggeration in the interview. While exaggeration is commonly identified as a type of deception, most of the behavioral indicators that were diagnostic of fabrication were not diagnostic of exaggeration. This is an important finding because some exaggeration is common in interviewing, and if such a system conflates it with fabrication, the value of its output may be diluted. Instead, the results suggest that exaggeration looks very different from fabrication when it comes to diagnostic behavioral indicators.

Additional analyses are underway. These focus on identifying the classification potential of this type of system but estimating AVIS's ability to predict deception. Though it is clear that deception creates behavioral anomalies, classification analyses will help provide an initial idea of how discriminatory and how useful the anomalies are.

References

1. DePaulo, B.M., Lindsay, J.J., Malone, B.E., Muhlenbruck, L., Charlton, K., Cooper, H.: Cues to deception. Psychol. Bull. **129**(1), 74–118 (2003)
2. Vrij, A.: Detecting Lies and Deceit: Pitfalls and Opportunities, 2nd edn. Wiley, London (2008)
3. Twyman, N.W., Elkins, A.C., Burgoon, J.K., Nunamaker Jr., J.F.: A rigidity detection system for automated credibility assessment. J. Manag. Inf. Syst. **31**(1), 173–202 (2014)
4. Twyman, N.W., Proudfoot, J.G., Schuetzler, R.M., Elkins, A.C., Derrick, D.C.: Robustness of multiple indicators in automated screening systems for deception detection. J. Manag. Inf. Syst. **32**(4), 215–245 (2015)
5. Derrick, D.C., Elkins, A.C., Burgoon, J.K., Nunamaker, J.F., Zeng, D.D.: Border security credibility assessments via heterogeneous sensor fusion. IEEE Intell. Syst. **25**(3), 41–49 (2010)
6. Twyman, N.W., Lowry, P.B., Burgoon, J.K., Nunamaker Jr., J.F.: Automated screening for detecting purposely concealed knowledge in individuals. J. Manag. Inf. Syst. **31**(3), 106–137 (2014)
7. Derrick, D., Jenkins, J.L., Nunamaker Jr., J.F.: Design principles for special purpose, embodied, conversational intelligence with environmental sensors (SPECIES). ACM Trans. Hum. Comput. Interact. **3**(2), 62–81 (2011)
8. Nunamaker, J.F., Derrick, D.C., Elkins, A.C., Burgoon, J.K., Patton, M.W.: Embodied conversational agent-based kiosk for automated interviewing. J. Manag. Inf. Syst. **28**(1), 17–48 (2011)
9. Levashina, J., Campion, M.A.: Measuring faking in the employment interview: development and validation of an interview faking behavior scale. J. Appl. Psychol. **92**(6), 1638 (2007)
10. Barrick, M.R., Shaffer, J.A., DeGrassi, S.W.: What you see may not be what you get: relationships among self-presentation tactics and ratings of interview and job performance. Am. Psychol. Assoc. **94**(6), 1394–1411 (2009)
11. Burgoon, J., Nunamaker, J.F., Metaxas, D.: Noninvasive measurement of multimodal indicators of deception and credibility. University of Arizona (2010)
12. Burgoon, J.K., Jensen, M., Twyman, N.W., Meservy, T.O., Metaxas, D.N., Michael, N., Elder, K., Nunamaker Jr., J.F.: Automated kinesic analysis for deception detection. In: Proceedings of the HICSS-43 Symposium on Credibility Assessment and Information Quality in Government and Business, Koloa, Hawaii, USA, 5–8 Jan 2010

13. Meservy, T.O., Jensen, M.L., Kruse, J., Burgoon, J.K., Nunamaker, J.F.: Automatic extraction of deceptive behavioral cues from video. In: Kantor, P., Muresan, G., Roberts, F., Zeng, D.D., Wang, F.-Y., Chen, H., Merkle, R.C. (eds.) ISI 2005. LNCS, vol. 3495, pp. 198–208. Springer, Cham (2005). https://doi.org/10.1007/11427995_16
14. Moffitt, K., Elkins, A.C., Burgoon, J.K., Nunamaker Jr., J.F.: Rapid noncontact credibility assessment via linguistic/vocalic analyses. In: Proceedings of the National Communication Association 96th Annual Convention, San Francisco, CA, USA (2010)
15. Ekman, P., Friesen, W.V.: Nonverbal leakage and clues to deception. Psychiatry 32(1), 88–106 (1969)
16. Buller, D.B., Burgoon, J.K.: Interpersonal deception theory. Commun. Theory 6(3), 203–242 (1996)
17. Elkins, A.C., Derrick, D.C., Gariup, M.: The voice and eye gaze behavior of an imposter: automated interviewing and detection for rapid screening at the border. In: Conference of the European Chapter of the Association for Computational Linguistics, Avignon, France (2012)
18. Moffitt, K.C., Giboney, J.S.: Structured Programming for Linguistic Cue Extraction (SPLICE). http://splice.cmi.arizona.edu/
19. De la Torre, F., Chu, W.-S., Xiong, X., Vicente, F., Ding, X., Cohn, J.F.: Intraface. In: IEEE International Conference on Automatic Face and Gesture Recognition (FG), Ljubljana, Slovenia (2015)
20. Pentland, S.J., Twyman, N.W., Burgoon, J.K., Nunamaker Jr., J.F., Diller, C.B.R.: A video-based screening system for automated risk assessment using nuanced facial features. J. Manag. Inf. Syst. 34(4), 970–993 (2017)

The Effects of 360-Degree VR Videos on Audience Engagement: Evidence from the New York Times

Guan Wang, Wenying Gu, and Ayoung Suh[✉]

School of Creative Media, City University of Hong Kong,
Hong Kong, China
guanwang3-c@my.cityu.edu.hk, wenyingu@um.cityu.edu.hk,
ahysuh@cityu.edu.hk

Abstract. This study examines the current application of 360-degree VR videos in the news industry. Both the advantages and challenges of 360-degree VR videos in enhancing audience experiences and engagement are discussed. To better understand the effects of immersive technology on audience engagement, this study selects the case of *The New York Times* (NYT). Data were crawled from 598 videos on the NYT YouTube account for analyses. The results showed that 360-degree VR videos generally performed worse than non-VR videos in enhancing audience engagement. An interaction effect was found between video format (360-degree VR or non-VR) and content genres.

Keywords: 360-degree VR videos · Audience engagement · Content genre

1 Introduction

Immersive technology is defined as technology that blurs the boundary between the physical and virtual worlds, thus enabling users to experience a sense of immersion [39]. Immersive technology, including augmented reality (AR) and virtual reality (VR), is becoming increasingly pervasive in education [26, 29], commerce [27, 28], and entertainment [11, 43]. For example, VR has been introduced into the news industry to enhance the audience's sense of presence related to an event and impart the illusion that the user is located in the place where the event occurred [17, 36]. By optimizing 360-degree videos in VR, news outlets can provide their audiences with immersive experiences [20, 70].

Previous studies have argued that 360-degree VR videos enhance audience engagement by increasing the audience's sense of presence, enjoyment, involvement, and empathy [63, 67]. While these immersive videos are gaining popularity, some researchers have pointed out that they may limit the user experience [62, 69]. Users have reported feeling sick, uncomfortable, bored, or distracted when watching 360-degree VR videos [45, 57, 74]. Inconsistent findings and anecdotal evidence regarding the effects of immersive technology on the user experience have led to the question of how 360-degree VR videos can enhance audience engagement. Despite the increasing scholarly attention toward this subject, little research has systematically

© Springer International Publishing AG, part of Springer Nature 2018
F. F.-H. Nah and B. S. Xiao (Eds.): HCIBGO 2018, LNCS 10923, pp. 217–235, 2018.
https://doi.org/10.1007/978-3-319-91716-0_17

examined the influence of immersive technology on audience engagement within the news industry. To fill this gap, the present study seeks to answer the research question: How do audiences engage with 360-degree VR videos compared to non-VR videos?

This study examines the case of *The New York Times* (*NYT*), which launched a VR project, called NYT VR, in collaboration with Google in 2015. The project distributed 1.3 million Google Cardboard VR headsets to *The NYT* subscribers for free [19], and several hundreds of 360-degree VR videos have been produced to date. To analyze the degree to which the audience has engaged with NYT VR videos, this study collected data from 598 videos updated to *The NYT*'s YouTube account, including 360-degree VR videos and non-VR videos, produced by *The NYT*. Several indicators, such as number of views, comments, likes, and dislikes, were compared for analysis.

2   Related Work

2.1   360-Degree VR Videos

Known for their spherical views, 360-degree VR videos allow viewers to observe a virtual environment in any direction [49]. They provide an innovative way to portray events and locations so that viewers feel they are present within the virtual space [47, 71]. Many applications have incorporated 360-degree VR videos captured by omni-directional cameras to offer users more realistic, navigable views. Such videos are becoming popular on video-streaming platforms, including YouTube and Facebook [72]. Recent advancements have made it possible to view 360-degree videos using several types of devices. Content can be viewed through head-mounted displays (HMDs) with stereoscopic capabilities, which enable users to experience full immersion as well as mobile devices that use a smartphone as a VR display, which enables users to experience partial immersion [70]. With HMDs, users control the camera's orientation and can turn their head at any time to view the surrounding environment. Users watching 360-degree VR videos through a mobile device can control the camera by physically moving the device or by tapping on the screen to pan around the virtual space [73]. Additionally, in desktop-based players, users can drag the video horizontally and vertically with their cursor to rotate the camera [56]. These viewing conditions represent a continuum of the degree of immersion; control of the viewport can be actuated through standard peripheral devices, such as a mouse and keyboard on desktop computers or sensors on a mobile device, either by manually moving it in sync with one's head movements to simulate real-life view changes [79]. While researchers have generally conclude that audiences are interested in and excited to explore their 360-degree surroundings, HMDs are crucial to enhancing the audience's sense of presence and immersion [21, 55, 73]. Each display device has a distinct advantage. For example, Magnus [49] found that while the use of an HMD increases the user's sense of presence, which is beneficial for navigational purposes, most users prefer using a mobile device due to its practicality. Van den Broeck et al. [74] also suggested that users may prefer watching 360-degree videos on their smartphones due to the simplicity of exploration and their familiarity with navigational controls.

2.2   360-Degree VR Videos in the News Industry

The proliferation of inexpensive devices and 360-degree VR videos brought VR to masses, thus giving rise to practical applications in various industries, such as education, entertainment, and news [9, 33, 61]. In the news industry, many organizations, such as *The NYT*, *The Guardian*, Euronews, CNN, and BBC, have adopted VR to produce news media, which allows their audiences to experience the incidents or situations described in their stories [17, 76]. The 2014 launch of Google Cardboard provided a low-cost solution to these organizations and allowed VR news to reach larger audiences. Additionally, video-streaming platforms (e.g., Facebook and You-Tube) began offering support for publishing and viewing 360-degree VR videos, which has shaped the development of VR technologies [31]. Watching 360-degree VR videos through Google Cardboard headsets become the most accessible form of immersive technology for broad audience consumption [24].

With the advent of VR technologies in the news industry, journalists had to develop new skills and innovative forms of storytelling. Currently, two types of 360-degree VR videos have been adopted by news organizations. The first type refers to documentary-style films, which are usually about 5 to 15 min, that are intended for audiences using VR headsets. The second type are short-form videos (under two minutes), typically intended for "magic window"/browser viewing, which are created with at low cost and with short production periods. Both types of videos are distributed on social media, such as YouTube 360 and Facebook [76]. By creating a sense of presence, 360-degree VR videos enable audiences to witness the emotions of others and thereby feel empathy for them, more so than other media forms [63]. Studies have found that audiences highly enjoy and become emotionally attached to the 360-degree VR videos they watch [9].

2.3   Current Features of 360-Degree VR Videos

Features unique to 360-degree VR videos compared to non-VR videos, include a wide field-of-view, partial control of viewing direction, multiple storylines, and a first-person perspective. First, 360-degree VR videos display a spherical viewing area (i.e., 360° horizontally and 180° vertically). Field-of-view refers to the extent of the observable area [59], and 360-degree videos offer a subset of the full field-of-view to give audiences a natural viewing experience. Second, the audience can control the camera orientation by manually rotating the display or turning their head to view the surrounding environment. Advanced 360-degree VR videos provide functions that zoom and enhance regions of interest [46]. Third, 360-degree VR videos can present multiple storylines simultaneously [40]. For video producers this feature brings both opportunities and challenges. Fourth, a 360-degree video offers a first-person perspective that makes the viewer feel like they are experiencing the depicted event or situation as a video producer would [17] (Table 1).

Table 1. Comparison between 360-degree VR videos and non-VR videos

	360-degree VR	Non-VR
Field of view	Wide	Narrow
View direction	Partially control	No control
Narrative	Multiple storylines simultaneously	Single storyline
First-person perspective	High	Low

2.4   Current Advantages of 360-Degree VR Videos

Compared to non-VR videos, 360-degree VR videos offer several advantages to enhancing audience experiences and engagement.

Sense of Presence. Presence refers to a psychological state in which the user feels they are in one place, even when they are physically situated in another place [28]. This sense of presence can be enhanced through 360-degree VR videos. First, a wider field-of-view raises the authenticity and realism of the viewing experience, which helps viewers develop greater spatial awareness [30, 44, 58]. Second, a first-person perspective within an event or situation also enhances the sense of presence [64]. Third, as the viewer has the ability to rotate the display and observe any point of their surroundings, 360-degree VR videos impart a greater sense of presence than non-VR videos [57, 71, 74]. It is noteworthy that only a partial sense of presence could be achieved in some studies, as the participants could not be separated from the real-world environment while watching 360-degree VR videos [9]. Research shows that the type of display device influences the sense of presence. For example, HMDs perform better than tablet and desktop displays in increasing the user's sense of presence [21, 55, 71, 74].

Empathy. Prior studies have shown that VR can increase the user's empathy toward characters presented in a virtual environment [22, 25], including 360-degree VR videos [66, 67] by conveying another person's experiences or feelings to the audience [65]. In VR environments, viewers may strongly empathize with another person's emotions or situation because they feel as if they are occupying the same physical space and are therefore close to that person [66]. Research has shown that viewers who experience stories through 360-degree VR videos outperform those who read the same stories via text and pictures, not only in terms of presence, but also empathy [71].

Emotion. As several studies have indicated, there are strong correlations between presence and emotions [18, 75] as well as between empathy and emotions [17, 63]. As first-person perspectives tend to draw out a deeper emotional response, 360-degree VR videos are more likely to elicit viewers' emotions and make viewers emotionally engaged with the content [63]. It has been also found that the viewer's dominant mood during watching the 360-degree VR videos was related to positive emotions (e.g., fun, happiness, surprise) [60].

Involvement. Involvement is a state of consciousness in which the audience's attention is attracted to the content [24]. Some researchers argue that, due to the increased display fidelity via an increased field of view and added stereoscopy, the use of 360-degree VR videos encourages more active involvement in the content [49, 50].

2.5   Current Challenges of 360-Degree VR Videos

Despite these advantages over non-VR videos, researchers suggest that 360-degree VR videos have their shortcomings, such as causing motion sickness and physical discomfort among users [32, 74].

Motion Sickness. Motion sickness is characterized by an adverse sense of discomfort, disorientation, nausea, and/or vomiting, which is common for users of contemporary HMD systems [15, 52]. The ailment typically occurs when there is a conflict between the motion of the video and the viewer's real-world perceptions, such as when the viewer is not in control of the protagonist's movements [51]. Moving the camera while capturing a 360-degree VR video is very likely to induce motion sickness in the viewer [24, 74]. Audiences may not view a 360-degree VR video for the same duration that they would a regular video, due to feeling uneasy or experiencing motion sickness [2].

Physical Discomfort. VR devices with HMDs have often been reported as uncomfortable. For devices with manual displays, discomfort occurs when users must hold up the device at the eye level to view the content. Devices that require other movements, such as uncomfortable hand postures and almost complete extension of the arm, can produce tiredness even after a relatively short time [16, 23].

Cognitive Barriers. The novelty of 360-degree VR videos may distract viewers from the content, thereby creating a cognitive barrier. Viewers who experience a greater sense of presence may focus on exploring the environment and fail to recall the key points [62]. Previous studies also found that although 360-degree VR videos with moving viewports elicit higher engagement from viewers and offer a superior viewing experience, these videos are cognitively demanding as they require the user's constant user attention [74].

Orientation and Attention. The viewer's ability to actively control the camera orientation creates a new challenge for 360-degree VR video producers. Because viewers can observe any part of the surrounding environment at any time, they may look in the wrong direction and miss important content [56]. Viewers may also be easily distracted by their surroundings and unintentionally lose track of the VR story [33]. This issue influences the audience's interest in 360-degree VR videos. Viewers often express concerns about whether they are looking in the correct direction [57]. Audience interest is also influenced by the desire to watch a video that follows a narrative or explores an environment [45]. Prior studies have proposed several reorientation techniques to help viewers return to the video's region-of-interest when their attentions are focused outside the intended field-of-view [45, 46, 56, 57].

Satiation. Satiation is a natural human response that occurs when a product is consumed repeatedly [13]. All consumers are likely to feel a decrease in their product enjoyment over time [13]. Repetitive viewing of 360-degree VR videos may cause audiences to lose their curiosity, along with other salient costs. It has been found that the 360-degree VR viewing experience becomes monotonous after several seconds (5–10 s) of initial exploration [74]. To overcome this effect, the information density of the content should be well designed.

Visual Quality. Another important shortcoming mentioned in prior studies is the lower resolution of existing 360-degree VR videos, which are constrained by the current capturing devices [33]. Low visual quality can have a negative effect on audience engagement, regardless of the level of visual realism [47, 55]. Higher quality videos require more storage space and greater network bandwidth for transmission, which introduces yet another challenge [79].

2.6   Audience Engagement in the NYT VR Project

Online content providers, such as news portals, constantly seek to keep their users engaged [38]. Previous studies have defined user engagement as the emotional, cognitive, and behavioral connection that exists between a user and a resource [4]. The connection between the audience and the news content is called audience engagement [14, 41]. The present study examines the audience's experiences and engagement with 360-degree VR videos published by *The NYT* on YouTube. In this study, audience engagement refers to online behavioral engagement in particular, which is measured through actions such as viewing, liking, disliking, and commenting [35]. Table 2 provides descriptions for these actions.

Table 2. Examples of online behavioral actions by YouTube audiences

Action	Description
View	YouTube offers a count based on the number of times a video is viewed
Like	A form of user vote or an expression of appreciation toward a video
Dislike	A form of user vote or an expression of disapproval toward a video
Comment	A form of text-based communication to express opinions about a video's topic(s)

Content Genres. Previous studies have demonstrated that content genres influence audience engagement [38]. Content-related factors can influence the VR user's sense of presence and may override the influence of technological factors [5, 6, 21]. Arapakis et al. [3] found that content sentimentality and polarity affected user engagement in online news. Koehler et al. [37] observed interacting effects between media format (i.e., video or text) and content genre. Extant literature also shows that the video content can influence the experience of 360-degree VR videos [8, 45]. Bleumers et al. [8] found that from a user perspective, certain genres are more suitable for 360-degree VR videos (e.g., hobbies, sports, or travel having scenes without change/with slow pacing). For instance, 360-degree VR videos enable multiple storylines, which can display sport or music events while allowing the audience to self-determine their focus (e.g., their favorite sports player or musician). In addition, as the audience can self-explore the environment by controlling the viewing direction, 360-degree VR videos are suitable for scenes in which the pacing is slow and display of the environment is the key motivation (e.g., documentaries and videos promoting tourism). While most immersive technologies are not suitable for news requiring high immediacy, due to the time- and resource-intensive nature of creating CG-based simulations, 360-degree VR videos can be rapidly captured and produced to meet the demand of immediacy [24]. Prior studies also suggest that different display devices should be adopted according to the content type [48].

360-degree VR videos may augment audience engagement by increasing sense of presence, empathy, emotion and involvement. In contrast, the audience may be less engaged in 360-degree VR videos because of motion sickness, physical discomfort, cognition barriers, orientation failure, satiation and low visual quality. One stream of extant studies stated that people might ignore the motion sickness when they had high sense of presence. For example, prior studies suggested that more presence and involvement could reduce motion sickness [34]. If the effects of advantages could override the disadvantages, 360-degree VR videos would better engage the audience than non-VR videos. Another stream of literature proposed that disadvantages like motion sickness could draw the audience's attention away, decreasing involvement and the sense of presence [53, 77]. If the disadvantages could dominate the user experience, 360-degree technology might decrease the audience's interest in the videos and the audience engagement would be worse than non-VR videos. Based on the extant literature, including the current advantages and challenges of 360-degree VR videos, the present researchers explored the following hypotheses:

Hypothesis 1a: 360-degree VR videos perform better than non-VR videos in enhancing audience engagement.
Hypothesis 1b: 360-degree VR videos perform worse than non-VR videos in enhancing audience engagement.
Hypothesis 2: The content genres of both 360-degree VR videos and non-VR videos influence audience engagement.

3 Method

3.1 Case Selection

In this study, the researchers selected the case of the NYT VR project because *The NYT* has pioneered the publishing of 360-degree VR videos on YouTube, including an experienced team for VR news production [76]. Considering that 360-degree VR video techniques are still in development, the present researchers chose the NYT VR project to ensure the overall quality of the videos. *The NYT* has published hundreds of 360-degree VR videos and non-VR videos to date, which provides the opportunity for comparison between these two types of videos using a sufficient data pool while controlling for publisher influences (e.g., [56, 71]). Figure 1 shows an example of a 360-degree VR video published by *The NYT* on YouTube.

Considering that 360-degree VR video techniques are still in development, the present researchers chose the NYT VR project to ensure the overall quality of the videos. *The NYT* has published hundreds of 360-degree VR videos and non-VR videos to date, which provides the opportunity for comparison between these two types of videos using a sufficient data pool while controlling for publisher influences.

Figure 1 shows an example of a 360-degree VR video published by *The NYT* on YouTube.

Fig. 1. An example of a 360-degree VR video

3.2 Sampling

360-Degree VR Videos. The researchers obtained a sample of 360-degree VR videos from an *NYT*-published YouTube playlist called "The Daily 360" [1], which contains all the 360-degree VR videos produced by *The NYT* since 2015. At the time of sampling, this playlist included 299 videos.

Non-VR Videos. To obtain the non-VR video sample, the researchers filtered all the videos published by *The NYT* on YouTube using several steps. First, to control for the impact of publication date, all videos published before 2015 were excluded. Next, all the 360-degree VR videos were excluded. These steps resulted in a total of 839 eligible non-VR videos. Finally, each video was tagged and 299 videos were randomly selected from the qualifying pool.

3.3 Data Collection

Data was collected from the two sample sets within one day, using Java 1.8 software. Each video was identified by its unique URL, along with the title, publication date, and other relevant information.

3.4 Content Coding

Professional editors at The NYT have identified the genre of each 360-degree VR video on their website (see Fig. 2). The present researchers combined some related genres and developed a more coarse-grained categorization, including seven genre subgroups: "U.S.," "World," "Culture," "Science," "Travel," "Sports," and "Politics." Within the non-VR video sample, 72 videos lacked an official genre and 23 videos had multiple genres. One researcher identified the genre of each non-VR video based on its original genre and the researcher's subjective judgment. The genres of all the videos were then recorded for further analysis.

Fig. 2. Categories of 360-degree VR videos on *The NYT* website

3.5 Measure

Eight indicators were used to measure the audience engagement, which contains three dimensions: popularity, engagement conversion, and audience preference. Popularity refers to the degree of audience reach, which was measured by the absolute number of views, likes, dislikes, and comments [7]. Engagement conversion refers to the conversion of views into active interactions, which was measured by the number of likes per view, dislikes per view, and comments per view [42]. Audience preference refers to the collective preference across audiences, which was measured by the proportion of dislikes (i.e., *dislikes/(likes + dislikes)*) [7, 54].

3.6 Data Analysis

Because extreme cases may cause bias, 15 outliers (VR: n = 6; non-VR: n = 9) whose number of views exceeded 300,000 (top 2.5% of the dataset) were excluded. Using the SPSS 20 software package, independent sample t-tests were conducted to compare the differences between the 360-degree VR videos and the non-VR videos. To further examine the effects of video content, independent sample t-tests were performed on each genre.

4 Results

4.1 Independent Sample T-Tests

Table 3 details the t-test comparisons between the mean figures of each indicator in both samples. The results show that the means of all the popularity indicators (i.e., views, likes, dislikes, and comments) of the 360-degree VR videos are significantly smaller than those of non-VR videos. For example, the mean views of the 360-degree VR videos is significantly smaller than that of the non-VR videos (t = −4.170, p < .000).

Table 3. Total sample t-test results for views, likes, dislikes, comments, likes/view, dislikes/view, comments/view, and dislikes/(likes + dislikes) of the 360-degree VR/non-VR videos

Indicator	Group					
	360-degree VR		Non-VR			
	M	SD	M	SD	t	p
T-test with a total sample (360-degree VR = 293, non-VR = 290)						
Views	12021.263	22248.708	22837.897	38222.456	−4.170	0.000*
Likes	75.218	188.005	217.576	408.256	−5.398	0.000*
Dislikes	14.478	22.412	67.824	276.844	−3.271	0.001*
Comments	11.570	24.527	77.035	155.962	−6.990	0.000*
Likes/view	0.009	0.006	0.014	0.008	−7.326	0.000*
Dislikes/view	0.002	0.003	0.004	0.007	−4.917	0.000*
Comments/view	0.002	0.002	0.004	0.004	−8.674	0.000*
Dislikes/(likes + dislikes)	0.190	0.145	0.203	0.196	−0.950	0.342

The means of all the engagement-conversion indicators (i.e., likes/view, dislikes/view, and comments/view) of the 360-degree VR videos are also significantly smaller than those of the non-VR videos. For example, the mean likes per view of the 360-degree VR videos is significantly smaller than that of the non-VR videos ($t = -7.326$, $p < .000$). The mean of the audience-preference indicator (i.e., proportion of dislike) does not differ between the two samples ($t = -0.950$, $p < .342$), which suggests that audiences do not have a preference toward 360-degree VR videos versus non-VR videos.

4.2   Genre Subgroups

Table 4 summarizes the seven subgroups based on the videos' content genres, including their respective frequencies within each sample. The three most frequent

Table 4. Description of Subgroups based on content genres

Genre	Video type	Frequency	Percentage
U.S.	360-degree VR	83	28%
	Non-VR	56	19%
World	360-degree VR	82	28%
	Non-VR	61	21%
Culture	360-degree VR	53	18%
	Non-VR	41	14%
Science	360-degree VR	17	6%
	Non-VR	11	4%
Travel	360-degree VR	31	11%
	Non-VR	2	1%
Sports	360-degree VR	13	4%
	Non-VR	14	5%
Politics	360-degree VR	14	5%
	Non-VR	105	36%

Table 5. Results of t-tests with subgroups for views, likes, dislikes, comments, likes/view, dislikes/view, comments/view and dislikes/(likes + dislikes) by 360-degree VR/non-VR

Indicator	Group					
	360-degree VR		Non-VR			
	M	SD	M	SD	t	p
U.S. (360-degree VR = 83, non-VR = 56)						
Views	7214.566	8928.142	23442.125	34902.116	−3.405	0.001*
Likes	47.458	37.600	240.196	358.567	−4.008	0.000*
Dislikes	12.590	17.902	48.107	71.292	−3.651	0.001*
Comments	11.916	16.001	96.196	178.914	−3.516	0.001*
Likes/view	0.010	0.006	0.015	0.010	−3.773	0.000*
Dislikes/view	0.003	0.003	0.004	0.004	−1.536	0.128
Comments/view	0.002	0.002	0.005	0.004	−4.053	0.000*
Dislikes/(likes + dislikes)	0.219	0.159	0.178	0.141	1.557	0.122
World (360-degree VR = 82, non-VR = 61)						
Views	11397.622	19314.361	30101.148	51802.428	−2.685	0.009*
Likes	57.146	48.093	182.213	291.991	−3.312	0.002*
Dislikes	12.707	16.653	64.295	123.891	−3.231	0.002*
Comments	9.061	8.834	103.016	153.240	−4.783	0.000*
Likes/view	0.010	0.006	0.012	0.009	−0.931	0.353
Dislikes/view	0.002	0.003	0.004	0.006	−1.507	0.135
Comments/view	0.002	0.002	0.005	0.005	−3.563	0.001*
Dislikes/(likes + dislikes)	0.170	0.137	0.203	0.183	−1.193	0.235
Culture (360-degree VR = 53, non-VR = 41)						
Views	15873.113	36290.103	21952.000	42940.833	−0.743	0.459
Likes	110.887	232.429	370.878	839.112	−1.928	0.060
Dislikes	14.019	20.211	12.951	18.562	0.263	0.793
Comments	10.566	29.625	26.610	72.796	−1.458	0.148
Likes/view	0.009	0.006	0.019	0.009	−6.224	0.000*
Dislikes/view	0.002	0.001	0.001	0.002	1.145	0.255
Comments/view	0.001	0.001	0.002	0.001	−3.978	0.000*
Dislikes/(likes + dislikes)	0.171	0.117	0.058	0.055	6.247	0.000*
Science (360-degree VR = 17, non-VR = 11)						
Views	18383.765	25838.557	14736.455	24880.724	0.373	0.713
Likes	61.647	54.031	211.273	225.505	−2.161	0.054
Dislikes	11.882	12.649	6.818	10.391	1.106	0.279
Comments	7.176	6.682	16.727	24.812	−1.518	0.141
Likes/view	0.008	0.006	0.018	0.008	−3.788	0.001*
Dislikes/view	0.001	0.001	0.001	0.001	1.023	0.316
Comments/view	0.001	0.001	0.001	0.001	−0.166	0.869
Dislikes/(likes + dislikes)	0.149	0.098	0.047	0.056	3.115	0.004*

(continued)

Table 5. (*continued*)

Indicator	Group					
	360-degree VR		Non-VR			
	M	SD	M	SD	t	p
Sports (360-degree VR = 13, non-VR = 14)						
Views	7957.538	12172.155	33196.857	34094.296	−2.597	0.019*
Likes	37.231	30.425	251.643	210.394	−3.771	0.002*
Dislikes	6.154	5.684	11.929	11.672	−1.652	0.115
Comments	4.000	3.512	26.143	22.497	−3.635	0.003*
Likes/view	0.008	0.006	0.011	0.006	−0.947	0.353
Dislikes/view	0.002	0.001	0.000	0.000	3.146	0.007*
Comments/view	0.001	0.001	0.001	0.002	−1.467	0.161
Dislikes/(likes + dislikes)	0.188	0.141	0.041	0.016	3.726	0.003*

genres within the 360-degree VR video sample are "U.S." (n = 83, 28%), "World" (n = 82, 28%), and "Culture" (n = 53, 18%). For the non-VR video sample, "Politics" (n = 105, 36%) is the most frequent content genre, followed by "World" (n = 61, 21%) and "U.S." (n = 56, 19%). Across these genres, "Travel" and "Politics" hold the largest discrepancies in frequency between the 360-degree VR videos and the non-VR videos (Travel: 31 vs. 2; Politics: 14 vs. 105). As "Travel" and "Politics" failed the assumptions of the t-tests, these two genres were excluded from the following analyses.

4.3   T-Tests for Subgroups

Table 5 details the t-test results for each subgroup. Regarding the popularity indicators, the results for "U.S." and "World" are congruent with the total sample results; that is, all the popularity indicators of the 360-degree VR videos under the "U.S." and "World" genres are significantly smaller than those of the non-VR videos under the same genres (p < 0.009). For 360-degree VR videos under the "Sports" genre, three of the four popularity indicators (excluding dislikes) are significantly smaller. Under "Culture" and "Science," none of the popularity indicators are significantly different between the two samples, which indicates that the popularity of these genres is similar.

Based on the total sample t-test results, all the engagement-conversion indicators (i.e., likes/view, dislikes/view, and comments/view) are significantly different between the two samples. However, engagement conversion is distinct across genres. Under "U.S." and "Culture," the results for dislikes/view are insignificant. Two of three engagement-conversion indicators are insignificant under "World" (i.e., likes/view and dislikes/view; p > 0.05), "Science" (i.e., dislikes/view and comments/view; p > 0.05), and "Sports" (likes/view and comments/view; p > 0.05).

The mean of the audience-preference indicator (i.e., proportion of dislikes) is not significantly different between 360-degree VR videos and non-VR videos under the "U. S." and "World" genres. However, under "Culture," "Science," and "Sports," the proportion of dislikes of the 360-degree VR videos is significantly larger than that of the non-VR videos.

5 Discussion

This study explored the differences in popularity, engagement conversion, and audience preference between 360-degree VR videos and non-VR videos published on YouTube by The NYT. The influence of each content genre was also investigated. The results reveal an interesting set of findings, as discussed in the following sections.

5.1 Popularity

360-Degree VR Videos vs. Non-VR Videos. The results indicate that 360-degree VR videos are not as popular as non-VR videos in general. Although the means of all the popularity indicators show that 360-degree VR videos are slightly more popular, the audience pool is smaller for 360-degree VR videos than for non-VR videos.

Content Genres. Across both samples, there are no significant differences between the popularity of "Culture" and "Science." These results are demonstrated by the relatively low popularity of the non-VR videos and the relatively high popularity of the 360-degree VR videos under both genres.

In accordance with Koehler et al. [37], the present findings suggest that there is an interaction effect between video type and content genre on popularity; that is, the popular genres differ between the two samples. Among the non-VR videos, "Sports" is the most popular genre, followed by "World" and "U.S." Prior studies found that the most popular genre on YouTube is sports, followed by news/politics, science, and travel [12], which is similar to the sequence in the present dataset. In contrast, "Culture" and "Science" are the most popular genres among the 360-degree VR videos. Previous literature may offer an explanation for this finding, as Bleumers et al. [8] suggested that 360-degree VR videos are most suitable for depicting scenes without any changes or with slow pacing. In the present study, "Culture" is a genre that involves the introduction of artwork, and most 360-degree VR videos under "Science" feature content related to the study of nature. Both genres require the audience to explore the content.

According to Bleumers et al. [8], the sports genre is also suitable for 360-degree VR videos; however, the present results do not support this statement. One explanation is that the overall quality of the 360-degree VR videos under "Sports" is problematic. Based on the present researchers' observations, the narratives behind these videos are not sufficiently convincing or engaging for audiences, possibly due to low information density, disordered splicing, and other issues.

5.2 Engagement Conversion

360-Degree VR Videos vs. Non-VR Videos. The results reveal that audiences are less engaged (e.g., liking, disliking, or commenting) after watching 360-degree VR videos than they are after watching non-VR videos. One possible explanation is that, as mentioned earlier, some shortcomings of 360-degree VR videos may decrease the quality of the audience's experience and reduce audience engagement due to low visual quality, physical discomfort, and motion sickness [15, 33, 74].

Another explanation is that the present measures for engagement conversion only considered traditional online actions (e.g., clicking and commenting). Behavioral actions indicating engagement conversion that are unique to 360-degree VR videos (e.g., rotating the mouse/screen/head) were not measured. The criteria for evaluating engagement conversion of 360-degree VR videos needs further discussion.

Content Genres. The interaction effect between video type and content genre on engagement conversion is more complex. Audiences had a similar probability to "like" a 360-degree VR video under the genres of "World" and "Sports" and to comment on a 360-degree video under the genres of "Science" and "Sports," compared to audiences watching non-VR videos under the same genres. One explanation for these findings is that audiences tend to click "Like" at less frequency or leave fewer comments on non-VR videos under these particular genres. Prior literature has also suggested that science videos gain the least amount of comments, followed by sports, travel, and news/politics [68].

For most genres (except "Sports"), audiences generally show no interest in clicking "Dislike," regardless of the video type, which is consistent with previous findings [10, 78]. For "Sports", audiences click much fewer dislikes than other genres after watching non-VR videos. In our sample, "Sports" for 360-degree VR videos seems to be not sufficiently convincing or engaging for audiences as stated. As a result, audiences are inclined to click more dislikes after watching 360-degree VR videos than non-VR videos under "Sports".

In general, we find that under "Culture" and "U.S.", 360-degree VR videos perform worse in engaging audiences than non-VR videos. Our findings support prior statements that news genres vary significantly in their content, and each type of content has different effects on to what extent to which audiences are engaged with the videos [3].

5.3 Audience Preference

Although the audiences showed no general preference toward either video type, the present study found that, under the genres of "Culture," "Science," and "Sports," the proportion of dislikes among the non-VR videos is significantly smaller than that of the 360-degree VR videos. This indicates that audiences are more inclined to click "Like" than "Dislike" after watching non-VR videos under these three genres.

6 Conclusion

This study contributes to the body of knowledge concerning how 360-degree VR videos enhance audience engagement compared to non-VR videos by clarifying the current advantages and challenges of 360-degree VR videos. Through the exploration of three dimensions (i.e., popularity, engagement conversion, and audience preference), this study shows how audience engagement with 360-degree VR videos manifests on YouTube. The findings indicate that 360-degree VR videos lack audience engagement, compared to non-VR videos. Further improvements to visual quality, as well as elements that induce physical discomfort and motion sickness among users, are required.

A few limitations must be acknowledged. First, the researchers did not control for the potential effects of device type on the viewing experience. There is no assurance that all audiences watched the videos using Google Cardboard or a more advanced headset, thereby receiving a fully immersive experience. Second, the sample size limited the researchers from exploring some genres (e.g., "Politics" and "Travel"). Third, the present measures of audience engagement are all objective. Subjective measures should be considered in the future to gain a more comprehensive understanding of the differences in audience engagement between 360-degree VR videos and non-VR videos. A new set of measures could be developed to capture the uniqueness of audience engagement with 360-degree VR videos on YouTube.

Acknowledgement. This research was supported by grant from the Centre for Applied Computing and Interactive Media (ACIM) of City University of Hong Kong and grant No. CityU 11531016 from the Research Grants Council of the Hong Kong SAR awarded to the third author.

References

1. The Daily 360 The New York Times (2018). https://www.youtube.com/playlist?list=PL4 CGYNsoW2iDN-xj9xxfgRLsqmAdY8J_W
2. Afzal, S., Chen, J., Ramakrishnan, K.: Characterization of 360-degree videos. In: Proceedings of the Workshop on Virtual Reality and Augmented Reality Network, pp. 1–6. ACM (2017)
3. Arapakis, I., Lalmas, M., Cambazoglu, B.B., Marcos, M.C., Jose, J.M.: User engagement in online news: under the scope of sentiment, interest, affect, and gaze. J. Assoc. Inf. Sci. Technol. **65**(10), 1988–2005 (2014)
4. Attfield, S., Kazai, G., Lalmas, M., Piwowarski, B.: Towards a science of user engagement. In: WSDM Workshop on User Modelling for Web Applications, pp. 9–12 (2011)
5. Baños, R.M., Botella, C., Alcañiz, M., Liaño, V., Guerrero, B., Rey, B.: Immersion and emotion: their impact on the sense of presence. CyberPsychol. Behav. **7**(6), 734–741 (2004)
6. Baños, R.M., Botella, C., Rubió, I., Quero, S., García-Palacios, A., Alcañiz, M.: Presence and emotions in virtual environments: the influence of stereoscopy. CyberPsychol. Behav. **11**(1), 1–8 (2008)
7. Baym, N.K.: Data not seen: the uses and shortcomings of social media metrics. First Monday **18**(10) (2013)
8. Bleumers, L., Van den Broeck, W., Lievens, B., Pierson, J.: Seeing the bigger picture: a user perspective on 360 TV. In: Proceedings of the 10th European Conference on Interactive TV and Video, pp. 115–124. ACM (2012)
9. Brautović, M., John, R., Potrebica, M.: Immersiveness of news: how croatian students experienced 360-video news. In: De Paolis, L.T., Bourdot, P., Mongelli, A. (eds.) AVR 2017. LNCS, vol. 10324, pp. 263–269. Springer, Cham (2017). https://doi.org/10.1007/978-3-319-60922-5_20
10. Buie, E., Blythe, M.: Meditations on YouTube. In: Proceedings of the 6th International Conference on Designing Pleasurable Products and Interfaces, pp. 41–50. ACM (2013)
11. Burrows, C.N., Blanton, H.: Real-world persuasion from virtual-world campaigns how transportation into virtual worlds moderates in-game influence. Commun. Res. **43**(4), 542–570 (2016)
12. Che, X., Ip, B., Lin, L.: A survey of current YouTube video characteristics. IEEE Multimedia **22**(2), 56–63 (2015)

13. Chugani, S.K., Irwin, J.R., Redden, J.P.: Happily ever after: the effect of identity-consistency on product satiation. J. Consum. Res. **42**(4), 564–577 (2015)
14. Couldry, N., Livingstone, S., Markham, T.: Media Consumption and Public Engagement: Beyond the Presumption of Attention. Springer, London (2016). https://doi.org/10.1057/9780230800823
15. Coxon, M., Kelly, N., Page, S.: Individual differences in virtual reality: are spatial presence and spatial ability linked? Virtual Real. **20**(4), 203–212 (2016)
16. Datcu, D., Lukosch, S., Brazier, F.: On the usability and effectiveness of different interaction types in augmented reality. Int. J. Hum.-Comput. Interact. **31**(3), 193–209 (2015)
17. De la Peña, N., Weil, P., Llobera, J., Giannopoulos, E., Pomés, A., Spanlang, B., Friedman, D., Sanchez-Vives, M.V., Slater, M.: Immersive journalism: immersive virtual reality for the first-person experience of news. Presence: Teleoperators Virtual Environ. **19**(4), 291–301 (2010)
18. Diemer, J., Alpers, G.W., Peperkorn, H.M., Shiban, Y., Mühlberger, A.: The impact of perception and presence on emotional reactions: a review of research in virtual reality. Front. Psychol. **6**(26), 1–9 (2015)
19. Doyle, P., Gelman, M., Gill, S.: Viewing the Future: Virtual Reality in Journalism. John S. and James L. Knight Foundation, Miami (2016)
20. Evgeny, K., David, P.: Next-generation video encoding techniques for 360 video and VR (2016). https://code.facebook.com/posts/1126354007399553/next-generation-video-encoding-techniques-for-360-video-and-vr/
21. Fonseca, D., Kraus, M.: A comparison of head-mounted and hand-held displays for 360° videos with focus on attitude and behavior change. In: Proceedings of the 20th International Academic Mindtrek Conference, pp. 287–296. ACM (2016)
22. Gillath, O., McCall, C., Shaver, P.R., Blascovich, J.: What can virtual reality teach us about prosocial tendencies in real and virtual environments? Media Psychol. **11**(2), 259–282 (2008)
23. Goh, D.H.L., Lee, C.S., Razikin, K.: Interfaces for accessing location-based information on mobile devices: an empirical evaluation. J. Assoc. Inf. Sci. Technol. **67**(12), 2882–2896 (2016)
24. Hardee, G.M., McMahan, R.P.: FiJi: a framework for the immersion-journalism intersection. Front. ICT **4**(Article 21), 1–18 (2017)
25. Hasler, B.S., Hirschberger, G., Shani-Sherman, T., Friedman, D.A.: Virtual peacemakers: mimicry increases empathy in simulated contact with virtual outgroup members. Cyberpsychol. Behav. Soc. Netw. **17**(12), 766–771 (2014)
26. Hsu, T.C.: Learning English with augmented reality: do learning styles matter? Comput. Educ. **106**, 137–149 (2017)
27. Huang, T.L., Liao, S.L.: Creating e-shopping multisensory flow experience through augmented-reality interactive technology. Internet Res. **27**(2), 449–475 (2017)
28. Huang, T.L., Liu, F.H.: Formation of augmented-reality interactive technology's persuasive effects from the perspective of experiential value. Internet Res. **24**(1), 82–109 (2014)
29. Hwang, G.J., Wu, P.H., Chen, C.C., Tu, N.T.: Effects of an augmented reality-based educational game on students' learning achievements and attitudes in real-world observations. Interact. Learn. Environ. **24**(8), 1895–1906 (2016)
30. IJsselsteijn, W., de Ridder, H., Freeman, J., Avons, S.E., Bouwhuis, D.: Effects of stereoscopic presentation, image motion, and screen size on subjective and objective corroborative measures of presence. Presence: Teleoperators Virtual Environ. **10**(3), 298–311 (2001)
31. Jones, S.: Disrupting the narrative: immersive journalism in virtual reality. J. Media Pract. **18**(2–3), 171–185 (2017)

32. Kasahara, S., Nagai, S., Rekimoto, J.: First person omnidirectional video: system design and implications for immersive experience. In: Proceedings of the ACM International Conference on Interactive Experiences for TV and Online Video, pp. 33–42. ACM (2015)
33. Kavanagh, S., Luxton-Reilly, A., Wüensche, B., Plimmer, B.: Creating 360° educational video: a case study. In: Proceedings of the 28th Australian Conference on Computer-Human Interaction, pp. 34–39. ACM (2016)
34. Keshavarz, B., Hecht, H.: Visually induced motion sickness and presence in videogames: the role of sound. In: Proceedings of the Human Factors and Ergonomics Society Annual Meeting, pp. 1763–1767. SAGE Publications, Los Angeles (2012)
35. Khan, M.L.: Social media engagement: what motivates user participation and consumption on YouTube? Comput. Hum. Behav. **66**, 236–247 (2017)
36. Kishore, S., Navarro, X., Dominguez, E., De La Peña, N., Slater, M.: Beaming into the news: a system for and case study of tele-immersive journalism. IEEE Comput. Graph. Appl., 1 (2016)
37. Koehler, M., Yadav, A., Phillips, M., Cavazos-Kottke, S.: What is video good for? Examining how media and story genre interact. J. Educ. Multimedia Hypermedia **14**(3), 249–272 (2005)
38. Lagun, D., Lalmas, M.: Understanding user attention and engagement in online news reading. In: Proceedings of the Ninth ACM International Conference on Web Search and Data Mining, pp. 113–122. ACM (2016)
39. Lee, H.-G., Chung, S., Lee, W.-H.: Presence in virtual golf simulators: the effects of presence on perceived enjoyment, perceived value, and behavioral intention. New Media Soc. **15**(6), 930–946 (2013)
40. Lescop, L.: Narrative Grammar in 360. In: IEEE International Symposium on Mixed and Augmented Reality (ISMAR-Adjunct), pp. 254–257. IEEE (2017)
41. Lewis, S.C., Holton, A.E., Coddington, M.: Reciprocal journalism: a concept of mutual exchange between journalists and audiences. Journal. Pract. **8**(2), 229–241 (2014)
42. Liikkanen, L.A., Salovaara, A.: Music on YouTube: user engagement with traditional, user-appropriated and derivative videos. Comput. Hum. Behav. **50**, 108–124 (2015)
43. Lin, J.-H.T.: Fear in virtual reality (VR): fear elements, coping reactions, immediate and next-day fright responses toward a survival horror zombie virtual reality game. Comput. Hum. Behav. **72**, 350–361 (2017)
44. Lin, J.-W., Duh, H.B.-L., Parker, D.E., Abi-Rached, H., Furness, T.A.: Effects of field of view on presence, enjoyment, memory, and simulator sickness in a virtual environment. In: Proceedings of IEEE Virtual Reality, pp. 164–171. IEEE (2002)
45. Lin, Y.-C., Chang, Y.-J., Hu, H.-N., Cheng, H.-T., Huang, C.-W., Sun, M.: Tell me where to look: investigating ways for assisting focus in 360° video. In: Proceedings of the 2017 CHI Conference on Human Factors in Computing Systems, pp. 2535–2545. ACM (2017)
46. Lin, Y.-T., Liao, Y.-C., Teng, S.-Y., Chung, Y.-J., Chan, L., Chen, B.-Y.: Outside-in: visualizing out-of-sight regions-of-interest in a 360 video using spatial picture-in-picture previews. In: Proceedings of the 30th Annual ACM Symposium on User Interface Software and Technology, pp. 255–265. ACM (2017)
47. Linder, Å.: Key factors for feeling present during a music experience in virtual reality using 360° video. In: KTH, School of Computer Science and Communication (CSC) (2017)
48. MacQuarrie, A., Steed, A.: Cinematic virtual reality: evaluating the effect of display type on the viewing experience for panoramic video. In: IEEE Virtual Reality, pp. 45–54. IEEE (2017)
49. Magnus, U.: Navigating using 360° panoramic video: design challenges and implications. In: School of Natural Sciences, Södertörn University (2017)

50. McMahan, R.P., Bowman, D.A., Zielinski, D.J., Brady, R.B.: Evaluating display fidelity and interaction fidelity in a virtual reality game. IEEE Trans. Vis. Comput. Graph. 18(4), 626–633 (2012)
51. Melo, M., Sampaio, S., Barbosa, L., Vasconcelos-Raposo, J., Bessa, M.: The impact of different exposure times to 360° video experience on the sense of presence. In: Computação Gráfica e Interação (EPCGI), 2016 23° Encontro Português de, pp. 1–5. IEEE (2016)
52. Munafo, J., Diedrick, M., Stoffregen, T.A.: The virtual reality head-mounted display Oculus Rift induces motion sickness and is sexist in its effects. Exp. Brain Res. 235(3), 889–901 (2017)
53. Nichols, S., Cobb, S., Wilson, J.R.: Health and safety implications of virtual environments: measurement issues. Presence: Teleoperators Virtual Environ. 6(6), 667–675 (1997)
54. Park, M., Naaman, M., Berger, J.: A data-driven study of view duration on YouTube. In: International Conference on Web and Social Media (ICWSM), pp. 651–654 (2016)
55. Passmore, P.J., Glancy, M., Philpot, A., Roscoe, A., Wood, A., Fields, B.: Effects of viewing condition on user experience of panoramic video. In: Proceedings of the 26th International Conference on Artificial Reality and Telexistence and the 21st Eurographics Symposium on Virtual Environments, pp. 9–16 (2016)
56. Pavel, A., Hartmann, B., Agrawala, M.: Shot orientation controls for interactive cinematography with 360 video. In: Proceedings of the 30th Annual ACM Symposium on User Interface Software and Technology, pp. 289–297. ACM (2017)
57. Philpot, A., Glancy, M., Passmore, P.J., Wood, A., Fields, B.: User experience of panoramic video in CAVE-like and head mounted display viewing conditions. In: Proceedings of the 2017 ACM International Conference on Interactive Experiences for TV and Online Video, pp. 65–75. ACM (2017)
58. Prothero, J., Hoffman, H.: Widening the field of view increases the sense of presence within immersive virtual environments. In: Virtual Environments Human Interface Technology Laboratory Technical report, University of Washington (1995)
59. Qian, F., Ji, L., Han, B., Gopalakrishnan, V.: Optimizing 360 video delivery over cellular networks. In: Proceedings of the 5th Workshop on All Things Cellular: Operations, Applications and Challenges, pp. 1–6. ACM (2016)
60. Ramalho, J., Chambel, T.: Immersive 360 mobile video with an emotional perspective. In: Proceedings of the 2013 ACM International Workshop on Immersive Media Experiences, pp. 35–40. ACM (2013)
61. Rhee, T., Petikam, L., Allen, B., Chalmers, A.: MR360: mixed reality rendering for 360° panoramic videos. IEEE Trans. Vis. Comput. Graph. 23(4), 1379–1388 (2017)
62. Rupp, M.A., Kozachuk, J., Michaelis, J.R., Odette, K.L., Smither, J.A., McConnell, D.S.: The effects of immersiveness and future VR expectations on subjec-tive-experiences during an educational 360° video. In: Proceedings of the Human Factors and Ergonomics Society Annual Meeting, pp. 2108–2112. SAGE Publications, Los Angeles (2016)
63. Sánchez Laws, A.L.: Can immersive journalism enhance empathy? Digit. Journal. 1–16 (2017)
64. Sheikh, A., Brown, A., Watson, Z., Evans, M.: Directing attention in 360-degree video. In: IET Conference Proceedings, p. 29. Institution of Engineering and Technology (2016)
65. Shin, D.-H.: The role of affordance in the experience of virtual reality learning: technological and affective affordances in virtual reality. Telematics Inform. 34(8), 1826–1836 (2017)
66. Shin, D.: Empathy and embodied experience in virtual environment: to what extent can virtual reality stimulate empathy and embodied experience? Comput. Hum. Behav. 78, 64–73 (2018)
67. Shin, D., Biocca, F.: Exploring immersive experience in journalism. New Media Soc. 19(11), 1–24 (2017)

68. Siersdorfer, S., Chelaru, S., Nejdl, W., San Pedro, J.: How useful are your comments?: analyzing and predicting YouTube comments and comment ratings. In: Proceedings of the 19th International Conference on World Wide Web, pp. 891–900. ACM (2010)
69. Smith, W.: Stop Calling Google Cardboard's 360-degree Video 'VR' (2015). https://www.wired.com/2015/11/360-video-isnt-virtual-reality/
70. Sreedhar, K.K., Aminlou, A., Hannuksela, M.M., Gabbouj, M.: Viewport-adaptive encoding and streaming of 360-degree video for virtual reality applications. In: Proceedings of IEEE International Symposium on Multimedia (ISM), pp. 583–586. IEEE (2016)
71. Sundar, S.S., Kang, J., Oprean, D.: Being there in the midst of the story: how immersive journalism affects our perceptions and cognitions. Cyberpsychol. Behav. Soc. Netw. 20(11), 672–682 (2017)
72. Tran, H.T., Ngoc, N.P., Bui, C.M., Pham, M.H., Thang, T.C.: An evaluation of quality metrics for 360 videos. In: 2017 Ninth International Conference on Ubiquitous and Future Networks (ICUFN), pp. 7–11. IEEE (2017)
73. Tse, A., Jennett, C., Moore, J., Watson, Z., Rigby, J., Cox, A.L.: Was i there?: impact of platform and headphones on 360 video immersion. In: Proceedings of the 2017 CHI Conference Extended Abstracts on Human Factors in Computing Systems, pp. 2967–2974. ACM (2017)
74. Van den Broeck, M., Kawsar, F., Schöning, J.: It's all around you: exploring 360 video viewing experiences on mobile devices. In: Proceedings of the 2017 ACM on Multimedia Conference, pp. 762–768 (2017)
75. Visch, V.T., Tan, E.S., Molenaar, D.: The emotional and cognitive effect of immersion in film viewing. Cogn. Emot. 24(8), 1439–1445 (2010)
76. Watson, Z.: VR for News: The New Reality? Digital News Publications: Reuters Institute for the Study of Journalism. Oxford University (2017)
77. Witmer, B.G., Singer, M.J.: Measuring presence in virtual environments: a presence questionnaire. Presence 7(3), 225–240 (1998)
78. Zhang, A.: Judging YouTube by its covers. Department of Computer Science and Engineering, University of California, San Diego, Technical report (2015)
79. Zhou, C., Li, Z., Liu, Y.: A measurement study of oculus 360 degree video streaming. In: Proceedings of the 8th ACM on Multimedia Systems Conference, pp. 27–37 (2017)

A Structure-Behavior Coalescence Systems Modeling Approach for Service Systems Design

Yu-Chen Yang[1](✉), Cheng-Ta Tsai[1], and William S. Chao[2]

[1] Department of Information Management, National Sun Yat-sen University, Kaohsiung, Taiwan
ycyang@mis.nsysu.edu.tw, tachengtsai@gmail.com
[2] Association of Chinese Enterprise Architects, Taipei, Taiwan
architectchao@gmail.com

Abstract. A service system is generally very complex that it includes several views, such as data, function, structure, behavior and so on. There are two different ways to model such many views. The model multiplicity approach for service systems design separately chooses a distinct model for every view. On the contrary, the model singularity approach for service systems design, instead of choosing many isolated models, will use only one single integrated model. In this paper, we proposed a structure-behavior coalescence (SBC) systems modeling approach for service systems design which is based on model singularity. The multiple models are un-related and therefore inconsistent with each other, which become the primary reason for the model multiplicity problems. Being able to think about a system in one single integrated model, the SBC systems modeling approach for service systems design truly avoids the model multiplicity problems.

Keywords: Structure-behavior coalescence · Systems modeling
Service systems design · Model multiplicity · Model singularity

1 Introduction

A service system is usually complex that it consists of many views such as data, function, structure, behavior, and so on. System modeling is an "artifact" created by humans to describe what a service systems design is. Without systems modeling, everyone has his own argument about a service systems design, never be able to reach a consensus. There are two approaches to model these different views. The model multiplicity approach such as Unified Modeling Language [1, 2] (UML) respectively uses a distinct model for each view. These multiple models for service systems design are separated and always inconsistent with each other, which becomes the primary cause for the model multiplicity problems [3–7], as shown in Fig. 1.

On the contrary, the model singularity approach such as Object-Process Methodology [3, 4] (OPM), instead of choosing many separated models, will use only one

The original version of this chapter was revised: The title of the contribution was changed and several typos were corrected. The correction to this chapter is available at https://doi.org/10.1007/978-3-319-91716-0_61

F. F.-H. Nah and B. S. Xiao (Eds.): HCIBGO 2018, LNCS 10923, pp. 236–249, 2018.
https://doi.org/10.1007/978-3-319-91716-0_18

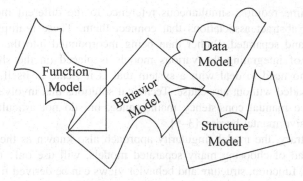

Fig. 1. The model multiplicity approach for service systems design

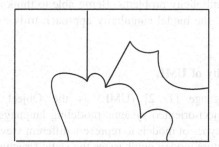

Fig. 2. The model singularity approach for service systems design

integrated model for service systems design, as shown in Fig. 2. All data, function, structure and behavior views can be derived from this single model.

Being able to think about a service systems design in an integrated model, the single model approach truly avoids the model multiplicity problems. In this paper, we proposed a structure-behavior coalescence (SBC) systems modeling approach for service systems design which is based on model singularity. The rest of this paper is organized as follows. Section 2 addresses related studies. A systematic method used to develop the SBC systems modeling approach for service systems design is described in Sect. 3. Section 4 presents the application of the SBC systems modeling approach for service systems design. The conclusion is in Sect. 5.

2   Literature Review

2.1   Model Multiplicity Versus Model Singularity

In general, a system is extremely intricate that it contains several aspects, or "views", such as data, function, structure, behavior, and so on. There are two approaches to model these different views. The model multiplicity approach, also known as the multi-model approach, respectively utilizes a distinct model for each view. In a multi-model environment, comprehending a system and the way it operates and changes over time requires simultaneous reference to the different models and the construction of abstract associations that connect them. These multiple models are heterogeneous and separated. Rather than being incorporated into the approach, the mental burden of integrating the various models is placed on the shoulder of the constructors who need to deal with a system that is intricate in itself, and they are mentally overloaded without any cause. Technical solutions that involve sophisticated tools can reduce manual consistency maintenance, but do not articulate the kernel issues of excessive mental burden [3–5].

On the contrary, the model singularity approach also known as the single model approach, instead of choosing many separated models, will use only one integrated model. All data, function, structure and behavior views can be derived from this single model.

The use of multiple models to delineate a system from different views is the major reason for the model multiplicity problems. Being able to think about a system in one single integrated model, the model singularity approach truly avoids the model multiplicity problems.

2.2   Model Multiplicity of UML

Unified modeling language [1, 2] (UML) is the Object Management Group (OMG) standard for object-oriented systems modeling language. UML model multiplicity uses at least two types of models to represent different views of the system under consideration. (A) Structure model: emphasizes the static structure of the system using objects, attributes, operations and relationships. This structure model includes object diagram, class diagram, deployment diagram, package diagram, composite structure diagram, component diagram, etc. (B) Behavior model: emphasizes the dynamic behavior of the system by showing collaborations among objects and changes to the internal states of objects. This behavior model includes use case diagram, activity diagram, state diagram, sequence diagrams, communication diagram, interaction overview diagram, timing diagram, etc.

In the UML multi-model environment, the straightforward intuition of thinking concurrently about the structure and behavior is seriously hindered by separating the structure and behavior models. These multiple models are isolated and always inconsistent with each other, which become the major cause for the UML model multiplicity problems [3–5].

2.3   Model Singularity of OPM

Object-Process Methodology [3, 4] (OPM), conceived and developed by Professor Dori, is a systems modeling paradigm that integrates the two things inherent in a system: its objects and its processes. This duality is recognized throughout the community that studies systems, and sometimes goes by labels such as systems structure/systems behavior. Objects are static things and have quantitative and qualitative properties such as value, density, piece and size, which define the object's state. Processes are dynamic things that can change the state of, transform, destroy, or create objects.

Being able to think about processes in parallel with objects, OPM delineates an excellent model singularity framework which avoids the model multiplicity problems [3–5] by integrating all the information within an integrated model and confining the complexity through a scaling mechanism.

2.4   Process Algebras

Process algebras (or process calculi) are a diverse family of related approaches to the study of concurrent systems. Their tools are algebraic languages for the high-level description of synchronizations, communications, and interactions between a collection of independent processes or agents. Process algebras also offer algebraic rules that permit process specifications to be analyzed and manipulated, and allow formal reasoning about equivalences and observation congruence between processes.

There are several leading algebraic approaches to modeling concurrent systems. Communicating Sequential Processes [8] (CSP) was first described in a 1978 paper by Hoare. Milner introduced the Calculus of Communicating Systems [9] (CCS) around 1980. Algebra of Communicating Processes [10] was originally conceived in 1982 by Bergstra and Klop.

3   The Structure-Behavior Coalescence Systems Modeling Approach

The structure-behavior coalescence (SBC) systems modeling approach uses SBC process algebra (SBC-PA) to accomplish the service systems design.

3.1   Channel-Based Value-Passing Integrations

An interaction (containing data, function, structure) represents an indivisible and instantaneous communication or handshake between two agents [11, 12]. In the channel-based value-passing approach as shown in Fig. 3, the caller agent (either external environment's actor or component) interacts with the callee agent (component) through the channel interaction.

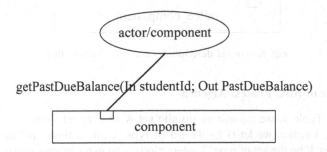

Fig. 3. Channel-based value-passing integrations

The external environment uses a "type-1 interaction" to interact with a component. We formally describe a channel-based value-passing type_1 interaction as a 3-tuple TYPE_1_INTERACTION = <actor, channel_formula, callee_component>, where "actor" stands for the name of an external environment's actor, "channel_formula" stands for a channel formula and "callee_component" stands for the name of a callee component as shown in Fig. 4.

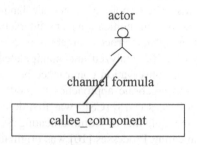

Fig. 4. Formal description of a type_1 interaction

Two components use a "type-2 interaction" to interact with each other. We formally describe a channel-based value-passing type_2 interaction as a 3-tuple TYPE_2_INTERACTION = <caller_component, channel_formula, callee_component>, where "caller_component" stands for the name of a caller component, "channel_formula" stands for a channel formula and "callee_component" stands for the name of a callee component as shown in Fig. 5.

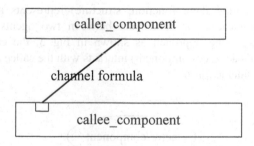

Fig. 5. Formal description of a type_2 interaction

3.2 Entities of SBC Process Algebra

As shown in Table 1, we assume an infinite set K of channel formulas, and use k to range over K. Further, we let G be the set of type_1 interactions, and use g to range over G. We let V be the set of type_2 interactions, and use v to range over V. We let Δ be the set of type_1_or_2 interactions, and use a, b to range over Δ. Further, we let X be the set of process variables, and use X, Y to range over X. We let Φ be the set of process Constants, and use A, B to range over Φ. We let Ψ be the set of process expressions, and use E, F to range over Ψ. Finally, we let Γ be the set of components, and use C, D to range over Γ.

Table 1. Entities of SBC process algebra.

Entity set	Entity name	Type of entity
K	$k,\ldots$	Channel formulas
G	$g,\ldots$	Type_1 interactions
V	$v,\ldots$	Type_2 interactions
Δ	$a, b,\ldots$	Type_1 or _2 interactions
X	$X, Y,\ldots$	Process variables
Φ	$A, B,\ldots$	Process constants
	$I, J,\ldots$	Indexing sets
Ψ	$E, F,\ldots$	Process expressions
Γ	$C, D,\ldots$	Components

3.3   Language Constructs of SBC Algebra

In the structure-behavior coalescence approach, the syntax of SBC process algebra is defined by the following BNF grammar, as shown in Fig. 6.

(1) <System> ::= "**fix** (" <Process_Variable> "="

"(" $\sum_{i \in I}$ <IFD$_i$> ") $\bullet$ " <Process_Variable> ")"

(2) <IFD> ::= <Type_1_Interaction> {"$\bullet$ " Type_1_Or_2_Interaction}

(3) <Type_1_Or_2_Interaction> ::= <Type_1_Interaction>

| <Type_2_Interaction>

Fig. 6. Backus-naur form of SBC process algebra

Rule 1 describes that the recursion (i.e. **fix**) of summation (i.e. $\Sigma_{i \in I}$) of one or more interaction flow diagram process expressions (i.e. IFD$_i$) defines the SBC process expression of a system.

Rule 2 describes that an interaction flow diagram process expression (i.e. IFD) is defined by a type_1 interaction process expression (i.e. Type_1_Interaction) followed by zero or more type_1_or_type_2 interaction process expressions (i.e. Type_1_Or_2_Interaction).

Rule 3 describes that the type_1_or_2 interaction process expression (i.e. Type_1_Or_2_Interaction) is either a type_1 interaction process expression (i.e. Type_1_Interaction) or a type_2 interaction process expression (i.e. Type_2_Interaction).

3.4   Transitional Semantics of SBC Process Algebra

In giving meaning to SBC process algebra, we shall use the following transition system $(\Psi, \Delta, \{\overset{a}{\to} : a \in \Delta\})$ which consists of a set Ψ of process expressions, a set Δ of transition type_1_or_2 interactions, and a transition relation $\overset{a}{\to} \subseteq \Psi \times \Psi$ for each $a \in \Delta$. The semantics for Ψ consists in the transition rules of each transition relation over Ψ. These transition rules will follow the construct of process expressions.

As shown in Fig. 7, we give the complete set of transition rules; the names Prefix, Sum, Recursion and Constant indicate that the rules are associated respectively with Prefix, Summation, and Recursion and with Constants.

$$\text{Prefix} \qquad \frac{}{a \bullet E \overset{a}{\to} E}$$

$$\text{Sum}_j \qquad \frac{E_j \overset{a}{\to} E'_j}{\sum_{i \in I} E_i \overset{a}{\to} E'_j} \ (j \in I)$$

$$\text{Recursion} \qquad \frac{E\{\mathbf{fix}(X=E)/X\} \overset{a}{\to} E'}{\mathbf{fix}(X=E) \overset{a}{\to} E'}$$

$$\text{Constant} \qquad \frac{E \overset{a}{\to} E'}{A \overset{a}{\to} E'} \ (A \overset{\text{def}}{=} E)$$

Fig. 7. Transition rules for SBC process algebra

The rule for Prefix can be read as follows: Under any circumstances, we always infer $a \cdot E \overset{a}{\to} E$. That is, an expression, with an interaction prefixed to it, will use this interaction to accomplish the transition.

The rule for Summation can be read as follows: If any one summand E_j of the sum $\Sigma_{i \in I} E_i$ has an interaction, then the whole sum also has that interaction. Finite summation, which is enough for many practical purposes, can be presented in a more convenient form. If $I = \{1, 2\}$ then we obtain two rules for $E_1 + E_2$, by setting $j = 1, 2$:

$$\frac{E_1 \overset{a}{\to} E_1'}{E_1 + E_2 \overset{a}{\to} E_1'} \quad \frac{E_2 \overset{a}{\to} E_2'}{E_1 + E_2 \overset{a}{\to} E_2'}$$

The rule for Recursion can be read as follows: This says that any interaction which may be inferred for the **fix** expression "unwound" once (by substituting itself for its bound variable) may be inferred for the **fix** expression itself.

The rule for Constants can be read as follows: the rule of Constants asserts that each Constant has the same transitions as its defining expression.

3.5   Summary of SBC Process Algebra

In SBC process algebra, the process of a service system is designed as **fix** $(X = (\Sigma_{i \in I} IFD_i) \cdot X)$ and the process of IFD_i is defined as $\bullet_{j \in J} a_{ij}$, where $a_{i1} = g_{i1}$ for all $i \in I$. To combine them together, we summarize that in SBC process algebra a service system is then formally designed as "**fix**$(X = (g_{111} \cdot a_{112} \cdot a_{113} \cdot \ldots + g_{121} \cdot a_{122} \cdot a_{123} \cdot \ldots + g_{1M1} \cdot a_{1M2} \cdot a_{1M3} \cdot \ldots \cdot a_{1MN}) \cdot X)$".

Examining SBC process algebra, we found that it consists of two parts. The first part of the SBC approach models the all interactions (containing data, function, structure) that occur in the process of a service systems design, as shown in Fig. 8.

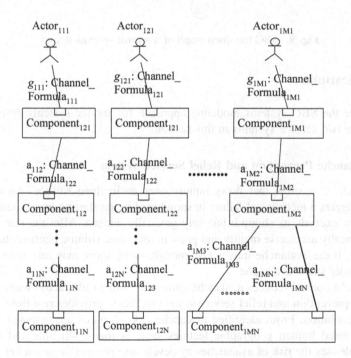

Fig. 8. SBC interactions of a service systems design

The second part of the SBC approach models the behavior of the entire service system. We use the SBC transition graph to design the behavior of the entire service system, as shown in Fig. 9.

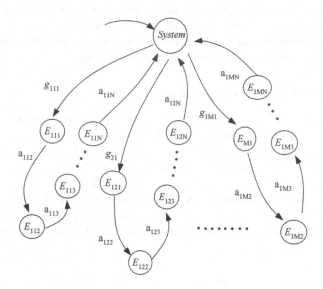

Fig. 9. SBC transition graph of a service systems design

4 Applications

To illustrate the SBC systems modeling approach for service systems design, let us demonstrate two service systems in this section.

4.1 Avalanche Prevention and Relief Service System

An avalanche is a snow that flows rapidly over an inclined surface. An avalanche typically triggers a mechanical failure in snowboard in the starting area when the force on the snow exceeds its strength but only gradually widens. After the start, the avalanches typically accelerate rapidly and grow in mass and volume because they entrain more snow. If the avalanche moves fast enough, some snow may mix with the air to form a powder snow avalanche.

Avalanche control reduces avalanche damage to human life, activity and property. Avalanche prevention and relief service system (APRSS) provides real-time avalanche monitoring solution. From identified avalanche risks, hazards are assessed by identifying threatened human geographic features such as roads, ski hills and buildings. APRSS addresses the risk of avalanches by developing prevention and relief plans that are then implemented in the winter. APRSS [13] directly intervenes in the evolution of the snowpack, or as soon as avalanches occur, avalanche effects are mitigated.

The SBC systems modeling of APRSS, E_{200}, is defined as "**fix**$(X = (g_{211} \cdot g_{212} \cdot v_{213} \cdot v_{214} + g_{221} \cdot v_{222} + g_{231} \cdot v_{232} \cdot g_{233} + g_{241} \cdot v_{242} + g_{251} \cdot v_{252}) \cdot X)$". All interactions (containing data, function, structure) of APRSS service systems design are shown in Fig. 10.

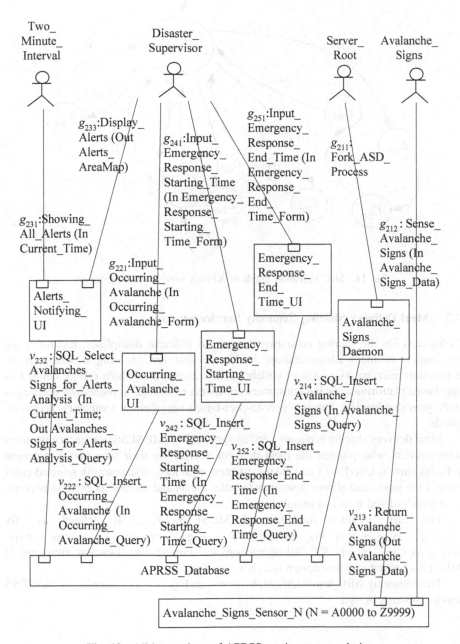

Fig. 10. All interactions of APRSS service systems design

The following SBC transition graph shows, in Fig. 11, the behavior of APRSS service systems design.

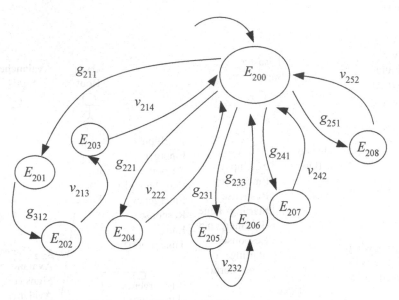

Fig. 11. SBC transition graph of APRSS service systems design

4.2   Meal Delivery Sharing Economy Service System

Definitions for the sharing economy come from different disciplines. Examples are economics, business administration, healthcare and law. Sharing economy is an expression referring to a form of collaborative consumption which can be defined as app-based platforms allowing consumers/borrowers to engage in monetized exchanges with providers/lenders through peer-to-peer-based services or temporary access to goods.

Meal delivery sharing economy service system [14] (MDSESS) connects customers with couriers who provide the meal delivery service on their own non-commercial vehicles such as UberEATS and ele.me, partners with local restaurants in selected cities around the world and allows customers to order meals and utilizes its existing network to deliver ordered meals in minutes.

The SBC systems modeling of MDSESS, E_{300}, is defined as "**fix** $(X = (g_{311} \cdot v_{312} + g_{321} \cdot v_{322} \cdot g_{323} \cdot g_{324} \cdot v_{325} + g_{331} \cdot v_{332} \cdot g_{333} \cdot g_{334} \cdot v_{335} + g_{341} \cdot v_{342} \cdot g_{343} + g_{351} \cdot v_{352}) \cdot X)$". All interactions (containing data, function, structure) of MDSESS service systems design are shown in Fig. 12.

The following SBC transition graph shows, in Fig. 13, the behavior of MDSESS service systems design.

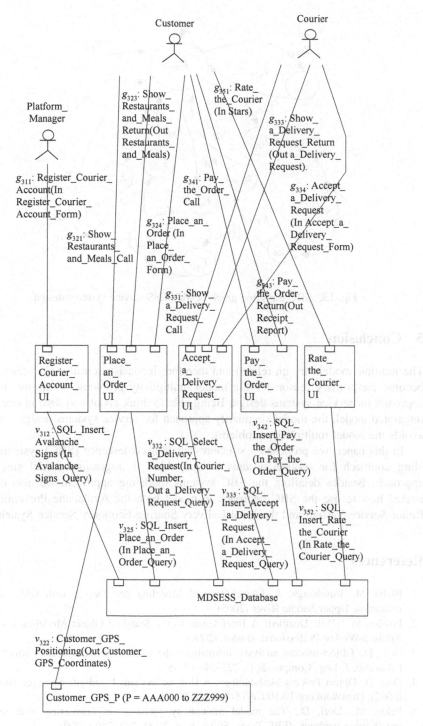

Fig. 12. All interactions of MDSESS service systems design

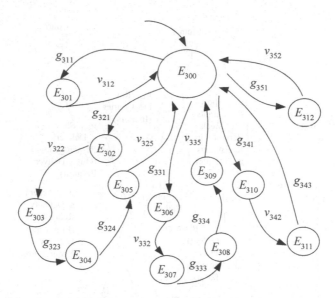

Fig. 13. SBC transition graph of MDSESS service systems design

5   Conclusion

The multiple models are un-related and therefore inconsistent with each other, which become the primary reason for the model multiplicity problems of the multi-model approach for service systems design. Being able to think about a system in one single integrated model, the model singularity approach for service systems design sincerely avoids the model multiplicity problems.

In this paper, we proposed a structure-behavior coalescence (SBC) systems modeling approach for service systems design which is a genuine model singularity approach. Besides detailing the SBC systems modeling approach, we also demonstrated how to use the SBC approach to model both the Avalanche Prevention and Relief Service System and the Meal Delivery Sharing Economy Service System.

References

1. Blaha, M., Rumbaugh, J.: Object-Oriented Modeling and Design with UML. Pearson Education, Upper Saddle River (2005)
2. Fowler, M.: UML Distilled: A Brief Guide to the Standard Object Modeling Language. Addison-Wesley Professional, Boston (2004)
3. Dori, D.: Object-process analysis: maintaining the balance between system structure and behaviour. J. Log. Comput. **5**(2), 227–249 (1995)
4. Dori, D.: Object-Process Methodology: A Holistic Systems Paradigm. Springer, New York (2002). https://doi.org/10.1007/978-3-642-56209-9
5. Peleg, M., Dori, D.: The model multiplicity problem: experimenting with real-time specification methods. IEEE Trans. Softw. Eng. **26**(8), 742–759 (2000)

6. Soderborg, N.R., Crawley, E.F., Dori, D.: System function and architecture: OPM-based definitions and operational templates. Commun. ACM **46**(10), 67–72 (2003)
7. Dori, D.: Model-Based Systems Engineering with OPM and SysML. Springer, New York (2016). https://doi.org/10.1007/978-1-4939-3295-5
8. Hoare, C.A.R.: Communicating sequential processes. Commun. ACM **21**(8), 666–677 (1978)
9. Milner, R.: Communication and Concurrency. Prentice Hall, New York (1989)
10. Bergstra, J.A., Klop, J.W.: ACPτ: a universal axiom system for process specification. CWI Q. **15**, 3–23 (1987)
11. Chao, W.S.: General Systems Theory 2.0: General Architectural Theory Using the SBC Architecture. CreateSpace Independent Publishing, North Charleston (2014)
12. Chao, W.S.: Generalized SBC Process Algebra for Communication and Concurrency: The Structure-Behavior Coalescence Approach. CreateSpace Independent Publishing, North Charleston (2016)
13. Chao, W.S.: Systems Architecture of Avalanche Prevention and Relief Cloud Applications and Services IoT System: General Systems Theory 2.0 at Work. CreateSpace Independent Publishing Platform, North Charleston (2016)
14. Chao, W.S.: Systems Architecture of Meal Delivery Sharing Economy Cloud Applications and Services IoT System: General Systems Theory 2.0 at Work. CreateSpace Independent Publishing Platform, North Charleston (2016)

Electronic Commerce and Consumer Behavior

Data Breaches and Trust Rebuilding: Moderating Impact of Signaling of Corporate Social Responsibility

Gaurav Bansal[✉]

University of Wisconsin – Green Bay, Green Bay, USA
bansalg@uwgb.edu

Abstract. Data breach is a serious global security and trust concern. Data breaches have both direct and indirect as well as a short-term and long-term financial implications for the victim organization. One of the significant long-term financial costs is the loss of consumer trust in the organization. It seems that the sheer number and size of data breaches, insider data breaches, in particular, is not about to slow down anytime soon. There is a need to heighten information security to prevent such breaches, and there is a need to deploy trust-building strategies to minimize the trust fallout from such breaches. There is plenty of evidence that consumers use corporate social responsibility (CSR) as a means of differentiating one company from another. In this paper, we examine if CSR strategies such as embracing a social cause (LGBT and nature) could assist in repairing organizational trust in the wake of a data breach.

Keywords: Data breaches · Trust rebuilding · Corporate social responsibility
LGBT issues

1 Introduction

Data breach is a serious global security and trust concern. According to Breach-levelindex.com (2017), more than 5 million records are lost or stolen every day. The site reports that India had 274 million records lost or stolen since 2003, while the US had 5.8 billion records lost or stolen during the same period. According to Infosecurity-magazine.com insider threats are responsible for 43% of all data breaches (Seals 2015). Data breaches have both direct and indirect as well as a short-term as well as long-term financial implications for the victim organization (Bansal et al. 2015, 2017). One of the significant long-term financial costs is the loss of consumer trust in the organization (Bansal and Zahedi 2015, Target 2015).

It seems that the sheer number and size of data breaches, insider data breaches, in particular, is not about to slow down anytime soon. There is a need to heighten information security to prevent such breaches, and there is a need to deploy trust-building strategies to minimize the trust fallout from such breaches. There is plenty of evidence that consumers use corporate social responsibility (CSR) as a means of differentiating one company from another. For instance, Gupta and Pirsch (2006) cite that around 80% of users trust organizations that back a social cause. However, to

© Springer International Publishing AG, part of Springer Nature 2018
F. F.-H. Nah and B. S. Xiao (Eds.): HCIBGO 2018, LNCS 10923, pp. 253–261, 2018.
https://doi.org/10.1007/978-3-319-91716-0_19

date, there has been no systematic examination of the results of perceived CSR activities on trust violation and repair. In this paper, we examine if CSR strategies such as embracing a social cause (LGBT and nature) could assist in repairing organizational trust in the wake of a data breach.

The remainder of this paper is organized as follows: the following section presents the research model and the hypotheses. Research methodology and results are presented next. The paper concludes by discussing the theoretical, practical, and social implications along with future research directions.

2 Theoretical Model

Ellen et al. (2006) grouped CSR efforts into four categories. First, egoistic driven motives – that exploit the cause rather than help it. Second, strategic driven motives – that support the attainment of business goals (e.g., create positive impressions) while supporting the cause. Third, stakeholder-driven motives – that support the cause primarily because of pressure from stakeholders. Last, values-driven motives – that pertain to benevolence-motivated giving. In this paper, we examine the signaling effect of social cause endorsement by a website using images (Zahedi and Bansal 2011). The use of website image in such a way could be argued to be a strategic or stakeholder driven CSR initiative (Ellen et al. 2006).

There is growing evidence that CSR activities help generate returns - in the form of increased purchase intentions as well as higher prices (Bhattacharya et al. 2009; Yoon et al. 2006). Such socially responsible organizations signal that they care for and are interested in healthy and enduring relationships with their stakeholders (Waddock and Smith, 2000). Gupta and Pirsch (2006) stated that "[i]ndividuals who support such companies satisfy their humanitarian desires and thus perceive they are obtaining additional value from their purchases" (p. 325).

Numerous theories have been brought to bear on the subject of CSR. Examples include agency theory, stakeholder theory, stewardship theory, RBV, institutional theory, and theory of the firm (see McWilliams and Siegel 2001). In this research, we examine CSR initiatives from an attribution theory perspective. Attribution theory suggests that if the behavior of the other party is consistent with prior expectations, then the cause of action is attributed internally to him/her. Otherwise, it is attributed to external situations (Jones and Nisbett 1971; Jarvenpaa et al. 2004). Thus, using an attribution theory perspective, we argue that in the case of a data breach and subsequent apology by a website, users would be more forgiving if the website comes across as more benevolent towards its stakeholders (Shankar et al. 2002). We argue that depicting images advocating and embracing a social cause would signal the strategic/stakeholder driven CSR efforts of the website. Such images, in turn, would make the users attribute the breach failure to external situational characteristics (instead of attributing it to the website), and thus dampen the effect of the data breach and enhance the effect of corporate apology. The research model is shown in Fig. 1 and discussed below.

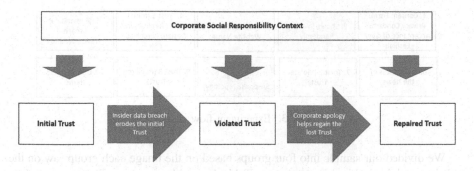

Fig. 1. Research model

Hypothesis 1. The level of initial trust is higher for websites signaling a higher level of social cause endorsements (such as LGBT and nature issues).

Hypothesis 2. The level of violated trust in the wake of an insider data breach is higher for websites signaling a higher level of social cause endorsements (such as LGBT and nature issues).

Hypothesis 3. The level of repaired trust in the wake of an insider data breach and a subsequent corporate apology is higher for websites signaling a higher level of social cause endorsements (such as LGBT and nature issues).

3 Research Methodology

We created four website home pages each with a different image – as shown in Fig. 2 below. We used Qualtrics to design an experimental survey to collect the data. Respondents were randomly assigned to view a website, and they were asked to answer questions about the website and also asked to provide individual traits and demographics. Figure 3 shows the flow process of the experiment. Respondents were quizzed to make sure that they had sifted through the website (homepage). Data were collected from students and families living in a Midwestern US region. 476 unique respondents completed the survey. Only 394 of the 476 respondents answered a quiz question about the website name correctly. We included only these 396 in our analysis.

Straight	Lesbian	Gay	Nature

Fig. 2. Images used for the website home pages

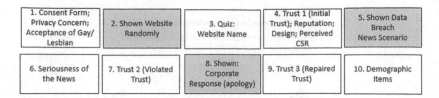

| 1. Consent Form; Privacy Concern; Acceptance of Gay/ Lesbian | 2. Shown Website Randomly | 3. Quiz: Website Name | 4. Trust 1 (Initial Trust); Reputation; Design; Perceived CSR | 5. Shown Data Breach News Scenario |
| 6. Seriousness of the News | 7. Trust 2 (Violated Trust) | 8. Shown: Corporate Response (apology) | 9. Trust 3 (Repaired Trust) | 10. Demographic Items |

Fig. 3. Experiment flow chart

We divided our sample into four groups based on the image each group saw on the website: straight, lesbian, gay or nature. Table 1 provides gender and mean age values for these four groups.

Table 1. Age and gender demographics

Scenario	N	Age				Gender		
		Min	Max	Mean	Std dev	Male	Female	Missing values
Straight	101	18	82	33.87	15.28	40	59	2
Lesbian	105	18	66	30.18	13.17	43	60	2
Gay	102	18	71	33.53	14.31	42	58	2
Nature	86	18	73	32.79	14.85	41	43	2

We used existing items wherever possible. Privacy concern (PC), trust (ability - ABL, benevolence - BEN, integrity - INT and overall trust), reputation (REP), design (DES), perceived seriousness of the breach news (SERIOUS), and trust propensity (TRPR) items were taken from Bansal and Zahedi (2015). Insider news and apology vignettes were taken from Bansal et al. (2017). Acceptance of LGBT (LGBT) items were adapted from Herek (1988), and perceived corporate citizenship (PCC) items were adapted from Lichtenstein et al. (2004).

We cleaned the data before conducting the analysis. We also performed exploratory factor analysis to identify the items that demonstrate high factor loadings and low cross-loadings. All items except for one reputation item demonstrated high loadings and low cross-loadings. We then averaged the items to generate the respective constructs (Shamir et al. 1998). All analyses were carried out with SPSS v 23.

4   Results

We analyzed the data using ANOVA. We carried out three different ANOVA tests to examine the three hypotheses. Results as shown in Tables 2, 3, and 4, and depicted graphically in Figs. 4, 5 and 6, reveal that H1 and H2 are not supported, H3 is supported at .05 level for overall trust and benevolence based trust, and at .10 level for ability-based trust. H3 is not supported for integrity based trust. We briefly discuss the results below.

Hypothesis 1 - Initial Trust: In the first step we examined whether the initial trust differed across the four website scenarios studied. We controlled for privacy concern, perceived website reputation, perceived website design, trust propensity, perceived corporate citizenship, user gender, and user age. We also controlled for one's acceptance of the LGBT community. The results showed that H1 is not supported. The p values are all higher than .05 for all trust types (as shown in Table 2). The graphs in Fig. 4 show that mean values for initial trust are slightly higher for the three websites depicting a social cause (LGBT and nature), especially for ability and benevolence based trust. However, the differences are not significant.

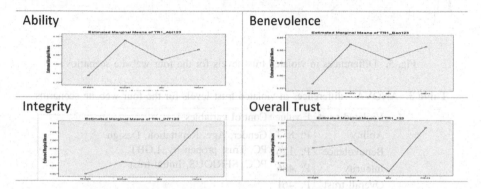

Fig. 4. Differences in initial trust levels for the four website scenarios

Table 2. ANOVA - differences in initial trust levels for the four website scenarios

Initial trust	P value	Control Variables
Ability	.709	Gender, Age, Reputation,
Benevolence	.851	Design, PC, TRPR,
Integrity	.733	LGBT, PCC
Overall trust	.929	

Hypothesis 2 - Violated Trust. In the second step, we examined whether the violated trust differed across the four website scenarios studied. We controlled for the perceived seriousness of the breach news along with the variables controlled in H1. We also controlled for the respective initial trust when examining the differences in violated trust. For instance, we controlled for initial integrity based trust when examining integrity based trust violation. The results (Table 3) show that H2 is not supported. The p values are higher than .05 for all trust types. The graphs in Fig. 5 show that mean values for violated trust are slightly lower for the websites depicting social cause endorsements (LGBT and nature) for benevolence based trust, however; the difference is not significant.

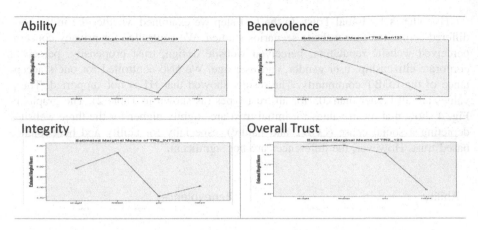

Fig. 5. Differences in violated trust levels for the four website scenarios

Table 3. ANOVA - differences in violated trust levels for the four website scenarios

Violated trust	P value	Control variables
Ability	P: .853	Gender, Age, Reputation, Design,
Benevolence	P: .126	PC, Trust propensity, LGBT,
Integrity	P: .486	PCC, SERIOUS, Initial trust
Overall trust	P: .461	

Hypothesis 3 - Repaired Trust. In the third and last step, we examined if the repaired trust differed across the four websites studied. In this step, we controlled for mean violated trust along with the control variables used in H2. Results support H3 for overall trust and benevolence trust at .05 level, and ability based trust at .10 level (Overall F test in Table 4). Results (Fig. 6) show that trust regained is higher for websites with "social responsibility" (except for integrity based trust).

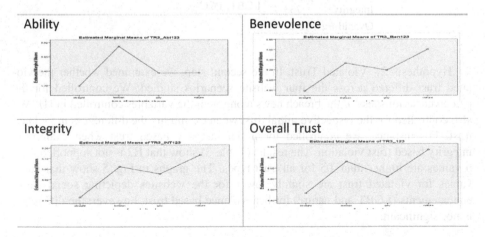

Fig. 6. Differences in repaired trust levels for the four website scenarios

Post hoc analysis (also in Table 4) suggests that the lesbian scenario garnered more trust (as compared to the straight scenario) for all four trust types. The analysis also shows that the nature scenario emerged as second best and improved trust for both benevolence based and overall trust. However, the gay scenario improved trust only for benevolence based trust. Thus, benevolence trust was regained across all three (lesbian, gay and nature) website scenarios (as compared to the straight scenario) followed by the overall trust which was regained significantly only for two scenarios (lesbian and nature).

Table 4. ANOVA - differences in repaired trust levels for the four website scenarios (S: Straight scenario, L: Lesbian scenario, G: Gay scenario, N: Nature scenario)

Repaired trust	Overall F test	Post hoc (P values)	Control variables
Ability	.062	L > S (.003); G = S (.261); N = S (.763)	Gender, Age, Reputation, Design, PC, TRPR, LGBT, PCC, SERIOUS, respective initial trust, respective violated trust
Benevolence	.012	L > S (.018); G > S (.082); N > S (.006)	
Integrity	.340	L > S (.072); G = S (.191); N = S (.183)	
Overall trust	.004	L > S (.006); G = S (.113); N > S (.013)	

5 Discussion

Even though researchers agree that CSR could provide a differentiation strategy (McWilliams and Kiegel 2001), "there exists little conceptual clarity regarding when, how, and why firms might be able to achieve their strategic goals, such as gaining a competitive advantage, through their CSR actions" (Du et al. 2011, p. 1528). Thus, this research serves two critical theoretical functions: it adds to our understanding of the role of CSR actions in achieving strategic goals, and it also provides additional insight into various strategies that could help mitigate a trust crisis following a data breach.

Prior research suggests that consumers are likely to view attributions of stakeholder and strategic driven motives negatively or unresponsively (Vlachos et al. 2009), as they believe the company is acting to avoid retribution from stakeholders or they suspect that the company is trying to get a strategic benefit in return. In this study, the unresponsiveness showed towards the initial and violated trust (p-value > .05) validates such apprehensions. However, the fact that the CSR initiatives did improve trust rebuilding (T3) shows that strategic and stakeholder driven CSR initiatives might not translate into immediate trust gains, but they do have the potential to supplement trust rebuilding efforts when followed by an apology. The fact that benevolence based trust scored higher than other trust types is consistent with the findings of Hegner et al. (2016) who found in their study using 304 Dutch respondents, that "rebuilding strategy has a more positive effect on benevolence-based than ability-based trust."

The work has managerial, theoretical, and social implications. The results suggest that managers may need to be aware of perceived CSR as a critical variable in rebuilding trust following a crisis, notably a data breach. Socially, the work shows that society in general, and the sample demographics (Midwestern US), are more accepting of two females raising a child and aptly reward the website with improved repaired trust following a data breach and subsequent corporate apology. Even though the US Supreme Court bars states from banning same-sex marriages, and courts in India recognize third-gender (Crocker 2017), US federal laws have no workplace protection for LGBT employees (Zapulla 2017) and there are minimal protections for transgender individuals in India (Crocker 2017); the results suggest that there might be economic returns to supporting such a cause.

This research shows that the LGBT driven CSR efforts could help in trust rebuilding efforts, especially in the Midwestern US region. However, it is known that CSR issues are country specific (e.g., Maignan and Ralston 2002). A social cause that is worth pursuing in one country might not be a noble goal in another country. For instance, two dozen countries allow same-sex marriages, mostly in Europe and the America (PEW 2017), and at the same time, in 74 countries, same-sex marriages are considered a criminal offense (Fenton 2016). The stakeholder theory of trust (Shankar et al. 2002) suggests that relationships and alliances with one stakeholder (say customers in the US) impacts trust with other stakeholders (say customers in India). In today's digital age many businesses have a global outreach. Several Indian IT businesses, for instance, drive revenues from western countries where same-sex marriages are now legal. It will be interesting to study the cross-cultural impact of LGBT endorsements and other CSR exercises on trust building/rebuilding by a multinational firm in two different countries in which it operates, one that legalizes the social cause, and the other that does not. Similarly, it would be of interest to examine the cross-cultural efficacy of different CSR social causes and different strategies of embracing them – strategic driven versus value driven for example (Ellen et al. 2006).

References

Bansal, G., Benzshawel, A., Estrada, D.: Insider data breaches and trust violation: the role of privacy concern, age and gender. In: Proceedings of 12th Midwest Association for Information Systems Conference. University of Illinois, Springfield (2017)

Bansal, G., Zahedi, F.M.: Trust violation and repair: the information privacy perspective. Decis. Support Syst. **71**, 62–77 (2015)

Bhattacharya, C.B., Korschun, D., Sankar, S.: Strengthening stakeholder-company relationships through mutually beneficial corporate social responsibility initiatives. J. Bus. Eth. **85**, 257–272 (2009)

Breachlevelindex.com: Data Breach Statistics (2017). http://breachlevelindex.com/. Accessed 27 July 2016

Crocker, L.: How India Embraces The 'Third Gender': Laxmi Narayan Tripathi at 'Women in The World', 4 July 2017. http://www.thedailybeast.com/how-india-embraces-the-third-gender-laxmi-narayan-tripathi-at-women-in-the-world. Accessed 26 July 2017

Du, S., Bhattacharya, C.B., Sen, S.: Corporate social responsibility and competitive advantage: overcoming the trust barrier. Manag. Sci. **57**(9), 1528–1545 (2011)

Ellen, P.S., Web, D.J., Mohr, L.A.: Building corporate associations: consumer attributions for corporate social responsibility programs. J. Acad. Mark. Sci. **34**(2), 147–157 (2006)

Fenton: LGBT relationships are illegal in 74 countries, research finds, 17 May 2016. http://www.independent.co.uk/news/world/gay-lesbian-bisexual-relationships-illegal-in-74-countries-a7033666.html. Accessed 27 July 2017

Gupta, S., Pirsch, J.: The company-cause-customer fit decision in cause-related marketing. J. Consum. Mark. **23**(6), 314–326 (2006)

Hegner, S.M., Beldad, A.D., Kraesgenberg, A.: The impact of crisis response strategy, crisis type, and corporate social responsibility on post-crisis consumer trust and purchase intention. Corp. Reput. Rev. **19**(4), 357–370 (2016)

Herek, G.M.: Heterosexuals' attitudes toward lesbians and gay men: correlates and gender differences. Journal Sex Res. **25**(4), 451–477 (1988)

Jarvenpaa, S.L., Shaw, T.R., Staples, D.S.: Toward contextualized theories of trust: the role of trust in global virtual teams. Inf. Syst. Res. **15**(3), 250–267 (2004)

Jones, E.E., Nisbett, R.E.: The Actor and the Observer: Divergent Perceptions of the Causes of Behavior. General Learning Press, Morristown (1971)

Lichtenstein, D.R., Drumwright, M.E., Braig, B.M.: The effect of corporate social responsibility on customer donations to corporate-supported nonprofits. J. Mark. **68**, 16–32 (2004)

Maignan, I., Ralston, D.A.: Corporate social responsibility in Europe and the U.S.: insights from businesses' self - presentations. J. Int. Bus. Stud. **33**, 497–514 (2002)

McWilliams, A., Siegel, D.: Corporate social responsibility: a theory of the firm perspective. Acad. Manag. Rev. **26**(1), 117–127 (2001)

PEW Research Center: Gay Marriage Around the World, 30 June 2017. http://www.pewforum.org/2017/06/30/gay-marriage-around-the-world-2013/. Accessed 27 July 2017

Seals, T.: Insider Threats Responsible for 43% of Data Breaches, 25 September 2015. https://www.infosecurity-magazine.com/news/insider-threats-reponsible-for-43/. Accessed 27 July 2016

Shamir, B., Zakay, E., Breinin, E., Popper, M.: Correlates of charismatic leader behavior in military units: subordinates' attitudes, unit characteristics, and superiors' appraisals of leader performance. Acad. Manag. J. **41**(4), 387–409 (1998)

Shankar, V., Urban, G.L., Sultan, F.: Online trust: a stakeholder perspective, concepts, implications, and future directions. J. Strateg. Inf. Syst. **11**, 325–344 (2002)

Target: 2015 Annual Report (2015). https://corporate.target.com/_media/TargetCorp/annualreports/2015/pdfs/Target-2015-Annual-Report.pdf. Accessed 27 July 2017

Vlachos, P.A., Tsamakos, A., Vrechopoulos, A.P., Avramidis, P.K.: Corporate social responsibility: attributions, loyalty, and the mediating role of trust. Acad. Mark. Sci. J. **37**(2), 170–180 (2009)

Waddock, S., Smith, N.: Relationships: the real challenge of corporate global citizenship. Bus. Soc. Rev. **105**(1), 47–62 (2000)

Yoon, Y., Gurhan-Canli, Z., Schwarz, N.: The effect of corporate social responsibility (CSR) activities on companies with bad reputations. J. Consum. Psychol. **16**(4), 377–390 (2006)

Zahedi, F.M., Bansal, G.: Cultural signifiers of web site images. J. Manag. Inf. Syst. **28**(1), 147–200 (2011)

Zappulla, A.: The simple reason why so many businesses support LGBT rights, 14 January 2017. https://www.weforum.org/agenda/2017/01/why-so-many-businesses-support-lgbt-rights/. Accessed 26 July 2017

The Effect of LOGO Location in Navigation Bar on Web Brand Recognition Based on Event-Related Potential

Yingying Dong, Chengqi Xue[✉], Ningyue Peng, and Yafeng Niu

School of Mechanical Engineering, Southeast University,
Nanjing 211189, China
ipd_xcq@seu.edu.cn

Abstract. In order to study the cognitive process of brand recognition in different positions (left, middle and right) of the web navigation bar, this paper adopts the Oddball experimental paradigm in event-related potentials combined with behavioral data for experimental investigation. An analytical comparison of the P300 amplitude of the LOGO located in three certain positions in the navigation bar is conducted. The LOGO placed on the left/right can generate larger amplitude than the LOGO placed on the middle. The experimental result shows that LOGO location in navigation bar have a great significance on brand recognition. From neural mechanism of visual cognition processing, ERP can objectively and effectively obtain the implicit feedback of web brand recognition from users, which provides a quantitative index for establishing an accurate evaluation model of web brand recognition.

Keywords: ERPs · Web brand recognition · LOGO location

1 Introduction

With the massive information and service content which tend to be homogenized filled in our daily life, the competitive pressures on websites are unprecedented. In order to help users to recognize brand and cultivate brand loyalty, the interactive system has increasingly become user's main way in brand recognition. Brand recognition will affect the user's purchase decisions and brand loyalty to a great extent. Howard pointed out that consumers' cognition of the brand and product is from the product information, which will be transformed into brand attitudes and will further influence the purchase intention and purchase behavior of the brand [1]. As a result, we now know that users tend to choose the product which has higher brand recognition when they do the purchase decisions. If the location of brand information appears more likely to be noticed, it can deepen user's cognition for brand and then promote user's brand recognition. As a result, website which has higher recognition can be easily distinguished from other websites and can occupy psychological position of users.

In recent years, many researchers have conducted brand recognition as follows: Kapferer suggested that the market had experienced the changes of brand image, brand positioning and brand personality, then an era of brand recognition will come. He put

© Springer International Publishing AG, part of Springer Nature 2018
F. F.-H. Nah and B. S. Xiao (Eds.): HCIBGO 2018, LNCS 10923, pp. 262–274, 2018.
https://doi.org/10.1007/978-3-319-91716-0_20

forward a hexagon prism model and brand pyramid theory in the book *Strategic Brand Management* [2]. Schniitt and Simonson proposed a brand recognition model from marketing aesthetics perspective. They considered brand recognition included four elements: properties, products, presentations and publications [3]. Aaker argued that brand identification should include soul of brand, core identity of brand and extended identity of brand in the book *Brand Leadership* [4]. Kotler studied brand recognition from the point of marketing communication and considered that brand was the means of communication. The information that company conveyed to consumers by brand was three-dimensional and all-around. It also included three-layer construction, namely, brand recognition, brand Image and brand personality [5]. Aaker proposed a 'four-level theory', he proposed that brand identification was composed of 12 elements in four levels: product identification (product area, product properties, quality value, usage, user, country of origin), brand organization (organizational nature, localization or globalization), personal brand (brand personality, relationship between the brand and customer) and symbolic brand (visual image/metaphor and brand tradition) [6]. Maria found the relationship among brand identification, brand image and brand preference in the network environment. He also verified that good brand recognition was beneficial to brand image and brand preference. Furthermore, offline influence had greater significance than online influence [7]. Bernd constructed a consumer psychology model through the integration of relevant research results, showing the consumer's brand awareness, judgments and related processes [8]. da Silveira et al. reconstructed the brand recognition model under the influence of many factors, such as time, consumer and so on [9].

The websites have the characteristic of content pre-guiding. Navigation bar which is the catalogue of the website content and has a higher utilization may directly influence user experience. Furthermore, users usually give priority concerns to the navigation bar when they enter the home page. In addition, the position of the navigation bar is fixed on the top of the page, which may help user to know where they are and can also play an important role in brand recognition. Therefore, this paper chooses the elements in navigation bar for brand recognition research.

At present, there are few researches on LOGO location in navigation bar. However, there are many papers on graphic and text design in LOGO. Li studied the elements of corporate culture, physical geography and environmental characteristics, the traditional cultural characteristics and the corresponding graphics and text in the hotel visual image LOGO design [10]. Wang argued that how to improve brand recognition from the perspective of LOGO attribute recognition and LOGO recognition in same class [11]. Niu discussed the importance of LOGO design in the brand and different design forms in LOGO design [12]. Xu found that lowercase wordmarks can increase perception of brand friendliness compared with the uppercase wordmarks. In addition, consumers felt that uppercase wordmarks were more authoritative [13]. Liu found the approach to combine traditional Chinese art elements with LOGO design [14]. Therefore, considering brand LOGO itself is not enough, no matter how good the brand is, if it cannot be recognized by the user, it will be nothing. If the application scenario of LOGO can be taken into account, in some way to enhance the user's brand cognition, it will attract more users and improve brand recognition.

In the past, the main method of brand recognition were subjective evaluation and physiological evaluation. The former obtains the brand recognition from users through questionnaire, user interview, etc. The latter is mainly used to obtain the physiological indexes to understand the degree of brand recognition from users, such as Electromyography (EMG), eye movement and so on. However, it still has some shortcomings: for subjective evaluation, it may lack reliable and repeatable objective indicators to evaluate; for physiological evaluation, it is easy to be disturbed by external factors. Event-related Potential (ERPs) uses brain-imaging techniques for positive and negative waves of the scalp-related potential in order to reflect the subtle brain cognitive activity. Moreover, it can describe and analyze the cognition process of digital interface, which directly reflect neuroelectricity activity and establishing the relationship between neurophysiology and cognitive process.

In the visual Oddball paradigm, the user's recognition process of target stimulus includes working memory, attention, stimulation evaluation and pattern matching, etc. The appearance of target stimulus may induce more significant effect on P300 component [15]. Hillyard proposed that during the selective attention process, P3 represented the response set, which represented the subsequent stage of the perceived information processing, and later it was confirmed that a larger P300 amplitude may appear when people pay more attention to something [16]. Donchin pointed out that the latency of the P300 reflected the speed and selection process of stimulus recognition when the memory was updated. In addition, he also believed that the content which induced higher amplitude of P300 was more likely to be remembered [17].

In this paper, the opinion that the brand recognition is not only dependent on the internal factors of the brand is put forward. From a new perspective, LOGO Location in the navigation bar is an important external factor that affects the web brand recognition, which can provide a more objective method for brand building. Oddball experimental paradigm is used to explore user's EEG psychological characteristics induced by the LOGO's different locations in the navigation bar. With the help of P300 amplitude changes and subjective evaluation results, the effect of LOGO location in navigation bar on web brand recognition can be revealed. If the brand appears more likely to be noticed, it can deepen user's cognition for brand and then promote user's brand recognition. What's more, it may help users recognize and choose websites rapidly according to LOGO location in navigation bar, enhancing the brand recognition and promoting brand loyalty of the website that have important influence on website building.

2 Experiment Design

2.1 Participants

Participants consist of 20 students who are between 22 and 27 years old with a ratio of one to one, right-handed. They all have corrected visual acuity over 1.0 and have no history of mental illness.

2.2   Experiment Method

ERP experiment

Experiment Materials. Oddball experimental paradigm is used in the experiment. According to the different LOGO locations, three sets of location relationship are established. Plan A places the LOGO on the left (Fig. 1), Plan B places the LOGO on the middle (Fig. 2), Plan C places the LOGO on the right (Fig. 3). Plan A, Plan B, Plan C are target stimuli, Fig. 4 is the standard stimulus. It is predicted that the target stimulus will induce significant P300 in the Oddball experimental paradigm.

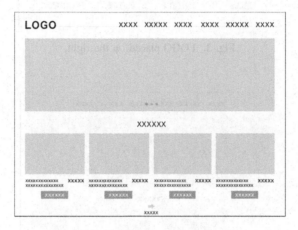

Fig. 1. LOGO placed on the left.

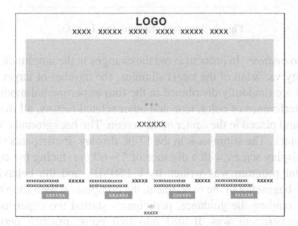

Fig. 2. LOGO placed on the middle.

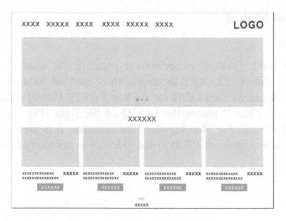

Fig. 3. LOGO placed on the right.

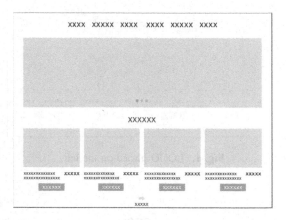

Fig. 4. Standard stimulus (no LOGO).

Experimental Procedure. In order to avoid the changes in the amplitude of P300 caused by the probability variation of the target stimulus, the number of target stimuli and the standard stimuli are randomly distributed in the four experimental modules. In order to eliminate the interference of color, icon and other related factors, all the stimuli images are desaturated and placed in the center of the screen. The background color is white and the stimulus is black. The stimulus is in the 17-in. display. Participants were asked to sit in front of the display screen with a distance of 55–60 cm, facing the computer screen. The experimental program was written by E-PRIME, and the behavioral data were collected. At the beginning of the experiment, the computer screen showed experimental guidance. After reading the guidance, participants started the experiment by pressing any key. The experiment was divided into two parts: practice period and formal experiment period. The cross-visual guidance appeared in the center of screen for 500 ms at first, then standard stimulus and target stimulus appeared at random. Azizian et al. set the stimulus presentation time to 500 ms to eliminate visual residuals [18]. The participants were told to respond at the fastest speed and press 'L' to respond to target stimulus. Throughout the testing process, the standard stimuli appeared 480 times in total (the number of standard stimuli account for 80%), each kind of target stimuli appeared 40 times (target stimuli account for 20%). The experiment procedure is shown below (Fig. 5).

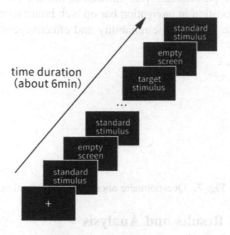

Fig. 5. Experiment procedure.

EEG Recording and Data Analysis. The experiment data collection and data analysis are conducted by BP EEG recording system. The brain waves induced by target stimuli are recorded by using EEG Recording Cap Set for 32 Channels (0.05–100 Hz band pass; 1 kHz/channel sampling rate). Electrode impedance is maintained below 5 kΩ throughout the experiment. According to the literature description and the total waveform of P300, the regions that have the highest brain activation between 0 ms and 800 ms are centro-parietal lobe, parietal lobe and occipital lobe [19], so CP5, CP1, CP2, CP6, P7, P3, Pz, P4, P8, POz, O1, Oz, O2 are selected (see Fig. 6). The amplitude

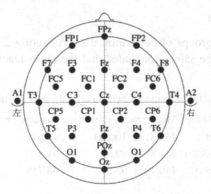

Fig. 6. Electrode diagram

and latency are compared by analysis of variance via SPSS. The p value of variance analysis is calibrated with the Greenhouse Geisser method.

2.3 Subjective Evaluation

After ERP experiment, participants were allowed to finish a questionnaire (see Fig. 7). The effect of LOGO location in navigation bar on web brand recognition was evaluated by 7-level Likert scale to verify the reliability and effectiveness of ERP.

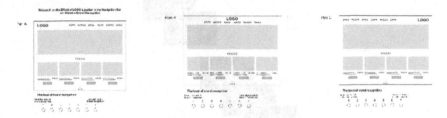

Fig. 7. Questionnaire about brand recognition

3 Experimental Results and Analysis

3.1 Subjective Evaluation Data

According to statistics, LOGO on the left was rated 5.36 points on average among 22 subjects; LOGO on the middle was rated 5.59 points; LOGO on the right was rated 3.37 points. Through further analysis of the results, we found that 57% subjects thought the LOGO placed on the middle had the highest brand recognition; 34% subjects thought the LOGO placed on the left had the highest brand recognition; only 9% subjects hold the view that the LOGO placed on the right had the highest brand recognition. Based on the subjective evaluation results, this paper will explore the relationship between LOGO location and brand recognition further.

3.2 Behavioral Data

Table 1 showed three groups of behavioral data, collecting 22 valid samples in total. From the table, it can be safely concluded that the mean reaction time in condition 1

Table 1. Descriptive statistics of behavioral data in 3 groups of experiments.

Condition	Mean reaction time/ms	Accuracy rate/%
1 (left)	446.81 ± 100.60	98.64%
2 (middle)	444.88 ± 99.59	98.52%
3 (right)	440.10 ± 93.82	98.75%

(LOGO on the left) was longer than condition 2 (LOGO on the middle) and condition 3 (LOGO on the right), and these three groups of mean reaction time had little dispersion degree. The accuracy of three experimental groups were more than 98%, which indicated that the subjects in the three experimental groups maintained high accuracy. Mean reaction time and accuracy in three experimental groups had little difference, so in-depth interactive effect analysis was not conducted.

3.3 EEG Data Analysis

Figure 8 showed the EEG waveforms of 13 electrodes CP5, CP1, CP2, CP6, P7, P3, Pz, P4, P8, POz, O1, Oz and O2 from 0 ms to 500 ms. The P2 and P3 components were all induced under the three experimental conditions (LOGO placed on the left, middle and right). The attention, repetition and stimulation may affect the amplitude of P2. This paper analyzed the P3 that appeared in 200–500 ms.

P300 Analysis. Tables 2, 3 and 4 showed the mean amplitude of CP5, CP1, CP2, CP6, P7, P3, Pz, P4, P8, POz, O1, Oz and O2 which appeared 200 ms to 500 ms after the target stimuli. With respect to P300 component, repeated ANOVA of mean amplitude for 200–500 ms in 3 (LOGO position: LOGO placed on the left, middle, right)) × 13 (electrode position: CP5, CP1, CP2, CP6, P7, P3, Pz, P4, P8, POz, O1, Oz, O2) was conducted. The statistical analysis results were shown in Table 5: (1) The main effect of the LOGO location was significant (F = 5.938, p = 0.005 < 0.01); The mean amplitude of LOGO placed on the right (3.59 μv) was slightly larger than LOGO placed on the left (3.48 μv); The mean amplitude of LOGO placed on the left/right was significantly larger than LOGO placed on the middle (2.58 μv); (2) The main effect of electrode position was marginal significant (F = 2.826, P = 0.052 > 0.05); (3) The interaction effect between LOGO location and electrode position was significant (F = 8.727, P = 0.000 < 0.01).

In order to explore the latency differences between the target and standard stimulus further, repeated ANOVA of mean latency in 3 (LOGO position: LOGO placed on the left, middle, right) × 13 (electrode position: CP5, CP1, CP2, CP6, P7, P3, Pz, P4, P8, POz, O1, Oz, O2) was conducted. The results were shown in Table 6 as follows: (1) The main effect of the LOGO location was significant (F = 6.373, p = 0.009 < 0.01); The latency of LOGO placed on the left (308 ms) < LOGO placed on the right (315 ms) < LOGO placed on the middle (331 ms); (2) The main effect of electrode position was significant (F = 3.613, P = 0.005 < 0.01); (3) The interaction effect between LOGO location and electrode position was significant (F = 5.242, P = 0.000 < 0.01).

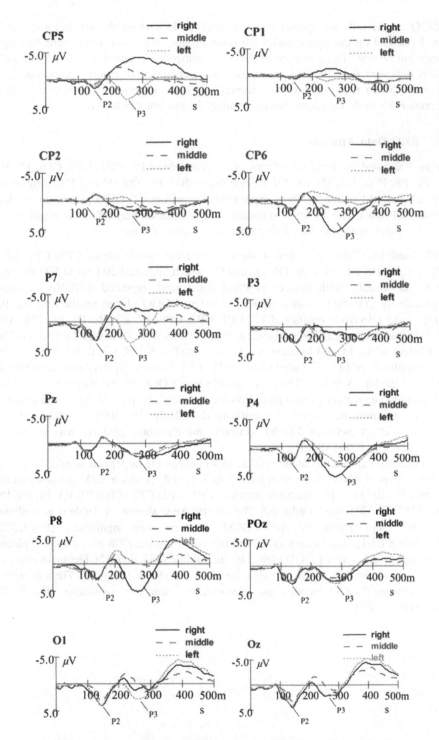

Fig. 8. Under condition of different types total mean ERP waveforms

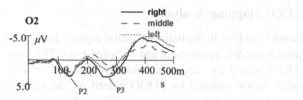

Fig. 8. (*continued*)

Table 2. The mean amplitude of P300 at different electrode positions (part 1).

Condition	CP5	CP1	CP2	CP6
1 (left)	4.48 ± 2.32	2.87 ± 1.79	2.73 ± 2.41	2.62 ± 2.53
2 (middle)	2.44 ± 1.89	2.07 ± 1.68	2.17 ± 1.20	3.29 ± 1.36
3 (right)	1.47 ± 1.83	2.36 ± 1.81	3.13 ± 2.08	5.87 ± 2.71

Table 3. The mean amplitude of P300 at different electrode positions (part 2).

Condition	P7	P3	Pz	P4	P8
1 (left)	4.28 ± 3.22	5.28 ± 3.13	3.42 ± 2.35	4.13 ± 2.52	2.27 ± 3.30
2 (middle)	2.40 ± 2.19	3.19 ± 1.94	2.28 ± 2.00	3.76 ± 2.26	2.32 ± 1.66
3 (right)	1.49 ± 1.88	3.38 ± 2.35	3.70 ± 2.37	5.23 ± 2.52	5.30 ± 4.36

Table 4. The mean amplitude of P300 at different electrode positions (part 3).

Condition	POz	O1	Oz	O2
1 (left)	3.88 ± 3.45	3.88 ± 3.45	2.55 ± 3.21	2.90 ± 2.96
2 (middle)	3.22 ± 2.21	2.45 ± 2.31	1.88 ± 1.89	2.09 ± 1.91
3 (right)	4.37 ± 3.25	3.21 ± 3.59	3.18 ± 3.53	3.96 ± 3.38

Table 5. The results of variance analysis for two factors (mean amplitudes).

	F	P
Logo position (L)	5.938	0.005
Electrode position (E)	2.826	0.052
L × E	8.727	0.000

Table 6. The results of variance analysis for two factors (mean latency).

	F	P
Logo position (L)	6.373	0.009
Electrode position (E)	3.613	0.005
L × E	5.242	0.000

3.4 EEG Mapping Analysis

As shown from Fig. 9, the brain activation regions induced by LOGO placed on the left appeared in the left hemisphere and occipital lobe; The brain activation region induced by LOGO placed on the middle mainly appeared in the occipital lobe; The brain activation region induced by LOGO placed on the right appeared in the right hemisphere and occipital lobe. According to the forementioned, brain activation region induced by LOGO placed on the right was the largest, brain activation region induced by LOGO placed on the left took second place and brain activation region induced by LOGO placed on the middle was the smallest. As time goes on, brain activation shifted to the front of brain, indicating that the brain had a deeper cognitive process for stimulation.

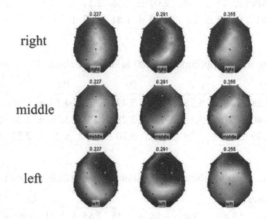

Fig. 9. Under condition of different types EEG Mapping

4 Discussion

In this experiment, the LOGO was placed on the left/middle/right under three different experimental conditions, all the target stimuli can induce significant P300. Donchin et al. considered that the P300 was related to the cognitive schema update. When the target stimulus deviated from the standard stimulus which stored in working memory, the P300 can be induced [17]. After analyzing the mean amplitude of p300 induced by the different LOGO locations, LOGO placed on the right can generate the largest p300 amplitude, LOGO placed on the left takes second place, LOGO placed on the middle generates the smallest P300 amplitude. Additionally, there was significant difference between LOGO placed on the left/right and middle, indicating that LOGO placed on the left/right can attract more attention than LOGO placed on the middle. The mean amplitude difference of P300 in the three experiments may be related to the brand recognition. The amplitude of P300 was proportional to the amount of psychological resources which users had invested in. The more attention resources users invested in the recognition of target stimuli from standard stimuli, the larger the amplitude of the

P300 was. The amplitude of P300 induced by target stimulus was proportional to brand recognition. The P300 appeared 300 ms to 600 ms after the target stimulus. In this paper, the mean latency of P300 is about 318 ms. Donchin et al. believed that the latency of P300 was only influenced by stimulus discriminability [20]. In this experiment, P300 induced by the user's recognition of the target stimulus was slightly delayed. After the latency of P300 was compared among three groups, the results showed that the experimental conditions had significant effect on the latency of P300 and the mean latency of LOGO placed on the left/right side was significantly shorter than the mean latency of the LOGO placed on the middle, indicating that LOGO placed on the left/right was conductive to brand recognition in navigation bar.

5 Conclusion

This paper first proposed the view that website brand recognition is influenced not only by the LOGO's image of the brand, but also its location in the web navigation bar. By analyzing the P300 amplitude of the LOGO located in three certain positions in the bar, namely on the left, on the middle and on the right side separately, result shows that the LOGO placed on the left/right can generate the largest p300 amplitude, occupying the most user's attention resources. This can further deepen users' awareness of the brand, thereby enhancing the website brand recognition as well as users' loyalty to the brand, which ultimately determines users' purchase decisions. Therefore, the company can promote customers' brand recognition with the ERPs technology in order to obtain better resources, to achieve a dominant position in market competitions, to erect barriers over the competitors, and finally to stand out among similar websites. Considering that this paper has only considered the impacts that LOGO location in the navigation bar on users' brand recognition, follow-up studies will look into more other factors of the websites, including the colors, the styles and so forth in the future.

References

1. Howard, J.A., Sheth, J.N.: The Theory of Buyer Behavior. Wiley, NewYork (1969)
2. Kapferer, J.N.: Strategic Brand Management: Creating and Sustaining Brand Equity Long Term, pp. 66–78. Kogan Page limited, London (1997)
3. Schmitt, B., Simonson, A.: Marketing Aesthetics: The Strategic Management of Brands, Identity, and Image, pp. 101–117. The Free Press, New York (1997)
4. Aaker, D.A.: Brand Leadership, pp. 48–73. Xinhua Publishing House, Beijing (2001). Translated by Y. Zeng
5. Kotler, L.P.: Marketing Management. Shanghai People's Publishing House, Shanghai (2003). Translated by R. Mei, 1–15, 22–24, 88–102
6. Aaker, D.A.: Building Strong Brands, pp. 45–68. China Labor and Social Security Publishing House, Beijing (2004)
7. Saakjarvi, M., Samiee, S.: Relationships among brand identity, brand image and brand preference: differences between cyber and extension retail brands over time. J. Interact. Mark. 25, 169–177 (2011)
8. Schmitt, B.: The consumer psychology of brands. J. Consum. Psychol. 22, 7–17 (2012)

9. da Silveira, C., Lages, C., Simoes, C.: Reconceptualizing brand identity in a dynamic environment. J. Bus. Res. **66**, 28–36 (2013)
10. Li, T.: Elements Analysis of Hotel Logo Design. Aagng Ngnrng **31**(4), 68–70 (2010)
11. Wang, C.: LOGO design in web design. Art Des. Theory **10**, 79–81 (2011)
12. Niu, H.: The importance of LOGO design in brand. Mod. Decorat. Theory **2015**(7), 118 (2015)
13. Xu, X., Chen, R., Liu, M.W.: The effects of uppercase and lowercase wordmarks on brand perceptions. Mark. Lett. **28**, 1–12 (2017)
14. Liu, B., Pang, R.: Inheritance and application of chinese traditional elements in modern logo design. In: International Conference on Education, Culture and Social Development (2017)
15. Potts, G.F., Tucker, D.M.: Frontal evaluation and posterior representation in target detection. Cogn. Brain. Res. **11**(1), 147–156 (2001)
16. Hillyard, S.A.: Elect rophysiology of human selective attention. Trends Neurosci. **8**, 400–405 (1985)
17. Donchin, E., Coles, M.G.H.: Is the P300 component a manifestation of context updating? Behav. Brain Sci. **11**(3), 357–427 (1988)
18. Azizian, A., Freitas, A.L., Watson, T.D., et al.: Electrophysiological correlates of categorization: P300 amplitude as index of target similarity. Biol. Psychol. **71**(3), 278–288 (2006). https://doi.org/10.1016/j.biopsycho.2005.05.002
19. Picton, T.W.: The P300 wave of the human event-related potential. J. Clin. Neurophysiol. **9** (4), 456–479 (1992)
20. Mccarthy, G., Donchin, E.A., McCarthy, G., Donchin, E.: Ametric for thought: a comparison of P300 latency and reaction time. Science **211**, 77–80 (1981)

Comparing Interface Influence on Users with Varying Expertise

Joel S. Elson$^{(\boxtimes)}$, Gina S. Ligon, and Doug C. Derrick

University of Nebraska, Omaha, NE 68182, USA
jselson@unomaha.edu

Abstract. The design of a system interface can impact user judgements among expert and novice users alike. With information systems, fundamental design choices can either augment or distract individuals in identifying patterns of converging data points. The goal of this effort was to compare the influence of Likert and categorical type rating scales in a system used to guide analysts through a content analysis process. While these scales have been examined in the context of psychological assessment literature, little has been said about their impact on decision makers from a human computer interaction perspective. We conducted a laboratory experiment to explore the effect of using Likert and categorical scales in an intelligence assessment task using unstructured data. The dependent variables included (1) Likert versus categorical type scales and (2) analyst experience (novice versus expert). Results indicated that expert and novices both had greater confidence and more creative, accurate responses in the interface utilizing Likert decision scaling.

Keywords: Interface design · Likert and categorical scaling
Novice and expert decision makers

1 Introduction

The design of decision support system interfaces has been studied in a number of different contexts and historically has shown mixed results in regards to their overall effectiveness [1, 2]. When designing these interfaces, it is important to realize that fundamental design choices can either augment or distract individuals in identifying patterns of converging data points. One such design consideration is the use of Likert and categorical type rating scales. While these scales have been examined in the context of psychological assessment literature, little has been said about their impact on decision makers when implemented in decision support systems from a human computer interaction perspective.

Leadership and organizational psychology literature suggests that novices versus experts consume and think about information differently from unstructured data about leader decision-making [3]. Moreover, when examining unstructured data in general, novices attend to ancillary information such as contextual dates, locations, and time frames, while experts tend to extract principles and concepts [4, 5]. This may be because experts, having more robust mental models based on experiences, have more working memory freed up when processing information that may be considered foreign

© Springer International Publishing AG, part of Springer Nature 2018
F. F.-H. Nah and B. S. Xiao (Eds.): HCIBGO 2018, LNCS 10923, pp. 275–284, 2018.
https://doi.org/10.1007/978-3-319-91716-0_21

or dense to novices [6]. It is important that decision aids be designed in a way that allows individuals with differing levels of experience and decision-making styles (e.g., tolerance for ambiguity, need for cognition) to quickly and accurately recognize patterns across unstructured data sources [7]. Decision support systems can do this by scaffolding the way individuals look and analyze data, drawing attention to information that experts consider important in an analysis task.

The goal of this effort was to compare the influence of an interface design used to guide an analyst through a content analysis process. To do this, we compared two types of common interfaces in psychological scaling: (1) Likert and (2) categorical. For the present effort, the following research question (RQ) was assessed via an experimental design.

RQ: What type of interface (e.g., categorical versus Likert scale) is most effective to assess the cognitive lens of leaders from a distance?

We designed a controlled laboratory experiment, using neurophysiological instrumentation, to assess the degree to which two interfaces impact decision-makers in assessing and interpreting leader intent from unstructured data. The experimental data resulted in recommendations about potential design considerations that could be offered to reduce the cognitive load of individuals interpreting intelligence indicators and recognizing patterns in unstructured data about an individual's likely interpretation of deterrence messaging.

1.1 Likert and Categorical Scales

Likert-based scales were first introduced by Likert [8], and can vary from 3, 5, or more options. When items are constructed to form a scale (e.g., confidence scale), they manifest an interval scale of measurement. One benefit of this is that it allows for multivariate analyses of analyst assessments. From a decision-making standpoint, Likert-based aids generally result in greater satisfaction and perceived ease of use in a host of populations when making judgments about unstructured data [9–11].

Conversely, categorical scales, usually represented by a bivariate response option (e.g., present versus absent) can result in faster decision-making [12], but incorporating fewer attributes may also reduce confidence and validity of responses in general [13]. In addition, the type of scales utilized by an interface has not been investigated in a population of intelligence professionals charged with making assessments from unstructured data.

1.2 Expertise in Decision Making

Expertise has been considered an important characteristic when studying decision making and judgment evaluation [14]. Expertise includes those skills and knowledge that are requisite in performing a specialized task and is developed through training and prior experience. Research in this area has been mixed, with expertise leading contributing to better decision outcomes as well as being a factor resulting in mistakes [14]. This may be explained by the fact that experts often rely on heuristics, or mental shortcuts, that enable experts to make decisions quickly and with less cognitive effort in comparison to domain novices [15]. Domain experts have been shown to consume information differently than novices, in addition domain experts engage in different processes or strategies when problem solving. Familiarity with a decision aid itself has also been shown to impact system users, requiring mastery of using a decision aid before functional area knowledge of an expert can be applied to a specific problem or task [16].

2 Methodology

An experiment was developed to assess the differences between scaling options in a decision support system and compared how expert and novice decision makers varied in their assessment of a foreign adversary. The experiment required participants to read background information and speech excerpts from a fictional foreign government leader then analyze his decision-making style using either a Likert type or categorical decision aid.

2.1 Experiment Development

Experimental materials were all developed based on actual background information about a real foreign leader, as well as literal speaking excerpts taken at two different points in the given leader's history. One speech excerpt was taken after an interview six-months prior to the bid for a major international sporting event, which was classified as a relatively neutral period in the leader's history (i.e., unmarked by subsequent escalation). This speech was thus labeled the "Neutral Speech." Another speech was selected at the same time point (six months) preceding a military event in a neighboring country. Given then subsequent regional conflict that ensued, this speech was labeled the "Escalatory Speech." The order the participants saw these speeches was counterbalanced in order to minimize bias across participants (e.g., participants were randomly assigned to read and assess the escalatory versus the neutral speech first). No significant differences were found based on this ordering. The speeches were the exact same length.

Subject matter expert feedback was obtained for each of these speeches and the materials were refined to conceal the actual identity of the foreign leader. This was done to minimize a priori biases participants may have held about the leader on which the materials were based.

There were two methods in which we varied the visual arrays: (1) the type of unstructured data from which analysts drew conclusions about the effectiveness of deterrence, and (2) the scaling options that were provided to support the decision-making of the analyst making the assessment (Fig. 1).

2.2 Participants

To assess differences in visual array processing that might arise given level of experience, two samples representing expert and novice decision makers were recruited for this effort. Analysts were recruited from the Department of Defense (DoD) via an

Fig. 1. Likert versus categorical scaling visual array format

email. This effort resulted in 43 individuals with varying levels of experience (a) assessing leader decision-making, (b) using all source intelligence, and (c) years working in the Department of Defense. Of these, 23 individuals reported having 10 or more years of analyst experience. The second sample was recruited from a participant pool at the University of Nebraska Omaha College of Business and consisted of both graduate and undergraduate students. The overwhelming majority of this sample had minimal or no experience (a) assessing leader decision-making, (b) using all source intelligence, or (c) years working in DoD. Thus, this second sample was used to represent novices. We considered those individuals with 10 or more years of experience to be experts, aligning with the definition of "expert" from Ericsson and Charness [17]. The following figure illustrates years of experience differences across the two samples (Fig. 2).

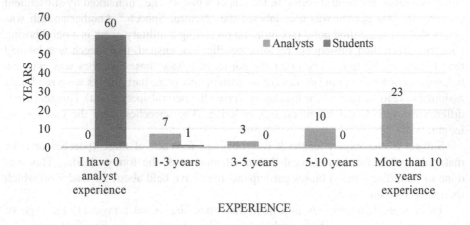

Fig. 2. Years of experience compared between analysts and students.

As previously mentioned, precautions were taken to conceal the identity of the foreign leader used in the development of the experimental task. Responses from participants indicated they were less familiar with exact backgrounds of leaders from this foreign country, and thus were unlikely to identify the characteristics and speeches of the actual identity of the leader.

2.3   Procedure

Participants first completed a battery of demographic information and the measures of problem solving style. Next, participants were assigned to one of four experimental conditions. Since the central research question of interest was to examine differences between two different interfaces among expert and novices, a 2 × 2 design was employed, varying decision-support array between conditions and type of unstructured data within condition.

To compare varying levels of expertise in assessing leader decision-making, two samples participated in an experiment at the University of Nebraska Omaha's Jack and Stephanie Koraleski Commerce and Applied Behavior Lab. Here, they participated in a series of individual difference measures (e.g., demographic survey about years of experience studying leaders from afar) and an experimental task. The process lasted anywhere from 45 min to 1.5 h, and all data was collected in the fall of 2017 on the university campus with IRB approval and was in compliance with the full HRPO human subjects' protection requirements.

In the experimental task itself, participants first read biographical information about the leader, and then answered four open-ended items about his decision-making style. After reading the biographical information, participants either first read the neutral or the escalatory speech excerpt and answered the same series of questions about each. Participants assessed the leader's decision-making style three times based on three types of unstructured data: (1) biographical data, (2) Neutral Speech, and (3) Escalatory Speech. Depending on whether they were assigned to the categorical or Likert condition, participants then completed 20-items related the attributes of the foreign leader. Specifically, participants judged, based solely on the background information available, the leader's likely cognitive lens through which he received and interpreted deterrence messages. For each of these items, participants also completed a confidence rating to provide some indication of the confidence they felt in their assessment.

2.4   Analysis

Prior to conducting analyses, several analytic steps were taken to prepare the data. First, open-ended responses to the three sets of analysis questions following the biographical data and speech excerpts were converted to quantitative scores to allow multivariate analyses. Four raters, unfamiliar with study hypotheses, were trained to assess responses on fluency, flexibility, complexity, and type of affect identified. Training lasted five hours, and raters achieved appropriate interrater reliability ($\alpha = 0.91$) across all scales.

For example, because participants were asked to provide a list of descriptors about the leader after reading through the stimulus materials, fluency was assessed by counting the total number of adjectives, while flexibility was assessed by counting the unique categories of adjectives for each participant (Table 1).

In addition, some index of accuracy of assessment was taken via the assessment of the responses for positive versus negative affect. Specifically, because the speech excerpts were selected during varying levels of escalatory activity, they manifested characteristics of positive versus negative affect. In the neutral speech, and particularly

Table 1. Fluency and flexibility scales.

	List as many adjectives as you can about the leader in this scenario…
Fluency (number of descriptors) = 8	Aggressive, dominant, powerful, commanding, commandeering, angry, experienced, bitter
Flexibility (number of different categories of descriptors) = 3	Aggressive, dominant, powerful, commanding, commandeering, angry, experienced, bitter

because the given leader was in a period of trying to influence the global community to host the Olympics in his country, the use of positive wording around decision-making far exceeded the use of negative wording. Conversely, prior to escalation activities of the invasion of Crimea, speech patterns turned more negative in affect, comparable to what has been seen in speeches of other leaders prior to escalation [18]. For this rating, a benchmark scale was developed to guide raters on assessing the primary Affect (or emotional valence) of a given response following either the neutral or the escalatory speech excerpt (Table 2).

Table 2. Affect benchmark scale.

Primary type of Affect of response. This is a 1–5 scale, use all points on the scale 1 (negative)–5 (positive)	
1	Response had all negative tone (e.g., annoyed, opportunistic, aggressive)
2	List was primarily negative in tone (e.g., hostile, angry, boasting)
3	Mix of negative and positive affect/balanced (e.g., powerful, defiant, fair, competitive)
4	List was primarily positive in tone (e.g., passionate, hard-working, achieving, angry)
5	Response had all positive tone (e.g., passionate, determined, strong)

Finally, responses were assessed for degree of complexity, or the amount of abstraction participants were able to complete based on the information available. Because decision support aids and visual arrays were meant to increase the analysts' capacity for abstraction to the cognitive lens of deterrence of a given leader, an assessment of participants capacity for abstraction was assessed using a 5-point behaviorally anchored benchmark scale. Particularly, since some leaders can perceive deterrence messaging as a direct affront to them personally [18], we assessed participant response to the item "Describe this leader's decision-making style when faced with what he perceives a personal betrayal" for complexity and capacity for abstraction to variables related to deterrence (Table 3).

3 Results

The guiding research question behind this work looked to see what type of interface scale (e.g. categorical verses Likert type) would be most effective to assess the cognitive lens of a foreign leader. We specifically looked at three facets of an analysts

Table 3. Complexity benchmark scale.

Degree of complexity/chunking of response. This is a 1–5 scale, use all points on the scale	
1–2	Response was organized by superficial groupings/characteristics; re-iterated only cues in the prompt; perceptually salient descriptors rather than abstract or complex ones *Participant Example: Angry*
3	Moderate level of Complexity; re-iterated some of the cues in the prompt, but also added new ones; ideas are moderately complex and convey multiple meanings with at least 1 word/concept *Participant Example: Leader would likely get mad and try punishing the personnel who betrayed him. Seeing as he has been in five physical altercations growing up he is quick-tempered so he may try fighting*
4	Response was organized by abstract/complex groupings/characteristics; conceptually combined 2 or more concepts; ideas are complex and convey multiple meanings with at least 2 words/concepts *Participant Example: Based on his rapid advancement in the KGB, this leader probably understands a certain level of restraint is necessary, but a clear message must be sent. He will likely take action based upon the severity of the slight against him and the organization, while calculating the perceived loyalty and value of the subordinate or person who has betrayed him. Those with potential and value will likely face less reprimand than someone who is a threat or a persistent problem to him. He does not want to make the punishment too overt or over-the-top, as this could draw negative attention and ire towards him from his superiors, whom he consistently seeks to please*
5	Response had all positive tone (e.g., passionate, determined, strong)

assessment: confidence in, complexity, and accuracy of assessments. The results of this endeavor found that interfaces utilizing Likert scaling outperformed categorical scaling interfaces on nearly every metric.

3.1 Confidence in Assessments

Decision confidence was first compared between individuals who used the Likert-type scaling (the Likert group, N = 43) and those who used the categorical scaling (the categorical group, N = 49). The two groups were comprised of individuals with both high experience (greater than 10 years of experience) and low experience (less than 10 years of experience). Confidence scores from the 72 items were summed to generate a total confidence score for each participant. A Welch's t-test was ran to compare the average confidence score between the two groups. There was a significant difference in the scores for the Likert (M = 232.33, SD = 22.52) and categorical (M = 209.86, SD = 29.16) conditions; (F (1, 90) = 16.75, p < 0.001). This means that individuals who used the Likert-type interface were more confident in their decision on average than individuals who used the categorical interface (Table 4).

Confidence in the decision task was also assessed between high experience (N = 19) and low experience (N = 73) raters, each group was comprised of individuals who utilized both the Likert-type and categorical type interfaces. A Welch's t-test was on the summed confidence scores for each individual. There was not a significant difference in the scores for the high experience group (M = 218.16, SD = 30.04) and

Table 4. Confidence by Likert vs categorical.

Type of question	Analyst mean (SD)	Student mean (SD)
Categorical	209.44 (21.92)	203.80 (32.75)
Likert	227.00 (28.83)	235.92 (14.38)

the low experience group (M = 220.93, SD = 28.22); (F (1, 90) = 0.14, p = 0.707). This means that there was no significant difference in decision confidence scores between individuals with high compared to low experience.

Confidence scores for users of the Likert-type interface were examined at the macro level to compare differences between users with high experience and low experience. There was not a significant difference in the scores for the high experience group (M = 226.92, SD = 25.76) and the low experience group (M = 234.42, SD = 21.23); (F (1, 41) = 0.96, p = 0.333). This means that for users of the Likert-type interface only; there was no significant difference in decision confidence scores between individuals with high experience compared to low experience.

Confidence scores for users of the categorical type interface were examined at the macro level to compare differences between users with high experience and low experience. There was not a significant difference in the scores for the high experience group (M = 203.14, SD = 32.76) and the low experience group (M = 210.98, SD = 28.80); (F (1, 47) = 0.43, p = 0.516). This means that for users of the categorical interface only, there was no significant difference in decision confidence scores between individuals with high experience compared to low experience.

Confidence scores for individuals with high previous experience were examined between users of the Likert-type interface and the categorical interface. There was not a significant difference in the scores for the Likert-type condition (M = 226.92, SD = 25.76) and the categorical type condition (M = 203.14, SD = 32.76); (F (1, 18) = 3.09, p = 0.097). This score is approaching significance and it is expected that with an increased sample size, users would have reported being more confident in the Likert-type condition.

Confidence scores for individuals with low previous experience were examined between users of the Likert-type interface and the categorical interface. There was a significant difference in the scores for the Likert-type condition (M = 234.42, SD = 21.23) and the categorical type condition (M = 210.98, SD = 28.80); (F (1, 71) = 14.64, p < 0.001). This means that individuals with low previous experience, those who used the Likert-type interface were more confident in their decision on average than individuals who used the categorical interface.

3.2 Complexity of Assessments

Complexity of assessments, as manifested by the nuanced interpretation of speech excerpts, varied between analysts and students, and also across speech type (escalatory versus neutral). However, the type of interface did not result in varied complexity of assessments. Analysts on average produced more complex responses when compared to students, but the type of decision-making aid provided did not impact the complexity of either student or analyst assessments (Table 5).

Table 5. Complexity by categorical vs. Likert (escalatory speech).

Type of question	Analyst mean (SD)	Student mean (SD)
Categorical	2.50 (1.41)	2.20 (1.13)
Likert	3.00 (1.36)	2.21 (1.01)

3.3 Accuracy of Assessments

While there are many metrics that could speak to the overall "accuracy" of the assessment, given the nature of the research question (what type of decision-making scale impacts accuracy of assessments), for the present effort we selected the degree to which participants could discern the affect manifested by a particular speech excerpt. Moreover, since one reliable indicator of a leader escalating aggression is his increased use of negative language (e.g., verbs, references to past grievances), participants' assessments in this study were assessed by the inference they were able to make about the effect, or the valence of the emotional imagery conveyed, identified in either the escalatory or the neutral speech. Through using this process, both the analyst and the student participants were able to accurately assess the affect in a given speech. Moreover, descriptors of the leader following the neutral speech—a time when the leader discussed engagement in the global community and hope for growth—were far more positive in affect (analyst $M = 3.09$, $SD = 1.49$ versus $M = 4.83$, $SD = 0.5$) in the categorical condition; ($M = 3.18$, $SD = 1.66$ versus $M = 4.95$, $SD = 1.16$) in the Likert condition.

4 Conclusion

Individuals who used Likert-style interface were more confident in their assessments. As user adoption of a new requirement (e.g., intent assessment) is an important element of training motivation, using this type of interface is recommended going forward for both experts and novices. Having the gradient-type response options may allow for great comfort when making decisions based on incomplete, unstructured raw data (e.g., speech excerpts). In addition, because assessing elements of a cognitive lens requires some comfort with ambiguity as well as a tenacious problem-solving style, using a priori categories of variables likely related to message interpretation can aid individuals in making connections between seemingly disparate data points.

When training both novices and experts, use of Likert-scaling interfaces to support analyst confidence, tolerance for ambiguity, and accuracy in assessments. Given that both analysts and students had greater confidence and more creative, accurate responses in the Likert interface conditions, it is not recommended that different scaling options be provided depending on the characteristics of the individual using them.

While the type of scaling appears to have less impact on judgments, it may be due to the nature of the speeches selected. Moreover, in pilot tests, speeches with the clearest differences were selected for the experimental materials. By doing this, we may have inadvertently made this component of the task too "clear" and less structured, possibly limiting the utility of the decision-making aids. However, more tests need to be run to vary the nature of the ambiguity in the speech presented in order to see if this is indeed a covariate.

References

1. Sharda, R., Barr, S.H., McDonnell, J.C.: Decision support system effectiveness: a review and an empirical test. Manag. Sci. **34**, 139–159 (1988)
2. Benbasat, I., Nault, B.R.: An evaluation of empirical research in managerial support systems. Decis. Support Syst. **6**, 203–226 (1990)
3. Ligon, G.S., Douglas, D.C., Elson, J.S., Mazgaj, M., d'Amato, A., O'Malley, D., Robinson, S.: Intelligence support to deterrence operations, Omaha, NE (2017)
4. Chase, W.G.: Visual Information Processing. Academic Press, New York (1973)
5. Larkin, J., McDermott, J., Simon, D.P., Simon, H.A.: Expert and novice performance in solving physics problems. Science **208**, 1335–1342 (1980)
6. Ericsson, K.A., Kirk, E.P.: The search for fixed generalizable limits of "pure STM" capacity: problems with theoretical proposals based on independent chunks. Behav. Brain Sci. **24**, 120–121 (2001)
7. Hermann, M.G.: Content analysis. In: Qualitative Methods in International Relations, pp. 151–167. Palgrave Macmillan, London (2008)
8. Likert, R.: A technique for the measurement of attitudes. Arch. Psychol. **22**(140), 55 (1932)
9. Boone, H.N., Boone, D.A.: Analyzing Likert data. J. Ext. **50**, 1–5 (2012)
10. van Laerhoven, H., van der Zaag-Loonen, H., Bhf, D.: A comparison of Likert scale and visual analogue scales as response options in children's questionnaires. Acta Paediatr. **93**, 830–835 (2004)
11. Lee, J.W., Jones, P.S., Mineyama, Y., Zhang, X.E.: Cultural differences in responses to a Likert scale. Res. Nurs. Health **25**, 295–306 (2002)
12. Redelmeier, D.A., Heller, D.N.: Time preference in medical decision making and cost-effectiveness analysis. Med. Decis. Mak. **13**, 212–217 (1993)
13. de Bekker-Grob, E.W., Ryan, M., Gerard, K.: Discrete choice experiments in health economics: a review of the literature. Health Econ. **21**, 145–172 (2012)
14. Shanteau, J., Stewart, T.R.: Why study expert decision making? Some historical perspectives and comments. Organ. Behav. Hum. Decis. Process. **53**, 95 (1992)
15. Logan, G.D.: Skill and automaticity: relations, implications, and future directions. Can. J. Psychol. Can. Psychol. **39**, 367 (1985)
16. Mackay, J.M., Elam, J.J.: A comparative study of how experts and novices use a decision aid to solve problems in complex knowledge domains. Inf. Syst. Res. **3**, 150–172 (1992)
17. Ericsson, K.A., Charness, N.: Expert performance: its structure and acquisition. Am. Psychol. **49**, 725 (1994)
18. Hermann, M.G.: Assessing leadership style: a trait analysis. Psychol. Assess. Polit. Lead. 178–212 (2005)

Initial Trust in Mobile Apps Based on Landing Page Information: Results of an Online Experiment

Thomas Fischer[1(✉)], Anja Obermüller[2], Andreas Auinger[1],
Harald Kindermann[1], and René Riedl[1,3]

[1] University of Applied Sciences Upper Austria, Steyr, Austria
{thomas.fischer,andreas.auinger,harald.kindermann,
rene.riedl}@fh-steyr.at
[2] Runtastic GmbH, Pasching, Austria
anja.obermueller@runtastic.com
[3] Johannes Kepler University, Linz, Austria

Abstract. We investigated the role of initial trust in an e-commerce context (hereafter e-Trust) that individuals perceive based on the information that is presented on the landing page of an app in an app store. In order to establish external validity, we collected data based on a set of realistic sport tracking apps and conducted an online experiment. Based on a sample of 2,042 individuals, we found that as in other online contexts (e.g., online shopping), e-Trust plays an important role in the context of mobile app transactions, significantly influencing an individual's decision to download or purchase an unfamiliar app. Interestingly though, we found that e-Trust has a different factor structure in this specific context compared to previous studies. In addition, not only individual disposition to trust was an important antecedent of e-Trust, but also gender, though in a different way than we expected. Men reported lower levels of e-Trust than women.

Keywords: Trust · Mobile apps · Transaction intention

1 Introduction

In the second quarter of 2017 about 340 million smartphones were sold according to IDC [1] and almost 2 billion smartphones will be sold worldwide throughout this year alone and the numbers are still rising [2]. The number of mobile apps that have been downloaded in this quarter is even more astonishing, with an estimated 25 billion downloads across all platforms in the second quarter of 2017 [3]. However, although the market that app vendors can target is huge, there is high risk for vendors of their apps not being downloaded or even found at all. On average, only 10–11 apps are used by individuals in the US per day and throughout a month this number only rises to about 35. Yet, if a vendor can make it into this exclusive selection, the benefits are tremendous as the interaction with those few apps reaches about 140 min per person per day in the US. It follows that intense competition exists among app vendors, and it is particularly difficult for unknown vendors to enter the market due to users' uncertainty perceptions.

© Springer International Publishing AG, part of Springer Nature 2018
F. F.-H. Nah and B. S. Xiao (Eds.): HCIBGO 2018, LNCS 10923, pp. 285–302, 2018.
https://doi.org/10.1007/978-3-319-91716-0_22

In the context of online transactions, previous research has shown that trust in the vendor and its products is essential as it can reduce the perceived risk of such a transaction (e.g., [4–7]). In the context of mobile apps we focus specifically on the landing page of an app in the app store as an important touchpoint where relevant information can be provided to potential users that is supposed to guide their purchase decision as elements of this page may build their trust in the app vendor. Based on these assumptions, we propose the following research question:

Does e-trust, formed based on elements of an app landing page, influence the intention of an individual to conduct a transaction (i.e., download or buy the app)?

In order to test the influence of trust in the app vendor based on information provided on the app landing page we conducted online experiments with a sample of potential users. In the next section, we outline our theoretical foundation including hypotheses derived from a review of previous research. Then, in Sect. 3, we provide details on our methods including the design of our stimulus material and the procedure of our online experiments. The results of our experiments are then described in Sect. 4, followed by a discussion and concluding remarks in Sect. 5.

2 Theoretical Foundation

Human interaction always entails a degree of uncertainty, as we are not able to predict with high certainty how our interaction partners will behave or what they intend to do. Even worse, it is almost impossible for us to do so, as individuals often act based on bounded rationality and may show behaviors that significantly deviate from how they may have behaved in comparable interactions before, without any explicit reasoning. Hence, it is often necessary to act based on assumptions, with one of the most profound assumptions being the trustworthiness of an interaction partner, which includes the expectation that the other party will act according to socially accepted standards.

Due to the particular importance of this scenario in the context of commercial transactions, trust has been a construct of research interest for many decades [8] and in the last two decades it has also become a primary construct in information systems (IS) research (e.g., [9–19]). Reichheld and Schefter [20] highlighted that trust has particular significance in online environments as there is (i) usually no contact between buyer and seller, (ii) there is no physical point-of-sale where individuals could check the quality of the product, (iii) decision-making is mostly based on descriptive information (e.g., textual descriptions and images of products), which is typically only provided by the selling party. Hence, there is much potential for consumers to be the victims of fraudulent behaviors such as misuse of provided data (e.g., credit card information), unfair pricing strategies (e.g., higher prices if they are not transparent across transactions), or incorrect information (e.g., unreliable visual depictions of the current state of a product) [4].

Despite the level of attention that trust has received in research thus far, no agreement on a common definition of trust has been reached. While Gefen [14] has defined trust as "…the confidence a person has in his or her favorable expectations of what other people will do, based, in many cases, on previous interactions" (p. 726) this definition is not completely applicable to our context, which is mostly characterized by one-time interactions. Therefore, Gefen et al. [4] later on proposed that trust is "...one's belief that the other party will behave in a dependable, ethical, and socially appropriate manner" which more clearly reflects our understanding of trust as a form of personal attitude towards another individual or group. Directly related to online transactions, Pavlou [6] provided a similar definition, stating that trust in electronic transactions is "...the subjective probability with which consumers believe that an online transaction with a Web retailer will occur in a manner consistent with their expectations." (p. 817). We posit that this subjective likelihood also drives the intention of individuals to complete an online transaction to download an app that is of interest to them [21, 22]. We therefore follow a notion by Reichheld and Schefter [20] who stated that "Price does not rule the Web; trust does." (p. 106).

In order to frame our investigation, we base our theoretical model on the conceptualization of trust in electronic transactions (e-Trust) provided by Gefen and Straub [15], which will be outlined in the next section.

2.1 E-Trust and Transaction Intention

Based on the empirical research by McKnight et al. [23], Gefen and Straub [15] proposed a theoretical framework to study trust in electronic environments. In this framework, trust is a multidimensional construct that comprises four components: integrity, benevolence, ability, and predictability.

Integrity refers to the perception that one's interaction partner will behave in accordance with what was promised beforehand. This basically boils down to the vendor being honest or dishonest about his later intentions to fulfill a made deal (e.g., whether product specifications are a true indication of what the product will actually be like [7]).

Benevolence refers to the individual perception that one's interaction partner actually cares about the well-being of his transaction partners. In the app vendor context high perceived benevolence results in the belief that the vendor is not only interested in one-time sales, but in a long lasting relationship with its customers.

Ability refers to the individual perception that one's interaction partner is capable of fulfilling a made deal. This component can be particularly important for innovative or complex products for which few vendors exist or previous vendors might have already failed. In our context, an app that is seemingly comparable to many others will not have a high threshold for its vendor to be perceived as able to deliver the expected functionalities or services.

Lastly, *predictability* refers to the individual perception that one's interaction partner will reliably deliver the promised product or service particularly in the case of repeated transactions. In the case of mobile apps this entails, for example, that potential users perceive the app vendor as being able to deliver an app that will work over a long period of time (e.g., an app that works despite frequent mobile operating system updates).

We expect that each of these components of e-Trust will be positively related to the transaction intention of a potential mobile app user. In our context, we use transaction intention to refer to the behavioral intention of an individual to download or even purchase a specific mobile app. We therefore posit H1 with sub-hypotheses for each of these components as follows:

H1a–d: Perceived integrity, benevolence, ability, predictability of an app vendor, based on the elements on an app landing page, is positively related to individual transaction intention.

We can also expect that, based on the context of a specific app, the degree of explained variance for each of these components will vary. For example, integrity may be more important in the context of apps that require a high level of data privacy (e.g., apps that are used to track medical issues); benevolence may be more important in the context of long lasting relationships (e.g., for apps that are intended to be used frequently and over a long period of time); ability may be more important in the context of novel or complex apps that make new promises with which potential users do not have experience (e.g., apps that use smartphone sensors to measure heart rate); and predictability may be more important in the context of apps that are costly.

As will be laid out in detail below, we focus on sport tracking apps and therefore surmise that integrity, in particular, will be of higher importance than the other e-Trust components in our specific context; hence, ability and predictability are of lower importance (i.e., cost-free apps that are offered with comparable functionality by many vendors).

2.2   Individual Characteristics

An individual characteristic that is an antecedent of perceived e-Trust and also used in the theoretical framework of Gefen and Straub [15] is an individual's disposition to trust other parties. This construct has previously been introduced into the study of trust in electronic environments by Gefen [14] who stated that "[d]isposition to trust is a general, i.e. not situation specific, inclination to display faith in humanity and to adopt a trusting stance toward others (...)." (p. 726). In the study by Gefen and Straub [15], trusting disposition was the strongest predictor for most components of e-Trust (with the exception of benevolence), though other studies did not find such a relationship (e.g., [18]). We are therefore interested in the investigation of this connection and posit that individuals high in trusting disposition will be more likely to show high levels of e-Trust. More specifically, we formulate the following hypotheses:

H2a–d: Individual trusting disposition is positively related to perceived integrity, benevolence, ability, predictability of an app vendor.

As trusting disposition is formed through life experiences and is therefore age-dependent [14], we further include age as an individual characteristic that will have an influence on e-Trust either directly or indirectly through its effect on individual trusting disposition (e.g., [24]). As individuals tend to become less likely to form initial trust due to their life experiences with age, we formulate the following hypotheses:

H3:   Trusting disposition is lower in older individuals than in younger individuals.

H4 a–d: Older individuals report lower levels of perceived integrity, benevolence, ability, predictability of an app vendor than younger individuals.

Finally, we also expect gender differences regarding trusting disposition and perceived e-Trust. For example, Riedl et al. [11] found that the brain activations (fMRI scans) for men and women differed when they had to evaluate trustworthy and untrustworthy Internet offers, with women showing activation in more brain areas overall and in limbic areas. This could be linked to a greater risk perception in women and we therefore posit that women will be less likely to show high levels of e-Trust or trusting disposition, according to the following hypotheses:

H5:   Trusting disposition is lower in women than in men.

H6 a–d: Women report lower levels of perceived integrity, benevolence, ability, predictability of an app vendor than men.

The resulting theoretical model that is the basis for our empirical investigation including the proposed hypotheses is shown in Fig. 1.

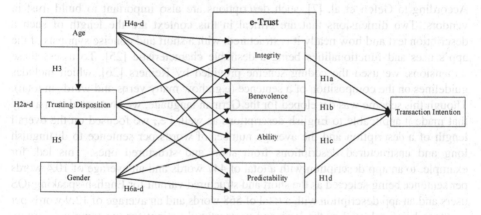

Fig. 1. Theoretical model and hypotheses

3 Methods

In order to test our hypotheses, we conducted an online experiment which aimed for high levels of external validity. To this end, we created a variety of stimuli based on actual mobile apps that are currently available in Google's Play Store (for Android devices) and Apple's App Store (for iOS devices). These stimuli were representative of the information that an app vendor as well as previous users can provide about a mobile app within the context of an app landing page in one of these app stores.

The development of these stimuli, the self-report instruments used to collect data on the respective constructs in our theoretical model and the procedure of our online experiment are laid out in the following sections.

3.1   Stimuli Development

For our stimuli we used exclusively real world examples drawn from sport tracking apps that are currently available in several mobile app stores. We chose sport tracking apps specifically, because there are currently many apps on the market that provide comparable functionality, with many of them provided by widely unknown vendors. We drew study material from the app landing pages of Runtastic Results[1], an app that is most popular in Europe, Runkeeper[2], an app that is most popular in North America, and Running for weight loss[3] as well as Freeletics bodyweight[4], apps that have a more international audience. To create variations of our stimulus material we targeted those aspects of an app landing page that could provide pivotal information to potential users. Specifically, we were interested in information provided by the app vendor (i.e., description of the app and pictures of the app) as well as other users (i.e., ratings and reviews).

App Descriptions. The description of an app is amongst the most informative elements for a potential user to get a feeling of what the capabilities of an app are [25]. According to Gefen et al. [7], such descriptions are also important to build trust in vendors. Two dimensions that are critical in this context are the length of such a description text and how neatly it is structured, with a short and concise synopsis of the app's uses and functionalities being a desirable characteristic [25]. To assess these dimensions, we used the coding scheme provided by Reiners [26], which includes guidelines on the composition of a sentence (e.g., how many verbs and words in total). Though this scheme was developed for the German language, we abstracted it in a way that made it applicable to English descriptions as well, i.e., we focused on the overall length of a description and the average number of words per sentence to distinguish long and unstructured descriptions from short and structured ones. This led, for example, to an app description with a total of 447 words and an average of 10.4 words per sentence being selected as the short and structured variant for English-speaking iOS users and an app description with a total of 568 words and an average of 12.9 words per sentence being selected as the long and unstructured variant for the same user group.

Visual Depictions. We chose three different types of pictures that are frequently used on app landing pages in this category. The first variation is a simple screenshot taken within the respective app that captures some major parts of its functionality (Fig. 2); the second variation also included an in-app screenshot combined with some advertising

---

[1] https://play.google.com/store/apps/details?id=com.runtastic.android.results.lite&hl=en-ca [10/26/2017].

[2] https://itunes.apple.com/us/app/runkeeper-gps-running-tracker/id300235330?mt=8 [10/26/2017].

[3] https://play.google.com/store/apps/details?id=com.grinasys.weightlossgoogleplay [10/26/2017].

[4] https://itunes.apple.com/at/app/freeletics-bodyweight/id654810212?mt=8 [10/26/2017].

message that is less informative to potential users (Fig. 3); and the third variation included an advertising image that does not include any actual footage from the mobile app, but is only used to promote its potential benefits (Fig. 4).

Fig. 2. Product screenshot   **Fig. 3.** Screenshot with text   **Fig. 4.** Advertising image

Ratings and Reviews. In previous research it has been found that also second-hand information in the form of user ratings and reviews of mobile apps can have an influence on their success [27]. Amongst these two elements, ratings (mostly scales of one to five stars) are usually assessed first, before the longer user reviews are examined [28]. Amongst a large number of potential mobile apps that offer comparable functionalities, those that received distinctly negative ratings are usually sorted out first [5, 29]. In the case of overall comparable ratings (e.g., several apps with high ratings), reviews are then used as a source of second-hand information by potential users [24], in particular to understand the benefits and functionalities of an app and perhaps to gather more information on the reasons for negative ratings [30].

To manipulate these elements of an app landing page, we gathered two actual reviews with ratings from the Runtastic Results app and changed the user name as well as the data of the review. The three variations we created here were (i) a five-star rating together with an overall negative review, (ii) a one-star rating together with an overall positive review, and (iii) a five-star rating together with a positive review of the app, which was intended to be the most useful variant as the information of rating and review supported each other.

For each of our eight stimulus variations (see Table 1) we created versions based on either Android or iOS versions of the landing pages of our selected apps. In addition, we created versions for each stimulus in English as well as in German. It has to be noted though that we removed the brand of each app and replaced it with the fictitious "FitnessApp". This was done because the brand can have significant influence on individual trust perceptions, particularly if individuals have had previous experiences with a certain brand [18]. As we were interested in initial trust formation in the absence of such experiences, we removed brand names and logos. An overview of our resulting 32 stimuli variations (Variations × Mobile Ecosystem × Language) can be found in Table 1.

Table 1. Overview of stimuli variations

Language	Mobile ecosystem	Trust element	Variations
English/German	iOS/Android	App store description	Structured – short
			Unstructured – long
		Visual depictions	Product screenshot
			Screenshot with text
			Advertising image
		Ratings and reviews	Positive – negative
			Negative – positive
			Positive – positive

3.2 Measurement Scales

The measurement scales that we used in our study to gather data on trusting disposition, e-Trust, and transaction intention were taken from Gefen and Straub [15] (see Table 2). We used a seven-point Likert scale ranging from (1) strongly disagree to (7) strongly agree.

Table 2. Overview of measurement scales and items used

Scales and items	Code
Integrity	
Promises made by FitnessApp are likely to be reliable	INTE1
I do not doubt the honesty of FitnessApp	INTE2
I expect that FitnessApp will keep promises they make	INTE3
I expect that the advice given by FitnessApp is their best judgment	INTE4
Benevolence	
I expect I can count on FitnessApp to consider how its actions affect me	BENE1
I expect that FitnessApp's intentions are benevolent	BENE2
I expect that FitnessApp puts customers' interests before their own	BENE3
I expect that FitnessApp is well meaning	BENE4
Ability	
FitnessApp is competent	ABIL1
FitnessApp understands the market it works in	ABIL2
FitnessApp knows about health and fitness applications	ABIL3
FitnessApp knows how to provide excellent service	ABIL4

(continued)

Table 2. (*continued*)

Scales and items	Code
Predictability	
I am quite certain about what FitnessApp will do	PRED1
I am quite certain what to expect from FitnessApp	PRED2
Transaction Intention	
I am very likely to download apps from FitnessApp*	TRANS1
I am very likely to purchase apps from FitnessApp	TRANS2
I would use my credit card to purchase from FitnessApp	TRANS3
Trusting disposition	
I generally trust other people	DISPO1
I tend to count upon other people	DISPO2
I generally have faith in humanity	DISPO3
I feel that people are generally well meaning	DISPO4
I feel that people are generally trustworthy	DISPO5
I feel that people are generally reliable	DISPO6

*Item was added to reflect that transactions in our context can also be free of cost.

Our demographic variables gender and age were both measured dichotomously. For age we used the two classes of "younger" and "older" individuals, where younger meant below 30 years and older meant 30 years or older. The reason for this specific split was that individuals younger than 30 years have mostly grown up with mobile phones or even smartphones (introduction of the iPhone in 2007) and are therefore likely more familiar with app transactions, while individuals older than 30 years may have more transaction experiences overall (traditional and electronic commerce in general), but not in this particular area.

3.3 Procedure

We conducted our online experiments from the end of May 2017 until the beginning of July 2017. We provided the link to the online survey tool (QuestionPro) on Click-worker[5] and Amazon's Mechanical Turk[6]. When starting the experiment, participants first indicated their language and which mobile operating system they mainly used and accordingly were only presented with the versions of our stimuli that were developed for their language and operating system. Our online experiment then followed a between-subjects design for each of the three components of the app landing page that we manipulated.

More specifically, participants saw one of the variations of the app description, one variation of our three types of visual depictions and one combination of ratings and reviews. The order in which these components appeared was randomized as was the

---

[5] https://www.clickworker.com/ [10/26/2017].

[6] https://www.mturk.com/mturk/welcome [10/26/2017].

selection of the individual variant that was presented to a participant. After each of these stimuli participants rated their perceived e-Trust and after all three of these evaluations they reported their individual trusting disposition, transaction intention, and demographic variables.

4   Results

In this section, we report the results of our empirical investigation. We first focus on the characteristics of our sample and data screening procedures, then we report the steps that we have taken to ensure the reliability and validity of our measures, and finally we present the results of the statistical analyses we applied to test the hypotheses.

4.1   Sample Characteristics

In total, 2,158 individuals completed our online experiment. We removed responses with low engagement across our self-report measures (i.e., a standard deviation of 0). This procedure led to 116 responses being removed which resulted in a sample of 2,042 responses being used for our further investigation (there were no significant outliers that had to be additionally removed). About half of our respondents are women (51%) and 61% of our respondents are 30 years or older.

4.2   Reliability and Validity Analyses

In accordance with the recommendations by Homburg and Giering [31], we first conducted an exploratory factor analysis (EFA) to test the factor structure of our constructs using SPSS version 24. We took this step particularly to test whether e-Trust in the specific context of our investigation also comprises four distinct factors. As extraction method we used principal component analysis with promax rotation (we used an oblique rotation method as our constructs are likely correlated).

Barlett's test for sphericity was significant indicating the appropriateness of an EFA for our data set and the KMO showed high potential for dimension reduction (.943). Including all self-report items, the initial EFA resulted in four factors explaining a total of 74.75% in variance of our data. In order to reduce crossloadings and to improve overall fit, we dropped items INTE1 and INTE2, which had the lowest loadings overall (INTE1: .580; INTE2: .544). This led to an improved overall explained variance of 75.83% and the factor structure depicted in Table 3.

Interestingly, we did not find a suitable solution where all four distinct factors of e-Trust could be kept. Instead, a solution with only two distinct factors formed, with one factor including the indicators used to measure benevolence and integrity and the other factor including the indicators used to measure ability and predictability. We call the first of these factors "trust in vendor intentions" as it comprises items that mainly measure an app vendors potential faithfulness to keep promises, while we call the second factor "trust in vendor capabilities" as it comprises items that mainly measure an app vendors capabilities to actual fulfill a transaction, independent of certain intentions.

However, this finding is in accordance with more recent studies investigating the factor structure of e-Trust such as the study by Barki et al. [32]. They found that the two main motivational determinants of trust are the "can do" and the "will do" of an interactional partner which corresponds well with our findings (i.e., "trust in vendor intentions" reflects the "will do" component while "trust in vendor capabilities" reflects the "can do" component).

In order to conduct further tests on our measurement model and structural model, we then used SmartPLS version 3. In accordance with the recommendations by Henseler et al. [33], we first calculated SRMR as an approximate measure of model fit. Our calculated resulted in an SRMR of .048, which is below even a conservative threshold for SRMR of .05. For internal consistency, we assessed composite reliability and Cronbach's α of our constructs. According to Bagozzi and Yi [34], composite reliability should exceed 0.60 and according to Nunnally and Bernstein [35], Cronbach's α should exceed 0.70 in order to ensure internal consistency. As shown in Table 3, these criteria are met for all constructs.

Table 3. Factor loadings, average variance extracted and composite reliability

Constructs	Items	Loadings	AVE	Cronbach's α
Trusting disposition (CR = 0.934)	DISPO1	0.782	0.704	0.934
	DISPO2	0.766		
	DISPO3	0.805		
	DISPO4	0.856		
	DISPO5	0.874		
	DISPO6	0.940		
Trust in vendor intentions (CR = 0.932)	BENE1	0.849	0.697	0.933
	BENE2	0.692		
	BENE3	0.879		
	BENE4	0.918		
	INTE3	0.885		
	INTE4	0.766		
Trust in vendor capabilities (CR = 0.928)	ABIL1	0.969	0.685	0.929
	ABIL2	0.730		
	ABIL3	0.792		
	ABIL4	0.964		
	PRED1	0.729		
	PRED2	0.742		
Transaction intention (CR = 0.852)	TRANS1	0.928	0.663	0.844
	TRANS2	0.844		
	TRANS3	0.644		

Note: INTE1 and INTE2 were dropped due to low factor loadings.

We then evaluated convergent validity and discriminant validity of our constructs. For convergent validity we followed the guideline by Fornell and Larcker [36] that all item loadings should exceed 0.70 and the guideline by Kline [37] that the values for the average variance extracted (AVE) of each construct should be at least 0.50. As shown in Table 3 as well, we can confirm that our constructs and items fulfill these criteria[7]. Finally, in order to confirm discriminant validity of our measures, we tested for the fulfillment of the Fornell-Larcker criterion [36], which includes comparing the square root of the AVE of each construct and its correlations with all other constructs. Further, as recommended by Henseler et al. [33], we also calculated the HTMT for all constructs as a measure of discriminant validity. As none of the construct inter-correlations exceeds the square root of the AVE, and none of the HTMT values comes close to one (in parentheses), we can assume sufficient discriminant validity of our measures (see Table 4).

Table 4. Discriminant validity test

	DISPO	INTE	CAPAB	TRANS
Trusting Disposition (DISPO)	*0.839*			
Trust in Vendor Intentions (INTE)	0.265 (0.264)	*0.835*		
Trust in Vendor Capabilities (CAPAB)	0.368 (0.365)	0.753 (0.749)	*0.828*	
Transaction Intention (TRANS)	0.398 (0.412)	0.372 (0.372)	0.423 (0.418)	*0.814*

Note: Diagonal elements (italic) are the square root of the AVE for each construct; Off-diagonal factors demonstrate the inter-correlations.

4.3 Hypotheses Testing

After confirming the quality of our measurement model, we then proceeded to test our structural model. As a prerequisite though, we first checked whether there were any multicollinearities between our independent variables (i.e., INTE and CAPAB) which could bias calculated path coefficients and as we collected all our data through self-reports we also checked for signs of common methods bias (CMB).

In order to test for multicollinearity we alternated our two independent variables and their dependent variable (transaction intention) in linear regressions in SPSS to see if their collinearity tolerances and VIF were acceptable (i.e., VIF values should be less than ten, while collinearity tolerances should be greater than 0.10 [38]). As VIF values ranged between 1.123 and 1.914 and collinearity tolerances between .522 and .891 we can assume that there are no signs of multicollinearity.

To test for common method bias, we applied Harman's single factor test [39] which involved an exploratory factor analysis in SPSS without rotation, aiming for one single factor. This single factor explained only 44.62% of the total variance (more than 50%

---

[7] Though the factor loading for TRANS3 and BENE 2 are slightly below the limit of .70, we did not remove them as the overall loadings for the constructs were still highly acceptable.

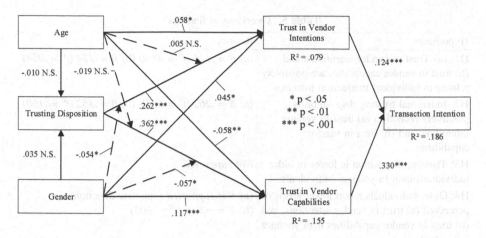

Fig. 5. Research model showing significance of relationships

would be indicative of CMB), so we can assume that common method bias is no significant threat to our analyses.

To test the significance of our structural paths we used the bootstrapping method in SmartPLS 3 with 5,000 subsamples [33]. To calculate the path coefficients we then used the PLS algorithm also with 5,000 iterations. The results are depicted in Fig. 5. It has to be noted here that we reorganized our model due to the two-factor structure we found for e-Trust in our study context.

Regarding our H1 which posited that components of e-Trust will predict transaction intention, we found support in both cases. Yet, the effect size is small in both cases (f^2 for INTE: .009, f^2 for CAPAB: .058) and only trust in vendor capabilities showed even a weak effect on individual transaction intention [40].

In accordance with H2, we found an influence of trusting disposition on e-Trust for both trust in vendor intentions (a weak effect with an f^2 of .079) and trust in vendor capabilities (a moderate effect with an f^2 of .160).

Interestingly, we found neither a direct effect of age nor gender on trusting disposition and therefore had to reject H3 and H4. As we were still interested in their potential effects on trusting disposition, we additionally investigated the possibility of moderating effects of age and gender on the relationship between trusting disposition and e-Trust. In both cases, the effect of age was not significant, though gender had a significant negative effect in both cases. This indicates that trusting disposition predicted e-Trust to a lesser degree in men than in women, though the effect size is negligible in both cases (f^2 of .003 for the effect on trust in vendor intentions and f^2 of .004 for the effect on trust in vendor capabilities).

Finally, we also investigated direct effects of age and gender on e-Trust. We found that all relationships in this context were significant, but only the relationship between age and trust in vendor capabilities conformed to H4. In all other cases, the opposite effect could be observed (i.e., older individuals reported higher levels of perceived trust in vendor intentions; women reported higher levels of e-Trust for both of its components). Hence, the data partially confirmed H4, while we have to reject H6. For most

Table 5. Overview of findings

Hypotheses	Results
H1: (a) Trust in vendor intentions, and (b) trust in vendor capabilities are positively related to individual transaction intention	(a) $\beta = .124$ ($f^2 = .009$) (b) $\beta = .124$ ($f^2 = .058$)
H2: Individual trusting disposition is positively related to (a) trust in vendor intentions, and (b) trust in vendor capabilities	(a) $\beta = .262$ ($f^2 = .079$) (b) $\beta = .362$ ($f^2 = .160$)
H3: Trusting disposition is lower in older individuals than in younger individuals	*Not supported*
H4: Older individuals report lower levels of perceived (a) trust in vendor intentions, and (b) trust in vendor capabilities than younger individuals	(a) *Not supported* (opposite direction) (b) $\beta = -.058$ ($f^2 = .005$)
H5: Trusting disposition is lower in women than in men	*Not supported*
H6: Women report lower levels of perceived (a) trust in vendor intentions, and (b) trust in vendor capabilities than men	(a) *Not supported* (opposite direction) (b) *Not supported* (opposite direction)
Additional Findings	
Moderating effect of gender on the relationships between trusting disposition and trust in vendor intentions; i.e. the effect of trusting disposition on reported e-Trust is smaller for women	$\beta = -.054$ ($f^2 = .003$)
Moderating effect of gender on the relationships between trusting disposition and trust in vendor capabilities; i.e. the effect of trusting disposition on reported e-Trust is smaller for women	$\beta = -.057$ ($f^2 = .004$)

parts the effect sizes were negligible though (f^2 of .004 for the direct effect of age on trust in vendor intentions; f^2 of .005 for the direct effect of age on trust in vendor capabilities; f^2 of .007 for the direct effect of gender on trust in vendor intentions), with the exception of the direct effect of gender on trust in vendor capabilities where we observed a small effect (f^2 of .020).We summarized our findings in Table 5.

5   Discussion and Concluding Remarks

The main goal of our research was to investigate the role of initial trust in the context of mobile apps. We therefore conducted online experiments with stimuli that aimed for high external validity and a sample that consisted of participants from two different countries. We found that initial trust in an app vendor based on information that is provided on the landing page of an app significantly influences the transaction intention of individuals (i.e., the likelihood that these individuals will download or even purchase an app). Hence, a practical implication would be that trust evaluations of landing pages for mobile apps should become a business routine including A/B testing to find those elements of the specific landing page that can successfully influence the trust of potential users.

An interesting finding of our research is that in this specific context, e-Trust does not comprise four distinct factors as in the theoretical framework we based our research on [15], which was previously applied in the context of e-commerce transactions (i.e., Amazon transactions). The two distinct factors that emerged during our research are focused on individual trust in the capabilities of an app vendor and the intentions of the vendor to stay faithful to a given deal. We can only assume the reasons for this result, but it is likely due to the specific context of an app transaction. For example, while e-commerce transactions in general often still involve physical products being shipped, app transactions only involve software being transferred, therefore constituting a type of transaction with fewer steps in its fulfillment. Also, app transactions can often be deemed "micro-transactions" as most apps are either free or cost only a small amount of money. For these reasons, and perhaps due to other characteristics of app transactions as well, integrity and benevolence did not emerge as separate factors as there is less risk involved than in usual e-commerce transactions (e.g., no shipment errors or delays, lesser chance of problems during payment) and particularly benevolence therefore seems not as distinctively important, as there are fewer potential points of interaction with an app vendor. For comparable reasons, predictability might not have emerged as a separate factor, as the transaction itself is virtually similar across vendors mostly due to common exchange platforms (Play Store or App Store). Importantly, our findings are in line with recent evidence showing that the relationship between ability, benevolence, and integrity is non-linear [32].

Due to the specific type of app that we used for our empirical investigation (i.e., sport tracking apps) and the type of data collected (i.e., health-related information), we originally expected that integrity, which is part of our first factor trust in app vendor intentions, would be the construct that explains most variance of an individual's transaction intention. However, this is not the case. Instead, trust in a vendor's capabilities is a far stronger predictor of transaction intentions. This result may be due to our experimental setting which provided information to potential users that allowed them to judge how useful a specific app could be to them and therefore emphasized the benefits and functionality of an app. Integrity of the vendor or information privacy measures were probably not of immediate importance and therefore received lower levels of consideration. In addition, it is possible that the so-called privacy paradox may have an effect on this type of judgement. In previous research on information privacy it was found that while people would rate information privacy as highly important to them if directly asked, they also easily exchange private information for some immediate benefit such as personalization of services or monetary rewards [41, 42].

Another unexpected finding was that men reported lower levels of e-Trust than women, though the size of the effect was small (avg. INTE for men: 4.79 vs avg. INTE for women: 4.90; avg. CAPAB for men: 4.73 vs avg. CAPAB for women: 4.97). Although we expected that women would be more risk averse and therefore not as trusting towards our fictitious vendor based on the given app information, men were less trusting in our specific context. We can assume that this effect was caused by the specific research context, as we found no general effect of gender on trusting disposition. One potential reason for this difference is that the advertising images that we used as part of our stimulus material only depicted women, which led to female participants reporting higher levels of trust as they were directly targeted by these images. Yet, only about one third of our participants saw this specific stimulus and this explanation is therefore not sufficient to explain our results. It would therefore be interesting to investigate this specific finding further in order to find out which specific individual or contextual characteristics might have caused this difference (e.g., by using different types of apps as stimulus and taking personality characteristics into account).

Like all research, ours also has its limitations, which will be detailed now. We designed our study as an online experiment and distributed it indiscriminately amongst German-speaking and English-speaking audiences. As cultural differences could have had an influence on our results, not asking about the respondents' nationality or dimensions of their cultural background can be regarded as a limitation. In addition, our research only focused on a small number of constructs in our investigation. Hence, future research could, for example, investigate the influence of further characteristics of a specific app and their influence on e-Trust such as the cost of apps [27]. In addition, the actual formation and level of initial trust could be clarified if apps from unknown vendors were directly compared to apps from vendors that were at least known based on their brand [18]. Still, despite these limitations, we can conclude that trust also plays an important role in the initial trust formation in the context of mobile app transactions.

It follows that future research should investigate the factors that drive e-Trust and that can be controlled by app vendors (e.g., the influence of the different landing page elements that we have included as well as further elements), but also contextual factors such as the influence of different cultures, experience with different mobile operating systems or the type of app that is advertised on the landing page.

References

1. IDC: Smartphone Volumes Decline Slightly in the Second Quarter of 2017 Amid Anticipation of Strong Second Half Product Launches, According to IDC. https://www.idc.com/getdoc.jsp?containerId=prUS42935817
2. Scarsella, A., Stofega, W.: Worldwide Mobile Phone Forecast Update, 2017–2021, September 2017. https://www.idc.com/getdoc.jsp?containerId=US43064517
3. Sydow, L.: Global App Downloads Soar: Q2 2017 Recap. https://www.appannie.com/en/insights/market-data/google-apple-app-stores-q2-2017/
4. Gefen, D., Karahanna, E., Straub, D.W.: Trust and TAM in online shopping: an integrated model. MIS Q. **27**, 51–90 (2003)
5. Ba, S., Pavlou, P.A.: Evidence of the effect of trust building technology in electronic markets: price premiums and buyer behavior. MIS Q. **26**, 243 (2002)
6. Pavlou, P.A.: Integrating trust in electronic commerce with the technology acceptance model: model development and validation. In: AIS (ed.) Proceedings of the Seventh Americas Conference on Information Systems (2001)

7. Gefen, D., Benbasat, I., Pavlou, P.: A research agenda for trust in online environments. J. Manag. Inf. Syst. **24**, 275–286 (2008)
8. Deutsch, M.: Trust and suspicion. J. Conflict Resolut. **2**, 265–279 (1958)
9. Javor, A., Ransmayr, G., Struhal, W., Riedl, R.: Parkinson patients' initial trust in avatars: theory and evidence. PLoS ONE **11**, e0165998 (2016)
10. Javor, A., Riedl, R., Kirchmayr, M., Reichenberger, M., Ransmayr, G.: Trust behavior in Parkinson's disease: results of a trust game experiment. BMC Neurol. **15**, 126 (2015)
11. Riedl, R., Hubert, M., Kenning, P.H.: Are there neural gender differences in online trust? An fMRI study on the perceived trustworthiness of eBay offers. MIS Q. **34**, 397–428 (2010)
12. Riedl, R., Javor, A.: The biology of trust: integrating evidence from genetics, endocrinology, and functional brain imaging. J. Neurosci. Psychol. Econ. **5**, 63–91 (2012)
13. Riedl, R., Mohr, P.N.C., Kenning, P.H., Davis, F.D., Heekeren, H.R.: Trusting humans and avatars: a brain imaging study based on evolution theory. J. Manag. Inf. Syst. **30**, 83–114 (2014)
14. Gefen, D.: E-commerce. The role of familiarity and trust. Omega **28**, 725–737 (2000)
15. Gefen, D., Straub, D.W.: Consumer trust in B2C e-Commerce and the importance of social presence: experiments in e-Products and e-Services. Omega **32**, 407–424 (2004)
16. Pavlou, P.A., Gefen, D.: Building effective online marketplaces with institution-based trust. Inf. Syst. Res. **15**, 37–59 (2004)
17. Pavlou, P.A.: Institution-based trust in interorganizational exchange relationships: the role of online B2B marketplaces on trust formation. J. Strateg. Inf. Syst. **11**, 215–243 (2002)
18. Lowry, P.B., Vance, A., Moody, G., Beckman, B., Read, A.: Explaining and predicting the impact of branding alliances and web site quality on initial consumer trust of e-commerce web sites. J. Manag. Inf. Syst. **24**, 199–224 (2008)
19. Vance, A., Elie-Dit-Cosaque, C., Straub, D.W.: Examining trust in information technology artifacts: the effects of system quality and culture. J. Manag. Inf. Syst. **24**, 73–100 (2008)
20. Reichheld, F.F., Schefter, P.: E-loyalty: your secret weapon on the web. Harvard Bus. Rev. **78**, 105–113 (2000)
21. Chang, T.-R., Kaasinen, E., Kaipainen, K.: What influences users' decisions to take apps into use? In: Rukzio, E. (ed.) Proceedings of the 11th International Conference on Mobile and Ubiquitous Multimedia, p. 1. ACM, New York, NY (2012)
22. Pavlou, P.A., Liang, H., Xue, Y.: Understanding and mitigating uncertainty in online exchange relationships: a principal-agent perspective1. MIS Q. **31**, 105–136 (2007)
23. McKnight, D.H., Choudhury, V., Kacmar, C.: Developing and validating trust measures for e-commerce. an Integr. Typology. Inf. Syst. Res. **13**, 334–359 (2002)
24. Li, X., Hess, T.J., Valacich, J.S.: Why do we trust new technology? A study of initial trust formation with organizational information systems. J. Strat. Inf. Syst. **17**, 39–71 (2008)
25. Albrecht, U.-V.: Transparency of health-apps for trust and decision making. J. Med. Internet Res. **15**, e277 (2013)
26. Reiners, L.: Stilfibel. Der sichere Weg zum guten Deutsch. Dt. Taschenbuch-Verl., München (2001)
27. Lee, G., Raghu, T.S.: Determinants of mobile apps' success: evidence from the app store market. J. Manag. Inf. Syst. **31**, 133–170 (2014)
28. Racherla, P., Furner, C., Babb, J.: Conceptualizing the implications of mobile app usage and stickiness: a research agenda. SSRN Electron. J. (2012)
29. Khalid, H., Shihab, E., Nagappan, M., Hassan, A.E.: What do mobile app users complain about? IEEE Softw. **32**, 70–77 (2015)
30. Song, J., Kim, J., Jones, D.R., Baker, J., Chin, W.W.: Application discoverability and user satisfaction in mobile application stores: an environmental psychology perspective. Decis. Support Syst. **59**, 37–51 (2014)

31. Homburg, C., Giering, A.: Konzeptualisierung und Operationalisierung komplexer Konstrukte – Ein Leitfaden für die Marktforschung. In: Hildebrandt, L., Homburg, C. (eds.) Die Kausalanalyse. Ein Instrument der empirischen betriebswirtschaftlichen Forschung, pp. 111–148. Schäffer-Poeschel, Stuttgart (1998)

32. Barki, H., Robert, J., Dulipovici, A.: Reconceptualizing trust. A non-linear Boolean model. Inf. Manag. **52**, 483–495 (2015)

33. Henseler, J., Hubona, G., Ray, P.A.: Using PLS path modeling in new technology research: updated guidelines. Industr. Manag. Data Syst. **116**, 2–20 (2016)

34. Bagozzi, R.P., Yi, Y.: On the evaluation of structural equation models. J. Acad. Mark. Sci. **16**, 74–94 (1988)

35. Nunnally, J.C., Bernstein, I.H.: Psychometric theory. McGraw-Hill, New York (1994)

36. Fornell, C., Larcker, D.F.: Evaluating structural equation models with unobservable variables and measurement error. J. Mark. Res. **18**, 39 (1981)

37. Kline, R.B.: Principles and Practice of Structural Equation Modeling. The Guilford Press, New York (1998)

38. Kline, R.B. (ed.): Principles and Practice of Structural Equation Modeling. The Guilford Press, New York (2005)

39. Podsakoff, P.M., MacKenzie, S.B., Lee, J.-Y., Podsakoff, N.P.: Common method biases in behavioral research: a critical review of the literature and recommended remedies. J. Appl. Psychol. **88**, 879–903 (2003)

40. Cohen, J.: A power primer. Psychol. Bull. **112**, 155–159 (1992)

41. Bélanger, F., Crossler, R.E.: Privacy in the digital age: a review of information privacy research in information systems. MIS Q. **35**, 1017–1041 (2011)

42. Smith, H.J., Dinev, T., Xu, H.: Information privacy research: an interdisciplinary review. MIS Q. **35**, 989–1015 (2011)

The Impact of Usability, Functionality and Sociability Factors on User Shopping Behavior in Social Commerce Design

Zhao Huang[✉]

School of Computer Science, Shaanxi Normal University, Xi'an 710119,
People's Republic of China
zhaohuang@snnu.edu.cn

Abstract. Usability, functionality and sociability have been found as the important factor in social commerce design. However, it is not clear about the influence of social commerce design to users shopping behavior, which needs to be further explored. It is arguable that such lacks of understanding may cause ineffective social commerce design and hamper users' online shopping behavior. Therefore, this study aims to explore the impact of social commerce design on user shopping decision-making. We believe that the results can provide a useful foundation for future social commerce research.

Keywords: Usability · Functionality · Sociability · Shopping behavior
Social commerce

1 Introduction

The development of social media applications has given rise to a new e-commerce paradigm called social commerce. It attracts users to participate actively in the buying and selling of products in online marketplaces and communities. Within it, users can receive a more social and collaborative online experience, where collective intelligence can be leveraged to help in better understanding of purchase, and in making more accurate decisions [1]. Business organizations can collect users' behaviors and preferences, which help them to provide more successful online services [2].

Studies of social media applications and Web 2.0 technologies in electronic business (e.g. [3]) and its impact on users' attitude (e.g. [4]) and their shopping behavior (e.g. [5]) have shown that design of a quality social commerce website is a key aspect of e-business [6]. It has a considerable effect on users' interaction with social commerce [7]. In particular, users' shopping behavior is largely determined by whether the design quality can be demonstrated through social commerce websites. This design quality can be greatly achieved by addressing usability, functionality and sociability. It is because that usability has been related with a number of important outcomes, such as ease of use, error reduction and positive attitudes [8], and has been shown to increase users' intention to purchase behavior [9]. As for functionality, it seems as a paramount factor that users most care about on social commerce design [7]. It appears to have a significant impact on user's decision and return [10]. Sociability is another major

© Springer International Publishing AG, part of Springer Nature 2018
F. F.-H. Nah and B. S. Xiao (Eds.): HCIBGO 2018, LNCS 10923, pp. 303–312, 2018.
https://doi.org/10.1007/978-3-319-91716-0_23

contributor towards social commerce design [11], linking to several critical impact on users engagement, and usage [12]. Hence, usability, functionality and sociability have been considered as the most important factors in social commerce design.

However, it is not clear about the influence of social commerce design to users purchase shopping behavior, which needs to be further explored. It is arguable that such lacks of understanding may cause ineffective social commerce design and hamper users online shopping behavior. Relevant studies indicate that a quality design of social commerce can be greatly achieved by addressing usability, functionality and sociability. However, existing research has not paid enough attention to them. Therefore, this study aims to explore the impact of social commerce design on user shopping decision-making. We believe that the results can provide a useful foundation for future social commerce research.

2 Study Background

Social commerce can be categorized as a subset of e-commerce [11]. However, a closer look at social commerce definitions in relevant research indicates that the social commerce concept has many inconsistencies, which may lead to some conceptual confusion. For example, Curty and Zhang [13] defined social commerce as a form of Internet-based social media application which enables companies to deliver commercial activities and services in online communities and marketplaces. However, this definition only looks at sellers to business organizations, lacking of enough attention to users. Huang and Benyoucef [11] explained social commerce as an online mediated application combining Web 2.0 technologies, such as Ajax and Really Simple Syndication (RSS) with interactive platforms, such as social networking sites and content communities in a commercial environment. Nevertheless, such definition limits the viewpoint to computer technology. Michaelidou et al. [14] defined social commerce as a type of social shopping, where users will be influenced by salient information cues from others within a network community when they do shopping online. But, such a definition limits stakeholders to individuals, excluding business organizations. These conceptual inconsistencies in defining social commerce, to some extent, bring a diversity of understandings of what social commerce are. Although there is no wide-ranging accepted definition, prior research identifies two major categories of social commerce. One is e-commerce on social network platforms, for instance Facebook or Twitter based sales platforms; the other is social media applications on e-commerce websites, such as Amazon, Groupon and eBay (these e-commerce websites contain a variety of social media applications).

Social interaction and commercial activities are delivered to users through social commerce websites. In other words, social commerce websites can be seen as a window for users to interact with online business. Regardless of the types of social commerce, democratic values underlying business organizational operations require that social commerce websites should aim for great quality design [15]. A well-designed user website has a significant effect on users shopping behavior [16]. Therefore, it is important to address the design of a quality social commerce website. Several studies have investigated various aspects of design quality on social commerce websites, and these design quality is extensively divided into usability, functionality and sociability factors.

Shopping behavior has been considered as the cognitive process, resulting in the selection of a product, service or a course of purchase action among several alternative possibilities [17]. Some studies conduct the assessment of the shopping processes using a variety of behavior models, frameworks and theories (e.g. [18]); some explores shopping behavior by looking at users' shopping attitude (e.g. [19]) and shopping expectations (e.g. [20]), others focus on users' perception of social commerce websites (e.g. [21]) using behavioral theory. For example, Simon [22] addressed decision making in a set of stage, including intelligence, design, choice and implementation. Intelligence refers to problems discovery; design is about solution discovery; choice is to make a choice of the best solution, and implementation is to evaluate the solution. Lai [23] extended shopping behavior to cognitive process, and suggested that shopping decision-making can be structured and ordered in a set of phases, covering intelligence, design and choice. Yadav et al. [24] explained shopping behavior within a social commerce context from a theoretical perspective, addressing that social commerce should consider design on all shopping stages rather than merely online transactions. Therefore, this study will focus on shopping behavior in a set of detailed stages, including product discovery, product evaluation and product purchase. The following sections will detail the importance of each design factor and their relevant influence to each stage of the user's shopping behavior.

3 Usability with Shopping Behavior

Usability is one of the most important factors of social commerce design [4]. It can be simply defined as capability of the software product to be understood, learned, operated, and attractive to the users [25]. Within a website context, usability refers to the extent to which website can be used by specified users to achieve specified goals to visit with effectiveness, efficiency and satisfaction in a specified context of website use [8]. Many studies employ multidimensional constructs to explain effectiveness, efficiency and satisfaction in website usability design. For example, usability reflects perceived simplicity, readability, consistency, learnability, interactivity, navigability, content relevance, supportability, credibility and telepresence [9]. Luna-Nevarez and Hyman [26] described six usability attributes in website design, including content quality, visual and presentation style, navigation, textual information, advertising and social media aids.

A number of usability features have a significant impact on various decision-making stages from literature. For example, Liu et al. [27] studied website attributes in online impulse purchase, and found that information quality, visual appeal and ease of use strongly influence users' emotion and personality in triggering online impulse shopping decision. Pallud and Straub [28] looked at the effect of store design on user shopping activities, and identified that providing easy start and clear navigation tools can facilitate website orientation and reduce users' cognitive load, which significantly aids users in products recognition during shopping decision-making. Likewise, Venkatesh et al. [29] found that website aesthetic and minimalist design directly affects user to recognize products. This can be achieved by providing visual appeal, such as consistent layout, corresponding graphics, clear text and hyperlinks [7]. Furthermore, the decision process of information search can be influenced by whether websites provide quality design in aspects of content organization [30], navigation [4], accessibility [31], ease of use [32], and information quality [33]. Gao et al. [34] indicated that user information search outcomes may be determined by information quality in aspects of completeness, usefulness, currency and relevance. Moreover, the usability attributes that influence user products evaluation include content presentation [35], contact information provision [23] and security of transaction [36], because these attributes can build user confidence and overcome perceptions of risk and uncertainty in decision-making [23]. Additionally, determinants that appears to be significant for affecting whether users may finally form shopping behavior in social commerce were empirically validated by offering visual aesthetics [37], well organized content [29], quality information display [38], ease of use [27], security [5] and credibility [9] (see Table 1).

Table 1. Usability features with shopping behavior

Usability features	Shopping behavior	References
Information quality, visual appeal and ease of use	Online purchase	[27]
Ease of start, navigation cues	Products recognition	[28]
Aesthetic and minimalist design	Products recognition	[29]
Content organization	Product search	[30]
Navigation	Product search	[4]
Accessibility	Product search	[31]
Ease of use, information quality	Product search	[32, 33]
Content presentation	Products evaluation	[35]

4 Functionality with Shopping Behavior

Functionality is a critical factor in social commerce design because it is about the quality of being functional on its websites [39]. It commonly refers to a set of functions and properties that satisfy consumers' requirements in their task completion, and contains a number of sub design elements, including suitability, accuracy, interoperability and security [40]. Specifically, suitability is about the ability to have the adequate functions for the required tasks; accuracy refers to the ability to provide the right results with the required degree of precision; interoperability is the ability to interact with one or more specified systems, and security is to prevent unauthorized access to services or data. Indeed, social commerce websites are composed of functional (e.g. search function, payment function) or non-functional (e.g. graphics presentation, multimedia, layout) components. Both of the functions and services constitute the basis of user interaction [41]. With higher level of functionality, users can better use social commerce websites, which in turn, achieve greater performance in interacting with information and services [42].

Prior study notes that a good design must provide adequate functional support to meet user requirements at each of their shopping decision. For example, Verhagen and van Dolen [43] described that website functional convenience and representational delight make profound impact on positive and negative shopping intentions, which in turn affect online shopping behavior. Liang and Lai [23] showed that stimulating the desire to purchase in aspects of offering online broadcasting, adding auction mechanism and showing the number of current visitors can be beneficial for products or services awareness. Yang et al. [32] implied that making a high level of search engine capability, customized information and navigation support can promote information search efficiency. Liang and Lai [23] found that functions of price comparison and functions enabling users to assess other users' comments directly affect consumer evaluation of alternative. More importantly, services of ordering, payment, delivering and login can be seen as the basic functions in social commerce design, which fundamentally support final purchasing [44]. These relevant literature has been summarized in Table 2.

Table 2. Functionality features with shopping behavior

Functionality features	Shopping behavior	References
Convenience and representational delight	Shopping intentions	[43]
Online broadcasting, auction	Products recognition	[23]
Search engine, customized information and navigation	Products search	[32]
Price comparison, users' comments	Product evaluation	[23]
Ordering, payment, delivering functions	Product purchase	[44]

5 Sociability with Shopping Behavior

Sociability has been recognized as another paramount contributor towards social commerce design [45]. It provides rich social experience that enables users to connect with their friends, to discover new friends with similar interests, to share product information and to communicate with others during shopping [32]. Sociability design is extensively studied in aspects of participation, conversations and community [46]. For instance, Bilgihan and Bujisic [47] claimed that participation fundamentally supports users in generating, sharing, editing, syndicating and disseminating information. To encourage user participation, a number of design features have been suggested by Bilgihan and Bujisic [47], including user generated content, information sharing, participation intensity, incentives provision and task creation. Conversation relates to establishing relationships among users, essentially assisting them in building peer communities. It can be achieved by developing design features in terms of interaction, communication and connection [48]. Without conversation, there is no multiplication of user generated content and no serious propagation of collective intelligence. While, community is about building networking effects and collaboration provision [49]. Constantinides et al. [2] suggested that communities can be quickly created based on special interest groups or consumers with common interests. It can largely support user collaboration and gather collective intelligence to solve problems and make decisions. Accordingly, social commerce leverage the power of abovementioned social features in a more collaborative and interactive way, encouraging networked communities to socially connect, and providing opportunities for utilizing the web to engage users more effectively [11].

The social aspect of design is seen as a major contributor towards social commerce, which provides users with social value [38]. Such value closely associates with word-of-mouth and user generated content, the core property of social commerce, which largely influences user decision-making process [50]. Hajli [3] argued that providing social support design, such as online social communities is an important part of social value, and positively affect users to recognize products or services provided on social commerce. This production awareness is also evidently achieved by offering other social media applications, such as reviews and rating [10], users' feedback [51], product sharing [52], and social recommendation [31]. Moreover, Sadovykh [53] explained clear advantages in aspect of information seeking during consumption decisions being made through social support. Count et al. [54] showed that providing virtual communities helps users to leverage social knowledge and experiences to support them in filtering their evaluation and choice, and in making more informed and accurate purchase decisions. Similarly, social features, such as content communities, chats, message boards, referrals, forum and social reviews intensely support user engagement with social commerce, enhancing probability of purchasing [44] (see Table 3).

Table 3. Sociability features with shopping behavior

Sociability features	Shopping behavior	References
User generated content	Shopping decision making	[50]
Online social communities	Products recognition	[3]
Reviews and rating, users' feedback	Products recognition	[10, 51]
Product sharing, social recommendation	Products recognition	[31, 52]
Social support	Products search	[53]
Virtual communities	Product evaluation	[54]
Content communities, chats, message boards,	Product purchase	[44]
Referrals, forum	Product purchase	[44, 54]

6   Research Model Development

To understand the effects of social commerce design on user shopping behavior and the underlying mechanism of quality design factors, our research model was developed. To be specific, social commerce design quality considers three key design factors, which are usability, functionality and sociability. User purchase behavior process focuses on three decision-making stages, namely product discovery, product evaluation and product purchase. Based on the literature, we believe that each quality design factor has a positively influence to each step of user shopping decision making. Accordingly, these are indicated in the model as shown in Fig. 1.

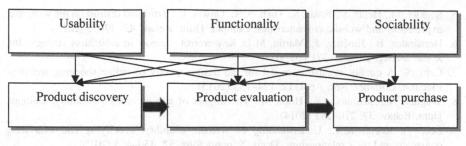

Fig. 1. Research model

The contributions of this study consist of exploring the impact of social commerce design on user decision-making behavior in a framework aimed at supporting social commerce researchers and developers. Our research model is developed. This confirms the explanatory power of our research model over shopping behavior process, which provides us with deep insights into the relationship between social commerce design and user shopping behavior. In fact, all social commerce design quality factors, including usability, functionality and sociability have the significant influences to user shopping behavior, namely product discovery, product evaluation and product purchase. Such results may evidently confirm the importance of these quality factors to social commerce design as well as to user shopping behavior. It benefits for understanding the core user shopping behavior in social commerce websites. Moreover, the relevant sub-element within each quality design factor provides deep insight into social commerce design, helping business organizations to develop social commerce to meet their desirable business goals. However, this study is just the first step of our research. A future empirical study will be conducted to investigate the effects of social commerce design on user shopping behavior, and identify certain design features that are more important than other on various shopping decision-making stages.

Acknowledgments. This study was supported by research grants funded by the "National Natural Science Foundation of China" (Grant No. 61771297), and "the Fundamental Research Funds for the Central Universities" (GK201803062, GK200902018).

References

1. Bai, B., Law, R., Wen, I.: The impact of website quality on customer satisfaction and purchase intentions: evidence from Chinese online visitors. Int. J. Hosp. Manag. **27**, 391–402 (2008)
2. Constantinides, E., Romero, L.R., Boria, M.A.G.: Social media: a new frontier for retailers? Eur. Retail Res. **22**, 1–28 (2008)
3. Hajli, M.N.: The role of social support on relationship quality and social commerce. Technol. Forecast. Soc. Chang. **87**, 17–27 (2014)
4. Hassanein, K., Head, M.: Manipulating perceived social presence through the web interface and its impact on attitude towards online shopping. Int. J. Hum.-Comput. Stud. **65**, 689–708 (2007)

5. Seckler, M., Heinz, S., Forde, S., Tuch, A.N., Opwis, K.: Trust and distrust on the web: user experiences and website characteristics. Comput. Hum. Behav. **45**, 39–50 (2015)
6. Hernández, B., Jiménez, J., Martín, M.J.: Key website factors in e-business strategy. Int. J. Inf. Manag. **29**, 362–371 (2009)
7. Cebi, S.: A quality evaluation model for the design quality of online shopping websites. Electron. Commer. Res. Appl. **12**, 124–135 (2013)
8. Wagner, N., Hassanein, K., Head, M.: The impact of age on website usability. Comput. Hum. Behav. **37**, 270–282 (2014)
9. Lee, Y., Kozar, K.A.: Understanding of website usability: specifying and measuring constructs and their relationships. Decis. Support Syst. **52**, 450–463 (2012)
10. Wu, Y.J., Shen, J., Chang, C.: Electronic service quality of Facebook social commerce and collaborative learning. Comput. Hum. Behav. **51**, 1395–1402 (2015)
11. Huang, Z., Benyoucef, M.: User preferences of social features on social commerce websites: an empirical study. Technol. Forecast. Soc. Chang. **95**, 57–72 (2015)
12. Curty, R.G., Zhang, P.: Website features that gave rise to social commerce: a historical analysis. Electron. Commer. Res. Appl. **12**, 260–279 (2013)
13. Curty, R.G., Zhang, P.: Social commerce: Looking back and forward. Proc. Am. Soc. Inf. Sci. Technol. **48**(1), 1–10 (2011)
14. Michaelidou, N., Siamagka, N.T., Christodoulides, G.: Usage, barriers and measurement of social media marketing: an exploratory investigation of small and medium B2B brands. Ind. Mark. Manag. **40**(7), 1153–1159 (2011)
15. Liang, T.P., Turban, E.: Introduction to the special issue – social commerce: a research framework for social commerce. Int. J. Electron. Commer. **16**, 5–14 (2011)
16. Fan, W.S., Tsai, M.C.: Factor driving website success: the key role of Internet customization and the influence of website design quality and Internet marketing strategy. Total Qual. Manag. Bus. **21**, 1141–1159 (2010)
17. Cheung, C.M.K., Thadani, D.R.: The impact of electronic word-of-mouth communication: a literature analysis and integrative model. Decis. Support Syst. **54**, 461–470 (2012)
18. March, J.G.: Bounded rationality, ambiguity, and the engineering of choice. Bell J. Econ. **9** (2), 587–608 (1978)
19. Li, C.: A tale of two social networking sites: how the use of Facebook and Renren influences Chinese consumers' attitudes toward product packages with different cultural symbols. Comput. Hum. Behav. **32**, 162–170 (2014)
20. Wang, J.C., Chang, C.H.: How online social ties and product-related risks influence purchase intentions: a Facebook experiment. Electron. Commer. Res. Appl. **12**, 337–346 (2013)
21. Liang, T.P., Ho, Y.T., Li, Y.W., Turban, E.: What drives social commerce: the role of social support and relationship quality. Int. J. Electron. Commer. **16**, 69–90 (2011)
22. Simon, H.A.: Theories of decision-making in economics and behavioral science. Am. Econ. Rev. **49**(3), 253–283 (1959)
23. Liang, T., Lai, H.: Effect of store design on consumer purchases: van empirical study of on-line bookstore. Inf. Manag. **39**, 431–444 (2002)
24. Yadav, M.S., de Valck, K., Hennig-Thurau, T., Hoffman, D.L., Spann, M.: Social commerce: a contingency framework for assessing marketing potential. J. Interact. Mark. **27**, 311–323 (2013)
25. Fernandez, A., Insfran, E., Abrahão, S.: Usability evaluation methods for the web: a systematic mapping study. Inf. Softw. Technol. **53**, 789–817 (2011)
26. Luna-Nevarez, C., Hyman, M.R.: Common practices in destination website design. J. Dest. Mark. Manag. **1**, 94–106 (2012)

27. Liu, Y., Li, H., Hu, F.: Website attributes in urging online impulse purchase: an empirical investigation on consumer perceptions. Decis. Support Syst. **55**, 829–837 (2013)
28. Pallud, J., Straub, D.W.: Effective website design for experience-influenced environments: the case of high culture museums. Inf. Manag. **51**, 359–373 (2014)
29. Venkatesh, V., Hoehle, H., Aljafari, R.: A usability evaluation of the Obamacare website. Gov. Inf. Q. **31**, 669–680 (2014)
30. Ranganathan, C., Ganapathy, S.: Key dimensions of business-to-consumer web sites. Inf. Manag. **39**, 457–465 (2002)
31. Kunst, K., Vatrapu, R.: Towards a theory of socially shared consumption: literature review, taxonomy, and research agenda. In: The 22nd European Conference on Information Systems, Israel (2014)
32. Yang, K., Li, X., Kim, H., Kim, Y.H.: Social shopping website quality attributes increasing consumer participation, positive eWOM, and co-shopping: the reciprocating role of participation. J. Retail. Consum. Serv. **24**, 1–9 (2015)
33. Vila, N., Kuster, I.: Consumer feelings and behaviours towards well designed websites. Inf. Manag. **48**, 166–177 (2011)
34. Gao, J., Zhang, C., Wang, K., Ba, S.: Understanding online purchase decision making: the effects of unconscious through, information quality, and information quantity. Decis. Support Syst. **53**, 772–781 (2012)
35. Kim, S., Park, H.: Effects of various characteristics of social commerce (s-commerce) on consumers' trust and trust performance. Int. J. Inf. Manag. **33**, 318–332 (2013)
36. Bélanger, F., Carter, L.: Trust and risk in e-government adoption. J. Strateg. Inf. Syst. **17**(2), 165–176 (2008)
37. Deng, L., Poole, M.S.: Aesthetic design of e-commerce web pages – webpage complexity, order and preference. Electron. Commer. Res. Appl. **11**, 420–440 (2012)
38. Park, C., Lee, T.M.: Antecedents of online reviews' usage and purchase influence: an empirical comparison of U.S. and Korean consumers. J. Interact. Mark. **23**, 332–340 (2009)
39. Pfleeger, N.F.: Software Metrics A Rigorous and Practical Approach. Thomson Computer Press, Stamford (1997)
40. Stefani, A., Xenos, M.: Weight-modeling of B2C system quality. Comput. Stand. Interfaces **33**, 411–421 (2011)
41. Chan, H., Raymond, L., Tharam, D., Chang, E.: E-Commerce Fundamentals and Applications. Wiley, Hoboken (2001)
42. Shaouf, A., Lü, K., Li, X.: The effect of web advertising visual design on online purchase intention: an examination across gender. Comput. Hum. Behav. **60**, 622–634 (2016)
43. Verhagen, T., van Dolen, W.: The influence of online store beliefs on consumer online impulse buying: a model and empirical application. Inf. Manag. **48**, 320–327 (2011)
44. Kim, H., Gupta, S., Koh, J.: Investigating the intention to purchase digital items in social networking communities: a customer value perspective. Inf. Manag. **48**, 228–234 (2011)
45. Guo, Y., Barnes, S.: Purchase behavior in virtual worlds: an empirical investigation in Second Life. Inf. Manag. **48**, 303–312 (2011)
46. Huang, Z., Benyoucef, M.: From e-commerce to social commerce: a close look at design features. Electron. Commer. Res. Appl. **12**, 246–259 (2013)
47. Bilgihan, A., Bujisic, M.: The effect of website features in online relationship marketing: A case of online hotel booking. Electron. Commer. Res. Appl. **14**, 222–232 (2015)
48. Ellahi, A., Bokhari, R.H.: Key quality factors affecting users' perception of social networking websites. J. Retail. Consum. Serv. **20**, 120–129 (2013)
49. Wang, X., Yu, C., Wei, Y.: Social media peer communication and impacts on purchase interactions: a consumer socialization framework. J. Interact. Mark. **26**, 198–208 (2012)

50. Moham, S., Choi, E., Min, D.: Conceptual modeling of enterprise application system using social networking and Web 2.0 'Social CRM System'. In: International Conference on Convergence and Hybrid Information Technology, pp. 237–244 (2008)
51. Ono, C., Nishiyama, S., Kim, K., Paulson, B.C., Cutkosky, M., Petrie, C.J.: Trust-based facilitator: handling word-of-mouth trust for agent-based e-commerce. Electron. Commer. Res. **3**, 201–220 (2003)
52. Chen, Y., Xie, J.: Third-party product review and firm marketing strategy. Mark. Sci. **24**, 218–240 (2005)
53. Sadovykh, V., Sundaram, D., Piramuthu, S.: Do online social networks support decision-making? Decis. Support Syst. **70**, 15–30 (2015)
54. Count, D., Elzinga, D., Mulder, S., Vetvik, O.J.: The consumer decision journey. McKinsey Q. **3**, 1–11 (2009)

Effect of Social Media Product Reviews
on Buying Decision When Presented
in Augmented Reality

Prateek Jain[(✉)], Adrienne Hall-Phillips, and Soussan Djamasbi

Worcester Polytechnic Institute, Worcester, MA, USA
{pjain, ahphillips, djamasbi}@wpi.edu

Abstract. Consumers are becoming dependent on online product reviews for making purchasing decisions. Although reviews are available directly on e-commerce websites. For better quality reviews consumers are using extensive resources like Google and Amazon. Social media could be a great resource for looking up product reviews as people post about their latest purchases on social media. However, it is hard to lookup reviews on social media and consolidate them. For in-store purchasing looking up reviews becomes challenging as there are very few reviews on in-store products. Consumers need to visit several websites while standing in front of the product to get reviews and consolidate all the information themselves to make a decision. Our proposed app will scan the product packaging, lookup reviews over different social media platforms, consolidate it and display reviews in augmented reality. Our results show that social media reviews are helpful in making buying decisions. Although augmented reality didn't make a big difference in improving the usability of the app, consumers still showed a positive inclination towards it.

Keywords: Social media · Buying behavior · Augmented reality
Product reviews · Decision making · Consumer behavior

1 Introduction

Online product reviews are becoming very crucial in supporting buying decisions of consumers. These reviews are also called electronic word of mouth because they are written online by customers who bought the product and used it. For an online review to be influential on a buying decision, it should be helpful to consumers. An online review is more helpful to consumers if it is written by customers than the experts [1]. However, in products with more technical outcomes consumers will likely seek information from experts [2]. To get reviews, consumers use search engines, e-commerce websites, blogs and vlogs for both online and in-store shopping.

Social media is also a great source for obtaining product reviews. It has an extensive collection of reviews of every type [3]. Moreover, social media has an impact on the buying behavior of consumers [4]. People may not want to post reviews on the Internet; however, they do so unconsciously when they share information about their latest purchase with their friends on social media platforms such as Facebook and Twitter. Social media posts also include the experiences consumers have had with the

© Springer International Publishing AG, part of Springer Nature 2018
F. F.-H. Nah and B. S. Xiao (Eds.): HCIBGO 2018, LNCS 10923, pp. 313–326, 2018.
https://doi.org/10.1007/978-3-319-91716-0_24

product, which can be less biased and more in-depth. More and more people are using social media for sharing their everyday experiences, making this source valuable for getting reviews. Consumers will use social media reviews because social media gives social position and a virtual community to consumers, which are the two motives for consumers to read reviews online [5]. Also, one of the primary motives for consumers posting product reviews online is because there is a social benefit in doing so [6]. Posting reviews on social media will give consumers maximum social benefit. Consumers who want to get reviews are either not aware of this or don't use social media because reviews are difficult to search for and are not available in a consolidated form.

There is no single platform on which consumers can get reviews from multiple channels. Specially for in-store shopping, when reviews are not available for products it is inconvenient to look for reviews online. Consumers are required to lookup different websites for getting reviews while standing in front of the product for a long time to make a buying decision. We are trying to consolidate reviews from multiple social media channels and present it in an augmented reality fashion.

Augmented reality is changing the way we see the world. Augmented reality is a technology which superimposes virtual objects in the real world and supplements reality [7]. Using augmented reality, information can be augmented on everyday objects and places to be viewed in an intuitive way using special applications. The interaction of the user with the real world and their perception of reality can be enhanced by the use of augmented reality [7]. We are using augmented reality in our research for displaying consolidated reviews from multiple social media channels to increase engagement and give a sense to consumers that they are directly interacting with the product.

In this paper, we are proposing an app that will scan the product packaging to grab keywords regarding the product using optical character recognition. It will then search for posts and comments regarding those keywords on various social media platforms and detect sentiments in the posts and comments. A report of reviews on social media will be generated and augmented over the product. To use the app, consumers will need to just scan the product using the application and reviews from different channels will be augmented on the product itself.

2   Theoretical Background

2.1   Product Reviews

Multiple studies have been done on knowing the effects of product reviews on the sales of the product [8–11]. Prior research showed evidence that customer reviews affect consumer buying behavior [8], which ultimately impacts sales. Researchers found that the volume of reviews has a greater influence on sales of experience products, while valance of reviews has influence on sales of search products [10]. Zhu and Zhang [9] found that when there is scarcity of information regarding a product, its reviews become important. Hu et al. [11] found that consumers pay attention to both quantitative and qualitative aspects of review. They also found that the impact of online reviews decreases with the increase in product age. There will be an overall effect but no unfavorable effect of positive and negative news.

There is some research that has been done on what makes a review helpful [1, 12, 13]. According to Pan and Zhang [12] characteristics of a product review, type of product and characteristics of a reviewer influences the helpfulness of a review. According to Li et al. [1] review helpfulness is a combination of perceived source credibility, perceived content diagnosticity and perceived vicarious expression. According to Liu et al. [13] the most important factors that affect the helpfulness of reviews are reviewer expertise, writing style and timeliness. Moreover, research suggests that consumers consider those reviews helpful which include both subjective and objective elements [14].

It is also important to know why consumers read and also post reviews. Hennig-Thurau and Walsh [5] identified five motives that entice consumers to lookup reviews online. Those motives are (1) getting information regarding a purchase, (2) establishing a social position, (3) being a member of a virtual community, (4) doing it in exchange of money and (5) learning to consume products. Along with this, consumers choose the sources that most cost effectively convey the information needed [15] and online reviews reduce the time to get information. Hennig-Thura et al. [6] also identified primary motives for posting reviews online, which are getting social benefits, getting paid, having concern for others, and self-enhancement.

2.2 Product Reviews on Social Media and Its Analysis

Wang and Chang [16] conducted a Facebook experiment to understand the influence of social ties and product related risk on purchase intentions when consumers see product review on social media. They found that reviews from a strong tie source (i.e. friend or family) have significant effect on consumers when product is high risk (i.e. expensive) and result in higher perceived diagnosticity of the information in the review. Another study [17] found that product reviews by peers on social media are positively associated with product attitude, which in return is positively associated with purchase intention.

Since Twitter is a large and popular microblogging platform, it is popular among researchers to study social media product reviews. Researchers consider tweets as "relatively new type of electronic word of mouth" [4]. Jansen et al. [18] found that 19% of tweets among all tweets in some way mention product or product brand. Also, out of those tweets that mentioned product brands, 20% contains sentiments or opinion regarding that brand, service or product and remaining 80% are seeking information regarding that brand. Promising results in research on Twitter shows that other social media platforms can reveal more benefits. Therefore, in our study we are focusing on Facebook and Amazon along with Twitter.

Analysis of online product reviews is done by sentiment detection. There are many research studies on different frameworks, model and approach for detecting and classifying sentiments. Some research investigates automatic sentiment analysis [19, 20], while others focus on speed of the analysis [21] and simplification [22]. Ghose and Ipeirotis [23] were able to identify helpfulness and the economic impact of the reviews using their model. They suggest to display helpful reviews first because they will be more useful. In another research, Ghose and Ipeirotis [14] designed two review ranking systems for consumers and manufacturers based on helpfulness and expected effect on sales, respectively. Liu et al. [24] came up with a framework for not only analyzing the reviews but also comparing reviews of competing products. Shaikh and Lobo [3] created a system to estimate sales performance by using online reviews. Kim and Hovy [25] developed a framework to automatically identify pros and cons in the reviews. Research was also performed on predicting utility of reviews [26]. All these analysis models and frameworks may fail if reviews are sarcastic. They may trigger a false negative. For this, Tsur et al. [27] presented a novel algorithm which can detect sarcastic sentences in product reviews.

2.3 Augmented Reality

Any system which combines the real world with the virtual world, provides possibility of real time interaction and works in a three-dimensional space is an augmented reality system [7]. Augmented reality systems evolved from see through head mounted display to handheld smartphones. Olsson and Salo [28], in their research discussed that there are two types of AR applications, one is an AR browser which shows content based on geolocation and the other is based on image recognition to detect markers and display content. They found more than expected positive experience of publicly available AR applications at the time of research. Their research shows that augmented reality enables users to do things better than before by helping them get a new perspective and obtain relevant information that is hard to find. They got mixed results on user interface and usability aspects of augmented reality but identified curiosity and novelty as main factors that influence users to install AR applications. Another study [29], although in different context also found that various underlying technological components affect the user experience of augmented reality and identified novelty as factor that facilitates positive user experience and emotions.

Augmented reality sometimes struggles with usability and user-friendliness aspects of the user experience. Research with augmented reality in the field of education shows that usability is a challenge for augmented reality which makes it difficult for students to use [30]. Kim et al. [31] studied failure of augmented reality applications in a Korean market. They suggest that while developing an app more focus should be on usefulness factors rather than enjoyment factors. They also found that information quality has great influence on perceived usefulness and enjoyment of an application. For improving the usability of augmented reality applications, Ko et al. [32] developed usability principles by identifying 22 usability problems. Duplicated expressions of information, providing limited information and unfamiliar icons were top three usability problems among all. For these problems, in their usability guidelines they suggested to display information actively using only a camera, providing additional information and designing universally understandable icons.

We also found research on an app similar to our proposed app, which runs in augmented reality by Balduini et al. [33] called BOTTARI. They used augmented reality to display recommendations related to point of interests around the geolocation of users using Twitter stream and static descriptions. Although, both apps revolve around augmented reality and social media recommendations, our app focuses on product reviews compared to point of interests. Moreover, the content of BOTTARI is based on geolocation while content of our app is based on image recognition and marker detection. The main difference is that their research was focused on how they designed BOTTARI and practical results they gained from it, while our research is focused on knowing the effect of social media product reviews on buying behavior and user experience aspects of augmented reality by conducting a research study.

2.4 Hypothesis

From our literature review it is evident that social media has potential to be used as a source of product reviews when presented in a consolidated form. We believe that consumers can make better decisions with the help of social media reviews and be more confident in their decision. Therefore, we hypothesize that

H1. There is an overall positive effect of social media product reviews on consumer buying behavior.
H2. Social media product reviews are useful to consumers.

Also, augmented reality is a promising technology to present information in an intuitive way as the literature indicates. We believe that displaying social media reviews in augmented reality will increase ease of use, engagement and overall experience with the app. Therefore, we hypothesize that

H3. Augmented reality increases overall experience of the app.
H4. Augmented reality increases usability of the app.

To test our hypothesis, we designed a controlled experiment to gauge consumer buying behavior and to see at what extent augmented reality helps in increasing experience compared to conventional information display methods. We will investigate current difficulty level of finding reviews and its impact on consumers in making their purchase decision. The following section discusses the methodology used in conducting the experiment.

3 Methodology

We conducted a between-subject research study to find the impact of social media reviews on the buying decision of consumers for a product when reviews are presented in augmented reality fashion in comparison to reviews presented on a static page. We will discuss more about it in this section.

3.1 App Design and Prototype

In our app design, we selected to show dummy product reviews from Facebook and Twitter in a consolidated form and dummy product ratings from Amazon. The app screen is divided into three parts, reviews from Facebook, reviews from Twitter and ratings from Amazon. Reviews from Facebook and Twitter include trends that shows percentages of positive and negative posts along with top positive comment and top negative comment. Ratings from Amazon include the number of people who have rated the product and their ratings. Dummy reviews and ratings were designed in a way to give a look and feel of actual social media accounts and posts.

We created three dummy product boxes of Bose portable bluetooth speakers to serve as products for purchase and placed them on a display shelf. These include SoundLink Color II, SoundLink Revolve and SoundLink Mini II. Using the same app design, we created two prototypes of our proposed app for each product. One is a static page containing reviews that will appear after scanning a QR code on a price tag and the other will augment reviews directly on the product after scanning it. Ratings and reviews for every product are different but both prototypes for each product contains identical information. For simplicity, we will call the prototype with reviews displayed on a static page as QR app and the prototype with reviews displayed in augmented reality as AR app in this research paper.

3.2 Participants, Method and Task

We recruited 20 participants for the study who are all students of a small university in the northeast United States. Participants were randomly divided into two groups. The first group was assigned AR app while second group was assigned QR app. We named the first group AR and second group QR. Therefore, one participant will work with only one of the prototypes making it between-subject study. We are conducting between-subject study to remove any biases that may come across if one participant will try both prototypes.

Before the task, participants were asked to answer pre-task questions regarding the difficulty in making purchasing decisions, decision factors, where they lookup reviews, frequency of looking up reviews and difficulty in finding reviews. After pre-task questions, participants were told a scenario for buying a portable Bluetooth speaker and were given a mobile device, which was the iPhone 6 plus with prototype app open for getting reviews of all the products placed on the display shelf. The AR group was asked to scan the product boxes directly while the QR group was asked to scan the QR code on the price tag. Participants were asked to come up with a product they will buy based on the reviews and rating available on the app. Participants were explicitly told that price should not be a factor in their buying decision.

After the task participants were asked interview questions regarding their buying decisions and factors considered in making their decision. Afterwards, survey questions were asked to rate confidence in purchase decision, usefulness of the app, ease of use, future use of the app, chance of recommendation to friend and overall experience with the app. At last, demographic questions regarding hours spent on social media, primary reason to use social media, online and in-store shopping frequency for electronics products, age and gender were asked. At the end of the survey, an open-ended question regarding their experience and suggestions for the app was asked.

4 Results

The sample had an age range of 19–27 years with an average age of 21.7 years. There were 8 females and 12 males. The participants reported an average of 2.34 hours per day spent on social media sites. The primary reasons participants listed for using social media is to know what their friends are up to, to interact with friends, for group messaging and to view new trends.

When analyzing the shopping behavior of the sample, we found that participants tend to purchase products online more compared to in-store for electronic goods. Out of 20, there were 11 participants who shop online between 7 times/year to more than 10 times/year and only 3 participants who shop in-store. While buying a product, about half of the time on average the participants have trouble deciding between two or more products. They lookup reviews of products about half of the time on average before and while purchasing a product.

It is slightly easy for them on average to find reviews about any product. To decide between different alternatives, they consider reviews as the top deciding factor (65% of participants) followed by price (40% of participants). Other deciding factors include features, quality and design. Amazon is the top choice (65% of participants) to lookup review, followed by looking up reviews directly on the website from where they are buying (55% of participants). Other places for looking up reviews include Google, YouTube and Reddit.

After performing the task, almost half of the participants in both groups selected SoundLink Revolve as the product they will buy. The prototype for SoundLink Revolve had more positive reviews compared to other two products. However, regardless of which speaker they selected, all of them considered positive and negative reviews, Amazon ratings and volume of ratings as factors for making their buying decision. Our aim was not to check which product they will buy, but to see if they are able to make a confident decision by looking at social media reviews.

Ratings of the prototype with reviews displayed in augmented reality were different compared to ratings of prototype with reviews displayed on a static page, but the difference is not statistically significant. Participants in both groups agree that they are confident in their purchase decision with 6.1 and 5.9 ratings in AR and QR groups respectively on average out of 7, shown in Fig. 1.

Participants in AR group agree that social media reviews were useful in making their buying decision with 5.5 rating out of 7 while the QR group somewhat agree that the reviews were useful with 5.4 rating out of 7 on average, shown in Fig. 2.

Participants in AR group agree that AR app was easy to use with 5.9 rating out of 7 while QR group strongly agree that QR app was easy to use with 6.6 rating out of 7 on average, shown in Fig. 3. Participants in both groups somewhat agree that they will use this app in future to get help in their purchase decision with 5.2 and 5.4 rating in AR and QR groups respectively on average out of 7, respectively. Participants rate their overall experience with the AR app to be 4.2 in the AR group and with the QR app to be 4.1 in the QR group on average out of 5, shown in Fig. 4.

Participants stated that, the overall experience of participants with the app was positive. For the QR app, participants liked the design, color coding of positive and

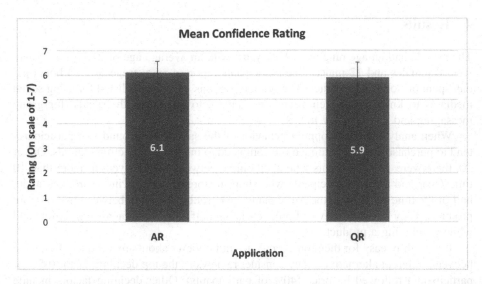

Fig. 1. Mean confidence rating of AR app compared to QR app, on scale of 1–7

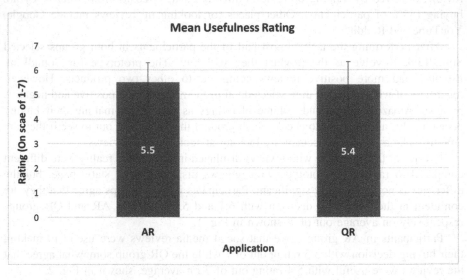

Fig. 2. Mean usefulness rating of AR app compared to QR app, on scale of 1–7

negative comments and ease of use. They also found it intuitive. For the AR app, some participants found it easy to use while others found it difficult to keep steady and hard to read text from the AR. Suggestions for the QR app include adding a filter for reviews, adding more and better quality of reviews, adding reviews from Amazon and clickable links with detailed reviews. Suggestions for the AR app include side by side

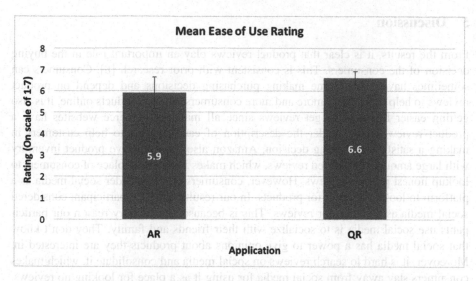

Fig. 3. Mean ease of use rating of AR app compared to QR app, on scale of 1–7

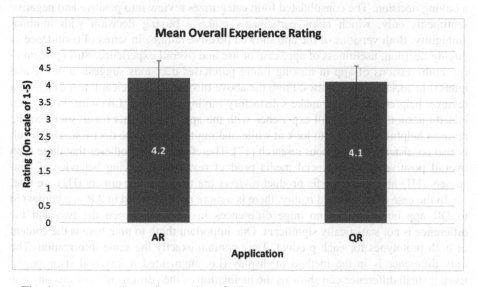

Fig. 4. Mean overall experience rating of AR app compared to QR app, on scale of 1–5

comparisons of reviews for multiple products, feature for making augmentation still after scanning, adding more reviews and, displaying reviews based on personal preference.

5 Discussion

From the results, it is clear that product reviews play an important role in the buying decision of the consumers. This is consistent with prior research [8]. Consumers can sometimes have a hard time making purchasing decisions and depend on product reviews to help them. With more and more consumers buying products online, it is also getting easier for them to get reviews since all major ecommerce websites have a product review section under the description of each product to help customers in making a satisfactory buying decision. Amazon also has extensive product inventory with large amounts of verified reviews, which makes it a favorite place of consumers to lookup honest product reviews. However, consumers don't consider social media as a platform to lookup reviews for products. In our results only one participant considered social media as a source for reviews. This is because, the primary reason our participants use social media is to socialize with their friends and family. They don't know that social media has a power to give opinions about products they are interested in. Moreover, it is hard to search reviews on social media and consolidate it, which makes consumers stay away from social media for using it as a place for looking up reviews.

When provided with social media reviews in a consolidated form using either version of our app, participants were successfully able to use it to help them in making a buying decision. The consolidated form categorizes review into positive and negative sentiments only, which helps participants make a buying decision with minimal ambiguity. Both versions of the app showed positive ratings, in terms of confidence in buying decision, usefulness of app, ease of use and overall experience. Strong intent to use both versions of app in making future purchases decisions suggests a desire and interest in social media reviews. From the above discussion, it is clear that social media reviews help consumers to make satisfactory buying decisions. Likewise, in an open ended question about overall experience with the app, participants found social media reviews helpful and useful to look at while making their purchase decision. This result is also consistent with previous research [17]. Therefore, our hypotheses that there is an overall positive effect of social media product reviews on buying behavior of consumers (H1) and social media product reviews are useful to consumers (H2) are true.

In the case of augmented reality, there is a more positive trend in AR app compared to QR app but there are no huge differences in ratings between the two and the difference is not statistically significant. One important thing to note here is the content of both prototypes for each product. They contain exactly the same information. The only difference is in the method of display (i.e. augmented reality and static page). Even a small difference can show us the inclination of the participants towards any one of the prototype.

Let's start with confidence in using the app. With exactly the same information in both app prototypes, participants are more confident in using AR app compared to QR app. This can be due to the advance and futuristic nature of the augmented reality app, which generated more confidence in purchase decision compared to QR app. Participants also consider AR app slightly more useful. Again, this can be due to their perception of augmented reality to be innovative and intuitive. The overall experience rating is slightly more for AR app than QR app. Since with augmented reality app, participants are experiencing something new for the very first time it is possible for them to give more rating to AR app compared to normal QR app. While the differences are not significant, the result show a supporting trend for our hypothesis that augmented reality increases overall experience of the app (H3).

Reasons for difference between ratings of AR app and QR app being not significant could be because of the small sample size. Since our study is formative we decided to go with small number of sample size. Also, our sample is composed of college students who are constantly exposed to new technologies like augmented reality. Therefore, participants might have considered augmented reality app normal and rated it almost the same as QR app.

However, when it comes to ease of use there is considerable difference between both prototypes. As augmented reality is known for positively transforming the user experience [28], it was assumed that it would be easier to use than QR app. But for participants, QR app was easier to use compared to AR app. Also, the participants are little more likely to use QR app in future than AR app. Therefore, our hypothesis that augmented reality increases usability of the app (H4) was not supported. Past research also shows that augmented reality struggles with usability [28, 30]. Answers to these differences lie in the responses to open ended questions. Participants found AR app tiring to use. For the continuous augmentation of reviews, it is required to hold phone still at the same position for the duration of the task. That was annoying for some participants. Moreover, dynamic nature of augmented reality resulted in non-steady augmentations which made reviews hard to read for some participants.

As for these challenges with the AR app, participants also provided solutions when asked for suggestions for the app. To make the app more stable and eliminate frustration in holding phone still, we can implement an augment and capture feature. This feature will make the screen still after information will augment and users don't need to hold the phone still anymore. This will also solve the problem of non-steady augmentation and increase the ease of use of the app.

6 Limitations and Future Research

In our research, we are proposing to analyze product reviews and display them based on sentiment analysis i.e. top positive and top negative comments from Facebook and Twitter. However, much better systems and mechanisms are available for the analysis of reviews based on expected helpfulness [14] and scoring based on utility of review [26]. Our analysis also doesn't include analysis of sarcastic product reviews [27], which may trigger false positive in analyzing sentiment of reviews. As Wang and Chang [16] showed, reviews from strong ties have a positive effect on consumers, therefore in future we can give preference to reviews posted by friends of the consumer.

We received many suggestions for the app from the participants in the study. In the future, we will implement those suggestions to make our app better. As shown in our results, augmented reality didn't show much difference and in fact has comparatively low ease of use rating, which is an aspect we need to improve on. Increasing the number of subjects in future research will also help in getting more generalizable results. We can use different categories of products instead of electronics, specially products for which consumers don't see reviews before buying. Improvements like side by side comparison feature along with augment and capture can be incorporated in a future version of the app to improve the usability of the app.

7   Conclusion

In this study, we proposed our novel app which combines product reviews, social media and augmented reality to have an impact on buying decision of consumers. The research study showed that our app has promising results and great potential to influence the buying intention of consumers. Social media reviews are found to be helpful in making decisions by consumers and augmented reality also increased overall experience of the app. Moreover, our results are also consistent with the previous research. By performing improvements in the app suggested by participants of the study, we will be able to overcome the usability issues of augmented reality encountered by participants while using the app.

References

1. Li, M., Huang, L., Tan, C.-H., Wei, K.-K.: Helpfulness of online product reviews as seen by consumers: source and content features. Int. J. Electron. Commer. **17**, 101–136 (2013). https://doi.org/10.2753/jec1086-4415170404
2. Zhang, J.Q., Craciun, G., Shin, D.: When does electronic word-of-mouth matter? A study of consumer product reviews. J. Bus. Res. **63**, 1336–1341 (2010). https://doi.org/10.1016/j.jbusres.2009.12.011
3. Shaikh, S.H., Lobo, L.M.R.J.: Revealing insights for sales based on analysis of Twitter product reviews. In: 2016 International Conference on Global Trends in Signal Processing, Information Computing and Communication (ICGTSPICC) (2016). https://doi.org/10.1109/icgtspicc.2016.7955303
4. Hodeghatta, U.R., Sahney, S.: Understanding Twitter as an e-WOM. J. Syst. Inf. Technol. **18**, 89–115 (2016). https://doi.org/10.1108/jsit-12-2014-0074
5. Hennig-Thurau, T., Walsh, G.: Electronic word-of-mouth: motives for and consequences of reading customer articulations on the internet. Int. J. Electron. Commer. **8**(2), 51–74 (2003)
6. Hennig-Thurau, T., Gwinner, K.P., Walsh, G., Gremler, D.D.: Electronic word-of-mouth via consumer-opinion platforms: what motivates consumers to articulate themselves on the Internet? J. Interact. Mark. **18**, 38–52 (2004). https://doi.org/10.1002/dir.10073
7. Azuma, R.T.: A survey of augmented reality. Presence Teleoperators Virtual Environ. **6**, 355–385 (1997). https://doi.org/10.1162/pres.1997.6.4.355
8. Chevalier, J., Mayzlin, D.: The effect of word of mouth on sales: online book reviews (2003). https://doi.org/10.3386/w10148
9. Zhu, F., Zhang, X.: Impact of online consumer reviews on sales: the moderating role of product and consumer characteristics. J. Mark. **74**, 133–148 (2010). https://doi.org/10.1509/jmkg.74.2.133
10. Cui, G., Lui, H.-K., Guo, X.: The effect of online consumer reviews on new product sales. Int. J. Electron. Commer. **17**(1), 39–58 (2012)

11. Hu, N., Liu, L., Zhang, J.: Do online reviews affect product sales? The role of reviewer characteristics and temporal effects. SSRN Electron. J. (2008). https://doi.org/10.2139/ssrn. 1324190

12. Pan, Y., Zhang, J.Q.: Born unequal: a study of the helpfulness of user-generated product reviews. J. Retail. **87**, 598–612 (2011). https://doi.org/10.1016/j.jretai.2011.05.002

13. Liu, Y., Huang, X., An, A., Yu, X.: Modeling and predicting the helpfulness of online reviews. In: 2008 Eighth IEEE International Conference on Data Mining (2008). https://doi. org/10.1109/icdm.2008.94

14. Ghose, A., Ipeirotis, P.G.: Designing novel review ranking systems: predicting the usefulness and impact of reviews. In: Proceedings of the Ninth International Conference on Electronic commerce - ICEC 2007 (2007). https://doi.org/10.1145/1282100.1282158

15. Ratchford, B.T., Talukdar, D., Lee, M.-S.: A model of consumer choice of the internet as an information source. Int. J. Electron. Commer. **5**, 7–21 (2001). https://doi.org/10.1080/ 10864415.2001.11044217

16. Wang, J.-C., Chang, C.-H.: How online social ties and product-related risks influence purchase intentions: a Facebook experiment. Electron. Commer. Res. Appl. **12**, 337–346 (2013). https://doi.org/10.1016/j.elerap.2013.03.003

17. Wang, X., Yu, C., Wei, Y.: Social media peer communication and impacts on purchase intentions: a consumer socialization framework. J. Interact. Mark. **26**, 198–208 (2012). https://doi.org/10.1016/j.intmar.2011.11.004

18. Jansen, B.J., Zhang, M., Sobel, K., Chowdury, A.: Twitter power: Tweets as electronic word of mouth. J. Am. Soc. Inf. Sci. Technol. **60**, 2169–2188 (2009). https://doi.org/10.1002/asi. 21149

19. Hangya, V., Farkas, R.: A comparative empirical study on social media sentiment analysis over various genres and languages. Artif. Intell. Rev. **47**, 485–505 (2016). https://doi.org/10. 1007/s10462-016-9489-3

20. Dave, K., Lawrence, S., Pennock, D.M.: Mining the peanut gallery: opinion extraction and semantic classification of product reviews. In: Proceedings of the Twelfth International Conference on World Wide Web - WWW 2003 (2003). https://doi.org/10.1145/775224. 775226

21. Sahni, T., Chandak, C., Chedeti, N.R., Singh, M.: Efficient Twitter sentiment classification using subjective distant supervision. In: 2017 9th International Conference on Communication Systems and Networks (COMSNETS) (2017). https://doi.org/10.1109/comsnets. 2017.7945451

22. Cui, H., Mittal, V., Datar, M.: Comparative experiments on sentiment classification for online product reviews. In: Proceedings of 21st Conference of the American Association for Artificial Intelligence. AAAI, Boston (2006)

23. Ghose, A., Ipeirotis, P.G.: Estimating the helpfulness and economic impact of product reviews: mining text and reviewer characteristics. IEEE Trans. Knowl. Data Eng. **23**, 1498–1512 (2011). https://doi.org/10.1109/tkde.2010.188

24. Liu, B., Hu, M., Cheng, J.: Opinion observer: analyzing and comparing opinions. In: Proceedings of the 14th International Conference on World Wide Web - WWW 2005 (2005). https://doi.org/10.1145/1060745.1060797

25. Kim, S.-M., Hovy, E.: Automatic identification of pro and con reasons in online reviews. In: Proceedings of the COLING/ACL on Main Conference Poster Sessions (2006). https://doi. org/10.3115/1273073.1273136

26. Zhang, Z., Varadarajan, B.: Utility scoring of product reviews. In: Proceedings of the 15th ACM International Conference on Information and Knowledge Management - CIKM 2006 (2006). https://doi.org/10.1145/1183614.1183626

27. Tsur, O., Davidov, D., Rappoport, A.: A great catchy name: semi-supervised recognition of sarcastic sentences in online product reviews. In: Proceeding of ICWSM of Context Dependent Opinions (2010)

28. Olsson, T., Salo, M.: Online user survey on current mobile augmented reality applications. In: 2011 10th IEEE International Symposium on Mixed and Augmented Reality (2011). https://doi.org/10.1109/ismar.2011.6162874

29. Olsson, T., Lagerstam, E., Kärkkäinen, T., Väänänen-Vainio-Mattila, K.: Expected user experience of mobile augmented reality services: a user study in the context of shopping centres. Pers. Ubiquit. Comput. **17**, 287–304 (2011). https://doi.org/10.1007/s00779-011-0494-x

30. Akçayır, M., Akçayır, G.: Advantages and challenges associated with augmented reality for education: a systematic review of the literature. Educ. Res. Rev. **20**, 1–11 (2017). https://doi.org/10.1016/j.edurev.2016.11.002

31. Kim, K., Hwang, J., Zo, H., Lee, H.: Understanding users' continuance intention toward smartphone augmented reality applications. Inf. Dev. **32**, 161–174 (2014). https://doi.org/10.1177/0266666914535119

32. Ko, S.M., Chang, W.S., Ji, Y.G.: Usability principles for augmented reality applications in a smartphone environment. Int. J. Hum.-Comput. Interact. **29**, 501–515 (2013). https://doi.org/10.1080/10447318.2012.722466

33. Balduini, M., Celino, I., Dell'Aglio, D., Valle, E.D., Huang, Y., Lee, T., Kim, S.-H., Tresp, V.: BOTTARI: an augmented reality mobile application to deliver personalized and location-based recommendations by continuous analysis of social media streams. Web Semant. Sci. Serv. Agents World Wide Web **16**, 33–41 (2012). https://doi.org/10.1016/j.websem.2012.06.004

Product Web Page Design:
A Psychophysiological Investigation of the Influence of Product Similarity, Visual Proximity on Attention and Performance

Carolane Juanéda[✉], Sylvain Sénécal, and Pierre-Majorique Léger

HEC Montreal, 3000 Chemin de la Côte-Sainte-Catherine, Montreal,
QC H3T 2A7, Canada
juanedacarolane@gmail.com

Abstract. This research examines attention to distracting products unrelated to the shopping goal and its impact on performance when making online decisions. An experiment was conducted with thirty-eight participants in a laboratory setting. The study used a 2 (product similarity: similar vs. non-similar) × 2 (visual proximity: near vs. far) within-subject design. The attention of participants was measured with eye tracking during an online decision task. The results showed a significant effect of distractors' visual proximity as participants spent more time on products that were near the target stimulus. In addition, the analysis yielded an interaction between product similarity and visual distance on users' attention. Finally, distractors that were similar to the focal stimulus positively influenced decisions accuracy. These findings contribute to theory by providing quantitative measures of the Gestalt law of proximity. In addition, the user experience has become a cornerstone for the success of firms and the conclusions have HCI design implications about effective product presentations in online shops.

Keywords: Visual attention · Visual distance · Product similarity
Consumer behavior · Ecommerce · Online design · Web pages
Inhibition

1 Introduction

Human activity is driven by impulses that are biochemically and psychologically stimulated, which come from conscious and unconscious activity of the brain. These psychological impulses appear suddenly and are accompanied by a persistent and powerful desire to immediately proceed to an action [1]. In order to control their behavior, individuals must respond only to aspects of the environment that are related to their objectives, by avoiding being distracted by stimuli that are irrelevant to the current task [2]. One of the mechanisms that reduce impulse temptations is the control of visual attention called selective attention, which is the ability to differentiate between relevant and non-relevant information. This system involves two components: the processing of relevant information (i.e., activation) and the active suppression of

© Springer International Publishing AG, part of Springer Nature 2018
F. F.-H. Nah and B. S. Xiao (Eds.): HCIBGO 2018, LNCS 10923, pp. 327–337, 2018.
https://doi.org/10.1007/978-3-319-91716-0_25

distracting information (i.e., inhibition) [3]. Thus, once a stimulus is identified as irrelevant, inhibition dampens activation and blocks its access to the response system, reducing interference from distractors [4]. The concept of cognitive inhibition explains an individual's ability to control his attention to a task, since it refers to mental processes in the attentional processing of stimuli [5]. When cognitive inhibition is activated, other cognitive and behavioral processes are facilitated, resulting in adjustments of goal-oriented actions. As a result, the ability to direct visual attention away from tempting stimuli avoids unexpected impulses [6].

When shopping online, attention is directed to a myriad of stimuli (e.g., products and ads) [7]. Given that the electronic commerce industry is highly competitive and continuously expanding, users expect a flawless online experience forcing firms to find new ways to attract consumers. Indeed, eMarketer indicates that online sales were $34.04 billion in Canada in 2017 and estimates that they will reach $71.05 billion in 2021, an increase of 109% compared to 2017 [8]. In order to stay competitive, the scientific literature demonstrated that both the first impression of a webpage and its appearance are crucial in capturing users' attention [9]. The mechanism of attention has been the subject of many scientific studies [10], yet, to the best of our knowledge, online attention has not been investigated in depth.

In light of this gap in the literature, this article investigates how stimuli affect individuals' attention and decisions in an online context. More precisely, the present research posits that individuals' attention is greater towards distractors that are visually near and conceptually similar to the target stimulus, impacting online decision-making. The discoveries would have HCI design implications as they would help web engineers to optimize the design of web pages in order to capture users' attention, a key element in ensuring a firm's prosperity.

2   The Proposed Model

In an online shopping context, the hypothesis that individuals pay more attention to distractors that are near the target stimulus rather than the target itself came from research on vision. Numerous psychological and neurophysiological studies on object-based attention have revealed that attention and perceptual grouping are closely tied to each other in biological visual systems [11]. According to the sensory enhancement theory, object-based attention arises from the spreading of attention along Gestalt grouping cues [11]. These principles were formulated since the mind has an innate disposition to structure the elements that the eye perceives. One principle is the law of proximity, which suggests that individuals first group together the points closest to each other in such a way that they tend to perceive objects close to one another as a single group with a relationship, while objects that are farther apart are placed in different groups [12]. Studies in e-commerce showed that the Gestalt principles strongly influence web page design [13]. Therefore, when a desired product is available online, other products have a significant advantage when placed next to it [14], supporting the law of proximity. Thus, in a shopping context, it is suggested that individuals' attention will be preferentially drawn towards close products relative to the target stimulus.

H1: Distractors close to the target stimulus attract more attention than distractors farther from the target stimulus.

We posit that a similar attentional bias exists for distractors that are conceptually similar to the target stimulus. This proposition arose from cognitive science research, namely the categorization process [15]. Product category schemas are organized prior knowledge structures stored in memory where a product matches a pattern. In order to identify objects and distinguish them from other categories, individuals unconsciously organize their memory. The categorization process helps to classify, interpret, and evaluate stimuli by defining all the alternatives with which a stimulus is compared [15]. It facilitates the assimilation and understanding of product-related information found in the environment [16]. The key concept that derives from categorization is similarity. Additionally, the perception of similarity is often seen as a primary influence on category representations [17]. Two types of categorization exist. First, there is the taxonomic categories, which is used to classify stimuli based on shared similar attributes. This suggests that people judge the similarity of one product to another based on common characteristics. Second, there are objective categories that are built ad hoc for a need sought in a consumption situation [18]. In comparison to objectives-related categorization, taxonomic categories are well-established in memory, making external similarities more accessible when considering a set of products. Therefore, through the activation in memory of objects associated with the target stimulus [19], attention is drawn to similar stimuli by information held in the working memory. Thus, in an e-commerce context, it is suggested that individuals' attention will be preferentially drawn towards products that are similar to the target stimulus.

H2: Distractors similar to the target stimulus attract more attention than distractors that are less similar to the target stimulus.

To prevent impulsive precursors from influencing behaviors, inhibitory control is necessary. Some consumers are less able to inhibit impulses, resulting in undesirable behavioral tendencies (e.g., impulsive purchase decisions) [20]. Hence, the shopping environment exposes consumers to many attractive products that grab their attention. Failed regulation in some people does not allow them to shift their visual attention away from stimuli [21]. Taken together, these findings indicate that the effect of visual distance and product similarity will trigger attentional bias.

H3: There is an interaction between product similarity and visual proximity on users' attention.

Moreover, in the literature, the definition of decision-making performance relates to rewards individuals obtained as a consequence of their choice. It was shown the stronger the activation of the attentional-control circuit, the better the decision [22]. This study suggested that individual' attention is drawn towards distractors that are similar and near the target stimulus, therefore these variables are expected to positively impact the performance of decisions.

H4: Distractors that are similar and near the focal product positively influence performance, i.e., product selection.

To test the hypotheses, we propose the following model (See Fig. 1).

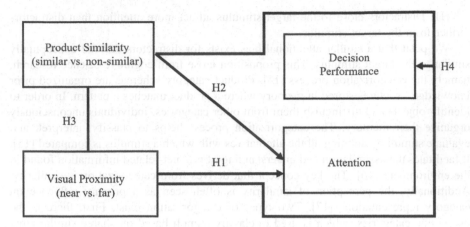

Fig. 1. Research model

3 Method

3.1 Participants and Design

An experiment was conducted in a laboratory using a 2 (similarity between the focal product and distractors: similar vs. non-similar) × 2 (proximity between the focal product and distractors: close vs. far) within-subject design. Thirty-eight students participated (Mage = 23.32, SD = 3.31) and received a $20 gift card for our University's store as compensation. The IRB of our institution approved this study. In the similar condition, the focal product and the distractors were conceptually close (e.g., cake vs. muffin), whereas in the non-similar condition they were far (e.g., cake vs. meat). In the near condition, the distance between all products was small (i.e., at the center of the screen), whereas in the far condition, the focal product was in the center of the screen and distractors were in the periphery.

3.2 Procedure and Measures

The study had two steps. First, participants accomplished two online shopping tasks separated between Scenario 1 and Scenario 2, in which the experimental factors were manipulated. The instructions indicated to focus on the target object. At first, instructions for Scenario 1 were displayed. It was about "Matthew", who needed to buy a birthday cake with fresh whole strawberries for his best friend. To reduce the variability of the response time that results from the distracted gaze of the subjects [23], it started with a fixation cross in the center of the screen. The latter was displayed during a random period of time (e.g., between 1000 ms and 3000 ms) to reduce a possible anticipatory effect. After the fixation cross, the screen that contained the distractors and the focal product was displayed for 4000 ms. It included one focal product and three distractors. When it disappeared, participants were asked to indicate if the focal product was a cake with or without strawberries. To increase the ecological validity and to limit stress, participants had no time limit to make the decision. The sequence always consisted of three screens in the following order: one screen with a fixing cross, one screen containing the distractors as well as the focal product and one screen with the question related to the previous screen. This order was repeated until the final trial. After participants completed thirty-two decisions, Scenario 2 instructions were displayed. Participants read about their niece "Sarah". As she celebrated her 7th birthday, they were asked to find her a pink dress. Subjects were informed that the dress would always be in the center of the screen. It started with a fixation cross in the center that was displayed during a random period of time (e.g., between 1000 ms and 3000 ms). Then, the screen that contained both the distractors and the focal product was displayed for 4000 ms. It included one focal product and four distractors. When it disappeared, they were asked to indicate if the dress was pink, without no time limit for answering. The sequence always consisted of three screens in the following order: one with a fixing cross, one containing the distractors and the focal product and one with the question related to the last screen. This order was repeated until the thirty-second decision. Second, once the main task was completed, we asked participants to fill in a questionnaire designed to assess their demographic profile.

Attention was measured using a computer monitor with an integrated SMI eye tracker (Model: RED 250, SensoMotoric Instruments GmbH, Teltow, Germany) that had a sampling rate of 60 Hz. Each participant was seated on a chair with a viewing distance of approximately 24 inches from the monitor. The equipment was individually calibrated using a five-point calibration method, producing a low tracking error (less than 0.4). The pixels area of the distractors was defined as separate areas of interest (i.e., AOI) [24]. To measure the allocation of attention, time spent on distractors was assessed and the milliseconds of net dwell time on distractors were used. As for decisions analysis performance, response time and accuracy of the answer given were monitored.

3.3 Stimuli

Given that impulsive individuals are less capable of self-controlling their domains of interest [25], we used stimuli from the food and the fashion industry. They were separated in two different scenarios known to trigger impulsive behaviors [26, 27] to simulate attentional bias.

For Scenario 1, the target product was a picture of a cake, whereas pictures of pastries, frozen desserts, chocolates, and sweet snacks served as similar product distractors (within-subject condition; Fig. 2). Pictures of cheeses, meats, alcoholic beverages, and fish were used as non-similar distractors (within-subject condition; Fig. 2).

For Scenario 2, the target product was a pink dress, whereas pictures of t-shirts, skirts, sweatshirts, and jackets served as similar distractors (within-subject condition; Fig. 3). For the non-similar distractors, pictures of swimwear, accessories, underwear, and shoes were presented (within-subject condition; Fig. 3).

Images had the same pixels size and appeared only once. Finally, to measure the visual distance effect, four image layouts were tested: all distant, all close, distance in x, and distance in y. Distances (e.g., x distance) were held constant across trials.

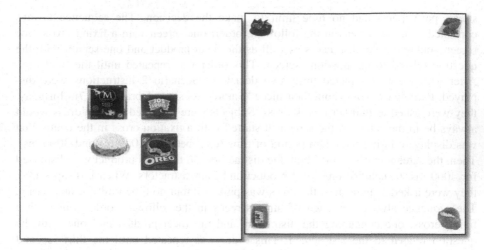

Fig. 2. Scenario 1 conditions: left panel: small distance - high similarity; right panel: far distance - low similarity)

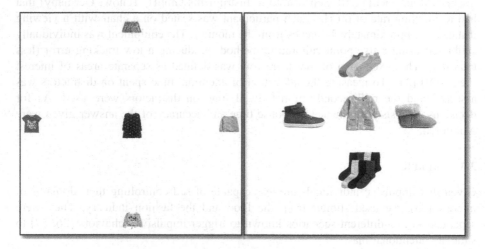

Fig. 3. Scenario 2 conditions: left panel: far distance - high similarity; right panel: small distance - low similarity (Color figure online)

4 Results

The experiment sought to investigate the influence of visual proximity and product similarity on online attention and decisions. To test the hypotheses, time spent on distractors was utilized as a dependent variable in a linear mixed-effects regression model [28]. The latter offers more information than ANOVAs about variance and covariance (i.e., variability of two random variables) [29]. The results of individuals' attention on distractors are summarized in Table 1. Moreover, to examine the performance of decisions, response time and accuracy of the answer were dependent variables measured in a mixed-effects logistic regression model. The results of individuals' decisions performance are summarized in Table 2. Finally, to avoid errors of multiple comparisons, the Holm-Bonferroni method was used.

Table 1. Distractors' proximity and similarity results

Model	Estimate	Std. error	t-value	p-value
Scenario 1				
Visual proximity	501	340	1.47	.140
Product similarity	−281	341	−0.82	.410
Visual proximity × Product similarity	120	23.2	5.17	<.000
Scenario 2				
Visual proximity	582	264	2.21	.027
Product similarity	1.85	268	0.010	.995
Visual Proximity × Product similarity	106	17.4	6.07	<.000

We hypothesized that individuals allocate more attention towards distractors that are near the target stimulus. The significant effect showed that participants spent more time on distractors that were near the focal product (t (4788) = 2.21, p = .027, d = 0.06, Table 1). Importantly, it emerged when the focal product was at the center of the screen (i.e., Scenario 2: prior knowledge of the focal stimulus position). In sum, this finding supports H1: participants allocate more attention to distractors that are close, but only for Scenario 2.

We postulated that individuals allocate more attention towards distractors that are similar to the target stimulus. For both scenarios, the effect was not significant (Table 1), therefore, H2 is rejected.

We further analyzed the visual distance x product similarity interaction using a least- squares means model for the comparison of multiple factors. The analysis yielded a significant effect (See Fig. 4). More precisely, in the non-similar products condition, attention was greater on distractors that were near the focal product (t (4788) = 6.07, p < .000, d = 0.18). The effect was obtained for both scenarios, confirming H3: an interaction exists between product similarity and their distance on users' attention.

Moreover, we supposed that similar distractors that are near the focal product influenced the performance of decisions. For Scenario 1, the answer is more likely to be accurate with similar stimuli rather than non-similar distractors (t (1161) = 3.39, p = .001, d = 0.20; Table 2). As for Scenario 2, the answer is more likely to be incorrect when distractors are far from the target product (t (1161) = −2.23, p = .026, d = 0.13; Table 2). Hence, distractors that are similar to the focal product lead to accuracy of the answer. No significant effect was found on response time, which partially confirmed H4: distractors that are similar to the focal product positively influence answer accuracy, but only for Scenario 1.

Table 2. Performance results

Model	Estimate	Std. error	t-value	p-value
Scenario 1: response time				
Visual proximity	2751	2180	1.26	.207
Product similarity	237	1546	0.15	.878
Scenario 1: accuracy				
Visual proximity	−14.4	−15.0	−0.96	.335
Product similarity	29.4	8.67	3.39	.001
Scenario 2: response time				
Visual proximity	−109	1445	−0.080	.940
Product similarity	96.3	1025	0.090	.925
Scenario 2: accuracy				
Visual proximity	−37.8	16.9	−2.23	.026
Product similarity	13.0	10.8	1.21	.227

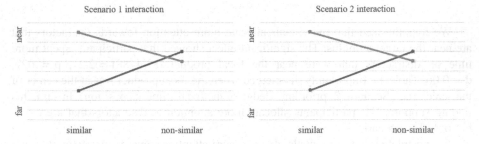

Fig. 4. Interaction effects

5 Discussion

An important finding of this research is that attentional bias is more pronounced when distractors are visually near the focal product. This supports our hypothesis that individuals are less successful in keeping their attention on the focal product when distractors are at a close distance. In addition, we discovered an interaction between visual proximity and product similarity on users' attention. Finally, distractors that are similar to the target stimulus positively impacted accuracy of the answer given during the decision task.

The results have theoretical contributions and managerial implications. First, this research quantitatively measures the Gestalt law of proximity (i.e., time spent on distractors) with attentional data (i.e., eye-tracking), thereby contributing to the general literature on vision through quantitative measurement [30]. Second, the user experience has become the cornerstone for designers and the concern of senior executives considering a great online experience has the potential to grow business revenues. Thus, understanding users' behavior is crucial to meeting their needs. The study provides relevant insights for web page design. For instance, the findings can guide recommendation system developers and web page designers about what type of products should be presented together and how far apart to capture and keep users' attention.

Two limitations should be noted. First, studies have shown cross-cultural variations in visual attention [27]. Thus, future research should consider adding this element as a control variable. Second, the main limitation stems from the artificial nature of the task. Because participants were not buying the product at the end, they could have been less capable of self-controlling their attention towards the focal product knowing that the goal was simulated.

Some results require further investigation. The discovery that individuals' attention to distractors that are near the focal product operated only for Scenario 2, can be explained by the top-down guidance theory of attention. The biased-competition model of visual attention suggests that objects are competing for access to higher levels of processing in the brain. The attention is controlled by the pre-activation of neural channels towards a relevant object [31]. Therefore, during a searching task, visual attention is guided to a stimulus matching the content in the working memory. Brain imaging studies showed that food-related stimuli are strongly represented in the working memory, thereby, it could generate attentional bias. Inhibiting food-related stimuli can be more challenging for individuals, since they are well represented in memory [32]. Consequently, the experiment scenario design (e.g., food industry) can explain the rejection of H2. Furthermore, this theory can give an explanation to the significant effect of answer accuracy for Scenario 1 only. Therefore, future research should consider combining eye tracking with electroencephalography signals (i.e., EEG) to measure cognitive load during the shopping task [33]. This would provide a timely alert for conveying high-attention level feedback against the distractors to gain additional information. Alpha waves' neural oscillations would be useful to measure attention and to analyze the brain activity [34] during the shopping task. Forthcoming research should also extend the participant pool to form gender groups to measure the level of attention against products that are known to trigger impulsivity in some groups [26]. Finally, regulating affective responses is harder for impulsive individuals [35], thereby, facial emotions could help to understand how emotions mediate visual attention.

Now that designers only have 50 ms to capture users' attention [36], web page design needs to be impeccable. One of the powerful factors influencing attention is the appearance of a website [9]. Despite the prevalence, a fairly limited scientific knowledge is available regarding online attention. With these facts, there is a relevance of pursuing research in this field.

References

1. Rook, D.W.: The buying impulse. J. Consum. Res. **14**, 189–199 (1987)
2. Allport, D.A.: Selection for action: some behavioral and neurophysiological considerations of attention and action. Perspect. Percept. Action **15**, 395–419 (1987)
3. Stevens, C., Bavelier, D.: The role of selective attention on academic foundations: a cognitive neuroscience perspective. Dev. Cogn. Neurosci. **2**, 30–48 (2012)

4. Moeller, B., Schächinger, H., Frings, C.: Irrelevant stimuli and action control: analyzing the influence of ignored stimuli via the distractor-response binding paradigm. J. Vis. Exp. JoVE **87** (2014)
5. Nigg, J.T.: On inhibition/disinhibition in developmental psychopathology: views from cognitive and personality psychology and a working inhibition taxonomy. Psychol. Bull. **126**, 220 (2000)
6. Serfas, B.G., Büttner, O.B., Florack, A.: Using implementation intentions in shopping situations: how arousal can help shield consumers against temptation. Appl. Cogn. Psychol. **30**, 672–680 (2016)
7. Etco, M., Senecal, S., Leger, P.M., Fredette, M.: The influence of online search behavior on consumers' decision-making heuristics. J. Comput. Inf. Syst. **57**, 344–352 (2017)
8. McNair, C.: Worldwide retail and ecommerce sales: emarketer's updated forecast and new mcommerce estimates for 2016–2021. Industry Report, eMarketing (2018)
9. Tuch, A.N., Presslaber, E.E., Stocklin, M., Opwis, K., Bargas-Avila, J.A.: The role of visual complexity and prototypicality regarding first impression of websites: working towards understanding aesthetic judgments. Int. J. Hum. – Comput. Stud. **70**, 794 (2012)
10. Pashler, H.E., Sutherland, S.: The Psychology of Attention, vol. 15 (1998)
11. Yu, J.-G., Xia, G.-S., Gao, C., Samal, A.: A computational model for object-based visual saliency: spreading attention along gestalt cues. IEEE Trans. Multimed. **18**, 273–286 (2016)
12. Reynolds, M., Kwan, D., Smilek, D.: To group or not to group an ecological consideration of the stroop effect. Exp. Psychol. **57**, 275–291 (2010)
13. Demangeot, C., Broderick, A.J.: Consumer perceptions of online shopping environments: a gestalt approach. Psychol. Mark. **27**, 117–140 (2010)
14. Breugelmans, E., Campo, K., Gijsbrechts, E.: Shelf sequence and proximity effects on online grocery choices. Mark. Lett. **18**, 117–133 (2007)
15. Barsalou, L.W.: Ideals, central tendency, and frequency of instantiation as determinants of graded structure in categories. J. Exp. Psychol. Learn. Mem. Cogn. **11**, 629 (1985)
16. Sujan, M., Bettman, J.R.: The effects of brand positioning strategies on consumers' brand and category perceptions: some insights from schema research. J. Mark. Res. **26**, 454–467 (1989)
17. Tversky, A.: Features of similarity. Psychol. Rev. **84**, 327 (1977)
18. Huffman, C., Houston, M.J.: Goal-oriented experiences and the development of knowledge. J. Consum. Res. **20**, 190–207 (1993)
19. Soto, D., Heinke, D., Humphreys, G.W., Blanco, M.J.: Early, involuntary top-down guidance of attention from working memory. J. Exp. Psychol. Hum. Percept. Perform. **31**, 248–261 (2005)
20. Strack, F., Deutsch, R.: Reflective and impulsive determinants of social behavior. Pers. Soc. Psychol. Rev. **8**, 220–247 (2004)
21. Serfas, B.G., Büttner, O.B., Florack, A.: Using implementation intentions in shopping situations: how arousal can help shield consumers against temptation. Appl. Cogn. Psychol. **30**, 672–680 (2016)
22. Laureiro-Martínez, D., Brusoni, S., Canessa, N., Zollo, M.: Understanding the exploration–exploitation dilemma: an fMRI study of attention control and decision-making performance. Strateg. Manag. J. **36**, 319–338 (2015). https://doi.org/10.1002/smj.2221
23. Eriksen, B.A., Eriksen, C.W.: Effects of noise letters upon the identification of a target letter in a nonsearch task. Percept. Psychophys. **16**, 143–149 (1974)
24. Riedl, R., Léger, P.-M.: Fundamentals of NeuroIS. Studies in Neuroscience, Psychology and Behavioral Economics. Springer, Heidelberg (2016). https://doi.org/10.1007/978-3-662-45091-8

25. Tsukayama, E., Duckworth, A.L., Kim, B.: Resisting everything except temptation: evidence and an explanation for domain-specific impulsivity. Eur. J. Pers. **26**, 318–334 (2012)
26. Dittmar, H., Beattie, J., Friese, S.: Objects, decision considerations and self-image in men's and women's impulse purchases. Acta Psychol. **93**, 187–206 (1996)
27. Zhang, B.Y., Seo, H.S.: Visual attention toward food-item images can vary as a function of background saliency and culture: an eye-tracking study. Food Q. Prefer. **41**, 172–179 (2015)
28. Magezi, D.A.: Linear mixed-effects models for within-participant psychology experiments: an introductory tutorial and free, graphical user interface (LMMgui). Front. Psychol. **6**, 2 (2015)
29. Kliegl, R., Wei, P., Dambacher, M., Yan, M., Zhou, X.: Experimental effects and individual differences in linear mixed models: estimating the relationship between spatial, object, and attraction effects in visual attention. Front. Psychol. **1**, 238 (2011)
30. Jäkel, F., Singh, M., Wichmann, F.A., Herzog, M.H.: An overview of quantitative approaches in Gestalt perception. Vis. Res. **126**, 3–8 (2016)
31. Tan, J., Zhao, Y., Wu, S., Wang, L., Hitchman, G., Tian, X., Chen, A.: The temporal dynamics of visual working memory guidance of selective attention. Front. Behav. Neurosci. **8**, 345 (2014). https://doi.org/10.3389/fnbeh.2014.00345
32. Higgs, S.: Cognitive processing of food rewards. Appetite **104**, 10–17 (2016)
33. Léger, P.-M., Sénecal, S., Courtemanche, F., de Guinea, A.O., Titah, R., Fredette, M., Labonte-LeMoyne, É.: Precision is in the eye of the beholder: application of eye fixation-related potentials to information systems research. J. Assoc. Inf. Syst. **15**, 651 (2014)
34. Chen, C.M., Wang, J.Y., Yu, C.M.: Assessing the attention levels of students by using a novel attention aware system based on brainwave signals. Br. J. Educ. Technol. **48**, 348–369 (2017)
35. Gross, J.J.: The emerging field of emotion regulation: an integrative review. Rev. Gen. Psychol. **2**, 271 (1998)
36. Lindgaard, G., Fernandes, G., Dudek, C., Brown, J.: Attention web designers: you have 50 milliseconds to make a good first impression. Behav. Inf. Technol. **25**, 115–126 (2006)

Emotions and Feelings: Some Aspects for the HCI-Community – A Work in Progress Paper

Harald Kindermann[1]([⊠]) and Franz Auinger[2]

[1] University of Applied Sciences Upper Austria, Steyr, Austria
`harald.kindermann@fh-steyr.at`
[2] University of Applied Sciences Upper Austria, Wels, Austria
`franz.auinger@fh-wels.at`

Abstract. Everyone has experienced emotions and everybody knows what they are – at least, we think we know. Asked for an explanation, the response will likely be something along the lines of "happiness is an emotion" or "if I'm scared of something, it is also an emotion." Such imprecise and in the narrower sense incorrect definitions are entirely sufficient for everyday use. But this is obviously not the case in science as well as in corporate practice. After all, important recommendations for the economy should be derived from well-founded studies. As a first step, this requires that the term "emotions" means the same to everybody. At the present time, this is wishful thinking. A steadily rising number of publications are produced within the HCI community, in which in part elaborate measuring techniques are used to account for emotions with different study designs. However, this approach appears to be problematic, because a standard definition of "emotions" has yet to be established. The purpose of this publication is to draw the attention of the HCI community to this issue and to start a worthwhile conversation with an attempt at providing a definition. It concludes with a specific recommendation as to which physiological measuring methods would be conducive for answering corporate research questions.

Keywords: Review · Emotions · Feelings · Somatic marker · Measurement

1 Introduction

Research efforts have long been aimed at understanding the decision-making behavior of consumers. Although the focus of corporate efforts after World War Two understandably revolved around the resolution of the rebuilding-related production bottleneck, merchandise was produced and stockpiled ever since this problem was resolved and the focus (again) shifted to the consumers' needs and all of the factors that contribute to fulfilling these needs. Given the enormous variety of product offerings, the often marginal performance differences between the products and the wealth of possibilities for how the desired product can be purchased, this topic has gained increasing importance. When analyzing the factors that influence the consumers' decision-making behavior, we generally resort to using different constructs, which are determined by

© Springer International Publishing AG, part of Springer Nature 2018
F. F.-H. Nah and B. S. Xiao (Eds.): HCIBGO 2018, LNCS 10923, pp. 338–350, 2018.
https://doi.org/10.1007/978-3-319-91716-0_26

means of empirical methods of measuring. Customer satisfaction, attitudes, trust as well as emotions are some examples of such constructs. They are measured and their impact on the purchasing behavior is verified by means of sophisticated mathematical models. They include a diverse set of structural equation modeling, regression or variance analyses. We refrain from mentioning publications at this point, because the bulk of the scientific literature dedicated to this topic is filled with such studies. The validity of these studies is tied directly to the correct measurement of the constructs, for which a plausible and clear definition of the used constructs is required in turn. Science has adequately achieved this with a number of constructs, but still has a long way to go when it comes to emotions. For example, Kleinginna and Kleinginna [1] counted more than one hundred different definitions in their review article. The publication by Kreibig [2] illustrates that this situation has not yet improved substantially by now, at least when it concerns the measurement of emotions.

Considering the significance of "emotions" for the corporate practice, it appears to be particularly problematic that many studies are based upon an incorrect or cursory definition of "emotions." It is often said that products/web pages and/or commercials should be "emotionalized" in order to promote sales, albeit without mentioning the term as such. In so doing, it is a problem that everyone has experienced emotions and everybody is capable of providing an explanation about what emotions are. Asked for an explanation, the response will likely be something along the lines of "happiness is an emotion" or "if I'm scared of something, it is also an emotion." Such imprecise and in the narrower sense incorrect definitions are certainly unproblematic for everyday use. However, if advertising campaigns in corporate practice are designed to "emotionalize" as mentioned above, the definition of "emotions" should be uniform and accurate – at least if the purpose is to spend the advertising dollars in an effective and efficient manner.

Publications aimed at determining emotions by means of in part elaborate measuring techniques can also be found at growing rates within the HCI and NeuroIS community. For this reason, it is also vital for this community to address this problem and to initiate a productive discussion process. Walla [3] has made an exciting contribution with his article. And we hope to inspire the dialog further with this paper.

It starts with a brief overview of the historic development of different theories on emotions, and concludes with the proposal of a model that suggests that the current definitions of emotions are much more similar than assumed. Substantial differences in part only exist with regard to the methods for whether and how emotions are measured. In light of these insights, recommendations on how to measure emotions are provided and put up for discussion.

2 A Historic Review of Important Explanatory Approaches

William James (1842–1910) and Carl Lange (1834–1900) virtually at the same time formulated a theory about emotions, which is indeed considered historic by now, but still serves as an important basis for current approaches. Because the two theoretical approaches were largely identical, this theory was referenced in the textbooks as "James-Lange theory." Both theories are based upon the basic premise that physiological reactions instigate the experience of emotion [4, 5]. It proposes that a physiological reaction is first caused by an external stimulus and that this reaction subsequently creates a perceivable emotional state. James writes: "...that the bodily changes follow directly the perception of the exciting fact, and that our feeling of the same changes as they occur IS the emotion." [pp. 189–190]. Accordingly, we are not afraid because we encounter a dangerous predatory animal, but the predatory animal instead elicits autonomous reactions within the body, in the muscle tone, the heart rate, blood pressure, etc., which are subsequently perceived as fear, a manifestation of an emotional state. It is important to note that James and Lange refer to this physiological reaction as the actual emotion and to the perception of the emotion as feeling [6, 7]. Another important aspect of this theory is that the perceived feelings differ with regard to the autonomous physiological reactions, and that these autonomous physiological reactions are always specific for the different perceived emotional states [6, 8]. The James-Lange theory was controversial in its time, as it was entirely contrary to the prevailing opinion. It was assumed that a dangerous stimulus instigates the feelings first, which subsequently lead to the physiological reactions [6]. This correlation is illustrated in Fig. 1.

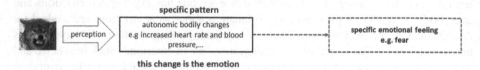

Fig. 1. The principle of the James-Lange-Theory

Walter Cannon (1871–1945) and his student Philip Bard (1898–1977) were the most vocal critics of the James-Lange theory. Their criticisms primarily concerned the aspect that emotional experience is associated with specific reaction patterns. According to them, feelings and physiological reactions are components of the emotion that are independent from one another, and it may well be that identical autonomous reactions result in different emotional states. This hypothesis was corroborated with experiments on cats, by severing the spinal cord of the laboratory animals. After the procedure, the cats had obviously lost the sensation in their body below the severed area, but the animals still displayed emotional states, such as for example hissing [7, 9–11].

Brain structures involving the thalamus and hypothalamus play a crucial role in the Cannon and Bard theory. Accordingly, perceived sensory stimuli arrive in these regions of the brain, leading to simultaneous changes in the body and to feelings. Consequently, it is not a specific autonomous reaction pattern, but rather a specific activation pattern in the mentioned cortical regions that is responsible for the perceived emotional state [6–8]. According to James-Lange, people are afraid of a predatory animal because the perception of one is associated with specific reactions of the body (e.g. escape or agonistic behavior and/or being scared stiff). According to Cannon-Bard, the reactions of the body triggered by a predatory animal are unspecific and not at all necessary for an emotional sensation. To experience an emotional state, it suffices when the thalamus is activated [7]. This correlation is illustrated in Fig. 2.

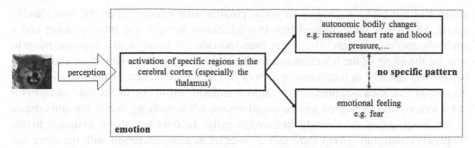

Fig. 2. The Cannon-Bard-Theory

In the 1960s, Stanley Schachter (1922–1997) and his student Jerome Everett Singer (1934–2010) formulated the so-called two-factor theory of emotions. It states that feelings develop when we perceive a physiological change (e.g. sweating, increased heart rate) and the physiological change is interpreted accordingly by the brain. In fact, our brain is looking for a possible and plausible cause for the perceived symptoms, in order to make a subsequent cognitive interpretation. Thus, it is not a specific arousal pattern in the autonomous nervous system (ANS) that is responsible for a certain emotional experience, but rather the same physical state of arousal can be attributed – cognitively labeled – to a pleasant or an unpleasant cause (cp. Fig. 3). As a result, ambiguous situations may be interpreted differently [12–14]. This theory gained particular significance because of a very well-known and often cited experiment we would like to introduce briefly below:

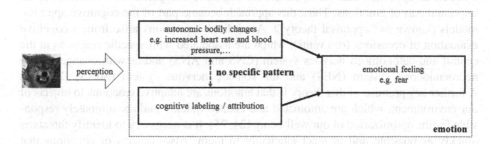

Fig. 3. Schachter-Singer-Theory

In this experiment, 185 participants were told that a "vitamin supplement" named Suproxin would be used to test their vision and that they would be injected with this active ingredient for this purpose. After consent for this procedure was obtained from 184 participants, three quarters of them were injected with adrenaline. The remaining quarter (=control group) received a saline solution. The persons who had been given adrenaline were divided into two equal groups. One group was told that the injection may cause rapid heartbeat, shaking, increased blood flow, etc. These effects are indeed expected following the injection of adrenaline. Another group was told that they may develop unexpected reactions, such as e.g. itching, headache and numbness. A third group was not told anything at all about possible side effects. After this first classification, all groups were divided into two additional sub-groups, into an anger and a euphoria condition group. They were then individually brought to a separate room to wait for the effect of the injection and for the planned vision test. However, another test person was already in that room, who was in fact a confederate of the investigator. If the person had been assigned to the "anger condition" group, he or she was asked to fill out a tedious and very provocative questionnaire while waiting, while the confederate of the investigator deliberately behaved angrily. In contrast, those assigned to the "euphoria condition" group were able to interact at their discretion with the other test person while waiting. Moreover, the confederate acted in an extremely positive manner.

Prior to the experiment, Schachter and Singer hypothesized that the misinformed or uninformed study participants would try to find a cognitive explanation for the physiological arousal resulting from the adrenaline injection, namely depending on whether the confederate in the room acted angrily or positively. In contrast, the manipulation of the confederate should only have a negligible effect on the correctly informed subjects and the control group, because they would be able to correctly attribute their physiological arousal to the injection.

Indeed, Schachter and Singer were able to confirm these hypotheses for the most part, but the experiment was criticized for its methodical errors [15, 16]. Furthermore, it was impossible to replicate the outcomes in subsequent similar experiments [17, 18]. On the other hand, the idea of the cognitive interpretation of emotions also obtained extensive empirical confirmation [19–21].

In summary, it can be concluded that the two-factor model by Schachter and Singer initiated an approach that incorporated the cognitive components of emotions as an important part of emotions. Thus, this approach became part of the cognitive appraisal models (known as "appraisal theory"). Accordingly, emotions arise from a cognitive evaluation of occasions (or events), which are associated with specific reactions in the central and autonomous nervous system (CNS and ANS) and/or with changes in the neuroendocrine system (NES) and the somatic nervous system (SoNS) [22, 23]. A further key premise of this theory is that emotions are adaptive reactions to objects of our environment, which are automated and elicited quickly and are ultimately responsible for the optimization of our well-being [24, 25]. It is necessary to identify threats as quickly as possible and to react efficiently to them. Also, objects or situations that contribute to well-being should be recognized as such. Klaus Scherer (born in 1943) is certainly one of the most important advocates of the appraisal theory. Magda Arnold (1960) and Richard Lazarus (1966) are other proponents and at the same time pioneers of the cognitive theories. A schematic overview of this theory is shown in Fig. 4.

In the recent past, neuroscientists also started to study this topic in more detail. Especially the so-called "somatic marker hypothesis" established by Damasio et al. [26] appears to be particularly noteworthy in this context. The starting point for this theory was established by the observation that patients with neurological deficits in the frontal lobe had difficulties with social decision-making situations, especially when these deficits affected ventral and medial areas. Moreover, these patients did not exhibit an appropriate social behavior. Damasio et al. attributed this to the lack of the ability to experience feelings in a way that would be expected in certain social situations.

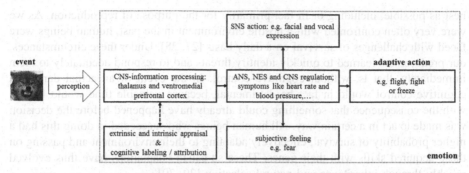

CNS=central nervous system; NES=neuroendocrine system; ANS=autonomic nervous system; SNS=somatic nervous system.

Fig. 4. Appraisal-Theory (referring to Scherer [22])

The research group postulated that an emotional event is positively or negatively labeled by an activation pattern in the ANS, which is elicited by a stimulus; they refer to these patterns as somatic markers (SMs). As a consequence, objects or situations are attributed a positive or negative value, which enables human beings to assess current or future events, allowing them to act adequately as a result. Damasio et al. argue that these SMs are processed in the ventromedial prefrontal cortex and stored in the amygdala [8, 26]. If no injuries are present in these areas, all human beings are capable of making socially acceptable and reasonable decisions based on the stored SM information, even in precarious and uncertain situations (Fig. 5).

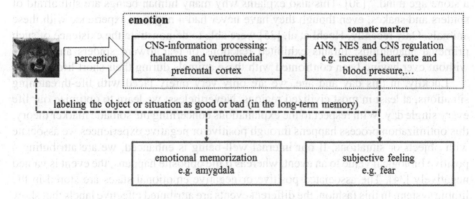

Fig. 5. Somatic-marker-hypothesis (referring to Damasio et al. [26])

3   A Consolidation of These Models

Looking at the models of emotion research introduced above, it becomes evident that the approaches of the appraisal theory and the model of somatic markers exhibit similarities and are based on approaches in evolutionary psychology. From an onto-genetic point of view, the principle applies that every organism strives to survive as best as possible, including or in fact primarily for the purpose of reproduction. As we were very often confronted with a hostile environment in the past, human beings were faced with challenges of survival on a daily basis [27, 28]. Under these circumstances, our predecessors learned to quickly identify threats and to respond adequately to them immediately, that is, without cognitive control. In the event of an actual danger, a cognitive control would in fact be detrimental, because valuable time would be lost with the consequence that something could already have happened before the decision was made to act in a certain way. All human beings who succeeded in doing this had a higher probability of survival, effectively adapting to their environment and passing on these acquired skills with their genes. These so-called adaptations have thus evolved reliably through inheritance and natural selection [29, 30].

Escape or the willingness to fend off the threat, often associated with a fight, are examples of adequate options for reacting to a threat (Taylor et al. 2000). For both possible actions, a human being requires among other things a sufficient amount of energy, which is made available in the form of glucose. This provision is achieved through reactions in the CNS, NES and ANS [31–33]. Similar processes likewise occur in the presence of states of deficiency, such as for example with hunger, thirst or respiratory distress [34].

Evolutionary psychologists point out that human beings have developed such adaptations over a period of approx. 1.8 million to 10,000 years. During this timeframe, they were organized in relatively small hunting and gathering societies, confronted primarily with predatory animals, venomous insects or dangerous parasites. It is argued that the human mind is therefore adapted to a stone-age rather than a modern environment. Cosmides and Tooby describe it in the following sense: "Our modern skulls house a stone age mind." [30]. This also explains why many human beings are still afraid of spiders and snakes, even though they have never had a negative experience with these animals. Only recently, Hoehl et al. [35] were able to demonstrate the existence of such primeval adaptations: Infants exhibited reactions of fear toward spiders and snakes without ever having been confronted with these animals during their short lifetime.

Luckily, in this day and age, we are only very rarely faced with life-threatening situations, at least in most civilized regions. Nevertheless, we learn to optimize our life every single day. With respect to the explanations concerning the somatic marker theory, this optimization process happens through positive or negative experiences we associate with objects or situations. If our internal well-being is enhanced, we are attributing a positive biological value to an event, whereas if the opposite happens, the event is valued negatively [34]. The associated positive or negative emotional states are stored in the limbic system. In this fashion, the different events are attributed affective labels that show us how positive or negative they were for our survival and whether they are beneficial or more of a hindrance for our reproduction efforts (="how" events should be assessed). In other words, we develop so-called appetitive or aversive behavior vis-à-vis the various events [36]. This behavior is associated with anticipated states of arousal, which elicit a pleasant feeling in connection with a positive value, interpreted for example as happy anticipation. As for negative events, we experience aversion, which is perceived as unpleasant feeling and may be interpreted as fear. However, feelings also show us the state of our internal environment. When everything is in a homeostatic balance, we experience a pleasant physical well-being. In the event of low blood sugar levels and/or high plasma osmolality (=the body's water and electrolyte balance), we feel hungry and/or thirsty. When a sharp object is pushed against our skin, this information is transmitted to the CNS via nociceptors and we feel pain that is perceived as an unpleasant, intense sensation [7, 37]. This demonstrates that feelings can be elicited by external events or by an imbalance in the internal environment.

These correlations are largely uncontested. But what exactly are emotions? An external event or deviations in the internal environment result in an activation of the CNS, which induces direct and measurable changes in the ANS, NES and SoNS. This may be, for example, a reflex action, a change in the pulse rate, increased levels of neurotransmitters and hormones, or a facial expression or gesture. The autonomous and quick reactions to an event are based upon innate action programs [34]. Action programs operate automatically, often exaggerating dangers and cannot be stopped willfully [38]. Damasio and Carvalho [34] refer to precisely these action programs as emotions and to the associated mental experiences as feelings. This definition is also consistent with the etymological definition of the terms emotion and feeling. Emotion is derived from the French word émouvoir (moving, arousing), which in turn is derived from the Latin root word emovere (moving out, stirring up) [39]. Feeling is derived from the late Middle High German root word gevūlichkeit and is associated directly with the verb feeling, which describes a sensation mediated by the nerves [40].

An "action program" thus comprises all of the components needed for an adequate reaction to an external event or, for example, a state of deficiency in the internal environment. Hence, this approach for the most part coincides with the cognitive theories of emotion. Feelings are an inherent part of emotions, although they can be labeled based on the involvement of cognitive processes and provide information about the underlying emotion and the reason for the emotion - the "what" of the event. Incorrect conclusions may indeed also be the reason why an autonomous activation of the ANS, NES and SoNS is attributed to a wrong root cause. This problem is not explicitly addressed by Damasio et al. [26, 34], but all the more thoroughly in the

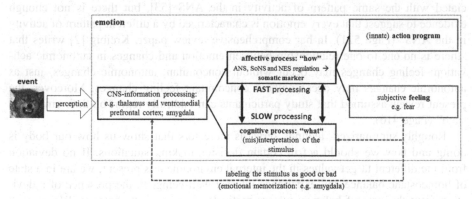

Stimulus: object or situation
ANS: autonomic nervous system (e.g. heart rates, pupillary response)
SoNS: somatic nervous system (e.g. reflexes)
NES: neuroendocrine system (e.g. hypothalamic–pituitary–adrenal axis; releasing or inhibiting hormones)
CNS: central nervous system (brain and spinal cord)

Fig. 6. Extended emotion model

appraisal theory. The cognitive evaluation of a stimulus takes place at a significantly slower speed than the associated, rapidly and autonomously occurring affective processes. Still, the cognitive component is capable of correcting the intuitive and perhaps exaggerated assessment of a threat by the affective processes [38].

It should be noted that feelings not only reflect processes in the ANS, NES and SoNS, but that they can also be feigned. Every actor is living proof of this possibility. Ambiguous situations can definitely lead to misinterpretations, an effect just mentioned above. In contrast, emotions cannot be feigned, because they are formed through autonomous, affective processes and are expressed outwardly and can be recognized by our environment [3] (Fig. 6).

4   Implication for the Measurement of Emotions

Now comes the time to answer the question whether emotions or feelings are associated with specific reaction patterns in the ANS and are thus measurable or whether this is not the case. Plenty of evidence supports the postulation of specific reaction patterns in the ANS [15, 41–48]. However, a current review article suggests that the reaction patterns in the ANS, which are elicited by different objects, are highly complex and also often inconsistent. For example, the pulse rate rises in equal measure in connection with negatively and positively perceived objects [2]. A specific reaction pattern that clearly corresponds with an experienced feeling is difficult to identify, if at all. The use of elaborate pattern recognition tools (pattern classification analysis, PCA [49] - Huberty [49] may enable the identification of certain reaction patterns that correspond with certain feelings [50]. Based on these challenges and the differences in empirical evidence, a compromise is often proposed these days. For example, Pinel and Pauli [51] report that "experimental findings suggest that the specificity of reactions in the ANS is somewhere between the extremes of absolute specificity and absolute generality [52]. There is plenty of evidence demonstrating that not all emotions are associated with the same pattern of activity in the ANS [53], but there is not enough evidence to suggest that every emotion is characterized by a different pattern of activity in the ANS" (Page 521). In her comprehensive review paper, Kreibig [2] writes that "there is no one-to-one relationship between emotion and changes in autonomic activation: feeling changes may occur without concomitant autonomic changes, just as autonomic changes may occur without concomitant feeling changes. Moreover, the present review assumed that study participants can faithfully report on their emotional state" (Page 410).

Roughly summarized, feelings serve as indicators that show us how our body is doing and how we should act in certain decision-making situations. If no deviation from the different target values in the internal environment is present, we are in a state of homeostatic balance and experience internal well-being. In the presence of a deviation from the state of balance, we are motivated to restore the balance. We want to drink or eat something or get rid of the root cause of our pain as quickly as possible. We react directly and autonomously to menacing external events. The associated changes in the ANS are detectable by means of electrophysiological measuring techniques (ECG, EDR, HRV, etc.), albeit they are not always specific and thus only attributable to a certain emotion or feeling to a limited extent. In addition, our actions give rise to a reaction from our social environment, which in turn causes changes in the ANS, NES and SoNS. We are praised or reprimanded, admired or laughed at, earn recognition or disrespect, etc. All of this leads to autonomous reactions that we experience as emotional states and mark the respective situations. Pronounced changes can be measured well, as they are potentially specific and associated with a direct reaction (e.g. startle reflex, but also laughing or crying). Small changes are less significant and probably remain unspecific. This approach is consistent with the prevailing opinions, which are based upon the fact that a range exists between specific measurable and unspecific and not clearly attributable changes in the ANS.

What do these findings mean for the often-performed measurements of emotions? First, we should establish that the focus of the corporate practice should not be on emotions, but rather on the feelings associated with the emotions. Based on the mentioned cognitive component, it is evident that these feelings can be surveyed directly, but there is a risk that the provided response is false or cursory. Therefore, the survey design is extremely important, and putting excessive strain on the participants by asking overly complicated questions should be avoided at all costs. We would like to describe an actual use case to help illustrate this problem: A company is planning to test an advertising design idea for its effect on consumers. For this purpose, the advertising design idea is presented to study participants to determine the effect of the design on the study participants. Specifically, this is about the nature (e.g. contentment, amusement or embarrassment, disgust) and strength of the elicited feelings.

The nature of feelings can be surveyed with relatively valid results from well-instructed study participants. The valence of the advertising material is determined already by the nature. The determination of the valence of feelings by means of startle reflex measurements certainly represents an interesting approach [3, 54]. This method would be a valuable addition to a questionnaire.

With respect to arousal, the problem certainly arises that it is generally only of mild nature, thereby exceeding the study participant's ability to distinguish, which is required for the completion of a questionnaire. A simple measurement of the electrical resistance of the skin (EDR) could be used as an alternative measurement [55, 56].

Physiological measurement techniques such as ECG, EDR and HRV are not suitable for measuring the strength of feelings, such as for example contentment or amusement. Contemplating the arousal patterns associated with emotions described in the review by Kreibig [2], conclusions about the valence of the feelings can only be drawn to a limited extent. For this reason, the use of these measuring techniques for this purpose should be discouraged all together, unless they are used for the basic research of this topic.

The IAT test [57] may become an innovative approach for measuring the associative strength between desired traits and markers. Early preliminary findings of a study conducted by Kindermann and Schreiner [58] and by Walla et al. [59] at least raise the hope that this method may become usable in corporate practice. Even though this approach is not measuring any feelings, but only the extent to which desired traits are associated with a label, this knowledge is often of greater relevance for corporate practice than e.g. the activation strength of an emotion.

One aspect that is completely absent in the proposed model is the influence of priming effects on our perceived feelings. A host of studies confirm that this influence is likewise important for the elicitation of emotions and should thus be considered in the model [60–63].

References

1. Kleinginna, P.R., Kleinginna, A.M.: A categorized list of emotion definitions, with suggestions for a consensual definition. Motiv. Emot. **5**, 345–379 (1981)
2. Kreibig, S.D.: Autonomic nervous system activity in emotion. A review. Biol. Psychol. **84**, 394–421 (2010)
3. Walla, P.: Affective Processing Guides Behavior and Emotions Communicate (2017)
4. James, W.: What is an emotion? Mind **9**, 188–205 (1884)
5. Lange, C.G.: The mechanism of the emotions. In: Dunlap, D. (ed.) The Emotions. Williams & Wilkins, Baltimore, pp. 33–92 (1885)
6. Friedman, B.H.: Feelings and the body. The Jamesian perspective on autonomic specificity of emotion. Biol. Psychol. **84**, 383–393 (2010)
7. Bear, M.F., Connors, B.W., Paradiso, M.A.: Neuroscience Exploring the Brain, pp. 744–786. Lipppincott Williams & Wilkins, Baltimore (2007)
8. Dalgleish, T.: The emotional brain. Nat. Revi. Neurosci. **5**, 583–589 (2004)
9. Bard, P.: Emotion. I. The neuro-humoral basis of emotional reactions (1934)
10. Cannon, W.B.: Again the James-Lange and the thalamic theories of emotion. Psychol. Rev. **38**, 281 (1931)
11. Cannon, W.B.: The James-Lange theory of emotions. A critical examination and an alternative theory. Am. J. Psychol. **39**, 106–124 (1927)
12. Schachter, S., Singer, J.: Cognitive, social, and physiological determinants of emotional state. Psychol. Rev. **69**, 379 (1962)
13. Schachter, S.: The interaction of cognitive and physiological determinants of emotional state. Adv. Exp. Soc. Psychol. **1**, 49–80 (1964)
14. Sinclair, R.C., Hoffman, C., Mark, M.M., Martin, L.L., Pickering, T.L.: Construct accessibility and the misattribution of arousal. Schachter and Singer revisited. Psychol. Sci. **5**, 15–19 (1994)
15. Fehr, F.S., Stern, J.A.: Peripheral physiological variables and emotion. The James-Lange theory revisited. Psychol. Bull. **74**, 411 (1970)
16. Plutchik, R., Ax, A.F.: A critique of determinants of emotional state by Schachter and Singer (1962). Psychophysiology **4**, 79–82 (1967)
17. Maslach, C.: Negative emotional biasing of unexplained arousal (1979)
18. Marshall, G.D., Zimbardo, P.G.: Affective consequences of inadequately explained physiological arousal. J. Pers. Soc. Psychol. **37**(6), 970–988 (1979)
19. Bzdok, D., Langner, R., Caspers, S., Kurth, F., Habel, U., Zilles, K., Laird, A., Eickhoff, S. B.: ALE meta-analysis on facial judgments of trustworthiness and attractiveness. Brain Struct. Funct. **215**, 209–223 (2011)
20. Meston, C.M., Frohlich, P.F.: Love at first fright. Partner salience moderates roller-coaster-induced excitation transfer. Arch. Sex. Behav. **32**, 537–544 (2003)
21. Dutton, D.G., Aron, A.P.: Some evidence for heightened sexual attraction under conditions of high anxiety. J. Pers. Soc. Psychol. **30**, 510 (1974)
22. Scherer, K.R.: What are emotions? And how can they be measured? Soc. Sci. Inf. **44**, 695–729 (2005)

23. Scherer, K.R., Schorr, A., Johnstone, T.: Appraisal Processes in Emotion: Theory, methods, research. Oxford University Press, Oxford (2001)

24. Ellsworth, P.C., Scherer, K.R.: Appraisal processes in emotion. Handb. Affect. Sci. **572**, V595 (2003)

25. Moors, A., Ellsworth, P.C., Scherer, K.R., Frijda, N.H.: Appraisal theories of emotion. State of the art and future development. Emot. Rev. **5**, 119–124 (2013)

26. Damasio, A.R., Everitt, B.J., Bishop, D.: The somatic marker hypothesis and the possible functions of the prefrontal cortex [and discussion]. Philos. Trans. Roy. Soc. Lond. Ser. B: Biol. Sci. **351**, 1413–1420 (1996)

27. Saad, G.: Evolutionary consumption. J. Consum. Psychol. **23**, 351–371 (2013)

28. Buss, D.M.: How can evolutionary psychology successfully explain personality and individual differences? Perspect. Psychol. Sci. **4**, 359–366 (2009)

29. Buss, D.M.: Evolutionary psychology: The new science of the mind. Allyn & Bacon (1999)

30. Cosmides, L., Tooby, J.: The modular nature of human intelligence. The origin and evolution of intelligence, 71–101 (1997)

31. Kindermann, H., Javor, A., Reuter, M.: Playing Counter-Strike versus Running: The Impact of Leisure Time Activities and Cortisol on Intermediate-term Memory in Male Students. Cognitive Systems Research, - (2016)

32. Wolf, O.T.: Stress and memory in humans: twelve years of progress? Brain Res. **1293**, 142–154 (2009)

33. Joëls, M., Baram, T.Z.: The neuro-symphony of stress. Nat. Rev. Neurosci. **10**, 459–466 (2009)

34. Damasio, A., Carvalho, G.B.: The nature of feelings: evolutionary and neurobiological origins. Nat. Rev. Neurosci. **14**, 143–152 (2013)

35. Hoehl, S., Hellmer, K., Johansson, M., Gredebäck, G.: Itsy Bitsy Spider... Infants React with Increased Arousal to Spiders and Snakes. Frontiers in Psychology **8**, 1710 (2017)

36. Birbaumer, N., Schmidt, R.F.: Biologische Psychologie.(6., vollständig überarbeitete und ergänzte Auflage). Springer, Heidelberg (2006). https://doi.org/10.1007/3-540-30350-2

37. Craig, A.D.: Interoception. The sense of the physiological condition of the body. Curr. Opin. Neurobiol. **13**, 500–505 (2003)

38. Kahneman, D.: Thinking, fast and slow. Macmillan (2011)

39. Drosdowski, G.: Das Herkunftswörterbuch. Etymologie der deutschen Sprache. Wissenschaftlicher Rat der Dudenredaktion 7, 2 (1989)

40. Scholze-Stubenrecht, W., Wermke, M.: Der Duden in zwölf Bänden. Das Standardwerk zur deutschen Sprache. 1. Duden-die deutsche Rechtschreibung. Dudenverlag (2006)

41. Christie, I.C., Friedman, B.H.: Autonomic specificity of discrete emotion and dimensions of affective space. A multivariate approach. Int. J. Psychophysiol. **51**, 143–153 (2004)

42. Stemmler, G.: Physiological processes during emotion. In: The Regulation of Emotion, pp. 33–70 (2004)

43. Stemmler, G.: The autonomic differentiation of emotions revisited. Convergent and discriminant validation. Psychophysiology **26**, 617–632 (1989)

44. Ekman, P., Levenson, R.W., Friesen, W.V.: Autonomic nervous system activity distinguishes among emotions. Science **221**, 1208–1210 (1983)

45. Wenger, M.A.: Studies of autonomic balance. A summary. Psychophysiology **2**, 173–186 (1966)

46. Lacey, J.I., Kagan, J., Lacey, B.C., Moss, H.A.: The visceral level. Situational determinants and behavioral correlates of autonomic response patterns. In: Expression of the Emotions in Man, vol. 9 (1963)

47. Ax, A.F., Bamford, J.L., Beckett, P.G.S., Domino, E.F., Gottlieb, J.S.: Autonomic response patterning of chronic schizophrenics. Psychosom. Med. **31**, 353–364 (1969)

48. Averill, J.R.: Autonomic response patterns during sadness and mirth. Psychophysiology **5**, 399–414 (1969)
49. Huberty, C.J.: Applied Discriminant Analysis. Wiley (1994)
50. Rainville, P., Bechara, A., Naqvi, N., Damasio, A.R.: Basic emotions are associated with distinct patterns of cardiorespiratory activity. Int. J. Psychophysiol. **61**, 5–18 (2006)
51. Pinel, J.P., Pauli, P.: Biopsychologie (8. Auflage Ausg.). Pearson Deutschland, Hallbergmoos (2012)
52. Levenson, R.W.: The search for autonomic specificity. In: The Nature of Emotion, pp. 252–257 (1994)
53. Ax, A.F.: The physiological differentiation between fear and anger in humans. Psychosom. Med. **15**, 433–442 (1953)
54. Lang, P.J., Bradley, M.M., Cuthbert, B.N.: Emotion, attention, and the startle reflex. Psychol. Rev. **97**, 377 (1990)
55. Senior, C., Russell, T., Gazzaniga, M.S.: Methods in mind. MIT press (2006)
56. Riedl, R., Kindermann, H., Auinger, A., Javor, A.: Computer breakdown as a stress factor during task completion under time pressure: identifying gender differences based on skin conductance. Adv. Hum.-Comput. Interact. **2013**, 7 (2013)
57. Greenwald, A.G., McGhee, D.E., Schwartz, J.L.K.: Measuring individual differences in implicit cognition. The implicit association test. J. Pers. Soc. Psychol. **74**, 1464 (1998)
58. Kindermann, H., Schreiner, M.: IAT measurement method to evaluate emotional aspects of brand perception—a pilot study. In: Davis, F.D., Riedl, R., vom Brocke, J., Léger, P.-M., Randolph, A.B. (eds.) Information Systems and Neuroscience. LNISO, vol. 25, pp. 167–173. Springer, Cham (2018). https://doi.org/10.1007/978-3-319-67431-5_19
59. Walla, P., Koller, M., Brenner, G., Bosshard, S.: Evaluative conditioning of established brands: implicit measures reveal other effects than explicit measures. J. Neurosci. Psychol. Econ. **10**(1), 24–41 (2017)
60. Vohs, K.D., Mead, N.L., Goode, M.R.: The psychological consequences of money. Science **314**, 1154–1156 (2006)
61. Lee, S.W.S., Schwarz, N.: Dirty hands and dirty mouths embodiment of the moral-purity metaphor is specific to the motor modality involved in moral transgression. Psychol. Sci. **21**, 1423–1425 (2010)
62. Zhong, C.-B., Liljenquist, K.: Washing away your sins: threatened morality and physical cleansing. Science **313**, 1451–1452 (2006)
63. Strack, F., Martin, L.L., Stepper, S.: Inhibiting and facilitating conditions of the human smile: a nonobtrusive test of the facial feedback hypothesis. J. Pers. Soc. Psychol. **54**, 768 (1988)

Are You Worried About Personalized Service?
An Empirical Study of the
Personalization-Privacy Paradox

Yi-Cheng Ku[✉], Peng-Yu Li, and Yi-Lin Lee

Fu Jen Catholic University, New Taipei City, Taiwan (R.O.C.)
{ycku,pyli,404316257}@mail.fju.edu.tw

Abstract. Many e-stores adopt personalized recommender systems to provide service for the customers nowadays, which they can rely on to predict customers' preferences based on the detailed individual customer information. Customers got better services provided by the personalized recommender systems. However, customers also concerned that the websites may steal, misuse or sell their information to a third party. Such situation causes the "personalization-privacy paradox". This study proposed a research model based on the privacy calculus theory to explore how the customers make decision between personalized service and privacy concern. An online survey was conducted to collect empirical data in order to test our research model. The results of PLS analysis indicate that personalized service is positively affects perceived benefit. Both information sensitivity and privacy concern positively affects perceived risk. However, when customers with low information sensitivity and low privacy concern, they are less likely to evaluate associated risks. Perceived value is influenced by perceived benefit and perceived risk and in term, affects customers' willingness to provide personal information. The findings of this study provide implications for both researchers and practitioners of using personalized recommender systems.

Keywords: Personalized service · Recommender system · Privacy concern

1 Introduction

Recently, the internet and e-commerce booming provide convenient life for the customers. However, large information providing from numbers of website causes customers face the difficulties of information processing when conducting purchase decision. The information overloading also results in the customers hard to make a decision between various options. Personalized recommender systems have been pay attention to provide more relevant information for the customers to facilities their purchase decision. Such personalized systems provide the benefits for customers to search personalized products and services in efficient ways. The companies also benefit from such system which predict consumer behavior more accurately and bring in higher sales volume and revenue.

Previous studies claimed that the success of personalized recommender systems rely on the companies' data collecting and processing capabilities. In addition,

© Springer International Publishing AG, part of Springer Nature 2018
F. F.-H. Nah and B. S. Xiao (Eds.): HCIBGO 2018, LNCS 10923, pp. 351–360, 2018.
https://doi.org/10.1007/978-3-319-91716-0_27

customers' willingness to share their personal information and obtain personalized services is vital to the development of personalized recommender systems [6]. In fact, companies need many information to be collected from the customers to provide personalized services for customers, however, the customers often have low willingness to share such personalized information with companies [2, 26]. The privacy issue is the largest concern of the customers to share the personalized information because a lot of personalized individuals information are collected, obtained, and sold inappropriately to the third parties. The privacy concern and the worry about the personal data are used in illegal ways cause the customers prefer to protect their personal data.

Such issue is largely drawn the attentions from previous studies [11, 28, 32]. Personalization-privacy paradox was incurred because the customers tend to get benefits from the personalized services which provided by the websites but are also afraid of their personal privacy are invaded [27]. Since personalization-privacy paradox is a very interesting phenomenon and an important research issue in personalized service, many previous studies have investigated this issue and provided insightful implications [27, 42]. However, prior studies are more focus on the causal effects among the related variables, but less studies focused on examining the influence of sensitivity in different level of personalized service and privacy concern on the willingness of sharing personal information. Hence, the purpose of this study is to explore the sensitive relationships between personalized service and privacy concern while an individual is using a personalized recommender system. The following sections are organized as follows. The theoretical foundations and hypotheses are proposed in the Sect. 2. In the Sect. 3, the experimental scenario design and empirical survey are described. Then, the results of statistical analysis are discussed in the Sect. 4. Finally, we make a brief conclusion in the Sect. 5.

2 Theoretical Foundations and Hypotheses

Privacy calculus theory claimed that the individuals' intention of disclosing personal information will depend on comparing perceived risks and anticipated benefits [12, 16]. Personal information is viewed as a tradable good between the customers and the websites. The consumer evaluate the benefit of providing information such as the privacy information and personal data and the risk of the concern of privacy invasion. Individuals will conduct a privacy calculation, which the customers compare the benefits and the risks of providing personal information to the websites and then decide the scope and the level of the privacy information they wants to expose.

Privacy calculation also is viewed as a cognitive process which indicates that the individuals make a decision based on measuring the potential cost and benefit of disclosing private information to others [5, 19]. If the foreseeable benefit is larger than (or equal to) the potential risk, the individuals will incline to disclose their personal information to exchange their desired products/services, such as financial incentives and personalized services [9, 13].

According to the prior research, the privacy calculation has been viewed as one kind of functional exchange between the customers and the companies. The customers will calculate how much higher quality services they can earn from the website and decide the level of the personal information that they are willing to offer [9]. The individual will evaluate the expected benefits and privacy risks of offering such private information to other people [22]. Once the individual perceived the benefits are higher than the risks of providing the information, they will have the higher willingness of sharing their personal information and preferences to others [8]. Hence, we propose hypothesis H1 as follows,

H1: The willingness of providing personal information will be positively affected by perceived value of personalized service

Previous studies found that when the consumer realized the benefit can generate from disclosing private information, they tend to behave lower concern of privacy issues. At this situation, the consumers prefer to release their individual information to exchange the potential benefits [12, 43]. Studies also found the evidences that the consumers have higher willingness to disclose their individual information if they can gain offerings or discounts from providing personal information [35]. In this study, perceived benefit is defined as the benefits of personalized service that the individuals can earn through disclosing their personal information. Thus, the hypothesis H2 is proposed here:

H2: Perceived value of personalized service will be positively affected by perceived benefit of information disclosure.

Privacy calculation theory also proposed that privacy risk will affect the likelihood of consumers' privacy intention and consumer behavior [21, 32]. For example, the uncertainty of using the Internet will force the consumers feel hesitate to disclose their personal information. The tendency of disclosing information will rely on the evaluation of risk and benefit. The perceived uncertainty results in the customers perceived risks of disclosing private information in inappropriately and unauthorized ways [24], such as internal personnel's use, intentionally access and selling to the third parties [15]. Such unauthorized information disclosing let the consumers suffer from possible risks because of exposing personal privacy under public without noticed. Therefore, we hypothesize that

H3: Perceived value of personalized service will be negatively affected by perceived risk of information disclosure.

Personalization provides the customized service to the customer, which let the customers can enjoy the services based on their personal preference and needs. Personalization also lets the consumers experience as serving by a customized salesperson during the purchase process [25]. Customer loyalty also is developed through satisfying the customers' personalized needs [18]. Recently, recommender system provides the personalized recommendations and information to the customers in helping their purchase decision in e-commerce websites [30]. Recommender systems can provide the relevant information and suggestions to the customers based on their preference and customer behaviors [1]. According to the prior purchasing history, the system recommends the products/services that may be interested by the customers. According, the customers can get accurate information and shorten the searching time in purchasing process. The personalization bring the benefits to the customers in reducing transaction cost and searching cost through providing useful information to the customers. The system are thereby can earn the loyalty and recognition from the customers. Therefore, we propose hypothesis H4 as follows,

H4: Perceived benefit will be positively affected by personalization.

The risk of disclosing information depends on the types of information. The higher sensitive information represents the higher level of closeness of information to the individuals. Prior studies pointed out that higher closeness of information disclosing will cause the higher risk of personal losing [23]. Consumers prefer to disclose their demographic information rather than the sensitive information such as financial or identification information [29]. Moreover, consumer will perceive higher risk if they are asked to provide more sensitive information [29, 31, 37]. Such perceived risk will cause the consumers have more negative attitude and intention toward disclosing their personal information [24]. Therefore, the hypothesis H5 is proposed here:

H5: Perceived risk of information disclosure is positively affected by the sensitivity of information.

Warren and Brandeis [38] claimed that privacy is related to the individuals' rights and capabilities to control their owned information, to occupy their personal space [4, 39], to have their personal life [3], and to control the personal message [39]. Flushing internet draws scholars' attention from avoiding personal privacy invasion to learning the ways to protect personal information. Scholars suggest that information privacy should address the importance of how the private information to be used and to be transferred to users [40].

Consumers concern about the possible loss and risks after disclosing their private information [32]. In particular, the development of technology in monitoring and in searching information causes the consumers have the higher awareness that the personal privacy is under-protected and is invaded [7, 36]. People concern about their personal information is being misused [44]. In addition, unauthorized information assessed by the other organizations is also a vital concern to the customers [10]. Thus, the consumers' fell the difficulties of controlling the information after disclosing private information [11].

Studies also found that the privacy invaded causes consumers perceived risks to provide personal information in the future purchase. The negative perception and experience will be incurred to the customers, which causes the customers incline to provide the information or correct information to the website. Even more, some customers will claim to the organization or the official authorities [34]. Prior studies also found evidence that the perceived risk of information disclosure is positively associated with privacy concern [12]. The higher risks perceived by the consumers will lead the customers have higher concern of information disclosure [17]. Hence, we hypothesize that:

H6: Perceived risk of information disclosure will be positively affected by privacy concern.

3   Research Method

A survey questionnaire was developed to test the proposed hypotheses. The conceptual definition and the source of the measurement items for each construct are listed in Table 1. All constructs were measured using items equivalent to those used by previous studies. This study adopted the Likert Scales, allowing participants to choose one of seven levels of agreement with anchors ranging from 1 (strongly disagree) to 7 (strongly agree) with the exception of the personalization construct which was measured by the perception of personalized degree.

In order to explore the sensitive reaction to varied degrees of personalized service and personal information disclosure, three scenarios were designed as Table 2. Then three type questionnaires were designed to collect empirical data. Each questionnaire includes three parts. In part 1, the purpose of survey and one of three scenario, i.e., S1, S2, or S3, was described. In part 2, all items of the research constructs were designed by seven-Likert scales based on previous studies. In part 3, some questions related to respondents' profile and shopping experience were designed.

After questionnaire pretesting and revision, we conducted an empirical survey in May 2017 and gave 2 US dollars e-coupon to respondents who had filled the questionnaire successfully as incentive. Finally, 475 questionnaires were collected but 41 questionnaires were invalid. The valid amounts of three scenarios are S1:148, S2:142, S3:144, respectively. There were more females (67.7%) than males (32.3%). The majority are students (68.7%). Most of them averagely did online shopping once per month (46.1%) while some of them averagely purchased 2 or 3 times per month (35.9%). Furthermore, Most of them averagely spent no more than 35 USD (48.8%).

4   Preliminary Findings and Further Analysis

Partial Least Squares (PLS) was used to test the research model and six hypotheses because PLS is more appropriate to measure research models which are in the early development stages and have not yet been extensively tested. This study utilized the SmartPLS[1] software to conduct PLS analysis. Reliability and discriminant validity were tested before the research model was tested.

As Table 3 shows, the Cronbach's Alpha of each construct was higher than 0.74. The composite reliability of each construct is higher than 0.85. Notably, each square root of AVE is higher than 0.817 and also higher than the inter-construct correlation coefficients. Hence, the indicators of reliability and validity for the measurement model (i.e., item reliability, convergent validity, and discriminant validity) are all acceptable. Then PLS was used to assess the structural model. All path coefficients and explained variances for the model (all sample) are shown in Fig. 1.

The preliminary results of PLS analysis with all sample show that the explanatory power (R^2) of willingness of providing personal information is 25.6%. The path coefficient from perceived value to willingness of providing personal information is

---

[1] C.M. Ringle, S. Wende and A. Will, SmartPLS 2.0 (M3) Beta, Hamburg 2005.

Table 1. Conceptual definition of each construct

Construct	Conceptual definitions	Number of measurement [Reference]
Willingness of providing personal information	The customers' willingness to provide information for obtain better personalized services	3 [42]
Perceived value	The values perceived by the individuals' after comparing the risks of information disclosure and the benefits of personalized service	3 [42]
Perceived benefit	The benefits of personalization that the individuals can earn through disclosing their personal information [41]	3 [14, 42]
Perceived risk	The possible loss and risk of disclosing personal information	3 [42]
Personalization	The recommender system provides the personalized services to the customers based on the users' preferences	3 [42]
Sensitivity of information	The level of individuals feel uncomfortable to disclosure their private information to a specific website [20]	3 [14]
Privacy concern	The individuals' concern about how the websites collect and use their personal information [33]	4 [12]

Table 2. Experimental scenario design

Scenario	Personalized service	Personal information disclosure
S1	Users can customize their personalized webpages	Users were required to provide their basic profile, including user ID and password, when they were registering
S2	Users will get discount coupon for their birthday gift every year	In addition to basic profile, users were required to provide their medium-sensitivity personal data, including name, birthday, and telephone number
S3	Users will get special discount based on their credit card type when they are shopping	In addition to basic profile and medium-sensitivity data, users were required to provide their high-sensitivity personal data, i.e., credit card number

0.506 ($p < 0.001$), which means that H1 is significantly supported. In addition, there is a significantly positive association between perceived benefit and perceived value ($b = 0.515$, $p < 0.001$), while the association between perceived risk and perceived value is significantly negative ($b = -0.164$, $p < 0.001$). Hence, both H2 and H3 are significantly supported. The explanatory power (R^2) of perceived value is 30.4%. There is also a significantly positive association between personalization and perceived

Table 3. Correlation matrix and average variance extracted for the principal constructs

Constructs	CR	α	WP	PV	PB	PR	PL	SI	PC
Willingness of Providing Personal Information (WP)	0.945	0.914	0.923						
Perceived Value (PV)	0.941	0.906	0.506	0.917					
Perceived Benefit (PB)	0.854	0.743	0.368	0.527	0.817				
Perceived Risk (PR)	0.938	0.901	-0.443	-0.201	-0.071	0.914			
Personalization (PL)	0.933	0.893	0.211	0.424	0.654	0.028	0.907		
Sensitivity of Information (SI)	0.896	0.825	-0.534	-0.224	-0.099	0.708	0.060	0.862	
Privacy Concern (PC)	0.957	0.940	-0.452	-0.199	-0.048	0.814	0.074	0.743	0.921

Note: The shaded numbers in the diagonal row are square roots of the average variance extracted.

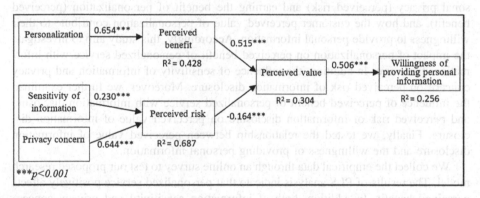

Fig. 1. Results of PLS analysis

benefit. Hence, H4 is significantly supported and 42.8% of the variance of perceived benefit can be explained by providing personalization. Finally, we found that perceived risk was significantly affected by sensitivity of information and privacy concern, $R^2 = 68.7\%$ means that the explanatory power is high. The test results of H1–H6 are listed in Table 4.

In addition, we found that when customers are asked for data with low information sensitivity and low privacy concern, they are less likely to evaluate associated risks by performing a cost-benefit analysis. Since three scenarios were designed in this study, further analysis is required to explore the sensitive relationships between perceived benefit and perceived risk.

Table 4. Test results

Path	Coefficient	T-statistic	Hypothesize	Results
Perceived value → Willingness of providing personal information	0.506	13.021	H1	Supported
Perceived benefit → Perceived value	0.515	13.435	H2	Supported
Perceived risk → Perceived value	−0.164	3.310	H3	Supported
Personalization → Perceived benefit	0.654	20.455	H4	Supported
Sensitivity of information → Perceived risk	0.230	5.523	H5	Supported
Privacy concern → Perceived risk	0.644	15.629	H6	Supported

5 Conclusion

This study proposes a research model based on the privacy calculus theory to explore the sensitive relationships between personalized service and privacy concern. i.e., how the users react when they perceived the decision dilemma between exposing the personal privacy (perceived risk) and earning the benefit of personalization (perceived benefit), and how the customer perceived value of personalization contribute to their willingness to provide personal information. Accordingly, this study aim to investigate the impact of personalization on perceived benefit of personalized service with information disclosure. In addition, the influence of sensitivity of information and privacy concern on perceived risk of information disclosure. Moreover, we further examined the influence of perceived benefit of personalized service with information disclosure and perceived risk of information disclosure on perceived value of information disclosure. Finally, we tested the relationship between perceived value of information disclosure and the willingness of providing personal information.

We collect the empirical data through an online survey to test our proposed research model. The results of PLS analysis indicate that personalized service positively affects perceived benefit. In addition, both of information sensitivity and privacy concern positively affect perceived risk. The results also indicate perceived value positively affected by perceived benefit but negatively affected by perceived risk. Moreover, perceived value will increase the customers' willingness to provide personal information. The findings of this study provide implications for both researchers and practitioners of personalized recommender systems.

Acknowledgment. This work was supported in part by the Ministry of Science and Technology of the Republic of China under the grant MOST 103-2410-H-030-087-MY3.

References

1. Adomavicius, G., Tuzhilin, A.: Personalization technologies: a process-oriented perspective. Commun. ACM **48**, 83–90 (2005)

2. Adomavicius, G., Tuzhilin, A.: Toward the next generation of recommender systems: a survey of the state-of-the-art and possible extensions. IEEE Trans. Knowl. Data Eng. **17**, 734–749 (2005)
3. Allen, A.L.: Uneasy Access: Privacy for Women in a Free Society. Rowman and Littlefield, Totowa (1988)
4. Altman, I.: The Environment and Social Behavior: Privacy, Personal Space, Territory, and Crowding. Brooks/Cole, Monterey (1975)
5. Angst, C.M., Agarwal, R.: Adoption of electronic health records in the presence of privacy concerns: the elaboration likelihood model and individual persuasion. MIS Q. **33**, 339–370 (2009)
6. Chellappa, R.K., Sin, R.G.: Personalization versus privacy: an empirical examination of the online consumer's dilemma. Inf. Technol. Manag. **6**, 181–202 (2005)
7. Culnan, M.J.: "How did they get my name?" An exploratory investigation of consumer attitudes toward secondary information use. MIS Q. **17**, 341–363 (1993)
8. Culnan, M.J., Armstrong, P.K.: Information privacy concerns, procedural fairness, and impersonal trust: an empirical investigation. Organ. Sci. **10**, 104–115 (1999)
9. Culnan, M.J., Bies, R.J.: Consumer privacy: balancing economic and justice considerations. J. Soc. Issues **59**, 323–342 (2003)
10. Culnan, M.J., Williams, C.C.: How ethics can enhance organizational privacy: lessons from the choicepoint and TJX data breaches. MIS Q. **33**, 673–687 (2009)
11. Dinev, T., Hart, P.: Internet privacy concerns and their antecedents- measurement validity and a regression model. Behav. Inf. Technol. **23**, 413–422 (2004)
12. Dinev, T., Hart, P.: An extended privacy calculus model for e-commerce transactions. Inf. Syst. Res. **17**, 61–80 (2006)
13. Dinev, T., Hart, P., Mullen, M.R.: Internet privacy concerns and beliefs about government surveillance–an empirical investigation. J. Strat. Inf. Syst. **17**, 214–233 (2008)
14. Dinev, T., Xu, H., Smith, J.H., Hart, P.: Information privacy and correlates: an empirical attempt to bridge and distinguish privacy-related concepts. Eur. J. Inf. Syst. **22**, 295–316 (2013)
15. Featherman, M.S., Pavlou, P.A.: Predicting e-services adoption: a perceived risk facets perspective. Int. J. Hum.-Comput. Stud. **59**, 451–474 (2003)
16. Hui, K.L., Teo, H.H., Lee, S.Y.T.: The value of privacy assurance: an exploratory field experiment. MIS Q. **31**, 19–33 (2007)
17. Laufer, R.S., Wolfe, M.: Privacy as a concept and a social issue: a multidimensional developmental theory. J. Soc. Issues **33**, 22–42 (1977)
18. Leppaniemi, M., Karjaluoto, H.: Factors influencing consumers' willingness to accept mobile advertising: a conceptual model. Int. J. Mob. Commun. **3**, 197–213 (2005)
19. Li, H., Sarathy, R., Xu, H.: Understanding situational online information disclosure as a privacy calculus. J. Comput. Inf. Syst. **51**, 62–71 (2010)
20. Li, H., Sarathy, R., Xu, H.: The role of affect and cognition on online consumer's decision to disclose personal information to unfamiliar online vendors. Decis. Support Syst. **51**, 434–445 (2011)
21. Li, Y.: Empirical studies on online information privacy concerns: literature review and an integrative framework. Commun. Assoc. Inf. Syst. **28**, 453–496 (2011)
22. Li, Y.: Theories in online information privacy research: a critical review and an integrated framework. Decis. Support Syst. **54**, 471–481 (2012)
23. Lwin, M., Wirtz, J., Williams, J.D.: Consumer online privacy concerns and responses: a power–responsibility equilibrium perspective. J. Acad. Mark. Sci. **35**, 572–585 (2007)
24. Malhotra, N.K., Kim, S.S., Agarwal, J.: Internet users' information privacy concerns (IUIPC): the construct, the scale, and a causal model. Inf. Syst. Res. **15**, 336–355 (2004)

25. Mittal, B., Lassar, W.M.: The role of personalization in service encounters. J. Retail. **72**, 95–109 (1996)
26. Murthi, B.P.S., Sarkar, S.: The role of the management sciences in research on personalization. Manag. Sci. **49**, 1344–1362 (2003)
27. Norberg, P.A., Horne, D.R., Horne, D.A.: The privacy paradox: personal information disclosure intentions versus behaviors. J. Consum. Aff. **41**, 100–126 (2007)
28. Pavlou, P.A.: State of the information privacy literature: where are we now and where should we go? MIS Q. **35**, 977–988 (2011)
29. Phelps, J., Nowak, G., Ferrell, E.: Privacy concerns and consumer willingness to provide personal information. J. Public Policy Mark. **19**, 27–41 (2000)
30. Resnick, P., Varian, H.R.: Recommender systems. Commun. ACM **40**, 56–58 (1997)
31. Sheehan, K.B., Hoy, M.G.: Dimensions of privacy concern among online consumers. J. Public Policy Mark. **19**, 62–73 (2000)
32. Smith, H.J., Dinev, T., Xu, H.: Information privacy research: an interdisciplinary review. MIS Q. **35**, 989–1016 (2011)
33. Smith, H.J., Milberg, S.J., Burke, S.J.: Information privacy: measuring individuals' concerns about organizational practices. MIS Q. **20**, 167–196 (1996)
34. Son, J.Y., Kim, S.S.: Internet users' information privacy-protective responses: a taxonomy and a nomological model. MIS Q. **32**, 503–529 (2008)
35. Sultan, F., Rohm, A.J., Gao, T.T.: Factors influencing consumer acceptance of mobile marketing: a two-country study of youth markets. J. Interact. Mark. **23**, 308–320 (2009)
36. Wang, H., Lee, M.K., Wang, C.: Consumer privacy concerns about internet marketing. Commun. ACM **41**, 63–70 (1998)
37. Wang, P., Petrison, L.A.: Direct marketing activities and personal privacy: a consumer survey. J. Direct Mark. **7**, 7–19 (1993)
38. Warren, S.D., Brandeis, L.D.: The right to privacy. Harv. Law Rev. **4**, 193–220 (1890)
39. Westin, A.F.: Privacy and Freedom. Athenaum, New York (1967)
40. Westin, A.F.: Social and political dimensions of privacy. J. Soc. Issues **59**, 431–453 (2003)
41. Wilson, D.W., Valacich, J.S.: Unpacking the privacy paradox: irrational decision-making within the privacy calculus, IS security and privacy. In: Proceedings of the 33rd International Conference on Information Systems, Orlando, FL (2012)
42. Xu, H., Luo, X.R., Carroll, J.M., Rosson, M.B.: The personalization privacy paradox: an exploratory study of decision making process for location-aware marketing. Decis. Support Syst. **51**, 42–52 (2011)
43. Xu, H., Teo, H.H., Tan, B.C., Agarwal, R.: The role of push-pull technology in privacy calculus: the case of location-based services. J. Manag. Inf. Syst. **26**, 135–174 (2009)
44. Zeng, S.Y., Wu, L.L., Chen, H.G.: Sharing private information online: the mediator effect of social exchange, service innovations for E-commerce. In: Proceedings of the 11th International Conference on Electronic Commerce, Taipei, Taiwan (2009)

Computers May Not Make Mistakes but Many Consumers Do

David Lewis[✉]

Ted Rogers School of Management, Ryerson University, Toronto, Canada
david.lewis@ryerson.ca

Abstract. Consumers regularly make decisions. Some of these decisions are relatively simple, such as a selecting a jam or a coffee, where the choice is entirely subjective. Others, such as investment decision-making, are risky, complex, consequential and there is a normatively optimal choice. Seeking advice from an expert is a reasonable solution in these circumstances and yet a minority of investors turn to a professional for advice. As an alternative to human advisors, technology is increasingly being harnessed to provide effective and low-cost advice to assist consumers in making decisions. In a retail context, these are shop bots and search engines often used on a mobile phone while shopping. In an investment context, these are frequently referred to as "robo-advisors". Examining consumer intention to seek advice in an investment context, the current study demonstrates that, among numerous factors examined, unfounded confidence was the best indicator of consumer reluctance to seek advice. Robo-advisors, as artificial intelligence agents providing financial literacy instruction and impartial expert advice, may offer a solution.

Keywords: Robo-advisors · Advice · Consumer decision-making

1 Introduction

Consumer decision-making regarding investments is an exemplary empirical context to study computer-based advice since investing is a complex, risky and consequential decision. These types of decisions cause uncertainty [1] and anxiety [2] and advice is a reasonable solution. An additional characteristic recommending investment decision-making as a context for studying advice is the fact that there is an objective and normatively optimal decision that maximizes investment returns for any given level of risk [3] in contrast with a low-risk inconsequential decision, (e.g. a subjective preference regarding jam or coffee) where it is difficult to argue that one decision is superior to another. With a normative ideal, the ability of an advisor to enhance decision-making outcomes can be evaluated objectively.

Investment decisions are clearly important since worries over money are the primary cause of stress in America [4]. Investing has become more relevant for a larger segment of society with accumulation of wealth in financial assets and increased participation in pension plans [5]. At the same time, the proliferation of investment products and financial innovation makes investment decision-making more difficult [6]. Seeking advice from an expert is one means of coping. When shopping, consumers

© Springer International Publishing AG, part of Springer Nature 2018
F. F.-H. Nah and B. S. Xiao (Eds.): HCIBGO 2018, LNCS 10923, pp. 361–371, 2018.
https://doi.org/10.1007/978-3-319-91716-0_28

often turn to store employees for assistance [7] and subsequently feel increased loyalty and choice satisfaction [8]. In an investment context, consumers enjoy benefits from expert advice by making more normatively optimal decisions that deliver superior investment returns with lower risk [9] and reduced stress [10]. Surprisingly, only 23% of working Americans and just 28% of retired Americans sought investment advice from a professional. Unfortunately, fewer still subsequently followed the advice [11]. Those most in need of advice were also those least likely to seek advice [12]. This pattern is puzzling. Despite the apparent benefits of advice in general and the curious hesitance to seek advice, understanding the decision to seek advice has not been studied and is an important gap in theory regarding consumer behavior [13].

A recent development in retail investment advisory services is the introduction of artificial intelligence to provide investment advice. Robo-advisors are computer applications that offer investment advice. Whereas human financial advisors are perceived as being expensive and subject to conflict of interest since their advice is influenced by own their compensation, robo-advisors are less expensive and less subject to conflict of interest since their compensation is product-neutral. As such, robo-advisors are likely to be very useful in assisting investors in making superior investment decisions [14].

Given the importance of investment decision-making to consumers' emotional and financial well-being and given the reluctance of consumers to seek financial advice from a human advisor, the question arises as to how investors will respond to offers of advice from a computer. Investment decision-making is an ideal context to study advice-seeking since there is a normatively optimal choice as opposed to merely a subjective preference and therefore the benefits of advice can be clearly identified. Understanding investment advice-seeking goes beyond intellectual curiosity and theory-building to addresses a serious risk to the wealth and happiness of large segments of society. The question of interest is: What factors are more or less likely to influence a consumer decision to seek advice from a robo-advisor?

2 Theoretical Background

The general consensus within the behavioral finance literature is that investors are subject to numerous emotional and cognitive biases (e.g. overconfidence) as well as limitations in cognitive ability [15]. Professional financial advisors offer a solution to the challenges of investment decision-making. When advice is sought and followed, the result is improved financial outcomes [16]. In examining how advice improves outcomes, Bluethgen et al. [17] attribute the results to improved preference identification, enhanced information search, and correction of cognitive errors and biases by the expert advisor.

In consideration of the apparent benefits, consumer reluctance to seek advice needs to be understood. Milner and Rosenstreich [18] identify a need for more research into financial decision-making and the factors affecting decisions regarding advice-seeking in particular. While research regarding the antecedents to advice-seeking is limited, there are some indications of likely factors that may influence the decision. As a complex, risky and consequential decision, there is an opportunity for advice to enhance decision-making. Morrin et al. [19] observed that some decisions, such as investing for retirement, are inherently more difficult due to the consequential nature of the decision. Leonard-Chambers and Bogdan [20] found that advice is perceived as a solution to the difficulty of the decision, therefore perceived difficulty is likely a factor influencing the decision regarding advice. Kimiyaghalam et al. [21] found that risk tolerance is associated with advice-seeking. While advice assists choosers facing difficult decisions, there are also indications that advice can be seen as a loss of control and a threat to self-esteem [22]. Countering this loss of personal agency, self-determination theory [23] suggests feelings of self-determination may not be compromised since individuals may recognize the positive benefits and choose to exercise their personal agency through a proxy (i.e. their advisor). Although there are conflicting perspectives, self-determination is likely to affect a decision regarding advice. Chooser expertise is also a likely factor but, contrary to the tempting notion that only novices need advice, Robb et al. [24] suggest that financial literacy and expertise are associated with more rather than less advice-seeking. Similarly, a study by Van Rooij et al. [25] suggests a role for confidence with more-confident rather than less-confident investors seeking advice. Bluethgen et al. [17] found that advice is associated with increased ability to identify preferences with those more able to identify preferences also more likely to seek advice. Finally, satisfaction with prior financial decisions will likely have an effect on the decision to seek advice. Grable and Joo [26] found that those with higher levels of satisfaction with prior financial decisions are also more likely to seek advice.

Extant research therefore suggests a number of potential factors that should be examined as possible factors affecting the decision to seek investment advice. The current study considers decision difficulty, perceived risk, self-determination, financial literacy, subjective expertise (hereafter referred to as expertise for brevity), ability to identify investment preferences, and decision-making satisfaction.

Of particular interest in the current study is the relationship between financial literacy, expertise and confidence. With investment decision-making being relatively infrequent and since the results of investment decisions are only known at some future point, individuals have few opportunities to receive an objective assessment of their own financial literacy. It is therefore entirely possible that subjective self-assessment of expertise and objective measures of financial literacy may diverge. Lusardi and Mitchell [27] found that individuals are likely to over-estimate their level of financial knowledge. The implications for risky, complex, consequential decisions are that consumers may be ill-equipped to make these decisions and unaware of their own need for advice. In what has been termed the Dunning-Kruger effect, Pennycook et al. [28] demonstrate that individuals who score lowest on the Cognitive Reflection Test tended to over-estimate their performance in advance. Individuals who scored highest, tended to underestimate their performance in advance. The proposed explanation is that those individuals who hold overly-favorable views of their decision-making ability also lack meta-cognitive awareness of their own limitations.

In the context of investment decision-making, individuals with lower financial literacy would benefit most from advice but may also be less likely to seek advice since they may over-estimate their own expertise. This divergence between financial literacy and expertise is conceptualized as overconfidence or under-confidence. Hypothesizing that confidence will make investors less likely to seek advice from a robo-advisor, the current study considers multiple factors as independent variables affecting the decision to seek advice and examines whether overconfidence leads individuals to refuse advice.

3 Method

Participants were tasked with allocating a hypothetical investment portfolio over a highly representative list of fifty equity and fixed income mutual funds drawn from the Morningstar mutual fund database. One hundred and seventy-one participants who were enrolled in a four-year Bachelor of Commerce program at a Canadian University volunteered for a student research pool experiment on investment decision-making. The respondents were not aware of the purpose of the study. Information regarding the investment choices included 1-year, 3-year, and 5-year returns for investment performance as well as standard deviation as a measure of risk. Fund names were disguised to avoid confounds resulting from brand awareness. Instead, fund names reflected the type of fund. For example, "Global Equity Fund" or "Short Term Bond Fund". The respondents considered the list of fifty funds and allocated their investment over the funds they selected. They were then offered advice in reviewing their investment decisions.

Respondents subsequently answered questions regarding their decision-making. From their responses, indexes were created for each of the factors and reliability was assessed with exploratory factor analysis using SPSS version 25. A perceived risk index was created from four items adapted from Cooper et al. [29] (Cronbach's alpha $(\alpha) = .71$). Five items creating an index for decision difficulty ($\alpha = .75$), four items creating an index for self-determination ($\alpha = .80$), three items creating an index for self-assessed expertise ($\alpha = .81$), three items creating an index for confidence ($\alpha = .87$), and three items creating an index for preference identification ($\alpha = .90$) were adapted from Lewis and Gill [30]. A single item measured satisfaction with the decision-making process.

In addition to self-assessed subjective expertise in investment decision-making above, respondents were also administered an objective test of their actual investment expertise or 'financial literacy'. The financial literacy questions were typical of basic financial literacy questions from the Rand American Life panel [31]. The questions were relatively simple such as, "Investments that are riskier tend to have lower returns over the long run." and required an answer of "True", "False" or "I Don't Know"; the latter which was considered an incorrect response. The objective measure of expertise was the number of correct answers out of 10.

4 Analysis and Results

Preliminary assessment comparing Spearman's rank-order correlation coefficient found a positive correlation between subjective expertise and confidence ($r_s = .62$, $p < .001$). Financial literacy shows very weak correlation to confidence ($r_s = .06$, $p = .452$). In turn, subjective expertise is only weakly correlated with financial literacy ($r_s = .32$,

$p < .001$). It is apparent that subjective assessment of one's own expertise regarding investment decision-making is positively correlated with confidence in one's ability to make investment decisions. In turn, financial literacy, the objective measure of investment expertise was only weakly related to both confidence and subjective expertise. These results suggest that, if respondents believed that they had expertise, they were confident even if the confidence was unfounded as indicated by low financial literacy. The confidence index noted above directly measured the extent of overconfidence. The index was created from the following questions, "I believe that I can earn above average returns compared to the overall market.", "I believe that I can earn above average returns compared to the average financial advisor.", and "I believe that I can earn above average returns compared to the average of my friends and family."

A mean split divided low and high subjective expertise as well as low and high financial literacy. Cross tabulation reveals the number of cases in one of two conditions: those whose subjective self-assessment of expertise is corroborated by their objective expertise in the form of their financial literacy score; and those whose self-assessment is at odds with their financial literacy score. Table 1 below shows how the sample of N = 171 is distributed among these cases.

Table 1. Distribution of objective and subjective expertise

	Subjective novices	Subjective experts	Total
Objective experts	51	41	92
Objective novices	30	49	79
Total	81	90	171

Those whose subjective assessment of their own expertise is at odds with their actual financial literacy are perhaps the most interesting. Those who believe they know less than they actually do have low subjective expertise and high financial literacy. Those who actually know less than they believe they do have low financial literacy and high subjective expertise. For the latter group, this "failure to recognize incompetence" [28, p. 1] manifests as unfounded confidence. These results are not atypical. A 2015 study of financial literacy found that two-thirds of global investors considered themselves to have advanced investment expertise and yet their average score on a financial literacy test was just 61% [15]. Similarly, Lusardi and Mitchell [32] found that only half of respondents were able to correctly answer simple financial literacy questions.

Hypothesizing that those with unfounded confidence will find a robo-advisor unappealing, binomial logistic regression was performed using SPSS version 25 to assess the relationship between advice-seeking behavior and confidence (M = 3.20, SD = 1.35, min = 1.00, max = 7.00) after controlling for a variety of other factors including perceived risk (M = 3.92, SD = 1.08, min = 1.00, max = 6.75), difficulty (M = 3.55, SD = .95, min = 1.00, max = 6.20), self-determination (M = 5.25, SD = 1.14, min = 2.25, max = 7.00), financial literacy (M = 5.40, SD = 1.77, min = 1.00, max = 10.00), subjective expertise (M = 3.32, SD = 1.36, min = 1.00, max = 6.33), preference identification (M = 3.75, SD = 1.25, min = 1.00, max = 7.00) and choice satisfaction (M = 4.60, SD = 1.32, min = 1.00, max = 7.00). The Box-Tidwell [33] procedure verified that the logit of the dependent variable (declining advice) is linearly related to each of the continuous independent variables. Using Bonferroni correction with testing at p < .003 [34], all 17 variables were accepted in the model.

The Hosmer Lemeshow test of goodness of fit is significant ($p = .53$) thus indicating that the model is not a poor fit. The logistic regression model is statistically significant $\chi2(9) = 27.51$, $p = .001$. The model explains 22.0% (Nagelkerke R^2) of the variance in accepting or refusing advice and correctly classifies 78.4% of cases. As shown in Table 2, of all the model variables, only confidence predicts whether a respondent will refuse advice (Exp(B) = 1.98, $p = .002$). Each unit increase in confidence makes a respondent 1.98 times more likely to refuse advice.

Table 2. Binomial logistic regression predicting the likelihood of refusing advice

	B	SE	Wald	Sig.	Odds
Preference identification	.00	.17	.00	.99	1.00
Satisfaction	.30	.21	2.00	.16	1.34
Difficulty	.00	.16	.00	.98	1.00
Self-determination	.22	.20	1.27	.26	1.25
Risk index	−.08	.25	.12	.73	.92
Objective expertise	.23	.13	3.16	.08	1.26
Expertise	−.25	.21	1.39	.24	.78
Confidence	.68	.22	9.92	<.01	1.98
Constant	−6.14	1.86	10.91	<.01	.00

Additional analysis considered the impact of refusing advice on the quality of decision-making measured by the extent to which the resultant portfolio allocation between equities and fixed income is normatively optimal. With floodlight analysis [35], regressing the ratio invested in equities on advice decision (accepted, refused), confidence, and their interaction reveals a significant effect for confidence (t (171) = 1.98, $p = .05$), and no significant interaction (t (171) = −1.15, $p = .25$). To decompose the results, we used the Johnson-Neyman technique to identify the range(s) of confidence for which the simple effect of refusing advice is significant. Figure 1 shows the results graphically.

This analysis reveals that there is a significant increase in the proportion invested in equities by those who refuse advice versus those who accept advice for levels of confidence above 2.60. Selecting the appropriate allocation between equities and fixed income is a critical determinant of long-term success when investing. Brinson et al. [36] found that 93.6% of the differences in investment returns for individual investors can be explained by allocation between asset classes (i.e. equity, fixed income, and un-invested cash). As confidence increases, the proportion invested in equities by those refusing advice rises to 85.9% thereby creating substantial excessive risk relative to the more optimal 58.9% mean ratio of equity to fixed income of the 100 top performing pension funds in the United States [37]. With confidence, individuals are more likely to refuse advice. Furthermore, as overconfidence increased, and respondents refuse

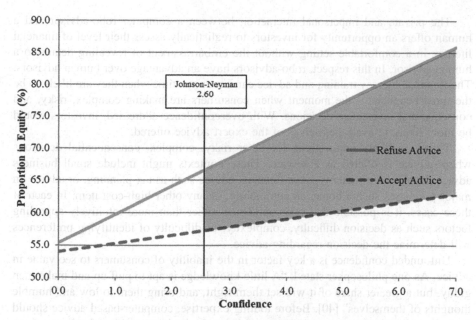

Fig. 1. Proportion invested in equity investments by confidence level

advice, the result is increasingly sub-optimal investment decision-making. Overconfident investors are taking much more risk than prudent experts recommend.

5 Discussion and Implications

Using a realistic investment decision-making scenario, the current study investigates investor reactions to the offer of advice and considers factors associated with refusing advice. Whereas low financial literacy and low expertise should ideally be associated with accepting advice, confidence, often unfounded, was the only significant factor affecting the decision to seek advice. This study demonstrates that overconfidence significantly reduces the likelihood of consumers seeking investment advice and the result is normatively sub-optimal investment decision-making with real potential for a negative impact on their long-term financial well-being.

The implications are that positioning a robo-advisor as delivering enhanced decision-making with lower cost and reduced conflict of interest substantially misses the mark among the target population. Robo-advisors would be more appealing and more effective at supporting financial well-being if they first addressed overconfidence. Willis identifies the need for personalized financial literacy training to reduce overconfidence and improve financial decision making but also describes the invasion of privacy in revealing details of "financial and emotional lives" [38, p. 431]. Colby et al. [39] identified a link between financial literacy training and shame as well as negative affect.

The private and impersonal interaction between a computer robo-advisor and a human offers an opportunity for investors to realistically assess their level of financial literacy in a comfortable setting without the embarrassment of revealing details to a human advisor. In this respect, robo-advisors have an advantage over human advisors. The financial literacy training and advice can occur at a time when they are likely to be the most beneficial – the moment when consumers are making complex, risky, and consequential investment decisions. With overconfidence addressed, investors would be more likely to avail themselves of the expert advice offered.

There are likely implications for other risky, complex, consequential decisions where advice is offered as a service. These contexts might include small business advice, legal advice, other types of financial advice such as tax planning, or advice on major purchases such a home, an automobile, or any other high-cost item. In each of these cases, it is possible that overconfidence rather than more intuitively appealing factors such as decision difficulty, complexity, or difficulty of identifying preferences will determine the decision regarding advice.

Unfounded confidence is a key factor in the inability of consumers to see value in advice. As one philosopher stated, "A little knowledge is apt to puff up and make men giddy, but a greater share of it will set them right, and bring them to low and humble thoughts of themselves" [40]. Before touting expertise, computer-based advice should first offer education to counteract overconfidence. In a private setting, after being given a better appreciation of their true level of expertise by a robo-advisor, consumers will be more willing to embrace computer-based advice and will then be more likely to make better decisions.

6   Limitations and Future Research

One potential limitation of this study is the reliance on a single respondent survey which introduces the potential for common method variance [41]. The study employs numerous procedural remedies to eliminate response cues and item context effects and also includes variation in response formats as a mitigant. It is also noted that refusing advice is a moderator of the effect of confidence on proportion invested in equites and common method variance would actually suppress any moderator effects [42] therefore the effect reported is actually, if anything, understated.

This research demonstrates the need to correct overconfidence in investment decision-making. It is also apparent that admitting the need for advice may result in feelings of shame for many consumers. It is suggested that a robo-advisor, as an inanimate artificial intelligence, may have an advantage over human advisors in providing financial literacy training to reduce overconfidence without the associated shame and negative affect. This intriguing potential benefit of human-computer interaction is worthy of future research. A future study might directly measure differences in shame, negative affect, and other outcomes within subjects and between conditions of an artificial intelligence advisor and a human advisor to establish the significance and magnitude of effects.

References

1. Markus, H.R., Schwartz, B.: Does choice mean freedom and well-being? J. Consum. Res. **37** (2), 344–355 (2010)
2. Song, H., Schwarz, N.: If it's difficult to pronounce, it must be risky: fluency, familiarity, and risk perception. Psychol. Sci. **20**(2), 135–138 (2009)
3. Benartzi, S., Thaler, R.H.: Heuristics and biases in retirement savings behavior. J. Econ. Perspect. **21**(3), 81–104 (2007)
4. American Psychological Association: Stress in America, Paying with our Health: American Psychological Association (2014). https://www.apa.org/news/press/releases/stress/2014/stress-report.pdf
5. Bernheim, B.D., Garrett, D.M.: The effects of financial education in the workplace: evidence from a survey of households. J. Public Econ. **87**(7), 1487–1519 (2003)
6. Ryan, A., Trumbull, G., Tufano, P.: a brief postwar history of US consumer finance. Bus. Hist. Rev. **85**(03), 461–498 (2011)
7. Beatty, S.E., Mayer, M., Coleman, J.E., Reynolds, K.E., Lee, J.: Customer-sales associate retail relationships. J. Retail. **72**(3), 223–247 (1996)
8. Reynolds, K.E., Arnold, M.J.: Customer loyalty to the salesperson and the store: examining relationship customers in an upscale retail context. J. Pers. Sell. Sales Manag. **20**(2), 89–98 (2000)
9. Bluethgen, R., Meyer, S., Hackethal, A.: High-quality financial advice wanted! SSRN 1102445 (2008)
10. Financial Planning Standards Council: The Value of Financial Planning, Toronto (2013). http://www.fpsc.ca/value-financial-planning
11. Helman, R., Adams, N.E., Copeland, C., Van Derhei, J.: 2013 retirement confidence survey: perceived savings needs outpace reality for many. In: E. B. R. Institute (eds.) EBRI Issue Brief, no. 384 (2013)
12. Bhattacharya, U., Hackethal, A., Kaesler, S., Loos, B., Meyer, S.: Is unbiased financial advice to retail investors sufficient? Answers from a large field study. Rev. Financ. Stud. **25** (4), 975–1032 (2012)
13. Brooks, A.W., Gino, F., Schweitzer, M.E.: Smart people ask for (my) advice: seeking advice boosts perceptions of competence. Manag. Sci. **61**(6), 1421–1435 (2015)
14. Kaya, O., Schildbach, J., Deutsche Bank AG, Schneider, S.: Robo-advice–a true innovation in asset management. Deutsche Bank Research (2017). https://www.dbresearch.com/prod/dbr_internet_en-prod/prod0000000000449010/Robo-advice_-_a_true_innovation_in_asset_managemen.pdf
15. Centre for Applied Research: The folklore of finance. Center for Applied Research Reports, State Street Corporation (2015). http://www.statestreet.com/ideas/articles/folklore-of-finance.html
16. Hilgert, M.A., Hogarth, J.M., Beverly, S.G.: Household financial management: the connection between knowledge and behavior. Fed. Reserve Bull. **89**, 309 (2003)
17. Bluethgen, R., Gintschel, A., Hackethal, A., Mueller, A.: Financial Advice and Individual Investors' Portfolios (2008). SSRN 968197
18. Milner, T., Rosenstreich, D.: A review of consumer decision-making models and development of a new model for financial services. J. Financ. Serv. Mark. **18**(2), 106–120 (2013). https://doi.org/10.1057/fsm.2013.7
19. Morrin, M., Inman, J.J., Broniarczyk, S.M., Nenkov, G.Y., Reuter, J.: Investing for retirement: the moderating effect of fund assortment size on the 1/N Heuristic. J. Mark. Res. (JMR) **49**(4), 537–550 (2012). https://doi.org/10.1509/jmr.08.0355

20. Leonard-Chambers, V., Bogdan, M.: Why do mutual fund investors use professional financial advisers? In: Investment Company Institute Fundamentals, vol. 16 (2007)
21. Kimiyaghalam, F., Safari, M., Mansori, S.: Who seeks a financial planner? A review of literature. J. Stud. Manag. Plan. 2(7), 170–189 (2016)
22. Usta, M., Häubl, G.: Self-regulatory strength and consumers' relinquishment of decision control: when less effortful decisions are more resource depleting. J. Mark. Res. 48(2), 403–412 (2011)
23. Deci, E.L., Ryan, R.M.: Self-determination theory: a macrotheory of human motivation, development, and health. Can. Psychol./Psychol. Can. 49(3), 182–185 (2008). https://doi.org/10.1037/a0012801
24. Robb, C.A., Babiarz, P., Woodyard, A.: The demand for financial professionals' advice: the role of financial knowledge, satisfaction, and confidence. Financ. Serv. Rev. 21(4), 291 (2012)
25. Van Rooij, M., Lusardi, A., Alessie, R.: Financial literacy and stock market participation. J. Financ. Econ. 101(2), 449–472 (2011)
26. Grable, J.E., Joo, S.-H.: A further examination of financial help-seeking behavior. J. Financ. Couns. Plan. 12(1), 55 (2001)
27. Lusardi, A., Mitchell, O.S.: The economic importance of financial literacy: theory and evidence. J. Econ. Lit. 52(1), 5–44 (2014). https://doi.org/10.1257/jel.52.1.5
28. Pennycook, G., Ross, R.M., Koehler, D.J., Fugelsang, J.A.: Dunning–Kruger effects in reasoning: theoretical implications of the failure to recognize incompetence. Psychon. Bull. Rev. 24(6), 1774–1784 (2017)
29. Cooper, W.W., Kingyens, A.T., Paradi, J.C.: Two-stage financial risk tolerance assessment using data envelopment analysis. Eur. J. Oper. Res. 233(1), 273–280 (2014)
30. Lewis, D., Gill, T.: Is there a mere categorization effect in investment decisions? Int. J. Res. Mark. 33(1), 232–235 (2016)
31. Hung, A., Parker, A., Yoong, J.K.: Defining and Measuring Financial Literacy. RAND Corporation Publications Department, Santa Monica (2009)
32. Lusardi, A., Mitchell, O.S.: Financial Literacy and Planning: Implications for Retirement Wellbeing: National Bureau of Economic Research. Working Paper No. 1078 (2011)
33. Box, G.E., Tidwell, P.W.: Transformation of the independent variables. Technometrics 4(4), 531–550 (1962)
34. Tabachnick, B.G., Fidell, L.S.: Using multivariate statistics, 6th edn. Pearson/Allyn & Bacon, Boston/Toronto (2012)
35. Spiller, S.A., Fitzsimons, G.J., Lynch Jr., J.G., McClelland, G.H.: Spotlights, floodlights, and the magic number zero: simple effects tests in moderated regression. J. Mark. Res. 50(2), 277–288 (2013)
36. Brinson, G.P., Hood, L.R., Beebower, G.L.: Determinants of portfolio performance. Financ. Anal. J. 51(1), 133–138 (1995)
37. Dyck, A., Lins, K.V., Pomorski, L.: Does active management pay? New international evidence. Rev. Asset Pricing Stud. 3(2), 200–228 (2013). https://doi.org/10.1093/rapstu/rat005
38. Willis, L.E.: The financial education fallacy. Am. Econ. Rev. 101(3), 429–434 (2011)
39. Colby, H., Erner, C., Trepel, C., Fox, C.R.: Financial Literacy Training Increases Implicit Preference for Spending 2014 Boulder Conference on Consumer Financial Decision-making (2014). https://www.encoreccri.org/wp-content/uploads/2014/06/Financial-Literacy-poster-Boulder-2014.pdf
40. Taylor, A.B., William: London: printed for T. Leigh, at the Peacock in Fleetstreet; and R. Knaplock, at the Angel and Crown in St. Paul's Church-Yard (1698)

41. Podsakoff, P.M., MacKenzie, S.B., Lee, J.-Y., Podsakoff, N.P.: Common method biases in behavioral research: a critical review of the literature and recommended remedies. J. Appl. Psychol. **88**(5), 879 (2003)
42. Siemsen, E., Roth, A., Oliveira, P.: Common method bias in regression models with linear, quadratic, and interaction effects. Organ. Res. Methods **13**(3), 456–476 (2010)

Keep Calm and Read the Instructions: Factors for Successful User Equipment Setup

Benjamin Maunier[1]([✉]), Juliana Alvarez[1], Pierre-Majorique Léger[1],
Sylvain Sénécal[1], Élise Labonté-LeMoyne[1], Shang Lin Chen[1],
Sylvie Lachize[2], and Julie Gagné[2]

[1] HEC Montréal, 3000 Chemin de la Côte-Sainte-Catherine, Montréal,
QC H3T 2A7, Canada
benjamin.maunier@hec.ca
[2] Vidéotron, 612 Rue St-Jacques, Montréal, QC H3C 1C8, Canada

Abstract. This paper explores the factors that predict a user' success at installing a home electronic device. Specifically, the objective of this paper is to investigate the effect of a range of attitudinal, psychophysiological, and behavioral factors on the success of an electronic equipment setup. Building upon an experiment conducted with 29 participants, two factors appears to have an impact on successful equipment setup: (i) when the user remains calm during the installation and (ii) when the user takes the time to read the instructions. These findings contribute to human-computer interaction research by high-lighting the importance pre-experience stages such as unboxing and installation as they may impact the overall experience of use.

Keywords: Installation · Equipment setup · Arousal · Instructions
Behavior · User experience · Emotion

1 Introduction

User Experience (UX) has become an important new focus for both practitioners in interaction design and researchers in the evaluation of Human Computer Interaction [18]. UX is defined as users' emotions, beliefs, preferences, perceptions, physical and psychological responses, behaviors and accomplishments that occur before, during and after use of a device (ISO 9241-210:2010). Thus, UX includes user experience before actual device usage. Factors impacting user experience before the actual use, such as installation of the product, are known to impact the perceptions and attitudes toward a digital product or service [17].

It is thus important to understand how users experience this initial interaction with the product and possibly identify the factors that influence a successful product installation. In addition, it has been shown that an unpleasant first experience can have negative consequences for the user's experience and perceptions of the brand [6].

This paper aims to empirically test factors that may explain a successful technology product installation. To this end, we use a controlled laboratory environment to investigate how users' perceptions, emotional and cognitive states, and behaviors influence successful product installation.

© Springer International Publishing AG, part of Springer Nature 2018
F. F.-H. Nah and B. S. Xiao (Eds.): HCIBGO 2018, LNCS 10923, pp. 372–381, 2018.
https://doi.org/10.1007/978-3-319-91716-0_29

2   Hypotheses : Factors Influencing Successful Electronic Equipment Setup

2.1   Attitudinal Factors

This study specifically focuses on two attitudinal factors that can potentially impact the performance of an installation: User motivation and self-efficacy. There are two main types of motivation : intrinsic and extrinsic [31]. Deci and Ryan [28] define extrinsic motivation as achieving a specific goal or reward. Intrinsic motivation is more related to a personal goal and a perception of pleasure [31]. Booth [4] suggests that with a high degree of motivation, people spend more effort in overcoming problems. Thus, a (intrinsically or extrinsically) motivated user should be more successful at setting up an electronic device. Thus, we posit a first hypothesis.

H1 : A user's motivation has a positive impact on installation success.

Self-efficacy is defined as people's beliefs and personal judgment about their abilities to perform different types of actions [2]. Self-efficacy plays a key role in the probability to accomplish different tasks and achieve goals. People who are reported high in self-efficacy think they have the capacity to succeed in a specific task [32]. Moreover, Bandura [3] suggests that people who believe they are self-efficient at performing a task will produce the necessary efforts to succeed. Because human motivation is generated cognitively and directly influences the user's self-efficacy, a high self-efficacy level plays an important role, especially when an individual has to face difficulties and obstacles.

H2 : A user's perceived self-efficacy has a positive impact on installation success.

2.2   State Factors

Concerning user state factors that can influence performance, we focused on arousal, cognitive engagement, and valence. Arousal is defined as general psychological and physiological activation. Thus, a user can move from a calm state to an excited state. Stress is defined as a state of physiological activation and arousal when people think they don't have the capacities to deal with threats or pressure [29]. Nixon [1] suggests a curvilinear relationship between stress and performance. Many researchers investigated the inverted-U relationship [9, 10, 12, 22] between arousal and performance. Until the inflexion point, an increase in arousal has a positive impact on performance, but passed this point, an increase in arousal has a negative impact on performance [23]. In a lab context where users are monitored, we expect that they may pass the inflexion point and observe that greater arousal leads to less successful installation. Thus, we posit the following hypothesis.

H3 : A user's arousal has a negative impact on installation success.

Blumenfeld and Paris [14] define cognitive engagement as the willingness to pursue efforts to achieve goals and comprehend complex ideas. In order to enhance the usability of interfaces and design new systems, cognitive engagement is essential to analyse the user's performance and reactions [21]. Greene et al. [16] and Charland et al. [8] show that cognitive engagement is tied to academic performance. In order to achieve goals such as an installation, cognitive and metacognitive strategies are necessary [14]. Metacognitive strategies are related to setting, planning goals when performing a task. Thus, cognitive engagement would be a useful factor in order to employ the best strategies to install the new electronic device.

H4 : A user's cognitive engagement has a positive impact on installation success.

Emotional valence is defined as the intensity of an emotion, positively or negatively [15] Emotional valence can be useful in order to understand performance during the installation. For example, it has been shown that pleasure and positive interactions with a product result when the activities or tasks are easily performed [13]. Moreover, emotion is directly related to the outcome. There is a sense of accomplishment that results for people when a goal is achieved and emotions help to evaluate this experience [13]. Thus, we posit a positive relationship between emotional valence and installation success.

H5 : A user's positive emotional valence has a positive impact on installation success.

2.3   Behaviors

Finally, we investigate the relationship between a specific behavior, reading installation instructions, and performance. On the one hand, research suggests a positive relationship between reading instructions and performance [20]. On the other hand, research suggests that users are generally not inclined to read instructions ([7, 24] especially for product that are perceive as easy to use [33]. Thus, we posit our final hypothesis.

H6 : Reading the installation instructions has a positive impact on installation success.

These hypotheses are depicted in Fig. 1 below.

3   Research Method

3.1   Design, Sample, and Procedure

We conducted a lab experiment with 29 participants (17 male, 12 female) between 20 and 70 years old with diverse backgrounds in terms of skills and motivation with regards to self-installation. In an experimental living room, each participant had to unbox a new entertainment electronic device, uninstall the old equipment and install the new device. Participants were provided with a short printed guide instructing them how to use a tablet on which they could access a step-by-step instruction mobile

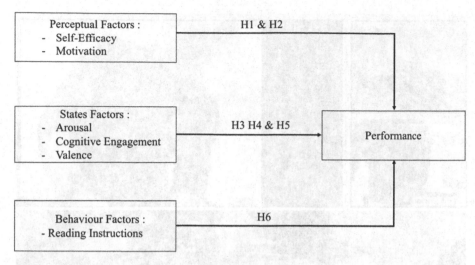

Fig. 1. Research model

application. They were free to conduct the task in whichever order they preferred. Consequently, the steps taken by participants did not all follow a linear pattern. The experiment ended when the participant believed to have completed the electronic device installation successfully. The study was approved by the ethics committee of our institution and each participant received a gift card as a compensation.

3.2 Experimental Setup and Stimuli

We deployed three cameras around the task area in order to ensure that every manipulation done by the user was recorded. Those cameras not only enabled us to observe the participant's reactions at every step of the experience, but also to observe all the actions that could be reported in synchronization with the other tools, in order to determine which specific moments were associated with varying levels of arousal and cognitive engagement. Synchronization was done based on Léger et al. [19] guidelines. We also strapped a GoPro camera on the user's chest to observe the way the manipulations were done. Furthermore, we measured the user's engagement level and emotional valence. To do so, the user wore a mobile EEG headset. All videos and neurophysiological signals were recorded and synchronized with Noldus Observer XT and Syncbox (Noldus Information Technology, Wageningen, The Netherlands) [Fig. 2].

3.3 Instrumentation

Dependent Variable

Installation task success was measured using many criteria (such as the completion of the task, the correctness of the wire connections, the firmness of the cable fastening).

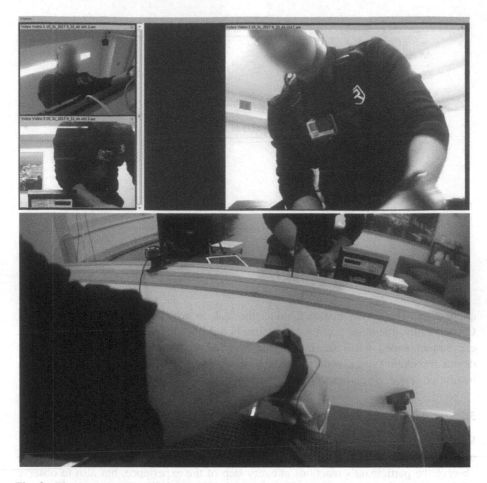

Fig. 2. Three cameras installed around the task area and a GoPro camera on the chest of the participant

Thus, success was achieved when the participant completed the installation with few or no mistakes.

Psychometric Measures

Motivation and perceived self-efficacy were assessed with a questionnaire. User installation motivation was measured using a single item question developed specifically for this study (ranging from 1 (low motivation) to 10 (high motivation). Perceived self-efficacy was assessed with a 6-item measure [30].

Psychophysiological Measures

Psychophysiological measures were used to measure arousal, valence, and cognitive engagement [27]. We used average electrodermal activity (EDA) during the task for each participant (Fig. 3) to assess arousal. Sensors (BIOPAC, Goleta, USA) were applied in the palm of the hand of participants to measure skin conductance during the experience. Electroencephalography (EEG) (Fig. 4) was used to measure participants' cognitive engagement [25] and valence [11] by means of a wireless EEG headset (Brainvision, Morrisville, USA).

Fig. 3. EDA sensors   **Fig. 4.** EEG headset

The EEG data was recorded from 32 Ag-AgCl preamplified electrodes mounted on the actiCap and with a brainAmp amplifier (Brainvision, Morrisville). The acquisition rate was 500 Hz and FCz was the recording reference. We used NeuroRT (Mensia, Rennes) software for the EEG processing of the data. Thus, preprocessing steps were performed in this order: down-sampling to 256 Hz, bandpass filtering with an infinite impulse response filter at 1–50 Hz, notch filtering at 60 Hz, blink removal through blind source separation, re-referencing to the common average reference, and artifact detection by computing the riemannian distance between the covariance matrix and the online mean. We used a filter bank to isolate the following bands: alpha (8–12 Hz), theta (4–8 Hz) and beta (12–30 Hz). Cognitive load was calculated with the formula beta/(alpha + theta) using the sum of channels F3, F4, O1, O2 [25]. Valence was calculated as frontal alpha asymmetry, i.e. the difference between F3 and F4 in the alpha band [11, 26]. These measures are summarized in the following Table 1.

Table 1. Psychophysiological measures

Variable	Measure	Instrument	References
Cognitive engagement	EEG	Brain Products sensors with a sampling rate of 500 Hz (BrainProducts, Germany)	Pope [25]
Valence	EEG	Brain Products sensors with a sampling rate of 500 Hz (BrainProducts, Germany)	Davidson [11]
Arousal	EDA	Biopac Sensors with a sampling rate of 500 Hz (Goleta, USA)	Boucsein [5]

4   Results

4.1   Attitudinal Factors

To test our hypotheses, success was used as the dependant variable in our statistical analysis. In order to test H1, suggesting a relationship between motivation and success, we used logistic regressions modelling the probability of success. Motivation was treated as binary variable (median split). Results presented in Table 2 show that motivation did not influence success. Thus, H1 was not supported. A similar test was performed for H2, which posits that users with greater self-efficacy are more successful at installing an electronic device. As no significant effect of self-efficacy was found on user success (Table 2), H2 was not supported.

Table 2. The impact of attitudinal factors on installation success

Response variable	Effect	DF	Estimate	p-value (one-tailed)
Success	Motivation level	1	−.1682	.3383
Success	Self-efficacy	1	−.2027	.29905

4.2   State Factors

Concerning user state factors, logistic regressions were performed to model the marginal effect of arousal, cognitive engagement, and valence on the probability of success. Results indicate that users with higher arousal (EDA levels) were less likely to succeed (p-value = .0322). Neither cognitive engagement, nor valence had an impact on successful installation (Table 3). Thus, only H3 was supported.

Table 3. The impact of user state on installation success

Response variable	Effect	DF	Estimate	p-value (one-tailed)
Success	Arousal (EDA)	1	−4.6876	.0322
Success	Cognitive engagement	1	.7019	.22805
Success	Valence	1	−.1833	.4524

4.3   Behavior Factor

A logistic regression was performed to model the effect of reading instructions at the beginning of the task on successful installation. Results indicate that users who read instructions at the beginning were more likely to succeed (p-value = .00215, Table 4). Thus, Hypothesis H6 is supported.

Table 4. The impact of user state on installation success

Response variable	Effect	DF	Estimate	p-value (one-tailed)
Success	Reading instructions	1	2.7568	.00215

In a *post hoc* analysis, we decided to analyze if the level of EDA may have an impact on the reading of instructions and thus, influence the success of the experience. Actually, it is interesting to understand if a person who was highly activated during the experience would completely forget to read instructions. We explored the relation between reading the instructions and arousal (EDA) using a linear regression. Arousal was negatively related to reading instructions (p-value = .0138) (Table 5).

Table 5. The impact of user state on installation success

Response variable	Effect	DF	Estimate	p-value (one-tailed)
EDA	Reading Instructions	1	−0, 2318	.0138

5 Discussion and Concluding Comments

This research is an exploratory attempt to analyze the first stages of the user experience with a product or service; i.e. unboxing, uninstalling and installing the product even before the configuration and usage. Our results show that attitudinal, state, and behavioral factors do not necessarily all have an impact on the successful installation of a product. Our results suggest three main findings: (1) Users' arousal negatively impacts their successful equipment installation, (2) Reading the installation instructions leads to more success, and (3) There is a relationship between reading the instructions and users' arousal level. All other variables investigated (motivation, perceived self-efficacy, emotional valence, cognitive engagement) did not discriminate between successful and unsuccessful participants.

This study contributes to human computer-interaction literature in different ways. First, we investigated user experience prior to the actual device usage, which is a relatively understudied area of UX. Second, the study illustrates the potential of using psychophysiological measures to capture automatic and unconscious states to inform UX research. Moreover, the non-linear nature of the task also required the recording in a synchronous manner using multiple cameras, including a chest camera, to track the user behavior at any time during the experiment.

Being an exploratory research, this study has several limitations and presents avenues for further research. First, the limited sample size may have contributed to some hypotheses not being supported. Thus, future research should be performed to improve the external validity of our findings. Moreover, additional variables or even additional relationships may be investigated in the future. For instance, the relationship between arousal and self-efficacy. Bandura [2] argues that performance is impacted by a state of high arousal and may have an impact on the individual's' perception of self-efficacy. There could be also a relationship between cognitive engagement and self-efficacy [32]. In addition, understanding the How and Why of the relationship between arousal and reading the instructions may help the design of a better experience and increase installation success rate. Methodologically, mobile eye tracking could be used to more precisely understand actual visual attention on instructions. Moreover, even if people interacted with different electronic devices (i.e., old and new ones), we did not investigate the actual use of the new device. It would be of interest to study if users' perception of the installation may have an impact on their first and future uses of the device.

To conclude, we tried to understand which attitudinal, psychophysiological, and behavioral factors can help a company in predicting successful electronic device installation. In the long run, this type of experience opens the door for new innovative modes of interaction and types of research in the field of User Experience and Human Computer Interaction.

Acknowledgments. We are thankful for the financial support of the Natural Sciences and Engineering Research Council of Canada. Authors want also to thank Brendan Scully for manuscript revision.

References

1. Maymand, M.M., Shakhsian, F., Hosseiny, F.S.: The effect of stress on flight performance. World Appl. Sci. J. **19**, 1381–1387 (2012). (Adapted from Nixon P, Practitioner 1979. The Performance level. AROUSAL STRESS)
2. Bandura, A.: Self-efficacy: toward a unifying theory of behavioral change. Psychol. Rev. Univ. **84**, 191–215 (1977). https://doi.org/10.1037/0033-295X.84.2.191
3. Bandura, A.: Perceived self-efficacy in cognitive development and functioning perceived self-efficacy in cognitive development and functioning. Educ. Psychol. **28**(2), 117–148 (1993). https://doi.org/10.1207/s15326985ep2802. Copyr o 1993, Lawrence Erlbaum Assoc Inc Perceived 1, 37–41
4. Booth, P.: An Introduction to Human-Computer Interaction. Lawrence Publishers, London (1989)
5. Boucsein, W.: Electrodermal Activity. Springer Science & Business Media, Berlin (2012). https://doi.org/10.1007/978-1-4614-1126-0
6. Brakus, J.J., Schmitt, B.H., Zarantonello, L.: Brand experience: what is it? How is it measured? Does it affect loyalty? J. Mark. **73**, 52–68 (2009). https://doi.org/10.1509/jmkg.73.3.52
7. Ceaparu, I., Lazar, J., Bessiere, K., Robinson, J., Shneiderman, B.: Determining causes and severity of end-user frustration. Int. J. Hum. Comput. Interact. **17**, 333–356 (2004). https://doi.org/10.1207/s15327590ijhc1703_3
8. Charland, P., Léger, P.-M., Mercier, J., Skelling, Y., Lapierre, H.G.: Measuring implicit cognitive and emotional engagement to better understand learners' performance in problem solving. le. Z Psychol. (2017)
9. Personality and the inverted-U relation: Corcoran, B.Y.D.W.J. Br. J. Psychol. **56**, 267–273 (1965)
10. Courts, F.A.: Relations between muscular tension and performance. Psychol. Bull. **39**, 347–367 (1942). https://doi.org/10.1037/h0060536
11. Davidson, R.J.: Emotion and affective style: hemispheric substrates. Psychol. Sci. **3**, 39–43 (1992). https://doi.org/10.1111/j.1467-9280.1992.tb00254.x
12. Duffy, E.: The psychological significance of the concept of "arousal" or "activation". Psychol. Rev. **64**, 265–275 (1957)
13. Forlizzi, J., Battarbee, K.: Understanding experience in interactive systems. Proc. DIS **2004**, 261–268 (2004)

14. Fredricks, J.A., Blumenfeld, P.C., Paris, A.H.: School engagement: potential of the concept, state of the evidence. Rev. Educ. Res. **74**, 59–109 (2004). https://doi.org/10.3102/00346543074001059

15. Frijda, N.H.: Emotion, cognitive structure, and action tendency. Cogn. Emot. **1**, 115–143 (1987). https://doi.org/10.1080/02699938708408043

16. Greene, B.A., Miller, R.B., Crowson, H.M., Duke, B.L., Akey, K.L.: Predicting high school students' cognitive engagement and achievement: contributions of classroom perceptions and motivation. Contemp. Educ. Psychol. **29**, 462–482 (2004). https://doi.org/10.1016/j.cedpsych.2004.01.006

17. Hartson, R., Pardha, S.P.: The UX Book: Process and Guidelines for Ensuring a Quality. Morgan Kaufmann, Los Altos (2012)

18. Hassenzahl, M., Tractinsky, N.: User experience - a research agenda. Behav. Inf. Technol. **25**, 91–97 (2006). https://doi.org/10.1080/01449290500330331

19. Léger, P.M., Sénecal, S., Courtemanche, F., de Guinea, A.O., Titah, R., Fredette, M., Labonte-LeMoyne, É.: Systems, precision is in the eye of the beholder: application of eye fixation-related potentials to information systems research. J. Assoc. Inf. Syst. **15**, 651 (2014)

20. Lim, K.H., Benbasat, I., Todd, P.A.: An experimental investigation of the interactive effects of interface style, instructions, and task familiarity on user performance. ACM Trans. Comput. Interact. **3**, 1–37 (1996). https://doi.org/10.1145/226159.226160

21. Longo, L.: Human-computer interaction and human mental workload: assessing cognitive engagement in the world wide web. In: Campos, P., Graham, N., Jorge, J., Nunes, N., Palanque, P., Winckler, M. (eds.) INTERACT 2011. LNCS, vol. 6949, pp. 402–405. Springer, Heidelberg (2011). https://doi.org/10.1007/978-3-642-23768-3_43

22. Malmo, R.B.: Anxiety and behavioral arousal. Psychol. Rev. **64**, 276–287 (1957). https://doi.org/10.1037/h0043203

23. Martens, R., Landers, D.: Motor performance under stress. J. Pers. Soc. **16**, 29–37 (1970). https://doi.org/10.1080/10671188.1968.10616565

24. Novick, D.G., Ward, K.: Why don't people read the manual? pp. 11–18 (2006)

25. Pope, A.T., Bogart, E.H., Bartolome, D.S.: Biocybernetic system evaluates indices of operator engagement in automated task. Biol. Psychol. **40**, 187–195 (1995). https://doi.org/10.1016/0301-0511(95)05116-3

26. Reuderink, B., Mühl, C., Poel, M.: Valence, arousal and dominance in the EEG during game play. Int. J. Auton. Adapt. Commun. Syst. **6**, 45 (2013). https://doi.org/10.1504/IJAACS.2013.050691

27. Riedl, R., Léger, P.-M.: Fundamentals of NeuroIS: Information Systems and the Brain (2015)

28. Ryan, R.M., Deci, E.L.: Intrinsic and extrinsic motivations: classic definitions and new directions. Contemp. Educ. Psychol. **25**, 54–67 (2000). https://doi.org/10.1006/ceps.1999.1020

29. Sanford, L.D., Suchecki, D., Meerlo, P.: Stress, arousal, and sleep. In: Meerlo, P., Benca, Ruth M., Abel, T. (eds.) Sleep, Neuronal Plasticity and Brain Function. CTBN, vol. 25, pp. 379–410. Springer, Heidelberg (2014). https://doi.org/10.1007/7854_2014_314

30. Sherer, M., Maddux, J.E., Mercandante, B., Prentice-dunn, S., Jacobs, B.: (1982) 1977, 1982. 663–671

31. Vallerand, R.J.: Toward a hierarchical model of intrinsic and extrinsic motivation. Adv. Exp. Soc. Psychol. **29**, 271–360 (1997). https://doi.org/10.1016/S0065-2601(08)60019-2

32. Walker, C.O., Greene, B.A., Mansell, R.A.: Identification with academics, intrinsic/extrinsic motivation, and self-efficacy as predictors of cognitive engagement. Learn. Individ. Differ. **16**, 1–12 (2006). https://doi.org/10.1016/j.lindif.2005.06.004

33. Wright, P., Creighton, P., Threlfall, S.M.: Some factors determining when instructions will be read. Ergonomics **25**, 225–237 (1982). https://doi.org/10.1080/00140138208924943

Measuring the Influence of User Experience on Banking Customers' Trust

Andrea Müller[1](✉), Selina Anke[1], Sabrina Herrmann[1], Pia Katz[1],
Christina Leuchtweis[1], Christina Miclau[1], Sandra Wörner[2],
and Oliver Korn[1]

[1] Offenburg University, Badstrasse 24, 77652 Offenburg, Germany
andrea.mueller@hs-offenburg.de, oliver.korn@acm.org
[2] Volksbank in der Ortenau, Okenstrasse 7, 77652 Offenburg, Germany
sandra.woerner@volksbank-ortenau.de

Abstract. Bank and trust – two words but one meaning in customers' minds. When interacting with financial service providers, customers are consistently looking for "trust signals" that comfort their decisions and "distrust signals" which create doubt. Therefore, service providers need a deep understanding of the customers' requirements and wishes. To identify trust and distrust signals, we combine established user experience research methods with a new testing procedure to gain helpful recommendations for optimizing the online appearance of banks. The contribution is divided into three parts: Firstly, we investigate current approaches in the financial service industry. Secondly, we provide a corpus describing the relationship between the customers' perception of a bank's website and trust. Thirdly, an empirical study based on qualitative user experience testing with banking website customers shows the value gained by optimizing the banks' virtual interface by enhancing "trust signals" and avoiding "distrust signals".

Keywords: Banking · Trust · Brand · User experience
Financial service providers · Customer expectations

1 Introduction: Changes in Financial Service Markets

In today's competitive banking industry, online-channels have an increasing relevance in customers' interaction behavior [1]. In the last years, several new competitors entered the financial market as pure online players, called FinTechs [2]. Customers perceive their online-specific competence and are pleased to have alternative service providers besides the traditional banking institutions.

Another trend is the introduction of virtual currencies, like Bitcoin, which revolutionize payment and gain a lot of attention in the stock markets [3]. Established banking companies already started to follow-up with own digital and safe currencies to seize their part of this new and fast growing investment business.

For many decades, banks held a convenient position in a very quiet and strongly regulated market. Thus the current development incite a challenging change management process for all financial service providers.

© Springer International Publishing AG, part of Springer Nature 2018
F. F.-H. Nah and B. S. Xiao (Eds.): HCIBGO 2018, LNCS 10923, pp. 382–395, 2018.
https://doi.org/10.1007/978-3-319-91716-0_30

The website of a company is often the first and sometimes sole contact point with potential customers. If potential customers visit a bank's website and gain the impression, that it is not trustworthy, they may never return. Customers feel the need to trust their financial institution [4] – but trust is built over time. A lack of customers' trust can have severe consequences for a financial institution [5]. To avoid these unwanted consequences, a bank continuously needs to put effort in the preservation of customers' trust [5]. However, to receive and maintain customers' trust, it is necessary to gain it first. Trust as a foundation serves the bank to strengthen its position and expand business [6]. To reach a position where the bank is perceived as an upright and trustworthy organization, a financial institution needs to follow several guidelines.

A survey of Ernst & Young Global Limited from 2016 conducted in the UK mentions "six actions that banks in the UK should take to preserve trust" [5] which will be presented shortly:

1. The whole institution needs to change its orientation towards the customer. All employees should be aware that gaining customers' trust is one of the key factors for corporate success [7].
2. It is indispensable that customers are offered complete transparency regarding transactions, products and services [8].
3. Customer data are the banks' most valuable treasure and must be protected at all costs to avoid fraud and suspicion [9].
4. For customers it is essential to receive consultancy that is unbiased and of high quality [10].
5. Customers do not accept errors in relation with their own financial well-being. For this reason, an operational excellence must be provided for the customer [11].
6. Customers prefer a full-service offer, therefore it is necessary that banks extend their businesses to consider non-financial services [12].

Even if all these action points are followed, there may still be situations when customers lose trust. Thus, the most important value in the finance service industry is trust. Therefore, potential barriers or obstacles need to be investigated to make sure customers feel comfortable and safe using the online services of a financial service provider. In this context, it is necessary for banks to identify and measure the influence of trust and distrust signals customers perceive while using a financial service website.

Our study aims to identify and measure the impact of bad user experience by trust and distrust signals on customers' trust before, while and after using banking websites. The four guiding research questions are:

1. How is customers' trust in banks characterized?
2. What are indicators of bad user experience?
3. Which trust and distrust signals do users perceive on a banking website?
4. How can a bad user experience be avoided?

In our study we address these research questions and provide recommendations for financial service providers.

2 Generating Trust on Financial Service Websites

The interaction between banking customers and financial services' online-channels is steadily gaining relevance. Therefore, the purpose of a website should not only be to inform potential customers about the company and its products and services, but also to offer a comfortable interaction experience between the user and the website. The aim of optimizing banking websites is to become perceived as a trustworthy partner for the financial service content and functions offered. Therefore, it is a valid approach to assess which elements of a website lead to a bad or a good user experience. Before describing these elements, we will briefly outline two important aspects of trust: The role of emotions in the economy and the meaning of trust in the banking industry. Triggered by stimuli and determined by direction, type and strength, emotions have a strong influence on the consumer information process [13], resulting in an intense impact on customers' attitude to a financial institution [14].

Addressing customers' emotions with marketing activities gains more and more attention from companies of all branches [15]. Products and services are increasingly replaceable in terms of content as well as function. Furthermore, consumers have almost absolute brand transparency due to the internet. Hence, the arousal of emotions by target group specific marketing activities is a great opportunity for the companies' marketing [16]. The image of a brand or a company is strongly determined by the emotions that arise in customers' minds while interaction with the company [17]. To improve the image, appropriate methods need to be used to incite positive emotions in the customers during as many activities related to the company or product as possible [18].

Working with emotions on financial products in the banking industry is an even greater challenge. The increasing competition in this sector makes financial products replaceable – and furthermore financial products are intangible and perceived as difficult to understand [19]. These special characteristics lead to a higher risk and an increased uncertainty among customers. Therefore, banking services strongly depend on the credibility of the business partners.

Currently, especially the German banking industry is losing the customers' trust. Research conducted by Statista in 2016 shows that the trust of nearly 50% of the German banking customers has slightly or strongly decreased over the past two years [20]. However, a study conducted by the Bundesverband Deutscher Banken (Fedeal Association of German Banks) revealed that nevertheless 82% of the customers had complete or at least moderate trust in their own bank. Thus the study shows a gap between the image of financial institutions in public and the customers' opinion and experiences with their personal bank [21]. This gap in customers' perception will be further evaluated in the study.

3 A Model of Trust in Banking

Trust is defined as the challenge of approaching others with positive expectations, despite someone's own vulnerability and uncertainty [22]. One party has the willingness to be exposed to the actions of another party, assuming that the other party is acting in their favor, regardless of the ability to control it. This leads to a further investigation of reliable signals of trustworthiness such as evaluated in the trust model of Mayer/Davis/Schoorman 1995: "ability", "benevolence" and "integrity" [22].

These three elements build the basic concept of our model for the evaluation of the influence of bad user experience on trust:

The first factor of perceived trustworthiness in Fig. 1 draws attention to the fact that trust is based on the ability to interact with its website. In this sense, the building of trust can be promoted by the establishment of user-friendly navigation and interaction patterns based on the seven principles of human centered design (DIN EN ISO 9241-210): suitability for the task, suitability for learning, suitability for individualization, conformity with user expectations, self-descriptiveness, controllability, and error tolerance [23].

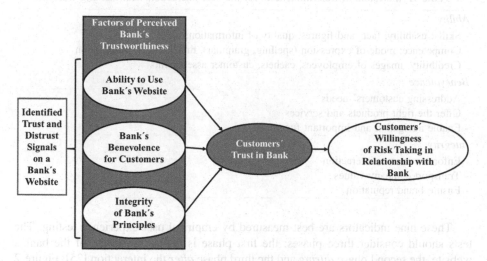

Fig. 1. Model of influence of user experience on users' trust in a bank (adapted from Mayer/Davis/Schoormann 1995).

The second factor states, that benevolence must be offered by banks to ensure customers that they are welcome and specific services are available to help them with financial problems and questions: trust develops as a result of reflection.

The third factor influences trust as a result of perception of strong principles the bank represents as a brand. Trust depends on the overlapping values of the both parties as well as their integrity as trustworthy partners based on bank specific criteria. To build trust, one must ensure that the trustor receives those specific criteria as reliable signals of trustworthiness [24].

These three trustworthiness factors can be measured by identifying trust and distrust signals on a bank's website:

- *Ability* is considered as a construct of skills, competences and credibility.
- *Benevolence* is understood as the perception of a positive orientation of the trustee towards the trustor [22]. Therefore, the trustor believes that the trustee wants his well-being by offering the right products and services meeting the customers' needs.
- *Integrity* involves the perception of the trusting person that the trustee complies with certain rules and principles that the trustor is comfortable with. Whether one is judged to possess integrity depends on the positive consistency of past activities and credible communication through third parties.

Table 1 compiles the nine identified indicators of trust influencers for banking websites.

Table 1. Indicators of trust influencers for the user interaction with banking websites

Ability
- Skills: usability, facts and figures, quality of information,
- Competence: mode of expression (spelling, grammar), timeliness of information
- Credibility: images of employees, cachets, customer assessments
Benevolence
- Addressing customers' needs
- Offer the right products and services
- Enable navigation and important functions
Integrity
- Enforce customer interaction
- Transport company values
- Ensure brand reputation

These nine indicators are best measured by empirical user experience testing. The tests should consider three phases: the first phase is *before* the usage of the bank's website, the second phase *during* and the third phase *after* the interaction [25]. Figure 2 illustrates the procedure and the applied methods.

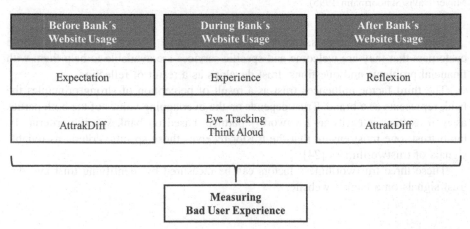

Fig. 2. Procedure, user activity, and applied methods of measuring bad user experience.

This model and the procedure of measuring the impact of bad user experience based on this theoretical background was evaluated in a case study with a top brand banking website in the German market: Volksbank in der Ortenau eG. The study is presented in the following chapter.

4 Study: Evaluating the User Experience Model

Based on the model of influence of bad user experience on users' trust presented above.

4.1 Background and Population

The Volksbank in der Ortenau eG was founded in 1864 and represents traditional values like trust, integrity, transparency and equity. To maintain long lasting and cooperative relationships, the bank ensures consistency and loyalty to its customers [26].

Volksbank aims to maintain an open and trustful communication. Therefore, the customers can reach out to the bank via a multi-channel strategy [27].

Seven banking website users from different age groups, which are not customers of our case study company Volksbank in der Ortenau, were invited to the Customer Experience Tracking lab located on Campus Gengenbach of Offenburg University.

4.2 Methods

Different methods were applied for the three outlined phases of the bad user experience testing process: before the usage of the banking website a person already has specific *expectations* on the presentation of the company in the online-communication-channel. We measured these by using AttrakDiff [28], a standardized online-survey to capture the expectations before and the reflection of the experience after the banking website usage. AttrakDiff examines the perceived *pragmatic quality* (attributes: useful, predictable, well-arranged), the *hedonic quality stimulation* (attributes: creative, inventive, challenging), the *hedonic quality identity* (attributes: people linking, professional, connectional) and the *attractiveness* (attributes: good, attractive, convenient) for interactive systems.

An additional interview ensured more information on the participants' opinions. The online-questionnaire and the interview helped to understand the users' experience by giving them the opportunity to reflect about it.

In the phase of usage, *eye-tracking* is suitable to evaluate the interaction of the user with the banking website. It is the central instrument for the determination of irritations and user behavior. Furthermore, the effects of communication instruments were identified [29]. This method-mix is applied to analyze and optimize the user experience of websites. It provides the owners of the website with optimization possibilities regarding content and design [30]. Also, unconscious behavior can be analyzed [31].

The user's gaze is captured in real-time by cameras with infrared technology. In case of a friction, the user's gaze remains longer at the hurdle and is shown as a fixation point. The longer the person looks at a specific spot, the larger the visualization of a fixation point becomes. The results are analyzed and interpreted in combination with the users' comments [32].

The *think-aloud* method provides information on the participant's thoughts and opinions of the tested system or product. Every participant comments on perceived aspects of the system while working on the given tasks. Think-aloud enables further insight into the users' minds by verbalizing their thoughts and feelings [33]. Even easy tasks can become hard to perform for different persons, so all experiences of negative aspects give insight into the system's frictions. In a pre-study, an expert evaluation identified possible irritations on the banking website. The results were ranked, so strong irritations could be focused the user experience testing.

4.3   Study Results

In the pre-study, we evaluated trust and distrust signals. Based on these, we defined the tasks the participants had to manage. The study started with a brief introduction on the background of the study followed by an explanation of the tasks they had to manage. Each test was conducted with a single participant, so they had to cope with the tasks on their own.

The first testing method before the usage phase was identifying the customers' expectations using the online-questionnaire tool AttrakDiff. After the usage phase, AttrakDiff was applied again to compare the users' expectations before dealing with the banking website and their experiences afterwards. Table 2 shows the trust and distrust signals identified:

Table 2. Overview of trust and distrust signals before and after the phase

Factor	Trust signal	Distrust signal
Pragmatic quality	Conventional	Not well-arranged
Hedonic quality stimulation	Safe	Not innovative Challenging Boring
Hedonic quality identity	Professional	
Attractiveness	Good	Demotivating

In the interview, the users answered questions on their experiences when dealing with the website and which signals they would classify as trustworthy in general.

In the analysis of the user behavior on the website, we found several trust and distrust signals. These signals could be identified by some characteristics like advancement on the website, statements and eye-movements. Using these characteristics, the trust and distrust signals presented in Table 3 were identified:

To determine the relevance of these signals, we analyzed the data gained with the help of our different instruments (AttrakDiff, eye-tracking and think-aloud). We evaluated all observations and peculiarities. If the majority of the participants, in this case at least four participants, noticed or stated the signal as important, we classified it as relevant.

Table 3. Overview of trust and distrust signals during the usage phase

Factor	Trust signal	Distrust signal
Ability	Convenient usability Many facts and figures Images of employees Cachets Customer assessments	Low quality, but high volume of information Untimely and useless information Low mode of expression
Benevolence	Right products and services Good navigation and important functions	Ignoring customers' needs
Integrity	Positive company values Good brand reputation	No or low customer interaction

However, the decisions were not only influenced by the statements of the participants. Also, the other methods such as the eye-tracking and AttrakDiff were crucial for the classification. Table 4 provides an overview of the most relevant trust signals based on our participants' behavior. The last column displays the ratio the classification is based on.

Table 4. Review of trust signals regarding their relevance for test participants

Trust signals	Ratio
1. Brand	6:1
2. Contact options	6:1
3. Images of employees	6:1
4. Images and videos	5:2
5. Privacy policy/general terms and conditions	4:3
6. Legal notice	4:3

Trust Signal 1: Brand
Six out of seven participants indicated that they rate the website and its content as reliable and competent, because they are familiar with the brand. Using eye-tracking, we could figure out that our participants did not look intensively at the brand's logo. They only glanced over and perceived it unconsciously. Therefore, it can be concluded, that the brand Volksbank and the presentation its logo is associated with a positive image which leads to a basic trust.

Trust Signal 2: Contact Options
Most of the participants evaluated the contact options as positive because they can connect with the bank in an easy way via multiple channels. The results of the eye-tracking demonstrated in Fig. 3, show that the participants considered only the prominent placed options. Furthermore, it shows that the fields of the contact form are well-structured.

Fig. 3. Result of the eye-tracking regarding the contact options.

Trust Signal 3: Images of Employees
Six out of seven participants indicated that images of well-known people, like their own bank advisors, convey a feeling of knowing which kind of people are acting in the background of the website. This creates affiliation and trust. Moreover, one participant expressed that pictures of employees testify that the company has nothing to hide and is proud of their employees.

Trust Signal 4: Images and Videos
Images and videos must be chosen carefully. With the help of the eye-tracking we could figure out, that our participants primarily had a look at the images of the website. Furthermore, videos were described as an easy method to gain information without reading the text. The website provokes different opinions among the participants. For some participants, the images and videos did not influence their emotions – but for others, images and videos with people had a positive impact on their feelings.

Trust Signal 5: Privacy Policy and General Terms and Conditions
Through the analysis of statements, we found out that our participants did not read the general terms and conditions or privacy policy, but they expect it to be found. This result is also confirmed by using the eye-tracking method. The participants were able to find the required information quickly because they have already developed routine and reflexivity. Regarding our model of trust, it can be assumed that the lack of such information let users doubt about the trustworthiness of the website provider.

Trust Signal 6: Legal Notice
Four out of seven participants were looking for the legal notice when asked to search for trust-building elements. The analysis of eye-tracking showed that our participants could find the information very purposefully. We therefore assume that they know that the publication is mandatory. As most of our participants were especially looking for the legal notice, its absence would cause distrust.

In Table 5, the most relevant distrust signals are listed:

Table 5. Review of distrust signals regarding their relevance for test participants

Distrust signals	Ratio
1. Complexity	6:1
2. Unstructured set-up	6:1
3. Information overload	6:1

Distrust Signal 1: Complexity
Six participants stated that the clarity of a website is important. Clarity illustrates the significance of getting quickly to a desired goal and being able to record information at the first glance. If this is not the case, the page is considered as confusing and participants become impatient that leads to distrust. The participants felt comfortable with the website. However, eye-tracking showed that the participants needed much time to get to the targeted information although there was a drop-down menu (Fig. 4).

Fig. 4. Result of the eye-tracking regarding the complexity.

Distrust Signal 2: Unstructured Set-Up
Six out of seven participants indicated that the structure of a website is a relevant aspect and therefore needs to be simple. Furthermore, the familiarity of a person with a website is important. Certain functions can be found in similar positions on every website.

The menu options following a routine ensure certainty to the website user. Routines, as stated in our model of trust, are perceived as risk reduction and promote trust. If a website does not follow this rules this may lead to a lack of trust.

Distrust Signal 3: Information Overload
Six out of seven participants got frustrated by the flush of information proved by their confused eye-movement while scanning the page. Indeed, three out of seven participants resigned by the first page after searching for the requested information. The evocation of frustration is memorized as a negative experience. This is likely to influence the image of the brand as a result of a bad user experience.

5 Recommendations

During the management of "trust" and "distrust" signals, the Volksbank website showed room for optimization on several layers: while factors such as brand, legal notice, general terms and conditions as well as the privacy policy are properly developed and placed, navigation and content management need improvement. As the Volksbank website is typical for banking websites, other banks will profit from adhering these optimizations, too. Six potential optimizations are below:

Recommendation 1: Improve Contact Options
The various contact possibilities of branch and contact search led to irritations: most participants wanted to contact directly the responsible counterpart. Therefore, we suggest to replace the prominently placed branch search by a search for counterparts.

Recommendation 2: Use Attractive Images and Videos
Images and videos are important to create a positive experience with a website. Currently, Volksbank uses generic images. Preference should be given to people and situations that convey a feeling of familiarity. Volksbank should use its regional character by presenting pictures with places and persons, which potential customers may already know. Videos are important, as they can explain complex products and issues. However, videos on a banking website should be kept concise and not exceed 30 s.

Recommendation 3: Implement Images of Real Employees and Customers
Images of employees are very important for a positive user experience and can be used to humanize a technical website. This insight can create both emotional and personal bonding which can lead to trust. Images of employees of Volksbank are often hard to get to and cannot be seen at first glance. An easy way to gain and increase trust, is to display images of the staff in proximity to the contact options to make them more visible on the website.

Recommendation 4: Reduce Complexity and Establish User Centered Structures
When designing a website, it is necessary to avoid complexity and unstructured buildup. Clarity and structure must dominate to avoid distrust. It should be possible to recognize important information without having to search for it. Although participants stated that Volksbank's website is clear and structured, some problems occurred: participants had to scroll due to long text sections. Instead, an interactive structure should be placed at the top of every side.

Recommendation 5: Avoid Information Overload
To reduce the stress level and the frustration of our users, the most valuable information need to be selected. Redundant information should be deleted. For example, users often perceive image texts as redundant information because they do not contain significant information. Furthermore, the most valuable information should be illustrated in graphics. For example, an overview of various products could be exemplified by graphics. When it is not possible to depict an information in graphics, it is even more important to select carefully the information relevant from the users' point of view.

Recommendation 6: Analyze and Satisfy Customer Expectations
A website is often consulted to get information about specific issues. It is necessary that a brand leaves a lasting positive impression. In contrast, a negative experience with the website causes a negative image in users' minds, which leads to a negative impact on customers' trust. Our study revealed that it is very important to meet the expectations of both future and existing customers. The reputation of the brand is a very important factor for the creation of trust in all marketing communication channels.

6 Conclusion

As pointed out in the introduction, this work aimed to identify the indicators of trust and distrust on banking websites. Based on important background aspects – the meaning of trust and fulfilling of user expectations in the banking industry – we proposed a model with specific criteria for the evaluation of trust, drawing from Mayer/Davis/Schoormann1995 [22].

We introduced a procedure and based on the three phases of usage where we combined different methods of user experience: the online-tool AttrakDiff, eye-tracking, think-aloud and an interview after the testing.

Based on the adapted model of trust, an expert evaluation identified frictions with a potential to negatively impact the user experience. We looked in detail at the Volksbank's website and carved out the main problems regarding trust.

After an expert analysis for apparent weaknesses, the testing was planned and prepared. Based on these, we defined the tasks the participants had to manage while we were evaluating the respective trust and distrust signals.

We started with a pre-test where every participant had to check the validity of the defined tasks. Each testing was conducted with one participant, so they had to cope with the tasks on their own. Using AttrakDiff and eye-tracking, we compared each user's expectations before dealing with the website and the experiences afterwards. The last part of the testing, we interviewed the participants. They were questioned on their experiences when dealing with the website and which signals they would classify as trustworthy in general.

The results show that the adapted model and the testing procedure is suited to describe and analyze trust and distrust signals on banking websites. Accordingly, we identified six most relevant trust signals and three distrust signals on banks' online presences. Based on the findings, we created six general recommendations to optimize the internet activities of banks.

7 Limitations and Future Work

It is important to point out that a bank cannot rely on its positive image to counterbalance a website which sends distrust signals. We are aware that the number of only seven participants needs to be increased to gain greater validity and reliability of the results. Nevertheless, the study clearly indicates that bad user experience also leads to negative effects on the banking customers' trust, when dealing with the bank's website.

To further evaluate the model of influence of user experience trust, additional qualitative and quantitative research work is necessary. For such future work, additional user experience analysis methods could be used. We are especially interested in additional physiological measurements, for example facial expressions, voice analysis, electro-dermal activity as well as motion and gesture tracking.

References

1. IfD Allensbach Bevölkerung in Deutschland nach Einstellung zu bzw. Kundschaft bei Direktbanken von 2013 bis 2017 (Personen in Millionen). https://de.statista.com/statistik/daten/studie/170960/umfrage/kunde-einer-direktbank—einstellung/
2. Bitconnect: What are the differences between Bitcoin and the traditional banking system? https://bitconnect.co/bitcoin-information/16/what-are-the-differences-between-bitcoin-and-the-traditional-banking-system
3. PWC: FinTechs: Banken gehen Kooperationen im Kreditgeschäft aus dem Weg. https://www.pwc.de/de/pressemitteilungen/2017/fintechs-banken-gehen-kooperationen-im-kreditgeschaeft-aus-dem-weg.html
4. Ansell, J.: The role of banking governance in consumer trust and confidence: a shared responsibility. In: Kim, K.K. (ed.) Celebrating America's Pastimes: Baseball, Hot Dogs, Apple Pie and Marketing? DMSPAMS, pp. 127–128. Springer, Cham (2016). https://doi.org/10.1007/978-3-319-26647-3_24
5. EYGM Limited: Customer trust: without it, you're just another bank: part of a series of articles exploring key themes from EY's Global Consumer Banking Survey (2016)
6. Frowen, S.F., McHugh, F.P.: Financial Competition, Risk and Accountability: British and German Experiences. Anglo-German Foundation for the Study of Industrial Society, p. 1. Palgrave Macmillan, London (2001)
7. Taleghani, M., Gilaninia, S., Mousavian, S.J.: The role of relationship marketing in customer orientation process in the banking industry with focus on loyalty: case study: banking industry of Iran. Int. J. Bus. Soc. Sci. 2(19 - Special Issue), 155–166 (2011)
8. Bahl, M.: The Business Value of Trust, p. 8. Cognizant
9. Joyner, E.: Detecting and Preventing Fraud in Financial Institutions, p. 1. Banking, Financial Services and Insurance (2011)
10. Knowles, G.: Quality Management, p. 171. Bookboon (2011)
11. Moenaert, R., Robben, H.S.J., Gouw, P.: Marketing Strategy & Organisation: Building Sustainable Business, 7th edn. LannooCampus, Leuven (2011)
12. Steinmann, T.: Vertrauen in Banken: Eine empirische Untersuchung von Determinanten und Konsequenzen. Zugl.: Frankfurt (Oder), Univ., Diss., Schriften zum europäischen Management. Springer, Wiesbaden (2013). https://doi.org/10.1007/978-3-658-01148-2
13. Trommsdorff, V., Teichert, T.: Konsumentenverhalten, 8., vollständig überarbeitete und erweiterte Auflage. Kohlhammer Edition Marketing. Verlag W. Kohlhammer, Stuttgart (2011)
14. Homburg, C.: Marketingmanagement: Strategie – Instrumente - Umsetzung – Unternehmensführung, 6, überarbeitete und erweiterte Auflage. Springer Gabler, Wiesbaden (2017). https://doi.org/10.1007/978-3-658-13656-7
15. Kreutzer, R.T., Merkle, W.: Die neue Macht des Marketing: Wie Sie Ihr Unternehmen mit Emotion, Innovation und Präzision profilieren. Betriebswirtschaftlicher Verlag Dr. Th. Gabler | GWV Fachverlage GmbH Wiesbaden, Wiesbaden (2008). https://doi.org/10.1007/978-3-8349-9562-9

16. Kapferer, J.-N.: The New Strategic Brand Management: Creating and Sustaining Brand Equity Long Term, 4th edn. Kogan Page, London (2011)

17. Carroll, C.E.: The Handbook of Communication and Corporate Reputation. Handbooks in Communication and Media, vol. 46. Wiley-Blackwell, Chicester (2013)

18. Bittner, G., Schwarz, E.: Emotion Selling: Messbar mehr verkaufen durch neue Erkenntnisse der Neurokommunikation, 2., überarb. Aufl. Springer Gabler, Wiesbaden (2015). https://doi.org/10.1007/978-3-658-04825-9

19. Spath, D.: Innovationen und Konzepte für die Bank der Zukunft. Springer Fachmedien, Wiesbaden (2009). https://doi.org/10.1007/978-3-8349-9880-4

20. Statista: Ist Ihr Vertrauen in die Bankenbranche in den letzten zwei Jahren gesunken oder gestiegen? https://de.statista.com/statistik/daten/studie/648176/umfrage/umfrage-zur-entwicklung-des-vertrauens-in-die-bankenbranche/

21. Bundesverband deutscher Banken: Vertrauensindex Banken 2016 zum Kunde-Bank-Verhältnis. https://de.statista.com/statistik/studie/id/47723/dokument/umfrage-zum-vertrauen-der-deutschen-in-ihre-kreditinstitute-2016/

22. Mayer, R.C., Davis, J.H., Schoorman, F.D.: An integrative model of organizational trust. Acad. Manag. Rev. **20**(3), 709–734 (1995)

23. DIN EN ISO 9241-210

24. Moellering, G.: Trust: Reason, Routine, Reflexivity. Emerald, Bingley (2006)

25. Müller, A., Gast, O.: Customer Experience Tracking – Online-Kunden conversion-wirksame Erlebnisse bieten durch gezieltes Emotionsmanagement. In: Keuper, F., Schmidt, D., Schomann, M. (eds.) Smart Big Data Management, Berlin (2014)

26. Volksbank in der Ortenau eG Unser Leitbild. https://www.volksbank-ortenau.de/wir-fuer-sie/ueber-uns/leitbild.html

27. Volksbank in der Ortenau eG Gemeinsam Zukunft gestalten seit 1864. https://www.volksbank-ortenau.de/wir-fuer-sie/ueber-uns/seit-1864.htm

28. Hassenzahl, M., Burmester, M., Koller, F.: AttrakDiff: Ein Fragebogen zur Messung wahrgenommener hedonischer und pragmatischer Qualität. In: Szwillus, G., Ziegler, J. (eds.) Mensch & Computer 2003, vol. 57, pp. 187–196. Vieweg+Teubner Verlag, Wiesbaden (2003). https://doi.org/10.1007/978-3-322-80058-9_19

29. Hofer, N., Mayerhofer, W.: Die Blickregistrierung in der Werbewirkungsforschung: Grundlagen und Ergebnisse. J. Mark. **49**(3–4), 143–169 (2010)

30. Naderer, G., Balzer, E.: Qualitative Marktforschung in Theorie und Praxis: Grundlagen - Methoden - Anwendungen, 2., überarbeitete Auflage. Gabler Verlag/Springer Fachmedien Wiesbaden GmbH Wiesbaden, Wiesbaden (2011). https://doi.org/10.1007/978-3-8349-6790-9

31. Romano Bergstrom, J., Schall, A.: Eye Tracking in User Experience Design. Morgan Kaufmann/Elsevier, Amsterdam (2014)

32. Norman, D.: Emotion & design: attractive things work better. Interactions **9**(4), 36–42 (2002). https://doi.org/10.1145/543434.543435

33. Jo, M.Y., Stautmeister, A.: Don't make me think aloud!: Lautes Denken mit eye-tracking auf dem Prüfstand. In: Brau, H., Lehmann, A., Petrovic, K., Schroeder, M.C. (eds.) Tagungsband UP11, pp. 172–177. German UPA e.V., Stuttgart (2011)

A Study of App User Behaviours: Transitions from Freemium to Premium

Christopher Mulligan[1], Carlito Vera Cruz[1], Donagh Healy[1],
David Murphy[1], Margeret Hall[2(✉)], Quinn Nelson[2],
and Simon Caton[1]

[1] National College of Ireland, Dublin, Ireland
[2] University of Nebraska-Omaha, Omaha, USA
mahall@unomaha.edu

Abstract. With the increased digitization of businesses and consumers, it is now not unusual for consumer businesses to solely engage with their customers through digital channels. Many such app driven businesses adopt a freemium business model, whereby use of the entry level service is free, whilst provision of premium content and services is for a fee. With no person to person contact with their customers, these businesses must rely on consumer data analytics to guide decisions on consumer marketing to incentivize users to adopt the premium services. This business scenario provides the motivation for this research project. In our research, using machine learning classification techniques, the team identified the key customer app usage attributes which were the main predictors of future paying subscribers.

Keywords: Data · Analytics · Computing · Machine learning
Mobile apps, finance

1 Introduction

With the pervasive adoption of smartphones and the ubiquitous availability of broadband, many companies engage with their customers through solely digital channels. This rapid adoption of app-powered businesses led Newsweek to coin the term App Economy in 2010 [1], referring to a growing digital economy.

Many of these businesses operate a freemium model; a tiered approach where the base application is free of charge whilst additional premium services are offered via in app purchases. This new business model has been operating for a number of years and generates a lot of user data. It is timely to review the data generated by such a business and to establish whether data mining and machine learning techniques can be applied to generate new insights to understand customer behavior, thereby enabling targeted customer marketing, and incentivisation.

In this paper, we have partnered with an industry partner: an App Economy company with a freemium investment app, but for reasons of confidentiality and data protection need to remain nameless. Their mission is to get the world investing successfully, for which they provide two apps, which we will refer to as "*Sandbox*", and "*Real*". The former helps users understand the fundamentals of investing in the absence

F. F.-H. Nah and B. S. Xiao (Eds.): HCIBGO 2018, LNCS 10923, pp. 396–412, 2018.
https://doi.org/10.1007/978-3-319-91716-0_31

of investor risk, and the latter is a showroom of recommended, hand-picked stocks by the Chief Investment Officer and an easy facility to track and invest in stocks.

This paper seeks specifically to understand which app usage behaviors in the Sandbox app correspond to (or indicate that) subscribers transitioning to the Real app stock advisory service. Aligned with this, there is to understand which customers in the non-paying cohort are most likely to subscribe to the premium Real service. This is a classification problem well suited for machine learning methods. App usage data is mined to identify what the leading App Usage indicators are for a user to subscribe, noting the significance of each indicator. Whilst there is some research literature in this area, there is no research as to how these classification algorithms can be applied for a freemium app of consumer investment advisory services.

Addressing this objective presents a number of challenges: (1) *Apps have many users, and vast amounts of data but not much information.* To remove barriers to adoption, no user profile or usage data is captured for the Sandbox App and limited user profile data is captured for the Real App. Hence, there is very limited demographic data on the user base. The primary data available is the Invest app event usage data. (2) *Data quality*: a number of fields in the user profile data have missing or inconsistent values. This is a common issue in freemium apps, where users often cloak or mis-represent their identity. The central challenge here corresponds to accurate building accurate user models and demographics. The underlying App Usage event data is considered to be more reliable. (3) *High volumes of usage data*: 10 million rows of event data. A user can generate one of over 200 events (e.g., saw stock details, favorited a stock). In isolation, each event record is meaningless. However, the vast array of data can be used to engineer meaningful features from the data, which can provide insight into user app engagement and service adoption patterns. (4) *Data imbalance*. The Real service for which we want to predict adoption has only been live since December 2016, whilst the App in general has been available for circa three years. Hence, naturally there is an imbalance in the data.

The Related Work section which follows describes other related research is this field, including how these challenges can be overcome. The insights from this research heavily influenced the approach and plan for this research project. In some cases, gaps in research are identified, some of which shaped the approach taken. These are set out in the methodology section which also details how the challenges are overcome. The Implementation section provides more details on the technical implementation of the project. An evaluation of the project results is provided, highlighting the algorithms which prove better for this situation. The report closes with conclusions and recommendations for future work in this field. Our industry partner will adopt the data mining and machine learning capability that was built for this research project and plan to address a number of the future work recommendations.

2   Related Work

There seems to be limited research conducted on data mining and machine learning to support transitioning users from freemium to premium in Apps. Other challenges such as feature engineering and managing imbalanced datasets are reviewed to help inform the data mining approach for this paper and to inform areas where research can be progressed through this work.

2.1 Freemium to Premium

Moving users from freemium to premium users is a key business objective, necessary for many companies to grow and sustain growth. Yet, there is limited research in this field. Sifa et al. [2] conducted research on predicting In-App purchase decisions in Mobile Free-to-Play games. Similar to our objective, they needed to manage class imbalance given that most users of these games have been non-paying. Using the Synthetic Minority Over-Sampling Technique-Nominal Continuous approach, they noted that Random Forest out-performed SVMs and Decision Trees with better recall (0.439) and precision (0.643) and F-Score (0.522). Unsurprisingly, models that ran with more data (e.g., 7 days of observations rather than 3) produced better results. Key important predictor variables of future purchases were noted as; number of previous purchases, amount spent previously, number of interactions with other players, levels progressed in game, device and playtime. The models provide insights into how to optimize marketing spend to a user's profile. Furthermore, the models provide valuable information for the design of the product itself (such as number of levels and other game specific features). Whilst the model included many pertinent features such as user engagement and frequency of engagement, the model did not include any recency measures.

2.2 Feature Engineering

As there are no (reliable) demographic attributes of note that could be used, feature engineering of the underlying event data is critical to derive relevant input variables of the user app usage behavior. Domingos [3] notes that the features used are the most important factor determining the success or failure of machine learning projects. He notes that the raw data is not often in the format that can be easily consumed by the Machine Learning algorithms and a very significant amount of work is required to create the appropriate features. He emphasizes that feature engineering and learning are largely inter-dependent steps and a significant degree of iteration is required to get the right results: creating the features, passing them through the learner, analyzing the results, tweaking the features and going again. Domingos notes the importance of feature selection, indicating that a typical approach is to only include the features that have the best information gain for the class. However, he also cautions that features that look unimportant in isolation may in fact be very important in combination with other features. Kelleher et al. [4] echo this approach - rank and prune with filters. They highlight some other alternatives, but conclude that the rank and prune approach is faster and typically delivers models with good accuracy.

2.3 Marketing Science to Inform the Identification of the Right Features

Our industry partner uses a database marketing approach, using push notifications for their customer communications. McCarty and Hastak [5] advocate a RFM (Recency

Frequency Monetary Value) model when high volume database marketing is used. It is based on the philosophy that the best customers to target with new offers are those who recently purchased from a marketer, those who purchase frequently from a marketer and those who spend money with a marketer. McCarthy et al. note that this model cannot be applied to new customers as there is no pre-existing transaction history. However, in our case, there is usage history. Hence, recency and frequency are considered to be key attributes to be engineered into our model.

2.4 Handling of Imbalanced Datasets

Our dataset has an imbalance of 0.85% Real users to 99.15% Sandbox only users, resulting in a need to manage this class imbalance. This extent of class imbalance problem falls into Weiss's Relative Rarity problem [6]. Weiss noted the challenges caused by rarity for data mining and set out a range of scenarios and possible solutions. He strongly discourages simple oversampling but also does not strongly support under-sampling. With under-sampling, potentially valuable data is lost from the model whereas oversampling both increases the time to build the classifier and can cause over-fitting. Chawla et al. [7] indicate that how much to over or under sample is usually established empirically. Burez and Van den Poel [8] note positive results from under-sampling, whilst recognizing that SMOTE for over-sampling might give better results. Based on mixed views in the literature, an under-sampling approach has been adopted.

2.5 Machine Learning Algorithms

Several works informed the choice of appropriate machine learning algorithms. Support Vector Machines (SVMs) were considered a good choice as they can capture much more complex relationships between data points. Cui and Curry [9] use SVMs to help predict customer intention in a marketing study and the algorithm outperformed all others. SVM is used in many customer churn prediction studies, which is analogous to the research question in this paper, i.e., prediction of future behavior based on analysis of customer's past actions. In their study of churn in the telecommunication field, Huang et al. [10] found that SVMs performed well on engineered features. This concurred with a similar study by Zhao et al. [11]. Xia and Jin [12] compare SVMs to several models and find they have the best accuracy and recall

Decision trees are also considered as they have been used in many customer prediction studies. Several studies have found that decision trees can deliver accurate churn prediction models by using customer data Hung et al. [13] and Bin et al. [14]. Decision trees have also been used in identifying high value customers with good results Han et al. [15]. GBM Gradient boosting is a machine learning method which builds an ensemble prediction model by combining weak prediction models. It is the idea of taking the wisdom of the crowd and averaging (or voting) across different models. It is often applied to decision trees. Van Wezel and PotHarst [16] show that GBM provides a large improvement over decision trees in customer choice prediction.

To better understand the dataset, clustering was applied to the majority class. Several studies have shown that under-sampling based on clustering performs better than other under-sampling methods such as Yen and Lee [17] and López et al. [18].

2.6   Model Evaluation

Lantz [19] advises that a good classification model finds a good balance between predicting in a very conservative way and being overly aggressive. He recommends a balanced set of measures including sensitivity (also known as recall), specificity and precision. These measures don't focus on aggregate accuracy of the model but accuracy for each of the classes. The F-measure combines precision and recall into a single performance measure. Rosset et al. [20] show that these measures can be used to compare results across different algorithms. These measures are used to measure the performance of the algorithms used in the research project.

3   Methodology

The paper is based on the Cross-Industry Standard Process for Data Mining (CRISP-DM) [21], as this methodology provides a particular focus on business engagement and understanding at the outset. With the goal to deploy models within business operations.

3.1   Business Understanding

Key to this research is the business context of the data, and correspondingly the objectives of the study: namely identifying transitional indicators of Sandbox only customers into premium customers that use the Real app. This corresponds to a supervised machine learning context, but where the overarching objective is not the prediction per se, but the ability to identify robust indicators of transitioning customers such that core business and marketing strategies (and correspondingly departments) can be informed.

3.2   Data Understanding

Our partner extract data from mixpanel.com, the primary system holding user-level and app usage data for each user. Upon receiving data it was reviewed and a preliminary data dictionary was agreed to ensure domain correspondence and context. The data was subsequently transformed and loaded into a Microsoft SQL Server database. Here, it was reviewed and missing value issues and inconsistencies between the user level and event level data were identified. Given the absence of demographic data and the data quality issues, we concluded that the user-level data does not provide reliable predictors. The event level data was identified as having the greatest potential, with initial analysis of the event data highlighting some interesting facts about user behavior. Users are more likely to subscribe in the early days after they have downloaded the app, with most users subscribing to Real after 40 calendar days and naturally for a slightly lower number of active days on the App (see Fig. 1).

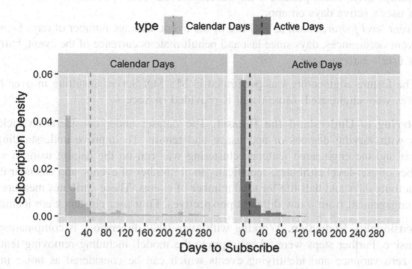

Fig. 1. Days to subscribe from initial app installation.

3.3 Data Preparation

Data Pre-processing. The event data is composed of events generated when the end-user takes an action in the Real app. There are 208 different event types captured, including events as trivial as App Opened and App Closed and other events such as Saw Stock Details. The app usage event data contained over 10 million rows. A domain expert at our industry partner, reviewed the list of possible events and identified events considered important for strategic decision marking. Correspondingly other events can be ignored, and thus reduces the breadth and by extension complexity of the data.

To maximize the relevance and focus of the study, users who had less than five events were filtered out as well as users who had obviously churned, i.e. a user who had not used the app in the last 90 days and had an event count of less than 10 events.

Feature Engineering. The individual events in isolation are meaningless for prediction purposes. Furthermore, the event data set is temporal in nature and as the event logs change over time, the events are difficult to encode and pass to a classification model. However, features can be engineered from the App usage event data and provided as input variables with the target classification algorithms. To achieve this, timestamped events were transformed into a matrix table with a row for each customer and the columns representing the possible events of two distinct types:

1. *Aggregate user level engagement features* such as total number of events, number of elapsed calendar days, number of active days, half-life for total number of events, average event count per active day, average event count per calendar day, half-life of user's active days on app.
2. *Event level features* such as half-life of the event, average number of days between event occurrences, days since last and penultimate occurrence of the event, half-life of user's activity days.

The feature engineering was performed in MS SQLServer, resulting in over 1000 features were engineered. More detail is provided in Sect. 4.

Clustering to Understand the Dataset. The dataset under consideration includes users with varying degrees of app usage and tenure. To improve understanding of dataset and the engineered features, clustering was run on the dataset using a small number of user-level attributes, specifically total number of events, app calendar days, app activity days and half-life for total number of events. These attributes measure app user engagement from a few different perspectives. Four user clusters were identified.

Dimensionality Reduction. Working with over 1000 dimensions is computationally expensive. Further steps were taken to prune the model, including removing features with zero variance and identifying events which can be considered as noise in the overall model such as App Opened and App Closed. These steps reduced the total number of feature engineered events to 382. Dimensionality reduction was a manual process. There are too many features to establish whether there is pairwise multi-collinearity in the dataset. The intention is to run the models, identify the subset of variables that are predictors and to perform pairwise multi-collinearity tests on this subset only.

Balancing the Data. As previously mentioned, the dataset is imbalanced: 0.85% Real users vs. to 99.15% Sandbox only users. Our objective is to predict membership of the Real user class. Whilst all Sandbox only users are in scope of the analysis, it is important that there is balance across the dataset with good representation from both user types. Correspondingly, Real customers are included in the sampling, and the Sandbox only customers were under-sampled to ensure the required balance achieved. Two sampling approaches were considered: randomized sampling and stratified sampling based on the clustering analysis. Whilst randomized sampling is considered adequate Kelleher et al. [4], stratified sampling was preferred as it guarantees to maintain the relative frequencies of the different clusters identified.

3.4 Modelling

This stage is where we build and run supervised machine learning classification models. The stratified dataset was split 70% for Training/Test (using cross-fold) and 30% for Validation. The classifiers were run on the Train/Test dataset using the standard ten-fold cross validation approach. Logistic Regression, C5.0 Decision Trees and Support Vector Machines classification algorithms are run.

3.5   Evaluation

Each model produced is run on the Validation dataset. As well as overall model accuracy, sensitivity is measured which gives the proportion of positive examples (transitioned customers) that were correctly classified. Likewise, specificity is measured which gives the proportion of negative examples (non-transitioned customers) that were correctly classified. The models are run under a number of conditions as presented in the Evaluation section. Here, engagement with our industry partner with respect to findings also commences.

4   Implementation

This section describes the general ETL strategy, feature engineering, clustering analysis, data balancing and application of k-fold cross validation, as shown in Fig. 2.

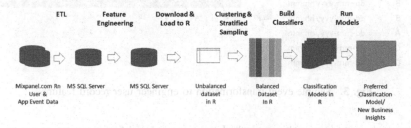

Fig. 2. General architecture.

4.1   Extracting, Transforming and Loading App Data

Two CSV data files are extracted from mixpanel.com corresponding to the data for this paper: user profile data file and app usage event. The user profile contained one record per user. This CSV file contained basic user data, such as their city, app version, user's iOS device. Emphasis is on the iOS app version as the Android version has only recently launched and there is insufficient usage data available. The app usage event data contains data for every event tracked by Mixpanel. The events can be either subscriber initiated, or platform initiated (i.e., push notifications).

4.2   Feature Engineering

Via SQL transformation, the features below were engineered and stored in a features table. Raw data was transformed into data that can be interpreted and consumed by the classification algorithms as depicted for example in Fig. 3. To provide a richer profile of users, several features were engineered: *Total event count:* the number of times an event was triggered for each user. *Total active days in app:* the number of days that the user has been active in the app. *Total calendar days:* number of elapsed days from when user was first seen to when the user was last seen. *Total event half-life:* The number of calendar days it takes a user to generate half of their total recorded events is also calculated. For example, if a user initiates 1000 events, the days between the first date any event was initiated and the date on which the 500th occurrence was observed is the half-life. *Average event count per active day:* The Total Event Count divided by the Total active days to give a measure of engagement per interaction day. *Average event count per calendar day:* The Total Event Count divided by the Total calendar days to give a sense of sparsity of interaction. Perhaps a user engages heavily when on the app but rarely actually opens the app. *Half-life of user's activity days:* The number of calendar days taken to reach half of their total active days on the app. For example, if a user has 10 active days, the half-life will be the number of days between the first active day and the day on which their fifth interaction day occurs.

Raw Event App Usage Data

User	Event	Timestamp
1	A	dd-mm-yyyy hh:mm
1	A	dd-mm-yyyy hh:mm
1	B	dd-mm-yyyy hh:mm
1	B	dd-mm-yyyy hh:mm
2	A	dd-mm-yyyy hh:mm
2	C	dd-mm-yyyy hh:mm
2	D	dd-mm-yyyy hh:mm

Feature Engineered User Record

User	Total Event Count	Event A Count	Event B Count	Event C Count	Event D Count	Total Event Half-Life	Etc...
1	4	2	2	0	0		
2	3	1	0	1	1		

Fig. 3. Sample event transformation to engineer user record features

For each event type within a user's dataset, event level features were generated. For example, if a user has 1000 events in the dataset containing 12 unique event types, features are engineered for the 12 unique events. *Average days between an events previous occurrence:* For each event, the number of days between the last time the event was triggered and the current observation of the event is computed. The sum of these time splits is divided by the number of times the event has occurred to provide a measure of event periodicity. The lower this value, the more it features within a user's session with the app. *Days since last and penultimate occurrence of the event:* The difference in days between the final occurrence and the penultimate occurrence of an event is also recorded. This essentially measures a recency effect for each event. The recency value can help the model discover the most frequent events in the model most recently. *Half-life of event:* This is the number of calendar days it takes for a user to generate half of the total occurrences of a specific event in their logs.

A key part of the feature engineering process is removing customer event data after they have successfully monetised to the premium service. A primary objective is to capture the set of events or features within a user's app usage that are predictive of them converting to the premium service. Therefore, the event data of a monetised customer becomes redundant after they sign on and deliver only noise to the model. Within the event logs, there are two events that initiate when a customer successfully signs up to the Invest Plus service. The time at which one of these events is captured for a user defines the monetisation point and any event beyond this moment is pruned from the feature engineering phase.

4.3   Clustering Analysis

Once the data cleaning and feature engineering was completed, K-means clustering was run on the data to increase understanding of the data and help stratify the data for the classification algorithms. A subset of the user-level engineered variables are chosen as the input variables for the clustering: Total Event Count, Event Count Half-Life, App Calendar Days and App Activity Days. As these variables have different measurement scales, the input variables are normalised to standardise them to have the same range. Clustering is run with k = 3, k = 4 and k = 5. Upon visual inspection of the clusters, and with the assistance of a scree plot k = 4 provided the most meaningful clusters.

Cluster 1, the *Old Fogeys*, represented light users who have used the app over the longest period (8%). Cluster 2, the *Tyre Kickers*, represented users who have been somewhat engaged with the app over a longer period of time (1%). Cluster 3, *Recent Casuals*, represents the most recent users who are less engaged than cluster 4 but more engaged than clusters 1 and 2 (59%). Finally, cluster 4, *Enthusiastic Beginners*, represents more recent users who are well engaged with the app when compared to the other clusters (32%). The standardised z-scores are included in Table 1.

Table 1. Standardized z-scores for k = 4 k-means clusters

	Standardised Z scores					
Cluster	Calendar days	Active days	Event halflife	Total event count	Count	Frequency
1	2.454944214	1.169908147	2.355675742	0.348069872	7.185	8%
2	2.299414046	3.459292577	0.901661924	7.081669032	958	1%
3	−0.290986133	−0.689131295	−0.27803878	−0.209295664	53.877	59%
4	−0.147334109	0.883744373	−0.0977158	0.069252587	28.751	32%

Here, Calendar Days is a measure of tenure, active days, a measure of user activity, total event halflife, measures the initial engagement (how long the user required to reach half their total number of events), and total number of events the degree of use. In each of these four cases, a positive number indicates above average, 0 is average, and a negative number, below average. Count and frequency indicate the proportion of the data captured within each cluster.

4.4   Mitigating Unbalanced Data

Running the classification algorithms without under-sampling the dominant class would lead to distorted results. Thus, we include the full positive class in the new dataset. Then clustered the dominant class to understand the component clusters, which identified four clusters as described above. Finally, we took stratified samples of the dominant class using the four clusters to form the Sandbox only part of the dataset, as illustrated in Fig. 4. The models are built and run for both 90:10 and 50:50 datasets, split between the two customer types.

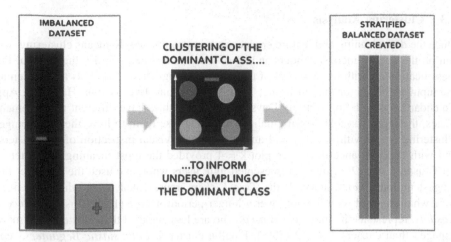

Fig. 4. Creating a stratified balanced dataset of 5 categorical user representations: 4 types non-premium users identified via k-means (Sandbox only) and 1 premium user type (Real).

4.5 Evaluating Machine Learning Models

To evaluate the machine learning models four steps are taken, as shown in Fig. 6: (1) The stratified dataset is split into Train/Test & Validation, with a 70:30 split. (2) 10 fold Cross-Validation is run on the Train/Test dataset. (3) The 30% validation dataset is passed into the models to test the accuracy. This step aided validation as the test data had been unseen by the model. (4) Key performance measures such as ROC, Sensitivity, Specificity are produced and examined. This process is repeated 10 times drawing samples from the overall dataset, and average measures are reported (Fig. 5).

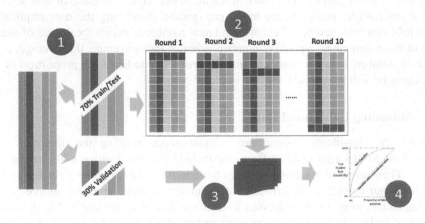

Fig. 5. Evaluation strategy

5 Model Evaluation and Results

A number of classification scenarios are taken to evaluate the research objective using the same feature engineered dataset. This section describes these models and their results in further detail. Five classification scenarios are picked to address the challenge with different parameters.

1. Baseline Model with random sampling of the dominate Sandbox only class (90/10 mix)
2. All Classification Models with 382 engineered features & stratified sampling with a 50/50 mix
3. All Classification Models with 382 engineered features & stratified sampling with a 90/10 mix
4. All Classification Models with "important input variables" (108 in total) & stratified sampling with a 90/10 mix
5. All Classification Models run for the top 7 most important engineered features identified by the other models to create an ensemble result

For 2, 3 and 4, the classification models used were logistic regression (GLM), Gradient Boosting Machine (GBM), C5.0 Decision Tree and a Support Vector Machine (SVM) using the Radial Base Function kernal. For scenarios 2 and 3, 382 engineered features are used, which is a subset of the total engineered features removing features with zero variance. For scenario 4, a subset of the engineered features are used based on the expertise of the business team. All models are evaluated through the ROC curve, Sensitivity and Specificity measures.

5.1 Baseline Models

A number of baseline models were built to establish the level of difficulty in the prediction problem. This is useful as it permits gauging the complexity of the machine learning problem, which given the significant class imbalance is useful. Essentially, these models mirror reasonable informed business categorizations by a human.

- **Top Activity:** predict "Yes", the user is a Real subscriber (if user event count in the top 5% event counts, i.e. the user has a large number of events in the app) and "No" if if user activity below top 5%.
- **Calendar Days:** predict "Yes", the user is a Real subscriber if user has had the App less than 28 calendar days and "No" otherwise. In this case, we treat all new users are potential subscribers.
- **Active Calendar:** predict "Yes", the user is a Real subscriber if user has the App less than 28 calendar days and activity in the top 5% event counts (A+B) and otherwise predict "No".

Top Activity and Active Calendar provide the highest accuracy (95.0 and 98.5% respectively), with Calendar Days achieving 21.9%. For sensitivity, Top Activity (0.579), Calendar Days (0.357), and Active Calendar (0.100) indicate that for Top Activity, approximately 58% of the time if a user will transition, they are correctly classified as such. For specificity, Top Activity achieves 0.953, Calendar Days 0.218, and Active Calendar 0.991, indicating that Active Calendar will correctly identify 99.1% users that will not transition. For such simple model, based mainly on human intuition, this is encouraging performance. However, note that the more critical performance measure is specificity, as it emphasizes a model's ability to correctly classify transitioning users.

5.2   Machine Learning Models

Tables 3, 4, 5 and 6 illustrate the performance results for each of the machine learning scenarios described above, consisting of a 10-fold cross validation evaluation reporting the average performance measure achieved across the 10 leave one out folds (Table 2).

Table 2. All classification models with 382 engineered features & stratified sampling with a 50/50 mix

Model	Sensitivity (Recall)	Specificity	Precision	F-score	AUROC
C50	0.94703	0.96920	0.96837	0.95758	0.991
GBM	0.93432	0.97511	0.97394	0.95372	0.992
GLM	0.61186	0.60127	0.60444	0.60813	0.607
SVM	0.93390	0.81055	0.83076	0.87931	0.957

The most important variables (i.e., the pre-engineered variables) were: (1) Stock: Did Tap On Favorite; (2) Showroom stock: tap stock; (3) Stock suggested; (4) Sign Up: Skip; (5) Link Broker: Tap (6) Link DriveWealth Account; (7) Saw Showroom: Couch Mark Sign Up: Success; (8) Stock Details: Graph Scrolled; (9) Sent to broker; (10) Stock Details: tap favorite.

Most important variables here in order of importance were: (1) Stock suggested; (2) Showroom stock: tap stock; (3) Sent to broker; (4) Sign Up: Success; (5) Showroom: tap BBN; (6) Order Popup: Tap fund; (7) Stock Details: Scroll; (8) Stock Details: tap favorite; (9) Stock Details: tap unfavourite; (10) DW: Order created

Most important variables here in order of importance were: (1) Stock Details: Graph Scrolled; (2) Stock Details: tap favorite; (3) Saw Store; (4) Broker: Order created; (5) Saw More; (6) Sent to broker; (7) Stock Details: tap invest now; (8) Saw Stock Details; (9) Store: did tap on purchase; (10) Order created.

Across each of these sampling methods with varying quantities of features, 7 appear consistently, namely: Stock Details: tap unfavorite_Total; Stock Details: Scroll_Total; Stock Details: tap favorite_Total; Stock suggested_Total; Stock Details: Graph Scrolled_Calendar; Stock: Did Tap On Favorite_Calendar; Stock Details: Graph Scrolled_Total. Thus, we include one modelling exercise using only these features (Table 6).

The most important reported engineered features as output by the models are present here. These are the top features across scenarios 2, 3 and 4 above. Sensitivity fell for this model though the specificity stayed high. Thus we can identify, that using stratified sampling and a rich (382 feature set) data set comprising of mostly engineered features, the C50 tree does well at identifying transitioning users.

Table 3. Aggregate performance across scenarios 2–5

Model	Sensitivity (Recall)	Specificity	Precision	F1
C50	0.78	0.99	0.91	0.84
GBM	0.78	0.99	0.91	0.83
GLM	0.59	0.88	0.66	0.60
SVM	0.51	0.95	0.83	0.58

Table 4. Classification model with the most engineered features (382) & stratified sampling with a 90/10 mix

Model	Sensitivity (Recall)	Specificity	Precision	F-score	AUROC
C50	0.89788	0.99453	0.93430	0.91573	0.994
GBM	0.91229	0.99390	0.92842	0.92028	0.994
GLM	0.78856	0.93339	0.50653	0.61684	0.781
SVM	0.32881	0.99236	0.78862	0.46411	0.963

Table 5. Classification models with "important input variables" (108) & stratified sampling with a 90/10 mix

Model	Sensitivity (Recall)	Specificity	Precision	F-score	AUROC
C50	0.53814	0.98824	0.79874	0.64304	0.931
GBM	0.50000	0.98861	0.79195	0.61299	0.923
GLM	0.22458	0.98677	0.59551	0.32615	0.826
SVM	0.13136	0.99669	0.77500	0.22464	0.835

Table 6. Models trained using only the top 7 most important variables identified by the other models

Model	Sensitivity (Recall)	Specificity	Precision	F score	AUROC
C50	0.74322	0.99467	0.92364	0.82367	0.986
GBM	0.75551	0.99625	0.94589	0.84005	0.987
GLM	0.73686	0.99658	0.94924	0.82968	0.973
SVM	0.62966	0.99566	0.92643	0.74975	0.949

To provide more depth with respect to classification performance specifically with respect to specificity and sensitivity Fig. 6 depicts the ROC curves for each of the 4 machine learning-based classification scenarios.

5.3 Summary

An aggregate of scenarios 2–5 is developed, calculating an average of the measures across the four scenarios: "Important Features at 50–50 Sample", "Full Feature Set", "Important Features at 90–10 Sample" and the "7 Variables". Taking the average across all approaches gives an overall measure of how robust the algorithm is when faced with different approaches in feature selection.

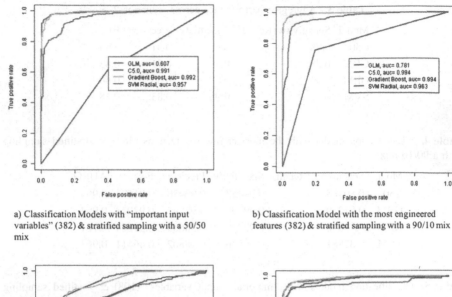

a) Classification Models with "important input variables" (382) & stratified sampling with a 50/50 mix

b) Classification Model with the most engineered features (382) & stratified sampling with a 90/10 mix

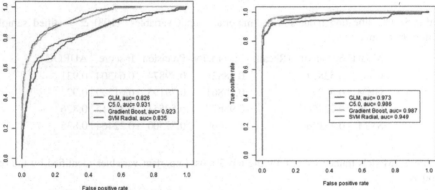

c) Classification Models with "important input variables" (108) & stratified sampling with a 90/10 mix

d) Models trained using only the top 7 most important variables identified by the other models

Fig. 6. ROC curves for each of the 4 machine learning scenarios.

C50 and GBM in general perform similarly, with the C50 having a slightly higher F1 score. Kelleher et al. [4] suggest that F1 is a good measure for prediction problems and place an emphasis on capturing the performance of a prediction problem on the positive level (the important level). Hence, we recommend the C50 model ahead of the GBM, not just based on the F-Score, but also in having demonstrated exceptional sensitivity performance (correctly identifying a transitioning user). For this business situation, we also need to evaluate the cost of getting the prediction wrong. All customer engagement is through push notifications. A false negative, i.e., predicting that a user will not transition when the user could be a potential premium user, is a lost business opportunity. A false positive (incorrectly predicting a transitioning user) is not such a serious issue for this business. However, correctly identifying transitioning users, or those that start to display key features indicative of transitioning users is highly relevant, and has been effectively demonstrated here.

6   Conclusion and Future Work

In this paper, we have demonstrated that machine learning approaches can both identify key user behavioral indicators of freemium users transitioning into premium users, i.e. paying subscribers, of trading service apps, as well as accurately predict these transitions. The data used in this paper corresponds to 10 million user events over a period of months for a production trading and investment mobile app. To facilitate our approach, we employed the CRISP data mining methodology, significant feature engineering, and subsequently dimensionality reduction techniques. We benchmarked our models against informed business user practices to gauge both problem complexity as well as a means to demonstrate the potential of the machine learning techniques (C50, GBM, Logistic Regression, and a Support Vector Machine) employed.

Our industry partner is keen to further develop the capabilities reported in this paper. They plan to hire a data scientist whose full-time job will be develop and run machine learning models, building on these initial findings. The insights gained will be used to in a number of different ways:

- to support targeted marketing to users who are at a certain stage in lifecycle
- as an early warning system when expected behaviors are not occurring (e.g., maybe a new app version has bugs)
- to support design enhancements to the product to enable easier display and use of the key predictive user events.

There are a couple of methodology limitations in our approach which can be addressed as future work:

- Test for pairwise multi-collinearity due to the volume of features and the relative computation complexity of this task
- Adopt alternate under-sampling and over-sampling mechanisms such as SMOTE and test for improvements

However, the key limitation of this work, justifying future work, is that the classification models did not distinguish between whether the user was going to make a one-off premium purchase (e.g. purchase a one-month subscription) or become a recurring user (e.g. annual subscription). Thus, there are significant further opportunities to extend our approach to predict the number of one-off purchases or annual subscriptions through regression models.

References

1. Burrows, P., MacMillan, D., Ante, S.E.: Inside the app economy (2009). https://www.scribd.com/document/273977882/Business-Week-App-Economy. Accessed 23 Apr 2017
2. Sifa, R., Hadiji, F., Runge, J., Drachen, A., Kersting, K., Bauckhage, C.: Predicting purchase decisions in mobile free-to-play games. In: Proceedings of AAAI AIIDE (2015)

3. Domingos, P.: A few useful things to know about machine learning. Commun. ACM **55**(10), 78–87 (2012)
4. Kelleher, J.D., Mac Namee, B., D'Arcy, A.: Fundamentals of Machine Learning for Predictive Data Analytics: Algorithms, Worked Examples, and Case Studies. MIT Press, Cambridge (2015)
5. McCarty, J.A., Hastak, M.: Segmentation approaches in data-mining: a comparison of RFM, CHAID, and logistic regression. J. Bus. Res. **60**(6), 656–662 (2007)
6. Weiss, G.M.: Mining with rarity: a unifying framework. ACM SIGKDD Explor. Newslett. **6**(1), 7–19 (2004)
7. Chawla, N., Japkowicz, N., Kolcz, A.: Special issue on learning from imbalanced datasets, sigkdd explorations. In: ACM SIGKDD (2004)
8. Burez, J., Van den Poel, D.: Handling class imbalance in customer churn prediction. Expert Syst. Appl. **36**(3), 4626–4636 (2009)
9. Cui, D., Curry, D.: Prediction in marketing using the support vector machine. Mark. Sci. **24**(4), 595–615 (2005)
10. Huang, B., Kechadi, M.T., Buckley, B.: Customer churn prediction in telecommunications. Expert Syst. Appl. **39**(1), 1414–1425 (2012)
11. Zhao, Y., Li, B., Li, X., Liu, W., Ren, S.: Customer churn prediction using improved one-class support vector machine. In: Li, X., Wang, S., Dong, Z.Y. (eds.) ADMA 2005. LNCS (LNAI), vol. 3584, pp. 300–306. Springer, Heidelberg (2005). https://doi.org/10.1007/11527503_36
12. Xia, G.-E., Jin, W.-D.: Model of customer churn prediction on support vector machine. Syst. Eng.-Theory Pract. **28**(1), 71–77 (2008)
13. Hung, S.-Y., Yen, D.C., Wang, H.-Y.: Applying data mining to telecom churn management. Expert Syst. Appl. **31**(3), 515–524 (2006)
14. Bin, L., Peiji, S., Juan, L.: Customer churn prediction based on the decision tree in personal handyphone system service. In: 2007 International Conference on Service Systems and Service Management, pp. 1–5. IEEE (2007)
15. Han, S.H., Lu, S.X., Leung, S.C.: Segmentation of telecom customers based on customer value by decision tree model. Expert Syst. Appl. **39**(4), 3964–3973 (2012)
16. van Wezel, M., Potharst, R.: Improved customer choice predictions using ensemble methods. Eur. J. Oper. Res. **181**(1), 436–452 (2007)
17. Yen, S.-J., Lee, Y.-S.: Under-sampling approaches for improving prediction of the minority class in an imbalanced dataset. In: Huang, D.S., Li, K., Irwin, G.W. (eds.) Intelligent Control and Automation, pp. 731–740. Springer, Heidelberg (2006). https://doi.org/10.1007/978-3-540-37256-1_89
18. López, V., Fernández, A., García, S., Palade, V., Herrera, F.: An insight into classification with imbalanced data: empirical results and current trends on using data intrinsic characteristics. Inf. Sci. **250**, 113–141 (2013)
19. Lantz, B.: Machine Learning with R. Packt Publishing Ltd., Birmingham (2013)
20. Rosset, S., Neumann, E., Eick, U., Vatnik, N., Idan, I.: Evaluation of prediction models for marketing campaigns. In: Proceedings of the Seventh ACM SIGKDD International Conference on Knowledge Discovery and Data Mining, pp. 456–461. ACM (2001)
21. Chapman, P., Clinton, J., Kerber, R., Khabaza, T., Reinartz, T., Shearer, C., Wirth, R.: CRISP-DM 1.0 step-by-step data mining guide (2000)

Influence of Color Perception on Consumer Behavior

Long Ren and Yun Chen[✉]

Huazhong University of Science and Technology,
Wuhan, People's Republic of China
longren@hust.edu.cn, yunchen92@foxmail.com

Abstract. With the intensified competition, attracting and retaining the customers has become a top concern for businesses. Color has been identified as one of most significant factors influencing consumers' purchasing behavior. The purpose of the research is to explore the ways color perceptions influence consumer behavior. A better understanding of influence of color perceptions enables them to direct marketing strategies design and implementation. In the research, the researcher makes an attempt to review relevant research papers and account for why color is important in capturing the interest of consumers. In the paper, consumer behaviors, influential factors and influence of colors on consumer behavior, color meanings and roles are reviewed and critically discussed. It is expected that the study can help better understand consumers' color perceptions and their potential influence on consumer behavior. The color psychology has become growingly significant in producing and packaging products. Colors, thus, accomplished prominence in marketing activities. The findings in the established literature can offer some great implications for businesses in terms of how to leverage color for creating distinct customer experience. The established literature also highlights colors have different meanings in different culture. That indicates the importance of considering cultural difference when exploring influence of color perceptions on consumer behaviors. The paper simply reviews the established literature, and these established findings remain to be empirically tested.

Keywords: Color · Color perceptions · Consumer behavior

1 Introduction

In the modern society, consumers dominate. The intensified globalization and competition prompts businesses to seek for alternative approaches to influencing consumers. Immaterial and intangible features of products influence consumers' purchasing decisions. Sensory marketing, under such circumstance, has become an innovative solution to generate emotional features of brand/product and capture strong relationship with consumers (Hultén 2011). The sensory marketing offers an excellent opportunity for using color as an approach to differentiate one product from another. Color may generate emotional link leading to product differentiation, competitiveness, strengthened customer loyalty, increased sales, reduced perception time for the brand, enhanced positive emotions and customer relationship (Aghdaie and Honari 2014).

© Springer International Publishing AG, part of Springer Nature 2018
F. F.-H. Nah and B. S. Xiao (Eds.): HCIBGO 2018, LNCS 10923, pp. 413–421, 2018.
https://doi.org/10.1007/978-3-319-91716-0_32

The researchers such as Cian and Cervai (2011); Kauppinen-Räisänen and Luomala (2010) argued that color is a cost-saving and effective approach to generate consumers' positive opinions. Color psychology is found to significantly influence human beings' lives in a variety of approaches. Many organizations worldwide have recruited color consultants to help figure out the best color for products so as to best capture consumers. It was found that 62–90% of purchasing decision was based on product color (Singh 2006). However, the established researches into color and its influence (Kareklas et al. 2014; Labrecque et al. 2013) are few. Little has been understood about the influence of color perception on consumer behavior. There is death of generalized material, in which information about color use in marketing would be explained in a systematic way. That allows the formulation of the research problem, "how does color perception influence consumer behavior?"

2   Consumer Behavior

According to Blackwell et al. (2006), consumer behavior refers to activities including obtaining products or service, consumption and product disposal. In marketing field, consumer behavior has captured interest of market-oriented marketers as it investigates into the ways consumers purchase and why they purchase. With insights into consumption behavior, marketers are capable of developing strategies for influencing consumers' purchasing behavior. Marketing activities no more flow from marketers to consumers. Instead, it is important for marketers to truly learn the ways consumers react to marketing efforts. Evans et al. (2006) develop model known as hierarchy of communication effects model, including seven stages, "exposure, attention, perception, learning, attitude, action, and post-purchase". Nevertheless, as other business model, it is unnecessary consumers observe sequence in the process of purchasing. However, the model offers marketers logical model for integrating psychological concepts into interpretation of why and how consumers react to marketing activities (Evans et al. 2006) (Fig. 1).

Fig. 1. Sequential effects of response to marketing (Evans et al. 2006)

3   Color

Color is differentiated in hue, brightness and saturation (Ogden et al. 2010). In terms of hue, colors can be categorized into cool color (e.g. orange and red) and warm color (e.g. violet, blue). Brightness and saturation are significant in color perception. Brightness plays an important role in determining lightness or darkness of color; saturation suggests purity of color. It was found that color is much more pleasant with enhanced attributes (Camgöz et al. 2002). According to Hemphill (1996), bright colors are linked with positive emotions like happiness, joy and hope. Likewise, Elliot and

Maier (2007) considers brighter colors as friendly, cultured, pleasant and beautiful. Conversely, dark color is associated with negative emotions like boredom and sadness (Camgöz et al. 2002). According to Elliot and Maier (2007), color may generate associations and responses, and they take meaning of color as bipartite. Meanings of colors are triggered by learned associations or shaped by the nature. Likewise, Tofle et al. (2004) also claimed emotional responses evoked by color as an outcome of learned associations on basis of culture and individual-related features. Cherry (2015) explores link between color and mood. Cool colors are linked with the moods as calm, serene and comfort. Conversely, arm colors are relevant to stressful and exciting moods. Furthermore, Valdez and Mehrabian (1994) confirms long-wave length color as much more arousing the short-wave length ones. Colors are capable of attracting attention. That indicates retailers are capable of leveraging color to elicit appropriate behaviors. Bellizzi and Hite (1992) identified people had higher willingness to stay and purchase products in environment with blue than environment with red.

In some case, "meaning" may represent a kind of mental stimulation (Osgood et al. 1957). Seahwa (2014) definitions colour meaning in her research: "Colour meaning is not about combinations that create pleasing responses (colour harmony), not about the processes with which people understand and react to colour (colour perception), and not about liking a particular colour among alternatives (colour preference). Instead, it is concerned with the meanings that are associated with certain colours."

The meanings linked with colors are different in different cultures. No absolute universal meanings are given to specific color. The most widely known studies on the feelings that different colors represent are mainly located in the context of North America. With expansion of North American culture, interpreting color meanings worldwide have been alternated and shown tendency of convergence. The color meanings identified in North America are presented in Table 1.

In addition to influence of culture, colors are different because of dependence on lighting conditions, observation position and surrounding especially the adjacent color. All these factors can shape the ways of perceiving a specific color. Moreover, even when people are exposed to the same color, the ways they perceive color, meanings and emotions incurred by the same color are different among people due to gender, age, educational and culture, childhood association and others (Scott-Kemmis 2013). A research by Choungourian (1969) into people from four countries identified variance in color preferences represents individual variation. It was found that the US consumers prefer red and blue, but least like blue-green. However, respondents from Iran and Kuwait preferred blue and green. As for gender, women tended to have different color preferences from men. Besides, many men in the western countries are red/green color blind, but marketers can use unisex colors like blue, red, black and white. There is a trend of shifting from bright and primary colors toward sophisticated color in form of patterns. Adults were found to be less open to experiment of new colors, but they adhered to the favorite color for lowing the risks. Regarding education, well-educated people are found to be much more complicated in color choice.

Table 1. Different colors and meanings (adapted from Scott-Kemmis 2013)

Color	Represent	Effects
Red	Energy, action, desire, low, passion	Stimulating, exciting, motivating, attention-capturing, assertive, aggressive
Orange	Adventure and risk taking; Social communication, interaction, friendship	Enthusiasm, rejuvenation, Simulation, courage, vitality , fun, playful
Yellow	Mind, intellectual; happiness and fun, communication of new ideas	Creative, quick decisions; anxiety; Producing; critical; non-emotional ; Light, warmth motivation
Green	Harmony, balance, growth, hope, wealth, health, prestige Serenity	Rejuvenation, nurturing; dependable Agreeable diplomatic, possessiveness; envy
Blue	Communication, peace and calm; honesty, authority, religion, wisdom	Conservative; Predictable; Trustworthy, trustworthy, secure, responsible
Purple	Inspiration; imagination, royalty, mystery, nostalgia, individuality	dignity Empathy ; controlled emotions Impractical Respectable
Pink	Unconditional love; compassion; nurturing; hope, girlish	Calming; non-threatening; Affectionate
Gray	Neutrality; compromise, control	Indecision, detached, depression, unemotional
White	Innocent, pure, new beginning, equal, unity, fairness	Impartial; rescuers, futuristic, clean, efficient, soft noble
Black	Black mystery; power and control; prestige; value; timelessness; sophisticated Formal, dignified and sophisticated	Formal, dignified and sophisticated Depressing Pessimistic

4 Roles of Color in Consumer Behavior

The established literature has been dedicated to exploring the relationship between colors and purchasing behaviors. It is found that packaging and color significantly and directly influence consumers' psyche (Raheem et al. 2014). Thus, it is significant to carry out the studies on relationship between colors and consumer behavior so as to distinguish color that mostly influence positively or negatively influence consumers' choice and thereby purchasing behavior. Brody et al. (1981), television advertising significantly influenced children consumerism. Thus, children without knowledge of substantial components may be fascinated by colors. That indicates advertising with good color was likely to attract children and purchasers. Color is taken as an important non-verbal sign in understanding consumer behavior (Kotler and Keller 2006). Consumers generally link specific color with specific product categories by understanding dependencies among different colors. Especially, colors play important in marketing and packing. Harmony, proper arrangement of colors can help to capture consumers' interest. A major factor influencing consumer perception is the type of color adopted in packaging. It is the color that captures consumers' attention (Hagtvedt 2016). Consumers get color of specific products on basis of relations they build up. on some occasions, having pleasant experience may result in favor of a specific color, and on other occasions consumers may acquire color on basis of relations (Luscher and Scott 2003).

Color is expected to be helpful for capturing consumers' attention as human beings are capable of quickly identifying colorful items. That is because the pre-attentive system of brain is designed and developed to easily spot color in the external environment, and what is more important sis that the system can immediately help select the items for following attentional processing. Nevertheless, color is not alone. In other words, it is hardly possible to perceive a specific color on its own, but a specific color is used with other adjacent colors. Therefore, adopting color for capturing consumers' interest may be inhibited by the surroundings where items with target colors are placed, and different colors have different values for capturing attention (Jansson-Boyd 2010). In addition, a recent research (Huang and Lu 2013) suggests that blue and red mediated the perception of healthiness perception of the food product.

Furthermore, relying on setting, a single color or combined color communicates symbolic meanings that can generate affective reactions and are adopted in marketing practices to figure out brands, categorize products, make assumptions and direct consumers' choices (Hanss et al. 2012). Ones' perception of color is based upon link between color and associated meanings. Consumer researches claim successful adoption of color significantly relies upon congruency between symbolic meanings of color and product attributes. Bottomley and Doyle (2006) conduct a research into brand logo and they found that cool colors such as blue and green are proper for utilitarian products, and warm colors such as red and orange are proper for products or services generating hedonic experience.

5 Practical Implications

The established literature has highlighted two important themes. First, it is highlighted that human beings have continued to be influenced by color psychically or mentally. How human beings are influenced by colors has remarkably psychological essence that indirectly affects norms, responses and individual consumer's behavior (Elm 2012). Second, it is highlighted that in different countries or cultures, colors are possessed with different meanings. That offers implications that mistakes in selecting color may discourage people from purchasing specific products. Colors, thus, accomplished prominence in marketing activities. The findings in the established literature can offer some great implications for businesses in terms of how to leverage color for creating distinct customer experience.

First, the established literature implies that marketers need to learn emotions and needs generated by each color for leveraging color in marketing activities. A good understanding of meanings of different colors is the prerequisite to successful use of color. For instance, cool colors such as blue and green are associated with attribute "pacifying", and warm colors such as red and orange can stimulate interest. Thus, if a business intends to stimulate consumers' interest, it is desirable to use warm colors.

Second, it is implied that businesses should capitalize on color for creating the customer experience that they intend to deliver to the customers. For attracting consumers, color has been taken as critical element. Learning well psychological influence of colors and its variance combination can help marketers a lot. However, color selection should be congruent with the business. For instance, brown, a color with the impression of being dull, can generate great effect in coffee shops or bakeries to enhance customer experience. Likewise, UPS, the leading shipping company worldwide, is renowned for its brown trucks. That indicates there is no formula for how to use different colors in creating customer experience.

6 Conclusion

Overall, the established literature has identified the great impact of color perceptions on consumer behaviors. The color psychology has become growingly significant in producing and packaging products. Colors, thus, accomplished prominence in marketing activities. Color can stimulate interest and enhance desire for purchasing a specific product or service. With the intensified competition, attracting and retaining the customers has become a top concern for businesses. Color has been identified as one of most significant factors influencing consumers' purchasing behavior. Color in marketing directly influences consumer behavior, which has been confirmed by lots of researches. Considers link color with different products, which increases difficulties of learning the ways people respond to colors. Each color must be deployed for suitable product in line with psychological features. The color psychology has become growingly significant in producing and packaging products. The established literature also highlights colors have different meanings in different culture. That indicates the importance of considering cultural difference when exploring influence of color perceptions on consumer behaviors. The paper simply reviews the established literature, and these established findings remain to be empirically tested.

References

Aghdaie, S.F.A., Honari, R.: Investigating the psychological impact of colors on process of consumer shopping behavior. Int. Rev. Manag. Bus. Res. **3**(2), 1244–1253 (2014)

Ahmed, S.: Understanding the use and reuse of experience in engineering design. Ph.D. thesis, Engineering Department, Cambridge University, Cambridge (2000)

Ahmed, S., Wallace, K.M., Blessing, L.S.: Understanding the differences between how novice and experienced designers approach design tasks. Res. Eng. Des. **14**, 1–11 (2003)

Albers, J.J., Wahl, P.W., Cabana, V.G., Hazzard, W.R., Hoover, J.J.: Quantitation of apolipoprotein AI of human plasma high density lipoprotein. Metabolism **25**(6), 633–644 (1976)

Ares, G., Deliza, R.: Studying the influence of package shape and colour on consumer expectations of milk desserts using word association and conjoint analysis. Food Qual. Prefer. **21**(8), 930–937 (2010)

Bannan-Ritland, B.: The role of design in research: the integrative learning design framework. Educ. Res. **32**(1), 21–24 (2003)

Bernard, H.R.: Research Methods in Anthropology: Qualitative and Quantitative Approaches, 3rd edn. AltaMira Print, Walnut Creek (2002)

Birren, F.: Color & Human Response, pp. 9–11. Wiley, New York (1978)

Blessing, L., Chakrabarti, A., Wallace, K.: A design research methodology. In: Proceedings of the 10th International Conference on Engineering Design (ICED 1995), Praha, Czech Republic, pp. 50–55 (1995)

Bottomley, P.A., Doyle, J.R.: The interactive effects of colors and products on perceptions of brand logo appropriateness. Mark. Theory **6**(1), 63–83 (2006)

Bryman, A., Teevan, J.J.: Social Research Methods: Canadian Edition. Oxford, Don Mills (2005)

Burchett, K.E.: Color harmony attributes. Color Res. Appl. **16**(4), 275–278 (1991)

Burchett, K.E.: Colour harmony. Color Res. Appl. **27**, 28–31 (2002)

Blackwell, R., Miniard, P., Engel, J.: Consumer Behavior, 10th edn. Thomson South-Western, Mason (2006)

Bellizzi, J.A., Hite, R.E.: Environmental color, consumer feelings, and purchase likelihood. Psychol. Mark. **9**(5), 347–363 (1992)

Brody, G.H., Stoneman, S., Lane, T.S., Sanders, A.K.: Television food commercials aimed at children, family grocery shopping, and mother-child interactions. Family Relat. **30**(3), 435–439 (1981)

Caivano, J.L.: Color and semiotics: a two-way street. Color Res. Appl. **23**(6), 390–401 (1998)

Camgöz, N., Yener, C., Güvenç, D.: Effects of hue, saturation, and brightness on preference. Color Res. Appl. **27**(3), 199–207 (2002)

Cardoso, C.: Design for inclusivity: assessing the accessibility of everyday products. Ph.D. thesis, The Department of Engineering and Design, Cambridge University, Cambridge (2005)

Case, D.O.: Looking for Information: A Survey of Research on Information Seeking, Needs and Behavior. Academic Press, Amsterdam (2008)

Cherry, K.: Color psychology: how colors impact moods, feelings, and behaviors. About Education (2015)

Chevreul, M.E.: The principles of harmony and contrast of colors. In: Birren, F. (ed.) (1987)

Chevreul, M.E.: The Principles of Harmony and Contrast of Colors, and Their Applications to the Arts. Reinhold, New York (1967)

Chuang, M.C., Ou, L.C.: Influence of a holistic color interval on color harmony. Color Res. Appl. **26**(1), 29–39 (2001)

Choungourian, A.: Color preferences: a cross-cultural and cross-sectional study. Percept. Mot. Skills **28**(3), 801–802 (1969)

Cifter, A.S.: An inclusive approach towards designing medical devices for use in the home environment. Ph.D. thesis, School of Engineering and Design, Brunel University, London (2011)

Creswell, J.W.: Research Design. Sage Publications, London (2009)

Creswell, J.W.: Qualitative Inquiry and Research Design: Choosing Among Five Traditions. Sage, London (1998)

Cross, N.: Design research: a disciplined conversation. Des. Issues **15**(2), 5–10 (1999)

Cross, N.: Designerly Ways of Knowing. Springer, London (2006). https://doi.org/10.1007/1-84628-301-9

Cian, L., Cervai, S.: The multi-sensory sort (MuSeS): a new projective technique to investigate and improve the brand image. Qual. Mark. Res. Int. J. **14**, 138–159 (2011)

Diane, T., Cassidy, T.: Colour Forecasting. Wiley, Hoboken (2009)

Dong, H.: Barriers to inclusive design in the UK. Ph.D. thesis, Department of Engineering, Cambridge University, Cambridge (2004)

Dorcus, R.M.: Color preferences and color associations. Pedagog. Semin. J. Genet. Psychol. **33**, 399–434 (1926)

Elliot, A.J., Maier, M.A.: Color and psychological functioning. Curr. Dir. Psychol. Sci. **16**(5), 250–254 (2007)

Evans, M., Jamal, A., Foxall, G.: Consumer Behaviour. Wiley, West Sussex (2006)

Fallman, D.: The interaction design research triangle of design practice, design studies, and design exploration. Des. Issues **24**(3), 4 (2008)

Feisner, E.A.: Colour: How to Use Colour in Art and Design. Laurence King Publishing, London (2006)

Fidel, R., Green, M.: The Many Faces of Accessibility: Engineers' Perception of Information Sources. Information Processing and Management (2004)

Frayling, C.: Research in Art and Design. Royal College of Art Research Papers, vol. 1, no. 1, pp. 1–5. Royal College of Art, London (1993)

Gage, J.: Colour and Meaning: Art, Science and Symbolism. Thames and Hudson, London (1999)

Goethe, J.W.: Theory of Colours. Dover Publications, Mineola (2006)

Granville, W.C.: Color harmony: what is it? Color Res. Appl. **12**(4), 196–201 (1987)

Guilford, J.P.: The affective value of color as a function of hue, tint, and chroma. J. Exp. Psychol. **17**(3), 342 (1934)

Guilford, J.P.: The prediction of affective values. Am. J. Psychol. **43**, 469–478 (1931)

Guilford, J.P., Smith, P.C.: A system of color-preferences. Am. J. Psychol. **72**(4), 487–502 (1959)

Gump, J.E.: The readability of typefaces and the subsequent mood or emotion created in the reader. J. Educ. Bus. **76**(5), 270–273 (2001)

Gupta, S.: Design and delivery of medical devices for home-use: drivers and challenges. Ph.D. thesis, Department of Engineering, Cambridge University, Cambridge (2007)

Hemphill, M.: A note on adults' color-emotion associations. J. Genet. Psychol. **157**(3), 275–280 (1996)

Hultén, B.: Sensory marketing: the multi-sensory brand-experience concept. Eur. Bus. Rev. **23**, 256–273 (2011)

Elm, N.: How color affects customer perception. Iran's industrial design (2012)

Hagtvedt, H.: The influence of product color on perceived weight and consumer preference. In: Groza, M.D., Ragland, C.B. (eds.) Marketing Challenges in a Turbulent Business Environment. DMSPAMS, p. 25. Springer, Cham (2016). https://doi.org/10.1007/978-3-319-19428-8_7

Hanss, D., Böhm, G., Pfister, H.-R.: Active red sports car and relaxed purple-blue van: affective qualities predict color appropriateness for car types. J. Consum. Behav. 11(5), 368–380 (2012)

Huang, L., Lu, J.: When color meets health: the impact of package colors on the perception of food healthiness and purchase intention. In: Botti, S., Labroo, A. (eds.) Advances in Consumer Research, vol. 41, pp. 625–626. Association for Consumer Research, Duluth (2013)

Jansson-Boyd, C.: Consumer Psychology. McGraw-Hill, Berkshire (2010)

Kareklas, I., Brunel, F.F., Coulter, R.A.: Judgment is not color blind: the impact of automatic color preference on product and advertising preferences. J. Consum. Psychol. 24, 87–95 (2014)

Kotler, P., Keller, K.L.: Marketing Management. Prentice Hall International, New Jersey (2006)

Kauppinen-Räisänen, H., Luomala, H.T.: Exploring consumers' product-specific colour meanings. Qual. Mark. Res. Int. J. 13, 287–308 (2010)

Labrecque, L.I., Patrick, V.M., Milne, G.R.: The marketers' prismatic palette: a review of color research and future directions. Psychol. Mark. 30, 187–202 (2013)

Luscher, M., Scott, I.: The Luscher Color Test. Random House, New York (2003)

Mullen, B., Johnson, C.: The Psychology of Consumer Behavior. Psychology Press, London (2013)

Ogden, J.R., Ogden, D.T., Akcay, O., Sable, P., Dalgin, M.H.: Over the rainbow - the impact of color on consumer product choice. J. Bus. Behav. Sci. 22(1), 65–72 (2010)

Raheem, A.R., Vishnu, P., Ahmed, A.M.: Impact of product packaging on consumer's buying behavior. Eur. J. Sci. Res. 122(2), 125–134 (2014)

Scott-Kemmis, J.: Target markets – using color psychology to attract your target markets (2013). http://www.empower-yourself-with-color-psychology.com/target-markets.html

Singh, S.: Impact of color on marketing. Manag. Decis. 44(6), 783–789 (2006)

Tofle, R.B., Schwartz, B., Yoon, S., Max-Royale, A.: Color in healthcare environments: a critical review of the research literature. The Coalition for Health Environments Research (CHER), California (2004)

Valdez, P., Mehrabian, A.: Effects of color on emotions. J. Exp. Psychol. Gen. 123(4), 394–409 (1994)

Inferring Consumers' Motivations for Writing Reviews

Dongning Yan, Lin Zhang, and Heshan Liu[⊠]

Mechanical Engineering School,
Shandong University, Jingshi Rd. 17923, Jinan, China
{yandongning, liuheshan}@sdu.edu.cn,
zhanglin209n@163.com

Abstract. In recent years, product reviews have taken an important role in helping consumers make online purchasing decisions, but only a small proportion of consumers post their reviews online. Researchers pointed out that consumers can be divided into distinct groups in terms of their motivations for eWOM (electronic word-of-mouth), and different strategies should be developed based on different motivation groups. However, the effort of explicitly acquiring motivations via questionnaire is unavoidably high, which may impede developing different strategies to different motivation groups. In this paper, we identified a set of consumers' motivations and behavior data. Then, we performed a user survey to validate whether the behavioral features are significantly correlated with consumers' motivations. These findings lay solid foundation to develop more adaptive design solutions for encouraging eWOM participation.

Keywords: E-commerce · Review writing · Electronic word-of-mouth
Motivation

1 Introduction

In recent years, product reviews have taken an important role in helping consumers make online purchasing decisions [3, 8]. According to statistics in [25], 84% of Americans rely on product reviews in their online purchasing process. Consulting reviews can effectively increase users' understanding for products [29, 32], reduce their decision uncertainty [16, 24] and make users' online purchasing process more enjoyable [18].

Given the important role of product reviews, merchants have tried to induce consumers to "spread the word" [17]. Actually, only a small proportion of consumers actively post their reviews online because consumers are social loafers rather than contributor [1]. It has been pointed out that consumers are more inclined to write reviews when they are very satisfied or disgruntled with the products, so that the reviews for a single item usually follow a bimodal distribution [20]. It can be inferred that reviews of a product sometimes can not reveal its true quality, which would mislead users' purchasing decisions.

With the purpose to proactively induce consumers to 'spread the word', researchers have utilized different approaches to sparking positive community participation, e.g.,

© Springer International Publishing AG, part of Springer Nature 2018
F. F.-H. Nah and B. S. Xiao (Eds.): HCIBGO 2018, LNCS 10923, pp. 422–430, 2018.
https://doi.org/10.1007/978-3-319-91716-0_33

using uniqueness and goal setting [2, 26]. In addition, some systems have been developed to provide authors real-time suggestions on what they may wish to write in terms of previous reviews [5, 12, 13, 21]. The results show that users feel they get support while writing reviews and would like to incorporate the suggestions into reviews. Furthermore, attention has been devoted to the forces that motivate consumers to write product reviews, e.g., economic incentives, concern for other consumers and social benefits, etc. [11, 14, 30, 31]. Hennig-Thurau et al. pointed out that consumers can be divided into distinct groups in terms of their motivations for posting electronic word-of-mouth (eWOM) [19]. Accordingly, it was suggested that different strategies should be developed based on different motivation groups. However, existing studies relied on traditional survey methodology to explicitly acquire consumers' eWOM motivations. From consumers' perspective, they may be unwilling to answer the survey for the sake of saving efforts or protecting their privacy.

In this paper, we focus on how to implicitly derive consumers' motivation for writing product reviews online from their behavior data. Specifically, we have identified a set of behavioral features that are significantly correlated with users' motivations through experimental validation.

In the following, we first introduce related work on WOM (word-of-mouth) motivations in Sect. 2. We then present the details of motivation and behavioral feature identification process in Sect. 3. In Sect. 4, we describe the correlations between consumers' motivations and their behavioral features. We finally conclude the work and indicate its future direction in Sect. 5.

2 Related Work

Considering that understanding the antecedents of online reviews is the foundation for enhancing users' willingness to write reviews [17], researchers have devoted attention to the drivers of contribution to online product review. For traditional WOM communication, Dichter first proposed four main motivations of providing positive WOM: product-involvement, self-involvement, other-involvement, and message-involvement [11]. Based on Dichter's findings, Engel et al. introduced dissonance reduction as an additional motivation [14]. Then, Sundaram et al. pointed out the motivations for generating positive and negative reviews should be different. According to 390 critical-incident reviews, they identified four motivations for positive WOM (i.e., altruism. product-involvement, self-enhancement, and helping the company) and the other four motivations for negative reviews (i.e., altruism, anxiety reduction, vengeance, and advice seeking) [30].

With the development of internet technology, users are provided with a variety of ways for sharing information and opinion (e.g., email, virtual community, web-based opinion paltforms, discussion forums, etc.) [4]. The communication of product reviews has been extended from the word-of-mouth between relatives to the electronic word-of-mouth among publics. Dholakia et al. pointed out the main motivations of virtual community participation are purposive value, self-discovery, maintaining interpersonal connectivity, social enhancement, and entertainment value [10]. Ma and Agarwal also indicated that knowledge contribution in online commnities is strongly linked to people's perceived identity verification [27]. Hennig-Thurau et al. investigated the motivations consumers may have in engaging in eWOM communication on web-based opinion paltforms. Through analyzing the responces of more than 2000 consumers, they extracted eight motivations: venting negative feelings, self-enhancement, concern for other consumers, helping the company, advice seeking, platform assistance, social benefits, and economic incentives [19]. In addition, some researchers pay attention to users' motivation for a specific type of product (e.g., movies [9], travel [33]). Table 1 summarizes the motivations of word-of-mouth communication identified in the literatures.

Table 1. Motivations of word-of-mouth communication identified in the literatures [9]

Dichter	Engel et al.	Sundaram et al.	Dholakia et al.	Hennig-Thurau et al.	Description
Product involvement	Product involvement	Product involvement; Vengeance; anxiety reduction		Venting negative feelings	Consumers feel urge to talk about for very good or bad products that trigger strong feelings
Self involvement	Self enhancement	Self enhancement	Self-discovery	Self-enhancement	WOM allows person to gain attention and show connoisseurship
Other involvement	Concern for others	Altruism; helping the company		Concern for other customers; helping the company	Consumers feel genuine need to help others make a better decision or to reward a company for a good product
Message involvement	Message intrigue		Purposive value		Discussion stimulated by advertisements or other marketing messages
	Dissonance reduction				Reduce cognitive dissonance (doubts) following a purchase decision
		Advice seeking		Advice seeking; platform assistance	Obtain advice on how to resolve problems
			Interpersonal connectivity; social enhancement; entertainment value	Social benefits	Enjoyment from engaging in the social experience of online WOM
				Economic incentives	Response to direct economic incentives for posting online reviews

Furthermore, Hennig-Thurau et al. analyzed how the eWOM motivations differ among consumers. The results show that consumers are not a homogeneous group in terms of their eWOM motivations, but can be divided into different groups [19]. For example, some customers are referred to as 'true altruism', as they are strongly motivated by helping other consumers and companies; while, some customers tend to be 'self-interested helpers', as they appear to be driven by economic incentives.

However, existing studies mainly rely on traditional questionnaires to measure users' motivations, which unavoidably demand a large amount of user efforts and hence impede the development of adaptive design solutions for encouraging eWOM participation. We are thus interested in exploring proper behavioral features to infer users' motivation for writing online reviews.

3   Method

3.1   Motivation Identification

In order to understand the motivations of writing online product reviews, our review of the literature has led us to suggest eight motivations [19], including: (1) economic incentives, (2) concern for other consumers, (3) helping the seller, (4) "advice seeking", (5) expressing positive feelings, (6) social benefits, (7) showing connoisseurship, and (8) obtaining prestige.

Then, through an informal discussion with consumers, we added the ninth and tenth dimension of motivations: (9) hard to refuse request and (10) reducing anxiety. Specifically, people usually find it hard to refuse a request made by a relative or friend, even though the benefit may remain unknown, lest being criticized as "lacking human feeling" [7]. Besides, some people also proposed that they feel anxiety or uncomfortable if they have unfinished work. Thus, when such people are informed that there are uncompleted reviews, they would write comments to prevent or reduce distress.

Table 2. Questions to measure consumers' motivations for writing reviews online

I write product reviews online because	
Economic incentives	I can accrue points or get a discount.
Concern for other consumers	I want to help others buy the right product with my own experience
Helping the seller	I am so satisfied with the seller's service or product that I want to help the seller
Advice seeking	I hope to receive reviews from other users when I buy products
Expressing positive feelings	I cannot help to share the joy of using the product
Social benefits	It is fun to talk about a product with other people
Showing connoisseurship	It allows me to show connoisseurship, assert superiority
Obtaining prestige	I can obtain prestige and esteem.
Hard to refuse requests	It is hard for me to refuse a request from relatives or friends for writing reviews
Reducing anxiety	I feel uncomfortable if I do not complete my review

In total, a list of 10 distinct motivations for writing online reviews was developed. To measure these motivations, a set of questions were pre-designed from existing studies, where they were tested and found to have strong content validity and reliability (see Table 2). Each question was responded on a five-point Likert scale ranging from 1 'strongly disagree' to 5 'strongly agree'. The higher the score, the stronger the motivation is.

3.2   Feature Identification

In terms of literature review, the behavioral features were assessed by five constructs: (1) demographic properties, (2) the valence of reviews, (3) the form of product reviews, (4) whether to answer potential consumers' questions, and (5) the likelihood of appending reviews.

Users' Demographic Properties. There are several demographic properties have been shown related to users' motivation. Young users are more likely to proactively interact with a social networking site and to be online content creators [22]. Males are traditionally driven by self-efficacy, self-assertion, and achievement orientation [28]. Yoo et al. found that females are more motivated by helping the company and experiencing enjoyment/positive self-enhancement. Also low-income groups are more motivated by desires to vent negative feelings and concerns for other consumers [33].

The Valence of Reviews. One of the most researched topics in WOM literature is the valence or polarity of messages. Researchers proposed that type of consumer's motivation does indeed influence the dissemination of the different valence of reviews (i.e., positive and negative) [23]. Specifically, a consumer with a utilitarian orientation (e.g., economic incentives, advice seeking) is more likely to spread negative information. In contrast, one with a hedonic orientation (e.g., social benefits) is more likely to spread positive information.

The Form of Product Reviews. Based on the findings of [6], it was concluded that motivation also influences the form of reviews (e.g., rating, textual comment or picture). Users with more of an other-directed (i.e., helping other consumers) motivation are more inclined to express themselves by combined use of text and rating. While those with a primarily self-directed motivation express by text only.

Whether to Answer Potential Consumers' Questions. In some online shopping websites (e.g., Amazon.com), potential consumers of a product can ask for help from people who have already bought it. We assume that whether to provide advice may vary with different motivations. For example, people with social sharing motivation are more inclined to feel a sense of urgency to connect with others and proactively answer the questions.

The Likelihood of Appending Reviews. Since the quality problem of some products will not appear in a short time, some online shopping websites (e.g., TaoBao.com) provide consumers with a second chance to post additional reviews after using a period of time. We can argue that consumers with different motivations will have different likelihood to append reviews.

3.3   User Survey Setup

To investigate the relation between motivations and behavioral features, we performed a user survey to collect consumers' motivations and behavior data. Of the 187 respondents, only those 110 individuals (54 females) who had previously written online reviews were included in data analysis. Table 3 gives the demographic profile of the final sample. All of them are Chinese, with different education backgrounds (51.6% with Bachelor, 35.9% with Master, and 12.5% with PhD) and age ranges (33.6% in the range of 20–30, 46.4% in the range of 30–40, and 20% in the range of above 40).

The behavioral features were concretely determined in the following ways. With respect to the valence of reviews, participants reported the percentages of positive, neutral and negative reviews they have given. Similarly, the form of product reviews was assessed via the average frequencies of posting rating, text and pictures. As for whether to answer potential consumers' questions, users were required to indicate *"Have you ever provided advice to other consumers online?"*. The likelihood of appending reviews was obtained by user's answer to the question *"I would like to provide additional comments after using a product."* (given on a five-point Likert scale from 1 'strongly disagree' to 5 'strongly agree').

Table 3. Demographic profile of participants in the user study

Gender	Female (54), male (56)
Education	Bachelor (57), Master (39), Phd (14)
Age	20-30 (37), 30-40 (51), >40 (22)
Major	Electronics, Engineering, Architecture, etc.
Internet usage	4.92 (daily/almost daily), *st.d.* = .42
E-commerce shopping experience	3.64 (1–3 times a month), *st.d.* = .91

Note: The scores for 'internet usage', and 'e-commerce shopping experience' were given on a 5-point Likert Scale from 1 'least frequent' to 5 'very frequent'.

4   Results

We employed Spearman's rank coefficient to validate whether the correlations between consumers' motivations and their behavioral features are significant correlated, because Spearman's rank coefficient can be applied to both numerical and ordinal variables [15]. The results are shown in Table 4.

Among users' demographic properties, on the contrary to literature, we observe that age is significantly correlated with 'Social benefits' in a positive way, which suggests that old people are more likely to share experience about a product with others than young people. Education is negatively correlated with users' motivation for economic incentives, indicating that people with higher education level show less interest in financial incentives. Consistent with the results in literatures, females are more motivated by experiencing enjoyment.

As for the valence of reviews, the proportion of neutral reviews is significantly positively correlated with 'Hard to refuse requests', which implies that people who are ashamed to refuse others' requests tend to preserve an attitude of neutrality. The proportion of negative reviews is negatively correlated with 'Concern for other consumers', suggesting that people possess altruistic motivation are not likely to provide positive reviews.

In terms of the form of product reviews, people who give ratings tend to possess the motivation of 'helping the seller' and 'obtaining social benefits'. Moreover, those who further post textual comments and pictures are more inclined to express delight, show connoisseurship and reduce anxiety.

Furthermore, people who once actively answered potential consumers' questions tend to be more motivated by 'Concern for other consumers', 'Expressing positive feelings', and 'Reducing anxiety'. With respect to the likelihood of appending reviews, it shows that people who post additional reviews after a period of time are subject to 'Helping the seller', 'Social benefits', 'Obtaining prestige', 'Hard to refuse requests' and 'Reducing anxiety'.

Table 4. Correlations between consumers' motivations and behavioral features ($^{*}p < 0.05$ and $^{**}p < 0.01$)

		M1	M2	M3	M4	M5	M6	M7	M8	M9	M10
		M1: Economic incentives M2: Concern for other consumers M3: Helping the seller M4: Advice seeking M5: Expressing positive feelings M6: Social benefits M7: Showing connoisseurship M8: Obtaining prestige M9: Hard to refuse requests M10: Reducing anxiety									
Demographic properties	Age	.100	.028	−.012	.066	.140	.356**	−.026	.055	−.052	.003
	Gender	.130	.129	.121	.035	.201*	.143	−.030	−.091	.086	−.028
	Education	−.256*	.197	−.064	−.117	−.021	.027	.009	−.220	.097	.066
The valence of reviews	Positive	−.025	.219	−.068	.031	−.212	−.242	.014	−.140	−.106	−.123
	Neutral	.109	.005	.083	.009	.241	.147	.081	.184	.264*	.131
	Negative	−.009	−.423**	−.079	−.122	.013	.184	.114	.142	−.091	.106
The form of product reviews	Rating	.192	.185	.342**	.175	.098	.209*	.033	−.163	.096	.084
	Text	.306**	.193	.096	.231*	.237*	.288**	.201*	.051	.269**	.310**
	Picture	.146	.083	.114	.077	.190	.171	.100	.112	.295**	.206*
Whether to answer others' questions		.015	.405**	.209	.143	.290*	.223	.053	−.140	.224	.302*
The likelihood of appending reviews		.161	.112	.202*	.041	.048	.234*	.168	.284*	.341**	.205*

5 Conclusion

In this paper, we presented an approach to implicitly deriving users' eWOM motivation from their behavior in online community. Specifically, we first identified a set of behavioral features. Then we have validated the significant correlations between multiple features and users' eWOM motivation through user survey.

In the future, we will combine all of these above significant features into a unified inference model to demonstrate that a consumer's motivation for writing online reviews can be inferred by his/her behavioral features. Concretely, we can compare three regression models: Gaussian Process, Pace Regression, and M5 Rules. These findings will lay solid foundation to develop more effective design solutions, which adaptively and accurately stimulate different consumers' motivations to encourage eWOM participation.

Acknowledgments. This research work was supported by the Fundamental Research Funds of Shandong University, China. We thank all participants who took part in our experiments.

References

1. Bakhshi, S., Kanuparthy, P., Shamma D.A.: Understanding online reviews: funny, cool or useful? In: Proceedings of the Conference on Computer Supported Cooperative Work & Social Computing, pp. 1270–1276. ACM (2015)
2. Beenen, G., Ling, K., Wang, X., Chang, K., Frankowski, D., Resnick, P., Kraut, R.E.: Using social psychology to motivate contributions to online communities. J. Comput. Mediat. Commun. **10**(4), 212–221 (2005)
3. Bickart, B., Schindler, R.M.: Internet forums as influential sources of consumer information. J. Interact. Mark. **15**, 31–40 (2001)
4. Blackshaw, P., Nazzaro, M.: Consumer-generated-media (CGM) 101: word-of-mouth in the age of the web-fortified consumer. http://www.nielsen-online.com/downloads/us/buzz/nbzm_wp_CGM101.pdf. Accessed 31 July 2006
5. Bridge, D., Healy, P.: The ghostwriter-2.0 case-based reasoning system for making content suggestions to the authors of product reviews. J. Knowl. Based Syst. **29**, 93–103 (2012)
6. Bronner, F., Hoog, R.D.: Vacationers and eWOM: who posts, and why, where, and what? J. Travel Res. **50**(1), 15–26 (2011)
7. Chang, H.C., Holt, G.R.: More than relationship: Chinese interaction and the principle of kuan-hsi. Commun. Q. **39**(3), 251–271 (1991)
8. Chevalier, J.A., Mayzlin, D.: The effect of word of mouth on sales: online book reviews. J. Mark. Res. **43**, 345–354 (2006)
9. Dellarocas, C., Narayan, R.: What motivates consumers to review a product online? A study of the product-specific antecedents of online movie reviews. In: Proceedings of WISE, pp. 1–6. ACM (2006)
10. Dholakia, U.M., Bagozzi, R.P., Pearo, L.K.: A social influence model of consumer participation in network- and small-group-based virtual communities. Int. J. Res. Mark. **21**(3), 241–263 (2004)
11. Dichter, E.: How word-of-mouth advertising works. Harvard Bus. Rev. **44**(Nov-Dec), 147–166 (1966)
12. Dong, R., McCarthy, K., O'Mahony, M.P., Schaal, M. and Smyth, B.: Towards an intelligent reviewer's assistant: recommending topics to help users to write better product reviews. In: Proceedings of the 2012 ACM International Conference on Intelligent User Interfaces (IUI 2012), pp. 159–168 (2012)
13. Dong, R., Schaal, M., O'Mahony, M.P., McCarthy, K., Smyth, B.: Harnessing the experience web to support user-generated product reviews. In: Agudo, B.D., Watson, I. (eds.) ICCBR 2012. LNCS (LNAI), vol. 7466, pp. 62–76. Springer, Heidelberg (2012). https://doi.org/10.1007/978-3-642-32986-9_7

14. Engel, J.F., Blackwell, R.D., Miniard, P.W.: Consumer Behavior, 8th edn. Dryden Press, Fort Worth (1993)
15. Field, A.: Discovering Statistics Using IBM SPSS Statistics. Sage, Beverley Hills (2013)
16. Ghose, A., Ipeirotis, P.: Towards an understanding of the impact of customer sentiment on product sales and review quality. Inf. Technol. Syst. **12**, 1–6 (2006)
17. Godes, D., Mayzlin, D., Chen, Y., et al.: The firm's management of social interactions. Mark. Lett. **16**(3–4), 415–428 (2005)
18. Gretzel, U., Yoo, K.H.: Use and impact of online travel reviews. Inf. Commun. Technol. Tourism **2008**, 35–46 (2008)
19. Hennig-Thurau, T., Gwinner, K.P., Walsh, G., Gremler, D.D.: Electronic word-of-mouth via consumer-opinion platforms: what motivates consumers to articulate themselves on the internet? J. Interact. Mark. **18**(1), 38–52 (2004)
20. Hu, N., Pavlou, P.A., Zhang, J.: Can online reviews reveal a product's true quality? Empirical findings and analytical modeling of online word-of-mouth communication. In: Proceedings of the 7th ACM Conference on Electronic Commerce, pp. 324–330. ACM (2006)
21. Huang, S.W., Tu, P.F., Fu, W.T., Amamzadeh, M.: Leveraging the crowd to improve feature-sentiment analysis of user reviews. In: Proceedings of the 2013 International Conference on Intelligent User Interfaces (IUI 2013), pp. 3–14 (2013)
22. iProspect: iProspect social networking user behavior study. http://www.iprospect.com/about/researchstudy_2007_socialnetworkingbehavior.htm. Accessed April 2007
23. Kim, N., Ulgado, F.: Motivational orientation for word-of-mouth and its relationship with WOM messages. J. Glob. Scholars Mark. Sci. **24**(2), 223–240 (2014)
24. Kim, Y., Srivastava, J.: Impact of social influence in e-commerce decision making. In: Proceedings of the Ninth International Conference on Electronic Commerce, pp. 293–302. ACM (2007)
25. Lee, J., Park, D.H., Han, I.: The different effects of online consumer reviews on consumers' purchase intentions depending on trust in online shopping malls: an advertising perspective. Internet Res. **21**, 187–206 (2011)
26. Ludford, P.J., Dan, C., Dan, F., Terveen, L.: Think different: increasing online community participation using uniqueness and group dissimilarity. In: Sigchi Conference on Human Factors in Computing Systems, pp. 631–638 (2004)
27. Ma, M., Agarwal, R.: Through a glass darkly: information technology design, identity verification, and knowledge contribution in online communities. Inf. Syst. Res. **18**(1), 42–67 (2007)
28. Meyers-Levy, J., Sternthal, B.: Gender differences in the use of message cues and judgments. J. Mark. Res. **28**, 84–96 (1991)
29. Ricci, F., Wietsma, R.T.: Product reviews in travel decision making. Inf. Commun. Technol. Tourism **2006**, 296–307 (2006)
30. Sundaram, D.S., Mitra, K., Webster, C.: Word-of-mouth communications: a motivational analysis. Adv. Consum. Res. **25**, 527–531 (1998)
31. Wang, Y., Fesenmaier, D.R.: Assessing motivation of contribution in online communities: an empirical investigation of an online travel community. Electron. Mark. **13**(1), 33–45 (2003)
32. Wu, J., Wu, Y., Sun, J., Yang, Z.: User reviews and uncertainty assessment: a two stage model of consumers' willingness-to-pay in online markets. Decis. Support Syst. **55**, 175–185 (2013)
33. Yoo, K.H.: What motivates consumers to write online travel reviews? Inf. Technol. Tourism **10**(4), 283–295 (2008)

An Assessment of Users' Cyber Security Risk Tolerance in Reward-Based Exchange

Xinhui Zhan[1(⊠)], Fiona Fui-Hoon Nah[1], and Maggie X. Cheng[2]

[1] Missouri University of Science and Technology, Rolla, MO, USA
{xzxpd, nahf}@mst.edu
[2] New Jersey Institute of Technology, Newark, NJ, USA
maggie.cheng@njit.edu

Abstract. This study examines users' risk-taking behavior in software downloads. We are interested in quantifying the degree of risks that users are willing to take in the cyber security context. We propose conducting an experiment using Amazon's Mechanical Turk to assess the degree of risks that people are willing to take for monetary gains when they download software from uncertified sources.

Keywords: Cyber security · Risk · Human factors · Decision-making

1 Introduction

Security and privacy threats are common on the Internet. To reduce cyber security risks and protect users' private information, mainstream browsers, such as Google Chrome, Safari, and Firefox, are working toward providing security warnings, security indicators, pop-up windows, and other types of warning systems when users are at risk of facing cyber security threats. Identification of security risks depends on user behavior and user response to such warnings [1, 2]. Users are expected to assess cyber security threats before they conduct online transactions, access a URL, or download files or applications.

Some of the previous studies on cyber threats have focused on comparing physical or structural cues and miscues [3, 4]. Researchers have looked at Internet users' ability to interpret cues and miscues that are embedded in webpages or emails. Researchers have also studied human factors, including individual differences, gender differences, human cognitive limitations, and factors influencing how users distinguish between legitimate and fraudulent messages [5, 6]. Awareness and vigilance of cyber threats among Internet users have increased; however, hackers and phishers have become more sophisticated and are able to fabricate content or display. As a result, some phishing websites can easily evade filters [7]. A recent work indicates that phishers framed their phishing messages as gains or benefits to induce users' responses [8]. Phishers and hackers exploit users' susceptibility to deception by providing potential monetary gains or by offering rewards. However, few studies have taken risks into consideration in examining how Internet users make trade-offs between the offered rewards and the risks involved

F. F.-H. Nah and B. S. Xiao (Eds.): HCIBGO 2018, LNCS 10923, pp. 431–441, 2018.
https://doi.org/10.1007/978-3-319-91716-0_34

when they make decisions. Therefore, the goal of this research is to fill this gap in the literature by quantifying users' perceived risks of cyber security threats.

2 Literature Review

2.1 Security Warnings and Cues/Miscues in Cyber Security Decision Making

Understanding human cognition and decision-making process is key to explaining user behavior when faced with cyber security threats. Hence, we need to open up the 'black box' in order to more fully understand users' cyber decisions, such as decisions to click through a link embedded in an email, downloading files from websites, or entering personal information on e-commerce websites or social media.

Several studies have focused on developing better interface and warning design to get users' attention to foster safe cyber security behavior. Security researchers have studied security warnings from multiple perspectives. In a laboratory study to assess the effectiveness of phishing warnings, it was found that more than 90% of the participants fell into the trap of phishing emails without any warnings [9]. On the contrary, when active warnings were popped up on the screen, 79% of the participants avoided the phishing attack. Based on the findings, it was recommended that warnings or indicators be provided to convey clear recommended actions to users even though they may interrupt the users' work. In a large-scale field study that assessed the effectiveness of browser security warnings on the Firefox and Chrome's telemetry platform, it was found that more participants entered personal information when there were no active warning indicators than when active warning indicators were provided [10]. The findings in another study indicate that opinionated framing or design increases adherence by users through decreasing the rate of click-through of SSL warnings [11].

Smith et al. examined user assessment of security levels in e-commerce by varying cues/miscues (i.e., HTTP vs. HTTPS, fraudulent vs. authentic URL, padlocks beside fields) presented on web pages [12]. They conducted an experiment and let users rate their perceived security, trustworthiness, and safety after examining e-commerce web pages that vary in these cues/miscues. They found that padlocks provided beside a field (i.e., miscues) do not affect user perceptions of security but primed subjects to look for more important security cues, such as HTTP vs. HTTPS.

2.2 Susceptibility to Cyber Threats

Human factors, such as past experience, culture, and concerns with Internet security, are expected to influence user security behaviors. In a study that investigated the relationship between demographic characteristics and phishing susceptibility, participants were asked to complete a background survey before they proceeded to a roleplay on phishing, where they were asked to click on a phishing link or enter personal information on phishing websites [13]. The results indicate that women were easier to fall into the phishing trap than men, and 18–25 year old individuals were found to be more susceptible to phishing. The authors provided a possible reason for the gender difference by suggesting that women tend to have less technical knowledge than men. The authors also considered the susceptible behavior to arise from lower levels of education and less experience on the Internet.

Flores et al. examined the influence of demographic, cultural, and personal factors on phishing [14]. Participants from nine organizations in Sweden, USA and India participated in their survey to compare user behavior in response to phishing attacks across users of different cultural backgrounds. The authors did not find any relationship between phishing and age or gender, but employees' observed phishing behavior, intention and security awareness have a significant effect on reactions to phishing. Additionally, the results show that subjects with the intention to resist social engineering and subjects with general security awareness and computer experience have higher resilience to phishing attacks.

In a study by Goel et al., phishing emails were sent to more than 7000 undergraduate students and their responses to the phishing attack were recorded [15]. The phishing message contained different rewards, such as gift cards, tuition relief, bank cards and registrations. The results show that susceptibility varies across users with different demographics (i.e., major and gender). Women were more likely to open phishing emails, with an overall rate of 29.9% as compared to 24.4% among men, but the rate varies based on content in the emails. Participants with business education backgrounds had the highest opening/clicking link rate than those with social science, business and STEM backgrounds. Based on the results, the authors suggest developing context-based education to decrease the susceptibility to phishing attacks on the Internet.

In another study that examined the effect of gender and personality on phishing, females were found to be more vulnerable to phishing [16]. 53% of women were phished as compared to 14% of men. The authors attributed the behavior to women being more comfortable with online shopping and digital communication than men. Moreover, they found women who fell into the phishing trap have a very high correlation with neuroticism. A possible explanation for it is that women tend to admit fears and are more sensitive to emotional needs, which could result in susceptibility to phishing attacks.

Vishwanath studied the influence of e-mail habits and cognitive processing on phishing [17]. Phishing emails were sent to college students to assess their response. They were later asked to complete a survey on their background and demographic information. It was found that heuristic processing and email habits have a positive effect on victimization.

2.3 Framing Effect and Prospect Theory

A key factor that is likely to influence users' cyber decision-making behavior relates to whether information is framed as a gain or a loss. Prospect theory suggests that decision-making under risk depends on whether the potential outcome is perceived as a gain or a loss [18]. Tversky and Kahneman proposed that the choice between options can be affected by the phrasing or framing of the options [19]. A well-known example is the "Asian disease problem," in which subjects were told that "the U.S. is preparing for the outbreak of an unusual Asian disease, which is expected to kill 600 people"

[20, p. 453]. Half of the subjects were given two positively framed options, which contained a certain outcome (i.e., 200 people will be saved) and a risky outcome (i.e., 1/3 probability of saving 600 people and 2/3 probability of saving none). 72% of subjects selected the certain outcome, suggesting that people are risk adverse in the positively framed scenario. In the other half of the subjects that were given two negatively framed options, one with a certain outcome (i.e., 400 people will die) and the other with a risky outcome (i.e., 1/3 probability that none will die and 2/3 probability that 600 will die), 78% chose the risky option, suggesting that people are risk seeking in the negatively framed scenario. Their findings indicate that losses have a greater impact on people's decision making than gains. Furthermore, they discovered two facts that influence people's high sensitivity to losses: reference points and loss aversion. Reference point refers to the status quo, in which people use the current situation as a reference and evaluates the outcome of options with uncertainty. People tend to attach subjective judgments to potential gains and losses. For example, they may associate gains with a positive value, such as a monetary reward, a free product, or a potential earning opportunity, and associate losses with a negative value, such as a penalty, a monetary cost, or a potential loss proposition. Loss aversion refers to the fact that people tend to avoid losses even if the risk is high. In other words, people perceive the value of a loss differently from the value of gaining the same amount. Prospect theory provides important implications for cybersecurity research. Phishing messages can provide incentives that influence users to change their status quo (reference point). To be more specific, hackers and phishers may indicate that they can help you save money, or offer complimentary products or service in order to deceive users.

2.4 Positive and Negative Framing in Cyber Decision-Making

Rosoff et al. [21] conducted an experiment to investigate whether and how human decision-making depends on gain-loss framing and the salience of a prior near-miss experience. They looked at one kind of near-miss experience, resilient near-miss, which refers to the case where a user had a near-miss experience on a cyber-attack [21]. They carried out a 2 by 2 factorial design and manipulated two levels of each of the two independent variables: frame (gain vs. loss framing) and previous near-miss experience (absence vs. presence). Their results show that users tend to follow a safe practice when they have prior experience with a near-miss cyber-attack. They also concluded that females are more likely to select a risky choice compared to men. More importantly, they discovered that framing has a strong influence on decision making.

There are two types of persuasion that have been investigated in the cyber context: reward-based and risk-based [22]. Persuasion techniques can be used to lure users to comply with a recommended course of action. Reward-based persuasion is designed to attract users by offering a reward or benefit. For example, emails that inform the recipient about winning a lottery. Risk-based persuasion is designed to scare people by describing a potential risk. It focuses on persuading people through the fear of threats, such as clicking a link to avoid an account from being suspended or downloading a software to prevent a loss.

Other empirical research on the framing effect has also been studied in the cyber context. Helander and Du examined how the gain-loss frame affects users' purchase intentions in e-commerce [23]. They found that perceiving the value of a product positively (gain frame) affects purchase intentions, and perceiving the risk of credit card fraud and price inflation (loss frame) does not negatively affect user's purchase intentions. Individuals tend to make decisions that are risk-adverse in a gain frame [24]. However, Valecha's study found that the presence of both reward-based persuasion (gain frame) and risk-based persuasion (loss frame) in phishing emails increase the likelihood of response [22]. The influence of framing effects also has some limiting conditions. When subjects were required to explain their choices, the framing effect tended to be reduced [25]. The framing effect can be eliminated if users are encouraged to think through the rationale underlying their choices [26]. Also, if users are experts in a particular area, the framing effect will be reduced [27]. Studies on prospect theory have shown that people tend to avoid risks under gain frames, but seek risks under loss frames [18].

2.5   Cyber Security Risk Assessment and Risk Taking

Assessing risks when making decisions is fundamental to cyber security. Risk taking is often associated with specific actions and environment. Chen, Gates, Li, and Proctor conducted three experiments on Amazon Mechanical Turk [28] to assess the influence of summary risk information on app-installation decisions. Their study focused on the security of the Android operating system because 99% of mobile malware is targeted at the Android system [29]. Risk information was framed as the amount of risk (negative framing) or amount of safety (positive framing) in the experimental conditions. The results suggest that summary information that was positively framed as safety has a greater effect on app-installation decisions than summary information that was negatively framed as risks. Hence, a valid risk index that is framed positively by focusing on safety can be developed to improve users' app-installation decisions.

Compared to adults, teens use the Internet extensively in terms of social networking sites, online shopping, and interactive communications. In a study on teens' perceived safety and risk taking behavior in online chat sites, it was found that teens with more social discomfort were less likely to take risks, and those who trusted their online friends were more likely to take risks [30].

Risk has been estimated using the formula: Risk = Threat × Vulnerability × Consequence [31]. The formula is based on the Risk Analysis and Management for Critical Asset Protection (RAMCAP) model with the definition of the terms provided in Table 1.

3   Research Methodology

A within-subject experiment is proposed to explore the relationship between cyber security risks and their associated monetary values. We will use a scenario-based survey [32] in the experiment to identify the users' trade-off decisions between cyber security risks and the minimum monetary value gains for users to take the associated risks. Furthermore, by varying the levels of cyber security risks that users face, we can

Table 1. Definitions of terms by RAMCAP

Term	RAMCAP definition
Risk	The potential for loss or harm due to the likelihood of an unwanted event and its adverse consequences
Consequence	The outcome of an event occurrence, including immediate, short- and long-term, and direct and indirect losses and effects. Losses may include human casualties, monetary and economic damages, and environmental impact, and may also include less tangible and therefore less quantifiable effects, including political ramifications, decreased morale, and reductions in operational effectiveness
Threat	Any indication, circumstance, or event with the potential to cause the loss of, or damage to, an asset or population. In the analysis of risk, threat is based on the analysis of the intention and capability of an adversary to undertake actions that would be detrimental to an asset or population
Vulnerability	Any weakness in an asset's or infrastructure's design, implementation, or operation that can be exploited by an adversary. Such weaknesses can occur in building characteristics, equipment properties, personnel behavior, locations of people, equipment and buildings, or operational and personnel practices

identify the minimum monetary value gains to entice users to take different levels of risks. We will recruit our research subjects through Amazon Mechanical Turk.

3.1   Research Design and Task/Scenarios

We are interested in quantifying the gains in monetary values associated with different levels of risks that users are willing to take. Through a series of scenarios, where subjects have to make a choice between two options given to them in each scenario, we will determine the threshold level for risk tolerance at which a user would not take any risk beyond that level. The threshold is the point at which the user would not risk any cyber threats for any amount of monetary value gain. Figure 1 shows an example of the threshold level for risk tolerance of a user. In this case, the user can tolerate up to 50% risk for a monetary value gain, but would not tolerate any risk beyond that level regardless of any amount of monetary value gain.

In order to determine the threshold level for risk tolerance, we use the scenario-based approach in which subjects have to make a selection between two choices for every scenario posed to them. An example of a scenario is as follows:

> *"You need to download a software named Accelerator that has a market price of $100 onto your primary computer.*
> *In this scenario, you have to make a choice between the following two options:*
> **Option A:** *Download Accelerator at the* **full price of $100** *with* **0% of cyber security risks.**
> **Option B:** *Download Accelerator at a* **discounted price of $90** *(i.e.,* **$10 or 10% saving)** *[varying monetary value] with* **5% of cyber security risks** *[varying risk level]."*
> Please indicate your choice (between option A and B): _____

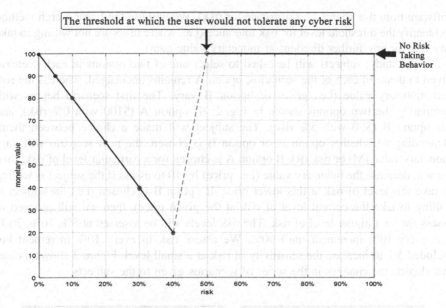

Fig. 1. Illustration of the threshold for risk tolerance

Figure 2 shows the design of a scenario-based question in which a subject needs to select a choice between two options.

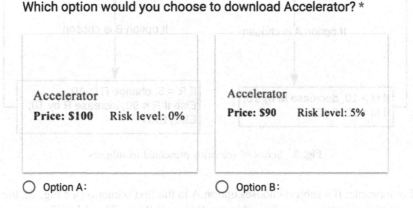

Fig. 2. Scenario-based question

3.2 Variables and Operationalizations

Two independent variables will be considered: monetary value gain and cyber security risk. The monetary value gain is the difference between the full and offering prices of the software. Risk is operationalized as the vulnerability of cyber threats (i.e. we use the percentage of users who reported virus/spyware/malware after downloading the software from this source as a surrogate for risk). We will use the linear search method to identify the threshold level for risk tolerance (i.e., where users are not willing to take any risk for any further discount or monetary value gain).

In the study, subjects will be asked to select one of two options in each scenario given to them. In each of the scenarios, option A remains unchanged, whereas the risk and monetary value (i.e., price) of option B vary. The first scenario begins with comparing the two options shown in Fig. 2: (i) option A ($100 with 0% risk), and (ii) option B ($90 with 5% risk). The subject will make a choice between them. Depending on whether option A or option B is chosen, the next scenario will vary monetary value (M) or risk (R). If option A is chosen for a particular level of risk, then we will decrease the monetary value (i.e., price) by 10 to assess if the subject is willing to take this level of risk at this lower price. If option B is chosen (i.e., the subject is willing to take the current level of risk at the given price), then we will proceed to assess the next higher level of risk. The risk levels will be assessed at 5%, 10%, 20%, and every 10% increment until 90%. We assess risk in every 10% increment but included 5% to increase the sensitivity of risk at a small level. Figure 3 shows a chart that depicts the changes in the series of scenarios given to the subjects.

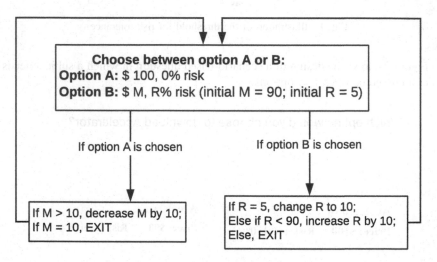

Fig. 3. Series of scenarios presented to subjects

For example: If a subject chooses option A in the first scenario (see Fig. 2), the next scenario of option B given to the subject will be as follows: The risk will remain at 5% and the monetary value will decrease by $10 from $90 to $80 in option B, which means the subject will need to make a choice between the following two options in the second scenario: option A ($100 with 0% risk) and option B ($80 with 5% risk). If the subject chooses A again, the previous step will repeat, and the following two options will be shown in the third scenario: option A ($100 with 0% risk) and option B ($70 with 5% risk). If option A is repeatedly chosen, this process will iterate until the monetary value equals $10 after which no more scenarios will be presented if option A is chosen when option B of monetary value (i.e., price) of $10 at 5% risk is presented. In this case, it can be said that this subject is intolerant of risks, even if the price is low (or the monetary value gain is high). On the other hand, if the subject chooses option A in the first scenario but option B in the second scenario, the monetary value (i.e., price) remains unchanged ($80) but the risk will be increased to the next level, which is 10%. In this case, the subject will be given the following two options in the third scenario: option A ($100 with 0% risk) and option B ($[previous value = 80] with 10% risk).

As another example, if the subject chooses option B in the first scenario (see Fig. 2), the monetary value is fixed at $90 and the risk will increase to 10%. Hence, the next or second scenario will show the following two options: option A ($100 with 0% risk) and option B ($90 with 10% risk). If the subject chooses B again, the previous step will iterate (i.e., risk level is increased) until the subject rejects the risky option and chooses option A.

In general, if the subject chooses option A and the monetary value (i.e., price) equals $10, the experiment ends. The experiment also ends if option B is chosen and risk is 90%.

We will include control variables in our survey as indicated below.

- Demographic factors
- Past cyber-attack experience, individual security concerns, Internet habits (potential moderating variables)

4 Expected Contributions

The main contribution of this research is to offer a better understanding of the trade-off decisions that users make between monetary value gains and risks of cyber security threats. The findings of the proposed study will not only provide a distribution of users' threshold levels for risk tolerance, but will also illustrate whether the distribution of the relationship between monetary value gains and cyber risks of users is linear, concave, or convex. With the knowledge gained from this research, we hope to design better mechanisms and warning systems to mitigate the risks taken by users. Additionally, the findings from this research could be useful for privacy policy design, security warning design, and user interaction design.

Acknowledgements. This research is supported by National Science Foundation grant CNS/1537538 and the Laboratory for Information Technology at Missouri University of Science and Technology.

References

1. Bresz, F.P.: People—often the weakest link in security, but one of the best places to start. J. Health Care Compliance **6**(4), 57–60 (2004)
2. Cranor, L.F.: A framework for reasoning about the human in the loop. In: Proceedings of the 1st Conference on Usability, Psychology, and Security, vol. 8, pp. 1–15 (2008)

3. Jakobsson, M., Ratkiewicz, J.: Designing ethical phishing experiments: a study of (ROT13) rOn1 query features. In: Proceedings of the 15th International Conference on World Wide Web, pp. 513–522. ACM (2006)
4. Darwish, A., Bataineh, E.: Eye tracking analysis of browser security indicators. In: International Conference on Computer Systems and Industrial Informatics, pp. 1–6 (2012)
5. Dhamija, R., Tygar, J.D., Hearst, M.: Why phishing works. In: Proceedings of the SIGCHI Conference on Human Factors in Computing Systems, pp. 581–590. ACM (2006)
6. Downs, J.S., Holbrook, M.B., Cranor, L.F.: Decision strategies and susceptibility to phishing. In: Proceedings of the Second Symposium on Usable Privacy and Security, pp. 79–90. ACM (2006)
7. Dong, L., Han, Z., Petropulu, A.P., Poor, H.V.: Improving wireless physical layer security via cooperating relays. IEEE Trans. Sig. Process. **58**(3), 1875–1888 (2010)
8. Wright, R.T., Jensen, M.L., Thatcher, J.B., Dinger, M., Marett, K.: Research note—influence techniques in phishing attacks: an examination of vulnerability and resistance. Inf. Syst. Res. **25**(2), 385–400 (2014)
9. Egelman, S., Cranor, L.F., Hong, J.: You've been warned: an empirical study of the effectiveness of web browser phishing warnings. In: Proceedings of the SIGCHI Conference on Human Factors in Computing Systems, pp. 1065–1074. ACM (2008)
10. Akhawe, D., Felt, A.P.: Alice in Warningland: a large-scale field study of browser security warning effectiveness. In: USENIX Security Symposium, vol. 13, pp. 257–272 (2013)
11. Felt, A.P., Ainslie, A., Reeder, R.W., Consolvo, S., Thyagaraja, S., Bettes, A., Harris, H., Grimes, J.: Improving SSL warnings: comprehension and adherence. In: Proceedings of the 33rd Annual ACM Conference on Human Factors in Computing Systems, pp. 2893–2902. ACM (2015)
12. Smith, S.N., Nah, F.F.-H., Cheng, M.X.: The impact of security cues on user perceived security in e-commerce. In: Tryfonas, T. (ed.) HAS 2016. LNCS, vol. 9750, pp. 164–173. Springer, Cham (2016). https://doi.org/10.1007/978-3-319-39381-0_15
13. Sheng, S., Holbrook, M., Kumaraguru, P., Cranor, L.F., Downs, J.: Who falls for phish? A demographic analysis of phishing susceptibility and effectiveness of interventions. In: Proceedings of the SIGCHI Conference on Human Factors in Computing Systems, pp. 373–382 (2010)
14. Flores, W.R., Holm, H., Nohlberg, M., Ekstedt, M.: Investigating personal determinants of phishing and the effect of national culture. Inf. Comput. Secur. **23**(2), 178–199 (2015)
15. Goel, S., Williams, K., Dincelli, E.: Got phished? Internet security and human vulnerability. J. Assoc. Inf. Syst. **18**(1), 22–44 (2017)
16. Halevi, T., Lewis, J., Memon, N.: Phishing, personality traits and Facebook. arXiv preprint arXiv:1301.7643 (2013)
17. Vishwanath, A.: Examining the distinct antecedents of e-mail habits and its influence on the outcomes of a phishing attack. J. Comput.-Mediat. Commun. **20**(5), 570–584 (2015)
18. Kahneman, D., Tversky, A.: Prospect theory: an analysis of decision under risk. Econometrica **47**(2), 263–291 (1979)
19. Tversky, A., Kahneman, D.: Evidential impact of base rates. No. TR-4. Stanford University, Department of Psychology (1981). http://www.dtic.mil/dtic/tr/fulltext/u2/a099501.pdf
20. Tversky, A., Kahneman, D.: The framing of decisions and the psychology of choice. Science **211**(4481), 453–458 (1981)
21. Rosoff, H., Cui, J., John, R.S.: Heuristics and biases in cyber security dilemmas. Environ. Syst. Decis. **33**(4), 517–529 (2013)

22. Valecha, R., Chen, R., Herath, T., Vishwanath, A., Wang, J.R., Rao, H.R.: Reward-based and risk-based persuasion in phishing emails. In: Proceedings of the 2016 Dewald Roode Workshop on Information Systems Security Research, IFIP WG8.11/WG11.13, pp. 1–18 (2016)

23. Helander, M.G., Du, X.: From Kano to Kahneman. A comparison of models to predict customer needs. In: Proceedings of the Conference on TQM and Human Factors, pp. 322–329 (1999)

24. Schroeder, N.J., Grimaila, M.R., Schroeder, N.: Revealing prospect theory bias in information security decision making. In: Emerging Trends and Challenges in Information Technology Management: Information Resources Management Association International Conference, pp. 176–179 (2006)

25. Larrick, R.P., Smith, E.E., Yates, J.F.: Reflecting on the reflection effect: disrupting the effects of framing through thought. In: Meetings of the Society of Judgment and Decision Making, November, St. Louis, MO (1992)

26. Takemura, K.: Influence of elaboration on the framing of decision. J. Psychol. **128**(1), 33–39 (1994)

27. Davis, M.A., Bobko, P.: Contextual effects on escalation processes in public sector decision making. Organ. Behav. Hum. Decis. Process. **37**(1), 121–138 (1986)

28. Chen, J., Gates, C.S., Li, N., Proctor, R.W.: Influence of risk/safety information framing on android app-installation decisions. J. Cogn. Eng. Decis. Mak. **9**(2), 149–168 (2015)

29. Cisco Systems, Inc.: Cisco 2014 annual security report. https://www.cisco.com/web/offer/gist_ty2_asset/Cisco_2014_ASR.pdf. Accessed 18 Feb 2014

30. McCarty, C., Prawitz, A.D., Derscheid, L.E., Montgomery, B.: Perceived safety and teen risk taking in online chat sites. Cyberpsychol. Behav. Soc. Netw. **14**(3), 169–174 (2011)

31. Cox Jr., L.A.: Some limitations of "risk = threat x vulnerability x consequence" for risk analysis of terrorist attacks. Risk Anal. **28**(6), 1749–1761 (2008)

32. Sheng, H., Nah, F., Siau, K.: An experimental study on u-commerce adoption: impact of personalization and privacy concerns. J. Assoc. Inf. Syst. **9**(6), 344–376 (2008)

Social Media and Social Communities in Business

Effect of Gamification on Intrinsic Motivation

Edna Chan[1], Fiona Fui-Hoon Nah[2], Qizhang Liu[3($\boxtimes$)], and Zhiwei Lu[2]

[1] Singapore Polytechnic, Singapore, Singapore
Edna_CHAN@sp.edu.sg
[2] Missouri University of Science and Technology, Rolla, MO, USA
{nahf,zlkh2}@mst.edu
[3] National University of Singapore, Singapore, Singapore
bizlqz@nus.edu.sg

Abstract. Gamification has been increasing in popularity in a variety of online context, including online learning. However, its impact on intrinsic motivation is still unclear. In this research, we carried out an experiment to assess the impact of providing two gamification features in an online learning system – point and leaderboard – on intrinsic motivation.

Keywords: Gamification · Points · Leaderboard · Intrinsic motivation
Online learning

1 Introduction

Gamification is defined as the use of game design elements in non-game contexts [1]. The term "gamification" was first used by a British computer programmer, Pelling, in late 2002. His original definition of gamification is to make electronic transactions enjoyable and fast through applying game-like accelerated user interface design [2]. Although the initial attempt ended in failure, the concept of gamification has become popular in both industry and academia [3]. Gamification has been applied in a variety of areas such as business and education to improve user experience and engagement [4].

Recently, gamification has attracted increasing interest across a wide range of contexts as a way to increase user engagement. Marketsandmarkets.com forecast the global gamification market to grow from USD 1.65 billion in 2015 to USD 11.10 billion by 2020 [5]. Companies are adopting gamification to enrich customer loyalty and employee productivity [6].

The rapid evolution in industry is mirrored in education. Students are becoming more technology-savvy, team-oriented, resourceful, and better at multi-tasking [7]. Motivation is considered as a key determinant, more important than ever, of engaging students in learning activities and allowing them to retain knowledge [8]. Part of educators' role is to motivate students, on top of knowledge transfer. However, this mission is becoming more challenging as students may now value rewards that are changed frequently to meet changing expectations and demands. Gamification has recently become a popular initiative adopted by educators worldwide as means of increasing motivation.

© Springer International Publishing AG, part of Springer Nature 2018
F. F.-H. Nah and B. S. Xiao (Eds.): HCIBGO 2018, LNCS 10923, pp. 445–454, 2018.
https://doi.org/10.1007/978-3-319-91716-0_35

However, the pros and cons of using gamification in education to capture students' interest and attention have been debated in the literature [9, 10]. Although gamification is expected to have a positive impact on engagement, participation, and learning behaviors, learner engagement needs to be understood in terms of intrinsic motivation to have a long-term effect [11, 12]. Hence, this research examines the effect of gamification on intrinsic motivation in online learning.

2   Background and Literature Review

The essential component of gamification is a reward system with points and leaderboards being two of the most basic patterns of rewards [6, 13]. A fun part of game playing is the failure and errors made in the process which lead to the final success. Therefore, the goal of gamification is not to punish failure but to associate a positive relationship with it by creating rapid feedback cycles and keeping the stakes for individual learning episodes low [9]. The ultimate objective is to nurture a positive learning behavior and enrich students' interest in learning. However, many have cautioned against the over-reliance on gamification elements, as they may diminish intrinsic interest in both game- and non-game contexts, ultimately leading users to stop interacting with the application or service altogether [14].

There are ten categories of motivational affordances in gamification: *Points, Leaderboards, Badges, Levels, Story/Theme, Clear Goals, Feedback, Rewards, Progress, and Challenge* [15]. *Points, Badges*, and *Leaderboards,* which are also called the PBL triad, are the most commonly used motivational affordances [6, 13, 16].

Points. Points are the heart of any gaming system – the accumulation of points is shared among players, or between the designer and the players. The point system includes experience points, redeemable points, skill points, karma points, and reputation points. Players can earn experience points based on specific activities in the system. Redeemable points serve as currencies in the virtual economy and can be in the form of coins, bucks, cash, etc. Players can earn redeemable points and exchange them for things they want. Skill points are assigned based on a player's level of competence in completing specific activities. Karma points are donated by others and they create a behavioral path for user reward and altruism. Reputation points act as a proxy for trust between two or more parties.

Badges. Badges offer encouragement and recognition to players. Badges are also used to indicate the completion of goals. Badges are sometimes used to replace levels.

Leaderboards. Leaderboards utilize a ranking system, which makes comparisons between players. There are two types of *leaderboards*: no-disincentive leaderboards and infinite leaderboards. The no-disincentive leaderboards will not show the players' literal ranking unless the players are in the top ranking; it can reduce the potential self-esteem damage. The infinite leaderboards show every player ordered by the rank. Players can slice and dice the leaderboard or display the leaderboard with a limited view. High rankings on the leaderboards can bring positive effects along with a high degree of pressure to continue to do well [17].

Gamification has been widely applied in several contexts, such as commerce, education/learning, health/exercise, work, innovation/ideation, data gathering, and marketing [15]. The motivational power of gamification in the education context has been gaining increasing attention in recent years. The reason for gamifying education is to increase the engagement of students and improve their performance/achievement, motivation, and sense of accomplishment [18–20]. Bunchball introduced game mechanics and game dynamics, where game mechanics are actions, behaviors, and control mechanisms to gamify an activity, and game dynamics relate to desires and motivations [21]. Table 1 shows the game dynamics identified by Bunchball for six game mechanisms: points, levels, challenges, virtual goods and spaces, leaderboards, and gifts/charity [21].

Table 1. Game mechanics and dynamics [21]

Game mechanics	Game dynamics
Points	Reward
Levels	Status
Challenges	Achievement
Virtual goods and spaces	Self-expression
Leaderboards	Competition
Gifts and charity	Altruism

Gamification in education can bring benefits to students and teachers as compared with traditional learning methods. In the school setting, information is usually applied out of the context of actual use or deviating from the user's purpose, while gamification provides information on demand in a just-in-time basis. Learning in traditional schools is designed based on the lowest common denominator; however, learning from games is challenging but do-able [22]. Gamification in education gives positive feedback to students, and students can be encouraged to push forward [18]. Simões et al. introduced a gamification framework, which allows teachers to create challenges based on the student's level of knowledge, achieve learning objectives through multiple ways, provide feedback and rewards, select the appropriate game mechanics, and use competitions to promote valuable behaviors [23]. Students also deal with failure as part of the learning process, explore new roles, and recognize and monitor their progress [23]. On the other hand, a study by Hanus and Fox on the use of a leaderboard and badges in a classroom setting found that the use of these game mechanics may damage educational outcomes [17]. Over time, students taking the gamified course have lower levels of intrinsic motivation, satisfaction, and empowerment than students from the non-gamified course. They concluded that the combination of leaderboards, badges, and competition mechanics will not improve educational outcomes [17]. Mekler et al. found that points, levels, and leaderboards increased user performance but has no effect on competence, autonomy or intrinsic motivation in carrying out an image annotation task [24, 25]. Hence, the literature has provided inconsistent findings from positive to neutral to negative effects of gamification.

3 Theoretical Foundation and Hypotheses

In this research, we will focus on studying the impact of using the leaderboard and point system in online education. Based on self-determination theory and cognitive evaluation theory [26–28], we will hypothesize the effects of using a leaderboard and the point system on intrinsic motivation in online education. Intrinsic motivation refers to people's interests and values that are in line with their basic psychological needs.

The self-determination theory is concerned with human motivation and personality [26–28]. It identifies three basic psychological or innate needs of humans that drive intrinsic motivation: competence, autonomy, and relatedness. Cognitive evaluation theory is a sub-theory within self-determination theory that focuses on competence and autonomy, and explains variability in intrinsic motivation by considering social and environmental factors [26, 27]. Factors that support or enhance the basic needs can contribute to intrinsic motivation and optimal functioning, while factors that thwart the basic needs can reduce intrinsic motivation and performance. In other words, external events, such as feedback, impact intrinsic motivation differently depending on whether they are considered informational or controlling. When an external event is perceived as informational, it enhances one's internal perceived locus of causality (or autonomy) and perceived competence, which in turn increase intrinsic motivation. When an external event is perceived as controlling, it enhances one's external perceived locus of causality (i.e., little or no autonomy), which reduces intrinsic motivation.

Because the point system is provided to learners as an informational feedback to support their learning process, we expect the point system to enhance the learners' internal perceived locus of causality and perceived competence, which in turn is expected to increase the learners' intrinsic motivation. Hence, the following hypothesis is proposed:

H1: The point system increases learners' intrinsic motivation.

A leaderboard typically displays only the scores and rankings of the top performers. The use of a leaderboard creates competition among learners, and rewards only the top performers. By creating a competition in an online learning environment, the leaderboard can be perceived to be controlling and can increase learners' perceived external locus of causality, which reduces their intrinsic motivation. Hence, the following hypothesis is proposed:

H2: The leaderboard decreases learners' intrinsic motivation.

Our research model is shown in Fig. 1.

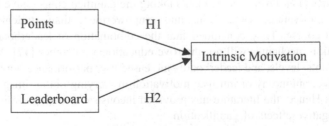

Fig. 1. Research model

4   Research Methodology

We used an experimental approach to study the effect of using a leaderboard and points on intrinsic motivation. The study was conducted on eight classes taking a bridging mathematics module in Singapore Polytechnic during semester 2 of the 2016/17 academic year. Students had access to a Learning Analytics Networked Tutoring System (LearningANTS), which is an online system that supports differentiated learning and facilitates learning analytics with in-system gamification features. They had access to the system for tutorial for over a period of one month. Two mathematics topics – solving trigonometric equations and rules of differentiation - were rolled out. The system adaptively released the topics to students. There were altogether four difficulty levels of learning achievement in LearningANTS – Beginner, Advanced Beginner, Competent, and Expert – for each topic. Starting from the Beginner level, students worked on questions and levelled up to the next achievement level when they performed well for the level. Students' progression through the difficulty levels for each topic were dependent on their own ability.

As illustrated in Fig. 2, LearningANTS automatically tracked students' learning progress and their learning progress was presented in a straight-forward way to help students monitor their own learning. Students could review all the questions that they had attempted, and communicate with their teachers via a feedback feature in the system if they needed help with the questions. At the same time, teachers could monitor the learning progress of their class through the system. Doing so facilitated the face-to-face tutorial sessions as teachers were then able to offer more targeted help to the class, for example, by going over questions with which a majority of the students had trouble, as well as dive down to help an individual student who was struggling to progress in the system.

The in-system gamification features – leaderboard and points – were set up for the eight classes using a 2 × 2 experimental design shown in Table 2.

For the study, all teachers were briefed prior to the deployment of the system that they should use the system for an hour during tutorial class for each planned topic. Since only two topics were planned, teachers were expected to use the system for two hours during face-to-face tutorials in total for the period of the study. Other than the deliberate use of the system in class for the two hours, all teachers were informed not to make any effort in requiring students to use the system during other times, whether on campus or outside campus.

At the end of the study, students completed a questionnaire that captured their intrinsic motivation using the following four questions adopted from [29].

1. I use LearningANTS because I think it is interesting.
2. I use LearningANTS because I think it is nice.
3. I use LearningANTS because I think it is fun.
4. I use LearningANTS because I feel good when I use it.

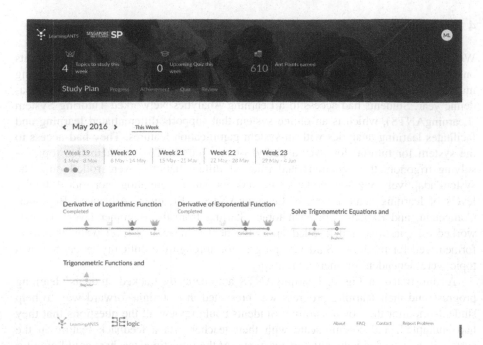

Fig. 2. Screen of student progress in LearningANTS

Table 2. Set-up of classes for gamification features - Leaderboard and Points

Gamification feature	No leaderboard	Leaderboard
No points	2 classes	2 classes
Points	2 classes	2 classes

4.1 LearningANTS

LearningANTS is an online learning system co-developed by Singapore Polytechnic and 3ELOGIC under the funding of Singapore Government's Public-Private Co-Innovation Partnership Fund. It was developed with two missions:

- To support data-driven differentiated learning, i.e., all students within a classroom can learn effectively, regardless of the difference in their abilities
- To enable fact-based teaching so that educators can teach more effectively with data collected on students' learning

Figure 3 shows a screen capture of LearningANTS from the viewpoint of Student Chenerd Soh. Student Soh has earned a total of 1890 points and is currently ranked first on the leaderboard. The leaderboard displays the name and corresponding points earned by the top five students.

Fig. 3. Screen of the Leaderboard in LearningANTS

5   Preliminary Results

We received a total of 67 completed questionnaires from the student subjects. The distribution of these responses across the four conditions is shown in Table 3.

Table 3. Distribution of completed responses across the four conditions

Gamification feature	No leaderboard	Leaderboard
No points	7 subjects	17 subjects
Points	27 subjects	16 subjects

Our Cronbach's alpha coefficient for the four-item measure of intrinsic motivation is 0.93, indicating that it has a very high internal consistency or reliability. From the data analysis carried out using ANOVA, the main effect for points is not significant ($p = 0.414 > 0.05$), thus H1 is not supported. The main effect for the leaderboard is significant ($p = 0.001 < 0.05$), thus H2 is supported. More interestingly, there is an observed interaction between points and the leaderboard ($p = 0.002$), where the condition with no point system and no leaderboard produced the highest intrinsic motivation among the four conditions, and the condition with the leaderboard but no point system produced the lowest intrinsic motivation.

The results suggest that gamification using the leaderboard in an online learning context can have a detrimental effect on intrinsic motivation of learners, especially when a point system is not available to provide feedback on the learning progress. The leaderboard can serve as a disincentive and be perceived as a 'controlling' factor due to the intense competition created, thus taking away intrinsic motivation from learners. When the leaderboard is not used, learners' intrinsic motivation is higher when there is no point system than when there is a point system. However, when a leaderboard is used, learners' intrinsic motivation is higher when there is a point system than when a point system is not used. Hence, the point system has a positive effect on intrinsic motivation when a leaderboard is present and a negative effect on intrinsic motivation when a leaderboard is not used. Overall, from the perspective of intrinsic motivation, it seems gamification using the leaderboard and the point system creates a negative effect on online learning.

6   Limitations and Future Research

One limitation of this research is that completing the questionnaire was optional and hence, not all students completed it. Hence, our results may be skewed toward students who tended to have high intrinsic motivation in learning. If the subjects were students with high intrinsic motivation in learning, offering gamification could be unnecessary and even detrimental to their motivation due to the gamification features being perceived as controlling. In future research, we may require all students to fill out the questionnaire.

The current research does not examine other variables such as end-of-semester performance in mathematics, actual time spent using the LearningANTS system, extrinsic motivation, user engagement, or student performance (points/levels) indicated by the LearningANTS system. It also does not consider covariates such as gender, age, GPA, motivation to learn, background, past or previous performance in mathematics, and involvement or interest in this course. We hope to incorporate these variables into our future research to provide a more complete understanding on the effect of gamification on students' learning. We are also interested to test a more complete set of gamification features in future research [15, 30].

Although this study was conducted in the field (i.e., an educational institution), we hope to further examine the use of the LearningANTS system in other educational institutions in order to extend the generalizability of the findings. We are also interested in examining the use of the LearningANTS system as a learning management system in organizational settings.

7   Conclusions

Our research findings suggest that highly motivated students may not need gamification. We also found that the use of leaderboards has a detrimental effect on intrinsic motivation in learning, especially when the point system is not provided as a form of feedback. Hence, educational institutions need to be very careful in implementing gamification in order not to negatively affect the intrinsic motivation of the learners. We also found that intrinsic motivation tends to be highest when both the leaderboard and point system are not provided. We believe that when both the leaderboard and the point system are not available, learners tend to adopt the mastery goal over the performance goal due to the lack of feedback on their overall performance. With a mastery goal in mind, students' intrinsic motivation is heightened. When a leaderboard is provided without a point system, learners may feel controlled or pressured to become a top performer, which decreases their intrinsic motivation. Hence, caution is needed to carefully analyze the impact of gamification in education.

References

1. Deterding, S., Dixon, D., Khaled, R., Nacke, L.: From game design elements to gamefulness: defining gamification. In: Proceedings of the 15th International Academic MindTrek Conference, pp. 9–15 (2011)
2. Pelling, N.: The (short) prehistory of "gamification" (2011). https://nanodome.wordpress.com/2011/08/09/the-short-prehistory-of-gamification
3. Huotari, K., Hamari, J.: Defining gamification: a service marketing perspective. In: Proceeding of the 16th International Academic MindTrek Conference, pp. 17–22 (2012)
4. Deterding, S., Sicart, M., Nacke, L., O'Hara, K., Dixon, D.: Gamification: using game-design elements in non-gaming contexts. In: CHI 2011 Extended Abstracts on Human Factors in Computing Systems, pp. 2425–2428 (2011)
5. Marketsandmarkets.com: Gamification market by solution (consumer driven and enterprise driven), applications (sales and marketing), deployment type (on-premises and cloud), user type (large enterprise, SMBs), industry and region - global forecast to 2020 (2016). https://www.marketsandmarkets.com/Market-Reports/gamification-market-991.html
6. Zichermann, G., Cunningham, C.: Gamification by Design: Implementing Game Mechanics in Web and Mobile Apps. O'Reilly Media, Sebastopol (2011)
7. Borges, N.J., Manuel, R.S., Elam, C.L., Jones, B.J.: Differences in motives between millennial and generation X medical students. Med. Educ. **44**, 570–576 (2010)
8. Brophy, J.E.: Motivating Students to Learn. Routledge, New York (2013)
9. Lee, J., Hammer, J.: Gamification in education: what, how, why bother? Acad. Exch. Q. **15** (2), 146–151 (2011)
10. Domínguez, A., Saenz-de-Navarrete, J., de-Marcos, L., Fernández-Sanz, L., Pagés, C., Martínez-Herráiz, J.-J.: Gamifying learning experiences: practical implications and outcomes. Comput. Educ. **63**, 380–392 (2013)
11. Deci, E.L., Koestner, R., Ryan, R.M.: Extrinsic rewards and intrinsic motivation in education: reconsidered once again. Rev. Educ. Res. **71**(1), 1–27 (2001)
12. Buckley, P., Doyle, E.: Gamification and student motivation. Interact. Learn. Environ. **24**(6), 1162–1175 (2016)
13. Zagal, J.P., Mateas, M., Fernandez-Vara, C., Hochhalter, B., Lichti, N.: Towards an ontological language for game analysis. In: Proceedings of International DiGRA Conference, pp. 3–14 (2005)
14. Deterding, S.: Situated motivational affordances of game elements: a conceptual model. In: Gamification: Using Game Design Elements in Non-gaming Contexts, a Workshop at CHI (2011)
15. Hamari, J., Koivisto, J., Sarsa, H.: Does gamification work? A literature review of empirical studies on gamification. In: Proceedings of the 47th Hawaii International Conference on System Sciences, pp. 3025–3034 (2014)
16. Nah, F.F.-H., Daggubati, L.S., Tarigonda, A., Nuvvula, R.V., Turel, O.: Effects of the use of points, leaderboards and badges on in-game purchases of virtual goods. In: Nah, F.F.-H., Tan, C.-H. (eds.) HCIB 2015. LNCS, vol. 9191, pp. 525–531. Springer, Cham (2015). https://doi.org/10.1007/978-3-319-20895-4_48
17. Hanus, M.D., Fox, J.: Assessing the effects of gamification in the classroom: a longitudinal study on intrinsic motivation, social comparison, satisfaction, effort, and academic performance. Comput. Educ. **80**, 152–161 (2015)
18. Muntean, C.I.: Raising engagement in e-learning through gamification. In: Proceedings of the 6th International Conference on Virtual Learning, pp. 323–329 (2011)

19. Nah, F.F.-H., Telaprolu, V.R., Rallapalli, S., Venkata, P.R.: Gamification of education using computer games. In: Yamamoto, S. (ed.) HIMI 2013. LNCS, vol. 8018, pp. 99–107. Springer, Heidelberg (2013). https://doi.org/10.1007/978-3-642-39226-9_12

20. Nah, F.F.-H., Zeng, Q., Telaprolu, V.R., Ayyappa, A.P., Eschenbrenner, B.: Gamification of education: a review of literature. In: Nah, F.F.-H. (ed.) HCIB 2014. LNCS, vol. 8527, pp. 401–409. Springer, Cham (2014). https://doi.org/10.1007/978-3-319-07293-7_39

21. Bunchball Inc.: Gamification 101: an introduction to the use of game dynamics to influence behavior. White Paper. Bunchball Inc. (2010). https://www.bunchball.com/gamification101

22. Gee, J.P.: What video games have to teach us about learning and literacy. Comput. Entertain. 1(1), 1–4 (2003)

23. Simões, J., Redondo, R.D., Vilas, A.F.: A social gamification framework for a K-6 learning platform. Comput. Hum. Behav. 29(2), 345–353 (2013)

24. Mekler, E.D., Bruhlmann, F., Opwis, K., Tuch, A.N.: Do points, levels and leaderboards harm intrinsic motivation? An empirical analysis of common gamification elements. In: Proceedings of Gamification, pp. 66–73 (2013)

25. Mekler, E.D., Bruhlmann, F., Tuch, A.N., Opwis, K.: Towards understanding the effects of individual gamification elements on intrinsic motivation and performance. Comput. Hum. Behav. 71, 525–534 (2017)

26. Deci, E.L., Ryan, R.M.: Intrinsic Motivation and Self-Determination in Human Behavior. Plenum, New York (1985)

27. Deci, E.L., Ryan, R.M.: The "what" and "why" of goal pursuits: human needs and the self-determination of behavior. Psychol. Inq. 11(4), 227–268 (2000)

28. Ryan, R.M., Deci, E.L.: Self-determination theory and the facilitation of intrinsic motivation, social development and well-being. Am. Psychol. 55(1), 68–78 (2000)

29. Guay, F., Vallerand, R.J., Blanchard, C.: On the assessment of situational intrinsic and extrinsic motivation: the situational motivation scale (SIMS). Motiv. Emot. 24, 121–175 (2000)

30. Nah, F., Eschenbrenner, B., Zeng, Q., Telaprolu, V., Sepehr, S.: Flow in gaming: literature synthesis and framework development. Int. J. Inf. Syst. Manag. 1(1/2), 83–124 (2014)

Role of Social Media in Public Accounting Firms

Brenda Eschenbrenner[1]($\boxtimes$), Fiona Fui-Hoon Nah[2], and Zhiwei Lu[2]

[1] University of Nebraska at Kearney, Kearney, NE, USA
eschenbrenbl@unk.edu
[2] Missouri University of Science and Technology, Rolla, MO, USA
{nahf, zlkh2}@mst.edu

Abstract. Social media has been widely used for both professional and personal communications. Businesses recognize the importance of social media and are using them to fulfill various business objectives. In this paper, we focus on analyzing the business objectives of public accounting firms that have both a firm-wide main page and a career page on Facebook. More specifically, we compare the business objectives they are achieving with their firm-wide main pages versus career pages. We not only find differences in the objectives that are being achieved, but also identify other objectives that are not actively being pursued on either page but may be considered in the future.

Keywords: Social media · Public accounting firms · Business objectives

1 Introduction

Social media refers to a wide range of Internet-based applications that facilitate the creation and exchange of user-generated content [1]. Social media provides a platform for content consumption and interaction [2]. The rise of social media has paved a new way for the expansion of social networking and communication, from which both individual and institutional users can benefit. Businesses are utilizing social media to revolutionize various aspects of their business, such as marketing, advertising, and promotions [3].

As professional service providers, public accounting firms strive to maintain long-lasting, beneficial relationships with clients and employees. The level of competency of their employees is important to their firms' success because it contributes to the quality of service and reputation of the firm. Public accounting firms have increased their social media presence in order to accomplish some of their objectives. To better realize their business objectives, it is common for a firm to manage different types of social media accounts on more than one social media platform, and some firms operate multiple accounts on one platform to reach different audiences.

In this paper, we examine the Big 4 public accounting firms' social media content to explore the business objectives associated with their use of social media. We chose Facebook for our analysis because Facebook is one of the most popular social media platforms used by Fortune 500 firms [4]. We compare the differences in social media usage between the main and career pages (or accounts) of three of the Big 4 firms that

© Springer International Publishing AG, part of Springer Nature 2018
F. F.-H. Nah and B. S. Xiao (Eds.): HCIBGO 2018, LNCS 10923, pp. 455–464, 2018.
https://doi.org/10.1007/978-3-319-91716-0_36

have both types of pages (or accounts) on Facebook. The results indicate that even though *Knowledge Sharing*, *Socialization and Onboarding*, and *Branding and Marketing* business objectives were the top three objectives fulfilled by the Facebook social medium, their usage differs between the firm-wide main pages and the career pages. For instance, more *Knowledge Sharing* messages were present on the firm-wide main pages than the career pages, but there were more *Socialization and Onboarding* and *Branding and Marketing* messages on the career pages than the firm-wide main pages.

2   Background and Review of Literature

Social media has brought substantial and pervasive changes to communication through functional elements such as identity, conversations, sharing, presence, relationships, reputation, and groups [5]. Organizations are experimenting in social media to communicate with internal and external stakeholders. Social media can be used to improve ways of serving customers, monitoring the market, attracting job candidates, and connecting partners in their value chain [6]. The utilization of social media can affect customer loyalty and brand identification.

Social media can also be used to support recruitment, build employee engagement, and facilitate communication. Employees also use social media as a knowledge-sharing platform [7]. Ployhart summarizes seven business objectives that organizations can achieve with social media. These seven business objectives are: *Recruitment and Selection*, *Socialization and Onboarding*, *Training and Development*, *Knowledge Sharing*, *Branding and Marketing*, *Creativity and Problem Solving*, and *Influencing Organizational Culture/Change* [7].

The *Recruitment and Selection* objective is intended to increase the speed of recruitment, the effectiveness in recruiting candidates, and the conversion rates [8]. The *Socialization and Onboarding* objective relates to enhancing employees' assimilation into the organization, as well as employee commitment and engagement [8]. The *Training and Development* objective relates to providing a platform where training can be carried out more efficiently and effectively [7]. The *Knowledge Sharing* objective refers to both reducing the cost of and accelerating the circulation of information and knowledge [7]. The *Branding and Marketing* objective enhances customer loyalty and promotes the brand to potential customers [7]. The *Creativity and Problem Solving* objective increases accuracy and velocity of resolving problems [7]. The *Influencing Organizational Culture/Change* objective refers to the strengthening of or modification to organizational culture [7].

Previous research has shown that *Knowledge Sharing*, *Branding and Marketing*, and *Socialization and Onboarding* business objectives were the top three objectives fulfilled by firm-wide main pages of Big 4 public accounting firms on Facebook [9, 10]. Other firms have also utilized social media to achieve business objectives. For example, SAP has been a prominent user of social media to communicate with customers and General Electric Co. has been utilizing social media to enhance and support its training programs [11]. Social media has been found to increase the performance of organizations in terms of enhancing customer relations and customer service activities, improving information accessibility, and reducing costs in marketing and customer service [12, 13]. An empirical relationship between social media usage and customer relationship performance has previously been demonstrated [14]. Also, the literature has found a relationship between social media usage and employees' performance that relates to creativity and problem solving [15, 16].

The American Institute of Certified Public Accountants and its Private Companies Practice Section team surveyed accounting firms to assess their top issues and challenges [17]. The top three issues for firms with 11 or more professionals included: (1) identifying qualified employees, (2) retaining qualified professionals, and (3) attracting new clients [10]. These issues are similar to some of the business objectives identified by Ployhart [7]. Identifying qualified employees is consistent with the *Recruitment and Selection* objective, retaining qualified professionals by increasing staff engagement is in line with the *Socialization and Onboarding* objective, and attracting new clients and maintain existing client relationships is related to the *Branding and Marketing* objective.

3 Hypothesis

Businesses may maintain multiple accounts on one social media platform to target different audiences and achieve different business objectives. For instance, three of the Big 4 public accounting firms have a firm-wide main page and a career page on Facebook. We are interested in examining differences in these firms' utilization of different social media account categories, and hypothesize that the business objectives are different between the main and career pages. Hence, our hypothesis can be stated as follows:

H: Business objectives differ between the main and career pages.

4 Methodology

In order to compare the business objectives of main and career pages, we conducted a case study using the content analysis approach. Since only three of the Big 4 firms, i.e., Ernst & Young, KPMG, PwC, have both main and career pages, we only compared the main and career pages across these three firms. In other words, Deloitte was not included in the analysis because it does not have a Facebook career page in the US. We collected all the Facebook messages posted on both the main and career pages of these three accounting firms in the year 2012, and coded each message into one of the seven categories of business objectives identified by Ployhart [7] based on the definitions provided in Table 1 [7, 10]. Two independent coders carried out a subset of the coding and attained a Kappa coefficient of 0.95, indicating a high level of agreement between them. Hence, the rest of the coding was completed by one of the two coders.

After coding all the messages, we used the Chi-square test to compare usage frequencies of the business objectives between the main and career pages.

Table 1. Business objectives of social media usage [7]

Business objective	Description
Recruitment and selection	Improve selection and recruiting of high-quality candidates
Socialization and onboarding	Increase allegiance to and identification with the organization
Training and development	Improve cost efficiencies and training effectiveness
Knowledge sharing	Accelerate dissemination of information and knowledge at low cost
Branding and marketing	Reach new customers, enhance customer loyalty, and increase brand value and marketing effort
Creativity and problem solving	Increase efficiency and accuracy in solving problems as well as innovativeness
Influencing organizational culture/change	Reinforce or change organizational culture

5   Findings

In this section, we will provide the social media usage frequencies of the firm-wide main pages in Sect. 5.1, and the social media usage frequencies of the career pages in Sect. 5.2. Section 5.3 will compare the social media usage frequencies between the main and career pages, and provide the result of the statistical analysis.

5.1   Social Media Usage of Firm-Wide Main Pages

All three firms, EY, PwC, and KPMG, maintain a firm-wide main page on Facebook. Table 2 shows the frequencies and normalized frequencies (or percentages) of Facebook usage by business objective. The *Knowledge Sharing* business objective took up the largest proportion (69%) of the messages, followed by *Branding and Marketing* (19.6%), and *Socialization and Onboarding* (10.1%). Figure 1 shows the distribution of messages across the different business objectives on a radar chart. Messages were focused on *Knowledge Sharing*, *Branding and Marketing*, *Socialization and Onboarding*, *Training and Development*, and *Recruitment and Selection* business objectives, and none of the messages were related to *Creativity and Problem Solving* or *Influencing Organization Culture/Change*. We believe the main reason that *Creativity and Problem Solving* and *Influencing Organization Culture/Change* business objectives were not present in the firm-wide main page of Facebook is that, unlike enterprise social media, the Facebook main pages are outward facing instead of inward facing. The *Creativity and Problem Solving* and *Influencing Organization Culture/Change* business objectives are more appropriate for enterprise (inward facing) social media.

5.2   Social Media Usage of Career Pages

All Big 4 firms, except Deloitte, have a US career page on Facebook. Table 3 summarizes the usage frequencies and normalized frequencies (or percentages) of career page messages by business objective. The *Socialization and Onboarding* business

Table 2. Facebook main page usage frequencies and normalized frequencies/percentages

Firm\objective	R&S	S&O	T&D	KS	B&M	C&PS	IOC/C
EY	0 (0.0%)	6 (5.3%)	3 (2.7%)	93 (82.3%)	11 (9.7%)	0 (0.0%)	0 (0.0%)
PwC	0 (0.0%)	10 (8.5%)	0 (0.0%)	89 (75.4%)	19 (16.1%)	0 (0.0%)	0 (0.0%)
KPMG	1 (1.3%)	15 (20.0%)	0 (0.0%)	29 (38.7%)	30 (40.0%)	0 (0.0%)	0 (0.0%)
Total	1 (0.3%)	31 (10.1%)	3 (1.0%)	211 (69.0%)	60 (19.6%)	0 (0.0%)	0 (0.0%)

* R&S = Recruitment and Selection; S&O = Socialization and Onboarding; T&D = Training and Development; KS = Knowledge Sharing; B&M = Branding and Marketing; C & PS = Creativity and Problem Solving; IOC/C = Influencing Organizational Culture/Change

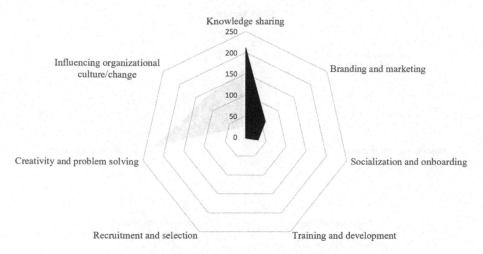

Fig. 1. Firm-wide main page messages coded by business objectives

objective took up the largest proportion (45.6%) of the messages, followed by *Knowledge Sharing* (28%), *Branding and Marketing* (23.3%), and *Recruitment and Selection* (3.1%). Figure 2 shows the distribution of business objectives on a radar chart. None of the messages were coded into *Training and Development*, *Creativity and Problem Solving*, and *Influencing Organizational Culture/Change* business objectives.

5.3 Social Media Usage: Main Page Versus Career Page

We performed the Chi-square test to assess if there is any difference between the main page usage and the career page usage on Facebook. An assumption of the Chi-square test is that expected frequencies should be at least 5, so we removed four business objectives from the analysis: *Recruitment and Selection, Training and Development, Creativity and Problem Solving*, and *Influencing Organizational Culture/Change*.

Table 3. Facebook career page usage frequencies and normalized frequencies/percentages

Firm\objective	R&S	S&O	T&D	KS	B&M	C&PS	IOC/C
EY	6 (5.0%)	22 (18.3%)	0 (0.0%)	49 (40.8%)	43 (35.8%)	0 (0.0%)	0 (0.0%)
PwC	8 (3.5%)	95 (42.0%)	0 (0.0%)	77 (34.1%)	46 (20.4%)	0 (0.0%)	0 (0.0%)
KPMG	1 (0.7%)	106 (74.1%)	0 (0.0%)	11 (7.7%)	25 (17.5%)	0 (0.0%)	0 (0.0%)
Total	15 (3.1%)	223 (45.6%)	0 (0.0%)	137 (28.0%)	114 (23.3%)	0 (0.0%)	0 (0.0%)

* R&S = Recruitment and Selection; S&O = Socialization and Onboarding; T&D = Training and Development; KS = Knowledge Sharing; B&M = Branding and Marketing; C & PS = Creativity and Problem Solving; IOC/C = Influencing Organizational Culture/Change

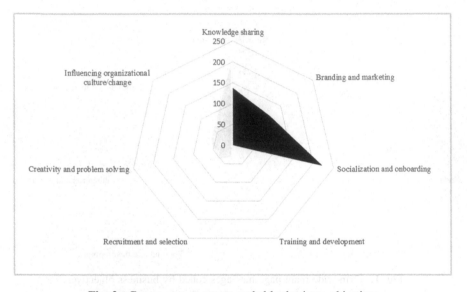

Fig. 2. Career page messages coded by business objectives

Table 4 shows the total frequencies of social media usage by main and career pages across *Socialization and Onboarding*, *Knowledge Sharing*, and *Branding and Marketing* business objectives.

The value of the Chi-square test statistic is 146.7 with a corresponding p-value of less than 0.001. Since the p-value is less than the significance level of $\alpha = 0.05$, the test result indicates a significant association between business objectives and social media page type, which suggests that firm-wide main and career pages serve different business objectives of public accounting firms, thus supporting the hypothesis for this research.

As shown in Fig. 3, public accounting firms used their career page for *Socialization and Onboarding* and *Branding and Marketing* objectives more frequently than on their firm-wide main page. On the contrary, more *Knowledge Sharing* messages were posted on the firm-wide main page than the career page.

Based on our analysis, Big 4 public accounting firms utilize Facebook to achieve the *Branding and Marketing*, *Knowledge Sharing*, and *Socialization and Onboarding* business objectives. The other four business objectives, *Creativity and Problem*

Table 4. Total frequencies of social media usage: main page vs career page

Page type	S&O	KS	B&M
Main page	31	211	60
Career page	223	137	114

* S&O = Socialization and Onboarding; KS = Knowledge Sharing; B&M = Branding and Marketing

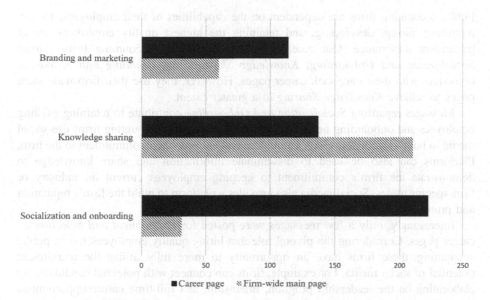

Fig. 3. Social media usage of firm-wide main page versus career page

Solving, Influencing Organizational Culture/Change, Recruitment and Selection, and *Training and Development*, were rarely addressed or not fulfilled. The business objective of *Recruitment and Selection* was pursued minimally, which may be due to Big 4 firms' use of other social media, such as LinkedIn, to achieve the business objective of recruitment. With regard to recruiting, employment-oriented social media like LinkedIn have a more professional appearance and targeted purpose than multipurpose social media such as Facebook. However, Facebook career pages have more messages on *Recruitment and Selection* as compared to Facebook main pages. This difference could be explained by the nature of career pages. Career pages provide a platform for sharing career information and attracting potential candidates.

The business objective *Knowledge Sharing* was achieved on both firm-wide main pages and career pages. However, *Knowledge Sharing* was realized to a greater extent on firm-wide main pages than career pages. Public accounting firms posted information and knowledge created or acquired (e.g., industry information). In comparison to the other objectives, a majority of the messages posted by public accounting firms on their main pages are related to *Knowledge Sharing*.

Career pages were utilized more extensively for *Socialization and Onboarding* and *Branding and Marketing*. *Socialization and Onboarding* is intended to improve employees' sense of belonging, loyalty, and commitment to the organization. *Branding and Marketing* is utilized to promote the brand to job applicants and outside parties.

6 Discussion

Public accounting firms are dependent on the capabilities of their employees. Hence, recruiting, hiring, developing, and retaining the highest quality employees are of paramount importance. Our research shows that public accounting firms pursue *Socialization and Onboarding*, *Knowledge Sharing*, and *Branding and Marketing* objectives with their Facebook career pages. However, they use their firm-wide main pages to achieve *Knowledge Sharing* to a greater extent.

Messages regarding *Socialization and Onboarding* contribute to retaining existing employees and onboarding newly hired employees. Public accounting firms use social media to build relationships with employees and enhance their commitment to the firm. Platforms can also be used to disseminate information and share knowledge to demonstrate the firm's commitment to keeping employees current on industry or firm-specific topics. Social media also provides a platform to build the firm's reputation and promote the firm's image.

Interestingly, only a few messages were posted for *Recruitment and Selection* on career pages. Considering the pivotal role that hiring quality employees has in public accounting, these firms have an opportunity to more fully utilize the recruitment potential of social media. For example, firms can connect with potential candidates by elaborating on the leadership program, internship, and full-time career opportunities they offer through social media. Recruiting is a very competitive process among the Big 4 firms, so they can also use social media to connect with potential candidates early in their careers by providing career advice such as information regarding changes in the CPA exam.

Although the Big 4 firms have utilized social media to achieve certain business objectives, they have an opportunity to further expand its use to achieve other objectives. For example, social media can provide training and development information to employees. In addition, firms can engage employees with interactive training tools that are made available on social media to allow them to acquire information and test their existing knowledge or understanding of a topic. These endeavors can assist employees in staying abreast of current changes as well as serve as a means of semi-formal training. They can also provide information regarding professional development, such as enhancing leadership or communication skills.

Based on our research, *Creativity and Problem Solving* and *Influencing Organizational Culture/Change* objectives were not evident on either firm-wide main or career pages. One possibility for *Creativity and Problem Solving* is that this objective is being pursued on different platforms, and possibly on private platforms. Considering the competitive nature of the industry and issues of confidentiality with client information, firms may best be served using an enterprise social network that restricts certain content to employees or clients only.

The Big 4 firms may consider utilizing social media to a greater extent to continuously reinforce their desired organizational culture or to institute changes. They may consider engaging a more diverse group of employees in their social media posts and communication exchanges in order to have the desired culture permeate all areas and levels of the organization. To do so, they may need to provide incentives to employees to participate, such as reward systems. Also, acknowledgements of employees' participation in social media can assist with making employees feel that their efforts and opinions are valued by the company. This may help strengthen the culture and also contribute to the objective of retaining employees.

7 Conclusion

Social media plays an important role in achieving business objectives by public accounting firms. The three key business objectives of social media usage are *Socialization and Onboarding*, *Knowledge Sharing*, and *Branding and Marketing*. We also found that firm-wide main pages and career pages are used to achieve different business objectives. The firm-wide main pages were used more extensively for *Knowledge Sharing*, while the career pages were used more extensively for *Branding and Marketing* and *Socialization and Onboarding*. Social media can present benefits and advantages to public accounting firms, and they are only at the cusp of tapping into its potential. For instance, public accounting firms can use it to connect with potential job applicants and disseminate information to existing employees as an informal training mechanism.

There are several limitations to our research. First, we analyzed the Facebook data for the year 2012. Social media has developed rapidly since 2012. Therefore, further research is warranted to collect messages of more recent years and extend the study to include other social media platforms such as Twitter and LinkedIn. Another limitation is that only three Big 4 public accounting firms were included in this research. Future research can extend the study to include other public accounting firms and assess how they differ from the Big 4. Future studies can also include more industries and compare social media use across different industries.

References

1. Kaplan, A.M., Haenlein, M.: Users of the world, unite! The challenges and opportunities of social media. Bus. Horiz. **53**(1), 59–68 (2010)
2. Obar, J.A., Wildman S.S.: Social media definition and the governance challenge: an introduction to the special issue (2015)
3. Hanna, R., Rohm, A., Crittenden, V.L.: We're all connected: the power of the social media ecosystem. Bus. Hori. **54**(3), 265–273 (2011)
4. Culnan, M.J., McHugh, P.J., Zubillaga, J.I.: How large US companies can use Twitter and other social media to gain business value. MIS Q. Exec. **9**(4), 243–259 (2010)

5. Kietzmann, J.H., Hermkens, K., McCarthy, I.P., Silvestre, B.: Social media? Get serious! Understanding the functional building blocks of social media. Bus. Hori. **54**(3), 241–251 (2011)
6. Nair, M.: Understanding and measuring the value of social media. J. Corp. Account. Financ. **22**(3), 45–51 (2011)
7. Ployhart, R.E.: Social media in the workplace: issues and strategic questions. SHRM Foundation Executive Briefing (2012). http://www.shrm.org/about/foundation/products/Documents/Social%20Media%20Briefing-%20FINAL.pdf
8. McFarland, L.A., Ployhart, R.E.: Social media: a contextual framework to guide research and practice. J. Appl. Psychol. **100**(6), 1653–1677 (2015)
9. Eschenbrenner, B., Nah, F.: Leveraging social media to achieve business objectives. Cut. IT J. **26**(12), 24–29 (2013)
10. Eschenbrenner, B., Nah, F., Telaprolu, V.R.: Efficacy of social media utilization by public accounting firms: findings and directions for future research. J. Inf. Syst. **29**(2), 5–21 (2015)
11. Kalman, F.: Social media: learning's new ecosystem. Chief Learn. Off. **11**(8), 42–45 (2012)
12. Parveen, F., Jaafar, N.I., Ainin, S.: Social media usage and organizational performance: reflections of Malaysian social media managers. Telematics Inf. **32**, 67–78 (2015)
13. Tajudeem, F.P., Jaafar, N.I., Ainin, S.: Understanding the impact of social media usage among organizations. Inf. Manag. Accepted and forthcoming
14. Trainor, K.J., Andzulis, J., Rapp, A., Agnihotri, R.: Social media technology usage and customer relationship performance: a capabilities-based examination of social CRM. J. Bus. Res. **67**, 1201–1208 (2014)
15. Ali-Hassan, H., Nevo, D., Wade, M.: Linking dimensions of social media use to job performance: the role of social capital. J. Strateg. Inf. Syst. **24**, 65–89 (2015)
16. Moqbel, M., Nah, F.: Enterprise social media use and impact on performance: the role of workplace integration and positive emotions. AIS Trans. Hum. Comput. Interact. **9**(4), 261–280 (2017)
17. PCPS CPA Firm Top Issues Survey (2017). https://www.picpa.org/docs/site/firm_liaisons doc/2017-pcps-top-issues-survey-commentary.pdf

Internet Use and Happiness: A Replication and Extension

Richard H. Hall[(⊠)]

Department of Business and Information Technology,
Missouri University of Science and Technology, Rolla, MO, USA
rhall@mst.edu

Abstract. This study is an extension of two previous studies, which explored the relationship between happiness and Internet use [1, 2]. An Internet Use Scale (IUS), developed in the initial study, was administered to college students along with the Flourishing Scale [3] and the Satisfaction with Life Scale [4]. I compared changes in the relationship between these measures, and their mean values, across the three samples; assessed the relationship between use factors and happiness over-all, combining data from all samples; and evaluated the relationship between individual usage scale items and happiness. Results indicated that those who reported spending less time on the Internet, and less time expressing negative emotions scored higher on measures of happiness. There was also some indication that those who spend time checking facts on the Internet are happier, but the effect was not as strong nor consistent.

Keywords: Happiness · Internet

1 Why Study Happiness and the Internet?

Following the dawn of the new millennium, research on happiness increased dramatically, largely spurred on by the fact that people increasingly rate happiness as a major life goal. For example, recent surveys have indicated that the strong majority of people across many countries rate happiness as more important than income [3]. Lyubomirsky [4] sums this research up, "…in almost every culture examined by researchers, people rank the pursuit of happiness as one of their most cherished goals in life" (p. 239).

In addition, there is a large body of evidence that suggests situational factors, in particular wealth, play a surprisingly small role in determining happiness. Some suggest that this may be the result of society moving into a post-materialistic phase, where basic needs have been largely met for many in industrialized countries, so pursuit of self fulfillment becomes more important [4].

Finally, there are number of studies that indicate that happy people, in general, have a positive effect on society. For example, there is evidence that happier people are more successful and socially engaged [5].

© Springer International Publishing AG, part of Springer Nature 2018
F. F.-H. Nah and B. S. Xiao (Eds.): HCIBGO 2018, LNCS 10923, pp. 465–474, 2018.
https://doi.org/10.1007/978-3-319-91716-0_37

2 What Is Happiness?

For the most part, researchers agree that happiness is inherently subjective, In fact, the term is often used interchangeably with "subjective well-being" (SWB) [6]. Myers [7], one of the leading researchers in the area, stated that happiness is "…whatever people mean when describing their lives as happy" (p. 57). Despite the potential for ambiguity with such a definition, there is considerable agreement, at least across Western culture, as to what happiness means [8]. Most people equate happiness with experiences of joy, contentment, and positive well being; as well as a feeling that life is good, meaningful, and worthwhile [9].

As a consequence, self-report measures have served as the primary measure of happiness. Examples include the Satisfaction with Life Scale (SLS), the Subjective Happiness Scale (SHS), and the Steen Happiness Index (SHI). Psychometric studies of these self-report measures indicate that they are, by and large, reliable over time, despite changing circumstances; they correlate strongly with friends and family ratings of happiness; and they are statistically reliable. Lyubomirsky [9] sums this up, "A great deal of research has shown that the majority of these measures have adequate to excellent psychometric properties and that the association between happiness and other variables usually cannot be accounted for by transient mood" (p. 239). These psychometric studies illustrate the general agreement among people as to what constitutes happiness.

One other interesting point, regarding the definition of happiness and its measurement, is that mean happiness is consistently above a mid-line point in most populations sampled [6]. For example, three in ten Americans say they are "very happy", only 1 in ten report that they are "not too happy", and 6 in 10 say they are "pretty happy" [7]. Therefore, there appears to be a positive set point, where most people appear to be moderately happy, and this is independent of age and gender [8].

3 Individual Difference and Happiness

Happiness is surprisingly stable over time [9] even with major changes in life circumstances [10], and there appears to be no time in life that is most satisfying [11]. These findings are consistent with research that indicates some individual difference traits are predictive of happiness. Further, happiness may also be strongly tied to genetic predisposition. We now turn to a discussion of this research.

Twin studies indicate that there is a strong genetic component in happiness [12, 13]. For example, Tellegen et al. [13] assessed the well being of twins at ages 20 and 30. They correlated the happiness scores between monozygotic twins at stage 1 with the score for their twin at stage 2 (cross time/cross twin) and found a correlation of .4, while the test-retest correlation where each twin's score was correlated with himself/herself was only .5. Further the cross twin/cross time correlation for dizygotic twins was only .07. Therefore, heritability appears to account for a large part of the stability in happiness.

As mentioned, some other individual difference measures have been found to consistently correlate with happiness, in particular extroversion. For example, in a cross-cultural study Lucas et al. found that extraversion correlated with positive affect in virtually all 40 nations they examine [15]. Extroversion, as a predictor of happiness, is strongly related to the literature to be discussed, which relates social interaction with happiness, in that there is a clear relationship between the number and quality of social relationships and happiness. One would expect that an extrovert would be more likely to seek out and form these types of relationships.

Religiosity is another variable that has been found to consistently predict happiness [7]. In addition, those who report higher levels of religiosity tend to recover greater happiness after suffering from negative life events [15]. This finding has been found for peoples' self reports of their degree of religiosity, and for behavioral measures such as Church attendance [7]. As with extroversion, the impact of religiosity may be, at least partly, explained by the importance of social interaction in determining happiness, in that those who attend Church regularly, and interact with others in a positive social environment, are more likely to be happy [17]. Further, people often derive meaning and purpose from religious practices, which is another important correlate of happiness [7].

In addition to behavioral tendencies, with respect to individual differences, the research of Lyubomirsky et al. provides substantial evidence that there are consistent differences between happy and unhappy people in the ways they process ("construe") information. For example, studies from Lyubomirsky's laboratory have found that happy people are less sensitive to social comparisons [18], tended to feel more positive about decisions after they were made [19], construed events more positively [19], and are less inclined to self-reflect and dwell on themselves [18]. This difference in information processing dispositions in happy vs. unhappy people is presumably one reason why the effects of circumstantial factors are relatively minimal.

Another individual difference factor, which has been identified as important in predicting happiness, is the autoletic personality, which refers to people who tend to regularly experience "flow" [20]. Flow refers to a kind of experience that is engrossing and enjoyable to such a degree that it becomes "autoletic" – worth doing for its own sake [21]. The autoletic personality and the flow concept are consistent with the views of happiness researchers who have suggested that engagement is a fundamental component of a happy life [22].

4   Happiness and the Internet

Studies that have examined the relationship between the Internet and happiness have been conducted at least since the relatively early days of the World Wide Web. Most of these have focused on communication/collaborative activities and the Internet. As we mentioned, these types of activities have been found in non-internet studies to be strongly related to happiness.

4.1   The Internet Paradox

In 1998 Kraut et al. reported the results of a reasonably extensive study of early World Wide Web users where they followed the activity of mostly first time Internet users over a period of years. Researchers administered periodic questionnaires and server logs indicating participant activity on the web. (Participants were provided with free computers and internet connections) [22].

Over all, the results showed that the Internet had a largely negative impact on social activity, in that those who used the Internet more communicated with family and friends less. They also reported higher levels of loneliness. Interestingly, they also found that email, a communication activity, constituted the participants main use of the Internet. The researchers coined the term "internet paradox" to describe this situation in which a social technology reduced social involvement.

These researchers speculated that this negative social effect was due to a type of displacement, in which their time spent online displaced face-to-face social involvement. Although they note that users spent a great deal of time using email, they suggest that this constitutes a low quality social activity and this is why they did not see positive effects on well being [22]. They find further support for this supposition in a study reported in 2002, where they found that business professionals who used email found it less effective than face-to-face communication or the telephone in sustaining close social relationships [23].

Since the time that this Internet paradox was identified, a number of studies over the next twelve years have found, fairly consistently, results that contradict the Kraut et al. results. More recent studies have indicated the potential positive social effects of the Internet and their relationship to well being. Further, the effect appears to be getting stronger as the Internet and the users mature.

In fact, one of the first challenges to this Internet paradox was provided by Kraut himself when he published follow up results for participants in the original Internet-paradox study, including data for additional participants. In this paper, "Internet Paradox Revisited," researchers report that the negative social impact on the original sample had dissipated over time and, for those in their new sample, the Internet had positive effects on communication, social involvement, and well being [24]. Therefore, it appears that the results of the original Kraut et al. study were largely due to the participants' inexperience with the Internet. Within just a few years, American society's experience with the Internet had increased exponentially. Further, the Kraut studies concentrated on email, whereas there are many other social communication tools available on the modern web.

4.2   Displacement Versus Stimulation Hypothesis

More recently, researchers have examined the relationship between on-line communication and users' over all social networks, explicitly addressing the question of whether or not on-line communication "displaces" higher quality communication, or "stimulates" it. Presumably, the former would negatively affect well being, while the latter would enhance it [25].

In one large scale study, over 1000 Dutch teenagers were surveyed regarding the nature of their on line communication activities, the number and quality of friendships, and their well being.

They found strong support for the stimulation hypothesis. More specifically, these researchers developed a causal model, which indicated that instant messaging lead to more contact with friends, which lead to more meaningful social relationships, which, in turn, predicted well being. Interestingly, they did not find this same effect for chat in a public chat room. They attributed this finding to the fact that participants reported that they interacted more with strangers in the chat room as compared to their interaction with friends with instant messaging [26].

4.3 The Internet and Social Connectedness

Despite studies, such as the one just mentioned, which have found a relationship between internet use and positive outcomes, there is still a great deal of press suggesting that the internet can effect users negatively, causing social isolation, and shrinking of social networks. This is purported to be especially true for adolescents [27].

Researchers with the Pew Internet and Daily Life Project set out to examine this concern directly in one of the most comprehensive studies of the effect of the Internet on social interaction, reported in 2009 [28]. Contrary to fears, they found that:

- A variety of Internet activities were associated with larger and more diverse core discussion networks.
- Those who participated most actively with social media were more likely to interact with those from diverse backgrounds, including race and political view.
- Internet users are just as likely as others to visit a neighbor in person, and they are more likely to belong to a local voluntary organization.
- Internet use is often associated with local activity in community spaces such as parks and restaurants, and Internet connections are more and more common in such venues.

Although these outcomes did not explicitly include happiness, they do support the contention that Internet activities can enhance the amount and quality of social relationships, which has been implicated in a number of studies as a strong and consistent predictor of happiness.

5 Research Overview

This study is a replication and extension of two previous studies conducted in 2016 [1] and 2017 [2], which also explored the relationship between Internet activities and happiness. In the 2016 study an internet-use-scale (IUS) was developed and subjected to initial psychometric analyses, and modified accordingly, resulting in a 13 item scale, representing three categories of internet use: Affective Expression, Information Gathering, and Total Time (spent on the internet). Results from both previous studies indicated that happiness measures were negatively related to the Time and Affective Expression categories, and positively related to Information Gathering. The current research extends these studies with a new sample, and some additional analyses, utilizing the larger data pool. I administered the Internet Use Scale, IUS and the same two happiness measures: Flourishing Scale [3] and the Satisfaction with Life [4] scale, as used in the previous studies.

6 Questions

6.1 Internet Use and Happiness

What is the relationship between Internet use and happiness?

6.2 Internet Use and Happiness Over Time

How does the relationship between happiness and Internet use, and the mean happiness and use scores differ between the 2016, 2017, and 2018 samples?

7 Research Method

7.1 Participants

Thirty-three students enrolled in an undergraduate course in digital media at a small Midwestern technological research University in the spring of 2018 served as the participants in this study.

7.2 Measures

The Internet use scale (IUS) [1] was administered to assess internet use. The 13-item scale represents three internet use categories: Affective Expression, Information Gathering, and Time Spent on the Internet. The Flourishing Scale (FS) [3], and the Satisfaction with Life Scale (SWLS) [4] were administered to represent happiness.

7.3 Procedure

Participants completed the survey on-line, which consisted of the measures delineated above.

8 Results

8.1 Relationship Between Internet Usage and Happiness

In order to assess the relationship between happiness and Internet use measures, and to compare the three samples (2016, 2017, and 2018), a series of zero-order correlations were computed among the happiness and internet use measures. These results appear in Table 1.

8.2 Internet Use, and Happiness as a Function of Time

In order to compare the three samples on their internet use and happiness, a series of one-way Analyses of Variance (ANOVA) were computed with the three internet usage factors, and two happiness scores as the dependent measures and time (2016 vs 2017 vs 2018) as the independent variable. Note that these scores were computed as means of

Table 1. Correlation between internet use and happiness as a function of year

Happiness	Factor								
	Affective expression			Info gathering			Time		
	2016	2017	2018	2016	2017	2018	2016	2017	2018
Flourishing	−.087	−.35*	−.52**	.46*	.53**	−.01	−.54**	−.54**	−.41*
SWLS	−.312	−.15	−.13	−.18	.18	−.40*	−.58**	−.30(*)	−.25

(*)p < .10; *p < .05; **p < .01

the items such that the Internet usage scores could range from −7 to +7 with higher scores representing more affective expression, information gathering, and time spent on the Internet. Scores on both happiness scales ranged from 1–7 with greater scores representing higher levels of happiness. These results are presented in Table 2.

Table 2. Internet usage and happiness as a function of sample year

Measure	2016	2017	2017
Affective expression**	.36	−.50	−.58
Info gathering	5.64	5.67	5.89
Time(*)	.26	−.43	−.13
Flourishing	5.31	5.57	5.55
SWLS(*)	4.33	4.90	4.38

(*)p < .10; *p < .05; **p < .01

8.3   Combining Years

In order to evaluate the over-all relationship between the use factors and happiness, a series of zero-order correlations were computed among the happiness and Internet use measures, using date from all three years combined. These results are listed in Table 3.

Table 3. Internet usage and happiness (combined data from all years)

Happiness	Factor		
	Affective expression	Info gathering	Time
Flourishing	−.31**	.36**	−.52**
SWLS	−.22*	−.15	−.40*

*p < .05; **p < .01

In order the explore the impact of individual scale items on happiness measures, a final series of correlations were computed between each scale item and the two happiness measures. Table 4 lists the correlations for all items, where the relationship was statistically significant at the p < .01 level for at least one happiness measure.

Table 4. Internet use scale items the significantly correlated with happiness (combined data from all years)

Item	Flourishing	SWLS
I spend more time on line than off line	−.37**	−.27**
I like to participate in off-line competitive games/sports	.30**	.25*
I feel better when I vent my anger online	−.34**	−.25*
I tend to write positive and supportive comments when I interact online	.36**	.147
I often use the internet for checking facts	.33**	.03
I spend a lot of my waking hours on the internet	−.26*	−.32**
I believe it is rude for someone to attend to a mobile device when participating in a face-to-face conversation	.42**	.21*
When I want to socialize, I'd rather interact face-to-face than online	.44**	.26*
The internet often distracts me from healthy physical activity like exercise	−.33**	−.26*
I rarely use the internet to post everyday things like what I had for lunch, or pictures of my pets	.27**	−.047
I would rather play a game/sport that requires physical activity and skill than play an on-line game	.48***	.32**
I spend a lot of time playing on-line games	−.32**	−.16

*p < .05; **p < .01; ***p < .001

9 Conclusions

These results were largely consistent with the studies from the previous two years [1, 2]. Taken together, the results paint a picture of the happy versus unhappy Internet user. First, those who spend more time on the Internet are less happy. This was demonstrated in the 2016 sample [1], replicated in the 2017 sample [2], and again in this sample. When all the data is combined, the time-on-the-internet factor is significantly and negatively correlated with both happiness measures.

Second, there is some indication that, when interacting with the Internet, those who report spending more time gathering information and carrying out research score higher on happiness measures. However, this relationship is not as strong or consistent as with the other factors, especially when considering the current research, where the only significant relationship between the information gathering factor and happiness was negative. Further, when using the entire data set, the information gathering factor was significantly related to the flourishing measure, but not satisfaction with life. However, the analyses of individual scale items, did find a significant relationship between the item "I often us the internet for checking facts" and the flourishing scale. Note that this usage factor refers to the degree to which someone is likely to spend time checking facts on the internet, but also the degree to which one is aware of the potential inaccuracy of information. One item scored positively on this sub-scale is "I'm skeptical of the accuracy of information I find on the internet". This was further supported by a qualitative analysis, carried out in the 2017 study where a number of those in with high-happiness scores reported that they found factual inaccuracy on the Internet as a major negative; while those with low-happiness scores did not mention it [2].

Third, those who use the Internet as a method for negative affective expression are less happy, consistently across the years and the analyses. Although this factor is not significantly related to the SWLS in this study, it is strongly and significantly related to flourishing, especially in the current sample. Further, when all the data was combined the relationship between the affective expression factor and both happiness measures were significantly and negatively related. In the qualitative analyses, carried out in the 2017 study, a common theme emerged with respect to what people liked least about the Internet, which was the aversion people have for negative-affective expression. Across both happiness groups users found it aversive when "people are jerks", as one participant put it [2].

Finally, we carried out some analyses to compare changes in the participants' views between the 2016, 2017, and 2018 samples, with respect to their happiness and Internet usage scores. The good news, in terms of what we've learned about the Internet and happiness, is that those in the 2017 sample report spending significantly less time online than the 2016 sample; when online are significantly less likely to participate in affective expression; and, perhaps consequently, scored significantly higher on the satisfaction with life scores; and this trend appears to be largely continuing with the 2018 sample.

References

1. Hall, R.H.: Internet use and happiness. In: Nah, F.-H., Tan, C.-H. (eds.) HCIBGO 2016. LNCS, vol. 9751, pp. 37–45. Springer, Cham (2016). https://doi.org/10.1007/978-3-319-39396-4_4
2. Hall, R.H.: Internet use and happiness: a longitudinal analysis. In: Nah, F.-H., Tan, C.-H. (eds.) HCIBGO 2017. LNCS, vol. 10294, pp. 213–222. Springer, Cham (2017). https://doi.org/10.1007/978-3-319-58484-3_17
3. Diener, E., Wirtz, D., Tov, W., Kim-Prieto, C., Choi, D., Oishi, S., Biswas-Diener, R.: New measures of well-being: flourishing and positive and negative feelings. Soc. Indic. Res. **39**, 247–266 (2009)
4. Diener, E., Emmons, R.A., Larsen, R.J., Griffin, S.: The satisfaction with life scale. J. Pers. Assess. **49**, 71–75 (1985)
5. Lyubomirsky, S., King, L., Diener, E.: The benefits of frequent positive affect: does happiness lead to success. Psychol. Bull. **6**, 803–855 (2005)
6. Diener, E.: Subjective well-being: the science of happiness and a proposal for a national index. Am. Psychol. **55**, 34–43 (2000)
7. Myers, D.G.: The funds, friends, and faith of happy people. Am. Psychol. **55**, 56–67 (2000)
8. Freedman, J.: Happy People: What Happiness Is, Who Has it, and Why?. Harcourt Brace Jovanovich, New York (1978)
9. Magnus, K., Diener, E.: A longitudinal analysis of personality, life events, and subjective well-being. In: Annual Meeting of the Midwestern Psychological Association, Chicago, IL (1991)

10. Costa, P.T., McCrae, R.R., Zonderman, A.B.: Environmental and dispositional influences on well-being: longitudinal follow-up of an American national sample. Br. J. Psychol. **78**, 299–306 (1987)

11. Myers, D.G., Diener, E.: Who is happy? Psychol. Sci. **6**, 10–19 (1995)

12. Lykken, D.T., Tellegen, A.: Happiness is a stochastic phenomenon. Psychol. Sci. **7**, 186–189 (1996)

13. Tellegen, A., et al.: Personality similarity in twins reared apart and together. J. Pers. Soc. Psychol. **54**, 1031–1039 (1988)

14. Lucas, R.E., et al.: Cross-cultural evidence for the fundamental features of extraversion. J. Pers. Soc. Psychol. **79**, 452–468 (2000)

15. McIntosh, D.N., Silver, R.C., Wortman, C.B.: Religion's role in adjustment to a negative life event: coping with the loss of a child. J. Pers. Soc. Psychol. **65**, 812–821 (1993)

16. Ellison, C.G., Gay, D.A., Glass, T.A.: Does religious commitment contribute to individual life satisfaction. Soc. Forces **68**, 100–123 (1989)

17. Lyubomirsky, S., Ross, L.: Hedonic consequences of social comparison: a contrast of happy and unhappy people. J. Pers. Soc. Psychol. **73**, 1141–1157 (1997)

18. Lyubomirsky, S., Ross, L.: Changes in attractiveness of elected, rejected, and precluded alternatives: a comparison of happy and unhappy individuals. J. Pers. Soc. Psychol. **76**, 988–1007 (1999)

19. Lyubomirsky, S., Tucker, K.L.: Implications of individual differences in subjective happiness for perceiving interpreting and thinking about life events. Motiv. Emot. **22**, 155–186 (1998)

20. Csikszentmihalyi, M.: If we are so rich, why aren't we happy? Am. Psychol. **54**(10), 821–827 (1999)

21. Seligman, E.P., et al.: Positive psychology progress: empirical validation of interventions. Am. Psychol. **60**(5), 410–421 (2005)

22. Kraut, R., et al.: Internet paradox: a social technology that reduces social involvement and psychological well-being? Am. Psychol. **53**(9), 1017–1031 (1998)

23. Cummings, J., Butler, B., Kraut, R.: The quality of online social relationships. Commun. ACM **45**, 103–108 (2002)

24. Kraut, R., Kiesler, S., Boneva, B., Cummings, J., Helgeson, V.: Internet paradox revisited. J. Soc. Issues **58**, 49–74 (2002)

25. Valkenburg, P.M., Peter, J.: Online communication and adolescent well-being: testing the stimulation versus the displacement hypothesis. J. Comput.-Mediat. Commun. **12**, 1169–1182 (2007)

26. Hampton, K.N., Sessions-Goulet, L., Her, E.J., Rainie, L.: Social Isolation and New Technology. Report of the Pew Internet and American Life Project (2009). http://www.pewinternet.org/2009/11/04/social-isolation-and-new-technology

27. Kuss, D.J., Griffiths, D.: Internet gaming addiction: a systematic review of empirical research. Int. J. Ment. Health Addict. **10**, 278–296 (2011)

How Do They Tag? Senior Adults' Tagging Behavior in Cultural Heritage Information

Ling-Ling Lai[✉]

Tamkang University, New Taipei City, Taiwan
llai@mail.tku.edu.tw

Abstract. This paper addresses the issue of social tagging, especially how the elderly give tags in digital resources. The connection between mental models and the principles of the elderly's tagging behavior is made. The research method used were two folds. First, two rounds of revised Delphi method were used to obtain the consensus of how the elderly provides tags after viewing a 10-min YouTube clip regarding cultural heritage information. The research team conducted in-depth interviews with 20 elderly citizens who are over 55 years old and are residents in northern Taipei, Taiwan. Each participant was interviewed for about 30 min. After interview sessions, the researcher asked each participant to draw a fishbone diagram with the purpose of grouping in more detailed manner the tags and sub-tags generated from interviews. The analysis of the interview and fishbone diagrams showed that the types of tags the elderly considered fall into three categories: concrete objects, emotion aspects, personal memory and related experience. In addition, the prompts the elderly considered when giving tags are based on explicit texts, buildings, and key people shown in the film. Lastly, the factors the elderly considered when giving tags are mainly because of repeated themes, concrete objects, as well as personal and communal memory from the past experience.

Keywords: Cultural heritage information · Digital humanities
Elderly · Mental model · Social tagging

1 Introduction

This paper describes a study that focuses on digital humanities; in particular, how senior adults tag cultural heritage information. The author reported the results of an empirical study that identified tagging behavior of elderly users. The results of the study can be used to identify tagging semantics for senior adults and clarify related interface design issues with regards to cultural heritage information presented in organizations such as archive, museum, and cultural centers.

As Collier stated, "Comparison is a fundamental tool of analysis. It sharpens our power of description, and plays a central role in concept-formation by brining into focus suggestive similarities and contrasts among cases" (p. 105) [1]. By making comparisons, one can further understand similarities and differences of the targeted phenomena. Most of the studies related to social tagging are not focused specifically on senior users; as a result, the interface design mostly targets towards users in general.

F. F.-H. Nah and B. S. Xiao (Eds.): HCIBGO 2018, LNCS 10923, pp. 475–484, 2018.
https://doi.org/10.1007/978-3-319-91716-0_38

This study sets out to understand the elderly's tagging behavior of multimedia cultural heritage information, with the purpose of possible comparisons with the general users. The research question is centered on the main question: What is senior adults' tagging behavior in cultural heritage information?

2 Related Literature

In this section, the author presents related literature from three areas, including the studies of mental models, social tagging, and cultural heritage information. Mental models describe how a person processes information and the associated behavior. In particular, mental models explain how and why a group of people do certain things. It is important to understand users from the perspective of mental models so that phenomena can be more easily understood. Social tagging has been studied from different perspectives and by scholars from various disciplines. With different perspectives come with the unique purposes and foci. For this study, the researcher is interested in the elderly and their ways of giving tags. In this section, the researcher looks into the fields of mental models, the history of tagging, recent development of social tagging in relation to the studies of the elderly. Lastly, concerning cultural heritage information the researcher focuses the discussion on the definition, the types of cultural heritage information, and the type that is specifically used in this study.

Even with the advancement of touch-based interface and technology, the art and science of searching and browsing still needs much effort from users' perspectives. With user studies, interface designers can better orient related design to better meet the user's needs. In this study, the research team sets out to identify the elderly's tagging behavior. When a specified and targeted audience is identified and their needs clarified, we believe that the overall searching experience would be enhanced.

2.1 Mental Models

It is generally believed that a mental model describes someone's thinking process about how something works in the real world. Since childhood, as we begin to understand the world, we construct numerous internal models in our minds. Child psychologist Jean Piaget and others believe that "a child constructs a mental model of the world." In essence, Piaget argued that intelligence was a not fixed trait, and regarded cognitive development as a process which occurs due to biological maturation and interaction with the environment" McLeod [2]. It is therefore reasonable to say that mental models shift states and shapes from a developmental stage to the next in a human's life.

Gentner and Stevens [3] edited a collection of chapters in a book titled *Mental Models*. They believed mental models are "people's views of the world, of themselves, of their own capabilities, and of the tasks that they are asked to perform, or topics they are asked to learn, depend heavily on the conceptualizations that they bring to the task." As a Design Researcher, Young [4] believes that a mental model is a thinking style about how an audience describes his/her behavioral aspect of achieving a certain goal. She uses mental model diagrams to understand her clients' thinking styles, so as to design the interface that suits the clients' real needs and their working styles. As

Magzan [5] stated that "mental models are very often hidden, and we are not consciously aware of our mental models or the effects they have on our behavior. Once created, they become fixed and reinforced in the mind, becoming difficult to change." This hidden and unconscious "framework" often guides us in carrying out things we set out to do in everyday life. DeBono [6] noted clearly that the function of mental models is to "mediate reality for our minds and help us categorize and organize an endless stream of information we take every day." In one way or another, it is positive that mental models are found in almost everything we do on the daily basis and are essential in understanding a particular group.

As described above, mental models change as we progress through life stages. In this paper, the research team is interested in understanding how senior adults tag differently from adults in other age groups. What is the mental model of the elderly and their thinking process as well as their decision making process in terms of tagging? With this in mind, the researcher aims to do two things. First, the researcher reports on the research results designed to examine the elderly's tagging behavior. Secondly, the elderly's tagging mental model is discussed to reveal its uniqueness.

2.2 Tagging and Social Tagging

Originated from the field of library and information science, tagging is a process of describing and categorizing objects, whether in forms of books, articles, archives, texts, images, or other types of multimedia resources. With the advances of technology, everyone who has access to the Internet can add tags to resources based on his/her own understandings of that resource. Social tagging describes how users provide tags collectively to a particular object, be it a piece of art, photo, an article, a blog post, etc. The user providing tags may include specialists and non-specialists. Folksonomy is the term that describes the results and the collection of social tagging. Unlike subject experts who assign subject terms for books in libraries and artifacts in museums and art centers, the nature of "folk taxonomy" (folksonomy) tends to be very user centered. Tsai et al. [7] stated that "user tags are much more subjective, reflecting the end-user's personal understanding of the content." Studies have shown that tagging provides two benefits. One is for the management purpose, and the other for the retrieval purpose. The tagging provided by the general public shows the essence of the object being described, which can reveal insights for the interface designer; on the other hand, from the user's perspective, accessing the collection using tags provided by the user enhances the retrieval effectiveness.

Nearly 10 years ago, Trant [8] reviewed 180 published research articles and noted that social tagging was a new area of research. In the review article, Trant stated that because the research area was new, theoretical perspectives and relevant research methods were just about to be defined. Ten years later now, the research has accumulated and flourished to a certain level, yet clarifying issues and applications of social tagging is still challenging. Essentially, social tagging relies on users rather than professional librarians to describe resources for management and retrieval purpose. People who share the same cultural context and belong to the same generation might act and think similarly, thus have similar ways of perceiving and processing the same piece of information represented at hand. In this research, the author intended to identify the mental model of the elderly's social tagging behavior.

2.3   Cultural Heritage Information

Cultural heritage information is discussed extensively among the *GLAM* community, which includes professionals in settings such as galleries, libraries, archives, and museums (GLAM). Cultural heritage information is defined in two categories, i.e., *tangible* (paintings, antiquities, artifacts, buildings, monuments, etc.) and *intangible* (dance, plays, music, stories, etc.) (Ruthven and Chowdhury) [9]. According to Culture in Development (CiD) [10], an organization with the mission to protect cultural heritage from any disaster, cultural heritage can be distinguished in the following ways:

- Built environment (buildings, townscapes, archaeological remains)
- Natural environment (rural landscapes, coasts and shorelines, agricultural heritage)
- Artifacts (books & documents, objects, pictures).

The concerns of this community, in terms of issues of human computer interaction (HCI), may focus more on the aspects relating to managing, accessing, and retrieving both tangible and intangible artifacts. From the digital humanities' point of view, the GLAM community cares about preserving and promoting the precious cultural and artistic objects and information to the public with sophisticated digital methods. In particular, with the assistance of technology, tagging provided by the general public can shed lights on the categorization and organization aspects of digital archives that GLAM professionals concern about.

In this research, Tamsui Wiki is the cultural heritage information that was studied and where the research data was collected. Built in 2013, Tamsui Wiki is a completely virtual cultural heritage collection and a collaborative effort made by the College of Liberal Arts in Tamkang University (TKU). The College of Liberal Arts is consisted of departments in both humanities and social sciences, including the Department of Chinese, the Department of History, the Department of Journalism, the Department of Information and Library Science, and the Department of Information and Communication. The collaborative research project received funding for digitally preserving the local cultural heritage. TKU is located in Tamsui, an early developed area where the western business first came in contact with Taiwan. In the 17th century, the Spanish arrived in the area of Tamsui; by the mid-19th century Tamsui had become the largest port in Taiwan. With the rich heritage influenced by diversified cultures, Tamsui has become a fascinating district of northern Taiwan that attracts many artists and visitors from local and abroad. Even in the present time, Tamsui plays a significant role in Taiwanese culture ("Tamsui District" n.d.) [11].

A vast amount of information and multimedia objects are collected from Tamsui Wiki, a digital humanities project built collaboratively by the five departments of TKU as mentioned above. Each department offers its scholarly expertise in different elements of the project. Essentially, the Department of History provided the rich oral history interviewed from the well-known local people; the Department of the Journalism provided valuable images and multimedia resources by filming stories of very important people who are Tamsui residents. Historic buildings, traditional shops, as well as cultural events focusing on Tamsui area are also included. After Tamsui Wiki accumulates its rich resources, the Department of Library and Information Science joined and centered its focus on the issue of organization, access, and retrieval of the diversified multimedia resources.

3   Research Method

This study sets out to examine the elderly's social tagging behavior. The research team used the revised Delphi method followed by a drawing session with 20 elderly citizens who are over 55 years old and are residents in northern Taipei.

Through a set of selection criteria, including the length of the film and the theme of the film (non-political and non-religious topics), a multimedia resource was selected by the research team from the digital humanities Wikipedia, Tamsui Wiki, as shown in Figs. 1 and 2. Each participant was interviewed for about 30 min after watching a 10-min film about a traditional bakery famous for its role as wedding engagement favors in Taiwan. The questions of the guided interviews mainly focus on the tags that the participant gave based on their understanding and knowledge of the film. Revised Delphi method was conducted for two rounds; with 10 elderly citizens each round, resulting in total number 20 seniors. The reason for carrying out multiple rounds of Delphi method is to seek consensus among the elderly on tagging principles. After the interview session, each participant was asked to draw a fishbone diagram with the

Fig. 1. The homepage of Tamsui Wiki, a cooperative effort of cultural heritage information (Source: http://tamsui.dils.tku.edu.tw/wiki/index.php/首頁)

Fig. 2. The testing video selected from Tamsui Wiki for the research purpose, a film about the legacy of a local bakery (Source: http://tamsui.dils.tku.edu.tw/wiki/index.php/大淡水地區全紀錄人物誌/淡水禮餅獻)

purpose of grouping in more detailed fashion the main tags and sub-tags with visual aid after giving the list of the tags during the interview session. With the knowledge of fishbone diagram being usually used for problem solving in various context, the researcher found such visual information particularly helpful l in assisting and clarifying the list of tags with the elderly. The process helped the elderly reexamine the classification of tags they perceived from watching the film.

4   Findings and Discussions

The findings of the study reveal three aspects: the *types* of tags the elderly consider, the *prompts* the elderly consider, and the *factors* the elderly consider. First, the analysis of the interview and fishbone diagram showed that the types of tags the elderly consider fall into three categories: concrete objects, emotion aspects, personal memory and related experience. The three categories were repeatedly shown in the elderly's tags. The very obvious examples in the category of concrete objects are names of the building, which fall in to the category of the definition of cultural heritage information, the built environment. Other examples are names of the street, the name of the shop, the name of the transportation stops, and also the name of the various goods filmed in the video. The second category, emotional aspects, means the overall perception that the elderly revealed through their tags. The sources of tags, such as "retro," "legacy," "preservation," etc. came from the scripts and the conversation in the film. The third category, personal memory and related experience, essentially means the hidden idea that the elderly caught after watching the film. For instance, the film's main idea was to preserve the emotional element of the traditional wedding cookies that usually a Taiwanese family would prepare for their bride-to-be as a wedding favor for the guests coming to the pre-marital engagement ceremony. Many Taiwanese people have experienced this sort of wedding customs more or less in their lives. This common knowledge and shared experience apparently influence the elderly's tagging.

Secondly, the prompts the elderly consider when giving tags are based on explicit texts, buildings, and people shown in the film. When the interviewee asked what prompted the elderly to give certain tags, the elderly shared the obvious texts shown in the film caught their attention. These texts, even appeared only a few and probably served as section titles in the film, became important prompts in the minds of the elderly when asked to provide tags regarding the film they have just watched. Again, repeated instances of seeing the same buildings and key people in the film seemed to bring emphasis as the elderly recalled what the film was about, and therefore became important prompts.

Lastly, the factors the elderly consider when giving tags are mainly because of repeated themes, concrete objects, as well as personal and communal memory from the past experience. When being asked of the possible reasons for tags and groupings of the tags in fishbone diagrams, the analysis showed the elderly easily picked up repeatedly conversed notions and words; they also perceived the importance of the concrete objects in the film. Also, it is important to note the communal memory is worthy of attention. After sharing the most important factors that helped coming up with tags about the film, the elderly's choices of tags then shifted to a rather subtle layer that was beneath the obvious ones. This layer is concerned with the shared memory of the same generation that no other generations perceived, or perhaps not as strongly perceived. Figures 3 and 4 are excerpts of tags obtained from the revised Delphi methods with weighted relevance marked by the participant.

Mental models change states and shapes during a person's maturity process; therefore, it is essential for researchers to understand how a group of users change in their state of mind as they interact with an interface. Collectively, studying the mental model of a certain group assists interface designers to more closely realize desired results. According to Wang et al. [12], "Current research on multimedia emotion tagging mainly consists of two steps: feature extraction and classification." The results of this study echoed the statement. The Delphi method combined with a drawing session revealed that upon watching a 10-min film concerning cultural heritage information, the elderly provided tags that first extracted from the facts and artifacts from the environment shown in the film, including buildings, people, and texts. After the first round of tagging, with the tool of fishbone diagrams, the elderly showed their thoughts on grouping of the tags. Emotion tagging comes after the factual tagging is completed, which brings implications for current tagging system. The interface designers are advised to extract the emotional aspects of the resources being described, especially for the elderly users, in order to enhance the efficiency and accuracy of information retrieval.

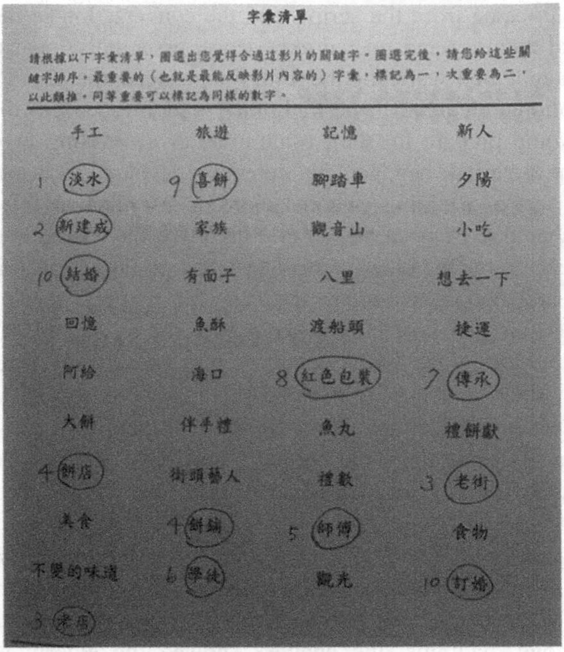

Fig. 3. Tags extracted from revised Delphi method, with numbered priorities

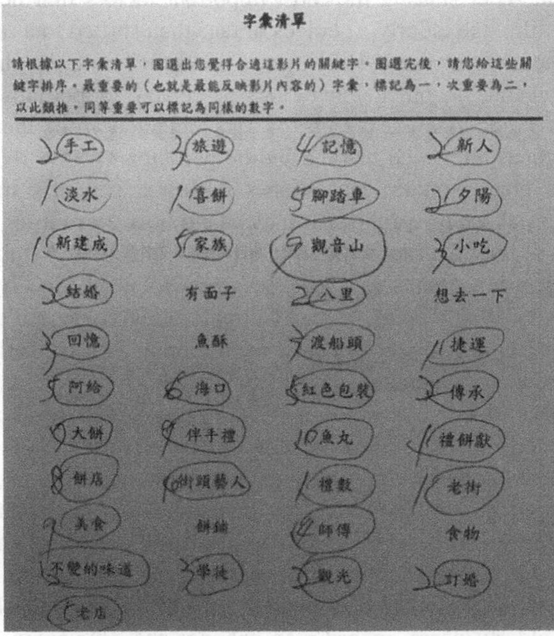

Fig. 4. Tags extracted from revised Delphi method, with numbered priorities from a different senior participant

5 Conclusion

Studying and analyzing senior adults' tagging behavior and their mental model provides insights for cultural heritage information for organizations such as museums and cultural centers to adjust interface design (in particular the searching and browsing aspects) to suit different generation of users. Searching the literature from the field of library and information science, human computer interaction, computer science, psychology, and social studies, past studies showed that mental models of different generations possibly reveal unique tagging principles and guidelines for the elderly.

The results of the study bring insights into the analysis of tagging semantics centered on senior users. The contribution of such results can help researchers, designers, stakeholders, and educators alike to understand the conceptual differences of tagging behavior, with the analysis of the mental models of users with age difference. The results of the study also help in designing the tag-based interface for senior users to ease the cognitive load when searching and choosing needed cultural heritage information in archive and museum settings. For future research focuses on the senior users, the author suggests innovative video tagging and retrieving options that include tagging principles that are revealed in this study. The concrete objects, the explicit texts, and key people repeatedly shown and mentioned in the video are the comparatively easy sources for tagging recommendations. For the aspect of past experience, shared memory, and the knowledge of the same generation that is found critical in the study, is primarily in the area of emotion tagging, the researcher believes more research studies are needed and expected in the long run, so we can better understand how emotion can be extracted and applied in retrieving multimedia resources in the most efficient and flexible way for the targeted user.

Acknowledgement. This project was supported by an internal research grant received from the College of Liberal Arts in Tamkang University. The author wishes to thank the Dean of College of Liberal Arts, Dr. Sinn-Cheng Lin, for creating and hosting the digital humanities project of Tamsui Wiki, as well as the faculty and students who contributed to the content of Tamsui Wiki. The link to the project is at http://tamsui.dils.tku.edu.tw/wiki/index.php/首頁.

References

1. Collier, D.: Comparative method (1993). http://polisci.berkeley.edu/sites/default/files/people/u3827/APSA-TheComparativeMethod.pdf. Accessed 2 Mar 2017
2. McLeod, S.A.: Jean Piaget (2015). https://www.simplypsychology.org/piaget.html. Accessed 2 Jan 2017
3. Gentner, D., Stevens, A.L.: Mental Models. Lawrence Erlbaum Associates, Hillsdale (1983)
4. Young, I.: The value of mental model diagrams. https://indiyoung.com/value/. Accessed 10 Dec 2017
5. Magzan, M.: Mental models for leadership effectiveness: building future different than the past. J. Eng. Manag. Compet. 2(2), 57–63 (2012)
6. DeBono, E.: I Am Right. You are Wrong. Penguin Books, London (1991)
7. Tsai, L.C., Hwang, S.L., Tang, K.H.: Analysis of keyword-based tagging behaviors of experts and novices. Online Inf. Rev. 35, 272–290 (2011)

8. Trant, J.: Studying social tagging and folksonomy: a review and framework. J. Digit. Inf. **10** (1) (2009)
9. Ruthven, I., Chowdhury, G.G.: Cultural Heritage Information: Access and Management. Neal-Schuman Publishers, Chicago (2015)
10. Culture in Development, What is cultural heritage? http://www.cultureindevelopment.nl/cultural_heritage/what_is_cultural_heritage. Accessed 4 Jan 2017
11. Tamsui District. https://en.wikipedia.org/wiki/Tamsui_District. Accessed 10 Jan 2018
12. Wang, S., Wang, Z., Ji, Q.: Multiple emotional tagging of multimedia data by exploiting dependencies among emotions. Multimed. Tools Appl. **74**(6), 1863–1883 (2013)

Digital Participation Roles of the Global Jihad: Social Media's Role in Bringing Together Vulnerable Individuals and VEO Content

Gina S. Ligon[✉], Margeret Hall, and Clara Braun

University of Nebraska Omaha, Omaha 68182, USA
{gligon, mahall, cbraun}@unomaha.edu

Abstract. The advent of the internet broadly changed the way society communicates. This is well-known and well-researched across standard populations. Niche or subpopulations, such as terrorist groups or other violent extremist organizations, are less well-understood and researched. However, as strategic outreach such as recruiting and advertising is more and more web-based, research's limited understanding of such groups is a detriment to effective management strategies. This work is a foundational attempt to ground violent extremist organization's internet usage into the theoretical lens of and discussion around digital participation and online communities. We analyze the spectrum of participation in violent extremist organizations' online communities and elucidate existing behaviors of individuals involved with terrorism in a series of mini case studies. This work's contribution is the expansion of the theoretical framework of digital participation in online violent extremist communities.

Keywords: Violent extremist organizations · Digital participation
Online communities · Social media

1 Introduction: The Internet's Facilitation of Violent Extremism

Violent Extremist Organizations (VEOs) have posed security challenges for decades. However, in the modern era, with the advent of more lethal weapons, global mobility, and improved communication methods (e.g., open social media), the span and impact of these groups grows from regional to worldwide via their online brand [1]. Thus, these cyber technologies have increased VEO lethality and messaging reach [2] and are becoming an ever-increasing part of the portfolios of VEOs [3]. Historically, access to resources allows wealthier nation-states and other large organizations to build and maintain infrastructures in comparison to their smaller, less prosperous counterparts. With the advent of participatory internet technologies and the promulgation of open and free internet architectures, however, less technical infrastructure is required for smaller or resource-poor organizations to communicate and conduct operations. While digitalization initially acted as a supply driver of this phenomenon, the advent of 'digital natives' (generally speaking, those born after 1980) reversed the equation and the move to ubiquitous online presence and content has become a demand-led necessity

© Springer International Publishing AG, part of Springer Nature 2018
F. F.-H. Nah and B. S. Xiao (Eds.): HCIBGO 2018, LNCS 10923, pp. 485–495, 2018.
https://doi.org/10.1007/978-3-319-91716-0_39

for groups communicating online [4]. This new paradigm of highly connected, low-cost communication technologies has simultaneously offered such organizations access to resources that further benevolent or malicious goals [2]. Terrorist groups use these technologies in a variety of ways, such as group decision-making, cyber facilitated financing, recruitment, enabled (remote-control) attacks, and propaganda dissemination [5].

VEO content sharing is neatly formatted for digital natives in a way that makes vulnerable youth feel like stars of their own action movies [6]. Yet despite its prominent place in public discourse, a basic understanding of how digital media content influences individuals to participate in propagating VEO content is lacking. Emerging qualitative approaches identify which digital media content influences individuals to adopt extremist beliefs and behaviors [2, 7]. This chapter proposes investigating the pathway to extremist beliefs and behaviors from the perspective of the digital participation lifecycle [8], considering the transition from viewing to actively participation in content dissemination. To illustrate the variety of roles users can play in digital communities, we highlight how a variety of individuals associated with Salafist-inspired Jihad have manifested roles spanning Lurkers to Creators.

2 Participation in Digital Communities

Broadly speaking, participation on the Internet and social media has a looped dependency. Individuals rely on connected technologies to receive content, where connected technologies rely on individuals to create the content that is propagated [9, 10]. Conceptually, content is created, then consumed. One issue in the current discourse scenario in social media as well as VEO research is that social media content is simultaneously treated as both an input and an output variable for measuring user behavior. A more mature theoretical lens investigates VEO social media from the perspective of how users engage or participate with the content. This allows practitioners and researchers to classify user behavior given their engagement with social media content. While the figure below (Fig. 1) may connote movement between the levels based on increasing commitment, individual differences (e.g., backgrounds in graphic design, degree of leadership) could drive individuals to move more quickly through the levels. The key consideration is that there are far more lurkers than there are creators in online digital communities [8]:

In the following discussion, we connect the literature on digital participation roles with the social media activities of violent extremists. In this discussion, we highlight notable individuals who manifest attributes described by Li and Bernoff [8].[1] This schema has alternatively been described as a ladder or a pyramid. There are progressively less active individuals the higher the level of participation is required; it should be noted that an individual can be differentially engaged in different communities and may find themselves in one of many roles simultaneously in different communities. By

---

[1] Inactives are not represented in this discussion as it is not possible to estimate the number of people in total who are online but have never had access to VEO content on the (social) web.

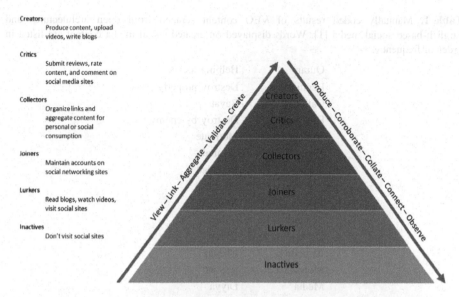

Fig. 1. Digital participation roles

linking content, behaviors, and users, it is possible to estimate escalating behaviors by mapping types of activities by individuals. Network science is a useful approach for mapping the escalation of individual behaviors.

3   Connecting the Digital Participation Lifecycle and VEO Social Media Content

Social media and content sharing technologies are ideal for groups with unknown followings, as it enables producers of content to have a one-to-many reach with potential followers [8]. VEOs (ISIL in particular) have capitalized on this by disseminating varying content types which are potentially relevant to an unknown, international, vulnerable audience. Derrick and colleagues classified 37 different content types produced and disseminated by ISIL in their advertising and recruitment campaigns (Table 1). The variety and frequency of the content types speaks to the sophistication of VEO content producers in disseminating enticing content for an unknown audience.

User-specific tailoring has become more important with the rise of social media outreach, as 'brands' that do not excite their audiences risk losing network traction. Followers who take an interest in social media content more thoroughly consume the presented information [11]. Content engagement is critical for growing support and recruitment through the internet.

Table 1. Manually coded results of VEO content scraped from open architectures and English-based social media [1]. Words displayed on created social media content are listed in order of frequency.

Quran	Helping locals
Legitimacy	Destroy property
Caliphate	Bayat
Education	Destroy by enemy
Violent items	Motivate
Mujahideen	Manuals
Apostate	Baghdad
Antiwest	Shame
Jihad	Apocbattle
Sharia	Cyber
Destroy by ISIS	Hijrah
Atrocities	Hisbah
Mohammed	Repent
Media	Diyya
Justify	Ribat
Leader	Training
Territory	Village ldr
Military ops	Lonewolf
Shahid (Martyr)	

3.1 Lurkers

The diversity of content types also indicates the variety of ways that groups can move passive content consumers (lurkers or spectators) into joiners. Lurkers are generally the largest of any online community. They are classified as content consumers who are otherwise inactive in radical behaviors. While an argument has been made that participation is dichotomous (thus any viewing of content should be considered active participation [10]), this is an oversimplification of the problem. Both in theory and practically, there is difference between an impact of seeing materials and using or propagating materials. Lurking and all forms of general exposure are tantamount to the material's reach and impressions count, and not clicks other return on investment metrics [11].

Due to their lack of engagement with the content (e.g., sharing, downloading, commenting), it is not possible to estimate the extent to which lurkers are consuming content for interest, values alignment, research or other motivations. Due to the nature of VEO content, it is also possible that lurkers are not stakeholders but may actually be intelligence agencies or competing groups. This fact drives the need for VEO content on the open social web to be attractive enough to further entice users' joining but not so specific to ongoing operations such that they may be disrupted. For this reason, much of the online planning and coaching that happens is done with encrypted services and not on the open social web [12]. In our technical report in 2017 to the Studies of

Terrorism and Responses to Terrorism (START, University of Maryland), we identi-fied that the majority of VEOs required some type of log-in to view content, which indicates that most members of Jihad digital communities quickly move to the Joiner stage [12].

3.2 Joiners

Joiners may either transition from lurking, or join the digital community directly. This is generally understood to be driven by user motivation and network structure. Moti-vation can be linked to interests or values. Specifically, the focus on religious content and community reflects values activation (see Table 1), whereas interests may be any combination of the content available or even driven by desire to digitally belong to a specific group affiliation [13]. Group affiliation is in this case an umbrella function which addresses both interests of the user and the network structure they belong in.

Network structures are highly pertinent to Joiners' transformation into active users. While the likelihood an individual will share increases monotonically with exposure, explicit feedback about how many friends have previously shared the same content increases the likelihood of an active response. Friends and 'influencers' (very active nodes in the social graph) activate other users, and have the highest impact on network ties and their behavior. The positioning of content on a user's interface strongly affects social contagion [11]. Estimating the propensity of one node in a graph to transition into an active node is feasible using Granovetter's theory of the strength of weak ties [14]. His theory has been used to track peer-based diffusion by identifying constrictions and contractions across nodes and edges [14]. These data reasonably can be, but have not been, extrapolated for online radicalization. Network models trace the spread individual influence. As such, network structures are useful to consider for discerning activation (as compared to lurking) along the participation spectrum.

One exemplar of a Joiner is *Saddam Mohamed Raishani* (aka *Adam Raishani*), who was arrested after attempting to flee the United States (Bucher 2017). Most of evidence related to this case involves audio recordings of Raishani discussing his allegiance to ISIS, his desire to travel overseas, and information about how he had helped another flee abroad as a foreign fighter. According to the criminal complaint related to Rais-hani's case[2], he had downloaded and used a web browser that allows the user to conceal online activities. During one of the recorded conversations with FBI agents, Raishani stated that he used the browser to view Jihadi videos. In a March meeting with undercover agents, Raishani was provided with a laptop where he covered the camera and microphone, wore gloves, and deleted all Jihadi content after viewing it. Beyond utilizing the web browser and downloading videos, Raishani's online footprint was minimal, indicating he fit the profile of a Joiner in his digital community.

---

[2] United States of America v Saddam Mohamed Raishani. 18 U.S.C. § § 2339B & 2.

3.3 Collectors

As opposed to seeing digital media content or joining a digital Jihad community, collecting, storing, owning and/or disseminating extremist materials is a direct violation of criminal statutes. This represents (knowingly or not) an escalation in radical behavior. Collectors transition from joiners: they are already activated by VEO content and now are actively working to further organize and disseminate it. Collectors are not creators. They do not generate new or original materials. Collectors are those who clone and fork digital repositories. They also collate collections of interest for the broader community to access. This is a particularly critical group for maintaining the pipeline of non-indexed websites (i.e., justpaste.it) [12], as well as for maintaining clear and open pathways to said content. Figure 1 contains a sample screenshot of how Collectors accomplish this pathway maintenance. Collectors are second only to creators in terms of maintaining the visibility of VEO content on the social web (Fig. 2).

The value of individual collectors (nodes) in the social network is contingent upon their betweeness and closeness with other high value individuals (nodes) in the social graph. Betweenness is the likelihood of a person to serve as the most direct route between two others. Closeness of nodes is a measurement of the speed by which information is disseminated in a network. Collectors with high betweenness and/or closeness scores are especially well-poised to broadly disseminate content. This propensity increases when they are connected to Creators with a high eigenvector score. Eigenvector scores measure how well connected an individual is to other well-connected individuals in a network. Those with high eigenvector scores will be well connected with suspects of terrorism investigations (Brooks 2011).

Collectors are critical for the forming of 'small world' networks. These are networks that appear almost random but exhibit significantly high clustering coefficients (i.e., nodes that tend to cluster locally) and a relatively short average path length (i.e., nodes that can be reached in a few steps). Such a network will have many sub-clusters but be joined by many bridges between clusters which shorten the average distances between individuals and other sub-networks. For these reasons, Collectors are strategically relevant targets for shutting down the pipeline of VEO content on the social web.

Khalid Ali-M Aldawsar exemplifies a Collector role (Bernstein 2011). During the time of his radicalization, Saudi immigrant Aldawsar was 20 years old and failing out of his chemical engineering program at Texas Tech. When he was arrested, he was a business student at South Plains College in Lubbock, TX. His Facebook posts progressed from being positive about his life, the United States, and liking girls to critically discussing U.S. and Israel foreign policy. One personal blog post explained how he excelled academically in high school, earned a scholarship that allowed him to be sent to America where he intended to learn English, learn to build explosives, and target U.S. citizens. Collecting behaviors ranged from accumulating guides and materials for making bombs and to acquiring information about selecting targets. Using three email addresses, he sent himself summaries and stored them in a common location before writing about them in his personal journal.

Fig. 2. An example of disseminating VEO content on the platform YouTube. Image taken from: "Upload Knights": How Terrorists Slip Beheading Videos Past YouTube's Censors. https:// motherboard.vice.com/en_us/article/xyepmw/how-terrorists-slip-beheading-videos-past-youtubes-censors

3.4 Critics

'Critics' as a stage in the participation lifecycle is a slight misnomer. While Critics may criticize, they are known for content evaluation or reviewing. Critics are also the 'experts' in mature social systems that set the standards of engagement and behaviors [15]. They are tantamount to moderators of subreddits or verified purchasers on e-Commerce sites. Critics take on the roles of discourse management in forums and posts. Discourse management or norm setting is a factor in establishing likeness (or homophily) within the group and for new entrants (lurkers and joiners). A strong established identity can lead to the formation of homogeneous groups (clusters) where facilitating direct relationships is easier. It must be remembered that Critics respond to content, rather than create content themselves. Critics shape and refine the messages and consequently influence its meaning.

They are the commenters on YouTube and the active retweeters of VEO 'influencers' on twitter. At this stage of activation Critics validate the organizations by interacting with VEO as it were any social media content. Critics comment, discuss, and evaluate VEO content in the same vein as the twitterati or redditors comment, discuss, and evaluate on their respective platforms. Content engagement at this level serves to make the social network denser. Density is a measure of the connections between nodes in a social network and serves as an indicator of popularity or influence. Density is a critical metric as information in dense networks can flow more quickly. In the case of non-indexed websites or content that is in violation of the Terms and Conditions of a platform, a swift flow of information can more quickly support Collectors in their dissemination of VEO content.

An example of a Critic is Nicholas Michael Teausant, who actively engaged across several social media platforms[3]. Teausant had accounts on several social media platforms, including Ask.fm, Google+, Facebook, Tumbler, and Instagram. During the time of his arrest, he was 20 years old and was a community college student in Stockton, CA. A National Guard dropout, Teausant communicated with an undercover FBI agent, stating he planned to bomb the Los Angeles subway system. His social media accounts were plagued with anti-Western messages, calling for violent action. He was arrested for attempting to flee to Canada in the hopes of making it abroad as a foreign fighter. Below are some of his Instagram comments:

> *May 31, 2013: user Assad Teausant bigolsmurfposted: @don-quad lol "don't get me wrong I despise america and want its down fall but yeah haha. Lol I been part of the army for two years now and I would love to join Allah's army but I don't even know how to start."*

> *August 5, 2013: user Assad Teausant bigolsmurf posted: Anyone know where I can get the "lone Mujahid pocket book" #alqaeda #jihadis t#jihad #islamicpridetimuslim#mashallah# islam#allah#AllahuAkbar#thelonemujahid*

3.5   Creators

There are far fewer content creators than consumers [8]. Social media's one-to-many content provision is built upon this model. Creators are the least common individuals in the digital participation lifecycle but are lynchpins to thriving content-based networks. Content creation entry points can include blogging, online fundraising, ideological campaigns, active recruitment, video or other media creation, or active participation in organizational decision-making. There is not a linear progression through the digital participation ladder or a known entry point for content creators, other than identity validation by the organization. Once validated, Creators directly engage in content creation. The more mature social network or digital communities are, the more they allow for this immediate progression. In other words, their skills may allow them to start at the top of the digital community pyramid.

Jose Pimentel exemplifies a Creator role (Goldstein and Rashbaum 2011). Pimentel maintained his own website (www.trueislam1.com) with bomb-making instructions from Inspire Magazine, and he also posted his own recipes. His personal website

---

[3] United States of America v. Nicholas Michael Teausant. Case no. 2:14-MJ-0064 DAD; 7 June 2016. California Man Sentenced to 12 Years I Prison for attempting to join ISIL. Department of Justice: Office of Public Affairs.

communicated anti-Western propaganda, ultimately calling for violent action against the United States. "Pimentel talked about killing U.S. military personnel returning home from Iraq and Afghanistan, particularly Marines and Army personnel," Mr. Kelly said. "He talked about bombing post offices in and around Washington Heights and police cars in New York City, as well as a police station in Bayonne, N.J. Once his bombing campaign began, Mr. Pimentel said the public would know that there were mujahideen in the city to fight Jihad here" (Goldstein and Rashbaum 2011).

4 Summary and Future Directions

Standard analytical models are built on the assumption that engagement with social media content is binary – content is created, and content is received [10]. Empirical and theoretical models increasingly show that participation in digital communities is actually a spectrum [8, 9]. This more nuanced view allows practitioners and researchers to better diagnose where individuals are in their engagement within communities by measuring their types of engagement, rather than the output of content created. It also corrects the current analytical issue in social media analysis, which is the use of social media content as an input and output factor of analysis. Analyzing the person in terms of which stage of participation they are currently in is more pertinent in terms of stopping the progression of extremist beliefs and behaviors. Whereas traditional analyses would suggest Creators should be the focus of disruption activities, this analysis suggests that there is an entire pathway of participation with VEO content. At each stage of participation there are entry (and exit) points which can effectively stop the flow of content and information dissemination. Escalating behaviors along with their qualifying activities help practitioners and researchers more accurately classify the differences between Lurkers and those who more actively create malevolent content.

Future work for scholars should address at least three critical issues. First, how robust are these roles in the context of violent extremism? As this taxonomy was originally developed to explain non-violent digital participation, it is critical that we further examine a sample of individuals participating in digital communities that are violent or prescribe violence to understand how these roles operate. Related, the second line of research should examine their online behaviors as they relate to these offline behaviors. While some assume that online recruitment is rampant in violent extremist groups, most extremism research indicates that offline relationships and roles are more important than online communications. However, this relationship has been investigated to date with small n sizes and scant data on online participation. Third, future scholarship in this area should examine how this participation is related to different types of outcomes. For example, given that creators and critics may have more of their personal identities invested in the generation of material in support of violent groups, it is may be that they also act in identity-congruent ways offline (e.g., higher levels of group participation and mobilization). However, it may also be that these individuals lack the skillset for greater levels of online participation, and thus lurkers and joiners have greater participation offline to compensate for these deficits. Without a large sample, it is impossible to understand how digital participation roles escalate coherently online and offline, or if they co-vary at all.

4.1   Limitations

While novel in its application of how online behavior relates to offline radicalization and engagement in violence, the present effort is not without limitations. First, the case examples from which we drew our exemplar behaviors were all individuals from the United States who endorsed a Jihadist ideology. Evidence suggests that online propaganda from the Far Right is much more prevalent online as of 2016, and thus, may yield different cases. Given that the focus of this effort was on the unique phenomenon of how Foreign Terrorist Organizations influence acts of terrorism in the United States, however, it should be noted that these findings only apply to that particularly unique domain. Extremist online behavior from the Far Right or Far Left may contribute different aspects to our understanding of online behaviors. Second, other digital narratives could be used to explain the online influence of this demographic as well. For example, the work on online communities in health care, branding, and knowledge-sharing could also be relevant to understanding how Jihadi-inspired individuals relate to virtual content. Specifically, word of mouth approaches to understanding network narratives in marketing can have significant value for understanding how the individuals described in the present effort related to each other and the narrative espoused by Foreign Terrorist Organizations. Despite these limitations, however, the present effort is at least a first attempt to apply an accepted framework for digital roles to actual offenders of Jihadist-inspired crimes in the United States, which holds promise for unpacking at least some drivers of violent ideological cyber influences.

References

1. Ligon, G.S., Harms, M., Derrick, D.C.: Lethal brands: how VEOs build reputations. J. Strateg. Secur. **8**, 27–42 (2015)
2. Derrick, D., Sporer, K., Church, S., Ligon, G.: Ideological rationality and violence: an exploratory study of ISIL's cyber profile. Dyn. Asymmetric Confl. **9**, 57–81 (2017)
3. Denning, D.E.: Terror's web: how the internet is transforming terrorism. In: Handbook of Internet Crime, pp. 194–213 (2010)
4. Niemeyer, C., Hall, M., Weinhardt, C.: Towards Digitally Native Online Participation Platforms (2016)
5. Derrick, D.C., Ligon, G.S., Harms, M., Mahoney, W.: Cyber-sophistication assessment methodology for public-facing terrorist web sites. J. Inf. Warf. **16**, 13–30 (2017)
6. Pape, R., Gunning, W.: ISIS and the Culture of Narcissism. http://www.wsj.com/articles/isis-and-the-culture-of-narcissism-1467069159?mg=id-wsj (2016)
7. Pelletier, I.R., Lundmark, L., Gardner, R., Ligon, G.S., Kilinc, R.: Why ISIS' message resonates: leveraging Islam, socio-political catalysts and adaptive messaging. Stud. Confl. Terror. **731**, 1–66 (2016)
8. Li, C., Bernoff, J.: Groundswell: winning in a world transformed by social technologies. Harvard Bus. Rev. Press. **26**, 286 (2011)
9. Bishop, J.: Increasing participation in online communities: a framework for human–computer interaction. Comput. Hum. Behav. **23**, 1881–1893 (2007)
10. Malinen, S.: Understanding user participation in online communities: a systematic literature review of empirical studies. Comput. Hum. Behav. **46**, 228–238 (2015)

11. Schacht, J., Hall, M., Chorley, M.: Tweet if you will – the real question is, who do you influence? In: WebSci, 15 p. (2015). Article 55
12. Ligon, G.S., Logan, M., Hall, M., Derrick, D.C., Fuller, J., Church, S.: The Jihadi Industry: Assessing the The Jihadi Industry, College Park, MD (2017)
13. Lindner, A., Hall, M., Niemeyer, C., Caton, S.: BeWell: a sentiment aggregator for proactive community management. In: CHI 2015 Extended Abstracts, pp. 1055–1060. ACM Press, Seoul, Korea (2015)
14. Granovetter, M.: The strength of weak ties. Am. J. Sociol. **78**, 1360–1380 (1973)
15. Lampe, C., Johnston, E., Arbor, A.: Follow the (Slash) dot: effects of feedback on new members in an online community. In: GROUP 2005, pp. 11–20 (2005)

Trust and the Flow Experience on Facebook: What Motivates Social Network Usage?

Soo Il Shin[1(✉)] and Dianne J. Hall[2]

[1] University of Wisconsin – Green Bay, Green Bay, WI 54301, USA
shins@uwgb.edu
[2] Auburn University, Auburn, AL 36849, USA

Abstract. Social networking sites (SNSs) have become one of the most frequently used communication media. While many studies have examined the motivations of SNS usage and visiting behaviors, this study mainly focuses on exploring the role of trust in an SNS and intrinsic motivational factors affecting continuous usage behaviors, using the flow theory. Using a web-based survey of 291 college students, the age group that most frequently uses SNSs, our research findings suggest theoretical insights. The flow experience—consisting of perceived enjoyment, perceived control, and concentration—serves as a salient antecedent to explaining SNS users' satisfaction, which in turn has a positive effect on continuous use of an SNS. Intent for continuous usage of an SNS mediates the relationships between satisfaction and actual use behaviors. Our research findings also reveal that trust in an SNS significantly affects all other constructs, including perceptions of SNS users, intentions, and actual behaviors. Further discussion is detailed, and the limitations of this research are addressed.

Keywords: Social networking sites · Trust · Flow theory
Partial least square (PLS)

1 Introduction

Among many types of computer-mediated communication (CMC), including email, chatting, blogging, and social networking sites (SNSs), SNSs are phenomenally popular. Prior literature defined SNSs as follows:

"Web-based services that allow individuals to (1) construct a public or semi-public profile within a bounded system, (2) articulate a list of other users with whom they share a connection, and (3) view and traverse their list of connections and those made by others within the system."
[5, p. 211]

Within a bounded system of premade personal profiles, two-way interaction with other SNS users bypasses a lack of physical coherence and the limitations of timing. Thus, SNSs help extend personal networking. Currently, Facebook is one of the most well-known SNSs; as of May 2016, it has more than 1.65 billion active monthly users, which is increasing by 15% each year [51]. Recent surveys also show that the average time of a Facebook visit in the U.S. is 40 min, the average Twitter visit is 34 min [43], and the largest group of Facebook users (30%) comprises those between 25 and 34 years old [51].

© Springer International Publishing AG, part of Springer Nature 2018
F. F.-H. Nah and B. S. Xiao (Eds.): HCIBGO 2018, LNCS 10923, pp. 496–512, 2018.
https://doi.org/10.1007/978-3-319-91716-0_40

Since the 1997 emergence of the first SNS, SixDegrees.com, this new, innovative medium of communication has been supported by Web 2.0 applications in the online network environment. As opposed to face-to-face (FtF) communication, where people have physical contact in a geographic location with one or more other people, CMC signifies social sharing and socio-emotional communication in an online environment through nonverbal cues with no physical expression (e.g., facial movement, eye contact, gestures). The literature indicates these nonverbal cues are easily adopted by communicators, thereby facilitating the development of effective relationships in an online communication environment [39]. As a type of CMC, SNSs are popularly regarded as representative of "online communities," a term stemming from the social perspective approach [24]. Such communities can be viewed from a social perspective if community members being motivated to build a network, share personal interests, and/or exchange useful information [50]. They can be viewed from a business perspective if community members' motivation is based on pursuit of goals reflecting their shared interests.

Regarding the impact of an SNS, such as Facebook (facebook.com) and Twitter (twitter.com), on the public as a new communication medium, earlier literature has revealed several important findings. First, research suggests that preferred SNSs differ according to ethnic and cultural background [21]. For instance, Mixi (mixi.jp) is the most popular SNS in Japan, with an estimated 14 million accounts [48]. Second, from a marketing perspective, the advertising effect has increased significantly between commercial companies and SNS users, resulting in rapidly increasing advertisement expenditures. Despite the significant marketing expenditure cutback in traditional media (i.e., advertising in printed media, radio and television decreased at least 22%) because of the recession, marketers are still apt to increase their advertising budget for online media [17]. Third, many researchers have found that the majority of SNS users are college-aged and young-adult people who lead the SNS culture by proffering their communication media, such as sharing multimedia content like photos and videos [40]. Interestingly, Muise et al. [36] found that Facebook usage induced feelings of jealousy between romantic partners because of a partner's dubious or ambiguous status, leading one to visit their significant other's page more often.

Regardless of the implications and findings of prior studies with respect to the influence of SNSs on public users, because of several critical issues, scholars are still debating whether SNS users are persistent or temporary. For example, in an early study of Facebook, profile owners' identity exposure and privacy concerns were important issues in terms of SNS users retaining continuous activities [29]. While Foster et al. [17] acknowledged the importance of motivation for user participation in online social networks, their research failed to delineate constructive relationships among motivation factors or illustrate how they combine to describe SNS users' visiting behaviors. Generally, SNS users are free from switching costs when moving from one SNS to another, so researchers have not been able to explain why some SNSs users are faithful to one SNS over others [25]. Consequently, the present study sheds special light on this area, raising the following research questions:

RQ1: What factors affect SNS users in such a way that they continue to use certain SNSs under the state of flow and flow experience?

RQ2: How does trust in an SNS affect users' continued usage behaviors?

This study is designed to identify factors that affect SNS users' continued use by integrating flow theory and concepts of trust into the research model. First, we argue that flow theory is the theoretical background to explain emotional pleasure and helps examine the intrinsic motivation of media use [27]. Flow theory is useful for capturing people's involvement in activities during which they feel nothing else matters [11]. Another aspect of our research is to employ the concept of trust in an SNS. Regarding shared profiles within a "friends" network in an SNS as a communication medium, trust in communicating parties and the communication platform itself is necessary [6]. It is true that greater trust in communication media induces more usage of such media, resulting in a greater feeling of effective communication and a closer relationship. Prior literature also identified that trust is an important determinant of building commitment and initiating enhanced relationships [35]. Unlike prior literature that measured the impact of trust on limited constructs, we examine the overall impact of trust on users' perception of continued use of an SNS. As primary antecedents, we also examined an influence of the status of flow on a user's satisfaction with SNS use, as well as the impact of satisfaction on continuous usage behaviors.

The Sect. 2 of this paper reviews the theoretical background and presents a research framework with hypotheses. The Sect. 3 describes research methods, and the Sect. 4 presents the data analysis and results. The Sect. 5 discusses the findings and implications, and the Sect. 6 contains the limitations of the current research, ideas for future research, and concluding remarks.

2 Theoretical Background and Hypothesis Development

2.1 The State of Flow and Flow Experience

In order to examine SNS usage behaviors, researchers have attempted to explain the reciprocal interactions between SNSs and their users by employing social psychological theories such as social capital theory, social influence, social network theory, and the behavior-chain model [8, 28, 44]. Along with those researchers' efforts to use social psychological theories, over the past couple of years, the concept of flow has been adopted by information systems (IS) researchers to examine users' total involvement while using a computer communication medium in the context of IS [27]. Unlike perceived usefulness, which is anchored in extrinsic motivation and defined as "the desire to perform an activity because it is perceived to lead to distinct and valued outcomes" [33, p. 31], the state of flow generally stems from intrinsic motivation, which is focused more on the inner desire to engage in an activity.

In the seminal research on the concept, Csikszentmihalyi [12] defined *flow* as "the state in which people are so involved in an activity that nothing else seems to matter" (p. 4). Similarly, Hsu and Lu [23] viewed the state of flow as an extremely enjoyable experience in the context of an online game. This implies that the intrinsic motivation of people in a flow state results in no awareness of themselves, a sense of control, and a loss of self-consciousness in an activity [1]. It is "a narrowing of the focus of awareness, so that irrelevant perceptions and thoughts are filtered out, by loss of self-consciousness, by responsiveness to clear goals and unambiguous feedback, and by a sense of control over the environment" [11, p. 72].

Although the concept of flow has been acknowledged in many academic disciplines as a state of absorbance in an activity and total involvement with no awareness, measuring state of flow is regarded as rather complex because of the term's unclear definition and the multiple dimensions addressed by many researchers [23]. Originally, Csikszentmihalyi [12] suggested four dimensions: intense concentration, a loss of self-consciousness, a sense of being in control, and a transformation of time. Afterward, Ghani and Deshpande [19] suggested two dimensions of flow: concentration and perceived enjoyment. Trevino and Webster [46] then developed four dimensions—control, curiosity, intrinsic interest, and attention focus—as characteristics of people in the flow state in the context of human-technology interaction. Using independently developed items, Webster et al. [49] empirically measured Trevino and Webster's [46] four dimensions of flow. However, their study had limitations in that their empirical test did not clearly identify intrinsic interest and curiosity because of the sample size [1]. Unlike other scholars, Hoffman and Novak [22] found that the four dimensions of the flow state served as antecedents rather than major dimensions in the context of a computer-mediated environment. Recently, Li and Browne's [30] research examined the effect of four dimensions—focused attention, control, temporal dissociation, and curiosity—on two personal aspects: cognition and mood. The findings indicated that only mood was significant related to the four dimensions. In extending the concept of flow, Agarwal et al. [2] introduced a new dimension, cognitive absorption, which incorporates Trevino and Webster's [46] four dimensions with computer playfulness and ease of use [24].

Among the suggested dimensions for measuring an individual's flow state, this study selected perceived enjoyment, perceived control, and concentration (or focused attention) to explain absorbance in SNS use and its association with actual continued use.

2.2   The Role of the State of Flow

Csikszentmihalyi [12] suggested four dimensions: intense concentration, a loss of self-consciousness, a sense of being in control, and a transformation of time. However, measuring the state of flow is still complex because of the term's unclear definition and the multiple dimensions addressed by many researchers [23]. Although multi-dimensional constructs of the state of flow have been applied to studying total involvement in an environment, our study adopts three constructs—perceived enjoyment, perceived control, and concentration—following Koufaris's [27] research.

First, concentration is an important dimension related to users' becoming absorbed in the state of flow; performing multiple simultaneous tasks distracts users' focused attention [37]. Li and Browne [30] asserted that a bad mood diminishes a user's focused attention in the HCI environment because it results in the user seeking external information to rectify a distressed internal state. Second, perceived enjoyment is defined as "the extent to which the activity of using a specific system is perceived to be enjoyable in its own right, aside from any performance consequences resulting from system use" [33, p. 32]. A number of prior studies have indicated that perceived enjoyment induced feelings of pleasure and fun in the CMC environment and had a positive effect on users' adoption of CMC technology [46]. Perceived enjoyment was also a key factor in the formation of loyalty in the context of online shopping [27] and of sellers returning to an auction marketplace [45]. Third, perceived control is defined as "the level of one's control over the environment and one's actions" [27, p. 208]. For example, SNS users is freed from the geographic and time restrictions of the communication environment because they do not need to make an appointment to talk to friends. Rather, they enjoy unlimited access to friends during log-in hours, all of which may lead them to feel more in control. This makes them expend less physical and mental effort to communicate and lets them take advantage of high-efficiency time management in their daily schedule.

Recently, many SNSs have provided user-friendly features for easier communication, such as convenient photo uploading, real-time chatting, and instant messaging services. Such web applications result in increasing levels of control and enjoyment on the part of SNS users. Therefore, we posit:

H1: An SNS user's concentration while using an SNS is positively associated with his or her satisfaction with an SNS.

H2: An SNS user's perceived enjoyment of an SNS is positively associated with his or her satisfaction with an SNS.

H3: An SNS user's perceived control of an SNS is positively associated with his or her satisfaction with an SNS.

2.3   The Role of Satisfaction in Intention and Continuous Use Behavior

Satisfaction is defined as "the summary psychological state resulting when the emotion surrounding disconfirmed expectation is coupled with the consumer's prior feelings about the consumption experience" [38, p. 29]. It means that after consuming products or rendering services, the customer determines the confirmation level. This is done in such a way that higher confirmation is achieved when greater gaps occur between the pre-purchase expectation of products or services and the post-purchase performance. Customer satisfaction is assessed via the level of confirmation: When post-purchase performance outweighs the customer's pre-purchase expectations, it is regarded as fulfillment of the customer's expectations, indicating positive customer satisfaction [3].

Prior literature supports the positive association between satisfaction and behavioral intention or actions. For example, Tsai et al. [47] found that an increase in a customer's satisfaction led to an increase in the rate of re-purchase. Eriksson and Nilsson [15] revealed that user satisfaction was one of the primary motivations behind continued usage. Bhattacherjee's [4] research found that actual continuance behavior is also associated with intention to continue. Placing the above discussion in the context of SNS, we posit:

H4: An SNS user's satisfaction is positively associated with his or her (a) intention to continue using the SNS and (b) actual continued use of an SNS.

H5: An SNS user's intention to continue using an SNS is positively associated with his or her actual continued use of an SNS.

2.4   The Role of Trust in SNS User Perceptions

Trust is defined as "the willingness of a party to be vulnerable to the actions of another party, with the expectation that the other will perform a particular action important to the trustor, irrespective of the ability to monitor or control that other party" [31, p. 1883]. Prior literature described trust in multiple ways depending on its use. For example, in early research, Zucker [52] categorized trust as three different types (1) characteristic-based trust, which relies on general (e.g., culture) or specific (e.g., family) similarities and commonalities; (2) process-based trust, which is anchored in the level of satisfaction of prior transactions or experience; and (3) institution-based trust, which depends on the third party's guarantee under a form of certification. Trust is a salient determinant for maintaining sustainable relationships because it plays a significant role in reducing the uncertainty and risk of a relationship, reduces anxiety about opportunism, and boosts mutuality among community members [50]. Accordingly, our study proposes the importance of trust for SNSs in that the combination of low associated risk and high trust increases willingness to conduct communicating behaviors, emotional motivation, and the development of intention. Additionally, trust affects people's satisfaction level [10]. For example, Deng et al. [14] research indicated that customers' recognition of poor service or an inferior product based on past experience had a negative effect on satisfaction, as well as that trust was a significant predictor of customer satisfaction in the context of mobile instant messaging services. Because trust alleviates uncertainty, we claim additionally that high levels of trust in an SNS directly influences visiting behaviors. Therefore, we posit:

H6: An SNS user's trust in an SNS will be positively associated with the user's (a) perceived control, (b) perceived enjoyment, (c) concentration, (d) satisfaction, (e) intention to continue use, and (f) actual continued use (Fig. 1).

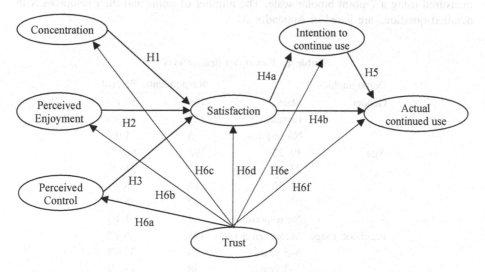

Fig. 1. Research model and hypotheses

3   Research Method

3.1   Research Context

We considered student participants for this study who currently use Facebook. We agreed that student samples are meaningful because students are already familiar with SNS use (e.g., instant messaging) as well as face-to-face conversation [40]. Other research has used students as survey participants for similar reasons, so this study administered a survey to college students to measure their intention to continue using SNSs and their actual usage behaviors [34]. First, we informed the participants regarding the purpose of the study and explained how to participate in the web-based survey, assuring them that it was completely anonymous. Afterward, an email containing the survey link was sent to the individual participants before they participated.

3.2   Selection of Measurement Items

A total of 7 constructs measured perceptions of the SNS, usage intention, and actual continued usage behaviors, using questionnaires modified to fit the research purpose. Four items for measuring satisfaction were adopted from Spreng et al. [42] and 3 items for intention to continued use were adopted from Bhattacherjee [3]. Three items for measuring actual continued use were adopted from Bhattacherjee et al. [4], and trust was measured by 4 items from Fogel and Nehmad [16]. In addition, some items were adopted from Koufaris [27]: 4 to measure perceived enjoyment, 3 to measure perceived control, and 4 to measure concentration. Four items measure the period of Facebook use. Gender and age were also measured. The survey items of trust, perceived enjoyment, perceived control, concentration, and intention were assessed via a 7-point Likert scale ranging from 1 (strongly disagree) to 7 (strongly agree). Satisfaction was measured using a 7-point bipolar scale. The number of items and their resources with detailed questions are listed in Appendix A.

Table 1. Participant descriptions

Demographics		Respondents	Percent
Gender	Male	165	56.7%
	Female	123	42.3%
	No response	3	1.0%
Age	19–22	192	66.0%
	23–27	62	21.3%
	28–32	16	5.5%
	32+	17	5.8%
	No response	4	1.4%
Facebook usage	More than 5 years	135	46.4%
	3–5 years	99	34.0%
	1–3 years	38	13.1%
	Less than 1 year	19	6.5%

3.3   Data Collection

In this study, 291 participants in Southeastern University in the U.S. participated in a web-based survey. Table 1 shows detailed demographic information: 80.4% of survey respondents have used Facebook for more than 3 years, and 54.3% visit Facebook at least 10 times per week.

4   Results

To analyze survey responses and test hypotheses, we used the partial least squares (PLS) statistical method using WarpPLS 5.0 [26]. All constructs are reflective.

4.1   Measurement Model Assessment

Convergent Validity. To examine the convergent validity of constructs, we considered the following four factors of each construct across all measured items: composite reliability, Cronbach's alpha, average variance extracted (AVE), and factor loadings (Table 2). First, all composite reliabilities ranged between 0.82 and 0.96, which qualifies them for the suggested criterion of 0.7 [20]. Second, Cronbach's alpha is over 0.68 for all constructs, which exceeds the minimum requirement suggested by prior literature [20]. Third, the average variance extracted (AVE) of all constructs was above the recommendation value of 0.5 [9]. Lastly, all pattern factor loadings and cross-loadings of measurement items (Table 3) ranged from 0.97 to 0.72, which qualifies them for the suggested the value of 0.7 and above [9]. Examining all four components, our measurement model achieves convergent validity.

Table 2. Convergent validity

Constructs	Composite reliability	Cronbach's alpha	AVE
Concentration	0.95	0.93	0.82
Perceived enjoyment	0.96	0.94	0.85
Perceived control	0.85	0.72	0.65
Satisfaction	0.92	0.88	0.73
Intention to continue use	0.82	0.68	0.61
Actual continued use	0.89	0.81	0.73
Trust	0.94	0.91	0.79

Discriminant Validity. The study also assessed discriminant validity via comparing the square root of each construct's AVE and correlations; the square root of each construct's AVE should be higher than the correlations [20]. Analysis results confirmed all construct correlations are higher than the square root of AVEs; discriminant validity is met under such criteria (see Table 4).

Table 3. Pattern factor loadings and cross-loadings

Constructs	Conc	Enj	Control	Sat	Int	Ac	Trust
Conc1	**0.86**	0.10	−0.04	−0.08	−0.02	0.13	−0.02
Conc2	**0.91**	−0.05	0.06	0.07	0.06	−0.11	−0.02
Conc3	**0.97**	−0.09	0.05	0.05	0.05	−0.12	0.02
Conc4	**0.89**	0.04	−0.07	−0.04	−0.08	0.11	0.02
Enj1	0.02	**0.91**	−0.09	0.06	0.02	−0.05	−0.01
Enj2	−0.06	**0.88**	0.13	−0.04	0.09	−0.03	0.00
Enj3	0.06	**0.94**	−0.08	0.01	−0.07	0.04	0.03
Enj4	−0.02	**0.96**	0.03	−0.03	−0.04	0.03	−0.02
Control1	0.04	0.03	**0.87**	−0.04	0.05	−0.09	−0.07
Control2	0.08	0.07	**0.82**	−0.12	0.03	−0.03	0.04
Control3	−0.14	−0.12	**0.72**	0.20	−0.11	0.14	0.04
Sat1	−0.05	0.03	0.04	**0.74**	0.11	−0.03	0.04
Sat2	−0.10	0.00	0.05	**0.94**	0.01	0.04	−0.04
Sat3	0.08	−0.09	0.03	**0.89**	−0.03	−0.03	−0.01
Sat4	0.07	0.06	−0.13	**0.85**	−0.08	0.01	0.01
Int1	−0.06	0.01	0.12	0.05	**0.76**	0.00	−0.04
Int2	−0.02	0.19	−0.22	−0.17	**0.73**	0.08	−0.01
Int3	0.07	−0.17	0.07	0.10	**0.85**	−0.06	0.05
Ac1	0.09	0.07	−0.11	−0.05	0.08	**0.75**	0.04
Ac2	−0.04	−0.05	0.06	0.02	−0.11	**0.97**	−0.02
Ac3	−0.04	−0.02	0.05	0.02	0.04	**0.83**	−0.02
Trust1	−0.02	−0.09	0.12	0.08	0.07	0.04	**0.77**
Trust2	−0.01	0.08	−0.05	0.03	−0.07	0.01	**0.91**
Trust3	0.00	0.01	−0.03	−0.01	−0.01	0.03	**0.93**
Trust4	0.03	−0.01	−0.03	−0.10	0.02	−0.08	**0.94**

Table 4. Discriminant validity

Constructs	Conc	Enj	Control	Sat	Int	Ac	Trust
Concentration	**0.91**						
Perceived enjoyment	0.55	**0.92**					
Perceived control	0.23	0.55	**0.81**				
Satisfaction	0.39	0.51	0.37	**0.86**			
Intention	0.29	0.44	0.34	0.47	**0.78**		
Ac	0.35	0.41	0.21	0.41	0.52	**0.85**	
Trust	0.33	0.35	0.18	0.40	0.32	0.35	**0.89**

Note: Conc: concentration, Enj: perceived enjoyment, Sat: satisfaction, Int: intention to continue use, Ac: actual continued usage

4.2 Structural Model Assessment and Hypothesis Testing

A summary of the hypothesis testing is provided in Fig. 2. Our analysis found that concentration, perceived enjoyment, and perceived control positively affected Facebook

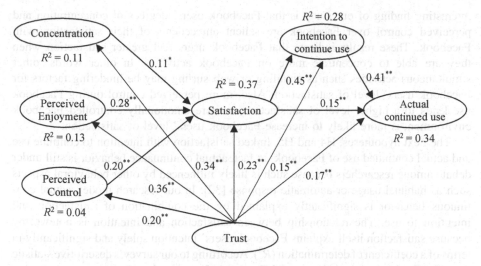

Fig. 2. Structural model - Hypothesis testing ($p^{**} < 0.001$, $p^* < 0.05$)

users' satisfaction with the SNS, which supports H1, H2 and H3. Facebook users' satisfaction was positively associated with both intention to visit Facebook continually and actual continued SNS use—thus, H4 is supported. The intention to continuously use Facebook and the actual continued use were shown to be positively associated with each other, which supports H5. Trust in Facebook is significantly associated with all other constructs, thus supporting H6.

Our research findings showed that each construct significantly explains variance-related constructs (see Fig. 2). Most noteworthy, trust in Facebook itself explained 13% of the total variance of perceived enjoyment and 11% of concentration. Satisfaction is explained 37% of the total variance by concentration, perceived enjoyment, and perceived control. Satisfaction and intention to continue use explained 34% of the total variance of actual continued usage. Satisfaction itself also accounts for 28% of the total variance of intention to continue use.

5   Discussion and Implications

By employing trust and the flow theory, we examined factors affecting SNS users' continued use in the context of Facebook. From the flow experience perspective, the hypothesis testing revealed that Facebook users' concentration (H1), perceived enjoyment (H2), and perceived control (H3) are significant predictors of satisfaction. The flow experience originates in intrinsic motivation, with a focus on "the desire to engage in an activity for no other reason than the process of performing it" [33, p. 31]. Therefore, our findings indicate that Facebook users communicate with others via Facebook who want not only the benefits of a Facebook visit, but also the fun and pleasure of communicating with their friends via Facebook activities. Additionally, the positive relationship between satisfaction and perceived enjoyment could be rooted in Facebook functionality itself, which our future research will focus on more. Another interesting finding of our study is that Facebook users' degrees of concentration and perceived control over Facebook are salient antecedents of their satisfaction with Facebook. These results indicate that Facebook users feel greater satisfaction when they are able to concentrate more on Facebook activities. In other words, other simultaneous activities such as emailing or web surfing may be hindering factors for Facebook users' level of satisfaction. Also, more perceived control during Facebook use leads to a higher level of satisfaction; a more emotionally controlled Facebook environment is more likely to increase Facebook users' level of satisfaction.

The next hypotheses, H4 and H5, linked satisfaction with intention to continue use and actual continued use of Facebook. In fact, actual continuance behavior is still under debate among researchers because such is likely influenced by other behavioral aspects such as habitual usage or automatic response [32]. In our research model, actual continuous behavior is significantly explained by the combination of satisfaction and intention to use. The relationship between satisfaction and intention is noteworthy because satisfaction itself explains Facebook users' intention solely and significantly in terms of a coefficient of determination (R^2). According to our survey's descriptive statistic that 80.4% of respondents have used Facebook for more than 3 years, we claim that satisfaction tends to be derived cumulatively from ongoing communicating activities instead of through temporal or transaction-specific satisfaction [7]. In long-term users, intention still pertains to their actual continuance behaviors, which are impacted by satisfaction.

Lastly, examining H6, trust in Facebook had positive and significant relationships with SNS users' perceptions, behavioral intentions, and actual continuance behavior. Interestingly, our analysis shows that trust explains 11% and 13% of the total variance of concentration and perceived enjoyment, respectively. Our research findings imply that the nature of trust in Facebook can be assessed differently given previous explorations of the root of trust derived from products or services. Trust in Facebook is fundamentally embedded in retaining ongoing relationships through continued use. In other words, the origin of trust in Facebook can be anchored in either (a) a user's friends trusting in Facebook as a safe communication tool or (b) trust of Facebook itself, through which a process of transferring trust from one entity (i.e., friends) to the other (i.e., Facebook) can be made. For further consideration of trust, a post-hoc analysis to examine any influence changes without the existence of trust in Facebook shows that all relationships were still supported positively. In addition, trust in Facebook shows an underlying effect on other relationships among constructs.

While the SNS has emerged as a popular communication medium, and many researchers have conducted SNS studies with varying aspects, this is a pioneer study examining SNS users' continued use of SNSs via flow theory and trust perspectives. This study provides several implications for researchers and practitioners.

First, drawing from flow theory, our study identified that perceived enjoyment, concentration, and perceived control serve as significant antecedents, explaining satisfaction with SNS use and continuous usage behaviors. Among those three constructs, perceived enjoyment is more influential than others, which indicates that a hedonic-oriented aspect is a strong motivator of continuous use of an SNS. Particularly, as prior literature noted [22], our findings also support that satisfaction with SNS use is accounted for by the fact that SNS users tend to filter out or escape any irrelevant thinking during access. As a result, they are able to entirely pay attention to interacting with other SNS friends, which our findings show motivates SNS users' continuous actual use. Second, our study extends prior adoption and intention studies by exploring flow experience as major antecedents, which differentiates our study from prior studies primarily by employing TRA, TPB, or TAM [13]. Our findings show that the construct of intention plays a salient role, not only as a dependent variable but also in explaining actual behaviors, which aligns with Bhattacherjee et al.'s [4] study in the context of communication IS artifacts. Going one step further than prior studies [4], our research findings indicate that intention for continuous use becomes a significant mediator between satisfaction and actual usage behaviors in the context of SNS. Thus, actual continued use is accounted for by both intention and satisfaction. From a practical perspective, our results imply that the hedonic use of SNSs is still a primary motivational factor in a user's actual continued use of an SNS.

From a practical perspective, according to survey responses, our study implies that hedonic-oriented perception is still dominant when using SNSs. In particular, we found that perceived enjoyment is a key driver for increasing the level of satisfaction. Therefore, SNS service providers' continuous attention to SNS users' flow experience should be important in maintaining SNS sustainability by providing a number of entertaining features. While many SNSs currently implement various features and tools to facilitate communication, such as games or blogs, prior study of flow theory also pointed out that an individual's perceived enjoyment of media usage should be balanced between his or her personal skills and the difficulty of media use, or an individual's feeling about the media's complexity [41]. Otherwise, media users feel bored or anxious if their skills, difficulty using media, or a lack of understanding prevents them from engaging with media, which results in ceasing to use such media. Therefore, SNS service providers may consider potential targets of SNS subscribers, especially if they seek SNS-specific content or features (e.g., virtual collaboration, multimedia contents). Additionally, our research findings emphasize the trustworthiness of SNS, which impacts all perceptions of SNS usage given in our survey responses. High trustworthiness can be achieved not only by implementing solid security countermeasures to prevent accidental exposure of personal information, but also by filtering unwanted information or spam. This would be beneficial to all SNS subscribers because social media spam targets one to one as well as one to many [18]. Furthermore, another report indicates that more than one-third of Facebook employees are fighting against spammers, but the rate of spam feeds such as "like-jacking" is rapidly increasing [18]. It is highly likely that many spam feeds or messages make SNS users inactive and distract from SNS usage.

6   Limitations and Future Research

The limitations of this study are as follows. First, the study participants were college students, thus limiting the scope of media users, even though college-aged students are one of the most experienced Facebook user groups. Also, Facebook is only one social networking site and may not represent all SNSs. Future research with varied groups of SNSs and users might provide distinguished perceptions. Second, the current research findings have not discussed any potential inverse relationship between trust, satisfaction, and high correlations among constructs related to longitudinal research design. For future research, we suggest identification of any perceptional changes to flow over the period of Facebook usage.

7 Conclusion

The purpose of this study is to examine the salient determinants affecting SNS users' continued usage behaviors by incorporating dimensions from flow theory and the concept of trust after a thorough review of prior literature. Unlike other prior studies, our research model includes the intention to continually use SNS as a mediator between satisfaction and actual SNS use. To test our hypotheses, data was collected from Facebook users who were currently studying at a university, as they were considered representative of the most frequent SNS users. The results of data analysis offer insights that flow experience, represented by concentration, perceived enjoyment, and perceived control—explained significantly the continual use of SNS via satisfaction with SNS use and intention to continue use. More interestingly, our findings suggest that trust plays an important role in explaining other constructs, which represents trust in SNS becoming an overarching perception for SNS usage. Further, our research findings show that SNS users' intention to continue use of an SNS serves as a mediator between the users' satisfaction and actual usage behavior. In conclusion, our research supports the notion that the flow experience serves as an important role in SNS users' continuous use behaviors. While hedonic-oriented constructs are key motivators of actual usage, perceived enjoyment is the strongest factor impacting satisfaction and, eventually, actual continuous SNS usage. It is worth noting that our study contributes a theoretical implication in terms of integrating flow theory and trust as a new perspective of IS users' actual continuance behaviors. More importantly, this study provided evidence that flow theory and its constructs explain sufficiently how IS users' continuance behaviors can be accounted for in the context of communication-based IS artifacts.

Appendix A. Measurement Items

Constructs	Items
Satisfaction	How do you feel about your overall experience of using Facebook? 1. Very dissatisfied – very satisfied 2. Very displeased – very pleased 3. Very frustrated – very contented 4. Absolutely terrible – absolutely delighted
Intention to continue use	1. I intend to continue using Facebook to interact with my friend(s) 2. My intentions are to continue using Facebook rather than any alternative means (e.g., email) 3. I plan to discontinue my use of Facebook. (Reverse coded)

(continued)

(*continued*)

Constructs	Items
Actual continued use	1. I use Facebook to interact with my friends very frequently (several times per days) 2. Number of times you currently use Facebook per week? (Choose only one) A. None, B. 1–3, C. 4–6, D. 7–9, E. 10–12, F. Over 12 3. In general, how much time do you spend on Facebook activities per week? (Choose only one) A. 0–5 min, B. 6–15 min, C. 16–60 min, D. Over 60 min
Trust	1. Facebook is a trustworthy social networking site 2. I can count on Facebook to protect my privacy 3. I can count on Facebook to protect personal information from unauthorized use 4. Facebook can be relied upon to keep its promises
Perceived enjoyment	During my last visit to Facebook.com … 1. I found my visit interesting 2. I found my visit enjoyable 3. I found my visit exciting 4. I found my visit fun
Perceived control	During my last visit to Facebook.com … 1. I felt calm 2. I felt in control 3. I felt frustrated (reverse coded)
Concentration	During my last visit to Facebook.com … 1. I was absorbed intensely in the activity 2. My attention was focused on the activity 3. I concentrated fully on the activity 4. I was deeply engrossed in the activity
Facebook usage	How long have you used Facebook? 1. More than 5 years 2. More than 3 years but less than 5 years 3. More than 1 year but less than 3 years 4. More than 6 months but less than 1 year 5. Less than 6 months
Gender	What is your gender? A. Male, B. Female
Age	What is your age? A. 18–22, B. 23–27, C. 28–32, D. 32+

References

1. Agarwal, R., Karahanna, E.: Time flies when you're having fun: cognitive absorption and belief about information technology usage. MIS Q. **24**(4), 665–694 (2000)
2. Agarwal, R., Sambamurthy, V., Stair, R.M.: Cognitive absorption and the adoption of new information technologies. In: The Academy of Management Annual Meetings, Boston, pp. 293–297. Academy of Management (1997)
3. Bhattacherjee, A.: Understanding information systems continuance: an expectation-confirmation model. MIS Q. **25**(3), 351–370 (2001)
4. Bhattacherjee, A., Perols, J., Sanford, C.: Information technology continuance: a theoretic extension and empirical test. J. Comput. Inf. Syst. **49**(1), 17–26 (2008)
5. Boyd, D.M., Ellison, N.B.: Social network sites: definition, history, and scholarship. J. Comput.-Mediat. Commun. **13**(1), 210–230 (2007). https://doi.org/10.1111/j.1083-6101.2007.00393.x
6. Brengman, M., Karimov, F.P.: The effect of web communities on consumers' initial trust in B2C e-commerce website. Manag. Res. Rev. **35**(9), 791–817 (2012)
7. Chang, H.H., Wang, Y.-H., Yang, W.-Y.: The impact of e-service quality, customer satisfaction and loyalty on e-marketing: moderating effect of perceived value. Total Qual. Manag. Bus. Excell. **20**(4), 423–443 (2009). https://doi.org/10.1080/14783360902781923
8. Cheung, C.M.K., Lee, M.K.O.: A theoretical model of intentional social action in online social networks. Decis. Support Syst. **49**(1), 24–30 (2010). https://doi.org/10.1016/j.dss.2009.12.006
9. Chin, W.W.: Issues and opinion on structural equation modeling. MIS Q. **22**, 1 (1998)
10. Chiou, J.S.: The antecedents of consumers' loyalty toward internet service providers. Inf. Manag. **41**(6), 685–695 (2004). https://doi.org/10.1016/j.im.2003.08.006
11. Csikszentmihalyi, M.: Beyond Boredom and Anxiety. Jossey Bass Publishers, San Francisco (1977)
12. Csikszentmihalyi, M.: Flow: The Psychology of Optimal Experience. Harper & Row, New York (1990)
13. Davis, F.D.: Perceived usefulness, perceived ease of use, and user acceptance of information technology. MIS Q. **13**, 319–340 (1989)
14. Deng, Z., Lu, Y., Wei, K.K., Zhang, J.: Understanding customer satisfaction and loyalty: an empirical study of mobile instant messages in China. Int. J. Inf. Manag. **30**(4), 289–300 (2010). https://doi.org/10.1016/j.ijinfomgt.2009.10.001
15. Eriksson, K., Nilsson, D.: Determinants of the continued use of self-service technology: the case of internet banking. Technovation **27**(4), 159–167 (2007). https://doi.org/10.1016/j.technovation.2006.11.001
16. Fogel, J., Nehmad, E.: Internet social network communities: risk taking, trust, and privacy concerns. Comput. Hum. Behav. **25**(1), 153–160 (2009). https://doi.org/10.1016/j.chb.2008.08.006
17. Foster, M.K., Francescucci, A., West, B.C.: Why users participate in online social networks. Int. J. e-Bus. Manag. **4**(1), 3–19 (2010)
18. Fowler, G.A., Shayndi, R., Efrati, A.: Spam finds new target; Facebook and Twitter build up their defenses as hackers attack social networks. Wall Str. J. (2012)
19. Ghani, J.A., Deshpande, S.P.: Task characteristics and the experience of optimal flow in human-computer interaction. J. Psychol. **128**(4), 381–391 (1994)
20. Hair, J., Joseph, F., Black, W.C., Babin, B.J., Anderson, R.E., Tatham, R.L.: Multivariate Data Analysis. Prentice Hall, Upper Saddle River (2006)

21. Hargittai, E.: Whose space? Differences among users and non-users of social network sites. J. Comput.-Mediat. Commun. **13**(1), 276–297 (2007). https://doi.org/10.1111/j.1083-6101. 2007.00396.x
22. Hoffman, D.L., Novak, T.P.: Marketing in hypermedia computer-mediated environments: conceptual foundations. J. Mark. **60**(3), 50–68 (1996)
23. Hsu, C.-L., Lu, H.-P.: Why do people play on-line games? An extended TAM with social influences and flow experience. Inf. Manag. **41**(7), 853–868 (2004). https://doi.org/10.1016/j.im.2003.08.014
24. Jin, B., Park, J.Y., Kim, H.-S.: What makes online community members commit? A social exchange perspective. Behav. Inf. Technol. **29**(6), 587–599 (2010). https://doi.org/10.1080/0144929x.2010.497563
25. Kefi, H., Mlaiki, A., Kalika, M.: Shy people and Facebook continuance of usage: does gender matter? In: The Americas Conference on Information Systems, Lima, Peru, pp. 1–13. AIS Electronic Library (2010)
26. Kock, N.: WarpPLS 5.0 user manual. ScriptWarp Systems, Laredo, April 2015
27. Koufaris, M.: Applying the technology acceptance model and flow theory to online consumer behavior. Inf. Syst. Res. **13**(2), 205–223 (2002)
28. Kwon, O., Wen, Y.: An empirical study of the factors affecting social network service use. Comput. Hum. Behav. **26**(2), 254–263 (2010). https://doi.org/10.1016/j.chb.2009.04.011
29. Lampe, C., Ellison, N., Steinfield, C.: A face(book) in the crowd: social searching vs. social browsing. Paper Presented at the Proceedings of the 2006 20th Anniversary Conference on Computer Supported Cooperative Work, Banff, Alberta, Canada (2006)
30. Li, D., Browne, G.J.: The role of need for cognition and mood in online flow experience. J. Comput. Inf. Syst. **46**(3), 11–17 (2006)
31. Liao, L.F.: Knowledge-sharing in R&D departments: a social power and social exchange theory perspective. Int. J. Hum. Res. Manag. **19**(10), 1881–1895 (2008). https://doi.org/10.1080/09585190802324072
32. Limayem, M., Hirt, S.G., Cheung, C.M.K.: How habit limits the predictive power of intention: the case of information systems continuance. MIS Q. **31**(4), 705–737 (2007)
33. Lu, Y., Zhou, T., Wang, B.: Exploring Chinese users' acceptance of instant messaging using the theory of planned behavior, the technology acceptance model, and the flow theory. Comput. Hum. Behav. **25**(1), 29–39 (2009). https://doi.org/10.1016/j.chb.2008.06.002
34. Miller, R., Parsons, K., Lifer, D.: Students and social networking sites: the posting paradox. Behav. Inf. Technol. **29**(4), 377–382 (2010). https://doi.org/10.1080/01449290903042491
35. Morgan, R.M., Hunt, S.D.: The commitment-trust theory of relationship marketing. J. Mark. **58**(3), 20–38 (1994)
36. Muise, A., Christofides, E., Desmarais, S.: More information than you ever wanted: does Facebook bring out the green-eyed monster of jealousy? CyberPsychol. Behav. **12**(4), 441–444 (2009). https://doi.org/10.1089/cpb.2008.0263
37. Novak, T.P., Hoffman, D.L., Yiu-Fai, Y.: Measuring the customer experience in online environments: a structural modeling approach. Market. Sci. **19**(1), 22 (2000)
38. Oliver, R.L.: Measurement and evaluation of satisfaction processes in retail settings. J. Retail. **57**(3), 25–48 (1981)
39. Riordan, M.A., Kreuz, R.J.: Emotion encoding and interpretation in computer-mediated communication: reasons for use. Comput. Hum. Behav. **26**(6), 1667–1673 (2010). https://doi.org/10.1016/j.chb.2010.06.015
40. Roblyer, M.D., McDaniel, M., Webb, M., Herman, J., Witty, J.V.: Findings on Facebook in higher education: a comparison of college faculty and student uses and perceptions of social networking sites. Internet High. Educ. **13**(3), 134–140 (2010). https://doi.org/10.1016/j.iheduc.2010.03.002

41. Sherry, J.L.: Flow and media enjoyment. Commun. Theory **14**(4), 328–347 (2004). https://doi.org/10.1111/j.1468-2885.2004.tb00318.x

42. Spreng, R.A., MacKenzie, S.B., Olshavsky, R.W.: A reexamination of the determinants of consumer satisfaction. J. Mark. **60**(3), 15–32 (1996)

43. Sproutsocial: 17 Powerful Facebook Stats for Marketers and Advertisers (2016)

44. Steinfield, C., Ellison, N.B., Lampe, C.: Social capital, self-esteem, and use of online social network sites: a longitudinal analysis. J. Appl. Dev. Psychol. **29**(6), 434–445 (2008). https://doi.org/10.1016/j.appdev.2008.07.002

45. Sun, H.: Sellers' trust and continued use of online marketplaces. J. Assoc. Inf. Syst. **11**(4), 182–211 (2010)

46. Trevino, L.K., Webster, J.: Flow in computer-mediated communication: electronic mail and voice mail evaluation and impacts. Commun. Res. **19**(5), 539–573 (1992). https://doi.org/10.1177/009365092019005001

47. Tsai, H.-T., Huang, H.-C., Jaw, Y.-L., Chen, W.-K.: Why on-line customers remain with a particular e-retailer: an integrative model and empirical evidence. Psychol. Mark. **23**(5), 447–464 (2006)

48. Vasalou, A., Joinson, A.N., Courvoisier, D.: Cultural differences, experience with social networks and the nature of "true commitment" in Facebook. Int. J. Hum. Comput. Stud. **68**(10), 719–728 (2010)

49. Webster, J., Trevino, L.K., Ryan, L.: The dimensionality and correlates of flow in human-computer interactions. Comput. Hum. Behav. **9**(4), 411–426 (1993). https://doi.org/10.1016/0747-5632(93)90032-n

50. Wu, J.-J., Chen, Y.-H., Chung, Y.-S.: Trust factors influencing virtual community members: a study of transaction communities. J. Bus. Res. **63**(9–10), 1025–1032 (2010). https://doi.org/10.1016/j.jbusres.2009.03.022

51. Zhephoria: The Top 20 Valuable Facebook Statistics, May 2016

52. Zucker, L.G.: Production of trust: institutional sources of economic structure. Res. Organ. Behav. **8**, 53–112 (1986)

The Impact of UI on Privacy Awareness
Connecting Online Polls and Social Media

Martin Stabauer$^{(\boxtimes)}$ (iD)

Johannes Kepler University, Linz, Austria
martin.stabauer@jku.at

Abstract. Online polls are considered a valuable method of collecting users' opinions, attitudes and preferences. They also help to increase user engagement, which is a goal of many online publishers, as they seek to understand their target audiences better and therefore want to collect and analyze user data. Gaining access to information from their users' social network accounts is seen as a significant advance and consequently social login functionality is becoming an increasingly common feature of various web applications. Users appreciate the convenience and benefits of this, but are often unaware of the privacy issues that arise. This study investigated the influence of different types of privacy alert on users' decisions whether to connect an online polling application to a social network, thereby granting access to their social media data in exchange for seeing their friends' votes. The method used live data from real polls in German-speaking countries and gives insights into user behavior when confronted with requests for Facebook data. Differences in privacy awareness and user decisions between our research and previous studies in laboratory settings are addressed as well.

Keywords: Online polls · Social media · Online profiling
Privacy awareness · Informed consent

1 Introduction

In 2001, Weill and Vitale stated: *"Information technology infrastructure and the information it contains, particularly customer information, will be a critical success factor for all e-business initiatives, thus raising the stakes for the management of the firm's IT investments and assets"* [1]. This prediction has since been fulfilled or even exceeded. The ability to collect, store and analyze personal data and user information has become the main asset of numerous IT giants of recent years and also a necessity in many other business fields.

However, this demand for personal data raises concerns for consumer privacy. Consumers give access to their personal data when the benefits they expect exceed their costs. We examined online polls – a type of Web 2.0 tool that publishers frequently employ to increase user engagement. We show how access to personal data from social networks is beneficial to the publishers utilizing this tool and discuss various strategies of convincing their users.

© Springer International Publishing AG, part of Springer Nature 2018
F. F.-H. Nah and B. S. Xiao (Eds.): HCIBGO 2018, LNCS 10923, pp. 513–525, 2018.
https://doi.org/10.1007/978-3-319-91716-0_41

The contribution of this research is twofold: It (a) explores general user awareness of the amount of personal information that is exposed to the web application when utilizing a social login functionality and (b) answers the question of whether consumers are less likely to provide access to their personal data when, at the time of making their decision, they are confronted with a clear statement of what use will be made of their data. Given that this information can be found in the general terms and conditions, the independent variable is a matter of the user interface.

1.1 Privacy

Privacy is a commonly discussed and widely researched topic. Influential publications include [2–4]. Two perspectives on privacy can be distinguished when discussing privacy awareness in the context of web applications and communities, both of which must be taken into account when designing new applications in this area [5]:

– Privacy of personal sphere as *"the right to be let alone"*, which was defined in the influential work "The Right to Privacy" from 1890 [6]. The definition includes (a) the secrecy of everyone's own thoughts, properties and actions and (b) the flow towards the individual of data regarding others, that might affect him or her.
– Privacy of personal data is the traditional viewpoint of computer scientists and refers to *"the right to select what personal information about me is known to what people"* [7]. The focus lies on control over information about oneself, one's conversations and actions. In contrast to the concept of solitude, privacy of personal data is actively determined by the individual.

1.2 Privacy Awareness

Awareness in general can be defined as an individual's attention, perception and cognition of both physical and non-physical objects. The two perspectives on privacy mentioned above suggest that, in the case of privacy awareness, this refers to [5]:

– whether information about oneself, one's conversations or one's actions has been received by others,
– what personal information is affected,
– how this information can or could be processed and used, and
– what amount of information about others flows towards, and might affect, one.

Information acting as stimuli for privacy awareness can be distinguished along two dimensions: Whether these means can be identical for each user and whether they are of a general nature or tailored to a specific application. Table 1 shows an overview with examples; obviously, intermediate levels and combinations also exist.

Table 1. Dimensions of privacy-awareness information [5]

	User-independent	User-dependent
Application-independent	Talks, campaigns, tutorials	Individual advice ("privacy commissioner")
Application-specific	Privacy disclaimers and info on website	Feedback from website's privacy evaluation

Various forms of measuring privacy awareness and the importance of information privacy have been described in the literature (e.g., [8,9]). In essence, users try to balance their benefits and costs, where benefits are derived from personalization and costs are the result of a function of consumer privacy concerns, previous privacy invasion experience, and consumer-rated importance of information transparency and privacy policies. This can be expressed by the utility function [10]:

$$U(X) = Benefit - Cost$$

The effects and relationships are shown in Fig. 3. Examples of both benefits and costs in the research areas of e-commerce and web communities are listed in Table 2.

Table 2. Benefits and costs of disclosure of personal data [5]

	Benefits	Costs
eCommerce	– Convenience	– Price discrimination
	– Automated processes	– Marketing spam
	– Price premiums	– Identity theft
	– Selected information	
Web communities	– Social exchange	– Identity theft
	– Relationships	– Marketing spam
	– Collaboration	– Stalking, Kidnapping
	– Reputation	– Negative reputation in other contexts

1.3 The Privacy Paradox

When people are more conscious of privacy issues, they can make more informed decisions, and one might assume that this would lead to less unintentional privacy-invasive behavior. In other words, people with an above-average level of privacy awareness who are conscious of their personal sphere and their personal data should act accordingly when facing various options. However, several studies have shown that this is often not the case: They compared people's intentions (e.g., their self-reported privacy preferences) with their actual behavior and found that people tend to disclose significantly larger amounts of personal information and data than they claim [11,12]. Regarding the utility function described in the previous section, another study showed that personalization is valued twice as high as the concern for privacy [13].

In this context, studies have shown that some privacy-concerned users refuse to join social media and networks. However, those who do decide to join share almost as much personal data as other members of the respective networks [14]. Many informed users know that social networks collect and store huge amounts of data and use them for targeted advertising. This knowledge does not keep them away from these communities, partly because the sector is highly monopolized and network effects play a crucial role [15].

2   Online Polls and Social Media

2.1   Online Polls

Contributing to a website's content and sharing one's opinion is becoming increasingly important to internet users. This can be observed in features such as comments sections in online newspapers [16]. Online polls were developed with this in mind and to increase user engagement at relatively low cost. The polls in our study achieved an interaction rate of 5.9985% (the proportion of all users who saw a poll who decided to vote in it). This is a satisfactory proportion in the context of online marketing applications. A typical poll consists of a single question with a minimum of two, and generally not more than five, answer options. Figure 1 shows the User Interface (UI) of such a poll.

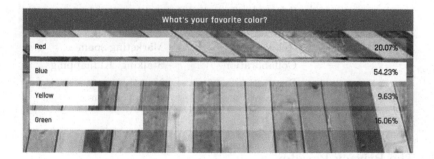

Fig. 1. Example online poll

A common issue with many current polling systems is that they do not make any further use of the collected data. Their main focus is on the basic functionality of showing polls to users and letting them pick an answer. However, previous studies showed that user opinions are an untapped source of knowledge, and have discussed possibilities and requirements of further usage [17]. Some of the potential benefits are:

- Extracting and aggregating private information about claims that cannot be verified is seen as valuable for market prediction [18].
- Combining the knowledge gained from votes on several independent polls can create more detailed and precise user profiles. Publishers can verify their current assumptions about their websites' users and target groups, and may also discover entirely new potential groups.
- Target groups can be used to create specific content as well as for *behavioral retargeting* advertising campaigns.
- Generally, polls cannot be narrowed down to a specific domain. Extracting their respective topics and clustering them into predefined categories can assist in automatically assigning polls to matching website content.

Hence, knowing more about their users can help publishers to monetize their content. The vast amounts of data and information users create in social networks thus promise to be very valuable when combined with knowledge from poll responses. Publishers are therefore trying to encourage users to connect to their social media accounts so they gain access to their data.

The study described in the following section sought to determine under what circumstances users allow access to their data from social networks in the context of online polls. Depending on the visualization of the poll (see e.g., [19]), we expected different user reactions to the request to provide access to more user data.

2.2   Social Login

Providing users with the ability to log in to a web application via their existing social network credentials can be defined as Social Login [20]. Such a single sign-on solution brings users the convenience of reducing the number of usernames and passwords needed and of automatically providing their information from social networks to other web applications. Figure 2 shows a Social Login (SL) process including a Social Network Service (SNS) provider and the user's Social Network Credentials (SNC).

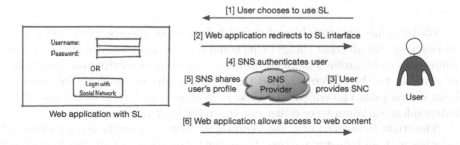

Fig. 2. Social Login [21]

Social Login can also be used to access the users' data stored in social networks, and users are often unaware of the amount of personal information that is exposed to the requesting application [22,23]. Although users are increasingly aware of the privacy settings of Facebook itself, there is still a lack of privacy awareness when accepting standardized requests for connecting with an SNS from within external web applications [24].

3   Study of Social Media Integration

3.1   Motivation

Extending the theoretical model by Awad and Krishnan [10] as illustrated in Fig. 3, we hypothesized that with a clearer message about the intended usage of user data, user privacy awareness would increase and users would tend not to allow the integration of social media data. The underlying model illustrates the influences of consumer demographics (Gender, Education, Income) and attitudes towards privacy (Previous Online Privacy Invasions, Privacy Concern, Importance of Privacy Policies) on the consumer-rated importance of information transparency and consequently on their willingness to participate in online profiling for the purposes of personalizing both service and advertising.

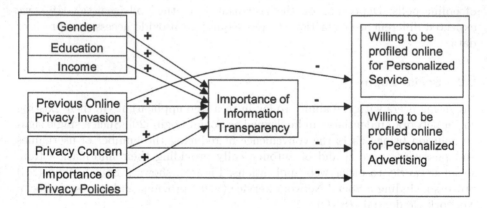

Fig. 3. Basic theoretical model [10]

We introduce the variables of actual Information Transparency and Setting and suggest that all other things being equal both are associated with a decreased willingness to be profiled online – both for personalized service and advertising. In contrast to the aforementioned theoretical study, we used actual live data from online polls embedded in online newspapers, and therefore some of the independent variables were either not controllable or not measurable.

The study forms part of a research project that is currently being carried out together with an industry partner. In earlier publications, we discussed applying a degree of intelligence by combining otherwise discrete online polls with semantic technologies and storing the knowledge gained in an RDF/OWL ontology [25]. We found that having more general knowledge about the pollees helps to classify the additional knowledge coming from their responses. Thus, the desire to identify users and gain access to their social media data arose.

3.2   Setting

All analyses within the aforementioned project are supported by a real-world data pool of more than 45k polls, 180k answer options and 10M answers given worldwide since 2015 as well as access to live polling data. This study of social media integration was conducted in the third and fourth quarters of 2017. Five popular online newspapers based in Austria and Germany that were already utilizing online polls to supplement their articles were selected.

The visitors to these newspaper websites were divided internally and randomly into two groups in accordance with the commonly used procedure of an A/B test. After voting in a poll, they were confronted with one of two different requests to connect the poll with their Facebook profile. The request of group A was *"How did your friends vote? Log in now and find out."*, while group B was additionally shown the message *"The deal: Your friends will see your vote, too."* These messages are illustrated in Figs. 4 and 5, respectively.

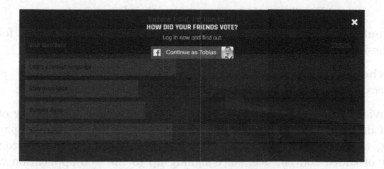

Fig. 4. Request after poll less explicit message

The benefit promised to users was that they could see their Facebook friends' votes on that poll. In the version with the more explicit message, they were made aware of the fact that their friends could in turn see their own answers, suggesting that their own social media data would be accessed. Users who accepted the request for access to their Facebook data saw a view as shown in Fig. 6. Obviously, users without a Facebook account were unable to connect the polls and were not taken into consideration. Previous studies were mostly laboratory-based experiments and showed an increase in privacy awareness when the participants

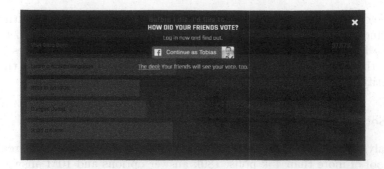

Fig. 5. Request after poll with more explicit message

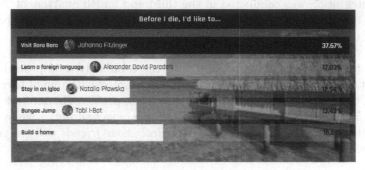

Fig. 6. Benefit to users: seeing their friends' votes

were confronted with a dedicated privacy alert [21]. This led to the following hypothesis:

Hypothesis 1 (H1).   *The willingness to participate in online profiling decreases significantly with a higher level of information transparency.*

Previous studies showed that, in laboratory situations, a majority of up to 76% of users tend to make use of social logins [24]. However, in our particular setting, we expected the proportion to be substantially lower, as there was no benefit of added convenience, since signing up to the web application was not required. The only advantage to connecting to Facebook was the ability to see their friends' answers. Additionally, in a real-world situation of voting in a poll, users often do not take the time to read messages shown after the poll. The aforementioned study by Egelman [24] revealed that a considerable proportion of users act intuitively; for instance, they leave the application before the alert has been displayed. Our second hypothesis was therefore:

Hypothesis 2 (H2).   *The willingness to participate in online profiling in the context of polling is significantly lower "in the wild" than in laboratory settings.*

Therefore, the basic theoretical model was extended by the two newly introduced variables. The relevant parts of this extension can be seen in Fig. 7. Hypothesis 1 can be measured by the effect of information transparency on the willingness to participate in online profiling; Hypothesis 2 can be measured by the effect of the real-world setting on the willingness to participate in online profiling.

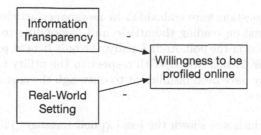

Fig. 7. Research model

3.3 Results

In total, 141,113 users responded to the polls under study and were shown one of the two messages listed above. The two groups A and B were of approximately the same size; the exact numbers are shown in Table 3. Group A was shown the less explicit message, while group B was shown the more explicit message and therefore confronted with a higher level of information transparency.

Table 3. Results

Group A	Connect: Yes	Connect: No
Total	120 (0.17%)	70462 (99.83%)
Male	71 (0.10%)	-
Female	49 (0.07%)	-
Gender unknown	-	70462 (99.83%)
Group B	Connect: Yes	Connect: No
Total	114 (0.16%)	70417 (99.84%)
Male	75 (0.11%)	-
Female	39 (0.05%)	-
Gender unknown	-	70417 (99.84%)

In both groups combined, the proportion of users accepting the request for a social login was 0.1658%, *Hypothesis* 2 was therefore corroborated. The explanation of this particularly low number is twofold:

– Immediately after answering a poll, users were presented a view of the preliminary results. Some users exited the application right after seeing these results and never saw the request for connecting their votes to their Facebook profiles. We cannot quantify this proportion as we operated in a real-world environment. Another group of users left even earlier in the process, specifically before seeing the results. Further, users without a Facebook account did not qualify.

- The polls in question were embedded in newspaper articles. Users typically spend more time on reading the article and responding to the poll than on what is offered after the poll. Additionally, the only benefit provided was information on their friends' votes. With respect to the utility function explained above, this may have been insufficient to outweigh the cost of granting access to personal data.

In group A, which was shown the less explicit message, 120 users (0.1700%) accepted the request, while in group B, which was shown the more explicit message, 74 users (0.1616%) signed in to their Facebook account. The difference between these groups is not significant (Pearson $\mathcal{X}^2 = 0.150$, $p = 0.699$), and therefore we can neither accept *Hypothesis* 1 nor reject the null hypothesis. The acceptance rate of group B with the higher level of information transparency was only slightly lower than that of group A. We discuss these results within the context of Friedman et al.'s six components of informed consent [26]:

- *Disclosure.* The presentation of information right after the poll obviously did not make any difference to the users' decisions. They may have believed to have a broad understanding of the implications of Facebook Connect from earlier exposures to similar messages. Further, the information in question could also be found in great detail in the general terms and conditions of the polling application. However, in total only 0.0096% of the users who voted in a poll opened the page with privacy information.
- *Comprehension.* Two of the online newspapers that took part in the study can be classified as tabloid press, which may have a less technically aware audience. The understanding of the value of their Facebook profiles and of what data would be transferred to the polling application is arguably less clear. The value proposition of connecting their votes to Facebook, however, can be understood more easily, and – considering this imbalance, an informed decision was improbable.
- *Voluntariness.* While our research cannot be directly compared to earlier studies that were conducted under different conditions, one distinctive difference is that in our study users were entirely free to accept the request in question without any further consequences. Additionally, the promised benefit may not have been convincing enough for some users.
- *Competence.* It is difficult to evaluate the competence of the participating users. The sample may have included children or badly informed adults. However, we assume that the majority of users fulfilled all requirements to give informed consent in our context.
- *Agreement.* Users were given a clear opportunity to accept or decline the request to connect to their Facebook profiles. As the request is implemented as an opt-in system, rejection was done implicitly by not accepting the request. Reconsidering this decision was possible in both directions: In the case of acceptance, the approval could be revoked within Facebook, and in the case of rejection, the permit could be given whenever the same or another poll was viewed.

– *Minimal Distraction*. This criterion was certainly not fulfilled as users in the middle of reading an online newspaper are often not willing to spend time on making an informed decision on whether their personal utility function considering the benefits and costs of the above-mentioned social login feature is positive or negative.

For these reasons, the variable of actual information transparency we introduced into the basic theoretical model cannot be validated in relation to its consequences for user willingness to be profiled online. While it may have an impact, the effects of disclosure, voluntariness and distraction confound its measurement.

4 Conclusion and Future Research Directions

The research presented was focused on investigating two questions: Are users in a real-world scenario aware of, and interested in, the implications of using a social login functionality and do they rate the benefit of knowing their friends' votes on a specific poll more highly than the cost of granting access to their own personal data? Do users act differently when they are confronted with a clearer privacy alert than just the standard information message? First, we gave a brief overview of the relevant concepts of Privacy, Privacy Awareness and the Privacy Paradox, and then we discussed the combination of online polls and social media and presented our general project of bringing more intelligence to online polls.

We subsequently introduced our study, which implemented a social login functionality in an online polling application. Five wide-coverage online newspapers based in Austria and Germany were chosen from among the current customers of the polling application under study. After responding to a poll from these publishers, users were offered the value proposition of seeing how their friends voted on the same poll. Following the widely used procedure of an A/B test, we divided them randomly into two groups, which were shown two different messages combined with the request to connect the poll to their Facebook profiles. We had expected that a higher proportion of people following this request would be found in the group with the less explicit message.

However, our results showed that different levels of information transparency had little effect on user decisions. In our study, the proportion of users accepting the request for personal data was generally very low. This is partly because (a) the tradeoff between the benefits and the costs involved was conceived to be negative, and (b) in the environment studied users obviously do not take the time to read and understand the messages they are shown.

Unlike in laboratory situations, some factors could not be measured due to the study design. One of these was the proportion of people who could be considered aware of the privacy implications of a social login feature, especially as only 0.0096% of users opened the page with the corresponding information. We conclude that the relevance of online polls and social login functionalities will increase, and it therefore seems worthwhile to overcome the limitations of this study within the scope of the ongoing research project by including qualitative studies in the preliminary results.

Acknowledgement. This research was funded in part by the Austrian Research Promotion Agency (FFG) within the scope of a joint project on *Poll Analytics*.

References

1. Weill, P., Vitale, M.R.: Place to Space: Migrating to Ebusiness Models. Harvard Business School Press, Boston (2001)
2. Newell, P.: Perspectives on privacy. J. Environ. Psychol. **15**(2), 87–104 (1995)
3. Andrade, E.B., Kaltcheva, V., Weitz, B.: Self-disclosure on the web: the impact of privacy policy, reward, and company reputation. Adv. Consum. Res. **29**, 350–353 (2002)
4. Manny, C.: European and american privacy: commerce, rights, and justice. Comput. Law Secur. Rep. **19**(1), 4–10 (2003)
5. Pötzsch, S.: Privacy awareness: a means to solve the privacy paradox? In: Matyáš, V., Fischer-Hübner, S., Cvrček, D., Švenda, P. (eds.) Privacy and Identity 2008. IAICT, vol. 298, pp. 226–236. Springer, Heidelberg (2009). https://doi.org/10.1007/978-3-642-03315-5_17
6. Warren, S., Brandeis, L.: The right to privacy. Harvard Law Rev. **4**, 193–220 (1890)
7. Westin, A.: Privacy and Freedom. Atheneum, New York (1967)
8. Bergmann, M.: Testing privacy awareness. In: Matyáš, V., Fischer-Hübner, S., Cvrček, D., Švenda, P. (eds.) Privacy and Identity 2008. IAICT, vol. 298, pp. 237–253. Springer, Heidelberg (2009). https://doi.org/10.1007/978-3-642-03315-5_18
9. Stewart, K.A., Segars, A.H.: An empirical examination of the concern for information privacy instrument. Inf. Syst. Res. **13**(1), 36–49 (2002)
10. Awad, N., Krishnan, M.: The personalization privacy paradox: an empirical evaluation of information transparency and the willingness to be profiled online for personalization. MIS Q. **30**(1), 13–28 (2006)
11. Norberg, P.A., Horne, D.R., Horne, D.A.: The privacy paradox: personal information disclosure intentions versus behaviors. J. Consum. Aff. **41**(1), 100–126 (2007)
12. Spiekermann, S., Grossklags, J., Berendt, B.: E-privacy in 2nd generation e-commerce: privacy preferences versus actual behavior. In: Proceedings of the 3rd ACM Conference on Electronic Commerce, EC 2001, pp. 38–47. ACM, New York (2001)
13. Chellappa, R.K., Sin, R.G.: Personalization versus privacy: an empirical examination of the online consumer's dilemma. Inf. Technol. Manag. **6**(2), 181–202 (2005)
14. Acquisti, A., Gross, R.: Imagined communities: awareness, information sharing, and privacy on the Facebook. In: Danezis, G., Golle, P. (eds.) PET 2006. LNCS, vol. 4258, pp. 36–58. Springer, Heidelberg (2006). https://doi.org/10.1007/11957454_3
15. Allmer, T., Fuchs, C., Kreilinger, V., Sevignani, S.: Social networking sites in the surveillance society: critical perspectives and empirical findings. In: Jansson, A., Christensen, M. (eds.) Media, Surveillance and Identity: Social Perspectives, pp. 49–70. Peter Lang, New York (2014)
16. Weber, P.: Discussions in the comments section: factors influencing participation and interactivity in online newspapers' reader comments. New Media Soc. **16**(6), 941–957 (2014)

17. Stabauer, M., Grossmann, G., Stumptner, M.: State of the art in knowledge extraction from online polls: a survey of current technologies. In: Proceedings of the Australasian Computer Science Week Multiconference, pp. 58:1–58:8. ACM (2016)
18. Jurca, R., Faltings, B.: Incentives for expressing opinions in online polls. In: Proceedings of the 9th ACM Conference on Electronic Commerce, pp. 119–128. ACM (2008)
19. Burgstaller, F., Stabauer, M., Morgan, R., Grossmann, G.: Towards customised visualisation of ontologies: state of the art and future applications for online polls analysis. In: Proceedings of the Australasian Computer Science Week Multiconference, ACSW 2017, pp. 26:1–26:10. ACM, New York (2017)
20. Brambilla, M., Mauri, A.: Model-driven development of social network enabled applications with WebML and social primitives. In: Grossniklaus, M., Wimmer, M. (eds.) Current Trends in Web Engineering, pp. 41–55. Springer, Berlin Heidelberg (2012). https://doi.org/10.1007/978-3-642-16985-4
21. Moey, L.K., Katuk, N., Omar, M.H.: Social login privacy alert: does it improve privacy awareness of Facebook users? In: 2016 IEEE Symposium on Computer Applications Industrial Electronics (ISCAIE), pp. 95–100, May 2016
22. Bauer, L., Bravo-Lillo, C., Fragkaki, E., Melicher, W.: A comparison of users' perceptions of and willingness to use Google, Facebook, and Google+ single-sign-on functionality. In: Proceedings of the 2013 ACM workshop on Digital Identity Management, pp. 25–36. ACM (2013)
23. Ibrahim, S.Z., Blandford, A., Bianchi-Berthouze, N.: Privacy settings on Facebook: their roles and importance. In: Proceedings of the 2012 IEEE International Conference on Green Computing and Communications, pp. 426–433 (2012)
24. Egelman, S.: My profile is my password, verify me!: the privacy/convenience trade-off of Facebook connect. In: Proceedings of the SIGCHI Conference on Human Factors in Computing Systems, pp. 2369–2378 (2013)
25. Stabauer, M., Mayrhauser, C., Karlinger, M.: Converting opinion into knowledge. In: Nah, F.F.-H.F.-H., Tan, C.-H. (eds.) HCIBGO 2016. LNCS, vol. 9751, pp. 330–340. Springer, Cham (2016). https://doi.org/10.1007/978-3-319-39396-4_30
26. Friedman, B., Lin, P., Miller, J.K.: Informed consent by design. In: Cranor, L.F., Garfinkel, S. (eds.) Security and Usability: Designing Secure Systems that People Can Use, pp. 495–521. O'Reilly Media (2005)

Why Blogger Sells: An Approach from the Attachment Theory

Wei Yang[1,2(✉)] and Choon Ling Sia[2]

[1] Xi'an Jiaotong University, Beilin District, Xi'an, China
[2] City University of Hong Kong, Kowloon, Hong Kong, China
wyang23-c@my.cityu.edu.hk, iscl@cityu.edu.hk

Abstract. This research studies the micro-celebrity endorsement effectiveness. To be more specific, we consider a typical social media enabled micro-celebrity: bloggers. This research asks two questions: 1, how does bloggers leverage the social media to recommend products; 2, what are the underlying psychological mechanisms? We adopt attachment theory to explain the research questions. We propose that factors that can fulfill the follower's self-enabling needs, self-enriching needs and self-gratifying needs are important to build attachment towards micro-celebrities. In advance, the attachment will lead to purchase behavior. A conceptual model is built and the further data collection will be conducted later.

Keywords: Micro-celebrity endorsement · Attachment theory

1 Introduction

1.1 A Subsection Sample

A new kind of word-of-mouth has emerged due to the prevalent use of Web2.0. Social media, such as Facebook, Instagram, Youtube and Microblog, provides opportunities for ordinary consumers to get thousands of followers [1]. Ordinary people who shows his or her talent on the social media can earn the fame and become influential in shaping the follower's perceptions and attitude. This new actor category through new media are named as "digital influencer", "social media influencer", "micro-celebrity" by scholars from media, communication, marketing and information systems [1–4]. Although no conclusive term is achieved by scholars yet, the "grass-root" and "niche" nature of those influencers are agreed by all scholars. The grass-root nature emphasizes that the influencer's "ordinary" origin, and the niche nature emphasizes that the influence of the micro-celebrity is effective only among the followers. Among them, the blogger is identified as an important kind of micro-celebrity.

A blogger endorses for multiple brands on social media and the economic value is huge [1, 4]. For example, Indy Clinton (Instagram account: indyclinton), a student is Austrilia, started to share her personal life on Instagram when she was 15 years old. Currently she has reached 104000 followers. She endorsed for the sponsored brands on Ins, and one piece of her endorsement post is charged for more than 750 dollars [5]. The endorsement phenomenon goes beyond the fashion context and nationality. Wenyi

© Springer International Publishing AG, part of Springer Nature 2018
F. F.-H. Nah and B. S. Xiao (Eds.): HCIBGO 2018, LNCS 10923, pp. 526–535, 2018.
https://doi.org/10.1007/978-3-319-91716-0_42

(micro-blog account: wenyi) is a food blogger in China's Microblog. The blogger was initially a housewife and received no academic training as a chef. She cultivates people how to cook home-made meals and shared her family lives with the followers. She is quite famous as she reaches more than 482000 fans. In 2015, Wenyi endorsed for a chopping board in her micro-blog, and 22.5 million RMB sales revenue in a single day is due to Wenyi's endorsement [6]. Given the success of blogger endorsement is new and of economic importance, it is important to understand why the blogger endorsement can be so effective.

Literature on attachment suggests that follower's intention to buy is influenced by celebrity attachment, which is built through the celebrity's frequently responses to the consumer's needs. As to celebrity attachment, we refer to the cognitive and emotional bonding with the celebrity [7, 8]. Followers who build strong attachment with celebrities are willing to allocate more resources to the celebrity, and the attachment outcomes are crucial for the endorsement effectiveness [8]. Thomson [9] suggests that strong attachment towards the celebrity is a key predictor of trusting relationships, and is parsimonious proxy for consumer-brand relations. Loroz and Braig [10] found that celebrity attachment is beneficial to commitment, trust on the endorsed brand, as well as intention to buy.

A few studies discuss the success of blogger endorsement effectiveness and identified several significant factors. Although those factors are useful to understand the success of blogger endorsement, they are pieces of findings and lacks of theoretical guidance. For instance, Gannon and Prothero [11] studies the influence of selfies on perceived authenticity on bloggers using an in-depth interview without theoretical implications. Furthermore, although current blogger studies mentioned blogger is a specific kind of celebrity, but much of the research hasn't combine the celebrity endorsement literature into their works. Among the few, Lee and Watkins [12] apply the celebrity attractiveness model into their study and discuss the influence of social attractiveness, physical attractiveness and attitude homophiles on blogger' intention to buy. In a word, the literature lacks of theoretical guidance and are pieces of findings on blogger endorsement studies.

This paper draws from attachment theory to illustrate how bloggers leverage social media to make the endorsement more effectiveness. Both the celebrity endorsement literature and blogger endorsement literature has made considerable progress in identifying important factors that may influence the endorsement effectiveness. For instance, in celebrity endorsement literature, attractiveness, credibility, fitness between the celebrity and the product, celebrity identification, role modeling is considered as the key factors of persuasion outcomes. In blogger endorsement studies, the social media enabled factors, such as blogger's self-disclosure, blogger's responsiveness, the blogger's selfies, attitude homophily are considered respectively. Although these findings are useful, theoretically based knowledge is underdeveloped yet. We review that enabling, enhancing and gratifying the follower's need of self can increase the attachment toward the blogger. Further, we show those characteristics derived from theory are important to generate attachment and follower's intention to buy.

To foreshadow this work, blogger's characteristics and activities are divided into three sub-groups: to fulfill follower's need of self-enabling, to fulfill follower's need of self-enriching and to fulfill follower's need of self-gratifying. To examine those features inspired by attachment theory, we summarized features into the enabling needs, enriching needs and gratifying needs respectively. We planned to conduct a survey to test whether the effects of these features are valid.

2 Theoretical Development

2.1 Attachment Theory and Relevant Studies

Attachment theory is developed from parent-infant relationship. Its main proposition is that when someone is in his childhood, survival is the basic need. He would like to seek for protection from environmental treats and maintain the sense of safety. As a result, he would like to build emotional bonding with people who are responsive to his needs [13]. Attachment also widely exists in a man's adulthood. When an object is responsive to one's specific needs, a satisfied and committed relationship is built then [9]. As human being have the tendency to maintain such intense relationship, they are mentally willing to allocate emotional, cognitive and behavioral resources towards the attachment target [14].

Although the original attachment theory stresses on close and intimate relationships, scholars from consumer psychology extends attachment study to marketing contexts. In marketing research, the attachment targets can be the target firm [15, 16], the employee [17], a specific brand [18–21], a human brand [9, 10, 22], or even a place [24]. For instance, Park et al. [18] considers brand as the attachment target. In this paper, they seperated "brand attachment" from "brand attitude strength" and empirically develops "brand-self connection" and "prominence" as two dimensions of brand attachment. Thomson [9] considers human brand as the attachment target. They study human brand attachment and proposed that need for autonomy, need for relatedness and need for competence are three antecedents of human brand attachment.

2.2 Consumers' Emotional Attachment to Bloggers

The terminology adopted in the literature regarding attachment varies. Some researchers used the term "emotional attachment" [10, 17, 24]. Some researchers used the term "attachment" [8, 20]. Some even use the terms "brand love", "intimacy" or "affection" [22, 25–27]. In our study, we adopt the term "emotional attachment" to refer to followers' emotional attachment towards bloggers.

Here we define blogger attachment as the strength of the emotional and cognitive bond linking the blogger with the follower' self. Although the terminology differs, the intensions and meanings those terms tend to express is identical. That is, they describe the extent to which the attachment target is linked to a person. To talk about attachment in general, Park et al. [18] stress on the "connection" nature of attachment, that is, to what extent is the attachment target part of the consumer. Emotional attachment emphasizes the emotional factors of this bond. The emotional attachment stream proposes that attachment is an emotion-laden and target specific bond. Thomson et al. [9] develop "connection", "passion" and "affection" as three dimensions to capture the emotional features of attachment.

According to Park et al. [18], attachment is the strength of bond connecting the individual and the targeted attachment group. Thomson et al. [9] suggests that emotional brand attachment reflects the bond between a consumer with a specific brand and the bond itself involves feelings toward the brand. Brand attachment consists of three emotional components: affection, passion and connection. Park et al. [8] extended the idea that brand attachment not only include the emotional bond but also the cognitive bond. Based on that notion, Park et al. [18] proposed brand attachment as the power of the bond linking the self with the brand. Brand-self connection and brand prominence are two critical factors to measure brand attachment.

Based on different theories, scholars find antecedents to predict attachment. Thomson [9] started by suggesting the fulfillment of three basic psychological needs (autonomy, relatedness and competence) as the predictors of attachment strength. Other studies [8, 15] found that enabling, gratifying and enriching the self are key antecedents of brand attachment. Orth et al. [28] considered human personality and brand personalities key antecedents of attachment. Malär et al. [19] suggest that self-congruence with brand personality has implications for consumers' emotional brand attachment.

2.3 EEG Needs

This paper aims to use attachment theory to explain why the blogger sells. More specifically, attachment theory propose that an individual will generate emotional attachment towards an object when the object is able to fulfill this individual's EEG needs (self-enabling needs, self-enriching needs, and self-gratifying needs). The underlying assumption is that individuals tend to link himself with people who is considered as responsive to their needs [29, 30]. Parallel, bloggers, who is trying to build emotional and cognitive bonding with the followers, must be highly responsive to followers' needs.

Part et al. [8] developed a conceptual framework to identify three kinds of needs (functional needs, symbolic needs and hedonic needs respectively) that is crucial to build the emotional and cognitive bonding. Functional needs (self-enabling needs) refers to a person's desire to enhance the self-efficacy and to achieve the mastery goal. Symbolic needs (self-enriching) needs means a person is willing to identify and express his real and ideal self [31]. Hedonic needs (self-gratifying needs) refers to a person's need to be involved in playful entertainment and hedonic pleasure [8].

Celebrity can provide varies resources to help the follower to fulfill the above desired needs. **First of all**, the blogger is an expert in a specific domain, thus he can offer credible information in this domain and cultivate people [32]. By following the blogger, the blogger can obtain more knowledge and feel more confident in this area. **Secondly**, the blogger is socially or physically attractive, his image is incorporated with some aspirational meanings for the follower. By following the celebrity, the follower's self will be expressed and enriched. **Thirdly**, the blogger will disclose himself, communicate with the follower and even share light-hearted jokes and videos. Thus, the followers can gain great pleasure and entertainment.

In this research, we adopt Part et al.'s [8] identification of needs, and build the research model based on self-enabling, self-enriching and self-gratifying. To be more specific, we recognize blogger's characteristics that is under the umbrella of the above three needs. We posit that:

- Credibility (i.e. expertise and trustworthiness) of the blogger is factor that enable the follower's self-enabling needs.
- Role-modeling of the blogger is factor that enable the follower's self-enriching needs.
- Blogger attractiveness, self-disclosure, responsiveness and light-hearted entertainment providing are factors that enable the follower's self-gratifying needs.

Figure 1 illustrates the proposed research model.

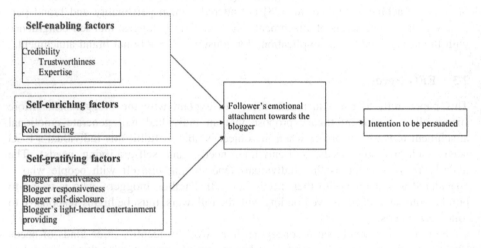

Fig. 1. Conceptual model

3   Hypotheses

3.1   Self-enabling Factors and Attachment Towards the Blogger

Learning from the knowledgeable and trustworthy blogger, the follower feels more confident on decision making and thus the need for enabling self is satisfied [33]. Thus, credibility of the blogger is a key self-enabling factor. A person feels enabled when a sense of efficacious and capable self is created [8]. Thus, any factor that is beneficial to create an efficacious and capable self could be considered as self-enabling factors. In the context of blogger endorsement, the blogger is considered as an expert in a specific domain and people believe in his authenticity [1, 33, 34]. When the blogger endorses in this specific domain, the follower will perceive the endorsement is based on professional knowledge and credible [35].

H1: Credibility of the blogger increases the follower's attachment towards the blogger.

3.2   Self-enriching Factors and Attachment Towards the Blogger

The blogger is considered as a role model by the follower. On the one side, the follower has the need to enhance himself and to be classified into a certain social group [1]. On the other side, the blogger is perceived to have huge similarities with the follower's ideal self [36]. The blogger is considered as a role model by the followers. In the process of learning from the blogger's taste and preference, the follower's self is enriched. Thus, Role modeling can be considered as a key factor of self-enabling.

H2: Role modeling of the blogger increases the follower's attachment towards the blogger.

3.3   Self-gratifying Factors and Attachment Towards the Blogger

Attractiveness includes both physical attractiveness and social attractiveness, such as personal traits, intellectual skills and lifestyles [12, 37]. The attractive of a blogger can make the follower release from heavy daily works and obtain positive emotions [38]. Thus, attractive blogger is able to gratify the follower, thus lead the follower to build physical connections with the blogger.

H3: Attractiveness of the blogger increases the follower's attachment towards the blogger.

Interpersonal communication is a key driver of attraction as it enhances a person's need for self-gratifying [39]. In the blogger-follower relationship context, blogger's responsiveness is a crucial aspect of communication [3, 40]. Responsiveness of the blogger refers to the blogger's response frequency and immediacy behaviors, such as a quick reply on the follower's comment. As the frequency of response increases, the follower is likely to perceived more communication willingness from the blogger. The follower enjoys the communication with the blogger, thus his gratifying needs is satisfied to some extent.

H4: Responsiveness of the blogger increases the follower's attachment towards the blogger.

Self-disclosure is another crucial aspect of interpersonal communication. It is defined as the exposure of one's information to another [41]. People tend to build intimate connections with another one who disclose a lot to himself [42]. This finding can be applied in many contexts, such as romantic relationships, consumer-brand relationships and also celebrity-follower relationships [43, 44]. In social media, the blogger releases diversified self-disclosure information to his followers, including personal lives, work-related things and attitudes on public affair [45]. By perceiving blogger's self-disclosure, the follower his attachment towards the blogger is strengthened.

H5: Self-disclosure of the blogger increases the follower's attachment towards the blogger.

For many people, to gain light-hearted entertainment is their motivation to follow a celebrity [38, 46]. In social media context, the blogger releases jokes, narrative stories and interesting videos, which can make the follower relax. Thus, the relaxed follower enjoys in the lighted-hearted entertainments, the need for gratification is satisfied.

H6: Light-hearted entertainment providing of the blogger increases the follower's attachment towards the blogger.

3.4   Attachment Towards the Blogger and Purchase Intention

People tend to allocation more resources to the attachment target [14, 47]. In the blogger endorsement context, when the follower builds cognitive and emotional attachment towards the blogger, he is more likely to generate positive attitudes on the blogger's behaviors, for example, endorsement. Thus, the intention to be persuaded will increase.

H7: The follower's attachment towards the blogger increases purchase intention.

4   Proposed Methodology

To test the research model, an online survey is planned to be conducted. A questionnaire will be designed to measure the independent and dependent variables. 20 bloggers will be selected randomly on microblog. For each blogger, 200 of their followers will be selected randomly to ask if they would like to participate in the online-survey.

5   Conclusion

This research tends to explore the question that why micro-celebrity endorsement is effective. To be more specific, we select blogger as a typical kind of micro-celebrity to conduct the following research. According to the attachment theory, we believed that a blogger who is capable to fulfill the followers' self-enabling, self-enriching and self-gratifying needs can encourage the followers to build strong emotional attachment with this blogger. Furthermore, the follower's emotional attachment towards the blogger can thus positively influence their purchase intention.

While the empirical test is under design in current stage, we propose that several results will be empirically tested. The credibility, including both expertise and trustworthiness dimension, is supposed to influence followers' attachment towards the blogger as self-enabling factors. The blogger's role modelling is supposed to influence followers' attachment towards the blogger as self-enriching factors. The blogger's attractiveness, self-disclosure, responsiveness and lighthearted entertainment providing are supposed to influence the follower's attachment towards the blogger as gratifying factors.

These findings will generate several theoretical and practical implications. This research is one of the first papers studying the blogger endorsement effectiveness. It focuses on the question that why blogger endorsement is effective by investigating the antecedents and the influencing mechanism. **In term of theoretical contribution**, this paper identified several unique antecedents of blogger endorsement effectiveness, which are different from the classical celebrity endorsement literature. Moreover, this research highlighted the importance of follower's emotional attachment towards the blogger, which is less mentioned in celebrity endorsement literature. **This research also has practical implications**. From the firm side, it provides important indicators for firms to identify suitable bloggers to endorse the products. From the blogger side, with the guidance from this research, the blogger can learn how to make use of their economic value strategically.

References

1. Mcquarrie, E.F., Miller, J., Phillips, B.J.: The megaphone effect: taste and audience in fashion blogging. J. Consum. Res. **40**(1), 136–158 (2013). https://doi.org/10.1086/669042
2. Vaast, E., Davidson, E.J., Mattson, T.: Talking about technology: the emergence of a new actor category through new media. MIS Q. **37**(4), 1069–1092 (2013). https://doi.org/10.25300/MISQ/2013/37.4.04
3. Marwick, A., Boyd, D.: To see and be seen: celebrity practice on Twitter. Convergence: Int. J. Res. New Media Technol. **17**(2), 139–158 (2011). https://doi.org/10.1177/13548565 10394539
4. Uzunoğlu, E., Kip, S.M.: Brand communication through digital influencers: leveraging blogger engagement. Int. J. Inf. Manag. **34**(5), 592–602 (2014). https://doi.org/10.1016/j.ijinfomgt.2014.04.007
5. Cross, J.: (2014). http://www.dailytelegraph.com.au/newslocal/northern-beaches/palm-beach-schoolgirl-indy-clinton-charges-up-to-750-for-instagram-selfies-of-surf-style/news-story/dad 1376436720736bde1e804eaabe061
6. Li, J.: (2016). http://news.pedaily.cn/201604/20160413395614.shtml
7. Thomson, M., MacInnis, D.J., Park, C.W.: The ties that bind: measuring the strength of consumers' emotional attachments to brands. J. Consum. Psychol. **15**(1), 77–91 (2005). https://doi.org/10.1207/s15327663jcp1501_10
8. Park, C.W., Macinnis, D.J., Priester, J.R.: Beyond Attitudes: Attachment and Consumer Behavior. Social Science Electronic Publishing, Rochester (2006)
9. Thomson, C.J., Rindfleisch, A., Arsel, Z.: Emotional branding and the strategic value of the doppelgänger brand image. J. Mark. **70**(1), 50–64 (2006)
10. Loroz, P.S., Braig, B.M.: Consumer attachments to human brands: the "Oprah Effect". Psychol. Mark. **32**(7), 751–763 (2015). https://doi.org/10.1002/mar.20815
11. Gannon, V., Prothero, A.: Beauty blogger selfies as authenticating practices. Eur. J. Mark. **50** (9/10), 1858–1878 (2016). https://doi.org/10.1108/EJM-07-2015-0510
12. Lee, J.E., Watkins, B.: YouTube vloggers' influence on consumer luxury brand perceptions and intentions. J. Bus. Res. **69**(12), 5753–5760 (2016). https://doi.org/10.1016/j.jbusres.2016.04.171
13. Bowlby, J.: The Making and Breaking of Affectional Bonds. Tavistock, London (1979)
14. Holmes, J.G.: Social relationships: the nature and function of relational schemas. Eur. J. Soc. Psychol. **30**(4), 447–495 (2000). https://doi.org/10.1002/1099-0992. (200007/08) 30:4% 3C447: AID-EJSP10%3E3.0.CO;2-Q
15. Vlachos, P.A., Theotokis, A., Pramatari, K.: Consumer-retailer emotional attachment: some antecedents and the moderating role of attachment anxiety. Eur. J. Mark. **44**(9/10), 1478–1499 (2008). https://doi.org/10.1108/03090561011062934
16. Moussa, S., Touzani, M.: Customer-service firm attachment: what it is and what causes it? Int. J. Qual. Serv. Sci. **5**(3), 337–359 (2013). https://doi.org/10.1108/IJQSS-01-2013-0002

17. Moussa, S., Touzani, M.: The moderating role of attachment styles in emotional bonding with service providers. J. Consum. Behav. https://doi.org/10.1002/cb.1605

18. Park, C.W., Macinnis, D.J., Priester, J.: Brand attachment and brand attitude strength: conceptual and empirical differentiation of two critical brand equity drivers. J. Mark. **74**(6), 1–17 (2010). https://doi.org/10.1509/jmkg.74.6.1

19. Malär, L., Krohmer, H., Hoyer, W.D.: Emotional brand attachment and brand personality: the relative importance of the actual and the ideal self. J. Mark. **75**(4), 35–52 (2011). https://doi.org/10.1509/jmkg.75.4.35

20. Proksch, M., Orth, U.R., Cornwell, T.B.: Competence enhancement and anticipated emotion as motivational drivers of brand attachment. Psychol. Mark. **32**(9), 934–949 (2015). https://doi.org/10.1002/mar.20828

21. Grisaffe, D.B., Nguyen, H.P.: Antecedents of emotional attachment to brands. J. Bus. Res. **64**(10), 1052–1059 (2011). https://doi.org/10.1016/j.jbusres.2010.11.002

22. Park, N., Jin, B., Jin, S.A.A.: Effects of self-disclosure on relational intimacy in Facebook. Comput. Hum. Behav. **27**(5), 1974–1983 (2011). https://doi.org/10.1016/j.chb.2011.05.004

23. Debenedetti, A., Oppewal, H., Arsel, Z.: Place attachment in commercial settings: a gift economy perspective. J. Consum. Res. **40**(5), 904–923 (2014). https://doi.org/10.1086/673469

24. Wan, J., Lu, Y., Wang, B.: How attachment influences users' willingness to donate to content creators in social media: a socio-technical systems perspective. Inf. Manag. **54**(7), 837–850 (2016). https://doi.org/10.1016/j.im.2016.12.007

25. Carroll, B.A., Ahuvia, A.C.: Some antecedents and outcomes of brand love. Mark. Lett. **17**(2), 79–89 (2006). https://doi.org/10.1007/s11002-006-4219-2

26. Albert, N., Merunka, D., Valette-Florence, P.: When consumers love their brands: exploring the concept and its dimensions. J. Bus. Res. **61**(10), 1062–1075 (2008). https://doi.org/10.1016/j.jbusres.2007.09.014

27. Yim, C.K., Tse, D.K., Chan, K.W.: Strengthening customer loyalty through intimacy and passion: roles of customer-firm affection and customer-staff relationships in services. J. Mark. Res. **45**(6), 741–756 (2008). https://doi.org/10.1509/jmkr.45.6.741

28. Orth, U.R., Limon, Y., Rose, G.: Store-evoked affect, personalities, and consumer emotional attachments to brands. J. Bus. Res. **63**(11), 1202–1208 (2010). https://doi.org/10.1016/j.jbusres.2009.10.018

29. Aron, A.P., Dutton, D.G., Aron, E.N., Iverson, A.: Experiences of falling in love. J. Soc. Per. Relat. **6**(3), 243–257 (1989). https://doi.org/10.1177/0265407589063001

30. Hazan, C., Shaver, P.R.: Attachment as an organizational framework for research on close relationships. Psychol. Inq. **5**(1), 1–22 (1994). https://doi.org/10.1207/s15327965pli0501_1

31. Kleine, S.S., Baker, S.M.: An integrative review of material possession attachment. Acad. Mark. Sci. Rev. **23**(1), 4–41 (2004)

32. Djafarova, E., Rushworth, C.: Exploring the credibility of online celebrities' Instagram profiles in influencing the purchase decisions of young female users. Comput. Hum. Behav. **68**, 1–7 (2017). https://doi.org/10.1016/j.chb.2016.11.009

33. Eisend, M., Langner, T.: Immediate and delayed advertising effects of celebrity endorsers' attractiveness and expertise. Int. J. Advertising **29**(4), 527–546 (2010). https://doi.org/10.2501/s0265048710201336

34. Spry, A., Pappu, R., Cornwell, T.B.: Celebrity endorsement, brand credibility and brand equity. Eur. J. Mark. **45**(6), 882–909 (2011). https://doi.org/10.1108/03090561111119958

35. Bergkvist, L., Hjalmarson, H., Mägi, A.W.: A new model of how celebrity endorsements work: attitude toward the endorsement as a mediator of celebrity source and endorsement effects. Int. J. Advertising **35**(2), 171–184 (2016). https://doi.org/10.1080/02650487.2015.1024384

36. Escalas, J.E., Bettman, J.R.: Connecting with celebrities: how consumers appropriate celebrity meanings for a sense of belonging. J. Advertising, 1–12. https://doi.org/10.1080/00913367.2016.1274925
37. Erdogan, Z.: Celebrity endorsement: a literature review. J. Mark. Manag. 15(4), 291–314 (1999). https://doi.org/10.1362/026725799784870379
38. Hung, K.: Why celebrity sells: a dual entertainment path model of brand endorsement. J. Advertising 43(2), 155–166 (2014). https://doi.org/10.1080/00913367.2013.838720
39. Festinger, L., Schachter, S., Back, K.: Social Pressures in Informal Groups; a Study of Human Factors in Housing. Harper, Oxford, England (1950)
40. Marwick, A.E., Boyd, D.: I tweet honestly, I tweet passionately: Twitter users, context collapse, and the imagined audience. New Media Soc. 20(1), 1–20 (2011). https://doi.org/10.1177/1461444810365313
41. Derlega, V.J., Chaikin, A.L.: Privacy and self-disclosure in social relationships. J. Soc. Issues 33, 102–115 (1977). https://doi.org/10.1111/j.1540-4560.1977.tb01885.x
42. Altman, I., Taylor, D.A.: Social Penetration: the Development of Interpersonal Relationships. Holt, Rinehart, & Winston, New York (1973)
43. Utz, S.: The function of self-disclosure on social network sites: not only intimate, but also positive and entertaining self-disclosures increase the feeling of connection. Comput. Hum. Behav. 45, 1–10 (2015). https://doi.org/10.1016/j.chb.2014.11.076
44. Lin, R., Utz, S.: Self-disclosure on sns: do disclosure intimacy and narrativity influence interpersonal closeness and social attraction? Comput. Hum. Behav. 7, 426–436 (2017). https://doi.org/10.1016/j.chb.2017.01.012
45. Kim, J., Song, H.: Celebrity's self-disclosure on Twitter and parasocial relationships: a mediating role of social presence. Comput. Hum. Behav. 62(C), 570–577 (2016). https://doi.org/10.1016/j.chb.2016.03.083
46. Hung, K., Chan, K.W., Caleb, H.T.: Assessing celebrity endorsement effects in China. J. Advertising Res. 51(4), 608–623 (2011). https://doi.org/10.2501/JAR-51-4-608-623
47. Fedorikhin, A., Park, C.W., Thomson, M.: Beyond fit and attitude: The effect of emotional attachment on consumer responses to brand extensions. J. Consum. Psychol. 18(4), 281–291 (2008). https://doi.org/10.1016/j.jcps.2008.09.006

Opinion Mining and Sentiment Analysis in Social Media: Challenges and Applications

Wenping Zhang[1], Mengna Xu[2(⊠)], and Qiqi Jiang[3]

[1] School of Information, Renmin University of China, Beijing, China
wpzhang@ruc.edu.cn
[2] School of Economics and Management, Hangzhou Normal University,
Hangzhou, China
xumena@163.com
[3] Copenhagen Business School, Frederiksberg, Denmark
qj.digi@cbs.dk

Abstract. It is a widely accepted truth there are great values embedded in the opinion and sentiment expressed by users on social media platforms. Nowadays, it is quite common for researchers or engineers to adopt opinion mining and sentiment analysis techniques to extract enriched emotional information from online text content. However, given the characteristics of social media, such as dynamic, short, informal and context dependent, applying general opinion mining and sentiment analysis techniques originally designed for static long text corpora would lead to serious bias. In many applications, even research that not specialized in opinion mining and sentiment analysis, this problem is ignored unintentionally or unintentionally. Such ignorance may contribute the failure of some designs or unexplainable results. In this paper, we summarized these challenges in social media sentiment analysis. Some potential solutions for these challenges are also discussed. Finally, we also introduced several state-of-the-art techniques in social media sentiment analysis.

Keywords: Opinion mining and sentiment analysis · Social media
Business applications

1 Introduction

There are 2.46 billion social media users worldwide up to 2017 (statistic 2018). There is no doubt that it is beneficial to analyze the content of social media. One of the most import analysis is to extract the opinion and sentiment expressed by users in social media posts. Many attempts haven been to make use of the public orientation expressed in social media to solve real social or business problems, such as election prediction (Agrawal and Hamling 2017), stock market analysis (Bollen et al. 2011) and personalized recommendation (Sun et al. 2015). However, due to characteristics of social media, like dynamic, short, informal and context dependent, it is risky to apply general opinion mining and sentiment analysis techniques directly to social media. There are several points that need special attentions and careful process when dealing with social media content. Ignorance of these points will bring serious bias in the analysis and finally lead to failure of some designs or unexplainable results.

© Springer International Publishing AG, part of Springer Nature 2018
F. F.-H. Nah and B. S. Xiao (Eds.): HCIBGO 2018, LNCS 10923, pp. 536–548, 2018.
https://doi.org/10.1007/978-3-319-91716-0_43

Given that most data in business practices are in text format, extracting emotions from text content plays a leading role in opinion mining and sentiment analysis. As a result, opinion mining and sentiment analysis generally can be considered as a branch of text mining. The situation is the same in social media. When referring to opinion mining and sentiment analysis in social media, we usually talking about extracting emotions from text content. Hence, it is necessary and important to make a deep understanding of text mining techniques before conducting opinion mining and sentiment analysis. However, there are some characteristics in social media content beyond the ability of common text mining. For instance, social media today is full of emoji, which is usually in non-text format but with rich emotions embedded. Emoji was treated as noise and removed directly in previous text mining (Kiritchenko et al. 2014). Apparently, it is not a suitable operation in up-to-date opinion mining and sentiment analysis in social media. Unfortunately, there is no good solution for emoji analysis due to its complexity and dynamics until recently. It is a challenge that we cannot bypass if we hope to make better understanding and usage of social media content.

In this paper, we summarize the points that need special attentions in opinion mining and sentiment analysis in social media. It is known to all that content in social media is short, meaningful and emotion enriched. Apparently, many statistics based opinion mining and sentiment analysis techniques that come from text mining don't work effectively anymore when applying directly to social media. If we treat each post in social media as one single document, and conduct analysis on it, there would be a large chance to get biased and inconsistent results (e.g. with large variance). Synonym is also one of the most well-known challenge in opinion mining and sentiment analysis. An opinion word may express different, even opposite, emotions in different places. Generally, the exact meaning can be deduced according to the context it affiliated. However, the context information is rather deficient when dealing with short social media posts, especially the method treating each post as an independent text fragment.

Finally, some typical applications of opinion mining and sentiment analysis in social media are provided. The use of opinion mining and sentiment analysis as a tool to assistant decisions in real world is not novel. However, the characteristics of social media could bring us unprecedented opportunities to do something important and interesting. For instance, the president election of U.S. in 2016 is one good example to show the power of public orientation analysis in social media. Compared with traditional methods, such as telephone questionnaire, it turns to be much faster and more accurate. We are in the era of social media. Catching opinions from social media could be a cheap, fast and effective way to collect feedbacks from users. In other words, there are great benefits contained in peoples' daily social media posts. The only problem is how to make good use of them.

All in all, this paper can be considered as a review that summarize work related to opinion mining and sentiment analysis. Besides these summarization, categorization and archive of existing work, we also discuss challenges that need special attentions when dealing with social media content. Some existing possible solutions are summarized to assist implementations in real business applications and research. We also provide some typical examples to support our introduction. We believe opinion mining and sentiment analysis techniques in social media could play a more important role in real business applications and research if handled properly.

2 Knowledge Foundation

2.1 Concept Foundation

Before the technical details of opinion mining and sentiment analysis, it is necessary to clarify some related basic concepts. Strictly speaking, there are certain differences between opinion mining and sentiment analysis. One evident difference is that opinion always has a holder and target, while sentiment doesn't have to. Intuitively, opinion mining is a process to identify someone's viewpoint (e.g. agree, disagree) to something. Sentiment analysis is to extract someone's attitude or feeling inside. Sometimes, it would be rather difficult to distinguish an opinion from a sentiment. One simple way is to image the possible responses. If one expression can be answered by "I agree/disagree", it must be an opinion. While if it can be responded by "I share your feeling/sentiment", it should be a sentiment. In most cases, it is not necessary to distinguish these two words explicitly. As a result, in most research and applications, these two terms are used alternatively. In this paper we also consider them as exchangeable if there is no special notifications.

Beside opinion and sentiment, three close terms are also worthy to be noticed: emotion, affection and mood. Compared with sentiment, emotion is more subjective. It can be described as mental activities reflected by degree of pleasure or displeasure. If someone express his/her feelings from the mental level, it would be reveal of emotions. Compared with above three widely used terms, affection and mood are not frequently to see in sentiment analysis yet. Affection can be defined as a state of mind that usually associated with a feeling (e.g. love). Mood usually stands for a conscious state of predominant emotion (e.g. in a good mood today). In most cases, it is unnecessary to distinguish these four terms. As a results, in many applications, these terms are considered as exchangeable during processing.

Nowadays, there is a trend that carrying study from group level to individual level. Along with this trend, emotion extract has become increasingly popular and important. In some specific research or application, it is necessary to extract peoples' emotions rather than general sentiments. For instance, in healthcare research, if we try to detect or predict depressions from users' social media, it is necessary and important to go to these delicate difference between emotion and opinion or sentiment. All in all, although there is no need to distinguish these four concepts in general applications, it is important to know the difference in case of any special situations.

2.2 Technology Foundation

Most business data are in text format (Breakthroughanalysis 2008). When referring to opinion mining, usually we mean extracting emotions from text content. Hence, here we have a brief introduction about text mining techniques. Similar to human comprehension processes, text mining techniques generally start with terms before analyzing the meaning of higher level structure (e.g. sentence, graph and document). Due to the characteristics of natural language, it is quite different for applying text mining techniques on different languages. Two typical ones are English and Chinese. Given that there are white space between sequential words in English, it is quite simple for the tokenization process for English text mining. The basic element of Chinese is word. However, the basic semantic element of Chinese is term, which is a combination of one to several words. Unfortunately, there is no white space for separation in Chinese. Hence, the first challenge in Chinese text mining is term segmentation. The performance of segmentation has a significant influence in the following analysis, e.g. opinion mining. However, it doesn't mean that English text mining is much easier that Chinese text mining. Since there are many derived word in English, it is always a problem to find their exact roots before further analysis. Such process is called stemmer. Without stemmer, same word in different formats would be considered as different ones. It will seriously decrease the performance of statistics based models.

3 Literature Review

3.1 General Techniques

Generally, sentiment analysis approaches can be classified into three categories: lexicon-based approach, linguistic-based approach and machine learning-based approach. In a lexicon-based approach, predefined sentiment lexicons that contain both positive indicators (term) and negative indicators are adopted to extract the number of corresponding sentiment indicators in a given text fragment (e.g. sentence, document) based on string matching (Pang and Lee 2008; Taboada et al. 2011). It has two remarkable advantages: ease of implementation and fast speed. Moreover, due to its intuitive outputs (e.g., a large number of positive terms indicates a strong positive orientation), the lexicon-based approach has been widely adopted in business practices and research (Liu et al. 2010). However, this method may suffer from low recall (the rate of detected targets on the total targets) because it strongly relies on the completeness of sentiment lexicons. Furthermore, it may cause confusions when dealing with synonymy and polysemy issues. One word may have different meanings (even opposite sentiment polarity) in different context. But in a lexicon, the meaning is fixed. In a machine learning-based approach, a set of labeled data (training data) is used to train classifiers to learn "rules" (Witten and Frank 2005). Then, these trained classifiers are used to predict the unlabeled data based on the "rules" they learned (Pak and Paroubek 2010; Pang et al. 2002). Such a process is generally carried on a text fragment level (e.g. sentence, document) instead of a word level. However, the overall learning rules or prediction processes are metaphorically described as a "black box" to users, which results in a dilemma when it comes to explaining or improving the algorithm. The principle of machine learning approach is that entrusting the machines, which is not easy to achieve in real business. In a linguistic approach, researchers have attempted to understand the semantic meaning of text and drew conclusions based on this meaning (Wilson et al. 2005). Such an approach is similar to the process of human cognition. However, due to the complexity and flexibility of human language (e.g., negation, idioms), this approach is not easily to implement in real-world applications.

Some researchers concentrated on improving detection accuracy of opinion mining from technical perspective. State of art machine learning techniques are adjusted and brought into the opinion mining tasks. For instance, Irsoy and Cardie (2014) applied recurrent neural networks (RNNs) for opinion mining tasks. Their experiments showed that the novel RNNs framework outperform previous conditional random field (CRF) based baselines. Similarly, Liu et al. (2015) developed a fine-grained token level opinion mining model that incorporating recurrent neural network. Cambria et al. (2015) adopted a vector space model—AffectiveSpace 2—to conduct concept-level sentiment analysis. Concept-level sentiment analysis concentrates on analyzing semantics of text utilizing web ontologies or semantic networks. Rather than gathering isolated opinion to an item, concept-level analysis allow for the inference of semantic and sentiment information associated with ontology features. In other words, it enables comparison of fine-grained features of items.

Although these advanced techniques could improve the accuracy of opinion mining significantly, these sophisticated models are still rare to see in the real business applications. One of the most important reason for such dilemma relates to model interpretability. In these machine learning models, the mining process is a black box for the users. It will lead to a feeling of "out-of-control", which prevent its applications in real business. As a result, the most widely used methods in real business is still lexicon-based approaches. As aforementioned, it is time and energy consuming to construct and maintain lexicons manually. As a result, low performance is one of the most serious weaknesses lexicon-based approaches must meet. To solve this problem, one possible solution is to construct lexicons automatically. One benefit along with these process is that context information can be incorporated in the sentiment lexicon construction or expansion process. Such context-aware sentiment lexicon, e.g. domain specific lexicon, could make contributions to increase opinion mining accuracy in certain applications. Losts of work has been done in this area. Du et al. (2010) developed a domain-oriented sentiment lexicon construction framework by adapting information bottleneck methods. Lu et al. (2011) proposed an optimization framework to combine different sources of information (e.g. context-dependent sentiment lexicons) by a unified and principled way. Huang et al. (2014) stated their constrained label propagation based domain-specific sentiment lexicon construction method.

Compared with automatic sentiment lexicon construction, one easier way is expanding and updating the existing widely used sentiment lexicon (e.g. SentiwordNet, HowNet, OpinionFinder). In practice, individuals tend to employ terms with similar or same meaning as alternatives in their expressions to avoid repetition. In other words, there will be a higher probability of co-occurrence for terms (words) with same or similar meaning in a short text fragment (e.g. a sentence, or a window). Based on this fact, sentiment lexicons can be expanded and updated incorporating context information. Generally, co-occurrence is not used directly in the expansion due to the problem of noise (e.g. frequently used but meaningless terms). Instead, a more advanced measure point-wise mutual information (PMI) are widely used (Read 2004; Su et al. 2006). PMI was defined as a measure of association between two objects (e.g. word) in information theory (see detail in Church and Hanks 1990). To calculate PMI, usually a slide window is used to catch the co-occurrence. There have been many applications that using PMI to expand sentiment lexicons and enhance analysis performance. For instance, Turney and Littman (2003) adopted PMI to extend positive and negative vocabulary. Khan et al. (2016) incorporated PMI to expand SentiWordNet to improve sentiment polarity detection. Manivannan and Kanimozhiselvi (2017) used PMI based integral classifier to conduct sentiment analysis cross domain.

Sentiment lexicon expansion using PMI could alleviate the domain dependence problem. However, it still suffer the problem of polysemy. The reason is that PMI is based on statistics and everything in statistic model is for certain (one word either belongs to one group or another). To solve this problem, probabilistic model could be one option. One typical method is topic modeling (e.g. latent Dirichlet allocation, LDA). In a topic model, terms with similar characteristics are probabilistically clustered into same topic trough sampling according to their context-aware co-occurrence (Blei et al. 2003). One word could belong to several topics with different probabilities. In this case, the exact meaning of a polysemous word could be inferred probabilistically according to the context it embedded. These unique characteristics of topic modeling are suitable for sentiment lexicon expansion. If the polarity of one topic is determined, then the words compose this topic would have a high probability to share the same polarity. The polarity of a topic can be indicated by a small sample of seeds (e.g. similarity to each kind of seeds). In real application, topic modeling users usually go one step further. Since a document can be seen as a distribution of topics, while a topic can be seen as a distribution of words. Once the polarities of topics are determined, the polarity of a document can be inferred according to the contributions of each kind of topics (positive, negative and neutral) to generate it. This method has become very popular in recent years. Li et al. (2014) proposed a supervised user-item based topic model for sentiment analysis. Nguyen and Shirai (2015) incorporated topic modeling based sentiment analysis on social media and used it for stock market prediction. Cao et al. (2016) designed a visual sentiment topic to extract sentiment from microblogs. Chen et al. (2017) utilized incremental hierarchical Dirichelt process (HDP) to conduct phrase level sentiment detection.

3.2   Challenges

There are several challenges to apply common opinion mining methods to social media. The first challenge refers to the length of the social media posts. Although the volume of social media is huge, each post is rather short. Usually, there are length limitations for each post on social media platforms, e.g. 140 characters for Tweets. Given the statistical information is rather limited in these short text, effective approaches suffer serious performance reduction when applying directly to social media. Generally, there are two ways to deal with these kind of short text. First, extracting the sentiment of each post, then calculate the overall sentiment according to the sentiment of each post. This method is very intuitive and explainable. But it would be very time consuming to process so many documents in real operation. Furthermore, the sentiment bias may be very large for each post, which will be reflected as a very large variance when calculating the overall sentiment. It will cast negative influence on the final analysis (e.g. weird or unexplainable results in the econometric analysis). Second, combining posts for a specific target in certain period as a "document" and extract the sentiment embedded in the "document". This is an easy but effective way that has been widely used the current social media analysis (Hong and Davison 2010).

The second challenge is social media content's strong context dependence. Social media posts usually are too short (even one or two words) to be self-explainable. It is quite common for people to look up the previous posts to catch the exact meaning of the current ones. In other words, the understanding of some terms seriously relies on the context they are in. Hence, it is important to handle context dependence problem in social media sentiment analysis. In machine learning-based approaches, this task is delivered to machines learning processes. The disadvantages is that we can never tell whether the context dependence problem is solved or not. In lexicon-based approaches, domain specific lexicon construction or expansion is effective to alleviate the context dependence problem. Thus widely used in social media sentiment analysis (e.g. Kouloumpis et al. 2011; Khan et al. 2015). Probabilistic topic models are also proved to be effective to this situation. However, this challenge is far from being solved due to the flexibility of social media. It is known to all that it is quite common for topic change in social media. A group of users may complain that some brand of notebook is too heavy. Here, "heavy" definitely expresses a negative sentiment. One moment later, they may be delighted to discuss the heavy investment that firm makes to improve their products. Here, "heavy" usually refers to a positive opinion. In this situation, even if we construct a domain specific lexicon on "computer" domain that can effectively recognize the polarity of "heavy" when refer to "notebook", it is helpless for the following "heavy" related to "investment". The key to handle this challenge is to catch the topic shift. One possible solution may be dynamic topic modeling (DTM) (Blei and Lafferty 2006). In DTM, topics evolves instead of static. Old topics may die while new topics are born with new data come (see detail in Blei and Lafferty 2006).

The third challenge is increasing usage of multimedia, such as emoji, image, and video. These non-text content has beyond the ability of traditional text mining based opinion mining techniques. In previous opinion mining, emoji usually was considered as noise and removed directly (Kiritchenko et al. 2014). With the popularity of emoji, this process is infeasible anymore. Nowadays, there is no surprise to see a conversation that only contains emoji but without one single word. Emoji is meaningful and cannot removed as noise anymore. Generally, emoji can be classified into three categories: coded emoji, static image emoji and dynamic image emoji. Coded emoji has their own character codes, usually released by large companies like Apple, Google, Samsung and Tecent. Since they have fixed codes as other words in the vocabulary, they can be simply processed as special words in text mining. Static image emoji is specially designed pictures, e.g. cartoon, and photo. Digital image processing techniques can be adopted to help processing this kind of emoji. Dynamic image emoji can be considered as a special kind of video (usually in gif format). While a video can be considered as a continuous display of sequential images. Hence, the key to solve such multimedia content is digital image processing. Additionally, audios are also very popular in social media. It is also a common phenomenon for a video to contain corresponding audio in it. The technology to handle audio refers to speech recognition, which has not been widely used in opinion mining.

Another challenge refers to the informal writing. It is quite common to see abbreviations and typos in social media expression. There is no problem for widely accepted common abbreviations. Due to the length limitation or just writing convenience, users may create their own abbreviations. Some of these abbreviations are difficult to recognize even for human beings no saying machines. Since there are no writing standards or following editing, typos are very common or inevitable. Some typos are even made deliberately to express some king of "cute". Currently, there has been no good solutions for this challenge. One possible option is to construct personalized knowledge graph for each user. This kind of personalized knowledge graph contains writing styles, expression habit, etc. of each user. When one unrecognized symbol (e.g. abbreviation, typo) comes, we can go to the personalized knowledge graph to search context information as supplement of their social media posts. Unfortunately, this kind of personalized knowledge graph is time and energy consuming to construct and maintain. As a result, it is not applicable in real business, at least in current stage.

4   Recent Developed Techniques

Nowadays, research and applications are no longer satisfied with the overall opinion. There is increasing demands to know details of the opinion. As aforementioned, each opinion should have a holder and a target. In real business, the opinion target is of great potential values. For instance, it is quite common for firms to collect firsthand customer feedbacks once they release a new product (Luo et al. 2013). An overall opinion only reflect general market response to this product. If they want to collect useful information for their further improvement, details, such as customer's feeling to one specific aspect of their product, are necessary and important. To meet this demand, aspect oriented sentiment analysis is proposed. Khan et al. (2015) combined lexicon-based and machine learning-based methods to achieve performance enhancement for entity-level Twitter sentiment analysis. This entity-level analysis could bring more detail to the related sentiment (e.g. product, brand). Lakkaraju et al. (2014) proposed a hierarchical deep learning framework to extract the sentiment and its associated aspect simultaneously. Poria et al. (2016) proposed a deep learning approach to extract aspect associated with each sentiment. More specifically, a 7-layer deep convolutional neural network is used to identify whether a word is an aspect or not. Lau et al. (2017) designed a parallel framework to accelerate the mining speed of product aspect and user's attitude to it. A parallel hierarchical Dirichlet process that incorporated Gamma-Gamma-Poisson process is proposed to keep the dependence of each processing. This design is especially suitable for large volume stream data (e.g. social media data).

There are increasingly more multimedia content used in social media. As a result, extracting sentiment from these multimedia content has become a challenging but promising task. Due to wide application prospects, many attempts has been made. You et al. (2015) adopted progressively trained and domain transferred deep networks to extract sentiment expressed by images. Wang et al. (2015) proposed an unsupervised sentiment analysis model for social media images to solve the challenge of lack of training data. As mentioned above, video can be considered as a continuous display of a sequence of related images. Based on this, Poria et al. (2016) proposed a temporal convolutional neural network (CNN) to deal with the time sequence problem of the video. Then a multiple kernel learning (MKL) method is used to select informative features and cluster them into groups. According to their experiments, MKL helped their model significantly outperform state-of-the-art other advanced multimodal emotion recognition and sentiment analysis on various dataset. Cao et al. (2016) designed a visual sentiment topic model to extract sentiment from images in microblog. Cai and Xia (2015) utilized convolutional neural network for multimedia sentiment analysis. Similarly, Luo et al. (2017) adopted deep neural network for social multimedia sentiment analysis.

5 Potential Applications

Sentiment expressed in social media reflects the public orientation. These public orientations are reveals of their true feelings about the event they involved. Profound prediction and analysis can be made utilizing these true feelings. Here I offer three examples to show the power of social media sentiment analysis.

5.1 Case 1: Election Prediction

In 2016, president election of United Sates, according to the polls conducted by traditional media, such as ABC News and Washington Post, the favorability of Clinton is always much higher than Trump (ABC News 2016). There are still a large gap just before the election. On the contrary, according to Twitter trend, Trump won more supports. Finally, the election result proved the power of the public orientation on social media. Inspired by this fact, much research has been done to mine the value behind this phenomenon (e.g. Agrawal and Hamling 2017; Bessi and Ferrara 2016; Schumacher et al. 2016).

5.2 Case 2: Stock Market Analysis

According to Keynes's famous castle-in-the-air theory, firms' stock prices reflect investors' confidence and expectations instead of their business performance in a long term (Lawlor 1998). It is exactly in the very center of the ability of social media sentiment analysis. Many attempt has been made to predict the stock market utilizing public opinions from the social media. One well-known and controversial study was carried by Bollen et al. in 2011 (Bollen et al. 2011). They extracted a set of Google-Profile of Mood States (GPOMS) that measured mood in terms of 6 dimensions (Calm, Alert, Sure, Vital, Kind, and Happy) to predict the changes in Dow Jones Industrial Average (DJIA) closing values. According to their experiments, they achieved 86.7% accuracy in predicting daily up and down changes. Although their work attracted many disputes from the supporters of Efficient Market Hypothesis (EMH), it did proved the power of social media sentiment analysis. Following their steps, more attempts have been made to incorporate the power of social media sentiment analysis to stock market prediction (e.g. Azar and Lo 2016; Chen et al. 2014; Nguyen and Shirai 2015).

5.3 Case 3: Personalized Recommendation

People are always free to express their true feelings on social media. Expressions like "The camera of my current cellphone is terrible. I really need a new one." are frequently to see in social media posts. These kinds of expressions reflect the real needs of potential customers. More accurate product recommendation can be made once this kind of information is extracted. Some attempts has been made to make use of such value information. For instance, Sun et al. (2015) developed a novel sentiment-aware social media recommendation framework that utilize collaborative filtering method to improve recommendation performance. Ashok et al. (2016) applied machine learning techniques to extract sentiment from social media content to enhance performance of personalized recommender system. From the application perspective, many ecommerce platforms have built partnership with social media platforms to make use of this kind of personal information. Although it is of great benefits to use these data, critics pointed out that it would be a serious threat for people's personal privacy.

6 Conclusion

In this paper, we made a brief review on sentiment analysis in social media. Applying common opinion mining techniques to social media would suffer serious performance reduction. Some simple operations could improve the performance obviously. For instance, when dealing with short social media posts, we can combine related ones as a document instead of processing them one by one to avoid serious bias. Common coded emoji can be processed as normal words, while more advanced multimedia processing techniques, such as digital image processing, speech recognition, are needed to deal with sophisticated emoji. It is also a popular and promising trend to leverage multimedia processing techniques to social media sentiment analysis.

With the development of advanced techniques, new business needs emerge. People are no longer satisfied with an overall sentiment. Aspect oriented sentiment analysis could help to specify the opinion target. This technology is beneficial for firms to collect first hand customer feedbacks online. Compared with traditional methods (e.g. survey), it is much faster and cheaper. Moreover, utilizing this kind of detail information could also contribute to more accurate personalized recommendation.

All in all, there are great values embedded in people's daily social media posts. However, it is a very challenging task to extract these useful information from large volume of dataset. Applying opinion mining techniques that perform well in other domain directly to social media is not a very wise idea. Adjustment and improvements are necessary to make these techniques effective. Emotions expressed in social media is a reflection of their true feelings. Once extracted, there will be unprecedented opportunities to carrying on significant social and business analysis utilizing this enriched information.

Acknowledgement. The work was fully supported by the following grants: Zhejiang Provincial Natural Science Foundation of China (No. LQ14G020012), Beijing brain research project of Beijing Municipal Science & Technology Commission (No. Z171100000117009), the Fundamental Research Funds for the Central Universities and the Research Funds of Renmin University of China (No. 17XNLF05), the National Nature Science Foundation of China (NSFC 71702133).

References

ABC News (2016). http://abcnews.go.com/Politics/clinton-trump-leaves-10-unhappy-contest-tightens-conventions/story?id=40615476

Agrawal, A., Hamling, T.: Sentiment analysis of tweets to gain insights into the 2016 US election. Columbia Undergrad. Sci. J. **11** (2017)

Ashok, M., Rajanna, S., Joshi, P.V., Kamath, S.: A personalized recommender system using machine learning based sentiment analysis over social data. In: 2016 IEEE Students' Conference on Electrical, Electronics and Computer Science (SCEECS), pp. 1–6. IEEE, March 2016

Azar, P.D., Lo, A.W.: Practical applications of the wisdom of Twitter crowds: predicting stock market reactions to FOMC meetings via Twitter feeds. Pract. Appl. **4**(2), 1–4 (2016)

Bessi, A., Ferrara, E.: Social bots distort the 2016 US presidential election online discussion (2016)

Blei, D.M., Lafferty, J.D.: Dynamic topic models. In: Proceedings of the 23rd International Conference on Machine Learning, pp. 113–120. ACM, June 2006

Blei, D.M., Ng, A.Y., Jordan, M.I.: Latent dirichlet allocation. J. Mach. Learn. Res. **3**(Jan), 993–1022 (2003)

Bollen, J., Mao, H., Zeng, X.: Twitter mood predicts the stock market. J. Comput. Sci. **2**(1), 1–8 (2011)

Breakthroughanalysis (2008). https://breakthroughanalysis.com/2008/08/01/unstructured-data-and-the-80-percent-rule/

Cai, G., Xia, B.: Convolutional neural networks for multimedia sentiment analysis. In: Li, J., Ji, H., Zhao, D., Feng, Y. (eds.) NLPCC 2015. LNCS (LNAI), vol. 9362, pp. 159–167. Springer, Cham (2015). https://doi.org/10.1007/978-3-319-25207-0_14

Cambria, E., Fu, J., Bisio, F., Poria, S.: AffectiveSpace 2: enabling affective intuition for concept-level sentiment analysis. In: AAAI, pp. 508–514, January 2015

Cao, D., Ji, R., Lin, D., Li, S.: Visual sentiment topic model based microblog image sentiment analysis. Multimed. Tools Appl. **75**(15), 8955–8968 (2016)

Chen, H., De, P., Hu, Y.J., Hwang, B.H.: Wisdom of crowds: the value of stock opinions transmitted through social media. Rev. Financ. Stud. **27**(5), 1367–1403 (2014)

Chen, Y., Lin, Y., Zuo, W.: Phrase-based topic and sentiment detection and tracking model using incremental HDP. KSII Trans. Int. Inf. Syst. **11**(12) (2017)

Church, K.W., Hanks, P.: Word association norms, mutual information, and lexicography. Comput. Linguist. **16**(1), 22–29 (1990)

Du, W., Tan, S., Cheng, X., Yun, X.: Adapting information bottleneck method for automatic construction of domain-oriented sentiment lexicon. In: Proceedings of the Third ACM International Conference on Web Search and Data Mining, pp. 111–120. ACM, February 2010

Hong, L., Davison, B.D.: Empirical study of topic modeling in Twitter. In: Proceedings of the First Workshop on Social Media Analytics, pp. 80–88 (2010)

Huang, S., Niu, Z., Shi, C.: Automatic construction of domain-specific sentiment lexicon based on constrained label propagation. Knowl.-Based Syst. **56**, 191–200 (2014)

Irsoy, O., Cardie, C.: Opinion mining with deep recurrent neural networks. In: Proceedings of the 2014 Conference on Empirical Methods in Natural Language Processing (EMNLP), pp. 720–728 (2014)

Khan, A.Z., Atique, M., Thakare, V.M.: Combining lexicon-based and learning-based methods for Twitter sentiment analysis. Int. J. Electron. Commun. Soft Comput. Sci. Eng. (IJECSCSE) 89 (2015)

Khan, F.H., Qamar, U., Bashir, S.: SentiMI: introducing point-wise mutual information with SentiWordNet to improve sentiment polarity detection. Appl. Soft Comput. **39**, 140–153 (2016)

Kouloumpis, E., Wilson, T., Moore, J.D.: Twitter sentiment analysis: the good the bad and the omg! Icwsm **11**(538–541), 164 (2011)

Lakkaraju, H., Socher, R., Manning, C.: Aspect specific sentiment analysis using hierarchical deep learning. In: NIPS Workshop on Deep Learning and Representation Learning (2014)

Lau, R.Y.K., Zhang, W., Xu, W.: Parallel aspect-oriented sentiment analysis for sales forecasting with big data. Prod. Oper. Manag. (2017)

Lawlor, M.S.: Keynes's uncertain revolution. Hist. Polit. Econ. **30**(4), 683–686 (1998)

Li, F., Wang, S., Liu, S., Zhang, M.: SUIT: a supervised user-item based topic model for sentiment analysis. In: AAAI, vol. 14, pp. 1636–1642, July 2014

Liu, P., Joty, S., Meng, H.: Fine-grained opinion mining with recurrent neural networks and word embeddings. In: Proceedings of the 2015 Conference on Empirical Methods in Natural Language Processing, pp. 1433–1443 (2015)

Liu, Y., Chen, Y., Lusch, R., Chen, H., Zimbra, D., Zeng, S.: User-generated content on social media: predicting market success with online word-of-mouth. IEEE Intell. Syst. **25**(1), 75–78 (2010)

Lu, Y., Castellanos, M., Dayal, U., Zhai, C.: Automatic construction of a context-aware sentiment lexicon: an optimization approach. In: Proceedings of the 20th International Conference on World Wide Web, pp. 347–356. ACM, March 2011

Luo, J., Borth, D., You, Q.: Social multimedia sentiment analysis. In: Proceedings of the 2017 ACM on Multimedia Conference, pp. 1953–1954. ACM, October 2017

Luo, X., Zhang, J., Duan, W.: Social media and firm equity value. Inf. Syst. Res. **24**(1), 146–163 (2013)

Manivannan, P., Kanimozhiselvi, C.S.: Pointwise mutual information based integral classifier for sentiment analysis in cross domain opinion mining. J. Comput. Theor. Nanosci. **14**(11), 5435–5443 (2017)

Nguyen, T.H., Shirai, K.: Topic modeling based sentiment analysis on social media for stock market prediction. In: Proceedings of the 53rd Annual Meeting of the Association for Computational Linguistics and the 7th International Joint Conference on Natural Language Processing, vol. 1, no. 1, pp. 1354–1364 (2015)

Pang, B., Lee, L.: Opinion mining and sentiment analysis. Found. Trends Inf. Retrieval **2**(1–2), 1–135 (2008)

Pang, B., Lee, L., Vaithyanathan, S.: Thumbs up?: sentiment classification using machine learning techniques. In: Proceedings of the Conference on Empirical Methods in Natural Language Processing, pp. 79–86 (2002)

Pak, A., Paroubek, P.: Twitter as a corpus for sentiment analysis and opinion mining. In: Proceedings of the Seventh Conference on International Language Resources and Evaluation, pp. 1320–1326 (2010)

Poria, S., Chaturvedi, I., Cambria, E., Hussain, A.: Convolutional MKL based multimodal emotion recognition and sentiment analysis. In: 2016 IEEE 16th International Conference on Data Mining (ICDM), pp. 439–448. IEEE, December 2016

Read, J.: Recognising affect in text using pointwise-mutual information. Unpublished M.Sc. Dissertation, University of Sussex, UK (2004)

Schumacher, R.P., Jarmoszko, A.T., Labedz Jr., C.S.: Predicting wins and spread in the premier league using a sentiment analysis of Twitter. Decis. Support Syst. **88**, 76–84 (2016)

Statistic 2018 https://www.statista.com/statistics/278414/number-of-worldwide-social-network-users/

Su, Q., Xiang, K., Wang, H., Sun, B., Yu, S.: Using pointwise mutual information to identify implicit features in customer reviews. In: Matsumoto, Y., Sproat, R.W., Wong, K.-F., Zhang, M. (eds.) ICCPOL 2006. LNCS (LNAI), vol. 4285, pp. 22–30. Springer, Heidelberg (2006). https://doi.org/10.1007/11940098_3

Sun, J., Wang, G., Cheng, X., Fu, Y.: Mining affective text to improve social media item recommendation. Inf. Process. Manag. 51(4), 444–457 (2015)

Taboada, M., Brooke, J., Tofiloski, M., Voll, K., Stede, M.: Lexicon-based methods for sentiment analysis. Comput. Linguist. 37(2), 267–307 (2011)

Turney, P.D., Littman, M.L.: Measuring praise and criticism: inference of semantic orientation from association. ACM Trans. Inf. Syst. (TOIS) 21(4), 315–346 (2003)

Wang, Y., Wang, S., Tang, J., Liu, H., Li, B.: Unsupervised sentiment analysis for social media images. In: IJCAI, pp. 2378–2379, July 2015

Wilson, T., Wiebe, J., Hoffmann, P.: Recognizing contextual polarity in phrase-level sentiment analysis. In: Proceedings of the Conference on Human Language Technology and Empirical Methods in Natural Language Processing, pp. 347–354 (2005)

Witten, I.H., Frank, E.: Data Mining: Practical Machine Learning Tools and Techniques. Elsevier Inc., Oxford (2005)

You, Q., Luo, J., Jin, H., Yang, J.: Robust image sentiment analysis using progressively trained and domain transferred deep networks. In: AAAI, pp. 381–388, January 2015

Social Innovation

The Role of Actor Capability in (Re)Defining Technology Affordances: The Case of Open Innovation Platform

Kaveh Abhari[1(✉)], Bo Sophia Xiao[2], and Elizabeth Davidson[2]

[1] San Diego State University, San Diego, CA 92182, USA
kabhari@sdsu.edu
[2] University of Hawaii at Manoa, Honolulu, HI 96822, USA
{boxiao, edavidso}@hawaii.edu

Abstract. Scholars have strived for more than two decades to understand and conceptualized technology affordances. While some claim that affordances should be at the core of the HCI discipline, there is limited consensus regarding how to define and operationalized this concept. In recent developments in the IS literature, perceived affordances are operationalized as the relationship between the actor's goal and the technology's features. In this research, we refine the concept of affordances by incorporating the new factor of 'actor capability' and test this claim by introducing and validating a three-way interaction between goal, capability, and feature in an open innovation context. Our contribution provides a more nuanced yet powerful way of understanding technology affordances from both theoretical and practical perspectives.

Keywords: Affordances · Actor capability · Open innovation platform

1 Introduction

The technology affordance lens has been broadly utilized to explore and understand technology use and its behavioral consequences. However, interpretations of the affordances are becoming increasingly incompatible with Norman's original definition. Norman defined affordances as "the perceived and actual properties of the thing, primarily those fundamental properties that determine just how the thing could possibly be used" (Norman 1999). Thus, the affordances of an artifact are the actor's mental representation of the artifact potential utilities (Faraj and Azad 2012). This cognitive process has been interpreted in IS discipline as the interaction between goal-oriented actor and an technical artifact (Majchrzak and Markus 2013; Markus and Silver 2008). While this interpretation could arguably denote the existence of functional affordances, it has limited relevance to design because of differentiating actors' perception merely based on their goals (Kaptelinin and Nardi 2012)

Furthermore, IS researchers argued that affordances could exist whether they are (immediately) perceived or not; however, affordances may not be actualized if actors do not perceive the existence of such affordances (e.g. Volkoff and Strong 2013). That means affordances are only potentials for actions and need to be perceived and then

© Springer International Publishing AG, part of Springer Nature 2018
F. F.-H. Nah and B. S. Xiao (Eds.): HCIBGO 2018, LNCS 10923, pp. 551–562, 2018.
https://doi.org/10.1007/978-3-319-91716-0_44

actualized by goal-oriented actors to achieve an outcome (Pozzi et al. 2014). This interpretation has been successfully used to explain actor behavior (Dong et al. 2016; Strong et al. 2014). Nevertheless, a few studies as yet focused on its limitations to inform design (e.g. Davis and Chouinard 2017).

In this paper, we argue that the interactions between technological features (defined by required functions) and actors' goals (defined by expected outcomes) cannot fully explain why so many designs fail while so few succeed. This fact calls for redefining affordances to meet the conceptual needs of new technology design and development. To this end, we first introduced a new approach to operationalize affordances based on the Norman's original interpretation. This new approach accounts for actors' capabilities in perceiving the potential utilities of an artifact. Then, we empirically verified this claim in the context of open innovation platform design. We concluded with a discussion of theoretical and practical implications of the findings.

2 Background

Norman was a pioneer who applied Gibson's affordance theory to technology design (Norman 1999). In his opinion, while actors do not necessarily participate in defining the properties of an artifact (designed affordances), they need to perceive the affordances of a design in order to actualize them (Norman 2013). Perceived affordances, or 'signifiers' in Norman's words, must be recognized by actors, else they fail to function (Norman 2013). Hence, perceived affordances is equally important, if not more than designed affordances, to achieve the design's goals (Fayard and Weeks 2014). Since then, evaluating the perceived affordances has become a common methodology in capturing actors' perception of technology and its applications (Bærentsen and Trettvik 2002; Pucillo et al. 2014).

In the IS field, perceived affordance is defined as a relational construct that depends on the interaction between a technological artifact and an actor's perception[1] (Leonardi 2013; Malhotra and Majchrzak 2012; Volkoff and Strong 2013). IS literature limited the relationship between actor and artifact to the actor's perception of action possibilities to achieve a particular goal (e.g. Markus and Silver 2008). Unfortunately, studies used the affordance lens for the purpose of system design did not typically account for diverse actor-artifact relations (Davis and Chouinard 2017). As a result, in these studies, an artifact either affords or do not afford a goal-oriented action regardless of the actor's capability in discovering or actualizing the affordances. One possible explanation for this false dilemma is the oversimplification of Norman's affordance concept. Researchers conceptualize affordance as a relational construct without accounting for the role of actors' capability or past experience in perceiving the possibilities (Norman 1999; Norman and Nielsen 2010). Lack of quantitative methods to examine the relationship between actors and technology features also limits researchers to highlight the relative value of each contributing factor (Michell 2013).

---

[1] In this paper, the term 'actor' is limited to individual user to emphasize the user active and central role in perceiving affordances.

Researchers argued that affordances should capture more accurately how actors perceive the action possibilities based on their past experience and current capability in technology-enabled environments (Bærentsen and Trettvik 2002; Pucillo et al. 2014). Each actor has a unique set of capabilities that could potentially influence how they perceive and actualize affordances (Cormier and Lewis 2015). However, previous studies failed to distinguish between 'capability to perceive' and 'capability to actualize' (Michell 2013). While we acknowledge that affordances exist independent from actualization (Anderson and Robey 2017), we argue their quality (not their existence) depend on actors' perception shaped by actors' goals as well as their capability. Therefore, the main goal of this paper is to propose and verify a quantitative method to model affordances beyond the relationship between goals and technology features by including actor capability in perceiving the affordances.

3   Research Context

In order to generate and empirically test affordance propositions, researchers argue that definition of affordances should be contextualized before applying the concept to a specific technological context (Malhotra and Majchrzak 2012). We chose open innovation context to verify the new definition since platform design is crucial to open innovation productivity and sustainability. Additionally, the existing models of affordances –mainly draw form collaboration literature– have not been evaluated to determine their applicability to the open innovation context (e.g. Sutcliffe et al. 2011). Therefore, using existing models may not support the design process and the results of such evaluation may not be comprehensive and valid. In response to these limitations, this paper verified the new operationalization in the context of open innovation platform. Due to the increasing adoption of social technologies in open innovation, this paper focus on the affordances of social product development platforms.

Open innovation business models democratize innovation by opening R&D process to creative crowds all over the world (Nambisan et al. 2017; Ramírez-Montoya and García-Peñalvo 2018). These distributed models of innovation have transformational capacity in helping businesses to develop and market new products within a short period of time (Barrett et al. 2015; Lee et al. 2012; Leenders and Dolfsma 2016). Open innovation platform is the key vehicle to recruit, organize, engage and motivate co-innovation teams (Hossain and Islam 2015). The study of open innovation platform affordances is an effective way to explain how actors perceive the co-innovation possibilities and realized the potential of open innovation environments (Abhari et al. 2017). This paper proposed a new way to operationalize affordance in order to evaluate the relationship between platform design and actor co-innovation activities. Drawing from Gloor's co-innovation model (Gloor 2006), we conceptualized co-innovation act as an actor's participation in ideation, collaboration, and socialization (Brown and Wyatt 2010; Cullen 2007; Füller et al. 2014; Kahnert et al. 2012; Piller et al. 2012). Open innovation platforms offer a variety of technology features affording these activities (Abhari et al. 2017; Gloor 2006; Sawhney et al. 2005). Therefore, we investigated three main affordances, namely ideation affordances, collaboration affordances, and socialization affordances.

Ideation affordances include the broad range of possible actions from submitting a new product idea to suggesting a new product updates. The ideation affordance is enabled by a group of features such as idea submission, revision, and resubmission forms, and idea development tools. Collaboration affordances relate to interdependent activities that allow for a large range of collaborative tasks from product development to product commercialization. Collaboration affordances rely on platform features such as evaluation and ranking forms, product improvement tools, and brainstorming tools. Lastly, socialization affordances enable activities such as discussing opinions, sharing knowledge, and asking for help or votes. Socialization affordances require social networking features such as profile creation and management pages, sharing and posting messages, and connecting and networking tools.

4 Hypothesis

A technology affordance was traditionally modeled as the interaction between the actors' goals and technology features (Wang et al. 2015). This approach is a well-established practice in both HCI and IS fields for measuring task-technology fit (e.g. Belanger et al. 2001). Wang et al. (2015) argued that researchers only need to measure the interaction between technology characteristics and individuals' goals to understand the influence of technology affordances on the consequences of technology use. We discussed that measuring technology affordances in this way represents a challenge to researchers since the relationship between goals and features are insufficient to explain the potential use and thereby misleading the design. In reality, we need not only goal-oriented actors but also qualified actors who will be able to perceive the potentials. This study tried to tackle this limitation by suggesting a third interacting variable. We named the new variable 'actor capability' that define how capable the actor is in discovering the potential use of an artifact.

The term capability is commonly referred to capacity to perform a task (e.g. Blomqvist and Levy 2006; Mathiesen et al. 2013; Michell 2013). From affordance perspective, actors should perceive a technology's potentials according to their goals and capabilities in order to create value (Michell 2013; Michell 2013; Ortmann and Kuhn 2010). Actor capability is defined by actors' past experience or prior knowledge about the environment or artifact affecting their perception (Norman 2013). Capability is different from 'goal' but it affects perceive affordances in the same way. This claim could be validated if the interaction between actors' goals, actors' capability and a particular group of features has a positive effect on the behavioral intention associated with those features. This three-way interaction suggests that the interplay between goals and technology features varies across different levels of the third variable, actor capability. In other words, the effect of technology features on actor behavior differs across various levels of goals as well as capability. From this perspective, affordance is still a relational construct between actor and artifact; however, actor can be conceptualized as an agent with different sets of goals and levels capabilities. For example, we can claim a platform affords ideation if the interaction between an actor's goals, her ideation capability, and platform ideation features perceived by actors has a positive effect on the ideation activity. At the same time, we do not expect the ideation affordances has a significant effect on other behavioral domains such as collaboration and socialization. Thus, we hypothesize the following three-way interactions (Fig. 1):

H_1: *Actor Capability* positively moderates the relationship between *Goals* × *Ideation Features* and *Continuous Intention to Ideate* (but not Continuous Intention to Collaborate or Socialize).

H_2: *Actor Capability* positively moderates the relationship between *Goals* × *Collaboration Features* and *Continuous Intention to Collaborate* (but not Continuous Intention to Ideate or Socialize).

H_3: *Actor Capability* positively moderates the relationship between *Goals* × *Socialization Features* and *Continuous Intention to Socialize* (but not Continuous Intention to Ideate or Collaborate).

5 Methods

We tested the proposed three-way interaction using a social product development platform through a survey study. The survey items derived from the literature were adapted and modified in the context for this study. The Partial Least Squares Modeling approach was used to test the effects and statistical significance of the hypothesized pathways in the structural mode.

5.1 Sample

The data for the field survey were collected from a random sample of Quirky members. Quirky is an open innovation platform soliciting new product ideas and sharing a portion of the sales revenue with the community of innovators who contribute to product ideation as well as product selection, design, development, and promotion. Quirky is one of the first companies to implement such a model on a social media platform (Piller et al. 2012; Roser 2013). Quirky compensates the individual contributors involved in the product's innovation process by paying community 50% of royalty revenue for each product. As of 2018, more than 1.2 million members had collaboratively developed 150 consumer products and collectively received about $11 million in royalties. This case demonstrated a prototypical and, at the same time, comprehensive model of open innovation due to the high levels of actor involvement and the variety of co-innovation processes and tools (Abhari et al. 2016).

5.2 Measurements

Goal construct was measured using a second-order construct with five dimensions: Financial gain, Recognition, Learning, Networking, Enjoyment, and Altruism. The items for these three dimensions were adopted from previous studies on open innovation networks (Abhari et al. 2018; Antikainen et al. 2010; Antikainen and Vaataja 2010; Battistella and Nonino 2012, 2013; Kahnert et al. 2012). Platform *features* were measured by three constructs developed especially for this study, in reference to the

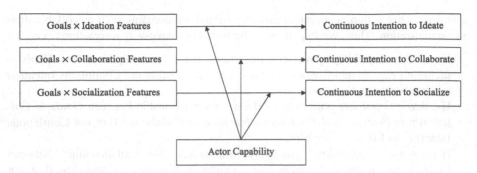

Fig. 1. Research model with three-way interactions between goals, features and capability (Other relationships are not presented for the sake of simplicity)

three key processes of social product development (i.e., ideation, collaboration, and socialization). Three constructs of *ideation features*, *collaboration features*, and *socialization features* were developed based on recent studies on sociotechnical features of collaborative virtual environments (Kreijns 2004; Sutcliffe et al. 2011; Wellman et al. 2003; Zebrowitz 2011). To emphasize the contextual nature of affordances, we slightly modified some items. The measurement items for three behavioral intention, were adapted from the studies on continuous behavioral intention in virtual collaborative communities (Bhattacherjee 2001; Chen 2007; Zhang et al. 2010). To model *actor capability*, we used actors' open innovation accumulated experience (self-report) as a proxy for their capability to perceive the potential uses of features. Actor goals, platform features, and continuous intention constructs were measured using seven-point scales using "strongly disagree" to "strongly agree" as the anchors.

5.3   Analysis

We used SmartPLS to test the effects and statistical significance of the hypothesized pathways in the structural model (Ringle et al. 2015). For estimating the second order construct (goal), we followed two-step process suggested by Anderson and Gerbing (1988) to estimate the latent variable and used these aggregate measures as indicators for the second order construct in the second step. To estimate the three-way interaction effects, we also estimated and saved the latent variable scores of the two-way effects, and then entered them as indicators of the associated two-way constructs in the model estimated. This analysis explained how affordances –as defined in this study– affect the behavioral intention by showing how the moderated relationships between goals and features behave under different scores of the second moderator (actor capability).

6   Findings

From 1000 randomly invited Quirky members, 261 members participated in this study. Demographic data analysis shows that respondents varying in gender, age, education, and employment were included in the sample. The comparison of sample's co-innovation experience and contributions with the population's indicated no nonresponse bias. Most respondents had participated in Quirky ideation (82%), collaboration (100%), and socialization (85%) activities. More women (59%) participated in the survey compared to men (41%). Most the respondents were between 26 and 65 years old (84%), and over 70% had at least some college education. Nearly 60% of the respondents were employed outside of their participation in open innovation network.

6.1 Measurement Model

The evaluation of measurement items was conducted first. All the loadings of measurement items on their latent constructs exceed 0.7, indicating acceptable item reliability (Hair et al. 2013). In addition, the Cronbach's alpha and composite reliability of all the constructs are higher than 0.7, indicating good internal consistency among the items measuring each construct (Hair et al. 2013). Three tests were conducted to determine convergent validity and discriminant validity: (1) all Average Variance Extracted (AVE) is higher than 0.50 (Hair et al. 2013); (2) the square root of the AVE of each constructs is larger than the correlations of this construct with the other constructs (Fornell and Larcker 1981); and (3) the correlations among all constructs (i.e., inter-construct correlations) are all well below the 0.90 threshold (Hair et al. 2013). The results of these tests suggest adequate convergent and discriminant validity. Because common method bias is a concern when utilizing a survey instrument to measure both independent and dependent variables, Harman's one-factor test was used to assess this potential problem. These results suggested common method bias was not a problem.

6.2 Structural Model

We focused on the comparisons between the current definition of affordances (Goals × Features) and the proposed definition (Goals × Features × Capability). Our results supported the baseline model as actors' goals and perception of platform feature positively influence the degree to which the actor intent to continuously ideate, collaborate, and socialize. However, explaining the variations in other relationships is not the main purpose of this paper.

H_1 proposed a three-way interaction of Goals, Ideation Features, and Capability on Continuous Intention to Ideate. As expected the empirical data show that this three-way interaction is positive and significant (b = 0.15, p < 0.05), thus supporting this hypothesis. The relationships between this three-way interaction and other two intention constructs (collaboration and socialization) were not supported. The results did not support the positive relationship between the two-way interaction of Goals and Ideation Features –as suggested by previous studies– on Continuous Intention to Ideate. Therefore, we conclude that Platform Ideation Affordances is a function of actors' goals, actor capability, and platform ideation features predicating actors' intention to ideate.

H_2 proposed a three-way interaction of Goals, Collaboration Features and Capability on Continuous Intention to Collaborate. As expected, the three-way interaction is positive and significant (b = 0.22, p < 0.001), thus supporting H2. However, the relationships between this three-way interaction and other two intention constructs were not supported. The results also did not support the positive relationship between the two-way interaction of Goals and Collaboration Features on Continuous Intention to Collaborate. Therefore, we conclude that Platform Collaboration Affordances is a function of actors' goals, actor capability, and platform collaboration features predicating actors' intention to collaborate.

H_3 proposed a three-way interaction of Goals, Socialization Features and Capability on Continuous Intention to Socialize. As expected, the three-way interaction is positive and significant ($b = 0.20$, $p < 0.01$), thus supporting H3. However, the relationships between this three-way interaction and other two intention constructs were not supported. The results did not support the positive relationship between the two-way interaction of Goals and Socialization Features on Continuous Intention to Socialize. Therefore, we conclude that Platform Socialization Affordances is a function of actors' goals, actor capability, and platform socialization features predicating actors' intention to socialize.

7 Discussion and Conclusion

We conducted an empirical investigation to theorize affordances in open innovation context. The review of the common approaches to modeling perceived affordances revealed that actor capability was typically overlooked in the operationalization of this concept. Nonetheless, capability is the major contributing factor to the perception of action possibility. We compared the predictive validity of a prototypical operationalization of affordances (interaction between goals and features) with our new model that includes the interaction between goal, capability, and features. Our results supported that the new operationalization could better capture the actor's perception of platform affordances and thereby predict their behavioral intention. The findings also provide a better understanding of platform design in the context of open innovation.

7.1 Theoretical Implications

We have introduced a new way to operationalize perceived affordances in order to explain regularities in actor behavior in the context of open innovation platforms. The results show that these effects are more complex than anticipated given the different results for two-way (Goal × Features) and three-way (Goal × Features × Capability) interactions. We found no support for a positive effect of affordances as traditionally defined (Goal × Features) on behavioral intention. A closer inspection reveals that capability affects the relationship between Goal × Features and behavioral intention constructs associated with the key features (i.e. ideation, collaboration, and socialization). A possible explanation for this result is that the goal-oriented actors with higher capabilities respond to the platform features with higher intention than their counterparts with lower capabilities because of ability to perceive the possibilities. This might imply that mere alignment between a platform's features and actor's goal would result in a platform full of features satisfying different goals rather than more participation. This is consistent with our argumentation that including actors' capabilities in defining a platform's affordances would ensure a better design by making right adjustments and customization of features.

In the context of this study, our results suggest that open innovation design strategy should entail a better understanding of the alignment between actors' goals and actors' capabilities in terms of knowledge, skills, qualifications and past experience. As open innovation platforms increasingly adopt social technologies to engage more actors, we call for further research drawing on affordance theory. This should result in a more user-centered design of the platforms and thereby the effectiveness of open innovation practices.

7.2 Practical Implications

Our use of capability to operationalize affordances represents a design perspective which argues designing features for satisfying goals is likely to result in superficial adoption and thus lower long-term application. This would benefit the practitioners towards a better understanding of platform design. We propose six-step process for platform design evaluation based on the findings of this study: (a) Identify existing system key features, (b) Identify actors' goals and capabilities, (c) Determine the two-way and three-way interactions between features, actors' goals and capabilities (d) Determine the associations between the interacting factors and behavioral intention constructs, and (e) Interpret the results using the following guide. We argue that positive two-way and three-way interaction coefficients demonstrate a proper alignment between the platform features and actors' goals and capability. No significant relationship suggests inconclusive results or inconsequential effect of affordances on user behavioral intention. In case of a negative coefficient, the platform owner may want to A/B testing the platform with new features or a new reward system depending on the coefficient of two-way interactions. A negative coefficient for Goals × Features suggests misalignment between goals and platform features. A negative coefficient for Goals × Capability suggests the necessity of improvement in the reward system. A negative coefficient for Capability × Features suggests misalignment between actors' capabilities and platform features. This approach would help platform owners to engage either the current actors with offering new features or new actors with a different set of goals and capabilities.

In the context of this study, our findings suggest that affordance lens can still contribute to our understanding of the effectiveness of platform design. However, our study shows that limiting affordances to the relationship between goal-directed actors and platform features can reduce open innovation platforms' ability to fully engage the actors in ideation, collaboration, and socialization. Open innovation platform designers, therefore, need to pay more attention to the actors' capabilities for evaluation of platform features. Misalignment between actors' goals and capabilities and platform features may jeopardize reaping benefits from open innovation platforms. That is why a significant number of platforms, even those with meticulously designed features, tend to gain less in co-innovation when they engage an inexperienced group of actors.

References

Abhari, K., Davidson, E.J., Xiao, B.: Taking open innovation to the next level: a conceptual model of social product development (SPD). In: The 22nd Americas Conference on Information Systems, San Diego (2016)

Abhari, K., Davidson, E.J., Xiao, B.: Co-innovation platform affordances: developing a conceptual model and measurement instrument. Ind. Manag. Data Syst. 117(5), 873–895 (2017)

Abhari, K., Davidson, E.J. Xiao, B.: Classifying motivations in social product development networks : a discriminant analysis of actor profiles. In: The 51st Hawaii International Conference on System Sciences (2018)

Anderson, C., Robey, D.: Affordance potency: explaining the actualization of technology affordances (2017)

Anderson, J.C., Gerbing, D.W.: Structural equation modeling in practice: A review and recommended two-step approach. Psychol. Bull. 103(3), 411–423 (1988)

Antikainen, M.J., Mäkipää, M., Ahonen, M.: Motivating and supporting collaboration in open innovation. Eur. J. Innov. Manag. 13(1), 100–119 (2010)

Antikainen, M.J., Vaataja, H.K.: Rewarding in open innovation communities–how to motivate members. Int. J. Entrep. Innov. Manag. 11(4), 440–456 (2010)

Bærentsen, K.B. Trettvik, J.: An activity theory approach to affordance. In: Proceedings of the Second Nordic Conference on Human-Computer Interaction, pp. 51–60 (2002)

Barrett, M., Davidson, E.J., Vargo, S.L.: Service innovation in the digital age: key contributions and future directions. MIS Q. 39(1), 135–154 (2015)

Battistella, C., Nonino, F.: What drives collective innovation? exploring the system of drivers for motivations in open innovation, web-based platforms. Inf. Res. 17(1), 1–33 (2012)

Battistella, C., Nonino, F.: Exploring the impact of motivations on the attraction of innovation roles in open innovation web-based platforms. Prod. Plann. Control 24(2–3), 226–245 (2013)

Belanger, F., Collins, R.W., Cheney, P.H.: Technology requirements and work group communication for telecommuters. Inf. Syst. Res. 12(2), 155–176 (2001)

Bhattacherjee, A.: Understanding information systems continuance: an expectation-confirmation model. MIS Q. 25(3), 351–370 (2001)

Blomqvist, K., Levy, J.: Collaboration capability–a focal concept in knowledge creation and collaborative innovation in networks. Int. J. Manag. Concepts Philos. 2(1), 31–48 (2006)

Brown, B.T., Wyatt, J.: Design thinking for social innovation. Stanf. Soc. Innov. Rev. 12(1), 30–35 (2010)

Cormier, P., Lewis, K.: An affordance-based approach for generating user-specific design specifications. Artif. Intell. Eng. Des. Anal. Manufact. 29(3), 281–295 (2015)

Chen, I.Y.L.: The factors influencing members' continuance intentions in professional virtual communities a longitudinal study. J. Inf. Sci. 33(4), 451–467 (2007)

Cullen, J.: Information work and the opportunity of innovation: from corporate to social product development. Bus. Inf. Rev. 24(3), 156–160 (2007)

Davis, J.L., Chouinard, J.B.: Theorizing affordances: from request to refuse. Bull. Sci. Technol. Soc. 36(4), 27046761771494 (2017)

Dong, X., Wang, T., Benbasat, I.: IT affordances in online social commerce : conceptualization validation and scale development full papers. In: AMCIS 2016 Proceedings, pp. 1–10 (2016)

Faraj, S., Azad, B.: The materiality of technology: an affordance perspective. In: Leonardi, P.M., Nardi, B.A., Kallinikos, J. (eds.) Materiality and Organizing: Social Interaction in a Technological World, pp. 237–258. Oxford University Press, Oxford (2012)

Fayard, A.L., Weeks, J.: Affordances for practice. Inf. Organ. 24(4), 236–249 (2014)

Fornell, C., Larcker, D.F.: Structural equation models with unobservable variables and measurement error: algebra and statistics. J. Mark. Res. **18**(3), 382 (1981)

Füller, J., Hutter, K., Hautz, J., Matzler, K.: User roles and contributions in innovation-contest communities. J. Manag. Inf. Syst. **31**(1), 273–308 (2014)

Gloor, P.A.: Swarm Creativity: Competitive Advantage Through Collaborative Innovation Networks. Oxford University Press, New York (2006)

Hair, J.F., Hult, G.T.M., Ringle, C., Sarstedt, M.: A Primer on Partial Least Squares Structural Equation Modeling (PLS-SEM). SAGE Publications, Thousand Oaks (2013)

Hossain, M., Islam, K.M.Z.: Ideation through online open innovation platform: dell ideastorm. J. Knowl. Econ. **6**(3), 611–624 (2015)

Kahnert, D., Menez, R., Blättel-Mink, B.: Coordination and motivation of customer contribution as social innovation: the case of crytek. In: Franz, H.W., Hochgerner, J., Howaldt, J. (eds.) Challenge Social Innovation: Potentials for Business, Social Entrepreneurship, Welfare and Civil Society, pp. 293–306. Springer, New York (2012). https://doi.org/10.1007/978-3-642-32879-4_18

Kaptelinin, V., Nardi, B.: Affordances in HCI: toward a mediated action perspective. In: Proceedings of the 2012 ACM Annual Conference on Human Factors in Computing Systems, pp. 967–976 (2012)

Kreijns, K.: Sociable CSCL Environments: Social Affordances, Sociability, and Social Presence. Datawyse Boek-Grafische producties, Maastricht (2004)

Lee, S.M., Olson, D.L., Trimi, S.: Co-innovation: convergenomics, collaboration, and co-creation for organizational values. Manag. Decis. **50**(5), 817–831 (2012)

Leenders, R.T.A.J., Dolfsma, W.A.: Social networks for innovation and new product development. J. Prod. Innov. Manag. **33**(2), 123–131 (2016)

Leonardi, P.M.: When does technology use enable network change in organizations? a comparative study of feature use and shared affordances. MIS Q. **37**(3), 749–776 (2013)

Majchrzak, A., Markus, M.L.: Technology affordances and constraint theory of MIS. In: Kessler, E. (ed.) Encyclopedia of Management Theory, pp. 832–835. Sage, Thousand Oaks (2013)

Malhotra, A., Majchrzak, A.: Use of collaborative technology affordances to innovate virtually. In: European Conference on Information Systems (ECIS), Barcelona (2012)

Markus, M.L., Silver, M.S.: A foundation for the study of IT effects: a new look at DeSanctis and Poole's concepts of structural features and spirit. J. Assoc. Inf. Syst. **9**(10/11), 609–632 (2008)

Mathiesen, P., Bandara, W., Watson, J.: The affordances of social technology: a BPM perspective. In: International Conference on Information Systems (ICIS 2013), pp. 3709–3719 (2013)

Michell, V.: The capability affordance model: comparing medical capabilities. In: Shishkov, B. (ed.) BMSD 2012. LNBIP, vol. 142, pp. 102–124. Springer, Heidelberg (2013). https://doi.org/10.1007/978-3-642-37478-4_6

Nambisan, S., Lyytinen, K., Majchrzak, A., Song, M.: Digital innovation management: reinventing innovation management research in a digital world. MIS Q. **41**(1), 223–238 (2017)

Norman, D.A.: Affordance, conventions, and design. Interactions **6**(3), 38–43 (1999)

Norman, D.A.: The Design of Everyday Things: Human Factors and Ergonomics in Manufacturing. Basic Books, New York (2013). https://doi.org/10.1002/hfm.20127

Norman, D.A., Nielsen, J.: Gestural interfaces: a step backward in usability. Interactions **17**(5), 46–49 (2010)

Ortmann, J., Kuhn, W.: Affordances as qualities. Front. Artif. Intell. Appl. **209**, 117–130 (2010)

Piller, F., Vossen, A., Ihl, C.: From social media to social product development: the impact of social media on co-creation of innovation. Die Unternehm. **65**(1), 7–27 (2012)

Pozzi, G., Pigni, F., Vitari, C.: Affordance theory in the IS discipline: a review and synthesis of the literature. In: 2014 Twentieth Americas Conference on Information Systems, Savannah, vol. 13, pp. 1–12 (2014)

Pucillo, F., Cascini, G., Milano, P., Giuseppe, V., Masa, L.: A framework for user experience, needs and affordances. Des. Stud. 35(2), 160–179 (2014)

Ramírez-Montoya, M.S., García-Peñalvo, F.-J.: Co-creation and open innovation: systematic literature review. Comunicar 26(54), 09–18 (2018)

Ringle, C., Wende, S., Becker, J.: SmartPLS 3, Boenningstedt: SmartPLS GmbH (2015). http://www.smartpls.com

Roser, T.: Managing your co-creation mix: co-creation ventures in distinctive contexts. Eur. Bus. Rev. 25(1), 20–41 (2013)

Sawhney, M., Verona, G., Prandelli, E.: Collaborating to create: the internet as a platform for customer engagement in product innovation. J. Interact. Mark. 19(4), 4–17 (2005)

Strong, D.M., Johnson, S.A., Tulu, B., Trudel, J., Volkoff, O., Pelletier, L.R., Bar-on, I., et al.: A theory of organization-EHR affordance actualization. J. Assoc. Inf. Syst. 15(2), 53–85 (2014)

Sutcliffe, A.G., Gonzalez, V., Binder, J., Nevarez, G.: Social mediating technologies: social affordances and functionalities. Int. J. Hum.-Comput. Interact. 27(11), 1037–1065 (2011)

Volkoff, O., Strong, D.: Critical realism and affordances: theorizing IT-associated organizational change processes. MIS Q. 37(3), 819–834 (2013)

Wang, N. (Tina), Carte, T., Schwarzkopf, A.: How should technology affordances be measured? an initial comparison of two approaches. In: Twenty-First Americas Conference on Information Systems, pp. 1–14 (2015)

Wellman, B., Quan-Haase, A., Boase, J., Chen, W., Hampton, K., De Diaz, I.I., Miyata, K.: The social affordances of the internet for networked individualism. J. Comput.-Mediated Commun. 8(3), 1–28 (2003)

Zebrowitz, L.A.: The affordances of immersive virtual environment technology for studying social affordances. Psychol. Inq. 13(2), 143–145 (2009)

Zhang, Y., Fang, Y., Wei, K.-K., Chen, H.: Exploring the role of psychological safety in promoting the intention to continue sharing knowledge in virtual communities. Int. J. Inf. Manag. 30(5), 425–436 (2010)

Theory and Practice of Social Innovation to Support Open ICT Ecosystems for Improved User Experience: The Case of UDRC

Kaveh Bazargan[✉], Ali Rezaeian, and Mohammad Taheri

Shahid Beheshti (National) University (of Iran), Tehran, Iran
{k_bazargan, a-rezaeian}@sbu.ac.ir,
m23taheri@gmail.com

Abstract. The dominant rhetoric of smart cities is mainly grounded in the large scale adoption and implementation of cutting-edge technological innovation by local governments and cities all over the world. Responsible context sensitive and social innovations are key complementary drivers to reduce digital divide within and between cities and promote dividends and human value such as dignity, inclusion, urban upgrading, participation and better user experience. This research reports on the continuous efforts performed at the Iranian Urban Development and Revitalization Corporation (UDRC), from February to August 2017, to implement social innovation for urban upgrading by redesigning it's website as open ICT ecosystems for improved user experience. The CUBI UX model is applied and continuous remote user research is conducted for three months to measure and understand the user experience of the old website. Then, after redesigning the old version of the website into a new one, interactive prototyping and implementation, user experience is being measured during the next three months. Finally, comparative analysis of user experience measures between the old and the new version of the website are presented and discussed.

Keywords: Social innovation · Open ICT ecosystems · User research
User experience · Web analytics

1 Introduction

The key concept of "innovation" and more specifically the importance of leveraging "social innovations" together with the informed usage of emergent "information and communication technologies" for creating "better living environments for all" have been highlighted more than 30 times in the New Urban Agenda adopted at the United Nations Conference on Housing and Sustainable Urban Development (Habitat III) in Quito, Ecuador, on 20 October 2016 and endorsed by the United Nations General Assembly on 23 December 2016. Adopting a lifelong learning approach and the wise application of the human computer interaction body of knowledge, including user experience research and user experience design, can be a great theoretical and practical enabler for professionals involved in the creation of more citizen/human/user-centric digital policies, strategies, ecosystems, platforms, services and tools. More specifically, professionals should learn how to address the challenges stated in the New Urban

© Springer International Publishing AG, part of Springer Nature 2018
F. F.-H. Nah and B. S. Xiao (Eds.): HCIBGO 2018, LNCS 10923, pp. 563–576, 2018.
https://doi.org/10.1007/978-3-319-91716-0_45

Agenda by setting measurable user experience target levels, goals, appropriating and implementing research-based user experience heuristics in the field of digital public sector systems design and digital innovations. This research illustrates how social innovation via user experience research and user experience design can support open ICT ecosystems towards continuously measuring and improving digital user experience by studying the domain specific case of the Iranian Urban Development and Revitalization Corporation (UDRC) website.

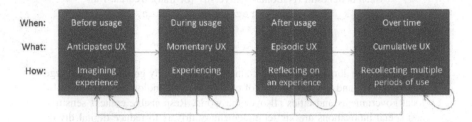

When:	Before usage	During usage	After usage	Over time
What:	Anticipated UX	Momentary UX	Episodic UX	Cumulative UX
How:	Imagining experience	Experiencing	Reflecting on an experience	Recollecting multiple periods of use

Fig. 1. Time span of UX based on key experience factors [2]

2 Review of Literature

2.1 Defining and Measuring the User Experience

The ISO [1] definition of User Experience (UX) states that: *UX is the person's perceptions and responses resulting from the use and/or anticipated use of a product, system or service. UX includes all the users' emotions, beliefs, preferences, perceptions, physical and psychological responses, behaviors and accomplishments that occur before, during and after use.*

Methods and tools used to measure UX should be selected based on the specific time spans in which the UX is actually being shaped. To this end, Roto et al. (2011) have classified UX in four distinct categories displayed in Fig. 1 [2]. Anticipated UX relates to the period before the first use of the system, or any of the three other time spans of UX, since a person may imagine a specific moment during interaction, a usage episode, or life after taking a system into use. UX can also refer to a specific change of feeling during interaction (momentary UX), appraisal of a specific usage episode (episodic UX), or views on a system as a whole, after having used it for a while (cumulative UX).

In this research we consider the definition of UX in the second time span (i.e. Momentary UX) that can be measured by relevant indicators linked to the online usage of the system. This definition is consistent with our past research studies on UX strategy maturity of Spatial Web-based Projects [3].

2.2 Open ICT Ecosystems and Socio-Technical Approach to Smart Cities

The Roadmap for Open ICT Ecosystems has been published by the Open ePolicy Group (2005) as user-friendly guide for policymakers and technologists offerings tools for understanding, creating, and sustaining open information and communication technologies ecosystems [4]. Some of the guiding principles of Open ICT Ecosystems are as follows:

Interoperable – allowing, through open standards, the exchange, reuse, interchangeability and interpretation of data across diverse architectures and platforms;
User-Centric – prioritizing services fulfilling and addressing user needs and requirements over perceived hardware or software constraints;
Collaborative – permitting governments, industry, and other stakeholders to create, grow and reform communities of interested parties that can leverage strengths, solve common problems, innovate and build upon existing efforts made by others;

Jha et al. (2016) have bult eKutir, a social business in India that leverages an information and communication technology (ICT) platform to progressively build a self-sustaining ecosystem to address multiple facets of smallholder farmer poverty [5]. The evolution displays a distinct pattern where the five elements of the ecosystem progressively evolve and reinforce each other to create a system that is economically sustainable, scalable, and can accelerate transformative change.

Smart cities, by definition, refer to the data economy, stimulation from ICTs and improved urban management from software algorithms integrated within the urban fabric. As highlighted by Han and Hawken (2017), a purely technocratic and techno-engineering focus on smart cities will not deliver the outcomes that are necessary to create more livable cities that innovate across all areas of society, from the environmental to social and economic areas [6]. According to the authors, future smart cities will rely on their distinctive informational ecosystems and multiple identities to address challenging and ever growing economic, social and environmental needs.

The Indian Housing and Land Rights Network (HLRN, 2017) has undertaken a comprehensive human factors review of the process and the guidelines of India's Smart Cities Mission as well as of the 60 selected smart city proposals [7]. The report recommends smart cities policies, programs and projects to adopt a more coherent and equitable socio-technical vision driven by Indian cities' realistic challenges, concerns, needs in order to holistically understand and address people's demands and concerns.

2.3 Social Innovation and Urban Upgrading Policies

Wehn and Evers (2015) have studied how advanced ICT-enabled citizen observatories can enable a two-way communication paradigm between citizens and decision makers, potentially resulting in profound changes to local environmental management processes and, as such, in social innovation processes and outcomes [8]. The specific case study discussed by the authors aims at illustrating how social innovation can result in increased eParticipation in local flood risk management.

Van der Have and Rubalcaba (2016) have performed a systematic analysis of available literature and identified that social innovation field is grounded in four distinct intellectual communities: (1) community psychology; (2) creativity research; (3) social and societal challenges; (4) local development [9]. Our research is mainly focused on the third community which aims at addressing social and societal challenges.

The I.R. of Iran Ministry of Roads and Urban Development has adopted the National Strategy Document for Revitalizing, Rehabilitation, Renovation and Enabling Deteriorated and Underserviced Urban Fabrics in 2014 [10]. The Iranian Urban Development and Revitalization Corporation (UDRC) key national mandate is to improve the cities' livability and citizens's quality of life by applying urban regeneration policy and the national strategy [11]. The eight key strategies adopted by this national strategy document are as follows [10]:

Strategy 1: A coordinated urban development policy framework giving priority to 'Endogenous Development';
Strategy 2: Real estate and capital market to correspond to demand by low-income urban strata;
Strategy 3: Improve quality of life and strengthen and nurture the identity of target urban areas and neighborhoods;
Strategy 4: Participation of residents;
Strategy 5: Facilitating investment and creating appropriate incentive structures aimed at the private sector;
Strategy 6: Improving economic, social, and environmental conditions for residents;
Strategy 7: Leveraging the physical, social, economic and environmental capacities;
Strategy 8: An appropriate financial system.

The Iranian UDRC has also signed more than 20 strategic alliance partnerships and collaborations agreements with national administrations, institutions and associations to facilitate the implementation of the national strategy.

The Regional Urban Upgrading Working Group (RUUWG) permanent secretariat is currently being hosted by the Iranian UDRC in the context of the Asia Pacific Ministerial Conference on Housing & Urban Development (APMCHUD) [10].

One of the key medium of communication and interaction between all stakeholders at different local, provincial and national scales is UDRC's main website which acts as an open Information and Communications Technology (ITC) platform that integrates online materials and is enriched with dedicated content for two way communications.

3   Research Methods

3.1   CUBI User Experience Model

Stern has proposed the CUBI User Experience Model to analysis interactive systems provided by businesses for user that includes four key components and four key process steps [12]. Figure 1 displays how each component intersects with others and how the four key processes are being shaped in each step.

As illustrated in Fig. 2, the intersection between business goals and content is called Attraction. Every experience will have initial touchpoints to engage users. Users will processes the signals they receive, react to these communications and quickly decide if it's something useful to them. Then, the reaction can motivate users to take action to complete a given goal or perform a given task. This could be prompted from a call to action, trigger and task list or by other relevant means. Finally, user actions then translate into business transactions. The types of transactions may include purchases, providing ratings on products or services, or other direct interactions with the business.

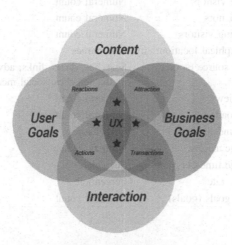

Fig. 2. CUBI User Experience Model and action cycle (Stern [12])

3.2 Remote User Research Tools

In order to fully understand and analyze UDRC website online user behavior, actions and reactions we used and integrated a combination of specialized remote user research tools such as Web Analytics, Web Optimization and Behavioral Analytics software packages including Google Analytics, Optimizely and Kissmetrics. Each relevant JavaScript tracking codes were automatically generated and embedded in all webpages with the assistance of UDRC web administrator and ACM SICHI Iran Chapter [13]. UDRC.IR website usage data and other relevant key metrics that are described in the next section were collected and analyzed during 6 months. The first time period for data collection started on the 16th February 2017 and ended on the 19th May 2017. The second time period for data collection ranged from the 20th May 2017 to the 20th August 2017.

3.3 Selecting Web Analytics Metrics and Dimensions

Selecting relevant web analytics metrics and dimensions is a key factor of success in using remote user research data to discover and formulate practical solutions to user experience challenges. Metrics represent quantitative measurements of different aspects of users' behavior, like the time period they spend viewing a webpage or the frequency at which users viewed a webpage. Dimensions qualify various attributes of users, their hardware, their internet browser, how they got to the website, or specific sections of the website that users visit, which can be used to divide website users into different user segments. Table 1 defines the list of selected web analytics metrics and dimensions used in this research.

Table 1. List of web analytics metrics, dimensions and measurement units

Metrics and dimensions	Measurement units
Unique visitors	Numeral count
New visitors	Numeral count
Returning visitors	Numeral count
Geographical location: city	City names
Visitor source (source)	Searches, direct, links, advertising, media searches, social media
Page views	Numeral count
Downloads	Numeral count
Outbound links	URL address
Average actions	Numeral count
Average time per visit	Seconds
Bounce rate	Percentage
Target goals (goals)	Numeral count

One the relevant JavaScript tracking codes are embedded into the website code, online specialized software packages such as Google Analytics, Optimizely and Kissmetrics provide an automated and systematic access to most of the metrics and dimensions listed in Table 4 based on collected and analyzed website log files. One exception are goals that must to be identified based on manual analysis of individual webpage content and usage frequency. Then, goals have to be manually added in order to get relevant measurements accordingly.

4   Results

4.1   Analyzing UDRC Old Website Users, Goals and Selection of Target Goals

We first explored all the data collected by the web analytics software packages during three months in a time span ranging from the 16.02.2017 to the 19.05.2017 in order to get some initial insights about visitors behavior and top geographical origins. The visitors originating cities were also of great importance due to specific target cities listed as top priority cities in ongoing urban regeneration programs and projects. Figure 3 (a) and (b) displays the UDRC old website homepage and associated heatmaps.

Table 2 presents UDRC old website visitor segmentation by top origin city for the time period ranging from the 16.02.2017 to the 19.05.2017. Visitors originated from Tehran for 51.1% of visits followed by Isfahan with 9.3%, Hamadan with 3.6%, Tarbriz with 3.3% and all others.

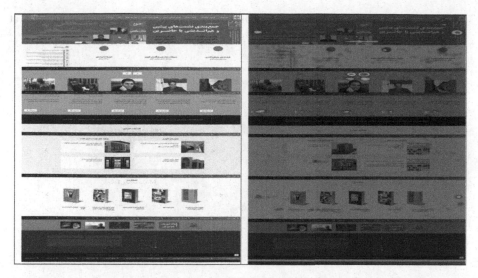

Fig. 3. (a) UDRC old website homepage and (b) heatmaps (16.02.2017–19.05.2017)

Table 2. UDRC old website visitor segmentation by top origin city (16.02.2017–19.05.2017)

City	Visitors ▼		Avg actions	Avg time	Total time	Bounce
⭐ ☲ Tehran, Iran	2,006	51.1%	3.1	5m 41s	7d 22h	17%
⭐ ☲ Isfahan, Iran	366	9.3%	3.3	6m 14s	1d 14h	9%
⭐ ☲ Hamadan, Iran	143	3.6%	2.4	3m 37s	8h 37m	23%
⭐ ☲ Tabriz, Iran	128	3.3%	3.5	4m 4s	8h 41m	12%
⭐ ☲ Karaj, Iran	115	2.9%	2.6	4m 15s	8h 9m	11%
⭐ ☲ Mashhad, Iran	95	2.4%	3.7	8m	12h 40m	5%
⭐ ☲ Yazd, Iran	95	2.4%	3.6	1m 43s	2h 43m	6%

4.2 Measuring UDRC Old Website UX and Target Goals Completion

We analyzed visitor statistics and key indicators such as pages visit statistics, entrance pages, exit pages, downloads and other relevant factors to understand user goals. Then, we requested UDRC board members to provide us with a list of top target goals that would expect website visitors to complete in each session. Then, target goals were manually coded into the web analytics software packages.

Figure 4 displays the UDRC old website visitor map by geographical location at national scale.

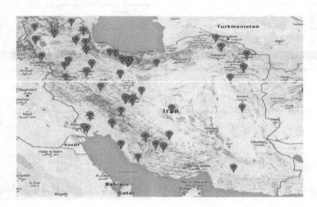

Fig. 4. Geographical locations of UDRC old website visitors at national scale

As shown in Table 3, more than half of the visitors originate from search engines with 56.2% followed by 33.3% of direct visits and 7.7% of visitors are redirected via links. The remaining rows display analytics for other relevant visitor sources.

Table 3. UDRC old website visitor segmentation by traffic source (16.02.2017–19.05.2017)

Source	Visitors ▼		Avg actions	Avg time	Total time	Bounce	Goals
Searches	9,240	56.2%	3.2	5m 45s	36d 21h	15%	4622
Direct	5,465	33.3%	7.8	23m 52s	90d 13h	23%	1709
Links	1,266	7.7%	2.8	5m 8s	4d 12h	20%	702
Advertising	415	2.5%	2.9	4m 37s	1d 7h	13%	189
Media searches	19	0.1%	5.3	10m 50s	3h 26m	15%	7
Social media	19	0.1%	1.2	1m 29s	28m 11s	20%	3
Syndication	7		6.0	9m 15s	1h 5m	0%	1
Total	16,431						7233

The last column in Table 4 displays the total number of target goal completion by origin city. Other UX metrics such as average actions, average visit time, total visit time and bounce rate are also presented.

Table 4. UDRC old website visitor segmentation by top origin city and target goal completion (16.02.2017–19.05.2017)

City	Visitors ▼		Avg actions	Avg time	Total time	Bounce	Goals	
☆ ═ Tehran, Iran	2,006	51.1%	3.1	5m 41s	7d 22h	17%	951	47.4%
☆ ═ Isfahan, Iran	366	9.3%	3.3	6m 14s	1d 14h	9%	236	64.5%
☆ ═ Hamadan, Iran	143	3.6%	2.4	3m 37s	8h 37m	23%	68	47.6%
☆ ═ Tabriz, Iran	128	3.3%	3.5	4m 4s	8h 41m	12%	96	75%
☆ ═ Karaj, Iran	115	2.9%	2.6	4m 15s	8h 9m	11%	80	69.6%
☆ ═ Mashhad, Iran	95	2.4%	3.7	8m	12h 40m	5%	68	71.6%
☆ ═ Yazd, Iran	95	2.4%	3.6	1m 43s	2h 43m	6%	76	80%

4.3   Imbedding Social Innovation into UDRC Proposed Website Prototype

Figure 5 shows the wireframe, components, user interface elements of the high fidelity interactive prototype made for the new UDRC website. This interactive prototype is the result of ongoing user research, usability testing sessions with actual users and joint meetings with key UDRC internal and external stakeholders and UDRC web editors and webmasters.

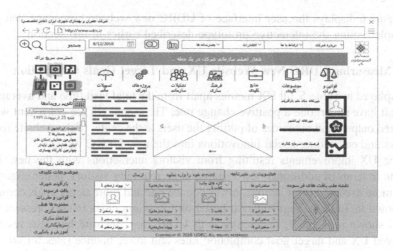

Fig. 5. UDRC new website interactive prototype

While designing the interactive prototype, we tried to redesign the original UDRC website home page, information architecture, navigation, content organization and interactions in a way that imbeds social innovations by following a localized version of the 75 GoodUI design patterns [14] and a localized adaptation of UX UK Awards innovation criteria and best public sector UX criteria localized with the support of

ACM SIGCHI Iran Chapter [3]. The original main UX UK Awards best public sector criteria are best innovation criteria are explained below [15]:

Best public sector criteria:

- **Engagement with the public** - how were members of the public (as well as public sector workers) engaged in the development of the product? User testing, interviews, persona development, workshops? Trials?;
- **Service to the public** - provides a valuable public service, possibly a new service or possibly improving on an existing service (that may have been offline previously);
- **Value to the public** - clearly brings value to users (members of the public) - not a wasting of public funds in its production; ideally able to demonstrate savings to the public purse as a result of developing the site/service/app, or able to demonstrate how the investment made is likely to benefit the public interest in years to come.

Best innovation criteria:

- **Novelty** - Some element of the design of the site/app/service is new; something we've not seen before, or very rarely seen it before.
- **Value** - Is it worthwhile innovation? Does it solve a problem, or does it bring real value, or is it just frivolous or "innovation for the sake of it"? This innovation should be good.
- **Pioneering** - Is this the future? Do we believe this innovation is clearly a game-changer, that in light of this site/app/service, others will follow and adopt what's novel here? Should others repeat and do as this? Sets the bar for where things will/should go in the future.

Figure 6 displays the user interface of UDRC new website homepage that results for implementing the interactive prototype described earlier in this section.

4.4   Measuring UDRC New Website UX and Target Goals Completion

As displayed in Table 5, all UX metrics apart from the total visit time and average time per visit have undergone a positive change rate. These changes are consistent with the expected outputs and outcomes of putting the users at the center of the website redesign process and embedding social innovations into the new UDRC website.

The UX improvements resulting from visitors interactions with the new UDRC website in terms of additional new visitors, more returning visitors, better engagement rates, more average visitor actions, lower bounce rate and more target goals completion are shown in Table 6. Segmentation based-on top origin cities is also presented.

As shown in Table 7, interacting with UDRC new website has also resulted in improved UX and target goal completion rates and lower bounce rates for all visitors across all sources during the selected time period ranging from the 20th May 2017 to the 20th August 2017.

Fig. 6. UDRC new website home page

Table 5. UDRC new website visitor data (20.05.2017–20.08.2017) compared to previous period

🦋 Visitors	19,325	+18%
Unique visitors	14,486	+16%
New visitors	7,330	+16%
Returning visitors	7,156	+15%
🍥 Actions	98,253	+51%
📄 Page views	92,185	+54%
⬇ Downloads	2,945	+8%
➡ Outbound links	3,123	+17%
🍥 Average actions	5.1	+28%
⏱ Total time	90d 11h	-7%
⏱ Average time per visit	6m 47s	-21%
⟳ Bounce rate	19%	-6%
🚩 Goals	8,456	+17%

Table 6. UDRC new website visitor segmentation by top origin city (20.05.2017–20.08.2017)

City	Visitors ▼		Avg actions	Avg time	Total time	Bounce	Goals		
⭐ 🇮🇷 Tehran, Iran	2,298	53.2%	3.2	5m 47s	9d 5h	13%	1266	55.1%	+15%
☆ 🇮🇷 Isfahan, Iran	363	8.4%	2.9	5m 43s	1d 10h	16%	219	60.3%	-1%
⭐ 🇮🇷 Tabriz, Iran	153	3.5%	3.5	6m 26s	16h 24m	16%	100	65.4%	+20%
☆ 🇮🇷 Mashhad, Iran	142	3.3%	2.5	7m 48s	18h 28m	14%	62	43.7%	+49%
⭐ 🇮🇷 Zanjan, Iran	121	2.8%	4.5	4m 8s	8h 20m	11%	47	38.8%	+116%
☆ 🇮🇷 Yazd, Iran	108	2.5%	3.3	3m 51s	6h 56m	23%	49	45.4%	+14%
⭐ 🇮🇷 Karaj, Iran	97	2.2%	3.1	4m 42s	7h 36m	6%	34	35.1%	-16%
☆ 🇮🇷 Hamadan, Iran	84	1.9%	3.6	5m 41s	7h 57m	17%	30	35.7%	-41%
⭐ 🇮🇷 Shiraz, Iran	69	1.6%	1.7	3m 2s	3h 29m	35%	20	29%	+23%

Table 7. UDRC new website visitor segmentation by traffic source (20.05.2017–20.08.2017)

Source	Visitors ▼		Avg actions	Avg time	Total time	Bounce	Goals		
Searches	10,067	52.1%	3.4	5m 53s	41d 3h	15%	5343	53.1%	-9%
Direct	7,396	38.3%	4.3	6m 30s	33d 9h	24%	2116	28.6%	+35%
Links	1,359	7%	3.2	6m 15s	5d 21h	19%	835	61.4%	-7%
Advertising	471	2.4%	3.6	5m 6s	1d 16h	24%	157	33.3%	+13%
Media searches	23	0.1%	1.2	2m 9s	49m 27s	34%	5	21.7%	+21%
Social media	9		1.0	17s	2m 33s	67%			-53%
Total	19,325						8456	43.8%	

5 Conclusion

This research aimed at understanding the theory and practice of social innovation for supporting open ICT ecosystems towards improving digital user experience. The case of the Iranian Urban Development and Revitalization Corporation (UDRC) website was selected in this study. First, remote user research was performed on old version of UDRC website for three months, from February to May 2017, in order to discover users profiles, what user goals are and define what expected target goals should be. Then, the UX and target goals completion rate for the old UDRC website were measured and selected. In the next phase, social innovation were embedded into the UDRC new website prototype and implemented accordingly. Finally, continuous remote user research was realized, from May 2017 to August 2017, in order to measure UX improvements and target goal completion rate for new UDRC website.

6 Limitations

The operational definition of UX adopted is this research is limited to *Momentary UX* which relates to the live usage of the UDRC website as explained in Sect. 1.1. It would therefore be of interest to consider other relevant types of UX and measure the evolution of relevant UX measures within different time spans in the context of additional longitudinal studies. In terms of the total time span for the data collection, this study is limited to six months. Extending the total time period for the user research from time six to twelve months would provide us richer data sets that shall be transformed into better user research insights and findings. Finally, the established concept of UX in a digital environment should be extended to more emerging concepts of city experience and urban experience in a mixed physical and digital smart city environment. In this respect, UNSECO learning cities [16] can provide relevant scenarios for future research studies blending build urban environments and digital environments.

References

1. ISO: ISO 9241-210:2010. Ergonomics of human system interaction - Part 210: Human-centred design for interactive systems (formerly known as 13407). International Organization for Standardization (ISO), Switzerland (2010)
2. Roto, V., Law, E., Vermeeren, A., Hoonhout, J., (eds.): User Experience White Paper: Bringing Clarity to the Concept of User Experience. Result from Dagstuhl Seminar on Demarcating User Experience, 15–18 September 2010 (2011). http://www.allaboutux.org/files/UX-WhitePaper.pdf. Accessed Feb 2017
3. Bazargan, K., Rezaeian, A., Hafeznia, H.: Measuring and evaluating the user experience strategy maturity of spatial web-based projects: a case study of Tehran web-based map. In: Kurosu, M. (ed.) HCI 2017. LNCS, vol. 10272, pp. 631–644. Springer, Cham (2017). https://doi.org/10.1007/978-3-319-58077-7_49
4. Open ePolicy Group: Roadmap for open ICT ecosystems. Berkman Center for Internet and Society, Cambridge, MA (2005). http://cyber.harvard.edu/epolicy/roadmap.pdf. Accessed Feb 2018
5. Jha, S.K., Pinsonneault, A., Dubé, L.: The evolution of an ICT platform-enabled ecosystem for poverty alleviation: the case of eKutir. MIS Q. 40(2), 431–445 (2016). https://doi.org/10.25300/MISQ/2016/40.2.08
6. Han, H., Hawken, S.: Introduction: innovation and identity in next-generation smart cities. City Cult. Soc. 12, 1–4 (2017). https://doi.org/10.1016/j.ccs.2017.12.003
7. HLRN: India's Smart Cities Mission: Smart for Whom? Cities for Whom? Housing and Land Rights Network, New Delhi (2017). http://hlrn.org.in/documents/Smart_Cities_Report_2017.pdf. Accessed Feb 2018
8. Wehn, U., Evers, J.: The social innovation potential of ICT-enabled citizen observatories to increase eParticipation in local flood risk management. Technol. Soc. 42, 187–198 (2015). https://doi.org/10.1016/j.techsoc.2015.05.002
9. van der Have, R.P., Rubalcaba, L.: Social innovation research: an emerging area of innovation studies? Res. Policy 45(9), 1923–1935 (2016). https://doi.org/10.1016/j.respol.2016.06.010
10. RUUWG: Regional Urban Upgrading Working Group oral presentation made at the World Urban Forum 9 by Dr. Farzin Fardanesh: Urban Upgrading Policies in the Islamic Republic of Iran (2018). http://www.ruuwg.org. Accessed Feb 2018
11. UDRC: Improving the Cities' Livability and Citizens' Quality of Life by Applying Urban Regeneration Policy. Iranian Urban Development and Revitalization Corporation Operation Report (2013–2017) (2018). http://www.udrc.ir. Accessed Feb 2018
12. Stern, C.: CUBI: a user experience model for project success (2014). http://cubiux.com/resources.php. Accessed Feb 2017
13. Bazargan, K., Kujala, T.: SIGCHI's Iran chapter: empowering local HCI to create a better shared sociotechnical future. Interactions 23(2), 86 (2016). https://doi.org/10.1145/2890102
14. GoodUI: The 75 Good User Interface ideas: Learn From What We Try And Test (2018). https://www.goodui.org. Accessed Feb 2018
15. UX UK Awards: User Experience (UX) United Kingdom's (UK) Awards (2017). http://www.uxukawards.com/judgingcriteria. Accessed Feb 2018
16. UNESCO: UNESCO Global Network of Learning Cities. UNESCO Institute for Lifelong Learning (UIL) (2018). http://uil.unesco.org/lifelong-learning/learning-cities/members. Accessed Feb 2018

User-Centered Taxonomy for Urban Transportation Applications

Jeremy Bowes(✉), Sara Diamond, Manpreet Juneja, Marcus Gordon,
Carl Skelton, Manik Gunatilleke, Michael Carnevale,
and Minsheng Davidson Zheng

Visual Analytics Lab, OCAD University, Toronto, Canada
jbowes@faculty.ocadu.ca, {sdiamond,mgordon}@ocadu.ca

Abstract. The widespread use of urban software and information technology infrastructure systems now demand new levels of complexity in data generation and data application across interoperating domains. Given this context, and discoveries in visual analytics research that reveal knowledge is created, verified, refined and shared through the interactive manipulation of the visualization (Pike et al. 2009), defining a taxonomy of visualizations can assist visualization system designers in understanding key visualization techniques that serve multiple linked user groups (Chengzhi et al. 2003). It could also be meaningful to others working in sectors that are now in the process of interoperating through the pervasive nature of digital economies. Understanding the potential components of a taxonomy for these forms of data visualization demands the identification of inter-relating and diverse user groups utilizing the same data for multiple tasks (Mahyar et al. 2015), the complexity of visualization processes, relevant task levels and interactions to supplement human insights. For example, a visualization displaying urban transit data might support the requirements of a wide array of users such as urban-designers, city-planners, data-scientists, engineers, transit-managers, pedestrians and transit users. This paper discusses the taxonomy design and prototype creation process for a user-centered taxonomy for urban transportation applications developed by the Visual Analytics Lab at OCAD University, as part of the VAL's research and design contribution to the iCity research project, a collaboration between academic researchers, industry partners, city transportation planning departments and transit authorities that seeks to develop software support systems for transportation planning.

Keywords: Taxonomy · Visualization · Transportation planning
Urban systems

1 Introduction: The iCity Project and Visual Analytics

Over the last decade, the adoption of smart urban software and information technology infrastructure have had profound economic and societal impacts, while multiplying the complexity of data and the variety of domains of practice called upon to interoperate within the ecosystem of modern cities. To address these challenges, the iCity project brings together the University of Toronto's urban simulation modelling capabilities, IBM's advanced software systems including their Cognitive Visualization lab, the

© Springer International Publishing AG, part of Springer Nature 2018
F. F.-H. Nah and B. S. Xiao (Eds.): HCIBGO 2018, LNCS 10923, pp. 577–593, 2018.
https://doi.org/10.1007/978-3-319-91716-0_46

visualization design capabilities of OCAD University, ESRI's GIS and GPS map modeling, city transportation planning departments and transit authorities (Toronto, Waterloo), Waterfront Toronto, and designers and policy analysts from the University of Toronto and the University of Waterloo to develop innovative new solutions for the design and management of urban transportation systems.

The project is based on the premise that the design of any one component of the city, such as transportation, affects not only this system but all the others with which it interacts: housing, the regional economy, etc. These systems, in turn have "feedback" effects on transportation (for example shifts in population affect travel demand and transport performance). A holistic, comprehensive approach to urban system design is therefore essential if major unintended consequences are to be avoided and if implemented policies and technologies are to cost-effectively achieve their intended outcomes with maximum benefit. Within the project cluster, the Visual Analytics Lab (VAL) at OCAD University (OCAD U) is tasked to develop relevant visualization and visual analytics tools that will enable the analysis and use of data outputs in evidence-based planning, predictive models and simulations, real-time decision making and outreach contexts; tools that can provide critical support in understanding and enabling transportation flows and human activities. This paper addresses the process the VAL followed to address the definition of categories that impact the design of such user-centered data visualization tools. The challenge is to ensure that diverse groups of users have appropriate levels of accessibility of data in usable forms. This requires understanding the visualization needs of user groups.

Research in visual analytics shows that knowledge is created, verified, refined and shared through the interactive manipulation of the visualization (Pike et al. 2009). There exists a relationship between human cognition and interaction with visualizations, whereby visualizations supplement human insights. Thus, the challenge is to ensure diverse groups of users have appropriate levels of accessibility to data in usable forms, which in turn requires understanding the visualization needs of multiple user groups.

As suggested by Simon (1969) we looked to a taxonomy as a first step towards understanding any phenomena, a taxonomy being "A systematic arrangement of objects or concepts showing the relations between them, especially one including a hierarchical arrangement of types" (Webster Online Dictionary 2006). For work in the diverse and still emerging field of data visualization, a taxonomy provides researchers with a common language with which to categorize and review existing systems, classify new ones and address gaps towards further development (Price et al. 1993).

A well-developed taxonomy of visualization types can help designers understand which visualization techniques (or combinations of them) best serve the goals and needs of user and stakeholder groups (Chengzhi et al. 2003). Our work on the taxonomy for urban transportation applications links to the ontological work on urban transportation systems led by the University of Toronto iCity team members which seeks to establish a hierarchy of terms. iCity seeks to serve expert technical users, researchers, urban planners, civic leaders and public users of urban-visualizations. Whether experts or casual users, different user groups can have varied information-seeking motivations and objectives, and desire diverse representations of urban data. Hence, in our proposed taxonomy we recognize the importance of user tasks and data type, and have framed this discussion in the relationship with use domains of the visualizations.

This paper outlines the design process and proposes a 'User-centered taxonomy for urban transportation applications' and outlines how we adapt Sorger et al.'s abstract and spatial data categories, integrating the three major components of *data, visual and navigation* into our visualization taxonomy prototype, along with Mahyar et al.'s levels of user engagement, to build a relationship between user engagement goals and visualization components.

2 Literature Review of Taxonomy

Our survey of a human-centered taxonomy for visualization provided an understanding of various methods through which researchers in the field of visual analytics propose the organization of data, user tasks and visual elements to create meaningful representations. Many taxonomies propose the organization of visualizations based on data type and user tasks, with most focusing on the quality of representation to suit a specific purpose. Shneiderman (1996) played a now canonical role in defining an early formulation of visual analytics, defining a task by data type taxonomy with seven data types and seven tasks. The seven data types include 1D, 2D, 3D, time, multi-dimension, tree, and network data in relation to the seven tasks of overview, zoom, filter, details-on-demand, relate, history, and extract. This taxonomy can be (1) data and view specification (visualize, filter, sort, and derive); (2) view manipulation (select, navigate, coordinate, and organize); and (3) analysis process and provenance (record, annotate, share, and guide), Shneiderman (1996). This approach relates task to data type as components of visualization, whereas Valiati et al. (2006) proposes a taxonomy of tasks in multidimensional visualization. Other user centric taxonomies like (Chignell 1990) specify the organization of data based on research in cognitive science which suggests that cognitive efficiency results from tying visualization tasks to the needs of defined user groups (Wang and Dunston 2011).

The most important categorization emerged when we saw that most approaches to establishing a visualization taxonomy essentially fell into three areas: *User Task, Level of Interaction or Engagement* and *Data Type* (Mahyar et al. 2015). We realized we must take into account all three aspects when thinking of visualizations. These three categories served as the foundation for our work towards defining a taxonomy for urban transportation applications. Subsequent sources gave us deeper insights into these categories as they are used in visual analytics.

User tasks can be defined and classified based on the context and scope of the tasks. Wehrend and Lewis (1990) defined 'visualization goals' as actions a user may perform on their data and presents nine such goals: identify, locate, distinguish, categorize, cluster, rank, compare, associate, and correlate. Amar et al. (2005) present a list of low-level tasks, such as retrieve value, filter, find extremum and sort. Zhou and Feiner (1998) define "visualization techniques" as low-level operations and "visual tasks" as interfaces between high-level presentation intents such as 'inform' and low-level visual techniques such as 'highlight' without describing 'how' an operation is performed. Brehmer and Munzer (2013) discuss tasks related to abstract visualizations, which focus on three questions: (1) why the task is performed (2) what the data inputs and data outputs are, and, (3) how the task is executed. Bertini et al. (2015) present a task taxonomy for cartograms, categorizing tasks along four dimensions, based on questions, why, how, what and where to address user goals, means, characteristics and cardinality. In the context of visualizations targeted to multiple user groups, the taxonomy of user engagement proposed by (Mahyar et al. 2015) is noteworthy, as it frames *user tasks* in relationship to *user interaction*, both 'types of interactions' and 'quality of interactions', also referred to as *engagements*. Mahyar et al. (2015) argue that there is a spectrum in the degree of engagement (user interaction) with the visualizations varying from a low level engagement, such as simply viewing a data visualization, to a high degree of engagement which requires analysis, synthesis and deriving decisions. The rating of levels of engagement enables the assessment of user engagement for various categories of user groups that we found can prove beneficial while designing visualizations targeted to these multiple user groups.

Tory and Moller (2002) invent a model based taxonomy which classify visualization algorithms based on whether the data being handled is discrete (a fixed and quantitative variable), continuous (a perpetual variable), or spatial. Their taxonomy framework is based on a data model to avoid ambiguity and streamlines conceptual biases of the designers that may influence the quality of data being represented. Although this taxonomy proposes a way of interpreting data based on data models and not data attributes themselves, it does not consider task based categories for complete visualization systems.

Chengzhi et al. (2003), proposed a taxonomy of visualization techniques and systems, enlisting analytical tasks based on data types for users and matching these to representation modes along with the details of interactions for developers. Their taxonomy elucidates a concept and process of visualization, yet limits task and interaction modes and does not elaborate the specifics of the user types nor their related levels of interactions. Sorger et al. (2015), in their paper on integration techniques for visualizations, suggest that almost all types of data can be understood within two categories, *abstract* or *spatial*. Abstract data lacks explicit spatial references (used for example in information visualizations); and spatial data types have inherent mapping coordinates, (used for example in scientific visualization and real-time rendering). Sorger et al.'s (2015) approach to a visualization taxonomy provides various integration techniques for spatial and non-spatial visualizations, to serve a broad spectrum of user needs. They structure visualization into three components: Data (what to visualize), Visual (how to visualize) and Navigation (viewing position and/or direction of the visual), and suggest permutations and combinations of these three components to cover all possible scenarios to build integrated visualizations. This categorization of visualization in our understanding and analysis of taxonomies was useful in its' application to urban data visualization. Pike et al. (2009), discuss the relationship between interaction and cognition and suggest a useful framework to understand the feedback between user goals and interaction components. Their framework embeds visualization into the context of interaction and positions various components of interaction as part of human knowledge creation.

This review of taxonomies led us to the conclusion that there was no single comprehensive framework that could be used to define the urban data visualization needs of diverse groups. Through the taxonomy development process, we have synthesized existing knowledge to propose a taxonomy for urban transportation applications that places user motivations and needs at the center of the design. In the iterative process that led to the creation of the first prototype and the final User-Centered Taxonomy for Urban Transportation Applications, we drew on Sorger et al.'s (2015) adaptation of the visualization pipeline, which helped us to scope the overall structure of the taxonomy at different stages, while Mahyar et al.'s (2015) breakdown of multiple levels of user engagement helped to inform the core categories that breakdown user engagement with applications. To address the complexity that arises from user interaction and cognitive processes, we draw on Pike et al.'s (2009) framework that takes in to account the variance in interaction based on goals of data use and levels of interaction. These components composed part of successive iterations of the visualization prototype and were modified through the steps explained in the following sections; comparing it against the environment scan of applications and toolsets used in the sector, understanding use case examples, and the design charrette with expert users.

Our effort with this research has been to synthesize existing knowledge to propose a taxonomy for urban transportation applications that is user-centered with user motivations and needs at the center of the design. For our taxonomy development process, we have drawn on the importance of the user's role in the visualization process; the significant relationship between interaction and cognition that reflects the feedback loops between user goals and interaction (Pike et al. 2009). This supports the detailed classification of interactive elements based on user tested needs for spatial and non-spatial data types (Sorger et al. 2015), and the need to segment User Task, User Engagement and User Interaction (Mayhar et al. 2015) to ensure that we address the levels of interaction that occur between users and the visualization spaces and processes.

3 Phase One of Taxonomy Development

To understand the data visualization environment within which we would be designing, we surveyed a wide range of software applications and tools being used in urban transportation focusing on tasks being performed by the users in transportation and related use domains. We did this in tandem with the literature review of taxonomies which helped us to define the evaluation criteria for the software applications we reviewed.

The environment scan provided a broad classification of *software applications and tools* (both of which from this point forward will be referred to as toolsets) serving urban transportation analysis, research, and planning along with the application of systems in related fields. The toolsets were categorized under the following headings: User-Centric Visualization, Transportation, Urban Design, Infrastructure Management, Mapping, Land Use, Big Data Analysis, and Simulation/Interaction/Games. Many of these headings catered to the specific research approach and mandate of the iCity project, resulting in the inclusion of categories such as Urban Design, including Built Environment and Neighborhood Planning; Infrastructure Management including Sustainability and Resilient Cities. This list provided us a baseline for the high-level categories in which to organize both currently listed and future listed toolsets and applications. This also provided us a starting list of *use domains* within urban transportation.

With this list, we created a comparative table/chart as a way of organizing and visualizing our findings, and this remains a core reference for visualization planning and other development with the VAL's iCity mandate. This chart helped us compare and contrast each toolset against similar criteria, thus understanding the nuances and major attributes that each toolset was programmed to serve. The process also helped us gather more information about the users being served by the toolsets, the tasks being performed and the data type, as well as other specifications such as the file formats, data formats, and differentiating features within the toolsets serving similar use cases. This chart (Table 1) became a master document for our reference.

Table 1. Survey of comparative software applications and toolsets used in urban transportation (partial view of larger table)

Type of Urban System Application	Software	Technology / Platform	Description / Application	User Type	Tasks (High Level)	Engagement Level	Interaction (low level tasks)	Data Visualization	Data Attributes
Selected Toolset / Methods									
Built environment, geodata, multi-player urban planning	Betaville	HTML / WebGL Three.JS, Postgres and PostGIS	an open-source multiplayer environment for real cities, in which ideas for new works of public art, architecture, urban design, and development can be shared, discussed, tweaked, and brought to maturity in context, and with the kind of broad participation people take for granted to open source software development.	designer, planners, architects, technicians, transportation engineers, citizens	modelling, navigation, visualization, search (exploration, analysis (geometrical), simulation, comment / query, multi-user collaboration (chat, collaborative work environment)	expose (viewing), involve (interacting), analyze (finding trends) synthesis (testing hypothesis), decide (deriving decisions)	orbit, walk/ fly-through, pan, scroll, zoom, filter, pivot, linking, select, annotate, transform (move, scale, rotate), measure	3D bar charts, 3D pie chart, 3D scatter plot, geo-data	nominal, ordinal, text, geo-spatial, periodic, dynamic, geometry
Qualitative and Quantitative Data Exploration and Analysis and Presentation Tool	StoryFacets	HTML, Javascript, D3 framework, Meteor, MongoDB	explore data through interaction, visual history, presentation, generate consumable overviews, high level-search /browse, visualization dashboard, visualization slide shows.	technicians, transportation engineers, citizens, business analysts	dataset/handle asset navigation, dataset visualization, dataset history and analysis history visualization, decision support	expose (consuming, learning and viewing), involve (interacting), analyze (finding trends), synthesis (testing hypothesis), decide (deriving decisions)	zooming inlet, brushing and linking, scrolling, panning, filter, pivot, compare	bar chart, pie chart, gather plot, markup language	categorical, ordinal, interval, provenance, audio, video, text, image
Transport, land use, demographics	ILUTE (XTMF)	.NET, XTMF	agent (person, business)-based micro-simulation multiyears (over the course of year, scenario)	planners, researchers	land use scenario forecasting (yearly currently) (min is to continuous simulation for multi years)	planner: interact, test hypothesis researcher: model development or submodel development	drag and drop, node based processing	(binary matrix) binary format (mtx) files, Excel (tabular data), csv data	relationships, all facets, comma + transportation network + (information about business characteristics, formological: based on model for e.g. marriage rate, birth rate, etc)

The intention of the environment scan and comparative chart of the available toolsets is to compare the needs of users, identify common toolsets and define a path towards developing a taxonomy that serves the needs of multiple users. This method helped us document the user groups, tasks, existing and required data types, source of the data, and the level of engagement or interaction the various applications currently provided. Although this environment scan will serve further stages of our research and support our work on dashboard design, it's primary role at this stage, is to confirm that users, user tasks, data types, data source and user engagement are critical attributes to be considered.

3.1 Expert Interviews

We followed the literature review and environment scan with a series of interviews with groups of experts from fields within the urban transportation sector to better understand their visualization needs and challenges. These included iCity transportation researchers, urban planners, and computer scientists. The interviews identified gaps in the existing visual representation of urban data in relation to user needs. The experts also shared visualization challenges they were struggling to address in their day-to-day visual analysis tasks. The interviews helped to map the landscape of visualization possibilities for different types of users, but we needed further clarity to understand the overlaps in requirements listed by various user groups. For example, our discussion with the transit research group indicated that they are currently unable to visualize scenarios such as accidents that may affect the route of a street car and therefore were constrained in their capacity to re-route streetcars and avoid delays. This was a specific use case, which in turn needed a very specific type of representation, yet it may be of limited usefulness for any other use domain. This highlighted the need to research use cases.

3.2   Use Cases

A use case is a series of related interactions between a user and a system that enables the user to achieve a goal; it is an effective method to capture the functional requirements of a system (Shrivathsan 2009).

A use case template was circulated to the group of iCity project researchers to identify user profiles that corresponded to specific user scenarios. The researchers had the freedom to include as many profiles as possible to illustrate their visualization challenges. Each Urban Informatics Use Case profile included an outline of a particular user, an application scenario, and a description of tasks to complete this use case. More detailed information around the preconditions for those tasks, required technology and assets required, provided a more comprehensive picture of the task interaction and required visualization functionality. The intention was to filter and aggregate user-types, user tasks and therefore existing and required visualization needs and techniques. This survey template is included in Fig. 1 below.

By the end of this process, we compiled a list of requirements, possible user groups and their visualization needs gathered from each research group, which provided enough information to create a tentative structure of classification for urban transit data that would serve all groups.

3.3   User-Centered Taxonomy

Guided by the literature review of data visualization taxonomies, the synthesis of our findings from the comparative applications and toolsets chart, the expert interviews, and use case mapping, we created our first iteration of a taxonomy for urban transportation applications. To test this first prototype we organized a design charrette with our actual user groups, with the objective of refining the categories used in the prototype.

This Taxonomy Prototype adopts the categories of Users, Tasks, Data representation and Type of Interaction, (Fig. 2) based on Sorger et al.'s (2015) and Mahyar et al.'s (2015) levels of user engagement. The visual layout of the prototype was influenced by Sorger et al.'s concept of the general visualization pipeline. Although we had identified Mahyar et al.'s level of engagement to be an essential category, we were unable to place it effectively in our initial taxonomy iteration, since it was still early in our design research.

| URBAN INFORMATICS USE CASE PROFILE | Case Number: C3 |
| | Date: January 30th, 2017 |

| User Type | Gender: Male   Age: 56   Nationality: Canadian   Occupation: Architectural Technician |
| | Laz is a Senior Architectural Technician working for city planning. His area of expertise is reviewing re-zoning applications and new development projects. |

Application Scenario

Laz is reviewing an application for a building re-zoning in the new West Don neighborhood. The applications have not included any parking statistical information, and Laz needs to ascertain whether the existing street and lot spaces will be overburdened by new users if the project proceeds. He must perform Quantitative Data Exploration and Analysis of existing parking resources, land use, and demographics, to evaluate and propose current and proposed parking against policy /regulations as documented in the city's geodata survey and 3D model resources. He needs to provide three documents of his findings:
- an explanatory presentation for an upcoming community meeting.
- a formal record of the application's parking implications, context and applicable
  regulations
- a recommended ruling based on the above

Description of Tasks

- Exploration of geodata & 3D model of existing conditions
- Record of parking inventory in defined area
- Calculation requirements with/without proposed changed
- Export of tabular data graphics
- Preparation of formal document and slide presentation for ruling recommendation
  decision
- Support/ justification/communication with decision makers and stakeholders

Preconditions

Knowledge of local study area, accessibility to platform, understanding of interface and functionality, availability of peak parking data on both street level and private areas etc.

| Technology | Software ArcGIS / CityEngine/ Insights |
| | Environments & Frameworks HTML5 / WebGL / Javascript |

| Assets | Formats online SHP, CSV, SLS, JSON, dwg, dmg files |
| | Functions 3D bar chart, geodata, bar chart, interactive digital maps with on/off information layer switching, call-out boxes |

| Task Interaction | How are you using this software / tool? |
| | orbit, walk/fly through, pan, scroll, zoom, select, annotate, measure, annotate measurement, zooming inset, scrolling, panning, compare, micro-simulation etc |

| Data Visualization | What is the visualization functionality of this software / tool? |
| | - Uses technological interface to visualize street segment, with displayed data of parking per location
- Statistical comparison
- Capture of generated data in a form that can be presented to others
- Access of demographic community data to project potential local patrons of future establishments.
Interface to select, analyze and prepare a visual summary of queried data on locations parking |

| Improvements | How could the software / tool be changed to support the required tasks? |
| | Real time 3D infographics, superimposed 3D map, highlighted statistical charts, prep of visual narrative |

Fig. 1. Use case template content describing requirements of city planning team member, *the architectural technician.*

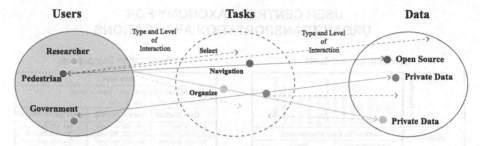

Fig. 2. Comparative categories of users, tasks, and data representation - first iteration of taxonomy

The design charrette helped us to rework the taxonomy categories based on the suggestions from the iCity research teams. For example, we combined user types with corresponding tasks and included levels of engagements; detailed data representation as a category to enhance understanding around the data type and the techniques of representations. We recognized a need to detail engagements in order to match intended tasks and the representations to the user. Since these users belonged to different domains, it highlighted the possibility to detail use domains further.

4 User-Centered Taxonomy for Urban Transportation Applications

Our proposed taxonomy (Fig. 3) mainly draws on Pike et al. (2009), Mahyar et al. (2015) and Sorger et al. (2015), to build a relationship between user engagement goals and visualization components.

4.1 User Engagement Goals

The study of use cases provided an understanding of users and their intended goals. It also helped to clarify various use domains within the urban transportation umbrella, which served as the core of this taxonomy. The users identified in our environment scan of urban transportation application systems included; Researcher, Hardware/Software vendor, Designer, Planner, Operator, Decision-maker/proponent, Politician, Real-estate - Developer, Advocate, City staff, Surveyor, Statistician, Engineer, Business user, Citizen/resident, Home-owner, Tenant, Guest/Tourist, Driver, Pedestrian, and Cyclist, etc. and the domains of Traffic, Transit, Roadways, Design, Cartography, Operations, Urban design, Urban Planning, Policy and regulations, Land Use, Services, Maintenance and Capital Facility Planning.

Interviews showed that different categories of users require varied levels of analytic tools. The design charrette provided us with a more comprehensive list of use domains. This expanded our chart headings from original environment scan to the following: Traffic, Transit, Roadways, Design, Cartography, Operations, Urban Design, Urban Planning, Policy and Regulations, Land Use, Services, Maintenance, and Capital Planning.

USER CENTRED TAXONOMY FOR
URBAN TRANSPORTATION APPLICATIONS

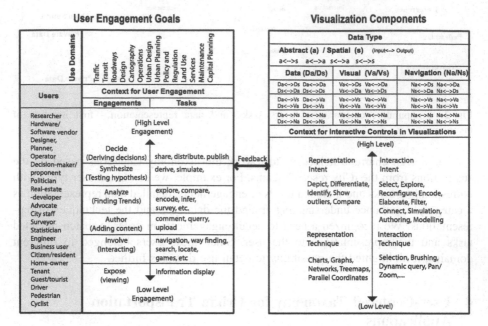

Fig. 3. User centered taxonomy for urban transportation applications

User engagement can be defined as the willingness to invest effort to explore and gain information from a visualization (Boy et al. 2015). Mahyar et al. (2015) define a taxonomy of engagement based on the level of user involvement with the visualizations. Designers can interpret these findings as an imperative to create meaningful and compelling visualizations that are equally useful – providing appropriate tools for non-expert and expert users. Mahyar et al.'s (2015) taxonomy outlines six stages of engagement from high to low level; Decide (deriving decision), Synthesize (testing hypothesis), Analyze (finding trends), Involve (interacting), and Expose (viewing). In our research with experts in the urban transportation applications we found that 'author' or authoring content is another type of user engagement missing in the list suggested by Mahyar et al. (2015). Authoring content may include activities like uploading 3D models on Google Earth etc. and hence we place this activity between 'involve' and 'analyze'. In our taxonomy, we include 'Author', that is authoring content as a crucial step that may indicate user involvement which is more than 'Interacting' but less than 'Analyze'. User tasks are listed next to their corresponding level of engagement for the clarity in understanding user intentions at each stage of engagement. It must be noted that the list of tasks in the proposed taxonomy are descriptive and not prescriptive.

4.2 Visualization Components

Our taxonomy builds on the categories suggested by Sorger et al. (2015) and utilizes their suggested framework of abstract data type and spatial data type to propose a comprehensive structure for representing data in urban transportation applications. They describe Data, Visual and Navigation as components of visualizations, and we use these categories to describe integration techniques between the inputs and outputs in a visualization. For example, if an Excel spread sheet containing statistics on the population of a city is 'Data' input, its representation as a bar chart is a 'Visual' output.

Another way of understanding the relationship between Data, Visual and Navigation proposed by Sorger et al. (2015) is through the concept of interactive controls defined as the control points or elements of interaction in any visualization, for example tool sets, menu options, etc. (Pike et al. 2009). Pike et al. explain the interactive controls of any display device should provide access to a set of low-level representation and interaction techniques that support higher-level intents. User tasks include low-level choices of manipulating interactive components and higher-level goals related to the problems investigated. These then form a feedback loop between the user and the visualization which they should be able to further manipulate based on their intent. For Pike et al., distinction between the techniques and intent helps in the development of analysis support tools, as a technique is never an end but a means to support the user's understanding of the data.

4.3 Example 1: The Architectural Technician

We take the example of an architectural technician above (Fig. 1) which is a use case from our research. A user group depicts the technician working on the review of a rezoning proposition for a new building. Two main tasks occupy this technician's work on such a project: (1) the exploration of datasets, and (2) analysis of land use, parking resources, and demographics. Using our aforementioned taxonomy chart, we can first classify our user engagement goals with the technician as *user* and urban planning as *use domain* (Fig. 4).

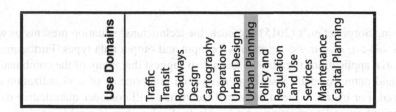

Fig. 4. Use domain of the architectural technician tasks

The scenario provided by this specific user group stipulates that the technician is required to perform quantitative data exploration and analysis in order to determine if the building application in question would create any issues with parking lot spaces being overwhelmed by new users. The taxonomy's user engagement context would classify this technicians' activity as *analysis* and the finding of trends, (Fig. 5) to unravel the patterns that will help the technician to generate decision support data for synthesis. On the side of the taxonomy regarding the visualization components, the technician's work in this use case involves geospatial data, making use of (a) abstract and (b) spatial data types. The use case also identifies the technician's use of geographical information systems (GIS) software, web, and graphic frameworks. Components of the ArcGIS software gives the technician the ability to explore abstract data in the form of information visualizations and provides the technician with a host of spatial navigation features.

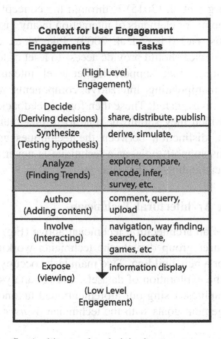

Fig. 5. Architectural technician's user engagement

Using Sorger et al.'s (2015) approach, the technicians' situation presents us with all *a<–>s, a<–>a, s<–>a, s<–>s* options for input and output data types. Furthermore, the geospatial applications used by the technician suggest that many of the combinations of input and output of data, visual and navigation components of a visualization can be achieved. For instance, the architectural technician will consider quantitative data sets of a neighborhood population, and is able to display this as a table of data or a 3D geospatial plot of that data, or combinations of both input and output formats. (*Da<–>Ds, Da<–>Da, Da<–>Vs, Da<–>Va, Da<–>Ns, Da<–>Na*).

This is essentially accomplished only by the input of abstract data (*Da*, such as a spreadsheet of the neighborhood populations) to produce either spatial data (*Ds*, an example being the plotting of the neighborhoods on a map) or other abstract data, to define spatial or abstract methods of viewing (*Vs* or *Va*), and also defines spatial or abstract positions and/or directions of the visuals (*Ns* or *Na*), (Fig. 6).

Data Type		
Abstract (a) / Spatial (s) (Input<--> Output) a<-->s a<-->a s<-->a s<-->s		
Data (Da/Ds)	**Visual (Va/Vs)**	**Navigation (Na/Ns)**
Da<-->Ds Da<-->Da Ds<-->Da Ds<-->Ds	Va<-->Ds Va<-->Da Vs<-->Da Vs<-->Ds	Na<-->Ds Na<-->Da Ns<-->Da Ns<-->Ds
Da<-->Vs Da<-->Va Ds<-->Va Ds<-->Vs	Va<-->Vs Va<-->Va Vs<-->Va Vs<-->Vs	Na<-->Vs Na<-->Va Ns<-->Va Ns<-->Vs
Da<-->Ns Da<-->Na Ds<-->Na Ds<-->Ns	Va<-->Ns Va<-->Na Vs<-->Na Vs<-->Ns	Na<-->Ns Na<-->Na Ns<-->Na Ns<-->Ns

Fig. 6. Source and target data types of use case example

In Sorger et al.'s (2015) model-based taxonomy, *integration* is triggered through interaction, a *source domain* is what the user interacts with, and in the architectural technician example, these include sheets, tables, maps and charts. The *target domain* is what is affected through the integration. If the source and target domains are the same, they are of *coordination* rather than *integration*, (Fig. 7). These tables, maps, and charts are both source and target domains in the case of the technician's GIS software used.

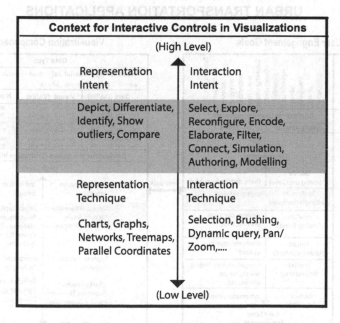

Fig. 7. Use case example's interaction model

4.4   Example 2: Traffic Operations Technical Support Person

In the example of traffic operations which is another use case from our research, a user group depicts the operations person analyzing the impact of weather events on the performance of a major thoroughfare in the greater Toronto area (GTA) traffic management operations. Three main tasks occupy this operations person's work on such a project: (1) the exploration of datasets to collect weather and traffic information, (2) classification of the weather data impact, and (3) analysis of the impact on road performance and travel times.

Using our taxonomy chart, (Fig. 8) we can first classify our user engagement goals with the operations person as *user* and traffic, roadways, and operations as *use domains*. The scenario provided by this specific user group stipulates that the operations person is required to perform quantitative data exploration and analysis in order to determine the severity of weather, and the impact on road performance (speed and flow rates) due to weather conditions. The taxonomy's user engagement context would classify this user's activity as *analysis* (the finding of trends) to unravel the patterns that will help the operation user to generate decision support data for synthesis. On the side of the taxonomy regarding the visualization components, the operations work in this use case involves geospatial data, making use of abstract (a) and spatial (b) data types.

The use case also identifies the operations person's use of historical weather conditions data (e.g. rain conditions, snow conditions, precipitation), historical

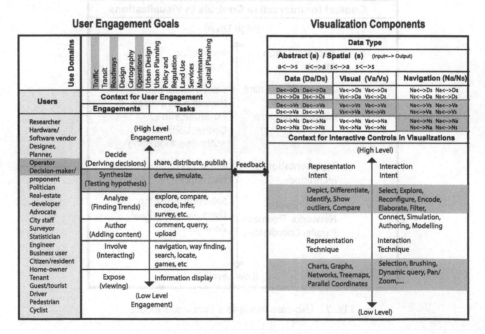

Fig. 8. Use case example of traffic operations task use case

highway data (e.g. flow-density-speed-relationships), highway characteristics (e.g. free flow speed-capacity) with regression analysis (statistical analysis), and spatiotemporal analysis, geographical information systems (GIS) software toolsets, web, and graphic frameworks. Components of the ESRI software could give the operations user the ability to explore abstract data in the form of information visualizations and will provide an understanding of the dynamics of the traffic system under differing conditions with a host of spatial navigation features.

This provides a variety of high level engagement contexts, analyze (find trends), synthesize (test hypothesis), and decide (deriving decisions) to publish or for action decision support. The operations user situation presents us with all $a<->s$, $a<->a$, $s<->a$, $s<->s$ options for input and output data types. Furthermore, the geospatial applications used by the operations user suggest that many of the combinations of input and output of data, visual and navigation components of a visualization can be achieved. For instance, the user will consider quantitative data sets of weather and roadways, and is able to display this as a table of data or a 3D geospatial plot of that data, or combinations of both input and output formats. ($Da<->Ds$, $Da<->Da$, $Da<->Vs$, $Da<->Va$, $Da<->Ns$, $Da<->Na$). This is accomplished only by the input of abstract data (Da, such as a spreadsheet of the weather data, and roadway data) to produce either spatial data (Ds, an example being the plotting of the roadways on a map) or other abstract data, to define spatial or abstract methods of viewing (Vs or Va), and also defines spatial or abstract positions and/or directions, and navigation of the visuals (Ns or Na).

As per Sorger et al.'s (2015) model-based taxonomy, *integration* is triggered through interaction, a *source domain* is what the user interacts with, and in the traffic operations example, these include data sets, spatial data charts and maps. The *target domain* is what is affected through the interaction, a synthesis of various data to be represented and integrated into an integration. In this case of the traffic operations' use of GIS software to depict, differentiate and compare at a high level of visualization control, then the domain is *integration* rather than *coordination*, as shown in the Fig. 8 above.

The use of the user-centred taxonomy in the two examples preceding serve to illustrate a level of understanding of the levels of task, data type, and user engagement necessary for particular use cases, and provide a guideline for the level of user interaction and visual representation necessary in the design of interactive controls, toolsets and visualization dashboards to serve them. Through a depiction of a variety of use cases in this way, commonalities of interactive controls and toolsets can be identified to serve the variety of users.

5 Conclusions

The literature review provided an understanding of the potential components of a taxonomy for this form of data visualization, and outlined the importance of identifying inter-relating and diverse user groups' needs, utilizing the same data for multiple tasks. Key articles researched also identified a variety of approaches to the complexity of visualization processes, relevant task levels and interactions necessary to consider supplementing human insights through visualization supports. Our survey of a taxonomy for visualization provided an understanding of the various methods through which researchers in the field of visual analytics propose the organization of data, user tasks and visual elements to create meaningful representations.

These findings focused our approach to establishing a visualization taxonomy into three areas: *User Task, Level of Interaction or Engagement* and *Data Type,* and the detailed classification of interactive elements based on user tested needs for *spatial and non-spatial data types* within our research groups. We tested this approach through Use Cases, and design consultation and charrettes with the users, identifying the contexts and levels of interactive visualization functionality desired by various users.

The research process led to the creation of a taxonomy that helps us to understand, analyze, and design urban transportation software application systems, while emphasizing the importance the role visualization plays within the understanding and design of these systems. This taxonomy is intended to help designers of urban transportation applications understand essential elements of visualizations and study their relationships. It also serves as a starting point for designers of urban transportation visualizations to address categories of users, their tasks, level of engagements, data types and interaction needs as part of a user centered approach.

5.1 Further Research

As next steps, we plan to conduct more extensive workshops with various user groups identified in the taxonomy to verify and refine the assumptions within the proposed framework. Further research will include surveys of varied user groups, to build, test and refine use cases, and the results of future processes will be shared with providers of software solutions for transportation planning. We will also utilize the results of the research towards our efforts to create visualization dashboards that serve the multiple user groups within the iCity research project.

Acknowledgements. The authors gratefully acknowledge the support of OCAD University and the Visual Analytics Lab, Canada Foundation for Innovation, the Ontario Ministry of Research & Innovation through the ORF-RE program for the iCity Urban Informatics for Sustainable Metropolitan Growth research consortium; IBM Canada and MITACS Elevate for support of post-doctoral research; NSERC Canada CreateDAV, and Esri Canada and MITACS for support of graduate internships; Artjem Disterhof at the Media2Culture (M2C) Institut für Angewandte Medienforschung at the University of Applied Sciences of Bremen for development work on the Betaville html5 prototype; the Rockefeller Foundation through its Cultural Innovation Fund; Microsoft Research; the Bundesministerium für Bildung und Forschung; and the department of Informatics of the City University of Applied Sciences, Bremen.

References

Amar, R., Eagan, J., Stasko, J.: Low-level components of analytic activity in information visualization. In: IEEE Symposium Proceedings, on Information Visualization, pp. 111–117 (2005)

Boy, J., Detienne, F., Fekete, J.D.: Storytelling in information visualizations: does it engage users to explore data? In: Proceedings of the 33rd ACM Conference on Human Factors in Computing Systems (CHI 2015), pp. 1449–1458. ACM (2015)

Brehmer, M., Munzner, T.: A multi-level typology of abstract visualization tasks. IEEE Trans. Vis. Comput. Graph. **19**(12), 2376–2385 (2013)

Chengzhi, Q., Chenghu, Z., Tao, P.: Taxonomy of visualization techniques and systems-concerns between users and developers are different. In: Asia GIS Conference Proceedings (2003)

Chignell, M.H.: A taxonomy of user interface terminology. ACM SIGCHI Bull. **21**(4), 27 (1990)

Fishkin, K.P.: A taxonomy for and analysis of tangible interfaces. Pers. Ubiquit. Comput. **8**(5), 347–358 (2004)

Haroz, S., Kosara, R., Franconeri, S.L.: Isotype visualization - working memory, performance, and engagement with pictographs. In: Proceedings of the 33rd Annual ACM Conference on Human Factors in Computing Systems, pp. 1191–1200. ACM (2015)

Mahyar, N., Kim, S.H., Kwon, B.C.: Towards a taxonomy for evaluating user engagement in information visualization (2015). http://www.vis4me.com/personalvis15/papers/mahyar.pdf

Nusrat, S., Kobourov, S.: Task taxonomy for cartograms. In: Bertini, E., Kennedy, J., Puppo, E. (eds.) Eurographics Conference on Visualization 2015 (EuroVis). https://www2.cs.arizona. edu/~kobourov/cartogram_taxonomy.pdf. Accessed 01 Feb 2018

Pike, W.A., Stasko, J., Chang, R., O'Connell, T.A.: The science of interaction – information visualization. Inf. Vis. **8**(4), 263–274 (2009). http://journals.sagepub.com/doi/abs/10.1057/ivs.2009.22?journalCode=ivia. Accessed 01 June 2018

Price, B.A., Ronald, M., Small, I.S.: A principled taxonomy of software visualization. J. Vis. Lang. Comput. **4**(3), 211–266 (1993)

Simon, H.A.: The Sciences of Artificial. MIT Press, Cambridge (1969)

Shneiderman, B.: The eyes have it - a task by data type taxonomy for information visualization. In: Proceedings of Australian Symposium on Information Visualization, IEEE Symposium on Visual Language, pp. 336–343 (1996)

Shrivathsan, M.: Use Cases - Definition (Requirements Management Basics). Pmblog. accompa.com: http://pmblog.accompa.com/2009/09/19/use-cases-definition-requirements-management-basics/. Accessed 08 Nov 2017

Sorger, J., Ortner, T., Piranger, H., Hesina, G., Groller, M.E.: A taxonomy of integration techniques for spatial and non-spatial visualizations. In: Bommes, D., Ritshel, T., Schultz, T. (eds.) Vision, Modeling and Visualization. Eurographics Association (2015). Cg.tuwien.ac: https://www.cg.tuwien.ac.at/research/publications/2015/sorger-2015-taxintec/. Accessed 01 May 2018

Taxonomy: Webster-Dictionary.org (2018). http://www.webster-dictionary.org/definition/Taxo nomy. Accessed 15 May 2018

Tory, M., Moller, T.: A model based visualization taxonomy (2002). Researchgate: https://www. researchgate.net/profile/Melanie_Tory/publication/2560256_A_Model-Based_Visualization_ Taxonomy/links/09e415090bb78aa0bf000000.pdf. Accessed 01 May 2018

Valiati, E.R., Pimenta, M.S., Freitas, C.M.: A taxonomy of tasks for guiding the evaluation of multidimensional visualizations. In: Proceedings 2006 AVI Workshop on Beyond Time and Errors: Novel Evaluation Methods for Information Visualization, pp. 1–6. ACM, May 2006

Wang, X., Dunston, P.S.: A user-centered taxonomy for specifying mixed reality systems for ACC industry. J. Inf. Technol. Constr. (ITcon) **16**(29), 493–508 (2011)

Wehrend, S., Lewis, C.: A problem-oriented classification of visualization techniques. In: Proceedings on the 1st Conference on Visualization 1990, pp. 139–143. IEEE Computer Society Press (1990)

Zhou, M.X., Feiner, S.K.: Visual task characterization for automated visual discourse synthesis. In: SIGCHI Conference on Human Factors in Computing Systems, pp. 392–399 (1998)

Identifying the Responsible Group for Extreme Acts of Violence Through Pattern Recognition

Mahdi Hashemi[✉] and Margeret Hall

College of Information Science and Technology, University of Nebraska Omaha,
Omaha, USA
m.hashemi1987@gmail.com, mahall@unomaha.edu

Abstract. The expansion of Internet has eased the broadcasting of data, information, and propaganda. The availability of myriads of social and televised media have turned the spotlight on violent extremism, widened the rift between different sides of the spectrum, and expanded the scope and impact of ideology-oriented acts of violence on citizens and nations. The human casualties and psychological impacts on societies make any study on such acts worthwhile, let alone attempting to detect patterns among them. This study focuses on mining the information about each violent act, including human casualties and fatalities, level of coordination and expertise, importance of the targeted process, and the extent of its impact on the process, to identify the responsible group. Decision tree, a non-linear classifier, reached 20% cross-validation accuracy in identifying the correct group among 38 groups. This is the highest accuracy achieved in comparison with other linear classifiers, including Perceptron, SVM, and least squares. Our results also underscored the human casualties and fatalities as the most important predictors. The other four variables, including level of coordination, level of expertise, importance of the targeted process, and the extent of the impact on the process were all partly correlated and less helpful. However, the single feature, generated by linear combination of these four features using PCA, was as good of a predictor as the human casualties and fatalities.

Keywords: Decision tree · Perceptron · SVM · Least squares
Feature selection · Machine learning

1 Introduction

The advance of technology, facility of satellite communications, and ubiquity of the Internet [1] have multiplied the extent and impact of ideology-, politically-motivated acts of violence, have expanded their scope beyond specific locales and regions, and have made them a growing threat against humanity, across the world [2]. In such violence, groups or individuals commit acts of unbelievable brutality against a leader, citizens, an entire city, or nation. The motivation behind it is usually a radicalized interpretation of defending a greater good, politics, or extreme ideology [3]. However, such acts of violence are always disturbing to people's minds and their everyday lives and destabilizing to societies and peace. They are associated with human and economic tolls, and challenge sustainable development in modern and third-world countries [4].

© Springer International Publishing AG, part of Springer Nature 2018
F. F.-H. Nah and B. S. Xiao (Eds.): HCIBGO 2018, LNCS 10923, pp. 594–605, 2018.
https://doi.org/10.1007/978-3-319-91716-0_47

In the age of information, there are more detailed datasets regarding such violent acts across the world. This information includes the human casualties and fatalities, the level of coordination and expertise, the targeted process, and how much the process was adversely affected. Groups and individuals committing such violent acts are usually associated with a Violent Extremist Organization (VEO) [5]. The purpose of this study is to investigate the possibility of recognizing the responsible VEO based on the information available about the violent act. We explore different machine learning models, appropriate based on the sample size, for this purpose. Section 2 describes our dataset and the features used as input to the machine. Section 3 explains the machine learning models selected for this study. Section 4 reports and discusses the results and Sect. 5 provides insight into our results along with future directions.

2 Data and Features

Information about violent acts carried out by VEOs across the world is provided to this study by Radical and Violent Extremism (RAVE) Laboratory at The University of Nebraska Omaha. They developed this dataset by first relying an open-source database on characteristics of extreme acts of violence, called GTD [6]. Violent acts are included in the GTD if they have a political, social, religious, or economic motive, are intended to coerce, intimidate, or publicize the cause, and/or if they violate international humanitarian law. Among other sources for their dataset are: historical accounts described in open-source data gathered from academic and government sources, scholarly case studies, public-records databases (e.g. Lexis-Nexis), and primary documents from VEOs themselves, such as propaganda and websites. Information were gathered by graduate students with expertise in criminology, industrial and organizational psychology, and information science and technology from a cross functional research center. Coders received 20 h of training prior to data collection on the nature of VEOs, extremist recruitment, and related manifestations in the context of extremism as well as on search tactics and filtering information.

There are six features associated with each violent act in our dataset, including: number of casualties, number of fatalities, level of coordination, level of expertise, importance of the process targeted by the violent act, and scope of the impact on that process. All features are numerical. Casualties range from 0 to 1500 with an average of 7, fatalities range from 0 to 1180 with an average of 5, and the other four variables range from 1 to 5.

Pattern recognition models require large number of training samples from each class, usually linear or exponential with respect to the number of features. Thus, VEOs with sample sizes smaller than 50 were removed. We also removed records containing unknown variables. Eventually our dataset contained 5,661 violent acts by 38 different VEOs from Jul 21st, 1972 until Dec 31st, 2016. The histogram in Fig. 1 shows the number of violent acts carried out by each VEO and the histogram in Fig. 2 shows the number of violent acts per year.

Table 1 shows the correlation coefficient between pairs of variables. Number of casualties and number of fatalities are not much correlated with each other or with other variables. However, the other four variables are partly correlated with each other. The

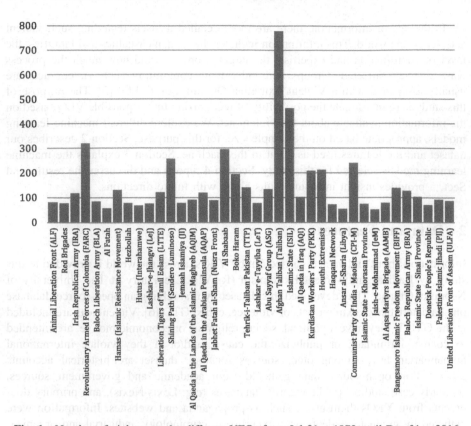

Fig. 1. Number of violent acts by different VEOs from Jul 21st, 1972 until Dec 31st, 2016.

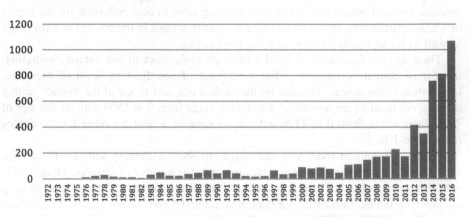

Fig. 2. Number of violent acts per year from Jul 21st, 1972 until Dec 31st, 2016.

largest correlation coefficient in Table 1 (0.71) means that when the targeted process is important, the chances are high that the impact on that process will be also high. The remaining correlation coefficients in Table 1 mean that, on one hand, the level of expertise and the level coordination are partly correlated which is not surprising, and on the other hand, when the level of coordination and expertise are high, the violent act usually targets an important process and results in large impacts on that process. In order to be able to investigate the importance of different features in prediction models, we will not use feature generation methods for now, despite the slight correlation among the last four features. However, all features are normalized to have a zero average and unit variance.

Table 1. Correlation coefficient between pairs of features.

	Number of casualties	Number of fatalities	Level of coordination	Level of expertise	Importance of the target	Scope of the impact
Number of casualties	1	0.27	0.14	0.16	0.11	0.17
Number of fatalities		1	0.14	0.10	0.11	0.17
Level of coordination			1	**0.52**	**0.40**	**0.36**
Level of expertise				1	**0.32**	**0.28**
Importance of the target					1	**0.71**
Scope of the impact						1

Figure 3 shows the boxplots of casualties in each of the 38 classes. Number of casualties is one of the six features. Each group is a class in this plot, represented by an individual box. The boxplot is a standardized way of displaying the distribution of data based on the five number summary: minimum, first quartile, median, third quartile, and maximum. More overlap among boxes means that feature is less diverse and less helpful in distinguishing among classes. The boxplots in Fig. 3 show that the values of this feature are well diversified across different classes (little overlap among boxes) and they can be effective in recognizing classes. Figures 4, 5, 6, 7 and 8 represent the same type of plot for the other five features. Little overlap among boxes, observed in these plots, similarly indicates their effectiveness in distinguishing among classes.

3 Prediction Models

Decision tree, SVM, least squares, and Perceptron are the four classifiers that we applied for our prediction purposes. Here we briefly explain each of them.

3.1 Least Squares

The output of the least squares (LS) predictor is $x^T w$ where w is the extended weight vector to include the threshold or intercept (w_0) and x is the extended feature vector to include a 1. The desired output is denoted with y_i. The weight vector will be computed so as to minimize the sum of square errors between the desired and true outputs [7], that is:

$$J(w) = \sum_{i=1}^{N} \left(y_i - x_i^T w\right)^2 \tag{1}$$

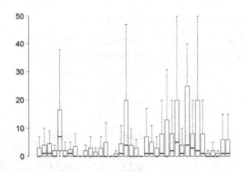

Fig. 3. Boxplot of number of casualties for different groups.

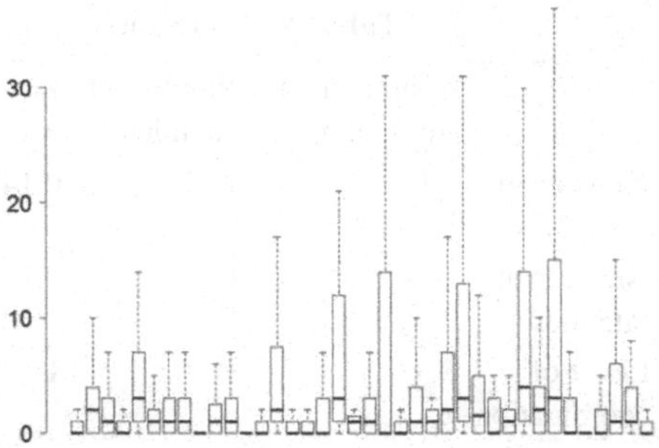

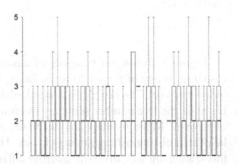

Fig. 4. Boxplot of number of fatalities for different groups.

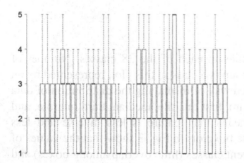

Fig. 5. Boxplot of level of coordination for different groups.

Fig. 6. Boxplot of level of expertise for different groups.

where N is the number of training samples. Minimizing the cost function in Eq. 1 with respect to w results in:

$$w = \left(X^T X\right)^{-1} X^T y \tag{2}$$

where X is an $N \times (l + 1)$ matrix whose rows are the feature vectors with an additional 1, l is the number of features, and y is a vector consisting of the corresponding desired responses:

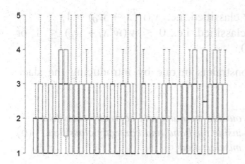

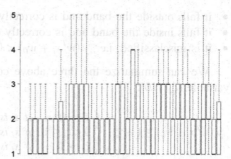

Fig. 7. Boxplot of importance of the process targeted by different groups.

Fig. 8. Boxplot of scope of the impact on processes for different groups.

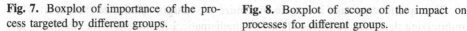

$$X = \begin{bmatrix} x_1^T \\ x_2^T \\ \vdots \\ x_N^T \end{bmatrix} = \begin{bmatrix} x_{11} & x_{12} & \cdots & x_{1l} & 1 \\ x_{21} & x_{22} & \cdots & x_{2l} & 1 \\ \vdots & \vdots & \ddots & \vdots & \vdots \\ x_{N1} & x_{N2} & \cdots & x_{Nl} & 1 \end{bmatrix} \quad and \quad y = \begin{bmatrix} y_1 \\ y_2 \\ \vdots \\ y_N \end{bmatrix} \tag{3}$$

3.2 Perceptron

The perceptron cost function is defined as [8]:

$$J(w) = \sum_{i=1}^{N} y_i w^T x_i, \quad y_i = \begin{cases} +1 & if \ wx_i > 0 \ but \ x_i \in \omega_2 \\ -1 & if \ wx_i < 0 \ but \ x_i \in \omega_1 \\ 0 & if \ wx_i > 0 \ and \ x_i \in \omega_1 \\ 0 & if \ wx_i < 0 \ and \ x_i \in \omega_2 \end{cases} \tag{4}$$

We can iteratively find the weight vector that minimizes the perceptron cost function using the gradient descent scheme [8, 9]:

$$w_{t+1} = w_t + \Delta w_t = w_t - \alpha \frac{\partial J(w)}{\partial w}\Big|_{w=w_t} = w_t - \alpha \sum_{i=1}^{N} y_i x_i \tag{5}$$

where w_t is the weight vector estimate at the t-th iteration and α is the training rate which is a small positive number.

3.3 SVM

SVM [10–12] maximizes the margin around the hyperplane separating the two classes. If the two classes are not linearly separable, then it is not possible to find an empty band separating them. Each training sample will have one of the following constraints:

- it falls outside the band and is correctly classified, i.e., $y_i(w^T x_i + w_0) > 1$,
- it falls inside the band and is correctly classified, i.e., $0 \leq y_i(w^T x_i + w_0) \leq 1$, or
- it is misclassified, i.e., $y_i(w^T x_i + w_0) < 0$.

We can summarize the three above constraints in one by introducing the slack variable (ξ_i) [10]:

$$y_i\left(w^T x_i + w_0\right) \geq 1 - \xi_i, \begin{cases} \xi_i = 0 & \text{if } x_i \text{ is outside the band and correctly classified} \\ 0 < \xi_i \leq 1 & \text{if } x_i \text{ is inside the band and correctly classified} \\ \xi_i > 1 & \text{if } x_i \text{ is misclassified} \end{cases} \quad (6)$$

The optimization task is now to maximize the margin (minimize the norm) while minimizing the slack variables [10]. The mathematical formulation for finding w and w_0 of the hyperplane follows:

$$\begin{cases} \text{minimize } J(w, w_0, \xi) = \frac{1}{2} \|w\|^2 + C \sum_{i=1}^{N} \xi_i = \frac{1}{2} w^T w + C \sum_{i=1}^{N} \xi_i & (7) \\ \text{subject to } y_i\left(w^T x_i + w_0\right) \geq 1 - \xi_i, \quad i = 1, 2, \ldots, N & (8) \\ \xi_i \geq 0, \quad i = 1, 2, \ldots, N & (9) \end{cases}$$

The smoothing parameter C is a positive user-defined constant that controls the trade-off between the two competing terms in the cost function.

3.4   Decision Tree

Ordinary binary decision trees (OBDTs) split the feature space into hyperrectangles with sides parallel to the axes [13]. Nodes in an OBDT are binary questions whose answers are either yes or no and the answer to these questions determines the path to a leaf which is equivalent to a response. Questions at nodes are of the form "is $x_k \leq \alpha$?" where x_k is the k-th feature and α is a threshold. To predict the response of an irresponsive sample, one needs to answer the question at each node and traverse to the left or right node based on the answer until a leaf is reached.

The best question to ask at a node is the one which maximizes the impurity decrease (ΔI) [13]:

$$\Delta I = I - \frac{N_Y}{N} I_Y - \frac{N_N}{N} I_N \quad (10)$$

where I is the impurity of the ancestor node, N is the number of training samples in the ancestor node, N_Y is the number of training samples in the descendant node corresponding with the answer "yes" to the question, N_N is the number of training samples in the descendant node corresponding with the answer "no" to the question, and I_Y and I_N are the impurities of the descendent nodes. Entropy of training samples at a node, in Eq. 11, is a common definition of node impurity in classification tasks ($I_{classification}$)

[13], where M is the number of classes, and $N(\omega_i)$ is the number of training samples from class ω_i at this node.

$$I_{classification} = -\sum_{i=1}^{M} \frac{N(\omega_i)}{N} log_2 \frac{N(\omega_i)}{N} \tag{11}$$

A node is considered a leaf if the maximum impurity decrease (ΔI_{max}) for that node is less than a user-defined threshold, although other alternative conditions have been used in the literature [13, 14]. The majority rule in case of classification is commonly used to determine the response at that leaf [13].

The relative importance of the k-th feature ($R(x_k)$) is the sum of the impurity decrease (ΔI) over all internal nodes (v_i, $i = 1,..., J$) for which x_k was chosen as the splitting variable:

$$R(x_k) = \sum_{i=1}^{J} \Delta I(v_i = x_k) \tag{12}$$

4 Results

A 10-fold cross validation of decision tree resulted in a generalization accuracy of 20%. Maximum impurity decrease (ΔI_{max}) was optimized to 0.055 using an internal cross-validation among training samples. This is a major improvement over a random classifier with an accuracy of 2.6%. Table 2 shows the recall and precision for each class. Larger values for both of these metrics indicate higher accuracies. While a small value for recall means that the classifier has not been able to identify all true samples from this class, a small value for precision means that only a small proportion of assigned samples to this class by the classifier truly belong to this class. In other words, a small value for recall means that the classifier is inaccurate and unfairly stingy to assign samples to this class, while a small value for precision means that the classifier is inaccurate and unfairly generous in assigning samples to this class. A zero value for both of these metrics means that no sample has been assigned to this class by the classifier. Rows shown with a bold font in Table 2 highlight the classes for whom the classifier performs more accurately and rows including a * in the beginning of the class name, indicate classes for whom the classifier performs less accurately. Class 4, 9, and 13 achieve the highest recall and precision which means the selected features in this study are very well capable of distinguishing these classes from others. This could also be inferred from the box plots in Figs. 3, 4, 5, 6, 7 and 8.

There is no meaningful correlation between recall and precision on one side and the size of classes (see Fig. 1) on the other side, which has also been observed by other researchers [15]. However, investigating the confusion matrix shows that largely represented classes among the training samples (e.g., class 22 and 23) have a higher systematic tendency to eat the samples from other classes during the classification. However, their precision stays at a reasonable rate because of their large size. For example, out of 5,661 test samples, 826 of them are assigned to class 22 by the classifier while only 205 of them truly belong to this class. Yet its recall and precision are 0.26 and 0.25 which is around the average among all classes. 371 samples were assigned to class 23 by the classifier, though only 88 of them truly belong to this class. The low recall for large classes, e.g. class 22 and 23, is surprising because it means many samples that truly belong to these classes (around 75% of them) are wrongly assigned to other classes by the classifier. This is mainly due to the large number of classes (38) and the overlap among classes in the feature space. While having more training samples might be helpful, finding features that are stronger in distinguishing among classes would certainly improve the accuracy. Besides, a larger sample size would allow the application of more nonlinear classifiers such as multi-layer Perceptron and kernel approaches such as kernel SVM and non-parametric Bayesian.

Table 2. Recall and precision for different classes obtained from 10-fold cross validation of decision tree.

#	Group name	Recall	Precision
1	Animal Liberation Front (ALF)	0.2805	0.2614
2	Red Brigades	0.2564	0.2273
3	Irish Republican Army (IRA)	0.2458	0.2231
4	**Revolutionary Armed Forces of Colombia (FARC)**	**0.5062**	**0.2651**
5	*Baloch Liberation Army (BLA)	0.0588	0.0505
6	*Al Fatah	0.0345	0.0513
7	*Hamas (Islamic Resistance Movement)	0.0763	0.0935
8	*Hezbollah	0.0759	0.0833
9	**Hutus (Interahamwe)**	**0.5652**	**0.4875**
10	Lashkar-e-Jhangvi (LeJ)	0.1558	0.1690
11	Liberation Tigers of Tamil Eelam (LTTE)	0.0902	0.1236
12	Shining Path (Sendero Luminoso)	0.3619	0.3780
13	**Jemaah Islamiya (JI)**	**0.5696**	**0.5172**
14	*Al Qaeda in the Lands of the Islamic Maghreb (AQIM)	0.0543	0.0556
15	Al Qaeda in the Arabian Peninsula (AQAP)	0.1667	0.1818
16	Jabhet Fatah al-Sham (Nusra Front)	0.1889	0.2099
17	Al Shabaab	0.2271	0.1882
18	Boko Haram	0.1333	0.1320
19	*Tehrik-i-Taliban Pakistan (TTP)	0.0638	0.0865
20	*Lashkar e-Tayyiba (LeT)	0.0385	0.0526
21	Abu Sayyaf Group (ASG)	0.2313	0.1512
22	Afghan Taliban (Taliban)	0.2632	0.2482
23	Islamic State (ISIL)	0.1905	0.2372
24	Al Qaeda in Iraq (AQI)	0.1068	0.1358
25	Kurdistan Workers' Party (PKK)	0.0913	0.1180
26	Houthi Extremists	0.1651	0.1215

(*continued*)

Table 2. (*continued*)

#	Group name	Recall	Precision
27	Haqqani Network	0.2740	0.3279
28	*Ansar al-Sharia (Libya)	0.0182	0.0385
29	Communist Party of India - Maoists (CPI-M)	0.1708	0.1640
30	*Islamic State - Khorasan Province	0	0
31	*Jaish-e-Mohammad (JeM)	0.0769	0.0870
32	*Al Aqsa Martyrs Brigade (AAMB)	0.0253	0.0645
33	Bangsamoro Islamic Freedom Movement (BIFF)	0.1223	0.1532
34	Baloch Republican Army (BRA)	0.1953	0.1953
35	*Islamic State - Sinai Province	0	0
36	Donetsk People's Republic	0.0704	0.1087
37	Palestine Islamic Jihadi (PIJ)	0.1613	0.1685
38	United Liberation Front of Assam (ULFA)	0.0795	0.1489

Table 3 shows how useful each feature has been in developing the decision tree. This can help in filtering out useless features or combining less useful features. Interestingly the number of casualties by itself makes a 41% contribution in developing the tree. The number of casualties and fatalities together from 64% of the decision nodes in the decision tree which means they are strong predictors of our classes. However, the other four features, together, only make a 36% contribution in developing the decision tree.

Table 3. Relative importance of different features in developing the decision tree.

Number of casualties	Number of fatalities	Level of coordination	Scope of the impact on that process	Level of expertise	Importance of the targeted process
0.4085	0.2276	0.1065	0.0928	0.0853	0.0792

Based on the correlation among the last four variables (see Table 2) and their relatively lower importance in the decision tree classifier, we combined them in one feature using principle component analysis (PCA). Table 4 shows the relative importance of new features in developing a decision tree. The new PCA-based feature is almost as good as all four original features combined.

Table 4. Relative importance of different features, after combining the last four features using PCA, in developing the decision tree.

Number of casualties	Number of fatalities	The first PCA component resulted from combining the last four features
0.4134	0.2078	0.3789

We used the number of casualties, fatalities, and the PCA-based feature to measure the accuracy of five different classifiers using 10-fold cross validation. These accuracies are reported in Table 5. Hyper-parameters for each classifier are optimized using cross-validation among training samples. While all classifiers outperform the random classifier, SVM is the least accurate and decision tree is the most accurate classifier. The fact that the only non-linear classifier, decision tree, outperforms all the other linear classifiers (SVM, least squares, and Perceptron), informs us of the complexity of the class distributions in the feature space which could be best separated by non-linear classifiers.

Table 5. Generalization accuracy of different classifiers obtained from 10-fold cross validation.

Classifier	Accuracy %	Description
Random classifier	3	Randomly assigns the test sample to a class
SVM	6	Smoothing parameter (C) = 0.05
Least squares	15	
Perceptron	15	Logistic activation function A maximum of 300 iterations during training Sum of squared errors as the cost function
Decision tree	19	Maximum impurity decrease (ΔI_{max}) = 0.055

5 Conclusions

This study was the first attempt to predict the responsible VEO for acts of violence based on human casualties and fatalities, level of coordination and expertise, importance of the targeted process, and the extent of its impact on the process. The two first features proved the best predictors while the last four features showed slight correlation and less predictive power. While decision tree, a non-linear classifier, outperformed other linear classifiers, its accuracy does not reach above 20% in identifying the correct group among 38 groups. The inability of classifiers to reach higher accuracies is the result of three shortcomings with respect to our dataset: (a) the features are not predictive enough of the classes, (b) the training sample size from different classes is imbalanced, and (c) the low number of training samples does not allow the application and proper training of non-linear classifiers. In our future work, we intend to investigate other features including weapon type, economical damage, location, and time [16] as additional predictors. These features are mostly unknown at the time. Additionally, we are going to apply more flexible classifiers, such as deep networks [17] and kernel methods, as our dataset is expanding.

References

1. Hashemi, M., Sadeghi-Niaraki, A.: A theoretical framework for ubiquitous computing. Int. J. Adv. Pervasive Ubiquit. Comput. **8**(2), 1–15 (2016)
2. Taylor, R., Fritsch, E., Liederbach, J.: Digital Crime and Digital Terrorism. Prentice Hall Press, Upper Saddle River (2014)

3. Martin, G.: Understanding Terrorism: Challenges, Perspectives and Issues. SAGE Publications, Thousand Oaks (2017)

4. Altier, M., Thoroughgood, C., Horgan, J.: Turning away from terrorism: lessons from psychology, sociology, and criminology. J. Peace Res. **51**(5), 647–661 (2014)

5. Ligon, G., Logan, M., Hall, M., Derrick, D., Fuller, J., Church, S.: The Jihadi Industry: Assessing the Organizational, Leadership, and Cyber Profiles. Final report, Department of Homeland Science and Technology Directorate's Office of University Programs, College Park, MD: START (2017)

6. LaFree, G., Dugan, L., Miller, E.: Global terrorism database. In: National Consortium for the Study of Terrorism and Responses to Terrorism (START). https://www.start.umd.edu/gtd

7. Leon, S.: Linear algebra with applications, 8th edn. Prentice Hall, Upper Saddle River (2010)

8. Rosenblatt, F.: The perceptron: a probabilistic model for information storage and organization in the brain. Psychol. Rev. **65**(6), 386–408 (1958)

9. Minsky, M., Papert, S.A.: Perceptrons, Expanded Edition. MIT Press, Cambridge (1988)

10. Cortes, C., Vapnik, V.: Support-vector networks. Mach. Learn. **20**(3), 273–297 (1995)

11. Vapnik, V.: The Nature of Statistical Learning Theory. Springer, New York (1995). https://doi.org/10.1007/978-1-4757-3264-1

12. Vapnik, V.: Statistical Learning Theory. Wiley, New York (1998)

13. Breiman, L., Friedman, J., Stone, C., Olshen, R.: Classification and Regression Trees. CRC Press, Boca Raton (1984)

14. Ripley, B.: Neural networks and related methods for classification. J. Roy. Stat. Soc. B **56**(3), 409–456 (1994)

15. Hashemi, M.: Intelligent GPS trace management for human mobility pattern detection. Cogent Eng. **4**(1), 1390813 (2017)

16. Hashemi, M.: Reusability of the Output of Map-Matching Algorithms Across Space and Time Through Machine Learning. IEEE Trans. Intell. Transp. Syst. **18**(11), 3017–3026 (2017)

17. Hashemi, M., Karimi, H.: A machine learning approach to improve the accuracy of GPS-based map-matching algorithms. In: Proceedings of the IEEE 17th International Conference on Information Reuse and Integration, Pittsburgh, PA, pp. 77–86 (2016a)

Short Paper: Psychosocial Aspects of New Technology Implementation

Dennis R. Jones[✉]

University of Wisconsin – Stout, Menomonie, WI 54751, USA
jonesde@uwstout.edu

Abstract. New technology is dramatically changing the workplace by allowing companies to increase efficiency, productivity, quality, safety, and overall profitability. An effective new technology implementation is required for companies to compete successfully in the marketplace. Time and money wasted on unsuccessful and improper new technology implementation is contrary to the overall goal of improving the competitiveness and profitability of the company. Teams and teamwork have been recommended as a way to improve efficiency, productivity, quality, safety, profitability, and employee satisfaction. New technology challenges the current implementation methods and techniques. To effectively utilize these new technologies it is best to consider all the factors involved in the implementation process; most importantly the individual human elements involved. It is recommended to utilize a cooperative team oriented approach to new technology implementation, which relies heavily on obtaining employee input and participation throughout the entire process. By doing this; it is hoped that the new technology can be implemented in the most effective way possible.

Keywords: Psychosocial · New technology · Teamwork · Efficiency
Productivity · Quality · Safety · Profitability · Employee satisfaction
Ergonomics

1 Teamwork

This paper proposes a technology implementation approach utilizing teams and teamwork. Teamwork has been recommended to organizations as a way to improve productivity, quality, and employee satisfaction [3].

2 The Model

The model to be utilized is based on achieving balance between the various implementation elements. This model is known as the Balance Model [6] and integrates the psychological and biological theories in an ergonomic framework. The factors involved in the implementation process are the new technology characteristics, organization structure, task factors, environmental characteristics, and the individual human factors involved. The Balance Theory Model is as follows (Fig. 1):

© Springer International Publishing AG, part of Springer Nature 2018
F. F.-H. Nah and B. S. Xiao (Eds.): HCIBGO 2018, LNCS 10923, pp. 606–610, 2018.
https://doi.org/10.1007/978-3-319-91716-0_48

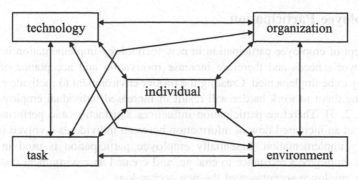

Fig. 1.

In the model these factors interact in a systematic fashion to determine the success and effectiveness of the new technology implementation. This is a total systems model, in that any one factor can influence and affect the other factors.

3 Team Advantages

Teamwork is one form of work organization that can have a positive effect on the various elements of the work organization; especially on the human elements; such as performance, productivity, motivation, attitudes, and health. Autonomous work groups (i.e. teams) have the authority to make work decisions, which resulted in increased personal commitment, improved cooperation, reduced absenteeism, and increased safety [7].

The advantages of using teams and employee involvement are to increase the potential for improving efficiency, productivity, quality, safety, profitability, employee satisfaction, and acceptance of change. Employee involvement affects the five major determinants of organizational effectiveness which are: motivation, satisfaction, acceptance of change, problem solving, and communication [2].

4 Participatory Ergonomics

Teamwork has been used in the implementation of participatory ergonomics in order to improve the working conditions for the employees. The use of teams to evaluate, design, and improve jobs is gaining widespread acceptance. Participatory ergonomics views the employee's participation and knowledge as critical [4]. Participatory ergonomics stresses worker's experience in problem solving. The employee's are in the best position to identify the problems in the work environment. The worker's involvement in the analysis and redesign of their work place leads to better solutions by utilization of the worker's knowledge to improve the process. Participatory ergonomics stresses employee empowerment and autonomy, by providing workers with more control over their work environment.

5 Employee Participation

The concept of employee participation in new technology implementation is to satisfy the employee's needs and therefore increase motivation and acceptance of the new technology to be implemented. Creating the proper environment to motivate employees and causing them to work harder will result in increased individual employee performance [1, 2, 5]. Therefore participation influences satisfaction and performance, and brings about an increased flow of information between individuals involved in the new technology implementation. Essentially employee participation is used in order to reduce the employee's resistance to change, and created an environment conducive to enhancing employee acceptance of the new technology.

6 Case Study

This model, involving teams and teamwork, was utilized on a new technology implementation in a manufacturing assembly facility. The project consisted of introduction of a new assembly method in a medium size manufacturing facility. This implementation of new technology consisted of the following project scope: (1) build a focus factory with capacity to produce 160 units per shift; (2) convert a 38,000 square foot warehouse into manufacturing space; (3) build a 5,000 square foot paint line building addition; and (4) initiate and complete the project within a four month time frame.

7 Case Study Project Items

This case study consisted of the following project items: (1) reinforce the existing building structure; (2) install welding ventilation; (3) install ¾ mile additional power and free paint conveyor; (4) install nine "new concept" robotic weld cells; (5) install a "new concept" overhead power conveyor system; (6) install a new powder paint robotic paint booth; (7) install three material paint drops, and (8) construct new offices, lunch room, bathrooms, and locker room facilities.

8 Case Study Highlights Summary

Throughout this new technology case study the following processes were implemented: information sharing, employee participation, employee involvement, planning for change, High Involvement Management [2], and the Balance Model [6].

The type of powered overhead conveyor system has never been utilized at the existing manufacturing facility. Therefore there was a high degree of uncertainty and uneasiness on the part of the management and employees in the manufacturing facility. Even though this powered overhead conveyor system has been proven to be successful in several similar mass production facilities. The current management and employees had to be convinced that a this was the best thing to do in order to ensure the long term profitability and survival of the organization.

In addition; the overall management and operational structure of the new assembly area was to be team oriented. This was a significant departure form the norm in regard to work group organization. Management had attempted to employ this team oriented approach in the past with very little success. It was thought that with this new conveyor and assembly method the time was right to attempt to employ a team oriented approach. This would be an empowered team oriented approach; in which the teams were empowered to run the entire assembly area. The team of employees working in the area would be empowered to make all day to day decisions related to the smooth operation of the area. All employees were already familiar with an employee incentive pay system, so therefore it was thought that total empowerment of the employees would result in greater employee satisfaction, improved employee motivation, and yield higher employee productivity and efficiency. The employees were also empowered to design their jobs in order to optimize their productivity and efficiency. The employees could therefore utilize peer pressure to attract like minded employees to their peer work group.

In regards to ergonomics; a participatory ergonomics approach was utilized in order to solve ergonomics problems in the assembly line environment. Participatory ergonomics consists of a small group of employees meeting in order to solve ergonomics problems which exist. Participatory ergonomics allows employees to be heard regarding ergonomic problems in the assembly area. Participatory ergonomics also give the employees the knowledge and access to expertise in order to solve the ergonomic problem. By listening to the employees opinions, and through cooperation between all the parties involved; ergonomics problems could be corrected in a timely proactive manner. The communication and sharing of information in critical to the successful utilization of participatory ergonomics. Participatory ergonomics is a useful tool to use to create employee participation and involvement, and also reduce the resistance to change with the implementation of new technology.

9 Conclusion

This model, involving teams and teamwork, explains a way in which new technology implementation can be successful; by the interaction of five different factors - technology, organization, task, environment, and individual. This model establishes a system to balance the bad aspects of new technology implementation with the good aspects of new technology implementation. The advantage of this model is that new technology can be implemented with a holistic "big picture" view of the project. Therefore all elements of the new technology implementation must be considered in order to determine the most effective implementation strategy for the new technology. Teamwork, participation, and employee involvement are critical to the successful implementation of new technology.

References

1. Coch, L., French, J.R.P.: Overcoming resistance to change. Hum. Relat. **1**, 512–532 (1948)
2. Lawler, E.E.: High Involvement Management. Josey Bass Publications, San Francisco (1986)
3. Lawler, E.E., Mohrman, S.A.: Quality circles: after the honeymoon. Organ. Dyn. **15**(4), 42–54 (1987)
4. Nora, K., Imada, A.: Participatory Ergonomics. Taylor & Francis, London (1991)
5. Smith, M.J., Carayon, P., Miezio, K.: VDT technology: pschosocial and stress concerns. In: Kave, B., Wideback, P.G. (eds.) Work with Display Units, vol. 86, pp. 695–712. Elsevier Science Publishers, The Netherlands (1987)
6. Smith, M.J., Sainfort, P.C.: A balance theory of job design for stress reduction. Int. J. Ind. Ergon. **4**, 67–79 (1989)
7. Trist, E.: The Evolution of Socio-Technical Systems. Ontario Ministry of Labor – Quality of Working Life Centre, Toronto (1981)

Visualizing and Analyzing Street Crimes in Kobe City Using Micro-level Demographic Data

Takuhiro Kagawa(✉), Sachio Saiki, and Masahide Nakamura

Graduate School of System Informatics, Kobe University,
1-1 Rokkodai, Nada, Kobe, Japan
kagawa@ws.cs.kobe-u.ac.jp, sachio@carp.kobe-u.ac.jp,
masa-n@cs.kobe-u.ac.jp

Abstract. In order to achieve the safety and security within a city, it is important for every citizen to understand when, where, and what kind of incident occurs frequently around oneself. Previously, many studies have been conducted to clarify relevant factors to street crimes. However, the previous studies mainly focus on the scale of city and ward, but do not consider the magnitude of town and town block. In this paper, we analyze street crimes within a Japanese city, Kobe, from *micro-viewpoints* rather than conventional *macro-viewpoints*. More specifically, we focus on the relation between population and street crimes. We use micro-level demographic data for each town block in Kobe city as population data. We also use incident data published by Hyogo Prefectural Police. Integrating these data, we conduct the fine-grained analysis of the relationship between population and street crimes. Furthermore, we develop a system that visualizes the frequency of street crime on the map. Using the system, we can see town blocks with frequently street crimes, and analyze the relationships between surrounding blocks.

1 Introduction

A street crime threatens safety and security our daily life. It is a major concern for every local government to prevent citizens from getting involved in the crimes. There are many incidents reported every day, including murder, robbery, snatching, groping, and observation of dangerous animals. In order for citizens to protect themselves, it is important to understand when, where, and what kind of incidents can occur around living areas.

There have been social studies that investigate relevant factors of street crimes. For instance, Hipp and Kane showed that cities with more population will experience larger increases in crime [2]. They also mentioned that cities with increasing population will experience larger decreases in crime.

Although their findings are interesting, the investigation is basically conducted at the magnification of city or ward level. Thus, the information is too coarse-grained for citizens to know the situation of individual living area.

© Springer International Publishing AG, part of Springer Nature 2018
F. F.-H. Nah and B. S. Xiao (Eds.): HCIBGO 2018, LNCS 10923, pp. 611–625, 2018.
https://doi.org/10.1007/978-3-319-91716-0_49

In recent years, due to the emerging trend of smart cities, motivated local governments are publishing fine-grained demographic data and information of street crimes as open data. Kobe, our local city, is one of such motivated cities in Japan.

The goal of this paper is to conduct micro-level analysis of street crimes in Kobe, using such fine-grained open data. Specifically, at a microscopic range of town blocks, we aim to answer the following three research questions:

RQ1: Does a town block with increasing population experience the decrease of street crimes?

RQ2: Does a town block with more population experience the increase of street crimes?

RQ3: How are occurrences of street crimes distributed and related among micro town blocks within the city?

In order to answer RQ1 and RQ2, we extensively use demographic open data published by Kobe city. The data include fine-grained population data of every ward, every town in the ward, every town block in the town, each of which is grouped by gender and age. Therefore, we can view the population in the region from various viewpoints. In addition, since the demographic open data is updated every quarter of the year, we can investigate the temporal transition of the population.

However, the original demographic data consists of a huge number of data items over multiple tables, which causes artificial complexity in retrieving necessary data. Therefore, we develop API, called *Kobe Demographics API*, which allows external tools and applications to easily access the large and complex demographic data. Using the API, one can efficiently query demographic data at various viewpoints and granularity, such as period, location, gender, and age.

As for the information of street crimes, we use data published by Hyogo Bouhan Net, which is a security information service operated by Hyogo prefectural Police. The service delivers recognized incident information within Hyogo prefecture (i.e., prefecture where Kobe city exists) by Web or e-mail.

In our previous research, we developed a security information service, called PRISM [3], which visualizes street crimes on a personalized security map. In developing PRISM, we implemented *incident API* to query the incident information from Hyogo Bouhan Net. Using the incident API, one can retrieve incident information by keywords, type, time, location, distance from central coordinates.

Combining the proposed Kobe demographics API, and the previous incident API, we can easily integrate fine-grained demographic data and incident information. Thus, we can conduct the micro-level analysis of population and street crimes to answer RQ1 and RQ2.

To address RQ3, we develop a new tool that visualizes fine-grained statistics of incidents on a map. The tool divides the whole region into multiple small square areas and calculates the frequency of street crimes in each area. The frequency is represented by a color of ten kinds, according to the number of crimes occurred within the area. The higher the frequency is, the deeper red is displayed. The lower the frequency is, the darker green is displayed. By using the tool, it is possible to see the distribution over micro town blocks, to know where street crimes frequently occur and its surroundings.

Analyzing the street crimes from a micro viewpoint, a local government can take precise policy actions based on the trends of individual town blocks. A police department can also benefit the micro-level analysis for efficient patrols within the area. Compared the conventional coarse-grained statistics, the fine-grained incident information give much more reality and impact to citizens, because the information of neighboring towns or town blocks directly influence to their daily life. For example, in areas where groping and exposure frequently occurs, a woman must be careful when she walks alone. Thus, we believe that the proposed micro-level analysis significantly contributes to citizens to achieve security and safety by themselves.

2   Preliminaries

2.1   Demographic Open Data of Kobe City

Open data refers to data that anyone can freely use and share without the permission of copyright. Recently, various governments and municipal bodies have published their data as open data. They aim to improve the quality of life of people, as well as the performance of business activities of enterprises [6].

Kobe city is operating a portal site of open data, where the city is disclosing various municipal data such as population, information of facilities, and time table of subway [5]. Among the various open data, *demographic open data* is quite interesting and informative. The data contains fine-grained population data for every town block within Kobe city, which is much more detailed than the magnitude of town or ward. Moreover, the population is grouped by gender and age for each ward, town, town block. Kobe city updates these data every quarter of the year. Thus, we can also see the transition of the fine-grained population for every quarter.

Although the open data is promising for digital innovation, it is not yet understandable by machines. The current major formats of open data are CSV (Comma-Separated Value), XLS format (Microsoft Excel), or PDF (Portable Document Format), which do not define machine-readable semantics for data items. Hence, to retrieve necessary data items, an application developer has to understand data structure and semantics, and implement proprietary program for parsing the data. This causes the *artificial complexity* in using open data, which is a barrier for private companies and general citizens to create new applications and services.

2.2   Security Information Service PRISM

In Japan, many local governments provide *security information service* for citizens. The service usually distributes information of crimes and incidents to residents using the Internet. Residents can make use of the information for avoiding crimes. For example, Hyogo Prefectural Police provides "Hyogo Bouhan Net", which distributes incident information recognized by the Police on the Web and e-mail. In these existing security information services, however, every incident information is uniformly delivered to all users. Hence, when much information is delivered in a day, a user may miss important information.

In our previous research, we have proposed a new security information service, called *PRISM (Personalized Real-time Information with Security Map)*, which personalizes the incident information based on living area of individual users. PRISM calculates the severity of each incident based on user's living area, current time, and type of incident. Then, PRISM visualizes weighted incidents on a heat map. Thus, a personalized and real-time security map is generated.

We used incident information provided by Hyogo Bouhan Net in PRISM. PRISM periodically obtains incident information from Hyogo Bouhan Net. It then analyzes the text written in natural language, structures the text into attributes, and inserts the attributes into the RDB. We also developed Web-API in order to access the DB. External applications can easily retrieve incident data using the API.

2.3   Related Work

Many studies have been conducted to clarify factors relevant to street crimes.

Hipp and Kane focused on the relationship between population and crime [2]. They state that cities with more population will experience larger increases in crime. They also state that cities with increasing population will experience larger decreases in crime. Morenoff and Sampson [7] investigated the relationship between the decrease of population and the violent crime. They also visualized changes in the population. Roncek [8] statistically examined how the characteristics of a region affect places of crimes, using actual data of San Diego and Cleveland. Stults and Hasbrouck [9] focused on the relationship between commuting and crime rates. They showed that a city with many workers commuting from outside tends to have higher crime rate, since the workers often become targets of a crime. Kester [4] analyzed and visualized the patterns of crimes, using Formal Concept Analysis.

Although the above findings are quite interesting, they mainly focus on interesting regions as a whole. In other word, the investigation is basically conducted at the magnification of city or ward level. Thus, the information is too coarse-grained for citizens to know the situation of individual living area.

As for the efficient use of open data, some motivated governments start to provide API (Application Program Interface) for developers. For instance, Japanese Cabinet Office is operating RESAS (Regional Economy Society Analyzing System) [1]. It aggregates and visualizes big data including industrial structure, demographic data, and flow of people. Since 2016, RESAS starts to provide API, with which anyone can easily access various data in RESAS. However, the API is not specifically designed for demographic data. It just returns the whole data of population. Also, the demographic data provided by RESAS is limited to the scale of city, and not grouped by age or gender. This is much coarser than the demographic open data of Kobe city.

3   Kobe Demographics API

3.1   Motivation

As we mentioned in Sect. 2.1, Kobe city is publishing demographic open data. To understand the data, we here explain the following terms, constructing the structure of Kobe city.

- **City:** a whole city of Kobe.
- **Ward:** a division of a city. There are 9 wards in Kobe city.
- **Town:** a populated area in a ward. Each ward consists of many towns.
- **Town Block:** an area of a town, usually surrounded by streets. Each town consists of many town blocks. A town block forms the basic unit of urban fabric in Kobe city, where several houses or building are built[1].

The demographic open data contains population for every town block within the city. Due to the above structure of the city, we can obtain different granularity of population at town, ward, and city levels. The population is also grouped by gender and ages.

The original demographic data is provided in the XLS format with a number of cells over multiple sheets. Therefore, when using the data for various purposes, we face with the problem of artificial complexity. To cope with the problem, we here develop *Kobe Demographics API*, which makes it easy to access the demographic data. In the following subsections, we will explain the flow of implementation of the API.

3.2   Inserting Data into Database

In order to develop the API, we first insert demographic data into a relational database (RDB).

To manage the demographic data, we create a database with two tables: *population*, and *town*. The population table is defined by the following data schema:

[Population]

- **blockCode:** a code identifying a town block
- **year:** year of census
- **month:** month of census
- **household:** the number of household
- **male:** the population of men
- **female:** the population of women

---

[1] Although a town block may have a name of street, a house is not addressed by a street but by a town block. This is different from Western addressing system.

- **total:** the total population in the block
- **0:** population of 0-year-old persons
- **1:** population of 1-year-old persons
- **2:** population of 2-year-old persons
- **... :** (columns for x-year-old persons)
- **99** population of 99-year-old persons
- **100** population of over-100-year-old persons

The town table manages information of town blocks, including address, town, and ward. In addition to them, for each town block, we associate latitude and longitude of the block. This is for convenience for external applications. The latitude and longitude are calculated from the address by using geographic information Web services. The town table is defined by the following data schema:

[**Town**]

- **blockCode:** a code identifying a town block
- **address:** the address of the town block
- **wardName:** the ward which the town block belongs to
- **blockName:** the name of town block
- **wardCode:** a code of the ward which the town block belongs to
- **longitude:** longitude of the town block
- **latitude:** latitude of the town block

We have used MySQL to implement the database. We also developed a set of Perl scripts, which automatically parse the original XLS files of demographic data, retrieve data items and structures, and insert the data items into the above tables of the database.

3.3 Developing Kobe Demographics API

We developed two API to access the demographic data stored in the databases.

The first API is **getPopulation()**, which returns fine-grained population of a designated town block with a set of parameters.

getPopulation(blockCode, wardCode, year, month, gender, from, to)

parameters:

- **blockCode:** specifies a town block to query
- **wardCode:** specifies a ward to aggregate the population by ward
- **year:** specifies a year of census
- **month:** specifies a month of census
- **gender:** specifies a gender to aggregate the population by gender
- **from, to:** specifies a range of age to aggregate the population by age

For example, when one likes to retrieve population from 0 to 10 years old, in the town with blockCode 101001001, in June 2017, executing getPopulation("101001000", -, 2017, 6, -, 0, 10) returns the desired result. The resultant JSON is as follows:

```
[JSON]....{"address":"1-chome Uozaki Kita-machi, Higashinada-ku, Kobe",
          "from":0,
          "gender":"total",
          "latitude":34.7181473,
          "longitude":135.2759896,
          "month":6,
          "population":83,
          "to":10,
          "blockCode":101001001,
          "blcokName":"1-chome Uozaki Kita-machi",
          "wardCode":28101,
          "wardName":"Higashinada-ku",
          "year":2017}
```

By changing these parameters, one can retrieve demographic data at various viewpoints and granularity such as period, location, gender, and age.

The API getPopulation() requires a block code as a parameter. However, it is not easy for a general user to specify the block code directly. Hence, we implemented **searchTown()**, which is the second API.

searchTown(address)

Parameters:
– **address:** specifies an address to query

This API returns a town block (or a set of town blocks involved) for the designated address. For a given address, searchTown() searches data items in the town table where the address contains the address. It then returns the information in JSON format. For example, when one likes to retrieve block code of "1-chome Uozaki Kita-machi", executing searchTown("1-chome Uozaki Kita-machi") returns the desired result. The resultant JSON is as follows:

```
[JSON]....{"address":"1-chome Uozaki Kita-machi, Higashinada-ku, Kobe",
          "latitude":34.7181473,
          "longitude":135.2759896,
          "townCode":101001001,
          "townName":"1-chome Uozaki Kita-machi",
          "wardCode":28101,
          "wardName":"Higashinada-ku"}
```

The above two API are deployed as Web service, so that applications running on various languages and platforms can easily consume the data.

3.4 Implementation

Techniques used in developing Kobe Demographics API are as follows:

– **Demographic Data:** Kobe Open Data - Basic Resident Register of Kobe city (Population per town blocks, per age)[2]

---

[2] http://www.city.kobe.lg.jp/information/data/statistics/toukei/jinkou/juukijinkou.
html.

- **Data Parsing Script:** Perl, Yahoo! GeoCoder API
- **Database:** MySQL
- **API:** Java JDK8, Jersey.

4   Micro-level Analysis of Street Crimes

To address the research questions introduced in Sect. 1, in this section, we investigate the relation between population and street crimes using the developed Kobe Demographics API.

4.1   Analyzing Relationship Between Population Change and Street Crime in Town Blocks

In order to answer RQ1, we here analyze the relationship between street crimes and the change in population for every town block in Kobe city. The procedure of the analysis consists of the following steps:

- **Step1:** Calculate *security index* of each town block
- **Step2:** Look up the increase and decrease of street crimes within each town block between two years
- **Step3:** Calculate population growth rate of each town block for two years
- **Step4:** Analyze the relation between the increase and decrease of crimes and the population growth rate.

In Step1, we define a metric called *security index*, indicating how often street crimes occurred within a town block compared to other blocks. Inspired by *ABC analysis* [10] in materials management, the security index divides town blocks into three categories: A (crimes rarely occur), B (crimes sometimes occur), or C (crimes frequently occur).

Let $SI(b, y)$ denote the security index of a town block b for a year y. To calculate $SI(b, y)$, we first count the number of incidents occurred (i.e., *frequency*) within every block b_i within the city for y, denoted by $f(b_i, y)$. Next, for each value of frequency $n(n = 1, 2, 3, \ldots)$, we count the number $B(n)$ of town blocks where $f(b_i, y) = n$. We then calculate the cumulative composition ratio of $B(n)$ for $n = [1 \ldots max(n)]$. This is to identify two thresholds n_1 and n_2 that determine categories A, B and C. There are no fixed thresholds for n_1 and n_2. However, for example, n_1 is determined at the point where approximately 70% of the town blocks are involved in category A. n_2 is determined at the point 20% of the rest belongs to B. Finally, $SI(b, y)$ is determined by:

$$SI(b, y) = \begin{cases} A \cdots (0 < f(b, y) \leq n_1) \\ B \cdots (n_1 < f(b, y) \leq n_2) \\ C \cdots (n_2 < f(b, y)) \end{cases}$$

Figures 1 and 2 respectively show the number of town blocks $B(n)$ w.r.t. the crime frequency n in year 2016 and 2017. The curve in the chart represents the cumulative composition ratio.

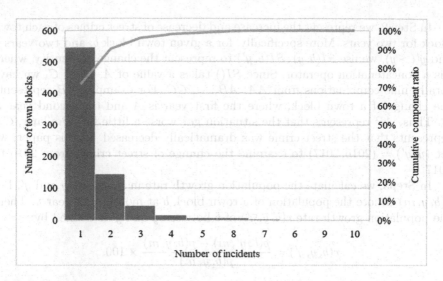

Fig. 1. Relationship between the incident frequency and the number of town blocks in Kobe in 2016

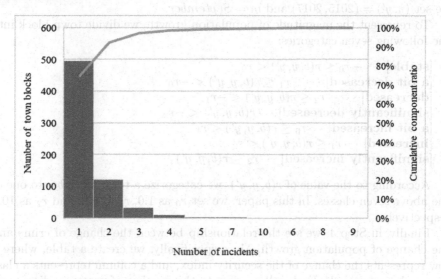

Fig. 2. Relationship between the incident frequency and the number of town blocks in Kobe in 2017

It can be seen in the figures that more than 70% town blocks with incidents has only one crimes. It is also seen that the number of town blocks exponentially decreases as the frequency increases. Based on the observation, we set $n_1 = 1$ and $n_2 = 2$. Thus, the security index divides the town blocks, where blocks with only one incident occurred in a year as A, blocks with two incidents as B, and blocks with three or more incidents as C.

In Step 2, we represent the increase and decrease of street crimes of each town block for two years. More specifically, for a given town block b, and two years y and $y'(> y)$, we use $SI(b, y) . SI(b, y')$ to represent the change of security, where . is a concatenation operator. Since $SI()$ takes a value of A, B, or C, we have totally nine combinations from AA, AB,..., CC. For example, AB represents the change of a town block, where the first year is A and the second year is B. Thus, AB represents that the situation got worse a little bit. Similarly, CA represents that the street crime was dramatically decreased. In this paper, we set $(y, y') = (2016, 2017)$ to examine the change of street crimes from 2016 to 2017.

In Step3, we calculate the population growth rate in two years y and y'. Let $p(b, y, m)$ denote the population of a town block b at month m of year y. Then, the population growth rate $r(b, y, y')$ of b between y and y' is defined by:

$$r(b, y, y') = \frac{p(b, y', m) - p(b, y, m)}{p(b, y, m)} \times 100$$

where m is a certain month. $p(b, y, m)$ and $p(b, y', m)$ can be easily obtained by $getPopulation()$ of Kobe Demographics API described in Sect. 3. In this analysis, we set $(y, y') = (2015, 2017)$ and $m = September$.

To represent the magnitude of population growth, we divide town block into the following seven categories:

- [stable] $\cdots - r_0 \leq r(b, y, y') < r_0$
- [a bit decreased] $\cdots - r_1 \leq r(b, y, y') < -r_0$
- [decreased] $\cdots - r_2 \leq r(b, y, y') < -r_1$
- [significantly decreased] $\cdots r(b, y, y') < -r_2$
- [a bit increased] $\cdots r_0 \leq r(b, y, y') < r_1$
- [increased] $\cdots r_1 \leq r(b, y, y') < r_2$
- [significantly increased] $\cdots r_2 \leq r(b, y, y')$

According to the value of $r(b, y, y')$, we categorize a town block b into one of the above seven classes. In this paper, we set r_0 as 1.0, r_1 as 5.0, and r_2 as 10.0 respectively.

Finally, in Step 4, we see the relationship between the change of crime and the change of population growth. More specifically, we create a table, where a row represents the change of the security index, and a column represents a class of population growth. Each cell represents the number of corresponding town blocks with respect to the security index and the population growth.

Table 1 summarizes the table. Rows AC, BC, AB represent the city blocks where the number of crimes increased from 2016 to 2017. Rows CC, BB, AA represent city blocks where the situations did not change. Rows BA, CB, CA represent city blocks where the number of crime decreased. From the table, the following facts can be observed:

- The number of town blocks belonging to BA, CB, CA is larger than the number of those belonging to AC, BC, AB. This indicates that the total number of recognized crimes decreased from 2016 to 2017.

Table 1. Relationship between change of the security index and the population growth

	Significantly decreased	Decreased	A bit decreased	Stable	A bit increased	Increased	Significantly increased
AC	0	2	2	0	2	0	0
BC	0	0	1	0	1	0	0
AB	2	9	43	4	23	7	6
CC	1	0	4	2	1	1	1
BB	0	2	3	1	6	4	1
AA	17	65	233	62	125	45	24
BA	5	8	38	10	26	8	5
CB	1	1	7	3	1	1	2
CA	0	2	18	5	8	2	3

- The number of town blocks with AA is large. It means that in a city block where the crimes rarely occurred in the previous year, the crimes rarely occur in the next year.
- In the town blocks where the population significantly increased (see the last column), the number of town blocks where crimes decreased is larger than those of increased.

4.2 Analyzing Relationship Between Population Size and Street Crime in Town Blocks

In order to answer RQ2, we analyze the relationship between the street crimes and population size for every town block in Kobe city. The procedure of the analysis consists of the following steps:

- **Step 1:** Calculate the security index of each town block in Kobe city
- **Step 2:** Look up the increase and decrease of street crimes within each town block between two years
- **Step 3:** Examine the population of each town block at a certain period
- **Step 4:** Analyze the relation between crimes and the population

Step 1 and Step 2 are same as Sect. 4.1. We calculate the security index of each town block in Kobe city, and represent changes in the security index by two letters of the alphabet.

In Step 3, we examine the population of each town block at month m of year y. Let $p(b, y, m)$ denote the population of a town block b at month m of year y. $p(b, y, m)$ can be easily obtained by *getPopulation*() of Kobe Demographics API described in Sect. 3. In this analysis, we set $y = 2017$ and $m = September$. Moreover, we divide town blocks into the following three categories:

- [large population] $\cdots p_0 \leq p(b, y, m)$
- [middle population] $\cdots p_1 \leq p(b, y, m) < p_0$
- [small population] $\cdots p(b, y, m) < p_1$

According to the value of $p(b, y, m)$, we categorize a town block b into one of the above three classes. In this paper, we set p_0 as 514, p_1 as 187 so that the number of town blocks included in the three classes becomes same.

Finally, in Step 4, we see the relationship between the change of crime and the population. In the same way as Sect. 4.1, we create a table, where a row represents the change of the security index, and a column represents a class of population. Each cell represents the number of corresponding town blocks with respect to the security index and the population. Table 2 summarizes the table.

Table 2. Relationship between security index and population in town blocks

	Large population	Middle population	Small population
AC	6	0	0
BC	1	0	2
AB	52	30	14
CC	6	0	3
BB	12	4	1
AA	293	186	99
BA	63	26	12
CB	9	4	2
CA	28	9	2

From the table, the following facts are observed:

- Overall, more town blocks with large population appear in the table than town blocks with small population. It turns out that crimes rarely occur in town blocks with small population.
- In town blocks with large population, there are more town blocks belongings to BA, CB, CA than AC, BC, AB.
- All of town blocks belongings to AC have large population.

4.3 Analyzing Distributed and Related Among Micro Town Blocks About Street Crimes

We think about RQ3 mentioned in Sect. 1. In order to answer to RQ3, we develop a system that divides Hyogo Prefecture into mesh-like areas and visualizes based on the frequency of street crimes in the area. We show a screenshot of the system in Fig. 3.

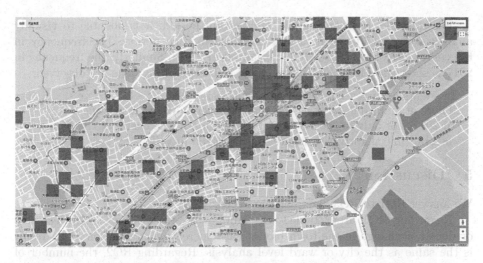

Fig. 3. A screenshot of prototype tool; showing occurrence of street crimes in Kobe area, since 2016-01-01 until 2016-12-31 (Color figure online)

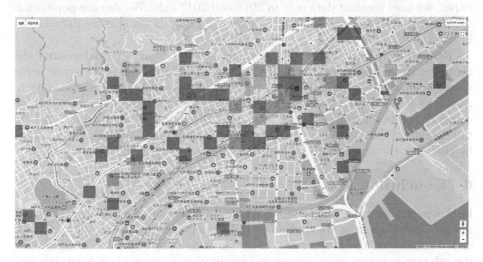

Fig. 4. Showing occurrence of street crimes in Kobe area, since 2016-01-01 until 2016-12-31 (Color figure online)

We explain the flow of visualization by the system. First, the system divides Hyogo Prefecture into mesh-like areas and counts the number of incident within each area. Next, the system colors each area with 10 colors according to the frequency. The area displayed in deep red has the high frequency in Fig. 3. The number of incident decreases in the order that the color changes to orange, yellow, yellowish green, and green. Incidents hardly occur in the uncolored areas. In the system, the user can specify aggregation period of the incident and the length of the side of areas.

For example, by changing the aggregation period, it is possible to visually analyze where incidents frequently occurred in each period. The frequency in the center of Kobe city in 2016 is visualized in Fig. 3. Similarly, the frequency in 2017 is shown in Fig. 4. From Figs. 3 and 4, the following facts are observed:

- Incidents occurred intensively in one area in 2016
- There are multiple areas where many incidents occurred in 2017
- In 2017, not only in the vicinity of the station in the center of the figure, but also in some slightly distant areas are colored in yellow.

5   Discussion

We answer RQ1 to RQ3 mentioned in Sect. 1.

Regarding RQ1, from Table 1, the number of street crimes often decreases or does not change in the town blocks with increasing population. This result is the same as the city or ward level analysis. Regarding RQ2, the number of street crimes has a tendency to decrease in the streets with large population from Table 2. It is the opposite result to RQ2. In analysis we conducted in this paper, we used incident data only in 2016 and 2017 only. We also use population data in two years. We would like to consider analysis using more data in the future.

Regarding RQ3, it is found that many street crimes occurred around the central station from Figs. 3 and 4. On the other hand, there are a few areas where many street crimes occurred even if the area is a little far from the station. Also, the location where many incidents occurred are quite different when we compare the two figures. However, we also used data only in 2016 and 2017 in this analysis. Therefore, it is necessary to use more data and conduct analysis by changing the aggregation period in the future.

6   Conclusion

In this paper, we analyzed the street crimes from a micro viewpoint by integrating incident data from Hyogo Prefectural Police and population data of Kobe city. Focusing on the number of street crimes in 2016 and 2017, we examined the relation between street crimes and population in town block level. We also develop a system that divides the area into mesh-like areas and visualizes the frequency of street crimes. Analyzing the street crimes from a micro viewpoint, a local government can take precise policy actions. A police department can also benefit the micro-level analysis for efficient patrolling within the area.

We used incident data and population data for two years at this time. We plan to conduct analysis using more data as a future work.

Acknowledgements. This research was partially supported by the Japan Ministry of Education, Science, Sports, and Culture [Grant-in-Aid for Scientific Research (B) (16H02908, 15H02701), Grant-in-Aid for Scientific Research (A) (17H00731), Challenging Exploratory Research (15K12020)], and Tateishi Science and Technology Foundation (C) (No.2177004).

References

1. RESAS: regonal economy society analyzing system. https://resas.go.jp
2. Hipp, J.R., Kane, K.: Cities and the larger context: what explains changing levels of crime? J. Crim. Justice **49**, 32–44 (2017). http://www.sciencedirect.com/science/article/pii/S004723521630160X
3. Kagawa, T., Saiki, S., Nakamura, M.: Developing personalized security information service using open data. In: 18th IEEE/ACIS International Conference on Software Engineering, Artificial Intelligence, Networking and Parallel/Distributed Computing (SNPD 2017), pp. 465–470, No. CFP1779A-USB, kanazawa, Japan. IEEE Computer Society and International Association for Computer and Information Science (ACIS), 2017 June
4. Kester, Q.: Visualization and analysis of geographical crime patterns using formal concept analysis. CoRR abs/1307.8112 (2013). http://arxiv.org/abs/1307.8112
5. Kobe City: Open Data Kobe (2017). https://data.city.kobe.lg.jp/
6. Molloy, J.C.: The open knowledge foundation: open data means better science. PLoS Biol. **9**(12), 1–4 (2011). https://doi.org/10.1371/journal.pbio.1001195
7. Morenoff, J.D., Sampson, R.J.: Violent crime and the spatial dynamics of neighborhood transition: Chicago, 1970–1990. Soc. Forces **76**(1), 31–64 (1997). https://doi.org/10.1093/sf/76.1.31
8. Roncek, D.W.: Dangerous places: crime and residential environment. Soc. Forces **60**(1), 74–96 (1981). https://doi.org/10.1093/sf/60.1.74
9. Stults, B.J., Hasbrouck, M.: The effect of commuting on city-level crime rates. J. Quant. Criminol. **31**(2), 331–350 (2015). https://doi.org/10.1007/s10940-015-9251-z
10. Vollmann, T.: Manufacturing Planning and Control Systems for Supply Chain Management: The Definitive Guide for Professionals. The McGraw-Hill/Irwin series in operations and decision sciences. McGraw-Hill Education, New York (2005). https://books.google.co.jp/books?id=1HrwqYad2WMC

Factors that Drive Successful Electronic Health Record Implementation Among Aging Nurses

Candice Mullings[1(✉)] and Ojelanki Ngwenyama[2(✉)]

[1] Ryerson University, Toronto, Canada
cmulling@ryerson.ca
[2] University of Cape Town, Cape Town, South Africa
ojelanki@ryerson.ca

Abstract. Objective: The purpose of this study is to identify the factors that drive EHR acceptance among nurses aged 55 years and older.

Design: A Technology Acceptance Model (TAM) based questionnaire was administered to the nursing staff of a Canadian healthcare facility that had adopted a new EHR system three years prior.

Results: A total of 126 nurses completed the survey (28% response rate). Using partial least squares analysis and multi-group comparison analysis, significant differences were found in acceptance factors among various age groups. The most significant factors for nurses 55+ were the subjective norms within the organization, the image/status the system could bring to the worker, and the perceived ease of use of the system.

Conclusions: To better tailor future EHR implementations to the increasing number of older nurses in the workforce, managers must: display clear support for the system themselves, as well as underscore the ease of the system and the status it can bring to the worker within the organization.

Keywords: Aging workforce · Electronic health records · Nursing Healthcare

1 Introduction

The consequences of Canada's aging population are numerous, not the least of which is the aging of Canada's workforce. Though the amount of workers aged 55 and older decreased steadily from 1976 to 1997, the trend has reversed sharply with their employment rate climbing from 22% in 1997 to 41.9% in 2017 [1, 2]. The reasons for this are varied, ranging from an increase in life expectancy and the amount of good-health years later in life, to the economic pressures of rising consumer and housing debt, as well as higher costs of living.

As companies seek to upgrade work processes with new technologies, the demographic composition of their staff will become an increasingly important issue. The difficulties of large-scale organizational change are well documented and the failure rates for major IS systems implementation averages around 70% [3]. The successful introduction of a new technology within an organization relies heavily on its acceptance among the workers and users themselves [4–6], and with such a significant

© Springer International Publishing AG, part of Springer Nature 2018
F. F.-H. Nah and B. S. Xiao (Eds.): HCIBGO 2018, LNCS 10923, pp. 626–644, 2018.
https://doi.org/10.1007/978-3-319-91716-0_50

amount of older workers in the workplace, special attention must be paid to how new technologies are best introduced to this segment of the workforce.

The use of new technologies is increasing rapidly in many sectors, though there has been a notable lag within Canada's healthcare industry, particularly in the area of electronic health record adoption. Currently, 78% of general practitioners use electronic health records and this rate drops to a disappointing 21% when considering only EHR systems with basic meaningful use functionalities, such as allowing for the exchange of health information with other providers, generating patient information, and providing routine decision support [7]. Clearly, there is still much work to be done in order to implement EHRs in facilities that do not yet use it and upgrade existing systems in those organizations that do not have the system functionalities to fully realize the benefits EHRs can provide. Both of these tasks required well-planned implementation techniques, tailored to the needs of the daily users, to be successful.

2   Literature Review

2.1   Measuring Implementation Success

Research has sought to better understand the factors driving technology implementation success through analyzing user satisfaction, professional identity, and user acceptance (see Table 1). User satisfaction is seen as an important aspect of EHR implementation and according to this theory, satisfied users are more likely to accept and use the technology as intended. When reviewing studies on user satisfaction, the positive or negative effects on satisfaction were most often tied to system functionalities. Lee et al. [8] designed a survey to assess user satisfaction of a newly implemented physician order entry system among physicians and nurses at a women's hospital. Efficiency was found to be the most influential factor, taking precedence over improvements in patient care [8]. Although, physicians reported greater satisfaction than nurses, revealing that there are significant differences between the two groups of users that must be addressed [8]. Lee et al. [8] also acknowledged the fact that the manner in which the technology was introduced also affected satisfaction. Clinical leadership, staff involvement, and customization to user needs were found to have a positive impact on user satisfaction [8].

Goorman and Berg [9] used observation and in-depth interviews to discover that the compatibility of a new health information system with current work processes was also an important aspect of user satisfaction. If the functionality of the system did not match with current process or if workflows were not adequately modified to suit the new system during implementation, satisfaction was very difficult to achieve [9]. Lee et al. [10] built on the theory of functionality being closely linked with user satisfaction by studying a group of intensive care nurses in Taiwan. Through staff interviews, Lee et al. [10] confirmed that efficiencies in information entry and paper consumption lead to user satisfaction, while slow information retrieval and lack of workload alleviation were found to lead to user dissatisfaction [10]. Likourezos et al. [11] also identified efficiency as a main driver in satisfaction. The improved entering and accessing of data EHR systems facilitated proved to be significant in the emergency setting and so resulted in high levels of user satisfaction [11].

Table 1. Healthcare technology implementation research from the individual perspective

Focus of study	Method of data collection	Method of data analysis	Citations
User satisfaction	Interviews and observations	Qualitative analysis	[9]
User satisfaction	Interviews	Qualitative analysis	[10]
User satisfaction	Survey questionnaire	Regression analysis	[11]
User satisfaction and usage patterns	Survey questionnaire	Regression analysis	[8]
Professional identity	Observation	Qualitative analysis	[12]
Professional identity	Interviews and observation	Qualitative analysis	[13]
User acceptance	Survey questionnaire	Regression analysis	[14]
User acceptance	Survey questionnaire	Regression analysis	[15]
User acceptance	Literature review	Qualitative analysis	[16]
User acceptance	Survey questionnaire	Regression analysis	[17]

While system functionality is undeniably important in the acceptance of health care technology, the above user satisfaction research overlooks the effect social constructions, such as professional identity, can have on acceptance. Prasad [12] explored the relationship between new technology in the healthcare sector and professional identity through the lens of symbolic interaction. According to Prasad, technology could take on meanings and become symbols of concepts and perspectives through the social interaction of those who used it [12]. The computerization of work within an American HMO studied by Prasad took on the meaning of professionalism for both physicians and nurses [12]. These healthcare providers felt their professionalism was validated through their work with computers and felt pride as well as a sense of increased organizational status as a result [12]. Prasad demonstrated that when new technologies became a symbol for social constructions that were important to the user, such as professionalism and status, acceptance became easier to achieve. Apesoa-Varano also explored the idea of professional identity among nurses, noting that historically, upgrades in skills and technical knowledge were often sought by the nursing profession in order to legitimize their status within the health care sector [13]. Since education and technological skill were seen as symbols of professionalism, nurses used them as tools to bring legitimacy to their occupation and increase their status within the organization. Quantitative measurement of exactly how much this process impacted nurse acceptance of new technologies, however, remained to be studied.

2.2 Targeting Further Understanding

Past research surrounding electronic health record implementation is abundant though incomplete. Earlier studies regarding the introduction of EHRs focused first on its benefits and how to best increase adoption rates [18–24]. Research addressing the processes and factors affecting implementation itself, while present, has had a narrow scope with little focus on the effect user age would have on acceptance. Furthermore, the majority of research on this subject addresses primarily physician acceptance and takes place within acute care settings or private clinics [9–11, 14, 25–28]. With the large role senior health care will play in the near future, studies that can establish EHR implementation best practices for long-term care facilities are needed.

Furthermore, the important user population of nurses has yet to be sufficiently addressed. Nurses are vital in all healthcare settings, often outnumbering other healthcare professionals. This is especially true in the field of long-term care, where patients and residents interact most with nursing staff. It is also important to note that 42% of all regulated nurses in Canada are over the age of 50, with 28% being 55 years of age or older [29]. In order to effectively introduce EHR systems, the factors that drive electronic health record acceptance among older nurses must be identified.

This research seeks to identify the factors necessary for the successful implementation of electronic health records among older nurses in health care facilities. Though electronic health record systems were introduced more than a decade ago, many facilities still face considerable challenges implementing them. Evidence of these challenges can be seen in the slow and incomplete adoption of EHR systems in North America and Canada especially. As the nursing workforce ages, these challenges become more varied, differing across age groups. By identifying predictive factors in EHR adoption and analyzing any changes in their significance among these groups, this research can help health care organizations tailor their implementation efforts effectively to their older nursing staff.

3   Method

This research used a hypothetico-deductive approach to investigate the user acceptance of an EHR system implemented in a long-term care facility. This study employed a modified version of the Technology Acceptance Model (TAM) questionnaire survey to collect empirical observations and the partial least squares method for its analysis.

3.1   Research Model

TAM has proven to be an effective model for examining technology acceptance within the workplace and the extended TAM2 model provided the framework necessary to better understand the more specific influences on this acceptance. Therefore, based on the goal of this study, a slightly modified TAM2 was chosen as the research model and can be seen in the Fig. 1 below. Within this framework, the variable of perceived usefulness is the measure of user acceptance. The determinants to be tested included experience, subjective norm, image, job relevance, output quality, result demonstrability, perceived usefulness, and perceived ease of use. For the purpose of this study, three factors present within the original TAM2 framework were excluded in the final research model: voluntariness, intention to use, and usage behaviour. Voluntariness was excluded, as the EHR system to be evaluated was not voluntary. For similar reasons, intention to use was also removed as all nurses must use and intend to use the

EHR system in the course of their patient care. As voluntariness and intention to use were inputs required to measure usage behaviour, this factor was excluded as well.

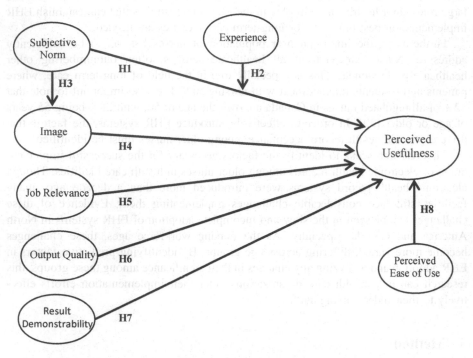

Fig. 1. Research model

3.2   Hypotheses

Based on the research model above, the following hypotheses were formulated: *Subjective norm* is a factor that was originally present in the Theory of Reasoned Action (TRA) and is defined as a "person's perception that most people who are important to him think he should or should not perform the behaviour in question" [30]. Within the workplace setting, this subjective norm can be viewed as the opinions of both management/superiors and peers towards the technology. The effect of subjective norm on technology acceptance has varied; with Mathieson [31] finding that subjective norm had no significant effect on usage, while others such as Taylor and Todd [32], Venkatesh and Davis [33], and Wu et al. [34] found that subjective norm did have significant effects. Though excluded from the original TAM model, Davis [35] stated that subjective norm could be more influential in settings where a system's use is mandatory. Users would feel compelled to use a system as result of managerial expectations as opposed to individual beliefs towards a system [35]. Electronic health records are often an organization-wide update in documentation processes and as a result subjective norm becomes an important variable to examine.

H1. Subjective norm will be positively associated with perceived usefulness.

Experience is defined as user history and interaction with the technology. Fuerst and Cheney [36] identified computer experience as a variable in the usage of information systems. Hartwick and Barki [37] continued with this concept stating that testing the effects of experience on IS use is an important subject of future study. Hartwick and Barki [37] theorized that the less experience a user had with a system, the more that user would rely on the opinions of others. Venkatesh and Davis [33] built on this view, concluding that experience would have a significant effect on the influence of subjective norm. The more experience one had with a system, the less subjective norm could influence one's perceptions [33] and the less experience one had, the more important subjective norm would become.

H2. Experience will moderate the influence of subjective norm on perceived usefulness.

While studying the factors affecting the diffusion of innovations, Rogers [38] stated that, "undoubtedly one of the most important motivations for almost any individual to adopt an innovation is the desire to gain social status." This motivation can readily be applied to the acceptance of new technology within the workplace. In the context of this research, *image* is defined as, "the degree to which use of an innovation is perceived to enhance one's ... status in one's social system" [39]. The importance of image in a healthcare setting was presented by Prasad [12] in her observations of HMO employees. New technology knowledge came to represent an increase in professional status, leading workers to more readily accept and learn new technologies in order to gain status within the organization. Therefore, the image of an EHR system should have a significant effect on how useful it is perceived to be. Additionally, the social nature of image suggests there is a close relationship with subjective norm and so the effect of subject norm on image is also the subject of further investigation.

H3. Subjective norm will be positively associated with image.
H4. Image will be positively associated with perceived usefulness.

The next three variables of job relevance, output quality, and result demonstrability focus on the instrumental rather than social characteristics of a new system. Bailey and Pearson [40] established that relevancy was one of the most important factors in determining user satisfaction. The more relevant the system to the task, the more positive the reaction to its use [40]. Even the most impressive functionalities are at best meaningless and at worst burdensome if it is not appropriate for a given task. Therefore, the more relevant a system is to the job, the more likely it will be viewed as useful and ultimately accepted by the user. The effects of output quality on technology acceptance in the workplace have been the subject of several research studies [4, 41–43]. Davis [4] examined output quality's effect on perceived usefulness and found it to be significant, though moderated by its task importance. Therefore, the higher the quality of the system output, the more useful the system is perceived to be. Lastly, result demonstrability is defined as, "tangibility of the results of using the innovation" [39]. New systems are most often introduced as a means to improve job/task performance. Should these improvements not present themselves in the course of the system's use, the perception of usefulness will most likely decrease. Agarwal and Prasad [44] and Mun et al. [45] both found evidence that result demonstrability was a significant determinant of perceived ease of use, concluding that a system's benefits must not just be talked about but readily identifiable to the user.

H5. Job relevance will be positively associated with perceived usefulness.

H6. Output quality will be positively associated with perceived usefulness.

H7. Result demonstrability will be positively associated with perceived usefulness.

Evidence of the effect of perceived ease of use on perceived usefulness has been well documented in a variety of studies [4, 6, 35, 46–49]. Not surprisingly, the easier a system is to use, the more useful it is perceived to be.

H8. Perceived ease of use will be positively associated with perceived usefulness.

3.3 Subject Selection

As the target population of this research is long-term care nursing staff, sample subjects chosen for this study were employees of a Canadian long-term care facility. At the time of study, the electronic health record system implementation had occurred three years prior. To test the proposed model hypotheses outlined above, data was collected through a program-wide questionnaire. Nursing staff members present during the implementation of the electronic health care system were eligible to participate. As the goal of this research is to highlight the needs of older nurses, nurses of all ages were invited to complete the survey in order to facilitate age comparisons.

3.4 Questionnaire Design

The survey created was composed of two distinct sections. The first consisted of questions relating directly to the constructs outlined in the research model. The validated Venkatesh and Davis [33] TAM2 survey questions were used as the basis of this questionnaire. The responses were measured on a 7-point Likert scale. The second section of the questionnaire reflected important demographic information relating to job status, job title, age, and experience that could then be used to compare survey results of various sub-groups within the sample. A copy of the questionnaire as well as the theoretical mapping of the questions can be found in the appendix.

3.5 Data Collection and Analysis

In order to collect the data necessary through questionnaires, voluntary sampling was used. The questionnaire was made available to all nursing staff both electronically through email and as hard copies from June 1st to July 3rd, 2014. A total of 126 completed questionnaires were submitted, resulting in a 28% response rate. The following chart details the descriptive statistics of the sample (Table 2).

Table 2. Descriptive statistics of sample

Demographic	Category	N	Percent
Job title	Registered Nurse (RN)	53	42%
	Registered Practical Nurse (RPN)	73	58%
Job status	Full-time	84	67%
	Part-time	42	33%
Age range	24–34 years old	16	13%
	35–54 years old	86	68%
	55+ years old	24	19%
Years of experience	3–5 years	31	25%
	5–10 years	29	23%
	10–20 years	35	28%
	20+ years	31	25%
Questionnaire version	Hard copy	67	53%
	Electronic copy	59	47%
Gender	Female	113	90%
	Male	13	10%

Analysis of the sample questionnaire data was done in four steps outlined below.

Step 1: Preliminary Review & Confirmatory Factor Analysis

After preliminary evaluation of the data collected, the overview of the sample and construct statistics were the following (Table 3):

Table 3. Sample mean and t-value statistics. *$p < 0.01$

Construct	Item	Weight	Mean	Standard error	T-value
Perceived usefulness	PUF1	0.341	4.937	0.012	27.419*
	PUF2	0.363	4.802	0.013	28.072*
	PUF3	0.398	5.556	0.033	12.222*
Perceived ease of use	PEU1	0.378	5.365	0.035	10.737*
	PEU2	0.347	5.556	0.027	13.098*
	PEU3	0.399	5.214	0.044	8.900*
Subjective norm	SN1	0.302	4.944	0.064	4.622*
	SN2	0.223	6.151	0.064	3.501*
	SN3	0.306	5.627	0.061	5.137*
	SN4	0.470	5.040	0.071	6.693*
Image	IM1	0.431	4.032	0.033	13.087*
	IM2	0.349	4.048	0.036	9.421*
	IM3	0.314	4.389	0.051	6.364*
Job relevance	JR1	0.404	6.325	0.043	9.305*
	JR2	0.314	6.135	0.034	9.309*
	JR3	0.401	5.937	0.058	6.917*
Output quality	OQ1	0.586	5.754	0.041	14.314*
	OQ2	0.462	5.571	0.035	13.257*
Result demonstrability	RD1	−0.174	5.587	0.533	1.019
	RD2	0.385	2.984	0.592	1.197
Experience	EX1	0.398	5.675	0.165	2.503
	EX2	0.565	5.683	0.163	3.548*
	EX3	0.263	3.571	0.220	1.288

After initial review of the sample statistics, formative construct validity could be assessed. Constructs result demonstrability as well as experience presented high standard error levels and low t-statistic values. The t-values indicate the significance of the difference between means, with statistical significance increasing the higher the t-value becomes. Those t-values over 2.58 are considered significant with a 99% confidence level. The low t-values of result demonstrability and experience indicated that these items were not measuring as significant, especially when compared to the other constructs of perceived usefulness, perceived ease of use, subjective norm, image, job relevance, and output quality.

To further examine the sample data, confirmatory factor analysis was conducted. The resulting cross-loadings of the factors can be seen below (Table 4). When assessing these factors, values above 0.6 are considered high and those below 0.4 considered low [50]. The high loadings of the factors within their own construct suggested the measurements fit the theoretical model well.

After this initial analysis, the partial least squares (PLS) method was used to further analyze the data collected.

Table 4. Construct cross-loadings

Item	Perceived usefulness	Perceived ease of use	Subjective norm	Image	Job relevance	Output quality	Result demonstrability	Experience
PUF1	**0.940**	0.474	0.627	0.378	0.446	0.500	−0.393	0.275
PUF2	**0.933**	0.486	0.618	0.397	0.495	0.572	−0.437	0.276
PUF3	**0.857**	0.532	0.537	0.436	0.602	0.625	−0.503	0.241
PEU1	0.495	**0.867**	0.574	0.206	0.561	0.514	−0.412	0.339
PEU2	0.455	**0.928**	0.579	0.238	0.478	0.502	−0.440	0.430
PEU3	0.517	**0.881**	0.559	0.254	0.456	0.552	−0.589	0.294
SN1	0.576	0.477	**0.675**	0.307	0.273	0.345	−0.347	0.234
SN2	0.386	0.695	**0.718**	0.230	0.515	0.449	−0.441	0.313
SN3	0.443	0.383	**0.759**	0.321	0.473	0.463	−0.336	0.196
SN4	0.538	0.471	**0.847**	0.488	0.556	0.600	−0.379	0.403
IM1	0.474	0.295	0.495	**0.940**	0.319	0.414	−0.300	0.220
IM2	0.377	0.244	0.400	**0.928**	0.297	0.383	−0.195	0.258
IM3	0.353	0.158	0.384	**0.858**	0.262	0.377	−0.299	0.074
JR1	0.545	0.566	0.578	0.294	**0.917**	0.733	−0.547	0.526
JR2	0.435	0.497	0.495	0.252	**0.889**	0.734	−0.552	0.434
JR3	0.544	0.439	0.548	0.315	**0.879**	0.801	−0.581	0.433
OQ1	0.658	0.572	0.662	0.469	0.835	**0.963**	−0.652	0.420
OQ2	0.527	0.546	0.530	0.340	0.773	**0.942**	−0.631	0.372
RD1	0.336	0.476	0.414	0.319	0.680	0.719	**−0.730**	0.269
RD2	−0.439	−0.401	−0.369	−0.169	−0.363	−0.400	**0.852**	−0.096
EX1	0.204	0.144	0.251	0.041	0.366	0.189	−0.054	**0.753**
EX2	0.287	0.475	0.431	0.258	0.538	0.503	−0.341	**0.868**
EX3	0.141	0.214	0.137	0.142	0.209	0.172	0.019	**0.663**

Step 2: Reliability Analysis

In this step, the reliability of the proposed construct measurements was determined. All the constructs within this study were tested for its Cronbach alpha value. Cronbach's alpha is continually used in statistical research as an index of reliability, with higher values being viewed as more reliable [51]. Acceptable values for the alpha threshold can vary from 0.7 to 0.95 [51]. For the purposes of this study, the constructs that resulted in values greater than 0.7 were considered a reliable measurement. Those constructs that resulted in Cronbach α values of less than 0.7 were omitted from further consideration. As can be seen below, experience failed to meet the criteria of reliability and was therefore excluded from further analysis (Table 5).

Table 5. Latent variable reliability

Construct	Cronbach alpha
Experience*	0.659
Image	0.895
Job Relevance	0.876
Output Quality	0.900
Perceived Ease of Use	0.871
Perceived Usefulness	0.897
Result Demonstrability	0.715
Subjective Norm	0.752

Step 3: Construct Validation

This step was used to validate the constructs of this study using convergent and discriminant validity. To establish convergent validity both composite reliability and average variance extracted (AVE) were analyzed. Those constructs with an AVE value greater than 0.5 and with a composite reliability reading greater than 0.7 demonstrated acceptable convergent validity and were included in further analysis. As result demonstrability did not meet the convergent validity threshold, it was omitted from further consideration. The results of this process can be seen below (Table 6).

Table 6. Latent variable parameters

Construct	Composite reliability	AVE
Image (IM)	0.9346	0.8268
Job Relevance (JR)	0.923	0.801
Output Quality (OQ)	0.952	0.908
Perceived Ease of Use (PEU)	0.921	0.796
Perceived Usefulness (PUF)	0.936	0.829
Result Demonstrability (RD)*	0.019	0.629
Subjective Norm (SN)	0.838	0.566

Discriminant validity was determined by evaluating whether or not an item loaded most heavily on its own construct. The items that met this condition were used in further analysis. The items that did not were omitted from further consideration. The results of this analysis are shown in Table 7 below. As all constructs that remained loaded most heavily within its own category, the validity of all remaining latent variables was confirmed.

Table 7. Latent variable correlations

	IM	JR	OQ	PEU	PUF	SN
IM	1.000					
JR	0.323	1.000				
OQ	0.431	0.846	1.000			
PEU	0.261	0.560	0.588	1.000		
PUF	0.447	0.573	0.628	0.551	1.000	
SN	0.474	0.607	0.632	0.640	0.651	1.000

4   Results

4.1   Sample Group Results

The PLS analysis of the five remaining latent variables (perceived ease of use, subjective norm, image, job relevance, output quality) resulted in an R^2 of 0.487. This indicated that 49% of the variance present in perceived usefulness can be explained by the five predictive variables within the model. The results of this analysis can be seen in the Fig. 2 below.

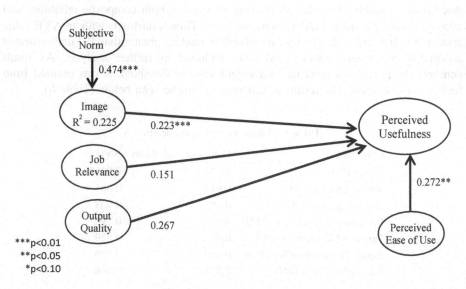

Fig. 2. Results of PLS model

Though nearly half of the variance in perceived usefulness can be explained by these variables, some were significant in their influence while others were not. The results of this analysis revealed that for all employees sampled only Hypotheses 3, 4, and 8 were adequately supported. Subjective norm was highly significant in determining image at a 99% confidence level. A positive subjective norm had a positive influence on image, supporting H3. Image itself was also highly significant in determining perceived usefulness at a confidence level of 99%. A positive image was shown to have a positive effect on perceived usefulness, supporting H4. Finally, perceived ease of use also proved to be a predictor of perceived usefulness at a 95% confidence level. Positive perceived ease of use had a positive effect on perceived usefulness, supporting H8. However, there was no evidence of job relevance (H5) or output quality (H6) having a significant effect of perceived usefulness. H5 and H6 did not reach an acceptable p value of less than 0.05, and therefore could not be classified as having any significant effect, positive or negative, on perceived usefulness.

4.2 Multi-group Comparison Results

Though certain conclusions may be drawn from the analysis of the entire sample as a whole, the goal of this study is to determine the success factors for mature, experienced workers. As a result, emphasis was placed on comparisons between older and younger nurses as well as those with less experience compared to those with more. In order to do these comparisons, the Stats Tool Package created by James Gaskin was used [52]. The path coefficients of the various groups were calculated by entering individual group data into SmartPLS and creating a bootstrap report. The sample mean and standard error were then entered into the following formula to determine the t-statistic:

$$t = \frac{Path_{sample\_1} - Path_{sample\_2}}{\left[\sqrt{\frac{(m-1)^2}{(m+n-2)} * S.E._{sample1}^2 + \frac{(n-1)^2}{(m+n-2)} * S.E._{sample2}^2}\right] * \left[\sqrt{\frac{1}{m} + \frac{1}{n}}\right]}$$

That t-statistic was then converted into its 2-tailed p-value using the Excel Stat Tools Package. If the resulting p-value was less than 0.05, the difference between the groups compared was considered statistically significant considered statistically significant.

Table 8. Path coefficient comparison 1

Hypothesis	Path	Comparison 1 - age								
		25–34	35–54	P $(b^{(1)} \neq b^{(2)})$	25–34	55+	P $(b^{(1)} \neq b^{(2)})$	35–54	55+	P $(b^{(1)} \neq b^{(2)})$
H3	SN → IM	1.159	7.871	0.343	1.159	10.476	0.424	7.871	10.476	0.608
H4	IM → PUF	0.942	2.383	0.776	0.942	6.791	**0.032***	2.383	6.791	**0.007***
H5	JR → PUF	0.412	0.442	0.668	0.412	1.007	0.765	0.442	1.007	0.818
H6	OQ → PUF	2.650	1.405	0.667	2.650	2.413	0.283	1.405	2.413	0.946
H8	PEU → PUF	2.290	2.281	0.757	2.290	1.652	**0.049***	2.281	1.652	0.084

The first comparison was that of the age ranges within the sample group (Table 8). The three sub groups within this comparison were ages 25 to 34 years old, 35 to 54 years old, and 55 years or older. These ages have been grouped to closely align with generational divisions. Those aged 25 to 34 fall within the Millennial generation, those 35 to 54 within Generation X, and those over 55 within the Baby Boomer generation [53]. There was no evidence of significant path coefficient differences between 25 to 34 year olds and 35 to 54 year olds. However, there was evidence of significant differences between nurses 25 to 34 years old and those 55 and older regarding the effect of perceived ease of use (H8) and image (H4) on perceived usefulness. Perceived ease of use was found to have significantly more influence with nurses 25 to 34 years old compared to nurses 55 years old and over, while image had a significantly stronger effect on nurses 55 and older compared to those aged 25 to 34. There was also evidence of significant path coefficient differences regarding image between 35 to 54 year olds and those over 55. Once again, image had a significantly stronger effect on nurses 55 and older compared to those age 35 to 54 years old.

Table 9. Path coefficient comparison 2, part 1

Hypothesis	Path	Comparison 2 – years of nursing experience								
		3–5	5–10	P $(b^{(1)} \neq b^{(2)})$	3–5	10–20	P $(b^{(1)} \neq b^{(2)})$	3–5	20+	P $(b^{(1)} \neq b^{(2)})$
H3	SN → IM	6.397	10.685	0.857	6.397	6.542	0.964	6.397	16.127	**0.018***
H4	IM → PUF	3.669	0.812	0.311	3.669	1.909	**0.027***	3.669	4.839	0.634
H5	JR → PUF	0.677	1.544	0.796	0.677	2.867	**0.038***	0.677	1.108	0.588
H6	OQ → PUF	3.517	0.710	0.202	3.517	7.480	**0.005***	3.517	0.436	**0.044***
H8	PEU → PUF	7.217	2.282	0.222	7.217	1.383	**0.000***	7.217	5.698	0.463

Table 10. Path coefficient comparison 2, part 2

Hypothesis	Path	Comparison 2 – years of nursing experience								
		5–10	10–20	P $(b^{(1)} \neq b^{(2)})$	5–10	20+	P $(b^{(1)} \neq b^{(2)})$	10–20	20+	P $(b^{(1)} \neq b^{(2)})$
H3	SN → IM	10.685	6.542	0.822	10.685	16.127	**0.004***	6.542	16.127	**0.020***
H4	IM → PUF	0.812	1.909	0.837	0.812	4.839	0.182	1.909	4.839	**0.003***
H5	JR → PUF	1.544	2.867	0.765	1.544	1.108	0.781	2.867	1.108	**0.014***
H6	OQ → PUF	0.710	7.480	**0.001***	0.710	0.436	0.340	7.480	0.436	**0.000***
H8	PEU → PUF	2.282	1.383	**0.023***	2.282	5.698	0.115	1.383	5.698	**0.000***

The second sub group comparison conducted measured significant differences among workers with varying years of nursing experience. As nurses within the sample entered the profession at varying ages, comparing sub groups based on experience could lead to differences not present among age groups. The results of this comparison can be found above (Tables 9 and 10). There was no evidence of any significant path coefficient differences between those with 3 to 5 years experience and those with 5 to 10 years experience. However, there was evidence of significant differences between nurses with 3 to 5 years experience and those with 10 to 20 years experience concerning Hypothesis 3, 4, 5, and 8. The influence of image (H4) and perceived ease of use (H8) on perceived usefulness were significantly stronger in those nurses with 3 to 5 years experience compared to those with 10 to 20 years. The influence of job relevance (H5) and output quality (H6) on perceived usefulness, however, was significantly lower in those nurses with 3 to 5 years experience compared to those with 10 to 20 years.

There was also evidence of many significant path coefficient differences between those with 10 to 20 years experience compared to those with over 20 years experience. The path coefficients from subjective norm to image (H3), image to perceived usefulness (H4), and perceived ease of use to perceived usefulness (H8) were all significantly more influential for those with more than 20 years of experience compared to those with 10 to 20 years. The path coefficients from job relevance (H5) and output quality (H5) to perceived usefulness were significantly more influential for those with 10 to 20 years experience compared to those with over 20 years experience.

When comparing the 3 to 5 years experience sub group to the over 20 years experience sub group, there was evidence of two statistically significant path coefficient differences. The positive influence of subjective norm on image (H3) was significantly higher with those having over 20 years experience compared with nurses who had 3 to 5 years experience, while the positive effect of output quality (H6) was significantly stronger for those with 3 to 5 years experience compared to nurses with over 20.

There was evidence of only two significant differences between nurses with 5 to 10 years experience and nurses with 10 to 20 years. The path of output quality to perceived usefulness (H6) was significantly more influential for nurses with 10 to 20 years experience compared to those with 5 to 10. However, the positive effect of perceived ease of use on perceived usefulness (H8) was significantly stronger for nurses with 5 to 10 years experience compared to 10 to 20 years.

Nurses with 5 to 10 years experience compared to those with over 20 showed evidence of significant differences regarding the path coefficients of subjective norm to image (H3). The effect of subject norm on image was significantly stronger among nurses with over 20 years experience compared to those with only 5 to 10 years experience.

The differences between the various age groups and levels of experience revealed that not only is it important to examine nurses separately from the larger group of clinicians, but also that there are significant differences among the nurse population itself that must be considered in order to effectively introduce new systems to older employees.

5   Discussion and Conclusions

The goal of this research study was to identify the factors that best predicted the successful adoption of an electronic health record system among older nurses within a long-term care facility. After analyzing the group sampled as a whole and then comparing various age groups, this study did reveal significant differences. The influence of image is significantly higher in the 55 and over age group compared to the other age groupings. This suggests that as nurses age, their professional identity and status begin to matter more. Older nurses hold their professional status within the organization in high regard and are, as a result, willing to more readily accept the introduction of new technology in order to secure and elevate this status.

The comparison of years of experience also resulted in significant differences. Image was significantly influential to those with the least experience as well as to those with the most, suggesting professional status was more important to nurses toward the beginning and end of their careers. While nurses in the beginning of their careers sought to establish their professional identities through acquiring technical knowledge, those towards the end of their careers sought to increase and secure the status they had already earned. Organizations can therefore call particular attention to the status benefits of the EHR system in question among older workers to facilitate their acceptance and support. The importance of subjective norm was also significantly higher in nurses with over 20 years experience compared to those with less, indicating that highly experienced workers also require strong leadership and support of their superiors to encourage the successful adoption of a new system.

The effect of perceived ease of use was also significantly different among various experience levels. Once again, nurses with the most experience as well as those with the least experience were influenced the most by ease of use. Older nurses reported having less experience with computer programs and this lack of experience can often lead to resistance in using newly implemented systems. These survey responses suggest, for nurses 55 and over, it is the lack of experience with computer programs that makes perceived ease of use so influential. The easier the program is to use, the more comfortable older nurses will feel using it, and the more likely they are to accept it in their well-established nursing routine.

Many health care facilities have recognized the benefits of electronic health record systems but the transition to such systems remains slow to such systems remains slow for some. Implementing new technologies in organizations as large and complex as long-term care facilities can be challenging, however this study has revealed that using subjective norms, image, and perceived ease of use as tools during implementation can greatly increase the likelihood of successful adoption among the increasing number of mature and experienced nurses in the health care system.

6   Limitations

Though it is believed the results of this study can make a significant contribution to the senior health care field, the conclusions may not be applicable to all long-term care facilities as a result of this study's inductive structure. The primary research is limited to one long-term care facility and there is a possibility that it is not representative of all the long-term care facilities across the province and country. Ideally, there will be an opportunity to conduct similar research in other facilities and verify these findings.

In terms of data collection, the risk of response bias – such as having a certain type of nurse be more likely to respond – is always present. There is also room for error in the interpretation of the survey as the responses available were limited, there was little opportunity to expand on answers, and respondents may have misunderstood the questions posed.

Appendix

TAM2 Theoretical Constructs and Mapping to Questionnaire

Construct	#	Code	Question
Intention to use	1.	INT1	Assuming I have access to the EHR system, I intend to use it
Perceived usefulness	2.	PUF1	Using the EHR system improves my performance in my job
	3.	PUF2	Using the system in my job increase my productivity
	4.	PUF3	I find the EHR system to be useful in my job
Perceived ease of use	5.	PEU1	My interaction with the EHR system is clear and understandable
	6.	PEU2	I find the EHR system to be easy to use
	7.	PEU3	I find it easy to get the system to do what I want it to do
Subjective norm	8.	SN1	People who are important to me think that I should use the EHR system
	9.	SN2	My managers/supervisors were supportive of the introduction of the EHR system
	10.	SN3	During its introduction, there was a PCC "champion" available to answer my questions about the features and use of the EHR system
	11.	SN4	My fellow nurses were enthusiastic during the introduction of the EHR system
Voluntariness	12.	VOL1	My use of the EHR system is voluntary
Image	13.	IM1	People in my organization/industry who use electronic health record systems have more prestige than those who do not
	14.	IM2	People in my organization/industry who use electronic health records systems have a high profile
	15.	IM3	Having the EHR system is a status symbol in my organization/industry
Job relevance	16.	JR1	In my job, usage of the EHR system is important
	17.	JR2	In my job, usage of the EHR system is relevant
	18.	JR3	I believe that the EHR system was a necessary update to paper charting
Output quality	19.	OQ1	The quality of the output I get from the EHR system is high
	20.	OQ2	I have no problem with the quality of the EHR system's output
Result demonstrability	21.	RD1	I have no difficulty telling others about the results of using the EHR system
	22.	RD2	I would have difficulty explaining why using the EHR system may be beneficial

(continued)

(continued)

Construct	#	Code	Question
Experience	23.	EX1	I have had previous experience with computers/computer programs during the course of my employment
	24.	EX2	I am very comfortable using new computer programs
	25.	EX3	I have used other electronic health record systems with other departments/employers
Demo-graphics	26.	DEM	___ Female ___ Male
	27.	DEM	Employee status (please, check one): full-time, temporary full-time, part-time, temporary part-time, casual
	28.	DEM	Current job title (i.e. RN, RPN): _____
	29.	DEM	Experience in current job title: 0–6 months, 6–12 months, 1–3 years, 3–5 years, 5–10 years, 10–20 years, 20+ years
	30.	DEM	Age: 18–24, 25–29, 30–34, 35–44, 45–54, 55+

References

1. Statistics Canada - Delayed retirement: a new trend. http://www.statcan.gc.ca/pub/75-001-x/2011004/article/11578-eng.htm. Accessed 6 June 2016
2. Statistics Canada - Labour force characteristics by age and sex, January 2018. http://www.statcan.gc.ca/tables-tableaux/sum-som/l01/cst01/labor20a-eng.htm
3. Drummond, H.: What we never have, we never miss? Decision error and the risks of premature termination. J. Inf. Technol. **20**(3), 170–176 (2005)
4. Davis, F.D.: Perceived usefulness, perceived ease of use, and user acceptance of information technology. MIS Q. **13**, 319–340 (1989)
5. Markus, M.L., Keil, M.: If we build it, they will come: designing information systems that people want to use. Sloan Manag. Rev. **35**(4), 11 (1994)
6. Hu, P.J., Chau, P.Y., Sheng, O.R., Tam, K.Y.: Examining the technology acceptance model using physician acceptance of telemedicine technology. J. Manag. Inf. Syst. **16**(2), 91–112 (1999)
7. National Physician Survey. http://nationalphysiciansurvey.ca/wp-content/uploads/2014/09/2014-FPGP-EN-Q10.pdf. Accessed 3 June 2014
8. Lee, F., Teich, J.M., Spurr, C.D., Bates, D.W.: Implementation of physician order entry: user satisfaction and self-reported usage patterns. J. Am. Med. Inform. Assoc. **3**(1), 42–55 (1996)
9. Goorman, E., Berg, M.: Modelling nursing activities: electronic patient records and their discontents. Nurs. Inq. **7**(1), 3–9 (2000)
10. Lee, T.T., Yeh, C.H., Ho, L.H.: Application of a computerized nursing care plan system in one hospital: experiences of ICU nurses in Taiwan. J. Adv. Nurs. **39**(1), 61–67 (2002)
11. Likourezos, A., Chalfin, D.B., Murphy, D.G., Sommer, B., Darcy, K., Davidson, S.J.: Physician and nurse satisfaction with an electronic medical record system. J. Emerg. Med. **27**(4), 419–424 (2004)
12. Prasad, P.: Symbolic processes in the implementation of technological change: a symbolic interactionist study of work computerization. Acad. Manag. J. **36**(6), 1400–1429 (1993)

13. Apesoa-Varano, E.C.: Educated caring: the emergence of professional identity among nurses. Qual. Sociol. **30**(3), 249–274 (2007)
14. Dansky, K.H., Gamm, L.D., Vasey, J.J., Barsukiewicz, C.K.: Electronic medical records: are physicians ready? J. Healthc. Manag. **44**(6), 440–454 (1999)
15. Carayon, P., Cartmill, R., Blosky, M.A., Brown, R., Hackenberg, M., Hoonakker, P., Hundt, A.S., Norfolk, E., Wetterneck, T.B., Walker, J.M.: ICU nurses' acceptance of electronic health records. J. Am. Med. Inform. Assoc. **18**(6), 812–819 (2011)
16. Boonstra, A., Broekhuis, M.: Barriers to the acceptance of electronic medical records by physicians from systematic review to taxonomy and interventions. BMC Health Serv. Res. **10**(1), 231 (2010)
17. Moody, L.E., Slocumb, E., Berg, B., Jackson, D.: Electronic health records documentation in nursing: nurses' perceptions, attitudes, and preferences. CIN: Comput. Inform. Nurs. **22**(6), 337–344 (2004)
18. Gans, D., Kralewski, J., Hammons, T., Dowd, B.: Medical groups' adoption of electronic health records and information systems. Health Aff. **24**(5), 1323–1333 (2005)
19. Hillestad, R., Bigelow, J., Bower, A., Girosi, F., Meili, R., Scoville, R., Taylor, R.: Can electronic medical record systems transform health care? Potential health benefits, savings, and costs. Health Aff. **24**(5), 1103–1117 (2005)
20. Chaudhry, B., Wang, J., Wu, S., Maglione, M., Mojica, W., Roth, E., Morton, S.C., Shekelle, P.G.: Systematic review: impact of health information technology on quality, efficiency, and costs of medical care. Ann. Intern. Med. **144**(10), 742–752 (2006)
21. Ford, E.W., Menachemi, N., Phillips, M.T.: Predicting the adoption of electronic health records by physicians: when will health care be paperless? J. Am. Med. Inform. Assoc. **13**(1), 106–112 (2006)
22. Tang, P.C., Ash, J.S., Bates, D.W., Overhage, J.M., Sands, D.Z.: Personal health records: definitions, benefits, and strategies for overcoming barriers to adoption. J. Am. Med. Inform. Assoc. **13**(2), 121–126 (2006)
23. Blumenthal, D., Tavenner, M.: The "meaningful use" regulation for electronic health records. N. Engl. J. Med. **363**(6), 501–504 (2010)
24. Jha, A.K.: Meaningful use of electronic health records: the road ahead. JAMA **304**(15), 1709–1710 (2010)
25. Ash, J.S., Bates, D.W.: Factors and forces affecting EHR system adoption: report of a 2004 ACMI discussion. J. Am. Med. Inform. Assoc. **12**(1), 8–12 (2005)
26. Gregory, K.: Implementing an electronic records management system: a public sector case study. Rec. Manag. J. **15**(2), 80–85 (2005)
27. Scott, J.T., Rundall, T.G., Vogt, T.M., Hsu, J.: Kaiser Permanente's experience of implementing an electronic medical record: a qualitative study. BMJ **331**(7528), 1313–1316 (2005)
28. Glaser, J.: Implementing electronic health records: 10 factors for success. Healthc. Finan. Manag. **63**(1), 50–54 (2009)
29. Canadian Institute for Health Information. https://secure.cihi.ca/free_products/Regulated_Nurses_EN.pdf. Accessed 7 June 2016
30. Fishbein, M., Ajzen, I.: Belief, Attitude, Intention and Behavior: An Introduction to Theory and Research. Addison-Wesley, Reading (1975)
31. Mathieson, K.: Predicting user intentions: comparing the technology acceptance model with the theory of planned behavior. Inf. Syst. Res. **2**(3), 173–191 (1991)
32. Taylor, S., Todd, P.A.: Understanding information technology usage: a test of competing models. Inf. Syst. Res. **6**(2), 144–176 (1995)
33. Venkatesh, V., Davis, F.D.: A theoretical extension of the technology acceptance model: four longitudinal field studies. Manag. Sci. **46**(2), 186–204 (2000)

34. Wu, J.H., Shen, W.S., Lin, L.M., Greenes, R.A., Bates, D.W.: Testing the technology acceptance model for evaluating healthcare professionals' intention to use an adverse event reporting system. Int. J. Qual. Health Care **20**(2), 123–129 (2008)
35. Davis, F.D.: User acceptance of information technology: system characteristics, user perceptions and behavioral impacts. Int. J. Man Mach. Stud. **38**(3), 475–487 (1993)
36. Fuerst, W.L., Cheney, P.H.: Concepts, theory, and techniques: factors affecting the perceived utilization of computer-based decision support systems in the oil industry. Decis. Sci. **13**(4), 554–569 (1982)
37. Hartwick, J., Barki, H.: Explaining the role of user participation in information system use. Manag. Sci. **40**(4), 440–465 (1994)
38. Rogers, E.M.: Diffusion of Innovations. Simon and Schuster, New York (2010)
39. Moore, G.C., Benbasat, I.: Development of an instrument to measure the perceptions of adopting an information technology innovation. Inf. Syst. Res. **2**(3), 192–222 (1991)
40. Bailey, J.E., Pearson, S.W.: Development of a tool for measuring and analyzing computer user satisfaction. Manag. Sci. **29**(5), 530–545 (1983)
41. Lucas Jr., H.C.: Performance and the use of an information system. Manag. Sci. **21**(8), 908–919 (1975)
42. O'Reilly, C.A.: Variations in decision makers' use of information sources: the impact of quality and accessibility of information. Acad. Manag. J. **25**(4), 756–771 (1982)
43. Swanson, E.B.: Information channel disposition and use. Decis. Sci. **18**(1), 131–145 (1987)
44. Agarwal, R., Prasad, J.: The role of innovation characteristics and perceived voluntariness in the acceptance of information technologies. Decis. Sci. **28**(3), 557–582 (1997)
45. Mun, Y.Y., Jackson, J.D., Park, J.S., Probst, J.C.: Understanding information technology acceptance by individual professionals: toward an integrative view. Inf. Manag. **43**(3), 350–363 (2006)
46. Horton, R.P., Buck, T., Waterson, P.E., Clegg, C.W.: Explaining intranet use with the technology acceptance model. J. Inf. Technol. **16**(4), 237–249 (2001)
47. Amoako-Gyampah, K., Salam, A.F.: An extension of the technology acceptance model in an ERP implementation environment. Inf. Manag. **41**(6), 731–745 (2004)
48. Pai, F.Y., Huang, K.I.: Applying the technology acceptance model to the introduction of healthcare information systems. Technol. Forecast. Soc. Chang. **78**(4), 650–660 (2011)
49. Lewis, T.L., Loker, S.: Technology usage intent among apparel retail employees. Int. J. Retail Distrib. Manag. **42**(5), 422–440 (2014)
50. Hair, J.F., Black, W.C., Babin, B.J., Anderson, R.E., Tatham, R.L.: Multivariate Data Analysis. Prentice Hall, Upper Saddle River (1998)
51. Tavakol, M., Dennick, R.: Making sense of Cronbach's alpha. Int. J. Med. Educ. **2**, 53 (2011)
52. StatWiki Main Page. http://statwiki.kolobkreations.com. Accessed 9 July 2014
53. Sydney, J., Fox, S.: Generations Online in 2009. Pew Internet & American Life Project (2009)

Implementing Connectivist Teaching Strategies in Traditional K-12 Classrooms

Robyn Rice(✉)

Grand Canyon University, Phoenix, USA
rjarice@gmail.com

Abstract. Connectivism is a learning theory that is designed for the digital age. Students in today's classrooms are digital natives who have unique learning styles. Connectivism has been studied primarily in online college classes and has been shown to increase motivation and student achievement. However, connectivism has not been widely explored in traditional K-12 classroom settings. Implementing connectivist learning strategies in traditional K-12 classrooms can bridge the gap between the needs of digital natives and K-12 education. The purpose of this paper is to present practical strategies for implementing connectivist learning strategies in the traditional K-12 classroom. Five strategies for implementing connectivism in the traditional K-12 classrooms are (1) shifting from teacher-centered to student-centered pedagogy, (2) incorporating technology with readily-available devices, (3) never providing information that students can access themselves, (4) incorporate and practice utilizing technology networks, and (5) incorporate and practice utilizing social networks.

Keywords: Connectivism · Connectivist learning · K-12
Traditional classroom · Technology integration · Social networks
Technology networks

1 Introduction

Technological advances have changed just about every aspect of modern society. However, education is one of the slowest areas to adapt to the change (Hung 2014). Connectivist learning strategies have been shown to be effective in online classroom settings at the tertiary level. In K-12 education, the standard in North American education remains based in traditional practices that focus on presenting academic information in print and text and do not allow students to interact with the material (Hicks and Sinkinson 2015). K-12 classrooms are knowledge-centric and view education as an individual achievement (Barsness and Kim 2015). Most current classrooms promote individual performance and learning (Saritas 2015). Unfortunately, students in the current K-12 classrooms are different from those of previous generations. Today's students learn best when they can network with one another and work in teams, so there is a disconnect between traditional classroom pedagogy and student needs.

'Digital natives' is a term that was coined in 2001 to describe students who were born and have grown up immersed in the current technological world (Prensky 2001).

© Springer International Publishing AG, part of Springer Nature 2018
F. F.-H. Nah and B. S. Xiao (Eds.): HCIBGO 2018, LNCS 10923, pp. 645–655, 2018.
https://doi.org/10.1007/978-3-319-91716-0_51

Current K-12 students are considered digital natives. Education needs new pedagogies that can adapt to changing technology, increase active learning, and provide authentic learning opportunities for digital natives (Hicks and Sinkinson 2015). Students today have constant access to information and have different learning styles that can be leveraged through an understanding of connectivism to help students be more successful. Digital natives have unique learning styles, communication styles, and are adept at multi-tasking and working in teams (Saritas 2015). Trnova and Trna (2015) stated that digital natives prefer to work in teams, learn through inquiry, and prefer to learn by doing rather than listening. Therefore, there needs to be a pedagogical change to learner participation instead of information retention (Downes 2010). Connectivism explains learning in the digital age, and views learning as the process of transforming information into meaning (Siemens and Training 2005). Implementing connectivist learning strategies in traditional K-12 classrooms will help to close the gap between student needs and classroom teaching. The purpose of this paper is to present practical strategies for implementing connectivist learning strategies in the traditional K-12 classroom.

2   Connectivism

Connectivism was developed to understand learning in the digital age. Siemens (2005) stated that the time to revise existing theories has passed, and a new theory to address the technological world is needed. The theories of behaviorism, cognitivism, and constructivism are no longer sufficient to address the type of learning that occurs in classrooms that are greatly impacted by technology (Siemens 2005). Connectivism is based on the idea that the world is changing rapidly, and new information is constantly being acquired. People need to be able to distinguish important and unimportant information. Connectivism acknowledges that knowledge can reside in non-human entities (Siemens 2005), like computers and technology networks. The individual is still the learning point, but knowledge entails a network. Knowledge, in connectivism, is not passive; knowledge is the transformation of information into meaning (Siemens and Training 2005). Connectivism is characterized by eight principles of learning. The eight principles of connectivism, developed by Siemens (2005) are:

1. "Learning and knowledge rests in diversity of opinions.
2. Learning is a process of connecting specialized nodes or information sources.
3. Learning may reside in non-human appliances.
4. Capacity to know more is more critical than what is currently known.
5. Nurturing and maintaining connections is needed to facilitate continual learning.
6. Ability to see connections between fields, ideas, and concepts is a core skill.
7. Currency (accurate, up-to-date knowledge) is the intent of all connectivist learning activities.
8. Decision-making is itself a learning process" (p. 4).

Connectivism views learning as a result of network connections. According to AlDahdouh et al. (2015), connectivism recognizes three types of networks: neural, conceptual, and external. Neural networks are connections of a neuron's axons and dendrites. The conceptual level consists of connections of concepts, ideas, and thoughts. The external networks involve people and technology (AlDahdouh et al. 2015). The external networks are social networks or technology networks that can be implemented in classrooms. Learning occurs through connections within these networks.

Schools no longer need brick and mortar buildings to provide quality education. With computer technology, knowledge can be acquired from non-human entities and networks (Siemens 2005). Computer and internet technology have changed higher education; classes have evolved from brick and mortar institutions with traditional teaching to online and distance learning classes. Implementing connectivist strategies in online college environments has helped increase student motivation, engagement, and achievement (Trnova and Trna 2015). In addition, college students report that learning in a connectivist environment allows them the freedom to learn through their preferred learning style which increases their achievement (Trnova and Trna 2015). The implementation of connectivist learning strategies lessens the gap between student learning needs and classroom pedagogy.

Unfortunately, connectivism has not entered the conversation in traditional classroom settings, likely because it is assumed that they are incompatible. Connectivism is a theory that explains how people acquire knowledge; therefore, connectivist networks should be present in all classroom environments. But, connectivism has not been discussed in relation to traditional K-12 education. One of the major tenets of connectivism is that learning occurs through networks, both using technology and face-to-face interaction with peers. Therefore, connectivist strategies are applicable to all classroom environments that are conducive to networks, including traditional classroom settings.

Most K-12 settings are still in traditional school settings with teacher-centered classrooms. So, little research and literature has been dedicated to connectivism in K-12 education. Connectivist classrooms in a K-12 setting will not look like online college classrooms that have traditionally been associated with connectivism. The strategies that are successful in online tertiary classrooms are not suitable for traditional K-12 classrooms with one teacher in the classroom with a group of students. However, that does not mean that connectivism cannot be successfully implemented into K-12 classrooms to meet the needs of digital natives.

3   Connectivist Strategies for Networked Learning

There are four strategies for learning in connectivist networked environments. The four strategies can be implemented in any classroom environment, including traditional classrooms. Four learning strategies utilized in connectivist environments are learner autonomy, resource openness, network connectivity, and opinion diversity (Smidt et al. 2017) which may be present in any classroom environment. Connectivist strategies can and should be implemented into all classrooms, including traditional K-12 classrooms.

Learner Autonomy. Students should be given choice regarding their learning resources and assignments. Students should be independent learners who set their own goals and outcomes. Learners become autonomous when they are given control over their learning (Smidt et al. 2017). Student choice can be increased through networking in the classroom.

Resource Openness. Students should have the opportunity to communicate in networks to gain and share knowledge (Smidt et al. 2017). Using networks allows students to access a variety of technological and social resources that were not previously available in classrooms.

Network Connectivity. Students should be encouraged to make connections with technological and social networks (Smidt et al. 2017). Students gain knowledge from their classmates, teachers, and online resources.

Opinion Diversity. Students should be given the opportunity to use their networks to gain different opinions and perspectives on various topics (Smidt et al. 2017). Connecting with other students promotes problem solving and social skills.

4   Strategies for Implementing Connectivism in Traditional K-12 Classrooms

When connectivism is successfully implemented into the traditional classroom, students benefit from learning through networks. The networks allow students to access, assimilate, and acquire knowledge. This paper presents five practical strategies that teachers in traditional K-12 classrooms can implement to incorporate the connectivist learning strategies of learner autonomy, resource openness, network connectivity, and opinion diversity.

4.1   Shift from Teacher-Centered to Student-Centered Pedagogy

Most K-12 classrooms are still following the traditional teacher-centered model of instruction. But the current generation of digital natives require a change in pedagogy to meet their unique needs as learners. Technology has changed the way that students think and learn, which has led to the need for a new approach to teaching and learning (Siemens 2005). Barsness and Kim (2015) asserted that the current Eurocentric model of pedagogy has limits and conflicts with current culture as it is knowledge-centric and views education as an achievement. Educators must rethink their current practices and pedagogies to prepare students for the real world (Barsness and Kim 2015). According to Bair and Stafford (2016), the instructor in the classroom should become the facilitator of the community of learners. Learning needs to be in the control of the learner, but the facilitator plays the important role of helping to guide the learning community and focus of the learners (Bair and Stafford 2016). To prepare students to be productive and successful in the 21st century, connectivism should be applied as a pedagogical approach that recognizes networks as tools for the distribution of knowledge, even in the traditional classroom model.

Full implementation of connectivism in the classroom shifts the pedagogy of the classroom away from the traditional classroom model and toward a more student-centered model. According to Hung (2014), the implementation of connectivist teaching will transform the traditional classroom. Connectivist learning networks place the responsibility for learning on the learner, increasing learner autonomy. Connectivist environments shift the control of learning away from the instructor and onto the learner (Siemens 2005). Learning occurs when students form connections that allow them to create their own learning (Siemens 2005). Conradie (2014) stated that connectivist learning allows students to create connections and develop networks, which promotes learner autonomy. The student should be the focus of the classroom in a connectivist environment rather than the teacher.

Connectivism promotes active learner engagement that increases student autonomy. Connectivist classrooms teach students to be autonomous learners by incorporating student choice and networking in the classroom. Students become more engaged in the learning process, and students who are engaged in the classroom are 75% more likely to have higher grades (Shan et al. 2014). Gillard et al. (2015) completed a study of undergraduate college students and found that autonomous students felt free to think for themselves, giving them the desire to learn for themselves. Autonomous students had a desire to master the task and provide their best work. Students who felt they were given autonomy, mastery, and purpose, become more intrinsically motivated to succeed. Shifting classroom pedagogy toward student-centered teaching focuses the learning environment on the needs of digital natives.

Beginning the process of shifting from a teacher-centered environment to a student-centered environment can be supported with technology. Incorporating software that enhances the student's control and freedom also increases student autonomy. Teachers should use a platform that allows students to access their assignments, manage their due dates, and communicate with the instructor. Several programs are available to K-12 instructors free of charge and can easily be implemented to increase learner control and autonomy.

4.2   Incorporate Technology with Readily-Available Devices

Successful implementation of technology can change the teaching and learning opportunities in the classroom. Traditionally, content was bounded by what was in the textbook, but the use of technology expands the content and curricula available to students (Hung 2014). Implementing technology has the effect of changing the teacher's practices from a teacher-centered environment to a more student-centered environment (Tondeur et al. 2016). When technology is fully integrated into instructional strategies, students are more satisfied in the classroom and believe that their academic performance is improved (Devasagayam et al. 2013). But, many teachers point to the lack of resources as a roadblock to technology integration because they do not have computers in their classrooms. Connectivist classrooms incorporate technology, but it does not require a class set of computers. Spring et al. (2016) stated that student smartphones are useful for integrating technology in the classroom, even without a class set of computers.

Most K-12 students have smartphones that can be utilized to implement technology in the classroom. Connectivist classrooms allow students to access and assimilate information from technology networks which can be done using smartphones, tablets, or computers. If this technology is not available in the classroom, teachers can request that parents, teachers, or community members donate their old cell phones that they are no longer using. These devices can easily be connected to the school Wi-Fi and used to meet the technology needs of the students.

Incorporating readily-available devices provides a link between the students' everyday experiences and their education. Allowing students to access technology through their personal devices increases resource openness, one of the strategies for connectivist learning. Incorporating technology that the students are familiar with will increase their comfort level and efficiency of use. Instead of struggling to learn foreign technology, students can focus on increasing their network sharing.

4.3   Never Provide Information that Students Can Access Themselves

A connectivist classroom has an instructor that facilitates the autonomous learning of students by providing expertise and guidance, but not directly providing information. The teacher directs the students to useful resources and poses questions to help organize and guide their research. Siemens and Training (2005) asserted that education should focus less on presenting information and more on building the learner's ability to navigate through the information. The ability to access information to acquire knowledge is more important than the retention of knowledge (Siemens 2005). Connectivist teachers no longer provide pre-determined knowledge, but instead provide a learning idea and guide students to use multi-media, diverse thinking, and networks to access and acquire knowledge (Foroughi 2015). The role of the instructor becomes that of a coach to help students learn how to work in a self-regulated environment (Conradie 2014). With the vast amount of knowledge available, people cannot acquire all of it. Students must learn how to assimilate information in a classroom environment.

A key component of interface design is to increase recognition, so the user minimizes their need for recall. Connectivist learning encourages knowledge acquisition, not memorization. Teachers should introduce students to programs that assist them in quickly and efficiently acquiring knowledge from valid sources. Learning to filter through information to acquire knowledge further increases learner autonomy.

4.4   Incorporate and Practice Utilizing Technology Networks

Accessing content through an online system is not the same as learning within a technology network. Utilizing technology networks is not the same thing as using a search engine to find knowledge. Technology networks involve websites, blogs, and connecting with people through technology. Using technology networks in the classroom empowers students to be autonomous learners. If students need information or clarification, they can access technology networks instead of asking the teacher. However, students do not automatically know how to interact with technology for educational purposes, so they require educational coaching from their teachers.

Dabbagh and Fake (2017) reported that most incoming college students do not know how to manage internet tools and use them for learning. This is because these skills are not being taught or practiced in K-12 education. While students are adept at using technology for informal learning and networking at home, the students must be taught how to create and manage technology networks that are useful for classroom learning (Dabbagh and Fake 2017). Most technological skills are acquired outside of school and may not be useful in the educational setting, so students must be taught the proper strategies and techniques for adapting their skills for educational networking (Laakkonen and Taalas 2015). Davidson (2017) explained that many schools and instructors assume that students already have the skills to successfully assimilate knowledge from technology networks, so they do not provide time to teach and allow students to practice these skills.

Instruction on developing and using technology networks should occur in three phases. Learning to acquire knowledge through technology resources requires three phases: the tool learning phase, the content learning phase, and the partner learning phase (Lu 2017). The tool learning phase involves learning how to use and integrate online resources. Students must learn how to effectively search for information and how to understand the information that is provided by a search engine. Often teachers assume that students know how to search for information, but the students may not know how to effectively use key words and phrases in their searches. Taking the time to teach students how to efficiently search for specific information will save the teachers and students time and frustration.

The content learning phase involves assimilating previous knowledge and newly acquired knowledge for the purpose of learning (Lu 2017). In traditional classrooms, this process is accomplished through direct instruction by the teacher; the teacher tells the students what information is important for them to know. In connectivist environments students must decipher which information they received from their research is important and which is unimportant. These are skills that require practice. Teachers should provide lessons that allow students to practice the content learning phase.

The last phase of acquiring knowledge through technology is the partner learning phase which incorporates social relationships to share knowledge. Social networks are as important as technological networks in the connectivist classroom. Aksal et al. (2013) found that students who shared experiences and knowledge through technology increased the skills that are known to contribute to educational success. However, like technology networks, students need to learn how to use social networks for educational purposes.

Helping students to learn to use and manage technology networks can be accomplished through various educational networking sites. An easy way to implement technology networks is to start a class networking site. The students can learn to network on the class site where the networking is managed on a small scale. As the students learn to manage their classroom networks, they will gain the confidence to explore networks on their own, increasing autonomy and network connectivity.

4.5 Incorporate and Practice Utilizing Social Networks

Social networks are the most important aspect of connectivist teaching in K-12 classrooms, and the easiest to implement. Manning (2015) asserted that knowledge is no longer acquired individually, but it is shared and distributed through networks. When achievements are shared among students, they are more motivated to improve their learning (Shan et al. 2014). Social networks focus on shared problem solving and increase the motivation of the members (Harding and Engelbrecht 2015). Social networks improve social skills and collaboration skills.

Hegedus et al. (2016) completed a study of 566 high school math students in traditional math classes. The experimental group was taught in a traditional classroom that integrated math software that encouraged student discourse, active learning, and group learning over teacher demonstration. Students in the technology-enhanced classroom showed more improvement from the pre-test to the post-test than traditional students. The results, however, were not due to the technology or software implementation. The main difference between the two groups of students was that the technology-enhanced classroom included communication and group work, so students could learn through networks (Hegedus et al. 2016). Students need to be given the opportunity to share the knowledge they gain from technology networks with others. Networked learning is applicable and can be implemented in the traditional classroom setting to meet the needs of digital natives.

Implementing social networks in the classroom moves learners from passive consumers of information to creators of knowledge and content because learning networks encourage meaningful learning and problem solving. Social networks are not controlled by the instructor; they are completely under the control of the learner and the goal is to help one another succeed (Harding and Engelbrecht 2015). Students learn through peer discussions and interacting with classmates (Aksal et al. 2013). In a study conducted by Khan and Madden (2016), 84% of students said they learned a moderate to high amount from their classmates and preferred to work with other students over working alone. Even students who are not comfortable speaking up in class are comfortable interacting in a discussion within their social networks (Ying and Yang 2017). When students are connected in networks, they are more willing to tackle challenging tasks because they know they can rely on peers for help.

Social networks are not the same thing as friendships or collaborative learning. Social networks are groups of people that a learner interacts with for the purpose of learning. Social networks are focused on knowledge distribution and not just social relationships. Social networks that exchange information are more influential than student friendships in increasing student autonomy (Alonso et al. 2015). To encourage student success, teachers need to encourage the formation of social networks, not just focus on classroom friendships or traditional collaborative learning.

Teachers are often concerned about students choosing to work with other students who are not going to benefit their learning. Contrary to expectations, Casquero et al. (2015) found that higher performing students do not network with only other high performers. In a successful social network, group interactions are more important than individual ability and all members contribute to the learning (Alonso et al. 2015). Students form groups that are heterogeneous, and higher performing students drive the interactions and discussions of the network (Casquero et al. 2015). Interactions in social networks are based on access to shared resources, and not focused on the academic performance of the individual. Therefore, high performers lead the discussion which has a positive impact on low performers but does not have a negative impact on high performers (Casquero et al. 2015). Encouraging connectivist networking in the classroom through social networks increases the success of all levels of students.

Teachers who seek to utilize social networks in the classroom need to coach their students on the formation and maintenance of networks. To ensure that students are forming social networks and not just working with their friends, the implementation and practice should be done in phases. First, the students need to have opportunities to interact with classmates who are not their friends. So, implementation should begin with short-term teacher-formed groups. The groups should be changed with every assignment, so the students have an opportunity to work with all the other students in the class in a relatively short period of time. After students have had the opportunity to work with their classmates on at least one occasion, the teacher should coach the students in forming their own networks. Social networks should eventually be in the control of the student, not the teacher, to promote learner autonomy.

5   Conclusion

Students today are growing up immersed in technology, and it has changed the way they think and learn. Unfortunately, most K-12 education remains based in traditional practices that do not benefit the digital natives in the classroom. Digital natives have unique learning styles and communication styles, and prefer to work in teams (Saritas 2015). The time has come for a new pedagogy to address the needs of these students. Connectivism is a learning approach for the digital age that is based on network learning. Four learning strategies utilized in connectivist environments are learner autonomy, resource openness, network connectivity, and opinion diversity (Smidt et al. 2017). This paper presented five practical strategies that teachers in traditional K-12 classrooms can incorporate to implement connectivist learning approaches. Five strategies for implementing connectivism in the traditional K-12 classrooms are (1) shift from teacher-centered to student-centered pedagogy, (2) incorporate technology with readily-available devices, (3) never provide information that students can access themselves, (4) incorporate and practice utilizing technology networks, and (5) incorporate and practice utilizing social networks. Implementing connectivism in the classroom will bridge the gap between traditional K-12 education and the needs of the learners in the classrooms.

References

Aksal, F.A., Gazi, Z.A., Bahçelerli, N.M.: Practice of connectivism as learning theory: enhancing learning process through social networking site (Facebook). Gaziantep Univ. J. Soc. Sci. 12 (2), 243–252 (2013). http://dergipark.gov.tr/jss

AlDahdouh, A.A., Osório, A.J., Caires, S.: Understanding knowledge network, learning and connectivism. Int. J. Instr. Technol. Distance Learn. 12(10), 3–21 (2015). http://www.itdl.org

Alonso, F., Manrique, D., Martínez, L., Viñes, J.M.: Study of the influence of social relationships among students on knowledge building using a moderately constructivist learning model. J. Educ. Comput. Res. 51(4), 417–439 (2015). https://doi.org/10.2190/EC.51.4.c

Bair, R., Stafford, T.: Connected and ubiquitous: a discussion of two theories that impact future learning applications. TechTrends 60(1), 129–135 (2016). https://doi.org/10.1007/s11528-016-0021-z

Barsness, R., Kim, R.D.: A pedagogy of engagement for the changing character of the 21st century classroom. Theol. Educ. **49**(2), 89–106 (2015). https://www.ats.edu

Casquero, O., Ovelar, R., Romo, J., Benito, M.: Reviewing the differences in size, composition and structure between the personal networks of high- and low-performing students. Br. J. Educ. Technol. **46**(1), 16–31 (2015). https://doi.org/10.1111/bjet.12110

Conradie, P.W.: Supporting self-directed learning by connectivism and personal learning environments. Int. J. Inf. Educ. Technol. Singap. **4**(3), 254–259 (2014). https://doi.org/10.7763/ijiet.2014.v4.408

Dabbagh, N., Fake, H.: College students' perceptions of personal learning environments through the lens of digital tools, processes and spaces. J. New Approach. Educ. Res. **6**(1), 28–38 (2017). https://doi.org/10.7821/naer.2017.1.215

Davidson, P.L.: Personal learning environments and the diversity of digital natives. Open Access Libr. J. **4**(5), 1–7 (2017). https://doi.org/10.4236/oalib.1103608

Devasagayam, P.R., Stark, N.R., Watroba, R.: Laptop technology in classrooms: how student perceptions shape learning and satisfaction. Atl. Mark. J. **2**(3), 14–23 (2013). http://digitalcommons.kennesaw.edu/amj/

Downes, S.: New technology supporting informal learning. J. Emerg. Technol. Web Intell. **2**(1), 27–33 (2010). https://doi.org/10.4304/jetwi.2.1.27-33

Foroughi, A.: The theory of connectivism: can it explain and guide learning in the digital age? J. High. Educ. Theory Pract. **15**(5), 12–34 (2015). http://www.na-businesspress.com/jhetpopen.html

Gillard, S., Gillard, S., Pratt, D.: A pedagogical study of intrinsic motivation in the classroom through autonomy, mastery, and purpose. Contemp. Issues Educ. Res. **8**(1), 1–6 (2015). https://doi.org/10.19030/cier.v8i1.9045

Harding, A., Engelbrecht, J.: Personal learning network clusters: a comparison between mathematics and computer science students. J. Educ. Technol. Soc. **18**(3), 173–184 (2015). http://www.ifets.info

Hegedus, S., Tapper, J., Dalton, S.: Exploring how teacher-related factors relate to student achievement in learning advanced algebra in technology-enhanced classrooms. J. Math. Teach. Educ. **19**(1), 7–32 (2016). https://doi.org/10.1007/s10857-014-9292-5

Hicks, A., Sinkinson, C.: Critical connections: personal learning environments and information literacy. Res. Learn. Technol. **23**(1), 1–12 (2015). https://doi.org/10.3402/rlt.v23.21193

Hung, N.M.: Using ideas from connectivism for designing new learning models in Vietnam. Int. J. Inf. Educ. Technol. **4**(1), 76–82 (2014). https://doi.org/10.7763/IJIET.2014.V4.373

Khan, A.A., Madden, J.: Speed learning: maximizing student learning and engagement in a limited amount of time. Int. J. Mod. Educ. Comput. Sci. **8**(7), 22–30 (2016). https://doi.org/10.5815/ijmecs.2016.07.03

Laakkonen, I., Taalas, P.: Towards new cultures of learning: personal learning environments as a developmental perspective for improving higher education language courses. Lang. Learn. High. Educ. **5**(1), 223–241 (2015). https://doi.org/10.1515/cercles-2015-0011

Lu, F.: The construction of personal learning network environment in the perspective of knowledge management. In: 3rd International Conference on Education and Social Development (ICESD) China, pp. 226–230 (2017). http://dpi-proceedings.com

Manning, C.A.: The construction of personal learning networks to support non-formal workplace learning of training professionals. Int. J. Adv. Corp. Learn. (iJAC) **8**(2), 4–12 (2015). https://doi.org/10.3991/ijac.v8i2.4367

Prensky, M.: Digital natives, digital immigrants. Horizon **9**(5), 1–6 (2001). https://doi.org/10.1108/10748120110424816

Saritas, M.T.: The emergent technological and theoretical paradigms in education: the interrelations of cloud computing (CC), connectivism and internet of things (IoT). Acta Polytech. Hung. **12**(6), 161–179 (2015). https://doi.org/10.12700/APH.12.6.2015.6.10

Shan, S., Li, C., Shi, J., Wang, L., Cai, H.: Impact of effective communication, achievement sharing and positive classroom environments on learning performance. Syst. Res. Behav. Sci. **31**(3), 471–482 (2014). https://doi.org/10.1002/sres.2285

Siemens, G.: Connectivism: a learning theory for the digital age. Int. J. Instr. Technol. Distance Learn. **2**(1), 3–10 (2005). http://www.itdl.org

Siemens, G., Training, C.: Connectivism: learning as network-creation. ASTD Learn. News **10** (1), 2–38 (2005). www.elearnspace.org

Smidt, H., Thornton, M., Abhari, K.: The future of social learning: a novel approach to connectivism. In: 50th Hawaii International Conference on System Sciences, Hawaii, pp. 2116–2125 (2017). http://aisel.aisnet.org

Spring, K.J., Graham, C.R., Hadlock, C.A.: The current landscape of international blended learning. Int. J. Technol. Enhanc. Learn. **8**(1), 84–102 (2016). https://doi.org/10.1504/IJTEL. 2016.075961

Tondeur, J., van Braak, J., Ertmer, P.A., Ottenbreit-Leftwich, A.: Understanding the relationship between teachers' pedagogical beliefs and technology use in education: a systematic review of qualitative evidence. Educ. Technol. Res. Dev. **65**(3), 555–575 (2016). https://doi.org/10. 1007/s11423-016-9482-3

Trnova, E., Trna, J.: Motivational effect of communication technologies in connectivist science education. Online J. Commun. Media Technol. **5**(3), 107–119 (2015). http://www.ojcmt.net

Ying, A.N.L., Yang, I.: Academics and learners' perceptions on blended learning as a strategic initiative to improve student learning experience. MATEC Web Conf. **87**(1), 1–7 (2017). https://doi.org/10.1051/matecconf/20178704005

Helping the Local Community
with Crypto-Currency: A Case Study

Norman Shaw[(⊠)]

Ryerson University, Toronto, Canada
norman.shaw@ryerson.ca

Abstract. Local currencies are a special form of digital cash that are used for payments within a contained geographical area. They are made feasible today with the aid of blockchain technology that assures their security, solves the double-spend problem and offers incentives for consumer participation. They can be attractive for small businesses, encouraging members of the community to engage in commercial transactions within the area. Consumers are motivated to support local merchants, while enjoying a simple way to pay and the possibility of earning rewards based on cryptocurrency. In this case study, key issues are explored in the local community of Tel Aviv.

Keywords: Local currency · Blockchain · Initial coin offerings
Case study

1 Introduction

Smartphones have changed the way people absorb news, listen to music and communicate with each other. With the aid of the digital wallet app, they are also changing the way we pay. By accessing digital versions of credit and debit cards that are stored in the wallet, the app makes payments easier and more convenient [1]. However, these payment cards, be they physical or digital, still depend on a central authorizing authority. With the aid of blockchain, the digital wallet is now being extended to store a digital version of cash, where the cryptocurrency does not require a centralized database. This additional functionality will help replace physical cash. Seventy eight percent of consumers in fifteen countries expect to go cashless within five years [2]. As an example, Sweden is a low cash society where the value of cash in circulation is 1.5% of GDP. Many Swedish banks have eliminated their ATMs and do not carry cash and some retail stores no longer accept cash [3].

A potential alternative to cash is Bitcoin [4]. At present, this is not linked to any fiat currency and only has speculative value. However, its introduction brought the blockchain into mainstream thinking. The blockchain technology facilitates the creation of a distributed public ledger with strong cryptography to assure security [5]. Transactions are stored on multiple networked computers to assure legitimacy [6]. Some central banks are considering issuing an electronic currency, which will substitute for cash. Unlike Bitcoin, it will be linked to fiat currency. Sweden is evaluating the e-krona [7] and the Bank of Canada published a white paper that suggested that the Bank should consider issuing a digital currency based on the blockchain [8].

© Springer International Publishing AG, part of Springer Nature 2018
F. F.-H. Nah and B. S. Xiao (Eds.): HCIBGO 2018, LNCS 10923, pp. 656–668, 2018.
https://doi.org/10.1007/978-3-319-91716-0_52

In his book, The Curse of Cash, Rogoff [9] describes the negative impacts of cash: transactions are anonymous and therefore can evade tax; and its non-traceability is valuable for funding illicit activities such as terrorism, the drug trade, human trafficking and corruption. In order to inhibit illegal activities, some central banks are withdrawing large denominations of banknotes [10]. Digital currencies based on blockchain could be a replacement for cash. Companies engaged in cryptocurrencies have increased in value, encouraged by Bitcoin's high valuation. Various platforms, such as Ethereum, provide distributed data recording, allowing other companies to build on their platform and offer alternatives to central record keeping [11].

One application is to provide a local currency, which can be used for payment within a specific geographical area. By basing this currency on a blockchain platform, such as Ethereum, transactions are secure without the need for any central financial institution. Merchants who sign on to accept this currency are able to advertise their location to consumers who have downloaded the local currency app to their smartphone. Incentives can be offered to attract customers. In addition, the merchant has no need to handle physical cash for smaller transactions. Bookkeeping is enhanced and time is saved because there is no cash to be counted. Consumers also enjoy advantages, which include the convenience of paying with their mobile phone, without the need to handle cash and worry about change.

Finland has introduced a form of local currency by partnering with MONI, who have provided a pre-paid MasterCard to refugees. These refugees lack documentation and are therefore unable to access the formal banking system. MONI has streamlined their sign-up allowing them to submit a photo of themselves with some authenticated proof of identity. Within minutes, they have an account. They can receive deposits to their account and the immigration services can keep track of them [12].

Local currencies have the potential to help communities by encouraging consumers to visit local stores. This paper seeks to answer the following research questions: Why would businesses adopt a local currency? Why would consumers adopt a local currency? Via a case study approach, we look at Colu [13], which is a company based in Tel Aviv. They have developed the technology for secure payments, which consumers can access via the Colu app. Their platform has been adopted in Tel Aviv, Haifa, Liverpool and East London.

2 Background on Colu

Colu [13] is an Israeli company whose head office is in Tel Aviv. They have a digital wallet app, which allows consumers to find local businesses and pay by simply clicking on the merchant's name and then transferring the amount to be paid electronically. No physical cash is exchanged. The merchant receives the funds via Colu and pays a small transaction fee that is less than the credit card fee. Merchants who subscribe to the service are able to promote their business via the app and can be easily located by consumers who are nearby. The local currency is securely implemented on the blockchain platform and can be used in any country. Currently, Colu is in Haifa and Tel Aviv in Israel plus Liverpool and East London in the United Kingdom.

The merchants have a number of benefits. As a 'local currency', the app is targeted to local businesses and helps them compete with the major national and international brands. Consumers are encouraged to support the local community. Transaction fees are less than visa and additional tools are made available, such as data analysis and bookkeeping. For the consumer, the Colu wallet is more convenient as there is no need to carry cash.

In Tel Aviv, one Colu currency is currently worth 1 Israeli shekel (US$0.28) and is immediately transferable. When they first sign up, consumers receive 25 shekels (US $7) and, when they top up, they receive an extra 10% in addition to their top up amount. These customer acquisition costs have been funded from an initial round of investment. Future plans are to replace these acquisition costs with crypto-tokens earned when the Colu local currency is used for payment. The tokens are sourced from an Initial Coin Offering (ICO) and their value will fluctuate based on supply and demand. As indicated in Colu's Whitepaper [14], the supply of tokens is finite and over time, as activity with the local currency increases, the value of the tokens is expected to rise, thereby encouraging more local currency activity.

Further details on blockchain and ICOs are provided in the Literature Review.

3   Literature Review

The local currency introduced by Colu is secured by blockchain technology. Initial financing has been raised via an Initial Coin Offering (ICO) and future plans are to provide digital tokens as rewards to participants. This literature review gives a brief overview of blockchain technology, followed by the increasing acceptance of ICOs by investors. In this paper, the theoretical framework for the spread of local currency is based on Rogers' Innovation Diffusion Theory (IDT) and propositions are developed based on IDT.

3.1   Digital Currency and Blockchain

Blockchain technology was first introduced in 2008 [15], followed a year later by the practical implementation with the first Bitcoin transaction taking place in February 2010 to purchase two pizzas. Blockchain is a decentralized distributed ledger that records all transactions on multiple networked computers [5]. With the aid of advanced cryptography, transactions are secured by digital signatures such that only the owners of the signatures can see the details of the transaction [16]. A block represents a group of prior transactions that has to be digitally related to previous blocks through a hash algorithm. This 'mining' mechanism, which is time consuming and requires significant computer resources, ensures that once a block is written it cannot be altered, due to its relationship with prior blocks. Instead of a central authority, transactions are shared across the network. The inherent nature of blockchain makes it secure and the mining resolves the 'double-spend' problem which is a risk of digital record keeping. Consequently, blockchain has become the foundation of digital currencies, the most notable being Bitcoin [17].

The success of Bitcoin has helped make 'blockchain' a household word, resulting in a proliferation of digital currencies, none of which, so far, have been linked directly to fiat money. The value of these cryptocurrencies has depended upon the market, which has meant large fluctuations. In the case of Bitcoin, its value was less than 1 US cent when first introduced and its highest valuation was close to US$20,000 in December 2017. This climb in value has created interest in blockchain technology in general and in cryptocurrencies in particular, with entrepreneurial companies raising funds via ICOs [18].

3.2 Initial Coin Offerings

When funds are invested via an ICO, the investor receives cryptocurrency in the form of tokens. Although it is a relatively new source of finance, it has become a popular one, with 253 ICOs in the period from 2014 to 2017 [17]. A blockchain token is a digital token created on a blockchain as part of a decentralized protocol [16]. Similar to an IPO disclosure, an ICO disclosure, typically in the form of a white paper, describes the underlying technology, the supply of tokens and the details of how the investment will be used. A percentage of the initial coin supply is distributed to early supporters. The tokens can be sold, or retained for future use to purchase products or services and, similar to share prices, the value of the token depends upon the market. An estimated $250M. was raised through ICOs in 2016 [19].

The token is a unit of account, representing a medium of exchange in a private group. With blockchain as the foundational technology, transactions are tamper-proof. The open decentralized network engenders trust in the security and integrity of the tokens [20]. Colu is selling CLN (Colu Local Network) tokens via an ICO token distribution between 14 February and 18 February 2018. The sale is for a minimum of 315 m. tokens to a maximum of 525 m. tokens at an offered price of US$0.095 per token [21].

3.3 Diffusion of Innovations

Innovation Diffusion Theory [22] argues that change occurs because products evolve to become a better fit. There are five characteristics that determine success: relative advantage, compatibility, complexity, trialability and observability. We develop propositions for each of these characteristics.

Relative Advantage. This is "the degree to which an innovation is perceived as being better than the idea it supersedes" [22]. Local currency is an alternative payment mechanism that can be used instead of credit, debit or cash. The success of a local currency depends upon two parties: the merchant and the consumer. The merchant desires a secure, fast, accountable payment medium. The consumer seeks convenience, speed and ease of use. In the past, local currencies have been printed, with some merchants offering their own loyalty coupons. Consumers had been rewarded with loyalty stamps allowing them to be traded for merchandise. However, such printed forms were not secure, were limited in their redemption value and were not easily transferable to other merchants. Paper based systems are being replaced by digital money, which can be offered as a local currency. Basing the currency on the blockchain technology ensures security and integrity. The app on the smartphone allows the consumer to have local currency readily available in the same way that cash in the pocket would be available. And the link to the merchant for payment, using standard Internet protocol, enables merchants to accept local currency without any major investment in technology. There is the potential that the relative advantage of local currency supersedes that of current payment mechanisms, typically focused on small amounts.

Proposition 1: local currency has a relative advantage over current payment options.

Compatibility. This is "the degree to which an innovation is perceived as consistent with the existing values, past experiences and needs of potential adopters" [22]. If an idea is incompatible, there is more effort required to persuade the individual to adopt it. However, local currencies are compatible. They act in a similar manner to cash. When the local currency has a value linked to fiat money, the amount in the digital wallet can be redeemed in a similar manner to cash. The valuation is compatible with existing currency. There is the necessity of using a smartphone instead of a wallet, but given the ubiquity of smartphone apps this is not an obstacle.

Proposition 2: local currency is compatible with current payment mechanisms.

Complexity. This is the "degree to which an innovation is perceived as relatively difficult to understand and use" [22]. The more complex the innovation, the less likely it will spread. The simpler the innovation, the more likely it will be adopted. Prior to understanding the benefits that could be gained, individuals are not willing to invest much time in learning how to use the innovation. Consumers are familiar with smartphones and use on average eight apps per day [23]. Adding an app is simple. Individuals are familiar with online banking and are comfortable checking their balances and performing certain banking tasks via their mobile device [24]. There has been a lot of publicity about the Google Wallet and Apple Pay such that the idea of having a digital wallet app is not new [25]. These apps have been designed such that they only require a few simple touches on the screen to effect payment.

Proposition 3: the use of a local currency app is simple to use.

Trialability. This is the "degree to which an innovation may be experimented with on a limited basis" [22]. Trialability refers to the ability of the innovation to co-exist with the current method of achieving the same goals. Users will therefore be able to try it on an experimental basis. Prior to the innovation being widely used, there are perceived risks. In the case of a wallet with local currency, consumers would want to exercise choice of payment and be able to select when to use the local currency and when to use other payment options. Consequently, trialability is important. Even the early adopters, who are more innovative [26], will want the option of accessing normal payment methods.

Proposition 4: the use of local currency can be trialed alongside current means of payment.

Observability. This is the "degree to which the results of an innovation are visible to others" [27]. Adopters can then assess whether it is worthwhile continuing with the innovation. Consumers are able to assess the advantages and disadvantages of using their smartphone to pay for merchandise with local currency loaded into their digital wallet. They can compare the convenience and speed in comparison with standard payment methods. In a similar manner, merchants can assess whether there are advantages to be gained.

Proposition 5: the advantages and disadvantages of using local currency can be observed.

Privacy. According to Westin, [28] privacy is the "claim of individuals, groups, or institutions to determine for themselves when, how, and to what extent information about them is communicated to others." When consumers download a mobile wallet app, they provide personal information and are requested to allow the app to access their location [29]. They are sensitive to the provision of such data, but they recognize that there are benefits to location-based services [30]. When using a local currency, the benefits include the ease of finding merchants nearby, any financial reward associated with the local currency and the social aspect of assisting the community. According to the privacy paradox, the risks of privacy loss are balanced against the benefits gained [31].

Proposition 6: Consumers are concerned about the privacy of their data when using local currency but balance these against the benefits.

4 Research Methodology

The methodology adopted for this research was qualitative. The availability of a local currency is limited to a select number of geographical locations and the application has only recently been introduced. There has not been a high rate of diffusion and currently, the users are the innovators and early adopters [32]. It would therefore be difficult to collect data to create a data set that would be meaningful to analyze statistically.

The case study approach was deemed appropriate as it allows the researcher to investigate in greater depth [33, 34]. Given the location of the Colu local currency, investigations can be carried out within a single setting. Data was collected by conducting interviews and reading documents about the company available on the Internet. Case study research method is "an empirical inquiry that investigates a contemporary phenomenon within its real-life context; when the boundaries between phenomenon and context are not clearly evident; and in which multiple sources of evidence are used" [35]. The method allows complex situations to be interpreted by the researcher [36].

Interviews were conducted with the founder of Colu, three merchants and a number of consumers. The merchants had signed up to Colu. The consumers were customers of the merchants. Some of them had used the Colu app, whilst others did not use it and some had not even heard of the app. The interviews were semi-structured and were recorded and transcribed for subsequent analysis. Statements made by participants are printed in italics in the next section.

5 Results

5.1 Proposition 1: Relative Advantage

Payment to merchants can be in the form of cash, debit card or credit card. The merchants preferred Colu to credit cards because the transaction fees to Colu were lower than those to the credit card companies

Commission is lower than with credit cards.

Colu also provides additional tools to the merchants helping them analyze their customer's spending behavior as well as balancing their Colu receipts without having to handle cash. This was not mentioned as an advantage, although the owners of two coffee bars did observe that Colu was more popular with takeout customers.

Currently, Colu is offering a monetary incentive to join and to top-up. Future plans are to offer a cryptocurrency token. When asked about the advantages of a digital token, one coffee bar owner was not that interested.

Not sure that tokens will be an advantage. I am not a Bitcoin guy. I am just a simple coffee roaster.

Customers have the choice of paying with cash, credit or debit. All customers interviewed had received the 25-shekel sign up bonus and were aware of the bonus of an extra 10% when topping up their Colu balance.

I like the 25-shekel sign up and the 10% top-up. It's free money.

They were also aware that they could receive a further 25 shekels if they were instrumental in signing up another person.

I like the incentive if you sign up someone.

Using a smartphone for payment also enhanced social image. It was 'cool' to pay with a smartphone.

It looks good, when you pay with your smartphone.

Some merchants and some customers were aware that Colu was local and that it was helping smaller independent businesses.

It supports the local community.

From these various responses, by both merchants and consumers, there were relative advantages in using Colu over the current mechanism of cash. Proposition 1 is supported.

5.2 Proposition 2 – Compatibility

The implementation of Colu for the merchant does not require any additional devices. The company, Colu, sets up an account for the merchants. Consumers use their smartphones by clicking on the name of the merchant, entering the amount and pressing send. The money is then deposited in the merchant's account with no additional activity.

Colu provides accounting and reconciliation reports to track the transfer of funds. The Colu local currency is convertible where one Colu equals one shekel.

> *When the customer pays with Colu, it is convertible to shekels.*
> *It is not like Bitcoin. It is like cash.*
> *Customers can pay with their credit card or pay with their phone.*

Consumers know when a merchant accepts Colu currency because the app displays the name of that merchant and because the merchant displays a sign in their window. Colu shekels can be used via the smartphone. Other forms of payment are still viable.

Colu is compatible with the payment options already in place. Other than the addition of the Colu app by the consumer and the linking of a bank account to Colu by the merchant, there are no changes. Proposition 2 is supported.

5.3   Proposition 3 – Simplicity

There is a 74% penetration of smartphones in Israel [37]. Apps are designed for ease of use and, given the constraints of the small screen with touch capabilities, often have similar characteristics [38]. Once the app is downloaded and the consumer allows access to the geo-location capabilities of the smartphone, Colu looks for merchants that are physically close to the consumer's location. Images of the merchant are displayed with descriptions of the merchandise. A map shows the distance and the route there. When arriving at the merchant, the icon of the merchant is clearly visible and with one touch, the consumer is ready to enter the amount owing into the app.

> *It is easier than taking out a credit card.*

Given that the smartphone is readily at hand, for some customers it is simpler than taking out a credit card from the wallet. Proposition 3 is supported.

5.4   Proposition 4 – Trialability

Merchants are able to accept payments via the Colu app while at the same time accepting cash, credit and debit. However, consumers only have access to those merchants that have signed up.

> *There are limited places where Colu can be used. I wish there were more in my area.*

For both the merchant and the consumer, it is easy to trial Colu as other means of payment are still viable. Proposition 4 is supported.

5.5   Proposition 5 – Observability

Colu provides the merchant with analytical tools that help them understand their customers.

> *Some customers want to pay with their smartphone.*
> *Younger customers like to use Colu.*
> *Colu is trendy.*
> *Older customers are less likely to have Colu on their smartphone.*

With the app on their phone, customers can find out which merchants nearby accept Colu. They can compare the convenience of Colu with other forms of payment.

> *It is faster than credit.*
> *Sometimes the credit card terminal is in use and I have to wait.*

Both merchants and consumers can observe the results of trialing Colu. Proposition 5 is supported.

5.6   Proposition 6 – Privacy

Customers know that they are disclosing personal information, but they are not concerned.

> *I am not concerned about privacy.*
> *There is already a lot of information about me out there.*

They enjoy the benefits of supporting the local community. In addition, Colu currently is giving a bonus when topping up or when signing up a friend. These benefits are worth the small risk of disclosing personal information.

> *Supporting the local community is important to me, so I don't mind letting them know where I am.*
> *It is easy to use and I receive free money when topping up or signing up a friend.*

One customer was a tourist from relatively cash-free Holland. She was concerned about privacy and did not feel that the benefits of smartphone usage outweighed those concerns.

> *I do not use my smartphone for any payments. I am from Holland where we do not use much cash. I prefer to use my debit and credit cards and not my phone.*

For those consumers who had adopted the local currency app, privacy was not a concern. Proposition 6 was supported.

6   Discussion

The speedy rise in the value of Bitcoin projected it into the public consciousness and created awareness of the underlying technology, the blockchain. Shared distributable databases can be created in a secure manner. Transactions are stored on multiple networked computers accessible by anyone, but digitally secured by public-private key cryptography. No central authority is required because the computers on the network write blocks of transactions each of which is linked to prior blocks, making it impossible to change a transaction already recorded. A number of companies now offer blockchain platforms that support the issuance of crypto-tokens. These digitally secure certificates can be exchanged for services or products.

Local currencies are new and their success depends upon their adoption and diffusion by merchants and consumers. According to Innovation Diffusion Theory [32], an innovation has to satisfy five characteristics in order to be successfully adopted: relative advantage, compatibility, complexity, trialability and observability. We proposed that local currencies do satisfy these five characteristics. In additon, because personal data is being shared, we proposed that the privacy protection is another important characteristic.

Colu is a company in Israel, which has extended the Ethereum platform to create a currency to be used within a geographical area. They have created local currencies in four areas: two in the United Kingdom and two in Israel. Our case study investigated the adoption in Tel Aviv. The Colu local currency is equivalent in value to one Israeli shekel (US$0.28). Consumers can buy local shekels and use them at member merchants via the Colu mobile wallet. Payments by local shekels are instead of cash or credit.

From semi-structured interviews with merchants and consumers, all propositions were supported. Consumers enjoyed the advantage of paying with their mobile phone, receiving a bonus for signing up and another bonus for topping up their local shekel balance. Merchants enjoyed the advantage of lower transaction fees when handling payments. They also were able to advertise their business via the Colu app, encouraging consumers to shop within the community. Payments via the Colu wallet were compatible with existing payment options. Merchants received full credit for the local currency they accepted. The mobile app was easy to use. Merchants were able to trial the local currency, while still accepting other payment mechanisms. Consumers were able to trial Colu on their mobile phone, while still being able to pay with cash, credit or debit if they so chose. All participants could observe the results of using Colu and make a decision to continue its use. Our propositions have been supported via the case study.

6.1 Limitations

This is a case study where the investigation was limited to one city. A limited number of interviews were conducted gathering opinions, which in turn were interpreted by the researcher. One of the findings was that relative advantage was a key influencing factor. Therefore there must be an understanding of what alternative payment methods are available. In the case of Tel Aviv, 'tap and pay'[1] is not readily available so consumers do not have the option of waving a plastic card or a smartphone over a terminal. Results may be different where tap and pay is an available means of payment. This qualitative study was limited in scope and results are not generalizable. However, they may be transferable to similar situations where a local currency is introduced within a defined geographical area.

6.2 Future Research

The focus of this research was on the use of a local currency in one specific market. Future researchers could extend this research by conducting a similar qualitative approach in other locations where local currencies are available. When the local

---

[1] 'Tap and Pay' refers to contactless payment cards, which can be placed in proximity of an enabled reader. The card does not have to be inserted or swiped by the reader.

currency wallet becomes more popular, users could be surveyed and sufficient sample size could be collected for quantitative analysis. Current rewards for using the local currency are in the form of extra funds that can be used for purchases. Future plans are to replace the acquisition bonus with crypto-tokens. Future research can then investigate consumer acceptance of these tokens as rewards for using local currency. Many countries are moving to having less cash in circulation [39]. The alternative to cash is digital money where payments can be made via a plastic card or a digital wallet on the smartphone. Both qualitative and quantitative studies of specific applications would assist practitioners in determining best practice to increase the rate of diffusion of their products.

7   Conclusion

Innovation Diffusion Theory can be used as a foundation to guide theory building around the adoption of local currencies. Because sensitive information concerning payments is involved, theory can be extended with the construct of privacy. In this case study, both merchant and consumer enjoyed a relative advantage. The merchant had transaction fees that were lower than credit card fees. Consumers were given a sign-up bonus and a top-up bonus – free money! Future plans are to reward participants with tokens, whose value will depend upon the local currency activity.

The implications for practitioners are that they should ensure that local currency is not viewed as something radically new, but rather as a simple extension of existing payment mechanisms. Merchants do not have to make major changes: they can accept local currencies while at the same time accepting all other forms of payments. Consumers can simply add the Colu mobile wallet to their smartphone, see the locations of local merchants, and choose to pay with local currency or existing forms of payment. The ability to trial and observe allows all parties to assess the relative advantages in order to make an adoption decision.

References

1. Adams, C.: Have Money, Will Travel: A Brief Survey of the Mobile Payments Landscape. Office of the Privacy Commissioner of Canada (2013)
2. ING International Survey, Mobile Banking 2017: All aboard for the cashless society (2017)
3. Skingsley, C.: How the Riksbank encourages innovation in the retail payments market. In: Annales des Mines-Réalités industrielles. FFE (2017)
4. Wonglimpiyarat, J.: The new Darwinism of the payment system: will bitcoin replace our cash-based society? J. Internet Bank. Commer. 21(S2), 1–15 (2016)
5. Mamun, S.A., Musa, S.: BLOCKCHAIN. Cost Manag. 45(5), 2–8 (2017)
6. Peck, M.E.: Blockchains: how they work and why they'll change the world. IEEE Spectr. 54 (10), 26–35 (2017)
7. Julin, E.: The Riksbank's e-krona project. The Riksbank, Stockholm (2017)
8. Engert, W., Fung, B.: Central Bank Digital Currency: Motivations and Implications. B.O. Canada, Ottawa (2017)
9. Rogoff, K.S.: The Curse of Cash. Princeton University Press, Princeton (2016). pages cm

10. The Economist: Why Big Banknotes May Be on the Way Out, in The Economist (Online). The Economist Newspaper NA, Inc., London (2016)
11. Wood, G.: Ethereum: a secure decentralised generalised transaction ledger. Ethereum Project Yellow Paper, 151 (2014)
12. Orcutt, M.: How Blockchain is Kickstarting the Financial Lives of Refugees. MIT Technology Review (2017)
13. Colu. Be a Local (2017). https://www.colu.com/. Accessed 10 Feb 2018
14. Colu. Colu Local Network: Whitepaper (2018). https://cln.network/pdf/cln_whitepaper.pdf. Accessed 10 Feb 2017
15. Nakamoto, S.: Bitcoin: a peer-to-peer electronic cash system (2008)
16. Conley, J.P.: Blockchain and the economics of crypto-tokens and initial coin offerings, Vanderbilt University Department of Economics (2017)
17. Adhami, S., Giudici, G., Martinazzi, S.: Why do businesses go crypto? An empirical analysis of Initial Coin Offerings (2017)
18. ICObench. ICObench Knowledge Base (2017). https://icobench.com/ico/colu-local-network. Accessed 10 Feb 2018
19. Smith and Crown. ICOs and crowdsales (2018). https://www.smithandcrown.com/icos-crowdsale-history/
20. Brühl, V.: Virtual currencies, distributed ledgers and the future of financial services. Intereconomics 52(6), 370–378 (2017)
21. Colu. Colu Local Network: Token Sale Summary (2017). https://cln.network/pdf/token_sale_summary.pdf. Accessed 10 Feb 2018
22. Rogers, E.M.: Diffusion of Innovations, 5th edn. Free Press, New York (2003). xxi, 551 p.
23. Statista. Average number of mobile apps used per day by users in the United States from June to December 2016 (2017). https://www.statista.com/statistics/681216/us-daily-smartphone-and-tablet-app-usage/. Accessed 10 Feb 2018
24. Dash, M., Bhusan, P.B., Samal, S.: Determinants of customers' adoption of mobile banking: an empirical study by integrating diffusion of innovation with attitude. J. Internet Bank. Commer. 19(3), 1–21 (2015)
25. de Kerviler, G., Demoulin, N.T., Zidda, P.: Adoption of in-store mobile payment: are perceived risk and convenience the only drivers? J. Retail. Consum. Serv. 31, 334–344 (2016)
26. Lee, S.Y.: Examining the factors that influence early adopters' smartphone adoption: the case of college students. Telematics Inform. 31(2), 308–318 (2014)
27. Adegoke, B.B.: Factors influencing the adoption of new information technology in the staffing industry, Capella University, United States – Minnesota (2007)
28. Westin, A.F.: Privacy and Freedom, 1st edn. Atheneum, New York (1967). xvi, 487 p.
29. Wang, T., Duong, T.D., Chen, C.C.: Intention to disclose personal information via mobile applications: a privacy calculus perspective. Int. J. Inf. Manag. 36(4), 531–542 (2016)
30. Zhang, R., Chen, J.Q., Lee, C.J.: Mobile commerce and consumer privacy concerns. J. Comput. Inf. Syst. 53(4), 31–38 (2013)
31. Lee, J.-M., Rha, J.-Y.: Personalization–privacy paradox and consumer conflict with the use of location-based mobile commerce. Comput. Hum. Behav. 63, 453–462 (2016)
32. Rogers, E.M.: Diffusion of Innovations. London Free Press, New York (1995)
33. Eisenhardt, K.M.: Building theories from case study research. academy of management. Acad. Manag. Rev. 14(4), 532 (1989)
34. Das, R.K., Singha, A.: Case study as a research method. Glob. Res. Methodol. J. 3, 1–6 (2011)
35. Yin, R.K.: Case Study Research: Design and Methods. Applied Social Research Methods Series, 160 p. Sage Publications, Beverly Hills (1984)

36. Stake, R.E.: The Art of Case Study Research. Sage Publications Inc., Thousand Oaks (1995). xv
37. Research, P.: Smartphone ownership and Internet usage continues to climb in emerging economies (2016). http://www.pewglobal.org/2016/02/22/smartphone-ownership-and-internet-usage-continues-to-climb-in-emerging-economies/. Accessed 14 Feb 2018
38. Iacob, C., Veerappa, V., Harrison, R.: What are you complaining about? A study of online reviews of mobile applications. In: Proceedings of the 27th International BCS Human Computer Interaction Conference. British Computer Society (2013)
39. Tee, H.-H., Ong, H.-B.: Cashless payment and economic growth. Financ. Innov. 2(1), 1–9 (2016)

Business Analytics and Visualization

Biometrics and Business Information Visualization: Research Review, Agenda and Opportunities

Dinko Bačić[✉]

University of Southern Indiana, Evansville, IN 47712, USA
dbacic@usi.edu

Abstract. Business Intelligence & Analytics' dashboards, data visualizations, and visual analysis systems are cognitive tools that heavily rely on our understanding of subconscious-level processing, human perception and cognitive processes overall. These cognitive tools are the focal point of data visualization subfield called Business Information Visualization (BIV). While the BIV field has seen calls for an increased need of deploying physiological sensing techniques and the use of biometric data, these calls have yet to translate to a more comprehensive evaluation of human response to visual displays and systems using business data. This research identifies and describes biometric sensors researchers should consider in BIV, provides a brief review of literature at the nexus of data visualization and biometrics, and identifies a biometric data-based research agenda and opportunities for BIV.

Keywords: Business Information Visualization · Information visualization
Biometrics · Physiological sensing · Eye tracking · EEG
Galvanic skin response · GSR · fNIRS · Facial muscle movement
FACS

1 Introduction

Business Intelligence & Analytics' (BI&A) dashboards, data visualizations, and visual analysis systems are cognitive tools that heavily rely on our understanding of subconscious-level processing, human perception and cognitive processes overall. These tools are the focal point of data visualization subfield called Business Information Visualization (BIV) or the use of computer-supported, interactive, visual representation of business data to amplify cognition [1] to achieve a better understanding of business (processes, data, and behaviors) to improve decision making [2]. While the literature suggests the role of cognitive processes in BIV [2, 3] and visualizations in general [4], research attempting to measure the physiological user response as correlates of those cognitive processes is scarce. The scarcity of BIV users' physiological response research is surprising given findings from psychology research that evaluating visual interface performance without measuring cognitive processes, such as workload, may lead to incorrect conclusions about the cognitive efficiency of an interface [5–7].

© Springer International Publishing AG, part of Springer Nature 2018
F. F.-H. Nah and B. S. Xiao (Eds.): HCIBGO 2018, LNCS 10923, pp. 671–686, 2018.
https://doi.org/10.1007/978-3-319-91716-0_53

For a field that declares to focus on cognition amplification, memory limits, preattentive attributes, and Gestalt psychology [8], the lack of more pronounced research inclusion of physiological measurements of a user response to visual capabilities of BI&A systems and processes represents a gap and an opportunity. In this research, I offer a starting path to close the gap and in the process, provide the following contributions: (i) identify and describe biometric sensors researchers should consider in BIV, (ii) provide a brief review of literature at the nexus of data visualization and biometrics, and (iii) identify a biometric-based research agenda and opportunities for BIV.

Organizations continue to make large investments in BI&A or "the techniques, technologies, systems, practices, methodologies, and applications that analyze critical business data to help an enterprise better understand its business and market and make timely business decisions" [9]. The visual layer and employee-facing interface of BI&A is often made available and delivered through visually intensive applications such as dashboards and other types of highly visual reporting and decision-supporting solutions that require insights from BIV, a field that is informed by and find its academic roots in interlinked subfields that literature labeled as Graphical display, Data Visualization, Information Visualization, and Visual Analytics. Despite BIV's significant impact and use within organizations, research focused on users' physiological response to BIV as a way of understanding users' and decision makers' perceptual and cognitive processes is still underdeveloped. The lack of progress is not limited to research only as "chartjunk" [8] design practices prevail in practice and are often enabled by both vendors and dashboard designers. Unfortunately, the visual layer of BI&A software too often gets in the way, interrupting and undermining the thinking process rather than complementing and extending it [10]. The frequent inappropriate use of information presentation formats [11] may lead to suboptimal decisions [12]. Further amplifying the practical significance of this research is the reality of users being asked to make decisions in the age of information overload, where the role of systems supporting visual analysis and data representation that filter and separate signal from noise is critical.

In the wider visualization field, others recognized the gap and offered an overview of available physiological sensing technology in evaluating information visualization systems [13], suggested the use of cognitive measures in related scientific visualization [14], evaluated research opportunities of using specific biometric sensor (eye tracking) [15], and made a call for more Information Systems research in BIV using biometrics [2]. This manuscript builds and extend their call by (i) documenting some of the progress in the last decade and (ii) suggesting BIV-system centric and user abilities centric lens that would benefit from applying those physiological sensing technologies.

The rest of the paper is organized as follows. Section 2 provides a brief historical and research summary of Business Information Visualization and introduces its critical elements. Section 3 provides an overview of biometric sensors that can provide value to BIV research and documents key literature at the nexus of broader visualization field and biometrics. Recommendations for future research design based on literature review are offered as well. Section 4 discusses the research agenda through the lens of critical BIV elements. The paper ends with concluding remarks in Sect. 5.

2 Business Information Visualization - Background

While the term Information Visualization has been coined in 1999 [1], it is important to recognize that the history of the field dates back long time before computers and information technology platforms. It was not until the 17th century and Renee Descartes [16] that two dimensional visual grids were first used purely to represent numbers. Through works of Heinrich Lambert and William Playfair (early 1800s), graphical design was at last no longer dependent on direct analogy to the physical world [17]. John Snow's famous cholera outbreak infographic and Minard's infographic showing Napoleon's march to Moscow and the consequent retreat represent some of the best visualization works of that era and beyond [8]. The innovative data visualization research remained effectively dormant in the first half of the 20th century, until a 'perfect storm' occurred with a call for recognition of data analysis as a separate discipline [18], the birth of computer technology and Bertin's [19] attempt to classify all graphic marks as expression of data. In 1970's, Management Information Systems' researchers are starting to explore presentation formats [20, 21] while statistical and quantitative themes continued in the 80s with Cleveland [22] and Tufte [8]. The cognitive perspective of information visualization came to the forefront in the same period with works by Kosslyn [23] and Tufte [24]. Some of the early notable Information Systems (IS) academic papers occurred in the same period [25–27] with emphasis on the analysis of computer graphics' implications on decision making. This research led to the introduction of the cognitive fit theory [3, 28], which attempts to explain the appropriateness of emphasizing the importance of task-representation match and resulting cognitive effort. With the emergence of Information Visualization (IV) and Business Intelligence (BI), a new discipline called Business Information Visualization came to life in the last 20 years, drawing from historical experiences, events and disciplines such as the ones described above.

Most of the existing IV and BIV research adopted the lens of information representation and interaction [29]. Information representation, or spatial representations that are derived from symbolic data [1], has been researched extensively. Historically, a large part of it centered on understanding the significance of representation formats (histograms, tables, bar charts, bullet graphs, and other formats) and layout/position. More recent research is exploring the implications of interactivity, exploration, storytelling, and user & data characteristics. Bačić and Fadlalla [30] revealed an essential link between visualization and decision making support through the emphasis of human visual abilities and suggested the need for BI's visualization components to assist human intelligence. They provided an organizing framework [2] identifying critical BIV elements aligned with five nonverbal (visual) mental abilities: interaction, exploration, business acumen, relevant data, analytics, statistics, representation, perception, cognition, cognitive effort, memory & storytelling (Table 1).

The next section provides a brief overview of biometric sensors researchers should consider deploying in the BIV context, followed by a review of existing research at the nexus of biometrics and BIV, and the larger data visualization field.

Table 1. Business information visualization elements

Human IQ dimensions	BIV elements
Fluid intelligence	Interaction
	Exploration
Domain-specific knowledge	Business acumen
	Relevant data
Quantitative reasoning	Analytics
	Statistics
Visual-spatial processing	Representation
	Perception
	Cognition
	Cognitive effort
Working and short term memory	Memory
	Storytelling

3 Biometrics and BIV Background

The understanding of user physiological response to a BI&A system, specifically its presentation layer is still in its infancy. While there are remaining significant challenges in interpreting physiological data, measurement validity concerns [13], and the issues stemming from BIV's complex and interactive setting, the experiments capturing user physiological response are becoming more accessible and insightful. Several human physiological responses may be measured effectively in experimental, yet realistic setting using biometric equipment and techniques. A select few particularly promising in the BIV context are eye gaze and pupil dilation (visual attention and effort), galvanic skin response (arousal), facial muscle movement (affective states and emotional engagement), and brain activity (brain workload and cognitive engagement).

3.1 Biometrics Overview

Driven in part by the 'eye-mind hypothesis' [31], eye tracking is considered effective in assessing user's attention and effort as it reveals how the user reads and scans the displayed information by capturing users' eye fixation, saccades, blink and pupil dilation-based metrics [32]. Fixations [33] (time spent looking at a specific location), saccades (the rapid eye movements between fixations) and pupil dilation [34, 35] responses have been linked to cognitive processes indicating various forms of attention, interest, mental effort, and cognitive load [36, 37]. Eye tracking-based metrics have been used across many disciplines measuring attention in reading, psycholinguistics, website usage, online gaming, writing, and language acquisition [38]. The standard metrics can be separated into three categories: fixation-derived metrics (fixation count, duration, time to first fixation), saccade-derived metrics, and scan path-derived metrics (fixation and saccades sequence, area-of-interest (AOI) revisits) [15]. Despite a very long track record of using eye tracking across numerous fields, the eye tracking-based research, while emergent and the most common biometric technique in visualization

[13], is still rare in BIV or represents a relatively small portion of system evaluation in broader data visualization field [15].

Galvanic skin response (GSR), also referred to as electrodermal activity (EDA), Skin Conductance (SC) or Psychogalvanic Reflex (PGR), is a measure of conductivity of human skin and measures sympathetic nervous system response as an indicator of general arousal. As participant's effort, engagement, excitement, or anxiety level changes, the sympathetic nervous system reacts by releasing small amounts of moisture (sweat secretion) in the skin (sweat glands). Highly sensitive GSR devices capture skin conductance using skin electrodes and researchers deploy them in detecting the arousal level of emotions [39, 40], stress [40, 41], and cognitive load [42]. The use of GSR-based biometric data is currently minimal in the evaluation of BIV systems.

Biometrics based on the facial muscle movement offers insights into users' affective states, more specifically, their emotional valance. Facial Action Coding System (FACS), a method designed to help classify human facial movements by their appearance on the face [43, 44] is used by facial expression technology vendors to identify and understand not only facial units but also combine them to capture emotional valence (positive, negative) and basic emotions (joy, disgust, contempt, confusion, frustration, surprise, anger) [38]. Simultaneous use of GSR and automated FACS is a particularly effective way of understanding both the valance and the arousal associated with an emotional response. The use of facial muscle movement offers promising potential in BIV, especially in assessing system's usability (valance) and aesthetics.

While there are several ways to capture biometric data based on brain activity, electroencephalograms (EEG) and functional near-infrared spectroscopy (fNIRS) are particularly useful to BIV as they are very effective and non-invasive methods[1]. These devices detect electrical activity in the brain through the placement of electrodes on the head. EEG devices detect fields (waves) of electrical activity or neuronal oscillations of neurons firing around our brains. These waves provide a signal in the form of waves at different frequencies: delta (<3.5 Hz), theta (4–7.5 Hz), alpha (8–13 Hz), and beta (14–18 Hz) frequency bands. Researchers found that a change in specific waves correlates to several cognitive processes [45]. EEG has been proven effective in detecting alertness, cognitive workload [46, 47], cognitive overload [48], insight generation [49], memory and new information encoding [45], various levels of engagement/boredom [47], approach/avoidance motivation [50], and emotions [51]. Although relatively non-invasive, high in temporal resolution and low cost, EEG sensors can take a long time to set-up, have low spatial resolution and are sensitive to interferences. fNIRS can overcome some of those limitations as they have high spatial resolution and are less sensitive to interferences (cite) [52]. fNIRS detect the brain activity by using near-infrared light to measure levels and oxygenation of the blood in the tissue at depths of 1–3 cm. Like EEG, fNIRS was used to detect cognitive workload [7], a potentially useful metric to assess BIV efficiency and effectiveness.

---

[1] Other brain imaging techniques have been used in visualization research and can be very useful (for example, functional magnetic resonance (fMRI) and positron-emission tomography (PET)) but are excluded from this discussion due to their invasive nature and limited or no ability to test the subjects in BIV-realistic setting.

3.2   Biometrics and BIV

The review of literature focused on information visualization in the business (i.e. BIV) context revealed only three research efforts [38, 53, 54] focused on using or integrating biometrics. However, since BIV is firmly rooted in IV field and the distinction between the two is not always clear or useful, this manuscript provides a brief literature summary of the research at the nexus of biometrics and broader visualization field, focused on manuscripts with findings more directly applicable to the business context.

Eye Tracking. Eye tracking, although underutilized [55], is the dominant physiological sensing technology used to evaluate data visualizations. In the context of bar and radial chart, eye tracking was used to evaluate the influence of individuals' perceptual speed and working memory on gaze behavior [56]. Eye tracking was applied to evaluate simple information graphics, such as bar charts & line graphs [57, 58] and tables using various sorting techniques [59, 60]. Related eye tracking study partially showed that the decision quality difference came from the changes in decision strategies while noting incapability of capturing peripheral vision as a limitation of the eye tracking method [61]. Another study used eye tracking to study how parallel coordinate visualizations are perceived, and compared the results to the optimal visual scan path required to complete the tasks [62]. While not traditionally used in business dashboards and other visual displays, node-link diagrams are becoming more common in analyzing networks in the business context as well. The research focused on understanding sequential characteristics of eye movement in node-link diagrams is robust [63–69] and should be considered when deploying in the BIV context.

Several studied using eye tracking focused on understanding the process of graph comprehension. A comparison of linear and radial charts found that tasks requiring value lookup on one or two dimensions are more efficiently achieved using linear graphs. In the process, the same study found evidence of a three-stage processing model leveraged by visualization readers (i) find desired data dimension, (ii) find its data point, and (iii) map the data point to its value [55]. On other hand, suggestions were made that graph comprehension proceeds in distinct stages [70] and in sequential order; readers interpret graphs by first focusing on the nodes and then by processing the lines between the nodes [71]. Others noted the complexity of graph comprehension and reported that users, instead of spending time on patterns, were spending time mostly relating graph lines to referents/data legends [72] or performing encoding-recoding strategies to compensate for memory limitations [58].

In a context of dashboards, research shows that visualizations with misuse and overuse of colors do not lead to poorer decision performance but rather decision makers using such dashboards experience more cognitive effort and take longer to make a decision [53]. Eye tracking was also used to assess several conventional qualitative dashboard design guidelines, including the role of title and the supporting text, the use of pictograms and their role in recognition, how redundancy understanding can improve recognition, and how redundancy and memorability help to effectively communicate the message [54]. The role of information scents and context clues was assessed in Hyperbolic Tree display format [73], while the efficiency or effectiveness of the two highlighting methods in the context of supporting the visual search for information in linked geo-displays [74].

The use of eye tracking in combination with interaction logs, and thinking-aloud protocols in the context of interactive visualizations and insight creation was proposed as valuable [75]. Related empirical research dealing with challenges of insight creation in visual analytics reports that think-aloud insight statement are accompanied by peaks in the pupil diameter, usually followed by a sharp drop while fixation duration are good indicators of higher cognitive effort with some slight delay in comparison with the pupil diameter [36]. Pupillary dilations were used to compare cognitive efforts across auditory and visual presentation tasks, suggesting that when that visual task presentation leads to lower cognitive load [37].

There is only study that attempted to suggest areas in which eye tracking could be useful in evaluating visual display of data and visual analytics and identify open research challenges [15]. The same study provided an overview of how eye tracking is currently used in the evaluation of visualization techniques, how cognitive models could be applied in our use of eye tracking for visual analytics, and provided a list of additional research efforts linking eye tracking with visual analytics.

Other Sensors (GSR, EEG and fNIRs). Despite calls for more use of biometric sensors in the context of data visualization [38, 76], the use of sensors other than eye trackers is limited. No relevant research was identified attempting to assess emotional engagement and valance through facial muscle movement and FACS. Similarly, only a small study [5] using GSR (and heart rate) attempted to test the correlates of Bertin's [19] efficiency ranking of visual variables. Five selected visual characterizations (angle, text, surface, framed rectangles and luminosity) were evaluated in an Air Traffic Control setting but the study failed to confirm the ranking. Only in the case of angle and text visual variables the difference in galvanic skin response was detected. Due to small sample, we should be very cautious in interpreting these results.

Although the use of relatively less invasive brain imaging techniques such as EEG and fNIRS in broader HCI field is not uncommon, their use in a narrower data visualization filed is still in infancy. However, promising findings from cognitive science found a unique pattern in brain activity that corresponds with the unique sensation of the "a-ha moment" [49], which was supported in a study using ManyEyes map-based visualizations where a connection between insight and frustration and excitement was detected [77]. Beyond insight generation response measurement, EEG-generated alpha and theta signals were analyzed to assess cognitive resource strain on users when using different methods of visualizing distribution data [78].

Researchers tested the possibility of measuring the impact of data representation using fNIRS [6] and confirmed the promising potential of fNIRS technology. Study participants reacted differently to pie charts and bar graphs at a cognitive level, but exhibited the same performance characteristics, raising further need to understand the impact of visual displays beyond traditional performance metrics (speed and accuracy).

Literature Review-Based Insights. This brief literature review provides several insights and recommendations regarding the use of biometric sensors in BIV. First, there is a need to start testing and implementing findings from broader HCI and visualization fields into BIV. However, as the research moves into business context, it is critical for experiments to use very realistic business tasks, problems, scenarios and systems. Second, multidisciplinary approaches and collaborations between domain experts (business, HCI, design, psychology, neuroscience, information systems, computer science, and other contextually relevant domains) is important for appropriate experimental design, data analysis and the interpretation of the findings. More cross-discipline and collaborative research is needed. Third, eye tracking sensing technology dominates physiological research in the context of this manuscript. Given the evidence across other biometric technologies as correlates of affective, perceptual, and cognitive processes, there is a need and an opportunity to encourage research using facial muscle movement, galvanic skin response and brain imaging. Fourth, we should encourage and support research that combines multi-sensor research design. Affective, perceptual and cognitive processes are complex, task and subject dependent; using only one biometric technology in an experiment may not reveal critical insights when dealing with such complex processes. Fifth, biometric research is not the 'silver bullet'. We should encourage research that combines simultaneous biometric, survey and behavioral data collection.

4   Business Information Visualization – Research Agenda

The framework introduced in Sect. 2 suggests that BIV, to be effective, needs to support and accentuate relevant human intelligence dimensions. This need requires software that seamlessly interacts with the brain to support and extend human cognitive and perceptual abilities [2]. Given framework's (a) explicit recognition of human cognitive and perceptual response, (b) comprehensiveness rooted in existing visualization literature, and (c) identification of critical components, this research will adopt Bacic and Fadlalla's framework [2] and its BIV elements as a lens through which BIV & Biometrics agenda and research opportunities will be presented.

4.1   Fluid Intelligence - Data Exploration and Interaction

Fluid reasoning/intelligence allows humans to solve new problems on the 'spot' through mental operations such as drawing inferences, concept formation, classification, generating and testing hypothesis, identifying relations, comprehending implications, problem-solving, extrapolating, transforming information, and recognizing patterns [79, 80]. In BIV literature, system capabilities of exploration and interaction with data emerged and are well positioned to support users' fluid reasoning. Exploration is defined as the examination of data without having an apriori understanding of what patterns, information, or knowledge it might contain [81]. Some of the common exploratory tasks include: observing specific data point, patterns or outliers, making inferences, comparing to one's prior knowledge, generating hypotheses and drawing analogies [82].

Interaction capabilities often facilitate exploration capabilities. The goal of interaction is to enable a user to understand information better by allowing the user to interact with the information. The extant literature offers several interaction taxonomies: low level interaction tasks (overview, zoom, filter, details-on-demand, relate, history, and extract) [83], user's intent (select, explore, reconfigure, encode, abstract/elaborate, filter, and connect) [84], and model-based reasoning (external anchoring, information forging and cognitive offloading) [85].

Mental operations performed by users during exploration and interaction are critical to sense making and insight creation. These mental operations require well designed interfaces to support users' visual perception and cognitive processes. Research focused on understanding the physiological response and biometric correlates to affective, perceptual and cognitive processes linked to data exploration and interaction design and deployment can significantly enhance existing knowledge and represents a promising research opportunity. Furthermore, without access to information one cannot explore nor interact with it. BIV is being delivered across multiple platforms including PDAs/smartphones, tablets, and traditional PCs. Multi-platform physiological sensing and biometric research in the context of fluid reasoning represents an opportunity for practical insights.

4.2 Domain-Specific Knowledge - Business Acumen and Data Relevancy

Domain specific knowledge has been defined as individual's breadth and depth of acquired knowledge in specialized (demarcated) domains [80] and is modifiable "software" aspect of the cognitive system [86]. A viewpoint referred to as knowledge-is-power hypothesis is being described as "one of the most influential ideas to emerge in cognitive psychology during the past 25 years and is based on the idea that domain knowledge, and not basic/global cognitive abilities, is the main determinant of success in cognition related tasks" [86].

Literature focused on visualization is yet to approach the topic of knowledge and business acumen in similar depth as in the fields of psychology and cognition. Since it is widely accepted that a significant level of domain knowledge is needed to achieve expertise, BIV usage or deployment by users across various levels of expertize and business acumen is an underdeveloped research area independent of research methodology, let alone in biometric-based research. Similarly, the effectiveness of BIV, even if efficiently deployed in every other aspect, will be eliminated if deployed using inappropriate data. Understanding how experts comprehend, view, process, explore, interact, achieve insights, select appropriate data and eliminate noise when dealing with BIV applications are only some of the research questions biometric-inclusive research should explore. Biometric data using physiological sensors discussed in this research can provide valuable answers focused on the role of domain knowledge, expertize and business acumen in the BIV context.

4.3 Quantitative Reasoning - Analytics and Statistics

The research defines Quantitative Reasoning as a person's wealth (breadth and depth) of acquired store of declarative and procedural quantitative knowledge [80]. In BIV, a system can enhance decision making through Quantitative Reasoning by offering ready-to-use, statistical functions and analytics capabilities. Examples include, on the fly summary statistics such as averages, medians, standard deviations, percentiles as well as more complicated algorithms, calculations, and data mining techniques such as regressions, clustering, and association analysis [2]. With the advent of more advanced analytics and its popularity in the context of Big Data, BI&A users are starting to expect higher integration of analytics capabilities and visual technologies as well. Analytics capabilities and the representation methods once reserved for individuals strong in declarative, procedural quantitative knowledge, and acquired mathematical knowledge (statisticians, modelers and data-scientists), such as box-plots, scatterplots, node-link graphs, decision trees, and tabular representations of statistical data, are increasingly being directed at business analysts [2].

Despite knowing very little how users are responding to these new capabilities, BI&A vendors are starting to incorporate significant statistical and analytics capabilities into their interfaces. Often, the new capabilities are complex and low in transparency, with a potential for users to face challenges, stress, frustration, reach insights and different levels of cognitive load. We know very little about users' neurophysiological responses to these BIV applications especially in the light of varying degrees of expertise in analytics, statistics or how to visually communicate complex results. The trend of adding more advanced capabilities and complex visual representations will most likely continue due to 'fashion-like' popularity of everything labeled 'analytics' or 'Big Data' and the research focused on understanding user response using biometric data offers relevancy and practical value.

4.4 Visual-Spatial Processing - Representation, Perception, Cognition, and Cognitive Effort

Visual Spatial Processing abilities are defined as having the ability to generate, retain, retrieve, and transform well-structured visual images [87]. A significant majority of visualization literature is focused on how to enable visual-spatial processing abilities through research focused on data representation (formats and features), and how visualization choices both impact and are impacted by human perception, cognition, and cognitive effort [2].

Information representation has been researched extensively and a large part of it centered on understanding the significance of representation format (tables vs graphs or comparison between similar versions of the same display type). In addition to representation methods, researchers created a significant body of knowledge around representation elements such as color, object depth and dimensionality and layout, symbols, labels, text, icons, lines, grids, and axes [88]. The design of those elements is often informed by our knowledge of human perception or the process of interpreting and recognizing sensory information [89]. Studies of human perceptual ability including visual imagery, cognitive fit, gestalt principles and preattentive attributes, have led to many design principles [8]. The assessment of the physiological user response to representation method choices, design of representation elements (some call that 'presentation'), the role of the gestalt principles and preattentive attributes, and the evaluation of numerous design principles advocated in research and practice community represent currently underdeveloped research area that would benefit from validating or challenging current practices in BIV.

Within greater discussion of cognition, a robust Information Systems' visualization literature stream emerged with focus on the role of cognitive effort. Over the last 25 years, the Cognitive Fit Theory [3, 28], a dominant theoretical lens, has been used in empirical studies to suggest a significant role of cognitive effort in user efficiency and effectiveness when dealing with data representations. Yet, BIV literature is limited in capturing, measuring or discussing cognitive effort directly [2, 30]. These gaps should be addressed in future by adopting the available correlates of cognitive effort, both perceptual and physiological, such as those advocated through physiological sensors (for example, eye tracker (fixation duration, pupil dilation) and EEG (cognitive workload) or fNIRS (cognitive load)).

4.5 Working and Short-Term Memory – Memory and Storytelling

Lastly, visual designs that minimize memory limitations of human brains have been discussed in visualization literature along with more recent research on storytelling [2]. The importance of memory and the efficient use of memory when visually presenting and processing information is widely acknowledged [90] and the use of design principles leveraging memory is well documented in literature evaluating representation methods [23]. The issue of limited amount of information storable in short term memory is central to many design constraints. Consequently a way to increase the amount of information in short-term memory called "chunking" was proposed [24]. Similarly, the appropriate choice of colors [26] and symbols [19] is often executed in consultation with the relevant memory and cognition-based literature.

Most recently, the relevant literature is beginning to recognize the vital role of storytelling and narrative play. This development is partially rooted in the recognition that report designers are not always decision makers, necessitating well organized and captivating communication [91]. The convergence of computer technology, art and media is now allowing for various storytelling techniques to be deployed in business context as well [92]. These techniques include: building the picture, using comics metaphor, animating, setting mood and place in time, conflict and ambiguity resolution, intentional omission, continuity, effective redundancy, and increasing attention [2]. In the context of BI&A and dashboards, a set of requirements for enhancing BI analysis was proposed consisting of fluid transition, integration, narrative visual aids, interactive visualization, appropriate BI story templates, reuse, and option playback [93].

Both the design principles based on users' memory limitations and the storytelling approaches can benefit from understanding comprehension, recall, insight generation, truth-telling, user affective states and the overall decision-making implications. The physiological sensing techniques and the biometric data discussed in this research can offer valuable insights into this dimension (memory) of enhancing human visual intelligence abilities in the BI&A context.

5 Conclusion

While the BIV field has seen calls for an increased need for the use of physiological sensing techniques and the resulting biometric data, these calls have yet to translate to a more extensive evaluation of human response to visual displays and systems using business data. To initiate the process of addressing the gap, this research offers the following three contributions to research and practice. First, this research identified and described human physiological responses that may be measured in experimental setting using biometric equipment and techniques in the BIV context; eye gaze and pupil dilation (visual attention and effort), galvanic skin response (arousal), facial muscle movement (affective states and emotional engagement), and brain activity (brain workload and cognitive engagement). Second, it provided a brief review of literature at the nexus of data visualization and biometrics leading to five recommendations concerning the more effective use of biometric sensors in BIV. Third, this research identified six focus areas for a more robust BIV research agenda.

In conclusion, current BIV research is manly focused on gathering behavioral and self-reported data. Despite BIV's reliance on the need to understand subconscious-level processing, human perception and cognitive processes overall; the use of biometric data is mainly absent in the BIV. The current state-of-the-research represents a considerable opportunity for both a theoretical and practical impact. This manuscript provides an initial roadmap of how and in which context BIV research should employ physiological sensors and the resulting biometric data.

References

1. Card, S., Mackinlay, J., Shneiderman, B.: Readings in Information Visualization: Using Vision to Think. Morgan Kaufmann, Burlington (1999)
2. Bačić, D., Fadlalla, A.: Business information visualization intellectual contributions: an integrative framework of visualization capabilities and dimensions of visual intelligence. Decis. Support Syst. **89**, 77–86 (2016)
3. Vessey, I.: Cognitive fit: a theory-based analysis of the graphs versus tables literature. Decis. Sci. **22**, 219–240 (1991)
4. Peck, E.M., Yuksel, B.F., Harrison, L., Ottley, A., Chang, R.: Towards a 3-dimensional model of individual cognitive differences: position paper. In: Proceedings of the 2012 BELIV Workshop: Beyond Time and Errors - Novel Evaluation Methods for Visualization, pp. 6:1–6:6. ACM, New York (2012)
5. Causse, M., Hurter, C.: The physiological user's response as a clue to assess visual variables effectiveness. In: Kurosu, M. (ed.) HCD 2009. LNCS, vol. 5619, pp. 167–176. Springer, Heidelberg (2009). https://doi.org/10.1007/978-3-642-02806-9_20
6. RS brain sensing to evaluate information visualization interfaces. In: Proceedings of the SIGCHI Conference on Human Factors in Computing Systems, pp. 473–482. ACM, New York (2013)
7. Hirshfield, L.M., Solovey, E.T., Girouard, A., Kebinger, J., Jacob, R.J.K., Sassaroli, A., Fantini, S.: Brain measurement for usability testing and adaptive interfaces: an example of uncovering syntactic workload with functional near infrared spectroscopy. In: Proceedings of the SIGCHI Conference on Human Factors in Computing Systems, pp. 2185–2194. ACM, New York (2009)
8. Tufte, E.: The Visual Display of Quantitative Information (1983)
9. Chen, H., Chiang, R.H.L., Storey, V.C.: Business intelligence and analytics: from big data to big impact. MIS Q. **36**, 1165–1188 (2012)
10. Few, S.: BizViz: The Power of Visual Business Intelligence (2006). http://www.b-eye-network.com/view/2470

11. Tractinsky, N., Meyer, J.: Chartjunk or goldgraph? effects of persenataion objectives and content desirability on information presentation: effects of presentation objectives and content desirability on information presentation. MIS Q. **23**, 397–420 (1999)
12. Amer, T.S., Ravindran, S.: The effect of visual illusions on the graphical display of information. J. Inf. Syst. **24**, 23–42 (2008)
13. Riche, N.H.: Beyond system logging : human logging for evaluating information visualization. In: 2009 CHI (2009)
14. Anderson, E.W.: Evaluating visualization using cognitive measures. In: Proceedings of the 2012 BELIV Workshop: Beyond Time and Errors - Novel Evaluation Methods for Visualization, pp. 5:1–5:4. ACM, New York (2012)
15. Kurzhals, K., Fisher, B., Burch, M., Weiskopf, D.: Eye tracking evaluation of visual analytics. Inf. Vis. **15**, 340–358 (2016)
16. Descartes, R.: La Geometrie (1637)
17. Tufte, E.: Visual Explanations. Graphics Press, Cheshire (1997)
18. Tukey, J.W.: The future of data analysis. Ann. Math. Stat. **33**, 1–67 (1962)
19. Bertin, J.: Graphics and Graphic Information Processing. deGruyter Press, Berlin (1981)
20. Dickson, G.W., Senn, J.A., Chervany, N.L.: Research in management information systems: the minnesota experiments. Manag. Sci. **23**, 913–934 (1977)
21. Benbasat, I., Schroeder, R.G.: An experimental investigation of some MIS design variables. MIS Q. **1**, 37–49 (1977)
22. Cleveland, W.: Visualizing Data (1985)
23. Kosslyn, S.M.: Understanding charts and graphs. Appl. Cogn. Psychol. **3**, 185–225 (1989)
24. Tufte, E.: Envisioning information. Graphics Press, Cheshire (1990)
25. Ives, B.: Graphical user interfaces for business information systems. MIS Q. **6**, 15–47 (1982)
26. Benbasat, I., Dexter, A.S., Todd, P.: An experimental program investigating color-enhanced and graphical information presentation: an integration of the findings. Commun. ACM **29**, 1094–1105 (1986)
27. DeSanctis, G.: Computer graphics as decision aids: directions for research*. Decis. Sci. **15**, 463–487 (1984)
28. Vessey, I., Galletta, D.: Cognitive fit: an empirical study of information acquisition. Inf. Syst. Res. **2**, 63–84 (1991)
29. Bačić, D., Henry, R.: The role of business information visualization in knowledge creation. In: 2012 AMCIS (2012)
30. Bačić, D., Fadlalla, A.: Business information visualization: a visual intelligence-based framework. In: 2013 AMCIS (2013)
31. Rayner, K.: Eye movements in reading and information processing: 20 years of research. Psychol. Bull. **124**, 372–422 (1998)
32. Eckstein, M.K., Guerra-Carrillo, B., Singley, A.T.M., Bunge, S.A.: Beyond eye gaze: what else can eyetracking reveal about cognition and cognitive development? Dev. Cogn. Neurosci. **25**, 69–91 (2017)
33. Just, M.A., Carpenter, P.A.: Eye fixations and cognitive processes. Cogn. Psychol. **8**, 441–480 (1976)
34. Granholm, E., Steinhauer, S.R.: Pupillometric measures of cognitive and emotional processes. Int. J. Psychophysiol. **52**, 1–6 (2004)
35. Beatty, J.D.: Task-evoked pupillary responses, processing load, and the structure of processing resources. Psychol. Bull. **91**, 276–292 (1982)
36. Smuc, M.: Just the other side of the coin? from error to insight analysis. Inf. Vis. **15**, 312–324 (2016)

37. Klingner, J., Tversky, B., Hanrahan, P.: Effects of visual and verbal presentation on cognitive load in vigilance, memory, and arithmetic tasks. Psychophysiology **48**, 323–332 (2011)
38. Bačić, D.: Understanding business dashboard design user impact: triangulation approach using eye-tracking, facial expression, galvanic skin response and EEG sensors. In: 2017 AMCIS, Boston, MA (2017)
39. Nakasone, A., Prendinger, H., Ishizuka, M.: Emotion recognition from electromyography and skin conductance. In: The Fifth International Workshop on Biosignal Interpretation (BSI-05), pp. 209–2012 (2005)
40. Boucsein, W.: Electrodermal Activity. Springer Science & Business Media, Boston (2012). https://doi.org/10.1007/978-1-4614-1126-0
41. Villarejo, M.V., Zapirain, B.G., Zorrilla, A.M.: A stress sensor based on galvanic skin response (GSR) controlled by ZigBee. Sensors (Basel). **12**, 6075–6101 (2012)
42. Shi, Y., Ruiz, N., Taib, R., Choi, E., Chen, F.: Galvanic skin response (GSR) as an index of cognitive load. In: CHI 2007 Extended Abstracts on Human Factors in Computing Systems, pp. 2651–2656. ACM, New York (2007)
43. Hjortsjö, C.H.: Man's Face and Mimic Language. Studen litteratur, Lund (1969)
44. Ekman, P., Friesen, W.V, Hager, J.C.: Facial action coding system: the manual. Research Nexus Devision of Network Information Research Corporation. Salt Lake City (2002)
45. Klimesch, W.: EEG alpha and theta oscillations reflect cognitive and memory performance: a review and analysis. Brain Res. Rev. **29**, 169–195 (1999)
46. Berka, C., Levendowski, D.J., Cvetinovic, M.M., Petrovic, M.M., Davis, G., Lumicao, M. N., Zivkovic, V.T., Popovic, M.V., Olmstead, R.: Real-time analysis of EEG indexes of alertness, cognition, and memory acquired with a wireless EEG headset. Int. J. Hum.-Comput. Interact. **17**, 151–170 (2004)
47. Berka, C., Levendowski, D.J., Lumicao, M.N., Yau, A., Davis, G., Zivkovic, V.T., Olmstead, R.E., Tremoulet, P.D., Craven, P.L.: EEG correlates of task engagement and mental\workload in vigilance, learning, and memory tasks. Aviat. Space Environ. Med. **78**, B231–B244 (2007)
48. Gevins, A., Smith, M.E.: Neurophysiological measures of working memory and individual differences in cognitive ability and cognitive style (2000)
49. Bowden, E.M., Jung-Beeman, M., Fleck, J., Kounios, J.: New approaches to demystifying insight. Trends Cogn. Sci. **9**, 322–328 (2005)
50. Harmon-Jones, E., Gable, P.A.: On the role of asymmetric frontal cortical activity in approach and withdrawal motivation: an updated review of the evidence. Psychophysiology **55**, e12879 (2018)
51. Cernea, D., Olech, P.-S., Ebert, A., Kerren, A.: EEG-based measurement of subjective parameters in evaluations. In: Stephanidis, C. (ed.) HCI 2011. CCIS, vol. 174, pp. 279–283. Springer, Heidelberg (2011). https://doi.org/10.1007/978-3-642-22095-1_57
52. Lee, J.C., Tan, D.S.: Using a low-cost electroencephalograph for task classification in HCI research. In: Proceedings of the 19th Annual ACM Symposium on User Interface Software and Technology, pp. 81–90. ACM, New York (2006)
53. Bera, P., Bera, B.Y.P.: How colors in business dashboards affect users' decision making. Commun. ACM **59**, 50–57 (2016)
54. Borkin, M.A., Bylinskii, Z., Kim, N.W., Bainbridge, C.M., Yeh, C.S., Borkin, D., Pfister, H., Oliva, A., Member, S., Oliva, A.: Beyond memorability: visualization recognition and recall. IEEE Trans. Vis. Comput. Graph. **22**, 519–528 (2016)
55. Goldberg, J., Helfman, J.: Eye tracking for visualization evaluation: reading values on linear versus radial graphs. Inf. Vis. **10**, 182–195 (2011)

56. Toker, D., Conati, C., Steichen, B., Carenini, G.: Individual user characteristics and information visualization : connecting the dots through eye tracking (2013)
57. Goldberg, J.H., Helfman, J.I.: Comparing information graphics: a critical look at eye tracking. In: Proceedings of the 3rd BELIV 2010 Workshop: BEyond Time and Errors: Novel evaLuation Methods for Information Visualization, pp. 71–78. ACM, New York (2010)
58. Peebles, D., Cheng, P.C.-H.: Modeling the effect of task and graphical representation on response latency in a graph reading task. Hum. Factors **45**, 28–46 (2003)
59. Hur, I., Yi, J.S.: SimulSort: multivariate data exploration through an enhanced sorting technique. In: Jacko, J.A. (ed.) HCI 2009. LNCS, vol. 5611, pp. 684–693. Springer, Heidelberg (2009). https://doi.org/10.1007/978-3-642-02577-8_75
60. Hur, I., Kim, S.-H., Samak, A., Yi, J.S.: A comparative study of three sorting techniques in performing cognitive tasks on a tabular representation. Int. J. Hum.-Comput. Interact. **29**, 379–390 (2013)
61. Kim, S.H., Dong, Z., Xian, H., Upatising, B., Yi, J.S.: Does an eye tracker tell the truth about visualizations?: findings while investigating visualizations for decision making. IEEE Trans. Vis. Comput. Graph. **18**, 2421–2430 (2012)
62. Siirtola, H., Laivo, T., Heimonen, T., Räihä, K.J.: Visual perception of parallel coordinate visualizations. In: 2009 13th International Conference Information Visualisation, pp. 3–9 (2009)
63. Burch, M., Andrienko, G., Andrienko, N., Höferlin, M., Raschke, M., Weiskopf, D.: Visual task solution strategies in tree diagrams. In: 2013 IEEE Pacific Visualization Symposium (PacificVis), pp. 169–176 (2013)
64. Burch, M., Heinrich, J., Konevtsova, M., Hoeferlin, M., Weiskopf, D.: Evaluation of traditional, orthogonal, and radial tree diagrams by an eye tracking study. IEEE Trans. Vis. Comput. Graph. **17**, 2440–2448 (2011)
65. Huang, W., Eades, P.: How people read graphs. In: Proceedings of the 2005 Asia-Pacific Symposium on Information Visualisation, vol. 45, pp. 51–58. Australian Computer Society, Inc., Darlinghurst (2005)
66. Jianu, R., Rusu, A., Hu, Y., Taggart, D.: How to display group information on node-link diagrams: an evaluation. IEEE Trans. Vis. Comput. Graph. **20**, 1530–1541 (2014)
67. Huang, W.: Using eye tracking to investigate graph layout effects. In: Asia-Pacific Symposium on Visualisation 2007 (APVIS), pp. 97–100, Sydney (2007)
68. Huang, W., Eades, P., Hong, S.-H.: A graph reading behavior: geodesic-path tendency. In: 2009 IEEE Pacific Visualization Symposium, pp. 137–144 (2009)
69. Pohl, M., Schmitt, M., Diehl, S.: Comparing the readability of graph layouts using eyetracking and task-oriented analysis. In: Proceedings of the Fifth Eurographics Conference on Computational Aesthetics in Graphics, Visualization and Imaging, pp. 49–56. Eurographics Association, Aire-la-Ville (2009)
70. Körner, C.: Sequential processing in comprehension of hierarchical graphs. Appl. Cogn. Psychol. **18**, 467–480 (2004)
71. Körner, C.: Eye movements reveal distinct search and reasoning processes in comprehension of complex graphs. Appl. Cogn. Psychol. **25**(6), 893–905 (2011)
72. Carpenter, P.A., Shah, P.: A model of the cognitive and perceptual processes in graphical display comprehension. J. Exp. Psychol. Appl. **4**, 75–100 (1998)
73. Pirolli, P., Card, S.K., Van Der Wege, M.M.: Visual information foraging in a focus + context visualization. In: Proceedings of the SIGCHI Conference on Human Factors in Computing Systems, pp. 506–513. ACM, New York (2001)
74. Griffin, A.L., Robinson, A.C.: Comparing color and leader line highlighting strategies in coordinated view geovisualizations. IEEE Trans. Vis. Comput. Graph. **21**, 339–349 (2015)

75. Blascheck, T., Ertl, T.: Towards analyzing eye tracking data for evaluating interactive visualization systems. In: Proceedings of the 2014 BELIV Workshop: Beyond Time and Errors - Novel Evaluation Methods for Visualization (2014)
76. Ba, D., Fadlalla, A.: Business information visualization intellectual contributions: an integrative framework of visualization capabilities and dimensions of visual intelligence. Decis. Support Syst. **89**, 77–86 (2016)
77. Cernea, D., Kerren, A., Ebert, A.: Detecting insight and emotion in visualization applications with a commercial EEG headset. In: 2011 SIGRAD, pp. 53–60 (2011)
78. Anderson, E.W., Potter, K.C., Matzen, L.E., Shepherd, J.F., Preston, G.A., Silva, C.T.: A user study of visualization effectiveness using EEG and cognitive load, vol. 30 (2011)
79. Cattell, R.B.: Theory of fluid and crystallized intelligence: a critical experiment. J. Educ. Psychol. **54**, 1–22 (1963)
80. McGrew, K.S.: CHC theory and the human cognitive abilities project: standing on the shoulders of the giants of psychometric intelligence research. Intelligence **37**, 1–10 (2009)
81. Tukey, J.W.: Exploratory Data Analysis. Addison-Wesley, Reading (1977)
82. Baker, J., Jones, D., Burkman, J.: Using visual representations of data to enhance sensemaking in data exploration tasks. J. Assoc. Inf. Syst. **10**, 533–559 (2009)
83. Kosara, R., Hauser, H., Gresh, D.L.: An interaction view on information visualization. In: 2003 State-of-the-Art Proceedings of EUROGRAPHICS (2003)
84. Yi, J.S., ah Kang, Y., Stasko, J., Jacko, J.: Toward a deeper understanding of the role of interaction in information visualization. IEEE Trans. Vis. Comput. Graph. **13**, 1224–1231 (2007)
85. Liu, Z., Stasko, J.: Mental models, visual reasoning and interaction in information visualization: a top-down perspective. IEEE Trans. Vis. Comput. Graph. **16**, 999–1008 (2010)
86. Hambrick, D.Z., Engle, R.W.: Effects of domain knowledge, working memory capacity, and age on cognitive performance: an investigation of the knowledge-is-power hypothesis. Cogn. Psychol. **44**, 339–387 (2002)
87. Lohman, D.: Spatial Ability. Macmillan, New York (1994)
88. Ware, C.: Information Visualization: Perception for Design. Morgan Kaufmann, San Francisco (2000)
89. Ashcraft, M.H.: Fundamentals of Cognition. Addison-Wesley Educational Publishers, New York (1998)
90. Miller, G.A.: The magical number seven, plus or minus two: some limits on our capacity for processing information (1956)
91. Kosara, R., Mackinlay, J.: Storytelling: the next step for visualization. Computer (Long. Beach. Calif.) **46**, 44–50 (2013)
92. Gershon, N., Page, W.: What storytelling can do for information visualization. Commun. ACM **44**, 31–37 (2001)
93. Elias, M., Aufaure, M.-A., Bezerianos, A.: Storytelling in visual analytics tools for business intelligence. In: Kotzé, P., Marsden, G., Lindgaard, G., Wesson, J., Winckler, M. (eds.) INTERACT 2013. LNCS, vol. 8119, pp. 280–297. Springer, Heidelberg (2013). https://doi.org/10.1007/978-3-642-40477-1_18

Mining Patent Big Data to Forecast Enterprise Performance

Yu-Jing Chiu[✉]

Chung Yuan Christian University, 200 Chung Pei Road, Chung Li District,
Taoyuan City 32023, Taiwan, R.O.C.
yujing@cycu.edu.tw

Abstract. With intellectual assets are more important, the enterprise pay higher attention. And the patent is an important indicator to measure the R&D results of the company. As China gradually became the leading national competition, this study will be based on Chinese listed companies for the study. Using Granger causality test to identify which patents indicators has a leading enterprise performance. Based on the difficulty of data collection, the study is only with four patent indicators and three enterprise performance indicators for verification of indicators. Patent index are including patent growth rate, patent approval rate, patent number and patent activities and enterprise performance index are net profit, return on assets (ROA) and return on net worth (ROE). Results from this study show that patents leading indicator of different industries have a great deal of difference, which also similar situations and economic leading indicator, therefore, the study recommends more industrial application of different patents leading indicator.

Keywords: Patent indicator · Lead index · Patent-based lead index
Enterprise performance index · Granger causality test

1 Introduction

The competitive advantage that brought to an enterprise by intangible assets would even be more important than tangible assets. Hence, patent rights also have decisive influence in market value of an enterprise. To the competition in an industry, patents have those strengths like enhancing bargaining power of our side, increasing entry barriers, establishing image of our side and striking at the other side. Furthermore, patent rights have a monopolizing character to change the situation of competition in an industry. As the importance of intangible assets on industrial competitive strategies growing with each passing day, every country raises the investment rate of intangible assets. According to [1] estimation, the United States invests about one trillion USD in intangible assets and the investment amount is almost equal to plants and equipment. Even though the rate that intangible assets accounting for net worth of enterprises would be affected by economic fluctuations, empirical data has proved that the long swings of enterprises' market-to-book ratio grow from small to big if we take the difference between market and book as the evaluated value for enterprises' intangible assets. And it can also prove the trend that intangible assets have become the core value

© Springer International Publishing AG, part of Springer Nature 2018
F. F.-H. Nah and B. S. Xiao (Eds.): HCIBGO 2018, LNCS 10923, pp. 687–698, 2018.
https://doi.org/10.1007/978-3-319-91716-0_54

of enterprises [2, 3]. In fact, tangible assets accounted market value for more than 80% and intangible assets accounted for less than 20% in enterprises in the United States as S&P500 showed in 1975. However, the ratio of intangible assets has risen to 81% as Fig. 1 showed in 2009.

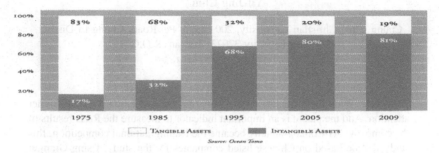

Fig. 1. Market values' component parts of S&P 500 index Source: WWW.OCEANTOMOIN DEXES.COM

To industry policies, patents are a means to improve industrial technique competitiveness; to firms, patents were regarded as monopoly in law so that it plays an important role in market strategy. In recent years of Taiwan, the quality and quantity of patents have greatly increased since government advocates it continually and research institutes, academic units and lots of enterprises fling themselves into it positively. After accumulating a larger quantity of intellectual assets, the needs of asset activation and circulation such as authorization, transaction, transfer, margin trading and securitization must derive from the follow-up of these intellectual assets. It shows that we can get royalties income through patent licensing. Besides, transactions of patent technology has been in a period of vigorous development and become an unmistakable trend. Furthermore, multi-national governments and privately owned enterprises also institute platforms for transactions of patent technology so that they can be a bridge of patent-circulation to fulfill the needs of patent transactions between patent suppliers and demanders.

In the past, the financial instruments of the United States were so highly developed, and they were also applied to IP. For instance, American Ocean Tomo cooperated with American Stock Exchange to announce an IP-based index that was called Ocean Tomo 300™ Patent Index (Ocean Tomo as following) so that people can participate in IP transaction market without investing and managing IP directly.

On the 13th September, 2006, Ocean Tomo activated the patent index, and this is the first stock index that took company's IP value as the base. This patent index stands for the combination of 300 companies' shares, and these 300 companies which owned the most patent value were assessed at the book value by Ocean Tomo. American Stock Exchange commented that the index is the first important Broad-Based Index after Dow Jones Industrial Average in 1896, Standard & Poor's 500 in 1957 and Nasdaq Composite Index in 1971. Ocean Tomo patent index uses the software of Patent Ratings System to assess every company's patent portfolios to calculate the patents registered at

United States Patent and Trademark Office, and that was recognized as relative attraction in IP industry. Besides, the process of screen stocks is in a way of regulation and quantification. Hence, the unique and innovation of Ocean Tomo patent index in financial market give people out of institutional investor a chance to use the important type of assets under knowledge economy and to offer a recognized index of assets management under knowledge economy.

Recently, Taiwan makes efforts in researches and rule-making for relative issues of intellectual property rights, but it still comes in significantly below America or other advanced countries. We can find that the index using patents as the base is feasible. Nevertheless, patent is Territoriality Principle. What's more, even though some scholars focus on intellectual assets securitization, most of the topics are about the difficult of intellectual assets securitization, interrelated law system, and the evaluation model of intellectual assets. As you can see from above-mentioned, it's important to set up the accountability and evaluation mechanisms before establishing the market of systematic intellectual assets transactions. Hence, Ocean Tomo 300™ index may be taken as a reference pattern to gradually establish intellectual assets transaction mechanisms for Taiwan's exclusive. However, in these numerous indexes, which indexes have the characteristic of lead index? For example, Baltic Dry Index (BDI) showed a premonition before financial crisis of 2008. Therefore, if these indexes with leading-characteristics can be extracted from numerous indexes, it can improve intellectual assets transaction market mechanisms. And that's the reason why the issue was worth studying. The research purpose of this study is to discuss what patent indicators have characteristics of lead index?

2 Literature Review

At first, the related literature of definition of patent will be mentioned in this part. Next, related literature of patent indicator will be discussed here.

2.1 Definition of Patent

World Intellectual Property Organization (WIPO) mentioned that a patent is an exclusive right granted for an invention, which is a product or a process that provides, in general, a new way of doing something, or offers a new technical solution to a problem. To get a patent, technical information about the invention must be disclosed to the public in a patent application. In another word, inventors create innovations on techniques and are willing to make it public to develop technologies so that laws give them exclusive rights for a period. According to our article 2 of Patent Act, The term "patent" referred to in this Act is classified into the following three categories: (1) Invention patents; (2) Utility model patents; and (3) Design patents. In U.S. patent classification, Utility model patents were called Little Invention patents, and Invention patents include Utility model patents and are collectively called Utility Patents. In these patents, Invention patents are the hardest one since they have to fit in with all the patentability of inventions like industrially applicable, **novelty and** non-obviousness; Utility model patents mean that the shape, structure and installation of an object are useful and improved; and Design patents indicate the shape, pattern and color of an object appearance are esthetic.

2.2 Patent Indicators

The values of patent rights include two sides: one is technique value and another one is right value. CHI Research Inc. develop a patent indicator system to evaluate the quality of patent right and analyze technique strength of a company through these seven Quantitative *index as following:* Number of patents, Patent growth percent in area, Cites per patent, Current impact index, Technology strength, Technology cycle time, Science linkage, and Science strength [4].

[5] investigated German patent values extensively in 1996 and took Patent Scope, Backward Citations, Forward Citations, Family Size and Oppositions against Patents as evaluation indicators for patent values according to the research results of this field. [6] took patent approved number as an indicator to discuss the relationship between patent approved number, the growing of sales and revenue rate. Also, [7] took patent application number as an indicator to discuss the relationship between patent application, approved number and sales. Besides, [8] mentioned that patent disclosure was taken as an indicator to discuss the influence of patent disclosure level on patent value. [9] indicated that it's not exactly to evaluate patent value by patent count directly since the levels of techniques in patents are not equal. Hence, it's better to evaluate patent value by Citation Frequency.

[10] mentioned that Family Size indicator can evaluate patent value. Furthermore, [11] integrated lots of patent indicators indicated before to develop many patent indicators for management, and these indicators include Patent Quality (PQ), Patent Strength (PS), Technology share, Relative Technology Share, Citation Frequency, International Scope, Technology Scope, Share of granted patents, Co-operation intensity, R&D Emphasis and Patent Activity (PA). [12] thought that previous studies about patent value almost focused on two parts: reference information (Foreign patents references, non-patent references and the total number of cited) and Classification Hierarchy (International Patent Classification, IPC and United States Patent Classification, USPC). Hence, they integrated some experts' opinions in this field and generalized 17 parameters that are relative to patent nature and can be used for quantitative statistics, and these parameters as patent evaluation indicators include Number of applicants, The number of inventors, Total number of items, The total number of independent items, US patents references, Foreign patents references, non-patent references, The total number of citations when filing a lawsuit, IPC classification number, USPC classification number, Numbers of global family size, Number of U.S. patent families, Office action times, The number of respondents/amendments, Patent examination time, Graphic number, and Prosecution time (from patent application to infringement prosecution time).

In the part of patent number analysis, [6] studied the relationship of patents granted to residents, the growing of sales and revenue rate with Patents Granted to Residents indexes. And the result shows that the patents made by a great deal of R&D activities can improve the turnover and profit of a company. [13] viewed patent information as an important indicator. And this scholar also viewed patent as an indicator for the output of invention activity and economic growth rate of America. Besides, [7] indicated Patents Granted to Residents index to discuss the relationship between patent application, patents granted to residents and sales. In their study, they took pharmaceutical firms as an example, and the result showed that a firm producing more patents by investing in more R&D activities will get better performances relatively.

[14] indicated that previous study results showed the patent citation will improve the performance of the firm (productivity or market value). However, these references studied the influence of science linkage in patent citation on performance of a firm in a system rarely. Therefore, they use Taiwan listed electronics companies' information about the granted patens in USPTO to evaluate the improvement of productivity form patent citation, and the result showed that the number of scientific publications quoted by manufacturers' patents has a negative impact on total factor productivity. Such finding can be explained that the paten with scientific patent references includes more complicated and originality knowledge [15–17] and there is still a gap between the application of the knowledge to produce and market [18]. Hence, it can't react to improve productivity directly and immediately. Otherwise, they also control the variables of patent quality (the speed of being cited of the patent) and other firms. They found that the higher patent quality of a firm will improve more productivity of it. In another word, patent quality of a firm can effect on the performance significantly. Also, scientific patent references will affect productivity of a firm besides other kind of citation. For example, scientific non-patent references and productivity of a firm are significantly positive, it means that scientific non-patent references is beneficial for performance of a firm; to cite the patents in USPTO or the patents in non-USPTO (including patents approved in any other country) makes different influence on performance of a firm (statistically non-significant relation between citing patents in USPTO and productivity; statistically significant negative relation between citing patents in non-USPTO and productivity.

As the above shows that different kinds of patent indicators have different purposes and meanings. In a conclusion, the numbers and the quality of a patent play an important role in the value and the effect of it; a patent indicator also plays an important role in the relative competitiveness of companies, industries and countries.

3 Methodology

The study uses Granger causality test testing the causality between the patent indicators and financial indicators. The Granger causality test is introduced as follows.

3.1 Granger Causality Test

Granger argues that when lack or incomplete of theoretical support, may seek positive complementary theoretical shortcomings and made after actual collection, reflecting information to the data itself, and its predicted effects to demonstrate the causal relationships between variables [19].

$$F(X_t|I_{t-1}) = F(X_t|I_{t-1}-), t = 1, 2 \tag{1}$$

$\{X_t\}$ and $\{Y_t\}$ are two bivariate linear stochastic process generated by stationary time series. $\{I_{t-1}\}$ is the message of the t−1 period collection. $F(X_t|I_{t-1})$ means the given conditional probability situations distribution and collection of composition $\{I_{t-1}\}$ means Y_t length L_y space to have a collection of messages, if (1) does not hold, on behalf of Y between X Granger causality and historical data help to predict the direction of Y (Liu 2012).

In a multivariate linear Gaussian system, if all the variables are observed, the change in the conditional distribution of a variable can be measured via linear regression. The regression formulation of Granger causality states that a variable X is the cause of another variable Y if the past values of X are helpful in predicting the future values of Y. Consider the following two regressions:

$$X_t = \sum_{j=1}^{L} a_j X_{t-j} + \sum_{j=1}^{L} b_j Y_{t-j} + e_t \tag{2}$$

$$Y_t = \sum_{j=1}^{L} c_j X_{t-j} + \sum_{j=1}^{L} d_j Y_{t-j} + f_t \tag{3}$$

where L is the maximal time lag. If Eq. (3) is a significantly better model than Eq. (2), we determine that time series X Granger causes time series Y. To this end, usually the noise variance in two models is compared with each other using a statistical significance test such as the Likelihood Ratio Test. Null hypothesis is as follows:

$$H_0 : b_1 = b_2 = \ldots = b_L = 0$$
$$H_1 : c_1 = c_2 = \ldots = c_L = 0 \text{ there is at least one.}$$

The reported *F-statistics* are the Wald statistics for the joint hypothesis:

$$\beta_1 = \beta_2 = \ldots = \beta_l = 0$$

for each equation. The null hypothesis is that x does not Granger-cause y in the first regression and that y does not Granger-cause x in the second regression.

3.2   Data Delimitation and Limitation

The research scope in this study is in Chinese market since the rise of Chinese market should not be underestimated. Especially in 2010, the amount of invention patent application in Chinese was more than 391,000 and ranked second in the world. At the same time, there were more than 3,000 enterprises applying 12,000 international patent applications through access to the treaty of patent cooperation and the amount of it increased more 56.2% than it in 2009. Besides, in 2010, the amount of effective invention patent applications within the territory of China was about 258,000 and the increment reached to 43%; the percentage of plant invention patent rose from 70.1% of 2006 to 81.3% of 2010. Furthermore, the advantage of owning patents are being turned to the advantage of economy transition in some developed economy regions of China, and lots of vantage enterprises with core technique patents and international competitiveness spring up, too. Now, both of GDP and the amount of PCT applications in China have ranked second in the world. Hence, intellectual asset rights can improve economy transition. For this reason, Chinese market was taken as the research scope in this study so that to understand the situation of China. Therefore, this study takes about 4138 listed companies in Shanghai Stock Exchange, Shenzhen Stock Exchange and Hong Kong Exchanges and Clearing Limited as the research objects to analyze present situation and the performance of patent indicator through all kinds of patent indicators.

3.3 Data Sampling

These samples of the study is distributed in the different industries, as well as shown in the following Table 1. Industries choose to patent more than 50 filter. Where industrial filters is the number of patents over 50 businesses. In relation to the Shenzhen Stock Exchange, companies' patents in Shanghai Stock Exchange are more widely distributed, while the Shenzhen Stock Exchange of patents is mainly concentrated in the manufacturing sector. These data screening processes are as shown in Fig. 2.

Table 1. Samples of the study

Stock exchange	Industry category	Number of companies
Shanghai Stock Exchange	All industries	261
	Petrifaction, chemistry & plastics	20
	Machinery, equipment & instrument	54
	Pharmaceutical & biotechnology	19
	Metal and nonmetal	22
	Information industry	15
	Manufacturing	106
	Others	25
Shenzhen Stock Exchange	All industries	257
	Manufacturing	255
	Others	2

3.4 Indicators

3.4.1 Patent Indicators

Because the number of patent indicators and the State Intellectual Property Office of the People's Republic of China's patent data can only be part of the patent search methods to do the search. After consider the time of data collection, the degree of difficulty and the data that can be collected, most of the indicators cannot be collected. In finally, the four patent indicators were selected as follows.

a. Patent Growth Percent in Area (GRA)

GRA refers to a business that year compared to percentage increases or decreases in the number of patents (CHI Research Company, 1995).

b. Share of Granted Patents (SGP)

SGP means approved by the company in its field is divided by the number of patents patent activities (Ernst, 1995).

c. Patent Activity (PA)

PA refers to the company in certain technical field of patent applications (Ernst, 1995).

d. Number of Patents (NP)

NP means a company within a certain period in the number of granted patents.

Stock Ex-change	Hong Kong Stock Exchange	**Shanghai Stock Exchange**	**Shenzhen Stock Exchange**
Number of Companies	delete	1044	1540

Screening of conditions: More than 50 patents		
Stock Exchange	Shanghai Stock Ex-chane	Shenzhen Stock Ex-change
Number of Companies	1044	1540

Screening of conditions: More than 50 patents and More than five years of financial information		
Stock Exchange	Shanghai Stock Ex-change	Shenzhen Stock Ex-change
Number of Companies	261	255

Fig. 2. The process of data screening

3.4.2 Indicators of Enterprise Value

In assessing the business value, most people use return on shareholders' equity (ROE), return on assets (ROA) and Net Profit from preparing financial statements, the present use these indicators, identifying patent indicators is influential.

a. ROE = Net Income/Shareholder Equity
b. ROA = Net Income/Total Asset
c. Net profit = Sales revenue − Total costs.

4 Results and Conclusions

According to the result of Granger causality test, we can know different industry has to refer to the implied information of different Leading Index. For example, petrochemical, plastic and plastics industries can use Patents Growth Rate to predict that whether net profit, return on assets ratio and return on net worth will rise up in the future. Furthermore, the sample size of manufacturing turns into 361 companies in total after the combination of two stock exchanges. Such combination shows that it has the highest reference value to manufacturing and the patent-based lead indexes are Number of Patents and Comprehensive Index. In addition, there is no suitable leading index for medical and bio-industry under the situation of the chosen four leading indexes. Hence, it can be inferred the chosen four leading indexes are not appropriate for both medical and bio-industry.

Companies would like to improve the value of the company through the information from patent indexes; investors also want to get some available information from them. However, there are too many numbers of patent indexes to choose. Consequently, the patent-based lead index that can predict the future, rise the value of a firm and are influential will be chosen from this study; moreover, Panel Data Model will be used to deal with cross-sectional data and time series analysis at the same time for the company from different kind of industry to analyze and compare with the result. Even though there were only 4 patent indexes chosen in this research, some of the 4 indexes are not suitable to predict the value of a firm during 2008 to 2012 as the result showed.

As Table 2 shows, the four chosen patent-based lead indexes in this research cannot offer a reference to all industries since the products and the technology cycle time of the companies in all industries are different, and it leads to the time of every company to rise value are different from each other. Also, it's worth taking it as a reference that to choose the patent index according to industrial characteristics. For instance, petrochemical, plastic and plastics industry are more appropriate to take Patents Growth Rate as the patent-based lead indexes of the industry according to the result of this study. Hence, these companies need to pay attention to whether the numbers of patents rise, besides, the numbers of growth will also affect the improvement of the firm's value in the future. On the other hand, mechanical, equipment, instrumental industry and information technology industry need to take more patent-based lead indexes as a reference. In addition, it was found that manufacturing can take Number of Patents as a reference for patent-based lead indexes after combing Shanghai Stock Exchange with Shenzhen Stock Exchange. Consequentially, all of the results prove that every patent index will not suit to all companies.

Table 2. Patent leading index in every industry

Stock Exchange	Industrial Type	The Value of an Enterprise								
		Net Profit			Return on Assets Ratio			Return on Net Worth		
		Patent Leading Index	Leading Period (Year)	P-Value	Patent Leading Index	Leading Period (Year)	P-Value	Patent Leading Index	Leading Period (Year)	P-Value
	All Companies									
Shanghai	Petrochemical, Plastic and Plastics Industries	Patents Growth Rate	4	0.0364**	Patents Growth Rate	4	0.0334**	Patents Growth Rate	4	0.0252**
		Comprehensive Index	1	0.0000***						
	Mechanical, Equipment, Instrumental Industry	Share of Granted Patent	3	0.0482**				Share of Granted Patent	1	0.0001***
		Patent Activity	3	0.0000***				Patent Activity	1	0.0000***
		Number of Patents	3	0.0013***						
		Comprehensive Index	1	0.0000***						
	Medical, Bioindustry									
	Metal, Non-metal	Comprehensive Index	1	0.0712*						
	Information Technology Industry	Patents Growth Rate	4	0.0006***				Patent Activity	2	0.0995*
		Number of Patents	4	0.0231**						
	Manufacturing	Comprehensive Index	3	0.0000***						
Shenzhen	Manufacturing									
	All Companies									
After Combination	Combined Manufacturing	Number of Patents	4	0.0000***	Number of Patents	4	0.0345**			
		Comprehensive Index	1	0.0000***	Comprehensive Index	1	0.0000***	Comprehensive Index	1	0.0132**

Remarks: 1.*** Significant at the 1% level；** Significant at the 5% level；* Significant at the 10% level. 2. Comprehensive Index were component of Number of Patents, Patent Activity, Patents Growth Rate and Share of Granted Patent.

This study offers not only a reference to develop strategies for a company through patent-based lead indexes but also the useful information to reduce risks for stakeholders of the company; besides, it also offers useful patent indexes to decrease in weakness and barriers to entry for those companies which have not entered the industry to compete. Furthermore, Share of Granted Patent cannot be a reference to most firms, and heterogeneity exists in different industry according to the result of fixed effect model. That means, the technique or the product life cycle of each industry may be different from each other so that different industry has to use different patent index. Hence, that's the reason some patent indexes have leading effect to some industries in the result of the study. In addition, it was found that the relation of Patent Activity to net profit is the most significant. For further discussing, the Patent Activity behind 2 periods and 3 periods are the best variable to explain the changes of net profit, but other patent indexes are not significant on it. Such finding also assists the information about patent-based lead indexes and offers more reference value for firms.

Although this research only takes 4 patent indexes as explanatory variables, we can still find that patent indexes need to be sieved to fit in the company if we only choose 3 variables from the indexes of company value. It's needed to sieve out more appropriate patent-based lead indexes from lots of patent indexes for each company and each industry in further researches. Besides, the choice of company value can stand on other indictors in further researches.

References

1. Nakamura, L.: Investing in intangible: is a trillion dollars missing from GDP? Bus. Rev. (Q4), 27–36 (2001)
2. Edvinsson, L., Malone, M.S.: Intellectual Capital: Realizing Your Company's True Value by Finding its Hidden Roots. HarperBusiness, New York (1997)
3. Booth, R.: The measurement of intellectual capital. Manag. Acc. 76(10), 26–28 (1998)
4. Thomas, P.: A relationship between technology indicators and stock market performance. Scientometircs 51, 319–333 (2001)
5. Harhoff, D., Scherer, F.M., Vopel, K.: Citations, family size, opposition and the value of patent rights. Res. Policy 32(8), 1343–1363 (2003)
6. Scherer, F.M.: Corporate inventive output, profits and growth. J. Polit. Econ. 73(3), 290–297 (1965)
7. Comanor, W.S., Scherer, F.M.: Patent statistics as a measure of technical change. J. Polit. Econ. 77(3), 392–398 (1969)
8. Green, J.R., Scotchmer, S.: On the division of profit in sequential innovation. RAND J. Econ. 26(1), 20–33 (1995)
9. Schankerman, M., Pakes, A.: Estimates of the value of patent rights in European countries during the post-1950 period. J. Econ. 96, 1052–1076 (1986)
10. Putnam, J.: The Value of International Patent Rights. Yale University, New Haven (1996)
11. Ernst, H.: Patent information for strategic technology management. World Pat. Inf. 25(3), 233–242 (2003)
12. Lai, Y.H., Che, H.C.: Modeling patent legal value by extension neural network. Expert Syst. Appl. 36, 10520–10528 (2009)
13. Schmookler, J.: Invention and Economic Growth. Harvard University Press, Cambridge (1966)
14. Hall, B.H., Jaffe, A., Trajtenberg, M.: Market value and patent citations. RAND J. Econ. 36 (1), 16–38 (2005)
15. Henderson, R., Orsenigo, L., Pisano, G.: The pharmaceutical industry and the revolution in molecular biology: interactions among scientific, institutional and organizational change. In: Mowery, D., Nelson, R. (eds.) The Sources of Industrial Leadership, pp. 267–311. Cambridge University Press, Cambridge (1999)

16. Mowery, D.C., Nelson, R.R., Sampat, B.N., Ziedonis, A.A.: The growth of patenting and licensing by US universities: an assessment of the effects of the Bayh-Dole act of 1980. Res. Policy **30**(1), 99–119 (2001)
17. Sampat, B.N., Mowery, D.C., Ziedonis, A.A.: Changes in university patent quality after the Bayh-Dole act: a re-examination. Int. J. Ind. Organ. **21**(9), 1371–1390 (2003)
18. Cassiman, B., Veugelers, R., Zuniga, P.: In search of performance effects of (in)direct industry science links. Ind. Corp. Change **17**(4), 611–646 (2008)
19. Granger, C.: Investigating causal relations by econometric models and cross-spectral methods. Econometrica **37**(3), 424–438 (1969)

Information Visualization and Responsiveness as Digital Capabilities to Improve Digital Business Performance

José Carlos da Silva Freitas Junior[1(✉)],
Antonio Carlos Gastaud Maçada[1], and Jie Mein Goh[2]

[1] Federal University of Rio Grande do Sul, Porto Alegre, Brazil
freitas.junior@ufrgs.br, acgmacada@ea.ufgrs.br
[2] Beedie School of Business, Simon Fraser University, Burnaby, BC, Canada
jmgoh@sfu.ca

Abstract. The digital economy has advanced from the growing investments in digital technologies by organizations in their digital transformation process. Furthermore, digital technologies are reshaping traditional business strategy leading to performance gains. In this study, we examine the notion of digital capabilities through a review of the literature. In particular, we focus on two digital capabilities, visualization and responsiveness, to examine the relationships between these digital capabilities and performance. We employed a qualitative approach to examine these relationships and interviewed 31 executives across a wide range of industries. The research makes several contributions through the conceptualization of digital capabilities and provides some preliminary results supporting our proposed conceptual framework. Our preliminary findings suggest that visualization and responsiveness, two digital capabilities, are key drivers of digital business performance.

Keywords: Digital capabilities · Visualization · Responsiveness

1 Introduction

Digital technologies have enabled firms to break out of their traditional paradigms of doing business and be open to the digital world. This is due to digital technologies that have the potential to transform traditional business models into digital business models [1]. Such transformation involves fundamental changes in business processes [2], operational routines [3], and organizational capabilities [4]. It is necessary for firms to possess new digital capabilities to improve their efficiency and agility, and to optimize relations with new customers and increase the speed of response to customer needs, especially where information plays a key role [5].

A Gartner survey conducted in 2017 reveals that 42% of CEOs have begun digital business transformation in their organizations. Furthermore, 47% of CEOs are being challenged by their boards of directors to make progress in digital business, and 56% said that their organizations have benefited from digital improvements through expanded profits [9]. According to Boulton [10], top-performing businesses which

© Springer International Publishing AG, part of Springer Nature 2018
F. F.-H. Nah and B. S. Xiao (Eds.): HCIBGO 2018, LNCS 10923, pp. 699–714, 2018.
https://doi.org/10.1007/978-3-319-91716-0_55

digitalization is already woven into their planning processes and their business models, are spending 34% of their IT budget on investments in digital transformations, with plans to increase that to 44% by 2018. Driven by consumers accustomed to such technologies such as mobile apps, smart appliances, and connected cars, the digital business shift is gaining traction.

Bock et al. [11] affirm that organizations which have undergone successful digital transformation, also known as "digital leaders", performed better than organizations that lagged behind i.e. the "digital laggards". This gap between digital leaders and laggards effectively creates a "digital divide" across organizations. This is a result of a significant capabilities possessed by digital leaders and the lack thereof in digital laggards. These transformations modify the processes and structures within and among businesses and other organizations, increasing the relevance and important role played by digital capabilities.

Recent studies have defined Digital Capabilities as the capabilities that build and develop an organization's capacity to develop, mobilize and efficiently use the organizational resources and improve its processes, (e.g. management of customers relationship, development of new products and collaboration) through the use of digital technologies [6]. In this study, we focused on two of these digital capabilities: Visualization and Responsiveness. Visualization is defined by Lyytinen et al. [7] as the capability to display visual business information and allows the organization to reduce the information complexity and uncertainty, delivering data and information in an appropriate format and with quality, thus improving the quality of information flows. Responsiveness refers to the managers' capacity to integrate, build and configure internal and external competencies to respond to environmental changes [8].

According to Aaker [12] and Yoo [13] companies are interested in the discussion on transformation in the digital age, thereby leading IS research to advance theoretically. However, there is still a lack of in-depth discussion regarding the skills and capabilities that can help organizations cope with these new challenges. Therefore, our study empirically examines the impact of two digital capabilities—visualization and responsiveness—on the business performance of e-commerce companies.

To fill this void, our research presents the results of the qualitative phase of a broader research program that has been conducted. The research objective of this study is to examine the relationships between key digital capabilities and digital business performance. Our study is expected to make several contributions. First, we complement the concept of digital capabilities based on the information systems literature. Second, our research advances in identifying the key digital capabilities required to make a digital business model successful, proposing a preliminary conceptual framework based on previous work. This research will be of practical value to executives in emphasizing the importance of digital capabilities in digital business performance.

In the next section, we present the theoretical development and initial propositions. This will be followed by the method, results and conclusions.

2 Theoretical Background

Digital capabilities have been associated with several theories including the theory of Dynamic capabilities (DC) which refers to the ability to integrate, reconfigure, gain, and release resources to match and even create market change. Dynamic capabilities explores the velocity of information, presenting its relationship with organizational processes and people [14]. In fact, Karimi and Walter [8] suggested that dynamic capabilities are positively associated with building digital capabilities. As such, the first step of this study entails a thorough examination of the literature with both the concepts of digital capabilities.

2.1 Literature Review Process

In developing our theoretical background, we conducted a full-text search for articles containing the terms "Digital Capability" and "Digital Capabilities." We followed the procedures suggested by Wolfswinkel et al. [15]. The search and selection of the papers occurred from July 2–18, 2017. The following search parameters were utilized: publications in the last 20 years and academic articles published on the Association for Information Systems electronic library (AISel), which is a central repository for research papers and journal articles relevant to the information systems academic community. During this step, each paper's abstract, keywords, and introduction were carefully read. In determining the inclusion/exclusion criteria, for an article to be included in the study, it must have been published in an IS journal and mentioned the keyword "digital capability" or its variants.

As a result, we identified 97 papers in the first round and excluded nine articles due to overlap, resulting in 91 papers. The second step was to verify the context of the studies. In our review, we only focused on papers situating their study in the business context. Subsequently, 37 articles were found, and after removing the duplicates, nine articles were disregarded, leaving 28 that were scrutinized.

Once the papers have been chosen, Wolfswinkel et al. [15] suggest to proceed to the analysis step, as well as to prepare the structure of the results. In this study, we used the software N'Vivo to support our analysis. First, we read all the papers, and then employed open coding to create tentative labels for chunks of data from the selected articles, to summarize our understanding. In particular, we paid special attention to articles discussing the definitions on digital capabilities, the capabilities required by digital business, the challenges for a digital business, and digital transformation.

During our review, we encountered many articles that only mentioned the term "digital capability," but do not offer definitions or further implications for this study. While we noted the articles for record, these papers were excluded from the final analysis. Next, we began axial coding to identify relationships among the open codes, and then we moved onto selective coding to identify the core variable that includes all the data. From these processes, we were able to relate the concept of digital capabilities with extant theories and understand the importance of visualization and responsiveness on digital business performance.

2.2   Digital Capabilities

From our review, we found five papers which provided an actual definition for digital capabilities among all the articles, most of which mention the term "digital capability" or "digital capabilities" without specifying the actual meaning of these capabilities. Of these five papers, Yoo et al. [16] defines Digital Capability as the organizational ability "used throughout the organization to support its different functions based on digital technology platforms." It is a business capability developed by the interaction of technology with a variety of complementary assets, such as process redesign, training, and incentive structures, that can be considered as sources of business value [17].

For Westerman et al. [18], digital capabilities are skills needed to go beyond pure IT to include specific technologies, such as social media or mobile, as well as analytic skills to drive value from big data. On the other hand, digital capabilities can be conceptualized as services that one system provides to another through value-creating, provider-user interactions [19].

The fifth definition presented by Tams et al. [6] suggests that digital capability is "an organization's focused deployment of information and communication technologies (ICTs), abilities to develop, mobilize, and use organizational resources effectively, for instance, customer relationship management, new product development, and knowledge collaboration."

As can be observed, the conceptualization of digital capability is quite broad and there is no standard definition. However, we notice that a commonality among these definitions is that digital capabilities allow organizations to give instant feedback, either internally or externally, by using digital technologies and digital platforms that generates value for the business.

From the five definitions of digital capability in the literature, we propose a new definition based on the analysis of these definitions with the objective of providing a synthesized definition which can be used in future studies. To do so, we enumerated the list of definitions found in the extant literature. Then, we conducted a cross-comparison of what has already been defined to formulate a precise, comprehensive definition for the term "digital capabilities."

Subsequently, we made a note on the terms which were considered key to constructing the definition in bold letters, as described next. From this analysis, we noticed that it is not clear whether the mere acquisition and possession of packages of resources will be adequate for a firm to achieve superior performance, especially when most of the firms have access to markets with similar factors. On the contrary, organizations should develop new capabilities by adding resources that would make them more valuable and inimitable. Several authors use the term "digital capability" and others the plural form, "digital capabilities." Digital capabilities can be better understood with existing theories in particular that of resource based theory and dynamic capablities theory. According to these two theories, a firms' capacity to integrate, build, and reconfigure the capabilities and internal and external resources to create superior capabilities that are incorporated into their social, structural, and cultural context [20, 21]. The mobilization of resources and new organizational capabilities becomes vital, focusing on people, facilities, structures, to ensure quality, speed, storage, and information flow, which will enable improvements in processes and client relationships and, thus, superior performance in the digital world.

Based on prior studies and these theories, we define digital capabilities as: "the combination of skills and processes of a Digital Business to develop, mobilize, and use organizational resources supported by Digital Technologies to respond to the environment and add value to the organization". This definition indicates that digital capabilities allow organizations to give instant answers either internally or externally by using digital channels that contribute to value generation for the company. These capabilities permit improvement in processes and customer relationships, thereby refining digital business, impacting operational and strategic fields [18], as we demonstrate in the following propositions.

In determining which resources and capabilities, when integrated and reconfigured, encompass digital capability, we examined the role of visualization and responsiveness on Digital Business Performance as suggested in the literature.

There are several ways to measure the performance of a business, for this study we follow the authors Rai et al. [3] that emphasize three areas of analysis to measure performance which should be observed about the relation of the performance of a company about its competition:

- operational excellence;
- revenue growth, and;
- the relationship with customers and other stakeholders involved in business processes.

Operational excellence is defined as the ability of a company to respond to customers and productivity improvements about its competitors [3]. To illustrate, one could cite the integration of the supply chains of e-commerce companies to improve the competitiveness of a firm based on time, compressing cycle times which improves business performance. The supply chains integrated into the business provide visibility, coordination, and streamlined flow of goods that shorten the time interval between a customer's request for a product and its delivery [22].

The relationship with customers and other stakeholders involved in business processes is an essential performance indicator [3]. Prior studies affirm that the decrease in time impacts the relationship with clients, and it is possible to broaden this view, with the satisfaction of all the actors involved in the processes both internally and externally.

Finally, the financial performance is also an indicator of performance. This performance can be analyzed by revenue growth, but also, by the return on investments and by the relation between the operating profit, as observed in the study of [23].

2.3 Visualization

According to Lyytinen et al. [7], digitization makes it possible to reconfigure and transform nearly all industrial-age products' design and production. From a digital capability perspective, a crucial capability which supports this reconfiguration and transformation is visualization. Visualization refers to the capability of a firm to represent their assets digitally. For instance, one specific function which supports the visualization capability is that of displaying business information and representing the information in a way that is readable, comprehensible, in the most efficient and effective way possible [16]. Further, visualization capability allows the organization to reduce information complexity and uncertainty, presenting data and information in an appropriate format [24].

Visualization also helps digital businesses deliver data and information about competitors, market trends and customers necessities in the proper format and time enabling business to compete in a digital world [25–27]. In addition, the visualization capability allows the organizations to maintain continuous contact, through new levels of digital sensing and tracking, producing big data that represent behaviors that were heretofore invisible [28].

Kohli and Grover [16] complement this idea and reiterate the importance of a "quick sense-and-respond to market demands by pricing, designing, sourcing, manufacturing, and distributing a product." Also, Drnevich and Croson [29] highlight the importance of monitoring competitors' actions and how it can improve business performance.

Considering the value of information for business, visualization capability allows the organization to reduce information complexity and uncertainty by delivering data and information in an appropriate, quality format, thus improving the quality of information flow [7].

Thus, the critical strength of Internet and digital technologies is the ability to provide information across time and space [30]. As defined in this capability's concept, it enables integration and reconfiguration of digital resources, contributing to better digital business results, thus maintaining the highlighted aspects of the dynamic capabilities theory. Therefore, we make the following proposition:

Proposition 1 (P1): Visualization is a digital capability that positively relates to digital business performance.

2.4 Responsiveness

Kohli and Grover [16] underscore responsiveness as a digital capability, defining it as the capacity to respond quickly to the firm's internal and external demands. Consequently, this digital capability can meet the digital economy's challenges [6–17]. Digital capabilities are a foundation upon which other firms can develop complementary products, technologies, and services [28]. In this context, responsiveness is an ability that requires velocity and flexibility of processes in an organization to allow the organization to quickly respond to a new customer need.

Tams et al. [6] citing the studies of Lavie [31] and Peppard et al. [32] emphasize that "Digital capabilities and practices have become increasingly important for organizations to improve organizational agility and responsiveness. As a result of the improvements in agility and responsiveness, firms can achieve greater performance and competitive advantage, even sustainable competitive advantage."

Müller et al. [26] also highlight the importance of being responsive to market responses, consumers, and other stakeholders and suggest the use of platforms and cloud computing. Fernandes et al. [33] emphasize that the organizations' response speed can imply an improvement in their performance. Therefore, we propose:

Proposition 2 (P2): *Responsiveness is a digital capability that positively relates to digital business performance.*

2.5 Conceptual Framework

Finally, what follows is the conceptual framework that illustrates the relationship between the Digital Capability propositions and Digital Business performance.

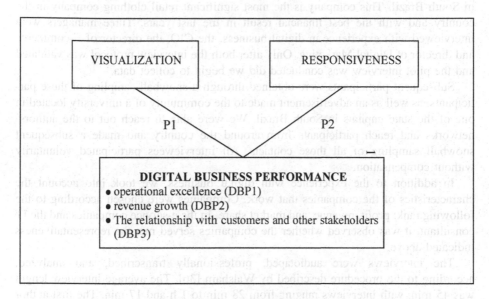

Fig. 1. Conceptual framework

As observed from our proposed conceptual framework, visualization and responsiveness are two digital capabilities that relate to the digital business performance of a digital business. This model emphasizes that a digital business requires extreme responsiveness and visualization [7, 24]. Next, we present the methods used in this research.

3   Methods

To answer our research question, we adopted a qualitative research method to explore our proposed model on digital capabilities. To do so, we conducted interviews with 31 managers and specialists who work in Digital Business. We selected respondents from native digital companies and traditional ones that started working with digital, such as e-commerce. This sampling of different-sized organizations from distinct industry sectors contributes to the study's analytical generalization [34]. The respondents are executives in IT, business, and company strategy.

3.1 Data Collection and Analysis

The interviewees were asked a series of questions based on a semi-structured instrument that was developed as Myers [35] suggests. Before the interview, we prepared an interview protocol with a list of questions derived from literature and our research question. In order to validate the protocol, we hired three specialists who went through the interview questions and conducted a pilot interview before initiating data collection.

The pilot interview was conducted at a multinational retail company headquartered in South Brazil. This company is the most significant retail clothing company in the country and with the best financial result in the last years. Three managers were interviewed with experience in digital business, the CIO, the director of E-commerce and director of Digital Marketing. Only after both the interview protocol was validated and the pilot interview was conducted did we begin to collect data.

Subsequent participants were obtained through a snowball sampling of these participants, as well as an advertisement made to the community of a university located in one of the state capitals in South Brazil. We were able to reach out to the authors' networks and reach participants from around the country and made a subsequent snowball sampling of all those contacts. All interviewees participated voluntarily without compensation.

In addition to the experience with digital business, we took into account the characteristics of the companies that work. Companies were chosen according to the following rank: profit, revenue, and market share. In the e-service companies and the IT consultant, it was observed whether the companies served met the representativeness indicated above.

The interviews were audiotaped, professionally transcribed, and analyzed, according to the procedure described by Walsham [36]. The average interview length was 45 min, with interviews ranging from 28 min to 1 h and 17 min. The first author conducted all the interviews. The average experience of the interviewees is 12 years in the area of IT or digital area, being the interviewee with less time has six years and the most experienced, 27 years. The descriptions of our 31 interviewees are summarized in Table 1.

Finally, we analyzed the results by utilizing the content analysis technique [37]. We analyzed the dataset with the use of the qualitative analysis software N'VIVO. This analysis was performed by all the researchers, following a qualitative coding analysis protocol developed for this research, which due to lack of space, could not be included here.

In summary, the data analysis codes were initially grouped into inductive themes based on the literature, while the data analysis revealed new categories. The analytical categories were established based on this set of issues. For this paper, we employed the categories that correspond to visualization and responsiveness. Next, we present our results.

Table 1. Characteristics of respondents

Nr	Interviewee position	Type of enterprise	Nr	Interviewee position	Type of enterprise
1	CEO	Retail E-commerce company: clothing	17	CIO	Shoes industry and e-commerce
2	CIO		18	IT manager	
3	E-commerce director		19	Digital marketing manager	
4	IT manager	Retail E-commerce company: accessories	20	CEO	e-Service
5	Digital marketing		21	IT director	
6	Financial manager	E-commerce retail stores groups: electronics	22	Digital services manager	
7	IT manager		23	Marketing manager	
8	Sales manager		24	IT director	Private bank
9	CEO	E-commerce retail stores groups: furniture	25	Sales manager	
10	IT manager		26	Digital marketing director	
11	CIO	E-business Ecosystem and marketplace	27	Digital business manager	
12	Sales manager		28	Sales manager	State bank
13	IT manager		29	IT manager	
14	Digital operations Manager		30	Digital operations manager	
15	IT manager	Household utensils industry	31	IT consultant	IT consulting
16	Digital marketing director				

Source: the authors

4 Data Analysis and Results

This section presents the results of our analysis of the interview data. The evidence of each digital capability is described through the interviewees' quotes, reinforcing the ideas of each category. Although many codes emerged from our analysis, we present themes that are mentioned frequently in the interviews. To do so, we consider the general theme, not literally the same words, but the general idea and the subcategorization using N'Vivo.

To examine the relations proposed in our conceptual model, we considered the digital business performance indicators presented in Sect. 2, and evaluated the relationship between the digital capability and each indicator. Thus, to help the analysis and discussion we named each of them as DBP1 - Operational excellence, DBP2 - Revenue growth, and DBP3 - The relationship with customers and other stakeholders.

4.1 Visualization and Digital Business Performance

In the Household Utensils Industry, it was possible to observe the managers have hourly sales reports, SMS, and e-mail. The IT Manager (Interviewee 15, i.e. I15) mentioned that every morning, he and other managers have access to all the previous day's sales volume, and those reports have graphs and are displayed on the managers' iPads. It helps to plan the actions to increase the sales and consequently increase the Revenue growth (DBP2).

In the banks, information visualization is essential for managers and clients. The interviewee I29 says "the bank has developed solutions for clients and our internal team." The Sales Manager pointed out they are always analyzing the market and says that "we need to provide information in an adequate format, because the FinTech's exists, and their DNA are digital, we need to be able to compete in the same level, showing the data and information the clients need".

Another aspect of visualization is information visibility. As an example, in the bank, for every transaction the client receives an SMS, so he can confirm if transactions actually went through, which increases the confidence of the client in the firm. This in turn improves the operational excellence (DBP1) and the relationship with customers and other stakeholders (DBP3).

In the Shoes Industry and E-Commerce, the CIO said that everyone involved in the ecosystem has access and, through the system could provide and receive input, participate and view information flow according to each role in the ecosystem, such as product development. I17 and I18 gave the same example: a Design Director went to a shoe fair in Milan. During the fair, he watched the trends, such as design and colors, and immediately sent photos from his cell phone to an internal communication system, where discussions to develop those shoe and color trends began along with participation from employees. The participation from everyone reduces time, costs and improves productivity. So, it the Shoes Industry and E-Commerce the visualization improves the digital business performance (DBP1, DBP2, and DBP3).

In another digital business, we find evidence for proposition 1, i.e. visualization improves digital business performance. In the E-business Ecosystem and marketplace, the CIO said he accesses information to the internal and external environment. According to I12 "we get clippings and various types of information from market analysts, BI, analytics area and social media. Also, some tools are used for each unit for monitoring customer and competitor actions". This way the managers at different decision levels and can act accordingly to the situation. Again, the DBS 1 and DBS 3 are improved by having the capability to perform visualization.

The evidence indicates that visualization is the capability to display business information visually, presenting data and information in an appropriate format, as defined by Yoo et al. [16]. Moreover, data and information are available in all adequate platforms such as laptops, mobile devices, and websites [38–40]. The relation to performance is evident in the declarations made by the CEO of Shoe E-Commerce. The bank directors also corroborated this finding.

The results from the observations and the respondents suggest that organizations are dealing with the challenges of the digital economy and the significant shifts that digital technologies have brought about. Hence, it is essential to monitor the market, customer demands, and any other data that can be useful for the business.

The relationship of visualization with digital business performance is evident, especially with performance indicators such as operational excellence, revenue growth and the relationship with customers and other stakeholders. The evidence and observations show the importance of monitoring the environment and displaying the data and information internally and externally, to the customers and stakeholder. I1, I4, I7, and I14 corroborated with this idea; they understand that analyzing the market and displaying the data and information is a critical business driver because it enables the surveillance of market trends and new technologies to sense and seize opportunities to show the data and information in the digital business [17].

4.2 Responsiveness and Digital Business Performance

I12 said that in the E-business Ecosystem and marketplace, his company tries to be fast in responding to clients and to adapt to the broader market. The company must capture the latest trend to beat competitors. Similarly, I13 affirmed that responsiveness is an important factor for digital business performance: "We have an area that looks at the client and another market intelligence area that looks at the competition. When we look at them internally, the latest trend must pass through various other sectors, such as styles, purchases, production, and even suppliers". We observed that the supplier must receive this same information in a nutshell since they must produce with agility and quickly make the product available to the client to ensure customer satisfaction. This way responsiveness capability improves customer satisfaction and this in turn improves business performance (DBP1 and DBP3).

In the private bank, the responsiveness capability is present in many ways including friendly navigation for mobile app and a responsive site. To I27, the Digital Business Manager, "we brought improvements to the user's navigation area and consequently the stakeholder users are more satisfied, and we measured that our sales through mobile and found that they increased by a significant amount." Again, the DBS 1 and DBS 3 are improved by the visualization.

In the Shoes Industry and e-commerce, we observed that the responsiveness of the companies in this industry requires the change in culture, when they seek to digitalize processes. One CIO (I17) gave an example, he said that "one of our clients decides to open a virtual store, so they need to load our products' data, such as images, videos, among others. Thanks to the agility that our resources provide, we can transmit all these data instantly, and [the data] can load up onto the site quickly and safely, without losing data, which demonstrates our excellent performance, helping our sales".

The CEO of an E-business Ecosystem and marketplace company pointed out that "a digital business must be agile and must always provide the client with a better experience, that's why we can obtain and deliver product information at any moment through systems and programs or BackOffice personnel." Additionally, we observed the documents and statistics that indicate they increase the revenue (DBP2) and improve the relationship with customers and other stakeholders (DBP 3).

Thus, as mentioned by Kohli and Grover [17], responsiveness refers to the capability whereby organizational process are adept and flexible which allows fast implementation of operational changes. Responsiveness is the ability to respond to both the market and internal dynamics of the company, according to Setia et al. [5] and Barenfanger and Otto [38].

We observed from our analyses that responsiveness, for both external facing and internal business processes, improves digital business performance. To illustrate an external facing responsiveness, the CIO and Director of Clothing and Accessories Retail E-Commerce, mentioned that a physical store can change its display window each season or, at most, once a month. A digital store varies every minute according to each client's characteristics. It is an example of the operational excellence and the relationship with customers, this way it is possible to improve the performance.

The IT Manager of Retail E-commerce company accessories (I4) complements this example by citing another example on customer service. In the past, clients had to go to the store in order to report an issue or make a complaint. With the digital transformation, the client can achieve the same goal by visiting the store's site. Given that digitization has enabled consumer empowerment, which has also facilitated the potential of negative sentiments among clients to go viral in seconds. Thus, a company who wants to have a strong brand will have to be more careful and agile, capable of responding instantly, immediately to the client's needs, whether good or bad. Again, it is another example of how to improve the relationship with customers and other stakeholders

Internally, responsiveness is often observed across the business such as decision making. A situation that exposes this internal agility is one related by the CIO, who said that on the day iPhone 7 was launched in Brazil, online sales were not being converted. The e-commerce platform's systems analysis verified that the clients were not buying because of delivery time, which was longer than that of the competition. Immediately, the CIO contacted the CEO and logistics Director and found an alternative to decrease delivery time, which was done on the site, and, minutes later, sales began to increase. All these activities reveal how responsiveness is a digital capability related to business performance, particularly in the factors operational excellence, revenue growth and the relationship with customers and other stakeholders.

4.3 Synthesis of the Findings and Contributions

From this study, we find that organizations are dealing with challenges arising from the digital economy and managing the changes that digital technologies have brought. These organizations find it essential to monitor the market, customer demands, and display the data that can be useful for the business.

From our analysis, we identified evidence supporting the relationship between the two digital capabilities and digital business performance. All digital capabilities analyzed are related to the performance indicators used in this study, operational excellence, revenue growth, and the relationship with customers and other stakeholders [3, 22, 23]. So, we find initial evidence for the proposed propositions, and that each capability influences more than one type of of business performance.

Most respondents highlight the importance of stakeholder integration and the ERP which is still the core technology. It is crucial to spot the market trends, to know the competitors, to monitor the environment and to look for business opportunities. The same way it is necessary to display the data and information with rapidly and precisely. Responsiveness increases all the stakeholders' satisfaction, mainly the clients, and speeds up decision making. This capability contributes to internal collaboration and improves the quality and security of data and information.

The contribution of this study is that we propose a preliminary conceptual framework between two digital capabilities and digital business performance, and demonstrates preliminary evidence from qualitative data to support our model. In particular, we find that visualization capability allows the companies to display business information visually, showing data and information in an appropriate format, helping the managers in many processes, such as decision making. Moreover, data and information must be available in all adequate platforms such as laptops, mobile devices, and websites. Responsiveness is also essential because digital business must respond quickly because it is necessary to know precisely the market demands, so visualization capability is fundamental to the responsiveness. Consequently, the relation of these two capabilities with the business performance is presented in many responses of the IT managers interviewed.

Thus, the findings contribute to companies that are considering their journey from traditional to digital businesses and those extant digital businesses, to improve their performance. While the investments in digital appear substantial, the results presented in this study suggest that digital business performance is associated with visualization and responsiveness capabilities.

In doing so, we hope that future research will be able to test our model with another kind of digital business and, improve it to check more digital capabilities.

5 Conclusions

To sum up this study, we aimed to examine the relationships between digital capabilities in digital business performance. Preliminary findings from this study show that visualization and responsiveness are digital capabilities which will drive digital business performance. Visualization capability is the capability to display business information visually, presenting data and information in an appropriate format. Moreover, data and information must be available in all adequate platforms such as laptops, mobile devices, and websites, as the evidence showed. Responsiveness capability is the ability of the company to act quickly which leads to the client's satisfaction and reduces operating times and costs.

Thus, it is essential for a firm to be connected and integrated into a digital ecosystem, which allows it to monitor the environment, to respond to the market and customer through business process supported by technology in order to achieve operational excellence and to achieve a satisfactory relationship with customers and other stakeholders, and consequently to have revenue growth.

This study contributes to the field by presenting an initial conceptual framework (Fig. 1) and preliminary results from testing this framework through a qualitative approach. The practical implication of this research rests on demonstrating the relationship between two specific digital capabilities, visualization and responsiveness, and the digital business performance. Additionally, this study may provide some insights for firms interested in sustaining their business and surviving in the digital economy.

One of the primary limitations of this study is that our results cannot be generalized as our interviewees were mainly based in the e-commerce industry in Brazil. Another limitation is that in this study, we are not able to capture the construct of digital capabilities quantitatively. Therefore, in future studies, verification of the model through quantitative research that identifies each digital capability's level of impact on Digital Business performance is suggested. It is also recommended that future studies examine other digital businesses and in other countries.

References

1. Matt, C., Thomas, H., Alexander, B.: Digital transformation strategies. Bus. Inf. Syst. Eng. **57**(5), 339–343 (2015)
2. Leonhardt, D., et al.: Reinventing the IT function: the role of IT agility and IT ambidexterity in supporting digital business transformation (2017)
3. Rai, A., Patnayakuni, R., Seth, N.: Firm performance impacts of digitally enabled supply chain integration capabilities. MIS Q. 225–246 (2006)
4. Tan, B., et al.: The role of IS capabilities in the development of multi-sided platforms: the digital ecosystem strategy of Alibaba.com. J. Assoc. Inf. Syst. **16**(4), 248 (2015)
5. Setia, P., Venkatesh, V., Joglekar, S.: Leveraging digital technologies: how information quality leads to localized capabilities and customer service performance. MIS Q. **37**(2), 565–590 (2013)
6. Tams, S., Grover, V., Thatcher, J.: Modern information technology in an old workforce: toward a strategic research agenda. J. Strateg. Inf. Syst. **23**(4), 284–304 (2014)
7. Lyytinen, K., Yoo, Y., Boland Jr., R.J.: Digital product innovation within four classes of innovation networks. Inf. Syst. J. **26**(1), 47–75 (2016)
8. Karimi, J., Walter, Z.: The role of dynamic capabilities in responding to digital disruption: a factor-based study of the newspaper industry. J. Manag. IS **32**(1), 39–81 (2015)
9. Gartner: Gartner Survey Shows 42 Percent of CEOs Have Begun Digital Business Transformation (2018). http://www.gartner.com/newsroom/id/3689017. Accessed 24 Jan 2017
10. Boulton, C.: CIOs move more dollars to digital transformation (2016). http://www.cio.com/article/3131927/cio-role/cios-move-more-dollars-to-digital-transformation.html?nsdr=true. Accessed 28 Feb 2017
11. Bock, R., Iansiti, M., Lakhani, K.R.: What the companies on the right side of the digital business divide have in common (2017). https://hbr.org/2017/01/what-the-companies-on-the-right-side-of-the-digital-business-divide-have-in-common. Accessed 28 Feb 2017

12. Aaker, D.: Four ways digital works to build brands and relationships. J. Brand Strategy 4(1), 37–48 (2015)
13. Yoo, Y.: The tables have turned: how can the information systems field contribute to technology and innovation management research? J. Assoc. Inf. Syst. 14(5), 227 (2013)
14. Eisenhardt, K.M., Martin, J.A.: Dynamic capabilities: what are they. Strateg. Manag. J. 21(1), 1105–1121 (2000)
15. Wolfswinkel, J.F., Furtmueller, E., Wilderom, C.P.M.: Using grounded theory as a method for rigorously reviewing literature. Eur. J. Inf. Syst. 22(1), 45–55 (2013)
16. Yoo, Y., et al.: Organizing for innovation in the digitized world. Organ. Sci. 23(5), 1398–1408 (2012)
17. Kohli, R., Grover, V.: Business value of IT: an essay on expanding research directions to keep up with the times. J. Assoc. Inf. Syst. 9(1), 23 (2008)
18. Westerman, G., Bonnet, D., Mcafee, A.: The Digital Capabilities Your Company Needs. MIT Sloan Management Review, Cambridge (2012)
19. Srivastava, S.C., Shainesh, G.: Bridging the service divide through digitally enabled service innovations: evidence from indian healthcare service providers. MIS Q. 39(1), 245–267 (2015)
20. Grant, R.M.: The resource-based theory of competitive advantage: implications for strategy formulation. Calif. Manag. Rev. 33(3), 114–135 (1991)
21. Sambamurthy, V., Bharadwaj, A., Grover, V.: Shaping agility through digital options: reconceptualizing the role of information technology in contemporary firms. MIS Q. 27(2), 237–263 (2003)
22. Hult, G.T.M., Ketchen, D.J., Slater, S.F.: Information processing, knowledge development, and strategic supply chain performance. Acad. Manag. J. 47(2), 241–253 (2004)
23. Chi, M., Zhao, J., Li, Y.: Digital business strategy and firm performance: the mediation effects of e-collaboration capability. In: WHICEB, p. 58 (2016)
24. Yoo, Y., Henfridsson, O., Lyytinen, K.: Research commentary—the new organizing logic of digital innovation: an agenda for information systems research. Inf. Syst. Res. 21(4), 724–735 (2010)
25. Aakhus, M., et al.: Symbolic action research in information systems: introduction to the special issue. MIS Q. 38(4), 1187–1200 (2014)
26. Müller, S.D., Holm, S.R., Søndergaard, J.: Benefits of cloud computing: literature review in a maturity model perspective. CAIS 37, 42 (2015)
27. Nambisan, S., et al.: Digital innovation management: reinventing innovation management research in a digital world. MIS Q. 41(1) (2017)
28. Barrett, M., et al.: Service innovation in the digital age: key contributions and future directions. MIS Q. 39(1), 135–154 (2015)
29. Drnevich, P.L., Croson, D.C.: Information technology and business-level strategy: toward an integrated theoretical perspective. MIS Q. 37(2) (2013)
30. Barua, A., et al.: An empirical investigation of net-enabled business value. MIS Q. 28(4), 585–620 (2004)
31. Lavie, D.: Capability reconfiguration: an analysis of incumbent responses to technological change. Acad. Manag. Rev. 31(1), 153–174 (2006)
32. Peppard, J., Galliers, R.D., Thorogood, A.: Information systems strategy as practice: micro strategy and strategizing for IS. J. Strateg. Inf. Syst. 23(1), 1–10 (2014)
33. Fernandes, C., et al.: The dynamic capabilities perspective of strategic management: a co-citation analysis. Scientometrics 112(1), 529–555 (2017)
34. Benbasat, I., Goldstein, D.K., Mead, M.: The case research strategy in studies of information systems. MIS Q. 369–386 (1987)

35. Myers, M.D., Newman, M.: The qualitative interview in IS research: examining the craft. Inf. Organ. **17**(1), 2–26 (2007)
36. Walsham, G.: Doing interpretive research. Eur. J. Inf. Syst. **15**(3), 320–330 (2006)
37. Bardin, L.: Content analysis. Editions Lisbon (1977)
38. Bacic, D., Fadlalla, A.: Business Information Visualization: A Visual Intelligence-Based Framework (2013)
39. Barenfanger, R., Otto, B.: Proposing a capability perspective on digital business models. In: 2015 IEEE 17th Conference on Business Informatics (CBI), vol. 1, pp. 17–25, 13–16 July 2015. https://doi.org/10.1109/cbi.2015.18
40. Tan, T.C.F., Tan, B., Pan, S.L.: Developing a leading digital multi-sided platform: examining IT affordances and competitive actions in Alibaba.com. CAIS **38**, 36 (2016)

Improving of User Trust in Machine Learning Recommender-Based Business Applications Through UI Design: A Case Study

Emily Mai JingWen$^{(\boxtimes)}$, Benjamin Yap$^{(\boxtimes)}$, and Steven Fu$^{(\boxtimes)}$

ML, Leonardo, SAP, Singapore, Singapore
mai.jingwen@gmail.com,
{benjamin.yap, steven.fu01}@sap.com

Abstract. Our work focuses on user trust and the impact of UI design on business professionals' level of engagement when using Machine Learning (ML) recommender applications to accomplish their business tasks. In order to achieve the purpose, the case study is Resume Matching; a web-based application which aims to provide recommendations of the best matched talents for recruiters. Due to the nature of the service provided by Resume Matching and its target users, we need to design its UI to engage recruiters to gain trust on the automatic recommendation. Till this end, we have created an iterative and incremental process of designing and testing the UI components of Resume Matching. This paper presents our design and testing processes, our findings and a set of guidelines on Machine Learning User Trust Improvement (ML-UTI) Research Model for increasing user trust level to end users through effective UI design.

Keywords: User experience design · User-centered research model
Trust · User acceptance · Human-industry application development
Machine learning (ML) recommender application design

1 Introduction

"A doctor or a patient will not be happy with a diagnosis that tells them they have a 75 percent likelihood of cancer and they should use drug X to treat it. They need to understand which pieces of information came together to create that prediction or answer."

- S. Somasegar and Daniel Li in a blog post (Techcrunch.com) dated July 6, 2016

In 2017, there is a trend that industry applications becoming more intelligent than they used to be [1]. A Machine Learning (ML) recommender system widely used in this area. ML recommender systems utilize data mining to make inferences about a user's interests as well as to filter out irrelevant content [2]. They build both predictive analytic applications and personalization systems [3]. ML recommender-based industry applications improves the efficiency of work produced. At a certain point of time, users would like to review the recommendation due to lack of trust [4, 5]. For example, in healthcare treatment prediction, the predictions made by ML systems are not useful to doctors without supporting information on why that prediction is made. If the displayed

© Springer International Publishing AG, part of Springer Nature 2018
F. F.-H. Nah and B. S. Xiao (Eds.): HCIBGO 2018, LNCS 10923, pp. 715–729, 2018.
https://doi.org/10.1007/978-3-319-91716-0_56

prediction cannot be justified by supporting evidence, especially when the prediction is different compared to human judgement, doctors will reject the suggested treatments and redo the research by themselves. Intelligent applications cannot improve the efficiency of our work unless it gains the trust from users, regardless of how accurate the recommendations are [5].

The user's trust will be gained when the explanations on the recommendation can meet certain expectations of the users [6, 7]. In particular, we require more explanation for the recommendation results on user interaction points, such as the UI [8, 9]. From 2005, many studies [2, 4, 10–12] have focused on user trust in consumers and they have shown ideal results on gaining user trust almost instantaneously. One good example is the header: "people who bought this also bought…" in an online shopping website. While UI designs for the ML model explanation flourished in consumer domain applications, their counterpart in industry applications have not enjoyed similar successes. This is due to the order-of-magnitude increase in complexities in both technical and management aspects of industrial class software applications. Working professionals such as doctors, bankers and recruiters, their thinking process of using business tool is extremely different in comparison to consumers'. Studies [13–15] shown that it is of equal importance to offer explanations for ML applications in industrial domain in order to explore behaviours of business professionals and user trust. In current ML application trend, UI is the most common interaction point for user to understand more information of the ML prediction. This study aims to explore the topic of increasing user trust level in ML recommender-based business applications through effective UI design.

This paper will focus on work efficiency through ML recommender applications for business professionals and the impact of its UI design. Resume Matching, an ML-based solution which ranks the quality of candidates' resumes based on a job description, will be used for this study. At its core, Resume Matching aims to provide recommendation of best matched talents for recruiters. Due to this application's nature, the UI needs to be designed in a way that it minimizes the time spent for searching the right talents when the recruiters view the automatic recommendations. This brings forth the iterative and incremental process created to test the UI components of Resume Matching.

It will also present our design, design process, testing process, our findings, and a set of compiled guidelines from both research literature and user feedback. A guideline of ML User Trust Improvement (ML-UTI) Research Model will be presented which is targeted for improving ML recommender applications' user trust level of business professionals through effective UI design.

2 User Trust Challenges in Machine Learning (ML) Recommender Applications for Business Professionals

We started by examining literature covering multiple impairments that will affect business professionals while they are using work related applications. Efficiency is one of the key measurements and desire for those applications. Utilizing visualizations is a vital process. ML recommender systems for business domains such as healthcare [16] will filter out irrelevant information and shorten the decision period for end users.

Accuracy is another significant parameter for users to measure the performance of the applications. When the accuracy of the system sways the trust of the user, it proves inadequate efficiency. Users will spend additional time to learn about the recommendation by studying the original data and review the irrelevant information until they determine its trustworthiness. Business professionals will rely on their own experience and lead to bias judgements [16].

Reviewing resulted lack of trust in the recommendation. User trust level will make credible impact on usability of the ML recommender system [17]. One way to measure the quality of usability is through "autonomy level" which refer to the ratio of user complete the tasks by themselves or by machine [18–22]. While the application is gaining trust from the user, the autonomy level will be reduced, along with increased efficiency.

User trust will be gained within a period of time when user adopt the system's repeated quality recommendations [23]. Presenting the information that meets the user's expectations can shorten this time span.

For user testing, we gave the users a task of shortlisting the top 3 candidates out of 25 submitted resumes for a particular job description. This task is repeated 20 times, each with a different set of resumes and job description. Amongst the 25 resumes for each task, the top 5 resumes are intentionally chosen to reflect suitable candidates, whereas the next 20 resumes are from unsuitable candidates. User experience was measured by the number of unnecessary clicks by the user in this shortlisting task. This metric can be used to find out the number of tasks needed for a particular user to minimize the number of unnecessary clicks. For example, a user may make 20 unnecessary clicks on his first task, and consistently make 4 unnecessary clicks after 12 tasks. In this case, we can infer that it takes 12 repetitions before the user reaches a low autonomy level. The shorter length of the period it takes for a user to reach a low autonomy level will indicate a faster confidence gain from the user.

Many UI guides [24–27] can help on designing corporate applications to achieve better user experience. Those guides are for presenting the information effectively with UI. Nonetheless, there is no research on how to understand the user expectation from the perspective of user trust.

By studying many web applications which are related to ML recommender systems, we outlined two UI design trends which can improve user trust level (Table 1). Displaying Probability [28] is most commonly seen as part of rating. Such as the rating of the movie is 4/5 stars, the chance of you like it will be 97%. "4/5 stars" and "97%" in these examples are probability ratings. Displaying Token [29] (explanation) helps the users understand more details about the recommendation, it functions as a summary of the recommendations or explanation of the calculation logic.

Ultimately when it comes to gaining user trust from business professionals, these two UI designs Displaying Probability and Displaying Token cannot shorten the time taken to gain users' trust despite the recommendations from ML systems are of satisfactory.

Table 1. UI design trend in ML recommender applications.

UI design pattern	Displaying probability	Displaying token (explanation)
Example	• Matching score displaying in Movie recommendation of Netflix • Job matching score displaying in LinkedIn	• Related content displaying in search result of Google • "people who bought this also bought" title displaying in shopping applications

These challenges, along with the compiled guidelines were included throughout the iterative design process; to ensure shortening of time spent gaining user trust and improve the productivity and effectiveness of ML recommendation applications.

3   Methodology

This study follows **mix-method research paradigm**. We adopted elicitation (interactive demo) and structured interview methods to inquiry participants' perspective on trust. During the study, participants are presented with variations of UI design and asked to comment on how such designs affected their sense of trust. We measure trust by several questions adapted from Steve Portigal [30].

3.1   Outline

The process began with the development of Resume Matching via wireframe prototyping. We created four designs based on two UI design trends, Displaying Probability and Displaying Token. Another two designs had been built after we applied ML User Trust Improvement (ML-UTI) Research Model. During development, hiring managers, developers, and researchers from out organization provided their expertise on the design and implementation of the test framework. Figure 1 is showing the research outline.

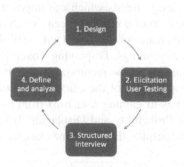

Fig. 1. Research outline.

After obtaining test users, we design the test framework in which the users would carry out the main activities next. Once the users give their feedback, further research on usability and engagement will commence. Changes will then be made within the site and were once again tested but by a different set of users in an iterative and incremental process.

The total time taken for each user test is estimated to be two hours. All users will be doing twenty separate tasks with different job descriptions.

3.2   Test Users

In order to accurately obtain the correct sample type representing the desired demographic, we studied the information about recruiters and interviewed recruiters from our organization. The targeted group is between 21 to 39 years old and need to read more than 30 resumes for one job posting.

A minimum of six users were used to test each of the six designs. The first part of the research is elicitation user testing where users would be observed while testing the design and verbally asked for their feedback. They are again questioned verbally for structured interview.

3.3   Measures and Validation Techniques

Qualitative and quantitative methods are part of measuring user trust.

Qualitative - Objective Observation: Two factors are used to measure level of user trust via number of unnecessary clicks and number of doubts raised by users when they are doing the test. For each factor, the number of tasks between the maximum and minimum number of occurrences will be measured.

Quantitative - Subjective Rating: Users rating their trust level towards the design(s).

As the quality of ML recommender system will affect the test results, we prepared sets of good quality recommendations from three senior recruiters to help us perform the test.

Six designs had been created based on different design guides (Table 2). Although the full design of the application displayed during the test for helping the users to have a more realistic experience, our observation is focused on the list design of recommendation (Figs. 2, 3, 4, 5, 6 and 7).

This straight-line list design is showing probability score of different categories. Such as matching score of education, matching score of skills and overall matching score.

This is a graphic presentation of probability score. The big number in the center of each circle is the overall matching score, followed by the small numbers which are probability score from different categories.

The summary of each recommendation has been shown in this design.

This design combines the summary of each recommendation and probability matching score of different categories.

Table 2. Design and design guide.

	Displaying probability	Displaying token	ML user trust design (ML-UTD) principle checklist
Design 1	X		
Design 2	X		
Design 3		X	
Design 4	X	X	
ML user trust improvement (ML-UTI) research model			
Design 5		X	X
Design 6			X

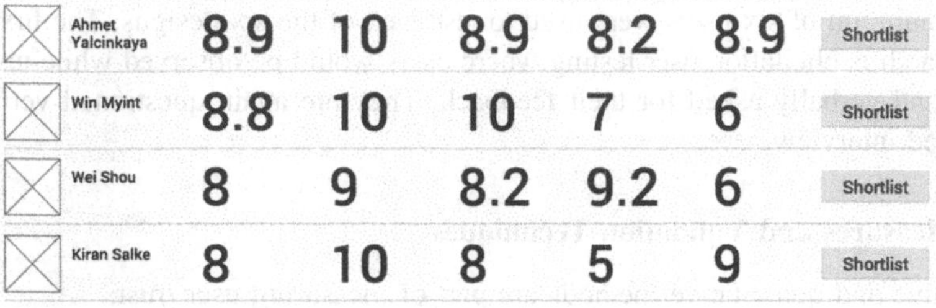

Ahmet Yalcinkaya
8.9
10
8.9
8.2
8.9
Shortlist
Win Myint
8.8
10
10
7
6
Shortlist
Wei Shou
8
9
8.2
9.2
6
Shortlist
Kiran Salke
8
10
8
5
9
Shortlist

Fig. 2. Design 1.

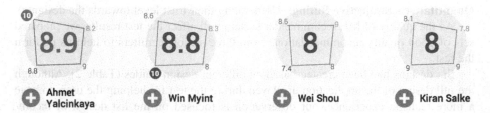

10
8.2
8.9
9
8.8
Ahmet Yalcinkaya
8.6
8.3
8.8
8
10
Win Myint
8.5
9
8
7.4
8
Wei Shou
8.1
7.8
8
9
9
Kiran Salke

Fig. 3. Design 2.

This design displays the information which follow the guide of ML-UTD Principle Checklist.

We used a conversation-like UI design to displays the information which follow the guide of ML-UTD Principle Checklist.

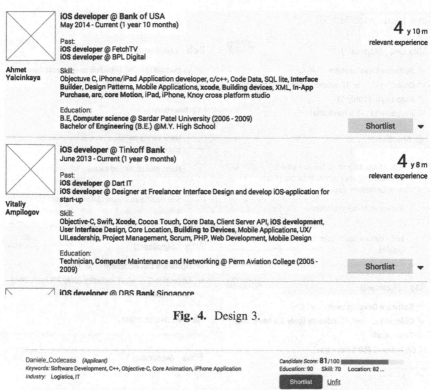

Fig. 4. Design 3.

Fig. 5. Design 4.

3.4 Testing Process

Users were informed of what they are expected to do throughout the test. Upon explanation, users could then decide if they are still positive on commencing the test. Each participant will be seated in front of a computer or paper prototype. There will be a list of tasks for them to complete. They are also provided with verbal guidance from the test coordinator when needed. Upon completion of all tasks, they commence short interview to get additional feedbacks. Prior to the start of the interview, users were given a brief introduction about the interview. Their answers will be recorded for further studies and research (Fig. 8).

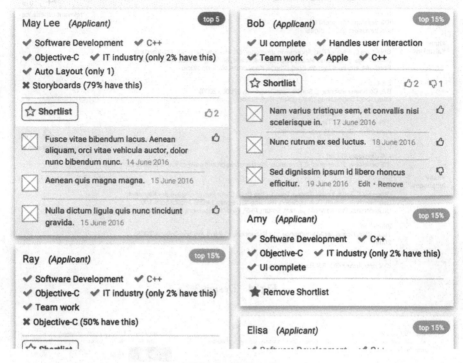

Fig. 6. Design 5.

Fig. 7. Design 6.

4   Findings

Business professionals tends to have high confidence based on their past experiences which resulted in them seeking for more explanation on automatic recommendation. Candidate score is not a proper way to describe or classify a candidate. "If this person is

Introduction

▼

Elicitation user test
User is required to complete a task. The key task is shortlist 3 job candidates for job 1 to job 20.

▼

Structured interview

▼

Acknowledgement

Fig. 8. Testing process.

not suitable to the job does not makes him a bad candidate" obtained by one of the feedbacks from user interview.

Test participants cannot relate the reason of the recommendation from the basic and summarized information (Result shown in Figs. 9 and 10). Most of the test participants mentioned, even it can shorten the resume reading time, but they still need to go through all the candidates' summary before they decide which is a better candidate. After around fourteen tasks, users finally trust the ML recommendation without review the details. These results prove that the effect on user trust level of different presentations (Displaying Probability and Displaying Token) of the information is insignificant.

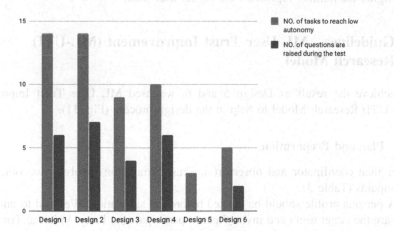

Fig. 9. Average user trust measurement.

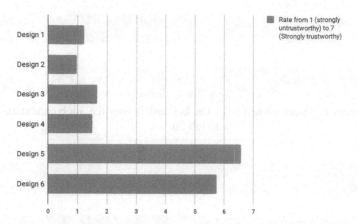

Fig. 10. Average rating on user trust Likert scale question.

Design 5 and 6 resulted in raised trust levels. Test participants do not question the information had being shown on the UI, and they gave a higher user trust score. To reach low autonomy only takes around five tasks. "I like that you are showing me the comparison information which is what I am looking for. I can relate it back to job description, and the suggestions are making sense." obtained by one of the feedbacks from user interview. The feedback from the users is matched with our finding from ML User Trust Improvement (ML-UTI) Research Model. The designs followed ML User Trust Design (ML-UTD) Principle checklist can accomplish a better result - user trust level is higher.

Average user trust measurement on number of tasks to reach low autonomy and number of questions are raised during the test. Lower the number represents the higher user trust.

Higher the number represents the higher user trust.

5   Guidelines - ML User Trust Improvement (ML-UTI) Research Model

To achieve the result as Design 5 and 6, we used ML User Trust Improvement (ML-UTI) Research Model to help in the design process (Fig. 11).

5.1   Plan and Preparation

Other than coordinator and observer(s), Trust Simulation involves two other major participants (Table 3).

A persona profile should be created before the simulation. We need to understand who are the target users and invite them to participate (as Party A) in the Trust Simulation. Meanwhile, we need to understand the objective of the ML application as it helps to create the right task for Party A. For example: Party A in Resume Matching Trust

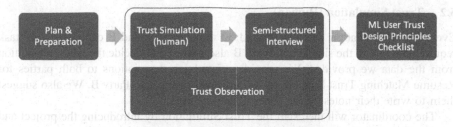

Fig. 11. ML-UTI Research Model.

Table 3. Trust Simulation participants.

Trust simulation participants	Description
Party A	Target user(s)
Party B	Assistant of Party A. The role of Party B in the Trust Simulation is doing as the ML application which will help Party A to finish their task

Simulation will be a recruiter who meets the profile of persona and one of the designed task for Party A is shortlist one job candidate among hundreds of job applicants.

Party B should be the domain expert who can give good recommendations to Party A.

Both Party A and B cannot work together or have close relationship as acquaintances, it will affect observation on the trust building process.

Two sets of interview questions had been designed before the Trust Simulation. Table 4 shows some examples of the questions.

Table 4. Example of survey questions.

Questions to Party A	
1	Why do you accept the suggestion from B?
2	How do you think about the suggestion?
3	How do you the suggestion is trustworthy? Please rate from 1 (strongly untrustworthy) to 7 (Strongly trustworthy)
4	How do you think B is trustworthy? Please rate from 1 (strongly untrustworthy) to 7 (Strongly trustworthy)
Questions to Party B	
1	How do you make the suggestion/recommendation?
2	Why do you choose this way to present your recommendation?
3	Why do you choose this suggestion?

5.2   Trust Simulation (Human)

Every Trust Simulation will take around 30 min. Party A and B can study their task requirement before the simulation. Party B also required to decide the recommendation from the data we provided. We provide printed job descriptions to both parties for Resume Matching Trust Simulation and 5 printed resumes to Party B. We also suggest them to write their notes on the paper if they needed.

The coordinator will then start the Trust Simulation by introducing the project and bringing all participant up to speed.

5.3   Semi-structured Interview

We designed questions adapted from Steve Portigal [30]. Most of the questions in the interview are open ended questions. We suggest doing the interview for both parties at the same time and direct them to have discussion. We can get more insight from this interview format. This can achieve similar effect as Focus Group Discussion.

5.4   Trust Observation

Some of the key observations we need to take notes during the Trust Simulation:

- Does Party B gain trust from Party A?
- How does Party B let Party A accept the suggestion?
- If Party A does not accept the suggestion, what is the reaction of Party B?
- What is the interaction between the two parties?
- What do they write on the notes?
- Table 5 shows our key findings in one of the simulations.

Table 5. Example of key findings.

	Key findings
1	Both parties did notes and highline on the resumes and job description (We study their notes after the simulation.)
2	Party B just provide 1 suggestion to Party A
3	Party B explain why he choose the candidate without questioning from Party A
4	Party B explain what makes the suggested candidate outstanding Party B used comparison method to explain his suggestion, compare candidates vs candidates, and candidates vs job description
5	Party B raise the hiring conditions when he think this is a good candidate but still is not a good match
6	Party A accepted the suggestion from party B without other questioning (trust level towards B from A is high)
7	No scoring or rating mentioned in the simulation

5.5   ML User Trust Design (ML-UTD) Principles Checklist

We observed the interaction between business professionals from the Trust Simulation and the study as well as the interview answers. We created a ML-UTD Principle Checklist based on the findings. Table 6 is an example of ML-UTD Principle Checklist for Resume Matching.

Table 6.   Example of ML-UTD Principle Checklist.

☑	Design principles	Example
	Do not give rating for each candidate	Cannot use: • 80 points to candidate 1 • 98% to candidate 2
	Highlight the best candidate(s)	
	Highlight the most convincing reasons for the recommendation	
	Requirement to present the convincing reasons: Compare candidates, compare candidates and job description	• 90% of candidates do not have this skill, but this is a needed skill that written in the job description
	Highlight the hiring condition(s)	
	Requirement to present the hiring conditions: Compare candidates, compare candidates and job description	• This candidate is a very good match with the job, however, he has 10 years of working experience but only looking for 2 years working experience or above

6   Conclusion

This case study kick-starts a movement to improve business professionals' level of engagement when using ML recommender applications to assist in their business tasks.

Based on our findings, the UI designs used ML-UTI Research Model and ML-UTD Principle Checklist as a guide can lead to a positive user experience. The UI expanded the explanation of the recommendations and this in turn is aligned with the thinking patterns of the user. This makes the UI design easily accepted. It also enables users to have a higher trust on the ML recommendations. It directs the user's attention to the top recommendations instead of reviewing the whole list again, causing period of gaining user trust to be greatly shortened. This results higher work efficiency when user uses the business application.

However, this project has its limitations based on the number of participants available and are mainly from Singapore. As such, we should not over-generalize our findings. Further investigations into users from different demographics could provide more in-depth insights. When user base of Resume Matching grows, more information could be gathered to verify if the findings could be applied to other mediums of communication in ML recommender applications, such as voice, chat and drawing. As the need of ML recommender applications for industry increases, consequently there will be increased need for investigations into ML recommender specific HCI and the multiplicity of possible future research streams that is highly anticipated to arise from this area of study.

References

1. Somasegar, S.: Key trends in machine learning and AI. https://techcrunch.com/2016/07/06/key-trends-in-machine-learning-and-ai/. Accessed 08 Feb 2018
2. Pazzani, M.J., Billsus, D.: Content-based recommendation systems. In: Brusilovsky, P., Kobsa, A., Nejdl, W. (eds.) The Adaptive Web. LNCS, vol. 4321, pp. 325–341. Springer, Heidelberg (2007). https://doi.org/10.1007/978-3-540-72079-9_10
3. Riddle, C.: The importance of big data and analytics in the era of digital transformation. http://www.itproportal.com/features/the-importance-of-big-data-and-analytics-in-the-era-of-digital-transformation/. Accessed 08 Feb 2018
4. O'Donovan, J., Smyth, B.: Trust in recommender systems. In: Proceedings of the 10th International Conference on Intelligent User Interfaces (IUI 2005), pp. 167–174. ACM, New York (2005)
5. McLellan, C.: Inside the black box: understanding AI decision-making. http://www.zdnet.com/article/inside-the-black-box-understanding-ai-decision-making/. Accessed 08 Feb 2018
6. Cosley, D., Lam, S.K., Albert, I., Konstan, J.A., Riedl, J.: Is seeing believing? How recommender system interfaces affect users' opinions. In: Proceedings of the SIGCHI Conference on Human Factors in Computing Systems, pp. 585–592. ACM (2003)
7. Herlocker, J.L., Konstan, J.A., Terveen, L.G., Riedl, J.T.: Evaluating collaborative filtering recommender systems. ACM Trans. Inf. Syst. (TOIS) 22(1), 5–53 (2004)
8. Bandyszak, T., Moffie, M., Goldsteen, A., Melas, P., Nasser, B.I., Kalogiros, C., Barni, G., Hartenstein, S., Giotis, G., Weyer, T.: Supporting coordinated maintenance of system trustworthiness and user trust at runtime. In: IFIP International Conference on Trust Management, pp. 96–112 (2016)
9. Nakayama, M., Medlin, B.D., Chen, C.C., Vannoy, S.A.: Key factors increasing the trust and intention to adopt standard cloud-based applications. In: PACIS, p. 229 (2016)
10. Pronin, E.: Perception and misperception of bias in human judgment. Trends Cogn. Sci. 11(1), 37–43 (2007)
11. Lieberman, H., Paternò, F., Klann, M., Wulf, V.: End-user development: an emerging paradigm. In: Lieberman, H., Paternò, F., Wulf, V. (eds.) End user development, pp. 1–8. Springer, Netherlands (2006). https://doi.org/10.1007/1-4020-5386-X_1
12. Nodder, C.: Gaining User Trust: Research and a Secret. http://uxpamagazine.org/gaining-user-trust-research-and-a-secret/. Accessed 08 Feb 2018
13. Mori, T., Nakanishi, M.: Application development for gathering "Inexperienced UX" data for planning next-generation products. In: Soares, M., Falcão, C., Ahram, T. (eds.) Advances in Ergonomics Modeling, Usability & Special Populations, pp. 15–25. Springer, Heidelberg (2017). https://doi.org/10.1007/978-3-319-41685-4_2
14. Hennes, J., Wiley, K., Anderson, J.B.: The trail reporter mobile application: methods for UX research and communication design as civic agency. In: Proceedings of the 34th ACM International Conference on the Design of Communication, p. 24. ACM (2016)
15. Lycett, M.: 'Datafication': making sense of (big) data in a complex world. Eur. J. Inf. Syst. 22(4), 381 (2013)
16. Duan, L.: Healthcare information systems: data mining methods in the creation of a clinical recommender system. http://www.tandfonline.com/doi/abs/10.1080/17517575.2010.541287. Accessed 08 Feb 2018

17. Krawczyk, H., Lubomski, P.: User trust levels and their impact on system security and usability. In: Gaj, P., Kwiecień, A., Stera, P. (eds.) CN 2015. CCIS, vol. 522, pp. 82–91. Springer, Cham (2015). https://doi.org/10.1007/978-3-319-19419-6_8
18. Kaniarasu, P., Steinfeld, A., Desai, M., Yanco, H.: Potential measures for detecting trust changes. In: Proceedings of the Seventh Annual ACM/IEEE International Conference on Human-Robot Interaction (HRI 2012), pp. 241–242. ACM, New York (2012)
19. Jian, J., Bisantz, A., Drury, C.: Foundations for an empirically determined scale of trust in automated systems. International J. Cogn. Ergon. 4(1), 53–71 (2000)
20. Guo, G.: Integrating trust and similarity to ameliorate the data sparsity and cold start for recommender systems. In: Proceedings of the 7th ACM conference on Recommender systems (RecSys 2013), pp. 451–454. ACM, New York (2013)
21. Guo, G., Zhang, J., Yorke-Smith, N.: A novel Bayesian similarity measure for recommender systems. In: Proceedings of the 23rd International Joint Conference on Artificial Intelligence, IJCAI (2013)
22. Xu, A., Dudek, G.: OPTIMo: online probabilistic trust inference model for asymmetric human-robot collaborations. In: Proceedings of the Tenth Annual ACM/IEEE International Conference on Human-Robot Interaction (HRI 2015), pp. 221–228. ACM, New York (2015)
23. Panniello, U., Gorgoglione, M., Tuzhilin, A.: Research note—In CARSs we trust: how context-aware recommendations affect customers' trust and other business performance measures of recommender systems. Inf. Syst. Res. 27(1), 182–196 (2016)
24. Kohno, I., Fujii, H.: User-centered approach for NEC product development. In: Stephanidis, C. (ed.) HCI 2011. CCIS, vol. 173, pp. 48–52. Springer, Heidelberg (2011). https://doi.org/10.1007/978-3-642-22098-2_10
25. Apple: iOS human interface guidelines. https://developer.apple.com/library/ios/documentation/UserExperience/Conceptual/MobileHIG/. Accessed 08 Feb 2018
26. Hartson, R., Pyla, P.S.: The UX Book: Process and Guidelines for Ensuring a Quality User Experience. Morgan Kaufmann, San Francisco (2012)
27. Miki, H., Suzuki, K., Suzuki, T.: User interface developing framework for engineers. In: Yamamoto, S. (ed.) HIMI 2016. LNCS, vol. 9734, pp. 433–441. Springer, Cham (2016). https://doi.org/10.1007/978-3-319-40349-6_41
28. Denker, J.S., Lecun, Y.: Transforming neural-net output levels to probability distributions. In: Advances in Neural Information Processing Systems, pp. 853–859 (1991)
29. Tokenization. https://nlp.stanford.edu/IR-book/html/htmledition/tokenization-1.html. Accessed 08 Feb 2018
30. Portigal, S.: Interviewing Users: How to Uncover Compelling Insights. https://www.goodreads.com/book/show/17869520-interviewing-users. Accessed 08 Feb 2018

Social Network Analysis: A Tool to Explore Intelligent Patterns of Commercial Data

Chien Hsiang Liao[✉]

Department of Information Management, Fu Jen Catholic University,
Taipei, Taiwan
jeffen@gmail.com

Abstract. Applying data-driven science to find out interesting patterns for enterprise has been the focus of research issues in recent years. With the advances in information technology and network infrastructure, huge amount of data can be instantly analyzed, interpreted, and visualized by scientists. Based on the existing literature in data science, the topics of most prior studies are emphasized on mathematical equations, algorithm evaluation, model development, and machine learning. Data science studies based on the application of social network are comparatively few. The purpose of this study is to elaborate the key concepts of social network analysis (SNA) and its plausible business applications for enterprise. SNA is not a novel application, in contrast, it is a mature tool and has been applied in the field of organizational behavior and management science. In general, SNA software (e.g., UCINET or Pajek) is often analyzed based on given or closed data. However, this study suggests that it can be developed as cloud service due to the progress of cloud computing. Most importantly, the notion of SNA can be applied as various applications in different industries, such as marketing, healthcare, and talent development. Its computations and applications need to be highlighted. This study aims to fill this gap and illustrate how to apply SNA to explore the intelligent patterns from data.

Keywords: Social network analysis · Intelligent pattern · Business application
Data science

1 Introduction

In the recent years, data science has increasingly become a hot topic. With the advances in scientific algorithms and calculations, data scientists extract unknown knowledge or interesting patterns from data. The data can be instantly analyzed and easily interpreted and understood via data visualization for users. Based on the existing literature in data science, the topics of most prior studies are emphasized on mathematical equations, algorithm evaluation, model development, and machine learning. Data science studies based on the application of social network are comparatively few. In other words, the hidden information in social networks might be neglected. A social network is constituted as a set of people, organizations or other social entities, connected by a set of socially meaningful relationships, such as friendship, transaction or co-working

© Springer International Publishing AG, part of Springer Nature 2018
F. F.-H. Nah and B. S. Xiao (Eds.): HCIBGO 2018, LNCS 10923, pp. 730–739, 2018.
https://doi.org/10.1007/978-3-319-91716-0_57

relations (Lea et al. 2006). The unknown patterns embedded in social network's architecture and relationships might be valuable for business and social members.

The purpose of this study is to elaborate the key concepts of social network analysis (SNA) and its plausible business applications for enterprise. SNA is not a novel application, in contrast, it is a mature tool and has been applied in the field of organizational behavior and management science. In general, SNA software (e.g., UCINET or Pajek) is analyzed and applied to the given or closed data. Nevertheless, this study proposes that SNA techniques can be developed as cloud service due to the progress of cloud computing. Most importantly, the notion of SNA can be applied as various applications in different industries, such as marketing, healthcare, and talent development. Its potential niches and applications need to be further discussed. This study aims to illustrate how to apply SNA to explore the intelligent patterns from data.

2 Theoretical Background

2.1 Social Network Analysis

In sociological research, some scientists use graph theory to represent the social structure of people. The words 'network' and 'graph' are synonymous, 'nodes' are often called 'actors', and a 'link' represents an 'edge' from one node to another (Otte and Rousseau 2002). SNA is a tool to map and measure relationships among social actors including people, groups, organizations, computers, and other social entities (Freeman 1979; Liao 2017). More precisely, SNA is based on the premise that the relationships among social actors can be described by a graph. The graph's nodes represent social actors, and the graph's edges connect pairs of nodes, and thus represent social interactions (Liu et al. 2005). SNA has been widely applied in many disciplines, including sociology, education, information systems and management science (Vidgen et al. 2007).

2.2 Concepts and Measures of SNA

In SNA, many network properties can be used to measure the relations among social actors. Tichy et al. (1979) conclude there are three sets of properties of network can be applied in business or commercial use. *Transactional content* (or *relational content*) is focused on the exchange content or relation between two connected actors, such as friendship, influence power, information exchange, and exchange of goods or services. *Nature of the links* refers to the linkages between pairs of individuals in terms of some characteristics, including the strength of the relation, reciprocity, and the role of social actors. *Structural characteristics* of network can be divided into four levels measured by external network, internal network, clusters or cliques within the network, and the characteristics of individual or specific social actor.

According to the context of research, these properties or measures have been widely treated as research variables by prior studies. For example, Brown and Reingen (1987) treat *nature of the links* as tie strength between two individuals and example its effect on word-of-mouth referral behavior. They found that individuals with strong tie are more likely to be activated for referral information. Likewise, Otte and Rousseau (2002) use three indicators to capture the notion of *structural characteristics* of social network, including density, cliques, and centrality. The *density* is an indicator of the general level of connectedness of the network (Borgatti et al. 2009; Chi et al. 2007). For instance, if every node is directly linked with every other node, that is a high density network. The *clique* or faction means a sub-network in which nodes are highly connected (Otte and Rousseau 2002; Thomas 2000). The centrality represents a node's structural position in the network (Freeman 1979; Scott 2017).

Since many available measures or strategies can be applied in SNA, it is difficult to explain the notions of all measures exhaustively here. This study only presents some commonly used measures, e.g., link analysis and structural analysis, and further show how to apply these measures in big data at the next section. The link analysis has been used to visualize connected structures or relationships of nodes (Kunegis et al. 2010; Ortega and Aguillo 2008; Xu and Chen 2005). In this vein, this study proposes that applying link analysis might be helpful to reveal multiple hierarchical associations and unknown relationships among nodes. In the link analysis, the distance among nodes in a network will be calculated. That is, the distance is the number of steps in the path from one node to another (Borodin et al. 2005; Cai et al. 2004).

For the structural analysis of social network, this study adopts *centrality* to measure a node's structural position in the network. Centrality is defined as a node's prominence in the network relative to others (Burkhardt and Brass 1990; Zemljič and Hlebec 2005) or whether a node occupies a strategically significant position in the overall structure (Troshani and Doolin 2007). The commonly used indicators of centrality are degree centrality, closeness centrality and betweenness centrality (Liao 2017; Opsahl et al. 2010; Otte and Rousseau 2002). *Degree centrality* is treated as the number of nodes linked with a node (Lu and Feng 2009). High degree centrality means a node has linked with many other nodes. The mathematical equation of degree centrality is illustrated in the following equation. The degree centrality, $d(i)$, of node i is the total number of linked nodes, where $m_{ij} = 1$ if there is a link between nodes i and j, and $m_{ij} = 0$ if there is no such link.

$$d(i) = \sum_{j} m_{ij}$$

The closeness and betweenness centrality measures both rely on the identification and length of the shortest paths among nodes in the network (Opsahl et al. 2010). *Closeness centrality* represents the mean distance of a node from the other nodes (Lu and Feng 2009). That is, a node with high closeness centrality means it has the shortest distance to all other nodes (Freeman 1979). If all links have the same weight in a network, this node could spread throughout the entire network via the smallest number of intermediary nodes or in the minimum time. The equation of closeness centrality is calculated as inverse total length of shortest distance to all other nodes, where s_{ij} is the number of links in the shortest path from node i to node j.

$$c_{std}(i) = \frac{N-1}{\sum_j s_{ij}}$$

Betweenness centrality is based on the number of shortest paths passing through a node (Opsahl et al. 2010). The betweenness centrality refers to a node's position to control resources or information passed to other nodes in the network (Freeman 1979). A node with high betweenness centrality plays the role of connecting different sub-groups or cliques. It captures the meaning of 'mediation' (Borgatti and Everett 2006), 'middlemen' (Phang et al. 2013), or 'broker' (Brandes et al. 2016) in a network. Otte and Rousseau (2002) proposed that betweenness centrality may be defined loosely as the number of times a node needs a given node to reach another node. Hence, the mathematical expression of betweenness centrality of node i, denoted as $b(i)$, is obtained as the following equation, where g_{jk} is the number of shortest paths from node j to node k $(j, k \neq i)$, and g_{ijk} is the number of shortest paths from node j to node k passing through node i.

$$b(i) = \sum_{j,k} \frac{g_{ijk}}{g_{jk}}$$

3 Data Analytics Using Social Network Analysis

To further elaborate the research idea, this study illustrates a case based on the application of customer marketing. This study adopts R programming language to develop algorithms according to the measures of SNA mentioned in the literature. This study designs a web-based system and an application interface (API) which can be applied in big data. More specifically, in the traditional SNA software, all nodes in a network are given in advance by researchers, then centrality values of all nodes can be calculated by SNA software functions. However, in the context of big data, this approach is inefficient and time-consuming because there may be millions or billions of social interaction data. If users only want to obtain the information of structural analysis of particular groups or individuals, it is very inefficient to calculate the centrality values of all nodes. In this vein, this study proposes that this problem can be overcome by improving the algorithm of calculation and using relational level or hierarchy. That is to say, the proposed algorithm merely analyzes individual social network based on the level of relationship hierarchy. For instance, if the level of relational level is three, the algorithm will analyze a particular person's network at the third level of relational hierarchy. Due to the page limits, this study only illustrates the modified algorithm of closeness centrality as an example. To make readers easy to understand the notion of the algorithm, Table 1 lists the pseudo code that does not contain too many mathematical formulas. Firstly, this algorithm will call a function to obtain total number of nodes and node's name in the network according to the value of relational level, i.e., store in TARGET array. Secondly, the algorithm will compute the summarized value of the shortest path lengths from a node to the other nodes in the network. Also, the summarized path lengths of each node will be standardized and divided by degree of freedom (i.e., nodes − 1). Finally, the values will be stored in *MCC* array. Specifically, the *MCC* array is a global variable and stores all nodes' closeness centrality values.

Table 1. The pseudo code of modified closeness centrality

```
Modified closeness centrality (level, N)
// level: relational level; N: starting node
{
    TARGET[nodes] = network(level, N);
// network() will return total number of nodes at the level of relationship hierarchy
    value = 0;
    for (int i = 1; i <= nodes; i++){
        for (int j = 1; j <= nodes; j++){
            value = value + Shortpath_length(TARGET [i], TARGET [j]);
// Shortpath_length () will return the shortest path length from node i to j
        }
        MCC[i] = value / (nodes-1);
    }
    return MCC[];
}
```

For the link analysis, the attributes, characteristics, or preferences of each node in the network can be set through data mining techniques, e.g., a node's age, gender, preferred goods, hobbies, socio-economic conditions and so on. Furthermore, while user entries a specific attribute as search condition, the algorithm of link analysis can help user find the targets, including the shortest path and optimal path analyses. In the traditional calculation of link analysis, the paths of all nodes are completely calculated. Again, this approach is inefficient in the context of big data. Hence, the modified link analyses are developed as well. The pseudo code of modified shortest path algorithm is explained in Table 2. The algorithm includes four input variables, the explanations of variables are denoted in the algorithm. It will search for nodes with attribute from starting node *N*, and end up according to value of relational level. As mentioned, if relational level is 5, the algorithm will search N's network at the fifth level of relationship hierarchy. It should be noteworthy that *S* array may exist multiple paths between *N* and target nodes *C*. Hence, the algorithm will sort S array according to path length and finally return *S* array values.

Table 2. The pseudo code of modified shortest path analysis

```
Shortest path analysis (level, r = 1, N, Att)

// level: relational level; r: current relational level; N: starting node; Att: attribute

{

    while node N is linked with node C {

        if (node C contain Att and node C is not in S[] array)

            S[] = (C, r); //if node C possesses attribute, then incorporate it into S array

        if (node C has other links and r less than level)

            Shortest path analysis (level, r ++, C, Att);

    }

    Sort (S[], r); // sort array order by r

    return S[];

}
```

In brief, this study not only develops the algorithms of structural analysis and link analysis which can be applied in big data, but also designs a web-based system for business. The aim of system is to help business to seek potential customers who might be interested in their products. The system functions include link analysis and analyze structural characteristics of customers in the network. Figure 1 illustrates the result of link analysis. Through this system, users or business managers can enter several attributes (e.g., Mac or laptop) and search potential customers who are interested in these attributes. The link analysis lists the target customers (i.e., brown color nodes) with the shortest path. In addition, the result lists all possible paths as path selection references for user. This function contributes some implications. For the enterprise, business managers can utilize this analysis tool to find out potential consumers who are interested in their products, and further promote their products via relationship marketing. This tool could be regarded as a new marketing channel or alternative way to sale products.

Likewise, this system also provides data analytics of structural characteristics, including seeking key persons who highly connected with others (high degree centrality), persons who have shortest path length to all persons (high closeness centrality), and persons who linked with two or more different sub-groups (high betweenness centrality). Figure 2 shows an example of closeness centrality analysis. The nodes with high closeness centrality are 'Gai', 'Iverson' and 'Marsharetea', implying he is located

Rank	Path				
1	5. Mars	→	10. Coco	→	14. Hank
2	5. Mars	→	9. Teresa	→	12. Des
3	5. Mars	→	9. Teresa	→	14. Hank
4	5. Mars	→	20. Lebron	→	21. Kobe
5	5. Mars	→	17. Guy	→	21. Kobe

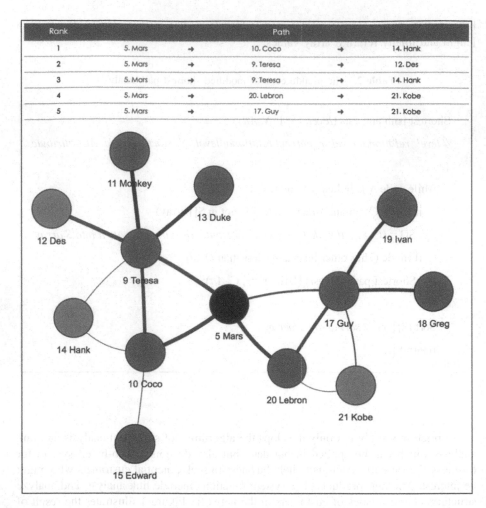

Fig. 1. Result of the shortest path analysis

in the center of whole network and has shortest path length to all nodes. Taking virus marketing or word-of-mouth as example, if the enterprise wants to launch a new product in the market, 'Kobe' will be a good first-mover because he can recommend product or deliver word-of-mouth to others with shortest path. This analysis technique helps managers to efficiently implement marketing strategies. For instance, managers could use the least or limited resources to achieve maximum efficiency. That is, spending the smallest contact costs to find out the correct target and contact with potential customers as many as possible.

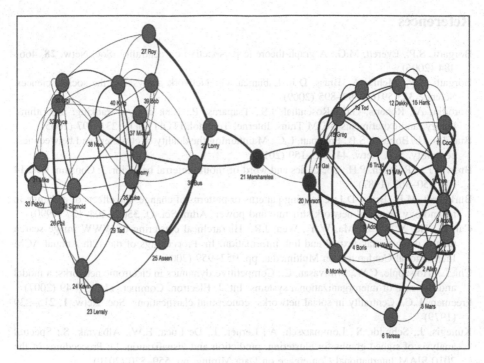

Fig. 2. Result of the closeness centrality analysis

4 Conclusions and Research Directions

This study reviews relevant literature about social network analysis and illustrates how to use some key measures of SNA in big data. Through the examples of link analysis and structural analysis, this study explains how to apply these results in marketing strategies. Based on the applications above, this study provides several research directions and propositions for future research.

First of all, although this study provides some examples of data analytics, the detailed system architecture and environment have not been mentioned and validated. Future research could develop system architecture by incorporating SNA and big data application. Such finding will be beneficial for the practical development. Second, this study merely uses some SNA measures, many indicators or strategies have not been mentioned. This study encourages future research could summarize more available indicators and conclude which indicator can be applied in big data or developed into a system. Finally, the measures of SNA can be applied to various practical applications in different companies and industries. Future researchers are encouraged to develop different practical or commercial applications by referring the examples in this study. For example, police department can use SNA to identify the associations between criminals and gang groups, thereby infer who is gangster boss behind the scenes and reduce crime rate, as suggested and highly recommended by prior studies (Van der Hulst 2009; Xu and Chen 2005).

References

Borgatti, S.P., Everett, M.G.: A graph-theoretic perspective on centrality. Soc. Netw. **28**, 466–484 (2006)

Borgatti, S.P., Mehra, A., Brass, D.J., Labianca, G.: Network analysis in the social sciences. Science **323**(5916), 892–895 (2009)

Borodin, A., Roberts, G.O., Rosenthal, J.S., Tsaparas, P.: Link analysis ranking: algorithms, theory, and experiments. ACM Trans. Internet Technol. (TOIT) **5**(1), 231–297 (2005)

Brandes, U., Borgatti, S.P., Freeman, L.C.: Maintaining the duality of closeness and betweenness centrality. Soc. Netw. **44**, 153–159 (2016)

Brown, J.J., Reingen, P.H.: Social ties and word-of-mouth referral behavior. J. Consum. Res. **14**(3), 350–362 (1987)

Burkhardt, M.E., Brass, D.J.: Changing patterns or patterns of change: the effects of a change in technology on social network structure and power. Adm. Sci. Q. **35**(1), 104–127 (1990)

Cai, D., He, X., Li, Z., Ma, W.Y., Wen, J.R.: Hierarchical clustering of WWW image search results using visual, textual and link information. In: Proceedings of the 12th Annual ACM International Conference on Multimedia, pp. 952–959 (2004)

Chi, L., Holsapple, C.W., Srinivasan, C.: Competitive dynamics in electronic networks: a model and the case of interorganizational systems. Int. J. Electron. Commer. **11**(3), 7–49 (2007)

Freeman, L.C.: Centrality in social networks: conceptual clarifications. Soc. Netw. **1**, 215–239 (1979)

Kunegis, J., Schmidt, S., Lommatzsch, A., Lerner, J., De Luca, E.W., Albayrak, S.: Spectral analysis of signed graphs for clustering, prediction and visualization. In: Proceedings of the 2010 SIAM International Conference on Data Mining, pp. 559–570 (2010)

Lea, B.-R., Yu, W.-B., Maguluru, N.: Enhancing business networks using social network based virtual communities. Ind. Manag. Data Syst. **106**(1), 121–138 (2006)

Liao, C.H.: Exploring the social effect of outstanding scholars on future research accomplishments. J. Assoc. Inf. Sci. Technol. **68**(10), 2449–2459 (2017)

Liu, X., Bollen, J., Nelson, M.L., Van de Sompel, H.: Co-authorship networks in the digital library research community. Inf. Process. Manag. **41**(6), 1462–1480 (2005)

Lu, H., Feng, Y.: A measure of authors' centrality in co-authorship networks based on the distribution of collaborative relationships. Scientometrics **81**(2), 499 (2009)

Opsahl, T., Agneessens, F., Skvoretz, J.: Node centrality in weighted networks: generalizing degree and shortest paths. Soc. Netw. **32**(3), 245–251 (2010)

Otte, E., Rousseau, R.: Social network analysis: a powerful strategy, also for the information sciences. J. Inf. Sci. **28**(6), 441–453 (2002)

Ortega, J.L., Aguillo, I.F.: Visualization of the Nordic academic web: link analysis using social network tools. Inf. Process. Manag. **44**(4), 1624–1633 (2008)

Phang, C.W., Zhang, C., Sutanto, J.: The influence of user interaction and participation in social media on the consumption intention of niche products. Inf. Manag. **50**(8), 661–672 (2013)

Scott, J.: Social Network Analysis. Sage, Thousand Oaks (2017)

Thomas, S.L.: Ties that bind: a social network approach to understanding student integration and persistence. J. High. Educ. **71**(5), 591–615 (2000)

Tichy, N.M., Tushman, M.L., Fombrun, C.: Social network analysis for organizations. Acad. Manag. Rev. **4**(4), 507–519 (1979)

Troshani, I., Doolin, B.: Innovation diffusion: a stakeholder and social network view. Eur. J. Innov. Manag. **10**(2), 176–200 (2007)

Van der Hulst, R.C.: Introduction to social network analysis (SNA) as an investigative tool. Trends Organized Crime **12**(2), 101–121 (2009)

Vidgen, R., Henneberg, S., Naudé, P.: What sort of community is the European conference on information systems? A social network analysis 1993–2005. Eur. J. Inf. Syst. **16**(1), 5–19 (2007)

Xu, J., Chen, H.: Criminal network analysis and visualization. Commun. ACM **48**(6), 100–107 (2005)

Zemljič, B., Hlebec, V.: Reliability of measures of centrality and prominence. Soc. Netw. **27**(1), 73–88 (2005)

Visualization of Zoomable 2D Projections on the Web

Michael Maus[1], Tobias Ruppert[2], and Arjan Kuijper[1,2]($\boxtimes$)

[1] Technische Universität Darmstadt, Darmstadt, Germany
[2] Fraunhofer IGD, Darmstadt, Germany
arjan.kuijper@igd.fraunhofer.de

Abstract. The objective of the work is the research and development of a web-based visualization system for the creation and testing of zoomable projection cards. The basic idea is to project a multidimensional data set onto two dimensions using projection methods to represent it on a 2D surface. Based on the Card, Mackinlay, and Shneiderman visualization pipeline, a data processing model has been developed. For data processing various distance metrics, dimension reduction methods, zooming approaches as well as presentation concepts are considered. The peculiarities and considerations of the respective technology are discussed. A zooming approach allows large amounts of data to be displayed on a limited area. In order to better visualize connections within the data, concepts of presentation are discussed. The data points are represented as glyph-based objects or using color maps, various shapes, and sizes. Best practices about colormaps are discussed. In order to display large amounts of data in real time, a separation of the generation and visualization process takes place. During generation, a tabular file and selected configuration execute computationally-intensive transformation processes to create map material. Similar to Google Maps, the generated map material is represented by a visualization. Management concepts for managing various map sets as well as their generation and presentation are presented. A user interface can be used to create and visualize map material. The user uploads a tabular file into the system and chooses between different configuration parameters. Subsequently, this information is used to generate map material. The maps and various interaction options are provided in the visualization interface. Using various application examples, the advantages of this visualization system are presented.

Keywords: Visualization · Zooming · Projection

1 Introduction and Motivation

Getting an overview of a tabular dataset is still a challenge. In addition to the classic representation of the dataset in tabular form (such as Excel), visual exploration offers alternative solutions. Visual projection methods (Multi-dimensional

© Springer International Publishing AG, part of Springer Nature 2018
F. F.-H. Nah and B. S. Xiao (Eds.): HCIBGO 2018, LNCS 10923, pp. 740–755, 2018.
https://doi.org/10.1007/978-3-319-91716-0_58

Scaling (MDS), Principal Component Analysis (PCA), etc.) make it possible to project multi-dimensional data sets on two dimensions, which are then displayed in 2D. Decisive advantages of visual projection methods are that relationships between the individual data sets are particularly well recognized. Relationships are expressed by distances based on topology-preserving approaches. Thus, "similar" data objects have a smaller distance from each other than "dissimilar" data objects, which have a large distance from each other and are therefore far from each other. In addition to the projection method, the choice of a suitable distance metric could influence the spatial arrangement of the objects. In addition, a heatmap for data visualization would be desirable. Heatmaps visualize the density of the object. A high density of objects exists when regions exist in which many objects are close to each other, whereas regions with few objects have a weak density of objects. Thanks to the different colors, the user is aware of the relationship with the object densities relatively quickly. Another challenge concerns the scalability of the visualization. Due to the limited display area, large amounts of data can hardly be displayed. The consequences would be overlapping data points, so that a clear assignment is impossible. Zoom-bare visual interfaces offer a solution for this. As the zoom level increases, the display area expands to allow more points to be displayed. Thus, large amounts of data could be represented by a suitable zoom approach. In addition, a client/server architecture with a web interface optimized for mobile devices would make sense. With the help of an Internet access, the visualization system of Anywhere (= client/server architecture) could be used to perform an exploratory data analysis. For optimization on mobile devices different display sizes, display resolutions have to be taken into account (= mobile first approach) [5]. Possible performance bottlenecks have to be overcome. The transfer of data between client and server, as well as the processing of the data on the mobile devices are critical processes that generate waiting times.

The aim of the work is the research and development of a web-based visualization system for the creation and testing of zoomable projection cards. The system should be based on the processing steps of the information visualization model of Card et al. [4]. Based on the model, the application should support the transformation process of the input data to map material, as well as their representation completely on the Web. In the app, the user selects a tabular text file. Panels set required configuration parameters. The user can manually set labels and features. Features are considered for the calculation of the X, Y coordinates. Labels describe characteristics that are displayed during a search. In addition, the user should choose between several similarity measures, projection method of his desired configuration. On the basis of a configuration and the file, map material is to be generated, which is displayed on request. Here, the configuration describes desired methods that are taken into account during processing. During processing, distances between the data objects are first calculated. With a selected dimension reduction method, the desired 2D data points are determined on the basis of the distances. The 2D data points are positioned on the map material. The map material is stored in the system and loaded on demand. The problem of visual scalability should be solved by using a zooming concept. The objects should be faded in or out at different zoom levels based on a user-definable measure of interest. To provide map material as quickly as possible, a caching concept is developed. After the described transformation process, map sections are generated and saved as image material. At the request of a client, the server transmits the stored images "on-demand". A web interface, similar to Google Maps, displays the footage. Related approaches to the testing of projection results were published this year by Stahnke et al. presented [14]. A related work for creating spatiotemporal maps based on 2D tiles has been described by Lins et al. [10].

2   Concept

The goal of the visualization system is to visually represent large multidimensional data sets. Configuration parameters are to be set via a user interface, whereby the user can choose between different configurations. In addition, the approach should enable usability on different devices (mobility). The system must: Load and process tabular files and generate suitable visual representations. A concept has been developed that allows the above-mentioned interactive visualization pipeline. Related work has described various models and approaches that help to solve the following problems: For the transformation of the data into a visual representation, a pipeline based on the visualization pipeline of Card et al. [4] has been developed. To ensure visual scalability of the data, a semantic zoom approach [2,3] has been taken into account. In order to consider device independence as well as multi-user scenarios, a client-server architecture based on the considerations of the ZOIL framework [15] has been developed. Pre-calculated maps are generated to prevent complex projections from being made on each client request. Large map material is unsuitable for transmission to the client because of the high transmission time. With a tiling approach, the map material is divided into tiles (so-called subsections), which have a small fixed size and are therefore transmitted faster.

Full results can be found in [11].

2.1   Projection Pipeline

The goal is to visually represent a tabular multidimensional record so that the user can explore the relationships within the data in an exploratory way [9]. The user is provided with a graphical representation in which relationships between the individual objects are better recognized than in a tabular representation (as in Excel). Objects are the individual line entries of the table. Instead of a table, the user is provided with a 2D scatterplot that visualizes the similarities between the different objects. Thus, a procedure model is needed to transform a tabular file into a 2D scatterplot representation.

The information visualization pipeline from Card et al. [4] describes, at a high level of abstraction, a model for transforming data over several levels into visual representations. Based on the Card et al. Visualization pipeline, we present a model that transforms multidimensional data. Starting from a data source, information is read, processed and visualized. The model performs 5 steps in succession. A data source reads the multidimensional data. From the multidimensional data, the relevant features are selected, with which a distance matrix is determined. The distance matrix contains all distances/distances between the individual objects. By using a projection method, the 2D data points are determined using the distance matrix and drawn on a scan plot. The following sections explain the considerations and special features involved in processing the individual steps.

2.2 Input

From a tabular file, multidimensional data is read and processed in further steps. The system must provide interfaces to read a tabular file. Within the scope of the work a calculation of the 2D data points using the projection methods is realized exclusively with numerical data. The focus is on numerical data that is interval scaled. A distance calculation of differently scaled data is limited possible. With similarity-based approaches, similarities between different strings or categorical data can be determined. Future work can take account of similarity-based approaches. Among other things, the pipeline is suitable for processing economic key figures as well as interval-scaled measurement data from research projects. The consideration of different data structures would be a meaningful extension and can be realized with relatively little effort. An extension would also allow the distance between hexcodes or dates to be determined.

For a suitable representation, relevant features must be identified and selected. Selecting features with no explanatory power will not recognize the context, or the result will be noisy. The choice of features can significantly affect the result of the projection. In order to avoid distortions or wrong connections, relevant features must be separated from irrelevant characteristics. For further processing within the pipeline, irrelevant features must be filtered. In order to determine suitable features, two strategies are suitable. In the first strategy, a simple model with few features is first set up, which is continuously expanded with additional features. In this procedure, characteristics for the model are successively selected. Irrelevant features distort the presentation and are therefore not included, whereas relevant features are included in the model and describe the desired context. Another approach is to include all variables except the non-numeric features in the model. In this procedure, individual characteristics are removed one after the other and a check is made as to whether an improvement is occurring. In the model, variables are removed until a desired relationship can be identified. In both strategies, as well as in general, an attempt is made to determine a compromise between overspecification by too many variables and a small explanatory power by too few variables.

2.3   Feature Selection

For a suitable representation, relevant features must be identified and selected. Selecting features with no explanatory power will not recognize the context, or the result will be noisy. The choice of features can significantly affect the result of the projection. In order to avoid distortions or wrong connections, relevant features must be separated from irrelevant characteristics. For further processing within the pipeline, irrelevant features must be filtered. In order to determine suitable features, two strategies are suitable. In the first strategy, a simple model with few features is first set up, which is continuously expanded with additional features. In this procedure, characteristics for the model are successively selected. Irrelevant features distort the presentation and are therefore not included, whereas relevant features are included in the model and describe the desired context. Another approach is to include all variables except the non-numeric features in the model. In this procedure, individual characteristics are removed one after the other and a check is made as to whether an improvement is occurring. In the model, variables are removed until a desired relationship can be identified. In both strategies, as well as in general, an attempt is made to determine a compromise between overspecification by too many variables and a small explanatory power by too few variables.

2.4   Distance Matrix

In order to map relationships between the objects, a suitable method is needed. Distances can be used to determine relationships between objects with numeric, metric-scaled features [13]. Metric scaling means that a ranking can be established and distances between the characteristic values can be measured. To achieve comparability between the various entries, normalization is required. Without a normalization, the entries would not be comparable, because the influence of certain features would be significantly larger than others. A min-max normalization unifies all features so that there are no size differences. When interpreting distances, it should be noted that distances with a higher value are farther apart and therefore less similar to one another, whereas a lower distance value describes a small distance between the objects and thus the objects are more similar to one another. Only numeric data are considered for the calculation. For a comparison of categorical data or strings special distance measures, also known as similarity measures, are needed, which are not part of this work. Supporting a variety of distance methods helps to create greater flexibility of graphical representations. Depending on the choice of the distance metric, it is possible in some cases for different representations to be generated. The distances between all objects are summarized in a distance matrix. Depending on the procedure, a distance matrix is optional or mandatory for the projection on 2D coordinates. In a PCA projection is often dispensed with a distance matrix, whereas in the MDS projection a distance matrix is mandatory.

2.5   Projection

Projection methods make it possible to use a given distance matrix to determine the desired 2D coordinates. In general, there is no central projection method that optimally explains all types or distributions of the data. Therefore, it is recommended to provide various projection methods in the visualization system.

PCA - also called *Principal Component Analysis* - describes a method for determining a linear projection of data that maps data to maximize variation in lower dimensional space. The goal is to explain the variation of the data with a small number of the most meaningful linear combinations ("main components"). The computation of the 2D coordinates does not necessarily require a distance matrix. Projection is also possible using the selected features of the multidimensional data set. The method is often used in linear relationships within the data. Thus, a linear relationship exists when the data is scattered around a straight line in the higher dimensional space. For non-linear relationships, the general PCA is inappropriate.

The *Kernel PCA* procedure describes an extension of the PCA, so that nonlinear relationships can be explained. It is useful if no meaningful representation of the data is generated with a PCA calculation. Using the Kernel PCA Trick, the input data is transformed using a selected function before the PCA calculation. Using the selected function, the data is transformed into a linear form and then the PCA projection is realized. With a Gaussian function, the data in the higher-dimensional space, which have a Gaussian distribution, can first be transformed into a linear form, in order then to carry out the PCA calculation. PCA, Kernel PCA Polynomial PCAs, and Kernel PCA Hellinger are unsuitable for imaging. Appropriate visualization is achieved using Kernel PCA Laplacian and Kernel PCA Gauss.

The *MDS* (*Multidimensional Scaling*) method describes a collection of analysis methods to represent objects based on their similarities in lower dimensional space. In contrast to the PCA method, a distance matrix is required. The MDS differentiates between ClassicalScaling and DistanceScaling. The Classical Scaling determines the 2D coordinates considering a distance matrix, using complex linear algebra. The distance matrix is transformed before the dimension reduction and then the desired coordinates are determined using a PCA projection. Distance Scaling uses an iterative approach and approaches a suitable representation in each iteration. First, the objects are randomly distributed in space and aligned in multiple iterations until an error threshold is reached. Objects that are more similar to each other are pushed toward each other, whereas objects that are more dissimilar are pushed away from each other.

The MDS methods are suitable for displaying objects based on their distances in the lower dimensional space. However, there are problems. As the number of entries increases, the distance matrix grows quadratically. From a size of more than 3000 entries memory leaks can occur. The required amount of data exceeds the main memory and errors occur. The ClassicalScaling should be preferred to DistanceScaling for metric scaled data. The DistanceScaling does not provide a consistent result, because with each new execution, the objects are randomly distributed in space. As a result, there is no globally uniform arrangement, but a local optimal arrangement. Due to the multiple iterations DistanceScaling offers a weaker performance compared to ClassicalScaling.

FastMap is suitable for big data processing. FastMap is an approximation of MDS that uses less memory and delivers higher performance than Classical MDS. The results of FastMap are not as accurate as those of the Classical MDS. FastMap integrates more disruptions. For the calculation of the 2D coordinates is dispensed with a square distance matrix and instead uses a distance matrix representation. On request, the desired distances are calculated on-the-fly. In summary, FastMap is suitable if a projection of large amounts of data (more than 3000 objects) is performed. If a memory leak occurs on the Classical MDS, FastMap should be used. FastMap dispenses with a distance matrix and is faster and more memory efficient than classical MDS.

Sammon mapping is a special case of the Distance Scaling MDS method. The goal is to consider smaller distances with the same relevance as larger distances.

ICA (Independent Component Analysis), describes a method to determine independent components. The method seeks to determine statistically independent factors that do not interfere with each other. The method is recommended if a clear separation of the individual components is required. The process removes all similarities between factors.

In summary:

- PCA: linear relationships of data from a data foundation are projected onto 2D coordinates. Distance matrix optional.
- Kernel PCA: Non-linear relationships are projected onto 2D coordinates. Distance matrix optional.
- MDS: 2D coordinates are determined on the basis of a distance matrix. For metric scaled data, ClassicalScaling should be preferred to DistanceScaling.
- FastMap: Heuristic variant of the MDS, suitable for MDS projections of large amounts of data.
- Sammon Mapping: Special case of MDS, trying to avoid favoring larger distances over smaller distances.
- ICA: Determination of statistically independent components that have no commonality.

2.6   Visualization

The 2D coordinates from the projection are drawn on a display surface. The representation is similar to a scatterplot. The similarities between the different objects are detected faster with this visualization than with the tabular representation. Similar objects are close together, whereas dissimilar objects are far apart.

Zooming Concept. Due to the limited display area, a large amount of data points can not be visualized. With large data sets of objects, objects may overlap or be drawn on top of each other, so that unambiguous assignment is not possible. One possible solution to prevent overplotting is to use a zooming concept. By using a zooming concept, the display area can be enlarged as required so that larger amounts of data can be visualized at the individual zoom levels. A semantic zoom concept allows you to visualize a large amount of data points without overplotting [12].

With a semantic zoom, the display area increases with increasing zoom level, so that more details, i.e. additional objects can be displayed without creating overlaps. Based on Pad [1], a zooming & panning concept is used. With zooming, the user enlarges the display area and with panning he navigates within the current zoom level on the display area. For the development of a suitable zooming approach, a compromise must be found between preventing overplotting and little loss of detail. An algorithm that does not represent objects, even though there is enough space on the canvas, would be inappropriate. The semantic zoom approach should use the display surface effectively and represent all data points if there is enough space. As the zoom level increases, the display area increases, leaving more room for more detail. Therefore, it is necessary that objects of lower zoom levels do not disappear, but are displayed and additional details appear [7,8]. Above all, it is important to rank the various objects in order to classify them as important or unimportant [6]. A suitable decision criterion for determining a ranking describes the measure of interest. Based on the measure of interest, the objects are sorted according to their importance in descending order. The measure of interest can be defined by the user by choosing an appropriate attribute. A metric scaled feature is selected and the feature's data is sorted in descending order of size. Objects of high importance are above the leaderboard, whereas unimportant objects are in the lower part of the leaderboard. The zooming processes take into account the ranking and distribute the objects at the different zoom levels. In this work, two zooming techniques have been developed, namely a bucketing approach and a neighbor approach.

Heatmap. The heatmap is a visualization technique to clarify relationships within the data. Heatmaps model the intensity or density between the data values. Depending on the intensity of the relationships, different colors are used. Often, warm colors are used for intense relationships (high density regions) and cold colors for weak relationships (low density regions). A heatmap makes it possible to visualize especially dense areas that create overplotting and interfere with a normal presentation. The heatmap is provided as an additional layer that can be hidden or hidden as needed. The variants static and dynamic heatmap exist for the representation of a heatmap. A static heatmap is displayed identically at all zoom levels, regardless of the zoom level, whereas a dynamic heatmap looks different at each zoom level. With a dynamic heatmap, a separate heatmap is created for each zoom level, which changes as the zoom level increases.

Presentation. This section describes concepts for the graphical design of the individual data points. In the visualization pipeline various techniques are described for generating a visual representation from a given data set. The graphical design of the individual data points is relevant to distinguish between individual objects. Black dots of equal size on a scatterplot are insufficient to illustrate relevant details. Although relationships between the individual objects are recognized, the objects do not visually differ from each other. The user does not recognize individual properties of the respective objects. Using a suitable visualization technique, data points could be customized so that individual properties of the objects are visible. Economic relationships between different countries could be visualized with the help of flags or air quality through objects of different colors. A red color describes a deficient air quality, whereas green indicates a good air quality. Therefore, approaches are useful in which objects in color, size, shape vary from each other and can be illustrated by different images. For this purpose, three approaches have been defined to adapt the data points in the simplest way. With a picture mapping every data point can be represented by a picture. The user is allowed to use images from web pages or local images from the computer. Another option is the Icon Wizard. By selecting different fields, different parameters can be set to visually represent objects. OData introduces an abstract modeling language that provides different configurations of the objects. This language can be used to assign different shapes or images to an object.

2.7 Optimizations

The model from sections generates a visual representation from a multidimensional tabular file. A presentation and a semantic zoom optimize the presentation of the data points. The basic problem is that the processing steps are complex and therefore do not generate the required map material in real time. However, it is required that the map material be provided to multiple users simultaneously in real time. Map Tiling is a concept in which the resulting maps are stored on the hard drive. The map material is divided into sections and can be loaded from the hard disk on request. The user would like to compare several combinations consisting of different features as well as different configurations. The concept of pre-calculated map sections is unsuitable for managing multiple configurations because only one configuration per map set can be created. With a large number of variations - created by using different tabular files and several different configurations - a large number of card sets are created under different names. Management using different names makes it difficult to understand large volumes of card sets. The Lazy Evaluation Approach introduces a complex file system for managing various feature combinations under a map set. As a result, different feature combinations can be created under a card name.

3   Usage Scenarios

3.1   Iris Dataset

The iris dataset is a popular dataset for testing classification methods. In a classification, the choice of relevant features tries to determine a correct assignment to the given classes. The dataset contains 50 objects with the explanatory variables sepal-width, sepal-length, petal-width, petal-length and the variable class to be determined. The goal is to use the four explanatory variables to determine the class. The variable class describes the three types of flowers Iris Setosa, Iris Versicolor and Iris Virginia. The flowers are presented in Fig. 2. The three flowers have a sepal (= sepal) and a petal (= petal). Based on Fig. 2, the sizes sepal and petal are described. In the picture sepal describes the yellow leaf and petal the green leaf of the flower. From the sizes petal and sepal, the width (= width) and height (= height) are recorded in the dataset. The table in Fig. 1 shows the structure of the data and describes part of the data set.

sepallength in cm	sepalwidth in cm	petallength in cm	petalwidth in cm	classes
5.1	3.5	1.4	0.2	Iris-setosa
6.3	3.3	6.0	2.5	Iris-virginica
7.0	3.2	4.7	1.4	Iris-versicolor
...	...	...	...	...

Fig. 1. Iris data set

Fig. 2. Left: sepal and petal. Right: flower types Iris (Color figure online)

The following section describes in several steps a procedure for analyzing the data record using the visualization system. After the iris dataset has been loaded into the system, a selection of all explanatory variables - sepal-length, sepal-width, petal-length and petal-width - is made to explain a classification of the different flower types. In a first test, an Euclidean distance is selected with a FastMap projection, without a semantic zoom, and the objects are represented by black dots. From Fig. 2 it can be seen that there are relationships between the objects but no differentiation of the different flower types is possible.

A picture mapping based on the three flower types could help to clarify the connections between the objects. The image mapping of the iris dataset is shown in Fig. 3. A better differentiation of the different flowers has been achieved only partially compared to the black dots. Because of the same color (purple), the minimum size of the images on the display and the related form, the flowers can not be clearly separated. In addition to the image mapping, there is the possibility to

Fig. 3. From left to right: default scatterplot. ImagePlot IconPlot (Color figure online)

vary an object in its color and size. An icon mapping could help. The iris dataset describes a classification problem, so it makes sense to consider the classes as categories. A qualitative color map is suitable for better visualizing relationships between different categories. Figure 3 uses a Qualitative Colormap to visualize the different flower classes. With the different colors a clear separation of the classes is visible. The iris-virginica (= green) differs from the iris-versicolor (= blue) and the iris-setosa (= red). The separation becomes visible because the objects of the identical flower varieties are close to each other, whereas different varieties of flowers are far apart are. Nevertheless, it can be seen that the iris-virginica is more similar to the iris-versicolor than the iris-setosa. Using a sequential color map and varying the size, numerical properties of objects can be highlighted. High numeric values are represented by larger or darker objects. Whereas a lower value is represented by a lighter or smaller object. The width (= width) and length (= length) characteristics can be used to represent the size and color of the objects. A comparison of sepal length and sepal width (see Fig. 2) shows that there is a relationship between the two variables. A longer sepal (= sepal) tends to imply a wider sepal. Another connection can be seen in the petal. With increasing length of the petal (= petal) increases the width (Fig. 4).

The visualization system allows for exploration of relationships within the iris dataset, taking appropriate procedures into account. The visualization system makes it possible to display a data record in just a few steps. Taking appropriate procedures into account, optimal representations of the data are generated so that relationships within the iris dataset become visible. The Iris dataset has been transformed into a visual representation considering the four features - sepal width, sepal length, petal width and petal length. In no time, the data was displayed on a scatterplot with black dots. This representation is difficult for the user to interpret. Relationships between the individual objects were not recognized. The presentation of the data set could be suitably displayed by changing the presentation. With the help of the icon option objects are displayed in a simple and understandable way. By varying the color and size and taking into account inuitive color maps, the objects are individually adapted. Through a

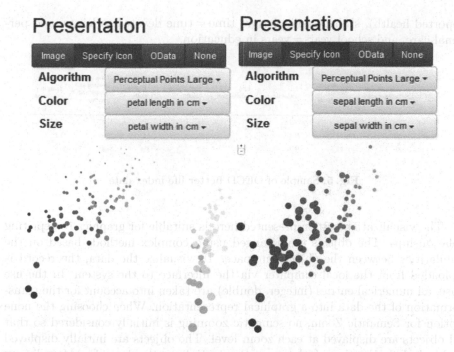

Fig. 4. Top: categorical and relationship presentation. Bottom: color sepal length & size: sepal width color - petal length & size: sepal width (Color figure online)

qualitative color map and constant size of the objects, connections have become visible. A clear separation of the different types of flowers became visible. The visualization system allows an analysis of relationships between two features of objects. Using a sequential colormap and the variation in size, relationships between the latitudes and lengths of sepal and petal have become apparent. A negative relationship between the width and length of the sepal, as well as a harmonious relationship between width and width of the petal were recognized.

3.2   OECD Dataset

The OECD dataset looks at the OECD Better Life Index The OECD Better Life Index makes it possible to compare well-being between different countries, considering eleven aspects. The eleven aspects are: "Common sense, education, environment, civic engagement, health, housing, income, employment, life satisfaction, security and work-life balance". The index describes the eleven aspects of the 34 OECD member countries, including Brazil and Russia. Every year the index is updated. Every year the data is collected. The Index provides citizens and scientists with information about people's quality of life and progress in society. The dataset (Fig. 5) contains 36 instances and is characterized by the characteristics of country, educational attainment, employee working hours (long hours), life expectancy, life satisfaction, health report (= self-assessment).

reported health), student skills, leisure time = time devoted to leisure and personal care, and school years = years in education.

Label	Educational attainment	Employees working very long hours	Life expectancy	Life satisfaction	Self-reported health	Student skills	Time devoted to leisure and personal care	Years in education
Brazil	43	10.74	73.4	7.2	69	402	14.97	16.3
Mexico	36	28.77	74.4	7.4	66	417	13.89	15.2
Chile	72	15.42	78.3	6.6	59	436	14.41	16.4

Fig. 5. Sample of OECD better life index data

The visualization system presented here is suitable for graphically depicting relationships. The objects are arranged using complex methods based on the similarities between the objects in space. To visualize the data, the record is uploaded from the local computer via the interface to the system. In the use case, all numerical entries (integer, double) are taken into account for the transformation of the data into a graphical representation. When choosing the none option for Semantic Zoom, no semantic zooming is initially considered so that all objects are displayed at each zoom level. The objects are initially displayed as black dots. For the calculation of the spatial coordinates a FastMap dimension reduction takes place, taking into account Euclidean distances. The selected configuration creates a scatterplot, as shown in Fig. 6. The similarities between the objects are recognizable, but a distinction between the objects is limited. On the black dot scatterplot in Fig. 6 countries can not be distinguished from each other. By means of a suitable visualization a differentiation is possible.

Fig. 6. Black dot scatterplot and image mapping

The OECD dataset compares countries with each other. A representation of the data points by their country flags allows the user to quickly capture relationships between countries. In Fig. 6, objects are visualized by their country flags. Compared to a black point scatter plot, interrelationships between countries are directly identifiable. The user sees at a glance which countries are related to each other. Figure 6 shows similarities between countries. Two countries are similar to each other when the distance is small. Countries between which a large distance exists are dissimilar and thus different from each other. There is a big gap between Russia and the rest of the country. In the distance calculation, all selected features are taken into account. Figure 7 compares Russia with other countries. The chart shows that the values of the characteristics Employees working very long hours, as well as Self-reported health are smaller compared to the other countries. The country Slovenia lists in the table compared to Russia a significantly higher value for the working time of the employees. The differences in size lead to large distances between Russia and the rest of the country. The countries Slovenia and Czech Republic are close to each other and are therefore similar to each other. The distance between the two countries is low because the values for life expectancy, self-reported health and student skills show little variation.

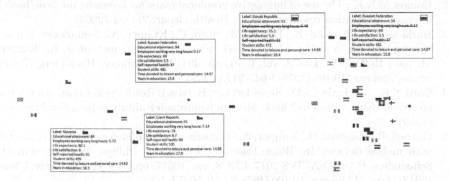

Fig. 7. Left: comparison of countries. Right: comparison between Russia and Slovakia

The distances between Russia and the rest of the countries exist because the characteristics of employees working very long hours and self-reported health deviate strongly. The visualization system allows a selection of different features so as not to consider them. For further consideration, the two features are removed from the further considerations. With the new feature combination a transformation is made with which a new representation of the ImagePlot is created. In the new illustration, Fig. 7, it can be seen that the distances between Russia and the other countries have narrowed. With the new feature combination Russia and the Slovak Republic are similar to each other. The gaps between the characteristics of "education attainment", "life satisfaction", "student skills" and "time devoted to leisure and personal care" are small, making Russia and Slovak Republic similar.

4   Conclusions

The aim of the work was to research and develop a web-based visualization system for creating and testing zoomable projection cards. The basic idea is to project a multidimensional dataset onto two dimensions using projection methods to represent it on a 2D scatterplot. For the development of the visualization system, several related papers were analyzed to identify the area of research and potentials. Required basic methods were elaborated to understand the peculiarities of the technologies used. Based on the methods and work, a concept has been developed to transform the data into visual representations. The implementation of the web-based visualization system was presented. Using various use cases, the advantages and potentials of the visualization system were presented using data examples.

References

1. Bederson, B.B., Hollan, J.D., Perlin, K., Meyer, J.M., Bacon, D., Furnas, G.W.: Pad++: a zoomable graphical sketchpad for exploring alternate interface physics. J. Vis. Lang. Comput. **7**, 3–32 (1996)
2. Boulos, M.N.K.: The use of interactive graphical maps for browsing medical/health internet information resources. Int. J. Health Geogr. **2**(1), 1 (2003)
3. Burkhardt, D., Nazemi, K., Breyer, M., Stab, C., Kuijper, A.: SemaZoom: semantics exploration by using a layer-based focus and context metaphor. In: Kurosu, M. (ed.) HCD 2011. LNCS, vol. 6776, pp. 491–499. Springer, Heidelberg (2011). https://doi.org/10.1007/978-3-642-21753-1_55
4. Card, S.K., Mackinlay, J.D., Shneiderman, B. (eds.): Readings in Information Visualization: Using Vision to Think. Morgan Kaufmann Publishers Inc., San Francisco (1999)
5. Gutbell, R., Kuehnel, H., Kuijper, A.: Texturizing and refinement of 3D city models with mobile devices. In: Blanc-Talon, J., Penne, R., Philips, W., Popescu, D., Scheunders, P. (eds.) ACIVS 2017. LNCS, vol. 10617, pp. 313–324. Springer, Cham (2017). https://doi.org/10.1007/978-3-319-70353-4_27
6. Kuijper, A.: On detecting all saddle points in 2D images. Pattern Recogn. Lett. **25**(15), 1665–1672 (2004)
7. Kuijper, A.: Using catastrophe theory to derive trees from images. J. Math. Imaging Vis. **23**(3), 219–238 (2005)
8. Kuijper, A., Florack, L.: The relevance of non-generic events in scale space models. Int. J. Comput. Vis. **57**(1), 67–84 (2004)
9. von Landesberger, T., Fiebig, S., Bremm, S., Kuijper, A., Fellner, D.W.: Interaction taxonomy for tracking of user actions in visual analytics applications. In: Huang, W. (ed.) Handbook of Human Centric Visualization, pp. 653–670. Springer, New York (2014). https://doi.org/10.1007/978-1-4614-7485-2_26
10. Lins, L., Klosowski, J.T., Scheidegger, C.: Nanocubes for real-time exploration of spatiotemporal datasets. IEEE Trans. Vis. Comput. Graph. **19**(12), 2456–2465 (2013)
11. Maus, M.: Definition und visualisierung von zoombaren 2D-projektionen im web. Technical report, TU Darmstadt (2016)

12. Nazemi, K., Breyer, M., Forster, J., Burkhardt, D., Kuijper, A.: Interacting with semantics: a user-centered visualization adaptation based on semantics data. In: Human Interface and the Management of Information. Interacting with Information - Symposium on Human Interface 2011, Held as Part of HCI International 2011, Orlando, FL, USA, 9–14 July 2011, Proceedings, Part I, pp. 239–248 (2011)
13. Pekalska, E., Duin, R.P.W.: The Dissimilarity Representation for Pattern Recognition: Foundations and Applications. Machine Perception and Artificial Intelligence. World Scientific Publishing Co., Inc., River Edge (2005)
14. Stahnke, J., Dörk, M., Müller, B., Thom, A.: Probing projections: interaction techniques for interpreting arrangements and errors of dimensionality reductions. IEEE Trans. Vis. Comput. Graph. **22**(1), 629–638 (2016)
15. Zöllner, M., Jetter, H.C., Reiterer, H.: ZOIL: a design paradigm and software framework for Post-WIMP distributed user interfaces. In: Gallud, J., Tesoriero, R., Penichet, V. (eds.) Distributed User Interfaces, pp. 87–94. Springer, London (2011). https://doi.org/10.1007/978-1-4471-2271-5_10

Operationalizing Analytics - A Composite Application Model

Neetu Singh[(⊠)]

University of Illinois at Springfield, Springfield, IL 62703, USA
nsing2@uis.edu

Abstract. Research on actionable data analytics has garnered considerable attention in recent times. Organizations are emphasizing on analytics as a competitive advantage enabler. Significant business and information systems research has been done to assess the value associated with analytics and to further its scope. Outcome of such research shows a need for organizations to effectively use analytics to generate, develop and use new insights in their operations. An active research area is reducing knowledge gap and bridging the action distance to realize an immediate value. To address this research gap, my focus is on operationalizing analytics to minimize action distance and bridge knowledge gap in the context of strategy and operations. Using design science research approach, this research aims to model how analytics can be used pervasively within an organization. This model is referred to as Composite Application Model for operationalizing analytics. The Composite Application Model for analytics will be helpful in minimizing the knowledge gap and action distance between the strategy and operations in organizations. This research contributes to expand the current practice of enterprise performance management and establishes a novel and intelligence based control within organizations.

Keywords: Actionable · Analytics · Action distance · Composite application
Data governance · Decision management · Knowledge gap
Organizational learning theory

1 Introduction

Organizations need to sustain and grow their business. Strategy provides a vision for the growth of an organization. In order to build strategic thinking, organizations need information and insights from within the business as well as the business environment [1, 2]. Analytics has become a key enabler for developing and sustaining an effective strategy. It has been observed that strategy does not provide a competitive advantage by itself [3, 4]. The operations need to be aligned with the strategy for success. The problem is how to achieve such alignment that is synergistic for the organization. Coupled with fact that every organization is different and employs systems and processes that may be unique to that organization, such problem cannot be answered without examining the theoretical basis and developing a design from theory.

Analytics has conventionally leveraged Relational and Multi-Dimensional OLAP (Online Analytical Processing) systems and played a strategic role in organizations

© Springer International Publishing AG, part of Springer Nature 2018
F. F.-H. Nah and B. S. Xiao (Eds.): HCIBGO 2018, LNCS 10923, pp. 756–766, 2018.
https://doi.org/10.1007/978-3-319-91716-0_59

answering questions arising from management by exception or objective [5]. From a taxonomical view, analytics is categorized as descriptive, predictive and prescriptive [6]. For organizations to gain competitive differentiation or sustain competitive advantage, knowing what happened and why it happened (Descriptive) is no longer adequate. What is happening now, what is likely to happen next (Predictive) and what actions should be taken to get the optimal results (Prescriptive) are prominent questions analytics must answer [5–9]. The expectations from analytics are sensory, insight and action.

Lavalle et al. [7] identified Process-Application-Data-Insight-Embed (PADIE) technique for organizations to successfully implement analytics-driven management and for rapidly creating business value. One of the major findings of this research specifies that the top two barriers to competitive advantage are "lack of understanding of how to use analytics to improve the business" and "lack of management bandwidth" [7]. However, how to supplement standard historical reporting of data with emerging approaches is still an unanswerable question. In other words, converting information into scenarios and simulations that make insights easier to understand and to act on is the area of research which is still unexplored [7]. To address this research gap my research focuses on operationalizing analytics to minimize action distance and bridge knowledge gap in the context of strategy and operations. The general research question is: How can organizations using analytics bridge strategic and operational knowledge gap and minimize action distance in organizations?

To address this research question, the design science approach is used which focuses on problem solving through the construction of artifact [10, 11]. This research aims to model how analytics can be used pervasively within an organization. The key objective is to (1) Minimize action distance and (2) Bridge knowledge gap for propagating strategy within operations. This research extends existing knowledge theory and develops a design theory method that eliminates the two identified problems. The goal of this research is to solve the problem of action distance and knowledge gap by approaching the two problems from an operational systems domain. The concept(s) outlined in this study will ultimately result in embedding analytics within the operational systems. This will provide a better perspective and help make informed decisions at the level of performance.

2 Literature Review

Business value of analytics is determined by the degree to which information produced is actionable [12] as shown in Fig. 1. Action distance is a measure of the effort required by the person responsible for a specific business situation to understand that information and to take proper action. The key aspects of action distance are alerting, informing and guiding. Therefore, minimizing action distance enables analytics to maximize its business value [12].

Knowledge gap is exhibited in the decision support system when the usefulness of intelligence generated is reduced because it did not present the context in which it can be used by the user. It also points to the ability to effectively manage knowledge and action [13] as represented in Fig. 2.

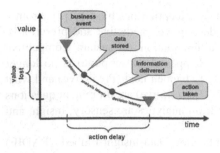

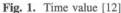

Fig. 1. Time value [12]

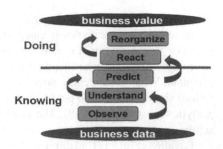

Fig. 2. Data value [13]

Organizational learning theory states that, to be competitive in a changing environment, organizations must change their goals and actions to reach those goals [14, 15] in a changing environment. The basic building block of this theory is the idea that all individuals need to become competent in acting and simultaneously reflecting on the action to learn from it. Salaway operationalized the organizational learning theory in the context of systems environment and offered a starting point for explicitly understanding the cause of errors in information systems development [1]. On the other hand, March [16] identifies that one of the major features of the social context of organizational learning is competitive ecology within which learning occurs and knowledge is used. The accumulation of knowledge affects the competitive advantage by linking learning, performance and position in ecology [16].

The concept of 'learning' has broad analytical value. Learning is a dynamic concept, and its use in theory emphasizes the continually changing nature of organization. Most research contribution to understanding organizational learning is limited to descriptive analyses of the outcomes of cumulative experience [17]. Dodgson [17] suggests using analytical concepts to have deeper understanding of organizational learning. In addition, Argyris and Schon [14] have great difficulties in finding organizations using double loop learning and could not find any example of organizations using deuteron loop for learning. As represented in Fig. 3, my research is leveraging the double loop learning to utilize feedback from user action and refining the knowledgebase for context generation in application.

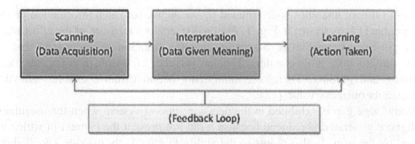

Fig. 3. Organization Learning Theory [14, 15]

3   Method

Design science attempts to create an artifact that serves needs of human beings. Multiple IT artifacts have been defined [11]. Design science research (DSR) consists of two activities at large: build and evaluate [18]. Building process refers to construction activities of an artifact that serves a certain need (e.g., problem solving and/or improvement), and evaluating process refers to assessment activities in terms of to what degree a created artifact serves its promised needs [18]. In addition, Vaishnavi and Kuechler [10] suggest that awareness of problem and suggestion should be preceded to development and evaluation. The effective solution of the problem is provided by developing a better interface [10]. The focus of design science is to understand the phenomenon, some or all of which may be created artificially instead of naturally occurring. This leads to artifact design and evaluation. Following the design science methodology, this research outlines the awareness of the problem, suggestions, develops a model and provides methods to evaluate the model. How can organizations leverage analytics to minimize the knowledge gap between strategic and operational systems to achieve and sustain competitive edge (Awareness of problem)? My research suggests that organizations can embed analytics into operations in a uniform manner by using a composite application model (Suggestion). I propose to develop a composite application model for analytics (Development) and then develop a prototype based on that model (Evaluation).

4   Artifact Description

Composite Application Model (CAM) for analytics (Fig. 4) is based on theoretical understanding of the problems of knowledge gap and action distance [19]. A composite application orchestrates independently developed programs, data and devices to deliver a new solution. I created a reference model for embedding analytics within operations and provide a logical view of the envisioned components and their interactions.

Composite application can govern the user interaction using operationalized analytics. As shown in Fig. 4, when user performs an action based on the intelligence from operationalized analytics, the action needs to be captured as pertaining to informed decision. The feedback is important for creating actionable knowledge base and refining it further for optimizing the recommendations.

The application needs to associate the operational information and insights and present it to the user. The problem to be solved at this stage is: how will application associate operational data with analytical insights. To solve this problem, an association between the operational transaction data and the analytics results using a context is needed.

When a transaction type that has an associated actionable analytics context gets committed in the operational system, with or without user interaction, it should also be able to classify the action as one of the recommended actions. Recommendations or guidance becomes a prominent aspect of actionable analytics. The action performed by user (action based on the recommendation or contrary to recommendation proposed) needs to be recorded by the intelligence system. Once data is in intelligence system,

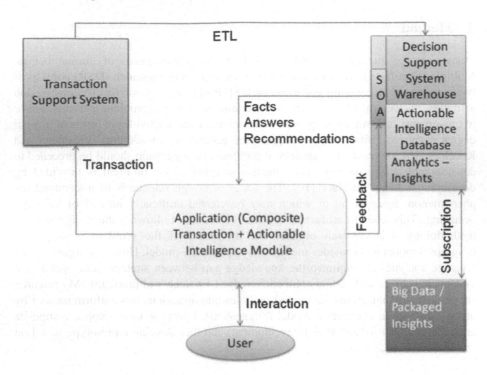

Fig. 4. Composite application model for analytics

analysis can be done and recommendations can be further optimized using feedbacks. All this can happen in near real time with current technologies in place.

As shown in Fig. 5, below activities will be performed for generating intelligence in actionable intelligence database:

1. Analyze use cases for analytics data.
2. Develop business process models to associate the use cases.
3. Identify context to associate the intelligence data in the business process model.
4. Identify methods to present the intelligence data to user as actionable insight.
5. Identify methods to capture and propagate the action performed by user based on the insight.

Composite Application Model for analytics is a reference model with a minimal set of unifying concepts and relationships within the problem domain, and is independent of specific standards, technologies, implementations, or other concrete details. This research examines the existing state of the designs and the modifications that can enable the desired state aligned with the design search process. It contributes to the existing knowledge base by developing a model of double loop learning in decision management system.

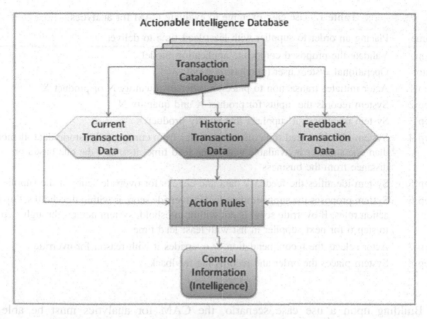

Fig. 5. Generating intelligence in actionable intelligence database

5 Evaluation

Design science research includes the building/design of an artifact as well as the evaluation of its use and performance [20]. The artifact will be further evaluated to demonstrate its worth with evidence addressing criteria such as validity, utility, quality, and efficacy [21]. I will evaluate and validate the artifact using prototype and use case (descriptive) [21, 22]. The ex-ante perspective, i.e., artificial evaluation methods will help us to control the potential confounding variables more carefully and to prove or disprove the design hypotheses, design theories, and the utility of the developed artifact [23]. Evaluation of an artifact based on a prototype facilitates the assessment of a solution's suitability for a certain problem by implementing the solution generically. In addition, evaluation with a prototype represents an adequate evaluation method for DSR artifacts [24].

To evaluate the model (CAM for analytics) being proposed in this research, a use case approach will be used as a formal proof [20–24] for preliminary evaluation. The model will be further evaluated using the domain expert interviews [25]. The insights from domain experts will further help in enhancing the composite application model for analytics.

The example of a use case for placing order to supplier with least lead time to deliver is as shown in Table 1.

Table 1. Use case example to evaluate CAM for analytics

Name	Placing an order to supplier with least lead time to deliver
Scope	Validate the proposed composite application model
Actor	Operational system user (purchasing user)
Step 1	Actor initiates transaction to place an order for quantity N of product X
Step 2	System records the inputs for product X and quantity N
Step 3	System identifies all suppliers that supply product X
Step 4	System identifies lead time of each supplier from current and historic data. If more than one supplier is available with same lead time, it selects the one based on distance from the business
Step 5	System identifies the feedback data and checks for override score of the supplier
Step 6	System proposes the supplier identified if override score is within threshold set up in action rules. If override score is not within threshold, system iterates through step 4 to step 6 for next supplier in list with least lead time
Step 7	Actor selects the recommendation or overrides it with reason for override
Step 8	System places the order and records the feedback

Building upon a use case scenario, the CAM for analytics must be able to demonstrate either through formal methods or by prototyping the following attributes: 1. Recommendation availability for the activity performed by user during interaction with application. 2. Availability of related intelligence results to the operational user based on context and use case. 3. Capture of action performed against recommendation in the analytics database. 4. Refinement of the recommendation and updated intelligence results upon reuse of the use case scenario based on prior interactions.

An approach is provided for the instantiation of this model for prototyping: 1. Recognize a leverageable event when it occurs. 2. Capture information about the event and the entity that caused it, and build a context for the event based on historical data or analytic scores drawn from a Data Warehouse. 3. Analyze the captured information to determine maximum leverage. 4. React to the event quickly and appropriately by delivering a response back to the source of the event, whether via software or human interaction, whether with latency or in real time.

To demonstrate that the research qualifies as design science research and not simple design, I examine the below aspects besides my own motivation to conduct design science research. The theory used in the study can be classified as 'Theory for Design and Action'. Composite Application Model for analytics is based on theoretical understanding of the problems of knowledge gap and action distance [19]. This contribution falls under improvement DSR (Fig. 6) as categorized by Gregor and Hevner [21].

The goal of DSR in the improvement quadrant is to create better solutions in the form of more efficient and effective products, processes, services, technologies, or ideas [21]. Improvement DSR is judged first on its ability to clearly represent and communicate the new artifact design (Composite Application Model for analytics). The presentation will show how and why the new solution differs from current solutions (Problems of Knowledge Gap and Action Distance reduces Business Value). The

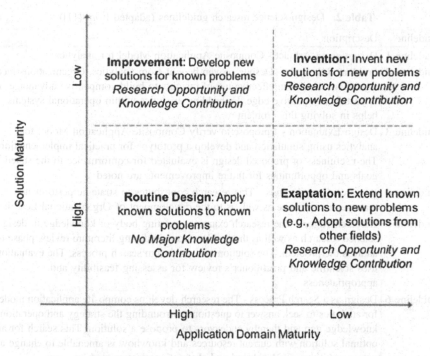

Fig. 6. DSR knowledge contribution framework (adapted from [21])

reasons for making the improvement should, desirably, be formally grounded in kernel theories from the knowledge base (Organization Learning Theory). Once the design improvement is described, then the artifact must be evaluated to provide convincing evidence of its improvement over current solutions (Simulation of Composite Application Model and Prototype for Instantiation). Improvement may be in the form of positive changes in efficiency, productivity, quality, competitiveness, market share, or other quality measures; depending on the goals of the research (Composite Application Model for Analytics improves business value of Analytics and helps attain competitive advantage). In the improvement quadrant, DSR projects make contributions to the knowledge base in the form of artifacts at one or more levels [21]. Contributions of this research to knowledge base will be at Level 2 as a Composite Application Model for Analytics.

This research attempts to address an unsolved problem by developing a theory based solution by following the design science research guidelines. The seven guidelines for design science research as outlined by Hevner is represented in Table 2 [11]. In addition, Table 2 describes how this design science research will conform to these guidelines.

Table 2. Design science research guidelines (adapted from [11])

Guideline	Description
Guideline 1	Design as an Artifact - Composite Application Model for analytics
Guideline 2	Problem Relevance - Despite proven benefit from analytics, Organizations face significant hurdles in effective use of insights to build competitive advantage or to sustain competitive edge. Embedding analytics within operational systems helps in solving this problem
Guideline 3	Design Evaluation - I propose to verify Composite Application Model for analytics using simulation and develop a prototype for practical implementation. The usefulness of proposed design is evaluated for conformance to the stated goals and opportunities for future improvements are noted
Guideline 4	Research Contributions - This research contributes to strategic performance management practice as well as to the development of Organizational Learning
Guideline 5	Research Rigor - The research examines existing body of knowledge in design science research as well as the problem domain during literature review phase to address the problem. The solution utilizes design search process. The evaluation uses scientific and practitioner's review for assessing feasibility and appropriateness
Guideline 6	Design as a Search Process - The research develops composite application model for analytics to seek answer to questions surrounding the strategy and operations knowledge gap and thereby endeavors to propose a solution. This search for an optimal solution with current resources and knowhow is amenable to change as new capabilities are developed and abstractions instantiated
Guideline 7	Communication of Research - The research can be disseminated to IS/IT researchers, as it solves a practice based problem and has sound theoretical basis. The capabilities arising from this design can be further developed by interested researchers

6 Discussion

Analytics is most valuable when used at the right place and the right time. Operationalizing analytics combines decision making knowledge with operational data to prompt users to immediately take actions to address issues and to ensure they apply best practices consistently across the enterprise. The model outlined in this study conforms to the notion that the value of analytics is most when used at the right place and the right time.

The CAM for analytics model is a generic model and requires domain specific customizations to build actionable intelligence database relevant to that domain. The accuracy of the results is dependent on the feedback being received in the intelligence database.

After the model is successfully implemented, two areas can be further studied: improving actionable knowledge classifications; and behavior analysis of user interactions when activity is controlled by decision making guidance. To present the theoretical and practical implications of this research, I apply 'Information Systems Research Framework' proposed by Hevner et al. [11] (Fig. 7).

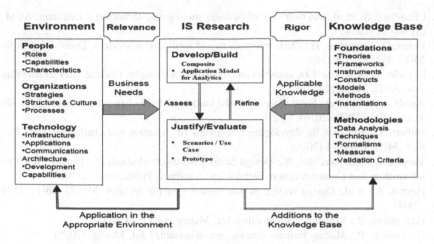

Fig. 7. Information system research framework (adapted from [11])

7 Conclusion

The Composite Application Model for analytics will be helpful in significantly minimizing the knowledge gap and action distance between the strategy and operations in organizations. It will allow future manifestation of decision management systems that can control how strategy propagates within operations and keep the two aligned.

This research contributes to expand the current practice of enterprise performance management. The targeted area of real time intelligence delivery is currently limited to strategic and tactical user groups. The field is expanding to include the operational users. The Composite Application Model for analytics aims at achieving this objective.

Operationalizing analytics combines decision making knowledge with real time operational data to prompt users to immediately take informed actions. The model outlined in this study aims at bridging the current gap in the application design to provide embedded intelligence within operational applications. It conforms to the notion that the value of analytics is most likely to be obtained when used at the right place and the right time. The CAM for analytics is a generic model and requires domain specific customizations to build actionable intelligence database relevant to the domain.

References

1. Salaway, G.: An organizational learning approach to information systems development. MIS Q. **11**(2), 245–264 (1987)
2. Bonn, I.: Developing strategic thinking as a core competency. Manag. Decis. **39**(1), 63–71 (2001)
3. Barney, J.: Firm resources and sustained competitive advantage. J. Manag. **17**(1), 99–120 (1991)
4. Ployhart, R.E., Hale Jr., D.: The fascinating psychological microfoundations of strategy and competitive advantage. Annu. Rev. Organ. Psychol. Organ. Behav. **1**(1), 145–172 (2014)

5. Chaudhuri, S., et al.: An overview of business intelligence technology. Commun. ACM **54** (8), 88–98 (2011)
6. Delen, D., Demirkan, H.: Data, information and analytics as services. Decis. Support Syst. **55**(1), 359–363 (2013)
7. LaValle, S., et al.: Big data, analytics and the path from insights to value. MIT Sloan Manag. Rev. **52**(2), 21–32 (2011)
8. Ransbotham, S., et al.: Beyond the hype: the hard work behind analytics success. MIT Sloan Manag. Rev. **57**(3) (2016)
9. Hilbert, M.: Big data for development: a review of promises and challenges. Dev. Policy Rev. **34**(1), 135–174 (2016)
10. Vaishnavi, V.K., Kuechler, W.: Design Science Research Methods and Patterns: Innovating Information and Communication Technology. Auerbach Publications (2007)
11. Hevner, A., et al.: Design science in information systems research. MIS Q. **28**(1), 75–105 (2004)
12. Hackathorn, R.: Real-time to real-value. Inf. Manag. **14**(1), 24 (2004)
13. Hackathorn, R.: Making business intelligence actionable? Inf. Manag. (2005)
14. Argyris, C., Schon, D.: Organizational Learning: A Theory of Action Perspective. Wesley, Massachusetts (1978)
15. Argyris, C., Schön, D.A.: Organizational learning: a theory of action perspective. Reis **77** (78), 345–348 (1997)
16. March, J.G.: Exploration and exploitation in organizational learning. Organ. Sci. **2**(1), 71–87 (1991)
17. Dodgson, M.: Organizational learning: a review of some literatures. Organ. stud. **14**(3), 375–394 (1993)
18. March, S.T., Smith, G.F.: Design and natural science research on information technology. Decis. Support Syst. **15**(4), 251–266 (1995)
19. Gregor, S.: The nature of theory in information systems. MIS Q. **30**(3), 611–642 (2006)
20. Pries-Heje, J., et al.: Soft design science research: extending the boundaries of evaluation in design science research. In: Proceeding of The 2nd International Conference on Design Science Research in IT (DESRIST), pp. 18–38 (2007)
21. Gregor, S., Hevner, A.R.: Positioning and presenting design science research for maximum impact. MIS Q. **37**(2), 337–356 (2013)
22. Cleven, A., et al.: Design alternatives for the evaluation of design science research artifacts. In: Proceedings of the 4th International Conference on Design Science Research in Information Systems and Technology, p. 19. ACM (2009)
23. Pries-Heje, J., et al.: Strategies for Design Science Research Evaluation (2008)
24. March, S.T., Storey, V.C.: Design science in the information systems discipline: an introduction to the special issue on design science research. Manag. Inf. Syst. Q. **32**(4), 6 (2008)
25. Parsons, J., Wand, Y.: Using cognitive principles to guide classification in information systems modeling. MIS Q. 839–868 (2008)

E-commerce Flow Management in Fulfillment Centers Through Data Visualization

Amith Tarigonda[✉], Bruce Hymes, and Alexei Nikonovich-Kahn

Williams-Sonoma, Inc., Memphis, TN, USA
amith.tarigonda@gmail.com

Abstract. Organizations face challenges in gathering, interpreting, and acting upon real-time data. To overcome the challenge of real time data interpretation, most retailers have built business dashboards to readily display key performance indicators (KPIs). The most critical element of a dashboard is the user interface and how KPIs are displayed to end users for interpretation. Given the importance of visual analytics and business dashboard design, Williams-Sonoma, Inc (WSI) tasked the supply chain solutions (SCS) team to develop a comprehensive strategy for gathering, interpreting, and acting upon real time data within its fulfillment centers. Prior to the implementation, operational leadership had limited visibility to people, processes, and systems within the fulfillment centers. Using a bottom-up design approach, the SCS team identified and bridged the gap between two order management systems and created end to end flow visibility. With an emphasis on providing visibility to the "right information at the right time" SCS created a Flow Management platform which predicts operational risks by intercepting real time order drops and worker activity. The flow management platform is a minute-by-minute supply chain monitoring system that displays a set of related KPIs from various stages (e.g. wave, pick, pack, ship) of the order fulfillment process. After the implementation, leadership of fulfillment centers had access to a business intelligence framework that linked two key order management systems and enabled them to develop an optimal strategy for best serving our customers. It also allowed leadership to identify gaps in the order fulfillment and prioritization process.

Keywords: Flow management · Visualization · Supply chain flow
E-commerce · Dashboard · Business intelligence · Decision making
Visual analytics · Warehouse management · Fulfillment centers
Supply chain solutions · Data analytics

1 Introduction

Supply chains have operated on the standard model of getting work done through sheer repetition and additional labor for years. Williams-Sonoma, Inc's (WSI) challenged the status quo and exemplified the spirit of innovation by exploiting data analytics. Most impressively, the Supply Chain Solutions (SCS) team accomplished this feat by channeling technical and human-computer interaction (HCI) skills less commonly associated with the supply chain into a flow management platform.

© Springer International Publishing AG, part of Springer Nature 2018
F. F.-H. Nah and B. S. Xiao (Eds.): HCIBGO 2018, LNCS 10923, pp. 767–778, 2018.
https://doi.org/10.1007/978-3-319-91716-0_60

The SCS team is rooted in an organization that fosters creativity and working collaboratively across sourcing, transportation, and operations to optimize the supply chain. With this culture, the SCS team was able to turn an idea into an innovative application that has empowered the business to evolve and build a strategic advantage in the marketplace. The operations team identified that a key issue within WSI's supply chain was a need to utilize data to provide an enhanced customer experience under high volume conditions. This necessity led to the SCS team to observe and analyze order prioritization and flow within the fulfillment center. This observation led to the concept of a flow management application that provides a powerful means to communicate KPIs and suggest optimal order release strategies through tailored displays. The platform would also provide executives the ability to monitor the performance of and adjust the execution of suggested strategies.

The Flow Management dashboard visualization enables integrated monitoring, real-time analysis, and controlled movement of supply chain processes, enhancing the limited analytical and data processing capacities of fragmented and redundant reporting systems. With powerful data visualization capabilities and a consistent, real-time, and transparent view into business operations, this centralized application provided a single source for real-time information and operational risk prediction.

2   Theoretical Foundation and Background

The dashboard design needs to go through an iterative process of identifying needs and priorities, designing the user experience, technical development, and usability studies in applying visual design [1]. The essential characteristic of a dashboard is that it displays information on a single screen [2]. Complex views of dashboard presentations can make a user puzzled and distracted in finding the functionality they need [3].

User interface design is crucial to the success of information analysis and is a key aspect of a user's experience [1]. There is no such thing as an objectively good user interface - quality and design depend on the context: who the user is and what the motivations are. The ideal dashboard interface to analytics should be simple yet comprehensive for the executives and should not lead to high cognitive load; otherwise, it would defeat the purpose of the business dashboard [4]. Users who chose preferred presentation formats made more accurate decisions for symbolic tasks [5]. We adopted the interaction perspective by viewing the dashboard as an immediate pleasurable subjective experience that is directed toward an object and not mediated by intervening factors [6]. Visual metaphors based on familiar colors and layouts serve as the design theme for business intelligence (BI) dashboards. The limited number of colors and menu options in the dashboard enables user to focus their attention on key information [7]. Responsive visualizations enable users not only to analyze data by interacting directly with the various visual representations like bar charts, line charts, heat maps, and geographic maps, but also to manipulate the charts with size, shape, color, and motion of the visual objects representing the aspects of data being analyzed [8].

3 Innovation

Why Was Visualization Important for Flow Management?

Visualization is important for the flow management platform because it presents 704 discrete data points to end users. Proper visualization enables accurate processing of every data point in context of the fulfillment center and highlights unexpected changes and fluctuations, and triggers responses to problematic areas based on real-time data.

Prior to the implementation of flow management, operations were being managed and monitored mostly through Excel spreadsheets and Access databases which lacked key visualization principles. Observing this, the SCS team started conversations on how data visualization is a powerful tool to simplify abstract ideas and complex processes. Through conversations with operations, the SCS team determined that graphical representations were the most absent visualization principle in existing reports.

Determined to design the flow management platform with geographical, proximal, closure, and similarity visualization principles absent in WSI's legacy reporting systems, the team began by benchmarking success factors in popular mobile applications – user friendliness, ease of understanding, and the use of intuitive and logical icons to represent key concepts. These factors led to a new idea, which was to design a platform that visually represented the physical reality of the fulfillment center as a building. Using a user interface akin to "Fitbit style" applications, where users feel empowered, end users of flow management would be able to click on a digital manifestation of any point of the fulfillment center and acquire actionable data.

WSI's centers contain several inter-connected, multi-level pick modules and are subdivided into zones. For context, a pick module is equal to the length of a FIFA soccer field, four stories tall, and houses roughly 8,200 unique products. Each product is in an individual location ready to be picked for customer orders. A zone is about 20 yards long and holds around 250 unique products. Orders can be routed through any number of zones to collect product(s) in the process of fulfilling a customer order. Once all products are collected (i.e. picked), orders are then routed to either the personalization department or packing lanes. Upon completion of packing, orders are routed to the proper shipping zone. This series of activities entails traveling miles of conveyor around a 1.2 million square foot facility processing upwards of 100,000 orders daily.

The coordination and prioritization of orders across each of these steps is generally referred to as "flow". The successful management of this flow hinges on complete and accurate data which was lacking in previous reports. Recognizing need for a complete, accurate, real time platform, the SCS team leveraged their technical expertise to build an eloquent data model connecting two critical fulfillment systems (warehouse management system and pick to lite order routing system) into a single geographical representation.

The final requirement for the platform was to not only go beyond fulfilling the existing operational needs, but also to provide a platform that encourages user engagement and analysis through visualization of potential issues and trend tracking.

4   Execution

With a new vision in place, the team started bringing their idea to life. Partnering with the engineering group, the team developed a simplified blueprint of WSI's largest fulfillment center Olive Branch 2 (OB2). The simplified, to scale, blueprint visually represents each area of the fulfillment center: pick modules, packing lanes and other important infrastructure such as conveyors and workstations. With a focus on geographical accuracy, objects and icons built in Adobe Photoshop and Adobe Illustrator were combined with the blueprint to build a layout for the platform.

Without the simple blueprint interface, the SCS team feared user acceptance would be low. The usability of a dashboard influences the perceived usefulness of operational and tactical support [9]. Dashboard visualizations focus on the design and evaluation of exploration views (EV), acting as a system for novice visualization users to easily build and customize data trends. Dynamic creation, re-organization, searching and exploration of visual data representations allow users to target the actionable areas [10]. These aspects aid users to better analyze, retrieve, experiment, understand and familiarize themselves with the business data.

End users need data, but they need the right data, in an actionable format. To provide this, the platform was designed for a six-monitor station. This empowered the end users by giving them visualization of both the entire fulfillment center and each key module, packing area, and other key infrastructure simultaneously.

Due to the need to combine multiple systems and provide different KPIs on each monitor, the SCS team elected to use a BI platform that is generally not used for visualization. Instead, a powerful BI tool intended to process and query data with a limited user interface was selected. Even still, the flow management platform stretched the bandwidth of both the platform and fulfillment center system servers during peak times. The SCS team's innovative approach to this was utilizing hundreds of custom created icons embedded with conditional formulas to display actionable data and geographically depict when and where problems were occurring in real time.

To accomplish real time data depiction, the SCS team created WSI's first multi-dimensional data model within the supply chain. The data model capitalizes on the concept of data bridges across multiple systems. Learning from previous operational reporting platforms which were reported on data silos, the SCS team started partnering with operations to develop a key understanding of what data was needed to make actionable decisions. In general terms, any data limited to one business or operational function is a data silo. In the context of flow management, a data silo impedes end users from viewing order patterns and employee productivity data simultaneously.

Through first-hand experience in operations and extensive interviews with operations leadership, the SCS team compiled a list of every data point needed across both systems. Required data ranged from order data (how much of each product, destination), inventory levels, fulfillment center employee performance, and average time elapsed on orders still within the building.

With each data point determined, it was clear that standardizing the data would be a critical process to bring data into a common format which allowed cross platform integration in large-scale analytics. To overcome the data silo and standardization hurdles, the SCS team adopted a bottom-up programming approach. This approach led to the creation of multiple data marts in-memory. When bridged together to create a single, broad data mart with in the flow management prototype, end users were able to view data across departments and systems.

To create an ideal data mart with WSI's supply chain data, the SCS team identified the need for a normalized data model. A normalized data model was designed to reduce data redundancy and improve data integrity. With this normalized approach, data is efficiently organized in the flow management platform's in-memory.

With the in-memory storage, every data mart could be rapidly reloaded. In addition, every data mart query was designed with cost based optimization in mind and the Structured Query Language (SQL) queries were optimized to 900% of their run time to provide a rapid reload. As query optimizing is the heart of SQL processing engine, the Cost Based Optimization technique is used to minimize the overall utilization of the CPU, Memory, and I/O executions. Computer programs were continually advanced to improve code quality and efficiency while maintaining the same data pull.

Cost based optimization within the flow management platform is achieved using two methods. First, the platform uses indexes in the SQL select operation which allowed quick read operations on data mart. Second, the platform severely limits nested query usage to leverage the parallel execution of queries on SQL engine. Combining these techniques allowed the entire platform to read across two separate systems and update 704 data points in under 75 s, which far exceeded the supply chain's original requirements.

The final requirement for successful execution of the flow management platform is data visualization. End users must be able to interpret and act upon the enormous data set near real time. In addition, visualization tools must identify trends and potential problems to assist end users with prioritization, without increasing the platforms reload time.

Vision is by far the most powerful sense [11]. Seeing and thinking are intimately connected. When data is presented in specific and intuitive ways, the patterns can be readily perceived [12]. To avoid the misuse of color in dashboard design, the team emphasized a relevant principle: some colors are soothing, and some are not (e.g., they could be glaring, loud or uncomfortable to look at). The team limited the use of extremely bright or fully saturated colors to act upon the data within the dashboard with an open mind, rather than to trigger stress due to the use of such colors.

Empirical validation of the Technology Acceptance Model (TAM) in the context of perceived aesthetics, interactivity and user engagement have been shown to have a strong impact on user adoption behavior [13, 14]. Morrissey [15] found that users were typically more involved in highly interactive applications than in applications with a single level of hierarchy. Using Google, Apple, Fitbit, and other dashboards as inspirations, the team developed an interface that encourages user engagement. In the flow management platform end users will find battery icons that slowly "charge" as product is stocked in the pick modules. Much like Apple Watch owners desire to close fitness rings, the operations team worked to achieve "100%" charge on each battery.

Understanding that minute details involving layouts, color schemes, and icons would create a desirable look and feel, Gestalt principles of visual perception -

Principles of Proximity, Similarity, Enclosure, Closure, Continuity, and Connection [16] - were embedded in the dashboard to provide a seamless flow of information to the user without interrupting warehouse order flow. For instance, fulfillment center wide performance could be found on the main screen. Performance details about specific departments are found by clicking on icons: forklift icons lead to performance details of individual forklift drivers, Similarly, cloud icons display the details of orders that are still in the queue, and inspector icons show metrics related to orders delayed due to inventory discrepancies.

Yee's [17] study suggests that color leads to the immersive and competitive components of the user to discover things in a game which other players do not know about. The SCS team extended this concept to leverage a color palette that provides insights on where to prioritize resources that end users may not notice with data alone.

Due to the volume of data presented and the end to end nature of the flow management platform, user engagement is critical to the platform's success. Users continue to engage in the application only if attention is maintained throughout the application [18]. To minimize attention required and promote engagement, the SCS team leveraged a 6-monitor set-up to minimize front end navigation and placed icons strategically to encourage end users to engage with all 6 monitors. Five of the monitors visualizes a key physical area or operation within the fulfillment center. Pick Modules 1–3 each have a dedicated monitor, Replenishment & Stocking are displayed on monitor 4, and Personalization on monitor 5. The sixth monitor provides an aerial view of the entire facility and executive summary or current performance.

Within each of the 6 monitors, data is presented with conditional formatting. By studying human perceptual capabilities and understanding how people find patterns and how they organize individual elements into structures and groups, visual layout and data bucketing techniques were integrated into the design level and the data structure level [19]. Following perception based rules, we can present our data in such a way that important and informative patterns stand out. End user's most critical pattern to perceive is the "in stock percentage" of each pick zone. However, with 118 zones, a simple number display was ineffective. The flow management platform instead combines the 4 KPIs that impact "in stock percentage" and colors each zone accordingly. Thus, zones ready for additional work are a deep green. Zones in need of attention are various shades of red, depending upon the severity of attention needed. Colors are also used in identifying whether the current employee in a zone can handle the incoming flow of orders to that zone based on the employee's performance over the last year.

In addition to applying design principles to the individual elements of the platform, the overall platform architecture uses advanced visualization techniques. Starting from the summarized graphical view (top layer), each successive layer provides additional details, views, and perspectives to help users to better understand a problem and identify the steps needed to solve it, as shown in Fig. 1 [9]. Eckerson [20] indicates that a performance dashboard often presents information in three different layers to effectively support its monitoring, analysis, and management functions.

The flow visualization screen not only enables executives to communicate strategy but also helps with coordination among the different groups to ensure that they are working toward the same goals or outcomes. The homepage provides an executive summary while the detailed transactional view provides front-line employees and their

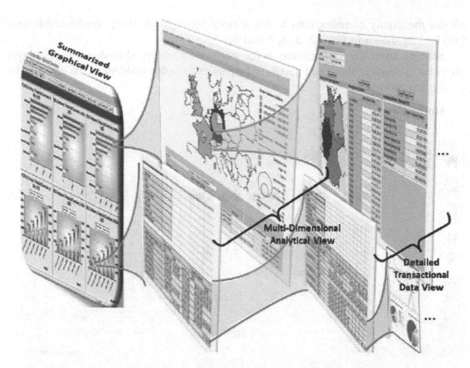

Fig. 1. Performance dashboard interconnected layers [9] (Color figure online)

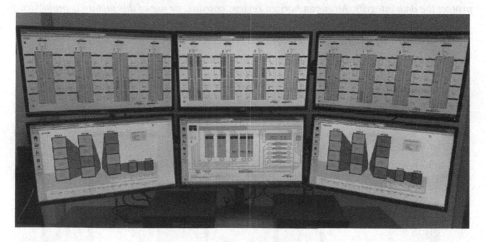

Fig. 2. Flow management integrated system (*Above picture is a property of WSI and is obscured to protect the data integrity. Any unauthorized review, copying, or use of this picture is prohibited.*)

supervisors may need a more detailed view to track performance of their specific operational processes and find the root cause of the problems specific to their processes.

The overall platform contains more than 2,000 lines of source code, 3,000 front end queries, and hundreds of images and icons. The result is a real-time application that allows the highly complex data to tell a story through an easily synthesizable user interface as shown in Figs. 2, 3, 4, 5 and 6.

Starting from the summarized home page view, every drill-down of the layer provides in-depth analysis and details to help users to better understand the entire order fulfillment process.

Home Page

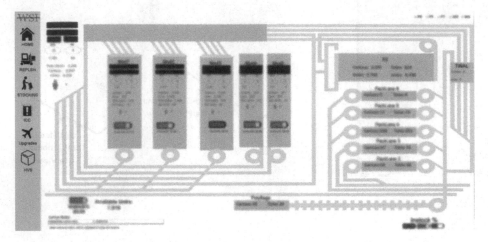

Fig. 3. Flow management home page (*Above picture is a property of WSI and is obscured to protect the data integrity. Any unauthorized review, copying, or use of this picture is prohibited.*)

Drill-Down of Home Page (1/8)

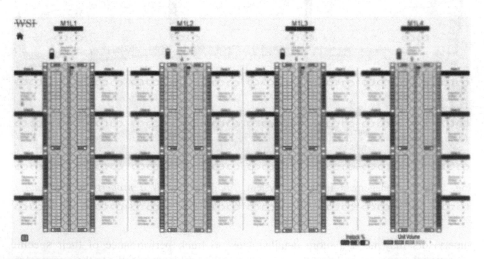

Fig. 4. An example of the drill-down pages in flow management (*Above picture is a property of WSI and is obscured to protect the data integrity. Any unauthorized review, copying, or use of this picture is prohibited.*)

Drill-Down of Home Page (4/8)

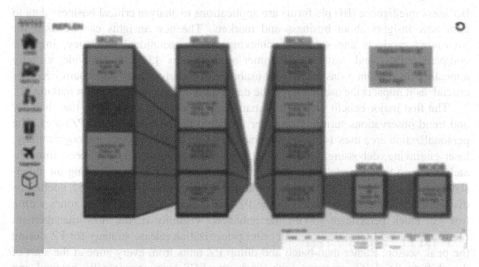

Fig. 5. One of the drill-down pages in flow management (*Above picture is a property of WSI and is obscured to protect the data integrity. Any unauthorized review, copying, or use of this picture is prohibited.*)

Drill-Down of Home Page (5/8)

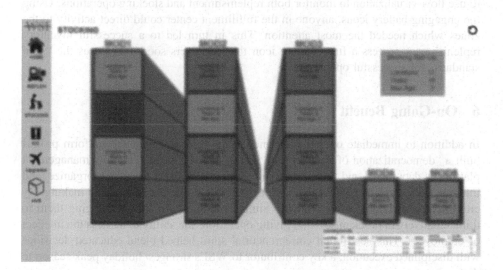

Fig. 6. One of the drill-down pages in flow management (*Above picture is a property of WSI and is obscured to protect the data integrity. Any unauthorized review, copying, or use of this picture is prohibited.*)

5 Benefits

Business intelligence (BI) platforms are applications to analyze critical business data to gain new insights about business and markets. The new insights can be used for improving products and services, achieving better operational efficiency, improve competitiveness, and fostering customer relationships [21]. To provide visually appealing displays in a dashboard, the usability of a performance dashboard becomes crucial, as it impacts the usefulness of the dashboard in supporting decision making [2].

The first major benefit of the flow management platform came from the visibility and trend observations surrounding order flow into the personalization (PZ) area. The personalization area uses 14 different personalization techniques (e.g. monogramming, laser engraving, debossing, etc.) to customize WSI products for customers. Immediately after go-live, the platform provided insight that PZ was experiencing an inconsistent flow of orders (i.e. Feast and Famine). Upon investigation, WSI operations discovered this was due to orders in the PZ queue being requested from zones with a low "in stock percentage." With the enhanced visibility of the flow management platform, the WSI team designed an order prioritization release strategy for PZ during the peak season. Rather than batch and dump PZ units from every zone at the start of the shift to flood PZ operators with work, the SCS team strategically batched and released a calculated number of units (based on available volume and employee productivity both in the pick modules and in the personalization area) over the course of the whole shift. This in turn assisted our outbound operations by improving the flow into our packing/shipping department rather than the traditional feast/famine execution.

After the successful analysis of the PZ Feast and Famine problem, WSI continued to use flow visualization to monitor both replenishment and stocking operations. Using the engaging battery icons, anyone in the fulfillment center could direct activity to the zones which needed the most attention. This in turn led to a successful inventory replenishment process a fully battery icon that end users soon adopted as the "gold standard" for successful operations.

6 On-Going Benefit

In addition to immediate operational benefits, the flow management platform project built a "democratization of data" culture within the SCS team. The flow management platform's data model and this new culture have enable users to collect, organize, and interpret complex data without the barriers that all too often stifle decision making. By empowering individual users with this simple platform, we are encouraging them to think creatively in problem solving, giving operations the ability to harness the intellect of employees. This new-found entrepreneurial spirit helped blend educated decisions with disciplined execution, a key contributor to WSI's strongest holiday peak season to date.

Flow management leads WSI to integrate wave management with operations management to determine the workload demand available as well as what needs to be made available to operations. Flow management oversees execution, thus waving control in the fulfillment center.

While we have yet to recognize the full value of this application, some notable results are listed below:

- Best in class "Click to Delivery" (customer order time to delivery) performance
- Improved decision-making process
- Minimized operational risks
- Better alignment with WSI strategy
- Increased customer fulfillments by 30%
- 80% reduction in Personalization queues
- 10% reduction in DC shrink
- 50% reduction in reprocessed orders
- Reduction in customer care call volume
- Streamlined/Centralized reporting
- Assess the flow of orders by location, by lines, by units.

References

1. Bors, P.A., Kemner, A., Fulton, J., Stachecki, J., Brennan, L.K.: HKHC community dashboard: design, development, and function of a web-based performance monitoring system. J. Public Health Manag. Pract. 21, S36–S44 (2015). https://doi.org/10.1097/PHH.0000000000000207
2. Few, S.: Dashboard confusion revisited. Vis. Bus. Intell. Newsl. 1–6 (2007). https://www.perceptualedge.com/articles/03-22-07.pdf
3. Read, A., Tarrell, A., Fruhling, A.: Exploring user preference for the dashboard menu design. In: 42nd Hawaii International Conference on System Sciences, pp. 1–10. IEEE, Waikoloa (2009). https://doi.org/10.1109/hicss.2009.213
4. Duval, E.: Attention please! Learning analytics for visualization and recommendation. In: 1st International Conference on Learning Analytics and Knowledge, pp. 9–17. ACM, New York (2011). https://doi.org/10.1145/2090116.2090118
5. Wilson, E.V., Zigurs, I.: Decisional guidance and end user display choices. Account. Manag. Inf. Technol. 9, 49–75 (1999). https://doi.org/10.1016/S0959-8022(99)00003-X
6. Moshagen, M., Thielsch, M.T.: Facets of visual aesthetics. Int. J. Hum.-Comput. Stud. 68, 689–709 (2010). https://doi.org/10.1016/j.ijhcs.2010.05.006
7. Marcus, A.: Dashboards in your future. Interactions 13, 48–60 (2006). https://doi.org/10.1145/1109069.1109103
8. Lapa, J., Bernardino, J., Figueiredo, A.: A comparative analysis of open source business intelligence platforms. In: Proceedings of the International Conference on Information Systems and Design of Communication, pp. 86–92. ACM, May 2014
9. Lea, B.-R., Nah, F.F.-H.: Usability of performance dashboards, usefulness of operational and tactical support, and quality of strategic support: a research framework. In: Yamamoto, S. (ed.) HIMI 2013. LNCS, vol. 8017, pp. 116–123. Springer, Heidelberg (2013). https://doi.org/10.1007/978-3-642-39215-3_14
10. Elias, M., Bezerianos, A.: Exploration views: understanding dashboard creation and customization for visualization novices. In: Campos, P., Graham, N., Jorge, J., Nunes, N., Palanque, P., Winckler, M. (eds.) INTERACT 2011. LNCS, vol. 6949, pp. 274–291. Springer, Heidelberg (2011). https://doi.org/10.1007/978-3-642-23768-3_23

11. Kölsch, M., Pavlović, V., Kisačanin, B., Huang, T.S.: Special issue on vision for human–computer interaction. Comput. Vis. Image Underst. **108**, 1–3 (2007). https://doi.org/10.1016/j.cviu.2007.01.002

12. Ware, C.: Information Visualization: Perception for Design, 3rd edn. Elsevier, Waltham (2012)

13. Moon, J., Kim, Y.: Extending the TAM for a world-wide-web context. J. Inf. Manag. Sci. **38**, 217–230 (2001). https://doi.org/10.1016/S0378-7206(00)00061-6

14. Few, S.: Dashboard design: taking a metaphor too far. Inf. Manag. **15**, 18 (2005)

15. Morrissey, R.: Tailoring performance dashboard content. Bus. Intell. J. **12**, 7 (2007)

16. Few, S.: Information Dashboard Design: The Effective Visual Communication of Data. O'Reilly Media Inc., Sebastopol (2006)

17. Yee, N.: Motivations for play in online games. Cyber Psychol. Behav. **9**, 772–775 (2006). https://doi.org/10.1089/cpb.2006.9.772

18. Lazzaro, N.: Why we play games: four keys to more emotion without story (2004). http://xeodesign.com/xeodesign_whyweplaygames.pdf

19. DeBusk, G.K., Brown, R.M., Killough, L.N.: Components and relative weights in utilization of dashboard measurement systems like the Balanced Scorecard. Br. Account. Rev. **35**, 215–231 (2003). https://doi.org/10.1016/S0890-8389(03)00026-X

20. Eckerson, W.W.: Performance Dashboards: Measuring, Monitoring, and Managing Your Business, 2nd edn. Wiley, Hoboken (2011)

21. Yigitbasioglua, O.M., Velcub, O.: A review of dashboards in performance management: implications for design and research. Int. J. Account. Inf. Syst. **13**, 41–59 (2012). https://doi.org/10.1016/j.accinf.2011.08.002

Correction to: A Structure-Behavior Coalescence Systems Modeling Approach for Service Systems Design

Yu-Chen Yang, Cheng-Ta Tsai, and William S. Chao

Correction to:
Chapter "A Structure-Behavior Coalescence Method
for Human-Computer Interaction System Requirements
Specification" in: F. F.-H. Nah and B. S. Xiao (Eds.):
HCI in Business, Government, and Organizations, **LNCS 10923,**
https://doi.org/10.1007/978-3-319-91716-0_18

The title of the originally published chapter was identical with a chapter by the same authors published in 2016. To avoid confusion it has been corrected to "A Structure-Behavior Coalescence Systems Modeling Approach for Service Systems Design". Additionally, typos were corrected in the legend of Figure 6 and in section 3.5.

The updated version of this chapter can be found at
https://doi.org/10.1007/978-3-319-91716-0_18

© Springer Nature Switzerland AG 2019
F. F.-H. Nah and B. S. Xiao (Eds.): HCIBGO 2018, LNCS 10923, p. C1, 2019.
https://doi.org/10.1007/978-3-319-91716-0_61

Author Index

Printed in the United States
By Bookmasters

Printed in the United States
By Bookmasters